JUSTICE STATISTICS

JUSTICE STATISTICS

AN EXTENDED LOOK AT CRIME IN THE UNITED STATES

Fifth Edition
2019

Edited by
Shana Hertz Hattis

Lanham • Boulder • New York • London

Bernan Press

Published by Bernan Press
An imprint of The Rowman & Littlefield Publishing Group, Inc.
4501 Forbes Boulevard, Suite 200, Lanham, Maryland 20706
www.rowman.com
800-462-6420

6 Tinworth Street, London SE11 5AL, United Kingdom

ISBN: 978-1-64143-376-1
eISBN: 978-1-64143-377-8

♾️™ The paper used in this publication meets the minimum requirements of
American National Standard for Information Sciences—Permanence of
Paper for Printed Library Materials, ANSI/NISO Z39.48-1992.

Contents

Part 7. Indicators of School Crime and Safety, 2018

INTRODUCTION

Bernan Press is pleased to present the fifth edition of its comprehensive collection of justice statistics in the United States. This volume provides a fresh look at the valuable information compiled by the Department of Justice, including its subsidiaries, the Bureau of Justice Statistics (BJS) and the Federal Bureau of Investigation (FBI).

The book brings together 12 key reports that fall under the general topic of "justice". Topics covered include criminal victimization, identity theft, crime in the United States, hate crimes, probation, parole, school violence, and law enforcement officers killed and assaulted. Tables in this volume provide a comprehensive account of each of these subjects; for more information, including full-scope methodologies and information about standard errors for each table, please see the full reports at the URLs listed below.

Each section contains statistical tables and figures highlighting the data, as well as a brief summary of the report's methodology and at-a-glance highlights of the most compelling information.

The reports:

Capital Punishment, 2016 discusses both prisoners on Death Row in the United States and prisoners executed in the applicable year. It can be found at https://www.bjs.gov/index. cfm?ty=pbdetail&iid=6246

Crime Against Persons with Disabilities, 2009–2015, presents estimates of nonfatal violent crime (rape or sexual assault, robbery, aggravated assault, and simple assault) against persons age 12 years or older with disabilities. Disabilities are classified according to six limitations: hearing, vision, cognitive, ambulatory, self-care, and independent living. The full report can be found on the BJS Web site at https://www.bjs.gov/ index.cfm?ty=pbdetail&iid=5986

Crime in the United States, 2017, provides an introduction to overall crime trends. This report is more fully presented in Bernan Press's companion volume, *Crime in the United States.* However, given the importance of this data in the understanding of justice and crime trends in the United States, its most relevant tables have been included in this volume. Once again appearing in this book, and not contained in the complementary *Crime* volume, is the full range of the UCR's expanded offense tables. Also included are three supplementary reports: *Federal Crime Data, Human Trafficking,* and *Cargo Theft.* The full report can be accessed at https:// www.bjs.gov/index.cfm?ty=pbdetail&iid=6467

Criminal Victimization, 2017, takes a close look at the victims of violent and property crime in the United States.

The full report is accessible at https://www.bjs.gov/index. cfm?ty=pbdetail&iid=6466

Federal Justice Statistics, 2015–2016, returns with an updated report to this volume. It describes the activities, workloads, and outcomes of the federal judicial system from arrest to conviction and imprisonment. It can be found at https://www.bjs.gov/ index.cfm?ty=pbdetail&iid=6506.

Hate Crime Statistics, 2017, details the hate crimes committed in the United States throughout 2015. It can be accessed at https://ucr.fbi.gov/hate-crime/2017

Indicators of School Crime and Safety, 2017 is an annual report that presents data on crime and safety at school from the perspectives of students, teachers, and principals. Conducted jointly by the Bureau of Justice Statistics and the National Center for Education Statistics, the report's data sources include the National Crime Victimization Survey (NCVS), the School Crime Supplement to the NCVS, the Youth Risk Behavior Survey, and the School Survey on Crime and Safety. The full report can be accessed at https://www.bjs.gov/index. cfm?ty=pbdetail&iid=5926

Jail Inmates in 2017, presents estimates of the inmate populations of jails based on various demographic characteristics. The full report can be accessed at https://www.bjs.gov/index. cfm?ty=pbdetail&iid=6547 Some tables are from the corresponding *Prisoners in 2017,* which uses much of the same data.

Law Enforcement Officers Killed and Assaulted, 2018 (LEOKA), is the primary resource for data about harm done to law enforcement officers. This volume provides a comprehensive sample of the report; further information can be obtained at https://www.bjs.gov/index.cfm?ty=pbdetail&iid=6547

Probation and Parole in the United States, 2016, details data about post-release inmates still in the legal system. The report can be accessed at https://www.bjs.gov/content/pub/pdf/ppus16.pdf

Update on Prisoner Recidivism: A 9-Year Follow-up Period (2005-2014) is expanded in this edition. It examines the rate, number, and percentage of prisoners who were arrested at least once during the nine years following their release. It can be found at https://www.bjs.gov/content/pub/pdf/18upr9yfup0514.pdf

Victims of Identity Theft, 2016, is new to this edition and analyses the ramifications of identity theft from judicial, financial, and relational persepctives. The full report can be found at https://www.bjs.gov/index.cfm?ty=pbdetail&iid=6467

ABOUT THE EDITOR

Shana Hertz Hattis is an editor with over a decade of experience in statistical and government research publications. Past titles include *State Profiles: The Population and Economy of Each U.S. State, Crime in the United States,* and *The Almanac of American Education.* She earned her bachelor of science in journalism and master of science in education degrees from Northwestern University.

PART 1

Capital Punishment, 2016

HIGHLIGHTS

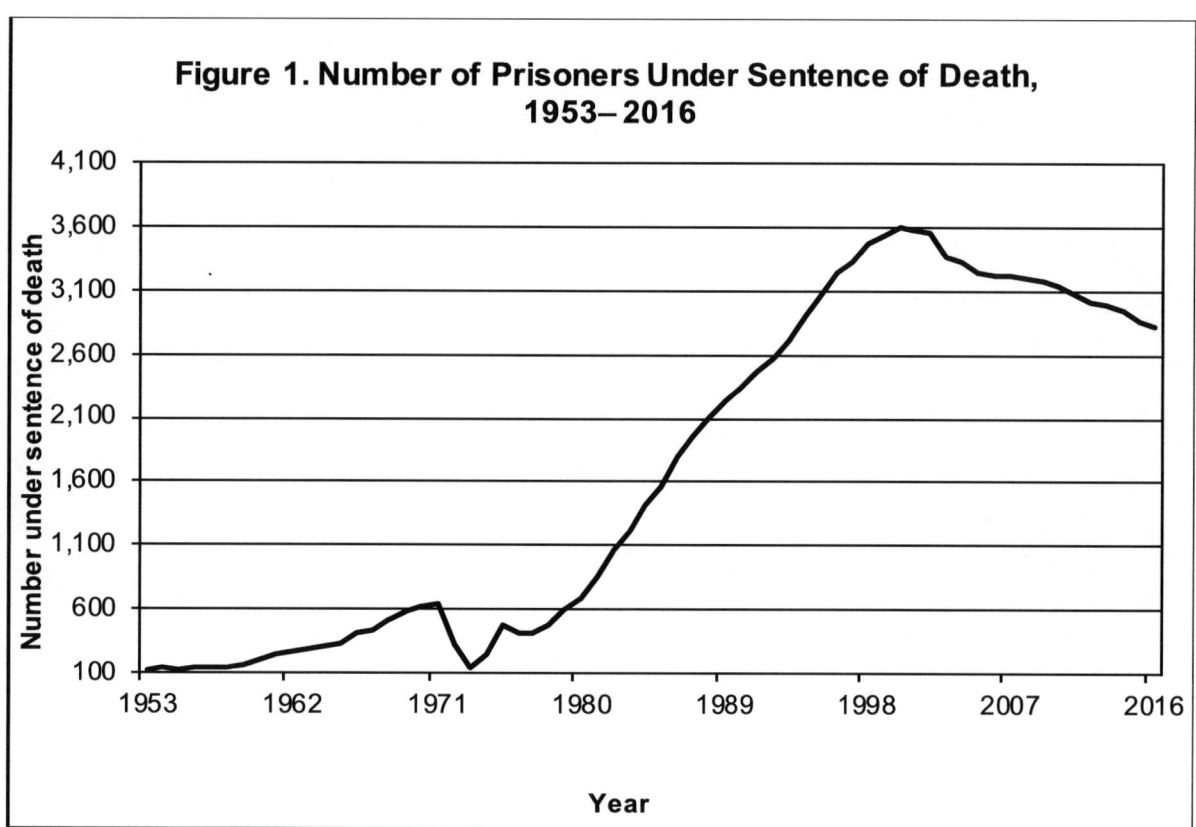

Figure 1. Number of Prisoners Under Sentence of Death, 1953–2016

- At yearend 2016, 32 states and Federal Bureau of Prisons (BOP) held 2,814 prisoners under sentence of death, 58 persons (2 percent) fewer than at yearend 2015. This was the 16th consecutive year in which this number has decreased.

- Twenty prisoners were executed in the United States in 2016; 18 were White and 2 were Black. Two prisoners were of Hispanic/Latino origin.

- The number of prisoners executed in 2016 represented the smallest number of executions since 1991, when 14 prisoners were executed.

- Thirteen states and the BOP held fewer prisoners under sentence of death at yearend 2016 than at yearend 2015, while 4 states held more prisoners and 16 states held the same number of prisoners.

- Approximately 55 percent of prisoners under sentence of death at yearend 2016 were White, while approximately 42 percent were Black and approximately 15 percent of were of Hispanic or Latino origin (in cases in which origin was known).

- Approximately 98 percent of prisoners under sentence of death were male.

- Nearly half (49 percent) of prisoners held under sentence of death were located in California (26 percent), Florida (14 percent), and Texas (9 percent). In 2016, Texas executed 7 prisoners; Florida, 1 prisoner; and California, no prisoners.

- Twelve states received a total of 32 prisoners under sentence of death in 2016; 17 states and the BOP removed 70 prisoners from under sentence of death by means other than execution.

Table 1. Status of the Death Penalty, 2015–2016

(Number.)

State	Executions		Number of prisoners under sentence of death on 12/31	
	2015	2016	2015	2016
Total	28	20	2,881	2,814
Alabama	0	2	187	183
Arizona	0	0	119	118
California	0	0	739	742
Federal Bureau of Prisons	0	0	59	58
Florida	2	1	390	382
Georgia	5	9	71	58
Louisiana	0	0	82	73
Mississippi	0	0	47	47
Missouri	6	1	NA	NA
Nevada	0	0	82	83
North Carolina	0	0	147	150
Ohio	0	0	137	140
Oklahoma	1	0	47	46
Pennsylvania	0	0	181	174
Tennessee	0	0	67	63
Texas	13	7	254	244
Virginia	1	0	NA	NA
Other jurisdictions	0	0	272 (19 jurisdictions)	253 (18 jurisdictions)

Note: Jurisdictions without the death penalty in 2016 include Alaska, Connecticut, District of Columbia, Hawaii, Illinois, Iowa, Maine, Maryland, Massachusetts, Michigan, Minnesota, New Jersey, North Dakota, Rhode Island, Vermont, and West Virginia. New Mexico repealed the death penalty for offenses committed after July 1, 2009. As of December 31, 2016, two males in New Mexico were under previously imposed death sentences.

Table 2. Prisoners Under Sentence of Death, by Region, Jurisdiction, and Race, 2015 and 2016

(Number.)

Region and jurisdiction	Prisoners under sentence of death, 12/31/15			Received under sentence of death, 2016			Removed from death row (excluding executions), 2016			Executed, 2016			Prisoners under sentence of death, 12/31/16		
	Total[1]	White[2,3]	Black[2]	Total[1]	White[2]	Black[2]	Total[1]	White[2]	Black[2]	Total[1]	White[2]	Black[2]	Total[1]	White[2]	Black[2]
U.S. Total	2,872	1,606	1,202	32	8	20	70	36	31	20	18	2	2,814	1,560	1,189
Federal[4]	59	30	28	0	0	0	1	0	1	0	0	0	58	30	27
State	2,813	1,576	1,174	32	8	20	69	36	30	20	18	2	2,756	1,530	1,162
Northeast	193	87	104	1	0	0	19	8	11	0	0	0	175	79	93
Connecticut[5]	11	5	6	0	0	0	11	5	6	0	0	0	0	0	0
New Hampshire	1	0	1	0	0	0	0	0	0	0	0	0	1	0	1
New York	0	0	0	0	0	0	0	0	0	0	0	0	0	0	0
Pennsylvania	181	82	97	1	0	0	8	3	5	0	0	0	174	79	92
Midwest	200	109	90	5	2	3	3	2	1	1	1	0	201	108	92
Indiana	13	10	3	0	0	0	0	0	0	0	0	0	13	10	3
Kansas	10	7	3	1	1	0	1	1	0	0	0	0	10	7	3
Missouri	26	18	8	0	0	0	0	0	0	1	1	0	25	17	8
Nebraska[3]	10	8	2	0	0	0	0	0	0	0	0	0	10	8	2
Ohio	138	63	74	4	1	3	2	1	1	0	0	0	140	63	76
South Dakota	3	3	0	0	0	0	0	0	0	0	0	0	3	3	0
South	1,413	742	651	17	4	12	41	21	17	19	17	2	1,370	708	644
Alabama	187	92	94	3	1	2	5	3	2	2	2	0	183	88	94
Arkansas[6]	35	16	19	1	1	0	1	1	0	0	0	0	35	16	19
Delaware	14	6	8	0	0	0	1	1	0	0	0	0	13	5	8
Florida[7]	389	235	153	3	1	2	9	3	6	1	1	0	382	232	149
Georgia	68	35	33	0	0	0	1	1	0	9	7	2	58	27	31
Kentucky	32	27	5	0	0	0	0	0	0	0	0	0	32	27	5
Louisiana	82	26	55	0	0	0	9	2	6	0	0	0	73	24	49
Mississippi	47	20	26	0	0	0	0	0	0	0	0	0	47	20	26
North Carolina	147	64	76	5	0	4	2	1	0	0	0	0	150	63	80
Oklahoma	47	23	20	1	0	1	2	1	0	0	0	0	46	22	21
South Carolina	40	17	23	0	0	0	3	1	2	0	0	0	37	16	21
Tennessee[7]	67	36	30	0	0	0	4	4	0	0	0	0	63	32	30
Texas[8]	251	141	106	4	1	3	4	3	1	7	7	0	244	132	108
Virginia	7	4	3	0	0	0	0	0	0	0	0	0	7	4	3
West	1,007	638	329	9	2	5	6	5	1	0	0	0	1,010	635	333
Arizona	119	96	18	1	0	0	2	2	0	0	0	0	118	94	18
California[3,6]	739	439	269	7	2	4	4	3	1	0	0	0	742	438	272
Colorado	3	0	3	0	0	0	0	0	0	0	0	0	3	0	3
Idaho	9	9	0	0	0	0	0	0	0	0	0	0	9	9	0
Montana	2	2	0	0	0	0	0	0	0	0	0	0	2	2	0
Nevada	82	49	31	1	0	1	0	0	0	0	0	0	83	49	32
New Mexico	2	2	0	0	0	0	0	0	0	0	0	0	2	2	0
Oregon[3]	33	29	3	0	0	0	0	0	0	0	0	0	33	29	3
Utah	9	7	1	0	0	0	0	0	0	0	0	0	9	7	1
Washington	9	5	4	0	0	0	0	0	0	0	0	0	9	5	4
Wyoming	0	0	0	0	0	0	0	0	0	0	0	0	0	0	0

Note: Some figures shown for yearend 2015 are revised from those reported in *Capital Punishment, 2014-2015 Statistical Brief* (NCJ 250638, BJS web, May 2017). The revised figures include 5 inmates who were either reported late to the National Prisoner Statistics program or were not in custody of state correctional authorities on December 31, 2015 (1 each in Ohio, Mississippi, Oklahoma, California, and Nevada), and exclude 14 inmates who were relieved of a death sentence before December 31, 2015 (3 each in Georgia and Texas; 2 in California; and 1 each in Missouri, Mississippi, Oklahoma, South Carolina, Tennessee, and Nevada).
[1]Includes American Indians and Alaska Natives, Asians, Native Hawaiians and Other Pacific Islanders, and persons of Hispanic/Latino origin for whom no other race was identified.
[2]Counts of White and Black inmates include persons of Hispanic/Latino origin.
[3]The race reported for 5 inmates has been revised from Hispanic to White (2 each in Nebraska and California and 1 in Oregon). The Hispanic/Latino origin for these inmates remains unchanged.
[4]Excludes persons held under Armed Forces jurisdiction with a military death sentence for murder.
[5]The Connecticut Supreme Court upheld a previous ruling that extended the repeal of the capital statute to include 11 males under a previously imposed death sentence. These prisoners will be resentenced to life in prison without the possibility of parole (State v. Peeler, 321 CONN. 375 (2016)).
[6]One inmate under sentence of death in Arkansas was erroneously reported as being under sentence of death in California in the 2014–2015 report.
[7]One inmate who was previously in the custody of Florida is now being reported in Tennessee where he is under a separate sentence of death.
[8]Two of the White prisoners executed were of Hispanic origin.

Table 3. Prisoners Removed from Under Sentence of Death, by Region, Jurisdiction, and Method of Removal, 2016

(Number.)

Region and jurisdiction	Not overturned by appeals court or higher court			Overturned by appeals court or higher court		
	Total	Execution	Other death[1]	Capital statute	Capital conviction[2]	Death sentence
U.S. Total..	90	20	19	11	15	25
Federal..	1	0	0	0	0	1
State..	89	20	19	11	15	24
Northeast...	19	0	0	11	3	5
Connecticut..	11	0	0	11	0	0
Pennsylvania...	8	0	0	0	3	5
Midwest..	4	1	1	0	1	1
Kansas...	1	0	1	0	0	0
Missouri...	1	1	0	0	0	0
Ohio...	2	0	0	0	1	1
South..	60	19	14	0	10	17
Alabama..	7	2	1	0	2	2
Arkansas...	1	0	0	0	1	0
Delaware...	1	0	0	0	1	0
Florida...	10	1	2	0	3	4
Georgia...	10	9	0	0	0	1
Louisiana...	9	0	3	0	3	3
North Carolina..	2	0	2	0	0	0
Oklahoma...	2	0	1	0	0	1
South Carolina..	3	0	0	0	0	3
Tennessee...	4	0	3	0	0	1
Texas...	11	7	2	0	0	2
West...	6	0	4	0	1	1
Arizona..	2	0	1	0	0	1
California...	4	0	3	0	1	0

[1]In 2016, all other deaths were due to natural causes.
[2]Includes capital conviction and sentence.

Table 4. Demographic Characteristics for Prisoners Under Sentence of Death, 2016

(Percent; number.)

Characteristic	Total yearend		Admissions		Removals	
	Number	Percent	Number	Percent	Number	Percent
Total	2,814	100.0	32	100.0	90	100.0
Sex						
Male	2,762	98.2	31	96.9	87	96.7
Female	52	1.8	1	3.1	3	3.3
Race[1]						
White	1,560	55.4	8	25.0	54	60.0
Black...	1,189	42.3	20	62.5	33	36.7
Other[2]...	65	2.3	4	12.5	3	3.3
Hispanic/Latino Origin[3]						
Hispanic/Latino	378	13.4	3	9.4	10	11.1
Non-Hispanic/Latino	2,175	77.3	24	75.0	68	75.6
Unknown...	261	9.3	5	15.6	12	13.3
Age						
18 to 19 years...	1	-	1	3.1	0	0.0
20 to 24 years...	8	0.3	0	0.0	0	0.0
25 to 29 years...	67	2.4	4	12.5	2	2.2
30 to 34 years...	167	5.9	9	28.1	3	3.3
35 to 39 years...	334	11.9	8	25.0	14	15.6
40 to 44 years...	441	15.7	4	12.5	14	15.6
45 to 49 years...	509	18.1	3	9.4	13	14.4
50 to 54 years...	448	15.9	1	3.1	9	10.0
55 to 59 years...	380	13.5	1	3.1	10	11.1
60 to 64 years...	233	8.3	1	3.1	9	10.0
65 years and older	226	8.0	0	0.0	16	17.8
Average Age (Years)						
Mean	49	X	38	X	51	X
Median	48	X	38	X	49	X
Education[4]						
8th grade or less...	275	9.8	3	9.7	20	22.2
9th to 11th grade	784	27.9	8	25.8	19	21.1
High school graduate/GED	983	34.9	6	19.4	33	36.7
Any college...	203	7.2	2	6.4	4	4.4
Unknown...	569	20.2	12	38.7	14	15.6
Median Education Level						
Grade	12th	X	11th	X	11th	X
Marital Status[5]						
Total	2,814	100.0	32	100.0	90	100.0
Married...	515	18.3	2	6.3	15	16.7
Divorced/separated...	477	17.0	2	6.3	21	23.3
Widowed	86	3.1	0	0.0	2	2.2
Never married	1,357	48.2	15	46.9	41	45.6
Unknown...	379	13.5	13	40.6	11	12.2

Note: Detail may not sum to total due to rounding.
X = Not applicable.
- = Less than 0.05 percent.
[1]Percentages for White, Black, and all other races include persons of Hispanic/Latino origin.
[2]At yearend 2016, prisoners of all other races consisted of 19 American Indians or Alaska Natives (AIANs), 40 Asians, and 6 Native Hawaiian or Other Pacific Islanders. During 2016, one AIAN prisoner and three Asian prisoners were admitted, while two AIAN prisoners and one Asian prisoner were removed.
[3]Excludes prisoners with unknown origin: 261 at yearend, 5 admissions, and 12 removals.
[4]Excludes prisoners with unknown education level: 569 at yearend, 13 admissions, and 14 removals.
[5]Excludes prisoners with unknown marital status: 379 at yearend, 13 admissions, and 11 removals.

Table 5. Advance Count of Executions, January 1–December 31, 2017

(Number.)

Year	Number of executions
Total	23
Texas	7
Arkansas	4
Alabama	3
Florida	3
Ohio	2
Virginia	2
Missouri	1
Georgia	1

Table 6. Authorized Method of Execution, by State, 2016

(Percent; number.)

State	Lethal injection	Electrocution	Lethal gas	Hanging	Firing squad	Nitrogen hypoxia
Total	34	8	3	3	2	1
Alabama	√	√				
Arizona[1]	√		√			
Arkansas[2]	√	√				
California	√					
Colorado	√					
Delaware[3]	√			√		
Florida	√	√				
Georgia	√					
Idaho	√					
Indiana	√					
Kansas	√					
Kentucky[4]	√	√				
Louisiana	√					
Mississippi	√					
Missouri	√		√			
Montana	√					
Nebraska	√					
Nevada	√					
New Hampshire[5]	√			√		
New Mexico[6]	√					
New York	√					
North Carolina	√					
Ohio	√					
Oklahoma[7]	√	√			√	√
Oregon	√					
Pennsylvania	√					
South Carolina	√	√				
South Dakota	√					
Tennessee[8]	√	√				
Texas	√					
Utah[9]	√				√	
Virginia	√	√				
Washington	√			√		
Wyoming[9]	√		√			√

Note: The method of execution of federal prisoners is lethal injection, pursuant to 28 C.F.R. Part 26. For offenses prosecuted under the Violent Crime Control and Law Enforcement Act of 1994, the execution method is that of the state in which the conviction took place (18 U.S.C. 3596).
[1]Authorizes lethal injection for persons sentenced after November 23, 1992; inmates sentenced before that date may select lethal injection or gas.
[2]Authorizes lethal injection for those whose offense occurred on or after July 4, 1983; inmates whose offense occurred before that date may select lethal injection or electrocution. Electrocution is the authorized method of use if lethal injection is invalidated by an unappealable court order.
[3]Authorizes hanging if lethal injection is held to be unconstitutional by a court of competent jurisdiction.
[4]Authorizes lethal injection for persons sentenced on or after March 31, 1998; inmates sentenced before that date may select lethal injection or electrocution.
[5]Authorizes hanging only if lethal injection cannot be given.
[6]Authorizes lethal injection for those whose capital offense occurred prior to July 1, 2009.
[7]Authorizes nitrogen hypoxia if lethal injection is held to be unconstitutional, electrocution if both lethal injection and nitrogen hypoxia are held to be unconstitutional, and firing squad if all other methods are held to be unconstitutional.
[8]Authorizes lethal injection for those whose capital offense occurred after December 31, 1998; inmates whose offense occurred before that date may select electrocution by written waiver. Electrocution is the authorized method if a court or the commissioner of corrections determines that lethal injection cannot be given.
[9]Authorizes firing squad if lethal injection is held unconstitutional. Inmates who selected execution by firing squad prior to May 3, 2004, may still be entitled to execution by that method.

Table 7. Number of Persons Executed Under Civil Authority in the United States, 1930–2016

(Number.)

Year	Executions
1930	155
1931	153
1932	140
1933	160
1934	168
1935	199
1936	195
1937	147
1938	190
1939	160
1940	124
1941	123
1942	147
1943	131
1944	120
1945	117
1946	131
1947	153
1948	119
1949	119
1950	82
1951	105
1952	83
1953	62
1954	81
1955	76
1956	65
1957	65
1958	49
1959	49
1960	56
1961	42
1962	47
1963	21
1964	15
1965	7
1966	1
1967	2
1968	0
1969	0
1970	0
1971	0
1972	0
1973	0
1974	0

(Number.)

Year	Executions
1975	0
1976	0
1977	1
1978	0
1979	2
1980	0
1981	1
1982	2
1983	5
1984	21
1985	18
1986	18
1987	25
1988	11
1989	16
1990	23
1991	14
1992	31
1993	38
1994	31
1995	56
1996	45
1997	74
1998	68
1999	98
2000	85
2001	66
2002	71
2003	65
2004	59
2005	60
2006	53
2007	42
2008	37
2009	52
2010	46
2011	43
2012	43
2013	39
2014	35
2015	28
2016	20

Table 8. Number of Persons Under Sentence of Death, 1953–2016

(Number.)

Year	Number of prisoners under sentence of death
1953	131
1954	147
1955	125
1956	146
1957	151
1958	147
1959	164
1960	212
1961	257
1962	267
1963	297
1964	315
1965	331
1966	406
1967	435
1968	517
1969	575
1970	631
1971	642
1972	334
1973	134
1974	244
1975	488
1976	420
1977	423
1978	482
1979	593
1980	692
1981	860
1982	1,066
1983	1,209
1984	1,420
1985	1,575
1986	1,800
1987	1,967
1988	2,117
1989	2,243
1990	2,346
1991	2,465
1992	2,580
1993	2,727
1994	2,905
1995	3,064
1996	3,242
1997	3,328
1998	3,465
1999	3,527
2000	3,601
2001	3,577
2002	3,562
2003	3,377
2004	3,320
2005	3,245
2006	3,228
2007	3,215
2008	3,210
2009	3,173
2010	3,139
2011	3,065
2012	3,011
2013	2,983
2014	2,942
2015	2,881
2016	2,814

Table 9. Admissions to and Removal from Under Sentence of Death, 1973–2016

(Number.)

Year	Admissions	Removals
1973	44	240
1974	161	55
1975	318	67
1976	249	317
1977	159	156
1978	211	150
1979	172	61
1980	202	101
1981	249	84
1982	287	79
1983	266	123
1984	305	90
1985	291	130
1986	320	109
1987	311	142
1988	317	165
1989	275	149
1990	270	152
1991	285	159
1992	300	173
1993	299	162
1994	330	153
1995	325	171
1996	323	155
1997	283	187
1998	310	174
1999	287	221
2000	235	173
2001	164	194
2002	172	191
2003	156	346
2004	140	198
2005	143	216
2006	125	145
2007	129	140
2008	122	136
2009	118	166
2010	116	143
2011	84	153
2012	85	128
2013	85	115
2014	68	111
2015	54	120
2016	32	90

Table 10. Number of Prisoners Under Sentence of Death, by Race, 1968–2016

(Percent; number.)

Year	White	Black	All other races
1968	243	271	3
1969	263	310	2
1970	293	335	3
1971	306	332	4
1972	167	166	1
1973	64	68	2
1974	110	128	6
1975	218	262	8
1976	225	195	0
1977	229	192	2
1978	281	197	4
1979	354	236	3
1980	424	264	4
1981	499	353	8
1982	613	441	12
1983	692	505	12
1984	806	598	16
1985	896	664	15
1986	1,013	762	25
1987	1,128	813	26
1988	1,235	848	34
1989	1,308	898	37
1990	1,368	940	38
1991	1,449	979	37
1992	1,511	1,031	38
1993	1,575	1,111	41
1994	1,653	1,203	49
1995	1,732	1,284	48
1996	1,833	1,358	51
1997	1,864	1,408	56
1998	1,917	1,489	59
1999	1,960	1,515	65
2000	1,989	1,541	71
2001	1,968	1,538	71
2002	1,931	1,554	72
2003	1,883	1,417	78
2004	1,856	1,390	74
2005	1,802	1,366	77
2006	1,806	1,353	74
2007	1,806	1,338	71
2008	1,795	1,343	72
2009	1,779	1,318	76
2010	1,743	1,309	87
2011	1,721	1,274	70
2012	1,684	1,258	69
2013	1,670	1,251	62
2014	1,647	1,233	62
2015	1,606	1,202	64
2016	1,560	1,189	65

METHODOLOGY

Capital punishment information is collected annually as part of the Bureau of Justice Statistics' (BJS) National Prisoner Statistics program (NPS-8). This data series is collected in two parts:

- Data on persons under sentence of death are obtained from the department of corrections in each jurisdiction currently authorizing capital punishment.

- The status of death penalty statutes is obtained from the Office of the Attorney General in each of the 50 states, the U.S. Attorney's Office in the District of Columbia, and Federal Bureau of Prisons for the federal government.

Data collection forms are available on the BJS website at www. bjs.gov.

The NPS-8 covers all persons under a state or federal civil sentence of death at any time during the year. This includes capital offenders transferred from prison to mental hospitals and those who may have escaped from custody. It excludes persons sentenced to death under the Uniform Code of Military Justice and those whose death sentences have been overturned by a court or executive action, regardless of their current incarceration status.

Statistics in this report may differ from data collected by other organizations for various reasons:

- The NPS-8 adds prisoners to the population under sentence of death not at sentencing, but at the time they are admitted to a state or federal correctional facility.

- If prisoners entered prison under a death sentence or were reported as being relieved of a death sentence in one year but the admission or removal had occurred in a previous year, counts are adjusted to reflect the actual dates of sentence or removal.

- NPS-8 counts are for the last day of the calendar year and will differ from counts for more recent periods.

DEFINITIONS

Aggravating factor—Specific elements of a crime defined by statute. When present, these factors may allow a jury to impose a death sentence for a person convicted of a capital offense. Sometimes these are also called aggravating circumstances.

Capital conviction—A formal declaration that a defendant is guilty of a capital offense, made by the verdict of a jury, the decision of a judge, or a guilty plea by the defendant in a court of law.

Capital offense—A criminal offense punishable by death. Offenses that are eligible for a death sentence are defined by statute in each jurisdiction that authorizes capital punishment. The most common is first-degree murder accompanied by at least one aggravating factor.

Lists of capital offenses by state and by federal can be found at the end of this section.

Capital punishment—The process of sentencing convicted offenders to death for the most serious crimes and carrying out that sentence. The specific offenses and circumstances which determine if a crime is eligible for a death sentence are defined by statute and are prescribed by Congress or a state legislature.

Capital statute—State or federal laws dictating specific crimes that are eligible for a death sentence and specific procedures to be followed in carrying out such sentences.

Civil authority— For the purposes of this report, the state or federal entities responsible for implementation and enforcement of capital punishment laws, excluding military authorities.

Commutation—Reduction of a death sentence by a governor or a board of advisors empaneled to review sentences. Criteria for granting a commutation vary by state. The new sentence can be to life or a term of years.

Death row—A slang term referring to the area of a prison in which prisoners under sentence of death are housed. Usage of the term "death row" continues despite the fact that many states do not maintain a separate unit or facility for prisoners under sentence of death.

Received under sentence of death—Persons admitted to prison after being sentenced to death by a court.

Removal from under sentence of death—A prisoner who was previously under sentence of death and is no longer included in the count of persons under sentence of death. An inmate can be relieved of a death sentence by several methods: execution, death by causes other than execution, commutation, or an overturned capital conviction or sentence.

Sentence of death—A sentence imposed by a court for a capital offense which authorizes the state to execute a convicted offender.

Yearend—As of December 31 of the calendar year.

Capital Offenses, by State, 2016

State	Offenses
Alabama	Intentional murder (Ala. Stat. Ann. 13A-5-40(a)(1)-(18)) with 10 aggravating factors (Ala. Stat. Ann. 13A-5-49).
Arizona	First-degree murder, including premeditated murder and felony murder, accompanied by at least 1 of 14 aggravating factors (A.R.S. ß 13-703(F)).
Arkansas	Capital murder (Ark. Code Ann. ß 5-10-101) with a finding of at least 1 of 10 aggravating circumstances; treason (Ark. Code Ann. ß 5-51-201).
California	First-degree murder with special circumstances; military sabotage; death in the course of train wrecking; treason; perjury resulting in execution of an innocent person; fatal assault by a prisoner serving a life sentence.
Colorado	First-degree murder with at least 1 of 17 aggravating factors; first-degree kidnapping resulting in death; treason.
Delaware	First-degree murder (11 Del. C. ß 636) with at least one statutory aggravating circumstance (11 Del. C. ß 4209).
Florida	First-degree murder with aggravating factors; felony murder.
Georgia	Murder with aggravating circumstances; rape, armed robbery, or kidnapping with bodily injury or ransom when the victim dies; aircraft hijacking; treason (O.C.G.A. ß 17-10-30).
Idaho	First-degree murder with aggravating factors; first-degree kidnapping; perjury resulting in the execution of an innocent person.
Indiana	Murder with 18 aggravating circumstances (I.C. 35-50-2-9).
Kansas	Intentional and premeditated killing of a person in one or more of seven different circumstances (K.S.A. 21-5401).
Kentucky	Capital murder with the presence of at least one statutory aggravating circumstance; capital kidnapping (K.R.S. 532.025).
Louisiana	First-degree murder with aggravating circumstances (La. R.S. 14:30); treason (La. R.S. 14:113).
Mississippi	Capital murder with aggravating circumstances (Miss. Code Ann. ß 97-3-19(2)); aircraft piracy (Miss. Code Ann. ß 97-25-55(1)).
Missouri	First-degree murder with at least 1 statutory aggravating circumstance (565.020 R.S.M.O. 2000).
Montana	Capital murder with one of nine aggravating circumstances (Mont. Code Ann. ß 46-18-303); aggravated kidnapping; felony murder; capital sexual intercourse without consent (Mont. Code Ann. ß 45-5-503).
Nebraska	First-degree murder with a finding of one or more statutory aggravating circumstances.
Nevada	First-degree murder with at least 1 of 15 aggravating circumstances (N.R.S. 200.030, 200.033, 200.035).
New Hampshire	Murder committed in the course of rape, kidnapping, drug crimes, or home invasion; killing of a police officer, judge, or prosecutor; murder for hire; murder by an inmate while serving a sentence of life without parole (R.S.A. 630:1, R.S.A. 630:5).
New Mexico	First-degree murder with at least one of seven aggravating factors (N.M.S.A. 1978 ß 31-20A-5). New Mexico enacted a prospective appeal of its capital statute as of July 1, 2009. Offenders who committed capital offenses prior to that date are eligible for the death penalty.
New York	First-degree murder with 1 of 13 aggravating factors (NY Penal Law ß125.27). The New York Court of Appeals has held that a portion of New York's death penalty sentencing statute (C.P.L. 400.27) was unconstitutional (People v. Taylor, 9 N.Y.3d 129 (2007)). No legislative action has been taken to amend the statute. As a result, capital cases are no longer pursued in New York.
North Carolina	First-degree murder (N.C.G.S. ß14-17) with the finding of at least 1 of 11 statutory aggravating circumstances (N.C.G.S. ß 15A-2000).
Ohio	Aggravated murder with at least 1 of 10 aggravating circumstances (O.R.C. 2903.01, 2929.02, and 2929.04).
Oklahoma	First-degree murder in conjunction with a finding of at least one of eight statutorily defined aggravating circumstances.
Oregon	Aggravated murder (O.R.S. 163.095).
Pennsylvania	First-degree murder with 18 aggravating circumstances.
South Carolina	Murder with at least 1 of 12 aggravating circumstances (ß 16-3-20(C)(a)).

South Dakota	First-degree murder with 1 of 10 aggravating circumstances (S.D.C.L. 23A-27A-1).
Tennessee	First-degree murder (Tenn. Code Ann. ß 39-13-202) with 1 of 15 aggravating circumstances (Tenn. Code Ann. ß 39-13-204).
Texas	Criminal homicide with one of nine aggravating circumstances (Tex. Penal Code ß 19.03).
Utah	Aggravated murder (Utah Code Ann. ß 76-5-202).
Virginia	Premeditated murder with 1 of 15 aggravating circumstances (VA Code ß 18.2-31(1-15)).
Washington	Aggravated first-degree murder.
Wyoming	First-degree murder; murder during the commission of sexual assault, sexual abuse of a minor, arson, robbery, burglary, escape, resisting arrest, kidnapping, or abuse of a minor under 16 (W.S.A. ß 6-2-101(a)).

Federal Capital Offenses, 2016

Statute	Description
8 U.S.C. 1342	Murder related to the smuggling of aliens.
18 U.S.C. 32-34	Destruction of aircraft, motor vehicles, or related facilities resulting in death.
18 U.S.C. 36	Murder committed during a drug-related drive-by shooting.
18 U.S.C. 37	Murder committed at an airport serving international civil aviation.
18 U.S.C. 115(b)(3) [by cross-reference to 18 U.S.C. 1111]	Retaliatory murder of a member of the immediate family of law enforcement officials.
18 U.S.C. 241, 242, 245, 247	Civil rights offenses resulting in death.
18 U.S.C. 351 [by cross-reference to 18 U.S.C. 1111]	Murder of a member of Congress, an important executive official, or a Supreme Court Justice.
18 U.S.C. 794	Espionage.
18 U.S.C. 844(d), (f), (i)	Death resulting from offenses involving transportation of explosives, destruction of government property, or destruction of property related to foreign or interstate commerce.
18 U.S.C. 924(i)	Murder committed by the use of a firearm during a crime of violence or a drug-trafficking crime.
18 U.S.C. 930	Murder committed in a federal government facility.
18 U.S.C. 1091	Genocide.
18 U.S.C. 1111	First-degree murder.
18 U.S.C. 1114	Murder of a federal judge or law enforcement official.
18 U.S.C. 1116	Murder of a foreign official.
18 U.S.C. 1118	Murder by a federal prisoner.
18 U.S.C. 1119	Murder of a U.S. national in a foreign country.
18 U.S.C. 1120	Murder by an escaped federal prisoner already sentenced to life imprisonment.
18 U.S.C. 1121	Murder of a state or local law enforcement official or other person aiding in a federal investigation; murder of a state correctional officer.
18 U.S.C. 1201	Murder during a kidnapping.
18 U.S.C. 1203	Murder during a hostage taking.
18 U.S.C. 1503	Murder of a court officer or juror.
18 U.S.C. 1512	Murder with the intent of preventing testimony by a witness, victim, or informant.
18 U.S.C. 1513	Retaliatory murder of a witness, victim, or informant.
18 U.S.C. 1716	Mailing of injurious articles with intent to kill or resulting in death.
18 U.S.C. 1751 [by cross-reference to 18 U.S.C. 1111]	Assassination or kidnapping resulting in the death of the President or Vice President.
18 U.S.C. 1958	Murder for hire.
18 U.S.C. 1959	Murder involved in a racketeering offense.
18 U.S.C. 1992	Willful wrecking of a train resulting in death.
18 U.S.C. 2113	Bank robbery-related murder or kidnapping.
18 U.S.C. 2119	Murder related to a carjacking.
18 U.S.C. 2245	Murder related to rape or child molestation.
18 U.S.C. 2251	Murder related to sexual exploitation of children.

18 U.S.C. 2280	Murder committed during an offense against maritime navigation.
18 U.S.C. 2281	Murder committed during an offense against a maritime fixed platform.
18 U.S.C. 2332	Terrorist murder of a U.S. national in another country.
18 U.S.C. 2332a	Murder by the use of a weapon of mass destruction.
18 U.S.C. 2340	Murder involving torture.
18 U.S.C. 2381	Treason.
21 U.S.C. 848(e)	Murder related to a continuing criminal enterprise or related murder of a federal, state, or local law enforcement officer.
49 U.S.C. 1472-1473	Death resulting from aircraft hijacking.

PART 2

Crimes Against Persons with Disabilities, 2009–2015

HIGHLIGHTS

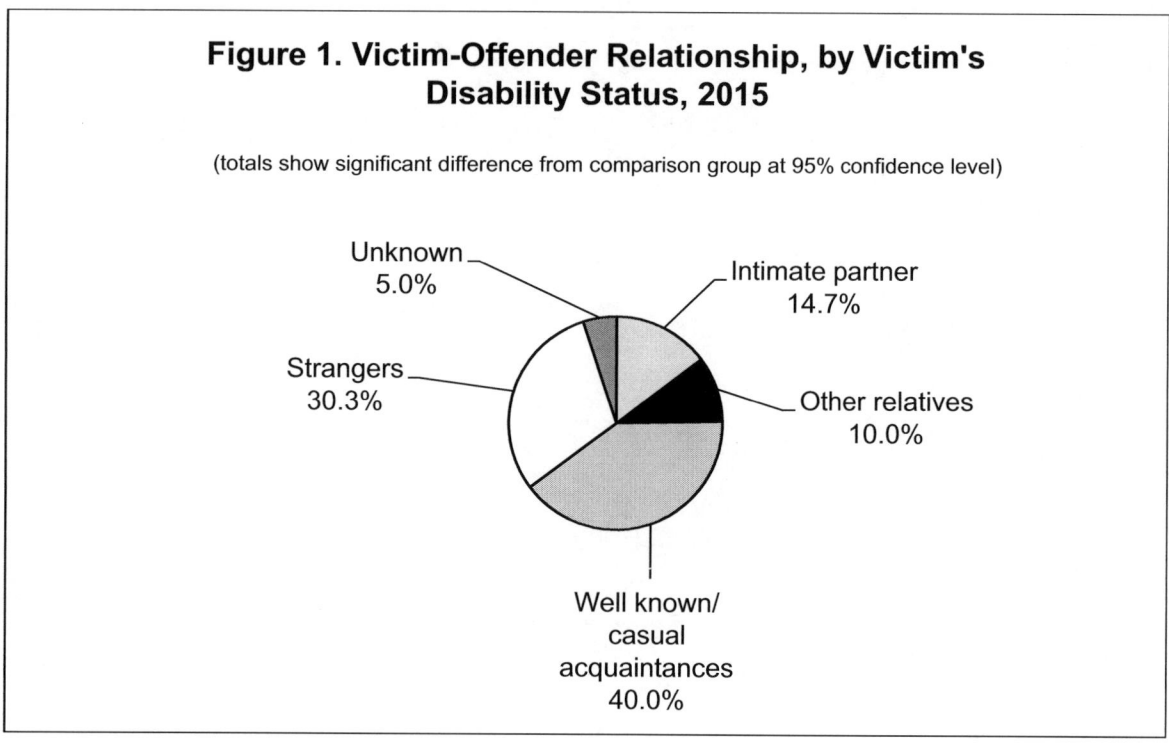

Figure 1. Victim-Offender Relationship, by Victim's Disability Status, 2015

(totals show significant difference from comparison group at 95% confidence level)

- Unknown 5.0%
- Intimate partner 14.7%
- Strangers 30.3%
- Other relatives 10.0%
- Well known/ casual acquaintances 40.0%

- In 2015, the rate of violent victimization against persons with disabilities (29.5 victimizations per 1,000 persons age 12 years or over) was 2.5 times the unadjusted rate for persons without disabilities. The rate for persons with disabilities has been at least double the rate for persons without disabilities for every year since 2009.

- Among those with disabilities, persons age 12 to 15 years (144.1 per 1,000 persons age 12 or older) had the highest rate of violent victimization among all age groups measured, while those age 65 years and over had no statistically significant difference between the rates of violent victimization by disability status.

- During the period from 2011 to 2015, persons with cognitive disabilities had the highest rates of total violent crime (57.9 per 1,000), serious violent crime (22.3 per 1,000), and simple assault (35.6 per 1,000) among the disability types measured. Persons with hearing disabilities (15.7 per 1,000) had the lowest rates of total violent victimization among the disability types examined.

- For each racial and ethnic group measured, persons with disabilities had higher violent victimization rates than persons without disabilities during the period from 2011 to 2015. Persons of two or more races had the highest rates of violent victimization among persons with disabilities (128.5 per 1,000) and without disabilities (33.6 per 1,000).

- The rate of violent victimization against males with disabilities was 31.8 per 1,000 males, compared to 14.1 per 1,000 males without disabilities. For females, the rate of violent victimization was 32.8 per 1,000, compared to 11.4 per 1,000 females without disabilities.

- A higher percentage of violence against persons with disabilities (40 percent) was committed by persons who knew the victims knew well or were casual acquaintances than against persons without disabilities (32 percent).

- Approximately 20 percent of violent crime victims with disabilities believed they were targeted due to their disability.

Table 1. Rate of Violent Victimization and Average Annual Number of Persons, by Victim's Disability Status and Age, 2011–2015

(Rate per 1,000 persons.)

Age of victim	Persons with disabilities		Persons without disabilities	
	Average annual number	Rate per 1,000 persons with disabilities[1]	Average annual number	Rate per 1,000 persons without disabilities*
Total	37,157,340	32.3	226,696,790	20.4
12–15..	938,300	144.1	15,682,970	38.8
16–19..	966,680	86.6	16,097,530	31.4
20–24..	1,276,180	83.4	20,982,730	29.6
25–34..	2,493,140	64.5	39,370,470	26.3
35–49..	5,387,430	58.2	56,038,570	19.7
50–64..	10,482,880	31.2	50,818,180	12.7
65 or older..	15,612,740	4.8	27,706,350	4.0

Note: Based on the noninstitutionalized U.S. residential population age 12 or older.
* = Comparison group.
[1]Significant difference from comparison group at 95% confidence level for all of the values in this column.

Table 2. Rates of Violent Victimization Against Persons With and Without Disabilities, by Type of Crime, 2011–2015

(Rate per 1,000 persons.)

Type of crime	Persons with disabilities[1]	Persons without disabilities*
Total crime	32.3	12.7
Serious violent crime..	12.7	4.0
Rape/sexual assault..	2.1	0.6
Robbery	4.7	1.3
Aggravated assault...	5.9	2.1
Simple assault..	19.6	8.7

Note: Based on the noninstitutionalized U.S. residential population age 12 or older. Rates for persons without disabilities were adjusted using direct standardization with the population with disabilities as the standard population.
* = Comparison group.
[1]Significant difference from comparison group at 95% confidence level for values in this column.

Table 3. Rates of Violent Victimization Against Persons With and Without Disabilities, by Victim Characteristics, 2011–2015

(Rate per 1,000 persons.)

Victim characteristic	Persons with disabilities[1]	Persons without disabilities[2]*
Total crime	32.3	12.7
Sex		
Male	31.8	14.1
Female	32.8	11.4
Race/Hispanic Origin[3]		
White...	30.8	12.0
Black...	31.0	18.2
Hispanic..	29.0	13.0
Other[4]..	28.0	6.4
Two or more races	128.5	33.6

Note: Based on the noninstitutionalized U.S. residential population age 12 or older.
* = Comparison group.
[1]Significant difference from comparison group at 95% confidence level.
[2]Rates for persons without disabilities were adjusted using direct standardization with the population with disabilities as the standard population.
[3]Excludes persons of Hispanic or Latino origin, unless specified.
[4]Includes persons identified as American Indian or Alaska Native and Asian, Native Hawaiian, or Other Pacific Islander.

Table 4. Rate of Violent Victimization Against Persons With Disabilities, by Disability Type and Type of Crime, 2011–2015

(Rate per 1,000 persons age 12 or older, except for independent living disabilities, which is per 1,000 persons age 15 or older.)

Disability type	Total violent crime	Serious violent crime	Simple assault
Hearing*..	15.7	7.8	7.9
Vision	28.8 A	11.3 A	17.6 A
Ambulatory...	29.4 A	13.1 A	16.3 A
Cognitive..	57.9 A	22.3 A	35.6 A
Self-care...	25.9 A	9.9	16.0 A
Independent living	30.8 A	12.1 A	18.8 A

Note: Based on the noninstitutionalized U.S. residential population age 12 or older. Includes persons with multiple disability types. Serious violent crime includes rape, sexual assault, robbery, and aggravated assault.
* = Comparison group.
A = Significant difference from comparison group at 95% confidence level.

Table 5. Rate of Violent Victimization, by Victim's Sex and Disability Type, 2011–2015

(Rate per 1,000 persons age 12 or older, except for independent living disability, which is per 1,000 persons age 15 or older.)

Disability type	Male*	Female
Hearing...	15.0	16.8
Vision	24.6	32.3
Ambulatory...	29.6	29.3
Cognitive..	55.4	60.3
Self-care...	24.7	26.8
Independent living	26.5	33.8 B

Note: Based on the noninstitutionalized U.S. residential population age 12 or older. Includes persons with multiple disability types.
* = Comparison group.
B = Significant difference from comparison group at 90% confidence level.

Table 6. Percent of Violence Against Persons with Disabilities, by Type of Crime and Number of Disability Types, 2011–2015

(Percent.)

Type of crime	Total	Single disability type*	Multiple disability types
Total	100.0	46.4	53.6 A
Serious violent crime............................	100.0	45.4	54.6 A
Rape/sexual assault.............................	100.0	34.6	65.4
Robbery	100.0	48.4	51.6
Aggravated assault..............................	100.0	46.7	53.3
Simple assault..	100.0	47.0	53.0 B

Note: Based on the noninstitutionalized U.S. residential population age 12 or older. For persons age 12 to 14, independent living disabilities is not included as a disability type.
A = Significant difference from comparison group at 95% confidence level.
B = Significant difference from comparison group at 90% confidence level.

Table 7. Rate of Violent Victimization, by Number of Disability Types and Type of Crime, 2011–2015

(Rate per 1,000 persons.)

Type of crime	Single disability type*	Multiple disability types
Total	29.6	35.2 A
Serious violent crime............................	11.4	14.1 A
Rape/sexual assault.............................	1.4	2.8 A
Robbery	4.5	5.0
Aggravated assault..............................	5.5	6.4
Simple assault..	18.2	21.1 B

Note: Based on the noninstitutionalized U.S. residential population age 12 or older. For persons age 12 to 14, independent living disabilities is not included as a disability type.
* = Comparison group.
A = Significant difference from comparison group at 95% confidence level.
B = Significant difference from comparison group at 90% confidence level.

Table 8. Victim-Offender Relationship, by Victim's Disability Status, 2011–2015

(Percent.)

Type of crime	Persons with disabilities	Persons without disabilities[1]*
Total	100.0	100.0
Intimate partner[1]...	14.7	12.8
Other relatives[2]	10.0 A	6.4
Well known/casual acquaintances..	40.0 A	32.5
Strangers	30.3 A	39.4
Unknown..	5.0 A	8.8

Note: Based on the noninstitutionalized U.S. residential population age 12 or older.
* = Comparison group.
A = Significant difference from comparison group at 95% confidence level.
[1]Includes spouses, ex-spouses, boyfriends, and girlfriends.
[2]Includes parents, children, and other relatives.

Table 9. Time Violent Crime Occurred, by Victim's Disability Status, 2011–2015

(Percent.)

Type of crime	Persons with disabilities	Persons without disabilities*
Total	100.0	100.0
Daytime (6 a.m.–6 p.m.)	57.1	53.6
Nighttime (6 p.m.–6 a.m.)..	38.2 B	42.7
Unknown..	4.8	3.7

Note: Based on the noninstitutionalized U.S. residential population age 12 or older.
* = Comparison group.
B = Significant difference from comparison group at 90% confidence level.

Table 10. Percent of Violent Crime Reported to Police, by Victim's Disability Status and Disability Type, 2011–2015

(Percent.)

Disability status and type	Reported to police
Persons without disabilities*	45.5
Persons with disabilities[1]	48.9
Single disability type	45.4
Multiple disability types	51.9 A
Disability type[2]	
Hearing...	51.1
Vision...	42.3
Ambulatory..	58.4 A
Cognitive	47.4
Self-care..	53.6 B
Independent living...	53.9 A

Note: Based on the noninstitutionalized U.S. residential population age 12 or older.
* = Comparison group.
A = Significant difference from comparison group at 95% confidence level.
B = Significant difference from comparison group at 90% confidence level.
[1]For persons ages 12 to 14, independent living disabilities are not included as a disability type.
[2]Includes persons with multiple disability types.

Table 11. Person Who Notified Police of Violent Crime, by Victim's Disability Status, 2011–2015

(Percent.)

Person who notified police	Persons with disabilities	Persons without disabilities*
Total	100.0	100.0
Victim	64.0	61.7
Other household member	6.2 A	10.4
Someone official	5.6 A	8.3
Someone else	19.6 A	10.7
Police were at the scene	2.5 A	6.0
Offender was a police officer	0.2 C	0.3
Police notified some other way	1.8	2.1

Note: Based on the noninstitutionalized U.S. residential population age 12 or older. Someone official includes a guard, apartment manager, school official, and other officials. In less than 1% of cases, the person who contacted police was unknown.
* = Comparison group.
A = Significant difference from comparison group at 95% confidence level.
C = Interpret with caution. Estimate is based on 10 or fewer sample cases or coefficient of variation is greater than 50%.

Table 12. Reasons for Not Reporting Violent Crime to Police, by Victim's Disability Status, 2011–2015

(Percent.)

Reason for not reporting crime to police	Persons with disabilities	Persons without disabilities*
Dealt with another way[1]	40.0	42.9
Other[2]	36.8	33.1
Police would not help[3]	20.8	18.8
Was not important enough to victim[4]	20.4	24.2
Police could not do anything[5]	3.0	3.3
Insurance would not cover	0.1 C	0.2 C

Note: Based on the noninstitutionalized U.S. residential population age 12 or older. Detail may sum to more than 100% because more than one response was allowed.
* = Comparison group.
[1]Includes reported to another official and private or personal matter.
[2]Includes did not want to get offender in trouble with the law, was advised not to report to police, was afraid of reprisal, reporting was too inconvenient, did not know why it was not reported, and other reasons.
[3]Includes police would not think it was important enough, police would be inefficient, police would be biased, and offender was a police officer.
[4]Includes minor or unsuccessful crime, offender was a child, and not clear if a crime occurred.
[5]Includes did not find out until too late, could not recover or identify property, and could not find or identify offender.

Table 13. Percent of Violent Crime Victims in Which Assistance from a Nonpolice Victim Services Agency Was Received, by Victim's Disability Status, 2011–2015

(Percent.)

Disability status of victim	Percent of violent victimizations
Persons with disabilities	12.3 A
Persons without disabilities*	8.3

Note: Based on the noninstitutionalized U.S. residential population age 12 or older.
* = Comparison group.
A = Significant difference from comparison group at 95% confidence level.

METHODOLOGY

About the Data

The use of age-adjusted rates: The differences in age distributions between the two populations must be taken into account when making direct comparisons of the violent victimization rate between persons with and without disabilities. The age distribution of persons with disabilities differs considerably from that of persons without disabilities, and violent crime victimization rates vary significantly with age. According to the U.S. Census Bureau's American Community Survey (ACS), persons with disabilities are generally older than persons without disabilities. The age adjustment standardizes the rate of violence to show what the rate would be if persons without disabilities had the same age distribution as persons with disabilities.

Survey Coverage

The National Crime Victimization Survey (NCVS) is an ongoing data collection conducted by the U.S. Census Bureau for the Bureau of Justice Statistics (BJS). The NCVS is a self-report survey in which interviewed persons are asked about the number and characteristics of victimizations they experienced during the prior 6 months. The NCVS collects information on nonfatal personal crimes (rape or sexual assault, robbery, aggravated and simple assault, and personal larceny) and household property crimes (burglary, motor vehicle theft, and other theft) both reported and not reported to police. In addition to providing annual level and change estimates on criminal victimization, the NCVS is the primary source of information on the nature of criminal victimization incidents. Survey respondents provide information about themselves (e.g., age, sex, race and Hispanic origin, marital status, education level, and income) and whether they experienced a victimization.

The NCVS collects information for each victimization incident about the offender (e.g., age, race and Hispanic origin, sex, and victim–offender relationship), characteristics of the crime (including time and place of occurrence, use of weapons, nature of injury, and economic consequences), whether the crime was reported to police, reasons the crime was or was not reported, and victims' experiences with the criminal justice system. The NCVS is administered to persons age 12 or older from a nationally representative sample of households in the United States. The NCVS defines a household as a group of members who all reside at a sampled address. Persons are considered household members when the sampled address is their usual place of residence at the time of the interview and when they have no usual place of residence elsewhere. Once selected, households remain in the sample for 3 years, and

eligible persons in these households are interviewed every 6 months either in person or over the phone, for a total of seven interviews. All first interviews are conducted in person with subsequent interviews conducted either in person or by phone. New households rotate into the sample on an ongoing basis to replace outgoing households that have been in the sample for the 3-year period. The sample includes persons living in group quarters (such as dormitories, rooming houses, and religious group dwellings) and excludes persons living in military barracks and institutional settings (such as correctional or hospital facilities) and persons who are homeless.

In 2007, the NCVS adopted questions from the U.S. Census Bureau's American Community Survey (ACS) to measure the rate of victimization against people with disabilities. The NCVS does not identify persons in the general population with disabilities. The ACS Subcommittee on Disability Questions developed the disability questions based on questions used in the 2000 Decennial Census and earlier versions of the ACS. The questions identify persons who may require assistance to maintain their independence, be at risk for discrimination, or lack opportunities available to the general population because of limitations related to a prolonged (i.e., 6 months or longer) sensory, physical, mental, or emotional condition. More information about the ACS and the disability questions is available on the U.S. Census Bureau website at http://www.census.gov/acs/www/.

Definitions of Disability Type

Disabilities are classified according to six limitations: hearing, vision, cognitive, ambulatory, self-care, and independent living.

Hearing limitation entails deafness or serious difficulty hearing.

Vision limitation is blindness or serious difficulty seeing, even when wearing glasses.

Cognitive limitation includes serious difficulty in concentrating, remembering, or making decisions because of a physical, mental, or emotional condition.

Ambulatory limitation is difficulty walking or climbing stairs.

Self-care limitation is a condition that causes difficulty dressing or bathing.

Independent living limitation is a physical, mental, or emotional condition that impedes doing errands alone, such as visiting a doctor or shopping.

PART 3

Crime in the United States, 2017

HIGHLIGHTS

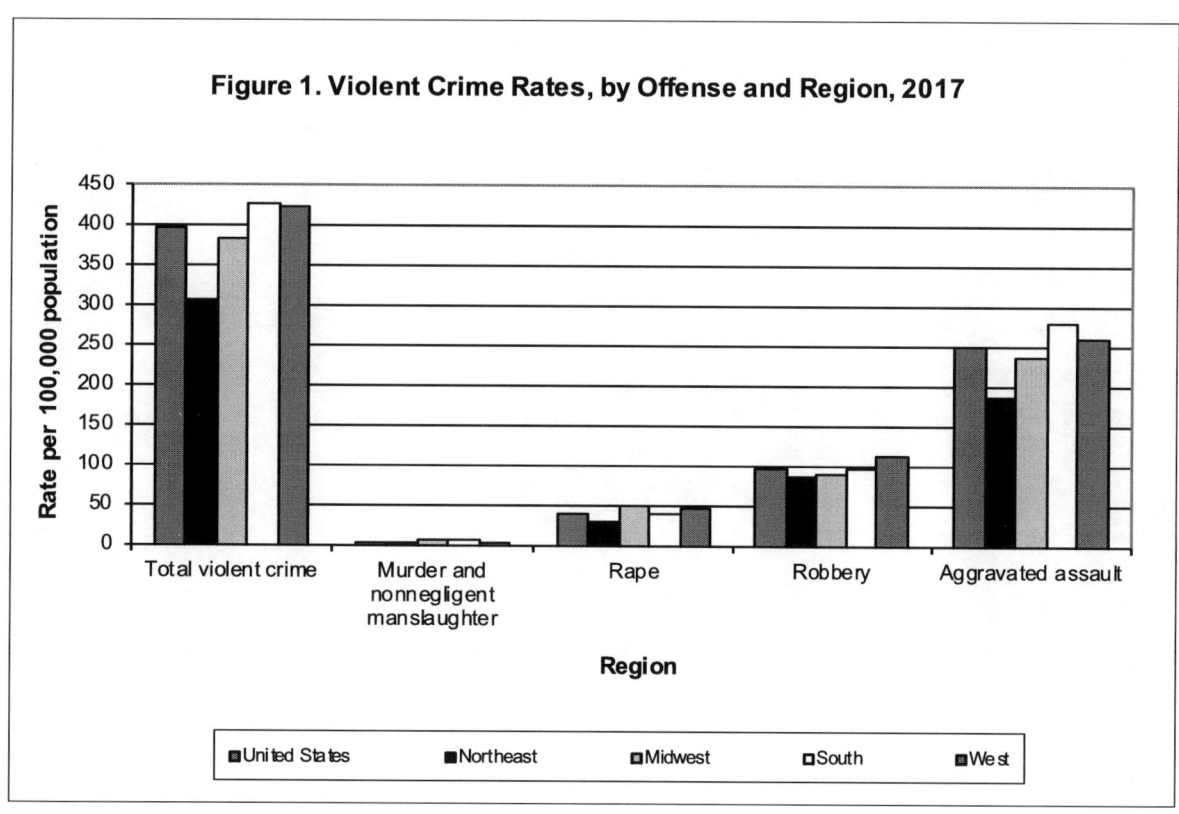

Figure 1. Violent Crime Rates, by Offense and Region, 2017

- An estimated 1,247,321 violent crimes occurred nationwide in 2017, a decrease of 0.2 percent from the 2016 estimate. Aggravated assaults accounted for 65.0 percent of violent crimes reported to law enforcement.

- The 2-year trend showed that property crime offenses (an estimated total of 7,694,086) declined 3.0 percent in 2017 when compared with the 2016 estimate. Larceny-theft accounted for 71.7 percent of all property crimes in 2016.

- In 2017, 45.6 percent of violent crimes (unchanged from 2016) and 17.6 percent of property crimes (a decrease of 0.7 percent from 2016) were cleared by arrest or exceptional means.

- Law enforcement made an estimated 10,554,985 arrests nationwide in 2017. Of these arrests, 518,617 were for violent crimes, and 1,249,757 were for property crimes. The highest number of arrests were for drug abuse violations (estimated at 1,632,921 arrests), driving under the influence (estimated at 990,678), and larceny-thefts (estimated at 950,357).

- Nationwide, the rate of sworn officers was 2.4 per 1,000 inhabitants. The rate of full-time law enforcement employees (civilian and sworn) per 1,000 inhabitants was 3.4. These numbers are unchanged from 2016.

Table 1. Crime in the United States, by Volume and Rate Per 100,000 Inhabitants, 1998–2017

(Number, rate per 100,000 population.)

Year	Population[1]	Violent crime[2] Number	Rate	Murder and nonnegligent manslaughter Number	Rate	Rape (revised definition)[3] Number	Rate	Rape (legacy definition)[4] Number	Rate	Robbery Number	Rate	Aggravated assault Number	Rate
1998	270,248,003	1,533,887	567.6	16,974	6.3	X	X	93,144	34.5	447,186	165.5	976,583	361.4
1999	272,690,813	1,426,044	523.0	15,522	5.7	X	X	89,411	32.8	409,371	150.1	911,740	334.3
2000	281,421,906	1,425,486	506.5	15,586	5.5	X	X	90,178	32.0	408,016	145.0	911,706	324.0
2001[5]	285,317,559	1,439,480	504.5	16,037	5.6	X	X	90,863	31.8	423,557	148.5	909,023	318.6
2002	287,973,924	1,423,677	494.4	16,229	5.6	X	X	95,235	33.1	420,806	146.1	891,407	309.5
2003	290,788,976	1,383,676	475.8	16,528	5.7	X	X	93,883	32.3	414,235	142.5	859,030	295.4
2004	293,656,842	1,360,088	463.2	16,148	5.5	X	X	95,089	32.4	401,470	136.7	847,381	288.6
2005	296,507,061	1,390,745	469.0	16,740	5.6	X	X	94,347	31.8	417,438	140.8	862,220	290.8
2006	299,398,484	1,435,123	479.3	17,309	5.8	X	X	94,472	31.6	449,246	150.0	874,096	292.0
2007	301,621,157	1,422,970	471.8	17,128	5.7	X	X	92,160	30.6	447,324	148.3	866,358	287.2
2008	304,059,724	1,394,461	458.6	16,465	5.4	X	X	90,750	29.8	443,563	145.9	843,683	277.5
2009	307,006,550	1,325,896	431.9	15,399	5.0	X	X	89,241	29.1	408,742	133.1	812,514	264.7
2010	309,330,219	1,251,248	404.5	14,722	4.8	X	X	85,593	27.7	369,089	119.3	781,844	252.8
2011	311,587,816	1,206,005	387.1	14,661	4.7	X	X	84,175	27.0	354,746	113.9	752,423	241.5
2012	313,873,685	1,217,057	387.8	14,856	4.7	X	X	85,141	27.1	355,051	113.1	762,009	242.8
2013	316,497,531	1,168,298	369.1	14,319	4.5	113,695	35.9	82,109	25.9	345,093	109.0	726,777	229.6
2014	318,907,401	1,153,022	361.6	14,164	4.4	118,027	37.0	84,864	26.6	322,905	101.3	731,089	229.2
2015	320,896,618	1,199,310	373.7	15,883	4.9	126,134	39.3	91,261	28.4	328,109	102.2	764,057	238.1
2016[6]	323,405,935	1,250,162	386.6	17,413	5.4	132,414	40.9	96,970	30.0	332,797	102.9	802,982	248.3
2017	325,719,178	1,247,321	382.9	17,284	5.3	135,755	41.7	99,856	30.7	319,356	98.0	810,825	248.9

Year	Property crime Number	Rate	Burglary Number	Rate	Larceny-theft Number	Rate	Motor vehicle theft Number	Rate
1998	10,951,827	4052.5	2,332,735	863.2	7,376,311	2729.5	1,242,781	459.9
1999	10,208,334	3743.6	2,100,739	770.4	6,955,520	2550.7	1,152,075	422.5
2000	10,182,584	3618.3	2,050,992	728.8	6,971,590	2477.3	1,160,002	412.2
2001[5]	10,437,189	3658.1	2,116,531	741.8	7,092,267	2485.7	1,228,391	430.5
2002	10,455,277	3630.6	2,151,252	747.0	7,057,379	2450.7	1,246,646	432.9
2003	10,442,862	3591.2	2,154,834	741.0	7,026,802	2416.5	1,261,226	433.7
2004	10,319,386	3514.1	2,144,446	730.3	6,937,089	2362.3	1,237,851	421.5
2005	10,174,754	3431.5	2,155,448	726.9	6,783,447	2287.8	1,235,859	416.8
2006	10,019,601	3346.6	2,194,993	733.1	6,626,363	2213.2	1,198,245	400.2
2007	9,882,212	3276.4	2,190,198	726.1	6,591,542	2185.4	1,100,472	364.9
2008	9,774,152	3214.6	2,228,887	733.0	6,586,206	2166.1	959,059	315.4
2009	9,337,060	3041.3	2,203,313	717.7	6,338,095	2064.5	795,652	259.2
2010	9,112,625	2945.9	2,168,459	701.0	6,204,601	2005.8	739,565	239.1
2011	9,052,743	2905.4	2,185,140	701.3	6,151,095	1974.1	716,508	230.0
2012	9,001,992	2868.0	2,109,932	672.2	6,168,874	1965.4	723,186	230.4
2013	8,651,892	2733.6	1,932,139	610.5	6,019,465	1901.9	700,288	221.3
2014	8,209,010	2574.1	1,713,153	537.2	5,809,054	1821.5	686,803	215.4
2015	8,024,115	2500.5	1,587,564	494.7	5,723,488	1783.6	713,063	222.2
2016[6]	7,928,530	2451.6	1,516,405	468.9	5,644,835	1745.4	767,290	237.3
2017	7,694,086	2362.2	1,401,840	430.4	5,519,107	1694.4	773,139	237.4

Note: Although arson data are included in the trend and clearance tables, sufficient data are not available to estimate totals for this offense. Therefore, no arson data are published in this table.
X = Not applicable.
[1] Populations are U.S. Census Bureau provisional estimates as of July 1 for each year except 2000 and 2010, which are decennial census counts.
[2] The violent crime figures include the offenses of murder, rape (legacy definition), robbery, and aggravated assault.
[3] The figures shown in this column for the offense of rape were estimated using the revised Uniform Crime Reporting Program's (UCR) definition of rape.
[4] The figures shown in this column for the offense of rape were estimated using the legacy UCR definition of rape.
[5] The murder and nonnegligent homicides that occurred as a result of the events of September 11, 2001, are not included in this table.
[6] The crime figures have been adjusted.

Table 1A. Crime in the United States, Percent Change in Volume and Rate Per 100,000 Inhabitants for 2 Years, 5 Years, and 10 Years, 2008–2017

(Percent change.)

Years	Violent crime		Murder and nonnegligent manslaughter		Rape (revised definition)[2]		Rape (legacy definition)[3]		Robbery	
	Number[1]	Rate	Number	Rate	Number	Rate	Number	Rate	Number	Rate
2008–2017	-10.6	-16.5	+5.0	-2.0	X	X	+10.0	+2.7	-28.0	-32.8
2013–2017	+6.8	+3.7	+20.7	+17.3	+19.4	+16.0	+21.6	+18.2	-7.5	-10.1
2016–2017	-0.2	-0.9	-0.7	-1.4	+2.5	+1.8	+3.0	+2.2	-4.0	-4.7

Table 2. Crime in the United States,[1] by Region, Geographic Division, and State, 2016–2017

(Number, rate per 100,000 population, percent.)

Area	Population[2]	Violent crime[3]		Murder and nonnegligent manslaughter		Rape[4]		Robbery	
		Number	Rate	Number	Rate	Number	Rate	Number	Rate
United States[5,6]									
2016	323,405,935	1,285,606	397.5	17,413	5.4	132,414	40.9	332,797	102.9
2017	325,719,178	1,283,220	394.0	17,284	5.3	135,755	41.7	319,356	98.0
Percent change	0.7	-0.2	-0.9	-0.7	-1.4	+2.5	+1.8	-4.0	-4.7
Northeast									
2016	56,359,360	178,406	316.6	1,977	3.5	16,763	29.7	52,958	94.0
2017	56,470,581	172,042	304.7	1,957	3.5	16,863	29.9	48,714	86.3
Percent change	0.2	-3.6	-3.8	-1.0	-1.2	+0.6	+0.4	-8.0	-8.2
New England									
2016	14,757,573	41,841	283.5	296	2.0	4,569	31.0	9,394	63.7
2017	14,810,001	40,519	273.6	346	2.3	4,833	32.6	8,918	60.2
Percent change	0.4	-3.2	-3.5	+16.9	+16.5	+5.8	+5.4	-5.1	-5.4
Connecticut									
2016	3,587,685	8,169	227.7	79	2.2	791	22.0	2,711	75.6
2017	3,588,184	8,180	228.0	102	2.8	837	23.3	2,813	78.4
Percent change	*	+0.1	+0.1	+29.1	+29.1	+5.8	+5.8	+3.8	+3.7
Maine									
2016	1,330,232	1,649	124.0	20	1.5	413	31.0	268	20.1
2017	1,335,907	1,617	121.0	23	1.7	473	35.4	249	18.6
Percent change	0.4	-1.9	-2.4	+15.0	+14.5	+14.5	+14.0	-7.1	-7.5
Massachusetts									
2016	6,823,721	25,975	380.7	135	2.0	2,141	31.4	5,365	78.6
2017	6,859,819	24,560	358.0	173	2.5	2,197	32.0	4,871	71.0
Percent change	0.5	-5.4	-5.9	+28.1	+27.5	+2.6	+2.1	-9.2	-9.7
New Hampshire									
2016	1,335,015	2,668	199.8	19	1.4	609	45.6	431	32.3
2017	1,342,795	2,668	198.7	14	1.0	663	49.4	419	31.2
Percent change	0.6	0.0	-0.6	-26.3	-26.7	+8.9	+8.2	-2.8	-3.3
Rhode Island									
2016	1,057,566	2,529	239.1	29	2.7	445	42.1	541	51.2
2017	1,059,639	2,460	232.2	20	1.9	445	42.0	474	44.7
Percent change	0.2	-2.7	-2.9	-31.0	-31.2	0.0	-0.2	-12.4	-12.6
Vermont									
2016	623,354	851	136.5	14	2.2	170	27.3	78	12.5
2017	623,657	1,034	165.8	14	2.2	218	35.0	92	14.8
Percent change	*	+21.5	+21.4	0.0	*	+28.2	+28.2	+17.9	+17.9
Middle Atlantic									
2016	41,601,787	136,565	328.3	1,681	4.0	12,194	29.3	43,564	104.7
2017	41,660,580	131,523	315.7	1,611	3.9	12,030	28.9	39,796	95.5
Percent change	0.1	-3.7	-3.8	-4.2	-4.3	-1.3	-1.5	-8.6	-8.8
New Jersey									
2016	8,978,416	21,861	243.5	378	4.2	1,454	16.2	8,940	99.6
2017	9,005,644	20,604	228.8	324	3.6	1,505	16.7	7,895	87.7
Percent change	0.3	-5.7	-6.0	-14.3	-14.5	+3.5	+3.2	-11.7	-12.0

Table 1A. Crime in the United States, Percent Change in Volume and Rate Per 100,000 Inhabitants for 2 Years, 5 Years, and 10 Years, 2008–2017—*Continued*

(Percent change.)

Years	Aggravated assault		Property crime		Burglary		Larceny-theft		Motor vehicle theft	
	Number	Rate	Number	Rate	Number	Rate	Number	Rate	Number	Rate
2008–2017...............	-3.9	-10.3	-21.3	-26.5	-37.1	-41.3	-16.2	-21.8	-19.4	-24.7
2013–2017...............	+11.6	+8.4	-11.1	-13.6	-27.4	-29.5	-8.3	-10.9	+10.4	+7.3
2016–2017...............	+1.0	+0.3	-3.0	-3.6	-7.6	-8.2	-2.2	-2.9	+0.8	*

X = Not applicable.
* = Less than one-tenth of one percent.
[1]The violent crime figures include the offenses of murder, rape (legacy definition), robbery, and aggravated assault.
[2]The figures shown in this column for the offense of rape were estimated using the revised UCR definition of rape.
[3]The figures shown in this column for the offense of rape were estimated using the legacy UCR definition of rape.

Table 2. Crime in the United States,[1] by Region, Geographic Division, and State, 2016–2017—*Continued*

(Number, rate per 100,000 population, percent.)

Area	Population[2]	Aggravated assault		Property crime		Burglary		Larceny-theft		Motor vehicle theft	
		Number	Rate	Number	Rate	Number	Rate	Number	Rate	Number	Rate
United States[5,6].................											
2016...............	323,405,935	802,982	248.3	7,928,530	2,451.6	1,516,405	468.9	5,644,835	1,745.4	767,290	237.3
2017...............	325,719,178	810,825	248.9	7,694,086	2,362.2	1,401,840	430.4	5,519,107	1,694.4	773,139	237.4
Percent change	0.7	+1.0	+0.3	-3.0	-3.6	-7.6	-8.2	-2.2	-2.9	+0.8	*
Northeast.........................											
2016...............	56,359,360	106,708	189.3	907,781	1,610.7	142,092	252.1	708,772	1,257.6	56,917	101.0
2017...............	56,470,581	104,508	185.1	880,154	1,558.6	127,908	226.5	695,447	1,231.5	56,799	100.6
Percent change	0.2	-2.1	-2.3	-3.0	-3.2	-10.0	-10.2	-1.9	-2.1	-0.2	-0.4
New England											
2016...............	14,757,573	27,582	186.9	242,151	1,640.9	41,835	283.5	182,176	1,234.5	18,140	122.9
2017...............	14,810,001	26,422	178.4	228,293	1,541.5	36,958	249.5	173,101	1,168.8	18,234	123.1
Percent change	0.4	-4.2	-4.5	-5.7	-6.1	-11.7	-12.0	-5.0	-5.3	+0.5	+0.2
Connecticut											
2016	3,587,685	4,588	127.9	64,875	1,808.3	10,107	281.7	47,642	1,327.9	7,126	198.6
2017	3,588,184	4,428	123.4	63,509	1,769.9	8,890	247.8	47,310	1,318.5	7,309	203.7
Percent change	*	-3.5	-3.5	-2.1	-2.1	-12.0	-12.1	-0.7	-0.7	+2.6	+2.6
Maine											
2016	1,330,232	948	71.3	21,908	1,646.9	4,001	300.8	17,131	1,287.8	776	58.3
2017	1,335,907	872	65.3	20,133	1,507.1	3,334	249.6	16,006	1,198.1	793	59.4
Percent change	0.4	-8.0	-8.4	-8.1	-8.5	-16.7	-17.0	-6.6	-7.0	+2.2	+1.8
Massachusetts..................											
2016	6,823,721	18,334	268.7	106,430	1,559.7	19,204	281.4	79,155	1,160.0	8,071	118.3
2017	6,859,819	17,319	252.5	98,575	1,437.0	17,089	249.1	73,946	1,078.0	7,540	109.9
Percent change	0.5	-5.5	-6.0	-7.4	-7.9	-11.0	-11.5	-6.6	-7.1	-6.6	-7.1
New Hampshire...............											
2016	1,335,015	1,609	120.5	20,323	1,522.3	2,989	223.9	16,454	1,232.5	880	65.9
2017	1,342,795	1,572	117.1	18,555	1,381.8	2,574	191.7	15,066	1,122.0	915	68.1
Percent change	0.6	-2.3	-2.9	-8.7	-9.2	-13.9	-14.4	-8.4	-9.0	+4.0	+3.4
Rhode Island											
2016	1,057,566	1,514	143.2	18,910	1,788.1	3,650	345.1	14,157	1,338.6	1,103	104.3
2017	1,059,639	1,521	143.5	18,561	1,751.6	3,217	303.6	13,861	1,308.1	1,483	140.0
Percent change	0.2	+0.5	+0.3	-1.8	-2.0	-11.9	-12.0	-2.1	-2.3	+34.5	+34.2
Vermont........................											
2016	623,354	589	94.5	9,705	1,556.9	1,884	302.2	7,637	1,225.1	184	29.5
2017	623,657	710	113.8	8,960	1,436.7	1,854	297.3	6,912	1,108.3	194	31.1
Percent change	*	+20.5	+20.5	-7.7	-7.7	-1.6	-1.6	-9.5	-9.5	+5.4	+5.4
Middle Atlantic											
2016...............	41,601,787	79,126	190.2	665,630	1,600.0	100,257	241.0	526,596	1,265.8	38,777	93.2
2017...............	41,660,580	78,086	187.4	651,861	1,564.7	90,950	218.3	522,346	1,253.8	38,565	92.6
Percent change	0.1	-1.3	-1.5	-2.1	-2.2	-9.3	-9.4	-0.8	-0.9	-0.5	-0.7
New Jersey											
2016	8,978,416	11,089	123.5	138,012	1,537.2	25,229	281.0	101,459	1,130.0	11,324	126.1
2017	9,005,644	10,880	120.8	140,086	1,555.5	23,891	265.3	104,025	1,155.1	12,170	135.1
Percent change	0.3	-1.9	-2.2	+1.5	+1.2	-5.3	-5.6	+2.5	+2.2	+7.5	+7.1

Table 2. Crime in the United States,[1] by Region, Geographic Division, and State, 2016–2017—*Continued*

(Number, rate per 100,000 population, percent.)

Area	Population[2]	Violent crime[3] Number	Violent crime[3] Rate	Murder and nonnegligent manslaughter Number	Murder and nonnegligent manslaughter Rate	Rape[4] Number	Rape[4] Rate	Robbery Number	Robbery Rate
New York									
2016	19,836,286	74,315	374.6	629	3.2	6,281	31.7	22,310	112.5
2017	19,849,399	70,799	356.7	548	2.8	6,324	31.9	20,108	101.3
Percent change	0.1	-4.7	-4.8	-12.9	-12.9	+0.7	+0.6	-9.9	-9.9
Pennsylvania									
2016	12,787,085	40,389	315.9	674	5.3	4,459	34.9	12,314	96.3
2017	12,805,537	40,120	313.3	739	5.8	4,201	32.8	11,793	92.1
Percent change	0.1	-0.7	-0.8	+9.6	+9.5	-5.8	-5.9	-4.2	-4.4
Midwest									
2016	67,978,168	258,949	380.9	3,956	5.8	32,271	47.5	64,138	94.4
2017	68,179,351	259,566	380.7	3,914	5.7	33,370	48.9	61,004	89.5
Percent change	0.3	+0.2	-0.1	-1.1	-1.4	+3.4	+3.1	-4.9	-5.2
East North Central									
2016	46,798,649	181,827	388.5	3,019	6.5	22,479	48.0	49,524	105.8
2017	46,885,244	180,826	385.7	2,859	6.1	23,210	49.5	46,605	99.4
Percent change	0.2	-0.6	-0.7	-5.3	-5.5	+3.3	+3.1	-5.9	-6.1
Illinois									
2016	12,835,726	56,054	436.7	1,061	8.3	5,003	39.0	17,829	138.9
2017	12,802,023	56,180	438.8	997	7.8	5,556	43.4	17,567	137.2
Percent change	-0.3	+0.2	+0.5	-6.0	-5.8	+11.1	+11.3	-1.5	-1.2
Indiana									
2016	6,634,007	26,516	399.7	431	6.5	2,449	36.9	7,291	109.9
2017	6,666,818	26,598	399.0	397	6.0	2,625	39.4	6,600	99.0
Percent change	0.5	+0.3	-0.2	-7.9	-8.3	+7.2	+6.7	-9.5	-9.9
Michigan									
2016	9,933,445	45,782	460.9	612	6.2	7,268	73.2	7,123	71.7
2017	9,962,311	44,826	450.0	569	5.7	7,031	70.6	6,488	65.1
Percent change	0.3	-2.1	-2.4	-7.0	-7.3	-3.3	-3.5	-8.9	-9.2
Ohio									
2016	11,622,554	35,759	307.7	683	5.9	5,754	49.5	12,574	108.2
2017	11,658,609	34,683	297.5	710	6.1	5,859	50.3	11,605	99.5
Percent change	0.3	-3.0	-3.3	+4.0	+3.6	+1.8	+1.5	-7.7	-8.0
Wisconsin									
2016	5,772,917	17,716	306.9	232	4.0	2,005	34.7	4,707	81.5
2017	5,795,483	18,539	319.9	186	3.2	2,139	36.9	4,345	75.0
Percent change	0.4	+4.6	+4.2	-19.8	-20.1	+6.7	+6.3	-7.7	-8.1
West North Central									
2016	21,179,519	77,122	364.1	937	4.4	9,792	46.2	14,614	69.0
2017	21,294,107	78,740	369.8	1,055	5.0	10,160	47.7	14,399	67.6
Percent change	0.5	+2.1	+1.5	+12.6	+12.0	+3.8	+3.2	-1.5	-2.0
Iowa									
2016	3,130,869	9,170	292.9	73	2.3	1,278	40.8	1,150	36.7
2017	3,145,711	9,230	293.4	104	3.3	1,234	39.2	1,253	39.8
Percent change	0.5	+0.7	+0.2	+42.5	+41.8	-3.4	-3.9	+9.0	+8.4
Kansas									
2016	2,907,731	11,665	401.2	132	4.5	1,618	55.6	1,757	60.4
2017	2,913,123	12,030	413.0	160	5.5	1,627	55.9	1,785	61.3
Percent change	0.2	+3.1	+2.9	+21.2	+21.0	+0.6	+0.4	+1.6	+1.4
Minnesota									
2016	5,525,050	13,365	241.9	101	1.8	2,349	42.5	3,730	67.5
2017	5,576,606	13,291	238.3	113	2.0	2,385	42.8	3,621	64.9
Percent change	0.9	-0.6	-1.5	+11.9	+10.8	+1.5	+0.6	-2.9	-3.8
Missouri									
2016	6,091,176	31,720	520.8	538	8.8	2,557	42.0	6,576	108.0
2017	6,113,532	32,420	530.3	600	9.8	2,729	44.6	6,351	103.9
Percent change	0.4	+2.2	+1.8	+11.5	+11.1	+6.7	+6.3	-3.4	-3.8
Nebraska									
2016	1,907,603	5,661	296.8	49	2.6	1,108	58.1	946	49.6
2017	1,920,076	5,873	305.9	43	2.2	1,191	62.0	968	50.4
Percent change	0.6	+3.7	+3.1	-12.2	-12.8	+7.5	+6.8	+2.3	+1.7
North Dakota									
2016	755,548	1,905	252.1	16	2.1	356	47.1	181	24.0
2017	755,393	2,125	281.3	10	1.3	399	52.8	183	24.2
Percent change	*	+11.5	+11.6	-37.5	-37.5	+12.1	+12.1	+1.1	+1.1
South Dakota									
2016	861,542	3,636	422.0	28	3.2	526	61.1	274	31.8

Table 2. Crime in the United States,[1] by Region, Geographic Division, and State, 2016–2017—*Continued*

(Number, rate per 100,000 population, percent.)

Area	Population[2]	Aggravated assault		Property crime		Burglary		Larceny-theft		Motor vehicle theft	
		Number	Rate	Number	Rate	Number	Rate	Number	Rate	Number	Rate
New York											
2016	19,836,286	45,095	227.3	305,224	1,538.7	39,850	200.9	250,990	1,265.3	14,384	72.5
2017	19,849,399	43,819	220.8	300,555	1,514.2	35,002	176.3	252,143	1,270.3	13,410	67.6
Percent change	0.1	-2.8	-2.9	-1.5	-1.6	-12.2	-12.2	+0.5	+0.4	-6.8	-6.8
Pennsylvania											
2016	12,787,085	22,942	179.4	222,394	1,739.2	35,178	275.1	174,147	1,361.9	13,069	102.2
2017	12,805,537	23,387	182.6	211,220	1,649.4	32,057	250.3	166,178	1,297.7	12,985	101.4
Percent change	0.1	+1.9	+1.8	-5.0	-5.2	-8.9	-9.0	-4.6	-4.7	-0.6	-0.8
Midwest											
2016	67,978,168	158,584	233.3	1,549,241	2,279.0	301,149	443.0	1,116,188	1,642.0	131,904	194.0
2017	68,179,351	161,278	236.5	1,505,278	2,207.8	275,410	403.9	1,092,608	1,602.5	137,260	201.3
Percent change	0.3	+1.7	+1.4	-2.8	-3.1	-8.5	-8.8	-2.1	-2.4	+4.1	+3.8
East North Central											
2016	46,798,649	106,805	228.2	1,034,821	2,211.2	208,077	444.6	742,456	1,586.5	84,288	180.1
2017	46,885,244	108,152	230.7	984,783	2,100.4	185,412	395.5	713,795	1,522.4	85,576	182.5
Percent change	0.2	+1.3	+1.1	-4.8	-5.0	-10.9	-11.1	-3.9	-4.0	+1.5	+1.3
Illinois											
2016	12,835,726	32,161	250.6	263,256	2,051.0	48,193	375.5	195,196	1,520.7	19,867	154.8
2017	12,802,023	32,060	250.4	257,497	2,011.4	43,459	339.5	193,157	1,508.8	20,881	163.1
Percent change	-0.3	-0.3	-0.1	-2.2	-1.9	-9.8	-9.6	-1.0	-0.8	+5.1	+5.4
Indiana											
2016	6,634,007	16,345	246.4	168,460	2,539.3	33,567	506.0	120,454	1,815.7	14,439	217.7
2017	6,666,818	16,976	254.6	161,132	2,416.9	30,140	452.1	115,591	1,733.8	15,401	231.0
Percent change	0.5	+3.9	+3.3	-4.3	-4.8	-10.2	-10.7	-4.0	-4.5	+6.7	+6.1
Michigan											
2016	9,933,445	30,779	309.9	190,249	1,915.2	39,738	400.0	130,249	1,311.2	20,262	204.0
2017	9,962,311	30,738	308.5	179,318	1,800.0	35,641	357.8	124,104	1,245.7	19,573	196.5
Percent change	0.3	-0.1	-0.4	-5.7	-6.0	-10.3	-10.6	-4.7	-5.0	-3.4	-3.7
Ohio											
2016	11,622,554	16,748	144.1	300,945	2,589.3	67,081	577.2	214,102	1,842.1	19,762	170.0
2017	11,658,609	16,509	141.6	282,034	2,419.1	58,573	502.4	203,208	1,743.0	20,253	173.7
Percent change	0.3	-1.4	-1.7	-6.3	-6.6	-12.7	-13.0	-5.1	-5.4	+2.5	+2.2
Wisconsin											
2016	5,772,917	10,772	186.6	111,911	1,938.6	19,498	337.7	82,455	1,428.3	9,958	172.5
2017	5,795,483	11,869	204.8	104,802	1,808.3	17,599	303.7	77,735	1,341.3	9,468	163.4
Percent change	0.4	+10.2	+9.8	-6.4	-6.7	-9.7	-10.1	-5.7	-6.1	-4.9	-5.3
West North Central											
2016	21,179,519	51,779	244.5	514,420	2,428.9	93,072	439.4	373,732	1,764.6	47,616	224.8
2017	21,294,107	53,126	249.5	520,495	2,444.3	89,998	422.6	378,813	1,779.0	51,684	242.7
Percent change	0.5	+2.6	+2.0	+1.2	+0.6	-3.3	-3.8	+1.4	+0.8	+8.5	+8.0
Iowa											
2016	3,130,869	6,669	213.0	65,888	2,104.5	15,306	488.9	45,580	1,455.8	5,002	159.8
2017	3,145,711	6,639	211.0	66,855	2,125.3	15,078	479.3	46,198	1,468.6	5,579	177.4
Percent change	0.5	-0.4	-0.9	+1.5	+1.0	-1.5	-2.0	+1.4	+0.9	+11.5	+11.0
Kansas											
2016	2,907,731	8,158	280.6	82,293	2,830.1	14,759	507.6	60,119	2,067.6	7,415	255.0
2017	2,913,123	8,458	290.3	81,593	2,800.9	13,931	478.2	59,816	2,053.3	7,846	269.3
Percent change	0.2	+3.7	+3.5	-0.9	-1.0	-5.6	-5.8	-0.5	-0.7	+5.8	+5.6
Minnesota											
2016	5,525,050	7,185	130.0	117,723	2,130.7	18,582	336.3	90,421	1,636.6	8,720	157.8
2017	5,576,606	7,172	128.6	122,212	2,191.5	18,787	336.9	93,446	1,675.7	9,979	178.9
Percent change	0.9	-0.2	-1.1	+3.8	+2.9	+1.1	+0.2	+3.3	+2.4	+14.4	+13.4
Missouri											
2016	6,091,176	22,049	362.0	170,661	2,801.8	31,716	520.7	120,649	1,980.7	18,296	300.4
2017	6,113,532	22,740	372.0	173,253	2,833.9	30,081	492.0	123,251	2,016.0	19,921	325.9
Percent change	0.4	+3.1	+2.8	+1.5	+1.1	-5.2	-5.5	+2.2	+1.8	+8.9	+8.5
Nebraska											
2016	1,907,603	3,558	186.5	43,197	2,264.5	6,459	338.6	32,009	1,678.0	4,729	247.9
2017	1,920,076	3,671	191.2	43,663	2,274.0	6,472	337.1	31,988	1,666.0	5,203	271.0
Percent change	0.6	+3.2	+2.5	+1.1	+0.4	+0.2	-0.4	-0.1	-0.7	+10.0	+9.3
North Dakota											
2016	755,548	1,352	178.9	17,451	2,309.7	3,248	429.9	12,249	1,621.2	1,954	258.6
2017	755,393	1,533	202.9	16,602	2,197.8	2,942	389.5	11,887	1,573.6	1,773	234.7
Percent change	*	+13.4	+13.4	-4.9	-4.8	-9.4	-9.4	-3.0	-2.9	-9.3	-9.2
South Dakota											
2016	861,542	2,808	325.9	17,207	1,997.2	3,002	348.4	12,705	1,474.7	1,500	174.1

Table 2. Crime in the United States,[1] by Region, Geographic Division, and State, 2016–2017—*Continued*

(Number, rate per 100,000 population, percent.)

Area	Population[2]	Violent crime[3] Number	Violent crime[3] Rate	Murder and nonnegligent manslaughter Number	Murder and nonnegligent manslaughter Rate	Rape[4] Number	Rape[4] Rate	Robbery Number	Robbery Rate
2017	869,666	3,771	433.6	25	2.9	595	68.4	238	27.4
Percent change	0.9	+3.7	+2.7	-10.7	-11.5	+13.1	+12.1	-13.1	-14.0
South[5,6]									
2016	122,423,457	528,273	431.5	8,027	6.6	49,829	40.7	129,408	105.7
2017	123,658,624	524,110	423.8	7,928	6.4	50,249	40.6	121,290	98.1
Percent change	1.0	-0.8	-1.8	-1.2	-2.2	+0.8	-0.2	-6.3	-7.2
South Atlantic[5,6]									
2016	63,991,523	259,114	404.9	4,126	6.4	22,502	35.2	66,916	104.6
2017	64,705,532	251,287	388.4	3,995	6.2	22,003	34.0	61,622	95.2
Percent change	1.1	-3.0	-4.1	-3.2	-4.2	-2.2	-3.3	-7.9	-8.9
Delaware									
2016	952,698	4,859	510.0	58	6.1	311	32.6	1,359	142.6
2017	961,939	4,361	453.4	54	5.6	334	34.7	1,082	112.5
Percent change	1.0	-10.2	-11.1	-6.9	-7.8	+7.4	+6.4	-20.4	-21.1
District of Columbia[5]									
2016	684,336	8,236	1,203.5	136	19.9	533	77.9	3,500	511.4
2017	693,972	6,974	1,004.9	116	16.7	444	64.0	2,623	378.0
Percent change	1.4	-15.3	-16.5	-14.7	-15.9	-16.7	-17.9	-25.1	-26.1
Florida									
2016	20,656,589	88,700	429.4	1,111	5.4	7.598	36.8	20,175	97.7
2017	20,984,400	85,625	408.0	1,057	5.0	7,940	37.8	18,597	88.6
Percent change	1.6	-3.5	-5.0	-4.9	-6.3	+4.5	+2.9	-7.8	-9.3
Georgia									
2016	10,313,620	40,268	390.4	682	6.6	3,381	32.8	12,114	117.5
2017	10,429,379	37,258	357.2	703	6.7	2,718	26.1	10,044	96.3
Percent change	1.1	-7.5	-8.5	+3.1	+1.9	-19.6	-20.5	-17.1	-18.0
Maryland									
2016	6,024,752	29,019	481.7	536	8.9	1,827	30.3	10,815	179.5
2017	6,052,177	30,273	500.2	546	9.0	1,691	27.9	11,200	185.1
Percent change	0.5	+4.3	+3.8	+1.9	+1.4	-7.4	-7.9	+3.6	+3.1
North Carolina[6]									
2016	10,156,689	37,767	371.8	678	6.7	2,847	28.0	9,336	91.9
2017	10,273,419	37,364	363.7	591	5.8	2,715	26.4	9,350	91.0
Percent change	1.1	-1.1	-2.2	-12.8	-13.8	-4.6	-5.7	+0.1	-1.0
South Carolina									
2016	4,959,822	25,137	506.8	358	7.2	2,491	50.2	4,071	82.1
2017	5,024,369	25,432	506.2	390	7.8	2,504	49.8	3,870	77.0
Percent change	1.3	+1.2	-0.1	+8.9	+7.5	+0.5	-0.8	-4.9	-6.2
Virginia									
2016	8,414,380	18,495	219.8	482	5.7	2,830	33.6	4,826	57.4
2017	8,470,020	17,632	208.2	453	5.3	2,862	33.8	4,332	51.1
Percent change	0.7	-4.7	-5.3	-6.0	-6.6	+1.1	+0.5	-10.2	-10.8
West Virginia									
2016	1,828,637	6,633	362.7	85	4.6	684	37.4	720	39.4
2017	1,815,857	6,368	350.7	85	4.7	795	43.8	524	28.9
Percent change	-0.7	-4.0	-3.3	0.0	+0.7	+16.2	+17.0	-27.2	-26.7
East South Central									
2016	18,931,477	87,200	460.6	1,404	7.4	7,748	40.9	18,320	96.8
2017	19,029,020	87,888	461.9	1,439	7.6	7,714	40.5	17,108	89.9
Percent change	0.5	+0.8	+0.3	+2.5	+2.0	-0.4	-0.9	-6.6	-7.1
Alabama									
2016	4,860,545	25,878	532.4	407	8.4	1,915	39.4	4,687	96.4
2017	4,874,747	25,551	524.2	404	8.3	2,028	41.6	4,217	86.5
Percent change	0.3	-1.3	-1.6	-0.7	-1.0	+5.9	+5.6	-10.0	-10.3
Kentucky									
2016	4,436,113	10,452	235.6	265	6.0	1,748	39.4	3,371	76.0
2017	4,454,189	10,056	225.8	263	5.9	1,661	37.3	2,958	66.4
Percent change	0.4	-3.8	-4.2	-0.8	-1.2	-5.0	-5.4	-12.3	-12.6
Mississippi									
2016	2,985,415	8,411	281.7	237	7.9	1,282	42.9	2,433	81.5
2017	2,984,100	8,526	285.7	245	8.2	1,091	36.6	2,071	69.4
Percent change	*	+1.4	+1.4	+3.4	+3.4	-14.9	-14.9	-14.9	-14.8
Tennessee									
2016	6,649,404	42,459	638.5	495	7.4	2,803	42.2	7,829	117.7
2017	6,715,984	43,755	651.5	527	7.8	2,934	43.7	7,862	117.1
Percent change	1.0	+3.1	+2.0	+6.5	+5.4	+4.7	+3.6	+0.4	-0.6

(Number, rate per 100,000 population, percent.)

Area	Population[2]	Aggravated assault		Property crime		Burglary		Larceny-theft		Motor vehicle theft	
		Number	Rate	Number	Rate	Number	Rate	Number	Rate	Number	Rate
2017.........................	869,666	2,913	335.0	16,317	1,876.2	2,707	311.3	12,227	1,405.9	1,383	159.0
Percent change........	0.9	+3.7	+2.8	-5.2	-6.1	-9.8	-10.7	-3.8	-4.7	-7.8	-8.7
South[5,6]**....................**											
2016............................	122,423,457	341,009	278.5	3,348,650	2,735.3	685,526	560.0	2,393,605	1,955.2	269,519	220.2
2017............................	123,658,624	344,643	278.7	3,227,423	2,609.9	629,601	509.1	2,323,145	1,878.7	274,677	222.1
Percent change	1.0	+1.1	+0.1	-3.6	-4.6	-8.2	-9.1	-2.9	-3.9	+1.9	+0.9
South Atlantic[5,6] **..............**											
2016............................	63,991,523	165,570	258.7	1,693,453	2,646.4	329,778	515.3	1,234,149	1,928.6	129,526	202.4
2017............................	64,705,532	163,667	252.9	1,620,766	2,504.8	295,702	457.0	1,195,134	1,847.0	129,930	200.8
Percent change	1.1	-1.1	-2.2	-4.3	-5.3	-10.3	-11.3	-3.2	-4.2	+0.3	-0.8
Delaware......................											
2016	952,698	3,131	328.6	26,370	2,767.9	5,028	527.8	19,812	2,079.6	1,530	160.6
2017	961,939	2,891	300.5	23,477	2,440.6	3,970	412.7	18,138	1,885.6	1,369	142.3
Percent change	1.0	-7.7	-8.6	-11.0	-11.8	-21.0	-21.8	-8.4	-9.3	-10.5	-11.4
District of Columbia[5]											
2016	684,336	4,067	594.3	32,377	4,731.2	2,361	345.0	27,089	3,958.4	2,927	427.7
2017	693,972	3,791	546.3	29,729	4,283.9	1,809	260.7	25,333	3,650.4	2,587	372.8
Percent change	1.4	-6.8	-8.1	-8.2	-9.5	-23.4	-24.4	-6.5	-7.8	-11.6	-12.8
Florida...........................											
2016	20,656,589	59,816	289.6	553,812	2,681.0	100,325	485.7	410,352	1,986.5	43,135	208.8
2017	20,984,400	58,031	276.5	527,220	2,512.4	88,853	423.4	395,453	1,884.5	42,914	204.5
Percent change	1.6	-3.0	-4.5	-4.8	-6.3	-11.4	-12.8	-3.6	-5.1	-0.5	-2.1
Georgia.........................											
2016	10,313,620	24,091	233.6	307,305	2,979.6	62,715	608.1	218,127	2,114.9	26,463	256.6
2017	10,429,379	23,793	228.1	298,298	2,860.2	55,374	530.9	216,661	2,077.4	26,263	251.8
Percent change	1.1	-1.2	-2.3	-2.9	-4.0	-11.7	-12.7	-0.7	-1.8	-0.8	-1.9
Maryland.......................											
2016	6,024,752	15,841	262.9	139,716	2,319.0	24,832	412.2	100,995	1,676.3	13,889	230.5
2017	6,052,177	16,836	278.2	134,496	2,222.3	23,508	388.4	97,420	1,609.7	13,568	224.2
Percent change	0.5	+6.3	+5.8	-3.7	-4.2	-5.3	-5.8	-3.5	-4.0	-2.3	-2.8
North Carolina[6]											
2016	10,156,689	24,906	245.2	277,765	2,734.8	72,082	709.7	190,377	1,874.4	15,306	150.7
2017	10,273,419	24,708	240.5	261,486	2,545.3	64,786	630.6	180,902	1,760.9	15,798	153.8
Percent change.............	1.1	-0.8	-1.9	-5.9	-6.9	-10.1	-11.1	-5.0	-6.1	+3.2	+2.0
South Carolina											
2016	4,959,822	18,217	367.3	161,534	3,256.9	33,149	668.4	114,455	2,307.6	13,930	280.9
2017	5,024,369	18,668	371.5	160,575	3,195.9	31,306	623.1	115,012	2,289.1	14,257	283.8
Percent change	1.3	+2.5	+1.2	-0.6	-1.9	-5.6	-6.8	+0.5	-0.8	+2.3	+1.0
Virginia											
2016	8,414,380	10,357	123.1	157,292	1,869.3	20,159	239.6	127,285	1,512.7	9,848	117.0
2017	8,470,020	9,985	117.9	151,855	1,792.9	18,468	218.0	123,215	1,454.7	10,172	120.1
Percent change	0.7	-3.6	-4.2	-3.5	-4.1	-8.4	-9.0	-3.2	-3.8	+3.3	+2.6
West Virginia...................											
2016	1,828,637	5,144	281.3	37,282	2,038.8	9,127	499.1	25,657	1,403.1	2,498	136.6
2017	1,815,857	4,964	273.4	33,630	1,852.0	7,628	420.1	23,000	1,266.6	3,002	165.3
Percent change	-0.7	-3.5	-2.8	-9.8	-9.2	-16.4	-15.8	-10.4	-9.7	+20.2	+21.0
East South Central											
2016................................	18,931,477	59,728	315.5	514,692	2,718.7	119,073	629.0	354,409	1,872.1	41,210	217.7
2017................................	19,029,020	61,627	323.9	518,062	2,722.5	115,098	604.9	356,724	1,874.6	46,240	243.0
Percent change	0.5	+3.2	+2.7	+0.7	+0.1	-3.3	-3.8	+0.7	+0.1	+12.2	+11.6
Alabama.........................											
2016	4,860,545	18,869	388.2	143,259	2,947.4	34,045	700.4	97,498	2,005.9	11,716	241.0
2017	4,874,747	18,902	387.8	144,160	2,957.3	31,477	645.7	99,842	2,048.1	12,841	263.4
Percent change	0.3	+0.2	-0.1	+0.6	+0.3	-7.5	-7.8	+2.4	+2.1	+9.6	+9.3
Kentucky.......................											
2016	4,436,113	5,068	114.2	97,713	2,202.7	20,932	471.9	66,833	1,506.6	9,948	224.3
2017	4,454,189	5,174	116.2	94,833	2,129.1	20,195	453.4	64,394	1,445.7	10,244	230.0
Percent change	0.4	+2.1	+1.7	-2.9	-3.3	-3.5	-3.9	-3.6	-4.0	+3.0	+2.6
Mississippi......................											
2016	2,985,415	4,459	149.4	82,521	2,764.1	23,489	786.8	54,725	1,833.1	4,307	144.3
2017	2,984,100	5,119	171.5	81,581	2,733.9	24,710	828.1	52,240	1,750.6	4,631	155.2
Percent change	*	+14.8	+14.9	-1.1	-1.1	+5.2	+5.2	-4.5	-4.5	+7.5	+7.6
Tennessee.......................											
2016	6,649,404	31,332	471.2	191,199	2,875.4	40,607	610.7	135,353	2,035.6	15,239	229.2
2017	6,715,984	32,432	482.9	197,488	2,940.6	38,716	576.5	140,248	2,088.3	18,524	275.8
Percent change	1.0	+3.5	+2.5	+3.3	+2.3	-4.7	-5.6	+3.6	+2.6	+21.6	+20.4

Table 2. Crime in the United States,[1] by Region, Geographic Division, and State, 2016–2017—*Continued*

(Number, rate per 100,000 population, percent.)

Area	Population[2]	Violent crime[3] Number	Rate	Murder and nonnegligent manslaughter Number	Rate	Rape[4] Number	Rate	Robbery Number	Rate
West South Central...........									
2016................................	39,500,457	181,959	460.7	2,497	6.3	19,579	49.6	44,172	111.8
2017................................	39,924,072	184,935	463.2	2,494	6.2	20,532	51.4	42,560	106.6
Percent change	1.1	+1.6	+0.6	-0.1	-1.2	+4.9	+3.8	-3.6	-4.7
Arkansas									
2016	2,988,231	16,563	554.3	217	7.3	2,214	74.1	2,125	71.1
2017	3,004,279	16,671	554.9	258	8.6	2,053	68.3	1,935	64.4
Percent change	0.5	+0.7	+0.1	+18.9	+18.3	-7.3	-7.8	-8.9	-9.4
Louisiana.........................									
2016	4,686,157	26,477	565.0	555	11.8	1,819	38.8	5,575	119.0
2017	4,684,333	26,092	557.0	582	12.4	1,867	39.9	5,358	114.4
Percent change	*	-1.5	-1.4	+4.9	+4.9	+2.6	+2.7	-3.9	-3.9
Oklahoma									
2016	3,921,207	17,855	455.3	247	6.3	2,100	53.6	3,174	80.9
2017	3,930,864	17,934	456.2	242	6.2	2,142	54.5	3,000	76.3
Percent change	0.2	+0.4	+0.2	-2.0	-2.3	+2.0	+1.7	-5.5	-5.7
Texas...............................									
2016	27,904,862	121,064	433.8	1,478	5.3	13,446	48.2	33,298	119.3
2017	28,304,596	124,238	438.9	1,412	5.0	14,470	51.1	32,267	114.0
Percent change	1.4	+2.6	+1.2	-4.5	-5.8	+7.6	+6.1	-3.1	-4.5
West..............................									
2016................................	76,644,950	319,978	417.5	3,453	4.5	33,551	43.8	86,293	112.6
2017................................	77,410,622	327,502	423.1	3,485	4.5	35,273	45.6	88,348	114.1
Percent change	1.0	+2.4	+1.3	+0.9	-0.1	+5.1	+4.1	+2.4	+1.4
Mountain									
2016................................	23,811,346	102,680	431.2	1,125	4.7	13,278	55.8	21,713	91.2
2017................................	24,158,117	105,943	438.5	1,220	5.1	13,868	57.4	21,876	90.6
Percent change	1.4	+3.2	+1.7	+8.4	+6.9	+4.4	+2.9	+0.8	-0.7
Arizona									
2016	6,908,642	32,542	471.0	389	5.6	3,304	47.8	7,045	102.0
2017	7,016,270	35,644	508.0	416	5.9	3,581	51.0	7,440	106.0
Percent change	1.5	+9.5	+7.9	+6.9	+5.3	+8.4	+6.7	+5.6	+4.0
Colorado..........................									
2016	5,530,105	19,030	344.1	189	3.4	3,635	65.7	3,525	63.7
2017	5,607,154	20,638	368.1	221	3.9	3,858	68.8	3,838	68.4
Percent change	1.4	+8.4	+7.0	+16.9	+15.3	+6.1	+4.7	+8.9	+7.4
Idaho									
2016	1,680,026	3,876	230.7	49	2.9	719	42.8	213	12.7
2017	1,716,943	3,888	226.4	32	1.9	707	41.2	196	11.4
Percent change	2.2	+0.3	-1.8	-34.7	-36.1	-1.7	-3.8	-8.0	-10.0
Montana...........................									
2016	1,038,656	3,886	374.1	37	3.6	598	57.6	268	25.8
2017	1,050,493	3,961	377.1	41	3.9	613	58.4	295	28.1
Percent change	1.1	+1.9	+0.8	+10.8	+9.6	+2.5	+1.4	+10.1	+8.8
Nevada.............................									
2016	2,939,254	19,924	677.9	228	7.8	1,729	58.8	6,338	215.6
2017	2,998,039	16,667	555.9	274	9.1	1,890	63.0	4,841	161.5
Percent change	2.0	-16.3	-18.0	+20.2	+17.8	+9.3	+7.2	-23.6	-25.1
New Mexico......................									
2016	2,085,432	14,585	699.4	139	6.7	1,527	73.2	2,737	131.2
2017	2,088,070	16,359	783.5	148	7.1	1,259	60.3	3,722	178.3
Percent change	0.1	+12.2	+12.0	+6.5	+6.3	-17.6	-17.7	+36.0	+35.8
Utah................................									
2016	3,044,321	7,406	243.3	74	2.4	1,560	51.2	1,528	50.2
2017	3,101,833	7,410	238.9	73	2.4	1,697	54.7	1,468	47.3
Percent change	1.9	+0.1	-1.8	-1.4	-3.2	+8.8	+6.8	-3.9	-5.7
Wyoming									
2016	584,910	1,431	244.7	20	3.4	206	35.2	59	10.1
2017	579,315	1,376	237.5	15	2.6	263	45.4	76	13.1
Percent change	-1.0	-3.8	-2.9	-25.0	-24.3	+27.7	+28.9	+28.8	+30.1
Pacific..............................									
2016................................	52,833,604	217,298	411.3	2,328	4.4	20,273	38.4	64,580	122.2
2017................................	53,252,505	221,559	416.1	2,265	4.3	21,405	40.2	66,472	124.8
Percent change	0.8	+2.0	+1.2	-2.7	-3.5	+5.6	+4.8	+2.9	+2.1

(Number, rate per 100,000 population, percent.)

Area	Population[2]	Aggravated assault Number	Aggravated assault Rate	Property crime Number	Property crime Rate	Burglary Number	Burglary Rate	Larceny-theft Number	Larceny-theft Rate	Motor vehicle theft Number	Motor vehicle theft Rate
West South Central..........											
2016....................	39,500,457	115,711	292.9	1,140,505	2,887.3	236,675	599.2	805,047	2,038.1	98,783	250.1
2017....................	39,924,072	119,349	298.9	1,088,595	2,726.7	218,801	548.0	771,287	1,931.9	98,507	246.7
Percent change	1.1	+3.1	+2.0	-4.6	-5.6	-7.6	-8.5	-4.2	-5.2	-0.3	-1.3
Arkansas.........................											
2016	2,988,231	12,007	401.8	98,092	3,282.6	23,814	796.9	67,091	2,245.2	7,187	240.5
2017	3,004,279	12,425	413.6	92,489	3,078.6	21,862	727.7	63,374	2,109.5	7,253	241.4
Percent change	0.5	+3.5	+2.9	-5.7	-6.2	-8.2	-8.7	-5.5	-6.0	+0.9	+0.4
Louisiana........................											
2016	4,686,157	18,528	395.4	154,511	3,297.2	34,689	740.2	109,492	2,336.5	10,330	220.4
2017	4,684,333	18,285	390.3	157,712	3,366.8	34,265	731.5	112,485	2,401.3	10,962	234.0
Percent change	*	-1.3	-1.3	+2.1	+2.1	-1.2	-1.2	+2.7	+2.8	+6.1	+6.2
Oklahoma........................											
2016	3,921,207	12,334	314.5	118,010	3,009.5	29,376	749.2	76,358	1,947.3	12,276	313.1
2017	3,930,864	12,550	319.3	113,066	2,876.4	28,608	727.8	72,207	1,836.9	12,251	311.7
Percent change	0.2	+1.8	+1.5	-4.2	-4.4	-2.6	-2.9	-5.4	-5.7	-0.2	-0.4
Texas.............................											
2016	27,904,862	72,842	261.0	769,892	2,759.0	148,796	533.2	552,106	1,978.5	68,990	247.2
2017	28,304,596	76,089	268.8	725,328	2,562.6	134,066	473.7	523,221	1,848.5	68,041	240.4
Percent change	1.4	+4.5	+3.0	-5.8	-7.1	-9.9	-11.2	-5.2	-6.6	-1.4	-2.8
West................................											
2016....................	76,644,950	196,681	256.6	2,122,858	2,769.7	387,638	505.8	1,426,270	1,860.9	308,950	403.1
2017....................	77,410,622	200,396	258.9	2,081,231	2,688.6	368,921	476.6	1,407,907	1,818.8	304,403	393.2
Percent change	1.0	+1.9	+0.9	-2.0	-2.9	-4.8	-5.8	-1.3	-2.3	-1.5	-2.4
Mountain..........................											
2016....................	23,811,346	66,564	279.5	676,849	2,842.5	123,130	517.1	475,693	1,997.8	78,026	327.7
2017....................	24,158,117	68,979	285.5	668,772	2,768.3	121,086	501.2	467,137	1,933.7	80,549	333.4
Percent change	1.4	+3.6	+2.1	-1.2	-2.6	-1.7	-3.1	-1.8	-3.2	+3.2	+1.8
Arizona											
2016	6,908,642	21,804	315.6	207,317	3,000.8	38,216	553.2	150,618	2,180.1	18,483	267.5
2017	7,016,270	24,207	345.0	204,515	2,914.9	37,627	536.3	147,830	2,107.0	19,058	271.6
Percent change	1.5	+11.0	+9.3	-1.4	-2.9	-1.5	-3.1	-1.9	-3.4	+3.1	+1.5
Colorado........................											
2016	5,530,105	11,681	211.2	152,146	2,751.2	23,825	430.8	108,680	1,965.2	19,641	355.2
2017	5,607,154	12,721	226.9	151,483	2,701.6	22,813	406.9	106,809	1,904.9	21,861	389.9
Percent change	1.4	+8.9	+7.4	-0.4	-1.8	-4.2	-5.6	-1.7	-3.1	+11.3	+9.8
Idaho											
2016	1,680,026	2,895	172.3	29,357	1,747.4	6,318	376.1	20,962	1,247.7	2,077	123.6
2017	1,716,943	2,953	172.0	28,079	1,635.4	5,655	329.4	20,278	1,181.1	2,146	125.0
Percent change	2.2	+2.0	-0.2	-4.4	-6.4	-10.5	-12.4	-3.3	-5.3	+3.3	+1.1
Montana											
2016	1,038,656	2,983	287.2	28,156	2,710.8	3,966	381.8	21,427	2,063.0	2,763	266.0
2017	1,050,493	3,012	286.7	27,225	2,591.6	3,615	344.1	21,018	2,000.8	2,592	246.7
Percent change	1.1	+1.0	-0.2	-3.3	-4.4	-8.9	-9.9	-1.9	-3.0	-6.2	-7.2
Nevada............................											
2016	2,939,254	11,629	395.6	75,922	2,583.0	18,816	640.2	43,949	1,495.2	13,157	447.6
2017	2,998,039	9,662	322.3	78,322	2,612.4	20,049	668.7	45,461	1,516.4	12,812	427.3
Percent change	2.0	-16.9	-18.5	+3.2	+1.1	+6.6	+4.5	+3.4	+1.4	-2.6	-4.5
New Mexico											
2016	2,085,432	10,182	488.2	81,930	3,928.7	17,280	828.6	52,907	2,537.0	11,743	563.1
2017	2,088,070	11,230	537.8	82,306	3,941.7	17,917	858.1	52,617	2,519.9	11,772	563.8
Percent change	0.1	+10.3	+10.2	+0.5	+0.3	+3.7	+3.6	-0.5	-0.7	+0.2	+0.1
Utah..............................											
2016	3,044,321	4,244	139.4	90,561	2,974.8	12,938	425.0	68,261	2,242.2	9,362	307.5
2017	3,101,833	4,172	134.5	86,238	2,780.2	11,817	381.0	64,892	2,092.1	9,529	307.2
Percent change	1.9	-1.7	-3.5	-4.8	-6.5	-8.7	-10.4	-4.9	-6.7	+1.8	-0.1
Wyoming											
2016	584,910	1,146	195.9	11,460	1,959.3	1,771	302.8	8,889	1,519.7	800	136.8
2017	579,315	1,022	176.4	10,604	1,830.4	1,593	275.0	8,232	1,421.0	779	134.5
Percent change	-1.0	-10.8	-10.0	-7.5	-6.6	-10.1	-9.2	-7.4	-6.5	-2.6	-1.7
Pacific...............................											
2016....................	52,833,604	130,117	246.3	1,446,009	2,736.9	264,508	500.6	950,577	1,799.2	230,924	437.1
2017....................	53,252,505	131,417	246.8	1,412,459	2,652.4	247,835	465.4	940,770	1,766.6	223,854	420.4
Percent change	0.8	+1.0	+0.2	-2.3	-3.1	-6.3	-7.0	-1.0	-1.8	-3.1	-3.8

Table 2. Crime in the United States,[1] by Region, Geographic Division, and State, 2016–2017—*Continued*

(Number, rate per 100,000 population, percent.)

Area	Population[2]	Violent crime[3]		Murder and nonnegligent manslaughter		Rape[4]		Robbery	
		Number	Rate	Number	Rate	Number	Rate	Number	Rate
Alaska..............................									
2016	741,522	5,966	804.6	52	7.0	1,053	142.0	850	114.6
2017	739,795	6,133	829.0	62	8.4	863	116.7	951	128.5
Percent change	-0.2	+2.8	+3.0	+19.2	+19.5	-18.0	-17.9	+11.9	+12.1
California..........................									
2016	39,296,476	174,796	444.8	1,930	4.9	13,702	34.9	54,789	139.4
2017	39,536,653	177,627	449.3	1,830	4.6	14,721	37.2	56,622	143.2
Percent change	0.6	+1.6	+1.0	-5.2	-5.8	+7.4	+6.8	+3.3	+2.7
Hawaii..........................									
2016	1,428,683	3,452	241.6	35	2.4	601	42.1	985	68.9
2017	1,427,538	3,577	250.6	39	2.7	567	39.7	1,077	75.4
Percent change	-0.1	+3.6	+3.7	+11.4	+11.5	-5.7	-5.6	+9.3	+9.4
Oregon[6]									
2016	4,085,989	10,983	268.8	116	2.8	1,784	43.7	2,307	56.5
2017	4,142,776	11,674	281.8	104	2.5	1,999	48.3	2,432	58.7
Percent change	1.4	+6.3	+4.8	-10.3	-11.6	+12.1	+10.5	+5.4	+4.0
Washington									
2016	7,280,934	22,101	303.5	195	2.7	3,133	43.0	5,649	77.6
2017	7,405,743	22,548	304.5	230	3.1	3,255	44.0	5,390	72.8
Percent change	1.7	+2.0	+0.3	+17.9	+16.0	+3.9	+2.1	-4.6	-6.2
Puerto Rico									
2016................................	3,406,520	7,643	224.4	679	19.9	169	5.0	3,201	94.0
2017................................	3,337,177	7,762	232.6	679	20.3	209	6.3	3,055	91.5
Percent change	-2.1	+1.6	+3.7	0.0	+2.1	+23.7	+26.2	-4.6	-2.6

Table 2. Crime in the United States,[1] by Region, Geographic Division, and State, 2016–2017—*Continued*

(Number, rate per 100,000 population, percent.)

Area	Population[2]	Aggravated assault		Property crime		Burglary		Larceny-theft		Motor vehicle theft	
		Number	Rate	Number	Rate	Number	Rate	Number	Rate	Number	Rate
Alaska............................											
2016	741,522	4,011	540.9	24,876	3,354.7	4,053	546.6	17,766	2,395.9	3,057	412.3
2017	739,795	4,257	575.4	26,204	3,542.1	4,171	563.8	17,775	2,402.7	4,258	575.6
Percent change	-0.2	+6.1	+6.4	+5.3	+5.6	+2.9	+3.2	+0.1	+0.3	+39.3	+39.6
California											
2016	39,296,476	104,375	265.6	1,002,070	2,550.0	188,304	479.2	637,010	1,621.0	176,756	449.8
2017	39,536,653	104,454	264.2	987,114	2,496.7	176,690	446.9	642,033	1,623.9	168,391	425.9
Percent change	0.6	+0.1	-0.5	-1.5	-2.1	-6.2	-6.7	+0.8	+0.2	-4.7	-5.3
Hawaii...........................											
2016	1,428,683	1,831	128.2	42,353	2,964.5	5,983	418.8	30,871	2,160.8	5,499	384.9
2017	1,427,538	1,894	132.7	40,392	2,829.5	5,549	388.7	29,574	2,071.7	5,269	369.1
Percent change	-0.1	+3.4	+3.5	-4.6	-4.6	-7.3	-7.2	-4.2	-4.1	-4.2	-4.1
Oregon[6]											
2016	4,085,989	6,776	165.8	121,716	2,978.9	16,919	414.1	91,507	2,239.5	13,290	325.3
2017	4,142,776	7,139	172.3	123,722	2,986.5	17,705	427.4	88,877	2,145.3	17,140	413.7
Percent change	1.4	+5.4	+3.9	+1.6	+0.3	+4.6	+3.2	-2.9	-4.2	+29.0	+27.2
Washington											
2016	7,280,934	13,124	180.3	254,994	3,502.2	49,249	676.4	173,423	2,381.9	32,322	443.9
2017	7,405,743	13,673	184.6	235,027	3,173.6	43,720	590.4	162,511	2,194.4	28,796	388.8
Percent change	1.7	+4.2	+2.4	-7.8	-9.4	-11.2	-12.7	-6.3	-7.9	-10.9	-12.4
Puerto Rico											
2016.................................	3,406,520	3,594	105.5	35,201	1,033.3	8,251	242.2	23,163	680.0	3,787	111.2
2017.................................	3,337,177	3,819	114.4	31,176	934.2	7,949	238.2	19,633	588.3	3,594	107.7
Percent change	-2.1	+6.3	+8.5	-11.4	-9.6	-3.7	-1.7	-15.2	-13.5	-5.1	-3.1

Note: Although arson data are included in the trend and clearance tables, sufficient data are not available to estimate totals for this offense. Therefore, no arson data are published in this table.
* = Less than one-tenth of 1 percent.
[1]The previous year's crime figures have been adjusted.
[2]Population figures are U.S. Census Bureau provisional estimates as of July 1, 2017.
[3]The violent crime figures include the offenses of murder, rape (revised definition), robbery, and aggravated assault.
[4]The figures shown in this column for the offense of rape were estimated using the revised Uniform Crime Reporting (UCR) definition of rape.
[5]Includes offenses reported by the Metro Transit Police and the District of Columbia Fire and Emergency Medical Services: Arson Investigation Unit.
[6]This state's agencies submitted rape data according to the legacy UCR definition of rape.

Table 3. Crime, by State and Area, 2017

(Number, percent, rate per 100,000 population.)

Area	Population	Violent crime[1]	Murder and nonnegligent manslaughter	Rape (revised definition)[2]	Robbery	Aggravated assault	Property crime	Burglary	Larceny-theft	Motor vehicle theft
Alabama										
Metropolitan statistical area	3,732,789									
Area actually reporting	99.0%	20,396	337	1,535	3,706	14,818	114,790	24,598	79,734	10,458
Estimated total	100.0%	20,585	340	1,548	3,738	14,959	116,031	24,809	80,666	10,556
Cities outside metropolitan areas	518,602									
Area actually reporting	94.3%	3,526	38	264	366	2,858	19,732	3,964	14,367	1,401
Estimated total	100.0%	3,715	40	277	385	3,013	20,642	4,169	15,000	1,473
Nonmetropolitan counties	623,356									
Area actually reporting	92.9%	1,162	22	189	87	864	6,954	2,321	3,879	754
Estimated total	100.0%	1,251	24	203	94	930	7,487	2,499	4,176	812
State total	4,874,747	25,551	404	2,028	4,217	18,902	144,160	31,477	99,842	12,841
Rate per 100,000 inhabitants		524.2	8.3	41.6	86.5	387.8	2,957.3	645.7	2,048.1	263.4
Alaska										
Metropolitan statistical area	348,650									
Area actually reporting	100.0%	3,859	38	418	830	2,573	18,698	2,453	12,750	3,495
Cities outside metropolitan areas	127,272									
Area actually reporting	97.2%	1,035	6	212	81	736	4,079	635	3,170	274
Estimated total	100.0%	1,064	6	218	83	757	4,197	653	3,262	282
Nonmetropolitan counties	263,873									
Area actually reporting	100.0%	1,210	18	227	38	927	3,309	1,065	1,763	481
State total	739,795	6,133	62	863	951	4,257	26,204	4,171	17,775	4,258
Rate per 100,000 inhabitants		829.0	8.4	116.7	128.5	575.4	3,542.1	563.8	2,402.7	575.6
Arizona										
Metropolitan statistical area	6,665,732									
Area actually reporting	99.6%	30,336	376	3,300	7,300	19,360	194,978	35,203	141,758	18,017
Estimated total	100.0%	30,412	376	3,310	7,316	19,410	195,650	35,305	142,278	18,067
Cities outside metropolitan areas	125,031									
Area actually reporting	96.9%	4,644	34	253	89	4,268	6,746	1,590	4,420	736
Estimated total	100.0%	4,790	35	261	92	4,402	6,958	1,640	4,559	759
Nonmetropolitan counties	225,507									
Area actually reporting	100.0%	442	5	10	32	395	1,907	682	993	232
State total	7,016,270	35,644	416	3,581	7,440	24,207	204,515	37,627	147,830	19,058
Rate per 100,000 inhabitants		508.0	5.9	51.0	106.0	345.0	2,914.9	536.3	2,107.0	271.6
Arkansas										
Metropolitan statistical area	1,870,966									
Area actually reporting	99.3%	11,887	171	1,250	1,614	8,852	64,624	14,487	44,777	5,360
Estimated total	100.0%	11,939	171	1,258	1,617	8,893	64,898	14,566	44,946	5,386
Cities outside metropolitan areas	515,402									
Area actually reporting	90.4%	2,565	46	396	252	1,871	16,666	4,271	11,542	853
Estimated total	100.0%	2,846	51	446	279	2,070	18,442	4,726	12,772	944
Nonmetropolitan counties	617,911									
Area actually reporting	93.5%	1,756	34	320	36	1,366	8,551	2,402	5,286	863
Estimated total	100.0%	1,886	36	349	39	1,462	9,149	2,570	5,656	923
State total	3,004,279	16,671	258	2,053	1,935	12,425	92,489	21,862	63,374	7,253
Rate per 100,000 inhabitants		554.9	8.6	68.3	64.4	413.6	3,078.6	727.7	2,109.5	241.4
California										
Metropolitan statistical area	38,706,996									
Area actually reporting	99.9%	173,634	1,778	14,252	56,127	101,477	968,957	171,705	631,712	165,540
Estimated total	100.0%	173,659	1,778	14,254	56,135	101,492	969,133	171,737	631,828	165,568
Cities outside metropolitan areas	263,117									
Area actually reporting	100.0%	1,641	13	182	296	1,150	9,240	1,950	6,070	1,220
Nonmetropolitan counties	566,540									
Area actually reporting	100.0%	2,327	39	285	191	1,812	8,741	3,003	4,135	1,603
State total	39,536,653	177,627	1,830	14,721	56,622	104,454	987,114	176,690	642,033	168,391
Rate per 100,000 inhabitants		449.3	4.6	37.2	143.2	264.2	2,496.7	446.9	1,623.9	425.9
Colorado										
Metropolitan statistical area	4,904,129									
Area actually reporting	99.9%	19,312	209	3,531	3,742	11,830	137,837	20,399	96,472	20,966
Estimated total	100.0%	19,326	209	3,533	3,743	11,841	138,023	20,421	96,613	20,989
Cities outside metropolitan areas	339,363									
Area actually reporting	96.6%	801	5	202	77	517	9,686	1,394	7,772	520
Estimated total	100.0%	829	5	209	80	535	10,024	1,443	8,043	538
Nonmetropolitan counties	363,662									
Area actually reporting	96.2%	465	7	112	14	332	3,305	913	2,071	321
Estimated total	100.0%	483	7	116	15	345	3,436	949	2,153	334

Table 3. Crime, by State and Area, 2017—*Continued*

(Number, percent, rate per 100,000 population.)

Area	Population	Violent crime[1]	Murder and nonnegligent manslaughter	Rape (revised definition)[2]	Robbery	Aggravated assault	Property crime	Burglary	Larceny-theft	Motor vehicle theft
State total....................	5,607,154	20,638	221	3,858	3,838	12,721	151,483	22,813	106,809	21,861
Rate per 100,000 inhabitants		368.1	3.9	68.8	68.4	226.9	2,701.6	406.9	1,904.9	389.9
Connecticut										
Metropolitan statistical area...................	2,967,056									
Area actually reporting	100.0%	7,739	95	732	2,745	4,167	59,420	8,014	44,567	6,839
Cities outside metropolitan areas.....................	112,933									
Area actually reporting	100.0%	125	1	24	22	78	1,532	206	1,215	111
Nonmetropolitan counties	508,195									
Area actually reporting	100.0%	316	6	81	46	183	2,557	670	1,528	359
State total....................	3,588,184	8,180	102	837	2,813	4,428	63,509	8,890	47,310	7,309
Rate per 100,000 inhabitants		228.0	2.8	23.3	78.4	123.4	1,769.9	247.8	1,318.5	203.7
Delaware										
Metropolitan statistical area...................	961,939									
Area actually reporting	100.0%	4,361	54	334	1,082	2,891	23,476	3,970	18,137	1,369
Cities outside metropolitan areas.....................	None									
Nonmetropolitan counties	None									
Area actually reporting	100.0%	0	0	0	0	0	1	0	1	0
State total....................	961,939	4,361	54	334	1,082	2,891	23,477	3,970	18,138	1,369
Rate per 100,000 inhabitants		453.4	5.6	34.7	112.5	300.5	2,440.6	412.7	1,885.6	142.3
District of Columbia[3]										
Metropolitan statistical area...................	693,972									
Area actually reporting	100.0%	6,974	116	444	2,623	3,791	29,729	1,809	25,333	2,587
Cities outside metropolitan areas.....................	None									
Nonmetropolitan counties	None									
District total....................	693,972	6,974	116	444	2,623	3,791	29,729	1,809	25,333	2,587
Rate per 100,000 inhabitants		1,004.9	16.7	64.0	378.0	546.3	4,283.9	260.7	3,650.4	372.8
Florida										
Metropolitan statistical area...............	20,272,180									
Area actually reporting	99.9%	82,152	1,013	7,675	18,321	55,143	512,472	84,699	385,742	42,031
Estimated total	100.0%	82,182	1,013	7,678	18,329	55,162	512,696	84,730	385,916	42,050
Cities outside metropolitan areas.....................	148,666									
Area actually reporting	96.5%	908	13	41	128	726	4,826	1,069	3,474	283
Estimated total	100.0%	940	13	42	133	752	5,002	1,108	3,601	293
Nonmetropolitan counties	563,554									
Area actually reporting	100.0%	2,503	31	220	135	2,117	9,522	3,015	5,936	571
State total....................	20,984,400	85,625	1,057	7,940	18,597	58,031	527,220	88,853	395,453	42,914
Rate per 100,000 inhabitants		408.0	5.0	37.8	88.6	276.5	2,512.4	423.4	1,884.5	204.5
Georgia										
Metropolitan statistical area...............	8,648,476									
Area actually reporting	98.7%	31,624	611	2,270	9,098	19,645	250,990	44,839	182,264	23,887
Estimated total	100.0%	31,963	617	2,294	9,194	19,858	253,813	45,376	184,272	24,165
Cities outside metropolitan areas.....................	644,485									
Area actually reporting	89.3%	2,543	43	190	607	1,703	23,153	4,446	17,875	832
Estimated total	100.0%	2,843	48	208	680	1,907	25,928	4,979	20,017	932
Nonmetropolitan counties	1,136,418									
Area actually reporting	93.9%	2,303	36	203	160	1,904	17,421	4,712	11,614	1,095
Estimated total	100.0%	2,452	38	216	170	2,028	18,557	5,019	12,372	1,166
State total....................	10,429,379	37,258	703	2,718	10,044	23,793	298,298	55,374	216,661	26,263
Rate per 100,000 inhabitants		357.2	6.7	26.1	96.3	228.1	2,860.2	530.9	2,077.4	251.8
Hawaii										
Metropolitan statistical area...............	1,156,252									
Area actually reporting	100.0%	2,886	34	380	975	1,497	33,206	4,237	24,556	4,413
Cities outside metropolitan areas.....................	None									
Nonmetropolitan counties	271,286									
Area actually reporting	100.0%	691	5	187	102	397	7,186	1,312	5,018	856
State total....................	1,427,538	3,577	39	567	1,077	1,894	40,392	5,549	29,574	5,269
Rate per 100,000 inhabitants		250.6	2.7	39.7	75.4	132.7	2,829.5	388.7	2,071.7	369.1
Idaho										
Metropolitan statistical area...............	1,262,172									
Area actually reporting	100.0%	3,067	20	563	170	2,314	22,617	4,422	16,514	1,681
Cities outside metropolitan areas.....................	185,424									
Area actually reporting	95.9%	407	6	63	18	320	2,943	587	2,180	176
Estimated total	100.0%	425	6	66	19	334	3,070	612	2,274	184

Table 3. Crime, by State and Area, 2017—*Continued*

(Number, percent, rate per 100,000 population.)

Area	Population	Violent crime[1]	Murder and nonnegligent manslaughter	Rape (revised definition)[2]	Robbery	Aggravated assault	Property crime	Burglary	Larceny-theft	Motor vehicle theft
Nonmetropolitan counties	269,347									
Area actually reporting	95.1%	377	6	74	7	290	2,275	591	1,417	267
Estimated total	100.0%	396	6	78	7	305	2,392	621	1,490	281
State total...	1,716,943	3,888	32	707	196	2,953	28,079	5,655	20,278	2,146
Rate per 100,000 inhabitants		226.4	1.9	41.2	11.4	172.0	1,635.4	329.4	1,181.1	125.0
Illinois										
Metropolitan statistical area................................	11,331,892									
Area actually reporting	97.1%	51,775	951	4,759	17,115	28,950	230,153	37,601	172,871	19,681
Estimated total	100.0%	52,451	958	4,868	17,292	29,333	235,187	38,399	176,814	19,974
Cities outside metropolitan areas........................	826,086									
Area actually reporting	83.5%	2,219	15	378	202	1,624	14,323	2,828	10,981	514
Estimated total	100.0%	2,661	18	455	242	1,946	17,164	3,389	13,159	616
Nonmetropolitan counties	644,045									
Area actually reporting	89.8%	955	19	205	30	701	4,621	1,501	2,859	261
Estimated total	100.0%	1,068	21	233	33	781	5,146	1,671	3,184	291
State total...	12,802,023	56,180	997	5,556	17,567	32,060	257,497	43,459	193,157	20,881
Rate per 100,000 inhabitants		438.8	7.8	43.4	137.2	250.4	2,011.4	339.5	1,508.8	163.1
Indiana										
Metropolitan statistical area................................	5,204,012									
Area actually reporting	85.1%	22,751	357	1,992	6,157	14,245	126,203	23,313	90,351	12,539
Estimated total	100.0%	24,167	370	2,212	6,390	15,195	137,437	25,342	98,436	13,659
Cities outside metropolitan areas........................	521,675									
Area actually reporting.............................	66.3%	814	6	87	99	622	9,615	1,356	7,640	619
Estimated total	100.0%	1,237	9	140	149	939	14,509	2,046	11,529	934
Nonmetropolitan counties	941,131									
Area actually reporting	55.8%	646	10	132	34	470	5,127	1,536	3,140	451
Estimated total	100.0%	1,194	18	273	61	842	9,186	2,752	5,626	808
State total...	6,666,818	26,598	397	2,625	6,600	16,976	161,132	30,140	115,591	15,401
Rate per 100,000 inhabitants		399.0	6.0	39.4	99.0	254.6	2,416.9	452.1	1,733.8	231.0
Iowa										
Metropolitan statistical area................................	1,875,128									
Area actually reporting	98.4%	5,814	79	768	1,098	3,869	47,559	9,932	33,401	4,226
Estimated total	100.0%	5,885	79	780	1,103	3,923	48,116	10,045	33,812	4,259
Cities outside metropolitan areas........................	599,405									
Area actually reporting	94.3%	2,343	13	307	132	1,891	13,785	3,177	9,759	849
Estimated total	100.0%	2,484	14	325	140	2,005	14,614	3,368	10,346	900
Nonmetropolitan counties	671,178									
Area actually reporting	99.3%	855	11	128	10	706	4,096	1,653	2,026	417
Estimated total	100.0%	861	11	129	10	711	4,125	1,665	2,040	420
State total...	3,145,711	9,230	104	1,234	1,253	6,639	66,855	15,078	46,198	5,579
Rate per 100,000 inhabitants		293.4	3.3	39.2	39.8	211.0	2,125.3	479.3	1,468.6	177.4
Kansas										
Metropolitan statistical area................................	1,983,302									
Area actually reporting	98.0%	9,009	126	1,241	1,554	6,088	59,437	9,265	43,779	6,393
Estimated total	100.0%	9,097	127	1,253	1,562	6,155	60,179	9,382	44,337	6,460
Cities outside metropolitan areas........................	599,197									
Area actually reporting	95.3%	2,092	23	298	192	1,579	16,577	3,109	12,542	926
Estimated total	100.0%	2,191	24	309	201	1,657	17,393	3,262	13,159	972
Nonmetropolitan counties	330,624									
Area actually reporting	96.9%	719	9	63	21	626	3,896	1,247	2,248	401
Estimated total	100.0%	742	9	65	22	646	4,021	1,287	2,320	414
State total...	2,913,123	12,030	160	1,627	1,785	8,458	81,593	13,931	59,816	7,846
Rate per 100,000 inhabitants		413.0	5.5	55.9	61.3	290.3	2,800.9	478.2	2,053.3	269.3
Kentucky										
Metropolitan statistical area................................	2,621,479									
Area actually reporting	100.0%	7,663	175	876	2,586	4,026	71,161	13,555	49,835	7,771
Cities outside metropolitan areas........................	542,756									
Area actually reporting	100.0%	915	20	206	247	442	13,481	2,757	9,686	1,038
Nonmetropolitan counties	1,289,954									
Area actually reporting	100.0%	1,478	68	579	125	706	10,191	3,883	4,873	1,435
State total...	4,454,189	10,056	263	1,661	2,958	5,174	94,833	20,195	64,394	10,244
Rate per 100,000 inhabitants		225.8	5.9	37.3	66.4	116.2	2,129.1	453.4	1,445.7	230.0

Table 3. Crime, by State and Area, 2017—*Continued*

(Number, percent, rate per 100,000 population.)

Area	Population	Violent crime[1]	Murder and nonnegligent manslaughter	Rape (revised definition)[2]	Robbery	Aggravated assault	Property crime	Burglary	Larceny-theft	Motor vehicle theft
Louisiana										
Metropolitan statistical area	3,929,950									
Area actually reporting	97.1%	22,131	539	1,662	4,971	14,959	135,775	28,709	97,204	9,862
Estimated total	100.0%	22,555	547	1,690	5,038	15,280	138,987	29,388	99,555	10,044
Cities outside metropolitan areas	249,151									
Area actually reporting	85.6%	1,691	12	69	206	1,404	9,884	2,459	7,129	296
Estimated total	100.0%	1,977	14	81	241	1,641	11,552	2,874	8,332	346
Nonmetropolitan counties	505,232									
Area actually reporting	97.0%	1,513	20	93	77	1,323	6,958	1,943	4,460	555
Estimated total	100.0%	1,560	21	96	79	1,364	7,173	2,003	4,598	572
State total	4,684,333	26,092	582	1,867	5,358	18,285	157,712	34,265	112,485	10,962
Rate per 100,000 inhabitants		557.0	12.4	39.9	114.4	390.3	3,366.8	731.5	2,401.3	234.0
Maine										
Metropolitan statistical area	793,252									
Area actually reporting	100.0%	949	6	273	189	481	12,182	1,815	9,917	450
Cities outside metropolitan areas	255,603									
Area actually reporting	100.0%	355	4	103	35	213	5,022	716	4,138	168
Nonmetropolitan counties	287,052									
Area actually reporting	100.0%	313	13	97	25	178	2,929	803	1,951	175
State total	1,335,907	1,617	23	473	249	872	20,133	3,334	16,006	793
Rate per 100,000 inhabitants		121.0	1.7	35.4	18.6	65.3	1,507.1	249.6	1,198.1	59.4
Maryland										
Metropolitan statistical area	5,901,111									
Area actually reporting	100.0%	29,897	545	1,666	11,135	16,551	131,261	22,726	95,128	13,407
Cities outside metropolitan areas	52,511									
Area actually reporting	100.0%	255	0	17	46	192	2,048	388	1,569	91
Nonmetropolitan counties	98,555									
Area actually reporting	100.0%	121	1	8	19	93	1,187	394	723	70
State total	6,052,177	30,273	546	1,691	11,200	16,836	134,496	23,508	97,420	13,568
Rate per 100,000 inhabitants		500.2	9.0	27.9	185.1	278.2	2,222.3	388.4	1,609.7	224.2
Massachusetts										
Metropolitan statistical area	6,760,988									
Area actually reporting	97.8%	23,749	171	2,099	4,786	16,693	95,258	16,466	71,455	7,337
Estimated total	100.0%	24,170	173	2,143	4,852	17,002	97,138	16,785	72,877	7,476
Cities outside metropolitan areas	91,409									
Area actually reporting	84.9%	327	0	46	16	265	1,220	258	908	54
Estimated total	100.0%	385	0	54	19	312	1,437	304	1,069	64
Nonmetropolitan counties	7,422									
Area actually reporting	98.8%	5	0	0	0	5	0	0	0	0
Estimated total	100.0%	5	0	0	0	5	0	0	0	0
State total	6,859,819	24,560	173	2,197	4,871	17,319	98,575	17,089	73,946	7,540
Rate per 100,000 inhabitants		358.0	2.5	32.0	71.0	252.5	1,437.0	249.1	1,078.0	109.9
Michigan										
Metropolitan statistical area	8,164,062									
Area actually reporting	99.8%	40,088	528	5,351	6,359	27,850	156,823	31,228	107,009	18,586
Estimated total	100.0%	40,136	528	5,361	6,366	27,881	157,112	31,273	107,231	18,608
Cities outside metropolitan areas	588,043									
Area actually reporting	98.0%	1,688	12	584	72	1,020	10,765	1,316	9,108	341
Estimated total	100.0%	1,723	12	598	73	1,040	10,980	1,342	9,290	348
Nonmetropolitan counties	1,210,206									
Area actually reporting	99.6%	2,955	29	1,068	49	1,809	11,178	3,013	7,551	614
Estimated total	100.0%	2,967	29	1,072	49	1,817	11,226	3,026	7,583	617
State total	9,962,311	44,826	569	7,031	6,488	30,738	179,318	35,641	124,104	19,573
Rate per 100,000 inhabitants		450.0	5.7	70.6	65.1	308.5	1,800.0	357.8	1,245.7	196.5
Minnesota										
Metropolitan statistical area	4,335,177									
Area actually reporting	100.0%	11,571	105	1,895	3,514	6,057	103,177	15,151	79,289	8,737
Cities outside metropolitan areas	557,001									
Area actually reporting	99.2%	1,077	5	294	79	699	12,204	1,667	9,934	603
Estimated total	100.0%	1,085	5	296	80	704	12,299	1,680	10,011	608
Nonmetropolitan counties	684,428									
Area actually reporting	100.0%	635	3	194	27	411	6,736	1,956	4,146	634

Table 3. Crime, by State and Area, 2017—*Continued*

(Number, percent, rate per 100,000 population.)

Area	Population	Violent crime[1]	Murder and nonnegligent manslaughter	Rape (revised definition)[2]	Robbery	Aggravated assault	Property crime	Burglary	Larceny-theft	Motor vehicle theft
State total...................................	5,576,606	13,291	113	2,385	3,621	7,172	122,212	18,787	93,446	9,979
Rate per 100,000 inhabitants		238.3	2.0	42.8	64.9	128.6	2,191.5	336.9	1,675.7	178.9
Mississippi										
Metropolitan statistical area.................	1,382,070									
Area actually reporting.....................	82.8%	3,251	113	386	1,010	1,742	33,658	7,787	23,607	2,264
Estimated total.............................	100.0%	3,633	124	429	1,088	1,992	38,696	8,952	27,189	2,555
Cities outside metropolitan areas..........	582,548									
Area actually reporting	43.1%	1,197	22	135	315	725	11,667	3,450	7,761	456
Estimated total.............................	100.0%	2,790	51	326	731	1,682	27,061	8,002	18,001	1,058
Nonmetropolitan counties	1,019,482									
Area actually reporting	31.4%	636	22	81	79	454	4,972	2,437	2,215	320
Estimated total.............................	100.0%	2,103	70	336	252	1,445	15,824	7,756	7,050	1,018
State total...................................	2,984,100	8,526	245	1,091	2,071	5,119	81,581	24,710	52,240	4,631
Rate per 100,000 inhabitants		285.7	8.2	36.6	69.4	171.5	2,733.9	828.1	1,750.6	155.2
Missouri										
Metropolitan statistical area.................	4,571,538									
Area actually reporting.....................	99.9%	27,993	535	2,278	6,095	19,085	141,180	23,237	100,277	17,666
Estimated total.............................	100.0%	27,996	535	2,278	6,095	19,088	141,230	23,244	100,315	17,671
Cities outside metropolitan areas..........	659,462									
Area actually reporting	99.2%	2,323	23	278	202	1,820	21,999	3,593	17,220	1,186
Estimated total.............................	100.0%	2,340	23	279	204	1,834	22,169	3,621	17,353	1,195
Nonmetropolitan counties	882,532									
Area actually reporting	99.7%	2,077	42	171	52	1,812	9,820	3,205	5,564	1,051
Estimated total.............................	100.0%	2,084	42	172	52	1,818	9,854	3,216	5,583	1,055
State total...................................	6,113,532	32,420	600	2,729	6,351	22,740	173,253	30,081	123,251	19,921
Rate per 100,000 inhabitants		530.3	9.8	44.6	103.9	372.0	2,833.9	492.0	2,016.0	325.9
Montana										
Metropolitan statistical area.................	370,184									
Area actually reporting.....................	100.0%	1,426	13	208	171	1,034	14,098	1,694	11,002	1,402
Cities outside metropolitan areas..........	225,508									
Area actually reporting	99.5%	1,238	12	234	101	891	6,820	803	5,482	535
Estimated total	100.0%	1,243	12	235	101	895	6,851	807	5,507	537
Nonmetropolitan counties	454,801									
Area actually reporting	99.9%	1,291	16	170	23	1,082	6,269	1,113	4,504	652
Estimated total.............................	100.0%	1,292	16	170	23	1,083	6,276	1,114	4,509	653
State total...................................	1,050,493	3,961	41	613	295	3,012	27,225	3,615	21,018	2,592
Rate per 100,000 inhabitants		377.1	3.9	58.4	28.1	286.7	2,591.6	344.1	2,000.8	246.7
Nebraska										
Metropolitan statistical area.................	1,253,777									
Area actually reporting.....................	99.4%	4,759	37	853	897	2,972	33,109	4,542	24,048	4,519
Estimated total.............................	100.0%	4,768	37	856	897	2,978	33,202	4,556	24,117	4,529
Cities outside metropolitan areas..........	338,896									
Area actually reporting	92.8%	740	3	235	57	445	7,711	1,255	6,037	419
Estimated total.............................	100.0%	802	3	258	61	480	8,312	1,353	6,507	452
Nonmetropolitan counties	327,403									
Area actually reporting	90.2%	272	3	68	9	192	1,938	508	1,230	200
Estimated total.............................	100.0%	303	3	77	10	213	2,149	563	1,364	222
State total...................................	1,920,076	5,873	43	1,191	968	3,671	43,663	6,472	31,988	5,203
Rate per 100,000 inhabitants		305.9	2.2	62.0	50.4	191.2	2,274.0	337.1	1,666.0	271.0
Nevada										
Metropolitan statistical area.................	2,724,009									
Area actually reporting.....................	100.0%	15,990	260	1,773	4,806	9,151	74,017	18,877	42,781	12,359
Cities outside metropolitan areas..........	48,711									
Area actually reporting.....................	100.0%	236	6	44	17	169	1,377	330	932	115
Nonmetropolitan counties	225,319									
Area actually reporting	100.0%	441	8	73	18	342	2,928	842	1,748	338
State total...................................	2,998,039	16,667	274	1,890	4,841	9,662	78,322	20,049	45,461	12,812
Rate per 100,000 inhabitants		555.9	9.1	63.0	161.5	322.3	2,612.4	668.7	1,516.4	427.3
New Hampshire										
Metropolitan statistical area.................	844,743									
Area actually reporting.....................	99.3%	1,728	9	378	312	1,029	10,940	1,439	8,935	566
Estimated total.............................	100.0%	1,736	9	380	313	1,034	11,008	1,447	8,992	569

Table 3. Crime, by State and Area, 2017—*Continued*

(Number, percent, rate per 100,000 population.)

Area	Population	Violent crime[1]	Murder and nonnegligent manslaughter	Rape (revised definition)[2]	Robbery	Aggravated assault	Property crime	Burglary	Larceny-theft	Motor vehicle theft
Cities outside metropolitan areas..........................	452,773									
Area actually reporting.............................	91.6%	804	5	241	95	463	6,579	933	5,345	301
Estimated total	100.0%	882	5	267	104	506	7,185	1,019	5,837	329
Nonmetropolitan counties	45,279									
Area actually reporting.............................	93.9%	46	0	14	2	30	340	101	223	16
Estimated total	100.0%	50	0	16	2	32	362	108	237	17
State total..	1,342,795	2,668	14	663	419	1,572	18,555	2,574	15,066	915
Rate per 100,000 inhabitants		198.7	1.0	49.4	31.2	117.1	1,381.8	191.7	1,122.0	68.1
New Jersey										
Metropolitan statistical area	9,005,644									
Area actually reporting.............................	100.0%	20,604	324	1,505	7,895	10,880	140,086	23,891	104,025	12,170
Cities outside metropolitan areas..........................	None									
Nonmetropolitan counties	None									
State total..	9,005,644	20,604	324	1,505	7,895	10,880	140,086	23,891	104,025	12,170
Rate per 100,000 inhabitants		228.8	3.6	16.7	87.7	120.8	1,555.5	265.3	1,155.1	135.1
New Mexico										
Metropolitan statistical area	1,392,948									
Area actually reporting	100.0%	12,153	102	898	3,409	7,744	63,392	12,665	40,610	10,117
Cities outside metropolitan areas..........................	398,213									
Area actually reporting.............................	95.9%	2,620	28	208	249	2,135	14,711	3,696	9,903	1,112
Estimated total	100.0%	2,734	29	220	260	2,225	15,333	3,852	10,322	1,159
Nonmetropolitan counties	296,909									
Area actually reporting.............................	97.4%	1,433	17	136	52	1,228	3,488	1,364	1,641	483
Estimated total	100.0%	1,472	17	141	53	1,261	3,581	1,400	1,685	496
State total..	2,088,070	16,359	148	1,259	3,722	11,230	82,306	17,917	52,617	11,772
Rate per 100,000 inhabitants		783.5	7.1	60.3	178.3	537.8	3,941.7	858.1	2,519.9	563.8
New York										
Metropolitan statistical area	18,471,765									
Area actually reporting	99.3%	67,860	522	5,260	19,828	42,250	274,714	31,348	230,558	12,808
Estimated total	100.0%	68,039	523	5,291	19,872	42,353	276,293	31,528	231,892	12,873
Cities outside metropolitan areas..........................	506,148									
Area actually reporting.............................	97.0%	1,221	11	269	181	760	15,094	1,514	13,362	218
Estimated total	100.0%	1,260	11	278	187	784	15,569	1,562	13,782	225
Nonmetropolitan counties	871,486									
Area actually reporting.............................	100.0%	1,500	14	755	49	682	8,693	1,912	6,469	312
State total..	19,849,399	70,799	548	6,324	20,108	43,819	300,555	35,002	252,143	13,410
Rate per 100,000 inhabitants		356.7	2.8	31.9	101.3	220.8	1,514.2	176.3	1,270.3	67.6
North Carolina[4]										
Metropolitan statistical area	8,060,478									
Area actually reporting.............................	96.9%	30,308	445	2,144	8,045	19,674	204,202	46,533	144,865	12,804
Estimated total	100.0%	30,803	450	2,184	8,154	20,015	209,340	47,782	148,496	13,062
Cities outside metropolitan areas..........................	650,145									
Area actually reporting.............................	89.5%	3,393	67	214	749	2,363	25,304	6,399	17,799	1,106
Estimated total..	100.0%	3,778	75	225	837	2,641	28,282	7,152	19,894	1,236
Nonmetropolitan counties	1,562,796									
Area actually reporting.............................	95.3%	2,652	63	291	342	1,956	22,746	9,390	11,926	1,430
Estimated total	100.0%	2,783	66	306	359	2,052	23,864	9,852	12,512	1,500
State total..	10,273,419	37,364	591	2,715	9,350	24,708	261,486	64,786	180,902	15,798
Rate per 100,000 inhabitants		363.7	5.8	26.4	91.0	240.5	2,545.3	630.6	1,760.9	153.8
North Dakota										
Metropolitan statistical area	376,890									
Area actually reporting..............................	100.0%	1,193	4	226	143	820	10,148	1,567	7,708	873
Cities outside metropolitan areas..........................	195,777									
Area actually reporting	99.6%	746	4	131	35	576	4,719	944	3,150	625
Estimated total	100.0%	748	4	131	35	578	4,739	948	3,163	628
Nonmetropolitan counties	182,726									
Area actually reporting.............................	100.0%	184	2	42	5	135	1,715	427	1,016	272
State total..	755,393	2,125	10	399	183	1,533	16,602	2,942	11,887	1,773
Rate per 100,000 inhabitants		281.3	1.3	52.8	24.2	202.9	2,197.8	389.5	1,573.6	234.7
Ohio										
Metropolitan statistical area	9,298,408									
Area actually reporting.............................	93.2%	30,217	628	4,676	10,754	14,159	227,171	47,926	161,354	17,891
Estimated total	100.0%	31,168	642	4,891	11,034	14,601	239,845	49,912	171,437	18,496

Table 3. Crime, by State and Area, 2017—*Continued*

(Number, percent, rate per 100,000 population.)

Area	Population	Violent crime[1]	Murder and nonnegligent manslaughter	Rape (revised definition)[2]	Robbery	Aggravated assault	Property crime	Burglary	Larceny-theft	Motor vehicle theft
Cities outside metropolitan areas..........................	1,044,126									
Area actually reporting	80.3%	1,609	29	439	338	803	22,829	3,952	18,105	772
Estimated total	100.0%	2,007	36	550	421	1,000	28,425	4,921	22,543	961
Nonmetropolitan counties	1,316,075									
Area actually reporting	93.9%	1,412	30	389	141	852	12,918	3,510	8,661	747
Estimated total	100.0%	1,508	32	418	150	908	13,764	3,740	9,228	796
State total...	11,658,609	34,683	710	5,859	11,605	16,509	282,034	58,573	203,208	20,253
Rate per 100,000 inhabitants		297.5	6.1	50.3	99.5	141.6	2,419.1	502.4	1,743.0	173.7
Oklahoma										
Metropolitan statistical area...................................	2,655,595									
Area actually reporting	100.0%	13,871	206	1,629	2,697	9,339	81,976	20,294	52,055	9,627
Cities outside metropolitan areas..........................	710,875									
Area actually reporting...............................	99.8%	2,998	28	389	265	2,316	23,644	5,703	16,208	1,733
Estimated total	100.0%	3,002	28	389	265	2,320	23,683	5,712	16,235	1,736
Nonmetropolitan counties	564,394									
Area actually reporting	97.9%	1,039	8	121	37	873	7,254	2,548	3,836	870
Estimated total	100.0%	1,061	8	124	38	891	7,407	2,602	3,917	888
State total...	3,930,864	17,934	242	2,142	3,000	12,550	113,066	28,608	72,207	12,251
Rate per 100,000 inhabitants		456.2	6.2	54.5	76.3	319.3	2,876.4	727.8	1,836.9	311.7
Oregon										
Metropolitan statistical area...................................	3,476,871									
Area actually reporting	99.1%	9,804	88	1,681	2,244	5,791	106,699	14,322	77,116	15,261
Estimated total	100.0%	9,878	89	1,701	2,257	5,831	107,527	14,417	77,746	15,364
Cities outside metropolitan areas..........................	311,774									
Area actually reporting	85.1%	857	3	135	122	597	9,390	1,519	6,996	875
Estimated total	100.0%	1,009	4	160	143	702	11,040	1,786	8,225	1,029
Nonmetropolitan counties	354,131									
Area actually reporting	82.1%	636	9	104	26	497	4,231	1,233	2,385	613
Estimated total	100.0%	787	11	138	32	606	5,155	1,502	2,906	747
State total...	4,142,776	11,674	104	1,999	2,432	7,139	123,722	17,705	88,877	17,140
Rate per 100,000 inhabitants		281.8	2.5	48.3	58.7	172.3	2,986.5	427.4	2,145.3	413.7
Pennsylvania										
Metropolitan statistical area...................................	11,340,583									
Area actually reporting	99.6%	37,306	693	3,610	11,526	21,477	193,204	28,135	152,753	12,316
Estimated total	100.0%	37,390	693	3,613	11,547	21,537	193,907	28,218	153,344	12,345
Cities outside metropolitan areas..........................	675,346									
Area actually reporting	96.0%	1,524	20	134	149	1,221	8,478	1,280	6,974	224
Estimated total	100.0%	1,585	21	137	155	1,272	8,829	1,333	7,263	233
Nonmetropolitan counties	789,608									
Area actually reporting	100.0%	1,145	25	451	91	578	8,484	2,506	5,571	407
State total...	12,805,537	40,120	739	4,201	11,793	23,387	211,220	32,057	166,178	12,985
Rate per 100,000 inhabitants		313.3	5.8	32.8	92.1	182.6	1,649.4	250.3	1,297.7	101.4
Puerto Rico[7]										
Metropolitan statistical area...................................	3,190,926									
Area actually reporting	100.0%	7,509	658	201	3,001	3,649	30,209	7,606	19,045	3,558
Cities outside metropolitan areas..........................	146,251									
Area actually reporting...............................	100.0%	253	21	8	54	170	967	343	588	36
Total	3,337,177	7,762	679	209	3,055	3,819	31,176	7,949	19,633	3,594
Rate per 100,000 inhabitants		232.6	20.3	6.3	91.5	114.4	934.2	238.2	588.3	107.7
Rhode Island										
Metropolitan statistical area...................................	1,059,639									
Area actually reporting	100.0%	2,436	19	432	473	1,512	18,507	3,217	13,809	1,481
Cities outside metropolitan areas..........................	None									
Nonmetropolitan counties	None									
Area actually reporting...............................	100.0%	24	1	13	1	9	54	0	52	2
State total...	1,059,639	2,460	20	445	474	1,521	18,561	3,217	13,861	1,483
Rate per 100,000 inhabitants		232.2	1.9	42.0	44.7	143.5	1,751.6	303.6	1,308.1	140.0
South Carolina										
Metropolitan statistical area...................................	4,279,294									
Area actually reporting	99.1%	21,049	312	2,109	3,344	15,284	134,276	24,630	97,240	12,406
Estimated total	100.0%	21,216	313	2,127	3,369	15,407	135,417	24,831	98,083	12,503
Cities outside metropolitan areas..........................	203,970									
Area actually reporting..............................	97.0%	1,861	25	133	270	1,433	10,587	2,175	7,930	482

Table 3. Crime, by State and Area, 2017—*Continued*

(Number, percent, rate per 100,000 population.)

Area	Population	Violent crime[1]	Murder and nonnegligent manslaughter	Rape (revised definition)[2]	Robbery	Aggravated assault	Property crime	Burglary	Larceny-theft	Motor vehicle theft
Estimated total	100.0%	1,919	26	137	278	1,478	10,918	2,243	8,178	497
Nonmetropolitan counties	541,105									
Area actually reporting	99.2%	2,279	51	238	221	1,769	14,130	4,199	8,684	1,247
Estimated total	100.0%	2,297	51	240	223	1,783	14,240	4,232	8,751	1,257
State total..........	5,024,369	25,432	390	2,504	3,870	18,668	160,575	31,306	115,012	14,257
Rate per 100,000 inhabitants		506.2	7.8	49.8	77.0	371.5	3,195.9	623.1	2,289.1	283.8
South Dakota										
Metropolitan statistical area................................	420,832									
Area actually reporting	98.9%	1,632	13	323	174	1,122	9,862	1,536	7,410	916
Estimated total	100.0%	1,638	13	324	174	1,127	9,929	1,548	7,460	921
Cities outside metropolitan areas........................	219,744									
Area actually reporting	91.2%	1,742	6	192	48	1,496	4,830	793	3,712	325
Estimated total	100.0%	1,914	7	213	53	1,641	5,297	870	4,071	356
Nonmetropolitan counties	229,090									
Area actually reporting	74.7%	159	4	39	8	108	815	216	520	79
Estimated total.........................	100.0%	219	5	58	11	145	1,091	289	696	106
State total..........	869,666	3,771	25	595	238	2,913	16,317	2,707	12,227	1,383
Rate per 100,000 inhabitants		433.6	2.9	68.4	27.4	335.0	1,876.2	311.3	1,405.9	159.0
Tennessee										
Metropolitan statistical area................................	5,208,587									
Area actually reporting	100.0%	37,597	479	2,443	7,498	27,177	163,250	30,730	117,262	15,258
Cities outside metropolitan areas........................	515,162									
Area actually reporting	100.0%	3,238	25	255	247	2,711	19,530	3,503	14,723	1,304
Nonmetropolitan counties	992,235									
Area actually reporting	100.0%	2,920	23	236	117	2,544	14,708	4,483	8,263	1,962
State total..........	6,715,984	43,755	527	2,934	7,862	32,432	197,488	38,716	140,248	18,524
Rate per 100,000 inhabitants		651.5	7.8	43.7	117.1	482.9	2,940.6	576.5	2,088.3	275.8
Texas										
Metropolitan statistical area................................	25,244,087									
Area actually reporting	99.5%	114,973	1,309	13,086	31,501	69,077	671,216	119,385	487,397	64,434
Estimated total	100.0%	115,298	1,311	13,133	31,573	69,281	673,378	119,794	488,952	64,632
Cities outside metropolitan areas........................	1,446,994									
Area actually reporting	96.5%	5,463	40	668	522	4,233	33,073	7,568	23,758	1,747
Estimated total	100.0%	5,655	41	695	539	4,380	34,188	7,824	24,561	1,803
Nonmetropolitan counties	1,613,515									
Area actually reporting.........................	99.1%	3,254	59	635	154	2,406	17,597	6,388	9,618	1,591
Estimated total.........................	100.0%	3,285	60	642	155	2,428	17,762	6,448	9,708	1,606
State total..........	28,304,596	124,238	1,412	14,470	32,267	76,089	725,328	134,066	523,221	68,041
Rate per 100,000 inhabitants		438.9	5.0	51.1	114.0	268.8	2,562.6	473.7	1,848.5	240.4
Utah										
Metropolitan statistical area................................	2,773,185									
Area actually reporting	99.4%	6,689	67	1,536	1,444	3,642	79,982	10,796	60,188	8,998
Estimated total	100.0%	6,719	67	1,544	1,450	3,658	80,375	10,856	60,471	9,048
Cities outside metropolitan areas........................	149,804									
Area actually reporting	87.2%	330	3	80	10	237	2,927	442	2,290	195
Estimated total	100.0%	378	3	92	11	272	3,357	507	2,626	224
Nonmetropolitan counties	178,844									
Area actually reporting	87.3%	274	3	54	6	211	2,186	396	1,566	224
Estimated total.........................	100.0%	313	3	61	7	242	2,506	454	1,795	257
State total..........	3,101,833	7,410	73	1,697	1,468	4,172	86,238	11,817	64,892	9,529
Rate per 100,000 inhabitants		238.9	2.4	54.7	47.3	134.5	2,780.2	381.0	2,092.1	307.2
Vermont										
Metropolitan statistical area................................	218,089									
Area actually reporting	100.0%	389	3	97	44	245	3,779	580	3,157	42
Cities outside metropolitan areas........................	202,042									
Area actually reporting	100.0%	394	2	82	34	276	3,551	623	2,864	64
Nonmetropolitan counties	203,526									
Area actually reporting	100.0%	251	9	39	14	189	1,630	651	891	88
State total..........	623,657	1,034	14	218	92	710	8,960	1,854	6,912	194
Rate per 100,000 inhabitants		165.8	2.2	35.0	14.8	113.8	1,436.7	297.3	1,108.3	31.1
Virginia										
Metropolitan statistical area................................	7,428,019									
Area actually reporting	99.9%	15,710	387	2,444	4,087	8,792	136,379	15,520	111,704	9,155

Table 3. Crime, by State and Area, 2017—*Continued*

(Number, percent, rate per 100,000 population.)

Area	Population	Violent crime[1]	Murder and nonnegligent manslaughter	Rape (revised definition)[2]	Robbery	Aggravated assault	Property crime	Burglary	Larceny-theft	Motor vehicle theft
Estimated total	100.0%	15,714	387	2,445	4,088	8,794	136,408	15,523	111,728	9,157
Cities outside metropolitan areas	256,861									
Area actually reporting	99.4%	710	26	90	157	437	6,832	951	5,550	331
Estimated total	100.0%	714	26	90	158	440	6,876	957	5,586	333
Nonmetropolitan counties	785,140									
Area actually reporting	100.0%	1,204	40	327	86	751	8,571	1,988	5,901	682
State total	8,470,020	17,632	453	2,862	4,332	9,985	151,855	18,468	123,215	10,172
Rate per 100,000 inhabitants		208.2	5.3	33.8	51.1	117.9	1,792.9	218.0	1,454.7	120.1
Washington										
Metropolitan statistical area	6,668,792									
Area actually reporting	99.9%	20,983	209	2,944	5,200	12,630	217,244	39,445	150,755	27,044
Estimated total	100.0%	20,983	209	2,944	5,200	12,630	217,252	39,446	150,761	27,045
Cities outside metropolitan areas	304,884									
Area actually reporting	96.0%	1,005	9	214	143	639	11,533	2,059	8,314	1,160
Estimated total	100.0%	1,045	9	221	149	666	12,014	2,145	8,661	1,208
Nonmetropolitan counties	432,067									
Area actually reporting	100.0%	520	12	90	41	377	5,761	2,129	3,089	543
State total	7,405,743	22,548	230	3,255	5,390	13,673	235,027	43,720	162,511	28,796
Rate per 100,000 inhabitants		304.5	3.1	44.0	72.8	184.6	3,173.6	590.4	2,194.4	388.8
West Virginia										
Metropolitan statistical area	1,123,324									
Area actually reporting	86.3%	3,837	59	494	413	2,871	22,338	5,066	15,252	2,020
Estimated total	100.0%	4,244	62	558	443	3,181	25,592	5,687	17,609	2,296
Cities outside metropolitan areas	186,093									
Area actually reporting	59.6%	359	5	42	29	283	2,086	351	1,608	127
Estimated total	100.0%	620	8	88	49	475	3,502	589	2,700	213
Nonmetropolitan counties	506,440									
Area actually reporting	97.1%	1,459	15	143	31	1,270	4,405	1,313	2,613	479
Estimated total	100.0%	1,504	15	149	32	1,308	4,536	1,352	2,691	493
State total	1,815,857	6,368	85	795	524	4,964	33,630	7,628	23,000	3,002
Rate per 100,000 inhabitants		350.7	4.7	43.8	28.9	273.4	1,852.0	420.1	1,266.6	165.3
Wisconsin										
Metropolitan statistical area	4,296,895									
Area actually reporting	99.3%	16,336	171	1,625	4,234	10,306	84,396	14,034	61,746	8,616
Estimated total	100.0%	16,365	171	1,632	4,237	10,325	84,630	14,080	61,920	8,630
Cities outside metropolitan areas	655,239									
Area actually reporting	99.7%	1,299	7	284	87	921	13,535	1,593	11,496	446
Estimated total	100.0%	1,303	7	285	87	924	13,578	1,598	11,533	447
Nonmetropolitan counties	843,349									
Area actually reporting	100.0%	871	8	222	21	620	6,594	1,921	4,282	391
State total	5,795,483	18,539	186	2,139	4,345	11,869	104,802	17,599	77,735	9,468
Rate per 100,000 inhabitants		319.9	3.2	36.9	75.0	204.8	1,808.3	303.7	1,341.3	163.4
Wyoming										
Metropolitan statistical area	178,138									
Area actually reporting	100.0%	465	6	94	55	310	4,881	784	3,678	419
Cities outside metropolitan areas	245,155									
Area actually reporting	95.7%	563	3	107	18	435	4,400	555	3,598	247
Estimated total	100.0%	589	3	112	19	455	4,597	580	3,759	258
Nonmetropolitan counties	156,022									
Area actually reporting	88.9%	285	5	49	2	229	1,002	204	707	91
Estimated total	100.0%	322	6	57	2	257	1,126	229	795	102
State total	579,315	1,376	15	263	76	1,022	10,604	1,593	8,232	779
Rate per 100,000 inhabitants		237.5	2.6	45.4	13.1	176.4	1,830.4	275.0	1,421.0	134.5

Note: Although arson data are included in the trend and clearance tables, sufficient data are not available to estimate totals for this offense. Therefore, no arson data are published in this table.
[1] The violent crime figures include the offenses of murder, rape (revised definition), robbery, and aggravated assault.
[2] The figures shown in the rape (revised definition) column were estimated using the revised Uniform Crime Reporting (UCR) definition of rape.
[3] Includes offenses reported by the Metro Transit Police and the Arson Investigation Unit of the District of Columbia Fire and Emergency Medical Services.
[4] This state's agencies submitted rape data according to the legacy UCR definition of rape.

Table 4. Crime, by Selected Metropolitan Statistical Area, 2017

(Number, percent, rate per 100,000 population.)

Area	Population	Violent crime	Murder and nonnegligent manslaughter	Rape[1]	Robbery	Aggravated assault	Property crime	Burglary	Larceny-theft	Motor vehicle theft
Abilene, TX MSA[2, 3]	170,995									
Includes Callahan, Jones, and Taylor Counties										
City of Abilene[2, 3]	122,981	636	4	100	138	394			2,605	260
Total area actually reporting	100.0%	753	7	120	143	483			2,938	301
Rate per 100,000 inhabitants		440.4	4.1	70.2	83.6	282.5			1,718.2	176.0
Akron, OH MSA[4]	703,907									
Includes Portage[4] and Summit Counties										
City of Akron	197,412	1,377	42	209	395	731	8,360	2,301	5,304	755
Total area actually reporting	96.3%	1,911	51	335	494	1,031	17,340	3,681	12,587	1,072
Estimated total	100.0%	1,952	52	344	506	1,050	17,886	3,764	13,024	1,098
Rate per 100,000 inhabitants		277.3	7.4	48.9	71.9	149.2	2,541.0	534.7	1,850.2	156.0
Albany, GA MSA	151,534									
Includes Baker, Dougherty, Lee, Terrell, and Worth Counties										
City of Albany	73,209	827	22	27	152	626	4,116	879	3,048	189
Total area actually reporting	96.0%	1,079	23	55	186	815	5,773	1,229	4,289	255
Estimated total	100.0%	1,101	23	57	192	829	5,966	1,259	4,436	271
Rate per 100,000 inhabitants		726.6	15.2	37.6	126.7	547.1	3,937.1	830.8	2,927.4	178.8
Albany, OR MSA[2]	124,014									
Includes Linn County[2]										
City of Albany[2]	53,701	56	0	8	20	28	1,406	158	1,137	111
Total area actually reporting	100.0%	196	2	41	26	127	3,159	489	2,368	302
Rate per 100,000 inhabitants		158.0	1.6	33.1	21.0	102.4	2,547.3	394.3	1,909.5	243.5
Albany-Schenectady-Troy, NY MSA	885,673									
Includes Albany, Rensselaer, Saratoga, Schenectady, and Schoharie Counties										
City of Albany	98,174	876	8	54	247	567	3,394	432	2,853	109
City of Schenectady	64,710	577	2	58	141	376	2,057	348	1,534	175
City of Troy	49,644	351	6	31	114	200	1,732	370	1,272	90
Total area actually reporting	100.0%	2,579	18	361	640	1,560	17,312	2,279	14,376	657
Rate per 100,000 inhabitants		291.2	2.0	40.8	72.3	176.1	1,954.7	257.3	1,623.2	74.2
Albuquerque, NM MSA	915,069									
Includes Bernalillo, Sandoval, Torrance, and Valencia Counties										
City of Albuquerque	561,375	7,686	70	473	2,930	4,213	41,350	6,996	26,670	7,684
Total area actually reporting	100.0%	9,928	81	607	3,180	6,060	50,319	9,056	32,128	9,135
Rate per 100,000 inhabitants		1,084.9	8.9	66.3	347.5	662.2	5,498.9	989.7	3,511.0	998.3
Alexandria, LA MSA	154,181									
Includes Grant and Rapides Parishes										
City of Alexandria	47,860	690	17	9	129	535	4,197	987	2,953	257
Total area actually reporting	85.8%	1,047	20	28	154	845	6,774	1,652	4,731	391
Estimated total	100.0%	1,124	21	33	167	903	7,345	1,777	5,142	426
Rate per 100,000 inhabitants		729.0	13.6	21.4	108.3	585.7	4,763.9	1,152.5	3,335.0	276.3
Allentown-Bethlehem-Easton, PA-NJ MSA	838,894									
Includes Warren County, NJ and Carbon, Lehigh, and Northampton Counties, PA										
City of Allentown, PA	120,823	557	16	70	269	202	3,302	634	2,362	306
City of Bethlehem, PA	75,336	594	0	29	61	504	1,359	187	1,124	48
Total area actually reporting	99.2%	1,980	26	176	496	1,282	13,889	1,934	11,166	789
Estimated total	100.0%	1,992	26	177	499	1,290	13,984	1,945	11,246	793
Rate per 100,000 inhabitants		237.5	3.1	21.1	59.5	153.8	1,667.0	231.9	1,340.6	94.5
Altoona, PA MSA	124,337									
Includes Blair County										
City of Altoona	44,366	120	0	33	31	56	918	167	708	43
Total area actually reporting	100.0%	252	0	67	41	144	1,765	249	1,447	69
Rate per 100,000 inhabitants		202.7	0.0	53.9	33.0	115.8	1,419.5	200.3	1,163.8	55.5
Amarillo, TX MSA	264,936									
Includes Armstrong, Carson, Oldham, Potter, and Randall Counties										
City of Amarillo	200,993	1,518	16	183	237	1,082	8,787	1,684	6,113	990
Total area actually reporting	100.0%	1,680	17	220	243	1,200	9,507	1,840	6,584	1,083
Rate per 100,000 inhabitants		634.1	6.4	83.0	91.7	452.9	3,588.4	694.5	2,485.1	408.8

Table 4. Crime, by Selected Metropolitan Statistical Area, 2017—*Continued*

(Number, percent, rate per 100,000 population.)

Area	Population	Violent crime	Murder and nonnegligent manslaughter	Rape[1]	Robbery	Aggravated assault	Property crime	Burglary	Larceny-theft	Motor vehicle theft
Ames, IA MSA...............................	98,260									
Includes Story County										
City of Ames.....................................	67,461	124	1	49	23	51	1,392	248	1,087	57
Total area actually reporting..................	93.1%	162	1	62	25	74	1,777	322	1,381	74
Estimated total..................................	100.0%	178	1	65	26	86	1,901	347	1,473	81
Rate per 100,000 inhabitants..................		181.2	1.0	66.2	26.5	87.5	1,934.7	353.1	1,499.1	82.4
Anchorage, AK MSA	313,465									
Includes Anchorage Municipality and Matanuska-Susitna Borough										
City of Anchorage..............................	296,188	3,564	27	391	778	2,368	16,041	2,216	10,721	3,104
Total area actually reporting..................	100.0%	3,645	28	392	789	2,436	17,057	2,283	11,495	3,279
Rate per 100,000 inhabitants..................		1,162.8	8.9	125.1	251.7	777.1	5,441.4	728.3	3,667.1	1,046.0
Ann Arbor, MI MSA............................	368,898									
Includes Washtenaw County										
City of Ann Arbor	121,930	259	0	57	53	149	2,108	278	1,731	99
Total area actually reporting..................	100.0%	1,206	11	233	179	783	6,029	864	4,753	412
Rate per 100,000 inhabitants..................		326.9	3.0	63.2	48.5	212.3	1,634.3	234.2	1,288.4	111.7
Anniston-Oxford-Jacksonville, AL MSA	113,915									
Includes Calhoun County										
City of Anniston.................................	21,955	754	14	47	71	622	1,352	542	700	110
City of Oxford..................................	16,937	48	1	0	7	40	884	94	756	34
City of Jacksonville.............................	12,573	113	2	10	12	89	489	137	325	27
Total area actually reporting..................	99.3%	976	17	71	98	790	3,242	955	2,095	192
Estimated total..................................	100.0%	980	17	71	99	793	3,267	959	2,114	194
Rate per 100,000 inhabitants..................		860.3	14.9	62.3	86.9	696.1	2,867.9	841.9	1,855.8	170.3
Appleton, WI MSA	235,528									
Includes Calumet and Outagamie Counties										
City of Appleton	74,660	203	1	39	17	146	1,155	136	996	23
Total area actually reporting..................	100.0%	331	2	55	30	244	2,905	340	2,479	86
Rate per 100,000 inhabitants..................		140.5	0.8	23.4	12.7	103.6	1,233.4	144.4	1,052.5	36.5
Asheville, NC MSA[4]	457,928									
Includes Buncombe, Haywood, Henderson, and Madison Counties[4]										
City of Asheville[4].............................	90,103		7		181	363	4,248	733	3,191	324
Total area actually reporting..................	99.2%		16		275	712	9,645	2,492	6,410	743
Estimated total..................................	100.0%		16		277	718	9,745	2,510	6,488	747
Rate per 100,000 inhabitants..................			3.5		60.5	156.8	2,128.1	548.1	1,416.8	163.1
Athens-Clarke County, GA MSA............................	207,610									
Includes Clarke, Madison, Oconee, and Oglethorpe Counties										
City of Athens-Clarke County	124,903	519	6	57	123	333	3,930	683	3,017	230
Total area actually reporting..................	100.0%	639	7	72	135	425	5,345	922	4,133	290
Rate per 100,000 inhabitants..................		307.8	3.4	34.7	65.0	204.7	2,574.5	444.1	1,990.8	139.7
Atlanta-Sandy Springs-Roswell, GA MSA	5,882,917									
Includes Barrow, Bartow, Butts, Carroll, Cherokee, Clayton, Cobb, Coweta, Dawson, DeKalb, Douglas, Fayette, Forsyth, Fulton, Gwinnett, Haralson, Heard, Henry, Jasper, Lamar, Meriwether, Morgan, Newton, Paulding, Pickens, Pike, Rockdale, Spalding, and Walton Counties										
City of Atlanta..................................	481,343	4,504	79	282	1,413	2,730	22,991	3,390	16,304	3,297
City of Sandy Springs..........................	107,740	126	0	12	56	58	2,263	377	1,708	178
City of Roswell..................................	95,602	108	2	15	32	59	1,616	229	1,278	109
City of Alpharetta	66,711	34	0	1	22	11	1,187	96	1,056	35
City of Marietta	61,646	215	4	14	102	95	2,209	327	1,700	182
Total area actually reporting..................	98.5%	21,357	392	1,514	6,715	12,736	166,368	27,784	120,804	17,780
Estimated total..................................	100.0%	21,627	397	1,534	6,791	12,905	168,586	28,218	122,365	18,003
Rate per 100,000 inhabitants..................		367.6	6.7	26.1	115.4	219.4	2,865.7	479.7	2,080.0	306.0
Atlantic City-Hammonton, NJ MSA	271,486									
Includes Atlantic County										
City of Atlantic City.............................	38,601	425	13	24	227	161	1,732	319	1,298	115
City of Hammonton............................	14,370	17	0	0	3	14	177	37	134	6
Total area actually reporting..................	100.0%	847	21	54	344	428	6,943	1,230	5,435	278
Rate per 100,000 inhabitants..................		312.0	7.7	19.9	126.7	157.7	2,557.4	453.1	2,001.9	102.4

Table 4. Crime, by Selected Metropolitan Statistical Area, 2017—*Continued*

(Number, percent, rate per 100,000 population.)

Area	Population	Violent crime	Murder and nonnegligent manslaughter	Rape[1]	Robbery	Aggravated assault	Property crime	Burglary	Larceny-theft	Motor vehicle theft
Auburn-Opelika, AL MSA..................................	162,152									
Includes Lee County										
City of Auburn...	64,831	217	4	17	30	166	1,711	156	1,454	101
City of Opelika...	30,476	223	5	21	47	150	1,399	220	1,091	88
Total area actually reporting..........................	100.0%	895	12	64	99	720	4,388	681	3,379	328
Rate per 100,000 inhabitants.........................		552.0	7.4	39.5	61.1	444.0	2,706.1	420.0	2,083.8	202.3
Augusta-Richmond County, GA-SC MSA[5]..........	600,734									
Includes Burke, Columbia, Lincoln, McDuffie, and Richmond										
Counties, GA and Aiken and Edgefield Counties, SC										
Total area actually reporting..........................	96.6%	1,800	39	190	419	1,152				1,330
Estimated total...	100.0%	1,891	40	199	432	1,220				1,386
Rate per 100,000 inhabitants.........................		314.8	6.7	33.1	71.9	203.1				230.7
Austin-Round Rock, TX MSA[2]............................	2,115,140									
Includes Bastrop, Caldwell, Hays, Travis, and Williamson										
Counties										
City of Austin...	971,949	4,032	25	834	987	2,186	31,001	4,380	24,542	2,079
City of Round Rock..	124,617	169	2	33	44	90	2,701	232	2,405	64
Total area actually reporting..........................	99.9%	6,476	52	1,345	1,316	3,763	49,566	7,377	38,969	3,220
Estimated total...	100.0%	6,479	52	1,345	1,317	3,765	49,588	7,380	38,986	3,222
Rate per 100,000 inhabitants.........................		306.3	2.5	63.6	62.3	178.0	2,344.4	348.9	1,843.2	152.3
Bakersfield, CA MSA..	891,188									
Includes Kern County										
City of Bakersfield..	381,154	1,827	41	92	753	941	15,507	3,667	9,063	2,777
Total area actually reporting..........................	100.0%	4,989	89	307	1,297	3,296	28,933	7,429	15,605	5,899
Rate per 100,000 inhabitants.........................		559.8	10.0	34.4	145.5	369.8	3,246.6	833.6	1,751.0	661.9
	2,811,573									
Baltimore-Columbia-Towson, MD MSA............	2,811,573									
Includes Anne Arundel, Baltimore, Carroll, Harford, Howard,										
and Queen Anne's Counties and Baltimore City										
City of Baltimore...	613,217	12,430	342	382	5,879	5,827	30,220	8,041	17,008	5,171
Total area actually reporting..........................	100.0%	22,001	413	1,048	8,454	12,086	76,837	14,673	53,711	8,453
Rate per 100,000 inhabitants.........................		782.5	14.7	37.3	300.7	429.9	2,732.9	521.9	1,910.4	300.7
Bangor, ME MSA..	151,887									
Includes Penobscot County										
City of Bangor..	31,814	48	1	8	14	25	1,209	181	1,004	24
Total area actually reporting..........................	100.0%	100	2	29	21	48	2,413	386	1,950	77
Rate per 100,000 inhabitants.........................		65.8	1.3	19.1	13.8	31.6	1,588.7	254.1	1,283.8	50.7
Barnstable Town, MA MSA................................	214,183									
Includes Barnstable County										
City of Barnstable	44,142	197	1	18	13	165	547	79	446	22
Total area actually reporting..........................	100.0%	761	3	91	39	628	2,930	731	2,078	121
Rate per 100,000 inhabitants.........................		355.3	1.4	42.5	18.2	293.2	1,368.0	341.3	970.2	56.5
Baton Rouge, LA MSA.......................................	836,722									
Includes Ascension, East Baton Rouge, East Feliciana,										
Iberville, Livingston, Pointe Coupee, St. Helena, West Baton										
Rouge, and West Feliciana Parishes										
City of Baton Rouge...	227,403	2,335	87	100	868	1,280	12,721	3,226	8,504	991
Total area actually reporting..........................	99.7%	4,565	140	240	1,211	2,974	32,865	6,853	24,185	1,827
Estimated total...	100.0%	4,575	140	241	1,212	2,982	32,946	6,868	24,248	1,830
Rate per 100,000 inhabitants.........................		546.8	16.7	28.8	144.9	356.4	3,937.5	820.8	2,898.0	218.7
Battle Creek, MI M.S.A.....................................	134,442									
Includes Calhoun County										
City of Battle Creek..	60,852	580	3	73	72	432	2,251	501	1,656	94
Total area actually reporting..........................	99.9%	920	4	147	99	670	3,977	811	2,994	172
Estimated total...	100.0%	920	4	147	99	670	3,978	811	2,995	172
Rate per 100,000 inhabitants.........................		684.3	3.0	109.3	73.6	498.4	2,958.9	603.2	2,227.7	127.9
Bay City, MI MSA..	104,519									
Includes Bay County										
City of Bay City...	33,286	242	1	57	35	149	998	223	716	59
Total area actually reporting..........................	100.0%	385	2	117	48	218	1,992	398	1,486	108
Rate per 100,000 inhabitants.........................		368.4	1.9	111.9	45.9	208.6	1,905.9	380.8	1,421.8	103.3

Table 4. Crime, by Selected Metropolitan Statistical Area, 2017—*Continued*

(Number, percent, rate per 100,000 population.)

Area	Population	Violent crime	Murder and nonnegligent manslaughter	Rape[1]	Robbery	Aggravated assault	Property crime	Burglary	Larceny-theft	Motor vehicle theft
Beaumont-Port Arthur, TX MSA[3]........................	410,600									
Includes Hardin, Jefferson, Newton, and Orange Counties										
City of Beaumont.................	118,456	1,259	16	86	304	853	5,136	1,259	3,472	405
City of Port Arthur.................	55,583	378	6	15	110	247	2,031	767	1,111	153
Total area actually reporting..........	99.9%	2,263	27	151	509	1,576			6,995	959
Estimated total..........	100.0%	2,264	27	151	509	1,577			7,004	960
Rate per 100,000 inhabitants.............		551.4	6.6	36.8	124.0	384.1			1,705.8	233.8
Beckley, WV MSA........................	119,499									
Includes Fayette and Raleigh Counties										
City of Beckley.................	16,862	117	1	22	19	75	1,006	172	791	43
Total area actually reporting..........	95.7%	360	6	51	36	267	2,466	564	1,720	182
Estimated total..........	100.0%	372	6	53	37	276	2,624	587	1,845	192
Rate per 100,000 inhabitants.............		311.3	5.0	44.4	31.0	231.0	2,195.8	491.2	1,543.9	160.7
Bellingham, WA MSA........................	220,105									
Includes Whatcom County										
City of Bellingham	88,652	258	2	56	73	127	4,151	552	3,435	164
Total area actually reporting..........	100.0%	496	4	121	96	275	6,526	1,116	5,080	330
Rate per 100,000 inhabitants.............		225.3	1.8	55.0	43.6	124.9	2,964.9	507.0	2,308.0	149.9
Bend-Redmond, OR MSA........................	185,760									
Includes Deschutes County										
City of Bend.................	93,786	154	0	33	24	97	1,960	177	1,680	103
City of Redmond.................	29,870	82	0	16	11	55	933	114	740	79
Total area actually reporting..........	100.0%	325	0	71	39	215	3,700	462	2,996	242
Rate per 100,000 inhabitants.............		175.0	0.0	38.2	21.0	115.7	1,991.8	248.7	1,612.8	130.3
Billings, MT MSA........................	171,334									
Includes Carbon, Golden Valley, and Yellowstone Counties										
City of Billings.................	111,317	549	2	76	87	384	6,076	783	4,451	842
Total area actually reporting..........	100.0%	680	4	96	92	488	7,156	951	5,229	976
Rate per 100,000 inhabitants.............		396.9	2.3	56.0	53.7	284.8	4,176.6	555.1	3,051.9	569.6
Binghamton, NY MSA........................	243,440									
Includes Broome and Tioga Counties										
City of Binghamton.................	45,399	362	4	42	90	226	1,983	370	1,557	56
Total area actually reporting..........	99.7%	743	4	179	138	422	5,284	865	4,248	171
Estimated total..........	100.0%	744	4	179	138	423	5,295	866	4,258	171
Rate per 100,000 inhabitants.............		305.6	1.6	73.5	56.7	173.8	2,175.1	355.7	1,749.1	70.2
Bismarck, ND MSA........................	131,352									
Includes Burleigh, Morton, Oliver, and Sioux Counties										
City of Bismarck.................	74,397	256	0	45	33	178	2,438	322	1,884	232
Total area actually reporting..........	100.0%	423	1	85	34	303	3,538	522	2,634	382
Rate per 100,000 inhabitants.............		322.0	0.8	64.7	25.9	230.7	2,693.5	397.4	2,005.3	290.8
Bloomington, IL MSA........................	189,116									
Includes DeWitt and McLean Counties										
City of Bloomington.................	78,203	343	3	73	45	222	1,334	220	1,037	77
Total area actually reporting..........	93.1%	525	5	135	67	318	2,753	424	2,212	117
Estimated total..........	100.0%	553	5	139	75	334	2,963	455	2,379	129
Rate per 100,000 inhabitants.............		292.4	2.6	73.5	39.7	176.6	1,566.8	240.6	1,258.0	68.2
Bloomington, IN MSA........................	167,618									
Includes Monroe and Owen Counties										
City of Bloomington.................	85,121	443	2	78	52	311	2,584	478	1,940	166
Total area actually reporting..........	87.6%	524	2	102	62	358	3,875	644	2,969	262
Estimated total..........	100.0%	554	2	107	66	379	4,108	698	3,121	289
Rate per 100,000 inhabitants.............		330.5	1.2	63.8	39.4	226.1	2,450.8	416.4	1,862.0	172.4
Bloomsburg-Berwick, PA MSA........................	84,669									
Includes Columbia and Montour Counties										
City of Bloomsburg Town	14,542	35	0	6	2	27	175	35	138	2
City of Berwick.................	10,080	22	1	2	2	17	195	23	167	5
Total area actually reporting..........	99.1%	164	1	45	6	112	960	150	787	23
Estimated total..........	100.0%	165	1	45	6	113	970	151	796	23
Rate per 100,000 inhabitants.............		194.9	1.2	53.1	7.1	133.5	1,145.6	178.3	940.1	27.2

Table 4. Crime, by Selected Metropolitan Statistical Area, 2017—*Continued*

(Number, percent, rate per 100,000 population.)

Area	Population	Violent crime	Murder and nonnegligent manslaughter	Rape[1]	Robbery	Aggravated assault	Property crime	Burglary	Larceny-theft	Motor vehicle theft
Boise City, ID MSA.....................	710,265									
Includes Ada, Boise, Canyon, Gem, and Owyhee Counties										
City of Boise	225,677	630	2	144	51	433	5,517	736	4,435	346
Total area actually reporting.................	100.0%	1,669	7	341	105	1,216	12,514	2,240	9,271	1,003
Rate per 100,000 inhabitants...............		235.0	1.0	48.0	14.8	171.2	1,761.9	315.4	1,305.3	141.2
Boston-Cambridge-Newton, MA-NH MSA	4,839,029									
Includes the Metropolitan Divisions of Boston, MA; Cambridge-Newton-Framingham, MA; and Rockingham County-Strafford County, NH										
City of Boston, MA.....................	682,903	4,570	57	290	1,404	2,819	14,266	2,109	10,952	1,205
City of Cambridge, MA..................	111,707	313	2	17	101	193	2,031	252	1,685	94
City of Newton, MA.....................	89,736	49	0	5	5	39	576	87	471	18
City of Framingham, MA.................	72,153	235	0	14	20	201	748	132	549	67
City of Waltham, MA....................	63,413	98	1	16	14	67	609	118	447	44
Total area actually reporting.................	98.6%	14,587	124	1,319	3,162	9,982	62,474	9,085	48,476	4,913
Estimated total..................	100.0%	14,775	125	1,339	3,191	10,120	63,317	9,227	49,115	4,975
Rate per 100,000 inhabitants...............		305.3	2.6	27.7	65.9	209.1	1,308.5	190.7	1,015.0	102.8
Boston, MA MD...................	2,014,011									
Includes Norfolk, Plymouth, and Suffolk Counties										
Total area actually reporting	97.1%	8,539	76	695	2,076	5,692	30,242	4,338	23,540	2,364
Estimated total	100.0%	8,706	77	713	2,102	5,814	30,985	4,464	24,102	2,419
Rate per 100,000 inhabitants.................		432.3	3.8	35.4	104.4	288.7	1,538.5	221.6	1,196.7	120.1
Cambridge-Newton-Framingham, MA MD......................	2,390,681									
Includes Essex and Middlesex Counties										
Total area actually reporting	99.7%	5,404	43	448	988	3,925	26,985	4,140	20,527	2,318
Estimated total	100.0%	5,424	43	450	991	3,940	27,075	4,155	20,595	2,325
Rate per 100,000 inhabitants.................		226.9	1.8	18.8	41.5	164.8	1,132.5	173.8	861.5	97.3
Rockingham County-Strafford County, NH MD...................	434,337									
Includes Rockingham and Strafford Counties										
Total area actually reporting	99.8%	644	5	176	98	365	5,247	607	4,409	231
Estimated total	100.0%	645	5	176	98	366	5,257	608	4,418	231
Rate per 100,000 inhabitants.................		148.5	1.2	40.5	22.6	84.3	1,210.4	140.0	1,017.2	53.2
Bowling Green, KY MSA.......................	173,283									
Includes Allen, Butler, Edmonson, and Warren Counties										
City of Bowling Green.............	66,317	225	4	61	82	78	3,089	436	2,476	177
Total area actually reporting..................	100.0%	295	5	86	93	111	4,201	799	3,129	273
Rate per 100,000 inhabitants..................		170.2	2.9	49.6	53.7	64.1	2,424.4	461.1	1,805.7	157.5
Bremerton-Silverdale, WA MSA.......................	267,867									
Includes Kitsap County										
City of Bremerton.................	41,173	216	3	26	29	158	1,670	264	1,206	200
Total area actually reporting..................	100.0%	685	11	132	67	475	6,178	1,196	4,406	576
Rate per 100,000 inhabitants..................		255.7	4.1	49.3	25.0	177.3	2,306.4	446.5	1,644.8	215.0
Bridgeport-Stamford-Norwalk, CT MSA.......................	930,673									
Includes Fairfield County										
City of Bridgeport.................	146,110	1,315	21	77	565	652	3,416	548	2,152	716
City of Stamford.................	130,189	292	0	30	91	171	1,986	241	1,488	257
City of Norwalk.................	88,849	255	3	11	40	201	1,505	160	1,188	157
City of Danbury	85,614	163	1	19	71	72	1,105	90	942	73
City of Stratford.................	52,263	89	2	10	50	27	1,117	137	826	154
Total area actually reporting..................	100.0%	2,298	28	181	889	1,200	13,459	1,713	9,951	1,795
Rate per 100,000 inhabitants..................		246.9	3.0	19.4	95.5	128.9	1,446.2	184.1	1,069.2	192.9
Brownsville-Harlingen, TX MSA[2]	424,158									
Includes Cameron County										
City of Brownsville.................	185,216	476	5	79	133	259	5,176	661	4,374	141
City of Harlingen.................	65,617	233	0	18	32	183	2,693	523	2,079	91
Total area actually reporting..................	100.0%	1,324	8	226	191	899	11,131	1,790	8,991	350
Rate per 100,000 inhabitants..................		312.1	1.9	53.3	45.0	211.9	2,624.3	422.0	2,119.7	82.5
Brunswick, GA MSA.......................	117,664									
Includes Brantley, Glynn, and McIntosh Counties										
City of Brunswick.................	16,500	170	4	10	44	112	866	265	557	44
Total area actually reporting..................	100.0%	418	13	29	91	285	3,617	990	2,428	199
Rate per 100,000 inhabitants..................		355.2	11.0	24.6	77.3	242.2	3,074.0	841.4	2,063.5	169.1

Table 4. Crime, by Selected Metropolitan Statistical Area, 2017—*Continued*

(Number, percent, rate per 100,000 population.)

Area	Population	Violent crime	Murder and nonnegligent manslaughter	Rape[1]	Robbery	Aggravated assault	Property crime	Burglary	Larceny-theft	Motor vehicle theft
Buffalo-Cheektowaga-Niagara Falls, NY MSA............	1,134,907									
Includes Erie and Niagara Counties										
City of Buffalo	256,169	2,611	40	142	857	1,572	9,827	2,356	6,638	833
City of Cheektowaga Town	77,576	187	1	14	82	90	2,296	300	1,908	88
City of Niagara Falls	48,385	544	3	36	150	355	2,336	458	1,738	140
Total area actually reporting............	100.0%	4,264	49	336	1,318	2,561	24,807	4,645	18,741	1,421
Rate per 100,000 inhabitants............		375.7	4.3	29.6	116.1	225.7	2,185.8	409.3	1,651.3	125.2
Burlington, NC MSA[4]............	161,435									
Includes Alamance County[4]										
City of Burlington[4]	52,986		4		114	381	2,016	502	1,402	112
Total area actually reporting............	100.0%		4		152	525	3,550	927	2,444	179
Rate per 100,000 inhabitants............			2.5		94.2	325.2	2,199.0	574.2	1,513.9	110.9
Burlington-South Burlington, VT MSA............	218,089									
Includes Chittenden, Franklin, and Grand Isle Counties										
City of Burlington	42,230	132	1	21	11	99	1,164	223	941	0
City of South Burlington	19,146	37	0	16	5	16	510	47	463	0
Total area actually reporting............	100.0%	389	3	97	44	245	3,779	580	3,157	42
Rate per 100,000 inhabitants............		178.4	1.4	44.5	20.2	112.3	1,732.8	265.9	1,447.6	19.3
California-Lexington Park, MD MSA............	113,700									
Includes St. Mary's County										
Total area actually reporting............	100.0%	214	1	22	47	144	1,973	479	1,444	50
Rate per 100,000 inhabitants............		188.2	0.9	19.3	41.3	126.6	1,735.3	421.3	1,270.0	44.0
Cape Coral-Fort Myers, FL MSA............	742,930									
Includes Lee County										
City of Cape Coral	184,346	235	3	16	41	175	2,888	570	2,148	170
City of Fort Myers	79,918	752	10	53	187	502	2,207	374	1,607	226
Total area actually reporting............	100.0%	2,297	45	249	541	1,462	11,268	2,294	8,018	956
Rate per 100,000 inhabitants............		309.2	6.1	33.5	72.8	196.8	1,516.7	308.8	1,079.2	128.7
Cape Girardeau, MO-IL MSA............	97,715									
Includes Alexander County, IL and Bollinger and Cape Girardeau Counties, MO										
City of Cape Girardeau, MO	39,887	234	5	24	51	154	1,523	252	1,189	82
Total area actually reporting............	100.0%	378	5	36	55	282	2,277	452	1,714	111
Rate per 100,000 inhabitants............		386.8	5.1	36.8	56.3	288.6	2,330.2	462.6	1,754.1	113.6
Carson City, NV MSA............	54,994									
Includes Carson City										
Total area actually reporting............	100.0%	198	1	0	18	179	908	175	649	84
Rate per 100,000 inhabitants............		360.0	1.8	0.0	32.7	325.5	1,651.1	318.2	1,180.1	152.7
Casper, WY MSA............	80,644									
Includes Natrona County										
City of Casper	60,034	91	1	29	14	47	1,727	318	1,281	128
Total area actually reporting............	100.0%	177	1	54	20	102	2,109	407	1,524	178
Rate per 100,000 inhabitants............		219.5	1.2	67.0	24.8	126.5	2,615.2	504.7	1,889.8	220.7
Cedar Rapids, IA MSA............	269,046									
Includes Benton, Jones, and Linn Counties										
City of Cedar Rapids	131,878	370	6	34	121	209	4,952	929	3,681	342
Total area actually reporting............	99.1%	580	8	70	138	364	6,439	1,350	4,636	453
Estimated total............	100.0%	585	8	71	138	368	6,484	1,359	4,669	456
Rate per 100,000 inhabitants............		217.4	3.0	26.4	51.3	136.8	2,410.0	505.1	1,735.4	169.5
Chambersburg-Waynesboro, PA MSA............	154,614									
Includes Franklin County										
City of Chambersburg............	20,757	56	2	4	19	31	601	72	512	17
City of Waynesboro	10,889	15	0	2	5	8	236	37	193	6
Total area actually reporting............	100.0%	200	2	48	41	109	2,140	374	1,704	62
Rate per 100,000 inhabitants............		129.4	1.3	31.0	26.5	70.5	1,384.1	241.9	1,102.1	40.1
Champaign-Urbana, IL MSA............	239,744									
Includes Champaign, Ford, and Piatt Counties										
City of Champaign............	87,543	634	5	83	109	437	2,623	446	2,054	123
City of Urbana	42,091	142	0	25	48	69	1,421	252	1,142	27
Total area actually reporting............	99.0%	1,011	6	154	194	657	5,527	1,029	4,300	198

Table 4. Crime, by Selected Metropolitan Statistical Area, 2017—*Continued*

(Number, percent, rate per 100,000 population.)

Area	Population	Violent crime	Murder and nonnegligent manslaughter	Rape[1]	Robbery	Aggravated assault	Property crime	Burglary	Larceny-theft	Motor vehicle theft
Estimated total..........................	100.0%	1,016	6	155	195	660	5,565	1,035	4,330	200
Rate per 100,000 inhabitants.................		423.8	2.5	64.7	81.3	275.3	2,321.2	431.7	1,806.1	83.4
Charleston, WV MSA[5]	215,067									
Includes Boone, Clay, and Kanawha Counties										
City of Charleston..........................	48,788	572	10	57	84	421	3,516	736	2,427	353
Total area actually reporting.........	91.6%	1,178	20	132	108	918				933
Estimated total..........................	100.0%	1,225	20	140	112	953				966
Rate per 100,000 inhabitants.................		569.6	9.3	65.1	52.1	443.1				449.2
Charleston-North Charleston, SC MSA[5]	778,783									
Includes Berkeley,[5] Charleston, and Dorchester Counties										
City of Charleston..........................	136,845	388	6	50	100	232	3,144	399	2,442	303
City of North Charleston..........................	111,305	1,026	35	74	305	612	6,291	919	4,687	685
Total area actually reporting.........	99.4%	3,190	64	301	668	2,157			15,340	2,043
Estimated total..........................	100.0%	3,209	64	303	671	2,171			15,466	2,054
Rate per 100,000 inhabitants.................		412.1	8.2	38.9	86.2	278.8			1,985.9	263.7
Charlotte-Concord-Gastonia, NC-SC MSA[4]	2,524,068									
Includes Cabarrus, Gaston, Iredell, Lincoln, Mecklenburg, Rowan, and Union Counties, NC4 and Chester, Lancaster, and York Counties, SC										
City of Charlotte-Mecklenburg, NC[4]..........................	914,609		86		2,017	3,965	34,894	6,416	25,856	2,622
City of Concord, NC[4]..........................	91,756		1		31	62	1,791	293	1,433	65
City of Gastonia, NC[4]..........................	76,191		4		158	405	3,714	587	2,865	262
City of Rock Hill, SC..........................	74,053	469	9	51	95	314	3,007	365	2,506	136
Total area actually reporting.........	97.7%	10,337	132	534	2,864	6,807	68,955	13,155	51,285	4,515
Estimated total..........................	100.0%	10,506	134	549	2,904	6,919	70,683	13,456	52,631	4,596
Rate per 100,000 inhabitants.................		416.2	5.3	21.8	115.1	274.1	2,800.4	533.1	2,085.2	182.1
Charlottesville, VA MSA	233,192									
Includes Albemarle, Buckingham, Fluvanna, Greene, and Nelson Counties and Charlottesville City										
City of Charlottesville..........................	47,446	185	3	31	22	129	1,036	145	820	71
Total area actually reporting.........	100.0%	409	11	103	43	252	3,147	395	2,535	217
Rate per 100,000 inhabitants.................		175.4	4.7	44.2	18.4	108.1	1,349.5	169.4	1,087.1	93.1
Chattanooga, TN-GA MSA	556,437									
Includes Catoosa, Dade, and Walker Counties, GA and Hamilton, Marion, and Sequatchie Counties, TN										
City of Chattanooga, TN..........................	178,753	1,905	31	120	330	1,424	10,700	1,540	7,818	1,342
Total area actually reporting.........	100.0%	3,101	37	202	426	2,436	18,886	3,182	13,510	2,194
Rate per 100,000 inhabitants.................		557.3	6.6	36.3	76.6	437.8	3,394.1	571.9	2,427.9	394.3
Cheyenne, WY MSA	97,494									
Includes Laramie County										
City of Cheyenne..........................	64,730	209	2	29	34	144	2,265	264	1,817	184
Total area actually reporting.........	100.0%	288	5	40	35	208	2,772	377	2,154	241
Rate per 100,000 inhabitants.................		295.4	5.1	41.0	35.9	213.3	2,843.3	386.7	2,209.4	247.2
Chicago-Naperville-Elgin, IL-IN-WI MSA[3, 4]	9,525,454									
Includes the Metropolitan Divisions of Chicago-Naperville-Arlington Heights, IL; Elgin, IL; Gary, IN; and Lake County-Kenosha County, IL-WI										
City of Chicago, IL..........................	2,706,171	29,737	653	1,762	11,887	15,435	88,324	12,912	63,834	11,578
City of Naperville, IL..........................	147,934	136	1	22	33	80	1,716	129	1,540	47
City of Elgin, IL..........................	112,767	224	2	38	56	128	1,579	195	1,310	74
City of Gary, IN..........................	75,808	471	48	32	192	199	2,581	678	1,481	422
City of Arlington Heights, IL..........................	75,586	44	0	9	14	21	654	77	550	27
City of Evanston, IL..........................	74,947	122	1	3	40	78	1,769	284	1,422	63
City of Schaumburg, IL..........................	74,471	79	2	13	31	33	1,244	92	1,103	49
City of Skokie, IL..........................	64,167	185	2	20	40	123	1,546	212	1,279	55
City of Des Plaines, IL..........................	58,089	61	1	7	10	43	565	79	454	32
City of Hoffman Estates, IL..........................	51,704	50	0	8	14	28	466	50	386	30
Total area actually reporting.........	97.3%		888	3,498	15,738		188,541	27,131	143,546	17,864
Estimated total..........................	100.0%		895	3,574	15,877		192,857	27,767	146,931	18,159
Rate per 100,000 inhabitants.................			9.4	37.5	166.7		2,024.6	291.5	1,542.5	190.6
Chicago-Naperville-Arlington Heights, IL MD	7,313,953									
Includes Cook, DuPage, Grundy, Kendall, McHenry, and Will Counties										

Table 4. Crime, by Selected Metropolitan Statistical Area, 2017—*Continued*

(Number, percent, rate per 100,000 population.)

Area	Population	Violent crime	Murder and nonnegligent manslaughter	Rape[1]	Robbery	Aggravated assault	Property crime	Burglary	Larceny-theft	Motor vehicle theft
Total area actually reporting....................	98.3%	37,400	780	2,888	14,501	19,231	154,261	22,184	116,450	15,627
Estimated total	100.0%	37,672	784	2,929	14,576	19,383	156,316	22,487	118,084	15,745
Rate per 100,000 inhabitants...................		515.1	10.7	40.0	199.3	265.0	2,137.2	307.5	1,614.5	215.3
Elgin, IL MD..	639,123									
Includes DeKalb and Kane Counties										
Total area actually reporting	98.3%	1,145	11	200	214	720	8,115	985	6,792	338
Estimated total	100.0%	1,169	11	204	221	733	8,296	1,012	6,936	348
Rate per 100,000 inhabitants...................		182.9	1.7	31.9	34.6	114.7	1,298.0	158.3	1,085.2	54.4
Gary, IN MD[3, 4]	700,701									
Includes Jasper, Lake, Newton, and Porter Counties										
Total area actually reporting	87.8%		73	141	637		14,518	2,131	10,968	1,419
Estimated total	100.0%		75	161	674		16,060	2,358	12,147	1,555
Rate per 100,000 inhabitants...................			10.7	23.0	96.2		2,292.0	336.5	1,733.5	221.9
Lake County-Kenosha County, IL-WI M.D.	871,677									
Includes Lake County, IL and Kenosha County, WI										
Total area actually reporting..................	96.2%	1,561	24	269	386	882	11,647	1,831	9,336	480
Estimated total	100.0%	1,633	25	280	406	922	12,185	1,910	9,764	511
Rate per 100,000 inhabitants...................		187.3	2.9	32.1	46.6	105.8	1,397.9	219.1	1,120.1	58.6
Chico, CA MSA..	227,777									
Includes Butte County										
City of Chico..	92,459	413	2	85	63	263	3,593	531	2,615	447
Total area actually reporting...................	100.0%	921	7	182	143	589	7,280	1,599	4,740	941
Rate per 100,000 inhabitants...................		404.3	3.1	79.9	62.8	258.6	3,196.1	702.0	2,081.0	413.1
Cincinnati, OH-KY-IN MSA[2, 4]	2,177,816									
Includes Dearborn, Ohio, and Union Counties, IN; Boone, Bracken, Campbell, Gallatin, Grant, Kenton, and Pendleton Counties, KY; and Brown, Butler, Clermont, Hamilton, and Warren Counties, OH										
City of Cincinnati, OH.............................	299,116	2,833	70	292	1,196	1,275	15,105	3,448	10,172	1,485
Total area actually reporting....................	94.9%	5,598	109	970	2,006	2,513	51,309	9,555	38,380	3,374
Estimated total.......................................	100.0%	5,770	111	1,001	2,045	2,613	53,156	9,874	39,779	3,503
Rate per 100,000 inhabitants...................		264.9	5.1	46.0	93.9	120.0	2,440.8	453.4	1,826.6	160.8
Clarksville, TN-KY MSA...............................	286,499									
Includes Christian and Trigg Counties, KY and Montgomery County, TN										
City of Clarksville, TN.............................	153,294	956	14	80	127	735	4,411	743	3,427	241
Total area actually reporting....................	100.0%	1,198	15	122	176	885	7,045	1,396	5,229	420
Rate per 100,000 inhabitants...................		418.2	5.2	42.6	61.4	308.9	2,459.0	487.3	1,825.1	146.6
Cleveland, TN MSA	122,405									
Includes Bradley and Polk Counties										
City of Cleveland	44,778	390	1	27	53	309	2,515	369	1,921	225
Total area actually reporting....................	100.0%	641	4	41	62	534	3,875	701	2,713	461
Rate per 100,000 inhabitants...................		523.7	3.3	33.5	50.7	436.3	3,165.7	572.7	2,216.4	376.6
Cleveland-Elyria, OH MSA[2,3,4]	2,057,704									
Includes Cuyahoga, Geauga, Lake,[3, 4] Lorain, and Medina Counties										
City of Cleveland	385,351	5,999	107	497	2,697	2,698	18,944	5,853	9,696	3,395
City of Elyria	53,586	191	3	39	64	85	1,146	248	842	56
Total area actually reporting....................	89.1%		143	812	3,480		38,814	9,416	24,784	4,614
Estimated total.......................................	100.0%		148	888	3,584		43,432	10,118	28,483	4,831
Rate per 100,000 inhabitants...................			7.2	43.2	174.2		2,110.7	491.7	1,384.2	234.8
Coeur d'Alene, ID MSA[3]...............................	158,326									
Includes Kootenai County[3]										
City of Coeur d'Alene	51,364	197	4	49	11	133	1,142	180	901	61
Total area actually reporting....................	100.0%	380	5	82	21	272			2,347	156
Rate per 100,000 inhabitants...................		240.0	3.2	51.8	13.3	171.8			1,482.4	98.5
College Station-Bryan, TX MSA[2]	259,198									
Includes Brazos, Burleson, and Robertson[2] Counties										
City of College Station.............................	115,357	230	1	53	49	127	2,304	300	1,887	117
City of Bryan..	84,438	363	4	53	69	237	2,028	348	1,557	123
Total area actually reporting....................	99.1%	734	8	136	128	462	5,474	903	4,283	288
Estimated total.......................................	100.0%	740	8	137	129	466	5,528	911	4,325	292
Rate per 100,000 inhabitants...................		285.5	3.1	52.9	49.8	179.8	2,132.7	351.5	1,668.6	112.7

Table 4. Crime, by Selected Metropolitan Statistical Area, 2017—*Continued*

(Number, percent, rate per 100,000 population.)

Area	Population	Violent crime	Murder and nonnegligent manslaughter	Rape[1]	Robbery	Aggravated assault	Property crime	Burglary	Larceny-theft	Motor vehicle theft
Colorado Springs, CO MSA............	720,520									
Includes El Paso and Teller Counties										
City of Colorado Springs..............	472,958	2,479	29	489	482	1,479	15,214	2,508	10,571	2,135
Total area actually reporting...........	99.9%	3,110	33	620	534	1,923	18,822	3,097	13,184	2,541
Estimated total..........................	100.0%	3,111	33	620	534	1,924	18,840	3,099	13,198	2,543
Rate per 100,000 inhabitants...........		431.8	4.6	86.0	74.1	267.0	2,614.8	430.1	1,831.7	352.9
Columbia, MO MSA.....................	179,032									
Includes Boone County										
City of Columbia.......................	122,585	610	9	115	117	369	3,597	505	2,826	266
Total area actually reporting...........	100.0%	735	10	128	129	468	4,672	641	3,673	358
Rate per 100,000 inhabitants...........		410.5	5.6	71.5	72.1	261.4	2,609.6	358.0	2,051.6	200.0
Columbia, SC MSA[5]	826,594									
Includes Calhoun, Fairfield, Kershaw, Lexington,5 Richland, and Saluda Counties										
City of Columbia.......................	134,957	991	10	66	273	642	7,134	954	5,389	791
Total area actually reporting...........	100.0%	4,620	59	372	808	3,381		4,831		3,425
Rate per 100,000 inhabitants...........		558.9	7.1	45.0	97.8	409.0		584.4		414.4
Columbus, GA-AL MSA	311,195									
Includes Russell County, AL and Chattahoochee, Harris, Marion, and Muscogee Counties, GA										
City of Columbus, GA..................	198,832	1,303	35	71	394	803	8,820	2,131	5,985	704
Total area actually reporting...........	96.3%	1,605	44	126	470	965	10,877	2,659	7,304	914
Estimated total..........................	100.0%	1,640	45	128	480	987	11,157	2,714	7,500	943
Rate per 100,000 inhabitants...........		527.0	14.5	41.1	154.2	317.2	3,585.2	872.1	2,410.1	303.0
Columbus, IN MSA[4]	82,293									
Includes Bartholomew County										
City of Columbus[4].....................	47,322		1		18	4	1,904	202	1,537	165
Total area actually reporting...........	100.0%	108	2	26	42	38	2,545	358	1,924	263
Rate per 100,000 inhabitants...........		131.2	2.4	31.6	51.0	46.2	3,092.6	435.0	2,338.0	319.6
Columbus, OH MSA	2,070,524									
Includes Delaware, Fairfield, Franklin, Hocking, Licking, Madison, Morrow, Perry, Pickaway, and Union Counties										
City of Columbus......................	872,205	4,478	142	919	1,963	1,454	34,408	7,111	23,121	4,176
Total area actually reporting...........	93.9%	5,836	161	1,310	2,369	1,996	56,924	10,722	41,013	5,189
Estimated total..........................	100.0%	6,018	164	1,351	2,421	2,082	59,333	11,122	42,904	5,307
Rate per 100,000 inhabitants...........		290.7	7.9	65.2	116.9	100.6	2,865.6	537.2	2,072.1	256.3
Corpus Christi, TX MSA................	458,865									
Includes Aransas, Nueces, and San Patricio Counties										
City of Corpus Christi..................	329,256	2,313	21	232	470	1,590	11,739	2,232	8,776	731
Total area actually reporting...........	100.0%	2,900	30	289	520	2,061	15,495	3,202	11,368	925
Rate per 100,000 inhabitants...........		632.0	6.5	63.0	113.3	449.2	3,376.8	697.8	2,477.4	201.6
Corvallis, OR MSA	90,142									
Includes Benton County										
City of Corvallis........................	57,576	75	2	20	13	40	1,440	153	1,229	58
Total area actually reporting...........	100.0%	125	3	34	19	69	2,115	226	1,803	86
Rate per 100,000 inhabitants...........		138.7	3.3	37.7	21.1	76.5	2,346.3	250.7	2,000.2	95.4
Crestview-Fort Walton Beach-Destin, FL MSA	273,416									
Includes Okaloosa and Walton Counties										
City of Crestview	24,022	117	0	17	16	84	868	189	605	74
City of Fort Walton Beach..............	22,413	73	1	14	16	42	617	92	460	65
Total area actually reporting...........	99.7%	904	7	117	93	687	5,970	1,216	4,336	418
Estimated total..........................	100.0%	907	7	117	94	689	5,993	1,219	4,354	420
Rate per 100,000 inhabitants...........		331.7	2.6	42.8	34.4	252.0	2,191.9	445.8	1,592.4	153.6
Cumberland, MD-WV MSA.............	98,718									
Includes Allegany County, MD and Mineral County, WV										
City of Cumberland, MD...............	19,842	150	1	7	41	101	1,240	248	976	16
Total area actually reporting...........	100.0%	280	2	24	62	192	2,518	535	1,923	60
Rate per 100,000 inhabitants...........		283.6	2.0	24.3	62.8	194.5	2,550.7	541.9	1,948.0	60.8
Dallas-Fort Worth-Arlington, TX MSA[2, 3]	7,365,764									
Includes the Metropolitan Divisions of Dallas-Plano-Irving and Fort Worth-Arlington										

Table 4. Crime, by Selected Metropolitan Statistical Area, 2017—*Continued*

(Number, percent, rate per 100,000 population.)

Area	Population	Violent crime	Murder and nonnegligent manslaughter	Rape[1]	Robbery	Aggravated assault	Property crime	Burglary	Larceny-theft	Motor vehicle theft
City of Dallas	1,338,551	10,369	167	831	4,377	4,994	42,634	9,874	24,847	7,913
City of Fort Worth	873,069	4,891	70	569	1,286	2,966	28,072	5,116	20,250	2,706
City of Arlington[2]	397,377	2,054	19	254	576	1,205	12,707	1,801	9,546	1,360
City of Plano	290,413	435	15	81	119	220	5,035	728	3,968	339
City of Irving	242,062	549	8	54	228	259	6,147	969	4,467	711
City of Denton	136,836	416	1	120	94	201	3,091	426	2,367	298
City of Richardson	115,824	193	3	25	97	68	2,295	389	1,717	189
Total area actually reporting	99.9%	27,188	380	3,485	8,869	14,454			122,870	20,323
Estimated total	100.0%	27,204	380	3,487	8,873	14,464			122,971	20,333
Rate per 100,000 inhabitants		369.3	5.2	47.3	120.5	196.4			1,669.5	276.0
Dallas-Plano-Irving, TX MD[2,3]	4,887,235									
Includes Collin, Dallas, Denton, Ellis, Hunt, Kaufman, and Rockwall Counties										
Total area actually reporting	99.9%	17,925	262	2,194	6,547	8,922			75,859	14,516
Estimated total	100.0%	17,938	262	2,196	6,550	8,930			75,944	14,524
Rate per 100,000 inhabitants		367.0	5.4	44.9	134.0	182.7			1,553.9	297.2
Fort Worth-Arlington, TX MD[2]	2,478,529									
Includes Hood,[2] Johnson, Parker, Somervell, Tarrant, and Wise Counties										
Total area actually reporting	99.9%	9,263	118	1,291	2,322	5,532	63,640	10,822	47,011	5,807
Estimated total	100.0%	9,266	118	1,291	2,323	5,534	63,661	10,825	47,027	5,809
Rate per 100,000 inhabitants		373.9	4.8	52.1	93.7	223.3	2,568.5	436.8	1,897.4	234.4
Includes Lawrence and Morgan Counties										
City of Decatur	55,836	112	0	7	25	80	2,451	434	1,883	134
Total area actually reporting	98.4%	246	2	36	40	168	3,660	791	2,631	238
Estimated total	100.0%	256	2	37	42	175	3,750	809	2,697	244
Rate per 100,000 inhabitants		166.9	1.3	24.1	27.4	114.1	2,445.5	527.6	1,758.8	159.1
Dalton, GA MSA	144,348									
Includes Murray and Whitfield Counties										
City of Dalton	34,228	108	0	16	17	75	981	126	782	73
Total area actually reporting	99.6%	315	2	38	23	252	2,941	566	2,147	228
Estimated total	100.0%	318	2	38	24	254	2,965	569	2,166	230
Rate per 100,000 inhabitants		220.3	1.4	26.3	16.6	176.0	2,054.1	394.2	1,500.5	159.3
Danville, IL MSA	77,582									
Includes Vermilion County										
City of Danville	31,368	546	10	36	88	412	1,833	456	1,306	71
Total area actually reporting	98.4%	696	10	87	96	503	2,651	728	1,817	106
Estimated total	100.0%	699	10	87	97	505	2,671	731	1,833	107
Rate per 100,000 inhabitants		901.0	12.9	112.1	125.0	650.9	3,442.8	942.2	2,362.7	137.9
Daphne-Fairhope-Foley, AL MSA	212,998									
Includes Baldwin County										
City of Daphne	26,669	34	0	1	9	24	556	74	464	18
City of Fairhope	20,180	52	0	6	4	42	606	89	490	27
City of Foley	18,032	47	0	4	9	34	782	65	693	24
Total area actually reporting	100.0%	532	4	42	54	432	4,662	716	3,694	252
Rate per 100,000 inhabitants		249.8	1.9	19.7	25.4	202.8	2,188.8	336.2	1,734.3	118.3
Davenport-Moline-Rock Island, IA-IL MSA	382,517									
Includes Henry, Mercer, and Rock Island Counties, IL and Scott County, IA										
City of Davenport, IA	103,063	750	13	90	203	444	5,249	1,108	3,586	555
City of Moline, IL	42,042	224	0	31	20	173	1,363	234	1,083	46
City of Rock Island, IL	38,079	133	3	5	10	115	1,060	198	754	108
Total area actually reporting	96.0%	1,520	18	212	266	1,024	10,659	2,175	7,613	871
Estimated total	100.0%	1,546	18	217	270	1,041	10,839	2,217	7,740	882
Rate per 100,000 inhabitants		404.2	4.7	56.7	70.6	272.1	2,833.6	579.6	2,023.4	230.6
Dayton, OH MSA[4]	802,856									
Includes Greene, Miami, and Montgomery Counties										
City of Dayton	140,171	1,232	30	122	393	687	6,083	1,779	3,688	616
Total area actually reporting	96.9%	2,326	42	439	722	1,123	19,998	4,079	14,356	1,563
Estimated total	100.0%	2,363	43	447	733	1,140	20,504	4,156	14,761	1,587
Rate per 100,000 inhabitants		294.3	5.4	55.7	91.3	142.0	2,553.9	517.7	1,838.6	197.7
Decatur, AL MSA	151,897									
Includes Lawrence and Morgan Counties										

Table 4. Crime, by Selected Metropolitan Statistical Area, 2017—*Continued*

(Number, percent, rate per 100,000 population.)

Area	Population	Violent crime	Murder and nonnegligent manslaughter	Rape[1]	Robbery	Aggravated assault	Property crime	Burglary	Larceny-theft	Motor vehicle theft
City of Decatur	54,958	199	9	20	53	117	2,284	431	1,680	173
Total area actually reporting	99.3%	463	11	45	61	346	3,423	791	2,345	287
Estimated total	100.0%	468	11	45	62	350	3,460	797	2,373	290
Rate per 100,000 inhabitants		308.1	7.2	29.6	40.8	230.4	2,277.9	524.7	1,562.2	190.9
Decatur, IL MSA	105,916									
Includes Macon County										
City of Decatur	72,153	443	10	52	106	275	2,394	731	1,571	92
Total area actually reporting	99.0%	503	10	66	113	314	2,818	818	1,896	104
Estimated total	100.0%	505	10	66	114	315	2,836	821	1,910	105
Rate per 100,000 inhabitants		476.8	9.4	62.3	107.6	297.4	2,677.6	775.1	1,803.3	99.1
Deltona-Daytona Beach-Ormond Beach, FL MSA	647,702									
Includes Flagler and Volusia Counties										
City of Daytona Beach	67,564	748	12	23	82	631	3,819	497	3,027	295
City of Ormond Beach	42,625	202	0	10	25	167	1,386	280	1,003	103
Total area actually reporting	100.0%	2,298	32	136	340	1,790	16,087	2,655	12,258	1,174
Rate per 100,000 inhabitants		354.8	4.9	21.0	52.5	276.4	2,483.7	409.9	1,892.5	181.3
Denver-Aurora-Lakewood, CO MSA[3]	2,895,448									
Includes Adams, Arapahoe, Broomfield, Clear Creek, Denver, Douglas, Elbert, Gilpin, Jefferson, and Park Counties										
City of Denver	706,616	4,774	59	699	1,232	2,784	25,912	4,331	16,021	5,560
City of Aurora	368,018	2,239	30	319	679	1,211	11,054	1,671	7,194	2,189
City of Lakewood	156,344	1,007	5	151	208	643	7,596	911	5,492	1,193
City of Broomfield	68,158	84	1	23	7	53	1,790	197	1,400	193
Total area actually reporting	99.9%	11,976	133	2,102	2,694	7,047			58,868	15,209
Estimated total	100.0%	11,985	133	2,104	2,695	7,053			58,944	15,222
Rate per 100,000 inhabitants		413.9	4.6	72.7	93.1	243.6			2,035.7	525.7
Detroit-Warren-Dearborn, MI MSA	4,309,631									
Includes the Metropolitan Divisions of Detroit-Dearborn-Livonia and Warren-Troy-Farmington Hills										
City of Detroit	670,792	13,796	267	697	2,639	10,193	30,458	8,258	14,045	8,155
City of Warren	135,303	681	7	125	97	452	2,900	659	1,804	437
City of Dearborn	93,889	256	0	38	51	167	2,272	218	1,776	278
City of Livonia	93,603	108	0	16	16	76	1,431	165	1,137	129
City of Troy	84,086	55	0	14	6	35	1,275	94	1,114	67
City of Farmington Hills	81,359	93	1	15	16	61	915	119	719	77
City of Southfield	73,324	151	1	18	37	95	2,032	315	1,454	263
City of Taylor	60,882	348	4	39	58	247	1,480	326	973	181
City of Pontiac	59,731	644	4	61	97	482	1,510	468	820	222
City of Novi	59,895	43	0	11	6	26	617	42	543	32
Total area actually reporting	100.0%	23,445	339	2,277	4,040	16,789	83,845	17,022	53,177	13,646
Rate per 100,000 inhabitants		544.0	7.9	52.8	93.7	389.6	1,945.5	395.0	1,233.9	316.6
Detroit-Dearborn-Livonia, MI MD	1,742,865									
Includes Wayne County										
Total area actually reporting	100.0%	17,965	304	1,257	3,360	13,044	51,921	11,710	29,411	10,800
Rate per 100,000 inhabitants		1,030.8	17.4	72.1	192.8	748.4	2,979.1	671.9	1,687.5	619.7
Warren-Troy-Farmington Hills, MI MD	2,566,766									
Includes Lapeer, Livingston, Macomb, Oakland, and St. Clair Counties										
Total area actually reporting	100.0%	5,480	35	1,020	680	3,745	31,924	5,312	23,766	2,846
Rate per 100,000 inhabitants		213.5	1.4	39.7	26.5	145.9	1,243.7	207.0	925.9	110.9
Dothan, AL MSA	148,079									
Includes Geneva, Henry, and Houston Counties										
City of Dothan	67,653	572	6	35	67	464	2,686	615	1,875	196
Total area actually reporting	99.4%	841	8	66	87	680	4,079	946	2,822	311
Estimated total	100.0%	845	8	66	88	683	4,107	951	2,843	313
Rate per 100,000 inhabitants		570.6	5.4	44.6	59.4	461.2	2,773.5	642.2	1,919.9	211.4
Dover, DE MSA	177,027									
Includes Kent County										
City of Dover	38,084	264	4	14	38	208	1,671	52	1,558	61
Total area actually reporting	100.0%	757	6	81	108	562	4,058	534	3,379	145
Rate per 100,000 inhabitants		427.6	3.4	45.8	61.0	317.5	2,292.3	301.6	1,908.7	81.9

Table 4. Crime, by Selected Metropolitan Statistical Area, 2017—*Continued*

(Number, percent, rate per 100,000 population.)

Area	Population	Violent crime	Murder and nonnegligent manslaughter	Rape[1]	Robbery	Aggravated assault	Property crime	Burglary	Larceny-theft	Motor vehicle theft
Dubuque, IA MSA	97,394									
Includes Dubuque County										
City of Dubuque	58,674	166	2	40	16	108	1,606	333	1,210	63
Total area actually reporting	100.0%	188	2	50	16	120	1,805	398	1,329	78
Rate per 100,000 inhabitants		193.0	2.1	51.3	16.4	123.2	1,853.3	408.6	1,364.6	80.1
Duluth, MN-WI MSA	280,022									
Includes Carlton and St. Louis Counties, MN and Douglas County, WI										
City of Duluth, MN	86,306	279	1	31	66	181	3,819	506	3,091	222
Total area actually reporting	100.0%	565	4	100	89	372	8,421	1,263	6,644	514
Rate per 100,000 inhabitants		201.8	1.4	35.7	31.8	132.8	3,007.3	451.0	2,372.7	183.6
Durham-Chapel Hill, NC MSA[4]	569,875									
Includes Chatham, Durham, Orange and Person Counties[4]										
City of Durham[4]	269,088		23		852	1,257	10,296	2,334	7,200	762
City of Chapel Hill[4]	59,553		1		40	38	1,284	251	980	53
Total area actually reporting	100.0%		31		1,003	1,679	16,298	3,967	11,324	1,007
Rate per 100,000 inhabitants			5.4		176.0	294.6	2,859.9	696.1	1,987.1	176.7
East Stroudsburg, PA MSA	165,582									
Includes Monroe County										
Total area actually reporting	100.0%	428	8	73	71	276	3,213	587	2,534	92
Rate per 100,000 inhabitants		258.5	4.8	44.1	42.9	166.7	1,940.4	354.5	1,530.4	55.6
Eau Claire, WI MSA[3]	167,499									
Includes Chippewa and Eau Claire[3] Counties										
City of Eau Claire	68,687	162	1	32	44	85	2,000	385	1,531	84
Total area actually reporting	100.0%		3	55	52		3,158	576	2,433	149
Rate per 100,000 inhabitants			1.8	32.8	31.0		1,885.4	343.9	1,452.5	89.0
El Centro, CA MSA	181,724									
Includes Imperial County										
City of El Centro	44,458	185	4	15	45	121	1,820	409	1,285	126
Total area actually reporting	95.9%	628	7	45	87	489	4,836	1,293	3,017	526
Estimated total	100.0%	653	7	47	95	504	5,012	1,325	3,133	554
Rate per 100,000 inhabitants		359.3	3.9	25.9	52.3	277.3	2,758.0	729.1	1,724.0	304.9
Elizabethtown-Fort Knox, KY MSA	149,535									
Includes Hardin, Larue, and Meade Counties										
City of Elizabethtown	30,065	61	1	11	13	36	469	169	244	56
Total area actually reporting	100.0%	169	5	31	37	96	1,810	519	1,098	193
Rate per 100,000 inhabitants		113.0	3.3	20.7	24.7	64.2	1,210.4	347.1	734.3	129.1
Elmira, NY MSA	86,084									
Includes Chemung County										
City of Elmira	27,740	80	2	2	29	47	863	126	717	20
Total area actually reporting	100.0%	143	4	28	32	79	1,417	185	1,198	34
Rate per 100,000 inhabitants		166.1	4.6	32.5	37.2	91.8	1,646.1	214.9	1,391.7	39.5
El Paso, TX MSA	847,071									
Includes El Paso and Hudspeth Counties										
City of El Paso	688,667	2,609	19	371	400	1,819	12,526	1,297	10,429	800
Total area actually reporting	100.0%	3,018	21	441	432	2,124	14,287	1,604	11,784	899
Rate per 100,000 inhabitants		356.3	2.5	52.1	51.0	250.7	1,686.6	189.4	1,391.1	106.1
Enid, OK MSA	62,575									
Includes Garfield County										
City of Enid	51,257	174	0	34	21	119	1,751	417	1,242	92
Total area actually reporting	100.0%	189	0	36	21	132	1,890	458	1,328	104
Rate per 100,000 inhabitants		302.0	0.0	57.5	33.6	210.9	3,020.4	731.9	2,122.3	166.2
Erie, PA MSA	275,639									
Includes Erie County										
City of Erie	98,071	306	6	32	98	170	2,258	531	1,619	108
Total area actually reporting	100.0%	643	12	66	114	451	4,907	911	3,814	182
Rate per 100,000 inhabitants		233.3	4.4	23.9	41.4	163.6	1,780.2	330.5	1,383.7	66.0
Eugene, OR MSA[2]	372,953									
Includes Lane County										

(Number, percent, rate per 100,000 population.)

Area	Population	Violent crime	Murder and nonnegligent manslaughter	Rape[1]	Robbery	Aggravated assault	Property crime	Burglary	Larceny-theft	Motor vehicle theft
City of Eugene	168,310	651	3	101	177	370	6,276	1,129	4,602	545
Total area actually reporting	99.1%	1,235	8	172	249	806	11,248	1,925	8,349	974
Estimated total	100.0%	1,242	8	174	250	810	11,334	1,935	8,414	985
Rate per 100,000 inhabitants		333.0	2.1	46.7	67.0	217.2	3,039.0	518.8	2,256.0	264.1
Evansville, IN-KY MSA	317,010									
Includes Posey, Vanderburgh, and Warrick Counties, IN and Henderson County, KY										
City of Evansville	119,371	825	20	75	185	545	5,979	863	4,641	475
Total area actually reporting	98.0%	1,167	26	117	231	793	8,672	1,442	6,569	661
Estimated total	100.0%	1,185	26	119	235	805	8,831	1,460	6,698	673
Rate per 100,000 inhabitants		373.8	8.2	37.5	74.1	253.9	2,785.7	460.6	2,112.9	212.3
Fairbanks, AK MSA	35,185									
Includes Fairbanks North Star Borough										
City of Fairbanks	32,937	205	10	24	40	131	1,493	164	1,121	208
Total area actually reporting	100.0%	214	10	26	41	137	1,641	170	1,255	216
Rate per 100,000 inhabitants		608.2	28.4	73.9	116.5	389.4	4,663.9	483.2	3,566.9	613.9
Fargo, ND-MN MSA	239,227									
Includes Clay County, MN and Cass County, ND										
City of Fargo, ND	123,430	497	3	83	68	343	3,870	593	2,975	302
Total area actually reporting	100.0%	670	4	133	85	448	5,755	902	4,370	483
Rate per 100,000 inhabitants		280.1	1.7	55.6	35.5	187.3	2,405.7	377.0	1,826.7	201.9
Farmington, NM MSA	112,964									
Includes San Juan County										
City of Farmington	40,940	519	3	62	54	400	1,971	492	1,326	153
Total area actually reporting	100.0%	1,250	5	133	66	1,046	3,144	792	2,110	242
Rate per 100,000 inhabitants		1,106.5	4.4	117.7	58.4	926.0	2,783.2	701.1	1,867.9	214.2
Fayetteville, NC MSA[4]	383,425									
Includes Cumberland and Hoke Counties[4]										
City of Fayetteville[4]	205,432		24		292	1,105	8,811	1,818	6,578	415
Total area actually reporting	96.5%		31		347	1,243	11,022	2,464	8,084	474
Estimated total	100.0%		31		356	1,265	11,401	2,533	8,378	490
Rate per 100,000 inhabitants			8.1		92.8	329.9	2,973.5	660.6	2,185.0	127.8
Flagstaff, AZ MSA	141,844									
Includes Coconino County										
City of Flagstaff	72,388	307	7	35	57	208	2,729	161	2,486	82
Total area actually reporting	100.0%	545	11	78	62	394	3,944	356	3,455	133
Rate per 100,000 inhabitants		384.2	7.8	55.0	43.7	277.8	2,780.5	251.0	2,435.8	93.8
Flint, MI MSA	406,927									
Includes Genesee County										
City of Flint	96,605	1,879	37	104	272	1,466	2,632	961	1,397	274
Estimated total	100.0%	2,902	48	293	412	2,149	7,752	1,901	5,274	577
Rate per 100,000 inhabitants		713.2	11.8	72.0	101.2	528.1	1,905.0	467.2	1,296.1	141.8
Florence, SC MSA	206,228									
Includes Darlington and Florence Counties										
City of Florence	38,449	487	5	27	61	394	2,728	353	2,242	133
Total area actually reporting	98.2%	1,707	48	111	208	1,340	8,997	1,981	6,454	562
Estimated total	100.0%	1,724	48	113	211	1,352	9,127	1,999	6,557	571
Rate per 100,000 inhabitants		836.0	23.3	54.8	102.3	655.6	4,425.7	969.3	3,179.5	276.9
Florence-Muscle Shoals, AL MSA	146,328									
Includes Colbert and Lauderdale Counties										
City of Florence	40,059	189	1	30	40	118	1,703	319	1,239	145
City of Muscle Shoals	13,939	81	1	3	5	72	637	121	458	58
Total area actually reporting	99.8%	488	2	68	65	353	3,601	749	2,499	353
Estimated total	100.0%	489	2	68	65	354	3,611	751	2,506	354
Rate per 100,000 inhabitants		334.2	1.4	46.5	44.4	241.9	2,467.7	513.2	1,712.6	241.9
Fond du Lac, WI MSA	102,243									
Includes Fond du Lac County										
City of Fond du Lac	42,929	110	1	28	19	62	901	82	788	31
Total area actually reporting	100.0%	148	2	42	19	85	1,225	150	1,027	48
Rate per 100,000 inhabitants		144.8	2.0	41.1	18.6	83.1	1,198.1	146.7	1,004.5	46.9

Table 4. Crime, by Selected Metropolitan Statistical Area, 2017—*Continued*

(Number, percent, rate per 100,000 population.)

Area	Population	Violent crime	Murder and nonnegligent manslaughter	Rape[1]	Robbery	Aggravated assault	Property crime	Burglary	Larceny-theft	Motor vehicle theft
Fort Collins, CO MSA..	345,764									
Includes Larimer County										
City of Fort Collins	167,633	369	6	45	42	276	4,250	457	3,586	207
Total area actually reporting....................	100.0%	829	6	147	76	600	7,755	937	6,394	424
Rate per 100,000 inhabitants...................		239.8	1.7	42.5	22.0	173.5	2,242.9	271.0	1,849.2	122.6
Fort Smith, AR-OK MSA.................................	281,048									
Includes Crawford and Sebastian Counties, AR and Le Flore and Sequoyah Counties, OK										
City of Fort Smith, AR	88,437	787	7	71	107	602	4,511	832	3,345	334
Total area actually reporting....................	99.7%	1,419	10	160	128	1,121	8,268	1,837	5,857	574
Estimated total...	100.0%	1,423	10	161	128	1,124	8,289	1,842	5,872	575
Rate per 100,000 inhabitants...................		506.3	3.6	57.3	45.5	399.9	2,949.3	655.4	2,089.3	204.6
Fort Wayne, IN MSA[4,5]	434,895									
Includes Allen, Wells, and Whitley Counties										
City of Fort Wayne.....................................	266,259	952	37	136	299	480	8,466	1,308	6,626	532
Total area actually reporting....................	92.7%	1,176	39	180	337	620		1,565		640
Estimated total...	100.0%	1,233	39	187	347	660		1,648		687
Rate per 100,000 inhabitants...................		283.5	9.0	43.0	79.8	151.8		378.9		158.0
Fresno, CA MSA...	986,951									
Includes Fresno County										
City of Fresno	526,371	2,974	56	174	958	1,786	20,220	3,649	13,782	2,789
Total area actually reporting....................	100.0%	5,747	85	336	1,214	4,112	30,470	6,757	19,322	4,391
Rate per 100,000 inhabitants...................		582.3	8.6	34.0	123.0	416.6	3,087.3	684.6	1,957.7	444.9
Gadsden, AL MSA	102,194									
Includes Etowah County										
City of Gadsden	35,665	613	3	23	63	524	2,641	497	1,914	230
Total area actually reporting....................	93.6%	800	6	41	68	685	3,648	780	2,528	340
Estimated total...	100.0%	834	7	44	73	710	3,864	817	2,690	357
Rate per 100,000 inhabitants...................		816.1	6.8	43.1	71.4	694.8	3,781.0	799.5	2,632.2	349.3
Gainesville, FL MSA....................................	284,282									
Includes Alachua and Gilchrist Counties										
City of Gainesville	132,777	952	4	164	176	608	4,778	500	3,915	363
Total area actually reporting....................	99.3%	1,670	9	249	296	1,116	7,465	1,158	5,779	528
Estimated total...	100.0%	1,678	9	250	298	1,121	7,524	1,166	5,825	533
Rate per 100,000 inhabitants...................		590.3	3.2	87.9	104.8	394.3	2,646.7	410.2	2,049.0	187.5
Gainesville, GA MSA....................................	199,799									
Includes Hall County										
City of Gainesville	40,836	157	2	19	34	102	1,404	209	1,091	104
Total area actually reporting....................	100.0%	442	5	71	70	296	3,654	622	2,663	369
Rate per 100,000 inhabitants...................		221.2	2.5	35.5	35.0	148.1	1,828.8	311.3	1,332.8	184.7
Gettysburg, PA MSA	102,366									
Includes Adams County										
City of Gettysburg	7,716	37	0	4	7	26	136	15	120	1
Total area actually reporting....................	100.0%	144	1	27	14	102	770	130	603	37
Rate per 100,000 inhabitants...................		140.7	1.0	26.4	13.7	99.6	752.2	127.0	589.1	36.1
Glens Falls, NY MSA.....................................	126,220									
Includes Warren and Washington Counties										
City of Glens Falls	14,268	29	2	1	3	23	190	28	156	6
Total area actually reporting....................	98.0%	179	5	77	13	84	1,372	200	1,134	38
Estimated total...	100.0%	182	5	77	14	86	1,409	204	1,166	39
Rate per 100,000 inhabitants...................		144.2	4.0	61.0	11.1	68.1	1,116.3	161.6	923.8	30.9
Goldsboro, NC MSA[4]	124,619									
Includes Wayne County[4]										
City of Goldsboro[4]	35,824		10		75	184	1,796	337	1,399	60
Total area actually reporting....................	97.7%		11		113	339	3,515	997	2,310	208
Estimated total...	100.0%		11		115	344	3,595	1,012	2,372	211
Rate per 100,000 inhabitants...................			8.8		92.3	276.0	2,884.8	812.1	1,903.4	169.3
Grand Forks, ND-MN MSA.............................	101,846									
Includes Polk County, MN and Grand Forks County, ND										
City of Grand Forks, ND............................	58,090	183	0	29	32	122	1,720	265	1,331	124

(Number, percent, rate per 100,000 population.)

Area	Population	Violent crime	Murder and nonnegligent manslaughter	Rape[1]	Robbery	Aggravated assault	Property crime	Burglary	Larceny-theft	Motor vehicle theft
Total area actually reporting.................................	100.0%	252	1	51	35	165	2,450	394	1,910	146
Rate per 100,000 inhabitants..............................		247.4	1.0	50.1	34.4	162.0	2,405.6	386.9	1,875.4	143.4
Grand Junction, CO MSA..................................	150,129									
Includes Mesa County										
City of Grand Junction..............................	62,352	361	2	71	25	263	2,849	356	2,324	169
Total area actually reporting..............	99.2%	610	4	137	41	428	4,405	680	3,407	318
Estimated total..	100.0%	613	4	138	41	430	4,438	684	3,432	322
Rate per 100,000 inhabitants..............		408.3	2.7	91.9	27.3	286.4	2,956.1	455.6	2,286.0	214.5
Grand Rapids-Wyoming, MI MSA......................	1,059,630									
Includes Barry, Kent, Montcalm, and Ottawa Counties										
City of Grand Rapids..................................	197,868	1,408	12	141	351	904	4,102	763	2,976	363
City of Wyoming.......................................	76,153	356	3	74	83	196	1,666	235	1,221	210
Total area actually reporting..............	99.6%	3,422	30	828	554	2,010	16,004	2,762	12,232	1,010
Estimated total..	100.0%	3,433	30	830	556	2,017	16,070	2,772	12,283	1,015
Rate per 100,000 inhabitants..............		324.0	2.8	78.3	52.5	190.3	1,516.6	261.6	1,159.2	95.8
Grants Pass, OR MSA[2]......................................	86,520									
Includes Josephine County[2]										
City of Grants Pass.....................................	38,082	103	0	17	15	71	1,627	156	1,264	207
Total area actually reporting..............	100.0%	191	5	28	18	140	2,044	265	1,415	364
Rate per 100,000 inhabitants..............		220.8	5.8	32.4	20.8	161.8	2,362.5	306.3	1,635.5	420.7
Great Falls, MT MSA...	81,700									
Includes Cascade County										
City of Great Falls	59,167	246	3	20	30	193	3,023	284	2,539	200
Total area actually reporting..............	100.0%	275	5	23	30	217	3,166	315	2,636	215
Rate per 100,000 inhabitants..............		336.6	6.1	28.2	36.7	265.6	3,875.2	385.6	3,226.4	263.2
Greeley, CO MSA...	301,211									
Includes Weld County										
City of Greeley..	105,906	449	5	75	57	312	2,714	428	2,020	266
Total area actually reporting..............	99.6%	769	9	113	85	562	5,205	848	3,812	545
Estimated total..	100.0%	772	9	114	85	564	5,239	852	3,838	549
Rate per 100,000 inhabitants..............		256.3	3.0	37.8	28.2	187.2	1,739.3	282.9	1,274.2	182.3
Green Bay, WI MSA[2]...	320,287									
Includes Brown, Kewaunee, and Oconto Counties										
City of Green Bay......................................	105,331	498	0	76	65	357	2,147	321	1,738	88
Total area actually reporting..............	91.2%	687	0	127	73	487	4,180	530	3,509	141
Estimated total..	100.0%	712	0	133	75	504	4,366	571	3,642	153
Rate per 100,000 inhabitants..............		222.3	0.0	41.5	23.4	157.4	1,363.2	178.3	1,137.1	47.8
Greensboro-High Point, NC MSA[4].................	763,106									
Includes Guilford, Randolph, and Rockingham Counties[4]										
City of Greensboro[4]	290,051		46		664	1,394	10,332	2,062	7,424	846
City of High Point[4]	112,368		20		206	530	4,161	754	3,127	280
Total area actually reporting..............	99.5%		83		1,017	2,448	21,988	4,800	15,692	1,496
Estimated total..	100.0%		83		1,020	2,455	22,100	4,820	15,779	1,501
Rate per 100,000 inhabitants..............			10.9		133.7	321.7	2,896.1	631.6	2,067.7	196.7
Greenville, NC MSA[4]	179,034									
Includes Pitt County[4]										
City of Greenville[4]	92,630		4		154	420	3,394	724	2,566	104
Total area actually reporting..............	97.5%		5		195	611	5,090	1,218	3,691	181
Estimated total..	100.0%		5		198	619	5,218	1,241	3,791	186
Rate per 100,000 inhabitants..............			2.8		110.6	345.7	2,914.5	693.2	2,117.5	103.9
Greenville-Anderson-Mauldin, SC MSA	896,199									
Includes Anderson, Greenville, Laurens, and Pickens Counties										
City of Greenville......................................	68,922	415	4	28	91	292	2,831	393	2,281	157
City of Anderson.......................................	27,728	181	2	14	20	145	1,666	229	1,310	127
City of Mauldin...	25,535	65	1	5	12	47	409	45	332	32
City of Easley	21,107	125	0	8	15	102	1,308	127	1,117	64
Total area actually reporting..............	100.0%	4,363	47	466	591	3,259	27,798	5,315	19,862	2,621
Rate per 100,000 inhabitants..............		486.8	5.2	52.0	65.9	363.6	3,101.8	593.1	2,216.2	292.5
Gulfport-Biloxi-Pascagoula, MS MSA[4]	393,581									
Includes Hancock, Harrison, and Jackson Counties										

Table 4. Crime, by Selected Metropolitan Statistical Area, 2017—*Continued*

(Number, percent, rate per 100,000 population.)

Area	Population	Violent crime	Murder and nonnegligent manslaughter	Rape[1]	Robbery	Aggravated assault	Property crime	Burglary	Larceny-theft	Motor vehicle theft
City of Gulfport	72,792	299	10	26	82	181	3,662	562	2,897	203
City of Biloxi	46,263	178	1	39	74	64	2,963	871	1,933	159
City of Pascagoula	21,928	72	0	25	22	25	1,450	246	1,135	69
Total area actually reporting............	93.2%	884	21	143	242	478	14,458	2,909	10,603	946
Estimated total.............................	100.0%	935	22	146	255	512	15,221	3,070	11,174	977
Rate per 100,000 inhabitants............		237.6	5.6	37.1	64.8	130.1	3,867.3	780.0	2,839.1	248.2
Hagerstown-Martinsburg, MD-WV MSA	264,967									
Includes Washington County, MD and Berkeley County, WV										
City of Hagerstown, MD	40,568	249	8	18	119	104	1,036	244	668	124
City of Martinsburg, WV	17,761	84	1	12	20	51	804	93	690	21
Total area actually reporting............	100.0%	784	12	76	194	502	4,391	940	3,144	307
Rate per 100,000 inhabitants............		295.9	4.5	28.7	73.2	189.5	1,657.2	354.8	1,186.6	115.9
Hammond, LA MSA............................	131,701									
Includes Tangipahoa Parish										
City of Hammond	20,712	308	2	24	64	218	2,006	655	1,272	79
Total area actually reporting............	96.6%	1,173	12	79	225	857	5,665	1,709	3,577	379
Estimated total.............................	100.0%	1,193	12	80	228	873	5,831	1,739	3,706	386
Rate per 100,000 inhabitants............		905.8	9.1	60.7	173.1	662.9	4,427.5	1,320.4	2,813.9	293.1
Hanford-Corcoran, CA MSA...............	149,193									
Includes Kings County										
City of Hanford............................	55,789	284	2	28	54	200	1,359	197	916	246
City of Corcoran	22,345	78	1	9	10	58	383	101	222	60
Total area actually reporting............	100.0%	754	9	88	104	553	2,935	620	1,786	529
Rate per 100,000 inhabitants............		505.4	6.0	59.0	69.7	370.7	1,967.3	415.6	1,197.1	354.6
Harrisburg-Carlisle, PA MSA...............	571,453									
Includes Cumberland, Dauphin, and Perry Counties										
City of Harrisburg	48,804	564	13	50	178	323	1,494	348	963	183
City of Carlisle	19,233	35	1	5	12	17	370	33	332	5
Total area actually reporting............	98.6%	1,598	25	266	365	942	8,576	1,337	6,853	386
Estimated total.............................	100.0%	1,612	25	267	368	952	8,691	1,351	6,949	391
Rate per 100,000 inhabitants............		282.1	4.4	46.7	64.4	166.6	1,520.9	236.4	1,216.0	68.4
Harrisonburg, VA MSA	133,939									
Includes Rockingham County and Harrisonburg City										
City of Harrisonburg	53,717	128	3	24	12	89	897	115	739	43
Total area actually reporting............	100.0%	194	4	49	14	127	1,498	222	1,190	86
Rate per 100,000 inhabitants............		144.8	3.0	36.6	10.5	94.8	1,118.4	165.7	888.5	64.2
Hartford-West Hartford-East Hartford, CT MSA...............	1,015,610									
Includes Hartford, Middlesex, and Tolland Counties										
City of Hartford	122,891	1,343	29	45	465	804	4,907	738	3,490	679
City of West Hartford......................	62,812	67	0	1	61	5	1,859	150	1,588	121
City of East Hartford	50,067	133	1	24	55	53	1,231	188	883	160
City of Middletown	46,363	49	0	6	8	35	730	68	591	71
Total area actually reporting............	100.0%	2,511	40	248	888	1,335	22,946	3,009	17,487	2,450
Rate per 100,000 inhabitants............		247.2	3.9	24.4	87.4	131.4	2,259.3	296.3	1,721.8	241.2
Hilton Head Island-Bluffton-Beaufort, SC MSA[5]..............	216,071									
Includes Beaufort5 and Jasper Counties										
City of Bluffton............................	20,024	41	0	6	5	30	330	33	275	22
City of Beaufort	13,612	92	1	3	21	67	667	98	536	33
Total area actually reporting............	100.0%	815	13	109	112	581				308
Rate per 100,000 inhabitants............		377.2	6.0	50.4	51.8	268.9				142.5
Homosassa Springs, FL MSA	144,428									
Includes Citrus County										
Total area actually reporting............	100.0%	399	3	42	40	314	2,037	431	1,472	134
Rate per 100,000 inhabitants............		276.3	2.1	29.1	27.7	217.4	1,410.4	298.4	1,019.2	92.8
Hot Springs, AR MSA	97,820									
Includes Garland County										
City of Hot Springs........................	36,956	218	8	20	59	131	2,518	838	1,514	166
Total area actually reporting............	100.0%	514	8	48	69	389	4,130	1,514	2,318	298
Rate per 100,000 inhabitants............		525.5	8.2	49.1	70.5	397.7	4,222.0	1,547.7	2,369.7	304.6
Houma-Thibodaux, LA MSA............................	211,101									
Includes Lafourche and Terrebonne Parishes										

(Number, percent, rate per 100,000 population.)

Area	Population	Violent crime	Murder and nonnegligent manslaughter	Rape[1]	Robbery	Aggravated assault	Property crime	Burglary	Larceny-theft	Motor vehicle theft
City of Houma.....................	34,083	123	2	20	18	83	1,245	168	1,027	50
City of Thibodaux..................	14,617	61	1	3	14	43	578	89	468	21
Total area actually reporting.........	100.0%	685	10	67	68	540	5,731	997	4,488	246
Rate per 100,000 inhabitants.........		324.5	4.7	31.7	32.2	255.8	2,714.8	472.3	2,126.0	116.5
Houston-The Woodlands-Sugar Land, TX MSA[2,5].........	6,914,428									
Includes Austin, Brazoria, Chambers, Fort Bend, Galveston, Harris, Liberty, Montgomery,[5] and Waller Counties										
City of Houston...................	2,338,235	25,609	269	1,366	9,773	14,201	96,532	17,108	67,828	11,596
City of Sugar Land................	89,790	71	0	15	36	20	1,289	158	1,075	56
City of Baytown...................	76,704	288	6	38	108	136	2,678	506	1,846	326
City of Conroe...................	85,534	249	4	54	65	126	1,931	276	1,479	176
Total area actually reporting.........	99.9%	40,846	438	2,938	14,152	23,318			132,783	
Estimated total...................	100.0%	41,008	440	2,958	14,187	23,423			133,368	
Rate per 100,000 inhabitants.........		593.1	6.4	42.8	205.2	338.8			1,928.8	
Huntington-Ashland, WV-KY-OH MSA[4].........	357,503									
Includes Boyd and Greenup Counties, KY; Lawrence County OH; and Cabell, Lincoln, Putnam, and Wayne Counties, WV										
City of Huntington, WV..............	47,933	428	16	54	120	238	2,082	599	1,303	180
City of Ashland, KY................	20,927	39	0	11	3	25	864	113	698	53
Total area actually reporting.........	81.8%	925	26	141	162	596	6,693	1,525	4,556	612
Estimated total...................	100.0%	1,097	28	167	173	729	7,842	1,775	5,344	723
Rate per 100,000 inhabitants.........		306.9	7.8	46.7	48.4	203.9	2,193.5	496.5	1,494.8	202.2
Huntsville, AL MSA.........	454,756									
Includes Limestone and Madison Counties										
City of Huntsville.................	195,173	1,766	22	172	360	1,212	9,232	1,428	6,758	1,046
Total area actually reporting.........	100.0%	2,532	33	256	441	1,802	14,229	2,550	10,229	1,450
Rate per 100,000 inhabitants.........		556.8	7.3	56.3	97.0	396.3	3,128.9	560.7	2,249.3	318.9
Idaho Falls, ID MSA.........	145,276									
Includes Bonneville, Butte, and Jefferson Counties										
City of Idaho Falls................	60,727	215	2	30	8	175	1,122	366	671	85
Total area actually reporting.........	100.0%	347	2	50	10	285	1,870	600	1,126	144
Rate per 100,000 inhabitants.........		238.9	1.4	34.4	6.9	196.2	1,287.2	413.0	775.1	99.1
Indianapolis-Carmel-Anderson, IN MSA[2,4].........	2,026,454									
Includes Boone, Brown, Hamilton, Hancock, Hendricks, Johnson, Madison, Marion, Morgan, Putnam, and Shelby Counties										
City of Indianapolis...............	870,788	11,616	156	668	3,485	7,307	38,418	8,945	24,569	4,904
City of Carmel...................	93,098	17	0	6	6	5	695	61	596	38
City of Anderson..................	54,959	260	1	82	101	76	2,418	408	1,786	224
Total area actually reporting.........	87.7%	13,657	164	923	3,878	8,692	55,047	10,992	37,679	6,376
Estimated total...................	100.0%	14,074	169	979	3,943	8,983	58,410	11,643	40,041	6,726
Rate per 100,000 inhabitants.........		694.5	8.3	48.3	194.6	443.3	2,882.4	574.6	1,975.9	331.9
Iowa City, IA MSA.........	171,405									
Includes Johnson and Washington Counties										
City of Iowa City..................	75,519	156	4	25	46	81	1,767	310	1,376	81
Total area actually reporting.........	100.0%	447	4	93	72	278	3,468	586	2,747	135
Rate per 100,000 inhabitants.........		260.8	2.3	54.3	42.0	162.2	2,023.3	341.9	1,602.6	78.8
Jackson, MI MSA.........	158,563									
Includes Jackson County										
City of Jackson...................	32,822	371	7	58	55	251	1,371	211	1,052	108
Total area actually reporting.........	98.7%	803	12	158	78	555	3,442	569	2,658	215
Estimated total...................	100.0%	809	12	159	79	559	3,479	575	2,686	218
Rate per 100,000 inhabitants.........		510.2	7.6	100.3	49.8	352.5	2,194.1	362.6	1,694.0	137.5
Jackson, MS MSA[4].........	579,463									
Includes Copiah, Hinds, Madison,[4] Rankin, Simpson, and Yazoo Counties										
City of Jackson[4]................	168,397		60		542	591	7,449	2,006	4,696	747
Total area actually reporting.........	76.4%	1,733	68	147	617	901	11,062	2,637	7,497	928
Estimated total...................	100.0%	1,957	75	166	666	1,050	14,139	3,335	9,710	1,094
Rate per 100,000 inhabitants.........		337.7	12.9	28.6	114.9	181.2	2,440.0	575.5	1,675.7	188.8
Jackson, TN MSA.........	129,687									
Includes Chester, Crockett, and Madison Counties										

Table 4. Crime, by Selected Metropolitan Statistical Area, 2017—*Continued*

(Number, percent, rate per 100,000 population.)

Area	Population	Violent crime	Murder and nonnegligent manslaughter	Rape[1]	Robbery	Aggravated assault	Property crime	Burglary	Larceny-theft	Motor vehicle theft
City of Jackson	67,031	655	7	28	91	529	2,917	497	2,271	149
Total area actually reporting	100.0%	907	8	41	104	754	3,729	744	2,772	213
Rate per 100,000 inhabitants		699.4	6.2	31.6	80.2	581.4	2,875.4	573.7	2,137.5	164.2
Jacksonville, FL MSA	1,505,471									
Includes Baker, Clay, Duval, Nassau, and St. Johns Counties										
City of Jacksonville	894,638	5,648	109	538	1,376	3,625	31,551	5,646	22,980	2,925
Total area actually reporting	100.0%	7,239	123	724	1,600	4,792	41,816	7,661	30,548	3,607
Rate per 100,000 inhabitants		480.8	8.2	48.1	106.3	318.3	2,777.6	508.9	2,029.1	239.6
Janesville-Beloit, WI MSA	161,894									
Includes Rock County										
City of Janesville	64,257	170	2	45	30	93	1,948	308	1,572	68
City of Beloit	36,724	156	1	32	34	89	1,114	211	863	40
Total area actually reporting	100.0%	391	4	105	70	212	3,774	664	2,966	144
Rate per 100,000 inhabitants		241.5	2.5	64.9	43.2	130.9	2,331.2	410.1	1,832.1	88.9
Jefferson City, MO MSA[3]	151,721									
Includes Callaway, Cole, Moniteau, and Osage Counties										
City of Jefferson City	42,989	152	4	16	38	94	1,254	164	1,032	58
Total area actually reporting	100.0%		6	57	47		2,757	512	2,080	165
Rate per 100,000 inhabitants			4.0	37.6	31.0		1,817.2	337.5	1,370.9	108.8
Johnson City, TN MSA	202,495									
Includes Carter, Unicoi, and Washington Counties										
City of Johnson City	67,193	267	2	26	42	197	2,831	377	2,296	158
Total area actually reporting	100.0%	663	8	54	65	536	5,653	958	4,342	353
Rate per 100,000 inhabitants		327.4	4.0	26.7	32.1	264.7	2,791.7	473.1	2,144.3	174.3
Johnstown, PA MSA	133,419									
Includes Cambria County										
City of Johnstown	20,946	157	9	10	27	111	634	190	419	25
Total area actually reporting	99.1%	246	11	27	40	168	1,835	345	1,435	55
Estimated total	100.0%	247	11	27	40	169	1,852	347	1,449	56
Rate per 100,000 inhabitants		185.1	8.2	20.2	30.0	126.7	1,388.1	260.1	1,086.1	42.0
Jonesboro, AR MSA	131,530									
Includes Craighead and Poinsett Counties										
City of Jonesboro	76,188	400	13	54	62	271	3,124	1,239	1,728	157
Total area actually reporting	92.8%	560	16	84	67	393	4,221	1,441	2,532	248
Estimated total	100.0%	597	16	89	69	423	4,406	1,500	2,638	268
Rate per 100,000 inhabitants		453.9	12.2	67.7	52.5	321.6	3,349.8	1,140.4	2,005.6	203.8
Joplin, MO MSA	178,239									
Includes Jasper and Newton Counties										
City of Joplin	52,412	317	3	44	61	209	3,729	487	2,918	324
Total area actually reporting	100.0%	713	5	92	81	535	6,971	1,020	5,370	581
Rate per 100,000 inhabitants		400.0	2.8	51.6	45.4	300.2	3,911.0	572.3	3,012.8	326.0
Kahului-Wailuku-Lahaina, HI MSA	165,868									
Includes Kalawao and Maui Counties										
Total area actually reporting	100.0%	446	2	95	67	282	5,729	906	4,016	807
Rate per 100,000 inhabitants		268.9	1.2	57.3	40.4	170.0	3,454.0	546.2	2,421.2	486.5
Kalamazoo-Portage, MI MSA	339,412									
Includes Kalamazoo and Van Buren Counties										
City of Kalamazoo	76,263	913	10	130	152	621	3,174	710	2,132	332
City of Portage	48,876	108	0	31	14	63	1,468	186	1,223	59
Total area actually reporting	99.7%	1,697	16	313	239	1,129	8,991	1,897	6,381	713
Estimated total	100.0%	1,699	16	313	239	1,131	9,006	1,899	6,393	714
Rate per 100,000 inhabitants		500.6	4.7	92.2	70.4	333.2	2,653.4	559.5	1,883.6	210.4
Kankakee, IL MSA	109,501									
Includes Kankakee County										
City of Kankakee	26,265	210	6	35	68	101	1,049	198	800	51
Total area actually reporting	91.5%	360	7	56	100	197	2,143	390	1,657	96
Estimated total	100.0%	380	7	59	106	208	2,294	412	1,777	105
Rate per 100,000 inhabitants		347.0	6.4	53.9	96.8	190.0	2,095.0	376.3	1,622.8	95.9
Kennewick-Richland, WA MSA	289,723									
Includes Benton and Franklin Counties										

Table 4. Crime, by Selected Metropolitan Statistical Area, 2017—*Continued*

(Number, percent, rate per 100,000 population.)

Area	Population	Violent crime	Murder and nonnegligent manslaughter	Rape[1]	Robbery	Aggravated assault	Property crime	Burglary	Larceny-theft	Motor vehicle theft
City of Kennewick..................	81,499	213	1	30	59	123	2,228	307	1,732	189
City of Richland....................	56,151	102	0	19	14	69	1,321	184	1,086	51
Total area actually reporting........	100.0%	594	2	85	123	384	5,926	1,040	4,383	503
Rate per 100,000 inhabitants........		205.0	0.7	29.3	42.5	132.5	2,045.4	359.0	1,512.8	173.6
Killeen-Temple, TX MSA	440,220									
Includes Bell, Coryell, and Lampasas Counties										
City of Killeen.....................	145,912	1,118	18	151	313	636	4,109	1,140	2,403	566
City of Temple.....................	74,794	238	5	63	65	105	2,130	409	1,483	238
Total area actually reporting........	99.3%	1,860	33	296	442	1,089	10,247	2,391	6,864	992
Estimated total.....................	100.0%	1,868	33	297	444	1,094	10,316	2,401	6,918	997
Rate per 100,000 inhabitants........		424.3	7.5	67.5	100.9	248.5	2,343.4	545.4	1,571.5	226.5
Kingsport-Bristol-Bristol, TN-VA MSA	306,090									
Includes Hawkins and Sullivan Counties, TN and Scott and Washington Counties and Bristol City, VA										
City of Kingsport, TN	52,810	381	3	17	58	303	2,884	377	2,303	204
City of Bristol, TN.................	27,176	110	2	14	8	86	915	137	704	74
City of Bristol, VA.................	16,795	54	0	15	3	36	562	86	428	48
Total area actually reporting........	100.0%	1,086	16	125	88	857	7,630	1,339	5,633	658
Rate per 100,000 inhabitants........		354.8	5.2	40.8	28.7	280.0	2,492.7	437.5	1,840.3	215.0
Kingston, NY MSA	179,106									
Includes Ulster County										
City of Kingston...................	23,110	73	1	5	22	45	449	53	392	4
Total area actually reporting........	100.0%	287	2	64	39	182	2,257	307	1,885	65
Rate per 100,000 inhabitants........		160.2	1.1	35.7	21.8	101.6	1,260.1	171.4	1,052.4	36.3
Knoxville, TN MSA	875,281									
Includes Anderson, Blount, Campbell, Grainger, Knox, Loudon, Morgan, Roane, and Union Counties										
City of Knoxville..................	187,539	1,676	33	145	371	1,127	10,211	1,665	7,510	1,036
Total area actually reporting........	100.0%	3,852	60	311	528	2,953	22,730	4,387	15,953	2,390
Rate per 100,000 inhabitants........		440.1	6.9	35.5	60.3	337.4	2,596.9	501.2	1,822.6	273.1
Kokomo, IN MSA.................	82,647									
Includes Howard County										
City of Kokomo	57,758	417	6	36	48	327	1,669	413	1,169	87
Total area actually reporting........	98.7%	487	6	41	48	392	1,871	473	1,291	107
Estimated total.....................	100.0%	490	6	41	49	394	1,898	476	1,313	109
Rate per 100,000 inhabitants........		592.9	7.3	49.6	59.3	476.7	2,296.5	575.9	1,588.7	131.9
La Crosse-Onalaska, WI-MN MSA	137,553									
Includes Houston County, MN and La Crosse County, WI										
City of La Crosse, WI..............	52,234	140	0	29	35	76	2,167	365	1,746	56
City of Onalaska, WI...............	18,847	15	0	4	0	11	532	26	495	11
Total area actually reporting........	100.0%	213	1	38	36	138	3,242	495	2,665	82
Rate per 100,000 inhabitants........		154.8	0.7	27.6	26.2	100.3	2,356.9	359.9	1,937.4	59.6
Lafayette, LA MSA[3, 5]	493,395									
Includes Acadia,[3] Iberia, Lafayette, St. Martin, and Vermilion Parishes										
City of Lafayette	128,691	721	22	21	175	503	5,863	1,011	4,555	297
Total area actually reporting........	85.2%	1,915	39	101	320	1,455		2,957		
Estimated total.....................	100.0%	2,169	44	119	361	1,645		3,371		
Rate per 100,000 inhabitants........		439.6	8.9	24.1	73.2	333.4		683.2		
Lafayette-West Lafayette, IN MSA	219,515									
Includes Benton, Carroll, and Tippecanoe Counties										
City of Lafayette	72,274	364	4	43	80	237	2,637	573	1,903	161
City of West Lafayette..............	46,541	49	0	8	5	36	466	49	397	20
Total area actually reporting........	85.9%	488	5	68	93	322	3,940	789	2,926	225
Estimated total.....................	100.0%	542	5	75	102	360	4,389	871	3,248	270
Rate per 100,000 inhabitants........		246.9	2.3	34.2	46.5	164.0	1,999.4	396.8	1,479.6	123.0
Lake Charles, LA MSA[2]	207,792									
Includes Calcasieu and Cameron Parishes										
City of Lake Charles................	77,647	638	9	45	146	438	3,524	1,836	1,429	259
Total area actually reporting........	96.9%	1,239	21	101	203	914	9,209	3,403	5,230	576
Estimated total.....................	100.0%	1,268	22	103	207	936	9,449	3,446	5,417	586
Rate per 100,000 inhabitants........		610.2	10.6	49.6	99.6	450.5	4,547.3	1,658.4	2,606.9	282.0

Table 4. Crime, by Selected Metropolitan Statistical Area, 2017—*Continued*

(Number, percent, rate per 100,000 population.)

Area	Population	Violent crime	Murder and nonnegligent manslaughter	Rape[1]	Robbery	Aggravated assault	Property crime	Burglary	Larceny-theft	Motor vehicle theft
Lake Havasu City-Kingman, AZ MSA[6]	205,868									
Includes Mohave County										
City of Lake Havasu City	53,937	120	0	21	6	93	1,164	245	848	71
City of Kingman	29,181	131	2	12	15	102	1,445	237	1,119	89
Total area actually reporting	97.7%		8	59	75		6,514	1,620	4,355	539
Estimated total	100.0%		8	61	78		6,644	1,640	4,455	549
Rate per 100,000 inhabitants			3.9	29.6	37.9		3,227.3	796.6	2,164.0	266.7
Lakeland-Winter Haven, FL MSA	679,166									
Includes Polk County										
City of Lakeland	107,927	307	1	73	89	144	4,021	574	3,237	210
City of Winter Haven	39,859	192	0	30	24	138	1,112	177	862	73
Total area actually reporting	100.0%	1,936	12	206	289	1,429	13,312	2,585	9,739	988
Rate per 100,000 inhabitants		285.1	1.8	30.3	42.6	210.4	1,960.1	380.6	1,434.0	145.5
Lancaster, PA MSA	541,945									
Includes Lancaster County										
City of Lancaster	59,199	530	5	97	141	287	1,999	205	1,689	105
Total area actually reporting	100.0%	1,126	15	198	241	672	7,196	959	5,923	314
Rate per 100,000 inhabitants		207.8	2.8	36.5	44.5	124.0	1,327.8	177.0	1,092.9	57.9
Lansing-East Lansing, MI MSA	478,097									
Includes Clinton, Eaton, and Ingham Counties										
City of Lansing	116,302	1,321	14	108	238	961	3,549	883	2,267	399
City of East Lansing	48,920	82	0	22	16	44	781	106	538	137
Total area actually reporting	100.0%	2,068	22	351	335	1,360	9,336	1,906	6,660	770
Rate per 100,000 inhabitants		432.5	4.6	73.4	70.1	284.5	1,952.7	398.7	1,393.0	161.1
Laredo, TX MSA	274,365									
Includes Webb County										
City of Laredo	260,669	839	10	114	154	561	6,474	874	5,430	170
Total area actually reporting	100.0%	890	10	125	156	599	6,715	931	5,610	174
Rate per 100,000 inhabitants		324.4	3.6	45.6	56.9	218.3	2,447.5	339.3	2,044.7	63.4
Las Vegas-Henderson-Paradise, NV MSA	2,203,346									
Includes Clark County										
City of Las Vegas Metropolitan Police Department	1,627,244	10,071	205	1,296	3,436	5,134	47,896	13,102	26,608	8,186
City of Henderson	299,285	554	10	86	240	218	5,486	1,089	3,756	641
Total area actually reporting	100.0%	13,395	238	1,543	4,286	7,328	61,236	16,496	34,468	10,272
Rate per 100,000 inhabitants		607.9	10.8	70.0	194.5	332.6	2,779.2	748.7	1,564.3	466.2
Lawton, OK MSA	126,813									
Includes Comanche and Cotton Counties										
City of Lawton	94,134	831	8	83	131	609	3,618	1,207	2,097	314
Total area actually reporting	100.0%	856	8	94	132	622	4,037	1,322	2,369	346
Rate per 100,000 inhabitants		675.0	6.3	74.1	104.1	490.5	3,183.4	1,042.5	1,868.1	272.8
Lebanon, PA MSA	139,840									
Includes Lebanon County										
City of Lebanon	25,771	89	2	6	34	47	538	126	389	23
Total area actually reporting	95.9%	250	3	34	50	163	1,775	303	1,416	56
Estimated total	100.0%	260	3	35	52	170	1,856	313	1,484	59
Rate per 100,000 inhabitants		185.9	2.1	25.0	37.2	121.6	1,327.2	223.8	1,061.2	42.2
Lewiston, ID-WA MSA	63,349									
Includes Nez Perce County, ID and Asotin County, WA										
City of Lewiston, ID	33,029	53	2	11	4	36	943	188	687	68
Total area actually reporting	100.0%	100	2	19	12	67	1,564	331	1,140	93
Rate per 100,000 inhabitants		157.9	3.2	30.0	18.9	105.8	2,468.9	522.5	1,799.6	146.8
Lewiston-Auburn, ME MSA	107,554									
Includes Androscoggin County										
City of Lewiston	36,067	98	0	24	31	43	788	164	582	42
City of Auburn	22,931	40	0	14	10	16	712	55	646	11
Total area actually reporting	100.0%	169	0	57	45	67	1,885	304	1,508	73
Rate per 100,000 inhabitants		157.1	0.0	53.0	41.8	62.3	1,752.6	282.6	1,402.1	67.9
Lexington-Fayette, KY MSA[3]	512,740									
Includes Bourbon, Clark, Fayette, Jessamine, Scott, and Woodford Counties										

Table 4. Crime, by Selected Metropolitan Statistical Area, 2017—*Continued*

(Number, percent, rate per 100,000 population.)

Area	Population	Violent crime	Murder and nonnegligent manslaughter	Rape[1]	Robbery	Aggravated assault	Property crime	Burglary	Larceny-theft	Motor vehicle theft
City of Lexington	322,332	1,131	29	200	547	355	12,191	2,087	8,831	1,273
Total area actually reporting	100.0%	1,401	34	260	656	451		3,109		1,634
Rate per 100,000 inhabitants		273.2	6.6	50.7	127.9	88.0		606.4		318.7
Lima, OH MSA[4]	103,577									
Includes Allen County										
City of Lima	37,220	275	5	52	81	137	1,982	569	1,334	79
Total area actually reporting	93.9%	326	6	72	96	152	3,145	804	2,230	111
Estimated total	100.0%	336	6	74	99	157	3,276	824	2,335	117
Rate per 100,000 inhabitants		324.4	5.8	71.4	95.6	151.6	3,162.9	795.5	2,254.4	113.0
Little Rock-North Little Rock-Conway, AR MSA	741,067									
Includes Faulkner, Grant, Lonoke, Perry, Pulaski, and Saline Counties										
City of Little Rock	199,314	3,256	55	175	502	2,524	13,817	2,378	10,309	1,130
City of North Little Rock	66,938	530	9	19	124	378	2,764	541	1,875	348
City of Conway	66,299	315	1	41	63	210	2,314	331	1,835	148
Total area actually reporting	100.0%	5,918	87	453	849	4,529	30,296	5,909	21,646	2,741
Rate per 100,000 inhabitants		798.6	11.7	61.1	114.6	611.1	4,088.2	797.4	2,920.9	369.9
Logan, UT-ID MSA	138,078									
Includes Franklin County, ID and Cache County, UT										
City of Logan, UT	51,059	48	1	23	1	23	678	94	547	37
Total area actually reporting	100.0%	110	4	55	4	47	1,251	207	945	99
Rate per 100,000 inhabitants		79.7	2.9	39.8	2.9	34.0	906.0	149.9	684.4	71.7
Longview, TX MSA	217,681									
Includes Gregg, Rusk, and Upshur Counties										
City of Longview	80,334	388	6	61	97	224	2,735	599	1,900	236
Total area actually reporting	98.0%	909	12	115	128	654	5,361	1,328	3,575	458
Estimated total	100.0%	921	12	117	131	661	5,461	1,343	3,652	466
Rate per 100,000 inhabitants		423.1	5.5	53.7	60.2	303.7	2,508.7	617.0	1,677.7	214.1
Longview, WA MSA	105,944									
Includes Cowlitz County										
City of Longview	37,424	112	2	46	21	43	1,360	262	956	142
Total area actually reporting	100.0%	259	3	96	31	129	2,698	564	1,867	267
Rate per 100,000 inhabitants		244.5	2.8	90.6	29.3	121.8	2,546.6	532.4	1,762.3	252.0
Los Angeles-Long Beach-Anaheim, CA MSA[2]	13,375,094									
Includes the Metropolitan Divisions of Anaheim-Santa Ana-Irvine and Los Angeles-Long Beach-Glendale										
City of Los Angeles	4,007,147	30,507	281	2,455	10,814	16,957	101,618	16,668	65,757	19,193
City of Long Beach	471,397	3,101	22	203	1,237	1,639	12,598	2,765	7,104	2,729
City of Anaheim	353,400	1,253	10	115	480	648	9,296	1,351	6,393	1,552
City of Santa Ana	335,699	1,640	21	188	605	826	7,017	929	4,108	1,980
City of Irvine	276,115	169	2	46	55	66	3,635	627	2,814	194
City of Glendale	202,381	274	3	32	127	112	3,118	498	2,303	317
City of Torrance	147,482	267	0	36	116	115	3,206	557	2,213	436
City of Pasadena	142,891	574	8	51	202	313	2,946	745	1,842	359
City of Orange	141,130	218	4	12	64	138	2,584	489	1,754	341
City of Costa Mesa	113,267	361	1	61	128	171	4,298	620	3,158	520
City of Burbank	104,622	253	0	20	86	147	2,944	355	2,344	245
City of Carson	92,992	475	8	20	166	281	2,250	479	1,261	510
City of Santa Monica	92,935	705	3	54	241	407	4,374	648	3,462	264
City of Newport Beach	86,910	124	0	31	21	72	2,123	361	1,630	132
City of Tustin	81,246	132	3	11	47	71	1,949	288	1,484	177
City of Monterey Park	61,210	112	1	10	55	46	1,613	439	955	219
City of Gardena	60,249	393	4	16	218	155	1,393	353	678	362
City of Arcadia	58,883	110	0	7	56	47	1,534	485	957	92
City of Fountain Valley	56,704	68	0	3	28	37	1,581	238	1,199	144
Total area actually reporting	100.0%	66,435	642	5,129	23,584	37,080	314,350	57,168	200,941	56,241
Rate per 100,000 inhabitants		496.7	4.8	38.3	176.3	277.2	2,350.3	427.4	1,502.4	420.5
Anaheim-Santa Ana-Irvine, CA MD	3,195,538									
Includes Orange County										
Total area actually reporting	100.0%	7,627	62	830	2,495	4,240	65,638	10,196	46,607	8,835
Rate per 100,000 inhabitants		238.7	1.9	26.0	78.1	132.7	2,054.1	319.1	1,458.5	276.5
Los Angeles-Long Beach-Glendale, CA MD[2]	10,179,556									
Includes Los Angeles County										

Table 4. Crime, by Selected Metropolitan Statistical Area, 2017—*Continued*

(Number, percent, rate per 100,000 population.)

Area	Population	Violent crime	Murder and nonnegligent manslaughter	Rape[1]	Robbery	Aggravated assault	Property crime	Burglary	Larceny-theft	Motor vehicle theft
Total area actually reporting	100.0%	58,808	580	4,299	21,089	32,840	248,712	46,972	154,334	47,406
Rate per 100,000 inhabitants		577.7	5.7	42.2	207.2	322.6	2,443.2	461.4	1,516.1	465.7
Louisville/Jefferson County, KY-IN MSA[4]	1,291,962									
Includes Clark, Floyd, Harrison, Scott, and Washington Counties, IN and Bullitt, Henry, Jefferson, Oldham, Shelby, Spencer, and Trimble Counties, KY										
City of Louisville Metro, KY	684,362	4,428	109	175	1,326	2,818	28,211	5,623	18,724	3,864
Total area actually reporting	91.4%	5,164	121	273	1,544	3,226	38,015	7,312	25,744	4,959
Estimated total	100.0%	5,396	123	299	1,590	3,384	39,982	7,608	27,239	5,135
Rate per 100,000 inhabitants		417.7	9.5	23.1	123.1	261.9	3,094.7	588.9	2,108.3	397.5
Lynchburg, VA MSA	261,147									
Includes Amherst, Appomattox, Bedford, and Campbell Counties and Bedford and Lynchburg Cities										
City of Lynchburg	80,890	287	4	33	42	208	1,886	224	1,522	140
Total area actually reporting	100.0%	502	7	78	66	351	3,995	544	3,156	295
Rate per 100,000 inhabitants		192.2	2.7	29.9	25.3	134.4	1,529.8	208.3	1,208.5	113.0
Macon-Bibb County, GA MSA	228,963									
Includes Bibb, Crawford, Jones, Monroe, and Twiggs Counties										
Total area actually reporting	99.6%	1,057	33	73	328	623	9,076	2,108	6,317	651
Estimated total	100.0%	1,060	33	73	329	625	9,113	2,113	6,346	654
Rate per 100,000 inhabitants		463.0	14.4	31.9	143.7	273.0	3,980.1	922.9	2,771.6	285.6
Madera, CA MSA	155,133									
Includes Madera County										
City of Madera	64,939	378	4	32	107	235	1,702	336	967	399
Total area actually reporting	100.0%	891	7	56	145	683	3,484	941	1,830	713
Rate per 100,000 inhabitants		574.3	4.5	36.1	93.5	440.3	2,245.8	606.6	1,179.6	459.6
Madison, WI MSA	656,500									
Includes Columbia, Dane, Green, and Iowa Counties										
City of Madison	255,850	958	11	95	212	640	6,811	927	5,452	432
Total area actually reporting	100.0%	1,501	15	193	301	992	11,988	1,712	9,552	724
Rate per 100,000 inhabitants		228.6	2.3	29.4	45.8	151.1	1,826.0	260.8	1,455.0	110.3
Manchester-Nashua, NH MSA	410,406									
Includes Hillsborough County										
City of Manchester	110,655	745	2	92	174	477	2,905	491	2,229	185
City of Nashua	88,102	150	1	53	30	66	1,190	115	1,003	72
Total area actually reporting	98.7%	1,084	4	202	214	664	5,693	832	4,526	335
Estimated total	100.0%	1,091	4	204	215	668	5,751	839	4,574	338
Rate per 100,000 inhabitants		265.8	1.0	49.7	52.4	162.8	1,401.3	204.4	1,114.5	82.4
Manhattan, KS MSA	97,562									
Includes Pottawatomie and Riley Counties										
Total area actually reporting	100.0%	277	2	60	24	191	1,801	301	1,395	105
Rate per 100,000 inhabitants		283.9	2.0	61.5	24.6	195.8	1,846.0	308.5	1,429.9	107.6
Mankato-North Mankato, MN MSA	100,926									
Includes Blue Earth and Nicollet Counties										
City of Mankato	42,047	107	0	24	17	66	1,301	183	1,067	51
City of North Mankato	13,664	16	0	2	1	13	162	32	119	11
Total area actually reporting	100.0%	166	0	49	20	97	1,856	312	1,451	93
Rate per 100,000 inhabitants		164.5	0.0	48.6	19.8	96.1	1,839.0	309.1	1,437.7	92.1
Mansfield, OH MSA	120,919									
Includes Richland County										
City of Mansfield	46,507	248	7	45	75	121	2,392	569	1,745	78
Total area actually reporting	99.3%	324	7	69	97	151	3,971	897	2,944	130
Estimated total	100.0%	325	7	69	97	152	3,990	900	2,959	131
Rate per 100,000 inhabitants		268.8	5.8	57.1	80.2	125.7	3,299.7	744.3	2,447.1	108.3
McAllen-Edinburg-Mission, TX MSA[2]	861,327									
Includes Hidalgo County										
City of McAllen	144,162	208	7	27	49	125	4,007	185	3,776	46
City of Edinburg	89,595	299	2	51	44	202	3,373	472	2,793	108
City of Mission	84,511	98	0	27	30	41	2,005	231	1,700	74

Table 4. Crime, by Selected Metropolitan Statistical Area, 2017—*Continued*

(Number, percent, rate per 100,000 population.)

Area	Population	Violent crime	Murder and nonnegligent manslaughter	Rape[1]	Robbery	Aggravated assault	Property crime	Burglary	Larceny-theft	Motor vehicle theft
Total area actually reporting..............	99.3%	2,506	38	411	361	1,696	21,519	3,229	17,509	781
Estimated total........................	100.0%	2,523	38	414	365	1,706	21,656	3,249	17,615	792
Rate per 100,000 inhabitants..............		292.9	4.4	48.1	42.4	198.1	2,514.3	377.2	2,045.1	92.0
Medford, OR MSA......................	219,042									
Includes Jackson County										
City of Medford........................	82,792	376	4	33	98	241	4,936	489	4,145	302
Total area actually reporting..............	100.0%	714	7	80	139	488	8,526	1,161	6,783	582
Rate per 100,000 inhabitants..............		326.0	3.2	36.5	63.5	222.8	3,892.4	530.0	3,096.7	265.7
Memphis, TN-MS-AR MSA[4]...........	1,346,961									
Includes Crittenden County, AR; Benton, DeSoto, Marshall, Tate, and Tunica4 Counties, MS; and Fayette, Shelby, and Tipton Counties, TN										
City of Memphis, TN....................	652,765	13,077	181	590	3,457	8,849	41,110	9,532	27,576	4,002
Total area actually reporting..............	97.1%	15,677	219	796	3,855	10,807	56,258	13,098	38,180	4,980
Estimated total........................	100.0%	15,737	220	803	3,865	10,849	56,959	13,270	38,659	5,030
Rate per 100,000 inhabitants..............		1,168.3	16.3	59.6	286.9	805.4	4,228.7	985.2	2,870.1	373.4
Merced, CA MSA......................	270,396									
Includes Merced County										
City of Merced........................	83,180	563	8	28	158	369	2,668	472	1,706	490
Total area actually reporting..............	100.0%	1,557	19	64	274	1,200	7,148	1,607	4,383	1,158
Rate per 100,000 inhabitants..............		575.8	7.0	23.7	101.3	443.8	2,643.5	594.3	1,621.0	428.3
Miami-Fort Lauderdale-West Palm Beach, FL MSA...........	6,167,945									
Includes the Metropolitan Divisions of Fort Lauderdale-Pompano Beach-Deerfield Beach, Miami-Miami Beach-Kendall, and West Palm Beach-Boca Raton-Delray Beach										
City of Miami.........................	463,009	3,338	52	105	978	2,203	18,586	2,440	14,311	1,835
City of Fort Lauderdale.................	180,972	1,072	15	81	429	547	10,006	1,657	7,424	925
City of West Palm Beach................	109,459	906	25	66	322	493	5,275	847	3,907	521
City of Pompano Beach.................	111,027	958	8	61	410	479	5,330	898	3,624	808
City of Miami Beach...................	92,571	884	4	101	308	471	7,587	706	6,431	450
City of Boca Raton....................	98,069	223	1	27	81	114	2,503	435	1,871	197
City of Deerfield Beach.................	80,552	324	3	35	111	175	2,360	328	1,771	261
City of Delray Beach...................	68,533	409	2	36	93	278	2,587	366	1,949	272
City of Jupiter........................	65,311	103	4	14	22	63	1,210	133	1,019	58
Total area actually reporting..............	100.0%	28,261	375	2,005	8,229	17,652	189,749	25,852	145,685	18,212
Rate per 100,000 inhabitants..............		458.2	6.1	32.5	133.4	286.2	3,076.4	419.1	2,362.0	295.3
Fort Lauderdale-Pompano Beach-Deerfield Beach, FL MD ...	1,942,468									
Includes Broward County										
Total area actually reporting..............	100.0%	7,546	95	581	2,523	4,347	57,397	8,191	43,253	5,953
Rate per 100,000 inhabitants..............		388.5	4.9	29.9	129.9	223.8	2,954.8	421.7	2,226.7	306.5
Miami-Miami Beach-Kendall, FL MD.................	2,756,549									
Includes Miami-Dade County										
Total area actually reporting	100.0%	14,460	188	874	4,032	9,366	92,712	11,628	72,384	8,700
Rate per 100,000 inhabitants..............		524.6	6.8	31.7	146.3	339.8	3,363.3	421.8	2,625.9	315.6
West Palm Beach-Boca Raton-Delray Beach, FL MD	1,468,928									
Includes Palm Beach County										
Total area actually reporting	100.0%	6,255	92	550	1,674	3,939	39,640	6,033	30,048	3,559
Rate per 100,000 inhabitants..............		425.8	6.3	37.4	114.0	268.2	2,698.6	410.7	2,045.6	242.3
Midland, MI MSA......................	83,632									
Includes Midland County										
City of Midland.......................	42,131	53	1	25	1	26	508	54	444	10
Total area actually reporting..............	100.0%	113	1	44	1	67	822	121	677	24
Rate per 100,000 inhabitants..............		135.1	1.2	52.6	1.2	80.1	982.9	144.7	809.5	28.7
Midland, TX MSA......................	172,994									
Includes Martin and Midland Counties										
City of Midland.......................	138,954	377	2	37	59	279	2,677	431	2,026	220
Total area actually reporting..............	98.2%	462	2	39	79	342	3,368	543	2,503	322
Estimated total........................	100.0%	470	2	40	81	347	3,437	553	2,557	327
Rate per 100,000 inhabitants..............		271.7	1.2	23.1	46.8	200.6	1,986.8	319.7	1,478.1	189.0
Milwaukee-Waukesha-West Allis, WI MSA...................	1,575,520									
Includes Milwaukee, Ozaukee, Washington, and Waukesha Counties										

(Number, percent, rate per 100,000 population.)

Area	Population	Violent crime	Murder and nonnegligent manslaughter	Rape[1]	Robbery	Aggravated assault	Property crime	Burglary	Larceny-theft	Motor vehicle theft
City of Milwaukee	595,168	9,507	118	434	2,919	6,036	22,569	5,518	11,548	5,503
City of Waukesha	72,565	119	0	43	25	51	1,007	126	845	36
City of West Allis	60,043	205	2	26	82	95	2,044	324	1,536	184
Total area actually reporting	100.0%	10,721	124	644	3,301	6,652	40,111	7,429	26,095	6,587
Rate per 100,000 inhabitants		680.5	7.9	40.9	209.5	422.2	2,545.9	471.5	1,656.3	418.1
Minneapolis-St. Paul-Bloomington, MN-WI MSA	3,597,545									
Includes Anoka, Carver, Chisago, Dakota, Hennepin, Isanti, Le Sueur, Mille Lacs, Ramsey, Scott, Sherburne, Sibley, Washington, and Wright Counties, MN and Pierce and St. Croix Counties, WI										
City of Minneapolis, MN	418,971	4,614	42	514	1,819	2,239	19,446	3,762	13,296	2,388
City of St. Paul, MN	306,696	1,996	22	217	697	1,060	10,935	2,274	6,577	2,084
City of Bloomington, MN	85,704	140	1	43	33	63	2,590	175	2,282	133
City of Plymouth, MN	78,356	63	0	16	15	32	964	181	755	28
City of Eagan, MN	66,805	58	2	18	14	24	1,270	100	1,128	42
City of Eden Prairie, MN	64,429	32	2	7	9	14	824	56	739	29
Total area actually reporting	99.9%	10,178	95	1,557	3,301	5,225	86,492	12,701	66,076	7,715
Estimated total	100.0%	10,182	95	1,558	3,302	5,227	86,540	12,706	66,117	7,717
Rate per 100,000 inhabitants		283.0	2.6	43.3	91.8	145.3	2,405.5	353.2	1,837.8	214.5
Missoula, MT MSA	117,150									
Includes Missoula County										
City of Missoula	73,304	352	2	71	45	234	3,342	325	2,843	174
Total area actually reporting	100.0%	471	4	89	49	329	3,776	428	3,137	211
Rate per 100,000 inhabitants		402.0	3.4	76.0	41.8	280.8	3,223.2	365.3	2,677.8	180.1
Mobile, AL MSA[7]	414,842									
Includes Mobile County										
City of Mobile[7]	248,431	1,839	50	142	440	1,207	13,549	3,023	9,267	1,259
Total area actually reporting	99.5%	2,558	64	178	568	1,748	18,832	4,476	12,462	1,894
Estimated total	100.0%	2,568	64	179	570	1,755	18,897	4,487	12,511	1,899
Rate per 100,000 inhabitants		619.0	15.4	43.1	137.4	423.1	4,555.2	1,081.6	3,015.8	457.8
Modesto, CA MSA	545,448									
Includes Stanislaus County										
City of Modesto	213,677	2,074	20	110	519	1,425	8,465	1,188	5,865	1,412
Total area actually reporting	100.0%	3,300	41	196	905	2,158	16,789	2,774	10,781	3,234
Rate per 100,000 inhabitants		605.0	7.5	35.9	165.9	395.6	3,078.0	508.6	1,976.5	592.9
Monroe, LA MSA[2]	179,088									
Includes Ouachita and Union Parishes										
City of Monroe[2]	49,354	1,098	13	35	214	836	4,063	848	3,011	204
Total area actually reporting	95.6%	1,640	17	66	272	1,285	8,231	2,217	5,580	434
Estimated total	100.0%	1,675	18	68	277	1,312	8,521	2,269	5,806	446
Rate per 100,000 inhabitants		935.3	10.1	38.0	154.7	732.6	4,758.0	1,267.0	3,242.0	249.0
Monroe, MI MSA	149,119									
Includes Monroe County										
City of Monroe	19,868	107	1	25	9	72	389	54	303	32
Total area actually reporting	97.3%	362	3	110	30	219	2,119	477	1,471	171
Estimated total	100.0%	373	3	112	32	226	2,188	488	1,524	176
Rate per 100,000 inhabitants		250.1	2.0	75.1	21.5	151.6	1,467.3	327.3	1,022.0	118.0
Montgomery, AL MSA	373,522									
Includes Autauga, Elmore, Lowndes, and Montgomery Counties										
City of Montgomery	199,099	1,277	38	52	346	841	8,800	2,129	5,827	844
Total area actually reporting	99.0%	1,794	50	111	436	1,197	13,068	2,997	8,844	1,227
Estimated total	100.0%	1,813	50	113	439	1,211	13,192	3,018	8,937	1,237
Rate per 100,000 inhabitants		485.4	13.4	30.3	117.5	324.2	3,531.8	808.0	2,392.6	331.2
Morgantown, WV MSA	138,881									
Includes Monongalia and Preston Counties										
City of Morgantown	31,215	83	0	10	16	57	480	88	369	23
Total area actually reporting	88.4%	354	0	46	36	272	1,523	331	1,105	87
Estimated total	100.0%	393	0	52	41	300	2,018	403	1,497	118
Rate per 100,000 inhabitants		283.0	0.0	37.4	29.5	216.0	1,453.0	290.2	1,077.9	85.0

Table 4. Crime, by Selected Metropolitan Statistical Area, 2017—*Continued*

(Number, percent, rate per 100,000 population.)

Area	Population	Violent crime	Murder and nonnegligent manslaughter	Rape[1]	Robbery	Aggravated assault	Property crime	Burglary	Larceny-theft	Motor vehicle theft
Morristown, TN MSA........	118,061									
Includes Hamblen and Jefferson Counties										
City of Morristown......	29,774	222	2	12	23	185	1,387	210	1,066	111
Total area actually reporting......	100.0%	477	3	34	39	401	3,031	599	2,176	256
Rate per 100,000 inhabitants......		404.0	2.5	28.8	33.0	339.7	2,567.3	507.4	1,843.1	216.8
Mount Vernon-Anacortes, WA MSA........	125,204									
Includes Skagit County										
City of Mount Vernon......	35,085	82	3	15	23	41	1,302	234	947	121
City of Anacortes......	16,838	19	0	4	0	15	470	64	386	20
Total area actually reporting......	100.0%	262	10	47	51	154	4,076	794	2,988	294
Rate per 100,000 inhabitants......		209.3	8.0	37.5	40.7	123.0	3,255.5	634.2	2,386.5	234.8
Muncie, IN MSA........	115,406									
Includes Delaware County										
City of Muncie......	68,814	246	3	38	85	120	2,491	422	1,794	275
Total area actually reporting......	100.0%	324	5	50	95	174	3,080	536	2,204	340
Rate per 100,000 inhabitants......		280.7	4.3	43.3	82.3	150.8	2,668.8	464.4	1,909.8	294.6
Muskegon, MI MSA........	174,084									
Includes Muskegon County										
City of Muskegon......	38,375	229	3	29	55	142	2,059	395	1,467	197
Total area actually reporting......	100.0%	702	9	150	118	425	5,838	909	4,562	367
Rate per 100,000 inhabitants......		403.3	5.2	86.2	67.8	244.1	3,353.6	522.2	2,620.6	210.8
Myrtle Beach-Conway-North Myrtle Beach, SC-NC MSA[4]	462,909									
Includes Brunswick County, NC[4] and Horry County, SC										
City of Myrtle Beach, SC......	33,167	523	5	60	146	312	4,331	378	3,608	345
City of Conway, SC......	23,806	142	2	21	18	101	936	100	769	67
City of North Myrtle Beach, SC......	16,422	72	0	22	13	37	1,278	197	976	105
Total area actually reporting......	98.2%	1,901	28	354	328	1,191	16,469	2,872	12,262	1,335
Estimated total......	100.0%	1,924	28	356	334	1,206	16,708	2,914	12,449	1,345
Rate per 100,000 inhabitants......		415.6	6.0	76.9	72.2	260.5	3,609.3	629.5	2,689.3	290.6
Napa, CA MSA........	142,919									
Includes Napa County										
City of Napa......	80,958	272	1	39	43	189	1,353	338	828	187
Total area actually reporting......	100.0%	597	1	60	61	475	2,225	560	1,384	281
Rate per 100,000 inhabitants......		417.7	0.7	42.0	42.7	332.4	1,556.8	391.8	968.4	196.6
Naples-Immokalee-Marco Island, FL MSA........	373,775									
Includes Collier County										
City of Naples......	22,244	23	1	3	3	16	389	57	323	9
City of Marco Island......	18,089	11	0	2	0	9	122	16	97	9
Total area actually reporting......	100.0%	996	7	82	155	752	4,392	712	3,447	233
Rate per 100,000 inhabitants......		266.5	1.9	21.9	41.5	201.2	1,175.0	190.5	922.2	62.3
Nashville-Davidson–Murfreesboro–Franklin, TN MSA	1,902,780									
Includes Cannon, Cheatham, Davidson, Dickson, Hickman, Macon, Maury, Robertson, Rutherford, Smith, Sumner, Trousdale, Williamson, and Wilson Counties										
City of Nashville Metropolitan......	674,942	7,682	110	492	2,046	5,034	25,769	4,261	18,943	2,565
City of Murfreesboro......	136,102	735	3	89	144	499	4,339	522	3,548	269
City of Franklin......	76,995	146	1	18	14	113	1,048	78	940	30
Total area actually reporting......	100.0%	11,890	149	894	2,486	8,361	48,684	7,912	36,448	4,324
Rate per 100,000 inhabitants......		624.9	7.8	47.0	130.7	439.4	2,558.6	415.8	1,915.5	227.2
New Bern, NC MSA[4]........	126,212									
Includes Craven, Jones, and Pamlico Counties[4]										
City of New Bern[4]......	30,191		1		47	92	1,005	198	792	15
Total area actually reporting......	88.7%		3		72	188	2,589	853	1,659	77
Estimated total......	100.0%		3		78	207	2,860	923	1,846	91
Rate per 100,000 inhabitants......			2.4		61.8	164.0	2,266.0	731.3	1,462.6	72.1
New Haven-Milford, CT MSA........	801,867									
Includes New Haven County										
City of New Haven......	129,953	1,100	7	52	378	663	5,211	840	3,728	643
City of Milford......	54,265	24	0	1	18	5	967	92	809	66
Total area actually reporting......	100.0%	2,465	23	200	856	1,386	19,355	2,776	14,223	2,356
Rate per 100,000 inhabitants......		307.4	2.9	24.9	106.8	172.8	2,413.7	346.2	1,773.7	293.8

Table 4. Crime, by Selected Metropolitan Statistical Area, 2017—*Continued*

(Number, percent, rate per 100,000 population.)

Area	Population	Violent crime	Murder and nonnegligent manslaughter	Rape[1]	Robbery	Aggravated assault	Property crime	Burglary	Larceny-theft	Motor vehicle theft
New Orleans-Metairie, LA MSA[2]................................	1,276,063									
Includes Jefferson, Orleans, Plaquemines, St. Bernard, St. Charles, St. James, St. John the Baptist, and St. Tammany Parishes										
City of New Orleans....................................	397,447	4,457	157	575	1,308	2,417	16,867	2,229	12,107	2,531
Total area actually reporting......................	100.0%	7,197	218	762	1,920	4,297	37,620	5,483	28,314	3,823
Rate per 100,000 inhabitants......................		564.0	17.1	59.7	150.5	336.7	2,948.1	429.7	2,218.9	299.6
New York-Newark-Jersey City, NY-NJ-PA MSA.................	20,306,398									
Includes the Metropolitan Divisions of Dutchess County-Putnam County, NY; Nassau County-Suffolk County, NY; Newark, NJ-PA; and New York-Jersey City-White Plains, NY-NJ										
City of New York, NY......................	8,616,333	46,433	292	2,375	13,995	29,771	124,815	11,104	107,976	5,735
City of Newark, NJ........................	283,673	2,543	77	116	1,070	1,280	6,794	1,202	3,200	2,392
City of Jersey City, NJ....................	267,906	1,365	21	123	534	687	4,841	1,119	3,231	491
City of White Plains, NY..................	58,461	103	0	9	26	68	982	34	916	32
City of New Brunswick, NJ...............	57,481	360	4	22	191	143	1,341	253	1,001	87
City of Lakewood Township, NJ........	102,759	95	1	4	30	60	931	216	689	26
Total area actually reporting...........	99.8%	67,519	571	4,002	21,803	41,143	270,484	30,904	221,682	17,898
Estimated total...........................	100.0%	67,600	571	4,012	21,826	41,191	271,205	30,986	222,294	17,925
Rate per 100,000 inhabitants...........		332.9	2.8	19.8	107.5	202.8	1,335.6	152.6	1,094.7	88.3
Dutchess County-Putnam County, NY MD..........................	393,569									
Includes Dutchess and Putnam Counties										
Total area actually reporting	99.2%	628	5	127	122	374	4,124	507	3,529	88
Estimated total	100.0%	634	5	128	124	377	4,173	513	3,570	90
Rate per 100,000 inhabitants..........		161.1	1.3	32.5	31.5	95.8	1,060.3	130.3	907.1	22.9
Nassau County-Suffolk County, NY MD............................	2,863,520									
Includes Nassau and Suffolk Counties										
Total area actually reporting	98.8%	3,270	39	146	1,094	1,991	31,111	2,731	26,639	1,741
Estimated total	100.0%	3,327	39	153	1,110	2,025	31,624	2,789	27,075	1,760
Rate per 100,000 inhabitants..........		116.2	1.4	5.3	38.8	70.7	1,104.4	97.4	945.5	61.5
Newark, NJ-PA MD...............................	2,523,572									
Includes Essex, Hunterdon, Morris, Somerset, Sussex, and Union Counties, NJ and Pike County, PA										
Total area actually reporting	100.0%	6,636	126	420	2,933	3,157	36,319	6,019	24,558	5,742
Rate per 100,000 inhabitants..........		263.0	5.0	16.6	116.2	125.1	1,439.2	238.5	973.1	227.5
New York-Jersey City-White Plains, NY-NJ MD..................	14,525,737									
Includes Bergen, Hudson, Middlesex, Monmouth, Ocean, and Passaic Counties, NJ and Bronx, Kings, New York, Orange, Queens, Richmond, Rockland, and Westchester Counties, NY										
Total area actually reporting	99.9%	56,985	401	3,309	17,654	35,621	198,930	21,647	166,956	10,327
Estimated total	100.0%	57,003	401	3,311	17,659	35,632	199,089	21,665	167,091	10,333
Rate per 100,000 inhabitants..........		392.4	2.8	22.8	121.6	245.3	1,370.6	149.1	1,150.3	71.1
Niles-Benton Harbor, MI MSA	153,925									
Includes Berrien County										
City of Niles...............................	11,202	67	1	16	9	41	265	57	169	39
City of Benton Harbor.....................	9,899	218	3	23	36	156	392	131	228	33
Total area actually reporting.............	100.0%	763	8	159	93	503	3,034	622	2,213	199
Rate per 100,000 inhabitants.............		495.7	5.2	103.3	60.4	326.8	1,971.1	404.1	1,437.7	129.3
North Port-Sarasota-Bradenton, FL MSA	805,941									
Includes Manatee and Sarasota Counties										
City of North Port	65,498	110	1	26	8	75	788	136	633	19
City of Sarasota	57,383	323	1	26	87	209	1,964	270	1,582	112
City of Bradenton	56,821	298	4	27	59	208	1,444	199	1,166	79
City of Venice	22,762	28	0	4	1	23	305	44	249	12
Total area actually reporting.............	100.0%	2,853	32	267	440	2,114	14,371	2,440	11,192	739
Rate per 100,000 inhabitants.............		354.0	4.0	33.1	54.6	262.3	1,783.1	302.8	1,388.7	91.7
Norwich-New London, CT MSA	176,834									
Includes New London County										
City of Norwich............................	39,393	103	0	21	33	49	601	134	428	39
City of New London.......................	26,880	132	4	24	33	71	741	98	541	102
Total area actually reporting.............	100.0%	397	4	83	95	215	3,239	418	2,620	201
Rate per 100,000 inhabitants.............		224.5	2.3	46.9	53.7	121.6	1,831.7	236.4	1,481.6	113.7

Table 4. Crime, by Selected Metropolitan Statistical Area, 2017—*Continued*

(Number, percent, rate per 100,000 population.)

Area	Population	Violent crime	Murder and nonnegligent manslaughter	Rape[1]	Robbery	Aggravated assault	Property crime	Burglary	Larceny-theft	Motor vehicle theft
Ocala, FL MSA..	353,029									
Includes Marion County										
City of Ocala..	59,731	468	4	54	117	293	3,172	482	2,537	153
Total area actually reporting...........................	100.0%	1,388	17	143	253	975	8,071	1,947	5,435	689
Rate per 100,000 inhabitants..........................		393.2	4.8	40.5	71.7	276.2	2,286.2	551.5	1,539.5	195.2
Ocean City, NJ MSA..	94,353									
Includes Cape May County										
City of Ocean City..	11,281	12	1	3	2	6	385	34	350	1
Total area actually reporting...........................	100.0%	192	2	18	42	130	2,696	468	2,164	64
Rate per 100,000 inhabitants..........................		203.5	2.1	19.1	44.5	137.8	2,857.4	496.0	2,293.5	67.8
Odessa, TX MSA..	160,996									
Includes Ector County										
City of Odessa	121,194	912	7	78	101	726	3,219	560	2,386	273
Total area actually reporting...........................	100.0%	1,079	12	85	121	861	4,734	858	3,411	465
Rate per 100,000 inhabitants..........................		670.2	7.5	52.8	75.2	534.8	2,940.4	532.9	2,118.7	288.8
Ogden-Clearfield, UT MSA	664,366									
Includes Box Elder, Davis, Morgan, and Weber Counties										
City of Ogden..	87,323	463	6	49	91	317	3,794	546	2,780	468
City of Clearfield..	30,994	41	1	7	9	24	615	73	492	50
Total area actually reporting...........................	98.1%	1,055	15	253	167	620	13,618	1,970	10,461	1,187
Estimated total...	100.0%	1,078	15	258	172	633	13,923	2,018	10,677	1,228
Rate per 100,000 inhabitants..........................		162.3	2.3	38.8	25.9	95.3	2,095.7	303.7	1,607.1	184.8
Oklahoma City, OK MSA	1,385,915									
Includes Canadian, Cleveland, Grady, Lincoln, Logan, McClain, and Oklahoma Counties										
City of Oklahoma City.....................................	648,260	5,104	81	474	1,120	3,429	24,326	6,105	15,421	2,800
Total area actually reporting...........................	100.0%	6,907	105	806	1,439	4,557	40,163	9,656	26,316	4,191
Rate per 100,000 inhabitants..........................		498.4	7.6	58.2	103.8	328.8	2,897.9	696.7	1,898.8	302.4
Olympia-Tumwater, WA MSA	279,936									
Includes Thurston County										
City of Olympia..	51,923	256	1	42	67	146	2,171	371	1,596	204
City of Tumwater..	22,961	71	1	13	10	47	691	142	453	96
Total area actually reporting...........................	100.0%	756	9	121	137	489	7,164	1,542	4,909	713
Rate per 100,000 inhabitants..........................		270.1	3.2	43.2	48.9	174.7	2,559.2	550.8	1,753.6	254.7
Omaha-Council Bluffs, NE-IA MSA....................	933,488									
Includes Harrison, Mills, and Pottawattamie Counties, IA and Cass, Douglas, Sarpy, Saunders, and Washington Counties, NE										
City of Omaha, NE..	449,388	2,909	31	410	625	1,843	17,437	2,088	11,849	3,500
City of Council Bluffs, IA	62,549	150	1	24	62	63	3,717	435	2,853	429
Total area actually reporting...........................	99.2%	3,573	35	556	741	2,241	25,674	3,317	17,906	4,451
Estimated total...	100.0%	3,589	35	559	742	2,253	25,810	3,343	18,007	4,460
Rate per 100,000 inhabitants..........................		384.5	3.7	59.9	79.5	241.4	2,764.9	358.1	1,929.0	477.8
Orlando-Kissimmee-Sanford, FL MSA	2,502,951									
Includes Lake, Orange, Osceola, and Seminole Counties										
City of Orlando..	283,982	2,113	23	183	605	1,302	15,490	2,388	11,715	1,387
City of Kissimmee...	71,130	350	7	32	88	223	2,104	314	1,633	157
City of Sanford...	59,457	415	9	53	95	258	2,476	398	1,944	134
Total area actually reporting...........................	99.9%	11,100	125	1,179	2,353	7,443	69,377	12,859	51,177	5,341
Estimated total...	100.0%	11,108	125	1,180	2,355	7,448	69,433	12,867	51,220	5,346
Rate per 100,000 inhabitants..........................		443.8	5.0	47.1	94.1	297.6	2,774.0	514.1	2,046.4	213.6
Oshkosh-Neenah, WI MSA	170,405									
Includes Winnebago County										
City of Oshkosh	66,652	157	0	4	28	125	1,363	177	1,116	70
City of Neenah...	25,983	50	0	7	2	41	496	40	444	12
Total area actually reporting...........................	100.0%	292	0	32	32	228	2,737	351	2,264	122
Rate per 100,000 inhabitants..........................		171.4	0.0	18.8	18.8	133.8	1,606.2	206.0	1,328.6	71.6
Owensboro, KY MSA	118,539									
Includes Daviess, Hancock, and McLean Counties										
City of Owensboro..	59,576	178	3	46	52	77	2,597	390	1,964	243

Table 4. Crime, by Selected Metropolitan Statistical Area, 2017—*Continued*

(Number, percent, rate per 100,000 population.)

Area	Population	Violent crime	Murder and nonnegligent manslaughter	Rape[1]	Robbery	Aggravated assault	Property crime	Burglary	Larceny-theft	Motor vehicle theft
Total area actually reporting..........................	100.0%	196	4	52	53	87	3,073	538	2,239	296
Rate per 100,000 inhabitants.............................		165.3	3.4	43.9	44.7	73.4	2,592.4	453.9	1,888.8	249.7
Oxnard-Thousand Oaks-Ventura, CA MSA	852,923									
Includes Ventura County										
City of Oxnard	209,513	908	15	65	430	398	5,328	787	3,848	693
City of Thousand Oaks...............	129,240	172	2	44	35	91	1,687	269	1,305	113
City of Ventura	110,006	460	2	63	111	284	3,638	585	2,717	336
City of Camarillo	67,714	107	1	8	42	56	1,086	182	826	78
Total area actually reporting..........................	100.0%	2,239	26	270	730	1,213	15,985	2,612	11,764	1,609
Rate per 100,000 inhabitants.............................		262.5	3.0	31.7	85.6	142.2	1,874.1	306.2	1,379.3	188.6
Palm Bay-Melbourne-Titusville, FL MSA	586,851									
Includes Brevard County										
City of Palm Bay.......................	111,275	561	7	41	50	463	2,120	445	1,524	151
City of Melbourne.......................	82,013	670	4	63	121	482	3,399	548	2,679	172
City of Titusville	46,425	289	1	35	55	198	1,631	387	1,071	173
Total area actually reporting..........................	100.0%	2,703	25	235	396	2,047	14,264	2,651	10,588	1,025
Rate per 100,000 inhabitants.............................		460.6	4.3	40.0	67.5	348.8	2,430.6	451.7	1,804.2	174.7
Total area actually reporting..........................	100.0%	649	17	60	142	430	3,382	1,281	1,867	234
Rate per 100,000 inhabitants.............................		685.4	18.0	63.4	150.0	454.1	3,571.5	1,352.8	1,971.6	247.1
Panama City, FL MSA	203,139									
Includes Bay and Gulf Counties										
City of Panama City.......................	38,135	332	5	4	53	270	2,352	395	1,752	205
Total area actually reporting..........................	100.0%	943	11	82	106	744	6,994	1,291	5,204	499
Rate per 100,000 inhabitants.............................		464.2	5.4	40.4	52.2	366.3	3,443.0	635.5	2,561.8	245.6
Parkersburg-Vienna, WV MSA	90,643									
Includes Wirt and Wood Counties										
City of Parkersburg.......................	30,475	221	4	26	11	180	1,431	413	905	113
City of Vienna.......................	10,409	22	0	3	0	19	352	25	318	9
Total area actually reporting..........................	96.7%	388	8	48	11	321	2,288	609	1,506	173
Estimated total.......................	100.0%	395	8	49	12	326	2,379	622	1,578	179
Rate per 100,000 inhabitants.............................		435.8	8.8	54.1	13.2	359.7	2,624.6	686.2	1,740.9	197.5
Pensacola-Ferry Pass-Brent, FL MSA	493,108									
Includes Escambia and Santa Rosa Counties										
City of Pensacola	54,072	319	0	29	69	221	2,073	302	1,680	91
Total area actually reporting..........................	100.0%	2,003	24	246	337	1,396	12,076	2,400	9,027	649
Rate per 100,000 inhabitants.............................		406.2	4.9	49.9	68.3	283.1	2,449.0	486.7	1,830.6	131.6
Peoria, IL MSA	375,998									
Includes Marshall, Peoria, Stark, Tazewell, and Woodford Counties										
City of Peoria	114,157	867	12	65	281	509	4,810	1,119	3,357	334
Total area actually reporting..........................	89.6%	1,421	14	189	321	897	8,311	1,931	5,872	508
Estimated total.......................	100.0%	1,488	14	203	333	938	8,785	2,036	6,212	537
Rate per 100,000 inhabitants.............................		395.7	3.7	54.0	88.6	249.5	2,336.4	541.5	1,652.1	142.8
Philadelphia-Camden-Wilmington, PA-NJ-DE-MD MSA ...	6,095,755									
Includes the Metropolitan Divisions of Camden, NJ; Montgomery County-Bucks County-Chester County, PA; Philadelphia, PA; and Wilmington, DE-MD-NJ										
City of Philadelphia, PA.......................	1,575,595	14,930	316	1,182	6,026	7,406	48,268	6,590	36,195	5,483
City of Camden County Police Department, NJ	74,299	1,462	23	75	410	954	2,526	583	1,393	550
City of Wilmington, DE	71,552	1,142	34	33	381	694	3,550	705	2,413	432
Total area actually reporting..........................	99.9%	26,128	496	2,024	9,313	14,295	125,286	18,104	97,216	9,966
Estimated total.......................	100.0%	26,131	496	2,024	9,314	14,297	125,306	18,106	97,233	9,967
Rate per 100,000 inhabitants.............................		428.7	8.1	33.2	152.8	234.5	2,055.6	297.0	1,595.1	163.5
Camden, NJ MD...................................	1,256,928									
Includes Burlington, Camden, and Gloucester Counties										
Total area actually reporting	100.0%	3,283	52	273	1,024	1,934	24,128	4,530	18,097	1,501
Rate per 100,000 inhabitants.............................		261.2	4.1	21.7	81.5	153.9	1,919.6	360.4	1,439.8	119.4
Montgomery County-Bucks County-Chester County, PA MD...................	1,972,157									
Includes Bucks, Chester, and Montgomery Counties										
Total area actually reporting	99.9%	2,513	33	307	714	1,459	25,532	2,636	21,847	1,049
Estimated total	100.0%	2,516	33	307	715	1,461	25,552	2,638	21,864	1,050

(Number, percent, rate per 100,000 population.)

Area	Population	Violent crime	Murder and nonnegligent manslaughter	Rape[1]	Robbery	Aggravated assault	Property crime	Burglary	Larceny-theft	Motor vehicle theft
Rate per 100,000 inhabitants		127.6	1.7	15.6	36.3	74.1	1,295.6	133.8	1,108.6	53.2
Philadelphia, PA MD	2,140,093									
Includes Delaware and Philadelphia Counties										
Total area actually reporting	100.0%	17,041	361	1,277	6,635	8,768	58,080	7,840	44,059	6,181
Rate per 100,000 inhabitants		796.3	16.9	59.7	310.0	409.7	2,713.9	366.3	2,058.7	288.8
Wilmington, DE-MD-NJ MD	726,577									
Includes New Castle County, DE; Cecil County, MD; and Salem County, NJ										
Total area actually reporting	100.0%	3,291	50	167	940	2,134	17,546	3,098	13,213	1,235
Rate per 100,000 inhabitants		452.9	6.9	23.0	129.4	293.7	2,414.9	426.4	1,818.5	170.0
Phoenix-Mesa-Scottsdale, AZ MSA	4,737,604									
Includes Maricopa and Pinal Counties										
City of Phoenix	1,644,177	12,511	157	1,142	3,293	7,919	60,353	12,801	39,899	7,653
City of Mesa	492,268	2,047	23	252	454	1,318	10,692	1,878	7,930	884
City of Scottsdale	251,840	396	5	103	100	188	5,470	878	4,346	246
City of Tempe	186,086	883	5	151	229	498	7,669	1,076	6,120	473
Total area actually reporting	99.9%	22,288	271	2,364	5,322	14,331	133,339	24,504	95,496	13,339
Estimated total	100.0%	22,293	271	2,365	5,323	14,334	133,380	24,510	95,528	13,342
Rate per 100,000 inhabitants		470.6	5.7	49.9	112.4	302.6	2,815.3	517.4	2,016.4	281.6
Pine Bluff, AR MSA	90,789									
Includes Cleveland, Jefferson, and Lincoln Counties										
City of Pine Bluff	43,040	795	22	34	133	606	2,378	812	1,282	284
Total area actually reporting	100.0%	914	27	55	143	689	3,200	1,107	1,717	376
Rate per 100,000 inhabitants		1,006.7	29.7	60.6	157.5	758.9	3,524.7	1,219.3	1,891.2	414.1
Pittsburgh, PA MSA	2,341,460									
Includes Allegheny, Armstrong, Beaver, Butler, Fayette, Washington, and Westmoreland Counties										
City of Pittsburgh	305,932	2,008	55	90	802	1,061	9,528	1,610	7,238	680
Total area actually reporting	99.3%	6,485	127	479	1,672	4,207	36,609	5,972	28,841	1,796
Estimated total	100.0%	6,514	127	482	1,679	4,226	36,833	5,999	29,029	1,805
Rate per 100,000 inhabitants		278.2	5.4	20.6	71.7	180.5	1,573.1	256.2	1,239.8	77.1
Pittsfield, MA MSA	126,293									
Includes Berkshire County										
City of Pittsfield	42,546	375	4	50	43	278	1,092	399	656	37
Total area actually reporting	90.3%	669	4	89	59	517	2,162	679	1,416	67
Estimated total	100.0%	705	4	93	65	543	2,320	706	1,535	79
Rate per 100,000 inhabitants		558.2	3.2	73.6	51.5	430.0	1,837.0	559.0	1,215.4	62.6
Pocatello, ID MSA	85,293									
Includes Bannock County										
City of Pocatello	54,800	243	1	13	9	220	1,609	295	1,194	120
Total area actually reporting	100.0%	257	1	13	12	231	2,077	339	1,601	137
Rate per 100,000 inhabitants		301.3	1.2	15.2	14.1	270.8	2,435.1	397.5	1,877.1	160.6
Portland-South Portland, ME MSA[2]	533,811									
Includes Cumberland, Sagadahoc, and York Counties										
City of Portland	67,079	186	2	48	55	81	1,767	166	1,504	97
City of South Portland	25,679	56	0	4	13	39	578	78	481	19
Total area actually reporting	100.0%	680	4	187	123	366	7,884	1,125	6,459	300
Rate per 100,000 inhabitants		127.4	0.7	35.0	23.0	68.6	1,476.9	210.7	1,210.0	56.2
Portland-Vancouver-Hillsboro, OR-WA MSA[2,5]	2,462,322									
Includes Clackamas, Columbia,[2] Multnomah, Washington, and Yamhill Counties, OR and Clark and Skamania Counties, WA										
City of Portland, OR	649,408	3,349	24	438	1,045	1,842	36,867	4,735	24,837	7,295
City of Vancouver, WA	176,884	652	9	154	122	367	5,469	749	3,657	1,063
City of Hillsboro, OR	107,433	268	1	80	60	127	2,144	209	1,714	221
City of Beaverton, OR	98,897	172	1	60	32	79	1,760	157	1,396	207
Total area actually reporting	98.8%	6,911	64	1,418	1,673	3,756			49,367	12,728
Estimated total	100.0%	6,974	65	1,432	1,685	3,792			49,932	12,820
Rate per 100,000 inhabitants		283.2	2.6	58.2	68.4	154.0			2,027.8	520.6
Port St. Lucie, FL MSA	473,556									
Includes Martin and St. Lucie Counties										
City of Port St. Lucie	188,652	186	2	13	31	140	2,126	309	1,730	87

Table 4. Crime, by Selected Metropolitan Statistical Area, 2017—*Continued*

(Number, percent, rate per 100,000 population.)

Area	Population	Violent crime	Murder and nonnegligent manslaughter	Rape[1]	Robbery	Aggravated assault	Property crime	Burglary	Larceny-theft	Motor vehicle theft
Total area actually reporting............	100.0%	1,106	13	156	195	742	7,964	1,450	6,114	400
Rate per 100,000 inhabitants.................		233.6	2.7	32.9	41.2	156.7	1,681.7	306.2	1,291.1	84.5
Prescott, AZ MSA	227,836									
Includes Yavapai County										
City of Prescott	42,975	157	0	11	15	131	903	121	757	25
Total area actually reporting............	100.0%	701	4	75	43	579	4,197	768	3,184	245
Rate per 100,000 inhabitants.................		307.7	1.8	32.9	18.9	254.1	1,842.1	337.1	1,397.5	107.5
Providence-Warwick, RI-MA MSA........................	1,619,966									
Includes Bristol County, MA and Bristol, Kent, Newport, Providence, and Washington Counties, RI										
City of Providence, RI	179,854	960	12	104	255	589	5,925	1,013	4,332	580
City of Warwick, RI	81,617	97	1	27	12	57	1,383	173	1,149	61
Total area actually reporting............	99.5%	4,756	32	637	1,002	3,085	27,304	4,963	20,182	2,159
Estimated total....................	100.0%	4,777	32	639	1,005	3,101	27,402	4,980	20,256	2,166
Rate per 100,000 inhabitants.................		294.9	2.0	39.4	62.0	191.4	1,691.5	307.4	1,250.4	133.7
Provo-Orem, UT MSA............	616,739									
Includes Juab and Utah Counties										
City of Provo	117,540	148	1	52	29	66	2,036	155	1,764	117
City of Orem	99,045	69	0	14	22	33	2,016	191	1,696	129
Total area actually reporting............	100.0%	492	7	163	92	230	9,436	1,051	7,857	528
Rate per 100,000 inhabitants.................		79.8	1.1	26.4	14.9	37.3	1,530.0	170.4	1,274.0	85.6
Pueblo, CO MSA...........	165,456									
Includes Pueblo County										
City of Pueblo....................	110,872	1,167	10	199	219	739	6,838	1,376	4,234	1,228
Total area actually reporting............	100.0%	1,201	11	200	226	764	8,004	1,562	5,072	1,370
Rate per 100,000 inhabitants.................		725.9	6.6	120.9	136.6	461.8	4,837.5	944.1	3,065.5	828.0
Punta Gorda, FL MSA............	182,274									
Includes Charlotte County										
City of Punta Gorda	19,181	16	0	0	5	11	246	23	208	15
Total area actually reporting............	100.0%	376	1	33	28	314	2,299	391	1,781	127
Rate per 100,000 inhabitants.................		206.3	0.5	18.1	15.4	172.3	1,261.3	214.5	977.1	69.7
Racine, WI MSA[2]............	195,139									
Includes Racine County										
City of Racine[2]	77,371	520	1	61	122	336	1,762	417	1,216	129
Total area actually reporting............	100.0%	673	2	79	143	449	2,961	579	2,197	185
Rate per 100,000 inhabitants.................		344.9	1.0	40.5	73.3	230.1	1,517.4	296.7	1,125.9	94.8
Rapid City, SD MSA	146,750									
Includes Custer, Meade, and Pennington Counties										
City of Rapid City....................	74,986	480	6	101	68	305	2,872	466	2,102	304
Total area actually reporting............	99.7%	705	7	173	72	453	3,865	685	2,795	385
Estimated total....................	100.0%	705	7	173	72	453	3,870	686	2,799	385
Rate per 100,000 inhabitants.................		480.4	4.8	117.9	49.1	308.7	2,637.1	467.5	1,907.3	262.4
Reading, PA MSA	415,562									
Includes Berks County										
City of Reading	87,487	624	9	60	219	336	2,106	631	1,278	197
Total area actually reporting............	100.0%	1,077	13	149	295	620	6,124	1,245	4,510	369
Rate per 100,000 inhabitants.................		259.2	3.1	35.9	71.0	149.2	1,473.7	299.6	1,085.3	88.8
Redding, CA MSA............	179,818									
Includes Shasta County										
City of Redding	92,127	654	2	64	150	438	3,841	690	2,360	791
Total area actually reporting............	100.0%	1,225	6	118	177	924	5,645	1,249	3,175	1,221
Rate per 100,000 inhabitants.................		681.2	3.3	65.6	98.4	513.9	3,139.3	694.6	1,765.7	679.0
Reno, NV MSA............	465,669									
Includes Storey and Washoe Counties										
City of Reno....................	248,531	1,674	19	142	382	1,131	7,669	1,347	4,890	1,432
Total area actually reporting............	100.0%	2,397	21	230	502	1,644	11,873	2,206	7,664	2,003
Rate per 100,000 inhabitants.................		514.7	4.5	49.4	107.8	353.0	2,549.7	473.7	1,645.8	430.1
Riverside-San Bernardino-Ontario, CA MSA[2]....................	4,572,004									
Includes Riverside and San Bernardino Counties										

Table 4. Crime, by Selected Metropolitan Statistical Area, 2017—*Continued*

(Number, percent, rate per 100,000 population.)

Area	Population	Violent crime	Murder and nonnegligent manslaughter	Rape[1]	Robbery	Aggravated assault	Property crime	Burglary	Larceny-theft	Motor vehicle theft
City of Riverside	328,023	1,669	12	166	544	947	10,032	1,673	6,629	1,730
City of San Bernardino	217,259	2,805	34	158	877	1,736	8,403	2,136	3,990	2,277
City of Ontario[2]	174,724	683	8	136	220	319	4,473	720	2,842	911
City of Corona	169,164	223	1	36	107	79	3,297	561	2,177	559
City of Victorville	123,284	862	14	54	267	527	3,318	830	1,839	649
City of Temecula	115,220	117	i	5	38	73	2,614	353	2,011	250
City of Chino	89,420	227	3	10	87	127	2,142	443	1,405	294
City of Redlands	71,707	216	1	36	69	110	2,629	426	1,910	293
Total area actually reporting	100.0%	17,525	209	1,396	5,208	10,712	113,833	23,358	69,876	20,599
Rate per 100,000 inhabitants		383.3	4.6	30.5	113.9	234.3	2,489.8	510.9	1,528.3	450.5
Roanoke, VA MSA	314,169									
Includes Botetourt, Craig, Franklin, and Roanoke Counties and Roanoke and Salem Cities										
City of Roanoke	100,027	402	16	41	79	266	4,493	487	3,719	287
Total area actually reporting	100.0%	722	26	113	121	462	7,507	863	6,147	497
Rate per 100,000 inhabitants		229.8	8.3	36.0	38.5	147.1	2,389.5	274.7	1,956.6	158.2
Rochester, MN MSA	218,186									
Includes Dodge, Fillmore, Olmsted, and Wabasha Counties										
City of Rochester	115,228	224	1	61	46	116	2,143	288	1,757	98
Total area actually reporting	100.0%	318	1	86	51	180	2,855	423	2,278	154
Rate per 100,000 inhabitants		145.7	0.5	39.4	23.4	82.5	1,308.5	193.9	1,044.1	70.6
Rochester, NY MSA	1,081,106									
Includes Livingston, Monroe, Ontario, Orleans, Wayne, and Yates Counties										
City of Rochester	208,591	1,872	27	141	707	997	7,934	1,337	5,981	616
Total area actually reporting	99.6%	3,052	40	467	951	1,594	20,785	3,039	16,662	1,084
Estimated total	100.0%	3,059	40	468	953	1,598	20,843	3,046	16,711	1,086
Rate per 100,000 inhabitants		283.0	3.7	43.3	88.2	147.8	1,927.9	281.7	1,545.7	100.5
Rockford, IL MSA	337,935									
Includes Boone and Winnebago Counties										
City of Rockford	146,768	2,331	18	113	427	1,773	5,236	1,383	3,403	450
Total area actually reporting	99.0%	2,762	21	194	471	2,076	8,148	1,991	5,580	577
Estimated total	100.0%	2,769	21	195	473	2,080	8,204	1,999	5,625	580
Rate per 100,000 inhabitants		819.4	6.2	57.7	140.0	615.5	2,427.7	591.5	1,664.5	171.6
Rocky Mount, NC MSA[4]	146,800									
Includes Edgecombe and Nash Counties[4]										
City of Rocky Mount[4]	55,098		15		95	270	1,984	554	1,310	120
Total area actually reporting	94.2%		22		130	371	3,230	1,043	2,017	170
Estimated total	100.0%		22		136	385	3,471	1,087	2,204	180
Rate per 100,000 inhabitants			15.0		92.6	262.3	2,364.4	740.5	1,501.4	122.6
Rome, GA MSA	96,700									
Includes Floyd County										
City of Rome	36,366	205	3	6	32	164	1,480	268	1,151	61
Total area actually reporting	100.0%	322	5	21	43	253	2,898	566	2,161	171
Rate per 100,000 inhabitants		333.0	5.2	21.7	44.5	261.6	2,996.9	585.3	2,234.7	176.8
Sacramento–Roseville–Arden-Arcade, CA MSA	2,318,414									
Includes El Dorado, Placer, Sacramento, and Yolo Counties										
City of Sacramento	499,997	3,378	39	99	1,100	2,140	14,683	2,888	9,077	2,718
City of Roseville	135,028	237	0	27	87	123	3,322	389	2,623	310
City of Folsom	78,155	64	0	21	21	22	1,229	257	847	125
Total area actually reporting	100.0%	8,977	99	614	2,568	5,696	52,147	9,747	34,682	7,718
Rate per 100,000 inhabitants		387.2	4.3	26.5	110.8	245.7	2,249.3	420.4	1,495.9	332.9
Saginaw, MI MSA	191,556									
Includes Saginaw County										
City of Saginaw	48,589	762	15	50	75	622	913	383	455	75
Total area actually reporting	100.0%	1,214	19	131	127	937	3,165	802	2,199	164
Rate per 100,000 inhabitants		633.8	9.9	68.4	66.3	489.2	1,652.3	418.7	1,148.0	85.6
Salem, OR MSA[4]	423,228									
Includes Marion4 and Polk Counties										
City of Salem	169,565	641	6	44	167	424	7,195	897	5,437	861
Total area actually reporting	100.0%	1,186	14	115	265	792	12,931	1,732	9,521	1,678
Rate per 100,000 inhabitants		280.2	3.3	27.2	62.6	187.1	3,055.3	409.2	2,249.6	396.5

Table 4. Crime, by Selected Metropolitan Statistical Area, 2017—*Continued*

(Number, percent, rate per 100,000 population.)

Area	Population	Violent crime	Murder and nonnegligent manslaughter	Rape[1]	Robbery	Aggravated assault	Property crime	Burglary	Larceny-theft	Motor vehicle theft
Salinas, CA MSA	437,962									
Includes Monterey County										
City of Salinas	158,313	1,021	28	71	358	564	4,795	964	2,589	1,242
Total area actually reporting	100.0%	1,802	43	168	547	1,044	10,043	1,937	6,026	2,080
Rate per 100,000 inhabitants		411.5	9.8	38.4	124.9	238.4	2,293.1	442.3	1,375.9	474.9
Salisbury, MD-DE MSA	404,765									
Includes Sussex County, DE and Somerset, Wicomico, and Worcester Counties, MD										
City of Salisbury, MD	33,558	326	7	21	94	204	1,784	273	1,443	68
Total area actually reporting	100.0%	1,592	16	192	320	1,064	10,313	2,001	7,973	339
Rate per 100,000 inhabitants		393.3	4.0	47.4	79.1	262.9	2,547.9	494.4	1,969.8	83.8
Salt Lake City, UT MSA[2]	1,203,339									
Includes Salt Lake and Tooele[2] Counties										
City of Salt Lake City	194,968	1,713	10	334	508	861	15,694	1,884	11,924	1,886
Total area actually reporting	99.9%	4,821	44	999	1,169	2,609	53,353	7,123	39,225	7,005
Estimated total	100.0%	4,821	44	999	1,169	2,609	53,363	7,124	39,233	7,006
Rate per 100,000 inhabitants		400.6	3.7	83.0	97.1	216.8	4,434.6	592.0	3,260.3	582.2
San Angelo, TX MSA	121,144									
Includes Irion and Tom Green Counties										
City of San Angelo	101,931	282	3	74	40	165	4,499	802	3,425	272
Total area actually reporting	100.0%	303	4	92	41	166	4,912	977	3,631	304
Rate per 100,000 inhabitants		250.1	3.3	75.9	33.8	137.0	4,054.7	806.5	2,997.3	250.9
San Antonio-New Braunfels, TX MSA[2,3]	2,476,620									
Includes Atascosa, Bandera, Bexar, Comal, Guadalupe, Kendall, Medina, and Wilson Counties										
City of San Antonio	1,520,712	10,759	124	1,270	2,298	7,067	73,676	11,722	55,090	6,864
City of New Braunfels	76,993	193	1	33	29	130	1,321	221	952	148
Total area actually reporting	99.9%	12,972	159	1,741	2,659	8,413			68,938	8,439
Estimated total	100.0%	12,976	159	1,742	2,660	8,415			68,960	8,441
Rate per 100,000 inhabitants		523.9	6.4	70.3	107.4	339.8			2,784.4	340.8
San Diego-Carlsbad, CA MSA	3,350,968									
Includes San Diego County										
City of San Diego	1,424,116	5,221	35	559	1,410	3,217	26,246	3,817	17,294	5,135
City of Carlsbad	115,344	247	0	30	46	171	2,209	432	1,638	139
Total area actually reporting	100.0%	11,296	81	1,098	3,013	7,104	56,816	9,134	37,951	9,731
Rate per 100,000 inhabitants		337.1	2.4	32.8	89.9	212.0	1,695.5	272.6	1,132.5	290.4
San Francisco-Oakland-Hayward, CA MSA[3]	4,732,078									
Includes the Metropolitan Divisions of Oakland-Hayward-Berkeley, San Francisco-Redwood City-South San Francisco, and San Rafael										
City of San Francisco	881,255	6,301	56	367	3,220	2,658	54,356	4,935	44,587	4,834
City of Oakland	424,915	5,521	69	400	2,676	2,376	25,422	2,622	17,305	5,495
City of Hayward	161,417	563	5	70	306	182	5,023	482	2,740	1,801
City of Berkeley	122,687	666	1	83	364	218	6,020	843	4,556	621
City of San Leandro	91,386	524	2	21	292	209	3,715	460	2,369	886
City of Redwood City	86,353	209	0	57	61	91	1,390	177	1,053	160
City of San Ramon	76,325	56	0	8	30	18	974	126	768	80
City of Pleasanton	84,440	99	0	13	53	33	1,661	137	1,406	118
City of Walnut Creek	69,953	105	1	2	39	63	2,304	243	1,871	190
City of South San Francisco	67,533	234	1	31	72	130	1,605	214	1,184	207
City of San Rafael	59,144	194	0	21	89	84	1,627	271	1,091	265
Total area actually reporting	100.0%	22,554	199	1,848	10,314	10,193		19,501		25,398
Rate per 100,000 inhabitants		476.6	4.2	39.1	218.0	215.4		412.1		536.7
Oakland-Hayward-Berkeley, CA MD[3]	2,817,472									
Includes Alameda and Contra Costa Counties										
Total area actually reporting	100.0%	13,753	132	1,104	6,317	6,200		11,086		18,442
Rate per 100,000 inhabitants		488.1	4.7	39.2	224.2	220.1		393.5		654.6
San Francisco-Redwood City-South San Francisco, CA MD	1,652,939									
Includes San Francisco and San Mateo Counties										
Total area actually reporting	100.0%	8,338	63	698	3,848	3,729	70,395	7,474	56,440	6,481
Rate per 100,000 inhabitants		504.4	3.8	42.2	232.8	225.6	4,258.8	452.2	3,414.5	392.1
San Rafael, CA MD	261,667									
Includes Marin County										

Table 4. Crime, by Selected Metropolitan Statistical Area, 2017—*Continued*

(Number, percent, rate per 100,000 population.)

Area	Population	Violent crime	Murder and nonnegligent manslaughter	Rape[1]	Robbery	Aggravated assault	Property crime	Burglary	Larceny-theft	Motor vehicle theft
Total area actually reporting	100.0%	463	4	46	149	264	5,006	941	3,590	475
Rate per 100,000 inhabitants........................		176.9	1.5	17.6	56.9	100.9	1,913.1	359.6	1,372.0	181.5
San Jose-Sunnyvale-Santa Clara, CA MSA	2,000,325									
Includes San Benito and Santa Clara Counties										
City of San Jose........................	1,037,529	4,188	32	571	1,376	2,209	25,323	3,926	13,329	8,068
City of Sunnyvale........................	154,919	182	1	29	56	96	2,682	512	1,872	298
City of Santa Clara........................	127,538	214	2	35	82	95	3,618	408	2,810	400
City of Mountain View........................	81,525	150	1	14	44	91	1,982	290	1,590	102
City of Milpitas........................	79,503	114	2	12	58	42	1,978	235	1,447	296
City of Palo Alto........................	67,441	90	0	11	39	40	1,783	214	1,478	91
City of Cupertino........................	60,970	77	2	9	21	45	970	164	756	50
Total area actually reporting........................	100.0%	6,178	48	827	1,931	3,372	45,510	6,972	28,107	10,431
Rate per 100,000 inhabitants........................		308.8	2.4	41.3	96.5	168.6	2,275.1	348.5	1,405.1	521.5
San Luis Obispo-Paso Robles-Arroyo Grande, CA MSA[5] ..	284,792									
Includes San Luis Obispo County[5]										
City of San Luis Obispo........................	47,934	178	0	44	23	111	1,782	172	1,516	94
City of Paso Robles........................	32,266	35	0	3	6	26	920	126	731	63
City of Arroyo Grande........................	18,239	32	0	3	5	24	311	53	226	32
Total area actually reporting........................	100.0%		2	96	85		5,812	1,038	4,345	429
Rate per 100,000 inhabitants........................			0.7	33.7	29.8		2,040.8	364.5	1,525.7	150.6
Santa Cruz-Watsonville, CA MSA........................	276,313									
Includes Santa Cruz County										
City of Santa Cruz........................	65,132	409	1	57	103	248	3,684	412	2,911	361
City of Watsonville........................	54,226	298	1	41	69	187	1,711	251	995	465
Total area actually reporting........................	100.0%	1,056	3	156	232	665	8,947	1,235	6,445	1,267
Rate per 100,000 inhabitants........................		382.2	1.1	56.5	84.0	240.7	3,238.0	447.0	2,332.5	458.5
Santa Fe, NM MSA	149,636									
Includes Santa Fe County										
City of Santa Fe........................	84,358	289	4	36	56	193	3,178	1,228	1,736	214
Total area actually reporting........................	100.0%	482	5	42	71	364	4,061	1,639	2,171	251
Rate per 100,000 inhabitants........................		322.1	3.3	28.1	47.4	243.3	2,713.9	1,095.3	1,450.9	167.7
Santa Maria-Santa Barbara, CA MSA	449,405									
Includes Santa Barbara County										
City of Santa Maria........................	107,424	476	3	58	155	260	2,354	446	1,231	677
City of Santa Barbara........................	92,508	377	0	67	80	230	2,499	327	1,968	204
Total area actually reporting........................	100.0%	1,532	8	257	327	940	8,742	1,663	5,825	1,254
Rate per 100,000 inhabitants........................		340.9	1.8	57.2	72.8	209.2	1,945.2	370.0	1,296.2	279.0
Santa Rosa, CA MSA	505,613									
Includes Sonoma County										
City of Santa Rosa........................	176,361	722	5	109	126	482	3,245	525	2,309	411
Total area actually reporting........................	100.0%	2,025	12	298	277	1,438	7,586	1,399	5,358	829
Rate per 100,000 inhabitants........................		400.5	2.4	58.9	54.8	284.4	1,500.4	276.7	1,059.7	164.0
Savannah, GA MSA[3]........................	390,752									
Includes Bryan, Chatham, and Effingham Counties										
City of Savannah-Chatham Metropolitan	242,941	1,124	35	100	381	608	8,336	1,335	6,061	940
Total area actually reporting........................	100.0%	1,534	38	130	440	926			8,601	1,142
Rate per 100,000 inhabitants........................		392.6	9.7	33.3	112.6	237.0			2,201.1	292.3
Scranton–Wilkes-Barre–Hazleton, PA MSA	554,189									
Includes Lackawanna, Luzerne, and Wyoming Counties										
City of Scranton........................	77,499	198	1	22	90	85	1,698	351	1,215	132
City of Wilkes-Barre........................	40,418	251	2	12	104	133	1,101	225	816	60
City of Hazleton........................	24,549	91	1	7	26	57	304	82	191	31
Total area actually reporting........................	98.5%	1,407	22	127	338	920	8,692	1,524	6,752	416
Estimated total........................	100.0%	1,422	22	128	342	930	8,813	1,538	6,854	421
Rate per 100,000 inhabitants........................		256.6	4.0	23.1	61.7	167.8	1,590.3	277.5	1,236.8	76.0
Seattle-Tacoma-Bellevue, WA MSA[3,4]	3,872,207									
Includes the Metropolitan Divisions of Seattle-Bellevue-Everett and Tacoma-Lakewood										
City of Seattle........................	721,365	4,564	27	266	1,515	2,756	37,934	7,805	26,499	3,630
City of Tacoma	213,504	1,737	10	171	403	1,153	11,901	2,073	7,742	2,086
City of Bellevue........................	143,703	144	0	24	55	65	4,175	592	3,274	309

Table 4. Crime, by Selected Metropolitan Statistical Area, 2017—*Continued*

(Number, percent, rate per 100,000 population.)

Area	Population	Violent crime	Murder and nonnegligent manslaughter	Rape[1]	Robbery	Aggravated assault	Property crime	Burglary	Larceny-theft	Motor vehicle theft
City of Everett....................	110,040	497	5	52	131	309	5,099	869	3,292	938
City of Kent....................	128,990	465	7	70	203	185	6,928	948	4,666	1,314
City of Renton	102,470	328	3	45	113	167	5,128	607	3,640	881
City of Auburn[3]....................	78,718	376	3	64	117	192			2,124	653
City of Lakewood....................	61,080	425	4	54	89	278	2,793	488	1,927	378
City of Redmond....................	63,889	96	2	11	33	50	2,077	271	1,695	111
Total area actually reporting....................	100.0%	13,695	115	1,451	3,955	8,174			94,652	18,627
Rate per 100,000 inhabitants....................		353.7	3.0	37.5	102.1	211.1			2,444.4	481.0
Seattle-Bellevue-Everett, WA MD[3,4]....................	2,996,781									
Includes King[4] and Snohomish Counties										
Total area actually reporting	100.0%	9,645	91	1,005	3,087	5,462			74,313	13,991
Rate per 100,000 inhabitants....................		321.8	3.0	33.5	103.0	182.3			2,479.8	466.9
Tacoma-Lakewood, WA MD[3]	875,426									
Includes Pierce County										
Total area actually reporting	100.0%	4,050	24	446	868	2,712			20,339	4,636
Rate per 100,000 inhabitants....................		462.6	2.7	50.9	99.2	309.8			2,323.3	529.6
Sebastian-Vero Beach, FL MSA....................	154,339									
Includes Indian River County										
City of Sebastian....................	25,277	48	0	3	8	37	381	51	312	18
City of Vero Beach....................	17,015	46	0	10	7	29	490	94	376	20
Total area actually reporting....................	100.0%	457	3	39	51	364	2,884	532	2,189	163
Rate per 100,000 inhabitants....................		296.1	1.9	25.3	33.0	235.8	1,868.6	344.7	1,418.3	105.6
Sebring, FL MSA....................	101,583									
Includes Highlands County										
City of Sebring....................	10,679	68	2	5	12	49	538	129	395	14
Total area actually reporting....................	100.0%	329	7	38	42	242	2,665	693	1,863	109
Rate per 100,000 inhabitants....................		323.9	6.9	37.4	41.3	238.2	2,623.5	682.2	1,834.0	107.3
Sheboygan, WI MSA....................	115,448									
Includes Sheboygan County										
City of Sheboygan	48,595	161	0	40	12	109	821	90	698	33
Total area actually reporting....................	100.0%	211	2	66	14	129	1,416	170	1,202	44
Rate per 100,000 inhabitants....................		182.8	1.7	57.2	12.1	111.7	1,226.5	147.3	1,041.2	38.1
Sherman-Denison, TX MSA	129,343									
Includes Grayson County										
City of Sherman....................	42,122	158	2	20	35	101	1,306	287	942	77
City of Denison....................	23,814	107	4	18	15	70	525	115	340	70
Total area actually reporting....................	97.1%	375	6	64	52	253	2,509	606	1,664	239
Estimated total....................	100.0%	385	6	66	54	259	2,596	619	1,731	246
Rate per 100,000 inhabitants....................		297.7	4.6	51.0	41.7	200.2	2,007.1	478.6	1,338.3	190.2
Shreveport-Bossier City, LA MSA	439,907									
Includes Bossier, Caddo, De Soto, and Webster Parishes										
City of Shreveport....................	193,937	1,850	52	152	498	1,148	10,813	2,256	7,673	884
City of Bossier City....................	69,632	535	4	48	79	404	3,283	451	2,549	283
Total area actually reporting....................	100.0%	2,670	62	218	598	1,792	16,859	3,438	12,082	1,339
Rate per 100,000 inhabitants....................		606.9	14.1	49.6	135.9	407.4	3,832.4	781.5	2,746.5	304.4
Sierra Vista-Douglas, AZ MSA....................	124,671									
Includes Cochise County										
City of Sierra Vista....................	42,859	191	0	24	23	144	1,287	225	998	64
City of Douglas....................	16,443	41	1	0	3	37	657	94	549	14
Total area actually reporting....................	89.6%	466	1	38	35	392	2,721	392	2,185	144
Estimated total....................	100.0%	504	1	42	43	418	3,071	445	2,456	170
Rate per 100,000 inhabitants....................		404.3	0.8	33.7	34.5	335.3	2,463.3	356.9	1,970.0	136.4
Sioux City, IA-NE-SD MSA....................	168,938									
Includes Plymouth and Woodbury Counties, IA; Dakota and Dixon Counties, NE; and Union County, SD										
City of Sioux City, IA....................	82,879	360	2	56	71	231	3,561	612	2,660	289
Total area actually reporting....................	98.5%	488	3	73	80	332	4,634	802	3,420	412
Estimated total....................	100.0%	492	3	74	80	335	4,671	809	3,447	415
Rate per 100,000 inhabitants....................		291.2	1.8	43.8	47.4	198.3	2,764.9	478.9	2,040.4	245.7
Sioux Falls, SD MSA	259,149									
Includes Lincoln, McCook, Minnehaha, and Turner Counties										

Table 4. Crime, by Selected Metropolitan Statistical Area, 2017—*Continued*

(Number, percent, rate per 100,000 population.)

Area	Population	Violent crime	Murder and nonnegligent manslaughter	Rape[1]	Robbery	Aggravated assault	Property crime	Burglary	Larceny-theft	Motor vehicle theft
City of Sioux Falls....................	177,888	801	4	121	100	576	5,083	655	3,959	469
Total area actually reporting............	99.3%	918	6	146	102	664	5,870	833	4,517	520
Estimated total....................	100.0%	921	6	147	102	666	5,895	837	4,536	522
Rate per 100,000 inhabitants............		355.4	2.3	56.7	39.4	257.0	2,274.8	323.0	1,750.3	201.4
South Bend-Mishawaka, IN-MI MSA[5]	321,506									
Includes St. Joseph County, IN and Cass County, MI										
City of South Bend, IN............	101,857	1,064	15	93	345	611	5,100	1,192	3,440	468
City of Mishawaka, IN[5]............	48,749	105	3	8	54	40		275		
Total area actually reporting............	96.9%	1,389	23	166	435	765		2,028		
Estimated total....................	100.0%	1,417	23	170	440	784		2,056		
Rate per 100,000 inhabitants............		440.7	7.2	52.9	136.9	243.9		639.5		
Spokane-Spokane Valley, WA MSA	563,140									
Includes Pend Oreille, Spokane, and Stevens Counties										
City of Spokane............	217,066	1,360	6	238	229	887	15,697	2,221	11,739	1,737
City of Spokane Valley............	97,430	200	2	48	29	121	4,417	606	3,376	435
Total area actually reporting............	99.9%	1,814	15	365	286	1,148	25,182	4,069	18,499	2,614
Estimated total....................	100.0%	1,814	15	365	286	1,148	25,190	4,070	18,505	2,615
Rate per 100,000 inhabitants............		322.1	2.7	64.8	50.8	203.9	4,473.1	722.7	3,286.0	464.4
Springfield, IL MSA	210,042									
Includes Menard and Sangamon Counties										
City of Springfield............	115,568	1,219	11	93	251	864	5,496	1,210	3,973	313
Total area actually reporting............	96.2%	1,462	13	135	266	1,048	6,599	1,506	4,682	411
Estimated total....................	100.0%	1,480	13	138	271	1,058	6,730	1,525	4,786	419
Rate per 100,000 inhabitants............		704.6	6.2	65.7	129.0	503.7	3,204.1	726.0	2,278.6	199.5
Springfield, MA MSA	631,954									
Includes Hampden and Hampshire Counties										
City of Springfield............	154,562	1,351	14	73	380	884	4,594	1,183	2,902	509
Total area actually reporting............	97.5%	3,138	22	312	637	2,167	13,512	2,875	9,609	1,028
Estimated total....................	100.0%	3,184	22	317	644	2,201	13,718	2,910	9,765	1,043
Rate per 100,000 inhabitants............		503.8	3.5	50.2	101.9	348.3	2,170.7	460.5	1,545.2	165.0
Springfield, MO MSA	462,905									
Includes Christian, Dallas, Greene, Polk, and Webster Counties										
City of Springfield............	168,654	2,258	14	352	382	1,510	14,932	2,236	10,727	1,969
Total area actually reporting............	100.0%	2,672	23	431	412	1,806	19,826	3,241	14,171	2,414
Rate per 100,000 inhabitants............		577.2	5.0	93.1	89.0	390.1	4,283.0	700.1	3,061.3	521.5
Springfield, OH MSA	134,569									
Includes Clark County										
City of Springfield............	58,843	370	9	25	177	159	4,024	1,040	2,691	293
Total area actually reporting............	94.7%	393	9	32	180	172	4,883	1,269	3,281	333
Estimated total....................	100.0%	403	9	34	183	177	5,030	1,291	3,399	340
Rate per 100,000 inhabitants............		299.5	6.7	25.3	136.0	131.5	3,737.9	959.4	2,525.8	252.7
State College, PA MSA	162,798									
Includes Centre County										
City of State College............	58,169	44	0	7	9	28	616	45	566	5
Total area actually reporting............	100.0%	152	3	56	19	74	1,685	173	1,490	22
Rate per 100,000 inhabitants............		93.4	1.8	34.4	11.7	45.5	1,035.0	106.3	915.2	13.5
Staunton-Waynesboro, VA MSA	121,588									
Includes Augusta County and Staunton and Waynesboro Cities										
City of Staunton............	24,423	35	0	7	8	20	551	77	456	18
City of Waynesboro............	22,004	40	0	13	10	17	528	46	459	23
Total area actually reporting............	100.0%	170	1	48	23	98	1,975	334	1,507	134
Rate per 100,000 inhabitants............		139.8	0.8	39.5	18.9	80.6	1,624.3	274.7	1,239.4	110.2
St. Cloud, MN MSA	197,461									
Includes Benton and Stearns Counties										
City of St. Cloud............	67,911	256	3	62	49	142	2,789	330	2,278	181
Total area actually reporting............	100.0%	361	4	93	53	211	4,515	579	3,662	274
Rate per 100,000 inhabitants............		182.8	2.0	47.1	26.8	106.9	2,286.5	293.2	1,854.5	138.8

Table 4. Crime, by Selected Metropolitan Statistical Area, 2017—*Continued*

(Number, percent, rate per 100,000 population.)

Area	Population	Violent crime	Murder and nonnegligent manslaughter	Rape[1]	Robbery	Aggravated assault	Property crime	Burglary	Larceny-theft	Motor vehicle theft
St. Joseph, MO-KS MSA....................................	126,515									
Includes Doniphan County, KS and Andrew, Buchanan, and DeKalb Counties, MO										
City of St. Joseph, MO	76,435	438	7	37	98	296	5,146	737	3,633	776
Total area actually reporting..........................	99.4%	524	8	42	104	370	5,827	907	4,067	853
Estimated total...	100.0%	525	8	42	104	371	5,847	910	4,082	855
Rate per 100,000 inhabitants........................		415.0	6.3	33.2	82.2	293.2	4,621.6	719.3	3,226.5	675.8
St. Louis, MO-IL MSA[2,5,6]	2,813,173									
Includes Bond, Calhoun, Clinton, Jersey, Macoupin, Madison, Monroe, and St. Clair Counties, IL and Franklin, Jefferson, Lincoln, St. Charles, St. Louis, and Warren Counties and St. Louis City, MO										
City of St. Louis, MO....................................	310,284	6,461	205	289	1,944	4,023	18,745	3,138	12,894	2,713
City of St. Charles, MO................................	69,804	158	2	23	35	98	1,765	181	1,450	134
Total area actually reporting..........................	97.9%		352	1,069	3,395		67,670	11,354	49,545	6,771
Estimated total...	100.0%		354	1,088	3,428		68,598	11,496	50,276	6,826
Rate per 100,000 inhabitants........................			12.6	38.7	121.9		2,438.5	408.6	1,787.2	242.6
Stockton-Lodi, CA MSA[2]	740,904									
Includes San Joaquin County										
City of Stockton[2]..	309,566	4,379	55	154	1,208	2,962	11,229	2,140	7,040	2,049
City of Lodi..	65,042	323	1	13	127	182	1,681	347	985	349
Total area actually reporting..........................	100.0%	5,991	68	247	1,671	4,005	21,751	3,925	13,965	3,861
Rate per 100,000 inhabitants........................		808.6	9.2	33.3	225.5	540.6	2,935.7	529.8	1,884.9	521.1
Sumter, SC MSA..	107,470									
Includes Sumter County										
City of Sumter	40,747	333	5	13	63	252	1,839	354	1,411	74
Total area actually reporting..........................	100.0%	736	8	36	99	593	3,812	990	2,575	247
Rate per 100,000 inhabitants........................		684.8	7.4	33.5	92.1	551.8	3,547.0	921.2	2,396.0	229.8
Syracuse, NY MSA......................................	656,920									
Includes Madison, Onondaga, and Oswego Counties										
City of Syracuse	143,069	1,009	20	98	284	607	4,817	1,145	3,301	371
Total area actually reporting..........................	100.0%	1,759	26	353	386	994	13,478	2,300	10,506	672
Rate per 100,000 inhabitants........................		267.8	4.0	53.7	58.8	151.3	2,051.7	350.1	1,599.3	102.3
Tallahassee, FL MSA...................................	382,480									
Includes Gadsden, Jefferson, Leon, and Wakulla Counties										
City of Tallahassee......................................	192,455	1,503	17	190	348	948	9,428	1,519	7,165	744
Total area actually reporting..........................	99.2%	2,316	25	286	409	1,596	13,446	2,521	9,957	968
Estimated total...	100.0%	2,327	25	287	412	1,603	13,532	2,533	10,024	975
Rate per 100,000 inhabitants........................		608.4	6.5	75.0	107.7	419.1	3,538.0	662.3	2,620.8	254.9
Tampa-St. Petersburg-Clearwater, FL MSA......................	3,083,660									
Includes Hernando, Hillsborough, Pasco, and Pinellas Counties										
City of Tampa	384,360	1,785	39	121	406	1,219	6,702	1,235	4,900	567
City of St. Petersburg..................................	263,712	1,842	20	136	499	1,187	11,373	1,772	8,623	978
City of Clearwater.......................................	115,295	578	3	85	141	349	3,652	494	2,909	249
City of Largo...	83,728	365	1	71	97	196	2,856	310	2,315	231
Total area actually reporting..........................	100.0%	10,273	111	1,137	2,104	6,921	64,807	10,650	49,151	5,006
Rate per 100,000 inhabitants........................		333.1	3.6	36.9	68.2	224.4	2,101.6	345.4	1,593.9	162.3
Texarkana, TX-AR MSA...............................	150,196									
Includes Little River and Miller Counties, AR and Bowie County, TX										
City of Texarkana, TX	37,882	478	3	31	86	358	1,889	311	1,457	121
Total area actually reporting..........................	100.0%	939	11	86	150	692	4,748	1,032	3,391	325
Rate per 100,000 inhabitants........................		625.2	7.3	57.3	99.9	460.7	3,161.2	687.1	2,257.7	216.4
The Villages, FL MSA..................................	130,154									
Includes Sumter County										
Total area actually reporting..........................	100.0%	305	6	24	24	251	1,158	310	782	66
Rate per 100,000 inhabitants........................		234.3	4.6	18.4	18.4	192.8	889.7	238.2	600.8	50.7
Toledo, OH MSA[2,5]	606,018									
Includes Fulton, Lucas, and Wood Counties										
City of Toledo[2,5]	277,116		35		780	1,834	11,095	3,103	7,247	745

Table 4. Crime, by Selected Metropolitan Statistical Area, 2017—*Continued*

(Number, percent, rate per 100,000 population.)

Area	Population	Violent crime	Murder and nonnegligent manslaughter	Rape[1]	Robbery	Aggravated assault	Property crime	Burglary	Larceny-theft	Motor vehicle theft
Total area actually reporting.........	94.9%		38		856	2,016	16,670	3,890	11,830	950
Estimated total.........	100.0%		39		870	2,038	17,309	3,987	12,342	980
Rate per 100,000 inhabitants.........			6.4		143.6	336.3	2,856.2	657.9	2,036.6	161.7
Topeka, KS MSA.........	232,643									
Includes Jackson, Jefferson, Osage, Shawnee, and Wabaunsee Counties										
City of Topeka.........	126,624	777	27	56	269	425	6,494	1,001	4,725	768
Total area actually reporting.........	98.0%	952	32	83	283	554	8,126	1,340	5,862	924
Estimated total.........	100.0%	962	32	85	284	561	8,223	1,352	5,938	933
Rate per 100,000 inhabitants.........		413.5	13.8	36.5	122.1	241.1	3,534.6	581.1	2,552.4	401.0
Trenton, NJ MSA.........	373,064									
Includes Mercer County										
City of Trenton.........	84,231	1,083	23	63	343	654	2,193	792	1,035	366
Total area actually reporting.........	100.0%	1,387	27	96	451	813	6,996	1,543	4,822	631
Rate per 100,000 inhabitants.........		371.8	7.2	25.7	120.9	217.9	1,875.3	413.6	1,292.5	169.1
Tucson, AZ MSA.........	1,021,012									
Includes Pima County										
City of Tucson.........	532,323	4,268	46	498	1,431	2,293	27,956	4,424	21,125	2,407
Total area actually reporting.........	99.4%	5,078	64	612	1,657	2,745	39,956	6,517	30,246	3,193
Estimated total.........	100.0%	5,095	64	614	1,661	2,756	40,107	6,540	30,363	3,204
Rate per 100,000 inhabitants.........		499.0	6.3	60.1	162.7	269.9	3,928.2	640.5	2,973.8	313.8
Tulsa, OK MSA.........	989,910									
Includes Creek, Okmulgee, Osage, Pawnee, Rogers, Tulsa, and Wagoner Counties										
City of Tulsa.........	404,868	4,214	70	423	964	2,757	22,088	5,574	13,054	3,460
Total area actually reporting.........	100.0%	5,600	90	655	1,098	3,757	33,968	8,320	20,791	4,857
Rate per 100,000 inhabitants.........		565.7	9.1	66.2	110.9	379.5	3,431.4	840.5	2,100.3	490.7
Tuscaloosa, AL MSA.........	243,131									
Includes Hale, Pickens, and Tuscaloosa Counties										
City of Tuscaloosa.........	101,124	474	9	54	168	243	4,174	814	3,161	199
Total area actually reporting.........	99.0%	853	16	87	211	539	6,863	1,460	4,983	420
Estimated total.........	100.0%	865	16	88	213	548	6,940	1,473	5,041	426
Rate per 100,000 inhabitants.........		355.8	6.6	36.2	87.6	225.4	2,854.4	605.8	2,073.4	175.2
Twin Falls, ID MSA.........	108,516									
Includes Jerome and Twin Falls Counties										
City of Twin Falls.........	48,912	210	0	44	9	157	1,287	196	1,006	85
Total area actually reporting.........	100.0%	344	0	65	17	262	1,976	435	1,375	166
Rate per 100,000 inhabitants.........		317.0	0.0	59.9	15.7	241.4	1,820.9	400.9	1,267.1	153.0
Tyler, TX MSA.........	227,621									
Includes Smith County										
City of Tyler.........	106,115	464	6	65	60	333	3,337	446	2,745	146
Total area actually reporting.........	99.9%	802	9	116	85	592	5,618	1,152	4,076	390
Estimated total.........	100.0%	802	9	116	85	592	5,622	1,153	4,079	390
Rate per 100,000 inhabitants.........		352.3	4.0	51.0	37.3	260.1	2,469.9	506.5	1,792.0	171.3
Urban Honolulu, HI MSA.........	990,384									
Includes Honolulu County										
Total area actually reporting.........	100.0%	2,440	32	285	908	1,215	27,477	3,331	20,540	3,606
Rate per 100,000 inhabitants.........		246.4	3.2	28.8	91.7	122.7	2,774.4	336.3	2,073.9	364.1
Utica-Rome, NY MSA.........	293,570									
Includes Herkimer and Oneida Counties										
City of Utica.........	60,395	337	3	42	78	214	1,986	376	1,543	67
City of Rome.........	32,200	71	1	10	13	47	563	109	440	14
Total area actually reporting.........	99.1%	839	5	237	114	483	5,047	816	4,076	155
Estimated total.........	100.0%	843	5	237	115	486	5,084	820	4,108	156
Rate per 100,000 inhabitants.........		287.2	1.7	80.7	39.2	165.5	1,731.8	279.3	1,399.3	53.1
Valdosta, GA MSA.........	145,652									
Includes Brooks, Echols, Lanier, and Lowndes Counties										
City of Valdosta.........	56,729	215	10	17	47	141	3,485	554	2,699	232
Total area actually reporting.........	99.4%	439	11	39	69	320	5,259	1,023	3,859	377
Estimated total.........	100.0%	442	11	39	70	322	5,294	1,028	3,886	380

Table 4. Crime, by Selected Metropolitan Statistical Area, 2017—*Continued*

(Number, percent, rate per 100,000 population.)

Area	Population	Violent crime	Murder and nonnegligent manslaughter	Rape[1]	Robbery	Aggravated assault	Property crime	Burglary	Larceny-theft	Motor vehicle theft
Rate per 100,000 inhabitants...		303.5	7.6	26.8	48.1	221.1	3,634.7	705.8	2,668.0	260.9
Vallejo-Fairfield, CA MSA	444,232									
Includes Solano County										
City of Vallejo	122,174	1,048	15	93	390	550	4,597	2,445	1,181	971
City of Fairfield	116,372	546	10	40	181	315	3,252	545	2,174	533
Total area actually reporting............................	100.0%	2,112	30	179	701	1,202	12,004	3,660	6,337	2,007
Rate per 100,000 inhabitants............................		475.4	6.8	40.3	157.8	270.6	2,702.2	823.9	1,426.5	451.8
Victoria, TX MSA	100,898									
Includes Goliad and Victoria Counties										
City of Victoria..	68,544	217	4	48	49	116	2,436	646	1,680	110
Total area actually reporting............................	100.0%	339	6	85	57	191	3,126	941	2,026	159
Rate per 100,000 inhabitants............................		336.0	5.9	84.2	56.5	189.3	3,098.2	932.6	2,008.0	157.6
Vineland-Bridgeton, NJ MSA.............................	153,970									
Includes Cumberland County										
City of Vineland...	60,477	298	2	24	93	179	2,414	472	1,883	59
City of Bridgeton...	24,937	272	5	22	147	98	994	245	710	39
Total area actually reporting............................	100.0%	802	11	70	300	421	5,472	1,109	4,213	150
Rate per 100,000 inhabitants............................		520.9	7.1	45.5	194.8	273.4	3,553.9	720.3	2,736.2	97.4
Virginia Beach-Norfolk-Newport News, VA-NC MSA[4]......	1,733,006									
Includes Currituck and Gates Counties, NC[4] and Gloucester, Isle of Wight, James City, Mathews, and York Counties and Chesapeake, Hampton, Newport News, Norfolk, Poquoson, Portsmouth, Suffolk, Virginia Beach, and Williamsburg Cities, VA										
City of Virginia Beach, VA................................	454,353	625	14	102	272	237	8,790	754	7,577	459
City of Norfolk, VA...	245,190	1,363	36	135	371	821	9,192	1,156	7,318	718
City of Newport News, VA................................	181,738	907	24	93	239	551	5,528	829	4,211	488
City of Hampton, VA..	134,929	407	17	26	185	179	4,364	551	3,481	332
City of Portsmouth, VA....................................	95,100	677	17	36	224	400	5,447	1,160	3,903	384
Total area actually reporting............................	99.3%	5,717	137	597	1,633	3,350	45,489	5,952	36,587	2,950
Estimated total..	100.0%	5,732	137	598	1,635	3,362	45,642	6,007	36,675	2,960
Rate per 100,000 inhabitants............................		330.8	7.9	34.5	94.3	194.0	2,633.7	346.6	2,116.3	170.8
Visalia-Porterville, CA MSA	462,877									
Includes Tulare County										
City of Visalia..	132,143	457	9	81	144	223	4,396	839	2,953	604
City of Porterville	59,245	247	4	10	58	175	1,535	338	925	272
Total area actually reporting............................	100.0%	1,665	33	162	386	1,084	11,770	2,367	7,184	2,219
Rate per 100,000 inhabitants............................		359.7	7.1	35.0	83.4	234.2	2,542.8	511.4	1,552.0	479.4
Waco, TX MSA[2]...	266,886									
Includes Falls and McLennan Counties										
City of Waco..	135,997	690	5	117	108	460	4,889	957	3,741	191
Total area actually reporting............................	92.3%	1,169	5	210	143	811	7,037	1,345	5,383	309
Estimated total..	100.0%	1,225	5	218	156	846	7,435	1,417	5,674	344
Rate per 100,000 inhabitants............................		459.0	1.9	81.7	58.5	317.0	2,785.8	530.9	2,126.0	128.9
Walla Walla, WA MSA...	64,684									
Includes Columbia and Walla Walla Counties										
City of Walla Walla	32,189	140	1	31	24	84	1,131	148	917	66
Total area actually reporting............................	100.0%	217	1	48	26	142	1,707	259	1,323	125
Rate per 100,000 inhabitants............................		335.5	1.5	74.2	40.2	219.5	2,639.0	400.4	2,045.3	193.2
Warner Robins, GA MSA	191,962									
Includes Houston, Peach, and Pulaski Counties										
City of Warner Robins......................................	75,323	385	5	34	132	214	4,107	805	3,072	230
Total area actually reporting............................	100.0%	722	12	46	187	477	7,153	1,313	5,434	406
Rate per 100,000 inhabitants............................		376.1	6.3	24.0	97.4	248.5	3,726.3	684.0	2,830.8	211.5
Washington-Arlington-Alexandria, DC-VA-MD-WV MSA[2]	6,207,972									
Includes the Metropolitan Divisions of Silver Spring-Frederick-Rockville, MD and Washington-Arlington-Alexandria, DC-VA-MD-WV										
City of Washington, D.C.	693,972	6,584	116	443	2,351	3,674	28,843	1,808	24,490	2,545
City of Alexandria, VA......................................	158,256	262	6	16	102	138	2,482	163	2,046	273

(Number, percent, rate per 100,000 population.)

Area	Population	Violent crime	Murder and nonnegligent manslaughter	Rape[1]	Robbery	Aggravated assault	Property crime	Burglary	Larceny-theft	Motor vehicle theft
City of Frederick, MD	70,860	468	1	28	87	352	1,298	148	1,107	43
Total area actually reporting	99.9%	16,953	280	1,782	5,895	8,996	108,091	9,688	89,168	9,235
Estimated total	100.0%	16,973	280	1,785	5,897	9,011	108,355	9,726	89,378	9,251
Rate per 100,000 inhabitants		273.4	4.5	28.8	95.0	145.2	1,745.4	156.7	1,439.7	149.0
Silver Spring-Frederick-Rockville, MD MD[2]	1,304,678									
Includes Frederick and Montgomery[2] Counties										
Total area actually reporting	100.0%	2,166	17	283	777	1,089	17,090	1,874	14,288	928
Rate per 100,000 inhabitants		166.0	1.3	21.7	59.6	83.5	1,309.9	143.6	1,095.1	71.1
Washington-Arlington-Alexandria, DC-VA-MD-WV MD	4,903,294									
Includes District of Columbia; Calvert, Charles, and Prince George's Counties, MD; Arlington, Clarke, Culpeper, Fairfax, Fauquier, Loudoun, Prince William, Rappahannock, Spotsylvania, Stafford, and Warren Counties and Alexandria, Fairfax, Falls Church, Fredericksburg, Manassas, and Manassas Park Cities, VA; and Jefferson County, WV										
Total area actually reporting	99.8%	14,787	263	1,499	5,118	7,907	91,001	7,814	74,880	8,307
Estimated total	100.0%	14,807	263	1,502	5,120	7,922	91,265	7,852	75,090	8,323
Rate per 100,000 inhabitants		302.0	5.4	30.6	104.4	161.6	1,861.3	160.1	1,531.4	169.7
Waterloo-Cedar Falls, IA MSA	170,137									
Includes Black Hawk, Bremer, and Grundy Counties										
City of Waterloo	67,855	341	5	34	53	249	1,927	532	1,253	142
City of Cedar Falls	41,744	86	1	27	6	52	822	128	666	28
Total area actually reporting	94.0%	517	6	77	62	372	3,226	833	2,184	209
Estimated total	100.0%	541	6	81	64	390	3,412	871	2,321	220
Rate per 100,000 inhabitants		318.0	3.5	47.6	37.6	229.2	2,005.4	511.9	1,364.2	129.3
Watertown-Fort Drum, NY MSA	113,858									
Includes Jefferson County										
City of Watertown	25,746	139	1	39	16	83	1,054	153	880	21
Total area actually reporting	99.1%	234	4	84	23	123	2,003	291	1,665	47
Estimated total	100.0%	235	4	84	23	124	2,019	293	1,678	48
Rate per 100,000 inhabitants		206.4	3.5	73.8	20.2	108.9	1,773.3	257.3	1,473.8	42.2
Wausau, WI MSA	135,895									
Includes Marathon County										
City of Wausau	38,832	123	0	32	14	77	736	90	620	26
Total area actually reporting	100.0%	217	4	58	18	137	1,442	195	1,206	41
Rate per 100,000 inhabitants		159.7	2.9	42.7	13.2	100.8	1,061.1	143.5	887.4	30.2
Weirton-Steubenville, WV-OH MSA	118,293									
Includes Jefferson County, OH and Brooke and Hancock Counties, WV										
City of Weirton, WV	18,870	21	0	3	5	13	188	39	134	15
City of Steubenville, OH	17,979	49	3	4	11	31	1,132	89	1,021	22
Total area actually reporting	84.8%	133	4	21	21	87	1,681	228	1,385	68
Estimated total	100.0%	167	4	27	28	108	2,131	294	1,744	93
Rate per 100,000 inhabitants		141.2	3.4	22.8	23.7	91.3	1,801.5	248.5	1,474.3	78.6
Wenatchee, WA MSA	119,117									
Includes Chelan and Douglas Counties										
City of Wenatchee	34,191	73	1	18	16	38	818	123	647	48
Total area actually reporting	100.0%	140	2	35	25	78	2,068	417	1,513	138
Rate per 100,000 inhabitants		117.5	1.7	29.4	21.0	65.5	1,736.1	350.1	1,270.2	115.9
Wheeling, WV-OH MSA	141,891									
Includes Belmont County, OH and Marshall and Ohio Counties, WV										
City of Wheeling, WV	27,196	332	2	15	31	284	584	153	407	24
Total area actually reporting	83.7%	465	5	42	38	380	1,467	314	1,063	90
Estimated total	100.0%	515	5	51	45	414	1,904	396	1,386	122
Rate per 100,000 inhabitants		363.0	3.5	35.9	31.7	291.8	1,341.9	279.1	976.8	86.0
Wichita, KS MSA[3]	646,209									
Includes Butler, Harvey, Kingman, Sedgwick,[3] and Sumner Counties										
City of Wichita	391,084	3,998	35	382	599	2,982	21,649	3,281	15,890	2,478
Total area actually reporting	99.4%	4,671	44	486	645	3,496			19,971	2,896
Estimated total	100.0%	4,680	44	488	646	3,502			20,036	2,903

Table 4. Crime, by Selected Metropolitan Statistical Area, 2017—*Continued*

(Number, percent, rate per 100,000 population.)

Area	Population	Violent crime	Murder and nonnegligent manslaughter	Rape[1]	Robbery	Aggravated assault	Property crime	Burglary	Larceny-theft	Motor vehicle theft
Rate per 100,000 inhabitants.................		724.2	6.8	75.5	100.0	541.9			3,100.5	449.2
Wichita Falls, TX MSA[2].................	150,431									
Includes Archer, Clay, and Wichita Counties										
City of Wichita Falls	104,706	374	4	78	127	165	3,257	725	2,294	238
Total area actually reporting.................	97.7%	491	6	103	132	250	4,020	926	2,784	310
Estimated total.................	100.0%	501	6	105	134	256	4,098	938	2,844	316
Rate per 100,000 inhabitants.................		333.0	4.0	69.8	89.1	170.2	2,724.2	623.5	1,890.6	210.1
Williamsport, PA MSA.................	115,169									
Includes Lycoming County										
City of Williamsport.................	28,743	107	2	12	27	66	880	119	741	20
Total area actually reporting.................	100.0%	211	2	29	35	145	1,887	292	1,557	38
Rate per 100,000 inhabitants.................		183.2	1.7	25.2	30.4	125.9	1,638.5	253.5	1,351.9	33.0
Wilmington, NC MSA[4].................	287,932									
Includes New Hanover and Pender Counties[4]										
City of Wilmington[4]	119,422		18		195	535	4,318	998	3,039	281
Total area actually reporting.................	99.1%		25		257	706	7,883	1,793	5,700	390
Estimated total.................	100.0%		25		259	710	7,955	1,806	5,756	393
Rate per 100,000 inhabitants.................			8.7		90.0	246.6	2,762.8	627.2	1,999.1	136.5
Winchester, VA-WV MSA.................	136,089									
Includes Frederick County and Winchester City, VA and										
Hampshire County, WV										
City of Winchester, VA.................	27,715	115	0	36	25	54	688	81	584	23
Total area actually reporting.................	84.3%	217	0	77	43	97	1,907	239	1,578	90
Estimated total.................	100.0%	277	1	86	46	144	2,214	319	1,769	126
Rate per 100,000 inhabitants.................		203.5	0.7	63.2	33.8	105.8	1,626.9	234.4	1,299.9	92.6
Worcester, MA-CT MSA.................	865,611									
Includes Windham County, CT and Worcester County, MA										
City of Worcester, MA.................	185,107	1,345	5	42	324	974	4,047	866	2,784	397
Total area actually reporting.................	94.7%	2,986	10	279	475	2,222	11,051	2,055	8,198	798
Estimated total.................	100.0%	3,118	11	293	496	2,318	11,636	2,154	8,641	841
Rate per 100,000 inhabitants.................		360.2	1.3	33.8	57.3	267.8	1,344.3	248.8	998.3	97.2
Yakima, WA MSA.................	251,281									
Includes Yakima County										
City of Yakima.................	94,375	593	13	70	150	360	4,306	901	2,841	564
Total area actually reporting.................	100.0%	893	22	105	211	555	8,128	1,760	5,230	1,138
Rate per 100,000 inhabitants.................		355.4	8.8	41.8	84.0	220.9	3,234.6	700.4	2,081.3	452.9
York-Hanover, PA MSA.................	445,423									
Includes York County										
City of York.................	43,857	472	14	10	191	257	1,288	251	885	152
City of Hanover.................	15,606	36	0	2	10	24	378	32	340	6
Total area actually reporting.................	100.0%	1,098	23	108	301	666	6,492	860	5,294	338
Rate per 100,000 inhabitants.................		246.5	5.2	24.2	67.6	149.5	1,457.5	193.1	1,188.5	75.9
Yuba City, CA MSA.................	172,545									
Includes Sutter and Yuba Counties										
City of Yuba City.................	67,042	255	0	23	82	150	2,207	380	1,448	379
Total area actually reporting.................	100.0%	667	4	55	146	462	4,919	1,160	2,785	974
Rate per 100,000 inhabitants.................		386.6	2.3	31.9	84.6	267.8	2,850.9	672.3	1,614.1	564.5
Yuma, AZ MSA.................	206,897									
Includes Yuma County										
City of Yuma.................	95,522	491	5	49	90	347	2,595	502	1,874	219
Total area actually reporting.................	100.0%	725	17	74	106	528	4,307	1,046	2,837	424
Rate per 100,000 inhabitants.................		350.4	8.2	35.8	51.2	255.2	2,081.7	505.6	1,371.2	204.9
Aguadilla-Isabela, Puerto Rico MSA.................	302,615									
Includes Aguada, Aguadilla, Anasco, Isabela, Lares, Moca, Rincon, San Sebastian, and Utuado Municipios										
Total area actually reporting.................	100.0%	495	19	15	96	365	1,857	715	1,062	80
Rate per 100,000 inhabitants.................		163.6	6.3	5.0	31.7	120.6	613.7	236.3	350.9	26.4

Table 4. Crime, by Selected Metropolitan Statistical Area, 2017—*Continued*

(Number, percent, rate per 100,000 population.)

Area	Population	Violent crime	Murder and nonnegligent manslaughter	Rape[1]	Robbery	Aggravated assault	Property crime	Burglary	Larceny-theft	Motor vehicle theft
Arecibo, Puerto Rico MSA	181,643									
Includes Arecibo, Camuy, Hatillo, and Quebradillas Municipios										
Total area actually reporting..................................	100.0%	321	15	9	92	205	1,180	319	760	101
Rate per 100,000 inhabitants.................................		176.7	8.3	5.0	50.6	112.9	649.6	175.6	418.4	55.6
Guayama, Puerto Rico MSA	76,166									
Includes Arroyo, Guayama, and Patillas Municipios										
Total area actually reporting..................................	100.0%	175	14	3	24	134	501	203	282	16
Rate per 100,000 inhabitants.................................		229.8	18.4	3.9	31.5	175.9	657.8	266.5	370.2	21.0
Mayaguez, Puerto Rico MSA	91,557									
Includes Hormigueros and Mayaguez Municipios										
Total area actually reporting..................................	100.0%	163	10	6	45	102	820	165	617	38
Rate per 100,000 inhabitants.................................		178.0	10.9	6.6	49.1	111.4	895.6	180.2	673.9	41.5
Ponce, Puerto Rico MSA	300,843									
Includes Guanica, Guyanilla, Juana Diaz, Penuelas, Ponce, Villalba, and Yauco Municipios										
Total area actually reporting..................................	100.0%	834	52	16	179	587	2,289	522	1,674	93
Rate per 100,000 inhabitants.................................		277.2	17.3	5.3	59.5	195.1	760.9	173.5	556.4	30.9
San German, Puerto Rico MSA	126,097									
Includes Cabo Rojo, Lajas, Sabana Grande, and San German Municipios										
Total area actually reporting..................................	100.0%	141	9	5	19	108	459	158	281	20
Rate per 100,000 inhabitants.................................		111.8	7.1	4.0	15.1	85.6	364.0	125.3	222.8	15.9
San Juan-Carolina-Caguas, Puerto Rico MSA	2,112,005									
Includes Aguas Buenas, Aibonito, Barceloneta, Barranquitas, Bayamon, Caguas, Canovanas, Carolina, Catano, Cayey, Ceiba, Ciales, Cidra, Comerio, Corozal, Dorado, Fajardo, Florida, Guaynabo, Gurabo, Humacao, Juncos, Las Piedras, Loiza, Luquillo, Manati, Maunabo, Morovis, Naguabo, Naranjito, Orocovis, Rio Grande, San Juan, San Lorenzo, Toa Alta, Toa Baja, Trujillo Alto, Vega Alta, Vega Baja, and Yabucoa Municipios										
Total area actually reporting..................................	100.0%	5,380	539	147	2,546	2,148	23,103	5,524	14,369	3,210
Rate per 100,000 inhabitants.................................		254.7	25.5	7.0	120.5	101.7	1,093.9	261.6	680.3	152.0

[1] The figures shown in this column for the offense of rape were reported using only the revised Uniform Crime Reporting (UCR) definition of rape.
[2] Because of changes in the state/local agency's reporting practices, figures are not comparable to previous years' data.
[3] The FBI determined that the agency's data were overreported. Consequently, those data are not included in this table.
[4] One or more agency(s) wihin this Metropolitan Statistical Area submitted rape data classified according to the legacy UCR definition.
[5] The FBI determined that the agency's data were underreported. Consequently, those data are not included in this table.
[6] The FBI determined that the agency did not follow national UCR Program guidelines for reporting an offense. Consequently, this figure is not included in this table.
[7] The population for the city of Mobile, Alabama, includes 55,819 inhabitants from the jurisdiction of the Mobile County Sheriff's Department.

Table 5. Offense Analysis, United States, 2013–2017

(Number.)

Classification	2013	2014	2015	2016[1]	2017[1]
Murder	14,319	14,164	15,883	17,413	17,284
Rape[2]	113,695	118,027	126,134	132,414	135,755
Robbery[3]	345,093	322,905	328,109	332,797	319,356
By location					
Street/highway	146,499	132,269	130,724	129,337	118,719
Commercial house	45,760	45,273	47,229	50,785	49,462
Gas or service station	8,354	8,072	8,916	9,708	9,566
Convenience store	17,103	17,380	18,661	20,656	20,967
Residence	57,372	54,120	54,142	55,102	51,062
Bank	6,512	5,939	5,691	5,914	5,420
Miscellaneous	63,495	59,853	62,747	61,296	64,161
Burglary[3]	1,932,139	1,713,153	1,587,564	1,516,405	1,401,840
By location					
Residence (dwelling)	1,428,448	1,253,915	1,136,664	1,054,470	942,734
Residence, night	395,604	349,441	328,736	311,805	286,338
Residence, day	756,617	669,364	594,668	543,930	476,123
Residence, unknown	276,227	235,111	213,260	198,735	180,273
Nonresidence (store, office, etc.)	503,691	459,238	450,900	461,935	459,106
Nonresidence, night	206,031	188,010	189,167	199,741	201,548
Nonresidence, day	183,380	167,749	159,177	159,630	157,915
Nonresidence, unknown	114,280	103,480	102,556	102,564	99,643
Larceny-theft (except motor vehicle theft)[3]	6,019,465	5,809,054	5,723,488	5,644,835	5,519,107
By type					
Pocket-picking	32,426	31,213	31,208	27,648	31,060
Purse-snatching	25,867	23,479	23,144	22,671	21,985
Shoplifting	1,199,157	1,247,199	1,276,575	1,179,137	1,146,216
From motor vehicles (except accessories)	1,405,858	1,332,924	1,373,720	1,477,587	1,479,321
Motor vehicle accessories	439,151	408,545	399,452	415,590	407,468
Bicycles	212,889	209,762	205,600	184,546	174,997
From buildings	740,092	712,073	664,381	605,765	587,261
From coin-operated machines	15,906	13,328	13,020	12,349	12,028
All others	1,948,120	1,830,531	1,736,388	1,719,542	1,658,771
By value					
Under $50	1,857,474	1,815,113	1,832,128	1,861,970	1,815,743
$50 to $200	1,342,473	1,306,350	1,278,027	1,221,246	1,170,907
Over $200	2,819,518	2,687,591	2,613,333	2,561,619	2,532,457
Motor vehicle theft	700,288	686,803	713,063	767,290	773,139

[1] The crime figures have been adjusted.
[2] The figures shown for this offense of rape were estimated using the revised Uniform Crime Reporting (UCR) definition of rape.
[3] Because of rounding, the number of offenses may not add to the total.

Table 6. Crime Trends, by Population Group, 2016–2017

(Number, percent change.)

Population group	Violent crime	Murder and nonnegligent manslaughter	Rape[1]	Robbery	Aggravated assault	Property crime	Burglary	Larceny-theft	Motor vehicle theft	Arson	Number of agencies	Estimated population, 2017
Total, All Agencies												
2016	1,227,452	16,651	117,581	323,903	769,317	7,541,358	1,430,698	5,372,029	738,631	41,870		
2017	1,227,262	16,617	121,745	310,861	778,039	7,320,839	1,321,995	5,254,838	744,006	41,171	15,426	310,003,377
Percent change	*	-0.2	+3.5	-4.0	+1.1	-2.9	-7.6	-2.2	+0.7	-1.7		
Total, Cities												
2016	988,373	12,987	88,310	285,013	602,063	6,002,396	1,056,562	4,349,999	595,835	31,894		
2017	989,231	13,191	91,715	274,251	610,074	5,846,576	983,667	4,264,233	598,676	31,974	11,205	211,301,356
Percent change	+0.1	+1.6	+3.9	-3.8	+1.3	-2.6	-6.9	-2.0	+0.5	+0.3		
Group I (250,000 and over)												
2016	474,307	6,949	33,468	160,290	273,600	2,073,439	372,144	1,428,206	273,089	12,467		
2017	474,713	6,794	34,842	154,648	278,429	2,053,980	355,012	1,426,420	272,548	12,826	83	62,030,546
Percent change	+0.1	-2.2	+4.1	-3.5	+1.8	-0.9	-4.6	-0.1	-0.2	+2.9		
1,000,000 and over (Group I subset)												
2016	201,743	2,691	14,045	71,655	113,352	742,376	125,318	517,249	99,809	4,226		
2017	200,277	2,473	14,809	68,685	114,310	735,685	119,624	518,657	97,404	4,176	11	27,835,810
Percent change	-0.7	-8.1	+5.4	-4.1	+0.8	-0.9	-4.5	+0.3	-2.4	-1.2		
500,000 to 999,999 (Group I subset)												
2016	149,231	2,253	10,365	48,418	88,195	732,805	133,169	506,671	92,965	4,351		
2017	152,639	2,358	10,839	47,894	91,548	728,714	130,372	504,515	93,827	4,831	24	17,571,403
Percent change	+2.3	+4.7	+4.6	-1.1	+3.8	-0.6	-2.1	-0.4	+0.9	+11.0		
250,000 to 499,999 (Group I subset)												
2016	123,333	2,005	9,058	40,217	72,053	598,258	113,657	404,286	80,315	3,890		
2017	121,797	1,963	9,194	38,069	72,571	589,581	105,016	403,248	81,317	3,819	48	16,623,333
Percent change	-1.2	-2.1	+1.5	-5.3	+0.7	-1.5	-7.6	-0.3	+1.2	-1.8		
Group II (100,000 to 249,999)												
2016	158,660	2,137	15,152	45,781	95,590	1,054,235	189,689	745,706	118,840	5,192		
2017	158,515	2,282	15,710	43,864	96,659	1,028,358	175,848	733,964	118,546	5,095	223	33,279,937
Percent change	-0.1	+6.8	+3.7	-4.2	+1.1	-2.5	-7.3	-1.6	-0.2	-1.9		
Group III (50,000 to 99,999)												
2016	117,544	1,283	11,884	31,586	72,791	884,845	154,139	649,430	81,276	4,353		
2017	117,529	1,376	12,310	31,025	72,818	853,912	140,936	631,474	81,502	4,478	484	33,749,285
Percent change	*	+7.2	+3.6	-1.8	*	-3.5	-8.6	-2.8	+0.3	+2.9		
Group IV (25,000 to 49,999)												
2016	90,162	1,055	10,063	21,811	57,233	739,484	126,324	562,060	51,100	3,292		
2017	90,057	1,100	10,513	20,834	57,610	706,705	113,898	540,864	51,943	3,250	875	30,423,643
Percent change	-0.1	+4.3	+4.5	-4.5	+0.7	-4.4	-9.8	-3.8	+1.6	-1.3		
Group V (10,000 to 24,999)												
2016	76,670	879	8,929	15,845	51,017	673,637	117,372	515,744	40,521	2,905		
2017	76,916	868	9,285	14,905	51,858	647,140	107,002	498,276	41,862	2,811	1,798	28,686,467
Percent change	+0.3	-1.3	+4.0	-5.9	+1.6	-3.9	-8.8	-3.4	+3.3	-3.2		
Group VI (under 10,000)												
2016	71,030	684	8,814	9,700	51,832	576,756	96,894	448,853	31,009	3,685		
2017	71,501	771	9,055	8,975	52,700	556,481	90,971	433,235	32,275	3,514	7,742	23,131,478
Percent change	+0.7	+12.7	+2.7	-7.5	+1.7	-3.5	-6.1	-3.5	+4.1	-4.6		
Metropolitan Counties												
2016	190,966	2,770	20,915	36,125	131,156	1,243,670	281,127	843,894	118,649	7,468		
2017	189,421	2,613	21,628	33,967	131,213	1,190,522	250,712	820,600	119,210	6,849	1,915	74,252,901
Percent change	-0.8	-5.7	+3.4	-6.0	*	-4.3	-10.8	-2.8	+0.5	-8.3		
Nonmetropolitan Counties[2]												
2016	48,113	894	8,356	2,765	36,098	295,292	93,009	178,136	24,147	2,508		
2017	48,610	813	8,402	2,643	36,752	283,741	87,616	170,005	26,120	2,348	2,306	24,449,120
Percent change	+1.0	-9.1	+0.6	-4.4	+1.8	-3.9	-5.8	-4.6	+8.2	-6.4		
Suburban Areas[3]												
2016	333,810	4,273	38,034	68,830	222,673	2,542,241	485,703	1,851,550	204,988	13,574		
2017	332,467	4,191	39,460	65,205	223,611	2,439,671	437,162	1,795,372	207,137	12,635	8,522	134,599,243
Percent change	-0.4	-1.9	+3.7	-5.3	+0.4	-4.0	-10.0	-3.0	+1.0	-6.9		

* = Less than one-tenth of one percent.
[1]The figures shown in the rape (revised definition) column include only those reported by law enforcement agencies that used the revised Uniform Crime Reporting (UCR) definition of rape.
[2]Includes state police agencies that report aggregately for the entire state.
[3]Suburban areas include law enforcement agencies in cities with less than 50,000 inhabitants and county law enforcement agencies that are within a Metropolitan Statistical Area. Suburban areas exclude all metropolitan agencies associated with a principal city. The agencies associated with suburban areas also appear in other groups within this table.

Table 7. Rate: Number of Crimes Per 100,000 Population, by Population Group, 2017

(Number, rate.)

Population group	Violent crime		Murder and nonnegligent manslaughter		Rape[1]		Robbery		Aggravated assault	
	Number of offenses known	Rate	Number of offenses known	Rate	Number of offenses known	Rate	Number of offenses known	Rate	Number of offenses known	Rate
Total, All Agencies..	1,221,775	400.0	16,446	5.4	125,591	42.4	308,936	101.2	770,802	252.4
Total, Cities	981,574	469.6	12,999	6.2	94,045	46.2	272,035	130.2	602,495	288.3
Group I (250,000 and over).........................	472,560	768.5	6,783	11.0	35,845	59.7	154,090	250.6	275,842	448.6
1,000,000 and over (Group I subset)	200,277	719.5	2,473	8.9	14,809	53.2	68,685	246.8	114,310	410.7
500,000 to 999,999 (Group I subset)	152,876	870.0	2,358	13.4	11,076	66.5	47,894	272.6	91,548	521.0
250,000 to 499,999 (Group I subset)	119,407	742.4	1,952	12.1	9,960	64.2	37,511	233.2	69,984	435.1
Group II (100,000 to 249,999).....................	152,713	473.2	2,121	6.6	15,434	49.0	42,351	131.2	92,807	287.6
Group III (50,000 to 99,999)	119,145	347.9	1,386	4.0	12,730	38.2	31,337	91.5	73,692	215.1
Group IV (25,000 to 49,999)........................	89,414	297.8	1,068	3.6	11,032	37.6	20,451	68.1	56,863	189.4
Group V (10,000 to 24,999)	77,009	269.6	873	3.1	9,714	35.0	14,860	52.0	51,562	180.5
Group VI (under 10,000)..............................	70,733	315.6	768	3.4	9,290	42.6	8,946	39.9	51,729	230.8
Metropolitan Counties	191,537	262.9	2,629	3.6	22,769	32.5	34,301	47.1	131,838	180.9
Nonmetropolitan Counties[2]	48,664	206.7	818	3.5	8,777	39.2	2,600	11.0	36,469	154.9
Suburban Areas[3]	335,122	252.9	4,208	3.2	41,219	32.1	65,527	49.4	224,168	169.1

(Number, rate.)

Population group	Property crime		Burglary		Larceny-theft		Motor vehicle theft		Number of agencies	Estimated population, 2017
	Number of offenses known	Rate	Number of offenses known	Rate	Number of offenses known	Rate	Number of offenses known	Rate		
Total, All Agencies......................................	7,265,640	2,378.9	1,310,687	429.1	5,212,721	1,706.7	742,232	243.0	14,815	305,422,610
Total, Cities	5,792,834	2,771.5	972,529	465.3	4,224,859	2,021.3	595,446	284.9	10,828	209,015,851
Group I (250,000 and over)..........................	2,034,977	3,309.4	351,565	571.7	1,412,427	2,297.0	270,985	440.7	81	61,490,148
1,000,000 and over (Group I subset)	735,685	2,642.9	119,624	429.7	518,657	1,863.3	97,404	349.9	11	27,835,810
500,000 to 999,999 (Group I subset)	728,714	4,147.2	130,372	742.0	504,515	2,871.2	93,827	534.0	24	17,571,403
250,000 to 499,999 (Group I subset)	570,578	3,547.7	101,569	631.5	389,255	2,420.3	79,754	495.9	46	16,082,935
Group II (100,000 to 249,999)	994,848	3,082.9	169,373	524.9	709,243	2,197.9	116,232	360.2	217	32,269,399
Group III (50,000 to 99,999)	868,714	2,536.3	143,162	418.0	643,254	1,878.0	82,298	240.3	491	34,251,807
Group IV (25,000 to 49,999)........................	695,293	2,316.1	112,415	374.5	531,582	1,770.7	51,296	170.9	864	30,020,188
Group V (10,000 to 24,999)	648,930	2,271.4	106,387	372.4	500,122	1,750.6	42,421	148.5	1,789	28,569,221
Group VI (under 10,000).............................	550,072	2,454.0	89,627	399.9	428,231	1,910.5	32,214	143.7	7,386	22,415,088
Metropolitan Counties	1,189,830	1,633.0	251,079	344.6	817,962	1,122.6	120,789	165.8	1,828	72,861,356
Nonmetropolitan Counties[2]	282,976	1,201.8	87,079	369.8	169,900	721.6	25,997	110.4	2,159	23,545,403
Suburban Areas[3]	2,435,027	1,837.3	437,119	329.8	1,788,884	1,349.8	209,024	157.7	8,245	132,531,489

[1]The figures shown in this column for the offense of rape were reported using only the revised Uniform Crime Reporting definition of rape.
[2]Includes state police agencies that report aggregately for the entire state.
[3]Suburban areas include law enforcement agencies in cities with less than 50,000 inhabitants and county law enforcement agencies that are within a Metropolitan Statistical Area. Suburban areas exclude all metropolitan agencies associated with a principal city. The agencies associated with suburban areas also appear in other groups within this table.

Table 8. Offense Analysis, Number and Percent Change, 2016–2017

(Number.)

Classification	Number of offenses, 2017	Percent change from 2016	Percent distribution[1]	Average value (dollars)
Murder..	15,094	-11.8	NA	X
Rape[2]	106,854	+3.7	NA	X
Robbery...	280,507	-4.3	100.0	$1,373
By location				
Street/highway..	104,277	-8.1	37.2	1,202
Commercial house	43,445	+0.1	15.5	1,284
Gas or service station	8,402	+3.3	3.0	1,087
Convenience store..	18,416	+5.6	6.6	957
Residence..	44,850	-7.3	16.0	1,732
Bank	4,761	-7.1	1.7	3,483
Miscellaneous...	56,356	-1.2	20.1	1,474
Burglary	1,250,983	-7.4	100.0	2,416
By location				
Residence (dwelling)...	841,283	-12.0	67.2	2,368
Residence, night..	255,524	-8.2	20.4	1,995
Residence, day...	424,886	-11.8	34.0	2,383
Residence, unknown.......................................	160,873	-11.6	12.9	2,924
Nonresidence (store, office, etc.)	409,700	+1.2	32.8	2,514
Nonresidence, night.......................................	179,859	+1.9	14.4	2,337
Nonresidence, day	140,921	+0.5	11.3	2,211
Nonresidence, unknown	88,920	-4.3	7.1	3,353
Larceny-theft (except motor vehicle theft).........................	4,917,272	-2.5	100.0	1,007
By type				
Pocket-picking..	27,673	+0.7	0.6	648
Purse-snatching..	19,588	-5.0	0.4	564
Shoplifting	1,021,226	-3.9	20.8	260
From motor vehicles (except accessories)	1,318,007	+0.5	26.8	879
Motor vehicle accessories	363,035	-1.1	7.4	505
Bicycles	155,914	-6.1	3.2	477
From buildings	523,223	-6.7	10.6	1,381
From coin-operated machines	10,716	-5.7	0.2	538
All others	1,477,890	-2.6	30.1	1,700
By value				
Over $200...	2,256,303	-1.9	45.9	2,137
$50 to $200..	1,043,225	-4.2	21.2	105
Under $50...	1,617,744	-2.4	32.9	13
Motor Vehicle Theft.......................................	705,254	+0.5	NA	7,708

NA = Not available.
X = Not applicable.
* = Less than one-tenth of one percent.
[1]Because of rounding, the percentages may not add to 100.0.
[2]The rape figure in this table is an aggregate total of the data submitted using both the revised and legacy Uniform Crime Reporting definitions. See the chapter notes for further explanation.

Table 9. Property Stolen and Recovered, by Type and Value, 2017

(Dollars, percent; 13,681 agencies; 2017 estimated population 282,407,733.)

Type of property	Value of property (dollars)		Percent recovered
	Stolen	Recovered	
Total	$13,505,923,310	$3,938,510,699	29.2
Currency, notes, etc.	1,366,020,962	26,879,881	2.0
Jewelry and precious metals	1,213,092,968	43,196,761	3.6
Clothing and furs	376,921,356	37,029,432	9.8
Locally stolen motor vehicles	5,562,733,246	3,289,374,602	59.1
Office equipment	451,608,653	24,186,462	5.4
Televisions, radios, stereos, etc.	394,508,873	24,585,471	6.2
Firearms	151,910,488	22,230,563	14.6
Household goods	266,677,409	10,389,743	3.9
Consumable goods	134,257,875	13,128,523	9.8
Livestock	18,251,205	2,755,916	15.1
Miscellaneous	3,569,940,275	444,753,345	12.5

Table 10. Number and Percent of Offenses Cleared by Arrest or Exceptional Means, by Population Group, 2017

(Number, percent.)

Population group	Violent crime	Murder and nonnegligent manslaughter	Rape[1]	Robbery	Aggravated assault	Property crime	Burglary	Larceny-theft	Motor vehicle theft	Arson[2]	Number of agencies	Estimated population, 2017
Total, All Agencies												
Offenses known	1,177,632	15,657	121,084	293,160	747,731	7,074,399	1,281,083	5,072,970	720,346	40,416	14,975	297,646,423
Percent cleared by arrest	45.6	61.6	34.5	29.7	53.3	17.6	13.5	19.2	13.7	21.7		
Total Cities												
Offenses known	942,624	12,288	90,329	257,523	582,484	5,646,734	951,113	4,113,790	581,831	31,105	10,968	202,173,273
Percent cleared by arrest	43.6	60.3	33.0	29.1	51.4	17.4	12.8	19.2	12.4	20.7		
Group I (250,000 and over)												
Offenses known	443,507	6,188	34,061	142,364	260,894	1,953,831	339,700	1,354,430	259,701	12,493	81	59,068,040
Percent cleared by arrest	39.0	59.6	33.6	26.5	46.0	11.9	10.0	12.9	9.2	15.1		
1,000,000 and over (Group I subset)												
Offenses known	170,598	1,878	13,047	56,798	98,875	647,361	106,712	454,823	85,826	3,662	10	25,129,639
Percent cleared by arrest	44.0	69.1	34.7	31.0	52.1	11.8	10.1	12.8	8.8	14.1		
500,000 to 999,999 (Group I subset)												
Offenses known	152,876	2,358	11,076	47,894	91,548	728,714	130,372	504,515	93,827	4,831	24	17,571,403
Percent cleared by arrest	35.2	57.1	35.2	22.9	41.0	10.4	9.1	11.1	8.5	15.5		
250,000 to 499,999 (Group I subset)												
Offenses known	120,033	1,952	9,938	37,672	70,471	577,756	102,616	395,092	80,048	4,000	47	16,366,998
Percent cleared by arrest	36.7	53.3	30.5	24.3	43.8	13.7	10.8	15.1	10.5	15.6		
Group II (100,000 to 249,999)												
Offenses known	152,832	2,162	15,091	42,443	93,136	993,919	168,996	707,837	117,086	4,811	213	31,855,061
Percent cleared by arrest	42.3	58.8	31.9	28.5	49.8	15.7	12.0	17.2	12.3	23.2		
Group III (50,000 to 99,999)												
Offenses known	115,050	1,322	12,256	30,104	71,368	840,693	138,454	621,712	80,527	4,429	469	32,747,541
Percent cleared by arrest	48.2	63.4	34.2	32.9	56.9	18.6	13.1	20.5	13.0	22.1		
Group IV (25,000 to 49,999)												
Offenses known	85,734	1,015	10,548	19,837	54,334	680,453	109,920	519,732	50,801	3,068	828	28,843,794
Percent cleared by arrest	48.1	63.5	32.0	34.1	56.0	22.2	14.5	24.5	15.4	23.9		
Group V (10,000 to 24,999)												
Offenses known	74,858	845	9,291	14,031	50,691	636,078	104,476	489,861	41,741	2,776	1,715	27,384,738
Percent cleared by arrest	51.9	63.3	33.9	36.4	59.2	24.7	16.4	27.0	18.8	26.4		
Group VI (under 10,000)												
Offenses known	70,643	756	9,082	8,744	52,061	541,760	89,567	420,218	31,975	3,528	7,662	22,274,099
Percent cleared by arrest	54.2	58.3	31.3	37.7	61.0	24.5	17.9	25.9	24.2	28.4		
Metropolitan Counties												
Offenses known	186,998	2,556	22,162	32,995	129,285	1,149,484	243,886	792,143	113,455	6,989	1,857	71,893,861
Percent cleared by arrest	52.5	64.7	39.6	33.3	59.4	17.9	15.3	18.7	17.4	23.8		
Nonmetropolitan Counties												
Offenses known	48,010	813	8,593	2,642	35,962	278,181	86,084	167,037	25,060	2,322	2,150	23,579,289
Percent cleared by arrest	56.6	71.2	36.7	42.8	62.1	19.4	17.0	19.8	25.6	27.5		
Suburban Areas[3]												
Offenses known	324,524	4,036	39,641	62,504	218,343	2,353,692	424,177	1,729,649	199,866	12,613	8,189	128,800,806
Percent cleared by arrest	52.1	63.9	37.1	34.5	59.6	20.4	15.5	21.9	17.1	24.6		

[1] The figures shown in the rape column include only those reported by law enforcement agencies that used the revised Uniform Crime Reporting definition of rape.
[2] Not all agencies submit reports for arson to the FBI. As a result, the number of reports the FBI uses to compute the percent of offenses cleared for arson is less than the number it uses to compute the percent of offenses cleared for all other offenses.
[3] Suburban area includes law enforcement agencies in cities with less than 50,000 inhabitants and county law enforcement agencies that are within a Metropolitan Statistical Area. Suburban area excludes all metropolitan agencies associated with a principal city. The agencies associated with suburban areas also appear in other groups within this table.

Table 11. Estimated Number of Arrests, 2017

(Number.)

Offense	Arrests
Total[1]	10,797,088
Violent crime[2]	505,681
Murder and nonnegligent manslaughter	11,092
Rape[3]	22,863
Robbery	95,572
Aggravated assault	376,154
Property crime[2]	1,463,213
Burglary	216,010
Larceny-theft	1,160,390
Motor vehicle theft	77,979
Arson	8,834
Other assaults	1,081,019
Forgery and counterfeiting	55,333
Fraud	133,138
Embezzlement	15,909
Stolen property; buying, receiving, possessing	88,576
Vandalism	191,015
Weapons; carrying, possessing, etc.	145,358
Prostitution and commercialized vice	41,877
Sex offenses (except forcible rape and prostitution)	51,388
Drug abuse violations	1,488,707
Gambling	4,825
Offenses against the family and children	94,837
Driving under the influence	1,089,171
Liquor laws	266,250
Drunkenness	405,880
Disorderly conduct	386,078
Vagrancy	25,151
All other offenses	3,218,880
Suspicion	1,389
Curfew and loitering law violations	44,802

[1] Does not include suspicion.
[2] Violent crimes are offenses of murder and nonnegligent manslaughter, rape, robbery, and aggravated assault. Property crimes are offenses of burglary, larceny-theft, motor vehicle theft, and arson.
[3] The rape figures in this table are an aggregate total of the data submitted using both the revised and legacy Uniform Crime Reporting definitions.

Table 12. Number and Rate of Arrests, by Geographic Region, 2017

(Number, rate per 100,000 inhabitants.)

Offense charged	United States total (12,606 agencies; population 253,634,894)		Northeast (3,233 agencies; population 45,428,011)		Midwest (3,082 agencies; population 49,278,965)		South (4,502 agencies; population 86,203,577)		West (1,789 agencies; population 72,724,341)	
	Total	Rate	Total	Rate	Total	Rate	Total	Rate	Total	Rate
Total[1]	8,246,901	3,251.5	1,257,202	2,767.5	1,569,268	3,184.5	3,084,662	3,578.3	2,335,769	3,211.8
Violent crime[2]	407,496	160.7	57,707	127.0	64,884	131.7	124,694	144.7	160,211	220.3
Murder and nonnegligent manslaughter	9,576	3.8	1,066	2.3	1,742	3.5	4,259	4.9	2,509	3.5
Rape[3]	18,289	7.2	3,221	7.1	4,162	8.4	5,865	6.8	5,041	6.9
Robbery	74,340	29.3	13,223	29.1	11,026	22.4	24,391	28.3	25,700	35.3
Aggravated assault	305,291	120.4	40,197	88.5	47,954	97.3	90,179	104.6	126,961	174.6
Property crime[2]	985,847	388.7	160,109	352.4	198,631	403.1	366,855	425.6	260,252	357.9
Burglary	156,465	61.7	21,099	46.4	22,020	44.7	56,384	65.4	56,962	78.3
Larceny-theft	750,750	296.0	131,267	289.0	161,587	327.9	287,753	333.8	170,143	234.0
Motor vehicle theft	71,452	28.2	6,682	14.7	13,771	27.9	20,542	23.8	30,457	41.9
Arson	7,180	2.8	1,061	2.3	1,253	2.5	2,176	2.5	2,690	3.7
Other assaults	833,396	328.6	143,010	314.8	160,928	326.6	321,278	372.7	208,180	286.3
Forgery and counterfeiting	43,534	17.2	7,775	17.1	7,737	15.7	18,294	21.2	9,728	13.4
Fraud	96,948	38.2	19,418	42.7	18,044	36.6	41,515	48.2	17,971	24.7
Embezzlement	12,532	4.9	1,367	3.0	2,383	4.8	6,621	7.7	2,161	3.0
Stolen property; buying, receiving, possessing	77,474	30.5	10,967	24.1	12,732	25.8	25,494	29.6	28,281	38.9
Vandalism	147,959	58.3	32,400	71.3	27,565	55.9	38,140	44.2	49,854	68.6
Weapons; carrying, possessing, etc.	129,210	50.9	15,608	34.4	26,392	53.6	45,379	52.6	41,831	57.5
Prostitution and commercialized vice	28,490	11.2	4,313	9.5	3,224	6.5	8,918	10.3	12,035	16.5
Sex offenses (except forcible rape and prostitution)	37,850	14.9	5,980	13.2	6,807	13.8	10,846	12.6	14,217	19.5
Drug abuse violations	1,275,812	503.0	228,158	502.2	232,060	470.9	477,504	553.9	338,090	464.9
Gambling	2,510	1.0	350	0.8	675	1.4	998	1.2	487	0.7
Offenses against the family and children	72,229	28.5	14,965	32.9	15,804	32.1	30,413	35.3	11,047	15.2
Driving under the influence	764,569	301.4	125,609	276.5	149,100	302.6	237,517	275.5	252,343	347.0
Liquor laws	161,277	63.6	20,672	45.5	56,259	114.2	42,387	49.2	41,959	57.7
Drunkenness	289,608	114.2	30,363	66.8	22,236	45.1	150,064	174.1	86,945	119.6
Disorderly conduct	276,987	109.2	72,124	158.8	84,750	172.0	73,728	85.5	46,385	63.8
Vagrancy	18,542	7.3	1,330	2.9	3,248	6.6	4,020	4.7	9,944	13.7
All other offenses (except traffic)	2,560,932	1,009.7	297,618	655.1	470,861	955.5	1,053,738	1,222.4	738,715	1,015.8
Suspicion	690	0.3	10	*	115	0.2	178	0.2	387	0.5
Curfew and loitering law violations	23,699	9.3	7,359	16.2	4,948	10.0	6,259	7.3	5,133	7.1

* = Less than one-tenth of one percent.
[1]Does not include suspicion.
[2]Violent crimes are offenses of murder and nonnegligent manslaughter, rape, robbery, and aggravated assault. Property crimes are offenses of burglary, larceny-theft, motor vehicle theft, and arson.
[3]The rape figures in this table are aggregate totals of the data submitted based on both the legacy and revised Uniform Crime Reporting definitions.

Table 13. Arrests, by State, 2017

(Number.)

State	Total, all classes[1]	Violent crime[2]	Property crime[2]	Murder and nonnegligent manslaughter	Rape[3]	Robbery	Aggravated assault	Burglary	Larceny-theft	Motor vehicle theft	Arson	Other assaults
Alabama												
Under 18	4,707	365	1,264	18	34	116	197	323	860	71	10	782
Total, all ages	153,285	6,005	18,366	317	344	1,140	4,204	3,223	14,030	994	119	16,455
Alaska												
Under 18	1,570	164	459	1	26	20	117	117	258	78	6	320
Total, all ages	29,152	2,374	3,695	46	126	289	1,913	623	2,356	694	22	4,478
Arizona												
Under 18	22,613	1,228	4,528	30	52	450	696	761	3,364	347	56	3,677
Total, all ages	277,698	12,832	34,919	261	339	2,085	10,147	3,974	29,142	1,590	213	26,801
Arkansas												
Under 18	7,878	459	1,562	15	46	101	297	386	1,083	88	5	1,443
Total, all ages	123,971	4,715	12,355	138	238	563	3,776	2,026	9,686	603	40	11,347
California												
Under 18	51,603	7,152	10,712	98	295	2,952	3,807	4,067	4,616	1,774	255	8,483
Total, all ages	1,093,363	109,117	105,757	1,499	2,561	16,942	88,115	38,094	46,602	19,501	1,560	80,248
Colorado												
Under 18	21,183	773	3,921	18	58	230	467	339	3,135	377	70	1,924
Total, all ages	234,409	7,721	27,157	176	442	1,203	5,900	2,389	21,737	2,766	265	17,009
Connecticut												
Under 18	8,133	436	1,858	6	22	197	211	287	1,222	324	25	1,961
Total, all ages	100,211	3,844	14,074	85	190	1,082	2,487	1,998	11,076	926	74	18,621
Delaware												
Under 18	3,360	284	661	1	18	84	181	146	462	35	18	911
Total, all ages	31,549	1,989	6,156	42	69	476	1,402	950	5,038	136	32	6,225
District of Columbia[5]												
Under 18	594	80	39	0	0	60	20	0	39	0	0	79
Total, all ages	17,986	133	101	0	0	84	49	1	95	5	0	333
Florida[6,7]												
Under 18	55,359	3,829	15,812	43	263	1,545	1,978	4,066	9,081	2,617	48	8,456
Total, all ages	713,085	36,251	91,063	635	1,873	6,398	27,345	16,483	66,033	8,306	241	78,943
Georgia												
Under 18	19,766	1,206	5,177	46	42	396	722	996	3,697	457	27	2,712
Total, all ages	230,640	10,843	31,080	380	284	1,697	8,482	4,035	25,397	1,499	149	20,268
Hawaii												
Under 18	3,084	135	597	2	15	56	62	60	494	36	7	440
Total, all ages	35,618	1,227	3,748	36	114	270	807	436	2,865	424	23	3,837
Idaho												
Under 18	6,260	184	1,246	0	49	19	116	172	974	80	20	744
Total, all ages	51,686	1,441	5,192	10	120	70	1,241	790	4,138	220	44	4,513
Illinois[6]												
Under 18	8,587	842	2,593	28	18	603	193	195	1,084	1,301	13	1,411
Total, all ages	64,552	3,823	11,653	272	259	1,464	1,828	882	7,599	3,113	59	13,083
Indiana												
Under 18	11,369	842	2,724	17	48	218	559	301	2,104	294	25	1,731
Total, all ages	147,199	8,345	17,546	182	208	1,386	6,569	2,016	13,829	1,629	72	11,260
Iowa												
Under 18	10,088	445	2,607	3	41	94	307	407	1,918	248	34	1,518
Total, all ages	94,485	4,709	12,280	53	192	341	4,123	1,594	10,029	565	92	7,296
Kansas												
Under 18	3,948	185	683	3	17	27	138	102	490	71	20	742
Total, all ages	61,144	2,198	4,958	62	112	204	1,820	608	3,887	412	51	8,456
Kentucky												
Under 18	5,273	393	1,414	26	24	212	131	326	911	171	6	1,029
Total, all ages	219,872	3,398	17,117	185	212	987	2,014	2,891	13,271	894	61	12,015

Table 13. Arrests, by State, 2017—*Continued*

(Number.)

State	Total, all classes[1]	Violent crime[2]	Property crime[2]	Murder and nonnegligent manslaughter	Rape[3]	Robbery	Aggravated assault	Burglary	Larceny-theft	Motor vehicle theft	Arson	Other assaults
Louisiana												
Under 18	17,571	1,149	4,603	36	95	265	753	1,173	2,914	475	41	3,124
Total, all ages	166,867	9,494	29,489	359	391	1,195	7,549	5,260	22,413	1,692	124	18,935
Maine												
Under 18	3,046	57	779	0	14	12	31	131	596	28	24	505
Total, all ages	40,675	780	5,578	14	70	128	568	607	4,683	225	63	4,889
Maryland												
Under 18	17,653	2,056	4,510	14	60	1,131	851	937	2,839	639	95	3,922
Total, all ages	165,877	9,692	21,726	286	352	3,299	5,755	4,323	15,337	1,756	310	18,261
Massachusetts												
Under 18	6,732	793	1,179	6	23	176	588	280	780	90	29	1,562
Total, all ages	118,676	9,257	13,671	62	296	1,211	7,688	2,141	10,837	608	85	19,372
Michigan												
Under 18	16,474	1,094	4,206	16	133	282	663	634	3,167	361	44	2,620
Total, all ages	244,417	11,798	24,692	261	750	1,306	9,481	3,190	19,983	1,280	239	27,788
Minnesota												
Under 18	20,871	969	4,981	12	122	384	451	475	4,071	399	36	2,403
Total, all ages	143,702	5,769	26,025	120	632	1,176	3,841	2,298	22,105	1,521	101	14,363
Mississippi												
Under 18	3,485	138	836	5	7	75	51	180	600	50	6	449
Total, all ages	78,239	1,492	8,677	109	58	403	922	1,249	7,034	350	44	6,393
Missouri												
Under 18	17,518	906	3,790	25	125	265	491	550	2,955	251	34	2,885
Total, all ages	228,042	9,371	31,387	342	551	1,553	6,925	3,815	24,973	2,473	126	21,141
Montana												
Under 18	4,313	113	881	0	11	15	87	48	778	46	9	612
Total, all ages	30,824	1,262	4,965	19	47	91	1,105	275	4,401	252	37	4,390
Nebraska												
Under 18	599	27	83	0	2	0	25	10	58	15	0	87
Total, all ages	5,708	161	523	1	12	5	143	53	424	44	2	617
Nevada												
Under 18	7,672	924	1,159	4	54	319	547	337	700	108	14	1,720
Total, all ages	112,004	6,506	8,946	157	321	1,388	4,640	2,572	5,658	671	45	15,438
New Hampshire												
Under 18	3,529	67	373	1	0	17	49	39	300	23	11	557
Total, all ages	47,516	896	3,642	8	52	168	668	319	3,143	152	28	5,306
New Jersey												
Under 18	15,950	1,123	2,709	6	62	510	545	478	2,093	89	49	1,312
Total, all ages	281,631	8,577	24,807	149	333	2,472	5,623	3,910	20,274	494	129	20,175
New Mexico												
Under 18	1,303	172	220	0	3	21	148	46	154	19	1	249
Total, all ages	40,552	2,708	4,340	25	43	344	2,296	613	3,546	170	11	6,223
New York[6]												
Under 18	18,426	1,508	4,873	22	180	623	683	877	3,542	358	96	2,413
Total, all ages	259,257	12,440	43,759	264	970	3,090	8,116	5,200	36,562	1,713	284	27,397
North Carolina												
Under 18	15,757	947	4,335	31	18	465	433	1,271	2,822	214	28	2,896
Total, all ages	240,365	11,630	34,918	464	229	2,571	8,366	7,836	25,826	1,066	190	31,024
North Dakota												
Under 18	4,581	69	653	0	12	8	49	59	528	61	5	439
Total, all ages	39,944	855	3,787	6	61	69	719	352	3,128	291	16	2,943

Table 13. Arrests, by State, 2017—Continued

(Number.)

State	Total, all classes[1]	Violent crime[2]	Property crime[2]	Murder and nonnegligent manslaughter	Rape[3]	Robbery	Aggravated assault	Burglary	Larceny-theft	Motor vehicle theft	Arson	Other assaults
Ohio												
Under 18	22,865	870	4,203	16	78	348	428	728	3,180	222	73	4,341
Total, all ages	224,423	8,084	33,068	224	406	1,987	5,467	4,115	27,904	764	285	31,736
Oklahoma												
Under 18	8,750	479	2,064	16	26	138	299	398	1,532	106	28	920
Total, all ages	106,731	4,820	14,352	161	179	719	3,761	2,267	11,226	713	146	8,226
Oregon												
Under 18	8,955	349	1,833	8	24	106	211	151	1,486	141	55	1,045
Total, all ages	124,851	3,687	17,578	65	166	696	2,760	1,376	14,118	1,883	201	10,263
Pennsylvania												
Under 18	43,800	3,049	5,821	19	238	1,071	1,721	952	4,355	426	88	5,184
Total, all ages	372,570	20,385	50,437	464	1,171	4,891	13,859	6,123	41,549	2,409	356	42,271
Rhode Island												
Under 18	2,218	109	373	1	16	38	54	87	251	20	15	406
Total, all ages	22,707	864	2,458	10	77	150	627	533	1,773	126	26	3,638
South Carolina												
Under 18	12,279	616	2,881	17	69	214	316	537	2,184	143	17	2,162
Total, all ages	153,573	6,500	23,848	253	378	1,133	4,736	3,149	19,592	1,006	101	14,146
South Dakota												
Under 18	6,656	131	809	1	8	13	109	108	591	106	4	544
Total, all ages	63,625	1,748	3,283	16	79	88	1,565	445	2,512	311	15	4,931
Tennessee												
Under 18	22,282	1,459	4,399	30	49	422	958	754	3,020	573	52	4,118
Total, all ages	350,912	14,682	38,394	358	351	1,839	12,134	5,143	29,649	3,422	180	32,076
Texas												
Under 18	57,417	3,723	12,398	63	355	1,477	1,828	2,156	9,144	995	103	10,027
Total, all ages	745,719	30,372	78,504	839	2,247	6,519	20,767	10,570	62,387	5,093	454	90,763
Utah												
Under 18	11,259	304	2,390	1	64	68	171	149	2,086	125	30	1,110
Total, all ages	104,741	2,252	14,526	48	204	404	1,596	882	13,064	519	61	7,870
Vermont												
Under 18	800	51	137	0	14	1	36	33	94	6	4	145
Total, all ages	13,969	664	1,683	10	62	31	561	268	1,370	29	16	1,341
Virginia												
Under 18	16,417	709	3,553	24	59	321	305	463	2,862	175	53	2,648
Total, all ages	258,878	7,068	26,582	337	430	1,633	4,668	2,698	22,662	1,032	190	30,360
Washington												
Under 18	11,818	890	2,692	17	77	334	462	480	1,986	180	46	2,939
Total, all ages	173,344	8,472	27,055	158	515	1,887	5,912	4,723	20,526	1,637	169	25,114
West Virginia												
Under 18	1,033	57	162	0	9	6	42	34	104	13	11	215
Total, all ages	39,296	1,832	5,077	31	103	123	1,575	751	4,018	272	36	4,320
Wisconsin												
Under 18	39,393	1,067	6,140	14	212	319	522	652	4,875	555	58	2,633
Total, all ages	252,142	8,023	29,429	203	900	1,447	5,473	2,652	25,214	1,368	195	17,314
Wyoming												
Under 18	3,046	35	449	0	6	3	26	26	379	34	10	417
Total, all ages	27,914	612	2,374	9	43	31	529	215	1,990	130	39	1,996

Table 13. Arrests, by State, 2017—*Continued*

(Number.)

State	Forgery and counterfeiting	Fraud	Embezzlement	Stolen property; buying, receiving, possessing	Vandalism	Weapons; carrying, possessing, etc.	Prostitution and commercialized vice	Sex offenses (except rape and prostitution)	Drug abuse violations	Gambling	Offenses against the family and children
Alabama											
Under 18	13	29	1	134	86	103	0	26	196	0	29
Total, all ages	1,189	3,258	161	2,484	1,413	1,963	2	550	11,267	0	822
Alaska											
Under 18	2	5	7	5	98	21	1	9	180	0	0
Total, all ages	113	219	77	105	1,004	369	5	256	1,004	0	159
Arizona											
Under 18	22	74	6	156	1,754	258	4	218	3,096	1	182
Total, all ages	1,201	2,076	457	1,410	10,287	3,090	303	1,289	33,230	12	2,680
Arkansas											
Under 18	15	29	5	144	287	126	0	18	876	0	6
Total, all ages	830	893	54	1,766	1,510	1,106	172	92	17,515	13	293
California											
Under 18	45	175	23	1,167	2,656	3,081	18	1,139	3,781	11	2
Total, all ages	4,440	6,903	990	17,398	16,883	28,547	7,056	9,244	212,025	287	227
Colorado											
Under 18	10	87	17	21	878	325	0	133	2,615	2	34
Total, all ages	734	2,400	126	496	5,508	2,309	521	471	16,626	19	3,235
Connecticut											
Under 18	11	30	4	125	451	181	2	46	585	0	25
Total, all ages	649	912	144	693	2,188	1,242	183	368	9,174	7	1,500
Delaware											
Under 18	0	60	4	73	154	82	0	37	335	1	0
Total, all ages	283	1,837	221	401	749	338	81	122	4,015	20	176
District of Columbia[5]											
Under 18	1	2	0	9	12	15	0	0	17	0	0
Total, all ages	2	8	0	21	54	47	0	13	237	0	4
Florida[6,7]											
Under 18	46	423	20	184	1,178	864	11	250	5,497	0	0
Total, all ages	2,040	11,613	1,057	1,841	6,371	6,306	2,468	3,001	124,487	71	4
Georgia											
Under 18	48	110	9	373	567	412	4	313	2,127	6	129
Total, all ages	2,241	3,028	292	2,881	3,633	3,317	379	2,434	40,608	58	2,805
Hawaii											
Under 18	3	2	1	48	75	13	0	32	436	0	0
Total, all ages	76	147	11	414	426	247	120	155	2,724	156	13
Idaho											
Under 18	3	31	3	18	236	95	0	67	969	0	13
Total, all ages	127	299	43	170	756	276	13	188	8,432	0	636
Illinois[6]											
Under 18	1	8	0	25	288	693	0	16	845	60	5
Total, all ages	108	224	1	71	2,076	4,290	141	235	10,915	457	277
Indiana											
Under 18	15	63	7	35	349	207	4	123	1,391	0	209
Total, all ages	1,234	1,885	266	343	1,200	2,283	305	673	26,364	14	1,059
Iowa											
Under 18	27	49	12	34	652	131	1	47	902	0	3
Total, all ages	664	743	79	212	1,995	900	46	* 125	9,645	7	1,059
Kansas											
Under 18	4	22	8	48	243	54	0	43	701	0	6
Total, all ages	263	580	111	584	1,697	742	127	167	9,594	0	228

Table 13. Arrests, by State, 2017—*Continued*

(Number.)

State	Forgery and counterfeiting	Fraud	Embezzlement	Stolen property; buying, receiving, possessing	Vandalism	Weapons; carrying, possessing, etc.	Prostitution and commercialized vice	Sex offenses (except rape and prostitution)	Drug abuse violations	Gambling	Offenses against the family and children
Kentucky											
Under 18..	13	16	8	347	164	94	0	39	533	0	5
Total, all ages.................................	1,102	1,370	390	2,992	1,167	967	166	292	26,397	3	5,216
Louisiana											
Under 18..	12	33	9	258	589	398	8	168	1,361	0	114
Total, all ages.................................	762	1,519	146	2,100	2,785	3,234	412	841	25,770	41	1,856
Maine											
Under 18..	3	11	2	10	225	6	0	35	350	0	6
Total, all ages.................................	199	518	41	93	1,067	130	119	182	3,409	3	122
Maryland											
Under 18..	15	51	4	6	845	598	8	147	1,948	41	9
Total, all ages.................................	423	893	77	73	2,332	3,215	748	578	28,992	117	860
Massachusetts											
Under 18..	16	17	3	134	345	169	1	52	215	1	45
Total, all ages.................................	455	1,271	122	1,202	2,534	1,328	530	425	9,791	6	1,406
Michigan											
Under 18..	30	220	25	243	535	289	2	133	2,126	3	1
Total, all ages.................................	650	3,931	1,174	1,806	2,815	4,590	233	626	33,090	42	2,766
Minnesota											
Under 18..	32	196	1	329	931	433	2	178	1,893	0	14
Total, all ages.................................	1,465	2,664	23	1,995	3,056	2,208	359	1,055	19,281	16	569
Mississippi											
Under 18..	2	9	4	76	70	84	0	16	285	1	254
Total, all ages.................................	333	854	383	815	678	1,110	25	198	10,268	67	2,298
Missouri											
Under 18..	16	73	16	256	847	277	6	265	2,266	1	88
Total, all ages.................................	1,239	1,950	290	2,876	3,868	3,537	368	1,242	39,979	96	2,548
Montana											
Under 18..	3	5	0	6	246	17	0	23	385	0	40
Total, all ages.................................	106	254	30	98	931	85	9	102	2,872	0	253
Nebraska											
Under 18..	0	1	0	2	34	4	0	3	87	0	1
Total, all ages.................................	18	67	3	35	95	65	1	28	843	0	76
Nevada											
Under 18..	40	31	2	166	217	171	44	47	741	0	6
Total, all ages.................................	488	1,404	201	1,681	1,365	1,885	2,532	695	8,923	9	702
New Hampshire											
Under 18..	5	19	6	33	194	5	0	24	507	0	10
Total, all ages.................................	292	787	120	503	1,247	139	79	99	7,656	12	202
New Jersey											
Under 18..	39	48	12	456	658	566	9	157	3,535	30	27
Total, all ages.................................	1,020	3,478	269	2,511	3,297	3,838	900	916	61,989	158	8,915
New Mexico											
Under 18..	2	3	1	51	35	14	1	2	99	0	11
Total, all ages.................................	138	230	74	1,165	684	179	35	31	2,377	0	680
New York[6]											
Under 18..	82	179	3	417	1,880	330	6	322	3,344	14	24
Total, all ages.................................	2,616	4,086	48	3,183	13,559	3,468	672	1,662	69,904	102	550
North Carolina											
Under 18..	37	174	20	392	629	546	6	90	1,519	2	18
Total, all ages.................................	1,326	6,720	1,185	3,356	3,958	5,147	374	806	25,902	61	4,294

Table 13. Arrests, by State, 2017—*Continued*

(Number.)

State	Forgery and counterfeiting	Fraud	Embezzlement	Stolen property; buying, receiving, possessing	Vandalism	Weapons; carrying, possessing, etc.	Prostitution and commercialized vice	Sex offenses (except rape and prostitution)	Drug abuse violations	Gambling	Offenses against the family and children
North Dakota											
Under 18	5	16	7	26	145	29	2	42	476	0	171
Total, all ages	156	421	53	311	479	313	38	120	5,646	1	654
Ohio											
Under 18	33	139	2	454	960	327	4	137	1,973	2	212
Total, all ages	918	2,179	21	2,800	3,454	3,681	1,122	516	37,022	4	1,714
Oklahoma											
Under 18	11	35	25	301	289	145	0	42	1,280	3	20
Total, all ages	607	1,489	408	2,843	1,270	2,207	15	458	20,024	51	539
Oregon											
Under 18	12	44	2	25	678	107	2	68	1,796	0	0
Total, all ages	648	1,868	49	587	3,976	2,077	364	436	15,682	0	333
Pennsylvania											
Under 18	64	799	20	336	1,779	848	3	495	3,524	0	51
Total, all ages	2,414	7,703	478	2,392	7,196	5,056	1,755	2,211	63,306	53	2,034
Rhode Island											
Under 18	3	16	3	37	188	105	0	20	111	0	27
Total, all ages	74	425	102	287	932	379	71	76	1,792	9	62
South Carolina											
Under 18	13	68	17	143	451	435	5	56	2,090	0	8
Total, all ages	1,138	3,200	358	1,952	2,552	2,247	381	295	32,266	39	1,139
South Dakota											
Under 18	5	53	2	49	211	74	0	28	979	0	653
Total, all ages	102	731	37	225	624	334	33	92	8,900	1	2,361
Tennessee											
Under 18	45	131	16	133	1,017	408	0	133	2,591	12	47
Total, all ages	1,802	5,336	664	1,496	4,571	3,081	955	621	47,826	148	4,289
Texas											
Under 18	107	222	109	192	1,558	858	40	459	9,997	17	190
Total, all ages	4,287	5,764	794	899	7,178	12,954	4,482	2,804	136,796	355	4,005
Utah											
Under 18	10	43	4	106	652	135	10	217	1,696	0	28
Total, all ages	746	957	32	1,225	2,364	896	379	656	17,556	4	1,426
Vermont											
Under 18	2	4	1	6	92	10	0	7	49	0	4
Total, all ages	56	238	43	103	380	28	4	41	1,137	0	174
Virginia											
Under 18	32	133	32	153	691	318	5	137	2,217	1	23
Total, all ages	1,700	4,845	1,371	994	3,621	4,099	617	653	42,060	25	1,664
Washington											
Under 18	12	28	1	193	856	225	7	123	1,224	0	9
Total, all ages	862	1,056	53	3,438	5,178	1,793	650	587	12,027	0	359
West Virginia											
Under 18	3	3	3	8	44	14	0	5	120	0	1
Total, all ages	258	486	116	410	634	342	109	88	7,277	0	149
Wisconsin											
Under 18	31	115	27	469	1,836	517	13	695	3,213	4	129
Total, all ages	920	2,669	325	1,474	6,206	3,449	451	1,928	30,781	37	2,493
Wyoming											
Under 18	1	3	5	15	150	31	0	11	501	0	6
Total, all ages	49	158	18	94	492	78	48	107	4,612	0	344

Table 13. Arrests, by State, 2017—*Continued*

(Number.)

State	Driving under the influence	Liquor laws	Drunkenness[4]	Disorderly conduct	Vagrancy	All other offenses (except traffic)	Suspicion	Curfew and loitering law violations	Number of agencies	Estimated population, 2017
Alabama										
Under 18	42	212	34	338	0	1,053	0	0	223	3,737,635
Total, all ages	7,194	2,064	6,165	2,018	56	71,853	0	0		
Alaska										
Under 18	23	80	10	14	0	172	0	0	32	736,205
Total, all ages	3,102	653	43	757	2	10,737	0	0		
Arizona										
Under 18	198	1,461	78	1,424	57	3,062	3	1,126	91	6,400,872
Total, all ages	24,195	8,935	15,574	15,505	616	81,016	144	1,126		
Arkansas										
Under 18	32	205	85	609	0	1,667	0	310	264	2,760,388
Total, all ages	5,988	1,475	6,247	2,469	315	54,506	0	310		
California										
Under 18	455	1,107	695	1,193	103	8,607	0	998	676	39,386,220
Total, all ages	122,961	7,079	63,278	3,530	6,773	289,622	0	998		
Colorado										
Under 18	239	1,282	11	1,729	0	6,130	0	1,052	198	5,083,702
Total, all ages	23,664	8,143	485	7,284	596	108,846	7	1,052		
Connecticut										
Under 18	28	27	0	1,406	1	953	0	3	105	3,538,025
Total, all ages	8,228	159	5	10,579	24	27,614	0	3		
Delaware										
Under 18	0	71	3	287	0	364	0	33	62	961,939
Total, all ages	347	635	377	1,339	226	5,979	0	33		
District of Columbia[5]										
Under 18	0	2	0	32	0	306	0	0	2	0
Total, all ages	22	1,174	72	284	10	15,471	0	0		
Florida[6,7]										
Under 18	96	529	0	1	0	18,158	0	5	605	20,971,216
Total, all ages	32,727	11,739	37	33	0	303,028	0	5		
Georgia										
Under 18	99	260	30	1,637	129	4,080	7	331	389	8,205,589
Total, all ages	17,436	3,458	1,457	13,334	1,285	69,459	13	331		
Hawaii										
Under 18	29	76	0	87	0	893	0	217	4	1,427,538
Total, all ages	5,968	467	0	919	0	14,744	2	217		
Idaho										
Under 18	48	198	31	254	2	1,979	2	137	82	1,534,173
Total, all ages	5,458	1,010	566	1,582	15	20,826	6	137		
Illinois[6]										
Under 18	1	22	0	669	0	1,057	0	51	2	2,852,941
Total, all ages	2,357	131	0	2,988	18	11,653	0	51		
Indiana										
Under 18	60	653	39	597	29	2,077	4	210	201	4,267,407
Total, all ages	13,263	3,792	3,820	3,453	347	49,499	38	210		
Iowa										
Under 18	83	661	75	991	0	1,598	0	252	190	2,686,879
Total, all ages	10,082	3,733	5,793	3,574	17	31,274	0	252		
Kansas										
Under 18	61	353	1	156	0	638	0	0	225	1,900,556
Total, all ages	5,443	2,353	138	1,613	0	21,892	0	0		
Kentucky										
Under 18	41	8	44	177	0	946	0	2	330	4,329,947
Total, all ages	15,143	72	13,722	3,949	70	114,322	0	2		

Table 13. Arrests, by State, 2017—*Continued*

(Number.)

State	Driving under the influence	Liquor laws	Drunkenness[4]	Disorderly conduct	Vagrancy	All other offenses (except traffic)	Suspicion	Curfew and loitering law violations	Number of agencies	Estimated population, 2017
Louisiana										
Under 18	26	191	30	2,307	32	2,909	4	246	170	3,747,239
Total, all ages	6,117	2,869	2,965	7,332	243	49,696	15	246		
Maine										
Under 18	39	386	4	83	0	528	0	17	135	1,335,907
Total, all ages	5,835	2,181	20	1,257	0	14,227	8	17		
Maryland										
Under 18	45	233	2	821	5	2,299	23	65	139	5,488,907
Total, all ages	14,385	3,755	29	4,202	82	55,260	112	65		
Massachusetts										
Under 18	29	231	24	447	0	1,467	0	2	321	6,522,173
Total, all ages	8,665	1,565	5,187	4,359	8	37,518	2	2		
Michigan										
Under 18	200	1,137	5	534	0	2,752	0	319	614	9,789,634
Total, all ages	26,558	8,729	349	5,989	139	86,333	0	319		
Minnesota										
Under 18	176	1,816	0	2,053	0	3,595	0	869	374	5,379,142
Total, all ages	19,171	7,535	2	8,665	42	28,570	0	869		
Mississippi										
Under 18	55	33	22	363	12	684	2	90	64	1,385,928
Total, all ages	7,642	971	3,888	4,070	105	27,846	36	90		
Missouri										
Under 18	147	707	12	1,176	4	3,136	0	644	361	5,626,134
Total, all ages	18,386	4,061	306	7,059	1,096	76,597	1	644		
Montana										
Under 18	44	575	0	398	0	659	0	306	100	1,037,591
Total, all ages	4,344	2,023	0	2,475	10	6,309	0	306		
Nebraska										
Under 18	19	90	12	38	0	95	0	16	54	233,437
Total, all ages	785	416	178	282	0	1,499	0	16		
Nevada										
Under 18	50	372	4	194	64	1,304	4	412	51	2,680,733
Total, all ages	9,470	1,950	241	1,353	1,648	45,968	187	412		
New Hampshire										
Under 18	36	371	313	133	0	865	0	11	176	1,292,643
Total, all ages	4,805	2,489	4,210	1,001	82	13,938	0	11		
New Jersey										
Under 18	76	682	0	1,281	25	2,613	0	592	490	8,521,517
Total, all ages	21,574	2,876	0	11,629	299	103,811	0	592		
New Mexico										
Under 18	25	31	28	41	0	318	0	0	23	823,584
Total, all ages	3,283	473	1,578	973	64	15,300	17	0		
New York[6]										
Under 18	82	198	0	504	9	2,238	0	0	510	10,121,830
Total, all ages	27,136	1,450	0	4,867	618	41,740	0	0		
North Carolina										
Under 18	190	278	0	1,173	0	2,487	0	18	213	6,457,952
Total, all ages	30,277	1,926	0	5,425	5	72,013	0	18		
North Dakota										
Under 18	37	554	4	706	0	1,093	0	107	106	749,938
Total, all ages	6,318	3,086	384	2,492	7	11,772	1	107		
Ohio										
Under 18	64	617	27	1,745	0	6,212	1	542	453	9,362,266
Total, all ages	15,032	5,196	4,327	12,296	208	60,497	6	542		

Table 13. Arrests, by State, 2017—*Continued*

(Number.)

State	Driving under the influence	Liquor laws	Drunkenness[4]	Disorderly conduct	Vagrancy	All other offenses (except traffic)	Suspicion	Curfew and loitering law violations	Number of agencies	Estimated population, 2017
Oklahoma										
Under 18	72	111	211	538	0	1,342	0	862	389	3,789,847
Total, all ages	9,599	1,394	12,799	2,096	58	22,612	2	862		
Oregon										
Under 18	97	777	0	592	0	1,089	0	439	143	3,745,046
Total, all ages	13,273	3,658	18	6,594	22	43,299	0	439		
Pennsylvania										
Under 18	349	2,426	191	8,290	38	3,810	0	6,723	1,383	12,552,431
Total, all ages	45,128	9,446	20,941	35,630	298	46,713	0	6,723		
Rhode Island										
Under 18	5	68	0	422	0	314	0	11	41	943,094
Total, all ages	1,788	394	0	1,979	1	7,365	0	11		
South Carolina										
Under 18	93	297	69	1,318	0	1,525	0	32	346	3,920,047
Total, all ages	15,446	4,239	6,113	8,330	484	28,868	0	32		
South Dakota										
Under 18	88	804	220	576	1	1,247	11	171	75	729,800
Total, all ages	8,164	4,999	6,939	3,596	565	15,720	69	171		
Tennessee										
Under 18	109	532	129	1,793	0	3,996	0	1,214	449	6,505,139
Total, all ages	19,495	3,836	15,073	6,749	5	148,599	0	1,214		
Texas										
Under 18	419	1,187	783	1,284	30	11,516	0	2,301	909	25,980,682
Total, all ages	64,784	8,775	62,434	8,477	872	218,119	0	2,301		
Utah										
Under 18	143	708	66	421	18	2,842	0	356	114	2,646,000
Total, all ages	7,980	3,570	2,672	2,201	38	37,023	12	356		
Vermont										
Under 18	18	49	0	100	0	125	0	0	72	600,391
Total, all ages	2,450	112	0	823	0	4,692	0	0		
Virginia										
Under 18	70	574	75	501	0	3,804	0	741	373	7,782,044
Total, all ages	19,323	4,852	17,864	2,870	177	87,392	0	741		
Washington										
Under 18	167	683	10	190	0	1,569	0	0	222	6,678,694
Total, all ages	25,392	2,018	78	2,402	124	56,680	6	0		
West Virginia										
Under 18	16	24	2	30	0	317	0	9	178	1,150,294
Total, all ages	4,282	890	822	751	27	11,417	0	9		
Wisconsin										
Under 18	239	2,271	0	7,282	24	10,921	0	1,767	427	5,700,831
Total, all ages	23,541	12,228	0	32,743	809	75,555	0	1,767		
Wyoming										
Under 18	28	416	16	106	0	761	5	90	53	543,983
Total, all ages	3,253	1,980	2,412	810	36	8,345	6	90		

Note: Because the number of agencies submitting arrest data varies from year to year, users are cautioned about making direct comparisons between 2017 arrest totals and those published in previous years' editions of *Crime in the United States.* Further, arrest figures may vary widely from state to state because some Part II crimes are not considered crimes in some states.
[1] Does not include traffic arrests.
[2] Violent crimes are offenses of murder and nonnegligent manslaughter, rape, robbery, and aggravated assault. Property crimes are offenses of burglary, larceny-theft, motor vehicle theft, and arson.
[3] The rape figures in this table are aggregate totals of the data submitted based on both the legacy and revised Uniform Crime Reporting definitions.
[4] Drunkenness is not considered a crime in some states; therefore, the figures vary widely from state to state.
[5] Includes arrests reported by the District of Columbia Fire and Emergency Medical Services: Arson Investigation Unit and the Metro Transit Police. These agencies have no population associated with them.
[6] See 2017 arrest data for details.
[7] The Florida arrest counts for offenses against the family and children, drunkenness, disorderly conduct, vagrancy, suspicion, and curfew and loitering law violations are included under the category All other offenses (except for the data submitted by two Bureau of Indian Affairs agencies that provided data using those specific breakdowns).

Table 14. Ten-Year Arrest Trends, 2008 and 2017

(Number, percent change; 9,983 agencies; 2017 estimated population 211,303,234; 2008 estimated population 197,634,622.)

Offense charged	Number of persons arrested								
	Total, all ages			Under 18 years of age			18 years of age and over		
	2008	2017	Percent change	2008	2017	Percent change	2008	2017	Percent change
Total[1]	8,867,758	6,878,929	-22.4	1,283,505	538,333	-58.1	7,584,253	6,340,596	-16.4
Violent crime[2]	377,743	333,604	-11.7	59,171	32,785	-44.6	318,572	300,819	-5.6
Murder and nonnegligent manslaughter ...	7,544	7,342	-2.7	716	530	-26.0	6,828	6,812	-0.2
Rape[3]	13,598	14,759	-	2,042	2,482	NA	11,556	12,277	NA
Robbery	77,452	57,018	-26.4	20,608	11,152	-45.9	56,844	45,866	-19.3
Aggravated assault	279,149	254,485	-8.8	35,805	18,621	-48.0	243,344	235,864	-3.1
Property crime[2]	1,106,503	837,773	-24.3	293,060	112,498	-61.6	813,443	725,275	-10.8
Burglary	202,929	130,615	-35.6	55,319	20,461	-63.0	147,610	110,154	-25.4
Larceny-theft	835,771	643,853	-23.0	218,758	80,944	-63.0	617,013	562,909	-8.8
Motor vehicle theft	58,356	57,203	-2.0	14,442	9,507	-34.2	43,914	47,696	+8.6
Arson...	9,447	6,102	-35.4	4,541	1,586	-65.1	4,906	4,516	-7.9
Other assaults..	825,595	690,444	-16.4	149,218	81,635	-45.3	676,377	608,809	-10.0
Forgery and counterfeiting........................	59,792	37,230	-37.7	1,803	834	-53.7	57,989	36,396	-37.2
Fraud...	155,657	83,654	-46.3	5,139	2,766	-46.2	150,518	80,888	-46.3
Embezzlement	14,477	10,501	-27.5	863	372	-56.9	13,614	10,129	-25.6
Stolen property; buying, receiving, possessing	75,402	66,036	-12.4	14,456	6,902	-52.3	60,946	59,134	-3.0
Vandalism...	186,293	127,131	-31.8	70,977	25,822	-63.6	115,316	101,309	-12.1
Weapons; carrying, possessing, etc.	110,133	102,571	-6.9	24,967	11,639	-53.4	85,166	90,932	+6.8
Prostitution and commercialized vice.........	34,487	18,132	-47.4	749	148	-80.2	33,738	17,984	-46.7
Sex offenses (except forcible rape and prostitution)..	48,889	31,007	-36.6	9,368	5,746	-38.7	39,521	25,261	-36.1
Drug abuse violations..............................	1,044,058	1,077,640	+3.2	112,037	64,203	-42.7	932,021	1,013,437	+8.7
Gambling..	2,431	1,440	-40.8	276	83	-69.9	2,155	1,357	-37.0
Offenses against the family and children ...	74,321	56,777	-23.6	3,568	2,558	-28.3	70,753	54,219	-23.4
Driving under the influence......................	974,968	654,775	-32.8	10,664	4,104	-61.5	964,304	650,671	-32.5
Liquor laws	410,755	137,829	-66.4	90,052	23,943	-73.4	320,703	113,886	-64.5
Drunkenness...	410,144	230,361	-43.8	10,984	2,743	-75.0	399,160	227,618	-43.0
Disorderly conduct..................................	439,410	232,936	-47.0	123,160	42,305	-65.7	316,250	190,631	-39.7
Vagrancy	16,039	13,953	-13.0	1,088	407	-62.6	14,951	13,546	-9.4
All other offenses (except traffic)...............	2,438,997	2,119,016	-13.1	240,241	100,721	-58.1	2,198,756	2,018,295	-8.2
Suspicion	805	201	-75.0	152	42	-72.4	653	159	-75.7
Curfew and loitering law violations...........	61,664	16,119	-73.9	61,664	16,119	-73.9	NA	NA	NA

NA = Not available.

[1]Does not include suspicion.

[2]Violent crimes are offenses of murder and nonnegligent manslaughter, rape, robbery, and aggravated assault. Property crimes are offenses of burglary, larceny-theft, motor vehicle theft, and arson.

[3]The 2008 rape figures are based on the legacy definition, and the 2017 rape figures are aggregate totals based on both the legacy and revised Uniform Crime Reporting definitions. For this reason, a percent change is not provided.

Table 15. Five-Year Arrest Trends, by Age, 2013 and 2017

(Number, percent change; 10,561 agencies; 2017 estimated population 218,341,582; 2013 estimated population 212,249,163.)

Offense charged	Total, all ages			Under 18 years of age			18 years of age and over		
	2013	2017	Percent change	2013	2017	Percent change	2013	2017	Percent change
Total[1]	7,713,977	7,088,331	-8.1	727,655	545,420	-25.0	6,986,322	6,542,911	-6.3
Violent crime[2]	330,719	338,485	+2.3	34,894	32,777	-6.1	295,825	305,708	+3.3
Murder and nonnegligent manslaughter	6,767	7,547	+11.5	478	536	+12.1	6,289	7,011	+11.5
Rape[3]	12,783	15,230	+19.1	2,061	2,577	+25.0	10,722	12,653	+18.0
Robbery	62,556	58,445	-6.6	11,723	11,165	-4.8	50,833	47,280	-7.0
Aggravated assault	248,613	257,263	+3.5	20,632	18,499	-10.3	227,981	238,764	+4.7
Property crime[2]	1,076,095	848,594	-21.1	169,180	114,243	-32.5	906,915	734,351	-19.0
Burglary	175,831	134,031	-23.8	29,366	20,855	-29.0	146,465	113,176	-22.7
Larceny-theft	849,570	651,332	-23.3	129,815	82,489	-36.5	719,755	568,843	-21.0
Motor vehicle theft	43,867	57,255	+30.5	7,524	9,382	+24.7	36,343	47,873	+31.7
Arson	6,827	5,976	-12.5	2,475	1,517	-38.7	4,352	4,459	+2.5
Other assaults	755,019	716,439	-5.1	99,293	82,433	-17.0	655,726	634,006	-3.3
Forgery and counterfeiting	41,814	38,137	-8.8	722	851	+17.9	41,092	37,286	-9.3
Fraud	96,273	84,446	-12.3	3,139	2,824	-10.0	93,134	81,622	-12.4
Embezzlement	11,223	11,150	-0.7	286	468	+63.6	10,937	10,682	-2.3
Stolen property; buying, receiving, possessing	66,787	67,437	+1.0	7,378	6,979	-5.4	59,409	60,458	+1.8
Vandalism	137,091	129,316	-5.7	32,316	25,800	-20.2	104,775	103,516	-1.2
Weapons; carrying, possessing, etc.	91,434	104,943	+14.8	13,236	11,628	-12.1	78,198	93,315	+19.3
Prostitution and commercialized vice	29,044	20,528	-29.3	500	182	-63.6	28,544	20,346	-28.7
Sex offenses (except forcible rape and prostitution)	39,259	32,872	-16.3	7,008	5,927	-15.4	32,251	26,945	-16.5
Drug abuse violations	1,016,496	1,120,121	+10.2	78,397	65,233	-16.8	938,099	1,054,888	+12.4
Gambling	2,259	1,754	-22.4	178	133	-25.3	2,081	1,621	-22.1
Offenses against the family and children	68,097	62,951	-7.6	1,992	2,471	+24.0	66,105	60,480	-8.5
Driving under the influence	799,032	682,771	-14.6	5,327	4,259	-20.0	793,705	678,512	-14.5
Liquor laws	238,043	141,109	-40.7	43,056	24,015	-44.2	194,987	117,094	-39.9
Drunkenness	325,493	242,478	-25.5	5,460	2,843	-47.9	320,033	239,635	-25.1
Disorderly conduct	314,330	236,027	-24.9	63,549	43,283	-31.9	250,781	192,744	-23.1
Vagrancy	17,653	16,581	-6.1	678	518	-23.6	16,975	16,063	-5.4
All other offenses (except traffic)	2,230,169	2,175,563	-2.4	133,419	101,924	-23.6	2,096,750	2,073,639	-1.1
Suspicion	431	155	-64.0	51	22	-56.9	380	133	-65.0
Curfew and loitering law violations	27,647	16,629	-39.9	27,647	16,629	-39.9	NA	NA	NA

NA = Not available.
[1] Does not include suspicion.
[2] Violent crimes are offenses of murder and nonnegligent manslaughter, rape, robbery, and aggravated assault. Property crimes are offenses of burglary, larceny-theft, motor vehicle theft, and arson.
[3] The 2013 rape figures are based on the legacy definition, and the 2017 rape figures are aggregate totals based on both the legacy and revised Uniform Crime Reporting definitions. For this reason, a percent change is not provided.

Table 16. Current Year Over Previous Year Arrest Trends, by Age, 2016 and 2017

(Number, percent change; 11,889 agencies; 2017 estimated population 245,794,668; 2016 estimated population 244,059,561.)

Offense charged	Number of persons arrested											
	Total, all ages			Under 15 years of age			Under 18 years of age			18 years of age and over		
	2016	2017	Percent change	2016	2017	Percent change	2016	2017	Percent change	2016	2017	Percent change
Total[1]	8,057,300	7,990,795	-0.8	180,936	176,559	-2.4	649,211	620,264	-4.5	7,408,089	7,370,531	-0.5
Violent crime[2]	391,723	394,928	+0.8	10,827	11,021	+1.8	39,519	39,862	+0.9	352,204	355,066	+0.8
Murder and nonnegligent manslaughter	8,899	9,177	+3.1	66	58	-12.1	663	685	+3.3	8,236	8,492	+3.1
Rape[3]	17,827	17,765	-0.3	1,135	1,148	+1.1	2,812	2,989	+6.3	15,015	14,776	-1.6
Robbery	73,298	71,599	-2.3	2,792	2,824	+1.1	14,711	14,703	-0.1	58,587	56,896	-2.9
Aggravated assault	291,699	296,387	+1.6	6,834	6,991	+2.3	21,333	21,485	+0.7	270,366	274,902	+1.7
Property crime[2]	1,025,497	956,839	-6.7	38,693	37,252	-3.7	140,060	129,488	-7.5	885,437	827,351	-6.6
Burglary	157,814	151,840	-3.8	7,290	7,425	+1.9	24,433	23,569	-3.5	133,381	128,271	-3.8
Larceny-theft	794,517	728,141	-8.4	27,654	25,846	-6.5	101,730	91,715	-9.8	692,787	636,426	-8.1
Motor vehicle theft	66,228	69,888	+5.5	2,664	2,983	+12.0	12,022	12,466	+3.7	54,206	57,422	+5.9
Arson	6,938	6,970	+0.5	1,085	998	-8.0	1,875	1,738	-7.3	5,063	5,232	+3.3
Other assaults	804,819	799,265	-0.7	37,144	36,996	-0.4	96,293	94,010	-2.4	708,526	705,255	-0.5
Forgery and counterfeiting	42,884	42,361	-1.2	109	132	+21.1	946	941	-0.5	41,938	41,420	-1.2
Fraud	96,571	94,916	-1.7	722	728	+0.8	3,468	3,646	+5.1	93,103	91,270	-2.0
Embezzlement	12,234	12,061	-1.4	41	38	-7.3	499	494		11,735	11,567	-1.4
Stolen property; buying, receiving, possessing	72,133	76,013	+5.4	1,789	1,661	-7.2	8,330	8,060	-3.2	63,803	67,953	+6.5
Vandalism	146,436	143,337	-2.1	11,759	11,353	-3.5	29,382	28,130	-4.3	117,054	115,207	-1.6
Weapons; carrying, possessing, etc.	118,396	125,051	+5.6	4,549	4,173	-8.3	14,635	14,088	-3.7	103,761	110,963	+6.9
Prostitution and commercialized vice	28,451	26,618	-6.4	48	30	-37.5	393	207	-47.3	28,058	26,411	-5.9
Sex offenses (except forcible rape and prostitution)	37,818	36,652	-3.1	3,078	3,235	+5.1	6,392	6,469	+1.2	31,426	30,183	-4.0
Drug abuse violations	1,183,896	1,233,598	+4.2	11,214	10,813	-3.6	73,810	72,334	-2.0	1,110,086	1,161,264	+4.6
Gambling	2,791	2,460	-11.9	24	28	+16.7	198	209	+5.6	2,593	2,251	-13.2
Offenses against the family and children	67,385	69,108	+2.6	1,096	958	-12.6	2,879	2,814	-2.3	64,506	66,294	+2.8
Driving under the influence	766,954	743,538	-3.1	87	88	+1.1	4,879	4,593	-5.9	762,075	738,945	-3.0
Liquor laws	174,484	156,573	-10.3	2,909	2,981	+2.5	27,744	25,580	-7.8	146,740	130,993	-10.7
Drunkenness	294,270	283,471	-3.7	458	420	-8.3	3,757	3,333	-11.3	290,513	280,138	-3.6
Disorderly conduct	284,037	269,318	-5.2	19,466	18,924	-2.8	50,883	48,293	-5.1	233,154	221,025	-5.2
Vagrancy	19,012	18,007	-5.3	140	140	0.0	583	547	-6.2	18,429	17,460	-5.3
All other offenses (except traffic)	2,460,814	2,483,220	+0.9	29,107	28,688	-1.4	117,866	113,705	-3.5	2,342,948	2,369,515	+1.1
Suspicion	590	588	-0.3	22	12	-45.5	70	50	-28.6	520	538	+3.5
Curfew and loitering law violations	26,695	23,461	-12.1	7,676	6,900	-10.1	26,695	23,461	-12.1	NA	NA	NA

NA = Not available.
* = Less than one-tenth of 1 percent.
[1]Does not include suspicion.
[2]Violent crimes are offenses of murder and nonnegligent manslaughter, rape, robbery, and aggravated assault. Property crimes are offenses of burglary, larceny-theft, motor vehicle theft, and arson.
[3]The rape figures in this table are aggregate totals of the data submitted based on both the legacy and revised Uniform Crime Reporting definitions.

Table 17. Full-Time Law Enforcement Employees,[1] by Region and Geographic Division and Population Group, 2017

(Number, rate per 1,000 inhabitants.)

Region/geographic division	Total (10,058 cities; population 193,187,549)	Group I (79 cities, 250,000 and over; population 60,607,956)	Group II (198 cities, 100,000 to 249,999; population 29,257,403)	Group III (431 cities, 50,000 to 99,999; population 30,031,331)	Group IV (775 cities, 25,000 to 49,999; population 26,916,000)	Group V (1,609 cities, 10,000 to 24,999; population 25,660,537)
Total						
Number of employees...................................	542,639	203,398	62,162	61,566	56,881	58,891
Average number of employees per 1,000 inhabitants.......	2.8	3.4	2.1	2.1	2.1	2.3
Northeast						
Number of employees...................................	151,357	66,618	8,462	15,835	18,335	18,655
Average number of employees per 1,000 inhabitants.......	3.3	5.6	2.9	2.4	2.2	2.1
New England						
Number of employees...................................	34,175	2,778	4,459	6,412	7,203	6,957
Average number of employees per 1,000 inhabitants.......	2.6	4.1	3.0	2.3	2.2	2.3
Middle Atlantic						
Number of employees...................................	117,182	63,840	4,003	9,423	11,132	11,698
Average number of employees per 1,000 inhabitants.......	3.6	5.6	2.9	2.4	2.2	2.0
Midwest						
Number of employees...................................	99,302	33,337	7,364	13,442	12,417	13,756
Average number of employees per 1,000 inhabitants.......	2.5	3.5	2.0	1.8	1.9	2.0
East North Central						
Number of employees...................................	65,367	25,790	3,636	8,873	9,251	8,228
Average number of employees per 1,000 inhabitants.......	2.6	3.8	2.0	1.9	1.9	2.0
West North Central						
Number of employees...................................	33,935	7,547	3,728	4,569	3,166	5,528
Average number of employees per 1,000 inhabitants.......	2.4	2.9	2.0	1.7	1.9	2.1
South						
Number of employees...................................	176,083	53,827	25,431	16,884	17,314	19,607
Average number of employees per 1,000 inhabitants.......	3.2	2.9	2.5	2.5	2.6	2.9
South Atlantic						
Number of employees...................................	89,454	23,853	14,310	9,661	9,288	9,854
Average number of employees per 1,000 inhabitants.......	3.5	3.7	2.6	2.5	2.7	3.1
East South Central						
Number of employees...................................	27,430	6,317	2,011	2,482	3,816	3,754
Average number of employees per 1,000 inhabitants.......	3.3	2.7	2.7	2.6	2.6	3.0
West South Central						
Number of employees...................................	59,199	23,657	9,110	4,741	4,210	5,999
Average number of employees per 1,000 inhabitants.......	2.7	2.4	2.2	2.4	2.3	2.7
West						
Number of employees...................................	115,897	49,616	20,905	15,405	8,815	6,873
Average number of employees per 1,000 inhabitants.......	2.2	2.4	1.7	1.6	1.7	2.0
Mountain						
Number of employees...................................	42,195	16,388	7,490	4,671	3,460	2,690
Average number of employees per 1,000 inhabitants.......	2.5	2.6	1.9	1.9	1.9	2.3
Pacific						
Number of employees...................................	73,702	33,228	13,415	10,734	5,355	4,183
Average number of employees per 1,000 inhabitants.......	2.0	2.3	1.6	1.6	1.6	1.9

[1] Full-time law enforcement employees include civilians.
[2] The designation county is a combination of both metropolitan and nonmetropolitan counties.
[3] Suburban areas include law enforcement agencies in cities with less than 50,000 inhabitants and county law enforcement agencies that are within a Metropolitan Statistical Area. Suburban areas exclude all metropolitan agencies associated with a principal city. The agencies associated with suburban areas also appear in other groups within this table.

Table 17. Full-Time Law Enforcement Employees,[1] by Region and Geographic Division and Population Group, 2017—Continued

(Number, rate per 1,000 inhabitants.)

Region/geographic division	Group VI (6,966 cities, under 10,000; population 20,714,322)	Total city agencies	2017 estimated city population	County[2] (3,070 agencies; population 88,792,091)	Total city and county agencies	2017 estimated total agency population	Suburban areas[3] (7,001 agencies; population 120,076,115)
Total							
Number of employees	99,741	10,058	193,187,549	414,302	13,128	281,979,640	450,252
Average number of employees per 1,000 inhabitants	4.8			4.7			3.7
Northeast							
Number of employees	23,452	2,614	45,196,822				
Average number of employees per 1,000 inhabitants	3.7						
New England							
Number of employees	6,366	781	12,920,841				
Average number of employees per 1,000 inhabitants	3.8						
Middle Atlantic							
Number of employees	17,086	1,833	32,275,981				
Average number of employees per 1,000 inhabitants	3.6						
Midwest							
Number of employees	18,986	2,616	39,587,170				
Average number of employees per 1,000 inhabitants	3.3						
East North Central							
Number of employees	9,589	1,382	25,468,923				
Average number of employees per 1,000 inhabitants	3.1						
West North Central							
Number of employees	9,397	1,234	14,118,247				
Average number of employees per 1,000 inhabitants	3.6						
South							
Number of employees	43,020	3,427	55,419,668				
Average number of employees per 1,000 inhabitants	6.8						
South Atlantic							
Number of employees	22,488	1,606	25,229,607				
Average number of employees per 1,000 inhabitants	8.0						
East South Central							
Number of employees	9,050	738	8,207,314				
Average number of employees per 1,000 inhabitants	6.1						
West South Central							
Number of employees	11,482	1,083	21,982,747				
Average number of employees per 1,000 inhabitants	5.6						
West							
Number of employees	14,283	1,401	52,983,889				
Average number of employees per 1,000 inhabitants	6.3						
Mountain							
Number of employees	7,496	640	16,919,843				
Average number of employees per 1,000 inhabitants	6.5						
Pacific							
Number of employees	6,787	761	36,064,046				
Average number of employees per 1,000 inhabitants	6.1						

[1] Full-time law enforcement employees include civilians.
[2] The designation county is a combination of both metropolitan and nonmetropolitan counties.
[3] Suburban areas include law enforcement agencies in cities with less than 50,000 inhabitants and county law enforcement agencies that are within a Metropolitan Statistical Area. Suburban areas exclude all metropolitan agencies associated with a principal city. The agencies associated with suburban areas also appear in other groups within this table.

Table 18. Full-Time Law Enforcement Officers, by Region and Geographic Division, and Population Group, 2017

(Number, rate per 1,000 inhabitants.)

Region/geographic division	Total (10,058 cities; population 193,187,549)	Group I (79 cities, 250,000 and over; population 60,607,956)	Group II (198 cities, 100,000 to 249,999; population 29,257,403)	Group III (431 cities, 50,000 to 99,999; population 30,031,331)	Group IV (775 cities, 25,000 to 49,999; population 26,916,000)	Group V (1,609 cities, 10,000 to 24,999; population 25,660,537)
Total						
Number of officers	422,869	155,692	47,814	47,850	45,672	47,866
Average number of officers per 1,000 inhabitants	2.2	2.6	1.6	1.6	1.7	1.9
Northeast						
Number of officers	119,962	48,868	7,188	13,201	15,436	15,893
Average number of officers per 1,000 inhabitants	2.7	4.1	2.5	2.0	1.8	1.8
New England						
Number of officers	28,038	2,205	3,831	5,409	5,985	5,628
Average number of officers per 1,000 inhabitants	2.2	3.2	2.6	2.0	1.8	1.8
Middle Atlantic						
Number of officers	91,924	46,663	3,357	7,792	9,451	10,265
Average number of officers per 1,000 inhabitants	2.8	4.1	2.4	2.0	1.8	1.8
Midwest						
Number of officers	82,591	28,201	6,130	10,896	10,069	11,343
Average number of officers per 1,000 inhabitants	2.1	3.0	1.6	1.5	1.5	1.7
East North Central						
Number of officers	55,403	22,440	3,127	7,232	7,554	6,862
Average number of officers per 1,000 inhabitants	2.2	3.3	1.7	1.6	1.5	1.7
West North Central						
Number of officers	27,188	5,761	3,003	3,664	2,515	4,481
Average number of officers per 1,000 inhabitants	1.9	2.2	1.6	1.4	1.5	1.7
South						
Number of officers	136,418	41,899	19,615	12,939	13,720	15,426
Average number of officers per 1,000 inhabitants	2.5	2.3	1.9	1.9	2.0	2.3
South Atlantic						
Number of officers	69,076	17,795	11,099	7,477	7,407	7,857
Average number of officers per 1,000 inhabitants	2.7	2.7	2.0	2.0	2.2	2.4
East South Central						
Number of officers	21,736	5,121	1,657	1,986	3,060	3,005
Average number of officers per 1,000 inhabitants	2.6	2.2	2.2	2.1	2.1	2.4
West South Central						
Number of officers	45,606	18,983	6,859	3,476	3,253	4,564
Average number of officers per 1,000 inhabitants	2.1	1.9	1.7	1.8	1.8	2.0
West						
Number of officers	83,898	36,724	14,881	10,814	6,447	5,204
Average number of officers per 1,000 inhabitants	1.6	1.8	1.2	1.2	1.3	1.5
Mountain						
Number of officers	30,266	11,612	5,493	3,300	2,618	2,077
Average number of officers per 1,000 inhabitants	1.8	1.8	1.4	1.3	1.4	1.8
Pacific						
Number of officers	53,632	25,112	9,388	7,514	3,829	3,127
Average number of officers per 1,000 inhabitants	1.5	1.8	1.1	1.1	1.2	1.4

[1] The designation county is a combination of both metropolitan and nonmetropolitan counties.
[2] Suburban areas include law enforcement agencies in cities with less than 50,000 inhabitants and county law enforcement agencies that are within a Metropolitan Statistical Area. Suburban areas exclude all metropolitan agencies associated with a principal city. The agencies associated with suburban areas also appear in other groups within this table.

Table 18. Full-Time Law Enforcement Officers, by Region and Geographic Division, and Population Group, 2017—Continued

(Number, rate per 1,000 inhabitants.)

Region/geographic division	Group VI (6,966 cities, under 10,000; population 20,714,322)	Total city agencies	2017 estimated city population	County[1] (3,070 agencies; population 88,792,091)	Total city and county agencies	2017 estimated total agency population	Suburban areas[2] (7,001 agencies; population 120,076,115)
Total							
Number of officers	77,975	10,058	193,187,549	247,410	13,128	281,979,640	298,444
Average number of officers per 1,000 inhabitants	3.8			2.8			2.5
Northeast							
Number of officers	19,376	2,614	45,196,822				
Average number of officers per 1,000 inhabitants	3.0						
New England							
Number of officers	4,980	781	12,920,841				
Average number of officers per 1,000 inhabitants	2.9						
Middle Atlantic							
Number of officers	14,396	1,833	32,275,981				
Average number of officers per 1,000 inhabitants	3.1						
Midwest							
Number of officers	15,952	2,616	39,587,170				
Average number of officers per 1,000 inhabitants	2.8						
East North Central							
Number of officers	8,188	1,382	25,468,923				
Average number of officers per 1,000 inhabitants	2.6						
West North Central							
Number of officers	7,764	1,234	14,118,247				
Average number of officers per 1,000 inhabitants	3.0						
South							
Number of officers	32,819	3,427	55,419,668				
Average number of officers per 1,000 inhabitants	5.2						
South Atlantic							
Number of officers	17,441	1,606	25,229,607				
Average number of officers per 1,000 inhabitants	6.2						
East South Central							
Number of officers	6,907	738	8,207,314				
Average number of officers per 1,000 inhabitants	4.7						
West South Central							
Number of officers	8,471	1,083	21,982,747				
Average number of officers per 1,000 inhabitants	4.2						
West							
Number of officers	9,828	1,401	52,983,889				
Average number of officers per 1,000 inhabitants	4.3						
Mountain							
Number of officers	5,166	640	16,919,843				
Average number of officers per 1,000 inhabitants	4.5						
Pacific							
Number of officers	4,662	761	36,064,046				
Average number of officers per 1,000 inhabitants	4.2						

[1] The designation county is a combination of both metropolitan and nonmetropolitan counties.
[2] Suburban areas include law enforcement agencies in cities with less than 50,000 inhabitants and county law enforcement agencies that are within a Metropolitan Statistical Area. Suburban areas exclude all metropolitan agencies associated with a principal city. The agencies associated with suburban areas also appear in other groups within this table.

Table 19. Full-Time Law Enforcement Employees, by Selected State and City, 2017

(Number.)

State/city	Population	Total law enforcement employees	Total officers	Total civilians
ALABAMA				
Adamsville	4,334	33	20	13
Addison	735	3	3	0
Albertville	21,588	69	45	24
Alexander City	14,744	68	51	17
Andalusia	8,958	43	32	11
Anniston	21,955	97	80	17
Arab	8,380	36	27	9
Ardmore	1,414	11	7	4
Arley	349	2	2	0
Ashville	2,285	9	9	0
Athens	26,004	59	48	11
Atmore	9,994	31	25	6
Attalla	5,835	27	22	5
Auburn	64,831	132	124	8
Bay Minette	9,483	27	21	6
Bayou La Batre	2,499	17	12	5
Berry	1,091	3	3	0
Bessemer	26,360	164	122	42
Boaz	9,748	36	25	11
Brent	4,916	6	6	0
Brewton	5,436	32	24	8
Bridgeport	2,325	11	7	4
Brundidge	1,955	14	9	5
Camden	1,905	11	10	1
Carrollton	974	2	2	0
Castleberry	545	2	1	1
Centreville	2,698	6	6	0
Chickasaw	5,879	27	22	5
Citronelle	3,882	9	7	2
Clanton	8,882	25	25	0
Columbiana	4,605	13	9	4
Creola	1,968	10	5	5
Cullman	15,613	72	51	21
Daleville	5,068	22	16	6
Daphne	26,669	68	43	25
Dauphin Island	1,265	27	12	15
Decatur	54,958	153	130	23
Dora	1,933	10	6	4
Dothan	68,894	237	165	72
East Brewton	2,405	10	5	5
Elberta	1,707	8	7	1
Eufaula	12,295	60	38	22
Eutaw	2,722	11	10	1
Evergreen	3,653	25	19	6
Flomaton	1,403	15	9	6
Florala	1,947	8	8	0
Florence	40,059	131	106	25
Foley	18,032	92	64	28
Fort Deposit	1,209	5	4	1
Fort Payne	14,098	40	35	5
Fultondale	9,207	32	26	6
Greensboro	2,345	10	9	1
Greenville	7,724	33	28	5
Guntersville	8,476	47	35	12
Hanceville	3,317	22	12	10
Hartford	2,640	12	8	4
Helena	18,965	28	23	5
Hoover	85,634	231	168	63
Irondale	12,362	41	34	7
Jacksonville	12,573	38	30	8
Jasper	13,940	66	46	20
Killen	974	4	4	0
Lafayette	2,963	12	11	1
Lanett	6,383	28	26	2
Leeds	11,964	33	25	8
Level Plains	1,994	5	5	0
Lexington	715	4	4	0
Lineville	2,293	13	9	4
Livingston	3,454	11	7	4
Luverne	2,831	14	13	1

(Number.)

State/city	Population	Total law enforcement employees	Total officers	Total civilians
Lynn	635	2	1	1
Madison	48,777	105	78	27
Margaret	4,668	1	1	0
Midland City	2,396	8	4	4
Monroeville	6,007	28	23	5
Montevallo	6,793	23	14	9
Muscle Shoals	13,939	45	35	10
New Brockton	1,159	2	2	0
Northport	25,337	85	67	18
Oneonta	6,721	19	18	1
Opelika	30,476	106	86	20
Opp	6,573	29	20	9
Orange Beach	6,073	75	51	24
Oxford	21,084	68	59	9
Ozark	14,559	45	34	11
Phenix City	37,841	101	80	21
Piedmont	4,633	18	13	5
Pine Hill	904	4	4	0
Pleasant Grove	10,191	22	17	5
Priceville	3,414	5	5	0
Prichard	22,119	60	39	21
Ragland	1,707	4	4	0
Rainbow City	9,517	34	22	12
Rainsville	5,025	18	14	4
Roanoke	5,970	29	22	7
Robertsdale	6,112	26	15	11
Russellville	9,810	24	20	4
Samson	1,908	6	6	0
Sardis City	1,782	4	4	0
Satsuma	6,198	17	13	4
Scottsboro	14,660	68	43	25
Silverhill	818	5	5	0
Snead	842	4	4	0
Southside	8,630	15	11	4
Spanish Fort	8,584	25	21	4
Springville	4,280	11	11	0
Steele	1,093	4	4	0
Stevenson	1,966	7	6	1
St. Florian	630	4	4	0
Sumiton	2,390	18	10	8
Summerdale	1,314	7	7	0
Tallassee	4,748	24	18	6
Tarrant	6,249	25	20	5
Thomasville	3,971	23	18	5
Trinity	2,176	7	7	0
Troy	19,360	76	55	21
Tuscaloosa	101,124	342	264	78
Tuskegee	8,549	26	17	9
Valley	9,363	30	28	2
Vestavia Hills	34,781	91	88	3
Warrior	3,195	20	13	7
Weaver	3,081	11	8	3
Wedowee	804	8	8	0
West Blocton	1,259	3	3	0
Woodstock	1,594	4	4	0
ALASKA				
Anchorage	296,188	555	408	147
Bethel	6,426	22	11	11
Bristol Bay Borough	874	9	4	5
Cordova	2,199	9	4	5
Craig	1,235	9	4	5
Dillingham	2,369	17	6	11
Fairbanks	32,937	44	39	5
Haines	2,472	10	5	5
Homer	5,735	21	12	9
Hoonah	743	8	4	4
Juneau	32,344	72	44	28
Kenai	7,852	25	18	7
Ketchikan	8,230	32	21	11
Klawock	802	3	3	0

(Number.)

State/city	Population	Total law enforcement employees	Total officers	Total civilians
Kodiak	6,198	38	17	21
Kotzebue	3,251	17	10	7
Nome	3,829	15	8	7
North Pole	2,248	14	13	1
North Slope Borough	9,539	74	46	28
Palmer	7,184	25	14	11
Petersburg	3,108	14	9	5
Sand Point	1,054	3	2	1
Seward	2,806	20	10	10
Sitka	8,736	26	14	12
Skagway	1,100	10	3	7
Soldotna	4,693	16	14	2
St. Paul	498	11	4	7
Unalaska	4,449	25	12	13
Valdez	3,842	11	11	0
Wasilla	10,093	52	23	29
Whittier	213	6	5	1
Wrangell	2,395	11	5	6
ARIZONA				
Apache Junction	40,672	89	59	30
Avondale	84,041	180	122	58
Benson	4,836	22	14	8
Bisbee	5,160	15	11	4
Buckeye	67,147	119	89	30
Bullhead City	40,039	109	67	42
Camp Verde	11,299	27	18	9
Casa Grande	55,530	102	80	22
Chandler	249,355	502	335	167
Chino Valley	11,324	31	24	7
Clarkdale	4,304	10	8	2
Clifton	3,817	11	5	6
Colorado City	4,818	8	6	2
Coolidge	12,645	40	28	12
Cottonwood	12,116	56	34	22
Douglas	16,443	45	33	12
Eagar	5,001	8	6	2
El Mirage	35,611	57	44	13
Eloy	17,552	36	23	13
Flagstaff	72,388	152	102	50
Florence	25,623	38	29	9
Fredonia	1,322	2	2	0
Gilbert	242,090	345	231	114
Glendale	249,273	551	423	128
Globe	7,349	18	15	3
Goodyear	79,419	139	99	40
Hayden	976	7	7	0
Holbrook	5,077	15	13	2
Huachuca City	1,725	12	5	7
Jerome	457	4	4	0
Kearny	2,096	9	6	3
Kingman	29,181	69	54	15
Lake Havasu City	53,937	112	71	41
Mammoth	1,534	5	4	1
Marana	45,123	119	91	28
Maricopa	47,466	85	65	20
Mesa	492,268	1,208	786	422
Miami	1,774	11	7	4
Nogales	19,878	65	50	15
Oro Valley	44,251	130	100	30
Page	7,632	31	19	12
Paradise Valley	14,629	45	35	10
Parker	3,022	13	10	3
Patagonia	872	3	3	0
Payson	15,504	41	26	15
Peoria	165,889	288	192	96
Phoenix	1,644,177	3,816	2,838	978
Pima	2,527	6	6	0
Pinetop-Lakeside	4,392	23	15	8
Prescott	42,975	76	65	11
Prescott Valley	43,891	93	73	20

Table 19. Full-Time Law Enforcement Employees, by Selected State and City, 2017—*Continued*

(Number.)

State/city	Population	Total law enforcement employees	Total officers	Total civilians
Quartzsite	3,638	12	11	1
Safford	9,617	24	21	3
Sahuarita	29,373	46	40	6
San Luis	32,823	51	34	17
Scottsdale	251,840	623	392	231
Sedona	10,457	37	26	11
Show Low	11,163	39	29	10
Sierra Vista	42,859	87	61	26
Snowflake-Taylor	10,025	21	13	8
Somerton	15,082	29	20	9
South Tucson	5,645	20	18	2
Springerville	2,000	9	7	2
St. Johns	3,581	9	6	3
Superior	3,026	10	9	1
Surprise	135,345	191	135	56
Tempe	186,086	495	356	139
Thatcher	5,054	13	12	1
Tolleson	7,289	48	30	18
Tombstone	1,287	12	10	2
Tucson	532,323	1,174	834	340
Wellton	2,981	7	6	1
Wickenburg	6,979	26	18	8
Willcox	3,471	18	10	8
Williams	3,181	21	13	8
Winslow	9,764	35	25	10
Yuma	95,522	252	168	84
ARKANSAS				
Alexander	2,810	9	7	2
Alma	5,699	22	14	8
Amity	698	1	1	0
Arkadelphia	10,810	29	23	6
Arkansas City	316	1	1	0
Ashdown	4,433	12	11	1
Ash Flat	1,075	4	4	0
Atkins	3,065	8	7	1
Augusta	1,993	6	6	0
Austin	4,091	4	4	0
Bald Knob	2,908	9	7	2
Barling	4,820	11	11	0
Batesville	10,806	25	24	1
Bay	1,819	3	3	0
Bearden	874	1	1	0
Beebe	8,258	24	17	7
Bella Vista	28,721	42	30	12
Benton	36,702	88	64	24
Bentonville	49,301	100	72	28
Berryville	5,390	13	11	2
Bethel Heights	2,564	7	6	1
Black Rock	615	1	1	0
Blytheville	14,184	41	30	11
Bono	2,304	4	4	0
Booneville	3,886	13	9	4
Bradford	759	5	4	1
Brinkley	2,740	16	11	5
Brookland	3,353	5	5	0
Bryant	20,593	53	44	9
Bull Shoals	1,944	3	3	0
Cabot	26,118	55	44	11
Caddo Valley	599	4	4	0
Camden	11,069	36	19	17
Cammack Village	742	4	3	1
Caraway	1,275	2	2	0
Carlisle	2,164	10	6	4
Cave City	1,891	4	4	0
Cave Springs	4,031	6	6	0
Cedarville	1,369	2	2	0
Centerton	13,521	23	21	2
Charleston	2,457	4	4	0
Cherokee Village	4,639	9	8	1
Cherry Valley	596	1	1	0

(Number.)

State/city	Population	Total law enforcement employees	Total officers	Total civilians
Clarendon	1,424	4	4	0
Clarksville	9,581	23	18	5
Clinton	2,505	8	7	1
Conway	66,299	170	127	43
Corning	3,078	12	8	4
Cotter	944	2	2	0
Crossett	5,069	27	17	10
Danville	2,450	7	6	1
Dardanelle	4,578	15	10	5
Decatur	1,803	6	6	0
Dell	201	1	1	0
De Queen	6,555	16	14	2
Dermott	2,711	12	6	6
Des Arc	1,617	4	4	0
De Valls Bluff	577	1	1	0
De Witt	3,120	15	9	6
Diamond City	787	1	1	0
Diaz	1,219	2	2	0
Dierks	1,093	3	3	0
Dover	1,404	5	5	0
Dumas	4,226	17	11	6
Dyer	864	1	1	0
Earle	2,253	2	2	0
El Dorado	18,257	68	51	17
Elkins	3,018	7	7	0
England	2,741	10	7	3
Etowah	318	1	1	0
Eudora	2,048	5	4	1
Eureka Springs	2,074	15	10	5
Fairfield Bay	2,232	17	7	10
Farmington	6,949	12	11	1
Fayetteville	85,592	175	127	48
Flippin	1,338	5	5	0
Fordyce	3,904	12	7	5
Forrest City	14,343	40	31	9
Fort Smith	88,437	174	134	40
Gassville	2,140	4	4	0
Gentry	3,777	10	8	2
Glenwood	2,128	2	1	1
Gosnell	3,175	7	7	0
Gravette	3,295	12	11	1
Greenbrier	5,488	15	9	6
Green Forest	2,784	14	11	3
Greenland	1,405	4	4	0
Greenwood	9,409	22	20	2
Greers Ferry	859	3	3	0
Gurdon	2,126	6	4	2
Guy	775	1	1	0
Hamburg	2,719	7	6	1
Hampton	1,249	4	4	0
Hardy	768	2	2	0
Harrisburg	2,315	6	5	1
Harrison	13,208	42	31	11
Haskell	4,516	8	8	0
Hazen	1,388	6	5	1
Heber Springs	7,071	25	15	10
Helena-West Helena	10,609	34	18	16
Higginson	668	1	1	0
Highfill	659	3	3	0
Highland	1,071	3	3	0
Hope	9,859	36	24	12
Hot Springs	36,956	135	105	30
Hoxie	2,661	4	4	0
Hughes	1,278	3	3	0
Huntington	622	1	1	0
Jacksonville	28,540	81	69	12
Jasper	448	2	2	0
Johnson	3,681	9	8	1
Jonesboro	76,188	185	157	28
Judsonia	2,002	4	3	1
Keiser	676	1	1	0

Table 19. Full-Time Law Enforcement Employees, by Selected State and City, 2017—*Continued*

(Number.)

State/city	Population	Total law enforcement employees	Total officers	Total civilians
Kensett	1,647	3	3	0
Lake City	2,462	4	4	0
Lakeview	722	2	2	0
Lake Village	2,357	15	9	6
Lamar	1,680	3	3	0
Lavaca	2,418	3	3	0
Leachville	1,800	3	2	1
Lepanto	1,818	7	3	4
Lewisville	1,134	2	2	0
Lincoln	2,455	5	5	0
Little Flock	2,842	6	6	0
Little Rock	199,314	627	509	118
Lonoke	4,234	16	11	5
Lowell	9,220	24	18	6
Luxora	1,059	2	2	0
Madison	681	4	4	0
Magnolia	11,568	24	22	2
Malvern	11,007	22	20	2
Mammoth Spring	959	2	2	0
Marianna	3,521	28	15	13
Marion	12,356	32	28	4
Marked Tree	2,496	9	5	4
Marmaduke	1,240	4	4	0
Marvell	990	7	4	3
Maumelle	18,278	46	36	10
Mayflower	2,469	9	9	0
McCrory	1,554	5	5	0
McGehee	3,839	25	12	13
McRae	663	3	2	1
Mena	5,624	15	14	1
Menifee	312	1	1	0
Mineral Springs	1,159	1	1	0
Monette	1,573	3	3	0
Monticello	9,775	28	21	7
Morrilton	6,715	26	23	3
Mountainburg	623	1	1	0
Mountain Home	12,347	34	26	8
Mountain View	2,880	10	9	1
Mulberry	1,641	3	3	0
Murfreesboro	1,571	3	3	0
Nashville	4,480	17	16	1
Newport	7,726	22	15	7
North Little Rock	66,938	225	186	39
Ola	1,227	5	4	1
Osceola	6,984	38	25	13
Ozark	3,555	12	10	2
Pangburn	602	2	2	0
Paragould	28,588	65	50	15
Paris	3,443	13	8	5
Parkin	1,035	1	1	0
Pea Ridge	5,506	15	14	1
Perryville	1,415	5	5	0
Piggott	3,574	9	8	1
Pine Bluff	43,040	155	130	25
Plainview	587	1	1	0
Plumerville	796	2	2	0
Pocahontas	6,447	16	15	1
Pottsville	3,146	8	6	2
Prairie Grove	5,511	11	11	0
Prescott	3,039	9	8	1
Quitman	730	4	4	0
Ravenden	447	1	1	0
Redfield	1,547	7	6	1
Rison	1,258	3	3	0
Rogers	66,626	141	102	39
Rose Bud	482	3	3	0
Russellville	29,786	60	53	7
Salem	1,622	4	3	1
Searcy	24,553	68	49	19
Shannon Hills	3,958	6	6	0
Sheridan	4,866	29	14	15

(Number.)

State/city	Population	Total law enforcement employees	Total officers	Total civilians
Sherwood	30,830	89	65	24
Siloam Springs	16,680	48	35	13
Springdale	79,876	200	140	60
Stamps	1,493	3	3	0
Star City	2,131	7	6	1
St. Charles	218	1	1	0
Stuttgart	8,882	33	24	9
Sulphur Springs	534	3	3	0
Swifton	739	2	2	0
Texarkana	30,334	91	81	10
Trumann	7,104	25	18	7
Tuckerman	1,722	4	4	0
Tyronza	739	2	2	0
Van Buren	23,456	58	44	14
Vilonia	4,595	9	9	0
Waldron	3,331	10	9	1
Walnut Ridge	4,638	8	8	0
Ward	5,007	11	9	2
Warren	5,719	18	11	7
Weiner	681	1	1	0
West Fork	2,588	6	6	0
West Memphis	25,126	100	79	21
White Hall	5,009	17	15	2
Wilson	847	2	2	0
Wynne	8,033	22	20	2
CALIFORNIA				
Alameda	79,761	111	79	32
Albany	19,880	32	24	8
Alhambra	85,865	116	77	39
Alturas	2,491	7	7	0
Anaheim	353,400	602	419	183
Anderson	10,281	26	20	6
Angels Camp	3,779	7	6	1
Antioch	112,252	132	96	36
Arcadia	58,883	93	66	27
Arcata	18,054	36	23	13
Arroyo Grande	18,239	29	25	4
Arvin	21,390	26	18	8
Atascadero	30,661	37	28	9
Atherton	7,256	25	18	7
Atwater	29,442	35	25	10
Auburn	14,069	25	18	7
Avenal	12,054	19	17	2
Azusa	50,202	87	59	28
Bakersfield	381,154	514	364	150
Baldwin Park	76,636	94	69	25
Banning	31,247	38	25	13
Barstow	24,028	54	37	17
Bear Valley	5,497	6	5	1
Beaumont	46,856	56	39	17
Bell	35,925	43	27	16
Bell Gardens	42,930	72	50	22
Belmont	27,285	43	29	14
Belvedere	2,131	8	7	1
Benicia	28,370	46	30	16
Berkeley	122,687	247	162	85
Beverly Hills	34,781	216	133	83
Bishop	3,767	17	12	5
Blythe	19,572	31	21	10
Brawley	26,342	49	35	14
Brea	43,000	92	58	34
Brentwood	62,120	94	64	30
Brisbane	4,764	18	15	3
Broadmoor	4,438	9	8	1
Buena Park	83,552	128	84	44
Burbank	104,622	239	157	82
Burlingame	30,551	59	39	20
Calexico	40,499	33	20	13
California City	13,753	26	16	10
Calistoga	5,336	16	11	5

Table 19. Full-Time Law Enforcement Employees, by Selected State and City, 2017—*Continued*

(Number.)

State/city	Population	Total law enforcement employees	Total officers	Total civilians
Campbell	41,192	68	44	24
Capitola	10,222	28	21	7
Carlsbad	115,344	160	115	45
Carmel	3,918	21	13	8
Cathedral City	54,506	74	51	23
Central Marin	35,060	45	40	5
Ceres	48,673	60	47	13
Chico	92,459	138	89	49
Chino	89,420	158	107	51
Chowchilla	18,174	27	18	9
Chula Vista	271,109	309	223	86
Citrus Heights	88,126	132	88	44
Claremont	36,246	60	37	23
Clayton	12,173	13	11	2
Clearlake	15,018	23	17	6
Cloverdale	8,830	21	13	8
Clovis	108,419	167	100	67
Coalinga	16,371	25	17	8
Colma	1,520	25	19	6
Colton	55,127	84	50	34
Colusa	5,930	10	9	1
Concord	129,789	205	152	53
Corcoran	22,345	29	16	13
Corning	7,511	20	11	9
Corona	169,164	217	154	63
Coronado	26,294	63	43	20
Costa Mesa	113,267	183	119	64
Cotati	7,485	15	10	5
Covina	48,674	87	57	30
Crescent City	6,529	11	10	1
Culver City	39,440	145	105	40
Cypress	49,064	65	50	15
Daly City	107,355	126	98	28
Davis	68,540	91	58	33
Delano	52,639	69	48	21
Del Rey Oaks	1,694	6	6	0
Desert Hot Springs	28,717	32	24	8
Dinuba	24,387	46	36	10
Dixon	20,049	26	21	5
Dos Palos	5,291	7	6	1
Downey	113,511	154	110	44
East Palo Alto	29,933	46	35	11
El Cajon	104,447	172	116	56
El Centro	44,458	66	47	19
El Cerrito	25,704	47	40	7
Elk Grove	172,620	222	137	85
El Monte	116,168	164	118	46
El Segundo	16,932	75	58	17
Emeryville	11,971	55	41	14
Escalon	7,587	11	10	1
Escondido	152,845	214	159	55
Etna	713	3	3	0
Eureka	27,230	68	47	21
Exeter	10,533	18	16	2
Fairfax	7,623	16	11	5
Fairfield	116,372	167	111	56
Farmersville	10,760	15	14	1
Ferndale	1,372	5	5	0
Firebaugh	8,436	15	11	4
Folsom	78,155	104	72	32
Fontana	211,782	281	179	102
Fort Bragg	7,289	21	15	6
Fortuna	12,154	27	17	10
Foster City	34,808	50	36	14
Fountain Valley	56,704	71	53	18
Fowler	6,475	15	14	1
Fremont	236,368	278	178	100
Fresno	526,371	1,059	786	273
Fullerton	141,637	213	141	72
Galt	25,971	51	30	21
Gardena	60,249	116	92	24

(Number.)

State/city	Population	Total law enforcement employees	Total officers	Total civilians
Garden Grove	175,466	222	162	60
Gilroy	56,163	99	62	37
Glendale	202,381	327	233	94
Glendora	52,133	83	52	31
Gonzales	8,508	13	10	3
Grass Valley	12,947	27	24	3
Greenfield	17,603	23	20	3
Gridley	6,588	19	14	5
Grover Beach	13,720	26	18	8
Guadalupe	7,360	14	12	2
Gustine	5,865	11	9	2
Hanford	55,789	82	54	28
Hawthorne	88,664	139	91	48
Hayward	161,417	301	189	112
Healdsburg	11,915	27	18	9
Hemet	85,166	108	77	31
Hercules	25,570	22	20	2
Hermosa Beach	19,836	64	37	27
Hillsborough	11,531	34	27	7
Hollister	38,310	37	31	6
Huntington Beach	202,244	327	208	119
Huntington Park	59,004	81	52	29
Huron	6,973	20	13	7
Imperial	17,629	18	15	3
Indio	90,055	99	63	36
Inglewood	110,811	219	175	44
Ione	6,915	7	7	0
Irvine	276,115	302	211	91
Irwindale	1,436	32	26	6
Jackson	4,683	9	8	1
Kensington	5,397	7	7	0
Kerman	14,760	24	21	3
King City	14,037	20	17	3
Kingsburg	11,874	18	15	3
Laguna Beach	23,261	88	48	40
La Habra	61,878	98	67	31
Lakeport	4,775	13	12	1
Lake Shastina	2,562	4	4	0
La Mesa	60,425	96	67	29
La Palma	15,811	24	18	6
La Verne	32,613	60	40	20
Lemoore	25,999	40	33	7
Lincoln	47,741	28	21	7
Lindsay	13,513	19	15	4
Livermore	90,485	138	90	48
Livingston	14,117	29	20	9
Lodi	65,042	95	65	30
Lompoc	43,948	65	41	24
Long Beach	471,397	1,180	799	381
Los Alamitos	11,671	26	23	3
Los Altos	30,816	46	31	15
Los Angeles	4,007,147	12,857	9,988	2,869
Los Banos	37,910	64	40	24
Los Gatos	30,720	53	36	17
Madera	64,939	75	55	20
Mammoth Lakes	7,956	13	10	3
Manhattan Beach	35,843	98	59	39
Manteca	78,564	90	62	28
Marina	22,030	33	27	6
Martinez	38,619	42	32	10
Marysville	12,275	25	18	7
McFarland	14,882	20	13	7
Mendota	11,459	13	11	2
Menlo Park	34,195	61	43	18
Merced	83,180	121	87	34
Mill Valley	14,423	27	21	6
Milpitas	79,503	99	81	18
Modesto	213,677	311	213	98
Monrovia	37,214	79	50	29
Montclair	39,318	64	46	18
Montebello	63,473	94	65	29

Table 19. Full-Time Law Enforcement Employees, by Selected State and City, 2017—*Continued*

(Number.)

State/city	Population	Total law enforcement employees	Total officers	Total civilians
Monterey	28,584	69	50	19
Monterey Park	61,210	102	70	32
Moraga	17,653	14	12	2
Morgan Hill	45,277	60	39	21
Morro Bay	10,716	21	17	4
Mountain View	81,525	134	87	47
Mount Shasta	3,276	11	8	3
Murrieta	113,016	127	85	42
Napa	80,958	120	72	48
National City	61,574	119	85	34
Nevada City	3,157	13	11	2
Newark	46,360	78	56	22
Newman	11,271	14	11	3
Newport Beach	86,910	217	135	82
Novato	56,698	80	54	26
Oakdale	22,886	33	22	11
Oakland	424,915	1,037	744	293
Oceanside	176,815	282	204	78
Ontario	174,724	373	273	100
Orange	141,130	219	153	66
Orange Cove	9,674	12	11	1
Orland	7,624	13	10	3
Oroville	19,091	35	19	16
Oxnard	209,513	350	238	112
Pacifica	39,353	36	33	3
Pacific Grove	15,716	30	19	11
Palm Springs	48,193	133	94	39
Palo Alto	67,441	142	77	65
Palos Verdes Estates	13,611	37	33	4
Paradise	26,610	32	19	13
Parlier	15,289	16	16	0
Pasadena	142,891	334	229	105
Paso Robles	32,266	45	33	12
Petaluma	60,957	83	58	25
Piedmont	11,464	25	18	7
Pinole	19,449	35	22	13
Pismo Beach	8,291	33	22	11
Pittsburg	71,944	98	79	19
Placentia	52,437	69	45	24
Placerville	10,732	26	18	8
Pleasant Hill	35,136	59	44	15
Pleasanton	84,440	109	76	33
Pomona	153,066	253	147	106
Porterville	59,245	85	56	29
Port Hueneme	22,374	29	22	7
Red Bluff	14,169	40	25	15
Redding	92,127	134	103	31
Redlands	71,707	116	78	38
Redondo Beach	68,051	158	99	59
Redwood City	86,353	113	85	28
Reedley	25,794	42	28	14
Rialto	103,980	137	102	35
Richmond	110,804	244	177	67
Ridgecrest	28,873	50	32	18
Rio Dell	3,414	5	5	0
Rio Vista	8,870	14	12	2
Ripon	15,659	31	22	9
Riverside	328,023	496	350	146
Rocklin	63,735	78	51	27
Rohnert Park	42,922	83	58	25
Roseville	135,028	191	125	66
Ross	2,475	8	8	0
Sacramento	499,997	925	644	281
Salinas	158,313	211	146	65
San Bernardino	217,259	378	236	142
San Bruno	43,274	64	47	17
Sand City	392	14	13	1
San Diego	1,424,116	2,282	1,752	530
San Fernando	24,899	40	28	12
San Francisco	881,255	2,935	2,332	603
San Gabriel	40,531	69	54	15

(Number.)

State/city	Population	Total law enforcement employees	Total officers	Total civilians
Sanger	25,126	41	37	4
San Jose	1,037,529	1,346	940	406
San Leandro	91,386	135	93	42
San Luis Obispo	47,934	80	57	23
San Marino	13,402	31	25	6
San Mateo	105,090	146	107	39
San Pablo	30,781	66	42	24
San Rafael	59,144	88	66	22
San Ramon	76,325	83	65	18
Santa Ana	335,699	537	325	212
Santa Barbara	92,508	204	140	64
Santa Clara	127,538	227	153	74
Santa Cruz	65,132	117	90	27
Santa Maria	107,424	171	115	56
Santa Monica	92,935	373	206	167
Santa Paula	30,496	34	27	7
Santa Rosa	176,361	251	173	78
Sausalito	7,155	26	20	6
Scotts Valley	11,985	27	19	8
Seal Beach	24,495	47	31	16
Seaside	34,519	43	31	12
Sebastopol	7,725	20	14	6
Selma	24,817	41	32	9
Shafter	19,284	35	25	10
Sierra Madre	11,080	20	16	4
Signal Hill	11,757	47	33	14
Simi Valley	126,635	181	123	58
Soledad	25,560	19	15	4
Sonora	4,811	16	9	7
South Gate	95,717	116	79	37
South Lake Tahoe	21,768	56	36	20
South Pasadena	25,961	43	32	11
South San Francisco	67,533	114	80	34
Stallion Springs	2,644	4	4	0
St. Helena	6,210	17	12	5
Stockton	309,566	645	441	204
Suisun City	29,738	37	25	12
Sunnyvale	154,919	273	212	61
Susanville	14,414	17	14	3
Sutter Creek	2,517	4	4	0
Taft	9,393	25	17	8
Tehachapi	12,210	24	15	9
Tiburon	9,210	14	10	4
Torrance	147,482	329	213	116
Tracy	90,263	127	85	42
Truckee	16,429	36	23	13
Tulare	63,349	109	72	37
Tulelake	988	2	2	0
Turlock	73,488	117	78	39
Tustin	81,246	138	94	44
Ukiah	15,859	51	33	18
Union City	76,311	100	76	24
Upland	77,154	88	61	27
Vacaville	99,293	155	102	53
Vallejo	122,174	148	107	41
Ventura	110,006	177	134	43
Vernon	113	52	38	14
Visalia	132,143	207	139	68
Walnut Creek	69,953	122	83	39
Watsonville	54,226	92	73	19
Weed	2,605	14	9	5
West Covina	108,128	152	94	58
Westminster	91,863	113	76	37
Westmorland	2,276	6	6	0
West Sacramento	53,703	92	71	21
Wheatland	3,831	9	8	1
Whittier	87,141	166	120	46
Williams	5,201	13	11	2
Willits	4,870	14	9	5
Winters	7,235	13	11	2
Woodlake	7,678	10	9	1

(Number.)

State/city	Population	Total law enforcement employees	Total officers	Total civilians
Woodland	59,676	79	64	15
Yreka	7,564	21	14	7
Yuba City	67,042	85	55	30
Alamosa	10,025	28	24	4
Arvada	119,346	233	176	57
Aspen	6,906	37	28	9
Ault	1,710	6	5	1
Aurora	368,018	804	649	155
Avon	6,551	19	17	2
Basalt	3,933	11	10	1
Bayfield	2,677	9	8	1
Black Hawk	129	34	23	11
Blue River	924	1	1	0
Boulder	109,722	261	171	90
Breckenridge	4,959	27	20	7
Brighton	39,099	91	66	25
Broomfield	68,158	209	104	105
Brush	5,397	14	11	3
Buena Vista	2,815	10	9	1
Burlington	4,178	9	8	1
Calhan	797	3	3	0
Canon City	16,723	42	36	6
Carbondale	6,844	16	14	2
Castle Rock	59,337	99	72	27
Cedaredge	2,215	8	6	2
Centennial	111,416	164	126	38
Center	2,232	17	7	10
Cherry Hills Village	6,685	27	22	5
Collbran	694	1	1	0
Colorado Springs	472,958	997	707	290
Columbine Valley	1,432	8	8	0
Commerce City	56,469	118	88	30
Cortez	9,095	51	27	24
Craig	8,869	22	17	5
Crested Butte	1,626	7	7	0
Cripple Creek	1,173	22	14	8
Dacono	5,261	13	9	4
De Beque	490	4	4	0
Del Norte	1,583	5	4	1
Delta	8,925	19	16	3
Denver	706,616	1,774	1,479	295
Dillon	970	11	10	1
Durango	18,801	63	52	11
Eagle	6,780	10	9	1
Eaton	5,212	10	9	1
Edgewater	5,350	16	15	1
Elizabeth	1,400	8	7	1
Englewood	34,709	109	77	32
Erie	23,660	32	28	4
Estes Park	6,435	32	20	12
Evans	22,153	40	36	4
Fairplay	708	1	1	0
Federal Heights	12,624	35	25	10
Firestone	13,416	28	23	5
Florence	3,953	14	13	1
Fort Collins	167,633	315	205	110
Fort Lupton	8,057	18	16	2
Fort Morgan	11,347	28	22	6
Fountain	29,203	56	48	8
Fowler	1,139	3	3	0
Fraser/Winter Park	2,293	12	11	1
Frederick	12,850	21	18	3
Frisco	3,154	13	10	3
Fruita	12,971	20	17	3
Georgetown	1,064	3	3	0
Glendale	5,362	40	27	13
Glenwood Springs	10,073	30	25	5
Golden	20,948	66	45	21
Granby	1,929	7	6	1
Grand Junction	62,352	186	108	78
Greeley	105,906	200	149	51

State/city	Population	Total law enforcement employees	Total officers	Total civilians
Greenwood Village	16,067	83	62	21
Gunnison	6,326	29	14	15
Gypsum	7,052	3	3	0
Haxtun	912	3	3	0
Hayden	1,887	6	4	2
Holyoke	2,195	4	4	0
Hotchkiss	912	3	3	0
Hudson	1,508	4	4	0
Hugo	748	2	2	0
Idaho Springs	1,751	9	8	1
Ignacio	728	6	6	0
Johnstown	16,552	20	18	2
Kersey	1,616	4	4	0
Kiowa	745	1	1	0
Kremmling	1,501	4	4	0
Lafayette	28,939	46	39	7
La Junta	6,900	20	14	6
Lakeside	8	5	4	1
Lakewood	156,344	432	279	153
Lamar	7,468	29	15	14
La Salle	2,153	8	8	0
La Veta	774	2	2	0
Leadville	2,711	9	8	1
Limon	1,967	5	4	1
Littleton	47,112	94	70	24
Lochbuie	5,889	10	8	2
Log Lane Village	863	3	3	0
Lone Tree	13,638	57	49	8
Longmont	93,979	214	142	72
Louisville	21,224	39	34	5
Loveland	78,671	155	101	54
Mancos	1,482	4	4	0
Manitou Springs	5,364	16	14	2
Manzanola	413	2	2	0
Meeker	2,336	6	5	1
Milliken	6,870	13	9	4
Monte Vista	4,235	15	12	3
Montrose	19,346	48	33	15
Monument	6,644	18	14	4
Morrison	437	10	9	1
Mountain View	531	8	8	0
Mountain Village	1,432	7	4	3
Mount Crested Butte	839	9	8	1
Nederland	1,548	4	3	1
New Castle	4,798	10	9	1
Northglenn	39,520	79	64	15
Oak Creek	920	3	3	0
Olathe	1,803	6	5	1
Ouray	1,038	5	5	0
Pagosa Springs	1,858	7	6	1
Palisade	2,645	9	8	1
Palmer Lake	2,672	2	2	0
Paonia	1,420	3	3	0
Parachute	1,119	5	4	1
Parker	52,179	118	72	46
Platteville	3,854	9	7	2
Pueblo	110,872	253	200	53
Rangely	2,359	10	5	5
Ridgway	994	2	2	0
Rifle	9,724	23	18	5
Rocky Ford	3,792	10	8	2
Salida	5,642	19	16	3
Sanford	862	1	1	0
Sheridan	6,103	33	30	3
Silt	3,116	6	6	0
Silverthorne	4,615	19	16	3
Simla	625	2	2	0
Snowmass Village	2,913	13	10	3
South Fork	363	2	2	0
Springfield	1,366	4	4	0
Steamboat Springs	12,799	33	23	10

Table 19. Full-Time Law Enforcement Employees, by Selected State and City, 2017—*Continued*

(Number.)

State/city	Population	Total law enforcement employees	Total officers	Total civilians
Sterling	13,955	29	22	7
Stratton	653	1	1	0
Telluride	2,481	16	11	5
Thornton	139,825	287	218	69
Timnath	3,806	8	7	1
Trinidad	7,961	32	23	9
Vail	5,516	68	32	36
Walsh	506	1	1	0
Westminster	115,155	265	190	75
Wheat Ridge	31,567	103	75	28
Wiggins	885	2	2	0
Windsor	23,523	33	29	4
Woodland Park	7,424	28	22	6
Wray	2,369	7	6	1
Yuma	3,593	21	6	15
Ansonia	18,647	50	43	7
Avon	18,397	39	30	9
Berlin	20,601	54	41	13
Bethel	19,796	50	37	13
Bloomfield	20,667	58	46	12
Branford	28,027	66	51	15
Bridgeport	146,110	441	388	53
Bristol	60,090	145	120	25
Brookfield	17,203	44	34	10
Canton	10,285	20	15	5
Cheshire	29,282	57	45	12
Clinton	12,915	37	27	10
Coventry	12,431	21	16	5
Cromwell	13,953	35	27	8
Danbury	85,614	144	139	5
Darien	21,910	57	49	8
Derby	12,586	36	34	2
East Hampton	12,855	18	16	2
East Hartford	50,067	159	125	34
East Haven	28,739	56	52	4
East Lyme	18,849	29	23	6
Easton	7,570	17	15	2
East Windsor	11,383	33	25	8
Enfield	44,321	113	92	21
Fairfield	61,402	108	102	6
Farmington	25,551	60	44	16
Glastonbury	34,606	77	56	21
Granby	11,241	21	16	5
Greenwich	62,531	180	153	27
Groton	9,093	35	28	7
Groton Long Point	506	5	5	0
Groton Town	29,524	68	63	5
Guilford	22,259	45	37	8
Hamden	61,042	133	107	26
Hartford	122,891	435	390	45
Ledyard	14,889	28	21	7
Madison	18,130	40	27	13
Manchester	57,808	140	109	31
Meriden	59,417	123	111	12
Middlebury	7,651	13	11	2
Middletown	46,363	128	114	14
Milford	54,265	133	115	18
Monroe	19,682	55	43	12
Naugatuck	31,310	71	60	11
New Britain	72,442	166	158	8
New Canaan	20,364	52	46	6
New Haven	129,953	476	427	49
Newington	30,402	61	50	11
New London	26,880	83	68	15
New Milford	26,993	53	42	11
Newtown	27,908	49	45	4
North Branford	14,163	27	22	5
North Haven	23,646	58	49	9
Norwalk	88,849	218	179	39
Norwich	39,393	101	84	17
Old Saybrook	10,070	25	17	8

(Number.)

State/city	Population	Total law enforcement employees	Total officers	Total civilians
Orange	13,904	56	46	10
Plainfield	15,011	22	18	4
Plainville	17,669	45	37	8
Plymouth	11,671	29	23	6
Portland	9,324	13	12	1
Putnam	9,293	19	15	4
Redding	9,223	23	17	6
Ridgefield	25,127	47	40	7
Rocky Hill	20,189	50	35	15
Seymour	16,555	41	39	2
Shelton	41,625	58	50	8
Simsbury	24,559	48	37	11
Southington	43,769	85	64	21
South Windsor	25,740	54	41	13
Stamford	130,189	333	283	50
Stonington	18,666	49	38	11
Stratford	52,263	111	104	7
Suffield	15,602	26	21	5
Thomaston	7,548	28	18	10
Torrington	34,372	90	80	10
Trumbull	36,265	89	78	11
Vernon	29,142	62	49	13
Wallingford	44,577	87	66	21
Waterbury	107,924	321	277	44
Waterford	19,034	50	45	5
Watertown	21,672	46	37	9
West Hartford	62,812	141	122	19
West Haven	54,342	133	118	15
Weston	10,320	17	16	1
Westport	28,079	77	64	13
Wethersfield	26,116	64	48	16
Willimantic	17,768	48	43	5
Wilton	18,643	48	44	4
Winchester	10,677	26	21	5
Windsor	28,836	65	52	13
Windsor Locks	12,513	33	26	7
Wolcott	16,632	31	22	9
Woodbridge	8,816	32	24	8
DELAWARE				
Bethany Beach	1,218	11	10	1
Blades	1,404	3	3	0
Bridgeville	2,345	7	7	0
Camden	3,492	9	8	1
Cheswold	1,435	4	4	0
Dagsboro	895	3	3	0
Delaware City	1,750	5	4	1
Delmar	1,794	14	13	1
Dewey Beach	386	10	8	2
Dover	38,084	139	98	41
Ellendale	430	1	1	0
Elsmere	6,102	13	9	4
Felton	1,426	3	3	0
Fenwick Island	434	7	6	1
Georgetown	7,338	25	20	5
Greenwood	1,105	5	3	2
Harrington	3,699	14	13	1
Laurel	4,238	18	17	1
Lewes	3,131	14	13	1
Middletown	21,213	38	32	6
Milford	11,223	41	30	11
Millsboro	4,366	16	15	1
Milton	2,932	9	8	1
Newark	33,722	88	70	18
New Castle	5,362	18	17	1
Newport	1,049	9	8	1
Ocean View	2,117	10	9	1
Rehoboth Beach	1,516	28	17	11
Seaford	7,880	36	25	11
Selbyville	2,466	7	6	1
Smyrna	11,593	30	23	7

Table 19. Full-Time Law Enforcement Employees, by Selected State and City, 2017—*Continued*

(Number.)

State/city	Population	Total law enforcement employees	Total officers	Total civilians
South Bethany	518	8	7	1
Wilmington	71,552	364	300	64
Wyoming	1,516	3	3	0
DISTRICT OF COLUMBIA				
Washington	693,972	4,473	3,836	637
FLORIDA				
Altamonte Springs	43,833	113	94	19
Apopka	50,833	142	104	38
Arcadia	7,992	19	15	4
Atlantic Beach	13,589	38	26	12
Atlantis	2,141	19	14	5
Auburndale	15,903	43	35	8
Aventura	38,039	121	81	40
Bal Harbour Village	3,114	37	24	13
Bartow	19,889	57	38	19
Bay Harbor Islands	6,049	28	22	6
Belleair	4,048	16	14	2
Belle Isle	6,973	17	16	1
Belleview	4,926	15	13	2
Biscayne Park	3,218	11	11	0
Blountstown	2,499	15	12	3
Boca Raton	98,069	302	205	97
Bowling Green	2,904	7	7	0
Boynton Beach	76,845	199	147	52
Bradenton	56,821	155	118	37
Bradenton Beach	1,278	10	10	0
Brooksville	8,047	28	25	3
Bunnell	2,900	10	8	2
Cape Coral	184,346	317	219	98
Carrabelle	2,742	5	5	0
Casselberry	27,218	60	51	9
Cedar Key	706	3	3	0
Chattahoochee	3,082	11	10	1
Chiefland	2,222	14	12	2
Clearwater	115,295	328	240	88
Clermont	34,412	74	68	6
Clewiston	7,735	21	13	8
Cocoa	18,265	90	62	28
Coconut Creek	60,533	130	96	34
Cooper City	36,694	77	59	18
Coral Gables	51,487	252	170	82
Coral Springs	131,558	305	211	94
Cottondale	890	3	3	0
Crescent City	1,544	7	6	1
Dade City	7,214	30	23	7
Dania Beach	31,718	75	68	7
Davenport	4,201	9	8	1
Davie	103,555	248	185	63
Daytona Beach	67,564	259	225	34
Daytona Beach Shores	4,518	38	30	8
Deerfield Beach	80,552	129	122	7
Deland	32,406	79	62	17
Delray Beach	68,533	222	162	60
Dunnellon	1,815	8	7	1
Eatonville	2,297	14	12	2
Edgewater	22,301	31	26	5
Edgewood	2,914	15	12	3
Eustis	21,161	52	39	13
Fellsmere	5,608	8	7	1
Flagler Beach	5,087	18	15	3
Florida City	12,215	41	31	10
Fort Lauderdale	180,972	655	503	152
Fort Myers	79,918	235	173	62
Fort Pierce	45,858	141	114	27
Fort Walton Beach	22,413	60	44	16
Fruitland Park	6,435	17	16	1
Gainesville	132,777	398	284	114
Graceville	2,202	8	7	1
Green Cove Springs	7,800	22	19	3

(Number.)

State/city	Population	Total law enforcement employees	Total officers	Total civilians
Gulf Breeze	6,586	28	18	10
Gulfport	12,473	33	29	4
Gulf Stream	860	12	12	0
Haines City	23,968	57	43	14
Hallandale Beach	39,896	129	95	34
Havana	1,678	15	10	5
Hialeah	238,260	347	281	66
Hialeah Gardens	24,192	55	39	16
High Springs	6,046	16	15	1
Holly Hill	12,226	28	24	4
Hollywood	153,893	391	302	89
Holmes Beach	4,364	23	16	7
Homestead	69,276	150	116	34
Howey-in-the-Hills	1,195	6	6	0
Indialantic	2,919	14	10	4
Indian Creek Village	92	13	9	4
Indian Harbour Beach	8,649	27	20	7
Indian River Shores	4,286	24	21	3
Jacksonville	894,638	3,094	1,665	1,429
Jacksonville Beach	23,740	85	64	21
Jasper	4,156	8	7	1
Jennings	873	4	4	0
Juno Beach	3,629	18	16	2
Jupiter	65,311	145	115	30
Jupiter Inlet Colony	462	5	5	0
Jupiter Island	916	21	16	5
Kenneth City	5,125	13	12	1
Key Biscayne	13,127	47	36	11
Key Colony Beach	861	10	5	5
Key West	27,399	120	94	26
Kissimmee	71,130	202	129	73
Lady Lake	15,151	32	27	5
Lake Alfred	5,899	16	12	4
Lake Clarke Shores	3,611	12	11	1
Lake Hamilton	1,409	8	7	1
Lake Helen	2,758	6	5	1
Lakeland	107,927	336	230	106
Lake Mary	16,636	58	43	15
Lake Placid	2,272	10	8	2
Lake Wales	16,150	51	45	6
Lantana	11,322	35	27	8
Largo	83,728	185	146	39
Lauderdale-by-the-Sea	6,589	26	24	2
Lauderdale Lakes	35,144	41	39	2
Lawtey	716	2	2	0
Leesburg	22,763	88	63	25
Lighthouse Point	11,277	41	32	9
Live Oak	6,984	19	16	3
Longboat Key	7,400	21	18	3
Longwood	15,254	41	37	4
Lynn Haven	21,262	36	26	10
Madison	2,823	16	15	1
Maitland	17,830	57	49	8
Manalapan	466	11	10	1
Marco Island	18,089	38	34	4
Margate	58,649	144	110	34
Marianna	9,346	25	18	7
Mascotte	5,613	13	12	1
Medley	844	48	39	9
Melbourne	82,013	210	153	57
Melbourne Beach	3,306	11	10	1
Melbourne Village	708	5	5	0
Miami	463,009	1,666	1,217	449
Miami Gardens	114,008	260	204	56
Miami Shores	10,808	45	37	8
Miami Springs	14,529	55	43	12
Midway	3,301	2	1	1
Milton	10,011	24	17	7
Miramar	141,328	293	214	79
Monticello	2,385	13	9	4
Mount Dora	14,104	47	33	14

(Number.)

State/city	Population	Total law enforcement employees	Total officers	Total civilians
Naples	22,244	102	70	32
Neptune Beach	7,388	28	20	8
New Port Richey	16,388	63	44	19
New Smyrna Beach	26,230	56	42	14
Niceville	15,380	33	23	10
North Bay Village	8,463	34	26	8
North Lauderdale	44,137	58	52	6
North Miami	62,543	149	114	35
North Miami Beach	44,269	136	102	34
North Palm Beach	13,160	36	31	5
North Port	65,498	120	88	32
Oakland	2,949	12	11	1
Oakland Park	44,814	95	84	11
Ocala	59,731	241	150	91
Ocean Ridge	1,946	19	15	4
Ocoee	46,501	86	74	12
Opa Locka	16,668	47	43	4
Orange City	11,478	27	21	6
Orange Park	8,848	29	22	7
Orlando	283,982	926	714	212
Ormond Beach	42,625	77	61	16
Oviedo	40,391	70	63	7
Palatka	10,439	37	31	6
Palm Bay	111,275	218	156	62
Palm Beach	8,779	95	62	33
Palm Beach Gardens	54,677	161	105	56
Palm Beach Shores	1,253	15	11	4
Palmetto	13,581	48	35	13
Palm Springs	24,300	60	43	17
Panama City Beach	12,987	78	59	19
Parker	4,667	10	9	1
Parkland	32,951	42	37	5
Pembroke Pines	170,923	327	241	86
Perry	7,051	22	20	2
Pinellas Park	52,635	125	104	21
Plantation	93,995	261	169	92
Plant City	38,798	83	66	17
Pompano Beach	111,027	235	208	27
Ponce Inlet	3,253	14	12	2
Port Orange	61,892	108	92	16
Port Richey	2,836	19	14	5
Port St. Joe	3,479	8	8	0
Port St. Lucie	188,652	297	231	66
Punta Gorda	19,181	47	31	16
Riviera Beach	34,536	139	108	31
Rockledge	27,432	69	50	19
Sanford	59,457	153	133	20
Sanibel	7,505	38	23	15
Sarasota	57,383	208	159	49
Satellite Beach	10,954	32	21	11
Sea Ranch Lakes	740	11	7	4
Sebastian	25,277	55	37	18
Sebring	10,679	38	32	6
Sewall's Point	2,212	11	10	1
Shalimar	820	4	4	0
South Daytona	12,882	34	28	6
South Miami	12,291	55	47	8
South Palm Beach	1,447	8	8	0
Springfield	9,593	23	18	5
Starke	5,413	20	19	1
St. Augustine	14,500	66	51	15
St. Cloud	49,791	123	80	43
St. Petersburg	263,712	756	556	200
Stuart	16,800	63	43	20
Surfside	5,849	34	28	6
Sweetwater	20,824	121	36	85
Tallahassee	192,455	446	375	71
Tamarac	65,988	94	77	17
Tampa	384,360	1,213	956	257
Tarpon Springs	25,104	64	51	13
Tavares	16,274	28	25	3

State/city	Population	Total law enforcement employees	Total officers	Total civilians
Temple Terrace	26,854	62	45	17
Tequesta	6,049	24	19	5
Titusville	46,425	138	84	54
Umatilla	3,808	10	9	1
Valparaiso	5,081	17	12	5
Venice	22,762	56	45	11
Vero Beach	17,015	72	51	21
Village of Pinecrest	19,644	66	46	20
Virginia Gardens	2,487	7	6	1
Wauchula	4,920	17	13	4
Welaka	681	1	1	0
West Melbourne	21,808	53	43	10
West Miami	7,742	23	18	5
Weston	70,796	99	78	21
West Palm Beach	109,459	357	268	89
West Park	15,272	40	37	3
White Springs	775	4	4	0
Wildwood	7,810	46	36	10
Williston	2,758	19	12	7
Wilton Manors	12,861	46	31	15
Winter Garden	43,295	100	73	27
Winter Haven	39,859	114	85	29
Winter Park	30,602	106	78	28
Winter Springs	35,995	64	50	14
Zephyrhills	15,145	47	32	15
GEORGIA				
Abbeville	2,736	5	5	0
Acworth	22,747	59	43	16
Adairsville	4,844	15	14	1
Adel	5,359	44	20	24
Alamo	3,437	4	4	0
Albany	73,209	177	153	24
Alma	3,570	13	10	3
Alto	1,163	5	2	3
Americus	15,668	41	34	7
Aragon	1,241	12	4	8
Arcade	1,811	3	3	0
Ashburn	3,674	17	15	2
Athens-Clarke County	124,903	291	227	64
Atlanta	481,343	2,087	1,621	466
Attapulgus	429	2	1	1
Auburn	7,698	21	16	5
Austell	7,224	27	19	8
Avondale Estates	3,183	13	13	0
Bainbridge	12,208	46	40	6
Baldwin	3,308	14	9	5
Ball Ground	2,003	4	4	0
Barnesville	6,696	20	19	1
Baxley	4,752	12	11	1
Berlin	560	2	2	0
Blackshear	3,620	16	13	3
Blairsville	569	8	7	1
Bloomingdale	2,729	16	14	2
Blue Ridge	1,400	9	8	1
Blythe	689	2	2	0
Bowdon	2,106	10	8	2
Braselton	10,761	17	16	1
Braswell	391	1	1	0
Bremen	6,453	22	20	2
Brookhaven	52,973	86	67	19
Brooklet	1,547	6	5	1
Brunswick	16,500	62	58	4
Buena Vista	2,132	5	5	0
Butler	1,854	5	4	1
Byron	5,228	21	17	4
Cairo	9,558	24	21	3
Calhoun	16,557	50	43	7
Canon	804	1	1	0
Carrollton	26,951	83	67	16
Cave Spring	1,145	1	1	0

Table 19. Full-Time Law Enforcement Employees, by Selected State and City, 2017—*Continued*

(Number.)

State/city	Population	Total law enforcement employees	Total officers	Total civilians
Cedartown	9,806	37	34	3
Centerville	7,689	20	17	3
Chamblee	28,558	82	62	20
Chatsworth	4,258	17	16	1
Clarkesville	1,777	7	6	1
Clarkston	12,849	22	17	5
Claxton	2,284	9	8	1
Clayton	2,285	12	12	0
Cleveland	3,912	14	13	1
Cochran	5,029	13	12	1
College Park	15,134	135	97	38
Colquitt	1,896	12	9	3
Commerce	6,826	23	19	4
Conyers	16,034	82	62	20
Coolidge	529	2	1	1
Cordele	10,812	37	27	10
Covington	14,122	66	55	11
Cumming	6,365	19	12	7
Dallas	13,373	27	19	8
Dalton	34,228	98	86	12
Danielsville	588	3	3	0
Darien	1,830	13	13	0
Davisboro	1,659	1	1	0
Dawson	4,249	17	11	6
Decatur	23,378	49	38	11
Demorest	2,094	7	7	0
Dillard	336	4	3	1
Doerun	769	5	4	1
Donalsonville	2,635	13	9	4
Doraville	10,593	60	43	17
Douglasville	33,640	114	96	18
Dublin	16,086	71	61	10
Duluth	29,795	71	56	15
Dunwoody	49,321	67	54	13
East Ellijay	561	13	8	5
Eastman	5,093	13	11	2
East Point	35,740	127	84	43
Eatonton	6,568	22	15	7
Edison	1,437	6	5	1
Elberton	4,397	23	20	3
Ellaville	1,856	5	4	1
Ellijay	1,705	11	11	0
Emerson	1,579	7	7	0
Enigma	1,300	4	3	1
Eton	896	3	3	0
Euharlee	4,320	10	9	1
Fairburn	14,370	45	38	7
Fayetteville	17,749	52	44	8
Fitzgerald	8,902	34	27	7
Flowery Branch	7,317	17	15	2
Folkston	4,795	7	6	1
Forest Park	19,948	88	68	20
Forsyth	4,169	18	14	4
Fort Oglethorpe	9,935	33	31	2
Fort Valley	8,465	35	25	10
Franklin	959	8	8	0
Franklin Springs	1,160	2	2	0
Gainesville	40,836	106	93	13
Garden City	8,932	46	37	9
Glennville	5,086	15	13	2
Gordon	1,943	11	6	5
Graham	300	2	1	1
Grantville	3,226	13	12	1
Gray	3,270	13	12	1
Greensboro	3,388	22	19	3
Greenville	852	8	7	1
Griffin	22,878	91	70	21
Grovetown	13,841	28	22	6
Guyton	1,928	3	3	0
Hahira	2,968	8	7	1
Hampton	7,623	20	18	2

State/city	Population	Total law enforcement employees	Total officers	Total civilians
Hapeville	6,665	36	22	14
Harlem	3,077	7	6	1
Hartwell	4,511	25	20	5
Hazlehurst	4,178	11	11	0
Helen	547	10	9	1
Hiawassee	921	5	5	0
Hiram	3,954	17	14	3
Hoboken	525	3	2	1
Hogansville	3,157	22	15	7
Holly Springs	11,653	30	29	1
Homeland	855	7	7	0
Homerville	2,451	9	8	1
Ivey	911	2	1	1
Jackson	5,071	13	12	1
Jasper	3,841	19	17	2
Jesup	10,170	28	26	2
Johns Creek	85,048	83	75	8
Jonesboro	4,731	38	32	6
Kennesaw	34,154	67	59	8
Kingsland	16,852	35	33	2
Kingston	657	2	1	1
LaGrange	30,981	106	89	17
Lake City	2,811	17	16	1
Lakeland	3,284	10	8	2
Lake Park	724	4	4	0
Lavonia	2,170	15	15	0
Lawrenceville	31,183	98	72	26
Leary	573	1	1	0
Leslie	380	4	3	1
Lilburn	12,844	37	28	9
Locust Grove	6,028	26	23	3
Loganville	11,887	32	29	3
Lookout Mountain	1,573	7	7	0
Ludowici	2,244	10	6	4
Lumber City	1,255	1	1	0
Madison	4,072	14	12	2
Manchester	4,034	17	12	5
Marietta	61,646	181	134	47
Marshallville	1,292	4	3	1
Maysville	1,901	7	3	4
McDonough	24,278	44	39	5
McIntyre	611	5	5	0
McRae-Helena	8,295	12	11	1
Metter	4,066	11	10	1
Midville	262	1	1	0
Milledgeville	19,051	67	43	24
Millen	2,853	10	10	0
Milton	39,388	43	37	6
Molena	371	2	1	1
Montezuma	3,095	11	9	2
Morrow	7,400	24	23	1
Moultrie	14,365	29	26	3
Nahunta	1,047	5	2	3
Nashville	4,849	16	13	3
Newnan	38,825	93	80	13
Norcross	17,060	57	43	14
Norman Park	968	4	2	2
Oakwood	4,200	15	13	2
Ocilla	3,630	14	14	0
Oxford	2,239	3	3	0
Palmetto	4,744	18	15	3
Patterson	758	2	2	0
Peachtree City	35,300	69	64	5
Pembroke	2,539	9	7	2
Perry	16,624	46	40	6
Pine Lake	767	4	3	1
Pine Mountain	1,385	11	9	2
Plains	727	3	3	0
Port Wentworth	8,452	35	30	5
Powder Springs	15,127	32	28	4
Quitman	3,884	15	14	1

(Number.)

State/city	Population	Total law enforcement employees	Total officers	Total civilians
Remerton	1,122	10	8	2
Reynolds	1,016	7	5	2
Richmond Hill	13,059	34	25	9
Rincon	10,101	23	21	2
Ringgold	4,403	11	11	0
Riverdale	16,435	49	36	13
Rochelle	1,101	8	6	2
Rockmart	4,317	20	18	2
Rome	36,366	98	88	10
Roswell	95,602	185	145	40
Sandersville	5,669	20	17	3
Sandy Springs	107,740	150	129	21
Sardis	971	5	5	0
Savannah-Chatham Metropolitan	242,941	812	620	192
Screven	778	2	2	0
Senoia	4,283	17	15	2
Shiloh	462	5	1	4
Smyrna	57,576	130	85	45
Snellville	19,982	56	44	12
Social Circle	4,490	15	14	1
Sparks	1,994	3	3	0
Sparta	1,264	14	7	7
Springfield	4,308	7	6	1
Stapleton	397	2	2	0
Statesboro	31,937	73	58	15
St. Marys	18,220	28	25	3
Stone Mountain	6,413	19	18	1
Summerville	4,337	17	15	2
Suwanee	20,186	48	37	11
Sylvania	2,514	11	9	2
Sylvester	6,042	24	18	6
Talbotton	834	4	2	2
Tallapoosa	3,189	11	10	1
Tallulah Falls	171	2	2	0
Temple	4,403	14	11	3
Tennille	1,914	4	4	0
Thomasville	18,866	54	48	6
Thunderbolt	2,710	9	8	1
Tifton	16,908	49	41	8
Trenton	2,248	8	8	0
Tybee Island	3,134	34	25	9
Tyrone	7,260	17	17	0
Union City	21,160	68	55	13
Valdosta	56,729	174	147	27
Vidalia	10,743	42	32	10
Vienna	3,652	8	7	1
Villa Rica	15,398	48	40	8
Warner Robins	75,323	142	104	38
Warrenton	1,786	6	6	0
Warwick	407	6	4	2
Watkinsville	2,866	8	8	0
Waverly Hall	763	5	4	1
Waycross	13,996	73	61	12
Waynesboro	5,669	27	20	7
West Point	3,821	23	13	10
Whigham	473	3	2	1
White	735	1	1	0
Willacoochee	1,367	6	5	1
Winder	16,006	41	37	4
Winterville	1,210	2	2	0
Woodbury	892	10	7	3
Woodstock	32,293	56	52	4
Wrens	2,020	8	7	1
Zebulon	1,166	6	6	0
HAWAII				
Honolulu	990,384	2,510	2,013	497
IDAHO				
Aberdeen	1,910	7	4	3
American Falls	4,286	9	7	2

State/city	Population	Total law enforcement employees	Total officers	Total civilians
Bellevue	2,315	1	1	0
Blackfoot	11,870	30	27	3
Boise	225,677	375	290	85
Bonners Ferry	2,574	6	6	0
Buhl	4,326	8	7	1
Caldwell	54,345	78	64	14
Cascade	974	5	4	1
Chubbuck	14,754	36	22	14
Coeur d'Alene	51,364	106	87	19
Cottonwood	919	1	1	0
Emmett	6,747	13	11	2
Filer	2,757	5	5	0
Fruitland	5,205	15	9	6
Garden City	11,708	33	26	7
Gooding	3,481	9	7	2
Grangeville	3,137	6	6	0
Hagerman	878	1	1	0
Hailey	8,267	13	12	1
Heyburn	3,306	8	7	1
Homedale	2,577	6	5	1
Idaho City	441	1	1	0
Idaho Falls	60,727	127	88	39
Jerome	11,380	22	18	4
Kamiah	1,292	3	3	0
Kellogg	2,074	7	7	0
Ketchum	2,760	13	11	2
Kimberly	3,812	9	8	1
Lewiston	33,029	69	45	24
McCall	3,338	13	12	1
Meridian	99,241	123	98	25
Middleton	7,486	7	7	0
Montpelier	2,492	6	5	1
Moscow	25,576	40	34	6
Mountain Home	13,772	32	28	4
Nampa	93,064	165	113	52
Orofino	3,039	7	6	1
Osburn	1,500	2	2	0
Parma	2,101	4	4	0
Payette	7,405	16	14	2
Pinehurst	1,571	2	2	0
Pocatello	54,814	129	91	38
Ponderay	1,158	7	6	1
Post Falls	32,583	72	44	28
Preston	5,372	8	7	1
Priest River	1,780	7	5	2
Rathdrum	8,113	16	14	2
Rexburg	28,698	40	32	8
Rigby	4,078	7	6	1
Rupert	5,849	12	11	1
Salmon	3,040	8	8	0
Sandpoint	8,090	22	19	3
Shelley	4,329	8	8	0
Shoshone	1,506	5	5	0
Soda Springs	2,970	7	7	0
Spirit Lake	2,207	6	5	1
St. Anthony	3,493	6	6	0
Sun Valley	1,441	11	10	1
Twin Falls	48,912	94	74	20
Weiser	5,383	14	11	3
Wendell	2,700	4	4	0
Wilder	1,697	5	5	0
ILLINOIS				
Alsip	19,137	48	39	9
Altamont	2,292	4	4	0
Amboy	2,308	4	4	0
Anna	4,244	7	7	0
Annawan	851	1	1	0
Antioch	14,242	30	27	3
Arlington Heights	75,586	130	107	23
Aroma Park	698	3	3	0

(Number.)

State/city	Population	Total law enforcement employees	Total officers	Total civilians
Arthur	2,265	5	5	0
Ashland	1,224	1	1	0
Assumption	1,094	1	1	0
Athens	1,944	4	4	0
Atwood	1,179	1	1	0
Aviston	2,119	1	1	0
Barrington Hills	4,221	20	16	4
Barry	1,260	1	1	0
Bartlett	41,167	69	54	15
Belleville	41,511	101	76	25
Bensenville	18,353	40	34	6
Berwyn	55,594	165	114	51
Bloomington	78,203	158	127	31
Bourbonnais	18,474	26	25	1
Bradley	15,405	46	33	13
Braidwood	6,145	19	16	3
Brookfield	18,715	34	29	5
Buffalo Grove	41,323	73	62	11
Burbank	28,876	52	43	9
Burr Ridge	10,813	31	26	5
Byron	3,604	7	6	1
Campton Hills	11,342	6	6	0
Carbondale	26,127	82	65	17
Carlinville	5,585	17	12	5
Carol Stream	40,118	90	67	23
Carpentersville	38,380	63	59	4
Carrollton	2,411	6	6	0
Carthage	2,537	3	3	0
Centreville	4,988	13	12	1
Champaign	87,543	147	124	23
Charleston	21,016	33	30	3
Chenoa	3,167	4	4	0
Cherry Valley	3,075	14	13	1
Chester	8,559	12	9	3
Chicago	2,706,171	13,566	12,383	1,183
Chicago Ridge	14,222	35	31	4
Chillicothe	6,225	11	11	0
Cicero	82,779	174	153	21
Coal City	5,409	10	9	1
Coal Valley	3,721	7	7	0
Cobden	1,119	3	3	0
Collinsville	24,487	60	42	18
Columbia	10,369	22	15	7
Cortland	4,331	5	5	0
Countryside	5,951	27	24	3
Crest Hill	21,223	32	30	2
Crete	8,151	17	16	1
Crystal Lake	40,228	70	62	8
Danvers	1,121	2	2	0
Danville	31,368	68	56	12
Decatur	72,153	181	150	31
Deer Creek	670	1	1	0
Deerfield	19,126	54	40	14
De Kalb	43,043	77	63	14
Delavan	1,625	4	4	0
De Pue	1,710	3	3	0
De Soto	1,559	4	3	1
Des Plaines	58,089	118	98	20
Downers Grove	49,563	87	71	16
Dupo	3,848	8	8	0
Du Quoin	5,808	15	11	4
Earlville	1,606	3	3	0
Edinburg	1,037	2	2	0
Effingham	12,710	40	26	14
Elburn	5,782	7	6	1
Elgin	112,767	233	182	51
Elk Grove Village	32,894	101	88	13
Elmwood Park	24,581	42	35	7
Elwood	2,252	10	9	1
Energy	1,141	4	4	0
Erie	1,526	3	3	0

(Number.)

State/city	Population	Total law enforcement employees	Total officers	Total civilians
Eureka	5,393	6	6	0
Evanston	74,947	225	164	61
Evergreen Park	19,600	81	62	19
Fairfield	5,004	14	10	4
Fairmount	604	1	1	0
Farmington	2,293	4	4	0
Fisher	1,943	2	2	0
Flossmoor	9,347	26	21	5
Fox Lake	10,432	29	24	5
Fox River Grove	4,628	10	10	0
Freeburg	4,211	10	9	1
Freeport	24,196	62	45	17
Galena	3,229	11	10	1
Georgetown	3,286	4	4	0
Gibson City	3,372	8	7	1
Glendale Heights	34,128	70	54	16
Glenview	47,944	75	70	5
Golf	494	1	1	0
Goodfield	1,004	1	1	0
Grafton	635	2	2	0
Grandview	1,420	3	3	0
Greenfield	982	2	2	0
Greenup	1,485	3	3	0
Greenville	6,713	14	10	4
Gurnee	30,902	95	62	33
Hampshire	6,367	12	12	0
Hanover Park	38,053	84	60	24
Hartford	1,370	5	4	1
Harvard	9,067	18	16	2
Hawthorn Woods	8,234	13	12	1
Henry	2,291	5	4	1
Hickory Hills	13,980	35	28	7
Highland	9,809	27	20	7
Hillsdale	503	1	1	0
Hillside	8,066	34	27	7
Hinckley	2,055	2	2	0
Hinsdale	17,765	24	22	2
Hodgkins	1,840	23	21	2
Hoffman Estates	51,704	103	88	15
Homer	1,176	1	1	0
Hoopeston	5,106	14	10	4
Hopedale	831	1	1	0
Island Lake	8,076	15	14	1
Jacksonville	18,615	41	37	4
Jerseyville	8,315	21	15	6
Johnsburg	6,251	13	11	2
Joliet	148,342	336	267	69
Justice	12,829	29	22	7
Kansas	729	1	1	0
Kenilworth	2,522	9	8	1
Kewanee	12,386	27	21	6
Kildeer	4,072	9	8	1
Kincaid	1,405	2	2	0
Kingston	1,160	2	2	0
Kirkland	1,730	2	2	0
La Grange	15,617	30	26	4
Lake Bluff	5,664	17	15	2
Lake Villa	8,800	18	17	1
Lakewood	3,878	8	8	0
Lake Zurich	20,012	51	32	19
La Salle	9,134	23	22	1
Le Roy	3,547	7	7	0
Lincolnshire	7,259	25	22	3
Lindenhurst	14,362	15	13	2
Lockport	25,280	44	38	6
Lombard	43,885	77	66	11
Lyons	10,601	13	9	4
Machesney Park	22,772	29	28	1
Macomb	18,200	27	24	3
Manhattan	7,625	12	10	2
Marengo	7,406	14	12	2

Table 19. Full-Time Law Enforcement Employees, by Selected State and City, 2017—*Continued*

(Number.)

State/city	Population	Total law enforcement employees	Total officers	Total civilians
Marissa	1,814	4	4	0
Marseilles	4,893	11	10	1
Maryville	7,968	14	13	1
Mattoon	17,942	42	37	5
McHenry	26,540	75	46	29
McLean	802	1	1	0
Mendota	7,124	17	15	2
Metropolis	6,238	18	14	4
Midlothian	14,678	29	27	2
Milledgeville	968	2	2	0
Mokena	20,321	30	27	3
Moline	42,042	96	76	20
Momence	3,155	10	10	0
Monee	5,064	17	15	2
Monmouth	9,172	28	18	10
Monticello	5,591	8	7	1
Morris	14,640	28	24	4
Morrison	4,092	6	6	0
Morton	16,287	28	22	6
Mount Carmel	6,950	16	11	5
Mount Carroll	1,593	3	3	0
Mount Morris	2,829	5	4	1
Mount Olive	1,985	6	4	2
Mount Prospect	54,162	99	80	19
Mundelein	31,547	73	54	19
New Athens	1,914	4	4	0
Newton	2,780	8	7	1
Niles	29,582	68	55	13
Nokomis	2,140	6	5	1
Northfield	5,459	21	19	2
North Riverside	6,585	25	25	0
Oak Brook	8,099	43	40	3
Oak Forest	27,761	55	43	12
Oak Lawn	56,178	120	104	16
Oak Park	51,753	133	112	21
Oakwood	1,495	1	1	0
Oblong	1,414	1	1	0
O'Fallon	29,085	65	47	18
Okawville	1,382	4	4	0
Olney	8,928	14	13	1
Onarga	1,294	2	2	0
Orland Park	59,227	134	98	36
Oswego	35,273	57	48	9
Palestine	1,313	2	2	0
Palos Hills	17,396	34	31	3
Paris	8,352	23	16	7
Park Forest	21,750	47	39	8
Park Ridge	37,492	62	49	13
Peoria Heights	5,913	21	13	8
Peotone	4,132	10	9	1
Peru	9,829	25	24	1
Petersburg	2,189	6	6	0
Pittsfield	4,452	7	7	0
Plainfield	43,450	67	53	14
Plano	11,438	22	20	2
Pleasant Hill	936	1	1	0
Polo	2,209	5	4	1
Pontiac	11,813	18	17	1
Pontoon Beach	5,572	20	15	5
Posen	5,920	18	17	1
Potomac	704	1	1	0
Princeton	7,550	18	17	1
Quincy	40,506	86	73	13
Raleigh	343	1	1	0
Rantoul	12,791	36	30	6
Red Bud	3,536	6	6	0
Richmond	1,899	4	4	0
Ridge Farm	833	1	1	0
Riverdale	13,371	35	29	6
Riverton	3,429	8	8	0
Riverwoods	3,633	8	7	1

(Number.)

State/city	Population	Total law enforcement employees	Total officers	Total civilians
Rockford	146,770	323	284	39
Rock Island	38,079	106	79	27
Roscoe	10,478	14	13	1
Round Lake	18,382	28	24	4
Round Lake Heights	2,701	5	5	0
Roxana	1,463	8	6	2
Royalton	1,122	3	3	0
Rushville	2,875	4	4	0
San Jose	604	1	1	0
Savanna	2,827	7	7	0
Schaumburg	74,471	147	114	33
Schiller Park	11,674	36	33	3
Seneca	2,267	6	5	1
Shawneetown	1,143	3	3	0
Shorewood	17,171	31	27	4
Silvis	7,596	21	14	7
Skokie	64,167	155	115	40
Sleepy Hollow	3,333	8	7	1
Smithton	3,766	6	6	0
South Barrington	4,973	21	17	4
South Beloit	7,613	12	11	1
South Elgin	22,504	32	28	4
South Pekin	1,108	2	2	0
Springfield	115,568	267	238	29
Spring Valley	5,216	11	10	1
St. Anne	1,201	2	2	0
St. Charles	32,780	64	54	10
Steger	9,436	16	15	1
St. Elmo	1,381	2	2	0
Stockton	1,747	6	5	1
Streator	13,049	26	24	2
Sycamore	17,925	32	29	3
Thornton	2,474	11	10	1
Tilton	2,562	4	4	0
Tinley Park	56,823	85	72	13
Tolono	3,433	3	3	0
Trenton	2,641	4	4	0
Vernon Hills	26,547	70	42	28
Villa Park	21,857	47	37	10
Warren	1,340	4	3	1
Warrenville	13,255	40	32	8
Waukegan	88,017	191	147	44
Westchester	16,536	34	29	5
West Chicago	27,219	49	43	6
Western Springs	13,464	24	21	3
Westmont	24,781	42	36	6
Westville	3,036	4	4	0
Wheaton	53,444	79	64	15
White Hall	2,328	7	5	2
Willowbrook	8,542	27	24	3
Willow Springs	5,645	9	6	3
Wilmette	27,242	54	41	13
Winnebago	2,986	6	6	0
Winnetka	12,451	31	26	5
Winthrop Harbor	6,777	16	10	6
Wood Dale	13,817	41	32	9
Wood River	10,187	24	18	6
Woodstock	25,127	41	37	4
Yorkville	19,155	33	30	3
INDIANA				
Albion	2,316	6	6	0
Alexandria	5,004	14	13	1
Anderson	54,959	126	105	21
Auburn	13,090	24	23	1
Aurora	3,678	11	10	1
Bargersville	7,441	13	12	1
Batesville	6,705	17	12	5
Bedford	13,330	39	30	9
Beech Grove	14,831	35	32	3
Bloomington	85,121	144	97	47

Table 19. Full-Time Law Enforcement Employees, by Selected State and City, 2017—*Continued*

(Number.)

State/city	Population	Total law enforcement employees	Total officers	Total civilians
Bluffton	10,011	20	20	0
Brownsburg	26,030	49	43	6
Cannelton	1,483	2	2	0
Carmel	93,098	137	113	24
Cedar Lake	12,286	20	18	2
Clinton	4,782	9	8	1
Columbia City	8,876	19	18	1
Crawfordsville	16,011	39	34	5
Crown Point	29,399	51	45	6
Cumberland	5,649	16	14	2
Decatur	9,541	18	16	2
Dyer	15,869	35	31	4
East Chicago	28,210	95	88	7
Edinburgh	4,592	12	11	1
Ellettsville	6,682	12	11	1
Elwood	8,386	17	16	1
Evansville	119,371	304	282	22
Fairmount	2,782	7	6	1
Fishers	92,367	121	110	11
Fort Wayne	266,259	522	462	60
Franklin	25,060	52	46	6
Gary	75,808	202	178	24
Goshen	33,195	69	62	7
Greenwood	57,484	72	64	8
Hammond	76,550	237	206	31
Hartford City	5,873	11	10	1
Highland	22,577	45	38	7
Hobart	28,066	75	65	10
Huntingburg	6,143	13	12	1
Huntington	17,116	34	33	1
Indianapolis	870,788	1,834	1,625	209
Jasper	15,577	29	21	8
Jeffersonville	47,459	90	85	5
Kendallville	9,915	25	17	8
Kokomo	57,758	110	90	20
Lafayette	72,274	190	142	48
Lake Station	11,852	22	22	0
Lawrence	48,174	79	60	19
Lawrenceburg	4,955	25	21	4
Linton	5,221	14	9	5
Logansport	17,700	41	40	1
Marion	28,385	78	62	16
Merrillville	34,999	55	54	1
Michigan City	31,108	91	83	8
Monticello	5,240	17	13	4
Mooresville	9,709	26	21	5
Muncie	68,814	114	100	14
Munster	22,701	45	42	3
New Haven	15,481	29	21	8
New Whiteland	6,117	9	8	1
North Vernon	6,837	20	18	2
Plainfield	32,067	51	46	5
Plymouth	9,936	24	22	2
Portage	36,447	68	61	7
Porter	4,843	14	11	3
Portland	6,154	16	12	4
Rushville	6,022	17	12	5
Sellersburg	8,836	18	16	2
Seymour	19,604	58	40	18
Shelbyville	19,047	60	44	16
South Bend	101,857	289	241	48
Speedway	12,150	49	34	15
St. John	17,128	22	20	2
Tipton	5,094	14	12	2
Valparaiso	33,329	55	50	5
Walkerton	2,283	10	6	4
Warsaw	14,850	39	34	5
Waterloo	2,250	7	7	0
West Lafayette	46,541	69	50	19
Whitestown	7,464	23	22	1
Whiting	4,805	21	19	2

Table 19. Full-Time Law Enforcement Employees, by Selected State and City, 2017—*Continued*

(Number.)

State/city	Population	Total law enforcement employees	Total officers	Total civilians
Winchester	4,718	13	12	1
IOWA				
Adel............	4,397	8	7	1
Albia............	3,787	7	6	1
Algona............	5,509	14	10	4
Altoona............	18,556	30	27	3
Ames............	67,461	77	54	23
Anamosa............	5,411	9	8	1
Ankeny............	61,090	65	57	8
Arnolds Park............	1,278	6	5	1
Atlantic............	6,588	13	12	1
Audubon............	1,939	4	4	0
Belle Plaine............	2,442	5	5	0
Belmond............	2,316	5	5	0
Bettendorf............	36,133	51	45	6
Bloomfield............	2,643	7	6	1
Blue Grass............	1,743	2	2	0
Boone............	12,607	19	18	1
Buffalo............	1,297	3	3	0
Burlington............	25,227	49	45	4
Camanche............	4,305	7	7	0
Carlisle............	4,311	6	5	1
Carroll............	9,920	16	15	1
Carter Lake............	3,783	10	9	1
Cedar Falls............	41,744	44	43	1
Cedar Rapids............	131,878	274	209	65
Centerville............	5,316	17	11	6
Chariton............	4,171	6	5	1
Charles City............	7,425	20	13	7
Cherokee............	4,954	9	8	1
Clarinda............	5,353	11	10	1
Clarion............	2,752	8	7	1
Clear Lake............	7,559	22	16	6
Clinton............	25,532	48	42	6
Clive............	17,913	28	24	4
Colfax............	2,034	4	4	0
Coralville............	20,652	38	34	4
Council Bluffs............	62,549	136	115	21
Cresco............	3,799	7	7	0
Creston............	7,829	15	11	4
Davenport............	103,063	179	160	19
Decorah............	7,883	21	13	8
Denison............	8,304	19	14	5
Des Moines............	217,277	455	350	105
De Witt............	5,218	12	11	1
Dubuque............	58,674	113	107	6
Dyersville............	4,217	6	6	0
Eldora............	2,650	4	4	0
Eldridge............	6,406	10	9	1
Emmetsburg............	3,736	8	7	1
Estherville............	5,877	13	13	0
Evansdale............	4,792	8	7	1
Fairfield............	10,337	21	14	7
Forest City............	3,993	8	8	0
Fort Dodge............	24,331	42	39	3
Garner............	3,068	5	5	0
Glenwood............	5,315	11	9	2
Grinnell............	9,141	15	14	1
Grundy Center............	2,683	4	4	0
Hampton............	4,202	8	7	1
Harlan............	4,904	9	8	1
Hawarden............	2,524	4	4	0
Hiawatha............	7,245	14	14	0
Humboldt............	4,538	7	7	0
Independence............	6,027	11	11	0
Indianola............	15,953	23	20	3
Iowa City............	75,519	103	81	22
Iowa Falls............	5,110	13	9	4
Jefferson............	4,140	8	8	0
Johnston............	21,816	29	27	2

Table 19. Full-Time Law Enforcement Employees, by Selected State and City, 2017—*Continued*

(Number.)

State/city	Population	Total law enforcement employees	Total officers	Total civilians
Keokuk	10,376	27	24	3
Knoxville	7,233	15	14	1
Lansing	944	3	3	0
Le Claire	4,012	8	7	1
Le Mars	9,955	13	12	1
Leon	1,866	3	3	0
Lisbon	2,219	3	3	0
Manchester	5,032	15	10	5
Maquoketa	5,954	18	11	7
Marengo	2,486	4	4	0
Marion	39,050	57	45	12
Marshalltown	27,287	57	41	16
Mason City	27,327	52	47	5
Mechanicsville	1,116	1	1	0
Missouri Valley	2,635	6	6	0
Monticello	3,843	7	6	1
Mount Pleasant	8,349	16	14	2
Mount Vernon	4,436	6	6	0
Muscatine	23,940	43	40	3
Nevada	6,805	13	11	2
New Hampton	3,401	6	6	0
New Sharon	1,286	1	1	0
Newton	14,999	28	23	5
North Liberty	19,491	23	21	2
Norwalk	10,874	17	16	1
Oelwein	5,999	15	10	5
Ogden	1,989	2	2	0
Onawa	2,848	4	4	0
Orange City	6,199	7	7	0
Osage	3,623	7	6	1
Osceola	5,051	11	10	1
Oskaloosa	11,525	18	16	2
Ottumwa	24,397	44	34	10
Pella	10,240	23	17	6
Perry	7,824	19	12	7
Pleasant Hill	9,910	19	17	2
Polk City	4,616	6	6	0
Postville	2,098	4	4	0
Prairie City	1,718	3	3	0
Princeton	949	1	1	0
Red Oak	5,437	11	9	2
Rock Valley	3,788	6	6	0
Sac City	2,086	4	4	0
Sergeant Bluff	4,606	9	8	1
Sheldon	5,102	7	7	0
Sigourney	1,976	4	4	0
Sioux Center	7,578	7	7	0
Sioux City	82,879	148	126	22
Spencer	11,125	29	19	10
Spirit Lake	5,124	10	9	1
Storm Lake	10,790	23	19	4
Story City	3,406	6	6	0
Tama	2,825	5	5	0
Tipton	3,217	7	6	1
Toledo	2,163	5	5	0
Urbandale	43,637	59	50	9
Vinton	5,125	9	8	1
Walcott	1,639	3	3	0
Washington	7,451	12	11	1
Waterloo	67,855	131	122	9
Waukee	20,359	23	21	2
Waverly	10,129	17	16	1
Webster City	7,708	17	11	6
West Branch	2,365	4	4	0
West Burlington	2,935	10	10	0
West Des Moines	65,940	82	69	13
West Union	2,381	5	5	0
Williamsburg	3,197	7	7	0
Windsor Heights	5,001	12	11	1
KANSAS				
Abilene	6,407	17	14	3

State/city	Population	Total law enforcement employees	Total officers	Total civilians
Alma	786	1	1	0
Altamont	1,036	4	3	1
Andale	1,003	3	3	0
Andover	13,183	34	26	8
Anthony	2,164	6	5	1
Argonia	478	1	1	0
Arkansas City	12,009	31	26	5
Assaria	406	2	2	0
Atchison	10,628	23	23	0
Attica	569	1	1	0
Atwood	1,213	2	2	0
Augusta	9,329	33	24	9
Baldwin City	4,703	11	10	1
Basehor	5,835	14	12	2
Baxter Springs	3,921	15	11	4
Bel Aire	7,819	13	12	1
Belle Plaine	1,585	4	4	0
Belleville	1,881	3	3	0
Beloit	3,761	5	5	0
Benton	875	3	3	0
Blue Rapids	963	2	2	0
Bonner Springs	7,717	28	25	3
Buhler	1,313	3	3	0
Burden	533	1	1	0
Burlingame	881	2	2	0
Burlington	2,600	9	7	2
Burrton	885	2	2	0
Caldwell	1,013	2	2	0
Caney	2,014	10	6	4
Canton	715	1	1	0
Carbondale	1,386	3	3	0
Cedar Vale	519	1	1	0
Chanute	9,143	18	16	2
Chapman	1,355	3	3	0
Cheney	2,176	6	6	0
Cherokee	712	1	1	0
Cherryvale	2,161	7	6	1
Chetopa	1,051	4	4	0
Claflin	620	1	1	0
Clay Center	4,025	7	6	1
Clearwater	2,524	7	6	1
Coffeyville	9,423	31	23	8
Colby	5,420	18	12	6
Coldwater	812	2	1	1
Columbus	3,072	9	8	1
Colwich	1,410	3	3	0
Concordia	5,144	18	11	7
Council Grove	2,041	8	7	1
Derby	23,821	56	46	10
Dodge City	27,447	61	44	17
Eastborough	759	6	6	0
Edwardsville	4,395	18	17	1
El Dorado	13,125	26	23	3
Elkhart	1,892	3	3	0
Ellinwood	2,022	5	5	0
Ellis	2,048	5	5	0
Ellsworth	3,034	7	6	1
Elwood	1,154	5	5	0
Emporia	24,804	48	41	7
Eudora	6,417	12	12	0
Fairway	3,986	11	9	2
Fort Scott	7,725	22	20	2
Fredonia	2,261	7	6	1
Frontenac	3,410	11	7	4
Galena	2,855	10	9	1
Galva	873	1	1	0
Garden City	26,728	92	63	29
Gardner	21,449	36	32	4
Garnett	3,241	7	7	0
Girard	2,741	7	6	1
Goddard	4,761	11	11	0
Goodland	4,433	10	9	1

Table 19. Full-Time Law Enforcement Employees, by Selected State and City, 2017—*Continued*

(Number.)

State/city	Population	Total law enforcement employees	Total officers	Total civilians
Grandview Plaza	1,579	7	7	0
Great Bend	15,459	31	27	4
Greensburg	768	1	1	0
Halstead	2,080	6	5	1
Harper	1,361	3	3	0
Haven	1,207	3	3	0
Hays	21,110	38	33	5
Haysville	11,314	28	21	7
Hesston	3,817	8	7	1
Hiawatha	3,048	9	8	1
Highland	998	2	2	0
Hill City	1,451	4	4	0
Hillsboro	2,870	5	5	0
Hoisington	2,567	7	6	1
Holcomb	2,145	4	3	1
Holton	3,278	7	7	0
Holyrood	434	1	1	0
Horton	1,690	10	6	4
Hoxie	1,170	2	2	0
Hugoton	3,819	8	6	2
Humboldt	1,831	6	5	1
Hutchinson	41,160	105	68	37
Independence	8,692	25	18	7
Inman	1,348	3	3	0
Iola	5,413	18	17	1
Junction City	24,240	63	44	19
Kansas City	152,573	431	341	90
Kechi	2,009	5	4	1
La Cygne	1,106	4	3	1
Lake Quivira	945	1	1	0
Lansing	11,941	18	17	1
Larned	3,875	8	8	0
Lawrence	96,629	173	149	24
Leavenworth	36,284	75	53	22
Leawood	35,029	80	58	22
Lenexa	53,717	122	79	43
Leon	701	1	1	0
Liberal	20,317	51	36	15
Lindsborg	3,319	7	6	1
Linn Valley	814	3	3	0
Little River	532	1	1	0
Louisburg	4,391	11	10	1
Lyndon	1,016	2	2	0
Lyons	3,658	7	6	1
Maize	4,621	13	12	1
Maple Hill	617	1	1	0
Marion	1,823	5	5	0
Marquette	606	1	1	0
Marysville	3,294	9	8	1
McLouth	842	2	2	0
McPherson	13,169	38	33	5
Meade	1,564	3	2	1
Merriam	11,278	37	32	5
Minneapolis	1,976	4	4	0
Mission	9,461	31	29	2
Mission Hills	3,616	3	3	0
Moran	511	1	1	0
Mound City	678	2	2	0
Moundridge	1,738	4	4	0
Mount Hope	806	2	2	0
Mulberry	519	1	1	0
Mulvane	6,343	21	15	6
Neodesha	2,293	7	6	1
Newton	19,095	43	38	5
North Newton	1,802	3	3	0
Norton	2,799	7	6	1
Norwich	453	1	1	0
Oakley	2,105	10	6	4
Oberlin	1,688	4	4	0
Olathe	137,070	200	171	29
Onaga	695	1	1	0

State/city	Population	Total law enforcement employees	Total officers	Total civilians
Osage City	2,820	7	7	0
Osawatomie	4,284	17	13	4
Oswego	1,729	4	4	0
Ottawa	12,307	36	29	7
Overbrook	1,018	1	1	0
Overland Park	191,566	311	251	60
Oxford	1,012	3	3	0
Paola	5,560	22	16	6
Park City	7,678	16	14	2
Parsons	9,815	33	24	9
Peabody	1,129	1	1	0
Perry	902	1	1	0
Pittsburg	20,384	72	46	26
Plainville	1,851	5	5	0
Pleasanton	1,170	2	2	0
Prairie Village	21,860	53	40	13
Pratt	6,762	22	15	7
Protection	500	1	1	0
Roeland Park	6,794	16	14	2
Rose Hill	4,029	8	7	1
Rossville	1,126	2	2	0
Russell	4,497	8	7	1
Sabetha	2,587	9	5	4
Salina	47,251	98	68	30
Scott City	3,901	13	8	5
Sedan	1,021	2	2	0
Sedgwick	1,695	3	2	1
Seneca	2,056	6	6	0
Shawnee	65,683	110	92	18
Smith Center	1,569	3	3	0
South Hutchinson	2,552	10	8	2
Spearville	793	1	1	0
Spring Hill	6,293	13	12	1
Stafford	968	4	4	0
Sterling	2,253	5	5	0
St. Francis	1,289	3	2	1
St. George	1,004	2	1	1
St. John	1,202	3	3	0
St. Marys	2,669	5	5	0
Stockton	1,292	5	5	0
Tonganoxie	5,379	13	12	1
Topeka	126,624	328	274	54
Troy	964	1	1	0
Udall	723	2	2	0
Valley Center	7,431	15	14	1
Valley Falls	1,142	3	3	0
Victoria	1,223	2	2	0
Wa Keeney	1,763	4	4	0
Wathena	1,304	1	1	0
Wellington	7,845	19	16	3
Wellsville	1,806	5	4	1
Westwood	2,285	8	7	1
Wichita	391,084	819	638	181
Winfield	12,274	26	21	5
Yates Center	1,341	3	3	0
KENTUCKY				
Adairville	873	1	1	0
Albany	2,010	9	9	0
Alexandria	9,486	23	20	3
Anchorage	2,438	15	11	4
Ashland	20,927	56	52	4
Auburn	1,348	2	2	0
Audubon Park	1,511	3	3	0
Augusta	1,172	3	3	0
Barbourville	3,169	12	11	1
Bardstown	13,325	26	25	1
Beattyville	1,199	5	5	0
Beaver Dam	3,672	6	6	0
Bellefonte	855	9	9	0
Bellevue	5,826	12	11	1

(Number.)

State/city	Population	Total law enforcement employees	Total officers	Total civilians
Benham	452	1	1	0
Benton	4,533	7	7	0
Berea	15,406	38	36	2
Booneville	75	1	1	0
Bowling Green	66,317	153	117	36
Brandenburg	2,904	5	5	0
Brownsville	831	3	3	0
Burgin	969	2	2	0
Burkesville	1,505	6	6	0
Burnside	902	6	5	1
Butler	591	1	1	0
Cadiz	2,629	10	9	1
Calvert City	2,544	8	7	1
Campbellsville	11,486	22	20	2
Caneyville	612	1	1	0
Carlisle	1,992	10	6	4
Carrollton	3,864	17	10	7
Catlettsburg	1,794	8	8	0
Cave City	2,440	7	7	0
Centertown	446	1	1	0
Central City	5,837	12	12	0
Clinton	1,312	5	5	0
Coal Run Village	1,538	3	3	0
Cold Spring	6,276	9	9	0
Columbia	4,940	13	12	1
Corbin	7,411	28	20	8
Covington	40,845	116	108	8
Crab Orchard	830	2	1	1
Cumberland	2,032	6	6	0
Cynthiana	6,375	13	12	1
Danville	16,891	31	29	2
Dawson Springs	2,712	6	5	1
Dayton	5,423	10	9	1
Dry Ridge	2,224	5	5	0
Eddyville	2,575	5	5	0
Edgewood	8,771	15	15	0
Edmonton	1,583	6	6	0
Elizabethtown	30,065	69	43	26
Elkhorn City	921	2	1	1
Elkton	2,134	7	7	0
Elsmere	8,541	14	13	1
Eminence	2,579	6	6	0
Erlanger	22,947	40	39	1
Evarts	828	3	3	0
Falmouth	2,127	8	7	1
Ferguson	942	1	1	0
Flatwoods	7,284	11	11	0
Fleming-Neon	708	2	2	0
Flemingsburg	2,866	7	7	0
Florence	32,866	68	64	4
Fort Mitchell	8,306	14	14	0
Fort Thomas	16,485	22	21	1
Fort Wright	5,780	13	13	0
Frankfort	27,975	59	56	3
Franklin	8,884	24	23	1
Fulton	2,174	9	8	1
Georgetown	34,184	77	51	26
Glasgow	14,690	34	31	3
Graymoor-Devondale	2,974	1	1	0
Grayson	4,030	12	10	2
Greensburg	2,123	5	5	0
Greenville	4,347	9	9	0
Guthrie	1,406	4	4	0
Hardinsburg	2,324	5	5	0
Harrodsburg	8,427	30	19	11
Hartford	2,787	6	6	0
Hawesville	1,020	1	1	0
Hazard	5,268	42	29	13
Henderson	28,846	81	60	21
Highland Heights	7,178	11	10	1
Hillview	8,942	14	14	0

(Number.)

State/city	Population	Total law enforcement employees	Total officers	Total civilians
Hodgenville	3,224	7	7	0
Hopkinsville	31,761	103	75	28
Hyden	348	2	1	1
Independence	27,400	32	30	2
Indian Hills	2,995	6	6	0
Inez	665	1	1	0
Irvine	2,385	6	6	0
Jackson	2,100	11	8	3
Jamestown	1,807	4	4	0
Jeffersontown	27,400	59	49	10
Jenkins	2,043	3	3	0
Junction City	2,308	2	2	0
La Center	982	2	2	0
La Grange	8,831	13	13	0
Lakeside Park-Crestview Hills	6,133	12	11	1
Lancaster	3,874	11	10	1
Lawrenceburg	11,211	22	14	8
Lebanon	5,656	24	15	9
Leitchfield	6,900	19	18	1
Lewisburg	793	1	1	0
Lexington	322,332	581	506	75
Livingston	224	1	1	0
London	8,184	35	32	3
Louisa	2,474	6	6	0
Louisville Metro	684,362	1,510	1,249	261
Loyall	631	2	2	0
Ludlow	4,521	12	11	1
Lynnview	948	3	3	0
Madisonville	19,316	65	46	19
Manchester	1,382	13	13	0
Marion	2,972	11	6	5
Martin	585	4	3	1
Maysville	8,841	33	25	8
Middlesboro	9,534	28	24	4
Millersburg	792	1	1	0
Monticello	6,070	12	11	1
Morehead	7,915	29	20	9
Morganfield	3,541	17	8	9
Morgantown	2,454	6	6	0
Mortons Gap	843	1	1	0
Mount Sterling	7,298	22	20	2
Mount Vernon	2,482	8	8	0
Mount Washington	14,511	19	18	1
Muldraugh	995	3	3	0
New Haven	902	1	1	0
Newport	15,202	41	39	2
Nicholasville	30,333	70	61	9
Oak Grove	7,347	20	15	5
Olive Hill	1,584	7	7	0
Owensboro	59,576	136	90	46
Owingsville	1,605	5	5	0
Paducah	25,169	79	71	8
Paintsville	4,198	10	10	0
Paris	9,845	23	22	1
Park Hills	3,001	7	7	0
Pewee Valley	1,565	1	1	0
Pikeville	7,121	29	21	8
Pineville	1,739	5	5	0
Pioneer Village	2,931	5	5	0
Pippa Passes	658	6	2	4
Powderly	732	2	2	0
Prestonsburg	3,517	13	13	0
Princeton	6,084	15	14	1
Prospect	4,905	7	6	1
Providence	3,088	6	6	0
Raceland	2,380	6	6	0
Radcliff	22,473	49	35	14
Ravenna	583	2	2	0
Richmond	35,161	61	47	14
Russell	3,229	12	12	0
Russell Springs	2,573	10	9	1

Table 19. Full-Time Law Enforcement Employees, by Selected State and City, 2017—*Continued*

(Number.)

State/city	Population	Total law enforcement employees	Total officers	Total civilians
Russellville	7,006	24	23	1
Salyersville	1,787	4	4	0
Scottsville	4,446	26	18	8
Sebree	1,569	1	1	0
Shelbyville	15,758	22	21	1
Shepherdsville	12,204	31	29	2
Shively	15,830	36	30	6
Silver Grove	1,119	1	1	0
Simpsonville	2,795	6	6	0
Smiths Grove	780	1	1	0
Somerset	11,531	46	40	6
Southgate	3,856	8	8	0
South Shore	1,080	1	1	0
Springfield	3,167	13	8	5
Stanford	3,654	13	13	0
Stanton	2,658	6	6	0
St. Matthews	18,163	39	33	6
Taylor Mill	6,774	11	10	1
Taylorsville	1,264	5	4	1
Tompkinsville	2,261	13	10	3
Uniontown	943	2	2	0
Vanceburg	1,421	6	6	0
Versailles	26,320	35	34	1
Villa Hills	7,494	8	8	0
Vine Grove	6,055	7	7	0
Warsaw	1,689	3	3	0
Wayland	397	1	1	0
West Buechel	1,280	11	11	0
West Point	860	4	4	0
Whitesburg	1,949	8	6	2
Wilder	3,077	12	12	0
Williamsburg	5,342	14	13	1
Williamstown	3,971	7	6	1
Wilmore	6,380	9	8	1
Woodburn	387	2	2	0
LOUISIANA				
Abbeville	12,491	36	33	3
Addis	5,117	12	11	1
Alexandria	47,860	183	150	33
Baker	13,584	32	27	5
Ball	4,011	7	5	2
Basile	1,811	10	7	3
Baton Rouge	227,403	813	641	172
Berwick	4,649	12	11	1
Blanchard	3,186	5	4	1
Bogalusa	11,865	52	33	19
Bossier City	69,632	199	159	40
Breaux Bridge	8,451	25	23	2
Broussard	12,125	32	28	4
Brusly	2,827	10	10	0
Bunkie	4,045	8	5	3
Carencro	8,944	29	27	2
Church Point	4,485	16	16	0
Clinton	1,571	22	15	7
Cottonport	1,945	6	5	1
Covington	10,571	41	36	5
Crowley	13,026	42	35	7
Denham Springs	10,329	39	31	8
De Ridder	11,116	32	26	6
Epps	825	2	1	1
Erath	2,108	11	7	4
Eunice	10,258	39	29	10
Farmerville	3,841	14	14	0
Ferriday	3,300	18	14	4
Fisher	222	1	1	0
Florien	616	3	3	0
Folsom	826	5	3	2
Franklinton	3,770	26	20	6
French Settlement	1,205	2	2	0
Georgetown	326	3	2	1

(Number.)

State/city	Population	Total law enforcement employees	Total officers	Total civilians
Golden Meadow	2,028	7	5	2
Gonzales	11,012	49	44	5
Gramercy	3,425	8	7	1
Greenwood	3,145	10	9	1
Gretna	17,923	195	100	95
Hammond	20,712	108	81	27
Harahan	9,373	26	19	7
Haughton	3,301	13	12	1
Hodge	445	4	4	0
Houma	34,083	96	80	16
Ida	211	1	1	0
Independence	1,910	8	8	0
Iowa	3,343	17	12	5
Jena	3,440	7	6	1
Jennings	10,074	32	26	6
Kenner	67,149	221	158	63
Kentwood	2,407	12	11	1
Killian	1,347	3	3	0
Kinder	2,430	15	12	3
Lafayette	128,691	321	264	57
Lake Arthur	2,747	10	6	4
Lake Charles	77,647	186	153	33
Lake Providence	3,648	13	8	5
Leesville	6,226	32	27	5
Lutcher	3,333	3	3	0
Mamou	3,178	12	11	1
Mandeville	12,503	45	33	12
Mansfield	4,900	15	15	0
Many	2,780	11	11	0
Marion	752	1	1	0
Minden	12,497	32	31	1
Monroe	49,354	161	124	37
Montgomery	723	3	3	0
Morgan City	11,530	55	43	12
Natchitoches	18,284	70	53	17
New Orleans	397,447	1,436	1,101	335
Oak Grove	1,620	7	7	0
Oil City	982	4	4	0
Olla	1,393	2	2	0
Patterson	6,053	24	24	0
Pearl River	2,575	20	13	7
Pineville	14,473	73	64	9
Plaquemine	6,727	28	20	8
Ponchatoula	7,317	28	22	6
Port Allen	5,085	20	19	1
Port Vincent	773	3	3	0
Rayne	8,167	22	22	0
Ruston	22,438	53	39	14
Scott	8,780	27	25	2
Shreveport	193,937	608	508	100
Sibley	1,169	3	3	0
Slidell	28,163	104	81	23
Springhill	5,012	18	18	0
Sterlington	2,731	8	8	0
St. Gabriel	7,298	19	12	7
Sulphur	20,247	69	44	25
Tallulah	6,970	14	11	3
Thibodaux	14,617	68	55	13
Tickfaw	768	6	6	0
Vidalia	4,015	38	29	9
Ville Platte	7,244	48	29	19
Walker	6,447	22	18	4
Welsh	3,232	14	14	0
West Monroe	12,891	72	72	0
Westwego	8,532	38	36	2
Youngsville	13,679	29	25	4
Zachary	17,072	46	44	2
Zwolle	1,945	8	6	2
MAINE				
Ashland	1,217	2	2	0

Table 19. Full-Time Law Enforcement Employees, by Selected State and City, 2017—*Continued*

(Number.)

State/city	Population	Total law enforcement employees	Total officers	Total civilians
Auburn	22,931	60	54	6
Augusta	18,394	57	45	12
Baileyville	1,433	3	3	0
Bangor	31,814	94	80	14
Bar Harbor	5,422	28	19	9
Bath	8,272	23	19	4
Belfast	6,644	17	15	2
Berwick	7,627	12	11	1
Biddeford	21,378	72	50	22
Boothbay Harbor	2,188	8	7	1
Brewer	9,048	20	18	2
Bridgton	5,414	10	9	1
Brunswick	20,711	46	32	14
Bucksport	4,924	12	8	4
Buxton	8,222	12	7	5
Calais	2,940	8	8	0
Camden	4,833	10	10	0
Cape Elizabeth	9,383	14	13	1
Caribou	7,666	16	15	1
Carrabassett Valley	781	1	1	0
Clinton	3,300	4	4	0
Cumberland	7,956	12	11	1
Damariscotta	2,166	6	5	1
Dexter	3,710	5	5	0
Dixfield	2,457	3	3	0
Dover-Foxcroft	4,045	5	5	0
East Millinocket	2,943	2	2	0
Eastport	1,243	4	4	0
Eliot	6,481	9	8	1
Ellsworth	7,940	21	18	3
Fairfield	6,560	11	10	1
Falmouth	12,260	27	18	9
Farmington	7,548	24	14	10
Fort Fairfield	3,294	4	4	0
Fort Kent	3,900	9	5	4
Freeport	8,520	16	14	2
Fryeburg	3,389	6	6	0
Gardiner	5,592	12	11	1
Gorham	17,554	26	24	2
Gouldsboro	1,750	1	1	0
Greenville	1,585	3	2	1
Hallowell	2,318	5	5	0
Hampden	7,363	12	11	1
Holden	3,049	4	4	0
Houlton	5,781	19	12	7
Islesboro	565	1	1	0
Jay	4,628	7	6	1
Kennebunk	11,406	22	20	2
Kennebunkport	3,604	17	12	5
Kittery	9,669	26	20	6
Lewiston	36,067	89	78	11
Limestone	2,165	3	3	0
Lincoln	4,944	6	5	1
Lisbon	8,820	18	12	6
Livermore Falls	3,104	6	6	0
Machias	2,087	4	4	0
Madawaska	3,760	6	5	1
Mechanic Falls	2,986	3	3	0
Mexico	2,584	4	4	0
Milbridge	1,277	2	2	0
Millinocket	4,267	6	6	0
Milo	2,256	3	3	0
Monmouth	4,036	4	4	0
Newport	3,224	6	6	0
North Berwick	4,690	9	8	1
Norway	4,902	10	9	1
Oakland	6,145	10	9	1
Ogunquit	922	11	10	1
Old Orchard Beach	8,842	24	22	2
Old Town	7,466	17	16	1
Orono	11,400	16	15	1

(Number.)

State/city	Population	Total law enforcement employees	Total officers	Total civilians
Oxford	4,037	9	8	1
Paris	5,119	8	7	1
Phippsburg	2,246	1	1	0
Pittsfield	4,076	6	6	0
Portland	67,079	209	147	62
Presque Isle	9,016	22	17	5
Rangeley	1,159	2	2	0
Richmond	3,412	4	4	0
Rockland	7,161	18	16	2
Rockport	3,389	6	6	0
Rumford	5,692	12	12	0
Sabattus	5,038	7	6	1
Saco	19,332	44	33	11
Sanford	20,963	43	39	4
Scarborough	20,215	60	40	20
Searsport	2,638	3	3	0
Skowhegan	8,255	16	14	2
South Berwick	7,469	13	9	4
South Portland	25,679	60	53	7
Southwest Harbor	1,780	9	5	4
Thomaston	2,772	5	5	0
Topsham	8,790	15	14	1
Van Buren	2,068	3	3	0
Veazie	1,827	4	4	0
Waldoboro	5,023	8	7	1
Washburn	1,558	2	2	0
Waterville	16,522	41	31	10
Wells	10,287	31	23	8
Westbrook	18,560	45	38	7
Wilton	3,944	6	6	0
Windham	18,175	30	27	3
Winslow	7,534	12	11	1
Winthrop	5,950	12	7	5
Wiscasset	3,680	3	3	0
Yarmouth	8,594	14	13	1
York	13,018	37	26	11
MARYLAND				
Aberdeen	15,720	49	39	10
Annapolis	39,596	146	114	32
Baltimore	613,217	2,937	2,516	421
Baltimore City Sheriff		201	156	45
Bel Air	10,109	41	30	11
Berlin	4,628	19	14	5
Berwyn Heights	3,300	7	7	0
Bladensburg	9,683	25	20	5
Boonsboro	3,521	5	4	1
Bowie	58,891	85	61	24
Brentwood	3,205	5	4	1
Brunswick	6,219	14	14	0
Cambridge	12,471	48	44	4
Capitol Heights	4,582	10	9	1
Centreville	4,753	12	12	0
Chestertown	5,056	15	14	1
Cheverly	6,517	15	12	3
Chevy Chase Village	2,080	17	11	6
Colmar Manor	1,474	3	2	1
Cottage City	1,378	3	3	0
Crisfield	2,616	14	11	3
Cumberland	19,842	53	50	3
Delmar	3,216	14	13	1
Denton	4,385	14	13	1
District Heights	6,064	12	11	1
Easton	16,598	54	41	13
Edmonston	1,528	7	5	2
Elkton	15,794	44	39	5
Fairmount Heights	1,579	1	1	0
Federalsburg	2,664	9	8	1
Forest Heights	2,597	6	4	2
Frederick	70,860	189	148	41
Frostburg	8,622	20	16	4

(Number.)

State/city	Population	Total law enforcement employees	Total officers	Total civilians
Fruitland	5,298	21	19	2
Glenarden	6,228	15	13	2
Greenbelt	24,099	60	47	13
Greensboro	1,876	1	1	0
Hagerstown	40,568	116	102	14
Hampstead	6,361	10	9	1
Hancock	1,552	5	4	1
Havre de Grace	13,610	45	36	9
Hurlock	2,019	11	10	1
Hyattsville	18,579	55	43	12
Landover Hills	1,821	5	4	1
La Plata	9,324	17	16	1
Laurel	25,997	85	64	21
Lonaconing	1,125	5	2	3
Luke	63	1	1	0
Manchester	4,820	6	6	0
Morningside	2,060	8	7	1
Mount Rainier	8,516	20	16	4
New Carrollton	12,971	26	20	6
North East	3,661	12	11	1
Oakland	1,867	2	2	0
Ocean City	6,982	123	94	29
Ocean Pines	12,263	20	16	4
Oxford	612	3	3	0
Perryville	4,432	12	11	1
Pocomoke City	4,088	24	15	9
Princess Anne	3,639	12	11	1
Ridgely	1,622	5	5	0
Rising Sun	2,800	4	4	0
Riverdale Park	7,358	28	20	8
Rock Hall	1,297	4	4	0
Salisbury	33,558	112	84	28
Seat Pleasant	4,806	20	17	3
Smithsburg	3,002	5	4	1
Snow Hill	2,065	5	5	0
St. Michaels	1,039	9	8	1
Sykesville	3,940	8	7	1
Takoma Park	17,933	56	39	17
Taneytown	6,762	15	14	1
Thurmont	6,584	14	11	3
University Park	2,677	9	8	1
Upper Marlboro	672	3	3	0
Westminster	18,682	55	42	13
MASSACHUSETTS				
Abington	16,369	27	25	2
Acton	23,937	54	43	11
Acushnet	10,547	21	18	3
Agawam	28,839	65	50	15
Amesbury	17,636	41	35	6
Amherst	40,313	49	47	2
Andover	35,898	68	49	19
Aquinnah	330	4	4	0
Arlington	45,449	83	68	15
Ashburnham	6,255	16	12	4
Ashby	3,248	11	7	4
Ashland	17,878	31	25	6
Attleboro	44,607	97	82	15
Auburn	16,563	48	37	11
Avon	4,560	17	12	5
Ayer	8,240	30	20	10
Barnstable	44,142	135	117	18
Barre	5,518	10	9	1
Becket	1,744	4	4	0
Bedford	14,607	37	28	9
Belchertown	15,097	24	19	5
Bellingham	17,121	40	32	8
Belmont	26,432	67	48	19
Berkley	6,745	8	8	0
Berlin	3,175	10	9	1
Bernardston	2,082	3	3	0

(Number.)

State/city	Population	Total law enforcement employees	Total officers	Total civilians
Beverly	41,678	71	67	4
Billerica	43,127	79	66	13
Blackstone	9,079	18	18	0
Bolton	5,272	12	11	1
Boston	682,903	2,778	2,205	573
Bourne	19,867	53	44	9
Boxborough	5,972	18	12	6
Boxford	8,333	12	12	0
Boylston	4,610	13	9	4
Braintree	37,579	116	77	39
Brewster	9,895	28	23	5
Brockton	96,016	201	180	21
Brookfield	3,399	5	5	0
Brookline	59,233	141	102	39
Buckland	1,843	2	2	0
Burlington	26,678	73	65	8
Cambridge	111,707	311	278	33
Canton	23,551	43	43	0
Carlisle	5,313	16	11	5
Carver	11,671	20	16	4
Chatham	6,158	25	21	4
Chelmsford	35,392	65	51	14
Chelsea	40,514	114	105	9
Cheshire	3,160	1	1	0
Chicopee	56,255	138	134	4
Clinton	13,839	37	28	9
Cohasset	8,598	19	18	1
Concord	20,193	40	33	7
Dalton	6,602	12	10	2
Danvers	28,168	56	44	12
Dartmouth	34,802	85	70	15
Dedham	25,358	60	57	3
Deerfield	4,971	9	8	1
Dennis	13,976	57	47	10
Dighton	7,617	12	11	1
Douglas	8,795	18	14	4
Dover	6,053	16	16	0
Dracut	31,685	46	40	6
Dudley	11,801	14	14	0
Dunstable	3,389	9	8	1
East Bridgewater	14,573	26	22	4
Eastham	4,899	22	16	6
Easthampton	16,061	34	28	6
East Longmeadow	16,288	29	27	2
Easton	24,176	45	35	10
Egremont	1,204	4	4	0
Erving	1,763	5	5	0
Essex	3,729	9	8	1
Everett	47,185	116	108	8
Fairhaven	16,188	37	31	6
Fall River	89,012	279	228	51
Falmouth	31,487	62	58	4
Fitchburg	40,445	96	77	19
Foxborough	17,636	47	35	12
Framingham	72,153	141	124	17
Franklin	33,397	53	48	5
Freetown	9,343	21	18	3
Gardner	20,491	45	33	12
Georgetown	8,715	15	11	4
Gill	1,489	2	2	0
Gloucester	29,980	64	57	7
Goshen	1,074	2	2	0
Grafton	18,763	24	20	4
Granby	6,379	13	9	4
Great Barrington	6,815	18	17	1
Greenfield	17,462	47	34	13
Groton	11,411	26	19	7
Groveland	6,838	11	10	1
Hadley	5,382	17	13	4
Hamilton	8,216	18	13	5
Hampden	5,217	14	11	3

Table 19. Full-Time Law Enforcement Employees, by Selected State and City, 2017—*Continued*

(Number.)

State/city	Population	Total law enforcement employees	Total officers	Total civilians
Hanson	10,860	26	21	5
Hardwick	4,031	5	5	0
Harwich	12,150	42	33	9
Haverhill	63,244	107	94	13
Hingham	23,392	50	48	2
Holbrook	11,064	23	22	1
Holland	2,502	2	2	0
Holliston	14,736	23	19	4
Holyoke	40,451	138	119	19
Hopedale	5,959	16	12	4
Hopkinton	17,348	33	23	10
Hudson	19,963	43	33	10
Ipswich	13,951	29	24	5
Kingston	13,615	32	24	8
Lakeville	11,502	22	18	4
Lancaster	8,212	12	11	1
Lanesboro	2,951	6	6	0
Lawrence	80,890	160	135	25
Leicester	11,369	20	19	1
Lenox	4,947	10	10	0
Leominster	41,846	88	72	16
Lexington	33,768	59	44	15
Lincoln	6,860	19	13	6
Littleton	10,196	25	19	6
Longmeadow	15,848	33	27	6
Lowell	111,294	302	220	82
Ludlow	21,529	49	40	9
Lunenburg	11,477	16	15	1
Lynn	93,140	186	168	18
Malden	61,098	108	102	6
Mansfield	23,847	49	37	12
Marblehead	20,618	41	32	9
Marion	5,124	15	15	0
Marlborough	39,919	76	64	12
Marshfield	25,929	45	42	3
Mashpee	14,272	39	31	8
Mattapoisett	6,354	19	19	0
Maynard	10,756	27	21	6
Medford	57,418	108	105	3
Medway	13,407	27	22	5
Melrose	28,101	48	48	0
Mendon	6,069	17	12	5
Methuen	50,396	116	97	19
Middleboro	25,084	47	41	6
Middleton	9,788	17	15	2
Milford	28,772	57	45	12
Millbury	13,626	24	19	5
Millville	3,254	7	6	1
Montague	8,211	16	16	0
Nahant	3,500	13	12	1
Natick	36,705	71	57	14
Needham	31,054	56	47	9
New Bedford	95,107	297	247	50
Newton	89,736	180	147	33
Norfolk	11,815	24	18	6
North Adams	12,948	33	24	9
Northampton	28,458	69	63	6
North Andover	31,035	54	41	13
North Attleboro	29,158	53	40	13
Northborough	15,109	27	22	5
Northbridge	16,711	27	20	7
North Reading	15,780	33	32	1
Norton	19,654	32	31	1
Norwell	11,150	28	23	5
Norwood	29,194	71	60	11
Orange	7,569	14	13	1
Orleans	5,837	28	22	6
Oxford	13,955	28	22	6
Palmer	12,136	26	19	7
Paxton	4,891	19	15	4
Peabody	52,721	115	95	20

(Number.)

State/city	Population	Total law enforcement employees	Total officers	Total civilians
Pelham	1,333	1	1	0
Pepperell	12,267	16	15	1
Phillipston	1,757	2	2	0
Pittsfield	42,546	110	89	21
Plymouth	59,803	137	120	17
Plympton	2,976	9	9	0
Princeton	3,472	7	6	1
Provincetown	2,993	26	19	7
Quincy	93,966	283	212	71
Randolph	33,837	62	58	4
Raynham	14,048	35	27	8
Reading	26,033	57	41	16
Rehoboth	12,153	29	24	5
Revere	53,425	111	103	8
Rochester	5,593	12	12	0
Rowley	6,378	17	12	5
Salem	43,385	107	96	11
Sandwich	20,362	36	35	1
Saugus	28,241	71	58	13
Scituate	18,687	36	34	2
Seekonk	15,521	40	38	2
Sharon	18,419	37	33	4
Sherborn	4,318	15	14	1
Shrewsbury	36,974	60	45	15
Somerset	18,239	37	33	4
Somerville	82,326	139	124	15
Southborough	10,148	22	17	5
Southbridge	16,860	43	36	7
South Hadley	17,804	31	25	6
Southwick	9,778	23	18	5
Spencer	11,920	21	17	4
Springfield	154,562	516	448	68
Stockbridge	1,919	7	6	1
Stoneham	22,077	45	38	7
Stoughton	28,678	72	60	12
Stow	7,196	10	10	0
Sturbridge	9,605	22	16	6
Sudbury	19,120	37	27	10
Sunderland	3,627	6	5	1
Sutton	9,401	20	16	4
Swampscott	15,016	32	31	1
Swansea	16,597	37	31	6
Taunton	57,047	120	114	6
Templeton	8,184	14	9	5
Tewksbury	31,245	73	58	15
Topsfield	6,604	13	12	1
Townsend	9,626	15	14	1
Truro	2,018	21	16	5
Wakefield	27,049	48	47	1
Walpole	25,312	50	42	8
Waltham	63,413	183	147	36
Wareham	22,743	55	44	11
Watertown	35,586	76	63	13
Wayland	13,976	32	23	9
Webster	16,883	31	30	1
Wellesley	29,434	59	44	15
Wellfleet	2,757	18	13	5
Wenham	5,242	11	10	1
Westborough	19,074	31	29	2
Westfield	41,735	87	82	5
Westford	24,639	46	42	4
Westminster	7,699	16	11	5
West Newbury	4,671	11	10	1
Weston	12,249	33	24	9
Westport	15,919	32	28	4
West Springfield	28,635	94	89	5
West Tisbury	2,920	10	9	1
Westwood	16,347	40	30	10
Weymouth	56,382	113	94	19
Whitman	15,000	27	26	1
Wilbraham	14,749	28	27	1

Table 19. Full-Time Law Enforcement Employees, by Selected State and City, 2017—*Continued*

(Number.)

State/city	Population	Total law enforcement employees	Total officers	Total civilians
Williamsburg	2,480	1	1	0
Williamstown	7,756	15	12	3
Wilmington	23,791	50	48	2
Winchendon	10,812	19	14	5
Winchester	23,059	47	38	9
Winthrop	18,319	36	35	1
Woburn	39,677	80	75	5
Worcester	185,107	505	453	52
Wrentham	11,838	22	21	1
Yarmouth	23,370	71	59	12
MICHIGAN				
Adrian	20,598	29	27	2
Akron	387	1	1	0
Albion	8,293	17	16	1
Allegan	5,085	10	9	1
Allen Park	27,062	44	40	4
Alma	9,113	14	12	2
Almont	2,780	8	7	1
Alpena	10,066	19	17	2
Ann Arbor	121,930	143	119	24
Argentine Township	6,544	6	5	1
Armada	1,742	2	2	0
Auburn Hills	23,034	53	48	5
Au Gres	848	1	1	0
Bangor	1,839	5	5	0
Bath Township	12,759	13	12	1
Battle Creek	60,852	130	108	22
Bay City	33,286	56	51	5
Beaverton	1,044	2	2	0
Belding	5,772	8	8	0
Bellaire	1,061	2	2	0
Bellevue	1,298	2	2	0
Benton Harbor	9,899	25	20	5
Benton Township	14,354	26	22	4
Berkley	15,322	34	28	6
Berrien Springs-Oronoko Township	9,039	9	8	1
Beverly Hills	10,504	24	23	1
Big Rapids	10,437	17	16	1
Birch Run	1,452	6	5	1
Birmingham	21,162	43	32	11
Blackman Township	36,908	35	34	1
Blissfield	3,229	5	5	0
Bloomfield Hills	4,021	26	23	3
Bloomfield Township	42,291	89	70	19
Breckenridge	1,296	1	1	0
Bridgeport Township	9,909	9	8	1
Bridgman	2,247	5	5	0
Brighton	7,631	19	17	2
Bronson	2,315	4	4	0
Brown City	1,246	2	2	0
Brownstown Township	31,102	39	32	7
Buchanan	4,314	10	9	1
Burton	28,439	39	36	3
Cadillac	10,473	17	15	2
Cambridge Township	5,643	4	4	0
Canton Township	90,294	119	82	37
Capac	1,834	1	1	0
Carleton	2,342	3	2	1
Caro	4,037	7	7	0
Carrollton Township	5,728	6	6	0
Carson City	1,107	3	3	0
Caspian-Gaastra	1,173	1	1	0
Cass City	2,322	4	4	0
Cassopolis	1,717	5	5	0
Center Line	8,304	25	20	5
Central Lake	929	1	1	0
Charlotte	9,053	17	16	1
Cheboygan	4,705	8	8	0
Chelsea	5,225	14	10	4
Chesterfield Township	45,212	53	40	13

Table 19. Full-Time Law Enforcement Employees, by Selected State and City, 2017—Continued

(Number.)

State/city	Population	Total law enforcement employees	Total officers	Total civilians
Chocolay Township	5,948	5	4	1
Clare	3,058	8	8	0
Clawson	11,994	18	17	1
Clayton Township	7,113	4	4	0
Clay Township	8,845	19	16	3
Clinton	2,253	4	4	0
Clinton Township	100,999	102	93	9
Clio	2,495	4	4	0
Coldwater	10,750	20	18	2
Coleman	1,191	2	2	0
Coloma Township	6,362	11	8	3
Colon	1,150	3	3	0
Columbia Township	7,379	6	6	0
Constantine	2,042	3	3	0
Corunna	3,386	3	3	0
Covert Township	2,831	9	9	0
Croswell	2,278	6	6	0
Crystal Falls	1,380	2	2	0
Davison	4,891	7	6	1
Davison Township	19,029	20	18	2
Dearborn	93,889	220	187	33
Dearborn Heights	55,454	95	83	12
Decatur	1,755	5	5	0
Denton Township	5,324	4	4	0
Detroit	670,792	3,084	2,499	585
Dewitt	4,754	7	6	1
Dewitt Township	14,799	17	16	1
Dowagiac	5,820	15	14	1
Dryden Township	4,767	4	4	0
Dundee	4,012	3	3	0
Durand	3,312	6	6	0
East Jordan	2,348	4	4	0
East Lansing	48,920	63	50	13
Eastpointe	32,712	41	37	4
Eaton Rapids	5,230	10	9	1
Eau Claire	613	1	1	0
Ecorse	9,132	18	16	2
Elk Rapids	1,610	5	5	0
Elkton	763	2	2	0
Emmett Township	11,619	15	13	2
Erie Township	4,359	4	3	1
Escanaba	12,280	41	30	11
Essexville	3,340	8	8	0
Evart	1,858	2	2	0
Fair Haven Township	1,037	1	1	0
Farmington	10,537	23	22	1
Farmington Hills	81,359	137	100	37
Fenton	11,306	22	13	9
Ferndale	20,131	48	38	10
Flat Rock	9,821	20	20	0
Flint	96,605	120	107	13
Flint Township	30,284	44	38	6
Flushing	7,972	9	9	0
Flushing Township	10,172	6	6	0
Forsyth Township	6,189	9	8	1
Fowlerville	2,922	7	6	1
Frankenmuth	5,159	7	7	0
Frankfort	1,291	3	3	0
Franklin	3,260	10	10	0
Fraser	14,645	44	34	10
Fremont	4,020	8	7	1
Fruitport Township	14,138	9	9	0
Gaines Township	6,139	1	1	0
Garden City	26,571	30	28	2
Garfield Township	812	1	1	0
Genesee Township	20,253	15	13	2
Gerrish Township	2,902	7	7	0
Gibraltar	4,472	8	7	1
Gladstone	4,767	11	10	1
Gladwin	2,865	4	4	0
Grand Beach	279	4	4	0

Table 19. Full-Time Law Enforcement Employees, by Selected State and City, 2017—*Continued*

(Number.)

State/city	Population	Total law enforcement employees	Total officers	Total civilians
Grand Blanc	7,904	18	15	3
Grand Blanc Township	36,630	46	39	7
Grand Haven	11,004	36	31	5
Grand Ledge	7,809	14	14	0
Grand Rapids	197,868	335	276	59
Grandville	16,108	26	24	2
Grant	879	1	1	0
Grayling	1,830	8	8	0
Green Oak Township	18,839	17	15	2
Greenville	8,418	19	17	2
Grosse Ile Township	10,084	24	17	7
Grosse Pointe	5,151	22	22	0
Grosse Pointe Farms	9,106	41	32	9
Grosse Pointe Park	11,061	38	33	5
Grosse Pointe Shores	2,904	18	18	0
Grosse Pointe Woods	15,566	34	29	5
Hamburg Township	21,897	17	16	1
Hampton Township	9,522	9	9	0
Hamtramck	21,654	35	30	5
Hancock	4,576	8	8	0
Harbor Beach	1,602	4	4	0
Harbor Springs	1,208	6	5	1
Harper Woods	13,653	33	30	3
Hart	2,080	5	5	0
Hastings	7,272	16	14	2
Hazel Park	16,551	37	32	5
Highland Park	10,757	8	6	2
Holland	33,613	66	58	8
Home Township	1,346	1	1	0
Hopkins	609	1	1	0
Houghton	8,031	10	9	1
Howell	9,538	19	17	2
Hudson	2,225	2	2	0
Huntington Woods	6,343	18	17	1
Huron Township	15,636	26	20	6
Imlay City	3,577	11	8	3
Inkster	24,324	29	25	4
Ionia	11,287	17	15	2
Iron Mountain	7,397	12	12	0
Ironwood	4,887	11	10	1
Ishpeming	6,471	11	10	1
Jackson	32,822	55	43	12
Jonesville	2,208	3	3	0
Kalamazoo	76,263	263	225	38
Kalamazoo Township	24,590	40	33	7
Kalkaska	2,043	5	4	1
Keego Harbor	3,030	4	4	0
Kentwood	52,197	77	66	11
Kingsford	5,003	17	17	0
Kinross Township	7,396	2	2	0
Laingsburg	1,284	1	1	0
Lake Angelus	297	1	1	0
Lake Linden	990	1	1	0
Lake Odessa	2,035	3	3	0
Lake Orion	3,058	5	4	1
Lakeview	1,011	2	2	0
Lansing	116,302	213	188	25
Lansing Township	8,150	16	15	1
Lapeer	8,735	22	20	2
Lathrup Village	4,126	8	8	0
Laurium	1,941	4	4	0
Lennon	498	1	1	0
Leslie	1,875	3	3	0
Lincoln Park	36,502	55	47	8
Lincoln Township	14,460	12	10	2
Linden	3,842	5	5	0
Litchfield	1,343	2	2	0
Livonia	93,603	186	147	39
Lowell	4,089	6	5	1
Ludington	8,068	15	14	1
Luna Pier	1,368	2	2	0

State/city	Population	Total law enforcement employees	Total officers	Total civilians
Mackinac Island	475	6	6	0
Mackinaw City	801	6	6	0
Madison Heights	30,152	56	45	11
Madison Township	8,470	5	5	0
Mancelona	1,359	1	1	0
Manistee	6,030	13	13	0
Manistique	2,890	8	8	0
Manton	1,438	1	1	0
Marenisco Township	1,599	1	1	0
Marine City	4,108	4	4	0
Marlette	1,762	4	4	0
Marquette	20,442	38	33	5
Marshall	7,028	14	14	0
Marysville	9,702	16	14	2
Mason	8,418	12	11	1
Mattawan	1,936	6	6	0
Melvindale	10,262	24	23	1
Mendon	854	2	2	0
Menominee	8,230	16	15	1
Meridian Township	42,878	42	37	5
Metamora Township	4,250	4	4	0
Metro Police Authority of Genesee County	20,001	28	24	4
Michiana	181	3	3	0
Midland	42,131	48	46	2
Milan	6,044	13	9	4
Milford	16,726	20	18	2
Monroe	19,868	43	38	5
Montague	2,358	5	5	0
Montrose Township	7,466	8	7	1
Morenci	2,174	2	2	0
Mount Morris Township	20,365	32	29	3
Mount Pleasant	26,366	34	28	6
Munising	2,232	4	4	0
Muskegon	38,375	82	74	8
Muskegon Heights	10,786	25	22	3
Muskegon Township	17,842	15	14	1
Napoleon Township	6,727	2	2	0
Nashville	1,644	4	4	0
Negaunee	4,576	9	9	0
Newaygo	2,045	6	5	1
New Baltimore	12,401	18	17	1
New Buffalo	1,870	6	5	1
Niles	11,202	26	17	9
Northfield Township	8,634	11	10	1
Northville	5,981	11	11	0
Northville Township	28,751	41	28	13
Norton Shores	24,402	32	30	2
Norway	2,757	6	6	0
Novi	59,895	84	62	22
Oak Park	29,698	61	49	12
Olivet	1,707	2	2	0
Ontwa Township-Edwardsburg	6,487	7	7	0
Orchard Lake	2,431	9	8	1
Oscoda Township	6,831	11	10	1
Otsego	4,005	7	6	1
Ovid	1,615	2	2	0
Owosso	14,587	20	18	2
Oxford	3,548	4	4	0
Paw Paw	3,435	9	8	1
Pentwater	839	3	3	0
Petoskey	5,764	20	19	1
Pigeon	1,143	1	1	0
Pinckney	2,463	6	6	0
Pinconning	1,249	1	1	0
Pittsfield Township	39,061	57	40	17
Plainwell	3,825	9	8	1
Plymouth	9,072	17	16	1
Plymouth Township	26,779	48	30	18
Portage	48,876	74	55	19
Port Austin	628	1	1	0
Port Huron	29,092	58	49	9

(Number.)

State/city	Population	Total law enforcement employees	Total officers	Total civilians
Portland	3,943	6	6	0
Potterville	2,634	2	2	0
Prairieville Township	3,452	2	2	0
Quincy	1,627	3	3	0
Reading	1,046	1	1	0
Redford Township	46,867	68	60	8
Reed City	2,379	5	4	1
Richfield Township, Genesee County	8,270	11	9	2
Richfield Township, Roscommon County	3,607	6	5	1
Richmond	5,893	11	9	2
River Rouge	7,417	20	18	2
Riverview	12,045	25	23	2
Rochester	13,068	30	22	8
Rockford	6,316	11	10	1
Rockwood	3,159	6	6	0
Rogers City	2,676	6	6	0
Romeo	3,616	11	8	3
Romulus	23,174	51	39	12
Roosevelt Park	3,826	5	5	0
Roseville	47,651	72	69	3
Royal Oak	59,303	111	78	33
Saginaw	48,589	61	53	8
Saginaw Township	39,319	48	43	5
Saline	9,207	17	13	4
Sandusky	2,545	6	5	1
Sault Ste. Marie	13,630	26	24	2
Schoolcraft	1,571	3	3	0
Scottville	1,222	2	2	0
Sebewaing	1,655	3	3	0
Shelby Township	79,217	85	66	19
Shepherd	1,516	2	2	0
Somerset Township	4,556	3	3	0
Southfield	73,324	145	105	40
Southgate	28,939	39	36	3
South Haven	4,362	21	17	4
South Lyon	11,777	17	16	1
South Rockwood	1,638	2	2	0
Sparta	4,370	6	6	0
Spring Arbor Township	7,974	2	2	0
Springport Township	2,134	2	2	0
Stanton	1,415	1	1	0
St. Charles	1,925	2	2	0
St. Clair	5,350	7	7	0
St. Clair Shores	59,782	85	80	5
Sterling Heights	132,882	163	141	22
St. Ignace	2,366	6	5	1
St. Johns	7,938	12	10	2
St. Joseph Township	9,813	12	11	1
St. Louis	6,994	7	6	1
Stockbridge	1,237	2	2	0
Sturgis	10,858	23	18	5
Sumpter Township	9,215	17	14	3
Sylvan Lake	1,841	4	4	0
Tawas	4,522	6	5	1
Taylor	60,882	90	74	16
Tecumseh	8,345	14	13	1
Thomas Township	11,450	8	8	0
Three Rivers	7,695	17	15	2
Tittabawassee Township	9,776	6	5	1
Traverse City	15,617	29	28	1
Trenton	18,161	35	34	1
Troy	84,086	150	106	44
Tuscarora Township	2,946	8	7	1
Ubly	811	1	1	0
Unadilla Township	3,435	3	3	0
Utica	4,960	18	14	4
Van Buren Township	27,911	55	40	15
Vassar	2,580	5	5	0
Vernon	752	1	1	0
Vicksburg	3,350	5	5	0
Walker	24,987	39	35	4

(Number.)

State/city	Population	Total law enforcement employees	Total officers	Total civilians
Walled Lake	7,104	6	6	0
Warren	135,303	235	196	39
Waterford Township	73,060	70	54	16
Watervliet	1,671	3	3	0
Wayland	4,228	7	6	1
Wayne	16,857	20	20	0
West Bloomfield Township	65,948	104	74	30
West Branch	2,052	6	5	1
Westland	81,158	105	81	24
White Cloud	1,372	2	2	0
Whitehall	2,726	8	8	0
White Lake Township	31,016	37	27	10
White Pigeon	1,509	4	4	0
Williamston	3,892	7	6	1
Wixom	13,801	23	20	3
Wolverine Lake	4,586	8	8	0
Woodhaven	12,397	29	27	2
Wyandotte	24,817	47	34	13
Wyoming	76,153	98	85	13
Yale	1,889	3	3	0
Ypsilanti	21,267	30	25	5
Zeeland	5,594	11	10	1
Zilwaukee	1,546	2	2	0
MINNESOTA				
Aitkin	1,987	8	7	1
Akeley	430	1	1	0
Albany	2,682	5	4	1
Albert Lea	17,608	29	26	3
Alexandria	13,756	28	24	4
Annandale	3,328	5	5	0
Anoka	17,439	39	28	11
Appleton	1,341	3	3	0
Apple Valley	52,439	59	51	8
Arlington	2,146	2	2	0
Atwater	1,118	1	1	0
Austin	24,692	37	34	3
Avon	1,550	4	3	1
Babbitt	1,513	5	5	0
Barnesville	2,578	5	5	0
Battle Lake	890	2	2	0
Baxter	8,298	15	14	1
Bayport	3,420	5	5	0
Becker	4,825	7	6	1
Belgrade/Brooten	1,516	2	2	0
Belle Plaine	7,066	11	9	2
Bemidji	15,054	35	33	2
Benson	3,080	8	7	1
Big Lake	10,730	14	12	2
Blackduck	778	2	2	0
Blaine	63,857	75	60	15
Blooming Prairie	1,986	3	3	0
Bloomington	85,704	152	123	29
Blue Earth	3,191	5	5	0
Bovey	802	2	2	0
Braham	1,774	4	4	0
Brainerd	13,307	30	24	6
Breckenridge	3,250	7	7	0
Breezy Point	2,368	7	6	1
Breitung Township	607	2	2	0
Brooklyn Center	30,989	61	49	12
Brooklyn Park	80,347	139	108	31
Brownton	730	1	1	0
Buffalo	16,206	21	17	4
Buffalo Lake	687	2	2	0
Burnsville	61,442	85	75	10
Caledonia	2,773	5	5	0
Cambridge	8,770	15	14	1
Canby	1,708	3	3	0
Cannon Falls	4,110	10	8	2
Centennial Lakes	10,956	18	16	2

Table 19. Full-Time Law Enforcement Employees, by Selected State and City, 2017—*Continued*

(Number.)

State/city	Population	Total law enforcement employees	Total officers	Total civilians
Champlin	24,417	31	26	5
Chaska	26,383	28	25	3
Chisholm	4,935	13	12	1
Clara City	1,316	2	2	0
Clearbrook	522	1	1	0
Cloquet	12,108	25	23	2
Cold Spring/Richmond	5,565	10	9	1
Coleraine	1,993	2	2	0
Columbia Heights	19,759	32	26	6
Coon Rapids	62,495	73	65	8
Corcoran	5,735	9	8	1
Cottage Grove	36,253	48	41	7
Crookston	7,789	17	15	2
Crosby	2,329	8	8	0
Crosslake	2,239	5	5	0
Crystal	23,173	38	33	5
Danube	454	1	1	0
Dawson/Boyd	1,564	3	3	0
Dayton	5,515	8	7	1
Deephaven	3,878	8	7	1
Deer River	932	4	4	0
Detroit Lakes	9,242	18	16	2
Dilworth	4,462	8	7	1
Duluth	86,306	168	143	25
Dundas	1,513	3	3	0
Eagan	66,805	83	70	13
Eagle Lake	3,099	2	2	0
East Grand Forks	8,713	25	23	2
East Range	3,635	9	9	0
Eden Prairie	64,429	93	69	24
Eden Valley	1,034	1	1	0
Edina	51,923	73	52	21
Elko New Market	4,714	4	4	0
Elk River	24,593	42	32	10
Ely	3,379	8	7	1
Eveleth	3,636	11	10	1
Fairfax	1,142	2	2	0
Fairmont	10,027	20	18	2
Faribault	23,713	43	35	8
Farmington	22,917	27	24	3
Fergus Falls	13,468	28	23	5
Floodwood	515	4	3	1
Foley	2,656	3	3	0
Forest Lake	19,804	27	25	2
Fridley	27,516	46	42	4
Fulda	1,218	2	2	0
Gaylord	2,221	4	4	0
Gilbert	1,789	7	7	0
Glencoe	5,478	9	8	1
Glenwood	2,563	6	5	1
Golden Valley	21,545	41	31	10
Goodhue	1,186	1	1	0
Goodview	4,116	5	4	1
Grand Rapids	11,270	23	20	3
Granite Falls	2,735	7	6	1
Hallock	922	1	1	0
Hastings	22,671	31	27	4
Hawley	2,215	4	4	0
Hector	1,047	2	2	0
Henning	799	2	2	0
Hermantown	9,455	18	15	3
Hibbing	16,051	28	25	3
Hill City	581	1	1	0
Hokah	556	1	1	0
Hopkins	18,189	39	31	8
Houston	979	2	2	0
Howard Lake	2,057	3	3	0
Hutchinson	13,846	35	23	12
International Falls	6,009	12	11	1
Inver Grove Heights	35,254	43	38	5
Isanti	5,641	10	9	1

(Number.)

State/city	Population	Total law enforcement employees	Total officers	Total civilians
Isle	800	3	3	0
Janesville	2,274	3	3	0
Jordan	6,261	11	9	2
Kasson	6,308	9	8	1
Keewatin	1,029	3	3	0
Kimball	782	3	3	0
La Crescent	4,816	8	7	1
Lake City	5,039	11	10	1
Lake Crystal	2,489	3	3	0
Lakefield	1,618	3	3	0
Lakes Area	9,544	15	13	2
Lake Shore	1,044	2	2	0
Lakeville	62,958	65	57	8
Lamberton	773	1	1	0
Le Center	2,436	3	3	0
Lester Prairie	1,680	3	3	0
Le Sueur	3,966	8	7	1
Lewiston	1,555	2	2	0
Lino Lakes	21,147	30	27	3
Litchfield	6,634	9	8	1
Little Falls	8,665	15	14	1
Long Prairie	3,313	6	6	0
Lonsdale	3,931	9	8	1
Madelia	2,229	4	4	0
Madison Lake	1,161	2	2	0
Mankato	42,047	66	57	9
Maple Grove	70,966	79	64	15
Mapleton	1,698	3	3	0
Maplewood	40,689	57	52	5
Marshall	13,660	24	21	3
Medina	6,498	11	10	1
Melrose	3,614	6	5	1
Menahga	1,329	3	3	0
Mendota Heights	11,314	17	16	1
Milaca	2,891	7	6	1
Minneapolis	418,971	1,034	847	187
Minneota	1,357	1	1	0
Minnesota Lake	649	1	1	0
Minnetonka	52,811	69	55	14
Minnetrista	9,965	15	13	2
Montevideo	5,181	10	9	1
Montgomery	2,899	5	4	1
Moorhead	42,999	74	58	16
Moose Lake	2,834	5	4	1
Morris	5,297	10	8	2
Mounds View	13,146	22	19	3
Mountain Lake	2,101	4	4	0
Nashwauk	956	3	3	0
New Brighton	22,772	33	28	5
New Hope	20,967	44	34	10
New Prague	7,685	12	10	2
New Richland	1,198	2	2	0
New Ulm	13,316	25	22	3
New York Mills	1,232	3	3	0
North Branch	10,349	13	11	2
Northfield	20,512	27	22	5
North Mankato	13,664	15	14	1
North St. Paul	12,545	18	16	2
Oakdale	28,181	40	32	8
Oak Park Heights	4,915	11	10	1
Olivia	2,328	5	5	0
Onamia	862	3	3	0
Orono	19,923	31	27	4
Ortonville	1,815	4	4	0
Osakis	1,713	3	3	0
Osseo	2,810	6	5	1
Owatonna	25,810	38	35	3
Parkers Prairie	1,005	2	2	0
Park Rapids	3,949	11	10	1
Paynesville	2,497	5	5	0
Pequot Lakes	2,278	6	5	1

(Number.)

State/city	Population	Total law enforcement employees	Total officers	Total civilians
Pike Bay	1,651	3	3	0
Pine River	926	3	3	0
Plainview	3,222	8	7	1
Plymouth	78,356	92	77	15
Preston	1,302	3	3	0
Princeton	4,701	13	11	2
Prior Lake	26,374	29	26	3
Proctor	3,059	8	7	1
Ramsey	26,643	27	24	3
Red Wing	16,539	34	29	5
Redwood Falls	4,976	12	10	2
Renville	1,188	3	3	0
Rice	1,375	3	3	0
Richfield	36,087	51	43	8
Robbinsdale	14,545	29	24	5
Rochester	115,228	200	138	62
Rogers	13,021	21	18	3
Roseau	2,778	6	5	1
Rosemount	24,255	27	24	3
Roseville	36,196	58	48	10
Rushford	1,715	3	3	0
Sartell	17,353	22	19	3
Sauk Centre	4,376	7	6	1
Sauk Rapids	13,769	18	17	1
Savage	31,491	42	30	12
Sebeka	678	2	2	0
Shakopee	41,176	58	48	10
Sherburn	1,084	4	4	0
Silver Bay	1,791	5	5	0
Silver Lake	802	2	2	0
Slayton	2,017	5	4	1
Sleepy Eye	3,421	7	7	0
South Lake Minnetonka	12,343	17	14	3
South St. Paul	20,235	31	28	3
Springfield	2,040	5	5	0
Spring Grove	1,290	2	2	0
Spring Lake Park	6,482	14	11	3
St. Anthony	9,159	23	20	3
Staples	2,880	7	6	1
Starbuck	1,255	4	4	0
St. Charles	3,717	5	5	0
St. Cloud	67,911	133	107	26
St. Francis	7,507	14	11	3
Stillwater	19,394	26	22	4
St. James	4,422	8	7	1
St. Joseph	6,772	10	9	1
St. Louis Park	49,355	71	56	15
St. Paul	306,696	822	645	177
St. Paul Park	5,398	8	8	0
St. Peter	11,779	19	14	5
Thief River Falls	8,824	19	17	2
Tracy	2,052	3	3	0
Tri-City	1,403	3	3	0
Trimont	700	1	1	0
Truman	1,049	2	2	0
Twin Valley	778	2	2	0
Two Harbors	3,533	9	8	1
Virginia	8,493	22	22	0
Wabasha	2,442	8	7	1
Wadena	4,142	9	8	1
Waite Park	7,455	19	16	3
Walker	931	3	3	0
Warroad	1,794	6	5	1
Waseca	9,018	18	16	2
Waterville	1,841	3	3	0
Wayzata	6,517	14	12	2
Wells	2,208	4	4	0
West Concord	771	1	1	0
West Hennepin	5,591	12	10	2
West St. Paul	19,778	34	31	3
Wheaton	1,331	3	3	0

(Number.)

State/city	Population	Total law enforcement employees	Total officers	Total civilians
White Bear Lake	26,065	36	29	7
Willmar	19,553	37	33	4
Windom	4,499	10	9	1
Winnebago	1,356	3	3	0
Winona	27,071	42	38	4
Winsted	2,285	4	4	0
Woodbury	69,978	82	69	13
Worthington	13,195	34	22	12
Wyoming	7,866	10	9	1
Zumbrota	3,431	6	6	0
MISSISSIPPI				
Amory	7,029	28	21	7
Batesville	7,380	52	42	10
Biloxi	46,263	177	125	52
Brandon	24,125	49	35	14
Brookhaven	12,334	46	38	8
Byram	11,549	40	29	11
Columbus	24,454	75	63	12
D'Iberville	11,852	41	37	4
Florence	4,438	25	15	10
Fulton	4,085	10	10	0
Gautier	18,451	48	37	11
Gulfport	72,792	215	162	53
Hattiesburg	47,116	147	94	53
Hernando	15,897	52	41	11
Holly Springs	7,682	27	21	6
Horn Lake	27,199	63	48	15
Iuka	2,983	11	8	3
Laurel	18,790	75	54	21
Madison	26,339	91	71	20
McComb	12,812	59	31	28
Meridian	38,778	118	94	24
Ocean Springs	17,698	51	39	12
Oxford	24,071	87	73	14
Pascagoula	21,928	92	64	28
Pass Christian	5,902	22	19	3
Petal	10,743	31	26	5
Poplarville	2,993	10	10	0
Ridgeland	24,551	86	66	20
Southaven	53,928	123	117	6
Starkville	25,852	67	57	10
Summit	1,642	6	5	1
Vicksburg	22,772	93	65	28
Waveland	6,426	18	18	0
West Point	10,817	28	24	4
Wiggins	4,567	23	16	7
MISSOURI				
Adrian	1,609	4	4	0
Advance	1,368	3	3	0
Archie	1,215	4	4	0
Arnold	21,399	55	47	8
Ash Grove	1,446	4	4	0
Ashland	3,902	7	6	1
Aurora	7,508	23	17	6
Ava	2,918	12	7	5
Ballwin	30,299	60	48	12
Bates City	219	1	1	0
Battlefield	6,127	9	9	0
Bella Villa	737	4	4	0
Belle	1,504	3	3	0
Bellefontaine Neighbors	10,678	30	27	3
Bel-Nor	1,461	5	5	0
Bel-Ridge	2,679	17	16	1
Belton	23,312	63	44	19
Berkeley	8,958	28	20	8
Bernie	1,928	8	5	3
Bertrand	768	1	1	0
Bethany	3,095	4	4	0
Billings	1,101	3	3	0

Table 19. Full-Time Law Enforcement Employees, by Selected State and City, 2017—*Continued*

(Number.)

State/city	Population	Total law enforcement employees	Total officers	Total civilians
Bismarck	1,482	3	3	0
Bloomfield	1,872	5	5	0
Blue Springs	54,727	140	95	45
Bolivar	10,873	29	22	7
Bonne Terre	7,185	11	11	0
Boonville	8,482	27	21	6
Bourbon	1,610	4	4	0
Bowling Green	5,541	11	8	3
Branson	11,571	61	46	15
Branson West	433	7	7	0
Braymer	849	1	1	0
Breckenridge Hills	4,655	16	15	1
Brentwood	7,991	28	26	2
Bridgeton	11,703	62	52	10
Brookfield	4,266	18	11	7
Buckner	3,052	8	7	1
Buffalo	3,043	6	5	1
Butler	4,056	13	9	4
Cabool	2,134	11	7	4
California	4,441	8	7	1
Calverton Park	1,283	8	8	0
Camdenton	3,980	18	15	3
Cameron	9,765	22	15	7
Canalou	304	1	1	0
Canton	2,377	5	4	1
Cape Girardeau	39,887	114	80	34
Carl Junction	7,822	17	12	5
Carrollton	3,574	10	10	0
Carterville	1,893	5	5	0
Carthage	14,292	37	28	9
Caruthersville	5,745	19	16	3
Cassville	3,343	13	13	0
Center	504	1	1	0
Centralia	4,220	14	9	5
Charleston	5,698	18	12	6
Chesterfield	47,687	107	94	13
Chillicothe	9,760	22	14	8
Claycomo	1,477	11	11	0
Clayton	16,743	56	47	9
Clever	2,711	4	3	1
Clinton	8,817	24	23	1
Cole Camp	1,112	3	3	0
Columbia	122,585	191	158	33
Concordia	2,375	6	6	0
Conway	776	1	1	0
Cottleville	5,612	8	8	0
Country Club Hills	1,264	8	8	0
Country Club Village	2,471	2	2	0
Crane	1,338	3	3	0
Crestwood	11,904	31	27	4
Creve Coeur	18,746	54	49	5
Crocker	1,042	4	4	0
Crystal City	4,817	23	17	6
Cuba	3,339	13	12	1
Delta	440	1	1	0
Desloge	4,910	12	11	1
De Soto	6,488	18	12	6
Des Peres	8,567	51	42	9
Dexter	7,935	23	18	5
Diamond	941	2	2	0
Dixon	1,457	9	5	4
Doniphan	1,990	9	6	3
Doolittle	594	1	1	0
Drexel	958	2	2	0
Duenweg	1,295	6	6	0
Duquesne	1,725	10	9	1
East Prairie	3,094	9	5	4
Edmundson	832	12	11	1
Eldon	4,657	12	11	1
El Dorado Springs	3,575	12	7	5
Ellington	958	2	2	0

Table 19. Full-Time Law Enforcement Employees, by Selected State and City, 2017—*Continued*

(Number.)

State/city	Population	Total law enforcement employees	Total officers	Total civilians
Ellisville	9,242	23	22	1
Ellsinore	449	2	2	0
Elsberry	2,002	3	3	0
Eminence	579	3	3	0
Eureka	10,588	27	23	4
Everton	302	1	1	0
Excelsior Springs	11,592	36	24	12
Fair Grove	1,456	6	6	0
Fair Play	465	1	1	0
Farmington	18,710	35	27	8
Fayette	2,697	7	7	0
Ferguson	20,789	49	41	8
Festus	12,187	32	24	8
Flordell Hills	802	9	9	0
Florissant	51,693	113	89	24
Fordland	829	3	3	0
Foristell	559	6	6	0
Forsyth	2,426	6	5	1
Fredericktown	4,108	13	12	1
Frontenac	3,859	22	21	1
Fulton	13,160	35	30	5
Galena	420	1	1	0
Gallatin	1,722	1	1	0
Garden City	1,627	3	3	0
Gerald	1,307	2	2	0
Gideon	1,011	2	2	0
Gladstone	27,390	61	45	16
Glasgow	1,089	3	3	0
Glendale	5,889	14	11	3
Goodman	1,226	2	2	0
Gower	1,494	3	3	0
Grain Valley	13,825	25	21	4
Granby	2,122	4	4	0
Grandview	25,308	65	55	10
Greenfield	1,312	3	3	0
Greenwood	5,733	9	9	0
Hallsville	1,546	3	3	0
Hamilton	1,710	4	4	0
Hannibal	17,791	49	37	12
Hardin	534	1	1	0
Harrisonville	10,043	29	24	5
Hartville	592	2	2	0
Hayti	2,684	9	8	1
Hazelwood	25,401	78	66	12
Henrietta	359	1	1	0
Herculaneum	4,050	12	11	1
Hermann	2,355	11	6	5
Higginsville	4,629	15	9	6
Hillsboro	3,178	9	7	2
Hillsdale	1,574	12	12	0
Holcomb	593	2	2	0
Holden	2,240	6	6	0
Hollister	4,499	15	9	6
Holts Summit	3,784	12	10	2
Houston	2,094	6	6	0
Howardville	359	3	1	2
Huntsville	1,508	1	1	0
Independence	117,055	260	184	76
Indian Point	512	3	3	0
Ironton	1,364	6	3	3
Jackson	15,252	31	24	7
Jasper	938	2	2	0
Jefferson City	42,989	127	89	38
Jonesburg	716	1	1	0
Joplin	52,412	134	100	34
Kahoka	1,995	2	2	0
Kansas City	484,948	1,819	1,299	520
Kearney	10,032	18	17	1
Kennett	10,505	30	23	7
Kimberling City	2,293	6	6	0
Kirksville	17,520	26	23	3

Table 19. Full-Time Law Enforcement Employees, by Selected State and City, 2017—*Continued*

(Number.)

State/city	Population	Total law enforcement employees	Total officers	Total civilians
Kirkwood	27,621	76	59	17
Knob Noster	2,737	11	6	5
Ladue	8,593	31	26	5
La Grange	929	5	5	0
Lake Lotawana	2,061	2	2	0
Lake Ozark	1,818	17	11	6
Lakeshire	1,412	3	3	0
Lake St. Louis	15,979	39	30	9
Lake Tapawingo	723	3	3	0
Lake Waukomis	916	2	2	0
Lake Winnebago	1,164	5	5	0
Lamar	4,338	16	14	2
La Plata	1,311	4	4	0
Lathrop	2,040	5	5	0
Laurie	932	5	5	0
Lawson	2,395	5	4	1
Leadington	510	4	4	0
Leasburg	332	1	1	0
Lebanon	14,739	42	31	11
Lee's Summit	96,855	193	140	53
Leeton	553	1	1	0
Lexington	4,560	7	6	1
Liberal	719	2	2	0
Liberty	30,850	52	40	12
Licking	3,115	5	5	0
Lincoln	1,179	3	3	0
Linn	1,424	3	3	0
Linn Creek	245	3	3	0
Lone Jack	1,179	5	5	0
Louisiana	3,269	11	5	6
Lowry City	608	1	1	0
Macon	5,360	13	11	2
Malden	4,030	17	14	3
Manchester	18,154	41	38	3
Mansfield	1,255	5	5	0
Maplewood	7,843	33	30	3
Marceline	2,112	8	8	0
Marionville	2,192	5	5	0
Marshall	12,867	32	26	6
Marshfield	7,341	11	10	1
Marston	461	1	1	0
Maryland Heights	27,083	97	78	19
Maryville	11,820	26	20	6
Matthews	614	3	3	0
Maysville	1,083	1	1	0
Memphis	1,860	2	2	0
Merriam Woods	1,770	1	1	0
Mexico	11,709	33	32	1
Milan	1,802	3	3	0
Miller	686	1	1	0
Moberly	13,838	40	29	11
Moline Acres	2,399	8	8	0
Monett	9,048	21	19	2
Monroe City	2,428	8	7	1
Montgomery City	2,692	6	6	0
Morehouse	899	2	2	0
Moscow Mills	2,620	6	6	0
Mound City	1,032	1	1	0
Mountain Grove	4,674	15	11	4
Mountain View	2,669	9	8	1
Mount Vernon	4,551	11	11	0
Neosho	12,237	27	25	2
Nevada	8,198	27	21	6
Newburg	444	1	1	0
New Florence	717	2	2	0
New Franklin	1,065	4	3	1
New Haven	2,090	7	7	0
New London	969	2	2	0
New Madrid	2,930	17	8	9
Niangua	420	1	1	0
Nixa	21,575	37	31	6

State/city	Population	Total law enforcement employees	Total officers	Total civilians
Noel	1,814	3	3	0
Normandy	7,544	32	31	1
North Kansas City	4,407	50	39	11
Northwoods	4,138	22	20	2
Oak Grove	8,019	20	19	1
Oakland	1,375	76	59	17
Oakview Village	396	3	3	0
O'Fallon	87,388	151	116	35
Old Monroe	287	2	2	0
Olivette	7,859	24	22	2
Oregon	759	1	1	0
Oronogo	2,490	6	6	0
Orrick	802	3	3	0
Osage Beach	4,474	34	22	12
Osceola	892	1	1	0
Overland	15,760	57	42	15
Owensville	2,609	8	8	0
Ozark	19,688	36	32	4
Pacific	7,244	25	17	8
Pagedale	3,289	16	15	1
Palmyra	3,619	8	7	1
Park Hills	8,637	17	16	1
Parkville	6,685	15	14	1
Peculiar	5,039	10	9	1
Perry	697	1	1	0
Perryville	8,493	30	24	6
Pevely	5,748	21	14	7
Piedmont	1,931	6	6	0
Pierce City	1,298	4	4	0
Pilot Grove	762	1	1	0
Pilot Knob	699	2	2	0
Pineville	786	7	7	0
Platte City	4,900	13	12	1
Platte Woods	407	8	7	1
Plattsburg	2,280	12	12	0
Pleasant Hill	8,496	17	12	5
Pleasant Hope	613	2	2	0
Pleasant Valley	3,084	14	9	5
Polo	534	1	1	0
Poplar Bluff	17,264	60	45	15
Potosi	2,641	10	9	1
Purdy	1,102	2	2	0
Queen City	589	1	1	0
Qulin	448	1	1	0
Raymore	21,110	42	27	15
Raytown	29,224	50	38	12
Reeds Spring	857	3	2	1
Republic	16,316	28	23	5
Rich Hill	1,322	1	1	0
Richland	1,788	5	5	0
Richmond	5,540	14	12	2
Richmond Heights	8,362	42	41	1
Risco	317	1	1	0
Riverside	3,276	31	23	8
Riverview	2,795	10	10	0
Rockaway Beach	868	3	2	1
Rock Hill	4,616	12	11	1
Rock Port	1,214	3	3	0
Rogersville	3,598	9	8	1
Rolla	20,147	55	34	21
Salem	4,918	17	12	5
Salisbury	1,532	4	3	1
Sarcoxie	1,287	3	3	0
Savannah	5,136	8	7	1
Scott City	4,480	22	17	5
Sedalia	21,501	60	45	15
Seligman	831	1	1	0
Senath	1,679	5	5	0
Seneca	2,419	4	4	0
Seymour	1,997	3	3	0
Shelbina	1,610	6	5	1

Table 19. Full-Time Law Enforcement Employees, by Selected State and City, 2017—*Continued*

(Number.)

State/city	Population	Total law enforcement employees	Total officers	Total civilians
Shrewsbury	6,135	21	19	2
Sikeston	16,324	78	61	17
Silex	307	1	1	0
Slater	1,797	5	4	1
Smithville	9,638	16	16	0
Southwest City	954	3	3	0
Sparta	1,883	3	3	0
Springfield	168,654	409	335	74
St. Ann	12,779	68	45	23
St. Charles	69,804	149	109	40
St. Clair	4,718	16	14	2
Steelville	1,692	6	6	0
Ste. Genevieve	4,508	9	8	1
St. James	4,102	12	11	1
St. John	6,378	22	21	1
St. Joseph	76,435	173	130	43
St. Louis	310,284	1,624	1,188	436
St. Marys	347	1	1	0
Stover	1,072	3	3	0
St. Peters	58,079	114	90	24
Strafford	2,341	7	7	0
St. Robert	6,020	25	18	7
Sugar Creek	3,298	22	18	4
Sullivan	7,132	25	18	7
Summersville	502	2	2	0
Sunset Hills	8,498	33	26	7
Sweet Springs	1,439	4	4	0
Tarkio	1,457	3	3	0
Thayer	2,208	10	6	4
Tipton	3,397	4	4	0
Town and Country	11,157	32	30	2
Trenton	5,920	16	10	6
Trimble	639	2	2	0
Troy	12,079	25	23	2
Truesdale	747	1	1	0
Union	11,447	27	25	2
University City	34,601	87	70	17
Urbana	410	2	2	0
Vandalia	4,344	6	5	1
Velda City	1,382	9	9	0
Verona	602	1	1	0
Versailles	2,452	11	10	1
Vienna	588	1	1	0
Vinita Park	11,061	46	44	2
Walnut Grove	812	2	2	0
Warrensburg	20,483	40	34	6
Warrenton	8,168	22	20	2
Warsaw	2,118	5	5	0
Warson Woods	1,936	8	8	0
Washington	14,073	31	28	3
Waverly	829	2	1	1
Waynesville	5,381	12	11	1
Weatherby Lake	1,957	5	5	0
Webb City	11,259	24	20	4
Webster Groves	22,968	47	45	2
Wellsville	1,154	3	3	0
Wentzville	38,876	87	67	20
Weston	1,771	4	4	0
West Plains	12,367	34	28	6
Wheaton	693	2	2	0
Willard	5,452	11	10	1
Willow Springs	2,146	7	6	1
Winona	1,289	8	4	4
Woodson Terrace	4,043	19	17	2
Wright City	3,584	11	10	1
Wyatt	303	1	1	0
MONTANA				
Baker	2,029	5	5	0
Belgrade	8,393	25	18	7
Billings	111,317	173	150	23

State/city	Population	Total law enforcement employees	Total officers	Total civilians
Boulder	1,239	3	3	0
Bozeman	46,728	68	60	8
Bridger	736	2	2	0
Chinook	1,238	4	4	0
Colstrip	2,326	12	7	5
Columbia Falls	5,337	8	7	1
Columbus	2,050	4	4	0
Conrad	2,544	5	5	0
Cut Bank	3,031	9	8	1
Deer Lodge	2,968	6	5	1
Dillon	4,277	9	8	1
East Helena	2,084	4	4	0
Ennis	900	1	1	0
Fort Benton	1,455	4	4	0
Fromberg	446	1	1	0
Glasgow	3,379	10	8	2
Glendive	5,402	16	10	6
Great Falls	59,167	130	88	42
Hamilton	4,739	15	14	1
Havre	9,900	25	19	6
Helena	31,668	74	54	20
Hot Springs	560	2	2	0
Kalispell	23,243	51	41	10
Laurel	6,887	17	13	4
Libby	2,684	6	6	0
Livingston	7,470	14	14	0
Manhattan	1,723	3	3	0
Miles City	8,690	14	14	0
Missoula	73,304	131	106	25
Plains	1,076	3	3	0
Polson	4,821	17	16	1
Red Lodge	2,256	7	6	1
Ronan City	2,036	5	5	0
Sidney	6,814	14	13	1
Stevensville	1,985	2	2	0
St. Ignatius	827	2	2	0
Thompson Falls	1,361	4	4	0
Troy	891	3	3	0
West Yellowstone	1,367	12	6	6
Whitefish	7,446	19	16	3
Wolf Point	2,840	8	6	2
NEBRASKA				
Albion	1,591	3	3	0
Alliance	8,393	23	17	6
Aurora	4,484	10	9	1
Bayard	1,122	3	3	0
Beatrice	12,311	36	22	14
Bennington	1,518	2	2	0
Blair	8,103	18	16	2
Broken Bow	3,537	7	6	1
Central City	2,900	6	5	1
Columbus	22,955	50	35	15
Cozad	3,775	8	8	0
Crete	7,071	12	11	1
Emerson	798	1	1	0
Fairbury	3,680	7	6	1
Falls City	4,196	13	9	4
Gering	8,333	18	16	2
Gordon	1,523	6	5	1
Gothenburg	3,459	7	6	1
Grand Island	51,980	101	83	18
Harvard	944	1	1	0
Hastings	24,958	50	38	12
Holdrege	5,565	16	10	6
Kearney	33,960	70	55	15
Kimball	2,385	4	4	0
La Vista	17,219	42	37	5
Lexington	9,967	23	21	2
Lincoln	284,063	466	330	136
McCook	7,498	19	14	5

(Number.)

State/city	Population	Total law enforcement employees	Total officers	Total civilians
Milford	2,115	4	4	0
Minatare	799	2	2	0
Minden	3,009	5	5	0
Mitchell	1,663	3	3	0
Nebraska City	7,355	15	14	1
Neligh	1,512	3	3	0
Norfolk	24,364	54	38	16
North Platte	24,011	65	42	23
Ogallala	4,512	11	10	1
Omaha	449,388	963	814	149
O'Neill	3,618	9	8	1
Plattsmouth	6,475	17	14	3
Ralston	7,564	15	13	2
Scottsbluff	16,023	37	31	6
Seward	7,259	13	11	2
Sidney	6,911	16	14	2
St. Paul	2,357	4	4	0
Superior	1,839	4	4	0
Sutton	1,396	2	2	0
Tekamah	1,715	4	4	0
Tilden	930	1	1	0
Valentine	2,815	7	6	1
Valley	2,225	5	5	0
Wahoo	4,495	6	6	0
Wayne	5,555	12	8	4
West Point	3,319	7	6	1
Wymore	1,392	3	3	0
York	7,876	23	17	6
NEVADA				
Boulder City	15,804	45	32	13
Carlin	2,299	7	5	2
Elko	20,807	39	34	5
Fallon	8,450	35	22	13
Henderson	299,285	613	364	249
Las Vegas Metropolitan Police Department	1,627,244	5,379	3,563	1,816
Lovelock	1,834	6	4	2
Mesquite	18,476	42	29	13
North Las Vegas	242,537	412	300	112
Reno	248,531	385	318	67
Sparks	99,732	153	109	44
West Wendover	4,236	20	12	8
Winnemucca	7,938	22	19	3
Yerington	3,147	7	6	1
NEW HAMPSHIRE				
Alexandria	1,620	2	2	0
Alstead	1,893	2	2	0
Alton	5,334	14	12	2
Amherst	11,250	19	18	1
Antrim	2,660	6	5	1
Ashland	2,056	5	5	0
Atkinson	6,876	7	6	1
Auburn	5,449	11	9	2
Barnstead	4,667	5	5	0
Barrington	8,981	10	9	1
Bartlett	2,755	2	2	0
Bedford	22,623	49	36	13
Belmont	7,293	19	16	3
Bennington	1,485	2	2	0
Berlin	10,489	30	22	8
Bethlehem	2,560	5	5	0
Boscawen	3,977	8	7	1
Bow	7,820	14	12	2
Bradford	1,678	3	3	0
Brentwood	4,743	6	6	0
Bristol	3,057	10	9	1
Brookline	5,304	9	8	1
Campton	3,286	8	7	1
Canaan	3,894	6	6	0
Candia	3,903	7	6	1

State/city	Population	Total law enforcement employees	Total officers	Total civilians
Canterbury	2,416	3	3	0
Carroll	741	4	4	0
Center Harbor	1,098	3	3	0
Charlestown	4,971	8	5	3
Chester	5,068	8	7	1
Chesterfield	3,523	7	6	1
Claremont	12,893	31	25	6
Colebrook	2,147	4	4	0
Concord	42,942	91	79	12
Conway	9,946	32	23	9
Danville	4,471	5	5	0
Deerfield	4,465	8	7	1
Deering	1,933	2	2	0
Derry	33,382	66	53	13
Dover	31,344	74	50	24
Dublin	1,522	4	3	1
Dunbarton	2,808	4	4	0
Durham	16,751	23	20	3
East Kingston	2,396	5	5	0
Effingham	1,439	2	2	0
Enfield	4,527	8	7	1
Epping	6,978	17	16	1
Epsom	4,701	6	5	1
Exeter	14,807	34	24	10
Farmington	6,858	14	13	1
Fitzwilliam	2,316	3	3	0
Franconia	1,102	3	3	0
Franklin	8,444	26	18	8
Freedom	1,488	2	2	0
Fremont	4,737	6	5	1
Gilford	7,191	24	18	6
Gilmanton	3,746	6	5	1
Goffstown	18,057	43	30	13
Gorham	2,592	11	7	4
Grantham	2,967	5	4	1
Greenland	3,966	8	8	0
Hampstead	8,625	9	9	0
Hampton	15,524	43	34	9
Hampton Falls	2,302	3	3	0
Hancock	1,628	3	3	0
Hanover	11,443	30	17	13
Haverhill	4,542	8	7	1
Henniker	4,947	9	8	1
Hillsborough	5,954	20	14	6
Hinsdale	3,835	10	9	1
Holderness	2,090	6	6	0
Hollis	7,838	16	15	1
Hooksett	14,274	38	27	11
Hopkinton	5,629	8	7	1
Hudson	25,212	64	47	17
Jackson	814	3	3	0
Jaffrey	5,211	11	10	1
Keene	23,386	51	40	11
Kensington	2,126	5	4	1
Kingston	6,185	7	6	1
Laconia	16,616	47	37	10
Lancaster	3,288	6	5	1
Lebanon	13,577	44	31	13
Lee	4,417	7	6	1
Lincoln	1,761	16	11	5
Lisbon	1,564	3	3	0
Litchfield	8,508	13	11	2
Littleton	5,871	14	11	3
Londonderry	26,254	74	61	13
Loudon	5,506	8	7	1
Lyndeborough	1,707	1	1	0
Madison	2,523	4	4	0
Manchester	110,655	291	236	55
Marlborough	2,040	3	3	0
Meredith	6,404	18	14	4
Merrimack	25,675	49	38	11

(Number.)

State/city	Population	Total law enforcement employees	Total officers	Total civilians
Middleton...	1,810	4	4	0
Milford	15,330	32	27	5
Milton..	4,592	8	7	1
Mont Vernon..	2,519	3	3	0
Moultonborough......................................	4,038	10	10	0
Nashua...	88,102	235	174	61
New Boston...	5,618	9	8	1
Newbury...	2,198	3	3	0
New Durham..	2,671	5	5	0
Newfields..	1,713	3	3	0
New Hampton...	2,217	6	6	0
Newington...	796	10	9	1
New Ipswich..	5,248	6	5	1
New London...	4,590	13	8	5
Newmarket..	9,003	20	13	7
Newport...	6,344	17	12	5
Newton	4,963	8	7	1
Northfield	4,814	10	9	1
North Hampton	4,447	9	8	1
Northumberland......................................	2,122	2	2	0
Northwood	4,281	7	6	1
Nottingham...	5,046	8	7	1
Ossipee..	4,246	10	9	1
Pelham...	13,513	28	20	8
Pembroke	7,115	14	12	2
Peterborough...	6,568	14	12	2
Pittsfield...	4,086	6	6	0
Plainfield	2,345	3	3	0
Plaistow	7,695	26	18	8
Plymouth	6,303	18	12	6
Portsmouth..	21,607	86	63	23
Raymond	10,347	26	17	9
Rindge	5,883	8	7	1
Rochester..	30,441	69	56	13
Rollinsford	2,552	5	5	0
Rye	5,425	11	10	1
Salem	29,013	75	62	13
Sanbornton..	2,996	6	5	1
Sandown	6,368	8	8	0
Sandwich	1,304	2	2	0
Seabrook	8,816	34	28	6
Somersworth	11,795	34	27	7
Springfield	1,319	2	2	0
Strafford	4,121	5	5	0
Stratham..	7,452	12	11	1
Sugar Hill	571	2	2	0
Sunapee	3,449	5	5	0
Thornton	2,491	6	5	1
Tilton	3,556	19	16	3
Troy	2,054	3	3	0
Tuftonboro	2,327	4	4	0
Wakefield	5,613	11	10	1
Warner	2,879	5	4	1
Washington...	1,108	1	1	0
Waterville Valley	245	7	6	1
Weare..	8,935	10	9	1
Webster..	1,906	1	1	0
Wilton	3,687	8	7	1
Winchester	4,146	8	7	1
Windham..	14,686	25	19	6
Wolfeboro	6,189	18	13	5
Woodstock	1,367	6	6	0
NEW JERSEY				
Aberdeen Township..................................	18,403	44	37	7
Absecon	8,261	32	28	4
Allendale	6,938	20	15	5
Allenhurst	486	12	9	3
Allentown	1,808	6	5	1
Alpine..	1,885	12	12	0
Andover Township...................................	5,962	17	12	5

State/city	Population	Total law enforcement employees	Total officers	Total civilians
Asbury Park	15,656	93	88	5
Atlantic City	38,601	371	253	118
Atlantic Highlands	4,281	19	14	5
Audubon	8,748	18	17	1
Avalon	1,270	29	21	8
Avon-by-the-Sea	1,775	11	11	0
Barnegat Township	22,652	47	46	1
Barrington	6,792	16	15	1
Bay Head	986	9	8	1
Bayonne	67,041	227	177	50
Beach Haven	1,181	14	13	1
Beachwood	11,296	20	18	2
Bedminster Township	8,285	18	16	2
Belleville	36,409	117	108	9
Bellmawr	11,505	24	22	2
Belmar	5,666	30	23	7
Belvidere	2,589	5	5	0
Bergenfield	27,891	54	46	8
Berkeley Heights Township	13,654	34	26	8
Berkeley Township	42,036	96	70	26
Berlin	7,619	18	17	1
Berlin Township	5,560	18	17	1
Bernards Township	27,219	42	38	4
Bernardsville	7,876	26	20	6
Beverly	2,506	8	8	0
Blairstown Township	5,767	7	6	1
Bloomfield	48,928	154	129	25
Bloomingdale	8,295	18	17	1
Bogota	8,595	21	16	5
Boonton	8,421	28	23	5
Boonton Township	4,395	13	13	0
Bordentown City	3,839	13	11	2
Bordentown Township	12,216	26	25	1
Bound Brook	10,537	29	24	5
Bradley Beach	4,236	20	18	2
Branchburg Township	14,822	30	26	4
Brick Township	75,566	203	138	65
Bridgeton	24,937	78	65	13
Bridgewater Township	45,417	87	79	8
Brielle	4,708	16	15	1
Brigantine	8,976	44	34	10
Brooklawn	1,937	7	7	0
Buena	4,432	9	8	1
Burlington City	9,854	36	32	4
Burlington Township	22,772	50	41	9
Butler	7,829	17	16	1
Byram Township	7,944	14	14	0
Caldwell	8,073	21	21	0
Camden County Police Department	74,299	398	354	44
Cape May	3,483	26	21	5
Carlstadt	6,295	30	28	2
Carney's Point Township	7,729	19	18	1
Carteret	24,283	68	60	8
Cedar Grove Township	12,674	31	30	1
Chatham	9,011	23	20	3
Chatham Township	10,515	23	21	2
Cherry Hill Township	71,747	163	135	28
Chesilhurst	1,644	10	9	1
Chesterfield Township	7,451	11	10	1
Chester Township	7,961	23	22	1
Cinnaminson Township	16,696	27	27	0
Clark Township	16,084	49	38	11
Clayton	8,722	16	16	0
Clementon	4,937	13	12	1
Cliffside Park	25,166	46	44	2
Clifton	86,472	185	148	37
Clinton	2,694	10	10	0
Clinton Township	12,748	23	22	1
Closter	8,788	20	20	0
Collingswood	14,080	30	26	4
Colts Neck Township	9,936	23	22	1

(Number.)

State/city	Population	Total law enforcement employees	Total officers	Total civilians
Cranbury Township	3,966	18	17	1
Cranford Township	24,442	68	52	16
Cresskill	8,848	26	22	4
Deal	730	22	18	4
Delanco Township	4,528	13	12	1
Delaware Township	4,443	8	7	1
Delran Township	16,609	34	30	4
Demarest	5,034	13	13	0
Denville Township	16,811	43	33	10
Deptford Township	30,727	74	68	6
Dover	18,339	33	29	4
Dumont	18,018	38	31	7
Dunellen	7,428	16	16	0
Eastampton Township	5,962	19	18	1
East Brunswick Township	49,019	111	83	28
East Greenwich Township	10,573	18	16	2
East Hanover Township	11,284	38	34	4
East Newark	2,811	8	8	0
East Orange	65,160	255	208	47
East Rutherford	10,064	34	33	1
East Windsor Township	27,571	49	43	6
Eatontown	12,258	45	37	8
Edgewater	12,183	34	29	5
Edgewater Park Township	8,726	14	13	1
Edison Township	102,699	228	181	47
Egg Harbor City	4,182	13	12	1
Egg Harbor Township	43,515	111	83	28
Elizabeth	129,726	390	293	97
Elk Township	4,140	13	12	1
Elmer	1,317	1	1	0
Elmwood Park	20,515	47	42	5
Emerson	7,747	24	21	3
Englewood	28,795	106	82	24
Englewood Cliffs	5,442	26	25	1
Englishtown	1,956	7	7	0
Essex Fells	2,135	13	13	0
Evesham Township	45,314	87	77	10
Ewing Township	36,161	102	83	19
Fairfield Township, Essex County	7,597	39	36	3
Fair Haven	5,953	13	13	0
Fair Lawn	33,759	69	60	9
Fairview	14,573	37	33	4
Fanwood	7,796	18	17	1
Far Hills	935	6	6	0
Flemington	4,627	14	14	0
Florence Township	12,755	27	25	2
Florham Park	11,818	36	32	4
Fort Lee	38,095	116	97	19
Franklin	4,773	16	15	1
Franklin Lakes	10,939	29	23	6
Franklin Township, Gloucester County	16,599	35	31	4
Franklin Township, Hunterdon County	3,223	6	6	0
Franklin Township, Somerset County	67,463	123	105	18
Freehold Borough	11,865	33	30	3
Freehold Township	35,531	71	67	4
Frenchtown	1,396	4	4	0
Galloway Township	36,672	87	57	30
Garfield	32,233	70	60	10
Garwood	4,384	20	16	4
Gibbsboro	2,253	10	10	0
Glassboro	20,134	50	44	6
Glen Ridge	7,694	29	23	6
Glen Rock	12,051	24	23	1
Gloucester City	11,366	33	31	2
Gloucester Township	64,094	151	129	22
Green Brook Township	7,273	24	23	1
Greenwich Township, Gloucester County	4,861	19	17	2
Greenwich Township, Warren County	5,501	12	12	0
Guttenberg	11,736	26	23	3
Hackensack	45,226	139	114	25
Hackettstown	9,520	19	18	1

(Number.)

State/city	Population	Total law enforcement employees	Total officers	Total civilians
Haddonfield	11,445	23	21	2
Haddon Heights	7,586	16	15	1
Haddon Township	14,731	27	26	1
Haledon	8,439	18	18	0
Hamburg	3,125	10	8	2
Hamilton Township, Atlantic County	26,482	70	52	18
Hamilton Township, Mercer County	88,723	203	169	34
Hammonton	14,370	37	30	7
Hanover Township	14,904	37	30	7
Harding Township	3,891	12	11	1
Hardyston Township	7,884	25	19	6
Harrington Park	4,848	11	11	0
Harrison	16,802	46	35	11
Harrison Township	13,128	21	20	1
Harvey Cedars	342	8	8	0
Hasbrouck Heights	12,286	32	30	2
Haworth	3,491	12	11	1
Hawthorne	19,041	32	31	1
Hazlet Township	19,938	50	43	7
Helmetta	2,228	4	4	0
High Bridge	3,524	7	7	0
Highland Park	14,287	34	27	7
Highlands	4,793	17	14	3
Hightstown	5,522	14	13	1
Hillsborough Township	40,369	62	51	11
Hillsdale	10,602	21	18	3
Hillside Township	22,125	79	70	9
Hi-Nella	869	13	13	0
Hoboken	55,348	155	135	20
Ho-Ho-Kus	4,169	20	16	4
Holland Township	5,113	7	6	1
Holmdel Township	16,576	48	40	8
Hopatcong	14,263	29	24	5
Hopewell Township	18,633	38	30	8
Howell Township	52,432	101	87	14
Independence Township	5,482	10	9	1
Irvington	54,728	207	151	56
Island Heights	1,659	5	5	0
Jackson Township	57,400	112	88	24
Jamesburg	6,088	18	14	4
Jefferson Township	21,505	43	35	8
Jersey City	267,906	1,038	890	148
Keansburg	9,782	40	33	7
Kearny	42,527	115	109	6
Kenilworth	8,271	31	26	5
Keyport	7,062	23	17	6
Kinnelon	10,275	17	16	1
Lacey Township	28,915	58	43	15
Lakehurst	2,716	12	10	2
Lakewood Township	102,759	163	133	30
Lambertville	3,795	12	9	3
Laurel Springs	1,888	7	7	0
Lavallette	1,837	14	12	2
Lawnside	2,927	10	9	1
Lawrence Township, Mercer County	32,929	62	58	4
Lebanon Township	6,053	10	9	1
Leonia	9,273	21	18	3
Lincoln Park	10,466	28	22	6
Linden	42,948	155	124	31
Lindenwold	17,516	45	42	3
Linwood	6,859	19	18	1
Little Egg Harbor Township	21,076	53	43	10
Little Falls Township	14,479	33	28	5
Little Ferry	11,017	31	26	5
Little Silver	5,881	20	16	4
Livingston Township	29,987	81	71	10
Lodi	24,981	48	45	3
Logan Township	5,977	20	19	1
Long Beach Township	3,067	48	37	11
Long Branch	30,748	130	83	47
Long Hill Township	8,784	25	23	2

Table 19. Full-Time Law Enforcement Employees, by Selected State and City, 2017—*Continued*

(Number.)

State/city	Population	Total law enforcement employees	Total officers	Total civilians
Longport	868	13	13	0
Lopatcong Township	8,298	16	15	1
Lower Alloways Creek Township	1,770	11	11	0
Lower Township	21,870	57	47	10
Lumberton Township	12,286	21	20	1
Lyndhurst Township	22,621	53	50	3
Madison	16,175	37	29	8
Magnolia	4,310	12	12	0
Mahwah Township	26,753	62	53	9
Manalapan Township	40,177	49	46	3
Manasquan	5,804	23	17	6
Manchester Township	43,916	85	68	17
Mansfield Township, Burlington County	8,593	15	14	1
Mansfield Township, Warren County	7,435	13	12	1
Mantoloking	247	9	8	1
Mantua Township	15,123	28	26	2
Manville	10,519	26	23	3
Maple Shade Township	18,797	34	30	4
Maplewood Township	24,863	73	61	12
Margate City	6,107	35	29	6
Marlboro Township	40,370	109	78	31
Matawan	8,838	23	22	1
Maywood	9,862	26	22	4
Medford Lakes	4,038	10	9	1
Medford Township	23,503	38	34	4
Mendham	5,006	13	12	1
Mendham Township	5,883	16	15	1
Merchantville	3,774	14	13	1
Metuchen	13,981	35	29	6
Middlesex Borough	13,897	34	31	3
Middle Township	18,542	66	53	13
Middletown Township	65,303	124	112	12
Midland Park	7,378	17	16	1
Millburn Township	20,421	59	53	6
Milltown	7,201	18	15	3
Millville	27,984	77	67	10
Monmouth Beach	3,213	10	9	1
Monroe Township, Gloucester County	37,174	73	66	7
Monroe Township, Middlesex County	45,722	78	60	18
Montclair	39,029	124	105	19
Montgomery Township	23,706	40	34	6
Montvale	8,653	26	24	2
Montville Township	21,818	43	37	6
Moonachie	2,815	21	18	3
Moorestown Township	20,534	38	33	5
Morris Plains	5,626	18	16	2
Morristown	19,199	61	57	4
Morris Township	22,701	45	41	4
Mountain Lakes	4,377	14	13	1
Mountainside	6,943	27	22	5
Mount Arlington	5,551	15	14	1
Mount Ephraim	4,643	14	13	1
Mount Holly Township	9,522	24	21	3
Mount Laurel Township	41,712	75	67	8
Mount Olive Township	29,410	61	52	9
Mullica Township	6,024	14	13	1
Neptune City	4,725	19	17	2
Neptune Township	27,757	88	78	10
Netcong	3,247	9	9	0
Newark	283,673	1,491	1,171	320
New Brunswick	57,481	175	141	34
Newfield	1,569	5	5	0
New Hanover Township	8,264	3	3	0
New Milford	16,894	42	36	6
New Providence	12,904	21	19	2
Newton	7,874	27	22	5
North Arlington	16,009	34	27	7
North Bergen Township	63,490	125	114	11
North Brunswick Township	42,780	101	84	17
North Caldwell	6,782	20	15	5
Northfield	8,376	22	21	1

(Number.)

State/city	Population	Total law enforcement employees	Total officers	Total civilians
North Haledon	8,537	23	19	4
North Hanover Township	7,562	11	10	1
North Plainfield	22,255	54	46	8
Northvale	5,003	14	14	0
North Wildwood	3,856	36	29	7
Norwood	5,904	17	16	1
Nutley Township	28,833	81	69	12
Oakland	13,243	27	24	3
Oaklyn	4,002	17	16	1
Ocean City	11,281	71	57	14
Ocean Gate	2,023	10	9	1
Oceanport	5,705	15	14	1
Ocean Township, Monmouth County	26,637	78	63	15
Ocean Township, Ocean County	9,187	28	18	10
Ogdensburg	2,273	6	6	0
Old Bridge Township	67,162	117	90	27
Old Tappan	6,069	15	14	1
Oradell	8,291	24	23	1
Orange City	30,752	128	101	27
Palisades Park	21,030	45	35	10
Palmyra	7,217	19	18	1
Paramus	27,075	111	86	25
Park Ridge	8,977	20	19	1
Parsippany-Troy Hills Township	53,478	117	102	15
Passaic	71,053	188	156	32
Paterson	147,690	494	400	94
Paulsboro	5,959	20	18	2
Peapack-Gladstone	2,624	9	8	1
Pemberton Borough	1,355	9	8	1
Pemberton Township	27,506	49	44	5
Pennington	2,576	6	5	1
Pennsauken Township	36,041	84	77	7
Penns Grove	4,844	15	14	1
Pennsville Township	12,564	22	22	0
Pequannock Township	15,472	39	34	5
Perth Amboy	52,978	164	134	30
Phillipsburg	14,379	37	36	1
Pine Beach	2,170	8	7	1
Pine Hill	10,616	23	21	2
Pine Valley	11	6	6	0
Piscataway Township	58,109	108	87	21
Pitman	8,886	17	16	1
Plainfield	50,983	148	120	28
Plainsboro Township	23,569	48	36	12
Pleasantville	20,530	64	51	13
Plumsted Township	8,604	15	14	1
Pohatcong Township	3,215	14	13	1
Point Pleasant	18,696	43	33	10
Point Pleasant Beach	4,552	24	22	2
Pompton Lakes	11,176	25	21	4
Princeton	31,845	69	54	15
Prospect Park	5,944	18	17	1
Rahway	29,930	83	73	10
Ramsey	15,273	39	32	7
Randolph Township	25,950	41	35	6
Raritan	8,273	20	19	1
Raritan Township	21,918	36	33	3
Readington Township	15,834	29	23	6
Red Bank	12,135	47	39	8
Ridgefield	11,457	31	29	2
Ridgefield Park	13,166	38	31	7
Ridgewood	25,729	48	45	3
Ringwood	12,470	26	21	5
Riverdale	4,398	20	16	4
River Edge	11,744	25	22	3
Riverside Township	7,897	15	15	0
Riverton	2,704	6	6	0
River Vale Township	10,270	21	19	2
Robbinsville Township	14,446	36	27	9
Rochelle Park Township	5,714	24	20	4
Rockaway	6,512	16	15	1

(Number.)

State/city	Population	Total law enforcement employees	Total officers	Total civilians
Rockaway Township	24,719	62	51	11
Roseland	5,916	26	26	0
Roselle	21,796	71	58	13
Roselle Park	13,747	41	34	7
Roxbury Township	23,472	45	42	3
Rumson	6,783	21	17	4
Runnemede	8,402	18	16	2
Rutherford	18,804	43	40	3
Saddle Brook Township	14,190	36	33	3
Saddle River	3,263	22	17	5
Salem	4,776	19	17	2
Sayreville	45,460	94	82	12
Scotch Plains Township	24,375	50	47	3
Sea Bright	1,375	11	11	0
Sea Girt	1,777	12	11	1
Sea Isle City	2,079	27	21	6
Seaside Heights	2,918	34	22	12
Seaside Park	1,556	14	13	1
Secaucus	20,481	82	67	15
Ship Bottom	1,146	12	11	1
Shrewsbury	4,178	21	16	5
Somerdale	5,591	15	14	1
Somers Point	10,504	37	30	7
Somerville	12,263	33	31	2
South Amboy	8,839	28	22	6
South Bound Brook	4,652	14	13	1
South Brunswick Township	46,280	111	82	29
South Hackensack Township	2,479	22	19	3
South Harrison Township	3,193	5	5	0
South Orange Village	16,407	52	45	7
South Plainfield	24,458	69	55	14
South River	16,399	42	32	10
South Toms River	3,799	13	12	1
Sparta Township	18,807	42	28	14
Spotswood	8,492	27	22	5
Springfield Township, Burlington County	3,301	11	10	1
Springfield Township, Union County	17,805	48	44	4
Spring Lake	2,958	13	13	0
Spring Lake Heights	4,597	14	14	0
Stafford Township	27,433	65	52	13
Stanhope	3,327	10	9	1
Stone Harbor	827	19	17	2
Stratford	7,024	15	15	0
Summit	22,195	51	46	5
Surf City	1,186	10	10	0
Teaneck Township	41,377	110	94	16
Tenafly	14,960	40	34	6
Tewksbury Township	5,809	12	11	1
Tinton Falls	17,761	42	41	1
Toms River Township	92,543	207	160	47
Totowa	10,964	32	28	4
Trenton	84,231	352	279	73
Tuckerton	3,406	13	12	1
Union Beach	5,479	18	15	3
Union City	70,053	205	165	40
Union Township	59,051	185	135	50
Upper Saddle River	8,385	21	17	4
Ventnor City	10,263	51	37	14
Vernon Township	22,193	41	32	9
Verona	13,584	35	30	5
Vineland	60,477	144	121	23
Voorhees Township	29,532	64	54	10
Waldwick	10,137	24	19	5
Wallington	11,794	24	23	1
Wall Township	25,956	87	69	18
Wanaque	11,925	30	25	5
Warren Township	16,264	36	29	7
Washington Township, Bergen County	9,432	22	20	2
Washington Township, Gloucester County	48,088	92	84	8
Washington Township, Morris County	18,793	32	29	3
Washington Township, Warren County	6,429	27	26	1

Table 19. Full-Time Law Enforcement Employees, by Selected State and City, 2017—*Continued*

(Number.)

State/city	Population	Total law enforcement employees	Total officers	Total civilians
Watchung..	6,010	36	30	6
Waterford Township........................	10,817	24	22	2
Wayne Township............................	54,903	144	117	27
Weehawken Township.....................	15,683	71	53	18
Wenonah..	2,252	6	6	0
Westampton Township.....................	8,775	28	24	4
West Amwell Township....................	2,753	7	7	0
West Caldwell Township..................	11,013	30	25	5
West Deptford Township..................	21,386	46	43	3
Westfield..	30,301	74	59	15
West Long Branch...........................	7,944	22	21	1
West Milford Township....................	26,769	51	44	7
West New York...............................	54,156	118	107	11
West Orange...................................	47,615	110	97	13
Westville..	4,214	13	12	1
West Wildwood..............................	563	5	5	0
West Windsor Township..................	28,495	60	48	12
Westwood.......................................	11,328	31	26	5
Wharton...	6,610	20	19	1
Wildwood.......................................	5,087	53	43	10
Wildwood Crest..............................	3,147	26	20	6
Willingboro Township.....................	31,726	74	65	9
Winfield Township..........................	1,519	10	10	0
Winslow Township..........................	39,406	81	74	7
Woodbridge Township.....................	102,129	239	198	41
Woodbury.......................................	9,970	31	28	3
Woodbury Heights..........................	3,011	8	7	1
Woodcliff Lake...............................	5,942	19	18	1
Woodland Park...............................	12,836	29	25	4
Woodlynne.....................................	2,951	9	7	2
Wood-Ridge....................................	8,808	25	21	4
Woodstown.....................................	3,482	10	8	2
Woolwich Township........................	12,798	25	24	1
Wyckoff Township..........................	17,373	26	26	0
NEW MEXICO				
Alamogordo....................................	31,386	83	54	29
Artesia...	12,388	51	30	21
Aztec...	5,836	14	12	2
Bernalillo.......................................	9,355	25	22	3
Bosque Farms.................................	3,805	14	13	1
Capitan..	1,372	3	3	0
Carlsbad...	29,397	89	59	30
Carrizozo.......................................	929	4	3	1
Cimarron..	881	4	3	1
Clayton..	2,729	13	7	6
Clovis..	39,561	78	55	23
Corrales...	8,625	18	15	3
Cuba..	741	5	4	1
Deming...	14,428	43	39	4
Dexter..	1,263	6	5	1
Edgewood.......................................	3,816	10	9	1
Estancia...	1,572	10	5	5
Eunice..	3,040	13	7	6
Farmington.....................................	40,940	166	125	41
Gallup..	22,815	81	66	15
Grants..	9,313	20	16	4
Hatch...	1,585	9	6	3
Hope..	107	1	1	0
Hurley..	1,232	5	3	2
Jal..	2,135	15	7	8
Las Cruces......................................	102,350	261	187	74
Las Vegas.......................................	13,160	49	35	14
Logan...	940	4	4	0
Lordsburg.......................................	2,415	13	9	4
Los Alamos.....................................	18,204	68	31	37
Los Lunas.......................................	15,527	43	39	4
Lovington.......................................	11,468	32	23	9
Magdalena......................................	892	3	3	0
Mesilla...	1,848	7	7	0
Milan...	3,235	9	8	1

Table 19. Full-Time Law Enforcement Employees, by Selected State and City, 2017—*Continued*

(Number.)

State/city	Population	Total law enforcement employees	Total officers	Total civilians
Moriarty	1,766	12	10	2
Peralta	3,548	6	5	1
Portales	11,928	27	22	5
Raton	5,983	22	14	8
Red River	477	10	4	6
Roswell	48,134	105	84	21
Ruidoso	7,729	33	23	10
Ruidoso Downs	2,543	11	7	4
Santa Clara	1,740	5	4	1
Santa Fe	84,358	215	167	48
Santa Rosa	2,652	13	8	5
San Ysidro	198	2	2	0
Socorro	8,547	25	16	9
Springer	911	4	4	0
Taos	5,771	27	20	7
Taos Ski Valley	69	3	3	0
Tatum	832	6	2	4
Texico	1,104	3	2	1
Truth or Consequences	5,949	16	11	5
Tularosa	2,920	11	6	5
NEW YORK				
Addison Town and Village	2,518	3	3	0
Akron Village	2,848	1	1	0
Albany	98,174	418	333	85
Albion Village	5,944	13	12	1
Alfred Village	4,041	5	5	0
Allegany Village	1,717	1	1	0
Altamont Village	1,724	1	1	0
Amherst Town	121,150	182	152	30
Amity Town and Belmont Village	2,169	1	1	0
Amityville Village	9,492	24	23	1
Amsterdam	17,737	43	40	3
Arcade Village	1,957	5	5	0
Ardsley Village	4,663	19	19	0
Asharoken Village	647	3	3	0
Attica Village	2,435	3	3	0
Auburn	26,686	72	66	6
Avon Village	3,276	4	4	0
Baldwinsville Village	7,656	12	11	1
Ballston Spa Village	5,302	4	4	0
Batavia	14,711	31	28	3
Bath Village	5,556	11	9	2
Beacon	14,212	37	35	2
Bedford Town	17,997	43	38	5
Binghamton	45,399	150	136	14
Blooming Grove Town	11,863	12	10	2
Brant Town	2,055	1	1	0
Briarcliff Manor Village	8,064	21	21	0
Brighton Town	36,596	46	40	6
Brockport Village	8,310	16	15	1
Bronxville Village	6,420	23	21	2
Buffalo	256,169	982	781	201
Cairo Town	6,422	1	1	0
Caledonia Village	2,115	3	3	0
Cambridge Village	1,810	1	1	0
Camden Village	2,181	2	2	0
Camillus Town and Village	24,696	27	24	3
Canajoharie Village	2,132	4	4	0
Canandaigua	10,337	25	23	2
Canastota Village	4,586	5	4	1
Canisteo Village	2,171	3	3	0
Canton Village	6,557	10	9	1
Carthage Village	3,425	4	4	0
Cazenovia Village	2,849	5	4	1
Centre Island Village	408	7	7	0
Cheektowaga Town	77,576	159	122	37
Chester Town	7,970	17	17	0
Chester Village	3,960	14	13	1
Chittenango Village	4,888	3	2	1
Clarkstown Town	81,810	170	145	25

Table 19. Full-Time Law Enforcement Employees, by Selected State and City, 2017—*Continued*

(Number.)

State/city	Population	Total law enforcement employees	Total officers	Total civilians
Clayton Village	1,877	3	3	0
Cobleskill Village	4,540	12	12	0
Coeymans Town	7,369	4	3	1
Cohoes	17,007	36	32	4
Colchester Town	1,988	1	1	0
Colonie Town	79,526	145	109	36
Corning	10,751	24	20	4
Cornwall-on-Hudson Village	2,915	3	3	0
Cornwall Town	9,544	12	9	3
Cortland	18,735	47	44	3
Crawford Town	9,183	10	9	1
Croton-on-Hudson Village	8,271	20	18	2
Cuba Town	3,061	4	4	0
Dansville Village	4,482	7	7	0
Deerpark Town	7,712	4	4	0
Delhi Village	3,147	4	4	0
Depew Village	15,150	34	28	6
Dewitt Town	25,405	46	42	4
Dobbs Ferry Village	11,127	28	26	2
Dolgeville Village	2,099	2	2	0
Dryden Village	2,115	5	5	0
Dunkirk	11,845	34	33	1
East Aurora-Aurora Town	13,806	20	15	5
Eastchester Town	20,052	48	46	2
East Fishkill Town	29,500	39	29	10
East Greenbush Town	16,461	31	22	9
East Hampton Town	19,937	94	69	25
East Hampton Village	1,121	26	22	4
East Rochester Village	6,613	10	9	1
Eden Town	7,644	5	4	1
Ellenville Village	4,032	11	10	1
Ellicott Town	5,093	12	12	0
Ellicottville	1,599	3	3	0
Elmira Heights Village	3,909	9	9	0
Elmira Town	5,714	4	4	0
Elmsford Village	5,072	20	20	0
Endicott Village	12,932	31	29	2
Evans Town	16,162	29	22	7
Fairport Village	5,415	11	10	1
Fallsburg Town	12,042	21	21	0
Floral Park Village	15,959	48	34	14
Florida Village	2,866	1	1	0
Fort Edward Village	3,282	6	6	0
Fort Plain Village	2,212	3	3	0
Frankfort Town	4,890	1	1	0
Frankfort Village	2,466	4	4	0
Fredonia Village	10,543	18	14	4
Freeport Village	43,343	113	99	14
Garden City Village	22,579	65	52	13
Gates Town	28,723	35	31	4
Geddes Town	10,245	17	15	2
Geneseo Village	8,179	8	8	0
Geneva	12,951	33	31	2
Glen Cove	27,400	55	51	4
Glens Falls	14,268	30	28	2
Glenville Town	21,650	24	22	2
Gloversville	14,832	37	34	3
Goshen Town	8,661	9	9	0
Goshen Village	5,354	20	17	3
Gouverneur Village	3,716	9	6	3
Granville Village	2,454	5	5	0
Great Neck Estates Village	2,847	15	12	3
Greece Town	96,219	103	97	6
Greene Village	1,463	1	1	0
Greenwich Village	1,725	1	1	0
Greenwood Lake Village	3,092	6	5	1
Guilderland Town	34,098	50	36	14
Hamburg Town	46,040	65	62	3
Hamburg Village	9,617	13	12	1
Hamilton Village	4,105	5	5	0
Harriman Village	2,469	6	6	0

Table 19. Full-Time Law Enforcement Employees, by Selected State and City, 2017—*Continued*

(Number.)

State/city	Population	Total law enforcement employees	Total officers	Total civilians
Harrison Town	28,480	70	60	10
Hastings-on-Hudson Village	7,987	21	21	0
Haverstraw Town	37,535	69	63	6
Hempstead Village	55,807	153	127	26
Herkimer Village	7,410	20	20	0
Highland Falls Village	3,805	10	8	2
Holley Village	1,709	2	2	0
Homer Village	3,120	6	5	1
Hoosick Falls Village	3,407	1	1	0
Hornell	8,213	23	22	1
Hudson Falls Village	7,093	11	11	0
Hunter Town	2,634	3	3	0
Huntington Bay Village	1,436	4	4	0
Ilion Village	7,801	19	17	2
Inlet Town	309	3	2	1
Irondequoit Town	50,393	64	53	11
Irvington Village	6,614	23	22	1
Ithaca	30,875	71	64	7
Jamestown	29,562	72	62	10
Johnson City Village	14,595	39	34	5
Johnstown	8,251	24	22	2
Kenmore Village	15,085	25	25	0
Kensington Village	1,179	6	6	0
Kingston	23,110	74	69	5
Kirkland Town	8,204	5	5	0
Lake Placid Village	2,424	15	12	3
Lake Success Village	3,127	28	24	4
Lakewood-Busti	7,326	11	10	1
Lancaster Town	37,458	63	48	15
Larchmont Village	6,161	29	26	3
Le Roy Village	4,227	7	7	0
Lewisboro Town	12,823	3	3	0
Lewiston Town and Village	15,974	12	11	1
Liberty Village	4,050	18	16	2
Little Falls	4,709	12	11	1
Liverpool Village	2,246	5	5	0
Lloyd Harbor Village	3,696	11	11	0
Lloyd Town	10,465	13	10	3
Lockport	20,369	49	47	2
Long Beach	33,771	87	70	17
Lowville Village	3,398	6	6	0
Lynbrook Village	19,577	57	49	8
Macedon Town and Village	8,977	8	7	1
Malone Village	5,650	13	13	0
Malverne Village	8,548	25	24	1
Mamaroneck Town	12,218	34	34	0
Mamaroneck Village	19,424	54	51	3
Manlius Town	24,550	37	37	0
Marlborough Town	8,633	10	8	2
Massena Village	10,394	25	20	5
Maybrook Village	3,513	4	4	0
Mechanicville	5,081	10	9	1
Medina Village	5,739	12	11	1
Menands Village	3,960	14	11	3
Middleport Village	1,766	4	4	0
Middletown	27,607	78	65	13
Mohawk Village	2,568	4	4	0
Monroe Village	8,636	22	18	4
Montgomery Village	4,713	4	4	0
Monticello Village	6,373	25	23	2
Moriah Town	3,536	2	2	0
Mount Hope Town	6,904	3	3	0
Mount Morris Village	2,850	5	5	0
Mount Vernon	68,507	253	191	62
Newark Village	8,878	18	17	1
New Berlin Town	1,522	1	1	0
Newburgh	28,080	92	80	12
Newburgh Town	30,862	59	49	10
New Castle Town	18,189	40	38	2
New Hartford Town and Village	20,313	24	20	4
New Paltz Town and Village	14,125	25	21	4

Table 19. Full-Time Law Enforcement Employees, by Selected State and City, 2017—*Continued*

(Number.)

State/city	Population	Total law enforcement employees	Total officers	Total civilians
New Rochelle	79,960	221	161	60
New Windsor Town	27,609	51	40	11
New York	8,616,333	52,079	36,378	15,701
New York Mills Village	3,278	3	3	0
Niagara Falls	48,385	176	157	19
Niagara Town	8,030	8	7	1
Niskayuna Town	22,541	29	27	2
Nissequogue Village	1,747	1	1	0
North Castle Town	12,406	30	28	2
North Greenbush Town	12,234	19	17	2
Northport Village	7,331	22	17	5
North Syracuse Village	6,796	11	10	1
North Tonawanda	30,452	52	48	4
Norwich	6,804	17	17	0
Ocean Beach Village	82	4	4	0
Ogdensburg	10,685	32	27	5
Ogden Town	20,321	14	12	2
Old Brookville Village	2,219	33	26	7
Old Westbury Village	4,747	31	26	5
Olean	13,694	39	34	5
Oneonta City	13,967	30	24	6
Orangetown Town	37,804	84	76	8
Orchard Park Town	29,725	41	32	9
Oswego City	17,510	53	47	6
Owego Village	3,774	3	2	1
Oyster Bay Cove Village	4,337	14	14	0
Palmyra Village	3,357	6	5	1
Peekskill	24,127	64	54	10
Pelham Manor Village	5,577	26	25	1
Pelham Village	7,037	26	25	1
Penn Yan Village	4,961	12	11	1
Perry Village	3,467	4	4	0
Piermont Village	2,573	8	8	0
Plattsburgh City	19,742	54	47	7
Pleasantville Village	7,172	21	21	0
Port Chester Village	29,616	62	60	2
Port Dickinson Village	1,573	5	4	1
Port Jervis	8,527	33	32	1
Port Washington	19,384	68	60	8
Poughkeepsie	30,159	122	88	34
Poughkeepsie Town	38,960	93	80	13
Pound Ridge Town	5,253	2	1	1
Quogue Village	1,006	14	13	1
Ramapo Town	94,019	121	99	22
Rensselaer City	9,331	31	26	5
Riverhead Town	33,649	106	89	17
Rochester	208,591	889	761	128
Rockville Centre Village	24,654	63	55	8
Rome	32,200	75	73	2
Rosendale Town	5,875	1	1	0
Rotterdam Town	29,586	43	40	3
Rye	16,021	40	35	5
Rye Brook Village	9,608	27	26	1
Sag Harbor Village	2,292	14	12	2
Sands Point Village	2,903	21	21	0
Saranac Lake Village	5,268	12	12	0
Saratoga Springs	27,962	80	69	11
Saugerties Town	19,033	28	24	4
Scarsdale Village	18,031	46	41	5
Schenectady	64,710	171	145	26
Schodack Town	11,685	11	10	1
Scotia Village	7,651	14	13	1
Seneca Falls Town	8,811	18	16	2
Shandaken Town	2,963	4	4	0
Shawangunk Town	14,018	5	5	0
Shelter Island Town	2,416	10	9	1
Sherrill	3,045	3	3	0
Sidney Village	3,672	8	7	1
Skaneateles Village	2,493	3	3	0
Sodus Village	1,725	2	2	0
Solvay Village	6,329	15	14	1

Table 19. Full-Time Law Enforcement Employees, by Selected State and City, 2017—*Continued*

(Number.)

State/city	Population	Total law enforcement employees	Total officers	Total civilians
Southampton Town	50,987	108	95	13
Southampton Village	3,309	46	31	15
South Glens Falls Village	3,567	5	5	0
South Nyack Village	3,532	6	6	0
Southold Town	19,990	71	51	20
Spring Valley Village	32,795	49	49	0
St. Johnsville Village	1,669	1	1	0
Stony Point Town	15,540	25	25	0
Syracuse	143,069	495	420	75
Tarrytown Village	11,577	35	32	3
Tonawanda	14,808	35	29	6
Tonawanda Town	57,223	151	106	45
Troy	49,644	134	123	11
Tuckahoe Village	6,636	25	22	3
Tupper Lake Village	3,521	8	8	0
Ulster Town	12,473	26	22	4
Utica	60,395	179	162	17
Vernon Village	1,163	1	1	0
Vestal Town	28,090	37	34	3
Walden Village	6,692	14	11	3
Wallkill Town	28,881	40	39	1
Walton Village	2,864	4	4	0
Wappingers Falls Village	5,510	4	1	3
Warsaw Village	3,327	5	5	0
Warwick Town	18,375	36	31	5
Washingtonville Village	5,752	14	12	2
Waterford Town and Village	8,506	8	8	0
Waterloo Village	4,996	9	8	1
Watertown	25,746	68	65	3
Watervliet	10,100	25	24	1
Watkins Glen Village	1,896	5	5	0
Waverly Village	4,151	10	9	1
Webb Town	1,811	6	6	0
Wellsville Village	4,454	11	10	1
Westfield Village	3,029	4	4	0
Westhampton Beach Village	1,774	16	14	2
West Seneca Town	45,597	78	65	13
White Plains	58,461	201	191	10
Whitesboro Village	3,651	6	6	0
Whitestown Town	9,207	6	6	0
Windham Town	1,679	1	1	0
Woodbury Town	11,017	23	19	4
Woodstock Town	5,812	10	10	0
Yonkers	201,554	689	607	82
Yorktown Town	37,142	65	56	9
Yorkville Village	2,605	3	3	0
NORTH CAROLINA				
Aberdeen	7,707	30	28	2
Ahoskie	4,970	18	17	1
Albemarle	16,022	56	47	9
Andrews	1,800	6	5	1
Angier	5,227	14	14	0
Apex	49,159	93	77	16
Archdale	11,664	31	25	6
Asheboro	26,253	82	74	8
Asheville	90,103	275	206	69
Atlantic Beach	1,491	17	16	1
Aurora	517	1	1	0
Ayden	5,215	22	18	4
Badin	1,967	4	4	0
Bailey	568	2	2	0
Bakersville	447	1	1	0
Bald Head Island	178	23	21	2
Banner Elk	1,166	8	7	1
Beaufort	4,223	17	16	1
Beech Mountain	321	14	10	4
Belhaven	1,572	8	7	1
Belmont	10,880	41	34	7
Benson	3,764	12	11	1
Bessemer City	5,586	14	13	1

(Number.)

State/city	Population	Total law enforcement employees	Total officers	Total civilians
Bethel	1,626	3	3	0
Beulaville	1,326	4	4	0
Biltmore Forest	1,482	14	13	1
Biscoe	1,676	9	8	1
Black Creek	762	2	2	0
Black Mountain	8,477	22	18	4
Bladenboro	1,683	6	6	0
Blowing Rock	1,297	12	11	1
Boiling Spring Lakes	6,026	13	12	1
Boiling Springs	4,715	9	9	0
Boone	19,138	47	36	11
Boonville	1,201	5	5	0
Brevard	7,846	31	24	7
Bridgeton	432	1	1	0
Broadway	1,247	4	4	0
Brookford	373	1	1	0
Bryson City	1,457	9	8	1
Bunn	362	2	2	0
Burgaw	4,135	12	11	1
Burlington	52,986	157	121	36
Burnsville	1,650	8	8	0
Butner	7,718	43	36	7
Candor	831	4	4	0
Canton	4,261	19	14	5
Cape Carteret	2,080	8	8	0
Carolina Beach	6,296	30	28	2
Carrboro	21,553	38	35	3
Carthage	2,463	11	10	1
Cary	166,986	227	187	40
Caswell Beach	435	4	4	0
Chadbourn	1,758	10	9	1
Chapel Hill	59,553	120	91	29
Charlotte-Mecklenburg[1]	914,609	2,341	1,754	587
Cherryville	6,112	19	14	5
China Grove	4,226	13	13	0
Chocowinity	801	3	3	0
Claremont	1,389	10	9	1
Clayton	21,012	46	43	3
Cleveland	879	2	2	0
Clinton	8,666	31	27	4
Clyde	1,270	5	5	0
Coats	2,487	6	6	0
Columbus	979	11	10	1
Concord	91,756	189	164	25
Conover	8,354	30	28	2
Conway	744	2	2	0
Cooleemee	966	3	3	0
Cornelius	29,153	75	61	14
Cramerton	4,461	16	16	0
Creedmoor	4,563	18	14	4
Dallas	4,780	19	14	5
Davidson	12,723	20	18	2
Dobson	1,591	6	6	0
Drexel	1,872	5	5	0
Duck	386	11	10	1
Dunn	9,965	40	35	5
Durham	269,088	677	505	172
East Bend	592	2	2	0
East Spencer	1,562	10	10	0
Eden	15,321	48	44	4
Edenton	4,823	21	19	2
Elizabeth City	17,802	69	59	10
Elizabethtown	3,529	17	16	1
Elkin	4,120	21	17	4
Elon	10,283	16	15	1
Emerald Isle	3,710	19	18	1
Enfield	2,378	10	9	1
Erwin	5,017	11	10	1
Fair Bluff	899	4	3	1
Fairmont	2,680	11	9	2
Farmville	4,759	22	17	5

(Number.)

State/city	Population	Total law enforcement employees	Total officers	Total civilians
Fayetteville	205,432	595	438	157
Fletcher	8,237	18	17	1
Forest City	7,278	33	31	2
Four Oaks	2,118	6	6	0
Foxfire Village	1,013	3	3	0
Franklin	4,008	18	17	1
Franklinton	2,151	9	9	0
Fremont	1,279	4	4	0
Fuquay-Varina	27,429	46	40	6
Garner	29,287	73	64	9
Garysburg	941	2	2	0
Gaston	1,030	3	3	0
Gastonia	76,191	189	166	23
Gibsonville	7,131	18	17	1
Glen Alpine	1,498	4	4	0
Goldsboro	35,824	102	92	10
Graham	14,771	39	36	3
Granite Falls	4,680	17	14	3
Granite Quarry	3,006	8	8	0
Greensboro	290,051	749	656	93
Greenville	92,630	228	183	45
Grifton	2,667	5	5	0
Hamlet	6,361	21	18	3
Havelock	20,157	32	24	8
Haw River	2,467	8	8	0
Henderson	15,131	50	41	9
Hendersonville	13,967	56	43	13
Hertford	2,122	8	7	1
Hickory	40,653	141	105	36
Highlands	944	13	12	1
High Point	112,368	279	232	47
Hillsborough	6,640	28	27	1
Holden Beach	656	8	8	0
Holly Ridge	2,466	11	10	1
Holly Springs	34,897	63	49	14
Hope Mills	16,325	41	36	5
Hot Springs	568	1	1	0
Hudson	3,717	15	13	2
Huntersville	56,279	95	87	8
Indian Beach	114	5	5	0
Jackson	466	1	1	0
Jacksonville	67,293	146	118	28
Jefferson	1,542	4	4	0
Jonesville	2,240	10	8	2
Kannapolis	48,754	108	81	27
Kenansville	867	3	3	0
Kenly	1,518	8	8	0
Kernersville	24,222	89	70	19
Kill Devil Hills	7,194	34	28	6
King	7,046	24	21	3
Kings Mountain	10,824	40	32	8
Kinston	20,791	71	62	9
Kitty Hawk	3,507	18	16	2
Knightdale	15,423	33	31	2
Kure Beach	2,125	13	12	1
Lake Lure	1,178	10	9	1
Lake Royale	2,701	3	3	0
Lake Waccamaw	1,440	5	5	0
Landis	3,127	10	10	0
Laurel Park	2,344	6	6	0
Laurinburg	15,398	43	41	2
Leland	19,786	36	34	2
Lenoir	17,932	66	50	16
Lewiston Woodville	486	1	1	0
Lexington	19,135	67	59	8
Liberty	2,694	11	10	1
Lilesville	496	1	1	0
Lillington	3,648	14	13	1
Lincolnton	10,823	35	30	5
Littleton	620	3	3	0
Locust	3,090	12	12	0

State/city	Population	Total law enforcement employees	Total officers	Total civilians
Long View	4,900	15	15	0
Louisburg	3,576	15	13	2
Lowell	3,727	9	9	0
Lumberton	21,484	98	87	11
Madison	2,173	17	16	1
Maggie Valley	1,316	12	11	1
Magnolia	947	2	2	0
Maiden	3,403	15	14	1
Manteo	1,421	9	8	1
Marion	7,819	26	25	1
Marshall	892	3	3	0
Mars Hill	2,239	4	4	0
Marshville	2,692	8	8	0
Matthews	32,255	70	55	15
Maxton	2,434	13	9	4
Mayodan	2,445	15	15	0
Maysville	973	3	3	0
Mebane	14,619	35	31	4
Micro	509	1	1	0
Middlesex	826	4	4	0
Mint Hill	26,868	34	31	3
Misenheimer	666	5	5	0
Mocksville	5,302	23	22	1
Monroe	35,153	95	85	10
Montreat	794	4	4	0
Mooresville	37,049	106	83	23
Morehead City	9,520	45	40	5
Morganton	16,630	88	54	34
Morrisville	25,904	40	38	2
Mount Airy	10,338	53	40	13
Mount Gilead	1,169	6	6	0
Mount Holly	14,640	40	31	9
Mount Olive	4,760	21	19	2
Murfreesboro	3,057	9	8	1
Murphy	1,648	11	9	2
Nags Head	2,943	25	23	2
Nashville	5,530	17	16	1
Navassa	1,841	2	2	0
New Bern	30,191	111	86	25
Newland	682	4	4	0
Newport	4,776	8	8	0
Newton	13,059	43	35	8
Newton Grove	565	2	2	0
Norlina	1,050	5	5	0
North Topsail Beach	732	12	11	1
Northwest	783	2	2	0
North Wilkesboro	4,228	24	23	1
Norwood	2,401	9	8	1
Oakboro	1,865	6	6	0
Oak Island	7,883	25	23	2
Ocean Isle Beach	627	14	13	1
Oriental	879	1	1	0
Oxford	8,887	31	26	5
Parkton	437	1	1	0
Pembroke	3,014	18	14	4
Pikeville	695	4	4	0
Pilot Mountain	1,438	8	7	1
Pinebluff	1,491	3	3	0
Pinehurst	16,145	30	25	5
Pine Knoll Shores	1,359	7	7	0
Pine Level	1,922	5	5	0
Pinetops	1,291	6	6	0
Pineville	8,788	43	33	10
Pink Hill	520	2	2	0
Pittsboro	4,355	13	12	1
Plymouth	3,551	14	13	1
Polkton	3,461	2	2	0
Princeton	1,327	4	4	0
Raeford	5,057	16	15	1
Raleigh	468,261	869	713	156
Ramseur	1,713	6	6	0

Table 19. Full-Time Law Enforcement Employees, by Selected State and City, 2017—*Continued*

(Number.)

State/city	Population	Total law enforcement employees	Total officers	Total civilians
Randleman	4,174	15	15	0
Ranlo	3,657	9	8	1
Red Springs	3,417	13	12	1
Reidsville	13,900	52	46	6
Richlands	1,702	8	8	0
Rich Square	873	1	1	0
River Bend	3,128	3	3	0
Roanoke Rapids	15,083	42	37	5
Robbins	1,189	5	5	0
Robersonville	1,402	7	7	0
Rockingham	9,005	38	33	5
Rockwell	2,148	6	6	0
Rocky Mount	55,098	198	160	38
Rolesville	7,709	19	18	1
Rose Hill	1,660	5	5	0
Rowland	1,043	7	6	1
Roxboro	8,348	32	28	4
Rutherfordton	4,134	14	13	1
Salisbury	34,085	77	71	6
Saluda	705	4	4	0
Sanford	29,295	105	81	24
Scotland Neck	1,919	9	7	2
Seagrove	229	1	1	0
Selma	6,678	26	24	2
Seven Devils	203	6	6	0
Shallotte	4,050	15	14	1
Sharpsburg	1,990	10	9	1
Shelby	20,254	83	70	13
Siler City	8,531	25	19	6
Smithfield	12,489	45	41	4
Snow Hill	1,551	5	5	0
Southern Pines	14,025	45	39	6
Southern Shores	2,919	13	12	1
Southport	3,774	11	11	0
Sparta	1,720	6	6	0
Spencer	3,315	12	11	1
Spindale	4,236	11	11	0
Spring Hope	1,313	6	6	0
Spring Lake	13,369	29	25	4
Spruce Pine	2,095	10	10	0
Stallings	15,656	26	23	3
Stanfield	1,489	5	5	0
Stanley	3,769	13	12	1
Stantonsburg	784	3	3	0
Star	867	4	4	0
Statesville	26,847	101	80	21
Stoneville	1,027	4	4	0
St. Pauls	2,402	16	11	5
Sugar Mountain	197	5	5	0
Sunset Beach	3,958	14	14	0
Surf City	2,342	19	18	1
Swansboro	3,261	12	11	1
Sylva	2,653	14	14	0
Tabor City	4,225	11	10	1
Tarboro	10,924	34	28	6
Taylorsville	2,103	10	10	0
Taylortown	826	3	3	0
Thomasville	27,071	70	64	6
Topsail Beach	428	10	9	1
Trent Woods	4,162	5	5	0
Troutman	2,610	14	14	0
Troy	3,399	12	11	1
Tryon	1,618	8	6	2
Valdese	4,477	13	12	1
Vanceboro	993	2	2	0
Vass	775	4	4	0
Wadesboro	5,413	27	20	7
Wagram	795	1	1	0
Wake Forest	42,019	85	69	16
Wallace	3,946	15	11	4
Walnut Creek	867	2	2	0

(Number.)

State/city	Population	Total law enforcement employees	Total officers	Total civilians
Warrenton	845	5	4	1
Warsaw	3,160	16	14	2
Washington	9,793	35	28	7
Waxhaw	15,089	25	23	2
Waynesville	9,977	44	34	10
Weaverville	4,034	15	14	1
Weldon	1,563	13	12	1
Wendell	6,901	18	17	1
West Jefferson	1,305	8	8	0
Whispering Pines	3,342	9	8	1
Whitakers	718	2	2	0
White Lake	767	6	6	0
Whiteville	5,534	24	23	1
Wilkesboro	3,554	24	22	2
Williamston	5,438	20	19	1
Wilmington	119,422	345	270	75
Wilson	49,686	123	108	15
Wilson's Mills	2,597	5	5	0
Windsor	3,795	9	9	0
Wingate	3,993	7	7	0
Winston-Salem	244,278	671	511	160
Winterville	9,476	19	18	1
Woodfin	6,444	13	13	0
Woodland	717	2	2	0
Wrightsville Beach	2,574	26	24	2
Yadkinville	2,918	14	13	1
Youngsville	1,317	11	10	1
Zebulon	5,288	21	20	1
NORTH DAKOTA				
Arnegard	161	2	2	0
Belfield	1,055	4	3	1
Berthold	502	1	1	0
Beulah	3,420	6	5	1
Bismarck	74,397	151	121	30
Bowman	1,724	4	4	0
Burlington	1,215	2	2	0
Carrington	2,039	5	5	0
Cavalier	1,231	3	3	0
Devils Lake	7,344	18	16	2
Dickinson	23,967	55	36	19
Ellendale	1,269	2	2	0
Emerado	430	1	1	0
Fargo	123,430	197	174	23
Fessenden	462	1	1	0
Grafton	4,240	10	9	1
Grand Forks	58,090	103	88	15
Harvey	1,737	3	3	0
Hazen	2,424	4	4	0
Hillsboro	1,584	1	1	0
Jamestown	15,439	36	31	5
Kenmare	1,053	2	2	0
Killdeer	1,268	5	5	0
Lamoure	913	6	5	1
Lincoln	3,935	4	4	0
Lisbon	2,121	3	3	0
Mandan	22,369	40	34	6
Medora	136	2	2	0
Minot	50,118	109	81	28
Napoleon	786	1	1	0
New Town	2,642	7	6	1
Northwood	913	2	2	0
Oakes	1,769	2	2	0
Powers Lake	296	2	2	0
Ray	838	1	1	0
Rolla	1,331	3	3	0
Rugby	2,806	5	5	0
Sherwood	250	1	1	0
South Heart	448	3	3	0
Stanley	2,974	4	4	0
Steele	707	1	1	0

Table 19. Full-Time Law Enforcement Employees, by Selected State and City, 2017—*Continued*

(Number.)

State/city	Population	Total law enforcement employees	Total officers	Total civilians
Surrey	1,453	4	4	0
Thompson	1,016	1	1	0
Tioga	1,607	8	6	2
Valley City	6,558	13	12	1
Wahpeton	7,841	16	14	2
Watford City	8,015	27	23	4
West Fargo	36,624	68	54	14
Williston	28,748	73	52	21
Wishek	945	2	2	0
OHIO				
Ada	5,551	9	8	1
Akron	197,412	469	435	34
Alliance	21,838	50	38	12
American Township	12,208	1	1	0
Amherst	12,090	26	20	6
Ashland	20,485	36	29	7
Ashville	4,211	10	10	0
Aurora	15,932	35	28	7
Austintown	35,303	54	42	12
Avon Lake	23,839	34	29	5
Barberton	26,050	44	42	2
Bath Township, Summit County	9,678	26	20	6
Bay Village	15,327	27	23	4
Bazetta Township	5,614	8	8	0
Beavercreek	46,572	64	48	16
Beaver Township	6,427	12	9	3
Bedford	12,641	35	30	5
Bedford Heights	10,558	29	27	2
Bellbrook	7,159	13	12	1
Bellville	1,864	4	4	0
Belpre	6,466	15	10	5
Berea	18,871	28	26	2
Bethel	2,791	6	5	1
Bexley	13,773	34	30	4
Blue Ash	12,248	40	33	7
Bluffton	4,157	8	8	0
Bolivar	986	2	2	0
Boston Heights	1,293	4	4	0
Bowling Green	31,779	55	40	15
Brecksville	13,432	38	30	8
Brookville	5,896	13	12	1
Brunswick	34,838	52	40	12
Butler Township	7,799	17	17	0
Cambridge	10,391	29	23	6
Canal Fulton	5,428	10	9	1
Canfield	7,246	23	16	7
Carey	3,566	14	11	3
Carlisle	5,395	8	7	1
Carroll Township	2,085	5	5	0
Catawba Island Township	3,504	5	5	0
Celina	10,310	21	16	5
Centerville	23,782	54	39	15
Chagrin Falls	3,991	13	12	1
Cincinnati	299,116	1,274	1,025	249
Circleville	13,972	29	21	8
Clayton	13,149	21	20	1
Clearcreek Township	15,531	16	15	1
Cleveland Heights	44,525	111	101	10
Clyde	6,191	18	14	4
Coldwater	4,519	9	8	1
Colerain Township	58,996	57	52	5
Columbus	872,205	1,937	1,551	386
Copley Township	17,280	23	22	1
Cortland	6,844	9	9	0
Covington	2,637	7	6	1
Crooksville	2,491	4	3	1
Cuyahoga Falls	49,145	86	71	15
Deer Park	5,665	14	10	4
Defiance	16,594	33	30	3
Delaware	39,315	60	53	7

(Number.)

State/city	Population	Total law enforcement employees	Total officers	Total civilians
Delhi Township	29,619	35	33	2
Delphos	6,979	11	11	0
Eastlake	18,056	32	21	11
East Palestine	4,503	8	6	2
Elida	1,836	9	6	3
Elyria	53,586	95	81	14
Englewood	13,504	26	19	7
Evendale	2,767	23	20	3
Fairborn	33,936	65	48	17
Fairfield	42,627	78	59	19
Fairfield Township	22,524	20	19	1
Fairlawn	7,467	34	26	8
Findlay	41,474	83	65	18
Forest Park	18,665	42	36	6
Fort Loramie	1,500	1	1	0
Fostoria	13,255	22	19	3
Franklin	11,779	31	24	7
Gahanna	35,243	71	56	15
Garrettsville	2,321	5	5	0
Geneva-on-the-Lake	1,199	5	5	0
Genoa Township	27,061	28	26	2
German Township, Montgomery County	2,876	5	5	0
Glenwillow	923	4	4	0
Grandview Heights	7,831	22	18	4
Greenhills	3,584	11	10	1
Green Springs	1,307	2	2	0
Greenville	12,772	30	22	8
Hamilton	62,094	131	121	10
Harrison	11,246	23	20	3
Heath	10,681	25	18	7
Highland Heights	8,434	30	23	7
Hilliard	36,144	63	53	10
Hinckley Township	7,970	10	9	1
Hiram	1,164	2	2	0
Holland	1,662	9	9	0
Hubbard	7,533	11	11	0
Huber Heights	37,996	69	50	19
Jackson Township, Mahoning County	2,018	5	5	0
Kent	30,270	55	41	14
Kenton	8,190	14	14	0
Kettering	55,152	109	82	27
Kirtland	6,759	15	10	5
Lake Township	8,287	16	15	1
Lakewood	50,151	111	94	17
Lancaster	40,026	84	67	17
Lexington	4,686	13	9	4
Lima	37,220	100	80	20
Lockland	3,427	16	15	1
Lorain	63,672	118	97	21
Lordstown	3,242	13	9	4
Loudonville	2,642	7	6	1
Lyndhurst	13,586	37	29	8
Macedonia	12,027	32	23	9
Maineville	1,070	2	2	0
Mariemont	3,435	11	10	1
Marlboro Township	4,374	5	4	1
Mason	33,406	47	43	4
Maumee	13,809	55	41	14
Medina Township	8,940	10	10	0
Mentor	46,663	110	80	30
Mentor-on-the-Lake	7,359	13	8	5
Miamisburg	19,928	39	37	2
Miami Township, Clermont County	42,352	43	40	3
Middletown	48,828	101	68	33
Mifflin Township	2,587	13	13	0
Milan	1,339	3	3	0
Milford	6,939	21	19	2
Milton Township	2,445	4	4	0
Minerva Park	1,318	10	9	1
Mogadore	3,829	7	7	0
Monroe	16,002	39	31	8

Table 19. Full-Time Law Enforcement Employees, by Selected State and City, 2017—*Continued*

(Number.)

State/city	Population	Total law enforcement employees	Total officers	Total civilians
Moraine	6,360	33	25	8
Mount Healthy	6,020	11	10	1
Mount Vernon	16,553	32	29	3
Navarre	1,901	6	6	0
New Albany	10,838	28	20	8
Newark	49,389	79	68	11
New Bremen	2,966	7	7	0
New London	2,363	5	5	0
Newtown	2,679	9	8	1
Niles	18,334	39	34	5
Northfield	3,669	15	14	1
North Olmsted	31,779	59	45	14
North Ridgeville	33,586	47	37	10
Norton	11,998	17	16	1
Norwalk	16,811	30	23	7
Oak Harbor	2,731	8	5	3
Oberlin	8,321	23	16	7
Olmsted Falls	8,898	10	10	0
Orrville	8,527	15	14	1
Ottawa	4,394	8	8	0
Ottoville	975	2	2	0
Oxford Township	2,181	3	3	0
Parma	79,340	125	109	16
Pepper Pike	6,256	16	16	0
Perkins Township	11,773	21	20	1
Perrysburg Township	12,784	28	23	5
Perry Township, Franklin County	3,758	12	11	1
Perry Township, Montgomery County	3,322	5	5	0
Pierce Township	11,623	17	16	1
Pioneer	1,412	3	3	0
Piqua	20,973	38	35	3
Plain City	4,379	9	9	0
Poland Township	11,921	12	12	0
Port Clinton	5,928	19	14	5
Powell	13,029	21	19	2
Reading	10,307	24	20	4
Reynoldsburg	37,704	70	54	16
Richmond Heights	10,432	27	21	6
Rittman	6,610	12	9	3
Rossford	6,609	15	14	1
Ross Township	8,755	1	1	0
Russellville	524	2	2	0
Salem	11,887	22	22	0
Sandusky	24,861	49	47	2
Seven Hills	11,668	16	15	1
Shaker Heights	27,380	89	64	25
Sharonville	13,796	49	40	9
Shawnee Hills	785	5	5	0
Shawnee Township	12,096	18	12	6
Sidney	20,466	45	35	10
Silver Lake	2,494	9	8	1
Solon	23,023	64	47	17
South Russell	3,819	9	9	0
South Zanesville	1,970	2	2	0
Springboro	18,632	30	26	4
Springfield	58,843	121	113	8
Springfield Township, Hamilton County	36,571	54	48	6
Springfield Township, Mahoning County	6,374	9	9	0
St. Clair Township	7,583	14	13	1
Steubenville	17,979	43	38	5
Stow	34,692	49	41	8
Streetsboro	16,308	36	28	8
Strongsville	44,758	85	71	14
Sugarcreek	2,222	6	6	0
Sugarcreek Township	8,300	18	16	2
Sylvania	18,908	42	35	7
Tallmadge	17,529	27	24	3
Thornville	997	1	1	0
Tiffin	17,481	40	31	9
Toledo	277,116	688	587	101
Trenton	12,906	20	15	5

Table 19. Full-Time Law Enforcement Employees, by Selected State and City, 2017—*Continued*

(Number.)

State/city	Population	Total law enforcement employees	Total officers	Total civilians
Troy	25,865	45	43	2
Uhrichsville	5,372	7	7	0
Union Township, Clermont County	48,214	62	48	14
Upper Arlington	35,214	54	50	4
Upper Sandusky	6,529	18	13	5
Urbana	11,351	18	18	0
Valley View, Cuyahoga County	2,007	22	20	2
Vandalia	15,022	37	28	9
Van Wert	10,713	29	21	8
Wadsworth	23,388	39	30	9
Walton Hills	2,308	15	11	4
Warren	39,643	64	59	5
Warren Township	5,255	6	6	0
Washington Court House	14,136	26	21	5
Waterville	5,518	12	11	1
Waterville Township	1,655	5	5	0
Wauseon	7,407	19	16	3
West Carrollton	12,898	24	22	2
West Jefferson	4,347	16	12	4
West Salem	1,493	2	2	0
Whitehall	18,835	62	47	15
Whitehouse	4,622	10	10	0
Wickliffe	12,679	39	29	10
Wilmington	12,416	30	21	9
Winchester	1,025	2	2	0
Wooster	27,172	44	40	4
Worthington	14,692	43	31	12
Wyoming	8,531	20	18	2
Xenia	26,331	69	44	25
Yellow Springs	3,713	10	7	3
Yorkville	1,031	3	3	0
Youngstown	63,889	193	152	41
Zanesville	25,457	92	55	37
OKLAHOMA				
Achille	521	4	3	1
Ada	17,455	38	34	4
Allen	935	3	2	1
Altus	19,054	53	40	13
Alva	5,149	10	10	0
Amber	460	2	2	0
Anadarko	6,756	21	17	4
Antlers	2,306	9	4	5
Apache	1,439	3	3	0
Ardmore	25,211	57	52	5
Arkoma	1,914	3	2	1
Atoka	3,056	16	15	1
Avant	314	1	1	0
Barnsdall	1,197	2	2	0
Bartlesville	36,788	82	61	21
Beaver	1,429	2	2	0
Beggs	1,244	5	3	2
Bernice	562	2	2	0
Bethany	19,620	41	30	11
Big Cabin	257	4	3	1
Binger	654	1	1	0
Bixby	26,131	40	32	8
Blackwell	6,765	22	16	6
Blanchard	8,649	14	9	5
Boise City	1,074	2	2	0
Bokoshe	493	1	1	0
Boley	1,183	3	3	0
Boswell	688	1	1	0
Bristow	4,251	15	11	4
Broken Arrow	108,823	184	131	53
Broken Bow	4,100	18	14	4
Burns Flat	2,001	4	4	0
Cache	2,857	6	5	1
Caddo	1,070	2	2	0
Calera	2,295	12	10	2
Caney	197	5	3	2

Table 19. Full-Time Law Enforcement Employees, by Selected State and City, 2017—*Continued*

(Number.)

State/city	Population	Total law enforcement employees	Total officers	Total civilians
Canton	600	3	3	0
Carnegie	1,711	9	4	5
Carney	664	1	1	0
Cashion	860	4	4	0
Catoosa	7,129	16	15	1
Cement	499	3	3	0
Chandler	3,194	13	9	4
Chattanooga	441	3	2	1
Checotah	3,207	13	9	4
Chelsea	1,972	3	3	0
Cherokee	1,553	3	3	0
Chickasha	16,489	38	28	10
Choctaw	12,556	18	16	2
Chouteau	2,088	9	8	1
Claremore	19,147	45	37	8
Clayton	780	9	4	5
Cleveland	3,217	8	8	0
Clinton	9,455	22	14	8
Coalgate	1,850	6	6	0
Colbert	1,207	2	1	1
Colcord	814	3	3	0
Collinsville	6,836	16	11	5
Comanche	1,595	6	5	1
Commerce	2,458	5	5	0
Cordell	2,852	4	3	1
Covington	547	1	1	0
Coweta	9,718	21	15	6
Coyle	367	3	2	1
Crescent	1,564	10	5	5
Cushing	7,790	22	14	8
Cyril	1,053	1	1	0
Davenport	826	3	2	1
Davis	2,822	11	9	2
Del City	22,046	42	31	11
Depew	482	1	1	0
Dewar	865	2	2	0
Dewey	3,513	11	10	1
Dibble	846	3	3	0
Dickson	1,253	4	3	1
Drumright	2,870	5	5	0
Duncan	22,909	62	46	16
Durant	17,871	43	38	5
Earlsboro	644	2	2	0
Edmond	92,876	153	115	38
Elgin	3,164	5	5	0
Elk City	12,057	33	24	9
Elmore City	708	3	3	0
El Reno	19,133	52	32	20
Enid	51,257	125	97	28
Erick	1,034	3	3	0
Eufaula	2,971	12	8	4
Fairfax	1,335	3	1	2
Fairland	1,051	3	3	0
Fairview	2,672	8	5	3
Fletcher	1,138	1	1	0
Forest Park	1,082	3	2	1
Fort Gibson	4,045	9	8	1
Fort Towson	491	1	1	0
Frederick	3,621	10	7	3
Geary	1,286	11	5	6
Glenpool	13,954	31	23	8
Goodwell	1,311	4	4	0
Gore	939	5	4	1
Grandfield	955	1	1	0
Granite	2,008	3	3	0
Grove	6,868	27	21	6
Guthrie	11,713	37	27	10
Guymon	11,733	24	15	9
Haileyville	762	4	4	0
Harrah	6,215	9	9	0
Hartshorne	1,966	5	5	0

Table 19. Full-Time Law Enforcement Employees, by Selected State and City, 2017—*Continued*

(Number.)

State/city	Population	Total law enforcement employees	Total officers	Total civilians
Haskell	1,960	6	6	0
Healdton	2,757	5	4	1
Heavener	3,328	10	9	1
Hennessey	2,219	8	4	4
Henryetta	5,737	18	12	6
Hinton	3,273	5	5	0
Hobart	3,567	13	7	6
Holdenville	5,663	9	6	3
Hollis	1,886	10	6	4
Hominy	3,485	10	5	5
Hooker	1,959	3	3	0
Howe	789	2	2	0
Hugo	5,205	16	16	0
Hulbert	607	4	4	0
Hydro	959	3	3	0
Idabel	6,940	25	19	6
Jay	2,520	14	9	5
Jenks	22,693	30	22	8
Jennings	359	1	1	0
Jones	3,067	7	7	0
Kellyville	1,147	3	3	0
Kiefer	1,968	4	4	0
Kingfisher	4,931	15	12	3
Kingston	1,634	6	6	0
Kiowa	676	7	5	2
Konawa	1,267	4	3	1
Krebs	1,928	8	6	2
Lahoma	645	1	1	0
Lamont	402	1	1	0
Langley	819	3	3	0
Langston	1,857	3	2	1
Lawton	94,134	239	182	57
Lexington	2,169	11	6	5
Lindsay	2,827	14	8	6
Locust Grove	1,401	8	4	4
Lone Grove	5,252	10	7	3
Luther	1,675	8	7	1
Madill	3,937	12	11	1
Mangum	2,848	11	6	5
Mannford	3,150	11	8	3
Marietta	2,782	8	7	1
Marlow	4,520	10	10	0
Maud	1,077	2	2	0
Maysville	1,233	5	4	1
McAlester	18,181	48	45	3
McCurtain	510	2	2	0
McLoud	4,656	11	10	1
Medicine Park	447	2	2	0
Meeker	1,179	4	3	1
Miami	13,470	41	30	11
Midwest City	57,772	125	94	31
Minco	1,649	4	4	0
Moore	62,476	93	88	5
Mooreland	1,240	3	2	1
Morris	1,464	3	3	0
Mounds	1,200	3	3	0
Mountain View	759	2	2	0
Muldrow	3,250	12	7	5
Muskogee	38,199	105	87	18
Mustang	21,392	35	24	11
Nash	202	1	1	0
Newcastle	10,011	18	17	1
Newkirk	2,217	4	4	0
Nichols Hills	3,940	21	16	5
Nicoma Park	2,473	5	5	0
Ninnekah	1,033	4	3	1
Noble	6,799	16	11	5
Norman	124,074	231	168	63
North Enid	922	4	4	0
Nowata	3,709	8	6	2
Oilton	1,015	2	2	0

Table 19. Full-Time Law Enforcement Employees, by Selected State and City, 2017—*Continued*

(Number.)

State/city	Population	Total law enforcement employees	Total officers	Total civilians
Okarche	1,343	4	4	0
Okemah	3,239	13	8	5
Oklahoma City	648,260	1,368	1,088	280
Okmulgee	12,183	26	24	2
Olustee	576	1	1	0
Oologah	1,182	5	5	0
Owasso	36,869	75	56	19
Paoli	616	1	1	0
Pauls Valley	6,225	20	15	5
Pawhuska	3,461	14	10	4
Pawnee	2,160	7	6	1
Perkins	2,841	8	8	0
Perry	5,000	21	13	8
Piedmont	7,738	12	9	3
Pocola	4,073	12	8	4
Ponca City	24,397	69	51	18
Pond Creek	854	2	2	0
Porum	707	3	3	0
Poteau	8,913	31	25	6
Prague	2,464	13	8	5
Pryor Creek	9,517	29	22	7
Purcell	6,483	23	20	3
Quinton	987	4	4	0
Ringling	989	1	1	0
Roland	3,720	11	8	3
Rush Springs	1,271	4	4	0
Salina	1,381	5	5	0
Sallisaw	8,548	28	21	7
Sand Springs	19,977	40	29	11
Sapulpa	21,062	53	41	12
Savanna	642	7	6	1
Sawyer	312	2	2	0
Sayre	4,644	12	7	5
Seminole	7,415	15	13	2
Shady Point	995	2	2	0
Shattuck	1,333	2	2	0
Shawnee	31,725	86	63	23
Skiatook	8,018	21	17	4
Snyder	1,326	3	3	0
South Coffeyville	758	5	5	0
Spencer	4,031	6	4	2
Sperry	1,292	4	3	1
Spiro	2,184	3	3	0
Sportsmen Acres	312	1	1	0
Stigler	2,760	13	9	4
Stillwater	50,159	120	75	45
Stilwell	4,062	20	13	7
Stonewall	476	2	2	0
Stratford	1,539	4	4	0
Stringtown	401	2	2	0
Stroud	2,792	13	8	5
Sulphur	5,105	10	8	2
Tahlequah	16,905	45	36	9
Talala	278	3	2	1
Talihina	1,094	10	5	5
Tecumseh	6,699	13	12	1
Texhoma	955	3	3	0
Thackerville	478	1	1	0
The Village	9,512	29	22	7
Thomas	1,235	2	2	0
Tipton	779	2	2	0
Tishomingo	3,119	8	7	1
Tonkawa	3,077	9	6	3
Tryon	505	1	1	0
Tulsa	404,868	946	777	169
Tupelo	313	1	1	0
Tushka	301	3	3	0
Tuttle	7,140	16	11	5
Tyrone	769	2	1	1
Union City	2,053	8	8	0
Valley Brook	779	11	9	2

(Number.)

State/city	Population	Total law enforcement employees	Total officers	Total civilians
Valliant	737	4	4	0
Velma	602	1	1	0
Verden	527	1	1	0
Verdigris	4,488	5	4	1
Vian	1,383	4	4	0
Vici	702	3	2	1
Vinita	5,532	22	15	7
Wagoner	8,931	20	15	5
Wakita	339	1	1	0
Walters	2,464	4	4	0
Warner	1,614	3	3	0
Warr Acres	10,480	33	26	7
Washington	655	3	2	1
Watonga	2,931	9	7	2
Watts	310	3	2	1
Waukomis	1,349	4	4	0
Waurika	1,960	4	4	0
Waynoka	960	3	3	0
Weatherford	12,178	38	23	15
Webbers Falls	593	4	3	1
Weleetka	981	7	5	2
West Siloam Springs	839	10	9	1
Westville	1,561	9	5	4
Wetumka	1,221	9	4	5
Wewoka	3,390	7	7	0
Wilburton	2,633	7	6	1
Wilson	1,721	4	4	0
Wister	1,067	4	3	1
Woodward	12,655	25	21	4
Wright City	733	1	1	0
Wyandotte	330	5	4	1
Wynnewood	2,227	6	5	1
Wynona	440	3	3	0
Yale	1,207	6	3	3
Yukon	26,971	63	46	17
OREGON				
Albany	53,701	97	65	32
Amity	1,676	9	2	7
Ashland	21,908	35	28	7
Astoria	9,857	23	13	10
Aumsville	4,141	7	6	1
Baker City	9,764	17	15	2
Bandon	3,146	7	7	0
Beaverton	98,897	179	139	40
Bend	93,786	123	96	27
Black Butte		7	6	1
Boardman	3,408	11	10	1
Brookings	6,560	21	14	7
Canby	17,823	28	24	4
Cannon Beach	1,710	9	7	2
Carlton	2,156	4	3	1
Central Point	18,525	31	25	6
Coburg	1,073	4	3	1
Columbia City	2,005	7	4	3
Condon	677	1	1	0
Coos Bay	16,347	32	22	10
Coquille	3,912	8	7	1
Corvallis	57,576	81	57	24
Cottage Grove	10,182	31	16	15
Dallas	16,152	26	20	6
Eagle Point	9,143	13	12	1
Enterprise	1,912	5	5	0
Eugene	168,310	307	188	119
Florence	8,857	23	16	7
Forest Grove	24,520	33	28	5
Gearhart	1,580	3	3	0
Gervais	2,710	6	5	1
Gladstone	12,220	19	17	2
Gold Beach	2,314	7	5	2
Grants Pass	38,082	87	55	32

(Number.)

State/city	Population	Total law enforcement employees	Total officers	Total civilians
Gresham	112,466	155	125	30
Hermiston	17,377	37	31	6
Hillsboro	107,433	177	130	47
Hood River	7,797	16	14	2
Hubbard	3,421	4	3	1
Independence	9,854	19	14	5
Jacksonville	2,917	6	5	1
John Day	1,662	10	10	0
Junction City	6,174	9	7	2
Keizer	39,397	45	38	7
King City	3,945	8	7	1
Klamath Falls	22,436	41	36	5
La Grande	13,252	31	18	13
Lake Oswego	39,318	59	43	16
Lebanon	16,826	39	27	12
Lincoln City	8,798	37	25	12
Madras	6,800	11	10	1
Malin	810	7	7	0
Manzanita	646	4	4	0
McMinnville	35,125	45	38	7
Medford	82,792	141	104	37
Milton-Freewater	7,011	17	11	6
Milwaukie	21,033	42	37	5
Molalla	9,245	17	14	3
Monmouth	10,282	15	12	3
Mount Angel	3,569	9	6	3
Myrtle Creek	3,494	7	7	0
Myrtle Point	2,550	6	5	1
Newberg-Dundee	26,769	49	35	14
Newport	10,465	26	22	4
North Bend	9,806	28	21	7
North Plains	2,158	4	4	0
Nyssa	3,174	8	7	1
Oakridge	3,254	7	5	2
Ontario	10,970	25	21	4
Oregon City	36,921	54	47	7
Pendleton	16,864	28	23	5
Philomath	4,691	10	9	1
Phoenix	4,614	10	9	1
Pilot Rock	1,508	3	3	0
Portland	649,408	1,174	925	249
Port Orford	1,163	6	5	1
Prineville	10,053	28	16	12
Rainier	1,968	6	5	1
Redmond	29,870	48	40	8
Reedsport	4,106	19	10	9
Rockaway Beach	1,387	4	4	0
Rogue River	2,289	8	5	3
Roseburg	22,505	42	38	4
Salem	169,565	337	189	148
Sandy	11,249	22	18	4
Scappoose	7,236	11	10	1
Seaside	6,726	25	19	6
Sherwood	19,473	26	23	3
Silverton	10,136	18	16	2
Springfield	62,318	96	64	32
Stayton	8,148	17	13	4
St. Helens	13,611	17	15	2
Sunriver		12	11	1
Sutherlin	8,027	15	12	3
Sweet Home	9,500	22	15	7
Talent	6,558	10	8	2
The Dalles	15,670	26	23	3
Tigard	52,524	89	72	17
Tillamook	5,214	10	10	0
Toledo	3,577	13	7	6
Tualatin	27,781	46	38	8
Turner	2,061	2	2	0
Umatilla	7,009	13	11	2
Vernonia	2,199	4	3	1
Warrenton	5,545	13	12	1

State/city	Population	Total law enforcement employees	Total officers	Total civilians
West Linn	27,153	29	26	3
Winston	5,436	9	8	1
Woodburn	25,848	38	30	8
Yamhill	1,167	9	3	6
PENNSYLVANIA				
Abington Township, Montgomery County	55,578	78	61	17
Adams Township, Butler County	13,876	14	14	0
Adams Township, Cambria County	5,651	3	3	0
Akron	3,999	5	5	0
Albion	1,457	3	3	0
Alburtis	2,598	4	4	0
Aldan	4,154	5	5	0
Aleppo Township	1,887	17	14	3
Aliquippa	9,048	17	16	1
Allegheny Township, Blair County	6,602	8	7	1
Allegheny Township, Westmoreland County	8,142	10	9	1
Allentown	120,823	234	212	22
Altoona	44,366	72	64	8
Ambler	6,509	13	12	1
Ambridge	6,744	8	8	0
Amity Township	12,921	13	12	1
Annville Township	4,940	10	8	2
Archbald	6,975	18	18	0
Arnold	4,904	8	8	0
Ashland	2,694	2	2	0
Ashley	2,691	4	4	0
Aspinwall	2,726	7	6	1
Aston Township	16,714	18	16	2
Athens	3,195	4	4	0
Athens Township	5,009	11	10	1
Avalon	4,582	5	5	0
Avoca	2,606	2	2	0
Avonmore Boro	967	1	1	0
Baden	3,976	3	3	0
Baldwin Borough	19,727	23	22	1
Baldwin Township	1,942	5	5	0
Bally	1,103	2	2	0
Bangor	5,179	11	10	1
Beaver	4,353	12	10	2
Beaver Falls	8,516	19	18	1
Beaver Meadows	831	1	1	0
Bedford	2,702	5	5	0
Bedminster Township	7,117	7	6	1
Bell Acres	1,392	3	3	0
Bellefonte	6,321	13	10	3
Bellevue	8,140	16	13	3
Bellwood	1,759	3	3	0
Ben Avon	1,754	17	14	3
Ben Avon Heights	375	17	14	3
Bensalem Township	60,310	127	100	27
Berlin	1,990	2	2	0
Bern Township	6,975	12	12	0
Bernville	946	2	1	1
Berwick	10,080	15	14	1
Bethel Park	31,842	44	38	6
Bethel Township, Berks County	4,122	3	3	0
Bethlehem	75,336	154	154	0
Bethlehem Township	23,973	36	35	1
Biglerville	1,207	2	2	0
Birdsboro	5,138	8	7	1
Birmingham Township	4,255	3	3	0
Blairsville	3,275	4	4	0
Blair Township	4,559	4	4	0
Blakely	6,244	6	6	0
Blawnox	1,398	3	3	0
Bloomsburg Town	14,542	23	18	5
Blossburg	1,504	2	2	0
Bonneauville	1,828	1	1	0
Boyertown	4,026	8	7	1
Brackenridge	3,167	4	4	0

Table 19. Full-Time Law Enforcement Employees, by Selected State and City, 2017—*Continued*

(Number.)

State/city	Population	Total law enforcement employees	Total officers	Total civilians
Braddock Hills	1,838	2	2	0
Bradford	8,307	18	18	0
Bradford Township	4,761	5	5	0
Branch Township	1,766	2	2	0
Brecknock Township, Berks County	4,626	5	5	0
Brentwood	9,386	15	13	2
Briar Creek Township	2,989	4	4	0
Bridgeport	4,562	8	7	1
Bridgeville	5,029	9	8	1
Bridgewater	682	2	2	0
Brighton Township	8,392	8	8	0
Bristol	9,503	14	12	2
Bristol Township	53,628	69	60	9
Brockway	2,016	3	2	1
Brookhaven	8,074	9	8	1
Brookville	3,820	7	7	0
Brownsville	2,260	2	2	0
Bryn Athyn	1,394	3	3	0
Buckingham Township	20,339	24	22	2
Buffalo Township	7,276	5	5	0
Buffalo Valley Regional	12,590	16	15	1
Bushkill Township	8,494	17	16	1
Butler	13,057	24	23	1
Butler Township, Butler County	16,690	23	21	2
Butler Township, Luzerne County	9,709	12	11	1
Butler Township, Schuykill County	5,389	4	4	0
Caernarvon Township, Berks County	4,079	8	7	1
California	6,840	8	7	1
Caln Township	14,137	18	17	1
Cambria Township	5,823	4	4	0
Cambridge Springs	2,556	3	3	0
Camp Hill	7,941	13	12	1
Canonsburg	8,859	18	16	2
Canton	1,883	3	3	0
Carbondale	8,435	9	9	0
Carlisle	19,233	34	31	3
Carnegie	7,904	14	13	1
Carrolltown	804	2	2	0
Carroll Township, Washington County	5,503	3	3	0
Carroll Township, York County	6,359	12	12	0
Carroll Valley	3,949	5	4	1
Castle Shannon	8,213	15	14	1
Catasauqua	6,562	9	8	1
Catawissa	1,490	3	3	0
Cecil Township	12,605	21	20	1
Center Township	11,628	20	19	1
Centerville	3,156	2	2	0
Central Berks Regional	9,416	15	14	1
Central Bucks Regional	15,330	28	25	3
Chambersburg	20,757	36	33	3
Charleroi Regional	6,556	7	7	0
Chartiers Township	7,985	12	12	0
Cheltenham Township	37,160	75	67	8
Chester	33,984	101	91	10
Cheswick	1,709	1	1	0
Chippewa Township	8,116	9	8	1
Churchill	2,946	9	9	0
Clairton	6,588	10	10	0
Clarion	5,361	9	8	1
Clarks Summit	6,294	6	6	0
Clearfield	5,940	11	7	4
Cleona	2,183	4	4	0
Clifton Heights	6,695	11	10	1
Clymer	1,283	1	1	0
Coaldale	2,172	3	3	0
Coal Township	10,349	12	11	1
Cochranton	1,101	2	2	0
Colebrookdale District	5,985	11	9	2
Collegeville	5,282	8	8	0
Collier Township	8,164	17	16	1
Collingdale	8,762	9	8	1

(Number.)

State/city	Population	Total law enforcement employees	Total officers	Total civilians
Colonial Regional	20,540	27	25	2
Columbia	10,352	19	16	3
Conemaugh Township, Cambria County	1,886	1	1	0
Conemaugh Township, Somerset County	6,900	6	6	0
Conewago Township, Adams County	7,184	10	9	1
Conewango Township	3,392	4	4	0
Conneaut Lake Regional	3,506	4	3	1
Connellsville	7,405	14	14	0
Conoy Township	3,483	16	14	2
Conshohocken	8,006	21	19	2
Conway	2,121	4	4	0
Conyngham	1,863	3	3	0
Coopersburg	2,494	7	7	0
Coplay	3,239	5	5	0
Coraopolis	5,513	13	9	4
Cornwall	4,318	7	6	1
Corry	6,321	11	10	1
Coudersport	2,433	4	4	0
Covington Township	2,250	4	4	0
Crafton	6,251	10	9	1
Cranberry Township	31,191	31	27	4
Crescent Township	2,574	4	4	0
Cresson	1,598	10	10	0
Cresson Township	2,574	5	4	1
Croyle Township	2,249	1	1	0
Cumberland Township, Adams County	6,225	6	6	0
Cumberland Township, Greene County	6,333	3	3	0
Cumru Township	15,341	25	24	1
Curwensville	2,443	2	1	1
Dallas	2,762	4	4	0
Dallas Township	9,252	10	10	0
Dalton	1,204	2	2	0
Danville	4,604	8	6	2
Darby	10,648	18	17	1
Darby Township	9,302	15	14	1
Decatur Township	4,804	1	1	0
Delmont	2,612	4	4	0
Derry	2,551	2	2	0
Derry Township, Dauphin County	25,082	58	39	19
Dickson City	5,794	7	7	0
Donegal Township	2,418	3	3	0
Donora	4,597	6	6	0
Dormont	8,347	14	13	1
Douglass Township, Berks County	3,584	4	4	0
Douglass Township, Montgomery County	10,534	12	11	1
Downingtown	7,907	19	16	3
Doylestown Township	17,538	22	20	2
Dublin Borough	2,157	3	2	1
Du Bois	7,504	13	13	0
Duboistown	1,200	1	1	0
Duncansville	1,186	1	1	0
Dunmore	13,047	17	17	0
Duquesne	5,507	15	14	1
Duryea	4,840	4	4	0
East Bangor	1,705	1	1	0
East Berlin	1,530	3	1	2
East Bethlehem Township	2,268	1	1	0
East Brandywine Township	8,721	16	15	1
East Coventry Township	6,738	8	7	1
East Deer Township	1,455	1	1	0
East Earl Township	6,838	8	8	0
Eastern Adams Regional	7,388	6	6	0
Eastern Pike Regional	4,607	11	10	1
East Fallowfield Township	7,539	7	7	0
East Franklin Township	3,917	1	1	0
East Greenville	2,983	2	2	0
East Hempfield Township	24,504	36	32	4
East Lampeter Township	17,084	39	36	3
East Lansdowne	2,654	5	3	2
East Marlborough Township	7,310	1	1	0
East McKeesport	2,644	3	3	0

Table 19. Full-Time Law Enforcement Employees, by Selected State and City, 2017—*Continued*

(Number.)

State/city	Population	Total law enforcement employees	Total officers	Total civilians
East Norriton Township	14,154	29	27	2
Easton	27,013	68	63	5
East Pennsboro Township	21,800	23	22	1
East Pikeland Township	7,360	9	9	0
East Pittsburgh	1,769	1	1	0
Easttown Township	10,609	14	13	1
East Union Township	1,593	2	2	0
East Vincent Township	7,065	7	7	0
East Whiteland Township	11,672	22	20	2
Ebensburg	3,137	4	4	0
Economy	9,338	14	13	1
Eddystone	2,397	10	9	1
Edgewood	3,026	9	9	0
Edgeworth	1,644	13	4	9
Edinboro	6,204	8	8	0
Edwardsville	4,684	5	5	0
Elizabeth	1,983	2	2	0
Elizabethtown	11,641	19	17	2
Elizabeth Township	13,079	12	12	0
Elkland	1,758	2	2	0
Ellwood City	7,476	12	10	2
Emmaus	11,424	22	20	2
Emporium	1,887	2	2	0
Emsworth	2,387	17	14	3
Ephrata	13,907	38	34	4
Erie	98,071	195	174	21
Etna	3,354	7	7	0
Evans City-Seven Fields Regional	4,554	3	3	0
Everett	1,731	3	3	0
Everson	765	1	1	0
Exeter Township, Berks County	25,830	34	32	2
Exeter Township, Luzerne County	2,344	1	1	0
Fairchance	1,904	1	1	0
Fairview Township, Luzerne County	4,479	6	6	0
Fairview Township, York County	17,393	16	13	3
Falls Township, Bucks County	33,618	60	53	7
Farrell	4,702	14	13	1
Fawn Township	2,330	1	1	0
Ferguson Township	19,630	24	22	2
Ferndale	1,524	2	2	0
Findlay Township	5,739	23	16	7
Fleetwood	4,070	6	6	0
Folcroft	6,623	12	11	1
Ford City	2,825	1	1	0
Forest City	1,742	2	2	0
Forest Hills	6,357	9	9	0
Forks Township	15,518	22	21	1
Forty Fort	4,079	4	4	0
Forward Township	3,300	1	1	0
Foster Township, McKean County	4,116	5	5	0
Fountain Hill	4,638	10	9	1
Fox Chapel	5,329	11	11	0
Frackville	3,651	5	5	0
Franconia Township	13,293	11	10	1
Franklin	6,181	23	17	6
Franklin Park	14,690	13	12	1
Franklin Township, Beaver County	3,934	3	3	0
Franklin Township, Carbon County	4,104	4	4	0
Franklin Township, Columbia County	581	4	4	0
Frazer Township	1,143	2	2	0
Freedom Township	3,385	3	3	0
Freeland	3,423	5	4	1
Freemansburg	2,619	3	3	0
Galeton	1,102	1	1	0
Gallitzin	1,807	6	6	0
Geistown	2,326	1	1	0
Gettysburg	7,716	12	11	1
Girard	2,978	4	4	0
Glassport	4,360	6	6	0
Glenolden	7,153	11	10	1
Granville Township	5,022	10	8	2

State/city	Population	Total law enforcement employees	Total officers	Total civilians
Greencastle	4,041	5	4	1
Greenfield Township, Blair County	4,035	1	1	0
Greensburg	14,356	38	28	10
Green Tree	5,020	11	10	1
Greenville	5,547	8	7	1
Grove City	8,029	12	11	1
Hamburg	4,394	7	6	1
Hampden Township	29,905	26	25	1
Hampton Township	18,451	19	18	1
Hanover	15,606	28	25	3
Hanover Township, Luzerne County	10,822	17	16	1
Harmar Township	3,064	9	8	1
Harmony Township	3,066	4	4	0
Harrisburg	48,804	161	135	26
Harrison Township	10,358	21	18	3
Harveys Lake	2,770	2	2	0
Hastings	2,178	2	2	0
Hatboro	7,445	17	14	3
Hatfield Township	20,927	29	27	2
Haverford Township	49,116	82	70	12
Hazleton	24,549	42	38	4
Hegins Township	3,440	2	2	0
Heidelberg	1,215	3	3	0
Heidelberg Township, Berks County	1,739	1	1	0
Hellam Township	8,646	10	8	2
Hellertown	5,819	11	10	1
Hemlock Township	2,260	6	6	0
Hempfield Township, Mercer County	3,655	7	6	1
Hermitage	15,782	32	29	3
Highspire	2,366	13	13	0
Hilltown Township	15,278	20	17	3
Hollidaysburg	5,751	10	8	2
Homer City	1,614	2	2	0
Homestead	3,160	14	13	1
Honesdale	4,132	5	5	0
Honey Brook	1,751	1	1	0
Hooversville	607	1	1	0
Hopewell Township	12,346	16	15	1
Horsham Township	26,723	47	40	7
Houston	1,240	2	2	0
Hughesville	2,076	3	3	0
Hummelstown	4,621	7	6	1
Huntingdon	6,974	12	12	0
Independence Township, Beaver County	2,419	2	2	0
Indiana	13,984	24	22	2
Indiana Township	7,225	10	10	0
Indian Lake	386	5	5	0
Ingram	3,235	4	4	0
Irwin	3,801	4	4	0
Jackson Township, Butler County	3,834	10	8	2
Jackson Township, Cambria County	4,130	2	2	0
Jackson Township, Luzerne County	4,631	2	2	0
Jeannette	9,180	17	14	3
Jefferson Hills Borough	11,418	20	19	1
Jefferson Township, Mercer County	1,846	2	2	0
Jenkins Township	4,447	3	3	0
Jenkintown	4,421	16	14	2
Jermyn	2,065	1	1	0
Jessup	4,423	4	4	0
Jim Thorpe	4,579	8	7	1
Johnsonburg	2,313	3	3	0
Johnstown	20,946	43	38	5
Kane	3,520	3	3	0
Kenhorst	2,852	189	167	22
Kennedy Township	8,213	10	8	2
Kennett Square	6,176	16	13	3
Kennett Township	8,312	7	7	0
Kidder Township	1,929	6	6	0
Kilbuck Township	710	17	14	3
Kingston	12,809	19	19	0
Kingston Township	6,924	11	11	0

Table 19. Full-Time Law Enforcement Employees, by Selected State and City, 2017—*Continued*

(Number.)

State/city	Population	Total law enforcement employees	Total officers	Total civilians
Kiskiminetas Township	4,565	9	9	0
Kittanning	3,818	9	8	1
Kline Township	1,380	2	1	1
Knox	1,076	2	2	0
Koppel	732	2	2	0
Kulpmont	2,812	1	1	0
Kutztown	5,019	14	12	2
Lake City	2,923	3	3	0
Lamar Township	2,562	2	2	0
Lancaster	59,199	163	140	23
Lancaster Township, Butler County	2,513	2	2	0
Langhorne Borough	1,583	1	1	0
Lansdale	16,561	30	23	7
Lansdowne	10,604	18	15	3
Lansford	3,740	7	7	0
Larksville	4,389	7	7	0
Latimore Township	2,604	1	1	0
Latrobe	7,950	14	13	1
Laureldale	3,868	4	4	0
Lawrence Park Township	3,793	9	8	1
Lawrence Township, Clearfield County	7,694	9	8	1
Lebanon	25,771	44	41	3
Leechburg	2,033	3	3	0
Leetsdale	1,182	4	4	0
Leet Township	1,600	5	5	0
Lehighton	5,241	12	11	1
Lehigh Township, Northampton County	10,400	13	12	1
Lehman Township	3,448	3	3	0
Lewistown	8,196	11	10	1
Liberty	2,489	1	1	0
Liberty Township, Adams County	1,246	1	1	0
Ligonier	1,523	2	2	0
Ligonier Township	6,463	6	6	0
Limerick Township	19,145	27	25	2
Lincoln	1,047	3	2	1
Linesville	988	7	7	0
Lititz	9,214	16	14	2
Littlestown	4,473	9	8	1
Lock Haven	9,514	16	14	2
Locust Township	1,400	4	4	0
Logan Township	12,547	18	16	2
Lower Allen Township	19,604	25	22	3
Lower Burrell	11,303	18	17	1
Lower Chichester Township	3,468	5	5	0
Lower Frederick Township	4,901	3	3	0
Lower Gwynedd Township	11,581	19	18	1
Lower Heidelberg Township	6,143	11	10	1
Lower Makefield Township	32,779	42	38	4
Lower Merion Township	58,354	158	141	17
Lower Moreland Township	13,246	27	22	5
Lower Paxton Township	48,971	66	59	7
Lower Pottsgrove Township	12,179	19	17	2
Lower Providence Township	26,813	33	31	2
Lower Salford Township	15,487	20	18	2
Lower Saucon Township	10,818	17	15	2
Lower Southampton Township	19,120	33	30	3
Lower Swatara Township	8,855	16	14	2
Lower Windsor Township	7,500	10	9	1
Lykens	1,746	1	1	0
Macungie	3,162	4	4	0
Mahanoy City	3,981	2	2	0
Mahanoy Township	3,322	1	1	0
Mahoning Township, Carbon County	4,188	6	6	0
Mahoning Township, Lawrence County	2,910	1	1	0
Mahoning Township, Montour County	4,207	7	6	1
Malvern	3,487	6	5	1
Manheim	4,855	18	17	1
Manheim Township	40,170	74	63	11
Manor	3,334	4	4	0
Manor Township, Armstrong County	4,164	1	1	0
Manor Township, Lancaster County	20,949	21	19	2

(Number.)

State/city	Population	Total law enforcement employees	Total officers	Total civilians
Mansfield..	3,147	5	5	0
Marcus Hook	2,388	5	4	1
Marietta..	2,603	15	13	2
Marion Township, Beaver County	889	2	2	0
Marlborough Township............................	3,347	3	3	0
Marple Township	23,838	32	29	3
Mars	1,636	1	1	0
Martinsburg...	1,884	2	2	0
Marysville...	2,531	2	2	0
Masontown	3,351	5	5	0
Mayfield	1,709	2	2	0
McAdoo	2,176	3	3	0
McCandless	28,788	30	28	2
McDonald Borough..................................	2,060	5	5	0
McKeesport	20,937	55	52	3
McKees Rocks	5,926	10	9	1
McSherrystown..	3,062	4	4	0
Meadville..	12,896	28	22	6
Mechanicsburg	9,012	15	14	1
Media...	5,354	22	14	8
Mercer..	1,896	3	3	0
Mercersburg..	1,553	2	2	0
Meshoppen	1,444	2	2	0
Middleburg...	1,305	3	2	1
Middlesex Township, Butler County	5,673	4	4	0
Middlesex Township, Cumberland County ...	7,422	10	9	1
Middletown...	9,279	11	10	1
Middletown Township	45,282	63	57	6
Midland	2,523	3	3	0
Mifflinburg	3,518	10	9	1
Mifflin County Regional	16,872	14	14	0
Milford	966	2	2	0
Millbourne	1,159	1	1	0
Millcreek Township, Erie County	53,806	81	64	17
Millcreek Township, Lebanon County.......	5,670	2	2	0
Millersburg	2,528	3	2	1
Millersville...	8,419	15	13	2
Millvale	3,638	6	6	0
Milton...	6,879	9	8	1
Minersville	4,185	5	5	0
Mohnton	3,044	4	4	0
Monaca	5,567	8	8	0
Monessen	7,364	12	11	1
Monongahela	4,129	8	7	1
Monroeville..	27,888	55	46	9
Montgomery...	1,537	10	1	9
Montgomery Township.............................	26,369	38	35	3
Montoursville...	4,497	7	6	1
Montour Township	1,302	3	3	0
Montrose	1,471	3	3	0
Moon Township..	25,818	35	29	6
Moore Township.......................................	9,294	11	10	1
Moosic..	5,759	10	10	0
Morris-Cooper Regional	5,514	1	1	0
Morrisville..	8,523	13	11	2
Morton	2,693	5	4	1
Moscow...	1,934	3	3	0
Mount Carmel	5,644	8	8	0
Mount Carmel Township	3,030	6	6	0
Mount Gretna Borough	203	7	6	1
Mount Holly Springs	2,042	2	2	0
Mount Joy	8,221	12	11	1
Mount Lebanon..	32,367	54	45	9
Mount Oliver	3,308	10	10	0
Mount Pleasant..	4,304	4	4	0
Mount Pleasant Township	3,497	4	4	0
Mount Union	2,385	5	5	0
Muhlenberg Township..............................	20,150	33	31	2
Muncy	2,441	3	3	0
Muncy Township	1,081	2	2	0
Munhall..	11,140	25	23	2

(Number.)

State/city	Population	Total law enforcement employees	Total officers	Total civilians
Murrysville	20,034	23	21	2
Nanticoke	10,144	15	14	1
Nanty Glo	2,540	1	1	0
Narberth	4,338	4	4	0
Nazareth	5,675	8	7	1
Neshannock Township	9,241	7	7	0
Nether Providence Township	13,790	16	15	1
Neville Township	1,052	17	14	3
Newberry Township	15,530	18	16	2
New Bethlehem	2,717	2	2	0
New Brighton	8,907	9	7	2
New Britain Township	11,220	13	12	1
New Cumberland	7,302	10	9	1
New Hanover Township	13,095	10	9	1
New Holland	5,443	15	14	1
New Hope	2,492	11	9	2
New Kensington	12,508	22	22	0
Newport Township	5,257	2	2	0
New Sewickley Township	7,367	11	10	1
Newtown	2,226	5	5	0
Newtown Township, Bucks County	22,903	32	28	4
Newtown Township, Delaware County	13,190	20	18	2
Newville	1,332	3	3	0
New Wilmington	2,183	5	5	0
Norristown	34,374	80	67	13
Northampton	9,854	14	12	2
Northampton Township	39,395	48	42	6
North Belle Vernon	1,871	2	2	0
North Braddock	4,721	3	3	0
North Catasauqua	2,828	5	5	0
North Cornwall Township	7,909	9	9	0
North Coventry Township	8,001	12	11	1
North East, Erie County	4,109	7	7	0
Northeastern Regional	11,728	13	12	1
Northern Berks Regional	13,282	15	14	1
Northern Cambria Borough	3,582	2	2	0
Northern Lancaster County Regional	35,500	26	24	2
Northern Regional	35,113	31	29	2
Northern York Regional	69,203	53	49	4
North Fayette Township	14,656	25	20	5
North Franklin Township	4,571	10	10	0
North Hopewell Township	2,803	2	2	0
North Huntingdon Township	30,687	32	26	6
North Lebanon Township	11,975	14	12	2
North Londonderry Township	8,525	10	9	1
North Middleton Township	11,625	11	10	1
North Sewickley Township	5,474	1	1	0
North Strabane Township	14,778	20	19	1
Northumberland	3,687	5	5	0
North Versailles Township	12,193	24	19	5
North Wales	3,244	4	4	0
Northwest Lancaster County Regional	19,758	21	19	2
Norwood	5,878	7	6	1
Oakmont	6,449	7	7	0
O'Hara Township	8,514	16	15	1
Ohio Township	6,665	17	14	3
Ohioville	3,422	2	2	0
Oil City	9,931	22	16	6
Old Forge	7,949	5	5	0
Old Lycoming Township	5,014	8	8	0
Oley Township	3,760	2	2	0
Olyphant	5,075	4	4	0
Orangeville Area	1,746	1	1	0
Orwigsburg	2,979	5	5	0
Overfield Township	2,785	1	1	0
Oxford	5,447	12	11	1
Palmerton	5,253	10	9	1
Palmer Township	21,598	36	34	2
Palmyra	7,541	9	8	1
Palo Alto	988	1	1	0
Parkesburg	3,772	9	8	1

State/city	Population	Total law enforcement employees	Total officers	Total civilians
Parkside	2,328	3	3	0
Parks Township	2,603	2	2	0
Patterson Township	2,930	4	4	0
Patton	1,641	2	2	0
Patton Township	16,100	19	17	2
Penbrook	2,955	7	7	0
Penn	468	6	6	0
Penndel	2,179	1	1	0
Penn Hills	41,425	53	50	3
Pennridge Regional	10,979	15	13	2
Penn Township, Butler County	4,910	4	3	1
Penn Township, Westmoreland County	19,510	23	21	2
Penn Township, York County	16,394	24	22	2
Perkasie	8,474	19	17	2
Perryopolis	1,709	2	2	0
Peters Township	22,297	23	21	2
Philadelphia	1,575,595	7,347	6,558	789
Phoenixville	16,955	32	30	2
Pine Creek Township	3,273	2	2	0
Pine Grove	2,095	2	2	0
Pitcairn	3,202	3	3	0
Pittsburgh	305,932	903	885	18
Pittston	7,581	9	9	0
Pittston Township	3,387	4	4	0
Plains Township	9,690	19	18	1
Pleasant Hills	8,175	20	18	2
Plum	27,440	30	24	6
Plumstead Township	13,906	18	16	2
Plymouth	5,766	4	4	0
Plymouth Township, Montgomery County	17,835	52	45	7
Pocono Mountain Regional	42,213	42	37	5
Pocono Township	10,706	19	18	1
Point Township	3,670	5	5	0
Polk	782	2	2	0
Portage	2,451	2	2	0
Port Allegany	2,037	3	3	0
Port Carbon	1,794	2	2	0
Portland	509	2	2	0
Port Vue	3,693	2	2	0
Pottstown	22,706	57	44	13
Pottsville	13,645	24	24	0
Prospect Park	6,475	9	9	0
Pulaski Township, Lawrence County	3,291	2	2	0
Punxsutawney	5,790	11	8	3
Pymatuning Township	3,120	10	7	3
Quakertown	8,768	20	18	2
Quarryville	2,771	4	4	0
Raccoon Township	2,967	4	4	0
Radnor Township	31,859	46	42	4
Ralpho Township	4,279	6	6	0
Rankin	2,060	1	1	0
Reading	87,487	189	167	22
Reading Township	5,840	2	2	0
Redstone Township	4,284	3	3	0
Reilly Township	692	2	2	0
Renovo	1,216	1	1	0
Reserve Township	3,260	4	4	0
Reynoldsville	2,676	1	1	0
Rice Township	3,545	6	6	0
Richland Township, Bucks County	13,225	15	13	2
Richland Township, Cambria County	12,153	22	21	1
Ridgway	3,799	6	5	1
Ridley Park	7,026	14	10	4
Ridley Township	31,082	37	32	5
Riverside	1,894	3	3	0
Roaring Brook Township	1,957	1	1	0
Roaring Creek Township	536	4	4	0
Roaring Spring	2,502	3	3	0
Robeson Township	7,379	6	5	1
Robinson Township, Allegheny County	13,777	31	29	2
Rochester	3,514	7	6	1

Table 19. Full-Time Law Enforcement Employees, by Selected State and City, 2017—*Continued*

(Number.)

State/city	Population	Total law enforcement employees	Total officers	Total civilians
Rochester Township	2,699	4	4	0
Rockledge	2,535	4	4	0
Ross Township	30,684	45	43	2
Rostraver Township	11,046	15	14	1
Royalton	1,039	5	5	0
Royersford	4,761	8	7	1
Rush Township	3,305	1	1	0
Sadsbury Township, Chester County	3,934	2	2	0
Salem Township, Luzerne County	4,178	5	5	0
Salisbury Township	13,807	21	19	2
Sandy Lake	642	1	1	0
Sandy Township	10,661	11	10	1
Saxonburg	1,473	1	1	0
Saxton	696	1	1	0
Sayre	6,335	13	10	3
Schuylkill Haven	5,166	8	8	0
Schuylkill Township, Chester County	8,580	13	11	2
Scottdale	4,184	6	6	0
Scott Township, Allegheny County	16,684	23	22	1
Scott Township, Columbia County	5,035	6	6	0
Scott Township, Lackawanna County	4,789	4	4	0
Scranton	77,499	170	150	20
Selinsgrove	5,930	7	6	1
Seward	468	1	1	0
Sewickley	4,370	8	8	0
Sewickley Heights	811	4	2	2
Shaler Township	28,207	28	26	2
Shamokin	7,056	11	10	1
Shamokin Dam	1,726	3	3	0
Sharon	13,305	29	28	1
Sharon Hill	5,683	10	9	1
Sharpsburg	3,352	6	6	0
Shenandoah	4,812	4	4	0
Shenango Township, Lawrence County	7,251	7	7	0
Shenango Township, Mercer County	3,761	8	8	0
Shillington	5,241	8	7	1
Shinglehouse	1,074	1	1	0
Shippensburg	5,567	10	9	1
Shippingport	209	1	1	0
Shiremanstown	1,584	2	2	0
Shohola Township	2,308	1	1	0
Silver Lake Township	1,604	1	1	0
Silver Spring Township	17,558	25	24	1
Sinking Spring	4,100	7	6	1
Slate Belt Regional	12,398	23	23	0
Slatington	4,289	6	6	0
Slippery Rock	3,572	4	4	0
Smethport	1,552	2	2	0
Smith Township	4,391	4	4	0
Solebury Township	8,583	16	14	2
Somerset	5,945	8	7	1
Souderton	6,927	6	5	1
South Abington Township	8,995	12	11	1
South Annville Township	2,972	2	2	0
South Beaver Township	2,632	4	4	0
South Buffalo Township	2,583	2	2	0
South Centre Township	4,197	4	4	0
South Coatesville	1,447	2	2	0
South Connellsville Borough	1,905	1	1	0
Southern Chester County Regional	14,900	16	15	1
Southern Regional Lancaster County	3,867	7	7	0
Southern Regional York County	11,488	16	14	2
South Fayette Township	15,772	18	17	1
South Fork	854	2	2	0
South Greensburg	2,020	2	2	0
South Heidelberg Township	7,359	9	9	0
South Lebanon Township	9,903	8	7	1
South Londonderry Township	8,110	10	8	2
South Park Township	13,371	15	14	1
South Pymatuning Township	2,587	2	2	0
Southwestern Regional	17,764	15	14	1

State/city	Population	Total law enforcement employees	Total officers	Total civilians
Southwest Greensburg	2,052	2	2	0
Southwest Regional, Fayette County	7,619	3	3	0
South Whitehall Township	19,893	37	35	2
South Williamsport	6,206	9	7	2
Spring City	3,297	3	3	0
Springdale	3,334	3	3	0
Springdale Township	1,598	3	3	0
Springettsbury Township	26,895	34	31	3
Springfield Township, Bucks County	5,030	5	5	0
Springfield Township, Delaware County	24,363	37	32	5
Springfield Township, Montgomery County	19,728	30	28	2
Spring Garden Township	13,044	21	18	3
Spring Township, Berks County	27,446	30	29	1
Spring Township, Centre County	7,712	8	7	1
State College	58,169	72	62	10
St. Clair Boro	2,855	4	4	0
Steelton	5,897	14	12	2
St. Marys City	12,413	15	14	1
Stoneboro	993	1	1	0
Stonycreek Township	2,661	3	3	0
Stowe Township	6,181	6	6	0
Strasburg	2,960	4	4	0
Stroud Area Regional	34,259	59	52	7
Sugarcreek	5,034	3	3	0
Sugarloaf Township, Luzerne County	4,029	4	4	0
Sugar Notch	963	1	1	0
Summerhill Township	2,321	2	2	0
Summit Hill	2,913	6	4	2
Sunbury	9,520	19	15	4
Susquehanna Regional	8,405	16	14	2
Susquehanna Township, Dauphin County	25,055	45	42	3
Swarthmore	6,246	9	9	0
Swatara Township	24,867	52	49	3
Sweden Township	840	1	1	0
Swissvale	8,734	14	14	0
Swoyersville	4,941	5	5	0
Sykesville	1,122	1	1	0
Tamaqua	6,748	10	9	1
Tarentum	4,401	8	7	1
Tatamy	1,131	1	1	0
Taylor	5,929	7	7	0
Telford	4,844	7	6	1
Throop	3,902	6	6	0
Tiadaghton Valley Regional	7,666	11	10	1
Tilden Township	3,575	4	4	0
Tinicum Township, Bucks County	3,936	5	5	0
Tinicum Township, Delaware County	4,105	19	17	2
Titusville	5,345	10	10	0
Towamencin Township	18,484	26	23	3
Towanda	2,839	7	7	0
Trafford	3,095	3	3	0
Trainer	1,840	4	4	0
Tredyffrin Township	29,435	48	42	6
Tremont	1,681	2	2	0
Troy	1,247	2	2	0
Tullytown	1,844	7	6	1
Tulpehocken Township	3,313	3	3	0
Tunkhannock	1,749	3	3	0
Tunkhannock Township, Wyoming County	6,212	6	6	0
Turtle Creek	5,200	5	5	0
Tyrone	5,273	14	11	3
Union City	3,167	4	3	1
Uniontown	9,875	22	21	1
Union Township, Lawrence County	4,937	8	8	0
Upland	3,243	6	5	1
Upper Allen Township	20,119	24	23	1
Upper Burrell Township	2,244	2	2	0
Upper Chichester Township	17,033	23	22	1
Upper Darby Township	82,601	145	126	19
Upper Dublin Township	26,329	46	40	6
Upper Gwynedd Township	16,042	23	20	3

(Number.)

State/city	Population	Total law enforcement employees	Total officers	Total civilians
Upper Leacock Township	8,904	39	36	3
Upper Macungie Township	24,535	32	30	2
Upper Makefield Township	8,425	15	14	1
Upper Merion Township	28,677	82	65	17
Upper Moreland Township	24,238	43	37	6
Upper Nazareth Township	6,891	9	8	1
Upper Perkiomen	3,870	9	8	1
Upper Pottsgrove Township	5,605	9	8	1
Upper Providence Township, Delaware County	10,497	15	15	0
Upper Providence Township, Montgomery County	24,315	31	28	3
Upper Saucon Township	16,746	22	21	1
Upper Southampton Township	15,022	25	22	3
Upper St. Clair Township	19,911	33	26	7
Upper Uwchlan Township	11,540	11	11	0
Upper Yoder Township	5,158	13	13	0
Uwchlan Township	19,128	22	21	1
Valley Township	7,800	6	6	0
Vandergrift	4,945	9	8	1
Vandling	713	2	2	0
Vernon Township	5,438	2	2	0
Verona	2,410	4	3	1
Versailles	1,477	2	2	0
Walnutport	2,084	4	4	0
Warminster Township	32,423	49	44	5
Warren	9,171	21	15	6
Warrington Township	24,360	32	29	3
Warwick Township, Bucks County	14,661	20	19	1
Washington, Washington County	13,435	33	31	2
Washington Township, Fayette County	3,714	4	4	0
Washington Township, Franklin County	14,678	11	9	2
Washington Township, Northampton County	5,232	5	5	0
Washington Township, Westmoreland County	7,170	7	7	0
Watsontown	2,293	5	5	0
Waverly Township	1,699	3	3	0
Waynesboro	10,889	22	20	2
Waynesburg	3,965	9	9	0
Weatherly	2,431	4	4	0
Wellsboro	3,277	7	7	0
Wesleyville	3,170	8	7	1
West Brandywine Township	7,451	8	7	1
West Brownsville	960	1	1	0
West Caln Township	9,067	2	2	0
West Carroll Township	1,222	2	2	0
West Chester	20,183	60	47	13
West Conshohocken	1,402	12	11	1
West Cornwall Township	2,017	7	6	1
West Deer Township	11,921	12	11	1
West Earl Township	8,368	6	6	0
Western Berks Regional	4,591	6	5	1
West Fallowfield Township	2,591	2	2	0
Westfield	1,039	2	2	0
West Goshen Township	23,237	34	30	4
West Hazleton	4,452	4	3	1
West Hempfield Township	16,540	24	21	3
West Hills Regional	10,167	12	11	1
West Homestead	1,902	7	6	1
West Kittanning	1,114	2	2	0
West Lampeter Township	16,080	16	15	1
West Mahanoy Township	2,749	3	3	0
West Manchester Township	18,865	30	27	3
West Manheim Township	8,438	9	9	0
West Mead Township	5,125	2	2	0
West Mifflin	19,856	39	33	6
West Newton	2,501	2	2	0
West Norriton Township	15,780	30	27	3
West Penn Township	4,331	2	2	0
West Pikeland Township	4,092	4	4	0
West Pike Run	1,547	1	1	0
West Pittston	4,720	2	2	0
West Pottsgrove Township	3,883	8	8	0
West Reading	4,169	15	13	2

(Number.)

State/city	Population	Total law enforcement employees	Total officers	Total civilians
West Sadsbury Township	2,469	4	4	0
West Salem Township	3,447	8	7	1
West Shore Regional	7,736	13	12	1
Westtown-East Goshen Regional	32,299	32	29	3
West View	6,598	13	11	2
West Vincent Township	5,172	7	6	1
West Whiteland Township	18,430	27	25	2
West York	4,550	8	8	0
Whitehall	13,717	25	20	5
Whitehall Township	27,536	49	44	5
White Haven Borough	1,090	3	3	0
Whitemarsh Township	17,866	41	36	5
White Oak	7,682	13	12	1
Whitpain Township	19,377	36	28	8
Wiconisco Township	1,184	1	1	0
Wilkes-Barre	40,418	85	76	9
Wilkes-Barre Township	2,891	15	14	1
Wilkinsburg	15,530	25	23	2
Wilkins Township	6,222	12	12	0
Williamsburg	1,202	1	1	0
Williamsport	28,743	55	51	4
Willistown Township	10,965	20	18	2
Wilson	7,768	13	12	1
Windber	3,901	3	2	1
Womelsdorf	2,854	1	1	0
Woodward Township	2,389	1	1	0
Wrightsville	2,280	4	4	0
Wyoming	3,001	5	5	0
Wyomissing	10,415	23	22	1
Yardley	2,455	3	3	0
Yeadon	11,499	14	13	1
York	43,857	120	105	15
York Area Regional	55,256	48	44	4
Youngsville	1,638	2	2	0
Zelienople	3,670	10	9	1
RHODE ISLAND				
Barrington	16,307	33	26	7
Bristol	22,255	48	39	9
Burrillville	16,441	27	21	6
Central Falls	19,389	48	39	9
Charlestown	7,764	25	20	5
Coventry	35,083	69	57	12
Cranston	81,337	180	149	31
Cumberland	34,973	54	43	11
East Greenwich	13,139	42	34	8
East Providence	47,502	104	86	18
Foster	4,736	13	9	4
Glocester	10,108	20	15	5
Hopkinton	8,104	19	14	5
Jamestown	5,483	19	14	5
Johnston	29,375	77	65	12
Lincoln	21,863	43	36	7
Little Compton	3,498	14	10	4
Middletown	15,993	44	40	4
Narragansett	15,556	52	39	13
Newport	24,812	99	81	18
New Shoreham	1,044	8	4	4
North Kingstown	26,069	53	44	9
North Providence	32,641	82	64	18
North Smithfield	12,447	27	26	1
Pawtucket	71,648	170	136	34
Portsmouth	17,381	39	35	4
Providence	179,854	528	431	97
Richmond	7,598	17	12	5
Scituate	10,631	25	17	8
Smithfield	21,884	55	41	14
South Kingstown	30,823	69	52	17
Tiverton	15,767	46	33	13
Warren	10,498	27	22	5
Warwick	81,617	221	169	52

Table 19. Full-Time Law Enforcement Employees, by Selected State and City, 2017—*Continued*

(Number.)

State/city	Population	Total law enforcement employees	Total officers	Total civilians
Westerly	22,629	60	50	10
West Greenwich	6,167	18	13	5
West Warwick	28,790	60	48	12
Woonsocket	41,543	112	92	20
SOUTH CAROLINA				
Aiken	31,158	111	80	31
Allendale	2,983	9	9	0
Anderson	27,728	129	93	36
Bamberg	3,300	11	9	2
Barnwell	4,508	12	11	1
Batesburg-Leesville	5,462	24	20	4
Beaufort	13,612	55	51	4
Belton	4,426	12	10	2
Bennettsville	8,127	32	30	2
Blacksburg	1,894	11	10	1
Blackville	2,242	7	6	1
Bluffton	20,024	52	52	0
Bonneau	476	5	3	2
Branchville	968	4	3	1
Briarcliffe Acres	568	1	1	0
Burnettown	2,819	2	2	0
Chapin	1,599	7	7	0
Charleston	136,845	533	439	94
Cheraw	5,770	29	21	8
Chester	5,452	23	21	2
Clemson	16,442	42	31	11
Clinton	8,473	50	43	7
Clio	674	3	3	0
Clover	6,098	27	18	9
Columbia	134,957	386	301	85
Conway	23,806	57	50	7
Cowpens	2,326	6	6	0
Darlington	6,090	35	32	3
Dillon	6,568	27	24	3
Due West	1,300	5	5	0
Duncan	3,405	20	19	1
Easley	21,107	54	45	9
Edisto Beach	419	7	7	0
Ehrhardt	491	3	2	1
Elgin	1,582	7	6	1
Florence	38,449	111	87	24
Forest Acres	10,563	33	26	7
Fountain Inn	8,666	29	21	8
Gaffney	12,982	39	36	3
Goose Creek	43,006	91	66	25
Greenville	68,922	244	197	47
Greenwood	23,329	63	57	6
Greer	29,585	80	55	25
Hampton	2,613	12	12	0
Hanahan	24,487	35	32	3
Hardeeville	6,328	25	23	2
Harleyville	693	6	6	0
Hartsville	7,769	31	27	4
Irmo	12,353	26	23	3
Isle of Palms	4,439	28	22	6
Iva	1,296	10	10	0
Jackson	1,794	4	4	0
Johnsonville	1,508	6	5	1
Johnston	2,342	8	8	0
Jonesville	852	5	4	1
Kingstree	3,204	10	9	1
Lake City	6,774	28	23	5
Latta	1,326	6	6	0
Lexington	21,434	59	56	3
Liberty	3,250	14	9	5
Loris	2,695	15	12	3
Lyman	3,513	11	10	1
Manning	4,031	18	17	1
Marion	6,677	21	18	3
Mauldin	25,535	59	48	11

(Number.)

State/city	Population	Total law enforcement employees	Total officers	Total civilians
McCormick	2,493	6	6	0
Moncks Corner	10,818	34	31	3
Mount Pleasant	87,216	168	147	21
Mullins	4,502	25	23	2
Myrtle Beach	33,167	304	219	85
Newberry	10,373	33	30	3
New Ellenton	2,160	4	4	0
North Augusta	23,198	89	64	25
North Charleston	111,305	411	339	72
North Myrtle Beach	16,422	148	82	66
Olar	234	1	1	0
Orangeburg	13,076	87	59	28
Pawleys Island	108	7	5	2
Pelion	710	3	2	1
Port Royal	13,161	23	22	1
Ridgeland	4,158	13	12	1
Ridge Spring	754	2	2	0
Ridgeville	1,751	2	2	0
Salem	149	2	2	0
Salley	424	1	1	0
Saluda	3,626	12	10	2
Scranton	861	2	1	1
South Congaree	2,427	7	6	1
Spartanburg	38,057	140	121	19
Springdale	2,817	8	8	0
Summerville	50,498	124	101	23
Sumter	40,747	179	109	70
Surfside Beach	4,488	30	20	10
Tega Cay	10,367	27	24	3
Travelers Rest	5,130	21	16	5
Union	7,940	31	28	3
Walterboro	5,275	33	26	7
Ware Shoals	2,184	9	8	1
Wellford	2,588	7	6	1
West Columbia	16,426	62	51	11
West Pelzer	934	3	3	0
Whitmire	1,480	5	4	1
Williston	2,975	10	9	1
Woodruff	4,209	10	9	1
York	8,108	38	31	7
SOUTH DAKOTA				
Aberdeen	28,800	51	42	9
Alcester	738	2	2	0
Avon	591	1	1	0
Belle Fourche	5,662	12	10	2
Beresford	1,962	4	4	0
Box Elder	9,623	12	11	1
Brandon	10,090	14	13	1
Brookings	24,198	46	34	12
Burke	583	1	1	0
Canton	3,437	6	6	0
Chamberlain	2,364	6	6	0
Clark	1,033	2	2	0
Deadwood	1,262	16	13	3
Eagle Butte	1,354	3	3	0
Elk Point	1,831	4	4	0
Faith	420	2	2	0
Flandreau	2,331	7	6	1
Freeman	1,308	1	1	0
Gregory	1,237	2	2	0
Groton	1,517	4	4	0
Hot Springs	3,540	8	7	1
Huron	13,204	34	24	10
Jefferson	501	1	1	0
Kadoka	716	1	1	0
Lead	2,990	6	5	1
Lennox	2,364	4	4	0
Madison	7,584	13	12	1
Martin	1,071	2	2	0
Menno	623	1	1	0

State/city	Population	Total law enforcement employees	Total officers	Total civilians
Milbank	3,180	7	7	0
Miller	1,409	4	4	0
Mitchell	15,806	43	27	16
Mobridge	3,587	15	7	8
North Sioux City	2,766	8	7	1
Parkston	1,510	3	3	0
Philip	764	2	2	0
Pierre	14,064	43	26	17
Platte	1,280	2	2	0
Rapid City	74,986	158	126	32
Rosholt	423	1	1	0
Scotland	816	1	1	0
Sioux Falls	177,888	293	258	35
Sisseton	2,426	6	6	0
Spearfish	11,697	31	21	10
Springfield	1,945	2	2	0
Sturgis	6,868	18	15	3
Summerset	2,499	3	3	0
Tea	5,261	6	6	0
Tripp	637	1	1	0
Vermillion	10,892	20	18	2
Viborg	773	1	1	0
Wagner	1,589	6	6	0
Watertown	22,283	55	37	18
Webster	1,795	5	5	0
Whitewood	931	3	3	0
Winner	2,850	10	9	1
Yankton	14,579	28	26	2
TENNESSEE				
Adamsville	2,207	8	7	1
Alamo	2,452	5	4	1
Alcoa	10,128	48	41	7
Alexandria	974	3	3	0
Algood	4,323	11	11	0
Ardmore	1,218	13	8	5
Ashland City	4,642	16	14	2
Athens	13,783	28	26	2
Atoka	9,197	19	18	1
Baileyton	434	3	3	0
Bartlett	58,895	155	121	34
Baxter	1,413	6	6	0
Bean Station	3,090	9	8	1
Belle Meade	2,975	23	16	7
Bells	2,423	5	5	0
Benton	1,307	7	6	1
Berry Hill	536	18	14	4
Big Sandy	533	1	1	0
Blaine	1,879	2	2	0
Bluff City	1,651	8	8	0
Bolivar	5,066	22	20	2
Bradford	989	4	4	0
Brentwood	43,468	77	61	16
Brighton	2,949	7	7	0
Bristol	27,176	87	72	15
Brownsville	9,698	39	34	5
Bruceton	1,427	2	2	0
Burns	1,475	1	1	0
Calhoun	498	3	3	0
Camden	3,546	16	12	4
Carthage	2,283	11	7	4
Caryville	2,161	6	6	0
Celina	1,487	8	6	2
Centerville	3,564	24	14	10
Chapel Hill	1,481	6	6	0
Charleston	678	3	3	0
Chattanooga	178,753	558	483	75
Church Hill	6,739	11	10	1
Clarksville	153,294	350	286	64
Cleveland	44,778	103	91	12
Clifton	2,653	7	7	0

State/city	Population	Total law enforcement employees	Total officers	Total civilians
Clinton	10,146	40	33	7
Collegedale	12,005	22	22	0
Collierville	49,790	137	101	36
Collinwood	963	4	4	0
Columbia	38,031	97	87	10
Cookeville	32,860	90	69	21
Coopertown	4,455	5	4	1
Cornersville	1,252	2	2	0
Covington	8,909	36	35	1
Cowan	1,678	3	3	0
Cross Plains	1,736	1	1	0
Crossville	11,555	46	43	3
Crump	1,390	2	2	0
Cumberland City	298	2	2	0
Dandridge	2,983	12	11	1
Dayton	7,262	18	18	0
Decatur	1,571	6	6	0
Decaturville	876	1	1	0
Decherd	2,426	13	12	1
Dickson	15,637	52	46	6
Dover	1,450	6	5	1
Dresden	2,825	8	7	1
Dunlap	5,185	14	12	2
Dyer	2,225	8	7	1
Dyersburg	16,612	63	55	8
Eagleville	674	2	2	0
East Ridge	21,351	48	43	5
Elizabethton	13,771	42	38	4
Elkton	541	1	1	0
Englewood	1,530	4	4	0
Erin	1,277	5	5	0
Erwin	5,894	14	14	0
Estill Springs	2,031	6	6	0
Ethridge	482	1	1	0
Etowah	3,512	10	9	1
Fairview	8,648	21	21	0
Fayetteville	7,099	28	26	2
Franklin	76,995	139	129	10
Friendship	658	1	1	0
Gainesboro	944	6	5	1
Gallatin	36,689	90	79	11
Gallaway	653	7	5	2
Gates	611	1	1	0
Gatlinburg	4,247	55	45	10
Germantown	39,086	125	99	26
Gibson	376	2	2	0
Gleason	1,381	4	4	0
Goodlettsville	17,119	54	39	15
Gordonsville	1,209	6	6	0
Grand Junction	275	2	2	0
Graysville	1,525	3	3	0
Greenbrier	6,853	16	15	1
Greeneville	15,065	55	52	3
Greenfield	2,077	7	6	1
Halls	2,148	6	5	1
Harriman	6,196	21	18	3
Henderson	6,589	15	15	0
Hendersonville	58,034	127	111	16
Henry	462	2	2	0
Hohenwald	3,666	16	15	1
Hollow Rock	685	1	1	0
Hornbeak	386	1	1	0
Humboldt	8,210	34	28	6
Huntingdon	3,899	16	12	4
Jacksboro	1,929	5	5	0
Jackson	67,031	253	211	42
Jamestown	1,964	9	9	0
Jasper	3,371	8	8	0
Jefferson City	8,351	31	29	2
Jellico	2,219	7	6	1
Johnson City	67,193	176	146	30

(Number.)

State/city	Population	Total law enforcement employees	Total officers	Total civilians
Jonesborough	5,378	21	16	5
Kenton	1,208	4	4	0
Kimball	1,387	9	9	0
Kingsport	52,810	154	117	37
Kingston	5,823	13	12	1
Kingston Springs	2,765	5	4	1
Knoxville	187,539	486	396	90
Lafayette	5,251	22	15	7
La Follette	6,897	34	25	9
La Vergne	35,480	69	56	13
Lawrenceburg	10,780	38	33	5
Lebanon	32,248	109	86	23
Lenoir City	9,187	26	24	2
Lewisburg	11,684	29	28	1
Lexington	7,792	32	27	5
Lookout Mountain	1,892	21	16	5
Loretto	1,760	4	4	0
Loudon	5,811	16	15	1
Madisonville	4,805	20	17	3
Manchester	10,702	35	31	4
Martin	10,656	37	28	9
Maryville	28,918	61	55	6
Mason	1,574	5	4	1
Maynardville	2,348	4	4	0
McEwen	1,712	7	5	2
McKenzie	5,610	23	18	5
McMinnville	13,786	38	35	3
Medina	4,290	10	10	0
Memphis	652,765	2,501	1,972	529
Middleton	641	3	3	0
Milan	7,780	31	24	7
Millersville	6,792	13	13	0
Minor Hill	519	2	1	1
Monteagle	1,169	8	7	1
Monterey	2,867	7	6	1
Morristown	29,774	90	83	7
Moscow	524	4	4	0
Mountain City	2,431	8	8	0
Mount Carmel	5,427	8	7	1
Mount Juliet	34,888	68	55	13
Mount Pleasant	4,902	20	14	6
Munford	6,079	16	16	0
Murfreesboro	136,102	275	228	47
Nashville Metropolitan	674,942	1,725	1,394	331
Newbern	3,288	12	12	0
New Johnsonville	1,909	5	5	0
Newport	6,816	31	27	4
Niota	724	5	4	1
Nolensville	7,889	4	4	0
Norris	1,645	7	7	0
Oakland	7,884	18	17	1
Oak Ridge	29,355	77	60	17
Obion	1,064	2	2	0
Oliver Springs	3,255	14	10	4
Oneida	3,716	17	12	5
Paris	10,194	37	26	11
Parsons	2,355	8	8	0
Pigeon Forge	6,254	70	58	12
Pikeville	1,656	3	3	0
Piperton	1,725	8	8	0
Pittman Center	582	5	5	0
Plainview	2,035	1	1	0
Pleasant View	4,382	6	6	0
Portland	12,710	35	31	4
Pulaski	7,742	26	23	3
Puryear	672	1	1	0
Red Bank	11,838	26	24	2
Red Boiling Springs	1,142	4	4	0
Ridgetop	2,061	7	7	0
Ripley	8,067	29	22	7
Rockwood	5,424	16	15	1

State/city	Population	Total law enforcement employees	Total officers	Total civilians
Rocky Top	1,779	10	7	3
Rogersville	4,367	17	13	4
Rossville	848	7	7	0
Rutherford	1,101	4	4	0
Rutledge	1,201	5	5	0
Savannah	7,023	21	19	2
Scotts Hill	986	2	2	0
Selmer	4,476	18	16	2
Sevierville	16,991	72	57	15
Sharon	897	1	1	0
Shelbyville	21,618	51	41	10
Signal Mountain	8,624	17	15	2
Smithville	4,717	15	14	1
Smyrna	50,091	98	78	20
Sneedville	1,340	1	1	0
Soddy-Daisy	13,264	37	30	7
Somerville	3,139	13	12	1
South Carthage	1,348	4	4	0
South Fulton	2,238	8	7	1
South Pittsburg	3,097	7	7	0
Sparta	5,101	16	15	1
Spencer	1,634	2	2	0
Spring City	1,990	9	9	0
Springfield	16,869	38	31	7
Spring Hill	39,366	54	50	4
Surgoinsville	1,785	1	1	0
Sweetwater	5,957	20	19	1
Tazewell	2,291	6	6	0
Tellico Plains	952	6	5	1
Tiptonville	4,331	7	7	0
Townsend	445	4	4	0
Trenton	4,116	23	17	6
Troy	1,275	4	4	0
Tullahoma	19,386	40	36	4
Tusculum	2,672	2	2	0
Union City	10,544	41	33	8
Vonore	1,506	9	9	0
Wartrace	658	2	1	1
Watertown	1,537	5	5	0
Waverly	4,139	14	13	1
Waynesboro	2,347	7	7	0
Westmoreland	2,328	7	6	1
White Bluff	3,483	5	5	0
White House	11,591	22	19	3
White Pine	2,270	11	10	1
Whiteville	4,481	6	6	0
Whitwell	1,720	6	6	0
Winchester	8,573	24	22	2
Woodbury	2,799	10	9	1
TEXAS				
Abernathy	2,756	5	5	0
Abilene	122,981	260	200	60
Addison	15,795	70	60	10
Alamo	19,351	41	30	11
Alamo Heights	8,507	33	20	13
Allen	101,779	184	127	57
Alpine	5,983	18	12	6
Alton	17,432	23	18	5
Alvarado	4,033	16	14	2
Andrews	14,032	20	19	1
Anna	12,716	15	14	1
Anthony	5,681	15	15	0
Aransas Pass	8,431	37	25	12
Argyle	4,145	11	10	1
Athens	12,826	32	26	6
Atlanta	5,634	17	12	5
Austin	971,949	2,366	1,808	558
Azle	12,266	34	25	9
Baird	1,516	2	2	0
Balch Springs	25,199	53	37	16

Table 19. Full-Time Law Enforcement Employees, by Selected State and City, 2017—*Continued*

(Number.)

State/city	Population	Total law enforcement employees	Total officers	Total civilians
Balcones Heights	3,386	25	21	4
Bangs	1,579	3	3	0
Bayou Vista	1,625	6	6	0
Baytown	76,704	214	164	50
Beaumont	118,456	320	250	70
Bedford	49,947	130	81	49
Beeville	13,317	33	25	8
Bellville	4,304	12	11	1
Belton	21,310	48	36	12
Benbrook	23,236	48	38	10
Big Sandy	1,388	6	6	0
Big Spring	28,747	50	37	13
Bishop	3,135	9	5	4
Blue Mound	2,514	12	7	5
Bogata	1,074	4	4	0
Bovina	1,762	3	3	0
Bowie	5,131	19	15	4
Boyd	1,399	5	5	0
Brady	5,414	17	10	7
Brazoria	3,080	12	7	5
Breckenridge	5,530	17	12	5
Brenham	17,187	38	34	4
Bridge City	8,219	21	15	6
Brookside Village	1,587	4	4	0
Brownwood	19,133	53	32	21
Bryan	84,438	177	143	34
Buda	16,857	21	19	2
Bulverde	5,101	17	16	1
Burkburnett	11,142	26	19	7
Burleson	46,531	79	60	19
Cactus	3,176	11	9	2
Caddo Mills	1,587	5	5	0
Calvert	1,135	4	4	0
Carrollton	135,823	219	167	52
Castle Hills	4,533	28	21	7
Castroville	3,058	10	9	1
Cedar Hill	48,904	90	63	27
Celina	8,388	19	18	1
Cibolo	29,323	38	33	5
Cisco	3,788	11	9	2
Cleburne	30,320	69	50	19
Clute	11,649	30	20	10
Cockrell Hill	4,294	19	15	4
Coleman	4,388	14	10	4
Colleyville	26,737	45	40	5
Collinsville	1,748	3	3	0
Colorado City	3,977	15	8	7
Combes	3,079	8	8	0
Commerce	9,269	22	16	6
Converse	23,510	58	39	19
Coppell	41,809	67	59	8
Copperas Cove	32,895	69	50	19
Corpus Christi	329,256	604	436	168
Corrigan	1,586	17	13	4
Corsicana	24,011	56	43	13
Crandall	3,415	17	17	0
Crowell	823	1	1	0
Crowley	15,340	36	26	10
Crystal City	7,394	15	10	5
Cuero	8,572	16	15	1
Dalhart	8,366	20	16	4
Dallas	1,338,551	3,658	3,053	605
Dalworthington Gardens	2,403	17	12	5
Dayton	7,815	31	20	11
De Kalb	1,652	5	5	0
Del Rio	35,994	77	56	21
Denison	23,814	48	43	5
Denton	136,836	232	171	61
Denver City	4,909	12	7	5
DeSoto	53,163	127	84	43
Devine	4,847	14	11	3

(Number.)

State/city	Population	Total law enforcement employees	Total officers	Total civilians
Diboll	5,363	19	13	6
Dickinson	20,303	48	32	16
Dilley	4,309	10	9	1
Donna	16,641	45	33	12
Driscoll	744	5	3	2
Duncanville	39,603	64	51	13
Eagle Lake	3,722	10	9	1
Early	3,026	10	8	2
Eastland	3,878	12	10	2
Edinburg	89,595	217	161	56
Electra	2,711	13	8	5
El Paso	688,667	1,269	1,043	226
Elsa	6,798	24	18	6
Ennis	19,331	44	36	8
Euless	55,345	131	87	44
Everman	6,417	18	15	3
Fairview	8,547	16	16	0
Farmersville	3,425	12	10	2
Farwell	1,309	3	3	0
Ferris	2,595	16	11	5
Floresville	7,677	19	17	2
Fort Worth	873,069	2,198	1,681	517
Friendswood	39,990	77	57	20
Frisco	172,804	267	173	94
Fulshear	8,350	18	17	1
Fulton	1,616	1	1	0
Gainesville	16,372	52	38	14
Galveston	51,021	197	142	55
Ganado	2,121	3	3	0
Garden Ridge	4,079	14	13	1
Garland	236,243	469	342	127
Georgetown	71,007	127	84	43
Gilmer	5,270	19	15	4
Gladewater	6,422	18	13	5
Glenn Heights	12,509	23	16	7
Godley	1,130	6	6	0
Gonzales	7,734	29	22	7
Grand Prairie	193,249	396	267	129
Grapevine	52,925	146	99	47
Greenville	27,434	66	50	16
Groves	15,701	24	20	4
Haltom City	44,685	85	70	15
Hamlin	2,024	8	5	3
Haskell	3,173	4	4	0
Hawkins	1,305	4	4	0
Hawley	611	1	1	0
Hedwig Village	2,681	23	17	6
Hemphill	1,224	4	4	0
Henderson	13,366	39	29	10
Hereford	14,832	33	27	6
Hewitt	14,443	35	25	10
Hickory Creek	4,413	11	11	0
Hidalgo	14,048	45	35	10
Hooks	2,734	7	7	0
Houston	2,338,235	6,334	5,221	1,113
Hughes Springs	1,777	4	4	0
Hutchins	5,693	25	18	7
Indian Lake	657	3	3	0
Ingleside	10,698	21	16	5
Ingram	1,843	7	6	1
Irving	242,062	490	341	149
Jefferson	2,034	7	6	1
Jersey Village	7,938	27	25	2
Josephine	1,328	2	2	0
Joshua	6,983	14	13	1
Jourdanton	4,404	11	10	1
Junction	2,445	4	4	0
Karnes City	3,400	9	8	1
Keller	47,892	84	49	35
Kenedy	3,401	12	11	1
Kennedale	8,032	22	20	2

Table 19. Full-Time Law Enforcement Employees, by Selected State and City, 2017—*Continued*

(Number.)

State/city	Population	Total law enforcement employees	Total officers	Total civilians
Kermit	6,459	19	13	6
Kerrville	23,610	66	49	17
Kilgore	15,074	48	36	12
Killeen	145,912	302	237	65
Kingsville	26,048	67	47	20
Kirby	8,746	26	13	13
Knox City	1,167	2	2	0
Kyle	41,189	63	38	25
La Feria	7,279	17	15	2
Lakeside	1,411	3	3	0
Lakeview, Harrison County	6,410	13	12	1
Lake Worth	4,921	31	23	8
La Marque	16,796	41	33	8
Lamesa	9,469	18	14	4
Lampasas	7,910	30	19	11
Laredo	260,669	549	470	79
La Vernia	1,484	7	7	0
Lavon	3,247	10	9	1
League City	105,351	155	110	45
Levelland	13,901	34	23	11
Lewisville	106,199	215	155	60
Liberty	9,308	25	19	6
Linden	1,971	6	5	1
Little Elm	46,097	53	49	4
Live Oak	16,214	46	32	14
Lone Star	1,524	7	4	3
Lytle	2,967	9	8	1
Magnolia	2,107	17	15	2
Mansfield	67,233	222	98	124
Manvel	9,756	23	18	5
Marshall	23,564	63	47	16
McAllen	144,162	413	282	131
McKinney	179,934	245	192	53
Melissa	9,270	11	11	0
Memorial Villages	12,319	43	31	12
Mercedes	16,762	38	29	9
Merkel	2,613	6	6	0
Mesquite	144,406	307	219	88
Midland	138,954	239	182	57
Midlothian	24,617	72	46	26
Mineola	4,756	17	13	4
Mineral Wells	14,534	39	28	11
Missouri City	75,863	125	97	28
Monahans	7,765	17	11	6
Montgomery	985	11	10	1
Muleshoe	5,160	14	9	5
Nassau Bay	4,073	14	13	1
Natalia	1,537	5	5	0
Navasota	7,604	26	17	9
Nederland	17,344	40	26	14
New Boston	4,667	18	12	6
Nixon	2,514	5	5	0
North Richland Hills	70,910	184	110	74
Oak Ridge	194	2	2	0
Odessa	121,194	210	160	50
Olmos Park	2,448	14	13	1
Olney	3,147	7	6	1
Omaha	993	2	2	0
Orange	19,552	59	44	15
Ovilla	4,060	10	9	1
Palacios	4,676	16	11	5
Palmer	2,081	11	10	1
Panhandle	2,358	4	4	0
Paris	24,978	81	57	24
Parker	4,541	10	9	1
Pasadena	154,000	358	263	95
Patton Village	1,953	9	8	1
Pearsall	10,222	16	14	2
Pecos	9,820	45	19	26
Penitas	4,935	18	16	2
Pinehurst	2,085	8	6	2

(Number.)

State/city	Population	Total law enforcement employees	Total officers	Total civilians
Plainview	20,641	39	33	6
Pleasanton	10,563	29	22	7
Port Aransas	4,156	28	20	8
Port Arthur	55,583	143	113	30
Port Isabel	5,017	23	18	5
Poteet	3,476	11	10	1
Pottsboro	2,330	10	8	2
Primera	4,860	8	7	1
Princeton	9,934	17	16	1
Prosper	20,442	33	24	9
Queen City	1,464	6	6	0
Rancho Viejo	2,504	8	8	0
Ranger	2,454	4	4	0
Raymondville	11,151	24	15	9
Red Oak	12,833	25	22	3
Reno	3,324	5	5	0
Richland Hills	8,176	20	16	4
Rio Grande City	14,592	43	31	12
Rio Hondo	2,650	7	7	0
River Oaks	7,793	24	18	6
Robinson	11,653	30	22	8
Rockport	10,870	29	26	3
Roma	10,345	37	28	9
Royse City	12,599	22	19	3
Sabinal	1,711	5	4	1
Sachse	25,907	44	27	17
Saginaw	22,994	45	37	8
San Angelo	101,931	201	172	29
San Antonio	1,520,712	2,929	2,305	624
San Benito	24,503	47	39	8
Sansom Park Village	4,904	14	9	5
Santa Fe	13,347	26	20	6
Schertz	40,830	71	53	18
Seabrook	13,958	42	32	10
Seagoville	16,290	32	23	9
Seagraves	2,892	7	5	2
Seguin	29,132	72	52	20
Selma	11,117	34	30	4
Seminole	7,795	14	12	2
Seymour	2,717	7	6	1
Shallowater	2,560	5	5	0
Shavano Park	3,801	19	18	1
Shenandoah	3,019	24	23	1
Sherman	42,122	87	65	22
Shiner	2,148	7	7	0
Shoreacres	1,617	6	6	0
Sinton	5,614	12	11	1
Sour Lake	1,835	8	7	1
South Houston	17,537	42	31	11
Southlake	31,778	76	70	6
South Padre Island	2,881	35	26	9
Southside Place	1,857	12	8	4
Spearman	3,332	4	4	0
Spring Valley	4,312	24	19	5
Stafford	18,530	74	57	17
Stamford	2,961	7	6	1
Stanton	3,069	5	5	0
Stratford	2,092	3	3	0
Sullivan City	4,223	12	8	4
Sulphur Springs	16,281	38	27	11
Sunset Valley	704	14	13	1
Sweeny	3,773	8	8	0
Sweetwater	10,726	30	24	6
Terrell	17,579	58	36	22
Texarkana	37,882	101	89	12
Texas City	48,774	105	83	22
The Colony	43,484	95	62	33
Three Rivers	1,956	11	10	1
Tioga	958	2	2	0
Tool	2,284	10	6	4
Trophy Club	12,999	20	16	4

Table 19. Full-Time Law Enforcement Employees, by Selected State and City, 2017—*Continued*

(Number.)

State/city	Population	Total law enforcement employees	Total officers	Total civilians
Tulia	4,673	17	9	8
Tye	1,260	5	5	0
Tyler	106,115	231	187	44
Universal City	20,668	41	31	10
University Park	25,218	53	39	14
Van Alstyne	3,700	12	8	4
Venus	3,535	12	12	0
Vernon	10,378	26	18	8
Waco	135,997	338	248	90
Waelder	1,133	4	4	0
Wake Village	5,448	9	8	1
Watauga	24,814	40	32	8
Webster	11,149	67	49	18
Weimar	2,173	8	7	1
Westover Hills	714	14	10	4
West University Place	15,676	35	25	10
Wharton	8,769	35	26	9
White Oak	6,343	20	16	4
White Settlement	17,385	44	33	11
Wichita Falls	104,706	275	193	82
Willis	6,450	18	16	2
Wills Point	3,622	11	10	1
Windcrest	5,939	35	26	9
Winnsboro	3,356	14	9	5
Wylie	48,772	67	62	5
Yoakum	6,055	18	12	6
UTAH				
Alta	388	8	4	4
American Fork/Cedar Hills	39,603	45	38	7
Big Water	480	1	1	0
Blanding	4,161	6	5	1
Bluffdale	12,718	11	11	0
Bountiful	44,312	53	36	17
Brian Head	90	5	5	0
Brigham City	19,150	28	25	3
Cedar City	31,624	44	39	5
Centerville	17,635	23	18	5
Clearfield	30,994	48	33	15
Clinton	21,860	20	17	3
Cottonwood Heights	34,400	52	43	9
Draper	48,197	48	39	9
East Carbon	1,555	4	4	0
Enoch	6,691	6	4	2
Ephraim	7,240	5	5	0
Fairview	1,296	1	1	0
Farmington	24,040	22	19	3
Garland	2,500	3	3	0
Grantsville	10,731	15	13	2
Gunnison	3,323	6	4	2
Harrisville	6,512	10	9	1
Heber	15,653	25	19	6
Helper	2,077	6	5	1
Hurricane	16,592	26	23	3
Kamas	2,155	6	6	0
Kanab	4,562	7	6	1
Kaysville	31,873	28	25	3
La Verkin	4,277	3	3	0
Layton	77,048	111	78	33
Lehi	63,605	64	54	10
Lindon	11,085	17	15	2
Logan	51,059	85	54	31
Lone Peak	29,691	25	20	5
Mapleton	9,772	9	8	1
Moab	5,266	16	11	5
Monticello	2,257	3	3	0
Moroni	1,491	1	1	0
Mount Pleasant	3,380	4	4	0
Murray	49,650	86	73	13
Myton	633	1	1	0
Naples	2,203	6	5	1

(Number.)

State/city	Population	Total law enforcement employees	Total officers	Total civilians
Nephi	5,859	12	10	2
North Ogden	19,021	23	19	4
North Park	15,658	12	10	2
North Salt Lake	21,053	27	22	5
Ogden	87,323	181	140	41
Orem	99,045	122	88	34
Park City	8,415	34	30	4
Parowan	3,018	6	5	1
Payson	20,010	25	22	3
Perry	4,902	8	7	1
Pleasant Grove	39,666	36	28	8
Pleasant View	10,036	10	9	1
Price	8,313	19	17	2
Provo	117,540	156	105	51
Richfield	7,755	16	15	1
Riverdale	8,745	22	19	3
Roosevelt	7,057	11	10	1
Roy	38,410	42	38	4
Salem	8,086	11	10	1
Salina	2,561	5	4	1
Salt Lake City	194,968	562	450	112
Sandy	96,957	144	109	35
Santa Clara/Ivins	15,615	17	14	3
Santaquin/Genola	12,900	13	12	1
Saratoga Springs	28,739	24	21	3
Smithfield	11,409	13	12	1
South Jordan	72,533	56	50	6
South Ogden	17,177	25	22	3
South Salt Lake	24,811	67	56	11
Spanish Fork	39,512	40	36	4
Springdale	577	10	8	2
Springville	33,617	37	26	11
St. George	84,007	147	104	43
Stockton	649	3	2	1
Sunset	5,246	9	8	1
Syracuse	29,114	25	23	2
Tooele	34,112	44	36	8
Tremonton	8,551	11	9	2
Washington	26,618	28	24	4
Wellington	1,596	2	2	0
West Bountiful	5,625	10	9	1
West Jordan	115,390	145	110	35
West Valley	137,762	239	197	42
Willard	1,818	3	3	0
Woods Cross	11,627	22	19	3
VERMONT				
Barre	8,655	20	20	0
Barre Town	7,768	8	7	1
Bellows Falls	2,996	10	9	1
Bennington	15,215	32	24	8
Berlin	2,789	8	7	1
Bradford	2,711	2	2	0
Brandon	3,778	7	6	1
Brattleboro	11,536	34	22	12
Brighton	1,170	1	1	0
Bristol	3,908	3	3	0
Burlington	42,230	139	98	41
Canaan	924	1	1	0
Castleton	4,528	5	5	0
Chester	3,039	6	5	1
Colchester	17,353	32	25	7
Dover	1,076	8	7	1
Essex	21,470	31	25	6
Fair Haven	2,572	4	4	0
Hardwick	2,862	8	7	1
Hartford	9,628	26	17	9
Hinesburg	4,561	5	5	0
Killington	777	2	2	0
Ludlow	1,894	9	5	4
Lyndonville	1,166	3	3	0

(Number.)

State/city	Population	Total law enforcement employees	Total officers	Total civilians
Manchester	4,299	13	9	4
Middlebury	8,681	17	15	2
Milton	10,825	17	16	1
Montpelier	7,484	24	16	8
Morristown	5,475	11	11	0
Newport	4,287	14	12	2
Northfield	6,014	7	6	1
Norwich	3,343	4	3	1
Pittsford	2,826	1	1	0
Randolph	4,712	5	5	0
Richmond	4,120	6	6	0
Rutland	15,462	50	38	12
Rutland Town	4,061	3	3	0
Shelburne	7,827	19	11	8
South Burlington	19,146	47	38	9
Springfield	8,993	23	17	6
St. Albans	6,772	30	23	7
St. Johnsbury	7,196	15	9	6
Stowe	4,440	13	13	0
Swanton	6,529	6	6	0
Thetford	2,576	3	3	0
Vergennes	2,593	7	7	0
Weathersfield	2,767	2	2	0
Williston	9,731	17	15	2
Wilmington	1,807	8	6	2
Windsor	3,398	9	9	0
Winhall	750	11	10	1
Winooski	7,105	20	16	4
Woodstock	2,938	9	6	3
VIRGINIA				
Abingdon	8,066	28	25	3
Alexandria	158,256	415	317	98
Altavista	3,470	13	13	0
Amherst	2,201	6	6	0
Appalachia	1,638	5	5	0
Ashland	7,722	29	26	3
Bedford	6,622	26	24	2
Berryville	4,324	9	8	1
Big Stone Gap	5,334	16	15	1
Blacksburg	45,443	75	63	12
Blackstone	3,427	12	11	1
Bluefield	4,894	21	16	5
Boykins	539	1	1	0
Bridgewater	6,119	9	9	0
Bristol	16,795	72	52	20
Broadway	3,889	5	5	0
Brookneal	1,117	2	2	0
Buena Vista	6,413	17	16	1
Burkeville	402	1	1	0
Cape Charles	1,044	6	6	0
Cedar Bluff	1,049	3	3	0
Charlottesville	47,446	151	123	28
Chase City	2,268	10	9	1
Chatham	1,473	3	3	0
Chesapeake	240,119	561	379	182
Chilhowie	1,712	6	6	0
Chincoteague	2,916	14	10	4
Christiansburg	22,272	65	60	5
Clarksville	1,181	8	7	1
Clifton Forge	3,689	12	10	2
Clintwood	1,285	4	4	0
Coeburn	1,970	5	5	0
Colonial Beach	3,577	13	11	2
Colonial Heights	17,820	57	53	4
Covington	5,442	29	18	11
Crewe	2,199	6	5	1
Culpeper	18,232	51	42	9
Damascus	796	4	4	0
Danville	41,680	131	120	11
Dayton	1,621	8	7	1

(Number.)

State/city	Population	Total law enforcement employees	Total officers	Total civilians
Dublin	2,710	8	7	1
Dumfries	5,219	9	9	0
Elkton	2,871	6	5	1
Emporia	5,201	35	24	11
Exmore	1,438	6	6	0
Fairfax City	24,406	77	58	19
Falls Church	14,278	42	33	9
Farmville	8,127	29	27	2
Franklin	8,250	34	26	8
Fredericksburg	29,016	93	65	28
Front Royal	15,270	47	36	11
Galax	6,728	39	23	16
Gate City	1,911	4	4	0
Glade Spring	1,446	2	2	0
Glasgow	1,117	1	1	0
Glen Lyn	118	1	1	0
Gordonsville	1,599	7	7	0
Gretna	1,231	3	3	0
Grottoes	2,821	6	6	0
Grundy	949	6	6	0
Halifax	1,240	3	3	0
Hampton	134,929	361	265	96
Harrisonburg	53,717	117	99	18
Haymarket	2,001	6	6	0
Haysi	473	2	2	0
Herndon	24,561	72	56	16
Hillsville	2,643	15	14	1
Honaker	1,352	4	3	1
Hopewell	22,723	82	63	19
Hurt	1,260	2	2	0
Independence	919	2	2	0
Jonesville	948	4	4	0
Kenbridge	1,214	3	3	0
Kilmarnock	1,431	5	5	0
La Crosse	581	1	1	0
Lawrenceville	1,019	6	6	0
Lebanon	3,260	14	13	1
Leesburg	54,393	93	77	16
Lexington	7,034	20	17	3
Louisa	1,665	6	6	0
Luray	4,804	13	12	1
Lynchburg	80,890	196	171	25
Manassas	41,995	114	90	24
Manassas Park	16,158	39	30	9
Marion	5,837	21	20	1
Martinsville	13,383	50	45	5
Middleburg	856	7	6	1
Middletown	1,345	4	3	1
Mount Jackson	2,048	6	6	0
Narrows	1,963	5	5	0
New Market	2,217	5	5	0
Newport News	181,738	579	431	148
Norfolk	245,190	799	713	86
Norton	3,842	25	17	8
Occoquan	1,082	1	1	0
Onancock	1,266	5	5	0
Onley	513	5	5	0
Orange	5,033	17	15	2
Parksley	841	3	3	0
Pearisburg	2,683	7	7	0
Pembroke	1,086	3	3	0
Pennington Gap	1,759	6	6	0
Petersburg	31,739	114	90	24
Poquoson	11,981	25	24	1
Portsmouth	95,100	297	222	75
Pound	945	5	5	0
Pulaski	8,799	32	28	4
Purcellville	9,779	17	15	2
Quantico	550	1	1	0
Radford	17,641	47	36	11
Remington	637	1	1	0

(Number.)

State/city	Population	Total law enforcement employees	Total officers	Total civilians
Rich Creek	752	1	1	0
Richlands	5,365	23	18	5
Richmond	226,236	835	695	140
Roanoke	100,027	302	254	48
Rocky Mount	4,801	21	19	2
Rural Retreat	1,480	1	1	0
Salem	25,624	86	62	24
Saltville	1,998	7	7	0
Shenandoah	2,328	6	5	1
Smithfield	8,492	23	19	4
South Boston	7,919	31	28	3
South Hill	4,449	22	20	2
Stanley	1,643	5	5	0
Staunton	24,423	62	49	13
Stephens City	1,990	4	4	0
St. Paul	899	6	6	0
Strasburg	6,613	18	17	1
Suffolk	89,922	249	188	61
Tangier	722	1	1	0
Tappahannock	2,386	10	9	1
Tazewell	4,320	15	13	2
Timberville	2,659	6	6	0
Victoria	1,663	3	3	0
Vienna	16,590	50	41	9
Vinton	8,207	24	22	2
Virginia Beach	454,353	984	805	179
Warrenton	9,901	27	25	2
Warsaw	1,483	4	3	1
Waverly	2,033	7	7	0
Waynesboro	22,004	52	42	10
Weber City	1,234	4	4	0
West Point	3,313	10	9	1
White Stone	340	2	2	0
Williamsburg	15,464	41	38	3
Winchester	27,715	80	72	8
Windsor	2,694	6	6	0
Wise	3,056	13	12	1
Woodstock	5,272	18	16	2
Wytheville	8,084	29	25	4
WASHINGTON				
Aberdeen	16,243	51	37	14
Airway Heights	8,460	19	18	1
Algona	3,177	8	7	1
Anacortes	16,838	33	26	7
Arlington	19,302	29	24	5
Asotin	1,302	3	3	0
Auburn	78,718	131	113	18
Bainbridge Island	24,635	25	22	3
Battle Ground	20,516	28	24	4
Bellevue	143,703	212	172	40
Bellingham	88,652	176	117	59
Black Diamond	4,422	10	9	1
Blaine	5,245	15	13	2
Bonney Lake	20,844	34	29	5
Bothell	45,357	84	59	25
Bremerton	41,173	67	54	13
Brewster	2,335	6	5	1
Brier	6,840	8	7	1
Buckley	5,234	11	9	2
Burien	51,479	74	52	22
Burlington	8,830	31	26	5
Camas	22,973	30	27	3
Carnation	2,032	3	2	1
Castle Rock	2,228	5	4	1
Centralia	17,048	37	28	9
Chehalis	7,538	23	18	5
Cheney	12,510	21	15	6
Chewelah	2,641	6	5	1
Clarkston	7,359	16	14	2
Cle Elum	2,895	8	7	1

(Number.)

State/city	Population	Total law enforcement employees	Total officers	Total civilians
Clyde Hill	3,316	10	8	2
Colfax	2,913	5	5	0
College Place	9,198	13	11	2
Colville	4,805	11	9	2
Connell	5,656	7	7	0
Cosmopolis	1,593	6	5	1
Coulee Dam	1,088	3	3	0
Coupeville	1,934	2	2	0
Covington	21,001	24	18	6
Des Moines	31,415	44	34	10
Dupont	9,721	13	11	2
Duvall	7,875	12	12	0
East Wenatchee	14,097	23	20	3
Eatonville	2,994	5	4	1
Edgewood	10,984	9	9	0
Edmonds	42,197	61	52	9
Ellensburg	20,026	37	29	8
Elma	3,044	8	7	1
Enumclaw	11,745	29	15	14
Ephrata	8,086	19	16	3
Everett	110,040	231	192	39
Everson	4,217	7	6	1
Federal Way	98,014	156	127	29
Ferndale	13,757	22	19	3
Fife	10,264	40	30	10
Fircrest	6,830	9	9	0
Forks	3,822	12	6	6
Gig Harbor	9,494	21	19	2
Goldendale	3,455	8	7	1
Grand Coulee	2,051	8	8	0
Grandview	11,203	23	18	5
Granger	3,803	6	6	0
Hoquiam	8,386	25	24	1
Issaquah	38,592	65	36	29
Kalama	2,509	7	6	1
Kelso	12,070	31	27	4
Kenmore	22,673	20	16	4
Kennewick	81,499	114	99	15
Kent	128,990	201	146	55
Kettle Falls	1,609	3	2	1
Kirkland	88,898	136	99	37
Kittitas	1,452	2	2	0
La Center	3,177	9	7	2
Lacey	48,597	62	49	13
Lake Forest Park	13,375	22	19	3
Lake Stevens	32,288	37	29	8
Lakewood	61,080	114	99	15
Langley	1,111	4	4	0
Liberty Lake	9,505	13	12	1
Long Beach	1,389	8	7	1
Longview	37,424	69	57	12
Lynden	14,302	19	15	4
Lynnwood	38,469	97	68	29
Mabton	2,292	5	5	0
Maple Valley	26,214	25	20	5
Marysville	68,950	92	66	26
Mattawa	4,423	5	5	0
McCleary	1,627	4	4	0
Medina	3,293	11	9	2
Mercer Island	25,553	35	31	4
Mill Creek	20,664	31	25	6
Milton	8,121	13	13	0
Monroe	18,596	42	30	12
Montesano	3,902	9	8	1
Morton	1,149	3	3	0
Moses Lake	22,985	40	32	8
Mountlake Terrace	21,402	34	27	7
Mount Vernon	35,085	55	42	13
Moxee	4,120	6	5	1
Mukilteo	21,662	36	29	7
Napavine	1,881	2	2	0

Table 19. Full-Time Law Enforcement Employees, by Selected State and City, 2017—*Continued*

(Number.)

State/city	Population	Total law enforcement employees	Total officers	Total civilians
Newcastle	11,775	13	10	3
Normandy Park	6,702	9	8	1
Oak Harbor	23,371	37	24	13
Ocean Shores	5,872	9	9	0
Odessa	863	2	2	0
Olympia	51,923	98	68	30
Omak	4,829	12	11	1
Oroville	1,673	6	5	1
Orting	7,863	12	11	1
Othello	8,225	25	16	9
Pacific	7,210	13	11	2
Palouse	1,053	3	3	0
Pasco	72,146	87	78	9
Pe Ell	645	1	1	0
Port Angeles	19,964	58	31	27
Port Orchard	14,253	24	22	2
Port Townsend	9,596	17	14	3
Poulsbo	10,600	23	19	4
Prosser	6,091	14	13	1
Pullman	33,897	43	29	14
Puyallup	41,242	78	55	23
Quincy	7,488	23	16	7
Raymond	2,872	7	6	1
Reardan	567	1	1	0
Redmond	63,889	124	82	42
Renton	102,470	151	121	30
Republic	1,069	2	2	0
Richland	56,151	77	63	14
Ridgefield	7,532	11	10	1
Ritzville	1,617	4	4	0
Roy	827	2	1	1
Royal City	2,203	3	3	0
Ruston	828	3	3	0
Sammamish	64,857	40	32	8
SeaTac	29,200	62	45	17
Seattle	721,365	1,963	1,448	515
Sedro Woolley	11,545	18	15	3
Selah	7,839	18	15	3
Sequim	7,025	22	19	3
Shelton	10,000	20	18	2
Shoreline	55,703	71	52	19
Snohomish	10,045	20	18	2
Snoqualmie	13,648	26	22	4
Soap Lake	1,574	5	4	1
South Bend	1,637	5	4	1
Spokane	217,066	409	319	90
Spokane Valley	97,430	127	97	30
Stanwood	7,142	13	11	2
Steilacoom	6,364	11	10	1
Sumas	1,426	6	5	1
Sumner	10,060	22	18	4
Sunnyside	16,480	53	28	25
Tacoma	213,504	372	334	38
Tenino	1,842	5	4	1
Tieton	1,292	3	2	1
Toledo	740	5	4	1
Tonasket	1,010	5	4	1
Toppenish	8,974	17	13	4
Tukwila	20,183	93	76	17
Tumwater	22,961	35	29	6
Twisp	957	3	3	0
Union Gap	6,104	24	22	2
University Place	33,662	16	15	1
Vancouver	176,884	254	205	49
Walla Walla	32,189	77	47	30
Wapato	5,073	14	11	3
Warden	2,722	5	4	1
Washougal	15,698	25	20	5
Wenatchee	34,191	48	38	10
Westport	2,027	8	7	1
West Richland	14,603	23	19	4

(Number.)

State/city	Population	Total law enforcement employees	Total officers	Total civilians
White Salmon	2,495	7	6	1
Winthrop	436	3	2	1
Woodinville	12,181	19	15	4
Woodland	6,022	11	9	2
Yakima	94,375	184	138	46
Yelm	9,304	15	13	2
Zillah	3,162	9	8	1
WEST VIRGINIA				
Alderson	1,171	3	3	0
Anmoore	747	1	1	0
Ansted	1,368	3	2	1
Athens	924	1	1	0
Barboursville	4,315	24	22	2
Barrackville	1,312	3	2	1
Beckley	16,862	69	50	19
Belington	1,908	3	3	0
Belle	1,181	4	4	0
Benwood	1,332	6	6	0
Berkeley Springs	608	2	2	0
Bethlehem	2,381	5	5	0
Bluefield	10,148	33	27	6
Bradshaw	290	1	1	0
Bramwell	350	2	2	0
Bridgeport	8,401	35	31	4
Buckhannon	5,610	11	10	1
Burnsville	494	2	2	0
Cameron	882	3	3	0
Capon Bridge	371	2	2	0
Cedar Grove	929	1	1	0
Ceredo	1,365	9	5	4
Chapmanville	1,161	5	5	0
Charleston	48,788	187	163	24
Charles Town	6,062	17	15	2
Chesapeake	1,469	3	3	0
Chester	2,456	6	5	1
Clarksburg	15,946	43	39	4
Clendenin	1,164	4	4	0
Danville	632	1	1	0
Davy	364	1	1	0
Delbarton	519	3	3	0
Dunbar	7,486	17	16	1
Eleanor	1,617	2	2	0
Elkins	7,188	14	12	2
Fairmont	18,604	39	33	6
Farmington	374	2	1	1
Fayetteville	2,839	10	10	0
Follansbee	2,816	7	7	0
Fort Gay	665	3	3	0
Gary	850	1	1	0
Gassaway	901	1	1	0
Gauley Bridge	580	1	1	0
Gilbert	407	2	2	0
Glasgow	865	4	4	0
Glen Dale	1,433	11	6	5
Glenville	1,512	3	3	0
Grafton	5,121	9	8	1
Grantsville	535	1	1	0
Grant Town	611	1	1	0
Granville	3,238	15	15	0
Hamlin	1,110	1	1	0
Handley	334	1	1	0
Harpers Ferry/Bolivar	1,339	3	2	1
Harrisville	1,731	1	1	0
Hartford City	589	1	1	0
Hinton	2,436	6	5	1
Huntington	47,933	100	97	3
Hurricane	6,658	18	16	2
Iaeger	261	1	1	0
Kenova	3,029	13	8	5
Kermit	366	1	1	0

Table 19. Full-Time Law Enforcement Employees, by Selected State and City, 2017—*Continued*

(Number.)

State/city	Population	Total law enforcement employees	Total officers	Total civilians
Keyser	5,163	15	10	5
Kimball	170	1	1	0
Kingwood	2,959	2	2	0
Lewisburg	3,935	14	12	2
Logan	1,572	11	8	3
Lumberport	856	1	1	0
Mabscott	1,341	5	3	2
Madison	2,831	8	6	2
Man	671	3	3	0
Mannington	2,058	4	4	0
Marmet	1,417	5	5	0
Martinsburg	17,761	52	43	9
Mason	927	7	6	1
Matewan	447	2	1	1
McMechen	1,802	5	4	1
Milton	2,648	8	7	1
Monongah	1,116	1	1	0
Montgomery	1,567	4	4	0
Moorefield	2,460	10	9	1
Morgantown	31,215	89	78	11
Moundsville	8,691	20	16	4
Mount Hope	1,341	5	4	1
Mullens	1,419	4	4	0
New Cumberland	1,043	2	2	0
New Haven	1,508	1	1	0
New Martinsville	5,151	15	11	4
Nitro	6,645	19	17	2
Nutter Fort	1,565	6	6	0
Oak Hill	8,490	19	15	4
Oceana	1,263	4	4	0
Paden City	2,465	4	3	1
Parkersburg	30,475	83	70	13
Parsons	1,416	1	1	0
Paw Paw	491	2	1	1
Pennsboro	1,055	1	1	0
Petersburg	2,601	2	2	0
Philippi	3,640	6	6	0
Piedmont	828	1	1	0
Pineville	611	3	3	0
Point Pleasant	4,219	9	8	1
Pratt	582	3	3	0
Princeton	5,935	21	19	2
Rainelle	1,465	5	4	1
Ranson	5,303	16	15	1
Ravenswood	3,817	11	10	1
Rhodell	166	2	1	1
Richwood	1,940	3	3	0
Ridgeley	638	1	1	0
Ripley	3,243	10	9	1
Rivesville	934	1	1	0
Romney	1,746	4	3	1
Ronceverte	1,731	6	6	0
Salem	1,533	3	3	0
Shepherdstown	1,965	6	5	1
Shinnston	2,154	8	8	0
Sistersville	1,313	4	4	0
Smithers	771	2	2	0
Sophia	1,306	2	2	0
South Charleston	12,756	47	44	3
Spencer	2,136	6	6	0
St. Albans	10,476	28	26	2
Star City	2,059	7	7	0
St. Marys	1,834	4	4	0
Stonewood	1,744	2	2	0
Summersville	3,411	17	16	1
Sutton	1,040	2	2	0
Sylvester	147	1	1	0
Terra Alta	1,493	2	2	0
Triadelphia	754	1	1	0
Vienna	10,409	24	20	4
War	735	2	2	0

State/city	Population	Total law enforcement employees	Total officers	Total civilians
Wayne	1,356	3	2	1
Webster Springs	715	5	4	1
Weirton	18,870	39	35	4
Welch	1,735	6	5	1
Wellsburg	2,634	7	6	1
West Liberty	1,430	1	1	0
West Logan	383	1	1	0
West Milford	613	2	2	0
Weston	4,035	9	7	2
Westover	4,283	13	12	1
Wheeling	27,196	77	66	11
White Hall	659	4	4	0
White Sulphur Springs	2,417	7	6	1
Whitesville	459	2	2	0
Williamson	2,883	6	5	1
Williamstown	2,946	8	7	1
Winfield	2,366	6	6	0
WISCONSIN				
Adams	1,878	5	5	0
Albany	1,010	3	3	0
Algoma	3,086	8	4	4
Alma	712	1	1	0
Altoona	7,624	15	14	1
Amery	2,825	6	6	0
Antigo	7,807	18	15	3
Appleton	74,660	133	107	26
Arcadia	3,077	4	4	0
Ashland	7,915	20	19	1
Ashwaubenon	17,326	57	50	7
Athens	1,090	1	1	0
Balsam Lake	975	1	1	0
Bangor	1,487	3	3	0
Baraboo	12,191	34	29	5
Barneveld	1,226	1	1	0
Barron	3,294	6	6	0
Bayfield	473	3	3	0
Bayside	4,398	13	12	1
Beaver Dam	16,525	35	31	4
Belleville	2,438	7	6	1
Beloit	36,724	81	70	11
Beloit Town	7,648	15	13	2
Berlin	5,371	12	11	1
Big Bend	1,324	5	4	1
Birchwood	425	1	1	0
Black River Falls	3,541	6	5	1
Blair	1,384	3	3	0
Bloomer	3,503	7	6	1
Bloomfield	6,295	8	8	0
Blue Mounds	967	2	2	0
Boscobel	3,137	6	6	0
Boyceville	1,099	1	1	0
Brillion	3,121	8	8	0
Brodhead	3,274	12	8	4
Brookfield	38,033	87	70	17
Brookfield Township	6,108	14	13	1
Brown Deer	12,015	34	31	3
Burlington	10,686	26	20	6
Butler	1,817	8	7	1
Caledonia	24,945	36	34	2
Campbellsport	1,971	1	1	0
Campbell Township	4,380	5	5	0
Cashton	1,100	2	2	0
Cedarburg	11,529	26	19	7
Chenequa	588	9	8	1
Chetek	2,155	5	4	1
Chilton	3,809	7	7	0
Chippewa Falls	14,141	27	23	4
Cleveland	1,455	2	2	0
Clinton	2,122	5	5	0
Clintonville	4,379	15	11	4

(Number.)

State/city	Population	Total law enforcement employees	Total officers	Total civilians
Colby-Abbotsford	4,079	8	7	1
Colfax	1,161	1	1	0
Columbus	5,035	11	9	2
Cornell	1,419	2	2	0
Cottage Grove	7,105	15	13	2
Crandon	1,850	4	3	1
Cross Plains	4,236	6	5	1
Cuba City	2,050	4	4	0
Cudahy	18,191	40	30	10
Cumberland	2,130	5	5	0
Darlington	2,365	5	5	0
Deforest	9,818	21	18	3
Delafield	7,563	18	16	2
Delavan	9,986	28	23	5
Delavan Town	5,333	12	11	1
De Pere	25,066	40	36	4
Dodgeville	4,737	10	10	0
Durand	1,833	3	3	0
Eagle River	1,423	7	6	1
Eagle Village	2,006	2	2	0
East Troy	4,283	7	7	0
Eau Claire	68,687	136	98	38
Edgar	1,450	1	1	0
Edgerton	5,574	11	10	1
Eleva	670	1	1	0
Elkhart Lake	965	3	3	0
Elkhorn	9,817	18	16	2
Ellsworth	3,220	5	5	0
Elm Grove	6,216	26	18	8
Elroy	1,354	3	3	0
Evansville	5,305	11	10	1
Everest Metropolitan	17,321	30	26	4
Fall Creek	1,304	2	2	0
Fall River	1,681	2	2	0
Fennimore	2,485	5	5	0
Fitchburg	29,535	62	50	12
Fond du Lac	42,929	81	73	8
Fontana	1,718	7	6	1
Fort Atkinson	12,566	25	19	6
Fox Lake	1,461	3	3	0
Fox Point	6,694	18	17	1
Fox Valley Metro	21,789	28	26	2
Franklin	36,248	75	59	16
Frederic	1,091	1	1	0
Freedom	6,132	2	2	0
Galesville	1,546	4	4	0
Geneva Town	5,049	8	7	1
Genoa City	3,019	7	6	1
Germantown	20,072	43	32	11
Gillett	1,328	3	3	0
Gilman	393	1	1	0
Glendale	12,763	49	43	6
Grafton	11,579	29	22	7
Grand Chute	22,667	36	31	5
Grand Rapids	7,392	8	6	2
Grantsburg	1,279	3	3	0
Green Bay	105,331	224	185	39
Greendale	14,242	38	29	9
Greenfield	36,882	75	57	18
Green Lake	933	3	3	0
Hales Corners	7,675	18	16	2
Hammond	1,886	4	3	1
Hartford	14,664	29	25	4
Hartland	9,229	18	16	2
Hayward	2,313	8	7	1
Hazel Green	1,241	2	2	0
Highland	836	1	1	0
Hillsboro	1,423	5	5	0
Hobart-Lawrence	14,231	10	9	1
Holmen	9,714	13	12	1
Horicon	3,657	8	7	1

(Number.)

State/city	Population	Total law enforcement employees	Total officers	Total civilians
Hortonville	2,739	6	5	1
Hudson	13,788	28	25	3
Hurley	1,448	7	6	1
Independence	1,336	3	3	0
Iron River	1,121	2	2	0
Jackson	6,960	12	11	1
Janesville	64,257	113	99	14
Jefferson	8,033	17	14	3
Juneau	2,703	5	4	1
Kaukauna	15,969	27	26	1
Kenosha	99,671	210	199	11
Kewaskum	4,122	8	8	0
Kewaunee	2,857	6	6	0
Kiel	3,697	8	7	1
Kohler	2,102	8	7	1
Kronenwetter	7,687	8	7	1
La Crosse	52,234	114	94	20
Ladysmith	3,149	8	7	1
Lake Delton	2,982	22	20	2
Lake Geneva	7,850	34	25	9
Lake Hallie	6,678	10	9	1
Lake Mills	5,857	12	10	2
Lancaster	3,742	9	8	1
Lena	542	1	1	0
Linn Township	2,401	6	6	0
Lodi	3,060	11	5	6
Lomira	2,356	4	3	1
Luxemburg	2,562	2	2	0
Lyndon Station	476	2	1	1
Madison	255,850	593	484	109
Manawa	1,290	3	3	0
Manitowoc	32,813	74	64	10
Maple Bluff	1,342	6	5	1
Marathon City	1,505	6	3	3
Marinette	10,655	28	24	4
Marion	1,199	3	3	0
Markesan	1,400	3	3	0
Marshall Village	3,950	9	8	1
Marshfield	18,366	45	37	8
Mauston	4,368	9	8	1
Mayville	4,907	8	7	1
McFarland	8,407	18	16	2
Medford	4,336	10	9	1
Menasha	17,899	36	29	7
Menomonee Falls	36,963	68	54	14
Menomonie	16,493	33	26	7
Mequon	24,250	48	39	9
Merrill	9,154	25	22	3
Middleton	19,369	48	38	10
Milton	5,585	13	11	2
Milwaukee	595,168	2,292	1,824	468
Mineral Point	2,489	6	6	0
Minocqua	4,447	17	12	5
Mishicot	1,402	2	2	0
Mondovi	2,612	4	4	0
Monona	8,285	24	20	4
Monroe	10,709	36	26	10
Montello	1,429	3	2	1
Mosinee	4,016	8	7	1
Mount Horeb	7,518	12	11	1
Mount Pleasant	26,387	53	48	5
Mukwonago	7,898	21	14	7
Mukwonago Town	8,141	7	6	1
Muscoda	1,241	3	3	0
Muskego	25,004	45	36	9
Neenah	25,983	51	41	10
Neillsville	2,425	7	6	1
Nekoosa	2,421	6	6	0
New Berlin	39,839	86	73	13
New Glarus	2,159	2	2	0
New Holstein	3,112	7	6	1

Table 19. Full-Time Law Enforcement Employees, by Selected State and City, 2017—*Continued*

(Number.)

State/city	Population	Total law enforcement employees	Total officers	Total civilians
New Lisbon	2,490	4	4	0
New London	7,150	19	17	2
New Richmond	8,987	17	16	1
Niagara	1,564	4	4	0
North Fond du Lac	5,038	10	9	1
North Hudson	3,825	5	4	1
Oak Creek	36,126	78	56	22
Oconomowoc	16,650	30	23	7
Oconomowoc Lake	589	6	6	0
Oconomowoc Town	8,670	12	11	1
Oconto	4,455	10	9	1
Oconto Falls	2,825	5	5	0
Omro	3,562	7	6	1
Onalaska	18,847	31	28	3
Oregon	10,426	20	18	2
Osceola	2,510	5	4	1
Oshkosh	66,652	110	95	15
Osseo	1,695	4	4	0
Palmyra	1,768	6	6	0
Park Falls	2,266	7	7	0
Pepin	786	1	1	0
Peshtigo	3,391	6	6	0
Pewaukee Village	8,171	20	18	2
Phillips	1,359	10	5	5
Platteville	12,769	26	20	6
Pleasant Prairie	20,904	44	33	11
Plover	12,627	21	18	3
Plymouth	8,544	16	16	0
Portage	10,372	26	22	4
Port Edwards	1,739	3	3	0
Port Washington	11,702	25	20	5
Poynette	2,492	5	4	1
Prairie du Chien	5,690	13	12	1
Prescott	4,223	7	6	1
Princeton	1,169	3	3	0
Pulaski	3,544	8	7	1
Racine	77,371	223	191	32
Reedsburg	9,583	27	20	7
Rhinelander	7,560	18	15	3
Rice Lake	8,406	17	17	0
Richland Center	4,986	13	11	2
Rio	1,043	4	2	2
Ripon	7,770	21	15	6
Ripon Town	1,391	1	1	0
River Falls	15,389	26	23	3
River Hills	1,591	10	10	0
Rome Town	2,710	6	6	0
Rosendale	1,035	1	1	0
Rothschild	5,361	12	10	2
Sauk Prairie	4,652	15	13	2
Saukville	4,473	13	11	2
Seymour	3,441	6	6	0
Shawano	9,014	22	20	2
Sheboygan	48,595	100	80	20
Sheboygan Falls	7,829	16	15	1
Shiocton	918	1	1	0
Shorewood	13,405	28	24	4
Shorewood Hills	2,131	8	6	2
Shullsburg	1,205	1	1	0
Siren	774	3	2	1
Slinger	5,320	12	11	1
South Milwaukee	21,039	39	33	6
Sparta	9,721	21	19	2
Spencer	1,909	3	3	0
Spooner	2,581	8	7	1
Spring Green	1,658	4	3	1
Spring Valley	1,347	1	1	0
Stanley	3,668	5	5	0
St. Croix Falls	2,050	6	5	1
Stevens Point	26,379	49	44	5
St. Francis	9,487	22	21	1

(Number.)

State/city	Population	Total law enforcement employees	Total officers	Total civilians
Stoughton	13,213	28	22	6
Strum	1,114	2	2	0
Sturgeon Bay	8,876	22	20	2
Sturtevant	6,931	11	10	1
Summit	4,871	10	10	0
Sun Prairie	33,385	71	52	19
Superior	26,352	60	55	5
Theresa	1,198	2	2	0
Thiensville	3,174	8	7	1
Thorp	1,631	3	3	0
Three Lakes	2,120	5	5	0
Tomah	9,441	21	19	2
Tomahawk	3,169	9	8	1
Town of East Troy	4,113	7	6	1
Town of Madison	6,953	15	14	1
Town of Menasha	18,872	32	27	5
Trempealeau	1,633	3	3	0
Twin Lakes	6,100	17	12	5
Two Rivers	11,190	28	25	3
Verona	13,390	25	22	3
Viroqua	4,402	11	9	2
Walworth	2,842	8	7	1
Washburn	2,034	5	5	0
Waterloo	3,333	9	8	1
Watertown	23,814	52	38	14
Waukesha	72,565	149	117	32
Waunakee	13,866	22	20	2
Waupaca	5,924	16	15	1
Waupun	11,332	18	17	1
Wausau	38,832	84	74	10
Wautoma	2,120	5	5	0
Wauwatosa	48,208	112	88	24
Webster	622	2	2	0
West Allis	60,043	154	125	29
West Bend	31,783	70	53	17
Westby	2,283	3	3	0
Westfield	1,226	4	2	2
West Milwaukee	4,169	25	20	5
West Salem	4,993	8	7	1
Whitefish Bay	13,952	25	24	1
Whitehall	1,609	4	4	0
Whitewater	14,538	32	22	10
Wild Rose	699	2	2	0
Williams Bay	2,598	8	7	1
Wilton	501	1	1	0
Winneconne	2,444	6	5	1
Wisconsin Dells	2,823	19	14	5
Wisconsin Rapids	17,807	39	35	4
Woodruff	1,977	6	5	1
WYOMING				
Afton	2,008	4	4	0
Buffalo	4,590	21	12	9
Casper	60,034	125	88	37
Cheyenne	64,730	124	106	18
Cody	9,885	24	22	2
Diamondville	744	4	3	1
Douglas	6,615	26	18	8
Evanston	12,044	29	23	6
Evansville	3,014	12	10	2
Gillette	32,826	77	51	26
Glenrock	2,599	12	7	5
Green River	12,289	31	26	5
Greybull	1,876	6	5	1
Hanna	808	1	1	0
Jackson	10,692	36	30	6
Kemmerer	2,792	6	6	0
Lander	7,672	19	18	1
Laramie	32,632	73	48	25
Mills	3,875	18	14	4
Moorcroft	1,072	4	3	1

Table 19. Full-Time Law Enforcement Employees, by Selected State and City, 2017—*Continued*

(Number.)

State/city	Population	Total law enforcement employees	Total officers	Total civilians
Newcastle	3,537	14	6	8
Pine Bluffs	1,155	1	1	0
Powell	6,422	23	16	7
Rawlins	9,050	27	17	10
Riverton	11,028	41	27	14
Rock Springs	23,886	56	43	13
Saratoga	1,686	9	4	5
Sheridan	18,036	45	29	16
Sundance	1,294	3	3	0
Thermopolis	2,925	12	7	5
Torrington	6,729	22	15	7
Wheatland	3,602	10	9	1
Worland	5,287	12	11	1

[1]The employee data presented in this table for Charlotte-Mecklenburg represent only Charlotte-Mecklenburg Police Department and exclude Mecklenburg County Sheriff's Office.

Table 20. Murder Victims, by Race, Ethnicity, and Sex, 2017

(Number.)

Race	Total	Sex		
		Male	Female	Unknown
Total	15,129	11,862	3,222	45
White	6,579	4,616	1,958	5
Black..	7,851	6,789	1,060	2
Other race	456	315	141	0
Unknown race	243	142	63	38
Hispanic or Latino[1]	2,354	1,899	454	1
Not Hispanic or Latino[1]	9,761	7,692	2,065	4
Unknown[1]	2,085	1,550	510	25

[1]Not all agencies provide ethnicity data, therefore the race and ethnicity totals will not equal.

Table 20A. Murder Victims, by Age, Sex, Race, and Ethnicity, 2017

(Number; percent; single victim/single offender.)

Age	Total	Sex			Race				Ethnicity[1]		
		Male	Female	Unknown	White	Black or African American	Other[2]	Unknown	Hispanic/ Latino	Not Hispanic/ Latino	Unknown
Total	15,129	11,862	3,222	45	6,579	7,851	456	243	2,354	9,761	2,085
Percent distribution[3].........................	100.0	78.4	21.3	0.3	43.5	51.9	3.0	1.6	16.6	68.7	14.7
Under 18[4]	1,208	864	341	3	512	642	33	21	215	754	178
Under 22[4]...................................	2,994	2,405	583	6	1,113	1,767	73	41	548	1,863	429
18 and over[4]................................	13,754	10,893	2,840	21	6,010	7,149	417	178	2,120	8,941	1,840
Infant (under 1).............................	167	93	74	0	85	74	6	2	25	103	31
1 to 4	248	150	97	1	127	108	7	6	41	153	41
5 to 8	91	56	35	0	44	41	5	1	15	59	11
9 to 12	61	29	31	1	31	22	1	7	9	36	11
13 to 16	365	298	67	0	136	218	10	1	77	226	46
17 to 19	1,132	985	146	1	373	734	16	9	204	712	156
20 to 24	2,428	2,055	369	4	827	1,513	54	34	453	1,532	311
25 to 29	2,457	2,059	397	1	840	1,526	63	28	379	1,557	317
30 to 34	1,790	1,441	348	1	719	983	68	20	282	1,188	230
35 to 39	1,508	1,191	315	2	637	810	44	17	259	958	216
40 to 44	1,077	834	242	1	521	507	37	12	187	672	141
45 to 49	928	684	238	6	479	393	31	25	134	610	125
50 to 54	832	622	204	6	475	310	30	17	101	549	120
55 to 59	691	515	176	0	426	235	24	6	75	483	89
60 to 64	456	324	132	0	286	143	21	6	47	318	63
65 to 69	314	206	108	0	204	97	11	2	29	219	53
70 to 74	151	91	60	0	100	41	9	1	6	113	14
75 and over.................................	266	124	142	0	212	36	13	5	12	207	43
Unknown......................................	167	105	41	21	57	60	6	44	19	66	67

[1]Not all agencies provide ethnicity data, therefore the race and ethnicity totals will not equal.
[2]Includes American Indian or Alaska Native, Asian, Native Hawaiian or Other Pacific Islander.
[3]Because of rounding, the percentages may not add to 100.0.
[4]Does not include unknown ages.

Table 21. Murder Offenders, by Age, Sex, Race, and Ethnicity, 2017

(Number; percent; single victim/single offender.)

Age	Total	Sex			Race				Ethnicity[1]		
		Male	Female	Unknown	White	Black or African American	Other[2]	Unknown	Hispanic/Latino	Not Hispanic/Latino	Unknown
Total	17,251	10,665	1,443	5,143	5,125	6,444	314	5,368	1,505	6,324	5,353
Percent distribution[3].........................	100.0	61.8	8.4	29.8	29.7	37.4	1.8	31.1	11.4	48.0	40.6
Under 18[4]	803	730	73	0	295	488	10	10	113	401	73
Under 22[4]	2,932	2,626	284	22	1,045	1,766	57	64	430	1,494	267
18 and over[4]	10,669	9,264	1,351	54	4,736	5,464	301	168	1,336	5,621	1,082
Infant (under 1)..............................	0	0	0	0	0	0	0	0	0	0	0
1 to 4	0	0	0	0	0	0	0	0	0	0	0
5 to 8	1	0	1	0	0	1	0	0	0	0	1
9 to 12	7	6	1	0	4	3	0	0	0	5	0
13 to 16	405	365	40	0	151	242	5	7	56	199	40
17 to 19	1,467	1,327	135	5	524	903	21	19	224	755	123
20 to 24	2,519	2,222	279	18	858	1,545	63	53	347	1,298	251
25 to 29	2,053	1,764	282	7	826	1,152	54	21	274	1,068	227
30 to 34	1,465	1,259	197	9	676	718	52	19	184	786	148
35 to 39	1,062	916	145	1	543	472	33	14	132	546	107
40 to 44	754	627	123	4	387	330	26	11	81	398	80
45 to 49	566	480	86	0	323	214	20	9	60	289	61
50 to 54	421	357	57	7	233	159	18	11	34	249	37
55 to 59	335	290	43	2	213	109	8	5	31	182	32
60 to 64	179	163	16	0	110	61	5	3	19	102	17
65 to 69	93	84	9	0	69	21	1	2	5	55	7
70 to 74	53	49	4	0	42	7	1	3	0	29	9
75 and over	92	85	6	1	72	15	4	1	2	61	15
Unknown..............................	5,779	671	19	5,089	94	492	3	5,190	56	302	4,198

[1]Not all agencies provide ethnicity data, therefore the race and ethnicity totals will not equal.
[2]Includes American Indian or Alaska Native, Asian, Native Hawaiian or Other Pacific Islander.
[3]Because of rounding, the percentages may not add to 100.0.
[4]Does not include unknown ages.

Table 22. Murder, by Victim/Offender Situations, 2017

(Number; percent; single victim/single offender.)

Situation	Total	Percent distribution (may not add to 100.0 due to rounding)
Total	15,129	100.0
Single victim/single offender	6,902	45.6
Single victim/unknown offender or offenders..............................	4,713	31.2
Single victim/multiple offenders	1,781	11.8
Multiple victims/single offender.............................	972	6.4
Multiple victims/unknown offender or offenders..........................	300	2.0
Multiple victims/multiple offenders.............................	461	3.0

Table 23. Murder Age of Victim, by Age of Offender, 2017

(Number; single victim/single offender.)

Age of victim	Total	Age of offender		
		Under 18 years	18 years and over	Unknown
Total	6,902	318	6,307	277
Under 18	543	85	450	8
18 and over	6,307	228	5,815	264
Unknown...	52	5	42	5

Note: This table is based on incidents where some information about the offender is known by law enforcement; therefore, when the offender age, sex, and race are all reported as unknown, these data are excluded from the table.

Table 24. Murder, Race, Ethnicity, and Sex of Victim by Race, Ethnicity, and Sex of Offender, 2017

(Number; single victim/single offender.)

Victim characteristic	Total	Sex			Race				Ethnicity		
		Male	Female	Unknown	White	Black or African American	Other[1]	Unknown	Hispanic/ Latino	Not Hispanic/ Latino	Unknown
Race											
White	3,567	2,861	576	59	71	3,144	352	71	758	1,600	1,209
Black or African American........................	2,970	264	2,627	17	62	2,598	310	62	104	1,767	1,099
Other race[1]	257	72	35	144	6	226	25	6	23	160	74
Unknown	108	55	25	3	25	78	5	25	4	25	79
Sex											
Male	4,862	2,074	2,523	153	112	4,235	515	112	607	2,567	1,688
Female........................	1,932	1,123	715	67	27	1,733	172	27	279	960	693
Unknown........................	108	55	25	3	25	78	5	25	3	25	80
Ethnicity											
Hispanic or Latino	824	668	126	10	20	748	56	20	583	211	30
Not Hispanic or Latino........................	2,886	1,103	1,626	118	39	2,560	287	39	211	2,594	81
Unknown........................	3,192	1,481	1,511	95	105	2,738	349	105	95	747	2,350

Note: This table is based on incidents where some information about the offender is known by law enforcement; therefore, when the offender age, sex, and race are all reported as unknown, these data are excluded from the table.
[1]Includes American Indian or Alaska Native, Asian, Native Hawaiian or Other Pacific Islander.

Table 25. Murder Victims, by Weapons, 2013–2017

(Number.)

Weapons	2013	2014	2015	2016	2017
Total	12,253	12,270	13,750	15,296	15,129
Total firearms	8,454	8,312	9,778	11,138	10,982
Handguns	5,782	5,673	6,569	7,204	7,032
Rifles	285	258	258	378	403
Shotguns	308	264	272	261	264
Other guns	123	93	177	187	187
Firearms, type not stated	1,956	2,024	2,502	3,108	3,096
Knives or cutting instruments	1,490	1,595	1,589	1,632	1,591
Blunt objects (clubs, hammers, etc.)	428	446	450	479	467
Personal weapons (hands, fists, feet, etc.)[1]	687	682	659	669	696
Poison	11	10	8	13	13
Explosives	2	7	1	1	0
Fire	94	71	84	114	103
Narcotics	53	70	75	122	97
Drowning	4	14	14	9	8
Strangulation	85	89	99	99	88
Asphyxiation	95	102	120	93	105
Other weapons or weapons not stated	850	872	873	927	979

[1] Pushed is included in personal weapons.

Table 26. Murder, by State, Types of Weapon, 2017

(Number.)

State	Total murders[1]	Total firearms	Handguns	Rifles	Shotguns	Firearms (type unknown)	Knives or cutting instruments	Other weapons	Hands, feet, fists, etc.[2]
Alabama[3]	2	1	0	0	0	1	0	1	0
Alaska	62	37	7	3	3	24	13	8	4
Arizona	404	249	162	8	9	70	50	93	12
Arkansas	250	168	92	11	4	61	23	52	7
California	1,830	1,274	886	37	34	317	258	195	103
Colorado	218	137	88	7	4	38	37	22	22
Connecticut	102	72	30	0	1	41	11	9	10
Delaware	52	44	20	0	1	23	3	4	1
District of Columbia	116	90	89	0	0	1	15	5	6
Georgia	672	542	490	15	5	32	37	85	8
Hawaii	39	4	1	1	0	2	9	10	16
Idaho	28	13	8	4	1	0	6	3	6
Illinois[3]	814	693	596	24	3	70	53	50	18
Indiana	360	291	147	14	6	124	20	39	10
Iowa	100	57	25	1	5	26	18	18	7
Kansas	129	79	44	4	7	24	16	26	8
Kentucky	263	192	128	6	6	52	25	33	13
Louisiana	566	460	216	23	12	209	46	42	18
Maine	23	12	4	0	0	8	3	4	4
Maryland	475	370	339	5	3	23	44	50	11
Massachusetts	170	99	34	0	0	65	36	29	6
Michigan	567	381	185	13	12	171	55	101	30
Minnesota	113	69	58	1	2	8	14	23	7
Mississippi	149	111	90	4	3	14	12	20	6
Missouri	596	514	224	22	8	260	25	48	9
Montana	41	17	10	2	1	4	12	5	7
Nebraska	43	31	27	2	2	0	4	5	3
Nevada	270	201	16	58	0	127	28	30	11
New Hampshire	14	7	4	0	1	2	5	1	1
New Jersey	324	242	175	7	4	56	42	29	11
New Mexico	113	71	20	2	0	49	20	19	3
New York	547	292	233	6	9	44	113	91	51
North Carolina	547	413	279	9	26	99	33	64	37
North Dakota	9	5	2	1	0	2	1	2	1
Ohio	682	485	226	5	11	243	46	128	23
Oklahoma	239	163	131	5	5	22	25	32	19
Oregon	100	58	34	2	2	20	17	22	3
Pennsylvania	735	567	452	11	8	96	63	73	32
Rhode Island	20	8	1	0	0	7	4	5	3
South Carolina	387	312	183	11	8	110	29	36	10
South Dakota	21	8	6	0	0	2	7	2	4
Tennessee	525	407	271	19	11	106	42	64	12
Texas	1,364	1,012	594	40	26	352	156	131	65
Utah	73	46	32	0	3	11	7	12	8
Vermont	14	6	1	0	0	5	6	1	1
Virginia	453	338	156	11	11	160	44	54	17
Washington	228	134	75	1	1	57	36	40	18
West Virginia	79	45	25	4	4	12	8	23	3
Wisconsin	186	149	111	4	2	32	11	17	9
Wyoming	14	6	5	0	0	1	3	3	2
Guam	1	0	0	0	0	0	0	1	0

[1] Total number of murders for which supplemental homicide data were received.
[2] Pushed is included in hands, fists, feet, etc.
[3] Limited supplemental homicide data were received.

Table 27. Justifiable Homicide by Weapon, Law Enforcement,[1] 2013–2017

(Number.)

Year	Total	Total firearms	Handguns	Rifles	Shotguns	Firearms, type not stated	Knives or cutting instruments	Other dangerous weapons	Personal weapons
2013...	471	467	334	46	9	78	0	3	1
2014...	453	451	331	45	4	71	1	1	0
2015...	459	458	315	43	7	93	0	1	0
2016...	444	438	320	51	5	62	0	5	1
2017...	429	423	276	57	1	89	1	5	0

[1] The killing of a felon by a law enforcement officer in the line of duty.

Table 28. Justifiable Homicide by Weapon, Private Citizen, 2013–2017

(Number.)

Year	Total	Total firearms	Handguns	Rifles	Shotguns	Firearms, type not stated	Knives or cutting instruments	Other dangerous weapons	Personal weapons
2013...	315	263	198	20	15	30	35	6	11
2014...	286	227	174	6	11	36	35	13	11
2015...	338	272	219	8	13	32	41	10	15
2016...	337	282	202	11	10	59	34	7	14
2017...	353	299	231	6	7	55	34	8	12

Table 29. Robbery, by State, Types of Weapons, 2017

(Percent.)

State	Total[1]	Firearms	Knives or cutting instruments	Other weapons	Strong-arm	Agency count	Population
Alabama	3,190	1,895	137	376	782	242	4,175,710
Alaska	949	294	88	134	433	32	736,205
Arizona	7,312	3,115	826	782	2,589	97	6,732,019
Arkansas	1,813	968	104	161	580	265	2,774,792
California	56,590	15,343	5,276	6,502	29,469	729	39,379,687
Colorado	3,734	1,615	326	434	1,359	202	5,221,193
Connecticut	2,813	936	308	263	1,306	106	3,569,335
Delaware	1,082	488	96	82	416	61	961,939
District of Columbia	2,623	946	209	187	1,281	3	693,972
Florida	18,584	7,724	1,174	1,706	7,980	603	20,971,216
Georgia	9,640	5,690	327	858	2,765	484	9,793,925
Hawaii	1,077	167	114	122	674	4	1,427,538
Idaho	182	61	30	24	67	82	1,533,625
Illinois[2]	427	217	22	45	143	1	146,770
Indiana	5,913	3,000	292	536	2,085	206	4,497,992
Iowa	1,204	532	95	132	445	200	2,839,614
Kansas	1,345	657	113	119	456	226	2,325,762
Kentucky	2,946	1,332	231	333	1,050	331	4,330,642
Louisiana	5,213	2,816	236	382	1,779	185	4,439,478
Maine	249	56	30	30	133	135	1,335,907
Maryland	11,125	5,002	1,047	958	4,118	146	5,810,386
Massachusetts	4,788	1,227	875	1,012	1,674	328	6,646,961
Michigan	6,449	2,992	367	576	2,514	619	9,803,009
Minnesota	3,619	1,199	251	571	1,598	387	5,539,575
Mississippi	1,264	806	49	121	288	69	1,482,371
Missouri	6,314	3,725	335	430	1,824	560	5,993,489
Montana	295	72	27	48	148	107	1,048,283
Nebraska	670	403	47	37	183	54	764,921
Nevada	4,841	2,154	443	561	1,683	57	2,998,039
New Hampshire	409	82	53	42	232	176	1,292,643
New Jersey	7,895	2,718	665	502	4,010	576	9,005,644
New Mexico	3,617	1,916	410	351	940	115	1,858,425
New York	19,946	3,806	2,391	1,952	11,797	525	19,173,006
North Carolina	7,161	4,018	469	624	2,050	277	7,655,991
North Dakota	182	41	24	30	87	106	749,938
Ohio	10,869	3,395	462	801	6,211	458	9,718,364
Oklahoma	2,995	1,449	257	231	1,058	394	3,872,459
Oregon	2,333	515	280	323	1,215	145	3,751,984
Pennsylvania	11,707	4,816	865	731	5,295	1,452	12,586,674
Rhode Island	474	125	87	51	211	49	1,059,639
South Carolina	3,378	1,946	241	252	939	350	4,075,266
South Dakota	224	68	25	31	100	76	732,566
Tennessee	7,823	4,489	419	956	1,959	458	6,609,070
Texas	31,526	17,752	2,201	2,554	9,019	951	26,883,394
Utah	1,448	438	202	151	657	122	2,956,234
Vermont	91	22	17	14	38	71	597,819
Virginia	3,774	1,968	343	297	1,166	394	8,118,165
Washington	5,161	1,289	518	659	2,695	237	7,259,162
West Virginia	460	161	50	70	179	183	1,321,158
Wisconsin	4,337	2,274	253	400	1,410	430	5,739,270
Wyoming	75	25	3	11	36	55	550,712

[1] The number of robberies from agencies that submitted 12 months of data in 2017 for which breakdowns by type of weapon were included.
[2] Limited data were received.

Table 30. Aggravated Assault, by State, Types of Weapon, 2017

(Percent.)

State	Total[1]	Firearms	Knives or cutting instruments	Other weapons	Personal weapons	Agency count	Population
Alabama	15,072	2,872	1,589	9,182	1,429	242	4,175,710
Alaska	4,236	1,015	712	1,314	1,195	32	736,205
Arizona	22,279	5,410	3,214	5,203	8,452	97	6,732,019
Arkansas	11,822	4,311	1,555	2,536	3,420	265	2,774,792
California	104,181	19,143	17,111	36,546	31,381	729	39,379,687
Colorado	12,237	3,919	2,950	2,997	2,371	202	5,221,193
Connecticut	4,424	700	1,000	1,544	1,180	106	3,569,335
Delaware	2,891	953	569	1,070	299	61	961,939
District of Columbia	3,791	937	1,048	1,327	479	3	693,972
Florida	57,986	17,697	10,415	20,289	9,585	603	20,971,216
Georgia	22,130	7,907	3,132	5,815	5,276	484	9,793,925
Hawaii	1,894	180	448	652	614	4	1,427,538
Idaho	2,735	508	459	774	994	82	1,533,625
Illinois[2]	1,773	1,036	146	260	331	1	146,770
Indiana	14,364	3,372	1,452	3,998	5,542	206	4,497,992
Iowa	6,160	921	946	1,279	3,014	200	2,839,614
Kansas	7,107	2,484	1,315	1,884	1,424	226	2,325,762
Kentucky	5,141	1,861	730	1,772	778	331	4,330,642
Louisiana	17,410	5,690	2,546	4,539	4,635	185	4,439,478
Maine	872	79	143	257	393	135	1,335,907
Maryland	16,528	2,933	3,552	6,384	3,659	146	5,810,386
Massachusetts	16,887	1,856	3,643	7,464	3,924	328	6,646,961
Michigan	30,457	8,591	5,314	10,182	6,370	619	9,803,009
Minnesota	7,091	1,640	1,229	1,793	2,429	387	5,539,575
Mississippi	2,650	996	327	620	707	69	1,482,371
Missouri	22,213	8,810	2,453	5,590	5,360	560	5,993,489
Montana	3,003	453	387	1,065	1,098	107	1,048,283
Nebraska	2,143	715	402	714	312	54	764,921
Nevada	9,651	2,579	2,025	2,954	2,093	57	2,998,039
New Hampshire	1,521	368	341	347	465	176	1,292,643
New Jersey	10,880	2,204	2,132	3,634	2,910	576	9,005,644
New Mexico	10,855	2,568	1,739	2,816	3,732	115	1,858,425
New York	43,350	4,608	10,837	13,292	14,613	525	19,173,006
North Carolina	18,990	8,676	2,822	3,984	3,508	277	7,655,991
North Dakota	1,430	46	178	414	792	106	749,938
Ohio	15,191	5,991	2,856	4,263	2,081	458	9,718,364
Oklahoma	12,443	2,786	1,991	4,156	3,510	394	3,872,459
Oregon	6,627	1,033	1,184	2,169	2,241	145	3,751,984
Pennsylvania	23,144	4,751	3,240	5,119	10,034	1,452	12,586,674
Rhode Island	1,521	298	417	490	316	49	1,059,639
South Carolina	15,666	6,725	2,433	3,741	2,767	350	4,075,266
South Dakota	2,697	217	451	586	1,443	76	732,566
Tennessee	32,148	12,019	5,689	11,476	2,964	458	6,609,070
Texas	71,942	22,234	14,195	22,760	12,753	951	26,883,394
Utah	3,992	760	974	1,176	1,082	122	2,956,234
Vermont	701	64	132	85	420	71	597,819
Virginia	9,244	2,854	1,501	2,453	2,436	394	8,118,165
Washington	13,254	2,871	2,073	3,842	4,468	237	7,259,162
West Virginia	4,187	1,191	485	937	1,574	183	1,321,158
Wisconsin	11,873	3,247	1,279	2,530	4,817	430	5,739,270
Wyoming	972	115	136	195	526	55	550,712

[1]The number of robberies from agencies that submitted 12 months of data in 2016 for which breakdowns by type of weapon were included.
[2]Limited data were received.

Table 31. Larceny-Theft and Motor Vehicle Theft, Percent Distribution by Region, 2017

(Percent.)

Region	Larceny-theft										Motor vehicle theft			
	Total (may not sum to 100.0 due to rounding)	Pocket-picking	Purse-snatching	Shoplifting	From motor vehicles (except accessories)	Motor vehicle accessories	Bicycles	From buildings	From coin-operated machines	All others	Total (may not sum to 100.0 due to rounding)	Autos	Trucks and buses	Other vehicles
Total	100.00	0.6	0.4	20.8	26.8	7.4	3.2	10.6	0.2	30.1	100.00	75.4	15.1	9.5
Northeast...........................	100.00	0.9	0.5	24.0	20.4	5.7	4.2	16.8	0.2	27.3	100.00	85.9	4.4	9.8
Midwest	100.00	0.5	0.4	22.3	20.3	7.6	2.8	13.3	0.2	32.7	100.00	78.8	12.5	8.7
South..................................	100.00	0.5	0.4	20.5	27.3	7.3	2.3	8.6	0.2	32.9	100.00	71.9	16.6	11.5
West...................................	100.00	0.6	0.4	18.8	32.8	8.1	4.3	9.5	0.2	25.3	100.00	75.3	16.7	8.0

Table 32. Crime Trends, by Population Group, 2016–2017

(Number; percent.)

Population group	Violent crime	Murder and nonnegligent manslaughter	Rape[1]	Robbery	Aggravated assault	Property crime	Burglary	Larceny-theft	Motor vehicle theft	Arson	Number of agencies	2017 estimated population
Total, all agencies												
2016	1,227,452	16,651	117,581	323,903	769,317	7,541,358	1,430,698	5,372,029	738,631	41,870		
2017	1,227,262	16,617	121,745	310,861	778,039	7,320,839	1,321,995	5,254,838	744,006	41,171	15,426	310,003,377
Percent change	*	-0.2	+3.5	-4.0	+1.1	-2.9	-7.6	-2.2	+0.7	-1.7		
Total, cities												
2016	988,373	12,987	88,310	285,013	602,063	6,002,396	1,056,562	4,349,999	595,835	31,894		
2017	989,231	13,191	91,715	274,251	610,074	5,846,576	983,667	4,264,233	598,676	31,974	11,205	211,301,356
Percent change	+0.1	+1.6	+3.9	-3.8	+1.3	-2.6	-6.9	-2.0	+0.5	+0.3		
Group I (250,000 and over)												
2016	474,307	6,949	33,468	160,290	273,600	2,073,439	372,144	1,428,206	273,089	12,467		
2017	474,713	6,794	34,842	154,648	278,429	2,053,980	355,012	1,426,420	272,548	12,826	83	62,030,546
Percent change	+0.1	-2.2	+4.1	-3.5	+1.8	-0.9	-4.6	-0.1	-0.2	+2.9		
1,000,000 and over												
2016	201,743	2,691	14,045	71,655	113,352	742,376	125,318	517,249	99,809	4,226		
2017	200,277	2,473	14,809	68,685	114,310	735,685	119,624	518,657	97,404	4,176	11	27,835,810
Percent change	-0.7	-8.1	+5.4	-4.1	+0.8	-0.9	-4.5	+0.3	-2.4	-1.2		
500,000 to 999,999												
2016	149,231	2,253	10,365	48,418	88,195	732,805	133,169	506,671	92,965	4,351		
2017	152,639	2,358	10,839	47,894	91,548	728,714	130,372	504,515	93,827	4,831	24	17,571,403
Percent change	+2.3	+4.7	+4.6	-1.1	+3.8	-0.6	-2.1	-0.4	+0.9	+11.0		
250,000 to 499,999												
2016	123,333	2,005	9,058	40,217	72,053	598,258	113,657	404,286	80,315	3,890		
2017	121,797	1,963	9,194	38,069	72,571	589,581	105,016	403,248	81,317	3,819	48	16,623,333
Percent change	-1.2	-2.1	+1.5	-5.3	+0.7	-1.5	-7.6	-0.3	+1.2	-1.8		
Group II (100,000 to 249,999)												
2016	158,660	2,137	15,152	45,781	95,590	1,054,235	189,689	745,706	118,840	5,192		
2017	158,515	2,282	15,710	43,864	96,659	1,028,358	175,848	733,964	118,546	5,095	223	33,279,937
Percent change	-0.1	+6.8	+3.7	-4.2	+1.1	-2.5	-7.3	-1.6	-0.2	-1.9		
Group III (50,000 to 99,999)												
2016	117,544	1,283	11,884	31,586	72,791	884,845	154,139	649,430	81,276	4,353		
2017	117,529	1,376	12,310	31,025	72,818	853,912	140,936	631,474	81,502	4,478	484	33,749,285
Percent change	*	+7.2	+3.6	-1.8	*	-3.5	-8.6	-2.8	+0.3	+2.9		
Group IV (25,000 to 49,999)												
2016	90,162	1,055	10,063	21,811	57,233	739,484	126,324	562,060	51,100	3,292		
2017	90,057	1,100	10,513	20,834	57,610	706,705	113,898	540,864	51,943	3,250	875	30,423,643
Percent change	-0.1	+4.3	+4.5	-4.5	+0.7	-4.4	-9.8	-3.8	+1.6	-1.3		
Group V (10,000 to 24,999)												
2016	76,670	879	8,929	15,845	51,017	673,637	117,372	515,744	40,521	2,905		
2017	76,916	868	9,285	14,905	51,858	647,140	107,002	498,276	41,862	2,811	1,798	28,686,467
Percent change	+0.3	-1.3	+4.0	-5.9	+1.6	-3.9	-8.8	-3.4	+3.3	-3.2		
Group VI (Under 10,000)												
2016	71,030	684	8,814	9,700	51,832	576,756	96,894	448,853	31,009	3,685		
2017	71,501	771	9,055	8,975	52,700	556,481	90,971	433,235	32,275	3,514	7,742	23,131,478
Percent change	+0.7	+12.7	+2.7	-7.5	+1.7	-3.5	-6.1	-3.5	+4.1	-4.6		
Metropolitan counties												
2016	190,966	2,770	20,915	36,125	131,156	1,243,670	281,127	843,894	118,649	7,468		
2017	189,421	2,613	21,628	33,967	131,213	1,190,522	250,712	820,600	119,210	6,849	1,915	74,252,901
Percent change	-0.8	-5.7	+3.4	-6.0	*	-4.3	-10.8	-2.8	+0.5	-8.3		
Nonmetropolitan counties[2]												
2016	48,113	894	8,356	2,765	36,098	295,292	93,009	178,136	24,147	2,508		
2017	48,610	813	8,402	2,643	36,752	283,741	87,616	170,005	26,120	2,348	2,306	24,449,120
Percent change	+1.0	-9.1	+0.6	-4.4	+1.8	-3.9	-5.8	-4.6	+8.2	-6.4		
Suburban areas[3]												
2016	333,810	4,273	38,034	68,830	222,673	2,542,241	485,703	1,851,550	204,988	13,574		
2017	332,467	4,191	39,460	65,205	223,611	2,439,671	437,162	1,795,372	207,137	12,635	8,522	134,599,243
Percent change	-0.4	-1.9	+3.7	-5.3	+0.4	-4.0	-10.0	-3.0	+1.0	-6.9		

* = Less than one-tenth of 1 percent.

[1]The figures shown in the rape column include only those reported by law enforcement agencies that used the revised Uniform Crime Reporting definition of rape.

[2]Includes state police agencies that report aggregately for the entire state.

[3]Suburban areas include law enforcement agencies in cities with less than 50,000 inhabitants and county law enforcement agencies that are within a Metropolitan Statistical Area. Suburban areas exclude all metropolitan agencies associated with a principal city. The agencies associated with suburban areas also appear in other groups within this table.

Table 33. Crime Trends, by Population Group, 2017

(Number; rate.)

Population group	Violent crime Number of offenses known	Violent crime Rate	Murder and nonnegligent manslaughter Number of offenses known	Murder and nonnegligent manslaughter Rate	Rape[1] Number of offenses known	Rape[1] Rate	Robbery Number of offenses known	Robbery Rate	Aggravated assault Number of offenses known	Aggravated assault Rate	Property crime Number of offenses known	Property crime Rate
Total, All Agencies..........................	1,221,775	400.0	16,446	5.4	125,591	42.4	308,936	101.2	770,802	252.4	7,265,640	2,378.9
Total, cities	981,574	469.6	12,999	6.2	94,045	46.2	272,035	130.2	602,495	288.3	5,792,834	2,771.5
Group I (250,000 and over).............	472,560	768.5	6,783	11.0	35,845	59.7	154,090	250.6	275,842	448.6	2,034,977	3,309.4
1,000,000 and over..................	200,277	719.5	2,473	8.9	14,809	53.2	68,685	246.8	114,310	410.7	735,685	2,642.9
500,000 to 999,999	152,876	870.0	2,358	13.4	11,076	66.5	47,894	272.6	91,548	521.0	728,714	4,147.2
250,000 to 499,999	119,407	742.4	1,952	12.1	9,960	64.2	37,511	233.2	69,984	435.1	570,578	3,547.7
Group II (100,000 to 249,999)........	152,713	473.2	2,121	6.6	15,434	49.0	42,351	131.2	92,807	287.6	994,848	3,082.9
Group III (50,000 to 99,999)	119,145	347.9	1,386	4.0	12,730	38.2	31,337	91.5	73,692	215.1	868,714	2,536.3
Group IV (25,000 to 49,999)...........	89,414	297.8	1,068	3.6	11,032	37.6	20,451	68.1	56,863	189.4	695,293	2,316.1
Group V (10,000 to 24,999)	77,009	269.6	873	3.1	9,714	35.0	14,860	52.0	51,562	180.5	648,930	2,271.4
Group VI (Under 10,000)	70,733	315.6	768	3.4	9,290	42.6	8,946	39.9	51,729	230.8	550,072	2,454.0
Metropolitan counties......................	191,537	262.9	2,629	3.6	22,769	32.5	34,301	47.1	131,838	180.9	1,189,830	1,633.0
Nonmetropolitan counties[2]	48,664	206.7	818	3.5	8,777	39.2	2,600	11.0	36,469	154.9	282,976	1,201.8
Suburban areas[3].............................	335,122	252.9	4,208	3.2	41,219	32.1	65,527	49.4	224,168	169.1	2,435,027	1,837.3

[1]The figures shown in the rape column include only those reported by law enforcement agencies that used the revised Uniform Crime Reporting definition of rape.
[2]Includes state police agencies that report aggregately for the entire state.
[3]Suburban areas include law enforcement agencies in cities with less than 50,000 inhabitants and county law enforcement agencies that are within a Metropolitan Statistical Area. Suburban areas exclude all metropolitan agencies associated with a principal city. The agencies associated with suburban areas also appear in other groups within this table.

Table 33. Crime Trends, by Population Group, 2017—*Continued*

(Number; rate.)

Population group	Burglary Number of offenses known	Burglary Rate	Larceny- theft Number of offenses known	Larceny- theft Rate	Motor vehicle theft Number of offenses known	Motor vehicle theft Rate	Number of agencies	2017 estimated population
Total, All Agencies.........................	1,310,687	429.1	5,212,721	1,706.7	742,232	243.0	14,815	305,422,610
Total, cities	972,529	465.3	4,224,859	2,021.3	595,446	284.9	10,828	209,015,851
Group I (250,000 and over).............	351,565	571.7	1,412,427	2,297.0	270,985	440.7	81	61,490,148
1,000,000 and over..................	119,624	429.7	518,657	1,863.3	97,404	349.9	11	27,835,810
500,000 to 999,999	130,372	742.0	504,515	2,871.2	93,827	534.0	24	17,571,403
250,000 to 499,999	101,569	631.5	389,255	2,420.3	79,754	495.9	46	16,082,935
Group II (100,000 to 249,999).........	169,373	524.9	709,243	2,197.9	116,232	360.2	217	32,269,399
Group III (50,000 to 99,999)	143,162	418.0	643,254	1,878.0	82,298	240.3	491	34,251,807
Group IV (25,000 to 49,999)............	112,415	374.5	531,582	1,770.7	51,296	170.9	864	30,020,188
Group V (10,000 to 24,999)	106,387	372.4	500,122	1,750.6	42,421	148.5	1,789	28,569,221
Group VI (Under 10,000)	89,627	399.9	428,231	1,910.5	32,214	143.7	7,386	22,415,088
Metropolitan counties......................	251,079	344.6	817,962	1,122.6	120,789	165.8	1,828	72,861,356
Nonmetropolitan counties[2]	87,079	369.8	169,900	721.6	25,997	110.4	2,159	23,545,403
Suburban areas[3]...............................	437,119	329.8	1,788,884	1,349.8	209,024	157.7	8,245	132,531,489

[1]The figures shown in the rape column include only those reported by law enforcement agencies that used the revised Uniform Crime Reporting definition of rape.
[2]Includes state police agencies that report aggregately for the entire state.
[3]Suburban areas include law enforcement agencies in cities with less than 50,000 inhabitants and county law enforcement agencies that are within a Metropolitan Statistical Area. Suburban areas exclude all metropolitan agencies associated with a principal city. The agencies associated with suburban areas also appear in other groups within this table.

Table 34. Offense Analysis, Number and Percent Change, 2016–2017

(Number; percent; dollars; 14,254 agencies; 2017 estimated population 291,413,377.)

Classification	Number of offenses, 2017	Percent change from 2016	Percent distribution[1]	Average value
Murder...	15,094	-11.8	100.0	X
Rape[2]..	106,854	+3.7	100.0	X
Robbery	280,507	-4.3	100.0	$1,373
By location				
Street/highway	104,277	-8.1	37.2	1,202
Commercial house..................................	43,445	+0.1	15.5	1,284
Gas or service station............................	8,402	+3.3	3.0	1,087
Convenience store..................................	18,416	+5.6	6.6	957
Residence	44,850	-7.3	16.0	1,732
Bank..	4,761	-7.1	1.7	3,483
Miscellaneous	56,356	-1.2	20.1	1,474
Burglary	1,250,983	-7.4	100.0	2,416
By location				
Residence (dwelling):	841,283	-12.0	67.2	2,368
Residence, night..................................	255,524	-8.2	20.4	1,995
Residence, day	424,886	-11.8	34.0	2,383
Residence, unknown	160,873	-11.6	12.9	2,924
Nonresidence (store, office, etc.):	409,700	+1.2	32.8	2,514
Nonresidence, night............................	179,859	+1.9	14.4	2,337
Nonresidence, day...............................	140,921	+0.5	11.3	2,211
Nonresidence, unknown	88,920	-4.3	7.1	3,353
Larceny-theft..	4,917,272	-2.5	100.0	1,007
By type				
Pocket-picking	27,673	+0.7	0.6	648
Purse-snatching	19,588	-5.0	0.4	564
Shoplifting...	1,021,226	-3.9	20.8	260
From motor vehicles (except accessories)	1,318,007	+0.5	26.8	879
Motor vehicle accessories......................	363,035	-1.1	7.4	505
Bicycles...	155,914	-6.1	3.2	477
From buildings..	523,223	-6.7	10.6	1,381
From coin-operated machines...............	10,716	-5.7	0.2	538
All others..	1,477,890	-2.6	30.1	1,700
By value				
Over $200	2,256,303	-1.9	45.9	2,137
$50 to $200	1,043,225	-4.2	21.2	105
Under $50..	1,617,744	-2.4	32.9	13
Motor vehicle theft	705,254	+0.5	100.0	7,708

X = Not applicable.
[1] Because of rounding, the percentages may not add to 100.0.
[2] The rape figure in this table is an aggregate total of the data submitted using both the revised and legacy Uniform Crime Reporting definitions.

Table 35. Offenses Known to Law Enforcement, by Selected Federal Agency, 2017

(Number.)

Agency and unit/office	Violent crime	Murder and nonnegligent manslaughter	Rape	Robbery	Aggravated assault	Property crime	Burglary	Larceny- theft	Motor vehicle theft	Arson
National Institutes of Health..................	0	0	0	0	0	78	0	78	0	0
United States Dept. of the Interior Bureau of Indian Affairs[1]										
Bureau of Land Management	10	0	0	0	10	561	10	517	34	3
Bureau of Reclamation...................	0	0	0	0	0	1	1	0	0	0
Fish and Wildlife Service..................	14	0	1	1	12	140	17	106	17	2
National Park Service	276	7	49	62	158	4,368	119	4,155	94	44

[1]The Bureau of Indian Affairs submits these statistics to the FBI Uniform Crime Reporting Program on a monthly basis throughout the calendar year and can be found at https://ucr.fbi.gov/crime-in-the-u.s/2017/crime-in-the-u.s.-2017/tables/table-9/table-9.xls/view

Table 36. Full-Time Law Enforcement Employees, by Selected Federal Agency, 2017

(Number.)

Agency and unit/office	Total law enforcement employees	Total officers	Total civilians
National Institutes of Health.................................	77	77	0
United States Dept. of the Interior			
Bureau of Indian Affairs[1]..............................	1,061	326	735
Bureau of Land Management	305	285	20
Bureau of Reclamation................................	100	87	13
Fish and Wildlife Service..............................	653	653	0
National Park Service	2,540	2,144	396

[1]Tribal figures represented in the table at this URL (https://ucr.fbi.gov/crime-in-the-u.s/2017/crime-in-the-u.s.-2017/tables/table-81/table-81.xls/view) may be included in the aggregated totals listed under the Bureau of Indian Affairs data.

Table 37. Number of Arrestees by NIBRS Offense Code, by Selected FBI Field Office, 2017

(Number.)

NIBRS Offense Code / NIBRS Offense Description	09A - 09C Homicide offenses	11A - 11D Sex offenses	13A - 13C Assault offenses	23A - 23H Larceny/ theft offenses	26A - 26G Fraud offenses	35A - 35B Drug/ narcotic offenses	39A - 39D Gambling offenses	40A - 40C Prostitution offenses	64A - 64B Human trafficking	100 Kidnapping/ abduction	120 Robbery	210 Extortion/ blackmail	250 Counterfeiting/ forgery
Grand Total, All Field Offices.	144	255	587	21	2,348	4,065	13	6	843	106	952	2	46
Albany	0	0	4	0	22	33	0	0	11	0	0	0	0
Albuquerque	13	30	25	0	11	46	0	0	0	4	7	0	0
Anchorage	1	1	1	1	7	36	0	0	10	0	6	0	1
Atlanta	0	3	11	0	63	98	0	1	27	0	13	0	0
Baltimore	1	3	0	1	27	29	0	0	9	0	13	0	0
Birmingham	0	0	0	0	9	56	0	0	1	1	2	0	0
Boston	0	1	1	1	53	61	3	0	15	4	63	0	2
Buffalo	0	0	6	0	27	99	0	0	16	0	15	0	0
Charlotte	0	5	10	1	50	116	0	0	14	0	25	0	0
Chicago	1.	0	1	1	63	30	0	0	13	3	47	0	0
Cincinnati	0	1	0	0	9	30	0	0	19	2	13	0	1
Cleveland	0	1	1	1	49	117	0	0	14	0	11	0	0
Columbia	0	0	4	0	8	164	0	0	10	1	16	0	1
Dallas	0	0	6	0	55	76	0	0	27	6	28	0	3
Denver	5	5	23	0	9	64	0	0	0	1	24	0	2
Detroit	0	5	28	0	127	94	0	0	53	3	14	0	4
El Paso	0	0	3	0	74	57	0	0	4	4	1	0	1
Honolulu	0	3	2	0	21	13	0	0	1	0	2	0	0
Houston	0	0	5	6	63	15	1	4	70	1	55	0	0
Indianapolis	5	0	0	0	25	58	0	0	19	1	11	0	1
Jackson	3	3	9	0	2	38	1	0	9	1	1	0	0
Jacksonville	0	0	2	0	21	6	0	0	10	2	2	0	2
Kansas City	1	0	5	0	14	31	0	0	23	6	14	0	0
Knoxville	0	1	1	0	10	121	0	0	2	2	6	0	0
Las Vegas	1	0	3	0	53	26	0	0	13	5	14	0	0
Little Rock	0	0	1	0	1	42	0	0	6	0	3	0	0
Los Angeles	0	3	12	1	72	100	0	0	5	2	40	1	2
Louisville	0	2	2	0	26	31	0	0	15	0	2	0	1
Memphis	0	0	7	0	31	22	0	0	13	1	13	0	0
Miami	1	5	5	0	244	93	0	0	23	0	45	0	1
Milwaukee	0	3	3	0	11	16	0	0	5	0	8	0	0
Minneapolis	14	61	49	0	66	78	0	0	20	0	13	0	0
Mobile	0	0	1	0	8	45	0	0	5	4	6	0	0
New Haven	0	0	1	0	20	49	0	0	2	4	9	0	1
New Orleans	3	0	6	0	9	77	0	0	4	0	14	0	0
New York	0	8	12	3	271	90	2	0	36	1	33	1	5
Newark	0	1	2	1	50	46	0	0	18	2	17	0	1
Norfolk	0	0	0	0	11	9	0	0	1	0	1	0	0
Oklahoma City	1	3	3	0	29	91	0	0	4	0	28	0	1
Omaha	2	19	35	1	11	38	0	0	16	0	45	0	0
Philadelphia	1	0	8	0	103	228	0	0	54	1	61	0	0
Phoenix	78	58	162	0	24	82	0	0	30	21	37	0	1
Pittsburgh	0	0	4	0	25	194	0	0	20	0	26	0	2
Portland	0	5	10	0	6	38	0	0	18	3	33	0	0
Richmond	0	0	2	0	21	17	0	0	5	0	1	0	1
Sacramento	0	1	4	1	36	74	5	0	20	0	2	0	1
Salt Lake City	10	14	34	0	35	92	0	0	14	3	24	0	2
St. Louis	0	0	0	0	43	38	0	0	23	1	5	0	0
San Antonio	0	2	22	2	61	155	0	1	3	0	9	0	2
San Diego	0	0	4	0	14	57	1	0	5	2	7	0	1
San Francisco	0	0	2	0	42	36	0	0	10	1	11	0	4
San Juan[1]	0	1	9	0	55	79	0	0	6	7	14	0	1
Seattle	3	7	18	0	10	56	0	0	11	0	4	0	0
Springfield	0	0	1	0	13	17	0	0	3	1	12	0	0
Tampa	0	0	3	0	22	517	0	0	15	0	5	0	1
Washington, DC	0	0	14	0	106	44	0	0	43	5	21	0	0

[1]Population for the San Juan Field Office is a combination of the U.S. Census Bureau's 2010 decennial population for the U.S. Virgin Islands and population estimation for Puerto Rico.

Table 37. Number of Arrestees by NIBRS Offense Code, by Selected FBI Field Office, 2017—*Continued*

(Number.)

NIBRS Offense Code / NIBRS Offense Description	270 Embezzlement	280 Stolen property offenses	290 Destruction/ damage/ vandalism of property	370 Pornography/ obscene material	510 Bribery	520 Weapon law violations	720 Animal cruelty	Count of arrestees for Group A Offenses	90J Trespass of real property	90Z All other offenses	Count of arrestees for Group B Offenses	Total number of arrestees	Population per field office
Grand Total, All Field Offices.	134	78	44	1,028	66	2,926	23	13,687	3	6,879	6,882	20,569	329,162,760
Albany	0	0	0	33	2	4	0	109	0	48	48	157	4,029,168
Albuquerque	0	1	0	5	0	93	0	235	1	123	124	359	2,088,070
Anchorage	0	0	0	16	0	23	0	103	0	19	19	122	739,795
Atlanta	4	0	0	11	13	62	0	306	0	232	232	538	10,429,379
Baltimore	0	4	7	13	0	53	0	160	0	179	179	339	7,014,116
Birmingham	2	0	0	8	0	14	0	93	0	24	24	117	2,874,079
Boston	0	0	0	11	2	17	1	235	0	69	69	304	10,598,160
Buffalo	4	0	3	32	0	24	0	226	0	50	50	276	2,804,099
Charlotte	2	0	0	33	0	99	0	355	0	173	173	528	10,273,419
Chicago	0	1	1	8	1	66	0	236	0	90	90	326	9,327,020
Cincinnati	2	1	1	23	0	63	0	165	0	58	58	223	5,928,861
Cleveland	0	2	2	17	0	77	0	292	0	135	135	427	5,729,748
Columbia	1	1	0	4	0	152	0	362	0	141	141	503	5,024,369
Dallas	1	0	1	21	0	45	0	269	0	172	172	441	10,773,377
Denver	7	0	0	5	0	20	0	165	0	119	119	284	6,186,469
Detroit	7	0	0	77	0	87	4	503	0	204	204	707	9,962,311
El Paso	0	0	5	6	2	18	0	175	0	83	83	258	1,279,350
Honolulu	4	0	3	3	0	5	0	57	0	43	43	100	1,427,538
Houston	7	0	0	48	2	24	0	301	0	122	122	423	8,633,769
Indianapolis	3	9	0	43	1	64	0	240	0	139	139	379	6,666,818
Jackson	1	1	0	6	0	21	0	96	0	50	50	146	2,984,100
Jacksonville	1	0	0	13	1	20	0	80	0	28	28	108	5,234,632
Kansas City	0	2	0	41	0	63	0	200	0	194	194	394	6,090,229
Knoxville	0	1	1	7	0	63	0	215	0	132	132	347	2,621,128
Las Vegas	0	4	0	28	2	33	0	182	0	89	89	271	2,998,039
Little Rock	0	0	0	9	0	19	0	81	0	80	80	161	3,004,279
Los Angeles	0	4	0	19	6	84	0	351	1	350	351	702	19,534,218
Louisville	2	0	0	26	2	35	0	144	0	62	62	206	4,454,189
Memphis	4	3	0	12	1	50	1	158	0	111	111	269	4,094,856
Miami	26	5	5	19	4	57	0	533	0	492	492	1,025	7,018,226
Milwaukee	1	1	0	7	0	32	0	87	0	24	24	111	5,795,483
Minneapolis	9	1	0	26	0	32	0	369	0	79	79	448	7,201,665
Mobile	3	1	1	8	0	87	3	172	0	24	24	196	2,000,668
New Haven	2	0	0	0	0	57	0	145	0	83	83	228	3,588,184
New Orleans	0	0	0	10	0	37	0	160	0	67	67	227	4,684,333
New York	4	3	4	30	3	227	0	733	0	752	752	1,485	13,639,789
Newark	1	0	0	10	3	40	2	194	0	157	157	351	8,136,581
Norfolk	0	0	0	14	0	22	0	58	0	55	55	113	1,766,518
Oklahoma City	3	1	2	28	4	30	0	228	0	73	73	301	3,930,864
Omaha	3	10	1	11	0	64	0	256	0	74	74	330	5,065,787
Philadelphia	2	1	1	43	0	93	0	596	0	190	190	786	9,934,958
Phoenix	4	1	3	20	3	75	0	599	0	94	94	693	7,016,270
Pittsburgh	0	1	0	23	0	30	0	325	0	95	95	420	5,555,499
Portland	1	2	0	20	0	27	0	163	0	35	35	198	4,142,776
Richmond	0	0	0	5	1	9	0	62	0	35	35	97	4,137,305
Sacramento	0	0	0	16	1	54	0	215	0	85	85	300	8,058,982
Salt Lake City	3	4	0	19	0	65	0	319	0	60	60	379	5,869,269
St. Louis	1	2	0	25	0	60	0	198	0	47	47	245	2,936,426
San Antonio	9	1	0	18	0	73	0	358	1	215	216	574	7,618,100
San Diego	1	0	0	15	2	16	1	126	0	52	52	178	3,532,692
San Francisco	0	0	2	16	1	68	0	193	0	76	76	269	8,410,761
San Juan[1]	5	0	1	4	6	137	0	325	0	131	131	456	3,443,582
Seattle	2	0	0	8	0	46	0	165	0	97	97	262	7,405,743
Springfield	0	4	0	21	0	24	11	107	0	35	35	142	3,475,003
Tampa	2	0	0	27	0	39	0	631	0	58	58	689	8,731,542
Washington, DC	0	6	0	7	3	27	0	276	0	375	375	651	3,260,169

[1]Population for the San Juan Field Office is a combination of the U.S. Census Bureau's 2010 decennial population for the U.S. Virgin Islands and population estimation for Puerto Rico.

Table 38. Number of Arrestees for Child Exploitation, by Selected FBI Field Office, 2017

(Number.)

Field office	Arrests	Population per field office
Albany	44	4,029,168
Albuquerque	23	2,088,070
Anchorage	24	739,795
Atlanta	29	10,429,379
Baltimore	23	7,014,116
Birmingham	9	2,874,079
Boston	24	10,598,160
Buffalo	48	2,804,099
Charlotte	46	10,273,419
Chicago	15	9,327,020
Cincinnati	38	5,928,861
Cleveland	25	5,729,748
Columbia	11	5,024,369
Dallas	45	10,773,377
Denver	10	6,186,469
Detroit	125	9,962,311
El Paso	9	1,279,350
Honolulu	7	1,427,538
Houston	66	8,633,769
Indianapolis	56	6,666,818
Jackson	16	2,984,100
Jacksonville	19	5,234,632
Kansas City	60	6,090,229
Knoxville	10	2,621,128
Las Vegas	39	2,998,039
Little Rock	14	3,004,279
Los Angeles	27	19,534,218
Louisville	43	4,454,189
Memphis	23	4,094,856
Miami	40	7,018,226
Milwaukee	11	5,795,483
Minneapolis	78	7,201,665
Mobile	13	2,000,668
New Haven	1	3,588,184
New Orleans	13	4,684,333
New York	57	13,639,789
Newark	29	8,136,581
Norfolk	15	1,766,518
Oklahoma City	35	3,930,864
Omaha	34	5,065,787
Philadelphia	76	9,934,958
Phoenix	85	7,016,270
Pittsburgh	36	5,555,499
Portland	35	4,142,776
Richmond	8	4,137,305
Sacramento	29	8,058,982
Salt Lake City	43	5,869,269
St. Louis	46	2,936,426
San Antonio	24	7,618,100
San Diego	18	3,532,692
San Francisco	21	8,410,761
San Juan[1]	11	3,443,582
Seattle	20	7,405,743
Springfield	24	3,475,003
Tampa	42	8,731,542
Washington, DC	23	3,260,169

[1] Population for the San Juan Field Office is a combination of the U.S. Census Bureau's 2010 decennial population for the U.S. Virgin Islands and population estimation for Puerto Rico.

Table 39. Number of Arrestees by NIBRS Offense Code, by Selected ATF Judicial District, 2017

(Number.)

NIBRS Offense Code NIBRS Offense Description	09A Murder and nonnegligent manslaughter	13A Aggravated assault	13C Intimidation	23H All other larceny	26A False pretenses/ swindle/ confidnece game	26E Wire fraud	35A Drug/ narcotic violations	35B Drug equipment violations	100 Kidnapping/ abduction	120 Robbery
Grand Total, All Judicial Districts	35	18	3	172	239	8	1,196	14	3	133
Alabama, Middle District	0	0	0	0	1	0	1	0	0	0
Alabama, Northern District	0	0	0	7	2	0	7	0	0	0
Alabama, Southern District	0	0	0	2	2	0	1	0	0	0
Alaska	0	0	0	2	1	0	5	0	0	0
Arizona	3	0	0	0	25	0	28	0	0	0
Arkansas, Eastern District	0	0	0	0	0	0	29	0	0	0
Arkansas, Western District	0	0	0	1	1	0	0	0	0	0
California, Central District	2	0	0	1	1	0	63	3	0	1
California, Eastern District	0	0	0	6	0	0	14	0	0	0
California, Northern District	0	0	0	3	0	0	47	0	0	1
California, Southern District	0	0	0	0	1	0	19	0	0	0
Colorado	3	1	0	9	2	0	7	0	0	1
Connecticut	0	0	0	0	0	1	11	0	0	1
Delaware	1	0	0	1	4	0	3	0	0	1
District of Columbia	0	0	0	0	2	0	5	0	0	0
Florida, Middle District	1	1	0	6	4	0	28	1	0	1
Florida, Northern District	0	0	0	1	1	0	28	0	0	0
Florida, Southern District	0	0	0	5	1	0	28	0	0	8
Georgia, Middle District	0	0	0	2	0	0	3	0	0	0
Georgia, Northern District	0	0	0	6	4	0	8	0	0	0
Georgia, Southern District	0	0	0	0	1	2	25	0	0	0
Guam[1]	0	0	0	0	0	0	0	0	0	0
Hawaii	0	0	0	1	0	0	0	0	0	2
Idaho	0	0	0	1	0	0	8	0	0	0
Illinois, Central District	2	0	0	0	1	0	3	0	0	1
Illinois, Northern District	0	2	0	5	5	0	56	0	0	4
Illinois, Southern District	1	0	0	0	0	0	6	0	0	0
Indiana, Northern District	0	0	0	6	6	0	11	0	0	0
Indiana, Southern District	0	0	0	2	0	0	7	2	0	20
Iowa, Northern District	0	0	0	2	1	0	2	0	0	0
Iowa, Southern District	1	0	0	4	0	0	16	0	0	3
Kansas	0	0	0	4	0	0	8	1	0	0
Kentucky, Eastern District	0	0	0	3	1	0	8	0	0	0
Kentucky, Western District	0	0	0	1	0	0	20	0	0	0
Louisiana, Eastern District	0	0	0	2	0	0	0	0	0	0
Louisiana, Middle District	0	0	0	0	0	0	1	0	0	0
Louisiana, Western District	0	0	0	0	1	0	0	0	0	0
Maine	0	0	0	0	3	0	1	0	0	1
Maryland	5	1	0	0	3	0	82	0	0	3
Massachusetts	0	0	0	0	1	0	30	0	3	0
Michigan, Eastern District	1	0	0	1	5	0	22	0	0	0
Michigan, Western District	0	0	0	9	2	0	17	0	0	1
Minnesota	0	0	0	1	3	0	4	0	0	1
Mississippi, Northern District	0	0	1	0	1	0	1	0	0	0
Mississippi, Southern District	0	0	0	0	0	0	1	0	0	0
Missouri, Eastern District	0	0	0	1	5	0	25	0	0	0
Missouri, Western District	0	0	0	0	1	0	17	0	0	1
Montana	0	0	0	0	0	0	2	0	0	0
Nebraska	0	1	0	5	5	0	11	0	0	0
Nevada	0	0	0	0	0	0	3	0	0	2
New Hampshire	0	0	0	0	4	0	1	0	0	0
New Jersey	0	0	0	0	3	0	7	0	0	4
New Mexico	0	0	0	0	0	0	17	0	0	1
New York, Eastern District	1	0	0	0	0	0	7	0	0	15
New York, Northern District	1	1	0	3	1	0	0	0	0	0

(Number.)

NIBRS Offense Code	200	270	280	520		90Z			
NIBRS Offense Description	Arson	Embezzlement	Stolen property offenses	Weapon law violations	Count of arrestees for Group A Offenses	All other offenses	Count of arrestees for Group B Offenses	Total number of arrestees	Population per judicial district
Grand Total, All Judicial Districts	90	1	48	7,027	8,987	559	559	9,546	329,376,001
Alabama, Middle District	0	0	0	66	68	2	2	70	1,151,840
Alabama, Northern District	1	0	3	119	139	0	0	139	2,878,062
Alabama, Southern District	0	0	0	31	36	0	0	36	844,845
Alaska	0	0	0	38	46	2	2	48	739,795
Arizona	3	0	1	143	203	26	26	229	7,016,270
Arkansas, Eastern District	0	0	0	54	83	0	0	83	1,641,446
Arkansas, Western District	0	0	0	8	10	0	0	10	1,362,833
California, Central District	1	0	0	161	233	13	13	246	19,520,355
California, Eastern District	0	0	0	57	77	2	2	79	8,094,481
California, Northern District	0	0	0	61	112	19	19	131	8,401,302
California, Southern District	5	0	0	55	80	9	9	89	3,520,515
Colorado	1	0	1	93	118	4	4	122	5,607,154
Connecticut	1	0	0	35	49	1	1	50	3,588,184
Delaware	1	0	0	33	44	2	2	46	961,939
District of Columbia	3	0	0	24	34	2	2	36	693,972
Florida, Middle District	3	0	1	198	244	5	5	249	12,117,428
Florida, Northern District	1	0	0	72	103	0	0	103	1,858,835
Florida, Southern District	3	0	0	188	233	35	35	268	7,008,137
Georgia, Middle District	0	0	0	17	22	0	0	22	2,011,173
Georgia, Northern District	1	0	0	57	76	2	2	78	6,831,493
Georgia, Southern District	1	0	0	109	138	9	9	147	1,586,713
Guam[1]	0	0	0	5	5	0	0	5	159,358
Hawaii	0	0	0	16	19	0	0	19	1,427,538
Idaho	0	0	1	66	76	2	2	78	1,716,943
Illinois, Central District	0	0	0	33	40	0	0	40	2,209,511
Illinois, Northern District	2	1	6	160	241	9	9	250	9,334,009
Illinois, Southern District	1	0	0	55	63	3	3	66	1,258,503
Indiana, Northern District	0	0	2	124	149	5	5	154	2,595,142
Indiana, Southern District	2	0	0	66	99	4	4	103	4,071,676
Iowa, Northern District	0	0	0	43	48	0	0	48	1,325,687
Iowa, Southern District	1	0	0	56	81	5	5	86	1,820,024
Kansas	0	0	0	85	98	0	0	98	2,913,123
Kentucky, Eastern District	2	0	1	62	77	17	17	94	2,211,234
Kentucky, Western District	0	0	1	76	98	4	4	102	2,242,955
Louisiana, Eastern District	1	0	0	26	29	0	0	29	1,687,314
Louisiana, Middle District	0	0	0	51	52	0	0	52	836,722
Louisiana, Western District	0	0	0	44	45	0	0	45	2,160,297
Maine	1	0	0	19	25	1	1	26	1,335,907
Maryland	1	0	1	155	251	53	53	304	6,052,177
Massachusetts	1	0	0	68	103	2	2	105	6,859,819
Michigan, Eastern District	6	0	0	136	171	24	24	195	6,450,976
Michigan, Western District	0	0	4	89	122	9	9	131	3,511,335
Minnesota	0	0	1	55	65	3	3	68	5,576,606
Mississippi, Northern District	0	0	0	17	20	1	1	21	1,113,255
Mississippi, Southern District	0	0	0	43	44	4	4	48	1,870,845
Missouri, Eastern District	0	0	1	192	224	7	7	231	2,936,329
Missouri, Western District	2	0	0	157	178	8	8	186	3,177,203
Montana	1	0	0	82	85	0	0	85	1,050,493
Nebraska	1	0	0	44	67	0	0	67	1,920,076
Nevada	2	0	0	79	86	2	2	88	2,998,039
New Hampshire	1	0	0	10	16	0	0	16	1,342,795
New Jersey	1	0	0	62	77	12	12	89	9,005,644
New Mexico	0	0	0	47	65	1	1	66	2,088,070
New York, Eastern District	1	0	0	67	91	11	11	102	8,352,340
New York, Northern District	6	0	0	20	32	5	5	37	3,405,511

Table 39. Number of Arrestees by NIBRS Offense Code, by Selected ATF Judicial District, 2017—*Continued*

(Number.)

NIBRS Offense Code / NIBRS Offense Description	09A Murder and nonnegligent manslaughter	13A Aggravated assault	13C Intimidation	23H All other larceny	26A False pretenses/swindle/confidnece game	26E Wire fraud	35A Drug/narcotic violations	35B Drug equipment violations	100 Kidnapping/abduction	120 Robbery
New York, Southern District	2	1	0	0	7	0	5	0	0	14
New York, Western District	0	1	0	0	0	0	19	0	0	0
North Carolina, Eastern District	0	0	0	0	0	0	16	1	0	2
North Carolina, Middle District	0	0	0	5	0	0	5	0	0	9
North Carolina, Western District	0	0	0	4	0	0	18	0	0	5
North Dakota	0	0	0	0	1	0	3	0	0	0
Northern Mariana Islands [1]	0	0	0	0	0	0	0	0	0	0
Ohio, Northern District	0	1	0	2	2	0	23	0	0	1
Ohio, Southern District	0	4	0	3	0	0	14	0	0	2
Oklahoma, Eastern District	0	0	0	0	0	0	0	0	0	0
Oklahoma, Northern District	0	0	0	0	0	0	1	1	0	1
Oklahoma, Western District	0	0	0	0	0	0	3	0	0	0
Oregon	1	0	0	0	1	0	3	0	0	0
Pennsylvania, Eastern District	0	1	0	3	22	0	14	0	0	0
Pennsylvania, Middle District	0	0	0	0	1	0	5	1	0	0
Pennsylvania, Western District	0	0	0	1	9	0	7	0	0	0
Puerto Rico	0	0	0	0	0	0	9	0	0	3
Rhode Island	0	0	0	0	0	0	2	0	0	0
South Carolina	0	0	0	1	2	0	34	0	0	1
South Dakota	0	0	0	1	0	0	7	0	0	1
Tennessee, Eastern District	0	0	0	2	1	0	22	0	0	0
Tennessee, Middle District	0	0	0	0	1	0	7	0	0	1
Tennessee, Western District	0	0	0	6	4	1	17	1	0	3
Texas, Eastern District	5	0	0	3	0	1	27	1	0	0
Texas, Northern District	0	0	0	2	3	0	28	1	0	0
Texas, Southern District	2	0	0	8	40	0	32	0	0	7
Texas, Western District	0	0	1	6	13	0	7	0	0	5
U.S. Virgin Islands	0	0	0	0	0	0	0	0	0	0
Utah	0	0	0	0	0	0	5	0	0	0
Vermont	1	0	0	1	0	0	22	0	0	1
Virginia, Eastern District	0	3	0	5	19	3	39	0	0	3
Virginia, Western District	1	0	0	9	4	0	21	0	0	0
Washington, Eastern District	0	0	0	0	0	0	8	0	0	0
Washington, Western District	0	0	0	1	2	0	3	0	0	0
West Virginia, Northern District	0	0	0	1	1	0	7	1	0	1
West Virginia, Southern District	0	0	0	4	0	0	5	0	0	0
Wisconsin, Eastern District	1	0	1	1	1	0	2	0	0	0
Wisconsin, Western District	0	0	0	0	0	0	1	0	0	0
Wyoming	0	0	0	0	0	0	1	0	0	0

(Number.)

NIBRS Offense Code	200	270	280	520		90Z			
NIBRS Offense Description	Arson	Embezzlement	Stolen property offenses	Weapon law violations	Count of arrestees for Group A Offenses	All other offenses	Count of arrestees for Group B Offenses	Total number of arrestees	Population per judicial district
New York, Southern District	4	0	0	98	131	50	50	181	5,287,449
New York, Western District	1	0	0	46	67	13	13	80	2,804,099
North Carolina, Eastern District	1	0	2	143	165	2	2	167	4,040,346
North Carolina, Middle District	0	0	0	118	137	0	0	137	2,982,908
North Carolina, Western District	0	0	0	86	113	3	3	116	3,250,165
North Dakota	3	0	0	40	47	0	0	47	755,393
Northern Mariana Islands [1]	0	0	0	0	0	0	0	0	53,883
Ohio, Northern District	0	0	1	147	177	1	1	178	5,729,748
Ohio, Southern District	0	0	0	94	117	5	5	122	5,928,861
Oklahoma, Eastern District	0	0	0	10	10	0	0	10	744,540
Oklahoma, Northern District	1	0	0	25	29	0	0	29	1,063,380
Oklahoma, Western District	0	0	0	15	18	0	0	18	2,122,944
Oregon	0	0	0	33	38	1	1	39	4,142,776
Pennsylvania, Eastern District	5	0	3	93	141	4	4	145	5,738,564
Pennsylvania, Middle District	0	0	1	50	58	11	11	69	3,327,331
Pennsylvania, Western District	1	0	1	55	74	3	3	77	3,739,642
Puerto Rico	1	0	0	178	191	4	4	195	3,337,177
Rhode Island	1	0	0	17	20	0	0	20	1,059,639
South Carolina	0	0	1	290	329	2	2	331	5,024,369
South Dakota	0	0	0	48	57	3	3	60	869,666
Tennessee, Eastern District	0	0	1	102	128	15	15	143	2,621,077
Tennessee, Middle District	0	0	0	65	74	6	6	80	2,522,866
Tennessee, Western District	0	0	2	122	156	12	12	168	1,572,041
Texas, Eastern District	1	0	0	117	155	7	7	162	3,975,190
Texas, Northern District	1	0	3	189	227	45	45	272	7,327,013
Texas, Southern District	0	0	1	197	287	17	17	304	9,779,201
Texas, Western District	0	0	3	147	182	4	4	186	7,223,192
U.S. Virgin Islands	0	0	0	2	2	0	0	2	106,405
Utah	1	0	0	36	42	1	1	43	3,101,833
Vermont	0	0	0	15	40	5	5	45	623,657
Virginia, Eastern District	3	0	0	146	221	9	9	230	6,151,524
Virginia, Western District	1	0	1	38	75	5	5	80	2,318,496
Washington, Eastern District	1	0	0	37	46	1	1	47	1,603,175
Washington, Western District	2	0	0	51	59	3	3	62	5,802,568
West Virginia, Northern District	1	0	4	80	96	0	0	96	865,333
West Virginia, Southern District	0	0	0	49	58	0	0	58	950,524
Wisconsin, Eastern District	3	0	0	44	53	1	1	54	3,408,621
Wisconsin, Western District	0	0	0	13	14	0	0	14	2,386,862
Wyoming	0	0	0	62	63	1	1	64	579,315

[1] The population figures for Guam, Northern Mariana Island, and U.S. Virgin Islands were gathered from the 2010 U.S. Census.

Table 40. Number of Arrestees from Federally Issued Warrants by NIBRS Offense Code, by Selected U.S. Marshals Service Judicial District, 2017

(Number.)

NIBRS Offense Code	09A-09C	11A-11D	13A-13C	23A-23H	26A-26G	35A-35B	36A-36B	39A-39D	40A-40C	64A-64B	100	120	200	210	220	240
NIBRS Offense Description	Homicide offenses	Sex offenses	Assault offenses	Larceny/theft offenses	Fraud offenses	Drug/narcotic offenses	Sex offenses, nonforcible	Gambling offenses	Prostitution offenses	Human trafficking	Kidnapping/abduction	Robbery	Arson	Extortion/blackmail	Burglary/breaking & entering	Motor vehicle theft
Grand Total, All Judicial Districts....	86	65	161	65	367	2,204	55	2	4	10	20	111	2	10	30	13
Alabama, Middle District....	0	0	1	1	3	11	0	0	0	0	0	0	0	0	0	0
Alabama, Northern District....	0	1	0	1	4	8	3	0	0	0	0	1	0	0	0	0
Alabama, Southern District....	0	0	1	1	0	13	1	0	0	0	0	0	0	0	0	0
Alaska....	0	0	0	0	0	5	0	0	0	0	1	0	0	0	0	0
Arizona....	3	1	3	0	12	31	0	0	0	0	0	2	0	0	0	0
Arkansas, Eastern District....	0	0	0	0	1	20	0	0	0	0	0	0	0	0	0	0
Arkansas, Western District....	0	0	1	0	0	5	2	0	0	0	0	2	0	0	1	0
California, Central District....	10	1	6	0	1	20	1	0	0	0	3	5	0	0	2	7
California, Eastern District....	0	0	1	0	10	25	0	0	0	0	1	2	0	0	0	1
California, Northern District....	0	0	0	2	2	20	1	0	0	0	0	0	0	0	0	0
California, Southern District....	0	1	3	1	3	94	0	0	0	2	0	0	0	0	0	0
Colorado....	0	0	0	1	2	27	0	0	0	0	0	0	0	0	0	0
Connecticut....	0	0	2	0	6	35	0	0	0	0	0	0	0	0	0	0
Delaware....	0	0	0	0	0	1	0	0	0	0	0	0	0	0	0	0
District of Columbia	55	33	83	10	12	18	2	0	1	1	4	38	1	1	17	1
Florida, Middle District....	0	0	0	4	7	26	0	0	0	0	0	0	0	0	0	0
Florida, Northern District....	0	0	0	0	0	4	0	0	0	0	0	0	0	0	0	0
Florida, Southern District....	1	0	0	2	28	48	0	0	0	0	1	3	0	0	0	0
Georgia, Middle District....	0	0	1	4	0	49	0	0	0	0	0	3	0	0	0	0
Georgia, Northern District....	0	0	1	0	4	16	0	0	0	0	0	0	0	0	0	0
Georgia, Southern District....	0	0	0	0	1	14	0	0	0	0	0	0	0	0	0	0
Guam[1]....	0	0	0	0	4	3	0	0	0	0	0	0	0	0	0	0
Hawaii....	0	0	1	0	19	11	3	1	0	0	0	3	0	0	0	0
Idaho....	0	0	0	1	2	10	0	0	0	0	0	0	0	0	0	0
Illinois, Central District....	0	0	1	0	0	9	0	0	0	0	0	2	0	0	0	0
Illinois, Northern District....	1	0	0	0	2	29	1	0	0	0	0	0	0	0	0	0
Illinois, Southern District....	0	0	0	0	1	23	0	0	0	0	0	0	0	0	0	0
Indiana, Northern District....	1	1	0	0	2	5	0	0	1	0	0	0	0	0	0	0
Indiana, Southern District....	0	0	0	0	1	11	0	0	0	0	0	1	0	0	0	0
Iowa, Northern District....	0	0	1	1	4	62	1	0	0	0	0	0	0	0	0	0
Iowa, Southern District....	0	0	0	0	0	13	0	0	0	0	0	0	0	0	0	0
Kansas....	0	1	1	1	2	22	0	0	0	0	0	2	0	0	0	0
Kentucky, Eastern District....	0	0	0	0	0	16	0	0	0	0	0	0	0	0	0	0
Kentucky, Western District....	0	0	0	0	0	8	0	0	0	0	0	0	0	0	0	0
Louisiana, Eastern District....	1	0	0	1	0	5	0	0	0	0	0	1	0	0	0	0
Louisiana, Middle District....	0	0	0	0	0	9	0	0	0	0	0	0	0	0	0	0
Louisiana, Western District....	0	0	0	0	0	7	0	0	0	0	0	0	0	0	0	0

Table 40. Number of Arrestees from Federally Issued Warrants by NIBRS Offense Code, by Selected U.S. Marshals Service Judicial District, 2017—Continued

(Number.)

NIBRS Offense Code / Description	250 Counterfeiting/forgery	270 Embezzlement	280 Stolen property offenses	290 Destruction/damage/vandalism of property	370 Pornography/obscene material	510 Bribery	520 Weapon law violations	720 Animal cruelty	Count of arrestees for Group A Offenses	90C Disorderly conduct	90D Driving under the influence	90F Family offenses, nonviolent	90J Trespass of real property	90Z All other offenses	Count of arrestees for Group B Offenses	Total number of arrestees	Population per judicial district
Grand Total, All Judicial Districts....	28	11	12	5	78	6	931	2	4,278	9	5	19	3	32,163	32,199	36,477	329,376,001
Alabama, Middle District..................	0	0	0	0	0	0	74	0	90	0	1	0	0	92	93	183	1,151,840
Alabama, Northern District..................	0	0	0	0	0	0	44	0	62	0	0	0	0	183	183	245	2,878,062
Alabama, Southern District..................	0	0	0	0	0	0	10	0	26	0	0	0	0	222	222	248	844,845
Alaska..................	0	0	0	0	0	0	3	0	9	0	0	0	0	159	159	168	739,795
Arizona..................	0	0	0	0	4	0	10	0	66	0	0	0	0	1,844	1,844	1,910	7,016,270
Arkansas, Eastern District..................	0	0	0	0	0	0	3	0	24	0	0	0	0	121	121	145	1,641,446
Arkansas, Western District..................	0	0	0	0	0	0	3	0	14	0	0	0	0	60	60	74	1,362,833
California, Central District..................	1	0	1	0	0	0	11	1	70	0	0	1	0	587	588	658	19,520,355
California, Eastern District..................	0	0	1	0	0	0	6	0	47	0	0	0	0	295	295	342	8,094,481
California, Northern District..................	0	0	0	0	0	0	0	0	25	0	0	0	0	372	372	397	8,401,302
California, Southern District..................	0	0	1	0	19	0	14	1	139	0	0	0	0	1,072	1,072	1,211	3,520,515
Colorado..................	0	0	0	0	0	0	7	0	37	0	0	0	0	230	230	267	5,607,154
Connecticut..................	0	0	0	0	0	0	1	0	44	0	0	0	0	97	97	141	3,588,184
Delaware..................	0	0	0	0	0	0	3	0	4	0	0	0	0	19	19	23	961,939
District of Columbia	1	0	0	0	1	0	15	0	294	2	0	0	3	3,232	3,237	3,531	693,972
Florida, Middle District..................	1	0	0	0	0	0	3	0	41	0	0	0	0	618	618	659	12,117,428
Florida, Northern District..................	0	0	0	0	0	0	1	0	5	0	0	0	0	128	128	133	1,858,835
Florida, Southern District..................	2	0	0	0	0	2	17	0	104	0	0	0	0	523	523	627	7,008,137
Georgia, Middle District..................	0	1	0	0	2	0	12	0	72	0	0	0	0	127	127	199	2,011,173
Georgia, Northern District..................	0	0	0	0	0	0	5	0	26	0	0	0	0	210	210	236	6,831,493
Georgia, Southern District..................	1	0	0	0	0	0	3	0	19	0	0	0	0	174	174	193	1,586,713
Guam[1]..................	0	0	0	0	0	0	1	0	8	0	0	0	0	33	33	41	159,358
Hawaii..................	0	2	0	0	1	0	7	0	48	0	0	0	0	135	135	183	1,427,538
Idaho..................	0	0	0	0	0	0	0	0	13	0	0	1	0	163	164	177	1,716,943
Illinois, Central District..................	0	0	0	0	0	0	2	0	14	0	0	0	0	217	217	231	2,209,511
Illinois, Northern District..................	0	0	0	0	0	0	0	0	33	0	0	0	0	178	178	211	9,334,009
Illinois, Southern District..................	0	0	0	0	0	0	1	0	25	0	0	0	0	201	201	226	1,258,503
Indiana, Northern District..................	0	0	0	0	0	0	1	0	11	0	0	0	0	144	144	155	2,595,142
Indiana, Southern District..................	0	0	0	0	0	0	0	0	13	0	0	0	0	153	153	166	4,071,676
Iowa, Northern District..................	1	1	1	0	8	0	23	0	103	0	0	0	0	201	201	304	1,325,687
Iowa, Southern District..................	0	0	0	0	9	0	2	0	24	0	0	0	0	265	265	289	1,820,024
Kansas..................	0	0	0	0	0	0	22	0	51	0	0	0	0	369	369	420	2,913,123
Kentucky, Eastern District..................	0	0	0	0	2	0	4	0	22	0	0	0	0	304	304	326	2,211,234
Kentucky, Western District..................	0	0	0	0	0	0	3	0	11	0	0	0	0	109	109	120	2,242,955
Louisiana, Eastern District..................	0	0	0	0	0	0	2	0	10	0	0	0	0	176	176	186	1,687,314
Louisiana, Middle District..................	0	0	0	0	0	0	11	0	20	0	0	0	0	51	51	71	836,722
Louisiana, Western District..................	0	0	0	2	0	0	2	0	11	0	0	0	0	65	65	76	2,160,297

Table 40. Number of Arrestees from Federally Issued Warrants by NIBRS Offense Code, by Selected U.S. Marshals Service Judicial District, 2017—Continued

(Number.)

NIBRS Offense Code	09A - 09C	11A - 11D	13A - 13C	23A - 23H	26A - 26G	35A - 35B	36A - 36B	39A - 39 D	40A - 40C	64A - 64B	100	120	200	210	220	240
NIBRS Offense Description	Homicide offenses	Sex offenses	Assault offenses	Larceny/theft offenses	Fraud offenses	Drug/narcotic offenses	Sex offenses, nonforcible	Gambling offenses	Prostitution offenses	Human trafficking	Kidnapping/abduction	Robbery	Arson	Extortion/blackmail	Burglary/breaking & entering	Motor vehicle theft
Maine	0	0	0	0	3	9	0	0	0	0	0	0	0	0	0	0
Maryland	0	0	0	0	0	29	0	0	0	0	1	0	0	1	1	0
Massachusetts	1	1	0	0	1	8	0	0	0	0	0	0	0	0	0	0
Michigan, Eastern District	0	0	2	0	7	19	2	0	0	0	0	0	1	0	0	0
Michigan, Western District	0	0	0	0	1	18	0	0	0	0	0	0	0	0	0	0
Minnesota	0	0	0	0	2	7	0	0	0	0	0	0	0	0	0	0
Mississippi, Northern District	0	0	0	0	1	4	0	0	0	0	0	0	0	0	0	0
Mississippi, Southern District	0	0	0	1	1	6	0	0	0	0	0	0	0	0	0	0
Missouri, Eastern District	0	0	0	5	19	84	7	0	0	0	1	5	0	0	0	0
Missouri, Western District	1	0	1	0	3	34	0	0	0	1	0	0	0	0	0	0
Montana	0	0	0	0	2	13	2	0	0	0	0	0	0	0	0	0
Nebraska	0	1	0	1	2	35	0	0	0	0	0	0	0	0	0	0
Nevada	0	1	2	0	2	13	0	0	0	0	0	0	0	0	0	0
New Hampshire	0	0	0	0	0	4	0	0	0	0	0	0	0	0	0	0
New Jersey	2	3	0	0	4	12	0	0	0	0	0	0	0	0	0	0
New Mexico	0	2	13	0	2	45	2	0	0	1	0	2	0	0	2	2
New York, Eastern District	3	12	3	1	52	40	11	0	1	0	0	7	0	1	2	0
New York, Northern District	0	0	0	0	3	14	1	0	0	0	0	0	0	0	0	0
New York, Southern District	2	0	1	5	9	48	1	0	0	0	0	8	0	3	0	0
New York, Western District	0	0	1	0	3	15	0	0	0	0	0	0	0	0	0	0
North Carolina, Eastern District	0	0	0	1	3	25	0	0	0	0	0	4	0	0	1	0
North Carolina, Middle District	0	0	0	1	0	0	0	0	0	0	0	0	0	0	0	0
North Carolina, Western District	0	0	0	0	4	6	1	0	0	0	0	0	0	0	0	0
North Dakota	0	1	1	0	0	12	0	0	0	0	0	0	0	0	0	0
Northern Mariana Islands[1]	0	0	0	0	0	0	0	0	0	0	0	0	0	0	0	0
Ohio, Northern District	1	0	1	0	7	63	0	0	0	0	0	1	0	0	0	0
Ohio, Southern District	0	0	1	1	2	8	0	1	0	0	1	1	0	0	0	0
Oklahoma, Eastern District	0	0	1	0	0	3	0	0	0	0	0	0	0	0	0	0
Oklahoma, Northern District	0	0	1	0	0	3	0	0	0	1	0	0	0	0	0	0
Oklahoma, Western District	0	0	0	0	4	17	0	0	0	0	2	0	0	0	0	1
Oregon	0	0	1	1	1	18	2	0	0	0	0	2	0	0	0	0
Pennsylvania, Eastern District	0	0	2	0	6	5	0	0	0	0	0	1	0	0	0	0
Pennsylvania, Middle District	0	1	2	1	1	13	0	0	0	1	0	1	0	0	0	0
Pennsylvania, Western District	1	0	0	0	4	20	0	0	0	0	0	0	0	0	0	0
Puerto Rico	0	0	0	1	6	39	0	0	0	0	0	1	1	0	0	0
Rhode Island	0	0	0	0	1	3	0	0	0	0	0	0	0	0	0	0
South Carolina	0	0	1	1	9	40	0	0	0	0	0	1	0	1	0	0
South Dakota	0	0	6	2	1	27	0	0	0	0	0	1	1	0	0	0
Tennessee, Eastern District	0	0	0	0	0	34	1	0	0	0	0	0	0	0	0	0
Tennessee, Middle District	0	0	0	0	1	4	0	0	0	0	0	0	0	0	0	0
Tennessee, Western District	0	0	1	0	1	7	0	0	0	0	0	0	0	0	0	0

Table 40. Number of Arrestees from Federally Issued Warrants by NIBRS Offense Code, by Selected U.S. Marshals Service Judicial District, 2017—*Continued*

(Number.)

NIBRS Offense Description	250 Counterfeiting/forgery	270 Embezzlement	280 Stolen property offenses	290 Destruction/damage/vandalism of property	370 Pornography/obscene material	510 Bribery	520 Weapon law violations	720 Animal cruelty	Count of arrestees for Group A Offenses	90C Disorderly conduct	90D Driving under the influence	90F Family offenses, nonviolent	90J Trespass of real property	90Z All other offenses	Count of arrestees for Group B Offenses	Total number of arrestees	Population per judicial district
Maine	0	0	0	0	0	0	5	0	17	0	0	0	0	113	113	130	1,335,907
Maryland	0	0	0	0	0	0	1	0	33	0	0	0	0	354	354	387	6,052,177
Massachusetts	0	0	0	0	0	0	0	0	11	0	0	0	0	282	282	293	6,859,819
Michigan, Eastern District	0	0	0	0	0	0	3	0	34	0	0	1	0	232	233	267	6,450,976
Michigan, Western District	0	0	0	0	0	0	5	0	24	0	0	0	0	175	175	199	3,511,335
Minnesota	0	1	0	0	0	0	6	0	16	0	0	0	0	246	246	262	5,576,606
Mississippi, Northern District	0	0	0	0	0	0	7	0	12	0	0	0	0	137	137	149	1,113,255
Mississippi, Southern District	0	0	0	0	0	0	17	0	25	0	0	0	0	139	139	164	1,870,845
Missouri, Eastern District	1	0	0	2	3	0	107	0	234	0	0	0	0	462	462	696	2,936,329
Missouri, Western District	0	0	0	0	2	0	18	0	60	0	0	0	0	420	420	480	3,177,203
Montana	1	0	0	0	0	0	10	0	28	0	0	0	0	334	334	362	1,050,493
Nebraska	1	0	0	0	11	0	23	0	74	0	0	0	0	365	365	439	1,920,076
Nevada	0	0	0	0	0	0	13	0	31	0	1	0	0	302	303	334	2,998,039
New Hampshire	0	0	0	0	0	0	1	0	5	0	0	0	0	85	85	90	1,342,795
New Jersey	0	0	0	0	0	0	8	0	29	0	0	0	0	212	212	241	9,005,644
New Mexico	3	0	0	0	0	0	9	0	83	0	0	4	0	810	814	897	2,088,070
New York, Eastern District	0	0	0	0	1	1	6	0	141	0	0	7	0	259	266	407	8,352,340
New York, Northern District	0	0	0	0	0	0	0	0	18	0	0	0	0	218	218	236	3,405,511
New York, Southern District	1	0	6	0	0	0	25	0	109	0	0	0	0	368	368	477	5,287,449
New York, Western District	0	0	0	0	0	0	0	0	19	0	0	0	0	290	290	309	2,804,099
North Carolina, Eastern District	0	0	0	0	1	0	21	0	56	0	0	0	0	308	308	364	4,040,346
North Carolina, Middle District	0	0	0	0	0	0	1	0	2	0	0	0	0	181	181	183	2,982,908
North Carolina, Western District	0	0	0	0	1	0	5	0	17	0	0	0	0	405	405	422	3,250,165
North Dakota	0	0	0	0	0	0	0	0	14	0	0	0	0	268	268	282	755,393
Northern Mariana Islands[1]	0	0	0	0	0	0	0	0	0	0	0	0	0	2	2	2	53,883
Ohio, Northern District	1	0	0	0	0	0	21	0	95	1	0	0	0	310	311	406	5,729,748
Ohio, Southern District	0	0	0	0	0	0	2	0	17	0	0	0	0	263	263	280	5,928,861
Oklahoma, Eastern District	0	0	0	0	0	0	2	0	6	0	0	0	0	49	49	55	744,540
Oklahoma, Northern District	0	1	0	0	0	0	0	0	6	0	0	0	0	135	135	141	1,063,380
Oklahoma, Western District	0	1	0	0	1	0	6	0	32	0	0	0	0	162	162	194	2,122,944
Oregon	0	0	0	0	0	0	3	0	28	0	0	0	0	487	487	515	4,142,776
Pennsylvania, Eastern District	0	0	0	0	2	0	1	0	17	0	0	0	0	253	253	270	5,738,564
Pennsylvania, Middle District	0	0	0	0	0	0	0	0	20	0	0	0	0	168	168	188	3,327,331
Pennsylvania, Western District	0	0	0	0	0	0	2	0	27	0	0	0	0	179	179	206	3,739,642
Puerto Rico	0	0	0	0	0	0	12	0	60	0	0	0	0	346	346	406	3,337,177
Rhode Island	0	0	0	0	0	0	0	0	4	0	0	0	0	53	53	57	1,059,639
South Carolina	0	1	0	0	0	0	8	0	62	0	0	0	0	514	514	576	5,024,369
South Dakota	0	0	0	0	1	0	11	0	50	0	0	5	0	589	594	644	869,666
Tennessee, Eastern District	2	0	1	0	0	0	11	0	49	0	0	0	0	524	524	573	2,621,077
Tennessee, Middle District	0	0	0	0	1	0	1	0	7	0	0	0	0	156	156	163	2,522,866
Tennessee, Western District	0	0	0	0	0	0	4	0	13	0	0	0	0	312	312	325	1,572,041

Table 40. Number of Arrestees from Federally Issued Warrants by NIBRS Offense Code, by Selected U.S. Marshals Service Judicial District, 2017—*Continued*

(Number.)

NIBRS Offense Code	09A - 09C	11A - 11D	13A - 13C	23A - 23H	26A - 26G	35A - 35B	36A - 36B	39A - 39 D	40A - 40C	64A - 64B	100	120	200	210	220	240
NIBRS Offense Description	Homicide offenses	Sex offenses	Assault offenses	Larceny/ theft offenses	Fraud offenses	Drug/ narcotic offenses	Sex offenses, nonforc- ible	Gam- bling offenses	Prostitu- tion offenses	Human traffick- ing	Kidnap- ping/ abduc- tion	Robbery	Arson	Extortion/ blackmail	Burglary/ breaking & enter- ing	Motor vehicle theft
Texas, Eastern District..................	0	0	1	0	6	45	0	0	0	0	0	0	0	0	0	0
Texas, Northern District..................	1	0	0	0	6	54	2	0	0	0	0	1	0	0	0	0
Texas, Southern District..................	1	0	3	0	6	122	3	0	1	1	1	1	0	1	0	0
Texas, Western District..................	0	1	3	6	7	90	1	0	0	0	1	2	0	2	3	0
U.S. Virgin Islands[1]..	0	0	0	0	2	5	0	0	0	0	0	0	0	0	0	0
Utah	0	2	2	2	7	29	0	0	0	0	0	1	0	0	1	0
Vermont	0	0	0	0	0	22	0	0	0	0	0	0	0	0	0	1
Virginia, Eastern District..................	0	0	0	3	10	27	0	0	0	0	0	1	0	0	0	0
Virginia, Western District..................	0	0	1	0	14	48	0	0	0	0	0	0	0	0	0	0
Washington, East- ern District..............	0	0	2	0	1	23	0	0	0	0	0	0	0	0	0	0
Washington, West- ern District..............	1	1	0	0	2	12	1	0	0	0	1	3	0	0	0	0
West Virginia, Northern District	0	0	1	0	3	105	1	0	0	0	0	1	0	0	0	0
West Virginia, Southern District	0	0	0	1	0	39	0	0	0	0	0	0	0	0	0	0
Wisconsin, Eastern District..................	0	0	0	0	1	8	0	0	0	1	0	1	0	0	0	0
Wisconsin, Western District..................	0	0	0	0	0	2	0	0	0	0	0	0	0	0	0	0
Wyoming...............	0	0	0	0	1	36	2	0	0	1	0	0	0	0	0	0

(Number.)

NIBRS Offense Code	250	270	280	290	370	510	520	720	Count of arrestees for Group A Offenses	90C	90D	90F	90J	90Z	Count of arrestees for Group B Offenses	Total number of arrestees	Population per judicial district
NIBRS Offense Description	Counter-feiting/forgery	Embezzle-ment	Stolen property offenses	Destruc-tion/damage/vandalism of property	Pornog-raphy/obscene material	Brib-ery	Weapon law vio-lations	Animal cruelty		Disor-derly con-duct	Driving under the influ-ence	Family offenses, nonvio-lent	Tres-pass of real prop-erty	All other offenses			
Texas, Eastern District	1	0	0	0	0	0	15	0	68	0	0	0	0	262	262	330	3,975,190
Texas, Northern District	0	0	0	0	1	0	41	0	106	0	0	0	0	467	467	573	7,327,013
Texas, Southern District	5	0	0	1	5	3	49	0	203	0	0	0	0	1,892	1,892	2,095	9,779,201
Texas, Western District	4	1	1	0	1	0	42	0	165	6	3	0	0	2,255	2,264	2,429	7,223,192
U.S. Virgin Islands[1]	0	0	0	0	0	0	3	0	10	0	0	0	0	14	14	24	106,405
Utah	0	0	0	0	0	0	24	0	68	0	0	0	0	403	403	471	3,101,833
Vermont	0	0	0	0	0	0	0	0	23	0	0	0	0	76	76	99	623,657
Virginia, Eastern District	0	1	0	0	1	0	15	0	58	0	0	0	0	309	309	367	6,151,524
Virginia, Western District	1	0	0	0	0	0	2	0	66	0	0	0	0	182	182	248	2,318,496
Washington, Eastern District	0	0	0	0	0	0	8	0	34	0	0	0	0	286	286	320	1,603,175
Washington, Western District	0	0	0	0	0	0	0	0	21	0	0	0	0	399	399	420	5,802,568
West Virginia, Northern District	0	0	0	0	0	0	24	0	135	0	0	0	0	378	378	513	865,333
West Virginia, Southern District	0	0	0	0	0	0	6	0	46	0	0	0	0	219	219	265	950,524
Wisconsin, Eastern District	0	1	0	0	0	0	0	0	12	0	0	0	0	235	235	247	3,408,621
Wisconsin, Western District	0	0	0	0	0	0	1	0	3	0	0	0	0	49	49	52	2,386,862
Wyoming	0	0	0	0	0	0	0	0	40	0	0	0	0	141	141	181	579,315

[1]Population for Guam, Northern Mariana Island, and U.S. Virgin Islands was gathered from the 2010 U.S. Census.

Table 41. Number of Arrestees from State-Issued Warrants by NIBRS Offense Code, by Selected U.S. Marshals Service Judicial District, 2017

(Number.)

NIBRS Offense Code	09A - 09C	11A - 11D	13A - 13C	23A - 23H	26A - 26G	35A - 35B	36A - 36B	39A - 39 D	40A - 40C	64A - 64B	100	120
NIBRS Offense Description	Homicide offenses	Sex offenses	Assault offenses	Larceny/ theft offenses	Fraud offenses	Drug/ narcotic offenses	Sex offenses, nonforcible	Gambling offenses	Prostitution offenses	Human trafficking	Kidnapping/ abduction	Robbery
Grand Total, All Judicial Districts	4,926	4,856	13,245	1,192	654	13,530	977	4	73	124	1,157	6,646
Alabama, Middle District.........................	68	77	168	3	0	168	2	0	2	6	21	127
Alabama, Northern District......................	59	138	190	29	7	196	29	0	1	6	17	150
Alabama, Southern District	45	49	57	21	6	184	12	0	0	0	6	46
Alaska..	1	6	2	0	0	1	4	0	0	0	4	0
Arizona..	90	50	240	18	22	232	11	0	1	3	30	142
Arkansas, Eastern District......................	23	15	57	18	0	30	1	0	0	0	3	36
Arkansas, Western District	6	8	14	0	1	26	2	0	0	0	4	5
California, Central District......................	375	157	320	26	27	227	34	0	2	2	46	214
California, Eastern District......................	77	25	48	1	4	18	6	0	2	5	13	26
California, Northern District	131	65	66	6	8	72	9	0	2	3	10	78
California, Southern District	68	95	227	19	40	177	41	0	6	1	31	92
Colorado	6	16	7	4	4	17	0	0	0	1	3	2
Connecticut..	18	38	92	4	1	13	0	0	0	0	3	39
Delaware..	10	7	36	13	1	22	1	0	0	0	3	33
District of Columbia	1	0	4	12	5	0	1	0	0	0	1	4
Florida, Middle District	113	136	267	5	5	152	19	1	1	3	20	141
Florida, Northern District........................	59	65	170	11	9	180	24	0	0	1	16	65
Florida, Southern District........................	228	68	301	20	11	201	38	0	4	1	16	318
Georgia, Middle District	51	58	165	7	1	142	6	0	0	0	12	72
Georgia, Northern District.......................	135	113	477	14	4	151	9	0	0	0	40	187
Georgia, Southern District......................	45	30	141	27	0	112	2	0	0	0	13	27
Guam[1]..	1	0	1	0	0	1	0	0	0	0	0	0
Hawaii	6	15	15	2	0	13	0	0	0	0	3	6
Idaho...	6	37	76	0	0	0	5	0	0	0	3	8
Illinois, Central District	66	26	157	58	13	389	8	0	0	1	6	68
Illinois, Northern District........................	135	213	332	25	20	149	17	0	0	1	16	217
Illinois, Southern District........................	25	8	58	3	2	104	0	0	1	0	5	40
Indiana, Northern District.......................	43	51	65	4	8	109	6	0	0	0	8	56
Indiana, Southern District.......................	75	37	65	2	6	215	6	0	0	1	4	52
Iowa, Northern District...........................	4	9	21	2	1	25	1	0	0	0	0	7
Iowa, Southern District...........................	6	4	15	3	0	12	1	0	0	0	4	6
Kansas...	35	16	68	1	5	40	6	0	0	0	2	15
Kentucky, Eastern District.......................	17	8	35	0	0	89	7	0	0	2	2	21
Kentucky, Western District......................	17	6	50	5	2	26	1	0	0	0	2	16
Louisiana, Eastern District.......................	117	84	153	9	8	59	8	0	1	3	20	111
Louisiana, Middle District	27	9	34	2	2	13	2	0	0	0	2	15
Louisiana, Western District......................	136	55	103	8	2	251	7	0	0	1	26	89
Maine..	1	8	17	0	0	20	4	0	0	0	3	3
Maryland..	167	57	349	9	4	196	13	0	0	2	11	174
Massachusetts	33	75	353	50	2	174	9	0	0	0	24	131
Michigan, Eastern District.......................	71	116	296	54	52	367	18	0	2	0	9	152
Michigan, Western District	26	82	118	5	12	305	10	0	3	4	5	29
Minnesota..	16	18	43	1	3	17	1	0	0	0	3	15
Mississippi, Northern District	49	25	136	13	7	212	9	0	0	2	12	61
Mississippi, Southern District..................	68	53	220	11	11	92	16	0	0	1	30	128
Missouri, Eastern District........................	14	17	58	1	2	125	4	0	0	1	2	24
Missouri, Western District	10	14	16	2	0	9	12	0	0	0	2	10
Montana...	5	12	70	30	1	226	4	0	0	0	1	16
Nebraska..	17	63	327	107	19	316	4	0	0	1	3	64
Nevada..	2	27	20	13	16	33	2	1	0	2	4	8
New Hampshire.....................................	0	9	12	16	3	45	0	0	0	0	0	6
New Jersey..	120	75	300	14	33	372	5	0	3	3	22	156
New Mexico..	22	17	81	3	7	97	11	0	1	0	7	16
New York, Eastern District.......................	58	14	87	35	17	181	3	0	1	1	4	71
New York, Northern District.....................	42	15	86	8	3	402	13	0	0	0	2	54

(Number.)

NIBRS Offense Code	09A - 09C	11A - 11D	13A - 13C	23A - 23H	26A - 26G	35A - 35B	36A - 36B	39A - 39D	40A - 40C	64A - 64B	100	120
NIBRS Offense Description	Homicide offenses	Sex offenses	Assault offenses	Larceny/theft offenses	Fraud offenses	Drug/narcotic offenses	Sex offenses, nonforcible	Gambling offenses	Prostitution offenses	Human trafficking	Kidnapping/abduction	Robbery
New York, Southern District....................	31	7	30	7	12	34	1	0	0	0	1	18
New York, Western District.....................	15	13	136	5	0	121	24	0	0	0	6	85
North Carolina, Eastern District..............	94	40	126	23	22	188	14	0	3	0	21	138
North Carolina, Middle District...............	48	9	54	0	0	73	12	0	5	0	18	68
North Carolina, Western District.............	14	12	37	6	10	197	14	1	0	2	8	31
North Dakota...................................	3	8	79	3	3	137	5	0	1	0	0	19
Northern Mariana Islands[1].....................	0	0	0	0	0	0	0	0	0	0	0	0
Ohio, Northern District..........................	148	148	551	50	13	649	24	0	3	3	37	252
Ohio, Southern District..........................	45	66	287	65	16	744	20	0	1	2	27	128
Oklahoma, Eastern District.....................	11	29	146	1	1	87	3	0	0	1	13	33
Oklahoma, Northern District	28	33	63	1	3	44	10	0	0	1	5	36
Oklahoma, Western District	31	21	37	1	4	59	3	0	1	1	5	17
Oregon...	29	46	45	4	3	95	47	0	3	3	7	20
Pennsylvania, Eastern District	56	30	166	13	4	50	6	0	0	0	5	67
Pennsylvania, Middle District...................	23	28	62	7	2	122	4	0	2	1	3	39
Pennsylvania, Western District................	58	34	147	13	7	75	4	0	1	1	4	81
Puerto Rico.....................................	42	13	30	2	2	43	1	0	0	0	4	22
Rhode Island....................................	4	18	30	8	4	21	1	0	0	1	4	14
South Carolina..................................	273	94	253	18	4	230	47	0	2	6	135	184
South Dakota...................................	4	21	52	3	1	249	4	0	0	1	3	14
Tennessee, Eastern District.....................	41	53	182	6	4	278	11	0	1	3	25	70
Tennessee, Middle District......................	24	54	52	0	0	113	8	0	0	0	10	24
Tennessee, Western District	93	65	149	30	11	99	22	0	1	1	20	74
Texas, Eastern District	41	146	242	29	17	258	17	0	3	1	9	98
Texas, Northern District.........................	150	398	845	32	5	307	52	0	4	3	30	312
Texas, Southern District.........................	182	275	1,197	25	34	345	35	1	7	5	30	551
Texas, Western District..........................	118	256	392	16	17	319	40	0	0	4	41	197
U.S. Virgin Islands[1]	0	1	0	0	0	0	0	0	0	0	0	0
Utah...	26	94	198	1	10	115	18	0	0	21	27	65
Vermont..	1	2	13	0	3	16	0	0	0	0	1	3
Virginia, Eastern District	93	112	200	7	7	166	12	0	0	0	39	148
Virginia, Western District.......................	26	58	145	29	3	857	15	0	0	3	27	47
Washington, Eastern District	19	29	98	4	1	17	3	0	0	0	12	50
Washington, Western District..................	38	73	144	4	0	78	20	0	0	0	7	27
West Virginia, Northern District..............	13	16	22	2	1	168	4	0	0	0	4	11
West Virginia, Southern District..............	19	35	13	20	1	95	1	0	0	0	4	13
Wisconsin, Eastern District	24	9	24	2	8	43	7	0	0	1	0	21
Wisconsin, Western District....................	12	18	110	1	2	23	2	0	2	1	6	20
Wyoming..	3	1	2	0	2	10	2	0	0	0	0	0

[1]Population for Guam, Northern Mariana Island, and U.S. Virgin Islands was gathered from the 2010 U.S. Census.

Table 41. Number of Arrestees from State-Issued Warrants by NIBRS Offense Code, by Selected U.S. Marshals Service Judicial District, 2017—Continued

(Number.)

NIBRS Offense Code / NIBRS Offense Description	200 Arson	210 Extortion/ blackmail	220 Burglary/ breaking & entering	240 Motor vehicle theft	250 Counterfeiting/ forgery	270 Embezzlement	280 Stolen property offenses	290 Destruction/ damage/ vandalism of property	370 Pornography/ obscene material	510 Bribery	520 Weapon law violations	720 Animal cruelty
Grand Total, All Judicial Districts	218	50	4,129	570	261	46	369	77	371	13	4,948	8
Alabama, Middle District	0	0	68	2	0	0	0	0	25	0	87	0
Alabama, Northern District	3	0	77	5	4	0	13	2	6	0	56	1
Alabama, Southern District	0	0	40	3	0	0	7	0	1	0	33	0
Alaska	0	0	1	0	0	0	0	0	1	0	0	0
Arizona	2	1	62	30	8	2	10	2	13	1	66	1
Arkansas, Eastern District	1	0	11	2	1	0	0	0	2	0	13	0
Arkansas, Western District	0	0	1	1	2	0	1	0	1	0	8	0
California, Central District	9	9	108	65	10	2	63	2	27	1	183	0
California, Eastern District	0	1	3	3	0	1	1	0	3	0	34	0
California, Northern District	1	1	40	6	1	1	4	0	3	0	85	0
California, Southern District	5	2	49	27	2	1	8	3	6	0	78	0
Colorado	0	0	4	4	0	0	0	0	0	1	0	0
Connecticut	3	1	12	0	0	0	0	0	3	0	18	0
Delaware	0	0	28	5	1	0	3	0	0	0	25	0
District of Columbia	0	0	2	0	0	0	0	0	0	0	0	0
Florida, Middle District	5	1	63	17	0	0	1	0	4	2	78	0
Florida, Northern District	1	1	34	8	0	0	2	0	7	0	49	0
Florida, Southern District	6	1	117	9	0	0	1	1	5	0	58	0
Georgia, Middle District	1	0	50	18	1	0	3	0	0	0	73	0
Georgia, Northern District	1	0	64	7	0	0	2	1	3	1	143	0
Georgia, Southern District	0	0	28	4	0	0	0	0	2	1	80	0
Guam[1]	0	0	0	0	0	0	0	0	0	0	0	0
Hawaii	0	0	5	5	2	0	1	0	1	0	0	0
Idaho	1	0	4	0	0	0	0	0	9	0	3	0
Illinois, Central District	5	0	79	5	20	0	3	4	0	0	156	1
Illinois, Northern District	3	0	108	4	13	0	2	3	2	0	71	0
Illinois, Southern District	1	0	22	5	2	0	1	1	2	0	205	0
Indiana, Northern District	1	0	38	2	3	1	6	0	3	0	21	0
Indiana, Southern District	2	0	52	3	1	0	5	0	0	0	33	0
Iowa, Northern District	0	0	5	1	1	0	0	0	0	0	4	0
Iowa, Southern District	0	0	3	0	0	0	0	0	1	0	2	0
Kansas	0	2	13	1	2	0	2	1	8	0	24	0
Kentucky, Eastern District	2	0	9	0	0	0	0	0	3	0	6	0
Kentucky, Western District	1	0	10	1	1	0	6	0	0	0	21	0
Louisiana, Eastern District	5	0	88	7	4	0	8	7	3	0	64	0
Louisiana, Middle District	0	0	6	0	0	0	0	0	0	0	6	0
Louisiana, Western District	1	0	98	11	5	0	11	8	3	0	158	1
Maine	0	0	0	0	0	0	0	0	5	0	6	0
Maryland	9	0	119	28	1	0	0	0	2	0	50	0
Massachusetts	4	1	26	0	2	0	5	0	5	0	69	0
Michigan, Eastern District	11	2	95	16	10	8	8	5	11	2	86	0
Michigan, Western District	1	0	34	2	1	0	2	0	3	0	36	0
Minnesota	1	0	7	0	0	0	1	0	0	0	36	0
Mississippi, Northern District	0	2	39	4	8	3	5	0	2	0	59	0
Mississippi, Southern District	5	0	101	18	14	9	17	3	2	1	56	0
Missouri, Eastern District	0	0	23	2	1	0	3	0	3	0	62	0
Missouri, Western District	0	0	6	2	2	0	0	0	1	0	5	0
Montana	2	0	27	1	6	1	1	2	3	0	0	0
Nebraska	4	0	52	25	15	1	3	1	4	0	55	0
Nevada	0	0	15	5	1	4	2	0	1	0	13	0
New Hampshire	2	0	2	1	4	0	2	1	0	0	4	0
New Jersey	8	0	130	1	2	0	19	1	2	1	198	0
New Mexico	1	0	32	5	0	0	1	0	4	0	17	0
New York, Eastern District	0	0	35	3	17	1	10	1	2	0	59	0
New York, Northern District	3	0	58	0	5	0	0	0	15	0	57	0

(Number.)

NIBRS Offense Code	200	210	220	240	250	270	280	290	370	510	520	720
NIBRS Offense Description	Arson	Extortion/ blackmail	Burglary/ breaking & entering	Motor vehicle theft	Counterfeiting/ forgery	Embezzlement	Stolen property offenses	Destruction/ damage/ vandalism of property	Pornography/ obscene material	Bribery	Weapon law violations	Animal cruelty
New York, Southern District	0	0	7	0	1	0	0	0	0	0	13	0
New York, Western District	4	0	129	1	0	0	2	0	0	0	57	0
North Carolina, Eastern District	1	0	82	9	0	2	8	3	5	0	113	0
North Carolina, Middle District	1	0	10	2	0	0	2	0	1	0	61	0
North Carolina, Western District	0	1	10	10	2	0	7	0	0	0	24	0
North Dakota	1	0	37	1	0	0	2	1	0	0	11	0
Northern Mariana Islands[1]	0	0	2	0	0	0	0	0	0	0	0	0
Ohio, Northern District	17	1	250	22	12	1	24	3	14	1	142	0
Ohio, Southern District	9	3	178	13	20	0	20	3	3	0	131	1
Oklahoma, Eastern District	3	1	22	2	0	0	4	0	1	0	50	0
Oklahoma, Northern District	2	0	11	2	0	1	4	1	1	0	46	1
Oklahoma, Western District	0	0	3	2	2	1	2	0	3	0	16	0
Oregon	1	0	10	2	0	0	0	0	5	0	20	0
Pennsylvania, Eastern District	3	0	21	5	3	0	3	0	1	0	25	0
Pennsylvania, Middle District	0	0	21	2	1	0	1	0	0	0	32	0
Pennsylvania, Western District	2	0	75	3	8	0	10	1	0	0	46	0
Puerto Rico	0	0	9	4	0	0	1	0	0	0	39	0
Rhode Island	2	1	12	3	0	1	0	0	1	0	4	0
South Carolina	5	5	119	2	0	0	2	0	3	0	298	0
South Dakota	0	0	46	0	2	0	0	0	5	0	2	0
Tennessee, Eastern District	2	0	24	2	2	1	0	1	2	0	39	1
Tennessee, Middle District	1	0	24	1	0	0	0	1	0	0	17	0
Tennessee, Western District	2	0	41	4	2	0	3	2	0	1	77	0
Texas, Eastern District	6	2	74	4	7	0	3	0	25	0	59	0
Texas, Northern District	15	1	95	12	1	1	2	4	19	0	68	0
Texas, Southern District	5	0	196	16	5	0	1	1	11	0	70	1
Texas, Western District	10	3	92	11	5	1	3	3	10	0	80	0
U.S. Virgin Islands[1]	0	0	0	0	0	1	0	0	0	0	0	0
Utah	3	1	46	10	4	0	9	0	4	0	70	0
Vermont	0	0	5	0	0	0	1	0	0	0	1	0
Virginia, Eastern District	2	0	76	11	3	1	0	0	18	0	208	0
Virginia, Western District	5	1	71	29	1	0	0	2	19	0	173	0
Washington, Eastern District	0	2	58	1	1	0	5	1	0	0	34	0
Washington, Western District	3	3	19	5	2	0	2	0	2	0	54	0
West Virginia, Northern District	0	0	6	0	0	0	1	0	0	0	8	0
West Virginia, Southern District	0	0	38	1	0	0	4	0	0	0	8	0
Wisconsin, Eastern District	1	0	2	2	2	0	0	1	2	0	15	0
Wisconsin, Western District	1	0	4	2	1	0	0	0	2	0	27	0
Wyoming	0	0	1	0	1	0	0	0	2	0	1	0

[1]Population for Guam, Northern Mariana Island, and U.S. Virgin Islands was gathered from the 2010 U.S. Census.

Table 41. Number of Arrestees from State-Issued Warrants by NIBRS Offense Code, by Selected U.S. Marshals Service Judicial District, 2017—*Continued*

(Number.)

NIBRS Offense Description	Count of arrestees for Group A Offenses	90B Curfew/ loitering/ vagrancy violations	90C Disorderly conduct	90D Driving under the influence	90F Family offenses, nonviolent	90G Liquor law violations	90H Peeping tom	90J Trespass of real property	90Z All other offenses	Count of arrestees for Group B Offenses	Total number of arrestees	Population per judicial district
Grand Total, All Judicial Districts	58,444	7	116	140	1,138	1	8	27	35,519	36,956	95,400	329,376,001
Alabama, Middle District........................	824	0	0	0	16	0	0	0	159	175	999	1,151,840
Alabama, Northern District.....................	989	0	0	0	32	0	0	0	630	662	1,651	2,878,062
Alabama, Southern District	510	0	0	0	21	0	0	0	204	225	735	844,845
Alaska..	20	0	0	0	0	0	0	0	27	27	47	739,795
Arizona..	1,037	0	4	3	10	0	0	1	1,556	1,574	2,611	7,016,270
Arkansas, Eastern District......................	213	0	0	0	0	0	0	0	193	193	406	1,641,446
Arkansas, Western District	80	0	0	0	0	0	0	0	29	29	109	1,362,833
California, Central District......................	1,909	0	4	19	46	1	0	1	838	909	2,818	19,520,355
California, Eastern District......................	271	0	0	0	2	0	0	0	226	228	499	8,094,481
California, Northern District	592	0	2	2	5	0	0	0	347	356	948	8,401,302
California, Southern District	978	0	3	18	64	0	0	1	2,681	2,767	3,745	3,520,515
Colorado	69	0	0	0	0	0	0	0	119	119	188	5,607,154
Connecticut	245	0	0	0	14	0	1	0	258	273	518	3,588,184
Delaware	188	0	0	0	0	0	0	0	190	190	378	961,939
District of Columbia...............................	30	0	0	0	0	0	0	0	11	11	41	693,972
Florida, Middle District	1,034	0	0	0	22	0	0	0	174	196	1,230	12,117,428
Florida, Northern District.......................	702	0	0	0	16	0	1	0	366	383	1,085	1,858,835
Florida, Southern District.......................	1,404	0	0	1	16	0	0	2	418	437	1,841	7,008,137
Georgia, Middle District	660	0	0	0	15	0	0	1	584	600	1,260	2,011,173
Georgia, Northern District......................	1,352	0	0	0	29	0	0	0	551	580	1,932	6,831,493
Georgia, Southern District......................	512	0	1	0	21	0	0	0	309	331	843	1,586,713
Guam[1]	3	0	0	0	1	0	0	0	169	170	173	159,358
Hawaii	74	0	0	0	0	0	0	0	184	184	258	1,427,538
Idaho..	152	0	0	0	0	0	1	0	58	59	211	1,716,943
Illinois, Central District	1,065	0	2	4	7	0	0	2	465	480	1,545	2,209,511
Illinois, Northern District........................	1,331	0	4	6	2	0	0	1	805	818	2,149	9,334,009
Illinois, Southern District........................	485	0	2	1	0	0	0	7	341	351	836	1,258,503
Indiana, Northern District.......................	425	0	1	3	6	0	0	0	179	189	614	2,595,142
Indiana, Southern District.......................	559	0	0	0	3	0	0	0	143	146	705	4,071,676
Iowa, Northern District...........................	81	0	1	0	0	0	0	1	109	111	192	1,325,687
Iowa, Southern District...........................	57	0	0	0	0	0	0	0	219	219	276	1,820,024
Kansas	241	0	0	0	2	0	0	0	1,214	1,216	1,457	2,913,123
Kentucky, Eastern District.......................	201	0	0	0	0	0	0	0	172	172	373	2,211,234
Kentucky, Western District......................	165	0	0	0	3	0	0	0	158	161	326	2,242,955
Louisiana, Eastern District......................	759	0	1	0	10	0	0	0	220	231	990	1,687,314
Louisiana, Middle District	118	0	0	0	3	0	0	0	138	141	259	836,722
Louisiana, Western District.....................	974	0	2	0	36	0	0	0	359	397	1,371	2,160,297
Maine	67	0	0	0	0	0	0	0	25	25	92	1,335,907
Maryland	1,191	0	0	0	23	0	0	0	556	579	1,770	6,052,177
Massachusetts	963	0	0	1	0	0	0	0	160	161	1,124	6,859,819
Michigan, Eastern District.......................	1,391	0	4	9	13	0	0	0	1,320	1,346	2,737	6,450,976
Michigan, Western District......................	678	0	0	1	3	0	0	0	783	787	1,465	3,511,335
Minnesota	162	0	0	0	0	0	0	0	153	153	315	5,576,606
Mississippi, Northern District	648	0	1	0	6	0	0	0	322	329	977	1,113,255
Mississippi, Southern District.................	856	0	0	0	5	0	1	0	298	304	1,160	1,870,845
Missouri, Eastern District........................	342	0	0	0	7	0	0	0	161	168	510	2,936,329
Missouri, Western District	91	0	0	0	8	0	0	0	116	124	215	3,177,203
Montana...	408	0	0	0	3	0	0	0	929	932	1,340	1,050,493
Nebraska..	1,081	0	0	17	10	0	0	1	218	246	1,327	1,920,076
Nevada...	169	0	0	2	2	0	0	0	220	224	393	2,998,039
New Hampshire	107	0	1	0	3	0	0	2	214	220	327	1,342,795
New Jersey..	1,465	0	1	0	29	0	0	0	1,116	1,146	2,611	9,005,644
New Mexico..	322	0	0	0	12	0	0	0	370	382	704	2,088,070
New York, Eastern District......................	600	0	1	6	1	0	0	1	130	139	739	8,352,340
New York, Northern District...................	763	0	0	2	1	0	0	0	436	439	1,202	3,405,511

(Number.)

NIBRS Offense Code / NIBRS Offense Description	Count of arrestees for Group A Offenses	90B Curfew/ loitering/ vagrancy violations	90C Disorderly conduct	90D Driving under the influence	90F Family offenses, nonviolent	90G Liquor law violations	90H Peeping tom	90J Trespass of real property	90Z All other offenses	Count of arrestees for Group B Offenses	Total number of arrestees	Population per judicial district
New York, Southern District	162	0	0	0	0	0	0	0	87	87	249	5,287,449
New York, Western District	598	0	0	0	2	0	0	0	260	262	860	2,804,099
North Carolina, Eastern District	892	0	0	0	1	0	0	0	425	426	1,318	4,040,346
North Carolina, Middle District	364	0	0	0	0	0	0	0	136	136	500	2,982,908
North Carolina, Western District	386	0	0	0	2	0	0	0	229	231	617	3,250,165
North Dakota	311	0	0	1	20	0	0	0	303	324	635	755,393
Northern Mariana Islands[1]	2	0	0	0	0	0	0	0	1	1	3	53,883
Ohio, Northern District	2,365	2	3	1	65	0	0	0	1,140	1,211	3,576	5,729,748
Ohio, Southern District	1,782	0	11	10	58	0	0	1	734	814	2,596	5,928,861
Oklahoma, Eastern District	408	0	2	0	38	0	0	0	226	266	674	744,540
Oklahoma, Northern District	293	0	0	2	21	0	0	0	94	117	410	1,063,380
Oklahoma, Western District	209	0	2	0	3	0	0	0	133	138	347	2,122,944
Oregon	340	0	0	0	2	0	1	0	203	206	546	4,142,776
Pennsylvania, Eastern District	458	0	0	0	0	0	0	0	503	503	961	5,738,564
Pennsylvania, Middle District	350	0	0	3	2	0	0	0	430	435	785	3,327,331
Pennsylvania, Western District	570	0	2	1	8	0	0	1	546	558	1,128	3,739,642
Puerto Rico	212	0	0	0	2	0	0	0	59	61	273	3,337,177
Rhode Island	129	0	0	0	0	0	0	0	228	228	357	1,059,639
South Carolina	1,680	0	3	0	70	0	0	0	187	260	1,940	5,024,369
South Dakota	407	0	0	0	19	0	0	0	40	59	466	869,666
Tennessee, Eastern District	748	0	0	0	13	0	0	0	345	358	1,106	2,621,077
Tennessee, Middle District	329	0	1	0	2	0	0	0	317	320	649	2,522,866
Tennessee, Western District	697	0	1	2	11	0	0	0	390	404	1,101	1,572,041
Texas, Eastern District	1,041	0	2	8	28	0	1	0	514	553	1,594	3,975,190
Texas, Northern District	2,356	0	9	1	45	0	0	0	559	614	2,970	7,327,013
Texas, Southern District	2,993	0	38	9	64	0	0	4	1,746	1,861	4,854	9,779,201
Texas, Western District	1,618	0	1	3	49	0	0	0	627	680	2,298	7,223,192
U.S. Virgin Islands[1]	2	0	0	0	0	0	0	0	1	1	3	106,405
Utah	722	5	1	1	10	0	1	1	86	105	827	3,101,833
Vermont	46	0	0	1	0	0	0	0	7	8	54	623,657
Virginia, Eastern District	1,103	0	1	0	11	0	0	0	349	361	1,464	6,151,524
Virginia, Western District	1,511	0	0	0	31	0	0	0	544	575	2,086	2,318,496
Washington, Eastern District	335	0	0	0	1	0	0	0	462	463	798	1,603,175
Washington, Western District	481	0	0	0	9	0	0	0	456	465	946	5,802,568
West Virginia, Northern District	256	0	1	0	3	0	0	0	112	116	372	865,333
West Virginia, Southern District	252	0	0	0	7	0	0	0	162	169	421	950,524
Wisconsin, Eastern District	164	0	3	1	8	0	0	0	206	218	382	3,408,621
Wisconsin, Western District	234	0	0	1	5	0	0	0	318	324	558	2,386,862
Wyoming	25	0	0	0	0	0	0	0	24	24	49	579,315

[1]Population for Guam, Northern Mariana Island, and U.S. Virgin Islands was gathered from the 2010 U.S. Census.

Table 41A. Number of Arrestees from State-Issued Warrants by NIBRS Offense Code, by Department of Justice Office of the Inspector General Judicial District, 2017

(Number.)

NIBRS Offense Code	11A - 11D	13A - 13C	23A - 23H	26A - 26G	35A - 35B	36A - 36B	250	270
NIBRS Offense Description	Sex offenses	Assault offenses	Larceny/theft offenses	Fraud offenses	Drug/narcotic offenses	Sex offenses, nonforcible	Counterfeiting/ forgery	Embezzlement
Grand Total, All Judicial Districts	10	3	3	20	12	2	1	2
Alabama, Middle District	0	0	1	0	0	0	0	0
Alabama, Northern District	0	0	0	0	0	0	0	0
Alabama, Southern District	0	0	0	0	0	0	0	0
Alaska	0	0	0	0	0	0	0	0
Arizona	0	0	0	2	0	1	0	0
Arkansas, Eastern District	0	0	0	0	0	0	0	0
Arkansas, Western District	0	0	0	0	0	0	0	0
California, Central District	0	1	0	3	0	0	0	0
California, Eastern District	0	0	0	0	1	0	0	0
California, Northern District	0	0	0	0	0	0	0	0
California, Southern District	0	0	1	0	0	0	0	0
Colorado	0	0	0	0	0	0	0	0
Connecticut	0	0	0	0	0	0	0	0
Delaware	0	0	0	0	0	0	0	0
District of Columbia	0	0	0	1	0	0	0	0
Florida, Middle District	0	0	0	0	0	0	0	0
Florida, Northern District	0	0	0	0	0	0	0	0
Florida, Southern District	0	0	0	1	0	1	0	0
Georgia, Middle District	0	0	0	0	0	0	0	0
Georgia, Northern District	0	2	0	0	0	0	0	0
Georgia, Southern District	0	0	0	0	1	0	0	0
Guam[1]	0	0	0	0	0	0	0	0
Hawaii	0	0	0	1	0	0	0	0
Idaho	0	0	0	0	0	0	0	0
Illinois, Central District	0	0	0	0	0	0	0	0
Illinois, Northern District	0	0	0	0	0	0	0	0
Illinois, Southern District	0	0	0	0	0	0	0	0
Indiana, Northern District	0	0	0	0	0	0	0	0
Indiana, Southern District	0	0	0	0	0	0	0	0
Iowa, Northern District	0	0	0	0	0	0	0	0
Iowa, Southern District	0	0	0	0	0	0	0	0
Kansas	0	0	0	0	0	0	0	0
Kentucky, Eastern District	0	0	0	0	1	0	0	0
Kentucky, Western District	0	0	0	0	0	0	0	0
Louisiana, Eastern District	0	0	0	0	1	0	0	0
Louisiana, Middle District	0	0	0	0	0	0	0	0
Louisiana, Western District	0	0	0	0	0	0	0	0
Maine	0	0	0	0	0	0	0	0
Maryland	0	0	0	1	0	0	0	1
Massachusetts	0	0	0	0	0	0	0	0
Michigan, Eastern District	0	0	0	0	0	0	0	0
Michigan, Western District	0	0	0	0	0	0	0	0
Minnesota	0	0	0	0	0	0	0	0
Mississippi, Northern District	0	0	0	0	0	0	0	0
Mississippi, Southern District	0	0	0	0	0	0	0	0
Missouri, Eastern District	0	0	0	0	0	0	0	0
Missouri, Western District	0	0	0	0	0	0	0	0
Montana	0	0	0	2	0	0	0	1
Nebraska	0	0	0	0	1	0	0	0
Nevada	0	0	0	0	0	0	0	0
New Hampshire	0	0	0	0	1	0	0	0
New Jersey	0	0	0	1	0	0	0	0
New Mexico	0	0	0	0	0	0	0	0
New York, Eastern District	3	0	0	0	4	0	0	0
New York, Northern District	0	0	0	0	0	0	0	0

Table 41A. Number of Arrestees from State-Issued Warrants by NIBRS Offense Code, by Department of Justice Office of the Inspector General Judicial District, 2017—Continued

(Number.)

NIBRS Offense Code	280	290	510	Count of arrestees for Group A Offenses	90Z	Count of arrestees for Group B Offenses	Total number of arrestees	Population per judicial district
NIBRS Offense Description	Stolen property offenses	Destruction/ damage/ vandalism of property	Bribery		All other offenses (includes all alcohol & tobacco offenses)			
Grand Total, All Judicial Districts	2	1	32	88	15	15	103	329,376,001
Alabama, Middle District....................	0	0	0	1	0	0	1	1,151,840
Alabama, Northern District....................................	0	0	1	1	0	0	1	2,878,062
Alabama, Southern District	0	0	0	0	0	0	0	844,845
Alaska...	0	0	0	0	0	0	0	739,795
Arizona...	1	0	1	5	1	1	6	7,016,270
Arkansas, Eastern District	0	0	0	0	0	0	0	1,641,446
Arkansas, Western District	0	0	0	0	0	0	0	1,362,833
California, Central District	0	0	0	4	0	0	4	19,520,355
California, Eastern District	0	0	0	1	0	0	1	8,094,481
California, Northern District	1	0	0	1	0	0	1	8,401,302
California, Southern District	0	0	0	1	0	0	1	3,520,515
Colorado...	0	0	0	0	0	0	0	5,607,154
Connecticut..	0	0	0	0	0	0	0	3,588,184
Delaware..	0	0	0	0	0	0	0	961,939
District of Columbia	0	0	0	1	0	0	1	693,972
Florida, Middle District	0	0	1	1	0	0	1	12,117,428
Florida, Northern District	0	0	0	0	0	0	0	1,858,835
Florida, Southern District	0	0	0	2	0	0	2	7,008,137
Georgia, Middle District	0	0	0	0	0	0	0	2,011,173
Georgia, Northern District....................................	0	0	0	2	1	1	3	6,831,493
Georgia, Southern District....................................	0	0	3	4	0	0	4	1,586,713
Guam[1]..	0	0	0	0	0	0	0	159,358
Hawaii	0	0	0	1	0	0	1	1,427,538
Idaho..	0	0	0	0	0	0	0	1,716,943
Illinois, Central District	0	0	0	0	0	0	0	2,209,511
Illinois, Northern District	0	0	0	0	0	0	0	9,334,009
Illinois, Southern District......................................	0	0	0	0	0	0	0	1,258,503
Indiana, Northern District	0	0	0	0	0	0	0	2,595,142
Indiana, Southern District......................................	0	0	1	1	0	0	1	4,071,676
Iowa, Northern District...	0	0	0	0	0	0	0	1,325,687
Iowa, Southern District...	0	0	0	0	0	0	0	1,820,024
Kansas...	0	0	0	0	0	0	0	2,913,123
Kentucky, Eastern District.....................................	0	0	3	4	1	1	5	2,211,234
Kentucky, Western District....................................	0	0	0	0	0	0	0	2,242,955
Louisiana, Eastern District.....................................	0	1	0	2	0	0	2	1,687,314
Louisiana, Middle District	0	0	0	0	0	0	0	836,722
Louisiana, Western District....................................	0	0	1	1	0	0	1	2,160,297
Maine..	0	0	0	0	0	0	0	1,335,907
Maryland..	0	0	0	2	0	0	2	6,052,177
Massachusetts	0	0	0	0	0	0	0	6,859,819
Michigan, Eastern District.....................................	0	0	1	1	0	0	1	6,450,976
Michigan, Western District....................................	0	0	0	0	0	0	0	3,511,335
Minnesota	0	0	0	0	0	0	0	5,576,606
Mississippi, Northern District................................	0	0	0	0	0	0	0	1,113,255
Mississippi, Southern District................................	0	0	2	2	0	0	2	1,870,845
Missouri, Eastern District......................................	0	0	0	0	0	0	0	2,936,329
Missouri, Western District	0	0	0	0	0	0	0	3,177,203
Montana...	0	0	0	3	0	0	3	1,050,493
Nebraska	0	0	0	1	0	0	1	1,920,076
Nevada	0	0	0	0	0	0	0	2,998,039
New Hampshire	0	0	0	1	0	0	1	1,342,795
New Jersey...	0	0	0	1	0	0	1	9,005,644
New Mexico..	0	0	1	1	0	0	1	2,088,070
New York, Eastern District.....................................	0	0	1	8	0	0	8	8,352,340
New York, Northern District...................................	0	0	2	2	2	2	4	3,405,511

Table 41A. Number of Arrestees from State-Issued Warrants by NIBRS Offense Code, by Department of Justice Office of the Inspector General Judicial District, 2017—Continued

(Number.)

NIBRS Offense Code	11A - 11D	13A - 13C	23A - 23H	26A - 26G	35A - 35B	36A - 36B	250	270
NIBRS Offense Description	Sex offenses	Assault offenses	Larceny/theft offenses	Fraud offenses	Drug/narcotic offenses	Sex offenses, nonforcible	Counterfeiting/ forgery	Embezzlement
New York, Southern District	0	0	0	0	0	0	0	0
New York, Western District	0	0	0	0	0	0	0	0
North Carolina, Eastern District	1	0	0	0	0	0	0	0
North Carolina, Middle District	0	0	0	0	0	0	0	0
North Carolina, Western District	0	0	0	0	0	0	0	0
North Dakota	1	0	0	0	0	0	0	0
Northern Mariana Islands[1]	0	0	0	0	0	0	0	0
Ohio, Northern District	0	0	0	0	0	0	0	0
Ohio, Southern District	0	0	0	0	0	0	0	0
Oklahoma, Eastern District	0	0	0	0	0	0	0	0
Oklahoma, Northern District	0	0	0	0	0	0	0	0
Oklahoma, Western District	1	0	0	1	0	0	0	0
Oregon	0	0	0	0	0	0	0	0
Pennsylvania, Eastern District	0	0	0	0	1	0	0	0
Pennsylvania, Middle District	0	0	0	0	0	0	0	0
Pennsylvania, Western District	0	0	0	0	0	0	0	0
Puerto Rico	0	0	0	0	0	0	0	0
Rhode Island	0	0	0	0	0	0	0	0
South Carolina	0	0	0	0	0	0	0	0
South Dakota	0	0	0	0	0	0	0	0
Tennessee, Eastern District	0	0	0	0	0	0	0	0
Tennessee, Middle District	0	0	0	0	0	0	0	0
Tennessee, Western District	0	0	0	0	0	0	0	0
Texas, Eastern District	0	0	0	0	1	0	0	0
Texas, Northern District	1	0	0	6	0	0	0	0
Texas, Southern District	0	0	0	0	0	0	0	0
Texas, Western District	3	0	0	0	0	0	0	0
U. S. Virgin Islands[1]	0	0	0	0	0	0	0	0
Utah	0	0	0	0	0	0	0	0
Vermont	0	0	0	0	0	0	0	0
Virginia, Eastern District	0	0	0	0	0	0	0	0
Virginia, Western District	0	0	0	0	0	0	1	0
Washington, Eastern District	0	0	1	0	0	0	0	0
Washington, Western District	0	0	0	0	0	0	0	0
West Virginia, Northern District	0	0	0	0	0	0	0	0
West Virginia, Southern District	0	0	0	0	0	0	0	0
Wisconsin, Eastern District	0	0	0	0	0	0	0	0
Wisconsin, Western District	0	0	0	1	0	0	0	0
Wyoming	0	0	0	0	0	0	0	0

Table 41A. Number of Arrestees from State-Issued Warrants by NIBRS Offense Code, by Department of Justice Office of the Inspector General Judicial District, 2017—*Continued*

(Number.)

NIBRS Offense Description	280 Stolen property offenses	290 Destruction/ damage/ vandalism of property	510 Bribery	Count of arrestees for Group A Offenses	90Z All other offenses (includes all alcohol & tobacco offenses)	Count of arrestees for Group B Offenses	Total number of arrestees	Population per judicial district
New York, Southern District	0	0	0	0	1	1	1	5,287,449
New York, Western District	0	0	0	0	0	0	0	2,804,099
North Carolina, Eastern District	0	0	0	1	0	0	1	4,040,346
North Carolina, Middle District	0	0	0	0	0	0	0	2,982,908
North Carolina, Western District	0	0	0	0	0	0	0	3,250,165
North Dakota	0	0	0	1	0	0	1	755,393
Northern Mariana Islands[1]	0	0	0	0	0	0	0	53,883
Ohio, Northern District	0	0	0	0	1	1	1	5,729,748
Ohio, Southern District	0	0	0	0	0	0	0	5,928,861
Oklahoma, Eastern District	0	0	0	0	0	0	0	744,540
Oklahoma, Northern District	0	0	0	0	0	0	0	1,063,380
Oklahoma, Western District	0	0	3	5	0	0	5	2,122,944
Oregon	0	0	0	0	1	1	1	4,142,776
Pennsylvania, Eastern District	0	0	0	1	0	0	1	5,738,564
Pennsylvania, Middle District	0	0	0	0	0	0	0	3,327,331
Pennsylvania, Western District	0	0	0	0	0	0	0	3,739,642
Puerto Rico	0	0	0	0	0	0	0	3,337,177
Rhode Island	0	0	0	0	0	0	0	1,059,639
South Carolina	0	0	1	1	3	3	4	5,024,369
South Dakota	0	0	0	0	0	0	0	869,666
Tennessee, Eastern District	0	0	0	0	0	0	0	2,621,077
Tennessee, Middle District	0	0	0	0	0	0	0	2,522,866
Tennessee, Western District	0	0	0	0	1	1	1	1,572,041
Texas, Eastern District	0	0	2	3	0	0	3	3,975,190
Texas, Northern District	0	0	2	9	0	0	9	7,327,013
Texas, Southern District	0	0	3	3	1	1	4	9,779,201
Texas, Western District	0	0	0	3	0	0	3	7,223,192
U. S. Virgin Islands[1]	0	0	0	0	0	0	0	106,405
Utah	0	0	0	0	0	0	0	3,101,833
Vermont	0	0	0	0	0	0	0	623,657
Virginia, Eastern District	0	0	0	0	0	0	0	6,151,524
Virginia, Western District	0	0	0	1	1	1	2	2,318,496
Washington, Eastern District	0	0	0	1	1	1	2	1,603,175
Washington, Western District	0	0	0	0	0	0	0	5,802,568
West Virginia, Northern District	0	0	2	2	0	0	2	865,333
West Virginia, Southern District	0	0	0	0	0	0	0	950,524
Wisconsin, Eastern District	0	0	0	0	0	0	0	3,408,621
Wisconsin, Western District	0	0	1	2	0	0	2	2,386,862
Wyoming	0	0	0	0	0	0	0	579,315

[1]Population for Guam, Northern Mariana Island, and U.S. Virgin Islands was gathered from the 2010 U.S. Census.

Table 42. FBI Employment, by Gender, 2017

(Number.)

Employee	Male	Female	Total
Total	20,665	16,024	36,689
Special agents	10,984	2,683	13,667
Professional staff	9,490	13,304	22,794
Police officers	191	37	228

Table 43. ATF Employment, by Gender, 2017

(Number.)

Employee	Male	Female	Total
Total	3,461	1,635	5,096
Special agents	2,248	358	2,606
Professional staff	1,213	1,277	2,490
Police officers	0	0	0

Table 44. USMS Employment, by Gender, 2017

(Number.)

Employee	Male	Female	Total
Total	3,940	1,249	5,189
Special agents	3,443	359	3,802
Professional staff	497	890	1,387
Police officers	0	0	0

Table 45. Human Trafficking, Offenses and Clearances by Participating State, 2017

(Number.)

State	Commercial sex acts			Involuntary servitude			Total		
	Offenses	Total cleared	Clearances under 18	Offenses	Total cleared	Clearances under 18	Offenses	Total cleared	Clearances under 18
Alabama[1]	0	0	0	0	0	0	0	0	0
Alaska	2	0	0	1	0	0	3	0	0
Arizona	92	37	3	7	4	0	99	41	3
Arkansas	0	0	0	0	0	0	0	0	0
California[1]	0	0	0	0	0	0	0	0	0
Colorado	49	14	0	7	0	0	56	14	0
Connecticut	8	0	0	0	0	0	8	0	0
Delaware	5	4	0	0	0	0	5	4	0
Florida	65	51	0	24	7	0	89	58	0
Georgia	0	0	0	0	0	0	0	0	0
Guam	0	0	0	0	0	0	0	0	0
Hawaii	2	1	0	0	0	0	2	1	0
Idaho[1]	0	0	0	0	0	0	0	0	0
Illinois	26	0	0	8	0	0	34	0	0
Indiana	2	0	0	1	0	0	3	0	0
Kansas	3	2	0	0	0	0	3	2	0
Kentucky	8	0	0	14	0	0	22	0	0
Louisiana	59	47	0	2	2	0	61	49	0
Maine	2	0	0	0	0	0	2	0	0
Maryland	0	0	0	0	0	0	0	0	0
Massachusetts	17	5	0	11	2	0	28	7	0
Michigan	11	2	0	11	0	0	22	2	0
Minnesota	173	147	1	0	0	0	173	147	1
Mississippi	0	0	0	0	0	0	0	0	0
Missouri	25	16	1	3	0	0	28	16	1
Montana	2	0	0	0	0	0	2	0	0
Nebraska[1]	0	0	0	0	0	0	0	0	0
Nevada	5	0	0	0	0	0	5	0	0
New Hampshire	2	2	0	0	0	0	2	2	0
New Mexico[1]	0	0	0	0	0	0	0	0	0
New York[1]	0	0	0	0	0	0	0	0	0
North Carolina[1]	0	0	0	0	0	0	0	0	0
North Dakota	10	0	0	1	0	0	11	0	0
Ohio	0	0	0	0	0	0	0	0	0
Oklahoma	25	17	2	0	0	0	25	17	2
Oregon	1	0	0	0	0	0	1	0	0
Puerto Rico	0	0	0	0	0	0	1	0	0
Rhode Island	12	3	0	1	1	0	13	4	0
South Carolina	26	2	1	4	0	0	30	2	1
South Dakota	3	0	0	0	0	0	3	0	0
Tennessee	75	11	1	4	0	0	79	11	1
Texas	193	82	4	119	59	16	312	141	20
Utah	1	0	0	0	0	0	1	0	0
Vermont	0	0	0	0	0	0	0	0	0
Washington	29	6	0	1	1	0	30	7	0
Wisconsin	59	16	0	6	2	0	65	18	0
Wyoming	2	2	1	0	0	0	2	2	1

[1] Data submitted through the Bureau of Indian Affairs.

Table 46. Human Trafficking Arrests, by Age and Participating State, 2017

(Number.)

State	Juvenile		Adult	
	Male	Female	Male	Female
Arizona				
Commercial sex acts	0	0	125	60
Involuntary servitude	0	0	1	0
Colorado				
Commercial sex acts	0	0	1	1
Involuntary servitude	0	0	2	0
Connecticut				
Commercial sex acts	0	0	5	0
Involuntary servitude	0	0	0	0
Delaware				
Commercial sex acts	0	0	1	0
Involuntary servitude	0	0	0	0
Hawaii				
Commercial sex acts	0	0	1	1
Involuntary servitude	0	0	0	0
Illinois				
Commercial sex acts	0	0	0	0
Involuntary servitude	0	0	1	0
Kentucky				
Commercial sex acts	0	0	1	0
Involuntary servitude	0	0	0	0
Louisiana				
Commercial sex acts	0	0	20	9
Involuntary servitude	4	1	16	14
Maine				
Commercial sex acts	0	0	0	1
Involuntary servitude	0	0	0	0
Maryland				
Commercial sex acts	0	0	22	10
Involuntary servitude	0	0	2	0
Massachusetts				
Commercial sex acts	0	0	5	3
Involuntary servitude	0	0	0	0
Minnesota				
Commercial sex acts	1	0	131	18
Involuntary servitude	0	0	2	0
Missouri				
Commercial sex acts	0	0	8	5
Involuntary servitude	0	0	1	0
Nevada				
Commercial sex acts	0	1	33	8
Involuntary servitude	0	0	0	0
North Dakota				
Commercial sex acts	0	0	1	0
Involuntary servitude	0	0	0	0
Ohio				
Commercial sex acts	0	0	0	1
Involuntary servitude	0	0	0	0
Oklahoma				
Commercial sex acts	0	1	7	2
Involuntary servitude	0	0	1	1
Oregon				
Commercial sex acts	0	0	1	0
Involuntary servitude	3	0	0	0

Table 46. Human Trafficking Arrests, by Age and Participating State, 2017—*Continued*

(Number.)

State	Juvenile		Adult	
	Male	Female	Male	Female
Rhode Island				
Commercial sex acts	0	0	7	1
Involuntary servitude	0	0	0	0
South Carolina				
Commercial sex acts	0	0	5	2
Involuntary servitude	0	0	3	1
Tennessee				
Commercial sex acts	0	0	21	3
Involuntary servitude	0	0	1	0
Texas				
Commercial sex acts	2	34	22	6
Involuntary servitude	1	0	13	1
Washington				
Commercial sex acts	0	0	3	0
Involuntary servitude	0	0	1	0
Wisconsin				
Commercial sex acts	0	1	23	6
Involuntary servitude	0	0	0	1
Wyoming				
Commercial sex acts	0	0	1	0
Involuntary servitude	0	0	0	0

Table 47. Human Trafficking Arrests, by Race and Participating State, 2017

(Number.)

State	Juvenile						Adult					
	White	Black or African American	American Indian/ Alaska Native	Asian	Native Hawaiian/ Other Pacific Islander	Total	White	Black or African American	American Indian/ Alaska Native	Asian	Native Hawaiian/ Other Pacific Islander	Total
Arizona												
Commercial sex acts	0	0	0	0	0	0	132	48	1	4	0	185
Involuntary servitude.........	0	0	0	0	0	0	1	0	0	0	0	1
Colorado												
Commercial sex acts	0	0	0	0	0	0	2	0	0	0	0	2
Involuntary servitude.........	0	0	0	0	0	0	1	1	0	0	0	2
Connecticut												
Commercial sex acts	0	0	0	0	0	0	4	1	0	0	0	5
Involuntary servitude.........	0	0	0	0	0	0	0	0	0	0	0	0
Delaware												
Commercial sex acts	0	0	0	0	0	0	1	0	0	0	0	1
Involuntary servitude.........	0	0	0	0	0	0	0	0	0	0	0	0
Hawaii												
Commercial sex acts	0	0	0	0	0	0	1	0	0	1	0	2
Involuntary servitude.........	0	0	0	0	0	0	0	0	0	0	0	0
Illinois												
Commercial sex acts	0	0	0	0	0	0	0	0	0	0	0	0
Involuntary servitude.........	0	0	0	0	0	0	0	1	0	0	0	1
Kentucky												
Commercial sex acts	0	0	0	0	0	0	1	0	0	0	0	1
Involuntary servitude.........	0	0	0	0	0	0	0	0	0	0	0	0
Louisiana												
Commercial sex acts	0	0	0	0	0	0	5	24	0	0	0	29
Involuntary servitude.........	1	4	0	0	0	5	21	8	1	0	0	30
Maine												
Commercial sex acts	0	0	0	0	0	0	1	0	0	0	0	1
Involuntary servitude.........	0	0	0	0	0	0	0	0	0	0	0	0
Maryland												
Commercial sex acts	0	0	0	0	0	0	6	26	0	0	0	32
Involuntary servitude.........	0	0	0	0	0	0	0	2	0	0	0	2
Massachusetts												
Commercial sex acts	0	0	0	0	0	0	2	5	0	1	0	8
Involuntary servitude.........	0	0	0	0	0	0	0	0	0	0	0	0
Minnesota												
Commercial sex acts	1	0	0	0	0	1	70	47	4	27	0	148
Involuntary servitude.........	0	0	0	0	0	0	1	1	0	0	0	2
Missouri												
Commercial sex acts	0	0	0	0	0	0	4	9	0	0	0	13
Involuntary servitude.........	0	0	0	0	0	0	1	0	0	0	0	1
Nevada												
Commercial sex acts	1	0	0	0	0	1	14	27	0	0	0	41
Involuntary servitude.........	0	0	0	0	0	0	0	0	0	0	0	0
North Dakota												
Commercial sex acts	0	0	0	0	0	0	1	0	0	0	0	1
Involuntary servitude.........	0	0	0	0	0	0	0	0	0	0	0	0
Ohio												
Commercial sex acts	0	0	0	0	0	0	1	0	0	0	0	1
Involuntary servitude.........	0	0	0	0	0	0	0	0	0	0	0	0
Oklahoma												
Commercial sex acts	0	1	0	0	0	1	2	6	1	0	0	9
Involuntary servitude.........	0	0	0	0	0	0	1	1	0	0	0	2

Table 47. Human Trafficking Arrests, by Race and Participating State, 2017—*Continued*

(Number.)

State	Juvenile						Adult					
	White	Black or African American	American Indian/ Alaska Native	Asian	Native Hawaiian/ Other Pacific Islander	Total	White	Black or African American	American Indian/ Alaska Native	Asian	Native Hawaiian/ Other Pacific Islander	Total
Oregon												
Commercial sex acts	0	0	0	0	0	0	0	1	0	0	0	1
Involuntary servitude	3	0	0	0	0	3	0	0	0	0	0	0
Rhode Island												
Commercial sex acts	0	0	0	0	0	0	2	6	0	0	0	8
Involuntary servitude	0	0	0	0	0	0	0	0	0	0	0	0
South Carolina												
Commercial sex acts	0	0	0	0	0	0	2	5	0	0	0	7
Involuntary servitude	0	0	0	0	0	0	3	1	0	0	0	4
Tennessee												
Commercial sex acts	0	0	0	0	0	0	14	7	0	0	0	21
Involuntary servitude	0	0	0	0	0	0	1	0	0	0	0	1
Texas												
Commercial sex acts	17	19	0	0	0	36	10	18	0	0	0	28
Involuntary servitude	1	0	0	0	0	1	9	5	0	0	0	14
Washington												
Commercial sex acts	0	0	0	0	0	0	2	1	0	0	0	3
Involuntary servitude	0	0	0	0	0	0	0	1	0	0	0	1
Wisconsin												
Commercial sex acts	0	1	0	0	0	1	11	14	3	0	0	28
Involuntary servitude	0	0	0	0	0	0	0	1	0	0	0	1
Wyoming												
Commercial sex acts	0	0	0	0	0	0	1	0	0	0	0	1
Involuntary servitude	0	0	0	0	0	0	0	0	0	0	0	0

Table 48. Human Trafficking Arrests, by Ethnicity and Participating State, 2017

(Number.)

State	Juvenile			Adult		
	Hispanic or Latino	Not Hispanic or Latino	Total	Hispanic or Latino	Not Hispanic or Latino	Total
Arizona						
Commercial sex acts	0	0	0	47	138	185
Involuntary servitude.........................	0	0	0	0	1	1
Colorado						
Commercial sex acts	0	0	0	1	1	2
Involuntary servitude.........................	0	0	0	1	1	2
Connecticut						
Commercial sex acts	0	0	0	0	4	4
Involuntary servitude.........................	0	0	0	0	0	0
Delaware						
Commercial sex acts	0	0	0	1	0	1
Involuntary servitude.........................	0	0	0	0	0	0
Illinois						
Commercial sex acts	0	0	0	0	0	0
Involuntary servitude.........................	0	0	0	0	1	1
Kentucky						
Commercial sex acts	0	0	0	0	1	1
Involuntary servitude.........................	0	0	0	0	0	0
Massachusetts						
Commercial sex acts	0	0	0	1	7	8
Involuntary servitude.........................	0	0	0	0	0	0
Maine						
Commercial sex acts	0	0	0	0	1	1
Involuntary servitude.........................	0	0	0	0	0	0
Maryland						
Commercial sex acts	0	0	0	0	22	22
Involuntary servitude.........................	0	0	0	0	2	2
Minnesota						
Commercial sex acts	0	1	1	31	117	148
Involuntary servitude.........................	0	0	0	0	2	2
Missouri						
Commercial sex acts	0	0	0	0	13	13
Involuntary servitude.........................	0	0	0	0	1	1
Nevada						
Commercial sex acts	0	0	0	2	32	34
Involuntary servitude.........................	0	0	0	0	0	0
North Dakota						
Commercial sex acts	0	0	0	1	0	1
Involuntary servitude.........................	0	0	0	0	0	0
Ohio						
Commercial sex acts	0	0	0	0	1	1
Involuntary servitude.........................	0	0	0	0	0	0
Oklahoma						
Commercial sex acts	0	1	1	0	9	9
Involuntary servitude.........................	0	0	0	0	2	2
Rhode Island						
Commercial sex acts	0	0	0	2	6	8
Involuntary servitude.........................	0	0	0	0	0	0
South Carolina						
Commercial sex acts	0	0	0	1	6	7
Involuntary servitude.........................	0	0	0	3	0	3
Tennessee						
Commercial sex acts	0	0	0	6	18	24
Involuntary servitude.........................	0	0	0	0	1	1

Table 48. Human Trafficking Arrests, by Ethnicity and Participating State, 2017—*Continued*

(Number.)

State	Juvenile			Adult		
	Hispanic or Latino	Not Hispanic or Latino	Total	Hispanic or Latino	Not Hispanic or Latino	Total
Texas						
Commercial sex acts	9	27	36	5	22	27
Involuntary servitude	1	0	1	6	8	14
Washington						
Commercial sex acts	0	0	0	0	1	1
Involuntary servitude	0	0	0	0	0	0
Wisconsin						
Commercial sex acts	0	0	0	3	21	24
Involuntary servitude	0	0	0	0	1	1
Wyoming						
Commercial sex acts	0	0	0	1	0	1
Involuntary servitude	0	0	0	0	0	0

Note: Not all agencies provide ethnicity data; therefore, the race and ethnicity totals will not equal.

Table 49. Cargo Theft by Participating State, by Incidents and Stolen/Recovered Values, 2017

(Number; dollars; percent.)

State	Number of agencies reporting an incident	Number of incidents reported	Value of property		Percent recovered
			Stolen	Recovered	
Total	145	736	$21,721,702	$5,731,104	26.4
Alaska	2	4	8,321	0	0.0
Arkansas	5	12	87,192	75,066	86.1
Colorado	7	11	263,629	104,081	39.5
Delaware	3	18	29,799	11,266	37.8
Florida	20	68	5,047,275	1,723,768	34.2
Georgia	3	10	88,350	45,000	50.9
Indiana	2	2	8,100	0	0.0
Maryland	1	9	25,227	0	0.0
Michigan	6	13	129,938	0	0.0
Nevada	1	2	25,650	0	0.0
North Dakota	2	2	9,787	22	0.2
Ohio	10	18	131,728	0	0.0
Oklahoma	1	1	2,318	0	0.0
Oregon	2	2	61,559	0	0.0
Tennessee	30	324	3,798,984	437,008	11.5
Texas	42	227	11,815,043	3,239,893	27.4
Virginia	7	12	188,552	95,000	50.4
West Virginia	1	1	250	0	0.0

Table 50. Cargo Theft Property Stolen and Recovered, by Type of Value, 2017

(Dollars; percent.)

Type of property	Value of property		Percent recovered
	Stolen	Recovered	
Total	$21,721,702	$5,731,104	26.4
Alcohol...	117,272	17,675	15.1
Artistic supplies, accessories	46,666	0	0.0
Automobile...	280,002	92,000	32.9
Building materials	910,118	213,501	23.5
Camping, hunting, fishing equipment, supplies............	10	0	0.0
Chemicals..	120,016	0	0.0
Clothes, furs	1,744,256	50,489	2.9
Collections, collectibles	1,600	0	0.0
Computer hardware, software	889,738	3,000	0.3
Consumable goods..	2,598,199	188,651	7.3
Crops...	25,765	16,000	62.1
Documents, personal or business[1]	0	0	
Drugs, narcotics	24,219	0	0.0
Farm equipment	110,000	10,000	9.1
Firearm accessories	56	0	0.0
Firearms...	11,538	0	0.0
Fuel	9,990	0	0.0
Household goods...	1,155,532	42,197	3.7
Identity documents[1]	0	0	
Industrial equipment	297,832	87,000	29.2
Jewelry, precious metals..	89,561	55,030	61.4
Lawn, yard, garden equipment	14,746	12,405	84.1
Medical, medical lab equipment..................................	5,000	0	0.0
Merchandise..	487,503	101,436	20.8
Metals, non-precious	246,847	15,000	6.1
Money..	3,764	0	0.0
Office equipment...	500,801	500,001	99.8
Other..	1,792,099	483,296	27.0
Other motor vehicles...	217,334	74,834	34.4
Pending inventory	9	0	0.0
Portable electronic communications	1,158,436	5,800	0.5
Purse, wallet	221	170	76.9
Radio, TV, VCR	655,626	15,200	2.3
Recreational Vehicle...	120,000	0	0.0
Recordings	9,150	0	0.0
Structure, storage	34,665	0	0.0
Tools..	643,585	0	0.0
Trailers...	2,569,404	1,644,926	64.0
Trucks..	3,494,104	2,072,005	59.3
Vehicle parts...	1,335,888	30,488	2.3
Watercraft equipment, parts, accessories	150	0	0.0

[1]According to Uniform Crime Reporting guidelines, the value of property stolen and/or recovered must be zero for this property description.

Table 51. Cargo Theft, by Location, 2017

(Number.)

Type of property	Total at location
Abandoned, condemned structure	1
Air, bus, train terminal	2
Bar, nightclub	1
Camp, campground	2
Church, synagogue, temple	1
Commercial office building	67
Construction site	3
Convenience store	59
Department, discount store	19
Dock, wharf, freight, modal terminal	42
Drug store, doctor's office, hospital	4
Farm facility	1
Field, woods	4
Government, public building	1
Grocery, supermarket	10
Highway, road, alley, street	115
Hotel, motel, etc.	6
Industrial site	15
Liquor store	5
Parking lot, garage	297
Park, playground	1
Rental storage facility	5
Residence, home	4
Rest area	3
Restaurant	4
School, college	2
Service, gas station	27
Shopping mall	1
Specialty store (TV, fur, etc.)	14
Other, unknown	45

Table 52. Cargo Theft, by Victim Type, 2017

(Number.)

Victim type	Total victims
Business	681
Financial	1
Government	7
Individual	80
Other	1
Society	1
Unknown	5

Table 53. Cargo Theft, by Offense, 2017

(Number.)

Type of property	Total at location
Grand total of offenses	791
Cargo theft applicable offenses	
All other larceny...	183
Burglary...	32
Credit card, automated teller machine fraud	1
Embezzlement	20
Extortion, blackmail	1
False pretenses, swindle, confidence game..	3
Motor vehicle theft	100
Robbery..	12
Theft from building..	6
Theft from vehicle..	418
Total cargo theft applicable offenses...	776
Other offenses occurring with cargo offenses	
Destruction of property..	12
Stolen property offense..	2
Weapon Law	1
Total other offenses occurring with cargo offense...	15

METHODOLOGY

Submitting Uniform Crime Reporting (UCR) program data to the Federal Bureau of Investigation (FBI) is a collective effort on the part of city, county, state, tribal, and federal law enforcement agencies to present a nationwide view of crime. Law enforcement agencies in 46 states and the District of Columbia voluntarily contribute crime data to the UCR program through their respective state UCR programs. For those states that do not have a state program, local agencies submit crime statistics directly to the FBI. The state UCR programs function as liaisons between local agencies and the FBI. Many states have mandatory reporting requirements, and many state programs collect data beyond the scope of the UCR program to address crime problems specific to their particular jurisdictions. In most cases, state programs also provide direct and frequent service to participating law enforcement agencies, make information readily available for statewide use, and help streamline the national program's operations.

A Note Regarding Rape

In 2013, the FBI UCR Program initiated collection of rape data under a revised definition within the Summary Reporting System. Previously, offense data for forcible rape was collected under the legacy UCR definition: the carnal knowledge of a female forcibly and against her will. Beginning with the 2013 data year, the term "forcible" was removed from the offense title, and the definition was changed. The revised UCR definition of rape is: Penetration, no matter how slight, of the vagina or anus with any body part or object, or oral penetration by a sex organ of another person, without the consent of the victim. Attempts or assaults to commit rape are also included; however, statutory rape and incest are excluded. For more information, please see https://www.fbi.gov/about-us/cjis/ucr/crime-in-the-u.s/2013/crime-in-the-u.s.-2013/rape-addendum/rape_addendum_final.

Criteria for State UCR programs

The criteria established for state programs ensure consistency and comparability in the data submitted to the national program, as well as regular and timely reporting. These criteria are:

1. A UCR Program must conform to the FBI UCR Program's submission standards, definitions, specifications, and required deadlines.

2. A UCR Program must establish data integrity procedures and have personnel assigned to assist contributing agencies in quality assurance practices and crime reporting procedures. Data integrity procedures should include crime trend assessments, offense classification verification, and technical specification validation.

3. A UCR Program's submissions must cover more than 50 percent of the law enforcement agencies within its established reporting domain and be willing to cover any and all UCR-contributing agencies that wish to use the UCR Program from within its domain. (An agency wishing to become a UCR Program must be willing to report for all of the agencies within the state.)

4. A UCR Program must furnish the FBI UCR Program with all of the UCR data collected by the law enforcement agencies within its domain.

These requirements do not prohibit the state from gathering other statistical data beyond the national collection.

Data Completeness and Quality

National program staff members contact the state UCR program in connection with crime-reporting matters and, when necessary and approved by the state, they contact individual contributors within the state. To fulfill its responsibilities in connection with the UCR program, the FBI reviews and edits individual agency reports for completeness and quality. Upon request, they conduct training programs within the state on law enforcement record-keeping and crime-reporting procedures. The FBI conducts an audit of each state's UCR data collection procedures once every three years, in accordance with audit standards established by the federal government. Should circumstances develop in which the state program does not comply with the aforementioned requirements, the national program may institute a direct collection of data from law enforcement agencies within the state.

Reporting Procedures

Offenses known and value of property–Law enforcement agencies tabulate the number of Part I offenses reported based on records of all reports of crime received from victims, officers who discover infractions, or other sources, and submit these reports each month to the FBI directly or through their state UCR programs. Part I offenses include murder and non-negligent manslaughter, forcible rape, robbery, aggravated assault, burglary, larceny-theft, motor vehicle theft, and arson. Each month, law enforcement agencies also submit to the FBI the value of property stolen and recovered in connection with the offenses and detailed information pertaining to criminal homicide.

Unfounded offenses and clearances—When, through investigation, an agency determines that complaints of crimes are unfounded or false, the agency eliminates that offense from its crime tally through an entry on the monthly report. The report also provides the total number of actual Part I offenses, the number of offenses cleared, and the number of clearances that involve only offenders under the age of 18. (Law enforcement can clear crimes in one of two ways: by the arrest of at least one person who is charged and turned over to the court for prosecution or by exceptional means—when some element beyond law enforcement's control precludes the arrest of a known offender.)

Persons arrested—In addition to reporting Part I offenses each month, law enforcement agencies also provide data on the age, sex, and race of persons arrested for Part I and Part II offenses. Part II offenses encompass all crimes, except traffic violations, that are not classified as Part I offenses.

Officers killed or assaulted—Each month, law enforcement agencies also report information to the UCR program regarding law enforcement officers killed or assaulted, and each year they report the number of full-time sworn and civilian law enforcement personnel employed as of October 31.

Editing Procedures

The UCR program thoroughly examines each report it receives for arithmetical accuracy and for deviations in crime data from month to month and from present to past years that may indicate errors. UCR staff members compare an agency's monthly reports with its previous submissions and with reports from similar agencies to identify any unusual fluctuations in the agency's crime count. Considerable variations in crime levels may indicate modified records procedures, incomplete reporting, or changes in the jurisdiction's geopolitical structure.

Evaluation of trends—Data reliability is a high priority of the FBI, which brings any deviations or arithmetical adjustments to the attention of state UCR programs or the submitting agencies. Typically, FBI staff members study the monthly reports to evaluate periodic trends prepared for individual reporting units. Any significant increase or decrease becomes the subject of a special inquiry. Changes in crime reporting procedures or annexations that affect an agency's jurisdiction can influence the level of reported crime. When this occurs, the FBI excludes the figures for specific crime categories or totals, if necessary, from the trend tabulations.

Training for contributors—In addition to the evaluation of trends, the FBI provides training seminars and instructional materials on crime reporting procedures to assist contributors in complying with UCR standards. Throughout the country, representatives from the national program coordinate with representatives of state programs and law enforcement personnel and hold training sessions to explain the purpose of the program, the rules of uniform classification and scoring, and the methods of assembling the information for reporting. When an individual agency has specific problems with compiling its crime statistics and its remedial efforts are unsuccessful, personnel from the FBI's Criminal Justice Information Services Division may visit the contributor to aid in resolving the problems.

UCR Handbook—The national UCR program publishes the *Uniform Crime Reporting (UCR) Handbook* (revised 2004), which details procedures for classifying and scoring offenses and serves as the contributing agencies' basic resource for preparing reports. The national staff also produces letters to UCR contributors, state program bulletins, and UCR newsletters as needed. These publications provide policy updates and new information, as well as clarification of reporting issues.

The final responsibility for data submissions rests with the individual contributing law enforcement agency. Although the FBI makes every effort through its editing procedures, training practices, and correspondence to ensure the validity of the data it receives, the accuracy of the statistics depends primarily on the adherence of each contributor to the established standards of reporting. Deviations from these established standards that cannot be resolved by the national UCR program may be brought to the attention of the Criminal Justice Information Systems Committees of the International Association of Chiefs of Police and the National Sheriffs' Association.

NIBRS Conversion

Thirty-three state programs are certified to provide their UCR data in the expanded National Incident-Based Reporting System (NIBRS) format. For presentation in this book, the NIBRS data were converted to the historical Summary Reporting System data. The UCR program staff constructed the NIBRS database to allow for such conversion so that UCR's long-running time series could continue.

Crime Trends

By showing fluctuations from year to year, trend statistics offer the data user an added perspective from which to study crime. Percent change tabulations in this publication are computed only for reporting agencies that provided comparable data for the periods under consideration. The FBI excludes from the trend calculations all figures except those received for common months from common agencies. Also excluded are unusual fluctuations of data that the FBI determines are the result of such variables as improved records procedures, annexations, and so on.

Caution to Users

Data users should exercise care in making any direct comparison between data in this publication and those in prior issues of *Crime in the United States*. Because of differing levels of participation from year to year and reporting problems that require the FBI to estimate crime counts for certain contributors, some data may not be comparable. In addition, this publication may contain updates to data provided in prior years' publications.

For information about the FBI's caution against ranking, including warnings about variables affecting crime and characteristics of jurisdictions, please see http://www.fbi.gov/about-us/cjis/ucr/ucr-statistics-their-proper-use.

Offense Estimation

Some tables in this publication contain statistics for the entire United States. Because not all law enforcement agencies provide data for complete reporting periods, the FBI includes estimated crime numbers in these presentations. The FBI estimates data for three areas: Metropolitan Statistical Areas (MSAs), cities outside MSAs, and nonmetropolitan counties; and computes estimates for participating agencies that do not provide 12 months of complete data. For agencies supplying 3 to 11 months of data, the national UCR program estimates for the missing data by following a standard estimation procedure using the data provided by the agency. If an agency has supplied less than 3 months of data, the FBI computes estimates by using the known crime figures of similar areas within a state and assigning the same proportion of crime volumes to nonreporting agencies. The estimation process considers the following: population size covered by the agency; type of jurisdiction; for example, police department versus sheriff's office; and geographic location.

Estimation of State-Level Data

In response to various circumstances, the FBI calculates estimated offense totals for certain states. For example, some states do not provide forcible rape figures in accordance with UCR guidelines. In addition, problems at the state level have, at times, resulted in no useable data. Also, the conversion of the National Incident-Based Reporting System (NIBRS) data to summary data has contributed to the need for unique estimation procedures.

Expanded Offense Tables

Expanded offense data are the details of the various offenses that the Uniform Crime Reporting Program collects beyond the count of how many crimes law enforcement agencies report. These details may include the type of weapon used in a crime, the type or value of items stolen, and so forth. Expanded homicide data provide supplemental details about murders such as the age, sex, and race of both the victim and the offender, the weapon used in the homicide, the circumstances surrounding the offense, and the relationship of the victim to the offender. In addition, expanded data includes trends (for example, 2-year comparisons) and rates per 100,000 inhabitants.

Expanded offense data, including expanded homicide data, are information collected in addition to the reports of the number of crimes known. As a result, law enforcement agencies can report an offense without providing the supplemental data about that offense.

Federal Crime Data

In past years, these agencies' data were included in various tables in *Crime in the United States*. *Federal Crime Data* signals the move to presenting federal data in a way more attuned with local, state, and tribal UCR data. Included are the federal agencies that have submitted traditional UCR data for some time.

A few agencies, such as the National Institutes of Health (NIH) and several agencies within the U.S. Department of the Interior (DOI), investigate and police in ways similar to local or state authorities. These federal agencies have long reported data to the UCR Program. However, other federal agencies, the FBI included, found it more difficult to fit into the UCR model. This annual report was originally designed as a stepping stone to finding ways to provide a similar transparency and access to federal crime data that the UCR Program has brought to local, state, and tribal crime data for nearly 90 years. The arrest data from the FBI, ATF, and USMS have all been mapped to correspond to the UCR's National Incident-Based Reporting System (NIBRS) offense codes. This makes the overlay of federal data with local and state data much easier.

Comparability of federal data to state and local data

The best approach to viewing the federal data offered is to use it to gain an overall impression of the intensity of certain types of offenses within a specific area by overlaying the federal arrests in conjunction with the local and state information. As developments in the data collection continue to occur, more details will become available from federal agencies, and these impressions will become more sharply focused.

Federal crime data are often different from local and state data, not only in their collection, but also in their generation. The UCR Program has built its traditional data collection on three triggering events that are common to local and state agencies. Offense information begins with either, first, a complaint of a victim/citizen or, second, the observation of a crime in progress by a law enforcement officer. A third trigger for data is when an arrest is made and information related to that occurrence is reported.

For federal agencies, the initiation of investigation may be prompted in different ways. Many crimes, such as human trafficking and hate crime and their associated data, are brought to the attention of the FBI in much the same fashion:

- Reports from victims

- Liaison with other law enforcement agencies

- Information about victims (e.g., human trafficking, hate crime) brought to the FBI by nongovernmental organizations

- Reports from the media

The decision to handle a crime as a federal investigation or as a local investigation is determined on a case-by-case basis. Some of the factors that enter into the decision for federal agencies to pursue an investigation are the available evidence, the availability of resources at the local level, and, in the case of hate crime, statutory provisions that determine whether the U.S. Attorney will accept the case as a federal one. In addition, some states do not have a hate crime statute under which to pursue a case.

Why federal numbers are smaller than those of other UCR agencies

As mentioned previously, federal investigations, by nature, often begin under different circumstances and proceed and conclude on different timeframes than investigations conducted by local and state agencies. Just as federal agencies often do not have traditional offenses known to report, they also typically do not have a number of offenses to report until a case has been built and an arrest or indictment has occurred. Perhaps most impactful on the federal numbers is the fact that federal agencies often play a collaborative role with local and state agencies in crime investigations. Because the UCR Program has the "most local reporting" rule, which specifies that the agency involved that is the most local jurisdiction should report the incident to the UCR Program, investigations and arrests that federal authorities have worked on often are reported by city, county, state, or tribal agencies.

The UCR Program defines law enforcement officers as individuals who ordinarily carry a firearm and a badge, have full arrest powers, and are paid from governmental funds set aside specifically to pay sworn law enforcement.

Civilian employees include full-time agency personnel such as clerks, radio dispatchers, meter attendants, stenographers, jailers, correctional officers, and mechanics.

Data were not included for arrests made in joint investigations with other agencies when local or state codes were used nor for

Human Trafficking cases when different provisions of the U.S. Code were used for the basis of arrest.

These data include arrests by the FBI or task forces for the following:

09A – 09C Homicide Arrests

Section
1111 – Murder
1112 – Manslaughter
1114 – Protection of officers and employees of the United States
3592(c) – Aggravating factors for homicide

11A – 11D Sex Offense Arrests

13A – 13C Assault Arrests
Section
2241 – Aggravated sexual abuse
2242 – Sexual abuse
2243 – Sexual abuse of a minor or ward
2244C – Abusive sexual contact
2251 – Sexual exploitation of children

Section
111 – Assaulting, resisting, or impeding certain officers or employees
113 – Assaults within maritime and territorial jurisdiction
844(e) – Whoever, through the use of mail, telephone, telegraph, or other instrument of interstate or foreign commerce willfully makes any threat
871 – Threats against President and successors to the President
875 – Interstate communications
876 – Mailing threatening communications
879 – Threats against former Presidents and certain other persons
1389 – Prohibition on attacks on United States servicemen on account of service
1501 – Assault on process server
1503 – Influencing or injuring officer or juror generally
1512 – Tampering with a witness, victim, or an informant
1841 – Protection of unborn children
2231 – Assault or resistance
2237 – Criminal sanctions for failure to heave to, obstruction of boarding, or providing false information
7212 – Attempts to interfere with administration of internal revenue laws
46504 – Interference with flight crew members and attendants

23A – 23H Larceny and Theft Arrests

26A – 26E Fraud Arrests

35A – 35 B Drug and Narcotics Arrests

849 – Transportation safety offenses drug abuse prevention and control
853 – Criminal forfeitures drug abuse prevention and control
856 – Maintaining drug-involved premises
859 – Distribution to persons under the age of twenty-one
860 – Distribution or manufacturing in or near schools and colleges
862 – Denial of federal benefits to drug traffickers and possessors
864 – Anhydrous ammonia
881 – Forfeitures drug abuse prevention and control
952 – Importation of controlled substances
959 – Possession, manufacture, or distribution of controlled substance
960 – Unlawful for any person to knowingly or intentionally import or export a controlled substance
70503 – While on board a covered vessel, an individual my not knowingly or intentionally manufacture or distribute, or possess with intent to manufacture or distribute, a controlled substance
70506 – A person shall be punished under the Comprehensive Drug Abuse Prevention and Control Act of 1970
70507 – Seizure of property described in the Drug Abuse Prevention and Control Act

39A – 39D Gambling Offenses Arrests

Section
1084 – Transmission of wagering information

64A – 64B Human Trafficking Arrests

Section
1324 – Bringing in and harboring certain aliens
1351 – Fraud in foreign labor contracting
1581 – Peonage; obstructing enforcement
1583 – Enticement into slavery
1584 – Sale into involuntary servitude
1589 – Forced labor
1591 – Sex trafficking of children or by force, fraud, or coercion
1592 – Unlawful conduct with respect to documents in furtherance of trafficking, peonage, slavery, involuntary servitude, or forced labor
1593A – Benefitting financially from peonage, slavery, and trafficking in persons
1594 – General provisions
1596 – Additional jurisdiction in certain trafficking offenses
1597 – Unlawful conduct with respect to immigration documents
2251A – Selling or buying children
2421 – Transportation generally
2422 – Coercion and enticement
2423 – Transportation of minors
2425 – Use of interstate facilities to transmit information about a minor

3271 – Trafficking in persons offenses committed by persons employed by or accompanying the federal government outside the United States

100 Kidnapping and Abduction Arrests

120 Robbery Arrests

200 Arson Arrests

Section
1201 – Kidnapping
1202 – Ransom money
1203 – Hostage taking
1204 – International parental kidnapping

Section
2113 – Bank robbery and incidental crimes

Section
81 – Arson within special maritime and territorial jurisdiction

210 Extortion and Blackmail Arrests

Section
875 – Interstate communications
892 – Making extortionate extensions of credit
893 – Financing extortionate extensions of credit
894 – Collection of extensions of credit by extortionate means

250 Counterfeiting and Forgery Arrests

Section
21 – Stolen or counterfeit nature of property for certain crimes
473 – Dealing in counterfeit obligations or securities
499 – Military, naval, or official passes
505 – Seals of courts; signatures of judges or court officers
514 – Fictitious obligations
642 – Tools and materials for counterfeiting purposes
1010 – Department of Housing and Urban Development and Federal Housing Administration transactions
1546 – Fraud and misuse of visas, permits, and other documents
2320 – Trafficking in counterfeit goods or services

270 Embezzlement Arrests

Section
153 – Embezzlement against estate
641 – Public money, property or records
654 – Officer or employee of United States converting property of another
656 – Theft, embezzlement, or misapplication by bank officer or employee
657 – Lending, credit and insurance institutions

659 – Interstate of foreign shipments by carrier; state prosecutions

664 – Theft or embezzlement from employee benefit plan

1163 – Embezzlement and theft from Indian tribal organizations

1168 – Theft by officers or employees of gaming establishments on Indian lands

280 Stolen Property Arrests

Section

2312 – Transportation of stolen vehicles

2314 – Transportation of stolen goods, securities, moneys, fraudulent state tax stamps, or articles used in counterfeiting

2315 – Sale or receipt of stolen goods, securities, moneys, or fraudulent state tax stamps

2321 – Trafficking in certain motor vehicles or motor vehicle parts

290 Destruction, Damage, and Vandalism of Property Arrests

Section

248 – Freedom of access to clinic entrances

1366 – Destruction of energy facility

1512(c) – Whoever corruptly alters, destroys, mutilates, or conceals a record, document, or other object, or attempts to do so, with the intent to impair the object's integrity or availability for use in an official proceeding

1703 – Delay or destruction of mail or newspapers

1705 – Destruction of letter boxes or mail

370 Pornography and Obscene Material Arrests

Section

1462 – Importation or transportation of obscene material

1465 – Production and transportation of obscene matters for sale or distribution

1466 – Engaging in the business of selling or transferring obscene matter

1470 – Transfer of obscene material to minors

2252 – Certain activities relating to material involving the sexual exploitation of minors

2252A – Activities relating to material constituting or containing child pornography

2260 – Production of sexually explicit depictions of a minor for importation into the United States

223 – Obscene or harassing telephone calls in the District of Columbia or in interstate or foreign communications

Section

201 – Bribery of public officials and witnesses

212 – Offer of loan or gratuity to financial institution examiner

215 – Receipt of commissions or gifts for procuring loans

224 – Bribery in sporting events

1510 – Obstruction of criminal investigation

Section

841 – "Person" means any individual, corporation, company, association, firm, partnership, society, or joint stock company

842 – Unlawful acts in explosive materials

843 – Licenses and user permits in explosive materials

844 – Penalties in explosive materials

846 – Additional powers of the Attorney General in explosive materials

847 – Rules and regulations in explosive materials

848 – Effect on State Law in explosive materials

921 – The term "firearm" means (A) any weapon (including a starter gun) which will or is designed to or may readily be converted to expel a projectile by the action of an

510 Bribery Arrests

520 Weapon Law Arrests

explosive; (B) the frame or receiver of any such weapon; (C) any firearm muffler or firearm silencer; or (D) any destructive device

922(a) – Unlawful for any person, other than a licensed importer, licensed manufacturer, licensed dealer, or licensed collector to transport into or receive in the state where he resides

922(c) – A licensed importer, licensed manufacturer, or licensed dealer may sell a firearm to a person who does not appear in person at the license's business premise' only if transferee submits a sworn statement

922(d) – Unlawful for any person to sell or otherwise dispose of a firearm or ammunition to any person knowing or having reasonable cause to believe that a person under indictment, a fugitive from justice, unlawful user of or addicted to a controlled substance, has been adjudicated as a mental defective or committed to a mental institution, is illegally in the United States, discharged from the Armed Forces under dishonorable conditions, has renounced his citizenship, subject to a court order that restrains such person from harassing, stalking or threatening an intimate partner, and has been convicted in any court of a misdemeanor crime of domestic violence.

922(e) – It shall be unlawful for any person knowingly to deliver or cause to be delivered to any common or contract carrier for transportation or shipment in interstate or foreign commerce, to person other than licensed importers, licensed manufacturers, license dealers, or licensed collectors, any package or other container in which there is any firearm

922(g) – Unlawful for any person who has been convicted in any court of, a crime punishable by imprisonment for a term exceeding one year

922(j) – It shall be unlawful for any person to receive, possess, conceal, store, barter, sell, or dispose of any stolen firearm or stolen ammunition, or pledge or accept as security for a loan any stolen firearm or stolen ammunition

922(k) – It shall be unlawful for any person knowingly to transport, ship, or receive, in interstate or foreign commerce, any firearm which has had the importer's or manufacturer's serial number removed, obliterated, altered

922(n) – It shall be unlawful for any person who is under indictment for a crime punishable by imprisonment for a term exceeding one year to ship or transport in interstate or foreign commerce

922(o) – It shall be unlawful for any person to transfer or possess a machine gun

923 – Licensing

924 – Penalties

928 – Separability

930 – Possession of firearms and dangerous weapons in federal facilities

3665 – Firearms possessed by convicted felons

5841 – Registration of firearms

5842 – Identification of firearms

5861 – Prohibited acts under machine guns, etc.

5861(c) – To receive or possess a firearm made in violation of the provisions of machine guns, etc.

5861(d) – To receive or possess a firearm which is not registered to him in the National Firearms Registration and Transfer Record

5861(f) – To make a firearm in violation of the provisions

5861(i) – To receive or possess a firearm which is not identified by a serial number as required

5861(l) – To make, or cause making of, a false entry on any application, return, or record required by this chapter, knowing such entry to be false

46505 – Carrying a weapon or explosive on an aircraft

720 Animal Cruelty Arrests

Section

2156 – Animal fighting venture prohibition

41 – Hunting, fishing, trapping; disturbance or injury on wildlife refuges

90G Liquor Law Arrests

47 – Use of aircraft or motor vehicles to hunt certain wild horses or burros; pollution of watering holes

49 – Enforcement of animal fighting prohibitions

Section

1156 – Intoxicants possessed unlawfully

3113 – Liquor law violations in Indian country

90Z All Other Offenses Arrests

Section

1229 – Initiation of removal proceedings

1325 – Improper entry by alien

1325(a) – Improper time or place; avoidance of examination or inspection; misrepresentation and concealment of facts

1326 – Reentry of removed aliens

84 – Interference with aids to navigation; penalty

506(a) – Any person who willfully infringes a copyright shall be punished

4 – Misprision of felony

13 – Laws of States adopted for areas within federal jurisdiction

39(a) – Aiming a laser pointer at an aircraft

42 – Importation or shipment of injurious mammals, birds, fish (including mollusks and crustacea), amphibia, and reptiles; permits, specimens for museums; regulations

219 – Officers and employees acting as agents of foreign principals

228 – Failure to pay legal child support obligations

243(b) – Exclusion of jurors on account of race or color

371 – Conspiracy to commit offense or to defraud United States

372 – Conspiracy to impede or injure officer

373 – Solicitation to commit a crime of violence

402 – Contempts constituting crimes

513 – Securities of the states and private entities

545 – Smuggling goods into the United States

554 – Smuggling goods from the United States

751 – Prisoners in custody of institution or officer

793(e) – Gathering, transmitting or losing defense information

831 – Prohibited transactions involving nuclear material

842(p) – Distribution of Information Relating to Explosives, Destructive Devices, and Weapons of Mass Destruction

931 – Prohibition on purchase, ownership, or possession of body armor by violent felons

951 – Agents of foreign governments

951(a) – Whoever, other than a diplomatic or consular officer or attaché, acts in the United States as an agent of a foreign government without prior notification to the Attorney General if required

952 – Diplomatic codes and correspondence

955 – Financial transactions with foreign governments

956 – Conspiracy to kill, kidnap, main, or injure persons or damage property in a foreign country

960 – Expedition against friendly nation

981 – Civil forfeiture

1030 – Fraud and related activity in connection with computers

1071 – Concealing person from arrest

1073 – Flight to avoid prosecution or giving testimony

1083 – Transportation between shore and ship; penalties

1117 – Conspiracy to murder

1349 – Attempt and conspiracy

1365 – Tampering with consumer products

1425 – Procurement of citizenship or naturalization unlawfully

1511 – Obstruction of state or local law enforcement

1512 – Tampering with a witness, victim, or an informant

1519 – Destruction, alteration, or falsification of records in federal investigations and bankruptcy

1621 – Perjury generally

1622 – Subornation of perjury
1623 – False declarations before grand jury or court
1651 – Piracy under law of nations
1692 – Foreign mail as United States mail
1791 – Providing or possessing contraband in prison
1801 – Video voyeurism
1831 – Economic espionage
1924 – Unauthorized removal and retention of classified documents or material
1960 – Prohibition of unlicensed money transmitting businesses
1992 – Terrorist attaches and other violence against railroad carriers and against mass transportation systems on land, on water, or through the air
2156 – Production of defective national-defense material, national-defense premises, or national defense utilities
2250 – Failure to register as a sex offender
2332 – Criminal penalties for terrorism
2332A – Use of weapons of mass destruction
2332B – Acts of terrorism transcending national boundaries
2332F – Bombings of places of public use, government facilities, public transportation systems and infrastructure facilities
2339 – Harboring or concealing terrorists
2339A – Providing material support to terrorists
2339B – Providing material support or resources to designated foreign terrorist organizations
2341 – Definitions for trafficking in contraband cigarettes and smokeless tobacco
2342 – Unlawful acts for trafficking in contraband cigarettes and smokeless tobacco
2342(a) – It shall be unlawful for any person knowingly to ship, transport, receive, possess, sell, distribute, or purchase contraband cigarettes or contraband smokeless tobacco
2344 – Penalties for trafficking in contraband cigarettes and smokeless tobacco
2401 – Renumbered 2441
2441 – War crimes
2442 – Recruitment or use of child soldiers
3062 – General arrest authority for violation of release conditions
3103 – Grounds for issuing search warrant
3122 – Application for an order for a pen register or a trap and trace device
3146 – Penalty for failure to appear
3184 – Fugitives from foreign country to United States
3290 – Fugitives from justice
3606 – Arrest and return of a probationer
3615 – Criminal default
7201 – Attempt to evade or defeat tax
7202 – Willful failure to collect or pay over tax
7203 – Willful failure to file return, supply information, or pay tax
5324 – Structuring transactions to evade reporting requirement prohibited
5332 – Bulk cash smuggling into or out of the United States
1311 – Effluent limitations

1319(c) – Enforcement of criminal penalties
2077 – Unauthorized dealings in special nuclear material
46312 – Transportation hazardous material

Child Exploitation Arrests

Section
1204 – International parental kidnapping
1462 – Importation or transportation of obscene matters
1466 – Engaging in the business of selling or transferring obscene matter
1470 – Transfer of obscene material to minors
2241 – Aggravated sexual abuse
2242 – Sexual abuse
2243 – Sexual abuse of a minor or ward
2244c – Sexual abuse offenses involving your children
2251 – Sexual exploitation of children
2252 – Certain activities relating to material involving the sexual exploitation of minors
2260 – Production of sexually explicit depictions of a minor for importation into the United States
2421 – Transportation generally
2422 – Coercion and enticement
2423 – Transportation of minors

Employee counts were as of December 2016 for both FBI and ATF.

Population estimation

Population estimates used in this table are the U.S. Census Bureau's published resident population estimates for counties for 2015. The U.S. Census Bureau calculates estimates based on the decennial census of 2010 and by applying measures of population changes. See https://factfinder.census.gov/faces/tableservices/jsf/pages/productview.xhtml?pid=PEP_2016_PEPANNRES&src=pt for further information on county breakdowns for each state.

Human Trafficking

As state participation has grown, the UCR Program has seen an increase in human trafficking data submissions. The program will continue efforts to expand, gather, and make available information regarding human trafficking incidents.

Trafficking Victims Protection Act

In January 2013, the national UCR Program began collecting offense and arrest data regarding human trafficking as authorized by the William Wilberforce Trafficking Victims Protection Reauthorization Act of 2008. The act requires the FBI to collect human trafficking offense data and to make distinctions between prostitution, assisting or promoting prostitution, and purchasing prostitution.

To comply with the Wilberforce Act, the national UCR Program created two additional offenses in the Summary Reporting System (SRS) and the National Incident-Based Reporting System (NIBRS) through which the UCR Program collects both offense and arrest data. The definitions for these offenses are:

Human Trafficking/Commercial Sex Acts: inducing a person by force, fraud, or coercion to participate in commercial sex acts, or in which the person induced to perform such act(s) has not attained 18 years of age.

Human Trafficking/Involuntary Servitude: obtaining of a person(s) through recruitment, harboring, transportation, or provision, and subjecting such persons by force, fraud, or coercion into involuntary servitude, peonage, debt bondage, or slavery (not to include commercial sex acts).

The data in the tables included in this report reflect the offenses and arrests recorded by state and local law enforcement agencies (LEAs) that currently have the ability to report the data to the national UCR Program. As such, they should not be interpreted as a definitive statement of the level or characteristics of human trafficking as a whole. The data declaration pages, which will help the user better understand the data, and the methodology used for the four following tables are located in the Data Declarations and Methodology section near the end of this report. In addition, a Question and Answer section about human trafficking data is provided as a supplement to this report.

Note: Regarding the data reported to the UCR Program, it is important to note that these data represent only one view of a complex issue—the law enforcement perspective. However, due to the nature of human trafficking, many of these crimes are never reported to the local, state, tribal, and federal LEAs that investigate them. In addition to the law enforcement facet in fighting these crimes, there are victim service organizations whose mission it is to serve the needs of the victims of human trafficking. In order to have the complete picture of human trafficking, it would be necessary to gather information from all of these sources.

Tables include the states that have added human trafficking offenses to their data collection and the number of agencies per state participating in the UCR Program. Even though a state program included human trafficking, the individual agencies in that state may or may not have added it to their collections. Indiana, Mississippi, and portions of Ohio have no UCR state program to manage the collection of UCR data within the state. Each law enforcement agency is responsible for reporting its crime data directly to the FBI.

For UCR purposes, juveniles are individuals under the age of 18 years. Adults are 18 years of age or older.

The data used in creating these tables were from law enforcement agencies submitting one or more human trafficking incidents for at least 1 month of the calendar year. Also included are zero data for states which have incorporated human trafficking offenses in their data collection where no 2016 human trafficking incidents were reported to the FBI UCR Program.

The published data, therefore, do not necessarily represent reports from each participating agency for all 12 months of the calendar year. When the FBI determines that an agency's data collection methodology does not comply with national UCR guidelines, the figure(s) for that agency's offense(s) will not be included in the table, and the discrepancy will be explained in a footnote.

Cargo Theft

The FBI's Uniform Crime Reporting (UCR) Program collects cargo theft data to inform the law enforcement community, state and federal legislators, academia, and the public at large about this particular crime. The data can be used to create awareness and to measure the impact cargo theft has on the economy and potential threats to national security. Often cargo theft offenses are part of larger criminal schemes and have been found to be components of organized crime rings, drug trafficking, and funding for terrorism. The UCR collection of cargo theft data is new with only 4 years of data published, but the number of agencies reporting cargo theft incidents has increased each year. As more agencies participate, future versions of this cargo theft report will depict a more complete account of the occurrences of cargo theft in the United States.

Due to the significant economic impact cargo theft has on the United States economy, and the potential for use by terrorist organizations, Congress mandated H.R. 3199, the USA Patriot Improvement and Reauthorization Act of 2005 on March 9, 2006. It required the Attorney General to "take the steps necessary to ensure that reports of cargo theft collected by Federal, State, and local officials are reflected as a separate category in the Uniform Crime Reporting System, or any successor system, by no later than December 31, 2006." In response to this mandate, the Criminal Justice Information Services (CJIS) Advisory Policy Board approved a definition for collecting cargo theft in December 2006. Creation of the data specifications required to capture cargo theft data in the UCR's Summary Reporting System as well as the National Incident-Based Reporting System were finalized in 2010 with the first publication of cargo theft data in 2013.

Cargo theft is defined as "The criminal taking of any cargo including, but not limited to, goods, chattels, money, or baggage that constitutes, in whole or in part, a commercial shipment of freight moving in commerce, from any pipeline system, railroad car, motor truck, or other vehicle, or from any tank or storage facility, station house, platform, or depot, or from any vessel or wharf, or from any aircraft, air terminal, airport, aircraft terminal or air navigation facility, or from any intermodal container, intermodal chassis, trailer, container freight station, warehouse, freight distribution facility, or freight consolidation facility. For purposes of this definition, cargo shall be deemed as moving in commerce at all points between the point of origin and the final destination, regardless of any temporary stop while awaiting transshipment or otherwise."

This definition was developed, not as a legal description for prosecutorial purposes, but to capture the essence of the national cargo theft problem in the United States. The legal elements of knowledge and intent were intentionally omitted.

Participation in the UCR Program is voluntary, and agencies or states may choose not to participate. In 2013, seven states participated in the first release of cargo theft data from the national UCR Program. In 2014, a total of 29 states and the Bureau of Indian Affairs submitted cargo theft data to the UCR Program. In 2015, a total of 31 states and the Bureau of Indian Affairs participated in submitting data to the UCR Program. In 2016, a total of 30 states, the Bureau of Indian Affairs, and the National Institute of Health submitted cargo theft data, although only 20 states had at least one cargo theft incident and were able to verify the submitted data as publishable. Participation in the cargo theft data has remained steady; however, several factors have been identified having a direct impact on this important data collection:

- States may not have the resources required to make the necessary technical changes or to align their local and state statutes with federal requirements.

- States may not have the necessary resources to conduct data quality checks on reported incidents associated with cargo theft, which could result in inaccurate data.

- States may not have adequate resources to train participants on how to recognize and properly record cargo theft incidents.

- States may not perceive cargo theft as a priority or a significant problem within their states and make decisions based on their immediate needs regarding resource allocation.

Quality data concerning cargo theft can help us better understand this crime and the threats associated with it. As more agencies choose to report their incidents, the FBI's UCR Program will be able to provide more information about cargo theft on a national scale. For additional information on the UCR Program's collection of cargo theft incidents, visit https://www.fbi.gov/about-us/cjis/ucr/ucr-program-data-collections.

Tables present by state the total number of agencies that submitted data about cargo theft incidents, the number of incidents reported, the reported value of stolen property, the value and percentage of recovered property for each submitting state.

Data used were from all law enforcement agencies submitting one or more cargo theft incidents for at least 1 month of the calendar year. The published data, therefore, do not necessarily represent reports from each participating agency for all 12 months of the calendar year. Based on UCR guidelines, the property descriptions of credit/debit cards, nonnegotiable instruments, documents/personal or business, and identity-intangible, must be submitted with zero value for stolen and/or recovered. In the Cargo Theft Program, the victim of a cargo theft may be an individual, a business, an institution, or society as a whole. The UCR Program counted one for each victim type reported in an incident.

Because cargo theft has been defined as "the criminal **taking of** any cargo . . .," there are specific crimes against property that apply to cargo theft. The applicable crimes against property include:

120 = Robbery
23D = Theft from building
23F = Theft from motor vehicle
23H = All other larceny
26A = False pretenses, swindle, confidence game
26B = Credit card, automatic teller machine fraud
26C = Impersonation
26E = Wire fraud
210 = Extortion, blackmail
220 = Burglary, breaking & entering
240 = Motor vehicle theft
270 = Embezzlement
510 = Bribery

In addition, cargo theft is not considered an offense by itself; all offenses that happen within a cargo theft incident are to be reported. Cargo theft data are derived by capturing the additional element of "theft of cargo" in incidents that contain any of the applicable offenses.

PART 4

Criminal Victimization, 2017

HIGHLIGHTS

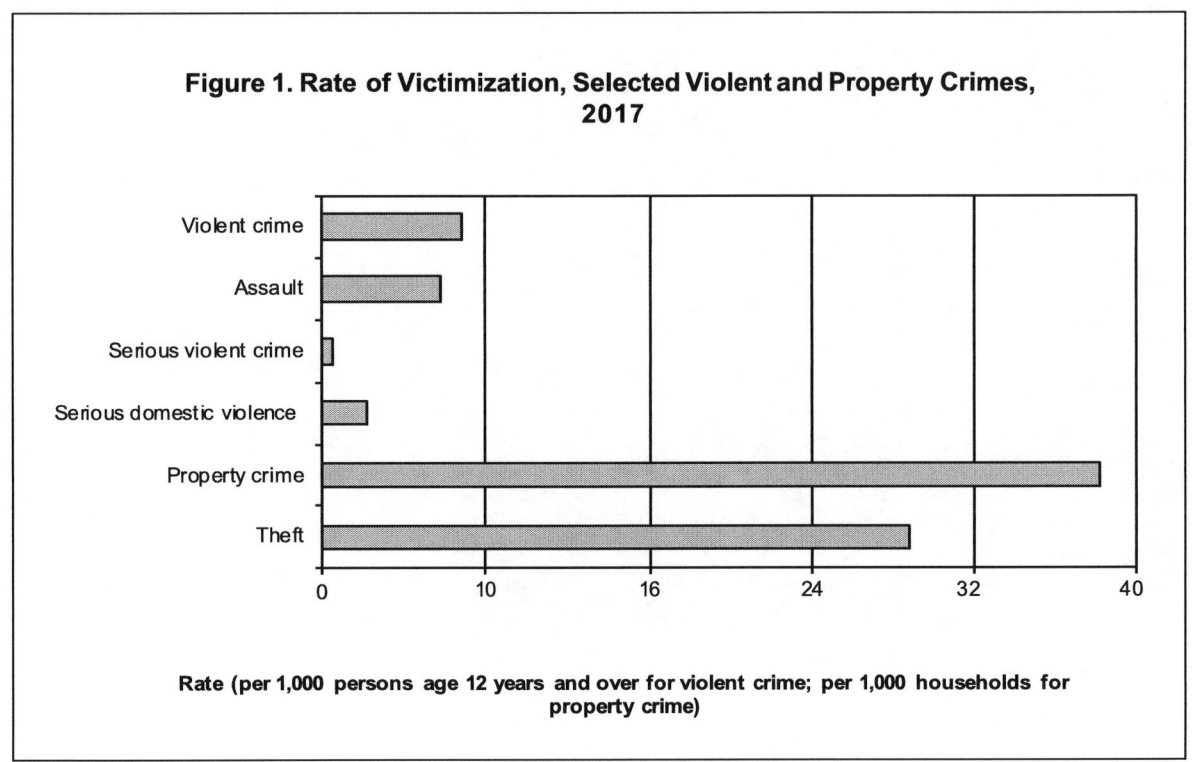

Figure 1. Rate of Victimization, Selected Violent and Property Crimes, 2017

Rate (per 1,000 persons age 12 years and over for violent crime; per 1,000 households for property crime)

- In 2017, U.S. residents age 12 years or older experienced approximately 5.6 million violent victimizations and 13.3 million property victimizations.

- Fewer than half of violent or property victimizations were reported to police (45 percent and 36 percent, respectively).

- The portion of persons age 12 or older who were victims of violent crime increased from 0.98 percent in 2015 to 1.14 percent in 2017.

- From 2015 to 2017, the percentage of persons who were victims of violent crime increased among the following groups: males, Whites, persons age 25 to 34 years, persons age 50 years old and over, and those who had never been married.

- From 2016 to 2017, the percentage of persons victimized by violent crime increased among the following groups: females, Whites, persons age 12 to 17 years, persons 65 years old and over, and those who were divorced or had never been married.

- From 2016 to 2017, the rate of overall property crime declined from 118.6 victimizations per 1,000 households to 108.4, while the burglary rate fell from 23.7 to 20.6.

Table 1. Nonfatal Violent Incidents, by Total Population, Victim, and Offender Demographic Characteristics, 2017

(Number; percent.)

Demographic characteristic	Population[1]		Victim		Offender[2]	
	Number of incidents	Percent	Number of incidents	Percent	Number of incidents	Percent
Total	272,468,480	100.0	5,179,800	100.0	5,179,800	100.0
Sex						
Male**	132,432,710	48.6	2,534,130	48.9	3,602,740	75.8
Female	140,035,770	51.4	2,645,670	51.1	959,200[B]	20.2[B]
Both male and female offenders	NA	NA	NA	NA	188,770[B]	4.0[B]
Race/Hispanic Origin[3]						
White**	171,454,370	62.9	3,247,940	62.7	2,230,910	49.2
Black	32,699,520	12.0	697,590[B]	13.5[B]	1,112,610[B]	24.5[B]
Hispanic	45,481,910	16.7	853,730[B]	16.5[B]	647,970[B]	14.3[B]
Asian	16,582,080	6.1	113,850[B]	2.2[B]	44,090[B]	1.0[B]
Other[4]	6,250,600	2.3	266,690[B]	5.1[B]	425,050[B]	9.4[B]
Multiple offenders of various races[5]	NA	NA	NA	NA	74,450[B]	1.6[B]
Age						
12 years or younger	NA	NA	NA	NA	109,280[B]	2.5[B]
12–17 years	24,911,170	9.1	785,080[B]	15.2[B]	667,620[B]	15.3[B]
18–20 years**	12,599,000	4.6	443,910	8.6	327,490	7.5
21–29 years	40,111,370	14.7	1,064,630[B]	20.6[B]	900,360[B]	20.6[B]
30 years or older	194,846,940	71.5	2,886,190[B]	55.7[B]	2,170,420[B]	49.6[B]
Multiple offenders of various ages	NA	NA	NA	NA	200,270[B]	4.6[B]

Note: Based on persons age 12 or older. Details may not sum to totals due to rounding and missing data for offender characteristics. An incident is a specific criminal act involving one or more victims or victimizations. Offender characteristics are based on the victims' perceptions of the offenders.
** = Comparison year.
B = Significant difference from comparison year at the 90% confidence level.
NA = Not available.
[1]NCVS population includes persons age 12 or older living in non-institutionalized residential settings in the United States.
[2]Includes incidents in which the perceived offender characteristics were reported. The sex of the offender was unknown in 8% of incidents, the race/Hispanic origin of offender was unknown in 12% of incidents, and the age of offender was unknown in 16% of incidents.
[3]Excludes persons of Hispanic/Latino origin, unless specified.
[4]Includes American Indians and Alaska Natives; Asians, Native Hawaiians, and other Pacific Islanders; and persons of two or more races.
[5]Victims perceived multiple offenders of various races or Hispanic origin.

Table 2. Violent and Property Victimization, by Type of Crime, 2015–2017

(Number; rate.)

Type of crime	2015* Number	2015* Rate per 1,000[1]	2017 Number	2017 Rate per 1,000[1]	2016* Number	2016* Rate per 1,000[1]	2017 Number	2017 Rate per 1,000[1]
Violent Crime[2]	5,006,620	18.6	5,612,670	20.6	5,353,820	19.7	5,612,670	20.6
Rape/sexual assault[3]	431,840	1.6	393,980	1.4	298,410	1.1	393,980	1.4
Robbery	578,580	2.1	613,840	2.3	458,810	1.7	613,840 A	2.3 A
Assault..	3,996,200	14.8	4,604,850 A	16.9	4,596,600	16.9	4,604,850	16.9
Aggravated assault............................	816,760	3	993,170	3.6	1,040,580	3.8	993,170	3.6
Simple assault	3,179,440	11.8	3,611,680	13.3	3,556,020	13.1	3,611,680	13.3
Domestic violence[4].............................	1,094,660	4.1	1,237,960	4.5	1,068,120	3.9	1,237,960	4.5
Intimate partner violence[5]..............	806,050	3	666,310	2.4	597,200	2.2	666,310	2.4
Stranger violence	1,821,310	6.8	2,034,100	7.5	2,082,410	7.7	2,034,100	7.5
Violent crime involving injury	1,303,290	4.8	1,248,480	4.6	1,220,640	4.5	1,248,480	4.6
Serious Violent Crime[6]	1,827,170	6.8	2,000,990	7.3	1,797,790	6.6	2,000,990	7.3
Serious domestic violence[4]	460,450	1.7	465,150	1.7	359,740	1.3	465,150	1.7
Serious intimate partner violence[5]	333,210	1.2	273,440	1	265,770	1	273,440	1.0
Serious stranger violence....................	690,550	2.6	784,370	2.9	780,580	2.9	784,370	2.9
Serious violent crime involving weapons....	977,840	3.6	1,260,810	4.6	1,203,200	4.4	1,260,810	4.6
Serious violent crime involving injury	658,040	2.4	643,760	2.4	668,230	2.5	643,760	2.4
Property Crime	14,611,040	110.7	13,340,220	108.4	15,815,310	118.6	13,340,220	108.4 B
Household burglary..............................	2,904,570	22.0	2,538,170	20.6	3,160,450	23.7	2,538,170	20.6 B
Motor vehicle theft	564,160	4.3	516,810	4.2	618,330	4.6	516,810	4.2
Purse-snatching	NA	NA	100,590	0.4	91,580	0.3	100,590	0.4
Other theft[7]	11,142,310	84.4	10,285,240	83.6	12,036,530	90.3	10,285,240	83.6 B

Note: Details may not sum to totals due to rounding. Violent crime classifications include rape or sexual assault, robbery, aggravated assault, and simple assault, and they include threatened, attempted, and completed crimes. Other violent crime categories in this table, including domestic violence and violent crime involving injury, are not mutually exclusive from these classifications. There were 269,526,470 persons age 12 or older living in non-institutionalized residential settings in the United States in 2015, 272,204,190 in 2016, and 272,468,480 in 2017. Total number of households was 131,962,260 in 2015, 133,365,270 in 2016, and 123,085,790 in 2017. The NCVS household weighting adjustment was updated for 2017, which decreased the estimated number of households, and the number of households experiencing property crime, by about 8%. As a result, readers should not compare the number of property crimes between 2016 and 2017. Property crime rates are unaffected by this change. See appendix table 5 for standard errors. See Methodology for details on the change in the household weighting adjustment in the NCVS.
* = Comparison year.
NA = Not available.
A = Significant difference from comparison year at the 90% confidence level.
B = Significant difference from comparison year at the 95% confidence level.
[1]For violent and serious violent crime, rate is per 1,000 persons age 12 or older. For property crime, rate is per 1,000 households.
[2]Excludes homicide because the NCVS is based on interviews with victims and cannot measure murder.
[3]See Methodology for details on the measurement of rape or sexual assault in the NCVS.
[4]Includes victimization committed by intimate partners and family members.
[5]Includes victimization committed by current or former spouses, boyfriends, or girlfriends.
[6]In the NCVS, serious violent crime includes rape or sexual assault, robbery, and aggravated assault.
[7]Involves other unlawful taking or attempted unlawful taking of property or cash without personal contact with the victim.

Table 3. Firearm Violence, 2015–2017

(Number; rate per 1,000 persons age 12 years or older; percent.)

Characteristic	2015*	2017	2016*	2017
Firearm incidents[1]	260,200	417,780 B	414,440	417,780
Firearm victimizations[2]	284,910	456,270 B	486,590	456,270
Rate of firearm victimizations[3]........................	1.1	1.7 B	1.8	1.7
Firearm victimizations reported to police				
Number..	217,850	254,910 B	314,500	254,910
Percent...	76.5	55.9 B	64.6	55.9

Note: Includes violent incidents and victimizations in which the offender possessed, showed, or used a firearm.
* = Comparison year.
B = Significant difference from comparison year at the 95% confidence level.
[1]An incident is a specific criminal act involving one or more victims or victimizations.
[2]Each victimization represents one person involved in an incident.
[3]Rate is per 1,000 persons age 12 or older.

Table 4. Rate of Crime Reported to Police in the Uniform Crime Reporting Program and National Crime Victimization Survey, 2017

(Rate.)

Type of crime	UCR rate per 1,000 residents[1]	NCVS rate per 1,000 persons age 12 or older (serious violent crime) or 1,000 households (property crime)
Serious Violent Crime[2]	3.8	3.8
Murder	0.1	X
Rape[3]	0.4	0.6
Robbery	1.0	1.1
Aggravated assault	2.5	2.1
Property Crime	23.6	38.7
Burglary	4.3	10.1
Motor vehicle theft	2.4	3.3

X = Not applicable.

[1]Includes crimes against persons age 11 or younger, persons who are homeless, persons who are institutionalized, and crimes against commercial establishments. These populations are out of sample for the NCVS.
[2]In addition to rape, robbery, and aggravated assault, the NCVS includes sexual assault.
[3]The NCVS estimate includes sexual assault. See Methodology for details on the measurement of rape or sexual assault in the NCVS. The UCR estimate is based on the revised definition of rape.

Table 5. Percent of Victimizations Reported to Police, by Type of Crime, 2016 and 2017

(Percent.)

Type of crime	2016*	2017
Violent Crime[1]	43.9	44.9
Rape/sexual assault[2]	23.2	40.4[B]
Robbery	57.0	49.0
Assault	43.9	44.7
Aggravated assault	59.8	57.2
Simple assault	39.3	41.3
Domestic violence[3]	52.2	47.2
Intimate partner violence[4]	49.0	47.5
Stranger violence	43.6	46.9
Violent crime involving injury	48.0	52.2
Serious Violent Crime[5]	53.0	51.4
Serious domestic violence[3]	52.5	48.3
Serious intimate partner violence[4]	47.1	51.8
Serious stranger violence	55.7	59.4
Serious violent crime involving weapons	60.8	52.5
Serious violent crime involving injury	53.4	54.4
Property Crime	35.2	35.7
Household burglary	49.0	49.1
Motor vehicle theft	73.2	79.0
Other theft[6]	29.6	30.2

Note: Violent crime classifications include rape or sexual assault, robbery, aggravated assault, and simple assault. Other violent crime categories in this table, including domestic violence and violent crime involving injury, are not mutually exclusive from these classifications.
* = Comparison year.
B = Significant difference from comparison year at the 95% confidence level.
[1]Excludes homicide because the National Crime Victimization Survey (NCVS) is based on interviews with victims and cannot measure murder.
[2]For details on the measurement of rape and sexual assault in the NCVS, see https://www.bjs.gov/content/pub/pdf/cv16.pdf
[3]Includes victimization committed by intimate partners and family members.
[4]Includes victimization committed by current or former spouses, boyfriends, or girlfriends.
[5]Includes rape or sexual assault, robbery, and aggravated assault.
[6]Includes the taking or attempted unlawful taking of property or cash without personal contact with the victim.

Table 6. Rate of Victimization Reported to the Police, by Type of Crime, 2016 and 2017

(Rates per 1,000 persons age 12 or older for violent crime and per 1,000 households for property crime.)

Type of crime	2016*	2017
Violent Crime[1]	8.6	9.2
Rape/sexual assault[2]	0.3	0.6 [B]
Robbery	1.0	1.1
Assault	7.4	7.6
Aggravated assault	2.3	2.1
Simple assault	5.1	5.5
Domestic violence[3]	2.0	2.1
Intimate partner violence[4]	1.1	1.2
Stranger violence	3.3	3.5
Violent crime involving injury	2.2	2.4
Serious Violent Crime[5]	3.5	3.8
Serious domestic violence[3]	0.7	0.8
Serious intimate partner violence[4]	0.5	0.5
Serious stranger violence	1.6	1.7
Serious violent crime involving weapons	2.7	2.4
Serious violent crime involving injury	1.3	1.3
Property Crime	41.7	38.7 [A]
Household burglary	11.6	10.1 [A]
Motor vehicle theft	3.4	3.3
Theft	26.7	25.3

Note: Violent crime classifications include rape or sexual assault, robbery, aggravated assault, and simple assault. Other violent crime categories in this table, including domestic violence and violent crime involving injury, are not mutually exclusive from these classifications.
* = Comparison year.
A = Significant difference from comparison year at the 90% confidence level.
B = Significant difference from comparison year at the 95% confidence level.
[1]Excludes homicide because the National Crime Victimization Survey (NCVS) is based on interviews with victims and cannot measure murder.
[2]For details on the measurement of rape and sexual assault in the NCVS, see https://www.bjs.gov/content/pub/pdf/cv16.pdf
[3]Includes victimization committed by intimate partners and family members.
[4]Includes victimization committed by current or former spouses, boyfriends, or girlfriends.
[5]Includes rape or sexual assault, robbery, and aggravated assault.

Table 7. Percent of Violent Victimizations in Which Victims Received Assistance from a Victim Service Agency, by Type of Crime, 2016 and 2017

(Percent.)

Type of crime	2016*	2017
Violent Crime[1]	9.3	8.3
Serious violent crime[2]	12.9	10.4
Simple assault	7.5	7.1
Intimate partner violence[3]	20.4	14.9
Violent crime involving injury	13.4	15.5
Violent crime involving weapon	12.4	9.8

* = Comparison year.
[1]Includes rape or sexual assault, robbery, aggravated assault, and simple assault. Includes threatened, attempted, and completed crimes. Excludes homicide because the National Crime Victimization Survey is based on interviews with victims and cannot measure murder.
[2]Includes rape or sexual assault, robbery, and aggravated assault.
[3]Includes victimization committed by current or former spouses, boyfriends, or girlfriends.

Table 8. Rate of Violent Victimization and Serious Violent Victimization, by Victim Demographic Characteristics, 2015–2017

(Rate per 1,000 persons age 12 years or older; percent.)

Victim demographic characteristic	Violent victimization[1]				Serious violent victimization[2]			
	2015*	2017	2016*	2017	2015*	2017	2016*	2017
Total	18.6	20.6	19.7	20.6	6.8	7.3	6.6	7.3
Sex								
Male..	15.9	20.4[B]	19.6	20.4	5.4	7.0	6.6	7.0
Female...	21.1	20.8	19.7	20.8	8.1	7.7	6.6	7.7
Race/Hispanic Origin[3]								
White	17.4	20.8	19.6	20.8	6.0	6.9	6.0	6.9
Black...	22.6	21.8	22.3	21.8	8.4	7.9	7.1	7.9
Hispanic..	16.8	20.7	18.2	20.7	7.1	9.5	7.9	9.5
Asian	8.2	6.9	12.1	6.9[B]	4.3	2.5	6.1	2.5[B]
Other[4]..	74.4	45.5[B]	38.6	45.5	27.3	15.4	12.5	15.4
Age								
12–17 years..	31.3	33.5	25.1	33.5[A]	7.8	10.4	5.9	10.4[B]
18–24 years..	25.1	34.7[B]	29.6	34.7	10.7	18.3[B]	11.9	18.3[B]
25–34 years..	21.8	26.3	28.4	26.3	9.3	8.5	12.5	8.5[B]
35–49 years..	22.6	20.1	22.3	20.1	7.8	7.4	6.3	7.4
50–64 years	14.2	16.3	15.0	16.3	5.7	4.4	4.7	4.4
65 years and over	5.2	6.5	5.3	6.5	1.5	1.8	1.1	1.8
Marital Status								
Never married	26.2	31.2	27.6	31.2	9.4	12.1	9.8	12.1
Married..	9.9	11.1	11.0	11.1	3.5	3.2	3.0	3.2
Widowed...	8.5	11.5	13.4	11.5	2.9	5.0	2.3	5.0[A]
Divorced	35.3	29.0	28.5	29.0	13.0	9.7	12.2	9.7
Separated	39.5	48.3	66.4	48.3	20.6	17.8	18.7	17.8
Household Income								
$9,999 or less.......................................	39.2	49.8	34.5	49.8[B]	17.7	22.0	15.1	22.0[A]
$10,000–$14,999....................................	27.7	21.9	30.8	21.9[A]	12.0	8.3	10.0	8.3
$15,000–$24,999....................................	25.9	26.3	30.6	26.3	8.2	9.2	13.5	9.2[A]
$25,000–$34,999....................................	16.3	24.5[B]	19.4	24.5	5.5	9.7[B]	6.0	9.7[A]
$35,000–$49,999....................................	20.5	18.8	19.2	18.8	7.1	7.6	6.6	7.6
$50,000–$74,999....................................	16.3	19.4	15.4	19.4	5.9	5.8	5.0	5.8
$75,000 or more	12.8	14.6	15.2	14.6	4.5	4.5	3.9	4.5

Note: Victimization rates are per 1,000 persons.
* = Comparison year.
A = Significant difference from comparison year at the 95% confidence level.
B = Significant difference from comparison year at the 90% confidence level.
[1]Includes rape or sexual assault, robbery, aggravated assault, and simple assault. Includes threatened, attempted, and completed crimes. Excludes homicide because the National Crime Victimization Survey is based on interviews with victims and cannot measure murder.
[2]Includes rape or sexual assault, robbery, and aggravated assault.
[3]Excludes persons of Hispanic/Latino origin, unless specified.
[4]Includes American Indians and Alaska Natives; Asians, Native Hawaiians, and other Pacific Islanders; and persons of two or more races.

Table 9. Number and Rate of Violent Victimizations, by Victim's Veteran, Citizenship, and Disability Status, 2017

(Number; rate per 1,000 persons age 12 years or older for violent crime; rate per 1,000 households for property crime.)

Household location	Violent victimization[1]		Population[3]
	Number	Rate per 1,000[2]	
Total	5,612,670	20.6	272,468,480
Veteran Status[4]			
Veteran[5]	348,520[B]	19.4	18,006,440
Non-veteran[6]**	4,384,410	19.3	227,110,790
Citizenship Status			
Born U.S. citizen[7]**	5,106,650	21.9	232,675,820
Naturalized U.S. citizen	197,820[B]	9.1[B]	21,840,640
Non-U.S. citizen	260,320[B]	16.2[B]	16,097,190
Disability Status			
Persons with disabilities[8]**	1,393,150[B]	40.4[B]	34,480,740
Cognitive	909,700[B]	76.0[B]	11,967,780
Ambulatory	560,060[B]	28.9[B]	19,381,790
Vision	208,940[B]	43.5[B]	4,798,100
Hearing	251,710[B]	23.2	10,831,970
Limited independent living[9]**	394,420[B]	31.8[B]	12,410,680
Limited self-care	202,760[B]	34.4[B]	5,901,130
Persons without disabilities**	4,177,410	17.7	235,898,220

Note: Victimization rates are per 1,000 persons age 12 or older for violent crime and per 1,000 households for property crime. Details may not sum to totals due to rounding and missing data.

** = Comparison group.

B = Significant difference from comparison group at the 95% confidence level.

[1]Includes rape or sexual assault, robbery, aggravated assault, and simple assault. Includes threatened, attempted, and completed crimes. Excludes homicide because the National Crime Victimization Survey (NCVS) is based on interviews with victims and cannot measure murder.

[2]Rate is per 1,000 persons age 12 or older.

[3]NCVS population includes persons age 12 or older living in non-institutionalized residential settings in the United States.

[4]Includes persons age 18 or older.

[5]Veterans include persons currently or previously on active duty. Because the NCVS is a household-based survey and veterans are more likely to be out of the household at the time of data collection, most veterans in the sample are former active duty.

[6]Non-veterans include persons who never served in the U.S. armed forces or who completed training in the Reserves or National Guard only.

[7]Includes persons born in the U.S., U.S. territory, or abroad to U.S. parents.

[8]Disabilities are classified according to six limitations: cognitive (serious difficulty in concentrating, remembering, or making decisions because of a physical, mental, or emotional condition), ambulatory (difficulty walking or climbing stairs), vision (blindness or serious difficulty seeing, even when wearing glasses), hearing (deafness or serious difficulty hearing), limited independent living (physical, mental, or emotional condition that impedes doing errands alone, such as visiting a doctor or shopping), and limited self-care (a condition that causes difficulty dressing or bathing).

[9]Includes persons age 15 or older.

Table 10. Number of Victims and Prevalence Rate, by Type of Crime, 2015–2017

(Number; percent.)

Type of crime	Number of victims[1]				Prevalence rate[2]			
	2015*	2017	2016*	2017	2015*	2017	2016*	2017
Violent Crime[3]	2,650,670	3,106,340 [B]	2,882,320	3,106,340	0.98	1.14 [B]	1.06	1.14
Rape/sexual assault	204,000	208,960	162,940	208,960	0.08	0.08	0.06	0.08
Robbery	375,280	402,430	312,310	402,430 [B]	0.14	0.15	0.11	0.15 [B]
Assault	2,175,520	2,595,780 [B]	2,497,500	2,595,780	0.81	0.95 [B]	0.92	0.95
Aggravated assault	560,720	646,540	680,770	646,540	0.21	0.24	0.25	0.24
Simple assault	1,690,190	2,024,880 [B]	1,903,860	2,024,880	0.63	0.74 [B]	0.70	0.74
Domestic violence[4]	493,310	559,820	514,350	559,820	0.18	0.21	0.19	0.21
Intimate partner violence[5]	310,090	308,560	273,890	308,560	0.12	0.11	0.10	0.11
Stranger violence	1,117,340	1,370,020 [B]	1,276,710	1,370,020	0.41	0.50 [B]	0.47	0.5
Violent crime involving injury	778,300	722,560	663,920	722,560	0.29	0.27	0.24	0.27
Serious Violent Crime[6]	1,099,400	1,225,800	1,123,190	1,225,800	0.41	0.45	0.41	0.45
Serious domestic violence[3]	212,690	243,740	183,230	243,740 [A]	0.08	0.09	0.07	0.09 [A]
Serious intimate partner violence[4]	141,530	152,650	120,760	152,650	0.05	0.06	0.04	0.06
Serious stranger violence	479,870	558,280	561,410	558,280	0.18	0.20	0.21	0.2
Serious violent crime involving weapons	644,370	776,770 [B]	767,320	776,770	0.24	0.29 [A]	0.28	0.29
Serious violent crime involving injury	399,360	398,900	395,300	398,900	0.15	0.15	0.15	0.15
Property Crime	10,030,500	9,145,690	9,825,060	9,145,690	7.60	7.43	7.37	7.43
Household burglary	2,175,380	1,842,730	2,037,320	1,842,730	1.65	1.50 [A]	1.53	1.5
Motor vehicle theft	465,650	438,860	470,880	438,860	0.35	0.36	0.35	0.36
Other theft[7]	7,941,030	7,330,960	7,803,350	7,330,960	6.02	5.96	5.85	5.96

Note: Details may not sum to totals because a person or household may experience multiple types of crime. Violent crime classifications include rape or sexual assault, robbery, aggravated assault, and simple assault, and they include threatened, attempted, and completed crimes. Other violent crime categories in this table, including domestic violence and violent crime involving injury, are not mutually exclusive from these classifications. There were 269,526,470 persons age 12 or older living in non-institutionalized residential settings in the United States in 2015, 272,204,190 in 2016, and 272,468,480 in 2017. Total number of households was 131,962,260 in 2015, 133,365,270 in 2016, and 123,085,790 in 2017. The NCVS household weighting adjustment was updated for 2017, which decreased the estimated number of households experiencing property crime by about 8%. As a result, readers should not compare the number of property crimes between 2016 and 2017. Property crime rates are unaffected by this change.
* = Comparison year.
A = Significant difference from comparison year at the 90% confidence level.
B = Significant difference from comparison year at the 95% confidence level.
[1]Number of persons age 12 or older who experienced at least one violent victimization during the year, and number of households that experienced at least one property victimization during the year.
[2]Percent of persons age 12 or older who experienced at least one violent victimization during the year, and percent of households that experienced at least one property victimization during the year.
[3]Excludes homicide because the National Crime Victimization Survey is based on interviews with victims and cannot measure murder.
[4]Includes victimization committed by intimate partners and family members.
[5]Includes victimization committed by current or former spouses, boyfriends, or girlfriends.
[6]Includes rape or sexual assault, robbery, and aggravated assault.
[7]Includes the taking or attempted unlawful taking of property or cash without personal contact with the victim.

Table 11. Prevalence of Violent Crime, by Victim Demographic Characteristics, 2015–2017

(Number; rate.)

Victim demographic characteristic	Number of victims[1]				Prevalence rate[2]			
	2015*	2017	2016*	2017	2015*	2017	2016*	2017
Total	2,650,670	3,106,340 [B]	2,882,320	3,106,340	0.98	1.14 [B]	1.06	1.14
Sex								
Male..	1,227,870	1,551,030 [B]	1,514,130	1,551,030	0.94	1.17 [B]	1.14	1.17
Female..	1,422,800	1,555,310	1,368,190	1,555,310 [B]	1.03	1.11	0.98	1.11 [B]
Race/Hispanic Origin[3]								
White	1,667,090	2,005,120 [B]	1,785,680	2,005,120 [B]	0.96	1.17 [B]	1.03	1.17 [B]
Black..	394,770	389,340	377,950	389,340	1.19	1.19	1.12	1.19
Hispanic.....................................	400,720	496,370	488,700	496,370	0.93	1.09	1.1	1.09
Asian	68,550	68,290	117,920	68,290 [B]	0.47	0.41	0.75	0.41 [B]
Other[4].......................................	119,530	147,220	112,080	147,220	2.27	2.36	2.03	2.36
Age								
12–17 years................................	407,850	459,160	313,470	459,160 [B]	1.64	1.84	1.25	1.84 [B]
18–24 years................................	445,760	495,760	461,310	495,760	1.46	1.66	1.52	1.66
25–34 years................................	476,630	659,150 [B]	689,590	659,150	1.09	1.49 [B]	1.56	1.49
35–49 years................................	686,380	647,610	706,000	647,610	1.13	1.06	1.15	1.06
50–64 years................................	497,800	607,520 [A]	541,330	607,520	0.79	0.97 [A]	0.85	0.97
65 years and over	136,250	237,140 [B]	170,640	237,140 [B]	0.29	0.48 [B]	0.36	0.48 [B]
Marital Status								
Never married.............................	1,343,010	1,610,610 [B]	1,422,600	1,610,610 [A]	1.44	1.67 [B]	1.49	1.67 [A]
Married.......................................	692,470	780,050	827,920	780,050	0.54	0.61	0.65	0.61
Widowed.....................................	92,330	105,930	88,310	105,930	0.62	0.71	0.59	0.71
Divorced.....................................	428,830	489,130	408,710	489,130 [A]	1.58	1.83	1.5	1.83 [A]
Separated...................................	84,370	108,890	119,150	108,890	1.65	2.21	2.37	2.21

Note: Detail may not sum to total due to rounding.
* = Comparison year.
A = Significant difference from comparison year at the 90% confidence level.
B = Significant difference from comparison year at the 95% confidence level.
[1]Number of persons age 12 or older who experienced at least one violent victimization during the year.
[2]Percentage of persons age 12 or older who experienced at least one violent victimization during the year.
[3]Excludes persons of Hispanic/Latino origin, unless specified.
[4]Includes American Indians and Alaska Natives; Native Hawaiians and Other Pacific Islanders; and persons of two or more races.

Table 12. Prevalence of Violent Crime, Burglary, or Motor Vehicle Theft, 2015–2017

(Rates per 1,000 persons age 12 or older for violent crime and per 1,000 households for property crime.)

Victim demographic characteristic	Number of persons victimized[1]				Prevalence rate[2]			
	2015*	2017	2016*	2017	2015*	2017	2016*	2017
Type of Crime, Total[3]	7,858,220	7,864,990	7,874,690	7,864,990	2.92	2.89	2.89	2.89
Violent Crime								
Rape/sexual assault	204,000	208,960	162,940	208,960	0.08	0.08	0.06	0.08
Robbery..	375,280	402,430	312,310	402,430 [B]	0.14	0.15	0.11	0.15 [B]
Assault...	2,175,520	2,595,780 [B]	2,497,500	2,595,780	0.81	0.95 [B]	0.92	0.95
Aggravated assault	560,720	646,540	680,770	646,540	0.21	0.24	0.25	0.24
Simple assault..................................	1,690,190	2,024,880 [B]	1,903,860	2,024,880	0.63	0.74 B	0.70	0.74
Property Crime								
Household burglary...........................	4,524,620	4,064,470 [A]	4,291,990	4,064,470	1.68	1.49 [B]	1.58	1.49
Motor vehicle theft	1,069,590	1,000,410	1,045,770	1,000,410	0.40	0.37	0.38	0.37

Note: Detail may not sum to total because a person may experience multiple types of crime. This prevalence measure is based on persons who experienced a violent victimization or whose households experienced a burglary or motor vehicle theft. Violent victimization includes rape or sexual assault, robbery, aggravated assault, and simple assault. This measure attributes a household's burglary to each person age 12 or older in the household. Motor vehicle thefts were attributed to persons only when they were the reference person for their household or were age 12 or older and related to the reference person. Classifications include threatened, attempted, and completed crimes.
* = Comparison year.
B = Significant difference from comparison year at the 95% confidence level.
[1]Number of persons age 12 or older who experienced at least one victimization (violent crime, burglary, or motor vehicle theft) during the year.
[2]Percentage of persons age 12 or older who experienced at least one victimization (violent crime, burglary, or motor vehicle theft) during the year.
[3]Includes persons age 12 or older who experienced at least one victimization (violent crime, burglary, or motor vehicle theft) during the year.

Table 13. Prevalence of Violent Crime, Burglary, or Motor Vehicle Theft, by Demographic Characteristics of Victims, 2016 and 2017

(Rates per 1,000 persons age 12 or older for violent crime and per 1,000 households for property crime.)

Victim demographic characteristic	Number of victims[1]		Prevalence[2]	
	2016*	2017	2016*	2017
Total	7,874,690	7,865,000	2.89	2.89
Sex				
Male..	3,947,420	3,845,990	2.98	2.90
Female..	3,927,270	4,019,010	2.81	2.87
Race/Hispanic Origin[3]				
White	4,546,190	4,778,580	2.63	2.79
Black..	1,185,100	1,125,020	3.52	3.44
Hispanic...	1,491,400	1,411,590	3.35	3.10
Asian	351,590	252,060 [A]	2.24	1.52 [B]
Other[4]...	300,410	297,740	5.45	4.76
Age				
12–17 years...	898,380	1,038,690	3.59	4.17 [A]
18–24 years...	1,182,860	1,040,430	3.90	3.48
25–34 years...	1,494,340	1,495,540	3.37	3.37
35–49 years...	1,832,960	1,795,620	3.00	2.95
50–64 years...	1,658,110	1,669,740	2.62	2.65
65 years and over	808,040	824,970	1.68	1.67
Marital Status				
Never married..	3,512,160	3,464,640	3.68	3.60
Married..	2,723,950	2,756,020	2.13	2.15
Widowed..	344,710	322,280	2.29	2.17
Divorced	987,380	1,040,980	3.63	3.89
Separated	263,420	243,060	5.25	4.92

Note: Details may not sum to totals due to rounding. This prevalence measure is based on persons who experienced a violent victimization or whose households experienced a burglary or motor vehicle theft. Violent victimization includes rape or sexual assault, robbery, aggravated assault, and simple assault. This measure attributes a household's burglary to each person age 12 or older in the household. Motor vehicle thefts were attributed to persons only when they were the reference person for their household or were age 12 or older and related to the reference person. Classifications include threatened, attempted, and completed crimes.
* = Comparison year.
A = Significant difference from comparison year at the 90% confidence level.
B = Significant difference from comparison year at the 95% confidence level.
[1]Number of persons age 12 or older who experienced at least one victimization (violent crime, burglary, or motor vehicle theft) during the year.
[2]Percentage of persons age 12 or older who experienced at least one victimization (violent crime, burglary, or motor vehicle theft) during the year.
[3]Excludes persons of Hispanic/Latino origin, unless specified.
[4]Includes American Indians and Alaska Natives; Asians, Native Hawaiians, and other Pacific Islanders; and persons of two or more races.

METHODOLOGY

Data are from the Bureau of Justice Statistics' (BJS) National Crime Victimization Survey (NCVS), which collects information on nonfatal crimes against persons age 12 or older from a nationally representative sample of U.S. households. The NCVS measures violent crimes, which include rape or sexual assault, robbery, aggravated assault, and simple assault. Property crimes include household burglary, motor vehicle theft, and theft. The survey also measures personal larceny, which includes pickpocketing and purse snatching. Unless otherwise noted, findings in this report are significant at the 95 percent confidence level. For additional estimates excluded from this report, see the NCVS Victimization Analysis Tool (NVAT) on the BJS Web site.

NCVS revised 2016 estimates

To permit cross-year comparisons that were inhibited by the 2016 sample redesign, BJS created a revised data file. Estimates for 2016 are based on the revised file and replace previously published estimates. For more information, see *Criminal Victimization, 2016: Revised* (NCJ 252121, BJS web, October 2018).

2016 NCVS Sample Redesign

To produce estimates on criminal victimization, the Bureau of Justice Statistics' (BJS) National Crime Victimization Survey (NCVS) collects information from a sample of U.S. households that represents the nation. The sample design is periodically changed to maintain the representativeness of the survey. In 2016, the NCVS sample was redesigned for two reasons:

1. To reflect changes in the U.S. population based on the 2010 Decennial Census

2. To make it possible to produce state- and local-level victimization estimates for the largest 22 states and specific metropolitan areas within those states

Every 10 years, the U.S. Census Bureau conducts the official population count of the United States. In 2016, a redesign of the NCVS sample was necessary to account for shifts in the population identified through the 2010 Decennial Census. From 2000 to 2010, the number of people residing in individual U.S. counties changed. Almost two-thirds of the nation's 3,143 counties gained population. Most counties along coastlines experienced population growth during this period, while others that lost population were clustered by region and were found in areas such as the Great Plains and Mississippi Delta. The NCVS sampling process involves selecting primary sampling units (PSUs), which are counties, groups of counties, or large metropolitan areas identified through the Decennial Census and the U.S. Census Bureau's American Community Survey. Within the PSUs selected, the sampling process identifies addresses to be included in the sample and interviews are conducted with persons and households at those addresses. Sampled households remain in the NCVS sample for seven waves (each wave is a 6-month period). The decennial sample update ensures that the sample reflects current population distributions. This process requires a phased shift of counties included in the 2000 sample design to those selected for the 2010 sample design, resulting in three types of counties in 2016: 1) continuing counties—those in both the 2000 and 2010 sample designs; 2) outgoing counties—those that were in the 2000 sample design, but not the 2010 sample design; and 3) new counties—those that were selected into the 2010 sample design, but were not in the 2000 sample design.

As part of ongoing efforts to enhance the usefulness and relevance of the NCVS, the sample also was expanded and redistributed to produce state and local estimates of victimization. Because the primary purpose of the NCVS has been to generate national estimates, the sample was initially designed to be representative of the United States as a whole and not individual states and local areas. To produce reliable estimates for the 22 most populous states and specific metropolitan areas within those states, it was necessary to change the NCVS sample design.

Implications of the 2016 Sample Redesign

When the 2016 NCVS data collection was complete, a comparison of the 2015 and 2016 victimization estimates showed that the violent and property crime rates had increased. Given recent patterns in NCVS data, these increases seemed too large to be a result of actual growth in crime, suggesting that the sample redesign may have affected the victimization rates. To better understand these results, the 2015 and 2016 victimization rates for new and continuing sample counties were examined separately. These comparisons showed that from 2015 to 2016 there were no statistically significant differences for continuing sample counties in the rates of total property crime, total violent crime, and total serious violent crime. In comparison, rates of total violent crime and total serious violent crime were higher in the new sample counties than in the outgoing sample counties.

Differences in Rates of Reporting to Police in the UCR and NCVS

For 2016, the Federal Bureau of Investigation's (FBI) Uniform Crime Reporting (UCR) program showed that 3.9 serious violent crimes per 1,000 persons and 24.5 property crimes per 1,000 persons were known to law enforcement. According to the Bureau of Justice Statistics' (BJS) National Crime Victimization Survey (NCVS), 3.6 serious violent crimes per 1,000 persons age 12 or older and 42.6 property crimes per 1,000 households were reported to law enforcement during this same year.

Because the NCVS and UCR measure an overlapping, but not identical, set of offenses and use different methodologies, congruity is not expected between estimates from these two data sources. Restricting the NCVS to serious violence reported to police keeps the measures as similar as possible. However, significant methodological and definitional differences remain between serious violent crimes in the NCVS and the UCR:

- The UCR includes homicide and commercial crimes, while the NCVS excludes these crime types.

- The UCR excludes sexual assault, which the NCVS includes.

- NCVS estimates are based on interviews with a nationally representative sample of persons in U.S. households. UCR estimates are based on counts of crimes reported by an incomplete census of law enforcement agencies and are weighted to compensate for the incomplete reporting.

- The NCVS excludes crimes against children age 11 or younger and persons in institutions (e.g., nursing homes and correctional institutions). It may also exclude highly mobile populations and persons who are homeless. Victimizations against these persons are included in the UCR.

Given these differences, the two measures of crime should not be compared but should be viewed as complementary sources, which together provide a more comprehensive picture of crime in the United States. For additional information about the differences between the two programs, see *The Nation's Two Crime Measures* (NCJ 246832, BJS web, September 2014).

Prevalence of Crime

Annual estimates of a population's risk for criminal victimization may be examined using victimization or prevalence rates. Historically, Bureau of Justice Statistics (BJS) reports based on National Crime Victimization Survey (NCVS) data rely on victimization rates, which measure the extent to which victimizations occur in a specified population during a specific time. For crimes affecting persons, NCVS victimization rates are estimated by dividing the number of victimizations that occur during a specified time (T) by the population at risk for those victimizations and multiplying the rate by 1,000.

Prevalence rates also describe the level of victimization but are based on the number of unique persons (or households) in the population experiencing at least one victimization during a specified time. The key distinction between a victimization and prevalence rate is whether the numerator consists of the number of victimizations or victims. For example, a person who experienced two robberies on separate occasions within the past year would be counted twice in the victimization rate but once in the prevalence rate. Prevalence rates are estimated by dividing the number of victims in the specified population by the total number of persons in the population and multiplying the rate by 100. This is the percentage of the population victimized at least once in a given period.

Victimization and prevalence rates may also be produced for household crimes, such as burglary. In these instances, numerators and denominators are adjusted to reflect households rather than persons. To better understand the percentage of the population that is victimized at least once in a given period, prevalence rates are presented by type of crime and certain demographic characteristics. (For further information about measuring prevalence in the NCVS, see *Measuring the Prevalence of Crime with the National Crime Victimization Survey*, NCJ 241656, BJS web, September 2013.)

Survey Methodology

NCVS is an annual data collection conducted by the U.S. Census Bureau for the Bureau of Justice Statistics (BJS). The NCVS is a self-report survey in which interviewed persons are asked about the number and characteristics of victimizations experienced during the prior 6 months. The NCVS collects information on nonfatal personal crimes (rape or sexual assault, robbery, aggravated and simple assault, and personal larceny) and household property crimes (burglary, motor vehicle theft, and other theft) both reported and not reported to police. In addition to providing annual level and change estimates on criminal victimization, the NCVS is the primary source of information on the nature of criminal victimization incidents. *Criminal Victimization* can be found here: http://www.bjs.gov/index.cfm?ty=pbdetail&iid=5804

Survey respondents provide information about themselves (e.g., age, sex, race and Hispanic origin, marital status, education level, and income) and whether they experienced a victimization. The NCVS collects information for each victimization incident about the offender (e.g., age, race and Hispanic origin, sex, and victim–offender relationship), characteristics of the crime (including time and place of occurrence, use of weapons, nature of injury, and economic consequences), whether the crime was reported to police, reasons the crime was or was not reported, and victim experiences with the criminal justice system.

The NCVS is administered to persons age 12 or older from a nationally representative sample of households in the United States. The NCVS defines a household as a group of persons who all reside at a sampled address. Persons are considered household members when the sampled address is their usual place of residence at the time of the interview and when they have no usual place of residence elsewhere. Once selected, households remain in the sample for 3 years, and eligible persons in these households are interviewed every 6 months either in person or over the phone for a total of 7 interviews.

All first interviews are conducted in person with subsequent interviews conducted either in person or by phone. New households rotate into the sample on an ongoing basis to replace outgoing households that have been in the sample for the 3-year period. The sample includes persons living in group quarters, such as dormitories, rooming houses, and religious group dwellings, and excludes persons living in military barracks and institutional settings such as correctional or hospital facilities, and persons who are homeless.

Nonresponse and Weighting Adjustments

The 2017 NCVS data file includes 145,508 household interviews. Overall, 76 percent of eligible households completed an interview. Within participating households, there were 239,541 personal interviews in 2017, representing an 84 percent response rate among eligible persons from responding households. Victimizations that occurred outside of the United States were excluded from this report. In 2017, less than 1 percent of the unweighted victimizations occurred outside of the United States.

Estimates in NCVS reports generally use data from the 1993 to 2017 NCVS data files, weighted to produce annual estimates of victimization for persons age 12 or older living in U.S. households. Because the NCVS relies on a sample rather than a census of the entire U.S. population, weights are designed to adjust to known population totals and to compensate for survey nonresponse and other aspects of the sample design.

NCVS data files include person, household, victimization, and incident weights. Person weights provide an estimate of the population represented by each person in the sample. Household weights provide an estimate of the U.S. household population represented by each household in the sample. After proper adjustment, both household and person weights are also typically used to form the denominator in calculations of crime rates. For personal crimes, the incident weight is derived by dividing the person weight of a victim by the total number of persons victimized during an incident as reported by the respondent. For property crimes, the incident weight and the household weight are the same, because the victim of a property crime is considered to be the household as a whole. The incident weight is most frequently used to calculate estimates of the number of crimes committed against a particular class of victim.

Victimization weights used in these analyses account for the number of persons victimized during an incident and for high-frequency repeat victimizations (i.e., series victimizations). Series victimizations are similar in type but occur with such frequency that a victim is unable to recall each individual event or describe each event in detail. Survey procedures allow NCVS interviewers to identify and classify these similar victimizations as series victimizations and to collect detailed information on only the most recent incident in the series.

The weighting counts series victimizations as the actual number of victimizations reported by the victim, up to a maximum of 10. Doing so produces more reliable estimates of crime levels than only counting such victimizations once, while the cap at 10 minimizes the effect of extreme outliers on rates. According to the 2017 data, series incidents accounted for 1.3 percent of all victimizations and 3.0 percent of all violent victimizations. Additional information on the enumeration of series victimizations is detailed in the report *Methods for Counting High-Frequency Repeat Victimizations in the National Crime Victimization Survey* (NCJ 237308, BJS web, April 2012).

Standard Error Computations

When national estimates are derived from a sample, as with the NCVS, caution must be used when comparing one estimate to another or when comparing estimates over time. Although one estimate may be larger than another, estimates based on a sample have some degree of sampling error. The sampling error of an estimate depends on several factors, including the amount of variation in the responses and the size of the sample. When the sampling error around an estimate is taken into account, estimates that appear different may not be statistically different.

One measure of the sampling error associated with an estimate is the standard error. The standard error may vary from one estimate to the next. Generally, an estimate with a small standard error provides a more reliable approximation of the true value than an estimate with a large standard error. Estimates with relatively larger standard errors are associated with less precision and reliability and should be interpreted with caution.

Generalized variance function (GVF) parameters and direct variance estimation methods were used to generate standard errors for each point estimate (e.g., counts, percentages, and rates) in this report. To generate standard errors around victimization and incidence estimates from the NCVS, the U.S. Census Bureau produces GVF parameters for BJS. To generate standard errors around prevalence estimates, BJS used direct variance estimation methods. The GVFs and direct variance estimation methods take into account aspects of the NCVS complex sample design and represent the curve fitted to a selection of individual standard errors based on the Balanced Repeated Replication (BRR) technique.

BJS conducted statistical tests to determine whether differences in estimated numbers, percentages, and rates in these reports were statistically significant once sampling error was taken into account. Using statistical analysis programs developed specifically for the NCVS, all comparisons in the text were tested for significance. The primary test procedure was the Student's t-statistic, which tests the difference between two sample estimates. Unless otherwise noted, the findings described in these reports as higher, lower, or different passed a test at the 0.05 level of statistical significance (95 percent confidence level) or at the 0.10 level of significance (90 percent confidence level). Readers should reference figures and tables in these reports for testing on specific findings. Caution is required when comparing estimates not explicitly discussed in these reports.

Readers may use the estimates and standard errors of the estimates provided in these reports to generate a confidence interval around the estimate as a measure of the margin of error. The following example illustrates how standard errors may be used to generate confidence intervals:

Based on the 2017 NCVS, the violent victimization rate among persons age 12 or older in 2017 was 20.6 victimizations per 1,000 persons. Using the GVFs, BJS determined that the estimated victimization rate has a standard error of 1.03. A confidence interval around the estimate is generated by multiplying the standard error by ± 1.96 (the t-score of a normal, two-tailed distribution that excludes 2.5 percent at either end of the distribution). Therefore, the 95 percent confidence interval around the 20.6 estimate from 2017 is 20.6 ± (1.03 x 1.96) or (18.59 to 22.61). In other words, if BJS used the same sampling method to select different samples and computed an interval estimate for each sample, it would expect the true population parameter (rate of violent victimization) to fall within the interval estimates 95 percent of the time.

For these reports, BJS also calculated a coefficient of variation (CV) for all estimates, representing the ratio of the standard error to the estimate. CVs provide another measure of reliability and a means for comparing the precision of estimates across measures with differing levels or metrics.

The 2017 NCVS weights include a new adjustment to control household weights to independent housing unit totals available internally within the Census Bureau. This new adjustment was applied only to household weights for housing units and does not affect person weights. Historically, the household weights were controlled to independent totals of the person population. This new weighting adjustment improves upon the historical one and better aligns the number of estimated households in the NCVS with other Census household survey estimates.

Because of this new adjustment, the 2017 NCVS household estimate is about 8 percent lower than the 2016 NCVS household estimate. As a result, the property crime estimate, or the number of households affected by property crime, is also about 8 percent lower. When making comparisons of property crime changes between 2016 and 2017, data users should compare victimization rates between the two years that are unaffected by this change in weighting adjustment. Comparisons of the number of property crime victimizations between 2016 and 2017 are not appropriate due to the change in weighting methodology. For more information on weighting in the NCVS, see Non-response and weighting adjustments section and *National Crime Victimization Survey, 2016 Technical Documentation* (NCJ 251442, BJS web, December 2017).

NCVS Measurement of Rape and Sexual Assault

Thee NCVS uses a two-stage measurement approach in the screening and classification of criminal victimization, including rape and sexual assault. In the first stage of screening, survey respondents are administered a series of "short-cue" screening questions designed to help respondents think about different experiences they may have had during the reference period (see NCVS-1 at https://www.bjs.gov/content/pub/pdf/ncvs15_bsq.pdf).

This design improves respondent recall of events, particularly for incidents that may not immediately come to mind as crimes, such as those committed by family members and acquaintances. Respondents who answer affirmatively to any of the short-cue screening items are subsequently administered a crime incident report (CIR) designed to classify incidents into specific crime types (see NCVS-2 at https://www.bjs.gov/content/pub/pdf/ncvs15_cir.pdf).

First stage of measurement. Two short-cue screening questions are specifically designed to target sexual violence:

1. Other than any incidents already mentioned, has anyone attacked or threatened you in any of these ways: (a) with any weapon, such as a gun or knife; (b) with anything like a baseball bat, frying pan, scissors, or stick; (c) by something thrown, such as a rock or bottle; (d) by grabbing, punching, or choking; (e) any rape, attempted rape, or other types of sexual attack; (f) any face-to-face threats; **or** (g) any attack or threat or use of force by anyone at all? Please mention it even if you are not certain it was a crime.

2. Incidents involving forced or unwanted sexual acts are often difficult to talk about. Other than any incidents already mentioned, have you been forced or coerced to engage in unwanted sexual activity by (a) someone you did not know; (b) a casual acquaintance; or (c) someone you knew well?

Respondents may screen into a CIR if they respond affirmatively to another short-cue screening question. For instance, a separate screening question cues respondents to think of attacks or threats that took place in specific locations, such as at home, work, or school. A respondent who recalled a sexual victimization that occurred at home, work, or school and answered affirmatively would be administered a CIR even if they did not respond affirmatively to the screening question targeting sexual violence.

Second stage of measurement. CIR is used to collect information on the attributes of each incident. Key attributes of sexual violence that are used to classify a victimization as a rape or sexual assault are the type of attack and physical injury suffered. Victims are asked if "the offender hit you, knock[ed] you down, or actually attack[ed] you in any way;" if "the offender TR[IED] to attack you;" or if "the offender THREATEN[ED] you with harm in any way?" Survey participant is classified as a victim of rape or sexual assault if he or she responds affirmatively to one of these three questions and then responds that the completed, attempted, or threatened attack was (a) rape; (b) attempted rape; (c) sexual assault; (d) verbal threat of rape; (e) verbal threat of sexual assault other than rape; (f) unwanted sexual contact with force (e.g., grabbing, fondling); or (g) unwanted sexual contact without force (e.g., grabbing, fondling).

Whether the victim selects one of these response options to describe the attack, he or she is also classified as a victim of rape or sexual assault if the injuries suffered as a result of the incident are described as: (a) rape; (b) attempted rape; or (c) sexual assault other than rape or attempted rape.

Coercion. Although the CIR does not ask respondents if psychological coercion was used, one screening question targeted to rape and sexual violence asks respondents if force or coercion was used to initiate unwanted sexual activity.

The final classification of incidents by the CIR results in the following definitions of rape and sexual assault used in the NCVS:

Rape. Coerced or forced sexual intercourse. Forced sexual intercourse means vaginal, anal, or oral penetration by the offender(s). This category could include incidents where the penetration was from a foreign object such as a bottle. Includes attempted rapes, male and female victims, and both heterosexual and same-sex rape. Attempted rape includes verbal threats of rape.

Sexual assault. A wide range of victimizations, separate from rape or attempted rape. These crimes include attacks or attempted attacks generally involving unwanted sexual contact between victim and offender. Sexual assaults may or may not involve force and include such things as grabbing or fondling. Sexual assault also includes verbal threats.

Comparison of NCVS Estimates to Other Survey Estimates

During the past several decades, a number of other surveys have also been used to study rape and sexual assault in the general population. BJS estimates of rape and sexual assault from the NCVS have typically been lower than estimates derived from other federal and private surveys. However, the NCVS methodology and definitions of rape and sexual assault differ from many of these surveys in important ways that contribute to the variation in estimates of the prevalence and incidence of these victimizations. Additional information about differences in self-report estimates of rape and sexual assault is available on the BJS website. BJS continues an active research program on the collection of rape and sexual assault data in an effort to improve the quality and accuracy of these estimates.

Despite the current differences in methods and estimates that exist between the NCVS and other surveys measuring rape and sexual assault, a strength of the NCVS is its capacity to be used to make comparisons between population subgroups and over time. Methodological differences that exist between the NCVS and the other surveys should not impact NCVS comparisons between groups or in trends over time.

PART 5

Federal Justice Statistics, 2015–2016

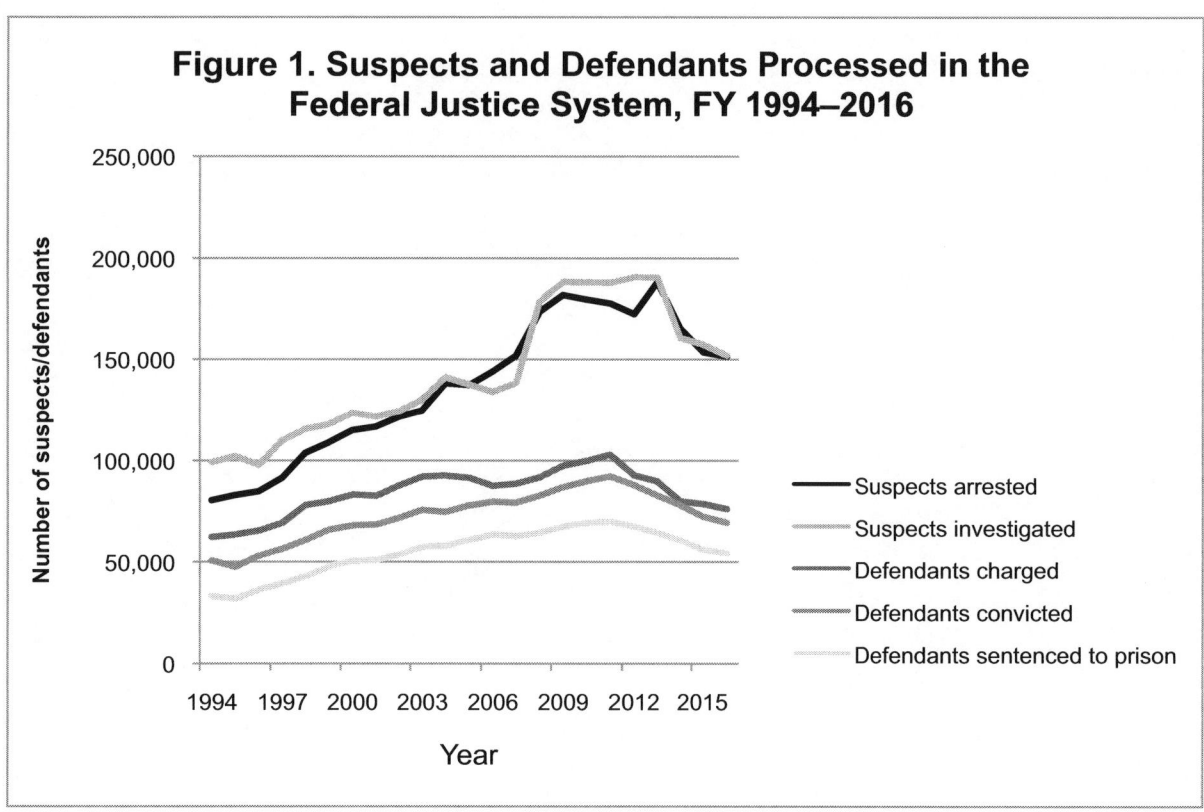

Figure 1. Suspects and Defendants Processed in the Federal Justice System, FY 1994–2016

- Federal law enforcement agencies made a total of 151,460 arrests in fiscal year (FY) 2016.

- More than half (58 percent) of all federal arrests in FY 2016 took place in the five federal judicial districts along the U.S.-Mexico border, up from 45 percent in FY 2006. These districts are listed individually in the tables in this section; these five districts also accounted for 52 percent of all suspects investigated and 41 percent of all offenders who were sentenced to federal prison.

- Forty-five percent of federal arrests in FY 2016 involved an immigration offense as the most serious arrest offense.

- In FY 2016, 41 percent of defendants charged in U.S. district courts were not U.S. citizens: 30 percent were Mexican citizens, 5 percent were from Central America, and 6 percent were citizens of other foreign nations.

Table 1. Offenders in Federal Confinement or under Federal Supervision in the Community, FY 2006, FY 2015, and FY 2016

(Number; percent.)

Characteristic	FY 2006		FY 2015		FY 2016	
	Number	Percent	Number	Percent	Number	Percent
Total	365,496	100.0	392,212	100.0	379,908	100.0
Secure confinement	224,661	61.5	236,512	60.3	222,964	58.7
Pre-trial detention	56,236	15.4	53,449	13.6	52,586	13.8
Federal Bureau of Prisons (post-sentencing)[1]	168,425	46.1	183,063	46.7	170,378	44.8
Community	140,835	38.5	155,700	39.7	156,944	41.3
Pre-trial release supervision	28,218	7.7	22,778	5.8	22,035	5.8
Post-sentencing supervision	112,617	30.8	132,922	33.9	134,909	35.5
Supervised release	85,317	23.3	112,567	28.7	115,843	30.5
Probation	24,879	6.8	19,126	4.9	17,938	4.7
Parole	2,421	0.7	1,229	0.3	1,128	0.3

Note: Federal offender populations are shown as of September 30, 2006, 2015, and 2016. Details may not sum to totals due to rounding.
[1]Federally sentenced prisoners in the custody of the Federal Bureau of Prisons (BOP). Counts exclude persons in federal prison for District of Columbia code offenses, military code offenses, treaty transfer cases, and as state boarders. Unsentenced federal offenders in the BOP are counted in pre-trial detention counts.

Table 2. Federal Arrests, by Most Serious Offense and Federal District, FY 2015 and FY 2016

(Number; percent.)

Characteristic	FY 2015		FY 2016		Percent change, 2015–2016
	Number	Percent	Number	Percent	
Total arrests	153,478	100.0	151,460	100.0	-1.3
Most serious offense at arrest					
Violent	3,437	2.0	3,463	2.3	0.8
Property	12,207	8.0	10,913	7.2	-10.6
Fraud	10,372	6.8	9,213	6.1	-11.2
Other	1,835	1.2	1,700	1.1	-7.4
Drug	23,655	15.0	23,566	15.6	-0.4
Public order	7,894	5.0	7,599	5.0	-3.7
Regulatory	288	0.2	276	0.2	-4.2
Other	7,606	5.0	7,323	4.8	-3.7
Weapons	7,420	4.8	8,008	5.3	7.9
Immigration	71,119	46.3	68,315	45.1	-3.9
Material witness	4,894	3.2	5,594	3.7	14.3
Supervision violations	22,715	14.8	24,000	15.8	5.7
Federal judicial district					
U.S./Mexico border district	90,135	58.7	88,448	58.4	-1.9
Arizona	24,967	16.3	21,702	14.3	-13.1
California Southern	6,373	4.2	6,562	4.3	3.0
New Mexico	5,540	3.6	6,215	4.1	12.2
Texas Southern	32,083	20.9	29,759	19.6	-7.2
Texas Western	21,172	13.8	24,210	16.0	14.3
Other	63,343	41.3	63,012	41.6	-0.5

Note: Suspects with more than one arrest are counted separately. Most serious arrest is determined by the deputy U.S. Marshal at booking. Federal district is the location of the federal court where booking takes place. Offense information was missing for 137 records in 2015 and for 2 records in 2016. Details may not sum to totals due to rounding.

Table 3. Suspects in Matters Opened by U.S. Attorneys, by Referring Authority, FY 2006, FY 2014, FY 2015, and FY 2016

(Percent; number.)

Department or authority	FY 2006	FY 2014	FY 2015	FY 2016
Justice...	31.3	25.0	28.2	29.7
Homeland Security............................	46.8	58.0	53.6	52.6
Treasury..	1.7	2.0	1.6	1.3
Interior..	1.6	2.0	1.9	2.0
Defense	3.7	2.0	2.5	2.0
Federal/state task forces..................	2.8	2.0	2.0	2.0
Other[1]..	12.2	9.0	10.2	10.4
Number of suspects.........................	133,935	160,505	157,313	151,994

Note: Department or authority is the entity making the referral for criminal action to the U.S. attorneys' offices. Percentages are based on records with non-missing referring authority information (268 records were missing the referring authority in 2006, 236 records in 2014, 71 records in 2015, and 41 records in 2016). The unit of count is a suspect in a matter referred to U.S. attorneys. Suspects in more than one matter are counted separately. A matter is opened when a federal prosecutor spends one hour or more investigating. Details may not sum to totals due to rounding.
[1]Includes departments of Agriculture, Commerce, Education, Energy, Health and Human Services, Labor, State, and Transportation; and state and local authorities.

Table 4. Outcome and Case Processing Time of Suspects in Matters Concluded, FY 2016

(Number; percent; days.)

Characteristic	Outcome				Prosecutor decision/case-processing time (median days)[1]			
	Number of suspects in matters concluded	Prosecuted in U.S. district court	Disposed of by U.S. magistrate	Declined to prosecute	Total	Decision to prosecute in U.S. district court	Decision to dispose of by U.S. magistrate	Decision to decline matter
Total	155,615	46.4	37.2	16.0	20	25	0	517
Lead charge[2]								
Violent..	4,746	59.0	8.6	32.3	70	28	117	341
Property..	20,382	51.0	7.7	41.9	336	136	112	659
Fraud..	17,962	50.1	7.0	43.2	371	172	135	674
Other..	2,420	53.5	15.0	31.9	90	23	79	526
Drug...	31,346	71.0	12.2	17.2	34	27	24	549
Public order..................................	18,539	44.0	16.9	39.3	146	36	92	461
Regulatory..................................	3,732	34.9	15.0	50.5	231	43	86	540
Other..	14,807	46.0	17.5	36.5	132	35	93	429
Weapons.......................................	10,316	74.0	3.7	21.9	36	26	83	256
Immigration	70,237	30.0	69.2	0.7	1	21	0	631
Federal judicial district								
U.S./Mexico border	81,131	34.0	63.5	2.9	3	23	0	469
Arizona......................................	19,720	24.9	72.0	3.6	0	26	0	477
California Southern....................	5,014	68.9	27.0	3.8	26	26	17	650
New Mexico	6,393	83.8	11.0	5.0	16	12	51	484
Texas Southern..........................	26,794	26.2	71.6	2.2	0	20	0	488
Texas Western	23,210	28.2	69.6	2.2	3	23	1	386
Other..	74,484	60.3	8.6	31.1	116	34	117	522

Note: The unit of count is a suspect in a matter referred to U.S. attorneys. Suspects investigated in more than one matter are counted separately. Lead charge was missing for 49 matters. Details may not sum to totals due to rounding.
[1]Prosecutor case-processing time reflects the time from receipt of a matter to the prosecutor's decision to prosecute as a case in U.S. district court, refer for disposal by a U.S. magistrate, or decline the matter, resulting in no further action. The median is the midpoint of processing time. A median of zero means that half of the suspects received a disposition on the same day as the matter was referred.
[2]Lead charge is the substantive statute that is the primary basis for referral. It is most often the charge with the greatest potential sentence, but not always.

Table 5. Demographic Characteristics of Defendants Charged in U.S. Federal District Court, by Sex of Defendant, FY 2016

(Number; percent.)

Defendant characteristic	All defendants		Male		Female	
	Number	Percent	Number	Percent	Number	Percent
Total	63,593	100.0	54,546	100.0	8,843	100.0
Race/Hispanic origin[1]						
White..	12,493	20.9	9,844	19.2	2,645	32.0
Black/African American	11,844	19.8	10,228	19.9	1,608	19.4
Hispanic/Latino..	33,248	56.0	29,675	57.8	3,558	43.0
American Indian/Alaska Native	1,329	2.0	1,026	2.0	303	3.7
Asian/Native Hawaiian/Other Pacific Islander	774	1.0	610	1.2	163	2.0
Age						
17 years or younger	34	0.0	32	0.1	2	--
18 to 19 years...	707	1.1	604	1.1	103	1.2
20 to 24 years...	7,546	12.0	6,392	11.7	1,151	13.0
25 to 29 years...	10,951	17.2	9,455	17.3	1,491	16.9
30 to 34 years...	11,517	18.1	10,094	18.5	1,419	16.0
35 to 39 years...	10,495	16.5	9,179	16.8	1,305	14.8
40 to 44 years...	7,763	12.2	6,712	12.3	1,039	11.8
45 to 49 years...	5,592	8.8	4,748	8.7	840	9.5
50 to 54 years...	3,751	5.9	3,159	5.8	586	6.6
55 to 59 years...	2,408	3.8	1,997	3.7	408	4.6
60 to 64 years...	1,392	2.2	1,123	2.1	268	3.0
65 years or older	1,274	2.0	1,044	1.9	230	2.6
Median age (years)	35 yrs.		35 yrs.		35 yrs.	
Citizenship						
U.S. citizen..	37,086	59.1	30,064	55.7	6,993	80.4
Legal alien	3,180	5.1	2,690	5.0	489	5.6
Illegal alien...	22,479	35.8	21,246	39.3	1,217	14.0
Country/region of citizenship						
North America	60,763	97.1	52,210	97.0	8,507	97.7
United States...	37,086	59.3	30,064	55.9	6,993	80.3
Mexico...	18,917	30.2	17,721	32.9	1,180	13.6
Canada...	104	0.2	81	0.2	23	0.3
Caribbean Islands[2]	1,349	2.2	1,226	2.3	123	1.4
Central America[2]	3,307	5.3	3,118	5.8	188	2.2
South America[2]	975	1.6	877	1.6	98	1.1
Asia and Oceania[2]	350	0.6	308	0.6	42	0.5
Europe[2]..	296	0.5	252	0.5	44	0.5
Africa[2]..	188	0.3	171	0.3	17	0.2

Note: The unit of count is a defendant in a case filed in U.S. district court. Defendants in more than one case filing are counted separately. Includes defendants charged in U.S. district court with a felony or Class A or B misdemeanor offense as the most serious charge. Data were missing for the following: sex (204), race/Hispanic origin (3,905), age (163), citizenship (848), and country/region of citizenship (1,021). Details may not sum to totals due to rounding.
-- = Less than 0.05 percent.
[1] Excludes persons of Hispanic/Latino origin, unless specified. Race/Hispanic origin are self-reported by the defendant during the pre-trial interview. Information collected for one race and one Hispanic origin category.
[2] Countries aggregated by region.

Table 6. Disposition and Case-Processing Time of Defendants in Cases Terminated in U.S. District Court, FY 2016

(Number; percent; days.)

Most serious offense at termination	Total cases terminated	Convicted			Not convicted		
		Total	Guilty plea	Bench/jury trial	Total	Bench/jury trial	Dismissed
All offenses...............................	76,639	91.0	89.0	2.0	9.3	0.4	8.9
Type of charge							
Felony..	67,996	94.0	92.0	2.2	6.3	0.4	5.9
Violent.......................................	2,474	91.0	84.2	7.0	8.8	1.1	7.7
Property.....................................	9,685	92.0	88.2	3.5	8.4	0.8	7.6
Fraud......................................	8,304	92.3	88.7	3.6	7.7	0.8	7.0
Other.....................................	1,381	87.6	84.9	2.6	12.5	1.2	11.3
Drug	22,024	92.3	90.3	2.0	7.7	0.3	7.4
Public order...............................	7,016	91.0	87.6	4.0	8.7	0.7	7.9
Regulatory..........................	834	86.2	82.9	3.4	13.8	2.9	10.9
Other...................................	6,182	92.0	88.2	3.8	8.0	0.5	7.5
Weapons.....................................	7,020	93.7	90.4	3.0	6.3	0.6	5.8
Immigration	19,777	97.5	97.3	0.0	2.5	0.1	2.4
Misdemeanor...............................	8,643	67.0	66.0	0.7	33.4	0.3	33.1
Federal judicial district							
U.S./Mexico border	27,834	96.0	95.0	0.6	4.1	0.1	4.0
Arizona.....................................	5,926	96.7	96.3	0.4	3.3	0.1	3.2
California Southern.....................	3,541	87.3	85.9	1.4	12.7	0.3	12.4
New Mexico	5,148	97.2	97.1	0.1	2.8	0.1	2.7
Texas Southern..........................	6,641	97.4	96.8	0.6	2.6	0.1	2.5
Texas Western	6,578	97.2	96.4	1.0	2.8	0.1	2.7
Other...	48,805	88.0	85.0	2.8	12.3	0.6	11.8
Median days from filing to disposition*	214 days	213 days	213 days	547 days	397 days	274 days	427 days

Note: Includes information on felony defendants, Class A misdemeanor (whether handled by U.S. district court judges or U.S. magistrates) and other misdemeanants provided they were handled by U.S. district court judges. Most serious offense at termination is determined by court personnel as the offense with the greatest statutory-maximum sentence. The unit of count is a defendant in a case terminated in U.S. district court. Defendants terminated in more than one case are counted separately. The median is the midpoint when processing time is sorted from slowest to fastest. A median of 214 days means that half of the defendants received a disposition in fewer than 214 days and half of the defendants received a disposition in more than 214 days. Details may not sum to totals due to rounding.

* = Includes the interval from the time a case is filed in U.S. district court through sentencing for those convicted and the interval from case filing through disposition for those not convicted or those whose cases were dismissed.

Table 7. Type and Length of Sentence Imposed for Convicted Offenders, by Offense and District, FY 2016

(Number; percent; months.)

Most serious offense at case termination	Number convicted	Type of sentence				Median sentence length (months)	
		Prison*	Probation only	Fine only	Suspended sentence	Prison	Probation
All offenses.................................	69,487	78.4	10.2	2.1	9.4	30	36
Type of charge							
Felony...	63,734	82.3	8.0	0.4	9.4	33	36
Violent......................................	2,256	93.1	3.4	0.2	3.3	81	37
Property	8,872	63.5	24.3	0.9	11.3	24	36
Fraud..................................	7,663	65.9	21.3	1.0	11.8	24	36
Other..................................	1,209	48.2	43.2	0.7	8.0	21	36
Drug	20,338	89.3	4.4	0.2	6.0	60	36
Public order..............................	6,407	78.3	14.4	0.9	6.5	51	36
Regulatory..........................	719	53.0	32.6	3.4	11.0	24	36
Other..................................	5,688	81.5	12.1	0.5	6.0	57	36
Weapons....................................	6,575	91.5	4.3	0.1	4.1	51	36
Immigration	19,286	80.3	4.0	0.2	15.5	12	36
Misdemeanor.................................	5,753	36.4	33.9	20.7	9.1	6	12
Federal judicial district							
U.S./Mexico border	26,689	84.4	5.3	0.3	10.0	15	36
Arizona.....................................	5,729	83.8	5.8	0.1	10.3	13	36
California Southern..................	3,092	81.2	5.1	0.1	13.6	24	60
New Mexico	5,006	98.1	1.7	--	0.2	2	24
Texas Southern	6,467	90.8	3.0	0.1	6.2	24	36
Texas Western	6,395	69.3	10.2	1.1	19.4	21	36
Other..	42,798	74.7	13.2	3.2	9.0	51	36

Note: The unit of count is a defendant in a case terminated with a conviction and sentence in U.S. district court. Defendants convicted and sentenced in more than one case are counted separately. The most serious offense is determined by court personnel as the offense with the greatest statutory maximum sentence. The median prison term is the midpoint of prison terms imposed. For example, a median of 30 months means that half of the defendants received a prison term of fewer than 30 months and half of the defendants received a prison term of more than 30 months. Sentence type was missing for 296 records in 2016. Details may not sum to totals due to rounding.
-- = Less than 0.05 percent.
* = Includes sentences to incarceration such as mixed (a prison term followed by a probation term) and life sentences.

Table 8. Demographic Characteristics of Federally Sentenced Offenders in the Custody of the Federal Bureau of Prisons, Fiscal Year-End 2006, 2015, and 2016

(Number; percent.)

Offender characteristic	2006 Number	2006 Percent	2015 Number	2015 Percent	2016 Number	2016 Percent	Average annual growth, 2006–2016[1]
All prisoners	168,425	100.0	183,063	100.0	170,378	100.0	0.2
Male	157,239	93.4	170,842	93.3	158,976	93.3	0.2
Female	11,186	6.6	12,221	6.7	11,402	6.7	0.3
Race/Hispanic origin[2]							
White	47,065	27.9	50,005	27.3	47,395	27.8	0.1
Black/African American	62,448	37.1	64,025	35.0	59,605	35.0	-0.4
Hispanic/Latino	53,461	31.7	63,010	34.4	57,608	33.8	0.9
American Indian/Alaska Native	2,960	1.8	3,460	1.9	3,443	2.0	1.5
Asian/Native Hawaiian/Other Pacific Islander	2,491	1.5	2,563	1.4	2327	1.4	-0.6
Age							
17 years or younger	27	0.0	9	--	2	--	--
18 to 19 years	361	0.2	235	0.1	246	0.1	-2.5
20 to 24 years	10,992	6.5	7,575	4.1	6,708	3.9	-4.7
25 to 29 years	28,687	17.0	21,080	11.5	19,163	11.2	-3.9
30 to 34 years	34,330	20.4	31,732	17.3	28,372	16.7	-1.8
35 to 39 years	30,429	18.1	35,006	19.1	32,817	19.3	0.8
40 to 44 years	23,459	13.9	29,399	16.1	27,561.00	16.2	1.7
45 to 49 years	17,115	10.2	21,728	11.9	20,740	12.2	2.0
50 to 54 years	10,633	6.3	15,599	8.5	14,653	8.6	3.3
55 to 59 years	6,560	3.9	9,931	5.4	9,645	5.7	4.0
60 to 64 years	3,333	2.0	5,709	3.1	5,442	3.2	5.1
65 years or older	2,498	1.5	5,060	2.8	5,028	3.0	7.3
Median age (years)	39		39		40		
Citizenship							
U.S. citizen	123,366	73.4	140,547	76.8	133,104	78.1	0.8
Non-U.S. citizen	44,629	26.6	42,483	23.2	37,242	21.9	-1.6
Country/region of citizenship							
North America	162,134	96.6	178,899	97.7	166,417	97.8	0.3
United States	123,366	73.5	140,547	74.2	133,104	78.2	0.8
Mexico	29,895	17.8	30,119	18.8	26,038	15.3	-1.1
Canada	335	0.2	299	0.2	236	0.1	-3.0
Caribbean Islands[3]	6,159	3.7	4,088	2.4	3,545	2.1	-5.3
Central America[3]	2,379	1.4	3,846[3]	2.2	3,494	2.1	4.3
South America[3]	3,435	2.0	2,073	1.2	2,037	1.2	-5.1
Asia and Oceania[3]	1,367	0.8	1,095	0.6	997	0.6	-3.0
Europe[3]	474	0.3	440	0.2	425	0.2	
Africa[3]	448	0.3	373	0.2	327	0.2	-2.8

Note: Includes prisoners sentenced in U.S. district court and excludes District of Columbia code offenders, military code offenders, foreign treaty transfers, state boarders, and pre-sentenced offenders. Citizenship data were missing in 2006 (430), 2015 (33), and 2016 (32). Country/region of citizenship data were missing in 2006 (567), 2015 (183), and 2016 (175). Details may not sum to totals due to rounding.
-- = Less than 0.05 percent.
[1] Calculated using each fiscal-year count from 2006 through 2016.
[2] Excludes persons of Hispanic/Latino origin, unless specified. Race/Hispanic origin are self-reported by the defendant during the pre-trial interview. Information collected for one race and one Hispanic origin category.
[3] Countries aggregated by region.

Table 9. Demographic Characteristics of Offenders Under Post-Sentencing Federal Supervision, FY 2016

(Number; percent.)

Offender characteristic	Total Number	Total Percent	Probation Number	Probation Percent	Supervised release Number	Supervised release Percent	Parole Number	Parole Percent
All prisoners	134,909	100.0	17,938	100.0	115,843	100.0	1,128	100.0
Male	111,347	82.7	11,102	62.8	99,140	85.6	1,105	98.0
Female	23,304	17.3	6,580	37.2	16,701	14.4	23	2.0
Race/Hispanic origin[1]								
White	46,198	35.1	7,794	45.8	38,058	33.5	346	32.5
Black/African American	47,168	35.8	4,611	27.1	41,986	36.9	571	53.6
Hispanic/Latino	32,223	24.4	3,383	19.9	28,719	25.3	121	11.4
American Indian/Alaska Native	2,846	2.2	444	2.6	2,382	2.1	20	1.9
Asian/Native Hawaiian/Other Pacific Islander	3,389	2.6	777	4.6	2,604	2.3	8	0.8
Age								
17 years or younger	22	--	21	0.1	1	--	0	^
18 to 19 years	113	0.1	90	0.5	23	--	0	^
20 to 24 years	3,734	2.8	1,213	6.9	2,514	2.2	7	0.6
25 to 29 years	13,015	9.7	2,224	12.6	10,739	9.3	52	4.6
30 to 34 years	19,251	14.3	2,279	12.9	16,899	14.6	73	6.5
35 to 39 years	23,597	17.5	2,222	12.6	21,311	18.4	64	5.7
40 to 44 years	21,073	15.7	2,005	11.3	18,965	16.4	103	9.1
45 to 49 years	17,346	12.9	1,927	10.9	15,310	13.2	109	9.7
50 to 54 years	13,245	9.8	1,776	10.0	11,313	9.8	156	13.8
55 to 59 years	9,840	7.3	1,467	8.3	8,215	7.1	158	14.0
60 to 64 years	6,325	4.7	1,065	6.0	5,103	4.4	157	13.9
65 years or older	7,095	5.3	1,399	7.9	5,448	4.7	248	22.0
Median age (years)		41.0		41.0		41.0		54.0
Citizenship								
U.S. citizen	124,662	93.2	15,620	88.9	108,015	93.8	1,027	95.6
Legal alien	4,567	3.4	1,008	5.7	3,551	3.1	8	0.7
Illegal alien	4,580	3.4	951	5.4	3,590	3.1	39	3.6
Country/region of citizenship								
North America	132,697	99.0	17,216	97.7	114,394	99.2	1,087	99.5
United States	130,089	97.0	16,747	95.0	112,278	97.3	1,064	97.4
Mexico	863	0.6	202	1.2	656	0.6	5	0.5
Canada	43	--	28	0.2	15	--	0	--
Caribbean Islands[2]	1,497	1.1	162	0.9	1,318	1.1	17	1.6
Central America[2]	205	0.2	77	0.4	127	0.1	1	0.1
South America[2]	195	0.2	58	0.3	133	0.1	4	0.4
Asia and Oceania[2]	704	0.5	219	1.2	483	0.4	2	0.2
Europe[2]	242	0.2	79	0.5	163	0.1	0	--
Africa[2]	245	0.2	57	0.3	188	0.2	0	--

Note: Details may not sum to totals due to rounding. Includes suspects for whom characteristics were unknown. The unit of count is an individual offender under federal supervision on September 30, 2016. Percentages are based on non-missing data. Citizenship and country/region of citizenship differ due to missing data. Data were missing for the following: age (253), sex (258), race/Hispanic origin (3,085), citizenship (1,100), and country/region of citizenship (826).
-- = Less than 0.05 percent.
^ = Estimate based on 10 or fewer cases.
[1]Excludes persons of Hispanic/Latino origin, unless specified. Race/Hispanic origin are self-reported by the defendant during the pre-trial interview. Information collected for one race and one Hispanic origin category.
[2]Countries aggregated by region.

METHODOLOGY

Federal Justice Statistics describes persons processed by the federal criminal justice system. Data are from the Federal Justice Statistics Program (FJSP). The FJSP collects, standardizes, and reports on administrative data received from six federal justice agencies: the U.S. Marshals Service, Drug Enforcement Administration, Executive Office for U.S. Attorneys, Administrative Office of the U.S. Courts, U.S. Sentencing Commission, and Federal Bureau of Prisons.

This report describes the annual activity, workloads, and outcomes of the federal criminal justice system from arrest to imprisonment. Findings are based on data from the U.S. Marshals Service, Drug Enforcement Administration (DEA), Executive Office for U.S. Attorneys, Administrative Office of the U.S. Courts, and Federal Bureau of Prisons. This report presents data on arrests and investigations by law enforcement agency and growth rates by type of offense and federal judicial district. It also examines trends on drug arrests by the DEA, and it includes the most recent available data on sentences imposed and their lengths by type of offense.

Definitions of Major Offense Categories

Violent—Includes murder, non-negligent or negligent manslaughter, aggravated or simple assault, sex abuse, robbery, kidnapping, and threats against the president.

Property—Includes fraudulent and other types of property offenses.

Fraudulent property—Includes embezzlement, fraud (including tax fraud), forgery, and counterfeiting.

Other property—Includes burglary, larceny, motor-vehicle theft, arson, transportation of stolen property, and other property offenses, such as destruction of property and trespassing.

Drug—Includes the manufacture, import, export, distribution, or dispensing of a controlled substance (or a counterfeit substance), or the possession of a controlled substance (or a counterfeit substance) with intent to manufacture or distribute.

Public order—Includes regulatory and other types of offenses.

Regulatory public order—Includes violation of agriculture, antitrust, labor, food and drug, motor carrier, and other federal regulations.

Other public order—Includes non-regulatory violations concerning tax law (tax fraud), bribery, perjury, national defense, escape, racketeering and extortion, gambling, liquor, mailing or transporting obscene materials, traffic, migratory birds, conspiracy, aiding and abetting, jurisdiction, and other offenses.

Weapons—Includes violations of any of the provisions of 18 U.S.C. §§ 922-923 concerning the manufacturing, importing, possessing, receiving, and licensing of firearms and ammunition.

Immigration—Includes offenses involving illegal entrance into the United States, illegally reentering after being deported, willfully failing to leave when so ordered, or bringing in or harboring any aliens not admitted by an immigration officer.

Supervision violations—Includes violation of bail, violation of pre-trial or post-sentencing supervision in the community (probation), and failure to appear.

Report Methodology

This report uses data from the Federal Justice Statistics Program (FJSP), a collection from the Bureau of Justice Statistics (BJS). The FJSP receives administrative data files from six federal criminal justice agencies. Data represent the federal criminal case processing stages from arrest to imprisonment. BJS standardizes this information to maximize comparability across and within agencies over time. This includes—

- counting each appearance of an individual in the data during a fiscal year (October 1 through September 30), whether it be for a criminal arrest, matter, case, or imprisonment stay

- delineating fiscal year as the period for reported events

- applying a uniform offense classification across agencies

- classifying disposition and sentences imposed

FJSP Data Sources

U.S. Marshals Service: The Justice Detainee Information System provides information on suspects arrested for federal offenses. Suspects may be counted more than once in a fiscal year if they are arrested multiple times during the period. This report uses most serious arrest offense as classified by the deputy U.S. Marshal at the time of booking. Each of the 94 federal judicial districts in the United States have a U.S.

Marshal. Deputy U.S. Marshals take federal suspects who have been charged with a crime into custody, which includes booking, processing, and detaining suspects. They also oversee court security and coordinate prisoner transportation, among other duties.

Drug Enforcement Administration (DEA): The Defendant Statistical System contains data on suspects arrested by DEA agents within the U.S. The data include information on characteristics of arrestees and the type of drug for which they were arrested. Suspects may be counted more than once in a fiscal year if they are arrested multiple times by the DEA during this period.

Executive Office for U.S. Attorneys: The Legal Information Office Network System database contains information on the investigation and prosecution of suspects in criminal matters received and concluded and criminal cases filed and terminated by U.S. attorneys. Suspects may be counted more than once in a fiscal year if they are involved in multiple matters received and concluded during the period. A matter is defined as a referral in which an attorney spends one hour or more investigating. The lead charge is used to classify the most serious offense at referral and is defined as the substantive statute that is the primary basis of referral.

Administrative Office of the U.S. Courts (AOUSC): The Criminal Master File contains information about the criminal proceedings against defendants whose cases were filed and terminated in U.S. district courts. It includes information on felony defendants, Class A misdemeanants—whether handled by U.S. district court judges or U.S. magistrates—and other misdemeanants provided they were handled by U.S. district court judges. A felony is classified as an offense for which the maximum term of imprisonment is more than one year in prison. Offenses classified as misdemeanors include those for which the maximum term of imprisonment is less than one year in prison. Class A misdemeanors include offenses for which the maximum term of imprisonment is one year or less but more than 6 months in prison. Class B misdemeanors include offenses for which the maximum term of imprisonment is 6 months or less but more than 30 days in prison.

Offenses are based on the most serious charged offense, as determined by the probation officer responsible for interviewing the defendant. The probation officer classifies the offense charged into AOUSC four-digit offense codes, which are maintained and updated by the AOUSC. For defendants charged with more than one offense on an indictment, the probation officer chooses as the charged offense the one carrying the most severe penalty or, in the case of two or more charges carrying the same penalty, the one with the highest offense severity. The offense severity level is determined by the AOUSC,

which ranks offenses according to the maximum sentence, type of crime, and maximum fine amount. These four-digit codes are then aggregated into the primary offense charges used for this report.

This report also uses AOUSC data from the Probation and Pretrial Services Automated Case Tracking System (PACTS), which contains information on defendants interviewed and supervised by pre-trial services. These data are used to describe background characteristics of defendants arraigned. Post-sentencing data from PACTS are used to describe persons under post-sentencing supervision in the community.

U.S. Sentencing Commission: The Monitoring Database contains information on criminal defendants sentenced pursuant to the provisions of the Sentencing Reform Act of 1984. Data files are limited to those defendants whose court records have been obtained by the U.S. Sentencing Commission. These data do not appear in this report.

Other Resources

Federal Bureau of Prisons (BOP): The SENTRY database contains information on all federally sentenced offenders admitted into or released from federal prison during a fiscal year and offenders in federal prison at the end of each fiscal year (September 30). The prisoner count reported by the FJSP differs from what is reported by the BOP although data are from the same source (SENTRY). For example, the BOP reports 192,170 prisoners as of September 30, 2016. The FJSP starts with data extracted from SENTRY that differs slightly (down 506) from this total (191,664). Of the 191,664 records, 15,759 records were dropped because the prisoner was not designated at an assigned BOP custodial facility. The excluded records included designations to community confinement, home confinement, hospital, Immigration and Customs Enforcement detention, material witness, and pre-sentence admission. Next, 439 records were excluded due to missing commitment offense, and 4,529 prisoners were dropped as they were sentenced by the District of Columbia Superior Court. Finally, 559 prisoner records were dropped because the prisoner was a state boarder, a treaty transfer, or serving a sentence from a military court commitment. Of the 191,664 prisoners reported by the BOP in custody on September 30, 2016, a total of 170,378 (89 percent of the total population) met the criteria as federally sentenced prisoners.

Detailed data tables will be available in *Federal Justice Statistics, 2015 - Statistical Tables* (NCJ 251771) and *Federal Justice Statistics, 2016 - Statistical Tables* (NCJ 251772), forthcoming in 2019 on BJS site. FJSP data are available in the Federal Criminal Case Processing Statistics Tool, an interactive BJS web tool that permits users to query the federal data and download the results as a spreadsheet. This tool is available on the BJS Web site. It provides statistics by stage of the federal criminal case process, including law enforcement, prosecution and courts, and incarceration. Users can generate queries using data for the years 1998 to 2016. Users can also generate queries by title and section of the U.S. criminal code.

For more information, please see: http://www.bjs.gov/index.cfm?ty=pbdetail&iid=6506

PART 6

Hate Crime Statistics, 2017

HIGHLIGHTS

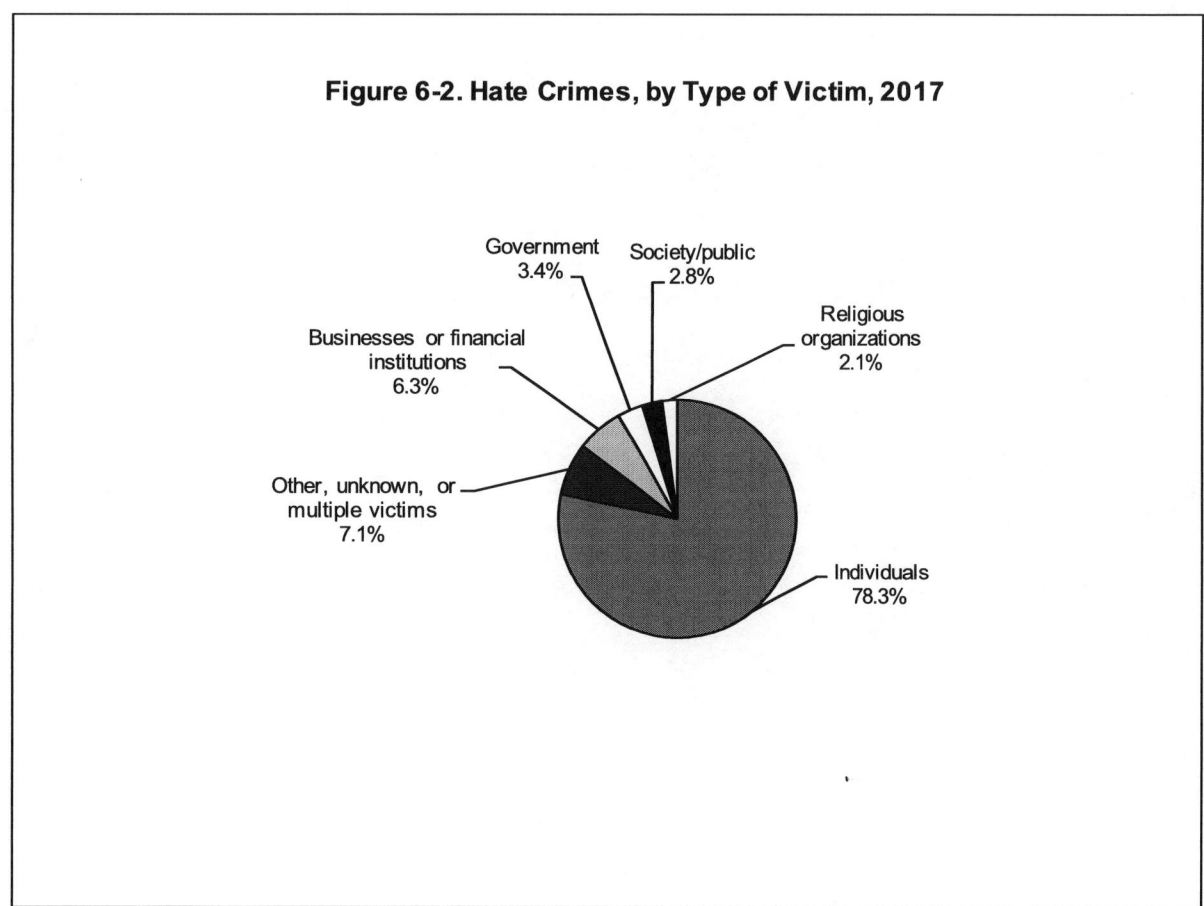

Figure 6-2. Hate Crimes, by Type of Victim, 2017

Government
3.4%

Society/public
2.8%

Religious
organizations
2.1%

Businesses or financial
institutions
6.3%

Other, unknown, or
multiple victims
7.1%

Individuals
78.3%

- In 2017, 16,149 law enforcement agencies participated in the Hate Crime Statistics Program. Of these agencies, 2,040 reported 7,175 hate crime incidents involving 8,437 offenses.

- There were 7,016 single-bias incidents that involved 8,126 offenses, 8,493 victims, and 6,307 known offenders. Among the 7,016 incidents, approximately 58.1 percent were racially/ethnically/ancestrally motivated, 15.9 percent resulted from sexual-orientation bias, 22.0 percent were motivated by religious bias, 1.7 percent were motivated by gender-identity bias, 1.6 percent were prompted by disability bias, and 0.6 percent (46 incidents) resulted from gender bias.

- The 69 multiple-bias incidents reported in 2017 involved 311 offenses, 335 victims, and 63 known offenders.

- The majority of the approximately 3,115 hate crime offenses that were crimes against property (74.6 percent) were acts of destruction/damage/vandalism; the remaining crimes against property (25.4 percent) consisted of robbery, burglary, larceny-theft, motor vehicle theft, arson, and other crimes.

- There were 238 offenses defined as crimes against society (e.g., drug or narcotic offenses or prostitution).

Table 1. Incidents, Offenses, Victims, and Known Offenders, by Bias Motivation, 2017

(Number.)

Bias motivation	Incidents	Offenses	Victims[1]	Known offenders[2]
Total	7,175	8,437	8,828	6,370
Single-Bias Incidents	7,106	8,126	8,493	6,307
Race/Ethnicity/Ancestry	4,131	4,832	5,060	3,747
Anti-White	741	844	864	758
Anti-Black or African American	2,013	2,358	2,458	1,742
Anti-American Indian or Alaska Native	251	281	321	228
Anti-Asian	131	152	165	108
Anti-Native Hawaiian or Other Pacific Islander	16	17	18	10
Anti-Multiple races, group	180	215	229	100
Anti-Arab	102	128	131	100
Anti-Hispanic or Latino	427	525	552	491
Anti-Other Race/Ethnicity/Ancestry	270	312	322	210
Religion	1,564	1,679	1,749	1,009
Anti-Jewish	938	976	1,017	523
Anti-Catholic	73	75	76	59
Anti-Protestant	40	40	40	15
Anti-Islamic (Muslim)	273	314	325	231
Anti-other religion	76	82	86	56
Anti-multiple religions, group	47	54	57	35
Anti-Mormon	15	15	15	8
Anti-Jehovah's Witness	7	13	13	6
Anti-Eastern Orthodox (Russian, Greek, Other)	23	23	27	14
Anti-Other Christian	27	31	32	18
Anti-Buddhist	8	9	12	10
Anti-Hindu	11	15	15	10
Anti-Sikh	20	24	26	18
Anti-atheism/agnosticism/etc.	6	8	8	6
Sexual orientation	1,130	1,303	1,338	1,250
Anti-gay (male)	679	758	774	778
Anti-lesbian	126	159	164	129
Anti-lesbian, gay, bisexual, or transgender (mixed group)	268	321	333	282
Anti-heterosexual	32	37	37	28
Anti-bisexual	25	28	30	33
Disability	116	128	160	124
Anti-physical	32	35	37	31
Anti-mental	84	93	123	93
Gender	46	53	54	40
Anti-male	22	25	26	21
Anti-female	24	28	28	19
Gender Identity	119	131	132	137
Anti-transgender	106	118	119	127
Anti-gender nonconforming	13	13	13	10
Multiple-Bias Incidents[3]	69	311	335	63

[1]The term victim may refer to a person, business, institution, or society as a whole.
[2]The term known offender does not imply that the identity of the suspect is known, but only that an attribute of the suspect has been identified, which distinguishes him/her from an unknown offender.
[3]A multiple-bias incident is an incident in which one or more offense types are motivated by two or more biases.

Table 2. Incidents, Offenses, Victims, and Known Offenders, by Offense Type, 2017

(Number.)

Offense type	Incidents[1]	Offenses	Victims[2]	Known offenders[3]
Total	7,175	8,437	8,828	6,370
Crimes Against Persons	4,090	5,084	5,084	4,442
Murder and nonnegligent manslaughter	12	15	15	15
Rape[4]	23	23	23	30
Aggravated assault	788	990	990	1,051
Simple assault	1,433	1,745	1,745	1,725
Intimidation	1,807	2,283	2,283	1,588
Human trafficking, commercial sex acts	1	1	1	0
Other[5]	26	27	27	33
Crimes Against Property	3,115	3,115	3,506	1,933
Robbery	157	157	171	288
Burglary	145	145	185	98
Larceny-theft	326	326	379	249
Motor vehicle theft	41	41	44	25
Arson	42	42	59	34
Destruction/damage/vandalism	2,325	2,325	2,585	1,182
Other[5]	79	79	83	57
Crimes Against Society[5]	238	238	238	284

[1]The actual number of incidents is 7,175. However, the column figures will not add to the total because incidents may include more than one offense type, and these are counted in each appropriate offense type category.
[2]The term victim may refer to a person, business, institution, or society as a whole.
[3]The term known offender does not imply the suspect's identity is known; rather, the term indicates some aspect of the suspect was identified, thus distinguishing the suspect from an unknown offender. The actual number of known offenders is 6,370. However, the column figures will not add to the total because some offenders are responsible for more than one offense type, and are, therefore, counted more than once in this table.
[4]The figures shown in this row for the offense of rape include only those reported by law enforcement agencies that used the revised Uniform Crime Reporting (UCR) definition of rape.
[5]Includes additional offenses collected in the National Incident-Based Reporting System.

Table 3. Offenses, Known Offender's Race and Ethnicity, by Offense Type, 2017

(Number.)

Bias motivation	Total offenses	Known offender's race							Known offender's ethnicity[1]				Unknown offender
		White	Black or African American	American Indian or Alaska Native	Asian	Native Hawaiian or Other Pacific Islander	Group of multiple races	Unknown race	Hispanic or Latino	Not Hispanic or Latino	Group of multiple ethnicities	Unknown ethnicity	
Total	8,437	3,228	1,217	58	46	3	281	1,132	350	1,294	56	3,085	2,472
Crimes Against Persons	5,084	2,491	999	49	37	3	215	445	278	1,067	50	2,064	845
Murder and nonnegligent manslaughter	15	6	7	0	0	0	0	1	0	3	0	7	1
Rape[2]	23	13	7	0	0	0	1	1	1	4	0	17	1
Aggravated assault	990	530	262	8	8	0	64	68	107	298	11	375	50
Simple assault	1,745	840	415	23	13	2	88	151	95	388	9	729	213
Intimidation	2,283	1,084	302	18	16	1	61	223	75	370	30	914	578
Human trafficking, commercial sex acts	1	0	0	0	0	0	0	0	0	0	0	0	1
Other[3]	27	18	6	0	0	0	1	1	0	4	0	22	1
Crimes Against Property	3,115	571	178	9	8	0	55	677	62	190	5	841	1,617
Robbery	157	49	55	1	0	0	20	16	16	36	2	58	16
Burglary	145	31	12	1	0	0	3	31	1	8	1	58	67
Larceny-theft	326	102	38	1	2	0	5	46	6	14	0	165	132
Motor vehicle theft	41	12	2	0	0	0	0	6	0	1	0	19	21
Arson	42	13	1	1	1	0	1	6	1	6	0	11	19
Destruction/damage/ vandalism	2,325	336	65	4	5	0	22	565	37	115	2	496	1,328
Other[3]	79	28	5	1	0	0	4	7	1	10	0	34	34
Crimes Against Society[3]	238	166	40	0	1	0	11	10	10	37	1	180	10

[1]The sum of offenses by the known offender's ethnicity does not equal the sum of offenses by the known offender's race because not all law enforcement agencies that report offender race data also report offender ethnicity data.
[2]The figures shown in the rape (revised definition) row include only those reported by law enforcement agencies that used the revised Uniform Crime Reporting (UCR) definition of rape.
[3]Includes additional offenses collected in the National Incident-Based Reporting System.

Table 4. Offenses, Offense Type, by Bias Motivation, 2017

(Number.)

Bias motivation	Total offenses	Crimes against persons						
		Murder and nonnegligent manslaughter	Rape[1]	Aggravated assault	Simple assault	Intimidation	Human trafficking, commercial sex acts	Other[2]
Total	8,437	15	23	990	1,745	2,283	1	27
Single-Bias Incidents	8,126	15	23	975	1,623	2,156	1	27
Race/Ethnicity/Ancestry	4,832	11	8	638	965	1,442	1	15
Anti-White	844	5	2	105	203	171	0	7
Anti-Black or African American....................	2,358	5	1	326	454	820	0	2
Anti-American Indian or Alaska Native..........	281	0	4	17	29	44	0	1
Anti-Asian	152	0	0	14	40	45	0	0
Anti-Native Hawaiian or Other Pacific Islander	17	0	0	1	2	3	1	1
Anti-Multiple Races, Group	215	0	0	8	27	65	0	2
Anti-Arab	128	0	1	24	37	37	0	2
Anti-Hispanic or Latino	525	1	0	105	124	167	0	0
Anti-Other Race/Ethnicity/Ancestry	312	0	0	38	49	90	0	0
Religion	1,679	1	1	55	184	331	0	2
Anti-Jewish	976	0	0	8	61	179	0	0
Anti-Catholic	75	0	0	1	3	4	0	0
Anti-Protestant	40	0	0	0	4	3	0	0
Anti-Islamic (Muslim)	314	0	0	28	77	110	0	0
Anti-Other Religion	82	0	0	2	10	21	0	0
Anti-Multiple Religions, Group	54	0	0	5	15	1	0	0
Anti-Mormon	15	0	0	0	0	2	0	0
Anti-Jehovah's Witness.............................	13	0	0	1	6	2	0	0
Anti-Eastern Orthodox (Russian, Greek, Other)	23	0	0	0	2	0	0	0
Anti-Other Christian	31	0	0	1	1	1	0	0
Anti-Buddhist.......................................	9	0	0	1	1	1	0	0
Anti-Hindu	15	0	0	4	1	4	0	1
Anti-Sikh	24	1	1	4	1	3	0	0
Anti-Atheism/Agnosticism/etc....................	8	0	0	0	2	0	0	1
Sexual Orientation	1,303	2	8	237	383	327	0	5
Anti-Gay (Male)	758	2	3	161	233	170	0	2
Anti-Lesbian	159	0	3	21	51	50	0	1
Anti-Lesbian, Gay, Bisexual, or Transgender (Mixed Group)..	321	0	1	44	83	95	0	2
Anti-Heterosexual..................................	37	0	0	5	8	8	0	0
Anti-Bisexual	28	0	1	6	8	4	0	0
Disability	128	1	3	12	32	23	0	2
Anti-Physical..	35	1	0	4	9	5	0	0
Anti-Mental...	93	0	3	8	23	18	0	2
Gender	53	0	3	5	12	8	0	3
Anti-Male	25	0	1	3	4	3	0	1
Anti-Female...	28	0	2	2	8	5	0	2
Gender Identity.....................................	131	0	0	28	47	25	0	0
Anti-Transgender	118	0	0	27	43	24	0	0
Anti-Gender Non-Conforming....................	13	0	0	1	4	1	0	0
Multiple-Bias Incidents[3]	311	0	0	15	122	127	0	0

[1] The figures shown in this column for the offense of rape include only those reported by law enforcement agencies that used the revised Uniform Crime Reporting (UCR) definition of rape.
[2] Includes additional offenses collected in the National Incident-Based Reporting System.
[3] A multiple-bias incident is an incident in which one or more offense types are motivated by two or more biases.

Table 4. Offenses, Offense Type, by Bias Motivation, 2017—*Continued*

(Number.)

Bias motivation	Total offenses	Crimes against property							Crimes against society[2]
		Robbery	Burglary	Larceny- theft	Motor vehicle theft	Arson	Destruction/ damage/ vandalism	Other[2]	
Total	8,437	157	145	326	41	42	2,325	79	238
Single-Bias Incidents	8,126	157	140	323	41	41	2,291	79	234
Race/Ethnicity/Ancestry	4,832	84	83	208	35	24	1,111	40	167
Anti-White	844	22	24	92	14	3	113	20	63
Anti-Black or African American.............	2,358	19	29	17	2	15	640	6	22
Anti-American Indian or Alaska Native........	281	2	12	60	14	0	26	10	62
Anti-Asian	152	0	4	8	1	0	38	0	2
Anti-Native Hawaiian or Other Pacific Islander	17	1	1	4	0	0	2	1	0
Anti-Multiple Races, Group	215	4	4	1	0	0	102	0	2
Anti-Arab	128	2	1	5	2	0	16	0	1
Anti-Hispanic or Latino	525	29	3	12	1	3	74	2	4
Anti-Other Race/Ethnicity/Ancestry	312	5	5	9	1	3	100	1	11
Religion	1,679	14	35	52	3	8	938	24	31
Anti-Jewish	976	4	11	11	0	2	696	2	2
Anti-Catholic	75	0	1	6	1	2	43	3	11
Anti-Protestant	40	0	2	6	0	0	22	1	2
Anti-Islamic (Muslim)	314	6	2	6	0	0	80	5	0
Anti-Other Religion	82	1	3	1	1	2	36	2	3
Anti-Multiple Religions, Group	54	1	4	4	0	1	21	0	2
Anti-Mormon	15	0	4	2	0	0	2	1	4
Anti-Jehovah's Witness	13	0	0	1	0	0	2	0	1
Anti-Eastern Orthodox (Russian, Greek, Other)	23	1	2	6	0	0	3	6	3
Anti-Other Christian	31	0	2	2	0	1	22	0	1
Anti-Buddhist	9	0	0	2	0	0	4	0	0
Anti-Hindu	15	0	1	1	0	0	2	1	0
Anti-Sikh	24	0	3	2	1	0	4	3	1
Anti-Atheism/Agnosticism/etc.	8	1	0	2	0	0	1	0	1
Sexual Orientation	1,303	52	15	38	1	7	207	3	18
Anti-Gay (Male).............................	758	42	11	9	1	3	115	1	5
Anti-Lesbian	159	0	0	5	0	0	26	0	2
Anti-Lesbian, Gay, Bisexual, or Transgender (Mixed Group).............................	321	9	3	18	0	4	60	0	2
Anti-Heterosexual	37	1	1	4	0	0	4	1	5
Anti-Bisexual	28	0	0	2	0	0	2	1	4
Disability	128	2	2	16	0	2	8	9	16
Anti-Physical.............................	35	0	0	5	0	0	2	2	7
Anti-Mental.............................	93	2	2	11	0	2	6	7	9
Gender	53	0	2	3	2	0	13	0	2
Anti-Male.............................	25	0	2	3	2	0	5	0	1
Anti-Female.............................	28	0	0	0	0	0	8	0	1
Gender Identity.............................	131	5	3	6	0	0	14	3	0
Anti-Transgender	118	4	2	4	0	0	13	1	0
Anti-Gender Non-Conforming...............	13	1	1	2	0	0	1	2	0
Multiple-Bias Incidents[3]	311	0	5	3	0	1	34	0	4

[1]The figures shown in this column for the offense of rape include only those reported by law enforcement agencies that used the revised Uniform Crime Reporting (UCR) definition of rape.
[2]Includes additional offenses collected in the National Incident-Based Reporting System.
[3]A multiple-bias incident is an incident in which one or more offense types are motivated by two or more biases.

Table 5. Offenses, Known Offender's Race, by Bias Motivation, 2017

(Number.)

Bias motivation	Total offenses	Known offender's race						
		White	Black or African American	American Indian or Alaska Native	Asian	Native Hawaiian or Other Pacific Islander	Group of multiple races	Unknown race
Total	8,437	3,228	1,217	58	46	3	281	1,132
Single-Bias Incidents	8,126	3,186	1,195	58	46	3	279	1,117
Race/Ethnicity/Ancestry	4,832	2,164	694	46	22	2	166	508
Anti-White	844	182	382	14	2	1	26	83
Anti-Black or African American	2,358	1,241	72	25	10	0	89	268
Anti-American Indian or Alaska Native	281	137	27	2	1	1	26	12
Anti-Asian	152	63	27	0	4	0	2	22
Anti-Native Hawaiian or Other Pacific Islander	17	7	3	0	0	0	0	0
Anti-Multiple Races, Group	215	76	14	0	0	0	1	29
Anti-Arab	128	54	30	0	2	0	5	16
Anti-Hispanic or Latino	525	274	107	3	0	0	9	43
Anti-Other Race/Ethnicity/Ancestry	312	130	32	2	3	0	8	35
Religion	1,679	409	87	1	13	0	25	443
Anti-Jewish	976	141	26	0	6	0	6	320
Anti-Catholic	75	28	8	0	1	0	2	16
Anti-Protestant	40	6	1	0	0	0	0	7
Anti-Islamic (Muslim)	314	139	30	0	1	0	8	44
Anti-Other Religion	82	18	2	0	2	0	5	19
Anti-Multiple Religions, Group	54	14	13	1	0	0	0	12
Anti-Mormon	15	6	1	0	0	0	0	1
Anti-Jehovah's Witness	13	11	0	0	0	0	0	1
Anti-Eastern Orthodox (Russian, Greek, Other)	23	9	3	0	0	0	1	0
Anti-Other Christian	31	10	1	0	0	0	0	8
Anti-Buddhist	9	3	1	0	1	0	1	2
Anti-Hindu	15	9	0	0	0	0	0	4
Anti-Sikh	24	10	1	0	1	0	2	7
Anti-Atheism/Agnosticism/etc.	8	5	0	0	1	0	0	2
Sexual Orientation	1,303	478	335	10	10	1	68	143
Anti-Gay (Male)	758	263	222	3	9	1	43	83
Anti-Lesbian	159	71	34	0	0	0	7	18
Anti-Lesbian, Gay, Bisexual, or Transgender (Mixed Group)	321	119	69	6	1	0	10	37
Anti-Heterosexual	37	10	6	0	0	0	6	2
Anti-Bisexual	28	15	4	1	0	0	2	3
Disability	128	66	28	0	0	0	2	6
Anti-Physical	35	18	7	0	0	0	2	1
Anti-Mental	93	48	21	0	0	0	0	5
Gender	53	28	8	0	1	0	0	8
Anti-Male	25	11	4	0	0	0	0	8
Anti-Female	28	17	4	0	1	0	0	0
Gender Identity	131	41	43	1	0	0	18	9
Anti-Transgender	118	37	40	1	0	0	17	9
Anti-Gender Non-Conforming	13	4	3	0	0	0	1	0
Multiple-Bias Incidents[2]	311	42	22	0	0	0	2	15

[1] The total number of offenses by the known offender's ethnicity do not equal the total number of offenses by the known offender's race because not all law enforcement agencies that report offender race data also report offender ethnicity data.

[2] A multiple-bias incident is an incident in which one or more offense types are motivated by two or more biases.

Table 5. Offenses, Known Offender's Race, by Bias Motivation, 2017—*Continued*

(Number.)

Bias motivation	Total offenses	Known offender's ethnicity[1]				Unknown offender
		Hispanic or Latino	Not Hispanic or Latino	Group of multiple ethnicities	Unknown ethnicity	
Total	8,437	350	1,294	56	3,085	2,472
Single-Bias Incidents	8,126	345	1,260	56	3,043	2,242
Race/Ethnicity/Ancestry	4,832	174	816	42	1,953	1,230
Anti-White	844	22	168	3	445	154
Anti-Black or African American	2,358	112	361	16	851	653
Anti-American Indian or Alaska Native	281	7	13	20	160	75
Anti-Asian	152	6	22	1	53	34
Anti-Native Hawaiian or Other Pacific Islander	17	0	3	0	4	7
Anti-Multiple Races, Group	215	9	25	0	67	95
Anti-Arab	128	4	19	0	59	21
Anti-Hispanic or Latino	525	6	160	2	190	89
Anti-Other Race/Ethnicity/Ancestry	312	8	45	0	124	102
Religion	1,679	40	140	2	433	701
Anti-Jewish	976	11	37	0	162	477
Anti-Catholic	75	9	6	0	30	20
Anti-Protestant	40	0	0	0	14	26
Anti-Islamic (Muslim)	314	10	48	1	120	92
Anti-Other Religion	82	2	8	0	30	36
Anti-Multiple Religions, Group	54	2	17	0	16	14
Anti-Mormon	15	0	2	0	6	7
Anti-Jehovah's Witness	13	0	6	0	6	1
Anti-Eastern Orthodox (Russian, Greek, Other)	23	0	7	0	6	10
Anti-Other Christian	31	0	3	0	11	12
Anti-Buddhist	9	0	2	0	4	1
Anti-Hindu	15	5	0	0	5	2
Anti-Sikh	24	1	4	1	15	3
Anti-Atheism/Agnosticism/etc.	8	0	0	0	8	0
Sexual Orientation	1,303	102	267	11	492	258
Anti-Gay (Male)	758	71	175	9	250	134
Anti-Lesbian	159	11	39	0	60	29
Anti-Lesbian, Gay, Bisexual, or Transgender (Mixed Group)	321	14	42	2	157	79
Anti-Heterosexual	37	2	6	0	12	13
Anti-Bisexual	28	4	5	0	13	3
Disability	128	4	17	0	76	26
Anti-Physical	35	2	6	0	19	7
Anti-Mental	93	2	11	0	57	19
Gender	53	1	3	0	41	8
Anti-Male	25	0	0	0	23	2
Anti-Female	28	1	3	0	18	6
Gender Identity	131	24	17	1	48	19
Anti-Transgender	118	22	16	1	43	14
Anti-Gender Non-Conforming	13	2	1	0	5	5
Multiple-Bias Incidents[2]	311	5	34	0	42	230

[1]The total number of offenses by the known offender's ethnicity do not equal the total number of offenses by the known offender's race because not all law enforcement agencies that report offender race data also report offender ethnicity data.
[2]A multiple-bias incident is an incident in which one or more offense types are motivated by two or more biases.

Table 6. Offenses, Victim Type, by Offense Type, 2017

(Number.)

Offense type	Total offenses	Victim type					
		Individual	Business/ financial institution	Government	Religious organization	Society/ public[1]	Other/ unknown/ multiple
Total	8,437	6,607	528	286	179	238	599
Crimes against persons[2]	5,084	5,084	NA	NA	NA	NA	NA
Crimes against property	3,115	1,523	528	286	179	0	599
Robbery	157	146	3	0	0	0	8
Burglary	145	94	28	3	10	0	10
Larceny-theft..................................	326	198	101	1	8	0	18
Motor vehicle theft..........................	41	36	3	0	0	0	2
Arson	42	31	4	0	4	0	3
Destruction/damage/vandalism..............	2,325	957	374	281	156	0	557
Other[2]	79	61	15	1	1	0	1
Crimes against society[2]	238	NA	NA	NA	NA	238	NA

NA = Not available.
[1] The victim type society/public is collected only in the National Incident-Based Reporting System (NIBRS).
[2] Includes additional offenses collected in the NIBRS.

Table 7. Victims, Offense Type, by Bias Motivation, 2017

(Number.)

Bias motivation	Total victims[1]	Total number of adult victims[2]	Total number of juvenile victims[2]	Crimes against persons Murder and nonnegligent manslaughter	Rape[3]	Aggravated assault	Simple assault	Intimidation	Human trafficking, commercial sex acts	Other[4]
Total	8,828	5,125	678	15	23	990	1,745	2,283	1	27
Single-Bias Incidents	8,493	5,027	674	15	23	975	1,623	2,156	1	27
Race/Ethnicity/Ancestry	5,060	3,086	465	11	8	638	965	1,442	1	15
Anti-White	864	566	72	5	2	105	203	171	0	7
Anti-Black or African American	2,458	1,437	263	5	1	326	454	820	0	2
Anti-American Indian or Alaska Native	321	155	27	0	4	17	29	44	0	1
Anti-Asian	165	100	4	0	0	14	40	45	0	0
Anti-Native Hawaiian or Other Pacific Islander	18	11	2	0	0	1	2	3	1	1
Anti-Multiple Races, Group	229	112	18	0	0	8	27	65	0	2
Anti-Arab	131	90	12	0	1	24	37	37	0	2
Anti-Hispanic or Latino	552	430	51	1	0	105	124	167	0	0
Anti-Other Race/Ethnicity/Ancestry	322	185	16	0	0	38	49	90	0	0
Religion	1,749	732	61	1	1	55	184	331	0	2
Anti-Jewish	1,017	317	28	0	0	8	61	179	0	0
Anti-Catholic	76	20	0	0	0	1	3	4	0	0
Anti-Protestant	40	16	1	0	0	0	4	3	0	0
Anti-Islamic (Muslim)	325	219	20	0	0	28	77	110	0	0
Anti-Other Religion	86	41	4	0	0	2	10	21	0	0
Anti-Multiple Religions, Group	57	32	0	0	0	5	15	1	0	0
Anti-Mormon	15	8	0	0	0	0	0	2	0	0
Anti-Jehovah's Witness	13	9	2	0	0	1	6	2	0	0
Anti-Eastern Orthodox (Russian, Greek, Other)	27	19	1	0	0	0	2	0	0	0
Anti-Other Christian	32	7	1	0	0	1	1	1	0	0
Anti-Buddhist	12	8	1	0	0	1	1	1	0	0
Anti-Hindu	15	12	0	0	0	4	1	4	0	1
Anti-Sikh	26	20	2	1	1	4	1	3	0	0
Anti-Atheism/Agnosticism/etc.	8	4	1	0	0	0	2	0	0	1
Sexual Orientation	1,338	978	116	2	8	237	383	327	0	5
Anti-Gay (Male)	774	577	50	2	3	161	233	170	0	2
Anti-Lesbian	164	124	19	0	3	21	51	50	0	1
Anti-Lesbian, Gay, Bisexual, or Transgender (Mixed Group)	333	245	37	0	1	44	83	95	0	2
Anti-Heterosexual	37	19	0	0	0	5	8	8	0	0
Anti-Bisexual	30	13	10	0	1	6	8	4	0	0
Disability	160	104	18	1	3	12	32	23	0	2
Anti-Physical	37	22	3	1	0	4	9	5	0	0
Anti-Mental	123	82	15	0	3	8	23	18	0	2
Gender	54	38	7	0	3	5	12	8	0	3
Anti-Male	26	14	6	0	1	3	4	3	0	1
Anti-Female	28	24	1	0	2	2	8	5	0	2
Gender Identity	132	89	7	0	0	28	47	25	0	0
Anti-Transgender	119	79	6	0	0	27	43	24	0	0
Anti-Gender Non-Conforming	13	10	1	0	0	1	4	1	0	0
Multiple-Bias Incidents[5]	335	98	4	0	0	15	122	127	0	0

Table 7. Victims, Offense Type, by Bias Motivation, 2017—*Continued*

(Number.)

Bias motivation	Crimes against property							Crimes against society[4]
	Robbery	Burglary	Larceny- theft	Motor vehicle theft	Arson	Destruction/ damage/ vandalism	Other[4]	
Total	171	185	379	44	59	2,585	83	238
Single-Bias Incidents	171	177	375	44	58	2,531	83	234
Race/Ethnicity/Ancestry	92	111	224	38	37	1,270	41	167
Anti-White	24	25	97	15	3	124	20	63
Anti-Black or African American	20	49	18	2	25	708	6	22
Anti-American Indian or Alaska Native	2	15	67	15	0	54	11	62
Anti-Asian	0	6	8	1	0	49	0	2
Anti-Native Hawaiian or Other Pacific Islander	1	1	5	0	0	2	1	0
Anti-Multiple Races, Group	4	4	1	0	0	116	0	2
Anti-Arab	2	1	6	3	0	17	0	1
Anti-Hispanic or Latino	34	3	13	1	6	92	2	4
Anti-Other Race/Ethnicity/Ancestry	5	7	9	1	3	108	1	11
Religion	16	41	58	3	10	990	26	31
Anti-Jewish	4	11	13	0	2	735	2	2
Anti-Catholic	0	1	6	1	2	43	4	11
Anti-Protestant	0	2	6	0	0	22	1	2
Anti-Islamic (Muslim)	6	5	8	0	0	86	5	0
Anti-Other Religion	1	4	1	1	2	38	3	3
Anti-Multiple Religions, Group	2	4	4	0	3	21	0	2
Anti-Mormon	0	4	2	0	0	2	1	4
Anti-Jehovah's Witness	0	0	1	0	0	2	0	1
Anti-Eastern Orthodox (Russian, Greek, Other)	2	3	7	0	0	4	6	3
Anti-Other Christian	0	2	3	0	1	22	0	1
Anti-Buddhist	0	0	2	0	0	7	0	0
Anti-Hindu	0	1	1	0	0	2	1	0
Anti-Sikh	0	4	2	1	0	5	3	1
Anti-Atheism/Agnosticism/etc.	1	0	2	0	0	1	0	1
Sexual Orientation	56	17	39	1	9	233	3	18
Anti-Gay (Male)	45	13	9	1	3	126	1	5
Anti-Lesbian	0	0	5	0	0	31	0	2
Anti-Lesbian, Gay, Bisexual, or Transgender (Mixed Group)	10	3	18	0	6	69	0	2
Anti-Heterosexual	1	1	4	0	0	4	1	5
Anti-Bisexual	0	0	3	0	0	3	1	4
Disability	2	2	45	0	2	10	10	16
Anti-Physical	0	0	7	0	0	2	2	7
Anti-Mental	2	2	38	0	2	8	8	9
Gender	0	2	3	2	0	14	0	2
Anti-Male	0	2	3	2	0	6	0	1
Anti-Female	0	0	0	0	0	8	0	1
Gender Identity	5	4	6	0	0	14	3	0
Anti-Transgender	4	3	4	0	0	13	1	0
Anti-Gender Non-Conforming	1	1	2	0	0	1	2	0
Multiple-Bias Incidents[5]	0	8	4	0	1	54	0	4

Note: The aggregate of adult and juvenile individual victims does not equal the total number of victims because total victims include individuals, businesses, institutions, and society as a whole. In addition, the aggregate of adult and juvenile individual victims does not equal the aggregate of victims of crimes against persons because not all law enforcement agencies report the ages of individual victims.
[1] A victim can be an individual, a business, an institution, or society as a whole.
[2] The figures shown in this column are individual victims only.
[3] The figures shown in this column for the offense of rape were reported using only the revised Uniform Crime Reporting definition of rape.
[4] Includes additional offenses collected in the National Incident-Based Reporting System.
[5] A multiple-bias incident is an incident in which one or more offense types are motivated by two or more biases.

Table 8. Incidents, Victim Type, by Bias Motivation, 2017

(Number.)

Bias motivation	Total incidents	Victim type					
		Individual	Business/ financial institution	Government	Religious organization	Society/ public[1]	Other/ unknown/ multiple
Total	7,175	5,373	515	282	168	220	617
Single-Bias Incidents	7,106	5,322	514	273	168	218	611
Race/Ethnicity/Ancestry	4,131	3,272	310	156	19	153	221
Religion	1,564	783	166	88	142	31	354
Sexual Orientation	1,130	1,034	20	20	6	16	34
Disability	116	89	7	2	0	16	2
Gender	46	40	3	1	0	2	0
Gender Identity	119	104	8	6	1	0	0
Multiple-Bias Incidents[2]	69	51	1	9	0	2	6

[1] The victim type society/public is collected only in the National Incident-Based Reporting System.
[2] A multiple-bias incident is an incident in which one or more offense types are motivated by two or more biases.

Table 9. Known Offenders,[1] by Known Offender's Race, Ethnicity, and Age, 2017

(Number.)

Race/ethnicity/age	Total
Race	6,370
White	3,227
Black or African American	1,359
American Indian or Alaska Native	49
Asian	42
Native Hawaiian or Other Pacific Islander	3
Group of multiple races[2]	475
Unknown race	1,215
Ethnicity[3]	5,131
Hispanic or Latino	454
Not Hispanic or Latino	1,284
Group of multiple ethnicities[4]	81
Unknown ethnicity	3,312
Age[3]	4,895
Total known offenders 18 and over	4,062
Total known offenders under 18	833

[1] The term known offender does not imply the suspect's identity is known; rather, the term indicates some aspect of the suspect was identified, thus distinguishing the suspect from an unknown offender.
[2] The term group of multiple races is used to describe a group of offenders of varying races.
[3] The total number of known offenders by age and the total number of known offenders by ethnicity do not equal the total number of known offenders by race because not all law enforcement agencies report the age and/or ethnicity of the known offenders.
[4] The term group of multiple ethnicities is used to describe a group of offenders of varying ethnicities.

Table 10. Incidents, Bias Motivation, by Location, 2017

(Number.)

Location	Total incidents	Bias motivation						Multiple- bias incidents[1]
		Race/Ethnicity/ Ancestry	Religion	Sexual orientation	Disability	Gender	Gender Identity	
Total	7,175	4,131	1,564	1,130	116	46	119	69
Abandoned/condemned structure	5	3	1	1	0	0	0	0
Air/bus/train terminal	118	84	13	15	1	0	4	1
Amusement park	3	2	0	1	0	0	0	0
Arena/stadium/fairgrounds/coliseum	7	3	0	3	1	0	0	0
ATM separate from bank	3	0	1	2	0	0	0	0
Auto dealership new/used	8	6	1	1	0	0	0	0
Bank/savings and loan	25	16	5	2	2	0	0	0
Bar/nightclub	99	52	5	37	2	0	2	1
Camp/campground	3	2	1	0	0	0	0	0
Church/synagogue/temple/mosque	292	44	234	12	0	0	1	1
Commercial office building	139	90	32	9	2	1	3	2
Community center	22	7	14	1	0	0	0	0
Construction site	25	19	3	2	1	0	0	0
Convenience store	105	71	13	14	3	1	1	2
Cyberspace	11	7	4	0	0	0	0	0
Daycare facility	6	4	0	1	1	0	0	0
Department/discount store	91	63	13	8	3	1	1	2
Dock/wharf/freight/modal terminal	3	1	1	0	0	0	1	0
Drug store/doctor's office/hospital	75	49	15	8	0	1	1	1
Farm facility	3	3	0	0	0	0	0	0
Field/woods	50	29	13	4	1	0	2	1
Gambling facility/casino/race track	3	3	0	0	0	0	0	0
Government/public building	117	78	19	17	2	1	0	0
Grocery/supermarket	75	57	11	4	1	0	2	0
Highway/road/alley/street/sidewalk	1,218	778	139	241	16	5	29	10
Hotel/motel/etc.	63	41	11	9	1	1	0	0
Industrial site	9	8	1	0	0	0	0	0
Jail/prison/penitentiary/corrections facility	59	42	3	13	1	0	0	0
Lake/waterway/beach	13	8	2	3	0	0	0	0
Liquor store	11	8	0	2	0	0	1	0
Military installation	1	1	0	0	0	0	0	0
Park/playground	128	67	33	20	1	0	1	6
Parking/drop lot/garage	419	271	62	66	7	2	4	7
Rental storage facility	14	9	4	0	1	0	0	0
Residence/home	1,971	1,133	360	366	46	24	22	20
Rest area	8	2	6	0	0	0	0	0
Restaurant	192	126	20	38	3	1	3	1
School/college[2]	199	85	87	22	3	0	2	0
School—college/university	214	129	45	29	1	1	6	3
School—elementary/secondary	340	207	67	42	7	2	9	6
Service/gas station	73	58	8	4	2	1	0	0
Shelter—mission/homeless	15	12	0	2	0	0	1	0
Shopping mall	21	10	5	3	0	0	3	0
Specialty store (TV, fur, etc.)	76	51	10	11	2	1	0	1
Other/unknown	822	381	299	115	5	1	20	1
Multiple locations	21	11	3	2	0	2	0	3

[1] A *multiple-bias incident* is an incident in which one or more offense types are motivated by two or more biases.
[2] The location designation School/college has been retained for agencies that have not updated their records management systems to include the new location designations of School—college/university and School—elementary/secondary, which allow for more specificity in reporting.

Table 11. Offenses, Offense Type, by Participating State, 2017

(Number.)

State	Total offenses	Crimes against persons						
		Murder and nonnegligent manslaughter	Rape[1]	Aggravated assault	Simple assault	Intimidation	Human trafficking, commercial sex acts	Other[2]
Total	8,437	15	23	990	1,745	2,283	1	27
Alabama............	9	0	0	0	1	7	0	0
Alaska..............	4	0	0	1	1	0	0	0
Arizona.............	328	0	2	52	62	111	0	0
Arkansas............	8	0	0	1	1	2	0	0
California...........	1,270	3	0	242	259	304	0	0
Colorado...........	136	0	1	22	30	39	0	1
Connecticut........	122	0	0	3	20	41	0	0
Delaware...........	30	0	0	1	5	15	0	0
District of Columbia....	207	0	0	30	72	40	0	0
Florida.............	166	0	0	37	35	22	0	0
Georgia............	230	0	0	5	108	112	0	0
Idaho..............	61	0	0	8	22	6	0	0
Illinois.............	94	0	0	22	24	19	0	0
Indiana.............	62	3	0	5	13	14	0	0
Iowa...............	12	0	0	3	1	6	0	0
Kansas.............	83	0	0	4	20	12	0	0
Kentucky...........	432	0	5	9	55	102	0	9
Louisiana...........	30	0	0	8	14	4	0	0
Maine..............	40	0	0	3	10	19	0	0
Maryland...........	53	1	0	10	13	2	0	0
Massachusetts.......	486	0	0	45	89	160	0	2
Michigan...........	515	0	3	55	110	131	0	3
Minnesota..........	169	0	1	19	27	64	0	0
Mississippi.........	4	0	0	0	0	4	0	0
Missouri............	133	0	0	45	32	23	0	0
Montana...........	18	0	0	5	7	0	0	0
Nebraska...........	46	0	0	1	5	3	0	0
Nevada............	7	0	0	3	1	0	0	0
New Hampshire......	16	0	0	3	7	2	0	0
New Jersey..........	502	0	0	6	6	310	0	0
New Mexico.........	14	0	0	5	7	0	0	0
New York...........	559	1	0	55	174	3	0	0
North Carolina......	230	0	0	20	54	81	0	0
North Dakota.......	17	0	0	2	2	10	0	0
Ohio...............	449	0	3	33	66	163	0	4
Oklahoma..........	49	0	0	14	8	12	0	2
Oregon............	169	0	2	20	25	37	0	2
Pennsylvania........	93	0	0	2	20	45	0	0
Rhode Island........	11	0	0	0	1	2	0	0
South Carolina......	94	0	0	10	19	10	0	1
South Dakota.......	19	0	0	3	6	6	0	0
Tennessee..........	179	1	0	38	39	42	0	1
Texas..............	219	1	2	43	50	36	1	0
Utah...............	94	1	0	8	23	7	0	1
Vermont............	36	0	1	1	5	3	0	0
Virginia............	214	2	2	14	44	40	0	0
Washington.........	613	1	1	72	134	183	0	1
West Virginia.......	34	1	0	0	8	0	0	0
Wisconsin..........	48	0	0	2	9	9	0	0
Wyoming...........	23	0	0	0	1	20	0	0

State	Crimes against property							Crimes against society[2]
	Robbery	Burglary	Larceny- theft	Motor vehicle theft	Arson	Destruction/ damage/ vandalism	Other[2]	
Total	157	145	326	41	42	2,325	79	238
Alabama	0	0	0	0	0	1	0	0
Alaska	0	0	0	0	0	2	0	0
Arizona	8	6	5	0	0	81	0	1
Arkansas	1	1	0	0	0	2	0	0
California	52	16	6	0	11	377	0	0
Colorado	3	0	3	0	1	36	0	0
Connecticut	2	1	10	2	0	39	2	2
Delaware	1	0	0	0	0	7	1	0
District of Columbia	9	0	1	0	0	55	0	0
Florida	0	2	2	1	1	66	0	0
Georgia	0	1	0	0	0	4	0	0
Idaho	0	1	5	0	0	10	2	7
Illinois	2	0	2	0	2	23	0	0
Indiana	0	1	4	0	1	12	1	8
Iowa	0	1	0	0	0	1	0	0
Kansas	0	2	8	1	2	28	1	5
Kentucky	6	20	71	11	0	67	9	68
Louisiana	0	1	0	0	0	1	1	1
Maine	0	0	0	0	0	8	0	0
Maryland	1	1	0	0	0	24	0	1
Massachusetts	1	7	8	2	0	167	5	0
Michigan	7	12	32	6	4	116	11	25
Minnesota	3	3	1	0	3	48	0	0
Mississippi	0	0	0	0	0	0	0	0
Missouri	2	2	2	0	2	24	0	1
Montana	0	0	1	0	0	5	0	0
Nebraska	0	3	2	0	0	27	1	4
Nevada	1	0	0	0	0	2	0	0
New Hampshire	0	0	0	0	0	4	0	0
New Jersey	4	0	1	0	2	173	0	0
New Mexico	1	0	0	0	0	1	0	0
New York	7	9	7	0	1	302	0	0
North Carolina	4	4	9	0	2	56	0	0
North Dakota	0	0	1	0	0	2	0	0
Ohio	8	12	45	3	2	82	4	24
Oklahoma	0	1	0	0	0	8	3	1
Oregon	1	2	5	0	0	69	3	3
Pennsylvania	1	0	1	0	3	19	1	1
Rhode Island	0	0	0	0	0	8	0	0
South Carolina	2	6	7	1	1	24	4	9
South Dakota	0	0	0	0	0	3	0	1
Tennessee	1	5	2	0	0	26	7	17
Texas	11	4	16	3	2	38	2	10
Utah	0	3	21	1	0	11	3	15
Vermont	0	0	4	0	0	18	1	3
Virginia	1	2	2	0	0	92	3	12
Washington	16	15	27	7	2	132	8	14
West Virginia	1	1	5	3	0	10	1	4
Wisconsin	0	0	10	0	0	12	5	1
Wyoming	0	0	0	0	0	2	0	0

[1]The figures shown in this column for the offense of rape include only those reported by law enforcement agencies that used the revised Uniform Crime Reporting (UCR) definition of rape.
[2]Includes additional offenses collected in the National Incident-Based Reporting System.

Table 12. Agency Hate Crime Reporting, by Participating State, 2017

(Number.)

State	Number of participating agencies	Population covered	Agencies submitting incident reports	Total number of incidents reported
Total	16,149	306,435,676	2,040	7,175
Alabama................................	334	2,918,324	3	9
Alaska....................................	32	736,205	3	4
Arizona..................................	87	6,755,795	20	264
Arkansas................................	292	2,836,240	4	7
California...............................	730	39,529,144	232	1,094
Colorado	221	5,575,629	43	106
Connecticut...........................	107	3,588,184	44	111
Delaware	63	961,939	11	29
District of Columbia	2	693,972	2	193
Florida	654	20,515,334	67	145
Georgia	509	8,948,013	8	27
Idaho	106	1,699,259	21	53
Illinois	741	12,270,234	32	82
Indiana	162	2,287,298	21	55
Iowa	240	3,104,739	8	11
Kansas...................................	364	2,620,785	38	75
Kentucky	409	4,444,239	132	378
Louisiana	145	3,764,930	15	26
Maine	132	1,335,907	10	32
Maryland	154	6,052,177	18	48
Massachusetts........................	360	6,703,220	102	427
Michigan	624	9,928,921	177	456
Minnesota	353	5,508,515	42	146
Mississippi.............................	28	682,046	1	1
Missouri.................................	610	6,109,596	32	105
Montana................................	110	1,050,005	11	15
Nebraska	238	1,865,845	9	45
Nevada	51	2,998,039	3	5
New Hampshire	177	1,295,556	13	13
New Jersey.............................	518	9,005,644	155	495
New Mexico............................	17	561,375	1	7
New York	567	19,685,625	74	552
North Carolina	527	10,271,767	44	166
North Dakota..........................	110	754,604	8	15
Ohio	572	9,703,884	137	380
Oklahoma..............................	412	3,916,111	27	37
Oregon..................................	214	3,902,529	29	146
Pennsylvania	1,488	12,730,580	23	78
Rhode Island..........................	49	1,059,639	4	11
South Carolina........................	438	4,996,532	46	87
South Dakota..........................	116	799,083	10	17
Tennessee..............................	466	6,715,984	57	136
Texas	1,009	28,096,894	75	190
Utah	126	3,056,326	27	78
Vermont	90	623,657	17	34
Virginia..................................	413	8,467,744	65	193
Washington............................	243	7,396,166	72	510
West Virginia..........................	245	1,591,058	20	31
Wisconsin..............................	437	5,767,235	24	46
Wyoming................................	57	553,149	3	4

Table 13. Hate Crime Incidents Per Bias Motivation and Quarter, by Selected State and Agency, 2017

(Number.)

State/agency	Number of incidents per bias motivation						Number of incidents per quarter				Population[1]
	Race/Ethnicity/Ancestry	Religion	Sexual orientation	Disability	Gender	Gender Identity	1st quarter	2nd quarter	3rd quarter	4th quarter	
ALABAMA											
Total	8	1	0	0	0	0					
Cities	7	1	0	0	0	0					
Hoover..	5	1	0	0	0	0	2	1	2	1	85,634
Ozark..	2	0	0	0	0	0	1			1	14,559
Universities and Colleges	1	0	0	0	0	0					
Jacksonville State University	1	0	0	0	0	0			1		8,514
ALASKA											
Total	3	1	0	0	0	0					
Cities	3	0	0	0	0	0					
Anchorage..	1	0	0	0	0	0	0	0	0	1	296,188
Juneau..	2	0	0	0	0	0	0	0	0	2	32,344
State Police Agencies...........................	0	1	0	0	0	0					
Alaska State Troopers	0	1	0	0	0	0	0	1			
ARIZONA											
Total	168	48	55	5	0	12					
Cities	160	47	52	5	0	12					
Avondale..	0	0	1	0	0	0	0	0	0	1	84,041
Chandler..	1	0	0	0	0	0	0	1	0	0	249,355
Cottonwood..	1	0	0	0	0	0	0	0	0	1	12,116
El Mirage..	1	0	0	0	0	0	0	1			35,611
Gilbert	2	1	0	0	0	0	0	1	1	1	242,090
Glendale..	3	2	0	0	0	0	0	1	2	2	249,273
Mesa..	4	1	0	0	0	0	1	0	1	3	492,268
Page..	1	0	0	0	0	0	0	0	1	0	7,632
Phoenix[2]..	142	41	44	4	0	12	49	57	48	65	1,644,177
Scottsdale..	2	1	1	0	0	0	4	0	0	0	251,840
St. Johns..	2	0	0	0	0	0	1	0	1	0	3,581
Tucson..	0	1	3	1	0	0	1	2	1	1	532,323
Wickenburg..	0	0	1	0	0	0	0	0	0	1	6,979
Yuma..	1	0	2	0	0	0	1	0	2	0	95,522
Universities and Colleges	1	1	1	0	0	0					
University of Arizona...........................	1	1	1	0	0	0	0	0	3		43,161
Metropolitan Counties	5	0	2	0	0	0					
Maricopa..	1	0	2	0	0	0	2	0	0	1	
Mohave..	1	0	0	0	0	0	0	0	1		
Pima..	2	0	0	0	0	0	2			0	
Yuma..	1	0	0	0	0	0	1	0	0	0	
Nonmetropolitan Counties.....................	2	0	0	0	0	0					
Apache..	2	0	0	0	0	0	0	0	0	2	
ARKANSAS											
Total	5	0	1	1	0	0					
Cities	5	0	1	0	0	0					
Benton..	1	0	0	0	0	0	0	0	1	0	36,702
Fayetteville..	0	0	1	0	0	0	0	0	0	1	85,592
Fort Smith..	4	0	0	0	0	0	0	1	1	2	88,437
Nonmetropolitan Counties.....................	0	0	0	1	0	0					
Boone..	0	0	0	1	0	0	0	1	0	0	
CALIFORNIA											
Total	603	207	248	4	4	29					
Cities	524	187	217	4	4	26					
Adelanto..	1	0	1	0	0	0	1	1	0	0	33,693

Table 13. Hate Crime Incidents Per Bias Motivation and Quarter, by Selected State and Agency, 2017—Continued

(Number.)

State/agency	Number of incidents per bias motivation						Number of incidents per quarter				Population[1]
	Race/ Ethnicity/ Ancestry	Religion	Sexual orientation	Disability	Gender	Gender Identity	1st quarter	2nd quarter	3rd quarter	4th quarter	
Alameda	6	1	2	1	0	0	0	0	7	3	79,761
Albany[2]	1	0	2	0	0	0	1	0	1	0	19,880
Alhambra	1	0	0	0	0	1	1	1	0	0	85,865
Aliso Viejo	1	0	0	0	0	0	1	0	0	0	51,984
Anaheim	0	0	1	0	0	0	0	0	0	1	353,400
Antioch	1	0	0	0	0	0	0	1	0	0	112,252
Apple Valley	0	1	0	0	0	0	0	0	1	0	73,105
Arcata	1	0	1	0	0	0	1	0	1	0	18,054
Atwater	1	0	0	0	0	1	1	0	1	0	29,442
Azusa	2	0	0	0	0	0	0	0	1	1	50,202
Bakersfield	4	0	3	0	0	0	0	3	0	4	381,154
Bell	0	1	0	0	0	0	0	0	0	1	35,925
Bellflower	0	1	0	0	0	0	0	0	0	1	77,984
Bell Gardens	1	0	0	0	0	0	0	0	1	0	42,930
Belmont	0	1	0	0	0	0	1	0	0	0	27,285
Benicia	1	0	0	0	0	0	0	1	0	0	28,370
Berkeley	13	4	6	0	0	0	7	6	4	6	122,687
Beverly Hills	2	0	0	0	0	0	0	0	1	1	34,781
Brentwood	1	0	0	0	0	1	0	1	1	0	62,120
Buena Park	1	0	0	0	0	0	0	1	0	0	83,552
Burbank	1	6	1	0	0	0	1	1	0	6	104,622
Camarillo	1	0	0	0	0	0	0	1	0	0	67,714
Capitola	1	0	0	0	0	0	0	0	0	1	10,222
Carlsbad	4	2	1	0	0	0	0	4	0	3	115,344
Carson	0	1	0	0	0	0	0	0	1	0	92,992
Central Marin	0	2	0	0	0	0	0	1	0	1	35,060
Chico	1	0	0	0	0	0	0	0	1	0	92,459
Chino	5	0	1	0	0	0	2	2	1	1	89,420
Chino Hills	1	0	0	0	0	0	1	0	0	0	79,480
Citrus Heights	1	0	1	0	0	0	1	0	1	0	88,126
Clearlake	0	1	1	0	0	0	1	1	0	0	15,018
Colma	0	0	1	0	0	0	0	1	0	0	1,520
Concord	0	0	1	0	0	0	0	0	1	0	129,789
Corcoran	1	0	0	0	0	0	0	1	0	0	22,345
Corning	1	0	0	0	0	0	0	1	0	0	7,511
Corona	1	0	1	0	0	0	0	0	2	0	169,164
Costa Mesa	2	0	0	0	0	0	1	0	0	1	113,267
Covina	0	0	1	0	0	0	0	1	0	0	48,674
Crescent City	1	0	0	0	0	0	0	0	0	1	6,529
Daly City	0	0	1	0	0	0	0	0	1	0	107,355
Davis	4	3	0	0	0	0	2	4	0	1	68,540
Desert Hot Springs	1	0	0	0	0	0	1	0	0	0	28,717
Duarte	2	0	0	0	0	0	2	0	0	0	21,877
Dublin	1	0	0	0	0	0	0	1	0	0	62,235
East Palo Alto	0	1	0	0	0	0	0	0	0	1	29,933
El Cajon	4	0	2	0	0	0	0	2	3	1	104,447
Elk Grove	4	0	0	0	0	0	0	1	2	1	172,620
El Monte	2	0	1	0	0	0	1	1	0	1	116,168
El Segundo	1	0	0	0	0	0	0	0	1	0	16,932
Escondido	5	0	0	0	0	0	3	0	1	1	152,845
Fairfield	3	0	0	0	0	0	0	1	1	1	116,372
Fontana	0	2	1	0	0	0	1	1	1	0	211,782
Fort Bragg	2	1	0	0	0	0	1	1	0	1	7,289
Foster City	0	1	0	0	0	0	1	0	0	0	34,808
Fremont	1	1	0	0	0	0	0	1	1	0	236,368
Fresno	7	1	4	0	0	1	1	3	6	3	526,371
Garden Grove	7	0	0	0	0	1	3	0	4	1	175,466
Glendora	1	0	0	0	0	0	0	0	0	1	52,133
Goleta	1	0	0	0	0	0	1	0	0	0	31,000
Gonzales	1	0	0	0	0	0	1	0	0	0	8,508
Hayward	3	1	0	0	0	0	2	1	0	1	161,417
Hesperia	3	0	0	0	0	0	2	0	0	1	94,292
Highland	1	0	0	0	0	0	1	0	0	0	55,229
Hollister	1	0	0	0	0	0	0	0	1	0	38,310
Huntington Beach	2	0	0	0	0	0	0	0	1	1	202,244
Huntington Park	1	1	0	0	0	0	1	1	0	0	59,004
Indio	1	0	0	0	0	0	0	0	1	0	90,055

(Number.)

State/agency	Number of incidents per bias motivation						Number of incidents per quarter				Population[1]
	Race/ Ethnicity/ Ancestry	Religion	Sexual orientation	Disability	Gender	Gender Identity	1st quarter	2nd quarter	3rd quarter	4th quarter	
Inglewood	2	0	0	0	0	0	0	1	0	1	110,811
Irvine	4	0	0	0	0	0	1	0	0	3	276,115
La Canada Flintridge	0	0	0	0	3	0	0	0	3	0	20,480
Laguna Beach	2	0	0	0	0	0	1	0	1	0	23,261
La Habra	1	0	0	0	0	0	1	0	0	0	61,878
Lake Elsinore	0	1	0	0	0	0	0	0	1	0	66,136
Lakeport	0	0	1	0	0	0	0	1	0	0	4,775
Lakewood	7	0	0	0	0	0	1	1	4	1	81,317
La Mesa	1	0	1	0	0	0	0	0	2	0	60,425
Lancaster	5	0	2	0	0	0	2	2	2	1	160,653
Lemon Grove	1	0	0	0	0	0	0	0	0	1	27,113
Livermore	2	0	0	0	0	0	0	0	2	0	90,485
Lodi	1	0	0	0	0	0	0	0	1	0	65,042
Loma Linda	1	0	0	0	0	0	1	0	0	0	24,265
Lomita	1	0	0	0	0	0	0	0	0	1	20,764
Long Beach	8	3	6	0	0	0	7	3	5	2	471,397
Los Angeles	126	43	82	0	1	11	65	72	70	56	4,007,147
Los Gatos	0	1	0	0	0	0	1	0	0	0	30,720
Malibu	2	0	0	0	0	0	1	0	1	0	12,918
Manhattan Beach	0	0	1	0	0	0	0	0	0	1	35,843
Manteca	2	2	0	0	0	0	1	0	3	0	78,564
Martinez	2	4	0	1	0	0	0	2	5	0	38,619
Marysville	3	0	0	0	0	0	0	0	3	0	12,275
Menifee	1	0	0	0	0	0	0	0	0	1	90,403
Merced	1	0	0	0	0	0	0	0	0	1	83,180
Modesto	6	1	3	0	0	0	6	1	2	1	213,677
Monterey	1	0	1	0	0	0	0	0	2	0	28,584
Monterey Park	3	1	0	0	0	0	1	0	1	2	61,210
Moreno Valley	1	0	2	0	0	0	1	0	1	1	207,418
Murrieta	1	0	0	0	0	0	0	1	0	0	113,016
National City	1	0	0	0	0	0	1	0	0	0	61,574
Newark	2	1	0	0	0	0	0	2	1	0	46,360
Newport Beach	1	0	0	0	0	0	0	0	0	1	86,910
Norco	0	1	0	0	0	0	0	1	0	0	26,654
Norwalk	1	0	1	0	0	0	0	0	1	1	106,278
Novato	2	0	0	0	0	0	1	0	1	0	56,698
Oakland	9	7	2	0	0	0	8	4	4	2	424,915
Oceanside	4	1	1	0	0	0	1	1	3	1	176,815
Ontario	1	0	0	1	0	0	1	1	0	0	174,724
Orange	1	0	0	0	0	0	0	0		1	141,130
Orland	1	0	0	0	0	0	0	1	0	0	7,624
Oxnard	2	4	1	0	0	0	0	2	5	0	209,513
Pacifica	1	0	1	0	0	0	1	0	1	0	39,353
Pacific Grove	0	1	0	0	0	0	0	1	0	0	15,716
Palmdale	3	0	0	0	0	0	2	1	0	0	158,094
Palm Springs	0	0	3	0	0	0	1	1	0	1	48,193
Palo Alto	2	3	0	0	0	0	4	0	1	0	67,441
Paradise	1	0	0	0	0	0	0	0	1	0	26,610
Pasadena	1	1	0	0	0	1	0	1	2	0	142,891
Petaluma	5	1	2	0	0	0	5	1	1	1	60,957
Pico Rivera	0	0	2	0	0	1	2	0	1	0	63,746
Piedmont	1	1	0	0	0	0	0	0	2	0	11,464
Placentia	1	0	0	0	0	0	0	1	0	0	52,437
Pleasant Hill	0	1	0	0	0	0	1	0	0	0	35,136
Pomona	1	1	1	0	0	0	0	2	1	0	153,066
Rancho Cordova	2	0	0	0	0	0	0	1	0	1	73,607
Red Bluff	0	0	1	0	0	0	0	0	0	1	14,169
Redding	11	0	4	0	0	0	4	3	5	3	92,127
Redlands	1	1	0	0	0	0	0	0	2	0	71,707
Redwood City	2	0	0	0	0	0	0	0	2	0	86,353
Reedley	0	1	0	0	0	0	0	0	0	1	25,794
Rialto	1	0	0	0	0	0	1	0	0	0	103,980
Richmond	3	0	2	0	0	0	1	0	2	2	110,804
Riverside	4	4	0	0	0	0	3	3	1	1	328,023
Roseville	12	6	1	0	0	0	7	6	5	1	135,028
Sacramento	2	2	0	0	0	1	1	2	1	1	499,997
Salinas	0	0	1	0	0	0	0	0	1	0	158,313

Table 13. Hate Crime Incidents Per Bias Motivation and Quarter, by Selected State and Agency, 2017—Continued

(Number.)

State/agency	Race/ Ethnicity/ Ancestry	Religion	Sexual orientation	Disability	Gender	Gender Identity	1st quarter	2nd quarter	3rd quarter	4th quarter	Population[1]
San Bernardino	4	0	4	0	0	0	4	2	2	0	217,259
San Clemente	1	0	0	0	0	0	0	1	0	0	65,596
San Diego	17	12	11	0	0	1	17	14	7	3	1,424,116
San Fernando	0	1	0	0	0	0	1	0	0	0	24,899
San Francisco	19	8	12	0	0	4	10	6	13	14	881,255
San Gabriel	1	1	0	0	0	0	1	0	0	1	40,531
San Jacinto	1	0	0	0	0	0	0	1	0	0	47,932
San Jose	26	11	7	0	0	1	10	8	16	11	1,037,529
San Leandro	6	0	3	1	0	0	3	5	1	1	91,386
San Luis Obispo	2	2	1	0	0	0	0	3	1	1	47,934
San Marcos	1	1	0	0	0	0	1	0	1	0	97,290
San Mateo	2	0	0	0	0	0	1	1	0	0	105,090
San Rafael	3	0	0	0	0	0	1	2	0	0	59,144
San Ramon	2	1	0	0	0	0	1	1	0	1	76,325
Santa Ana	1	2	0	0	0	0	0	1	1	1	335,699
Santa Clara	1	0	0	0	0	0	0	0	1	0	127,538
Santa Clarita	5	5	3	0	0	0	1	6	5	1	216,350
Santa Cruz	5	1	3	0	0	0	2	3	2	2	65,132
Santa Monica	2	0	1	0	0	0	0	0	2	1	92,935
Santa Rosa	1	0	1	0	0	0	0	1	1	0	176,361
Santee	1	0	0	0	0	0	0	1	0	0	58,563
Simi Valley	0	2	1	0	0	0	1	0	2	0	126,635
South Gate	1	0	0	0	0	0	1	0	0	0	95,717
South Lake Tahoe	1	0	4	0	0	0	4	1	0	0	21,768
South San Francisco	1	0	1	0	0	0	0	0	0	2	67,533
St. Helena	2	0	0	0	0	0	0	1	1	0	6,210
Stockton	2	3	1	0	0	0	3	0	2	1	309,566
Sunnyvale	1	0	0	0	0	1	1	1	0	0	154,919
Taft	1	0	0	0	0	0	0	0	0	1	9,393
Thousand Oaks	0	1	0	0	0	0	0	1	0	0	129,240
Torrance	4	0	1	0	0	0	2	2	0	1	147,482
Turlock	3	0	0	0	0	0	0	0	2	1	73,488
Tustin	1	0	0	0	0	0	0	0	0	1	81,246
Union City	2	0	0	0	0	0	0	0	0	2	76,311
Vacaville	2	2	0	0	0	0	2	1	0	1	99,293
Ventura	4	0	0	0	0	0	2	0	1	1	110,006
Vernon	0	1	0	0	0	0	0	0	1	0	113
Victorville	1	0	1	0	0	0	0	1	1	0	123,284
Visalia	1	0	0	0	0	0	1	0	0	0	132,143
Vista	4	1	1	0	0	0	0	3	2	1	103,004
Walnut	1	0	0	0	0	0	0	1	0	0	30,189
West Covina	0	3	0	0	0	0	3	0	0	0	108,128
West Hollywood	5	0	4	0	0	0	4	1	2	2	37,093
Westminster	2	2	0	0	0	0	0	2	2	0	91,863
Wildomar	1	0	0	0	0	0	0	1	0	0	36,683
Windsor	0	0	1	0	0	0	1	0	0	0	27,679
Yorba Linda	0	1	0	0	0	0	0	0	1	0	68,889
Yucca Valley	1	0	0	0	0	0	0	0	0	1	21,806
Universities and Colleges	19	7	6	0	0	0					
California State University											
Dominguez Hills	2	0	0	0	0	0	0	1	1	0	14,731
Long Beach	1	2	0	0	0	0	1	1	1	0	37,776
Monterey Bay	1	0	1	0	0	0	0	1	0	1	7,274
San Bernardino	1	0	0	0	0	0	1	0	0	0	20,767
Riverside Community College	2	0	0	0	0	0	0	0	0	2	38,677
San Diego State University	0	1	0	0	0	0	0	0	0	1	34,688
San Francisco State University	0	0	1	0	0	0	0	0	1	0	29,045
State Center Community College District	3	0	0	0	0	0	0	0	0	3	39,661
University of California											
Berkeley	3	0	2	0	0	0	3	0	1	1	40,154
Los Angeles	3	1	1	0	0	0	1	0	3	1	43,548
San Diego	0	0	1	0	0	0	0	0	0	1	34,979
San Francisco	0	2	0	0	0	0	0	2	0	0	3,145
Santa Barbara	2	0	0	0	0	0	0	2	0	0	24,346
Medical Center, Sacramento[3]	0	1	0	0	0	0	0	1	0	0	
Ventura County Community College District	1	0	0	0	0	0	0	0	1	0	33,976

Table 13. Hate Crime Incidents Per Bias Motivation and Quarter, by Selected State and Agency, 2017—*Continued*

(Number.)

State/agency	Race/ Ethnicity/ Ancestry	Religion	Sexual orientation	Disability	Gender	Gender Identity	1st quarter	2nd quarter	3rd quarter	4th quarter	Population[1]
Metropolitan Counties	51	12	17	0	0	3					
Alameda.........	1	0	1	0	0	0	0	1	1	0	
Contra Costa........	1	0	0	0	0	0	0	0	0	1	
El Dorado............	2	0	0	0	0	0	0	0	1	1	
Fresno............	1	0	1	0	0	0	1	0	1	0	
Kern............	2	0	0	0	0	0	0	1	0	1	
Los Angeles........	6	5	4	0	0	0	2	5	5	3	
Marin...........	0	1	0	0	0	0	1	0	0	0	
Monterey........	1	0	0	0	0	0	0	1	0	0	
Riverside........	1	0	0	0	0	0	0	1	0	0	
Sacramento	8	1	1	0	0	1	4	0	4	3	
San Bernardino	2	1	0	0	0	0	1	2	0	0	
San Diego........	7	0	7	0	0	0	3	4	4	3	
San Luis Obispo	3	0	0	0	0	0	0	1	1	1	
San Mateo............	0	1	0	0	0	0	0	0	1	0	
Santa Barbara	2	0	2	0	0	0	1	3	0	0	
Santa Clara........	1	0	0	0	0	2	1	1	0	1	
Santa Cruz........	1	1	0	0	0	0	0	0	2	0	
Solano........	1	0	0	0	0	0	0	0	0	1	
Sonoma........	4	0	1	0	0	0	2	2	1	0	
Stanislaus.........	1	0	0	0	0	0	0	0	1	0	
Sutter........	0	1	0	0	0	0	0	0	0	1	
Ventura........	2	1	0	0	0	0	0	0	2	1	
Yuba.........	4	0	0	0	0	0	3	1	0	0	
Nonmetropolitan Counties......................................	3	1	2	0	0	0					
Calaveras.........	1	0	0	0	0	0	0	0	0	1	
Lake.........	0	1	1	0	0	0	0	0	0	2	
Mendocino.........	1	0	0	0	0	0	1	0	0	0	
Nevada.........	0	0	1	0	0	0	0	1	0	0	
Plumas.........	1	0	0	0	0	0	0	0	1	0	
Other Agencies.......................................	6	0	6	0	0	0					
Department of Parks and Recreation											
Marin County	1	0	0	0	0	0	0	0	1	0	
Oceano Dunes.........	0	0	1	0	0	0	0	1	0	0	
Los Angeles Transportation Services Bureau	3	0	3	0	0	0	2	3	1	0	
Port of San Diego Harbor.........	0	0	1	0	0	0	0	0	0	1	
San Francisco Bay Area Rapid Transit											
Alameda County.........	1	0	0	0	0	0	0	0	0	1	
San Francisco County.........	1	0	1	0	0	0	1	0	1	0	
COLORADO											
Total	61	26	18	1	1	1					
Cities	49	16	13	1	1	1					
Arvada.........	1	0	1	0	0	0	2	0	0	0	119,346
Aspen........	1	0	0	0	0	0	0	1	0	0	6,906
Aurora.........	14	3	1	0	0	0	8	7	2	1	368,018
Boulder.........	2	1	0	0	0	0	2	1	0	0	109,722
Brighton	0	0	1	0	0	0	0	0	1	0	39,099
Broomfield.........	1	0	0	0	0	0	1	0	0	0	68,158
Canon City	0	1	0	0	0	0	1	0	0	0	16,723
Castle Rock	2	0	0	0	0	0	0	1	0	1	59,337
Centennial	2	0	0	0	0	0	1	0	1	0	111,416
Colorado Springs	0	1	0	0	0	0	0	0	1	0	472,958
Delta[2]	0	0	0	1	1	0	0	0	0	1	8,925
Denver.........	9	2	6	0	0	0	4	7	1	5	706,616
Durango	0	1	0	0	0	0	0	0	1	0	18,801
Englewood	2	0	0	0	0	0	0	1	1	0	34,709
Fruita	0	0	1	0	0	0	1	0	0	0	12,971
Golden	1	0	0	0	0	0	0	0	0	1	20,948
Grand Junction	0	1	1	0	0	0	1	1	0	0	62,352
Greeley.........	3	0	0	0	0	0	1	0	1	1	105,906
Idaho Springs.........	1	0	0	0	0	0	0	0	0	1	1,751
Lafayette.........	0	1	0	0	0	0	0	0	1	0	28,939

(Number.)

State/agency	Number of incidents per bias motivation						Number of incidents per quarter				Population[1]
	Race/ Ethnicity/ Ancestry	Religion	Sexual orientation	Disability	Gender	Gender Identity	1st quarter	2nd quarter	3rd quarter	4th quarter	
Lakewood	3	0	1	0	0	0	3	1	0	0	156,344
Littleton	0	3	0	0	0	0	1	2	0	0	47,112
Longmont[2]	1	0	0	0	0	1	0	0	1	0	93,979
Loveland	1	0	1	0	0	0	0	1	1	0	78,671
Monument	1	0	0	0	0	0	1	0	0	0	6,644
Northglenn	0	1	0	0	0	0	0	1	0	0	39,520
Pueblo	2	0	0	0	0	0	0	0	1	1	110,872
Steamboat Springs	0	1	0	0	0	0	1	0	0	0	12,799
Trinidad	1	0	0	0	0	0	0	0	0	1	7,961
Windsor	1	0	0	0	0	0	0	0	0	1	23,523
Universities and Colleges	3	1	0	0	0	0					
Colorado State University, Fort Collins	3	0	0	0	0	0	0	0	0	3	31,856
University of Colorado, Boulder	0	1	0	0	0	0	1	0	0	0	33,977
Metropolitan Counties	9	8	3	0	0	0					
Adams	1	0	0	0	0	0	0	0	0	1	
Arapahoe	3	3	0	0	0	0	2	2	1	1	
Boulder	0	3	0	0	0	0	3	0	0	0	
Douglas	1	0	0	0	0	0	1	0	0	0	
El Paso	2	0	1	0	0	0	1	0	1	1	
Jefferson	1	1	1	0	0	0	1	0	1	1	
Larimer	0	1	0	0	0	0	0	1	0	0	
Mesa	1	0	1	0	0	0	0	0	0	2	
Nonmetropolitan Counties	0	1	2	0	0	0					
Garfield	0	0	1	0	0	0	0	0	0	1	
Huerfano	0	1	0	0	0	0	0	1	0	0	
Routt	0	0	1	0	0	0	0	0	1	0	
CONNECTICUT											
Total	66	23	22	0	0	1					
Cities	60	23	19	0	0	1					
Avon	1	0	0	0	0	0	1	0	0	0	18,397
Berlin	1	2	0	0	0	0	1	1	0	1	20,601
Bethel	3	0	0	0	0	0	0	0	0	3	19,796
Bloomfield	0	0	2	0	0	0	0	2	0	0	20,667
Bridgeport[2]	5	0	2	0	0	0	1	1	1	3	146,110
Brookfield	1	0	0	0	0	0	1	0	0	0	17,203
Cheshire	0	0	2	0	0	0	1	0	0	1	29,282
Clinton	1	0	0	0	0	0	0	0	1	0	12,915
Danbury	4	0	1	0	0	0	2	2	1	0	85,614
Darien	1	0	0	0	0	0	0	1	0	0	21,910
East Haven	1	0	0	0	0	0	0	1	0	0	28,739
East Windsor	1	0	0	0	0	0	0	1	0	0	11,383
Enfield	1	0	0	0	0	0	1	0	0	0	44,321
Groton	1	0	0	0	0	0	0	1	0	0	9,093
Groton Town	1	0	0	0	0	0	1	0	0	0	29,524
Guilford	0	0	1	0	0	0	0	0	1	0	22,259
Hartford	2	1	1	0	0	0	1	1	0	2	122,891
Manchester	2	0	2	0	0	0	1	2	1	0	57,808
Meriden	0	0	1	0	0	0	0	1	0	0	59,417
Middletown	5	2	1	0	0	0	2	1	3	2	46,363
New Britain	0	1	0	0	0	0	0	1	0	0	72,442
New Haven	4	2	3	0	0	1	0	4	4	2	129,953
New London	0	0	1	0	0	0	0	1	0	0	26,880
New Milford	1	0	0	0	0	0	0	0	1	0	26,993
North Branford	0	1	0	0	0	0	0	0	1	0	14,163
North Haven	0	0	1	0	0	0	0	0	0	1	23,646
Norwich	0	1	0	0	0	0	0	0	1	0	39,393
Old Saybrook	3	0	0	0	0	0	1	0	2	0	10,070
Orange	2	1	0	0	0	0	0	1	1	1	13,904
Rocky Hill	2	0	0	0	0	0	0	1	1	0	20,189
Southington	1	0	0	0	0	0	0	1	0	0	43,769
Stamford	3	3	0	0	0	0	1	0	3	2	130,189
Torrington	4	1	0	0	0	0	2	2	0	1	34,372

(Number.)

State/agency	Number of incidents per bias motivation						Number of incidents per quarter				Population[1]
	Race/ Ethnicity/ Ancestry	Religion	Sexual orientation	Disability	Gender	Gender Identity	1st quarter	2nd quarter	3rd quarter	4th quarter	
Trumbull	4	4	1	0	0	0	4	2	1	2	36,265
Waterbury	0	1	0	0	0	0	0	0	1	0	107,924
West Hartford	1	0	0	0	0	0	0	0	0	1	62,812
Westport	1	0	0	0	0	0	0	0	1	0	28,079
Willimantic	1	0	0	0	0	0	0	0	1	0	17,768
Wilton	1	2	0	0	0	0	0	0	2	1	18,643
Windsor	1	0	0	0	0	0	0	1	0	0	28,836
Woodbridge	0	1	0	0	0	0	0	1	0	0	8,816
Universities and Colleges	3	0	0	0	0	0					
Yale University	3	0	0	0	0	0	1	0	2	0	12,458
State Police Agencies	2	0	3	0	0	0					
Connecticut State Police	2	0	3	0	0	0	0	1	0	4	
Tribal Agencies	1	0	0	0	0	0					
Mohegan Tribal	1	0	0	0	0	0	0	1	0	0	
DELAWARE											
Total	14	8	6	0	0	1					
Cities	2	0	4	0	0	1					
Dewey Beach	0	0	1	0	0	0	0	1	0	0	386
New Castle	0	0	1	0	0	0	1	0	0	0	5,362
Rehoboth Beach	1	0	1	0	0	1	0	0	3	0	1,516
Wilmington	1	0	1	0	0	0	0	0	0	2	71,552
Universities and Colleges	4	1	1	0	0	0					
University of Delaware	4	1	1	0	0	0	3	0	1	2	23,009
Metropolitan Counties	2	4	0	0	0	0					
New Castle County Police Department	2	4	0	0	0	0	4	0	0	2	
State Police Agencies	4	2	0	0	0	0					
State Police											
Kent County	2	1	0	0	0	0	0	2	1	0	
New Castle County	2	1	0	0	0	0	1	1	1	0	
Other Agencies	2	1	1	0	0	0					
Fish and Wildlife	1	0	0	0	0	0	0	0	1	0	
River and Bay Authority	1	0	0	0	0	0	0	0	1	0	
State Capitol Police	0	1	1	0	0	0	1	0	1	0	
DISTRICT OF COLUMBIA											
Total	108	14	57	1	0	13					
Cities	87	12	56	1	0	13					
Washington	87	12	56	1	0	13	27	40	45	57	693,972
Other Agencies	21	2	1	0	0	0					
Metro Transit Police	21	2	1	0	0	0	6	8	3	7	
FLORIDA											
Total	70	43	32	0	0	0					
Cities	42	33	26	0	0	0					
Boca Raton	0	1	0	0	0	0	0	0	0	1	98,069
Clearwater	1	0	0	0	0	0	1	0	0	0	115,295
Cooper City	0	1	0	0	0	0	0	0	0	1	36,694
Coral Gables	1	0	0	0	0	0	0	0	0	1	51,487
Davie	4	3	0	0	0	0	3	1	1	2	103,555
Deerfield Beach	2	0	0	0	0	0	0	1	0	1	80,552
Delray Beach	0	1	0	0	0	0	1	0	0	0	68,533
Fort Lauderdale	2	2	2	0	0	0	0	2	3	1	180,972

(Number.)

State/agency	Number of incidents per bias motivation						Number of incidents per quarter				Population[1]
	Race/Ethnicity/Ancestry	Religion	Sexual orientation	Disability	Gender	Gender Identity	1st quarter	2nd quarter	3rd quarter	4th quarter	
Fort Myers	1	1	1	0	0	0	1	1	0	1	79,918
Gainesville	0	1	0	0	0	0	0	0	1	0	132,777
Hollywood	0	0	1	0	0	0	1	0	0	0	153,893
Homestead	1	1	2	0	0	0	0	1		3	69,276
Jacksonville	3	2	1	0	0	0	1	0	2	3	894,638
Key Biscayne	0	0	1	0	0	0	1	0	0	0	13,127
Key West	0	0	1	0	0	0	1	0	0	0	27,399
Lake City	1	0	0	0	0	0	1	0	0	0	12,326
Largo	1	2	0	0	0	0	2	0	1		83,728
Lauderdale-by-the-Sea	1	0	0	0	0	0			1		6,589
Leesburg	1	0	0	0	0	0	1	0	0	0	22,763
Mangonia Park	0	0	1	0	0	0	0	0	0	1	2,009
Miami Beach	0	7	9	0	0	0	8	6	1	1	92,571
Miami Gardens	0	2	0	0	0	0	2	0	0	0	114,008
New Port Richey	1	0	0	0	0	0	0	0	1	0	16,388
North Miami	1	0	0	0	0	0	1	0	0	0	62,543
Oakland Park	2	1	1	0	0	0	1	1	1	1	44,814
Ocala	0	0	1	0	0	0	1	0	0	0	59,731
Orlando	2	0	3	0	0	0	1	2	1	1	283,982
Palm Bay	1	0	1	0	0	0	0	1	1	0	111,275
Pompano Beach	2	1	0	0	0	0	0	0	1	2	111,027
Port St. Lucie	0	0	1	0	0	0	0	1	0	0	188,652
Rockledge	1	0	0	0	0	0	1	0	0	0	27,432
St. Augustine	1	0	0	0	0	0	0	1	0	0	14,500
Sunrise	1	1	0	0	0	0	0	0	0	2	95,342
Tampa	3	0	0	0	0	0	2	0	0	1	384,360
Titusville	5	0	0	0	0	0	0	0	5	0	46,425
Weston	1	2	0	0	0	0	0	0	1	2	70,796
West Palm Beach	2	0	0	0	0	0	1	1	0	0	109,459
Wilton Manors	0	3	0	0	0	0	0	1	2	0	12,861
Winter Park	0	1	0	0	0	0	0	1	0	0	30,602
Universities and Colleges	1	2	1	0	0	0					
Florida Gulf Coast University	0	1	0	0	0	0	0	0	0	1	14,821
Tallahassee Community College	0	1	0	0	0	0	0	0	1	0	12,200
University of South Florida, Tampa	1	0	0	0	0	0	1	0	0	0	42,861
University of West Florida	0	0	1	0	0	0	0	0	0	1	12,966
Metropolitan Counties	25	8	5	0	0	0					
Alachua	1	0	0	0	0	0	0	0	1	0	
Broward	1	0	0	0	0	0	1	0	0	0	
Charlotte	1	0	0	0	0	0	0	1	0	0	
Clay	1	1	0	0	0	0	0	0	0	2	
Collier	0	1	0	0	0	0	0	0	0	1	
Hillsborough	0	1	0	0	0	0	0	1	0	0	
Lake	1	0	0	0	0	0	1	0	0	0	
Lee	4	1	1	0	0	0	2	3	0	1	
Leon	1	0	0	0	0	0	1	0	0	0	
Martin	1	0	0	0	0	0	0	1	0	0	
Miami-Dade	0	0	1	0	0	0	0	0	0	1	
Okaloosa	1	0	0	0	0	0	0	1			
Orange	2	0	0	0	0	0	2	0	0	0	
Osceola	2	1	1	0	0	0	2	0	1	1	
Palm Beach	1	1	0	0	0	0	1	1	0	0	
Pasco	3	0	0	0	0	0	0	0	3	0	
Pinellas	0	1	0	0	0	0	1	0	0	0	
Santa Rosa	0	0	1	0	0	0	1	0	0	0	
Sarasota	0	1	0	0	0	0	0	0	1	0	
Seminole	1	0	1	0	0	0	0	0	1	1	
St. Johns	3	0	0	0	0	0	1	2	0	0	
Volusia	1	0	0	0	0	0	1	0	0	0	
Nonmetropolitan Counties	2	0	0	0	0	0					
Hendry	1	0	0	0	0	0	1	0	0	0	
Monroe	1	0	0	0	0	0	1	0	0	0	
GEORGIA											
Total	19	5	4	0	0	0					

Table 13. Hate Crime Incidents Per Bias Motivation and Quarter, by Selected State and Agency, 2017—Continued

(Number.)

State/agency	Number of incidents per bias motivation						Number of incidents per quarter				Population[1]
	Race/Ethnicity/Ancestry	Religion	Sexual orientation	Disability	Gender	Gender Identity	1st quarter	2nd quarter	3rd quarter	4th quarter	
Cities	5	1	3	0	0	0					
Atlanta	0	1	2	0	0	0	2	1	0	0	481,343
Columbus	3	0	1	0	0	0	1	2	1		198,832
Warner Robins	1	0	0	0	0	0	1	0	0	0	75,323
Woodstock	1	0	0	0	0	0	0	1	0	0	32,293
Universities and Colleges	2	0	0	0	0	0					
University of Georgia	2	0	0	0	0	0	1	0	1	0	36,574
Metropolitan Counties	12	4	1	0	0	0					
Cobb County Police Department	9	2	1	0	0	0	1	5	3	3	
Forsyth	1	0	0	0	0	0	1	0	0	0	
Gwinnett County Police Department[2]	2	2	0	0	0	0	1	2	0	0	
IDAHO											
Total	30	17	4	2	0	0					
Cities	24	15	4	2	0	0					
Boise	7	6	2	0	0	0	1	5	6	3	225,677
Bonners Ferry	0	1	0	0	0	0	0	0	1	0	2,574
Caldwell	2	0	0	0	0	0	1	1	0	0	54,345
Coeur d'Alene	2	0	0	0	0	0	0	1	1	0	51,364
Heyburn	0	1	0	0	0	0	1	0	0	0	3,306
Kimberly	2	0	0	0	0	0	0	0	1	1	3,812
Lewiston	3	0	0	0	0	0	0	1	1	1	33,029
Middleton	1	0	0	0	0	0	0	0	1	0	7,486
Moscow	1	0	0	0	0	0	0	1	0	0	25,576
Mountain Home	2	0	0	0	0	0	0	1	0	1	13,772
Nampa	2	1	1	0	0	0	2	1	1	0	93,064
Pocatello	0	1	0	0	0	0	1	0	0	0	54,814
Preston	0	3	0	0	0	0	1	1	1	0	5,372
Soda Springs	1	0	0	0	0	0	0	0	0	1	2,970
Spirit Lake	1	0	0	0	0	0	0	0	0	1	2,207
Twin Falls	0	2	1	2	0	0	0	1	0	4	48,912
Metropolitan Counties	0	1	0	0	0	0					
Kootenai	0	1	0	0	0	0	0	0	1	0	
Nonmetropolitan Counties	5	0	0	0	0	0					
Cassia	3	0	0	0	0	0	1	0	2	0	
Idaho	1	0	0	0	0	0	0	0	1	0	
Teton	1	0	0	0	0	0	0	0	1	0	
State Police Agencies	1	1	0	0	0	0					
Idaho State Police	1	1	0	0	0	0	0	1	1	0	
ILLINOIS											
Total	39	27	14	1	0	1					
Cities	37	23	14	1	0	1					
Aurora	2	0	0	0	0	0	1	1	0	0	201,599
Berwyn	1	1	1	0	0	0	1	0	1	1	55,594
Bloomington	1	0	0	0	0	0	0	1	0	0	78,203
Chicago	16	17	7	0	0	1	18	5	10	8	2,706,171
Decatur	1	0	0	0	0	0	0	0	1	0	72,153
De Kalb	0	1	0	0	0	0	0	0	0	1	43,043
East Peoria	1	0	0	0	0	0	1	0	0	0	22,856
Forest Park	0	0	1	0	0	0	0	0	1	0	13,950
Fox Lake	1	0	0	0	0	0	0	1	0	0	10,432
Fox River Grove	1	0	0	0	0	0	0	0	0	1	4,628
Homewood	2	0	0	0	0	0	0	1	1	0	19,150
Manhattan	1	0	0	0	0	0	0	0	0	1	7,625
Mount Prospect	0	2	0	0	0	0	0	0	2	0	54,162
New Lenox	0	0	0	1	0	0	1	0	0	0	26,529
Oak Park	1	0	0	0	0	0	0	0	1	0	51,753
Pekin	1	0	0	0	0	0	0	0	0	1	32,866
Peoria	0	0	1	0	0	0	0	1	0	0	114,157
Plainfield	0	1	0	0	0	0	0	0	1	0	43,450

Table 13. Hate Crime Incidents Per Bias Motivation and Quarter, by Selected State and Agency, 2017—*Continued*

(Number.)

State/agency	Number of incidents per bias motivation						Number of incidents per quarter				Population[1]
	Race/ Ethnicity/ Ancestry	Religion	Sexual orientation	Disability	Gender	Gender Identity	1st quarter	2nd quarter	3rd quarter	4th quarter	
Pontiac	1	0	0	0	0	0	0	1	0	0	11,813
Rockford	2	0	2	0	0	0	0	2	1	1	146,770
Sandoval	1	0	0	0	0	0	0	0	1	0	1,211
Skokie	1	0	0	0	0	0	0	1	0	0	64,167
Springfield	2	0	1	0	0	0	0	0	3	0	115,568
Urbana	1	0	0	0	0	0	0	1	0	0	42,091
West Chicago	0	0	1	0	0	0	0	0	1	0	27,219
Wheaton	0	1	0	0	0	0	0	1	0	0	53,444
Universities and Colleges	0	1	0	0	0	0					
Illinois State University	0	1	0	0	0	0	0	0	0	1	21,039
Metropolitan Counties	2	3	0	0	0	0					
Lake	0	1	0	0	0	0	1	0	0	0	
Macon	1	0	0	0	0	0	0	0	1	0	
Peoria	1	0	0	0	0	0	0	0	0	1	
Will	0	1	0	0	0	0	0	1	0	0	
Winnebago	0	1	0	0	0	0	0	0	0	1	
INDIANA											
Total	32	13	9	1	0	0					
Cities	27	4	7	0	0	0					
Bloomington	6	2	2	0	0	0	1	4	3	2	85,121
Fishers	2	0	0	0	0	0	0	0	1	1	92,367
Fort Wayne	2	0	2	0	0	0	0	2	1	1	266,259
Hammond	2	0	1	0	0	0			2	1	76,550
Lafayette	8	0	1	0	0	0	2	5		2	72,274
Lawrence	2	1	0	0	0	0	0	1	2	0	48,174
Michigan City	1	0	0	0	0	0	0	0	0	1	31,108
Plainfield	1	0	1	0	0	0	1	1	0	0	32,067
South Bend	3	0	0	0	0	0	2		0	1	101,857
Whitestown	0	1	0	0	0	0	0	0	1	0	7,464
Universities and Colleges	1	0	0	0	0	0					
Purdue University	1	0	0	0	0	0	1				41,513
Metropolitan Counties	2	0	0	0	0	0					
Vigo	2	0	0	0	0	0	0	0	1	1	
State Police Agencies	2	9	2	1	0	0					
State Police											
Crawford County	0	1	0	0	0	0	1	0	0	0	
Floyd County	0	1	0	0	0	0	0	0	0	1	
Marion County	1	2	1	1	0	0	1	1	3	0	
Miami County	0	1	0	0	0	0	0	0	1	0	
Monroe County	0	1	0	0	0	0	0	0	0	1	
Posey County	0	1	0	0	0	0	0	0	0	1	
Scott County	0	2	0	0	0	0	0	0	1	1	
Vanderburgh County	1	0	0	0	0	0	0	0	0	1	
Washington County	0	0	1	0	0	0	1	0	0	0	
IOWA											
Total	9	1	1	0	0	0					
Cities	9	1	1	0	0	0					
Altoona	1	0	0	0	0	0	1	0	0	0	18,556
Ames	1	0	0	0	0	0	0	0	1	0	67,461
Clinton	1	0	0	0	0	0	0	1	0	0	25,532
Dubuque	1	0	0	0	0	0	0	1	0	0	58,674
Iowa City	3	0	0	0	0	0	2	0	1	0	75,519
Marshalltown	0	1	0	0	0	0	1	0	0	0	27,287
Urbandale	1	0	0	0	0	0	0	0	0	1	43,637
Waukee	1	0	1	0	0	0	1	0	1	0	20,359
KANSAS											
Total	39	16	11	9	0	0					

(Number.)

State/agency	Race/Ethnicity/Ancestry	Religion	Sexual orientation	Disability	Gender	Gender Identity	1st quarter	2nd quarter	3rd quarter	4th quarter	Population[1]
Cities	28	11	9	7	0	0					
Arma	0	0	1	0	0	0	0	0	1	0	1,438
Coffeyville	1	1	0	0	0	0	1	0	0	1	9,423
Dodge City	1	3	0	1	0	0	1	0	3	1	27,447
Edwardsville	1	0	0	0	0	0	0	0	1	0	4,395
El Dorado	0	1	0	0	0	0	0	1	0	0	13,125
Emporia	1	1	0	0	0	0	2	0	0	0	24,804
Garden City	2	1	0	0	0	0	0	0	3	0	26,728
Haven	1	0	0	0	0	0	0	1	0	0	1,207
Hays	0	1	0	0	0	0	0	1	0	0	21,110
Haysville	1	0	0	0	0	0	0	1	0	0	11,314
Herington	0	0	1	0	0	0	1	0	0	0	2,336
Hutchinson	1	0	0	1	0	0	0	1	0	1	41,160
Junction City	1	0	0	0	0	0	0	1	0	0	24,240
Liberal	0	0	0	1	0	0	0	0	0	1	20,317
Lindsborg	0	0	1	1	0	0	1	0	0	1	3,319
Mulvane	1	0	0	0	0	0	1	0	0	0	6,343
Newton	2	0	0	0	0	0	2	0	0	0	19,095
Norton	1	0	1	1	0	0	3	0	0	0	2,799
Ottawa	3	1	0	0	0	0	2	1	1	0	12,307
Salina	4	1	2	1	0	0	2	2	2	2	47,251
Sedgwick	1	0	0	0	0	0	0	0	0	1	1,695
Shawnee	1	0	0	0	0	0	0	1	0	0	65,683
Tonganoxie	0	0	0	1	0	0	0	1	0	0	5,379
Topeka	1	0	0	0	0	0	1	0	0	0	126,624
Valley Center	2	0	0	0	0	0	0	2	0	0	7,431
Wichita	2	1	3	0	0	0	2	3	0	1	391,084
Universities and Colleges	1	0	0	0	0	0					
Kansas State University	1	0	0	0	0	0	1	0	0	0	23,779
Metropolitan Counties	8	2	1	1	0	0					
Doniphan	0	0	0	1	0	0	0	0	1	0	
Johnson	1	0	0	0	0	0	0	0	1	0	
Riley County Police Department	3	1	0	0	0	0	0	0	3	1	
Sedgwick	2	0	0	0	0	0	0	0	1	1	
Shawnee	2	1	1	0	0	0	0	2	0	2	
Nonmetropolitan Counties	2	3	1	0	0	0					
Barton	0	1	0	0	0	0	0	0	1	0	
Crawford	0	1	1	0	0	0	1	0	1	0	
Ford	0	1	0	0	0	0	0	0	0	1	
Labette	1	0	0	0	0	0	0	1	0	0	
Saline	1	0	0	0	0	0	0	0	0	1	
State Police Agencies	0	0	0	1	0	0					
Highway Patrol, Troop E	0	0	0	1	0	0	0	0	0	1	
KENTUCKY											
Total	283	38	27	12	16	3					
Cities	186	21	17	6	7	3					
Alexandria	1	2	0	0	0	0	1	2	0	0	9,486
Ashland	0	0	1	0	0	0	1	0	0	0	20,927
Barbourville	1	0	0	0	1	0	0	1	0	1	3,169
Bowling Green	18	2	2	2	1	0	3	4	10	8	66,317
Cadiz	0	0	1	0	0	0	1	0	0	0	2,629
Carrollton	2	0	0	0	0	0	1	1	0	0	3,864
Cold Spring	1	0	0	0	0	0	0	0	0	1	6,276
Corbin	2	0	0	0	0	0	0	0	0	2	7,411
Covington	4	1	1	0	0	0	1	2	0	3	40,845
Cynthiana	1	0	0	0	0	0	0	0	1	0	6,375
Danville	3	0	0	0	0	0	0	1	1	1	16,891
Dayton	2	0	0	0	0	0	0	1	0	1	5,423
Elizabethtown	4	0	0	0	0	0	0	1	2	1	30,065
Elsmere	1	1	0	0	0	0	2	0	0	0	8,541
Erlanger	1	0	0	0	1	0	0	0	2	0	22,947

(Number.)

State/agency	Number of incidents per bias motivation						Number of incidents per quarter				Population[1]
	Race/ Ethnicity/ Ancestry	Religion	Sexual orientation	Disability	Gender	Gender Identity	1st quarter	2nd quarter	3rd quarter	4th quarter	
Falmouth	1	0	0	0	0	0	0	0	1	0	2,127
Florence	19	1	0	0	1	0	8	6	5	2	32,866
Fort Mitchell	1	0	0	0	0	0	0	1	0	0	8,306
Frankfort	5	1	0	0	1	0	1	2	0	4	27,975
Franklin	3	0	1	0	0	0	0	2	0	2	8,884
Fulton	0	0	1	0	0	0	0	0	1	0	2,174
Georgetown	2	0	0	0	0	1	1	1	0	1	34,184
Glasgow	6	0	0	0	0	0	0	3	1	2	14,690
Greensburg	1	0	0	0	0	0	0	0	0	1	2,123
Hillview	1	0	0	0	0	0	0	1	0	0	8,942
Hopkinsville	2	0	0	0	0	0	1	0	0	1	31,761
Independence	1	0	0	0	0	0	1	0	0	0	27,400
Irvine	0	0	0	1	0	0	0	0	0	1	2,385
La Center	0	0	1	0	0	0	1	0	0	0	982
La Grange	1	0	0	0	0	0	0	0	0	1	8,831
Lawrenceburg	2	0	0	0	0	0	0	1	0	1	11,211
Leitchfield	1	0	0	0	0	0	0	0	1	0	6,900
Lexington	20	3	3	0	0	1	7	6	9	5	322,332
London	1	0	0	0	0	0	0	0	1	0	8,184
Louisville Metro	11	2	0	1	0	0	5	0	7	2	684,362
Madisonville	1	1	0	0	0	0	0	1	0	1	19,316
Mayfield	6	0	1	0	0	0	0	1	3	3	9,991
Maysville	8	0	0	0	1	0	0	3	3	3	8,841
Middlesboro	1	0	0	0	0	0	0	0	0	1	9,534
Morehead	1	0	0	0	0	0	0	0	1	0	7,915
Mount Sterling	2	0	0	0	0	0	1	0	0	1	7,298
Mount Washington	1	0	0	0	0	0	0	1	0	0	14,511
Murray	2	0	1	0	1	0	0	1	3	0	19,205
Newport	1	0	0	0	0	0	0	1	0	0	15,202
Nicholasville	4	0	0	0	0	0	1	0	1	2	30,333
Owensboro	5	1	1	0	0	0	2	0	3	2	59,576
Paducah	10	2	1	0	0	1	4	5	3	2	25,169
Paris	2	0	1	0	0	0	1	1	1	0	9,845
Park Hills	1	0	0	0	0	0	0	0	1	0	3,001
Princeton	0	1	0	0	0	0	0	0	0	1	6,084
Providence	1	0	0	0	0	0	1	0	0	0	3,088
Radcliff	3	0	0	0	0	0	0	1	0	2	22,473
Richmond	5	0	1	0	0	0	1	2	1	2	35,161
Russell Springs	1	0	0	0	0	0	0	0	0	1	2,573
Russellville	0	0	0	1	0	0	0	0	0	1	7,006
Scottsville	1	0	0	0	0	0	0	1	0	0	4,446
Shelbyville	2	0	0	1	0	0	0	1	1	1	15,758
Shively	2	0	0	0	0	0	0	1	0	1	15,830
St. Matthews	4	1	0	0	0	0	1	2	0	2	18,163
Versailles	0	1	0	0	0	0	0	1	0	0	26,320
Villa Hills	1	0	0	0	0	0	1	0	0	0	7,494
Wilmore	1	0	0	0	0	0	0	0	1	0	6,380
Winchester	1	0	0	0	0	0	0	1	0	0	18,478
Worthington	0	1	0	0	0	0	0	0	0	1	1,565
Universities and Colleges	6	2	4	0	0	0					
Eastern Kentucky University	1	0	4	0	0	0	2	2	0	1	16,881
Kentucky State University	2	0	0	0	0	0	0	1	1	0	1,736
University of Kentucky	2	2	0	0	0	0	3	1	0	0	29,781
Western Kentucky University	1	0	0	0	0	0	0	1	0	0	20,271
Metropolitan Counties	31	6	2	1	0	0					
Boone	14	1	0	0	0	0	6	3	5	1	
Boyd	0	1	0	0	0	0	0	0	0	1	
Bullitt	0	0	1	0	0	0	0	0	1	0	
Campbell County Police Department[2]	2	2	1	0	0	0	0	1	2	1	
Christian	0	1	0	0	0	0	1	0	0	0	
Clark	3	0	0	0	0	0	1	2	0	0	
Daviess	1	0	0	0	0	0	0	0	0	1	
Grant	0	1	0	0	0	0	0	0	0	1	
Greenup	1	0	0	0	0	0	0	0	1	0	
Hardin	1	0	0	0	0	0	0	1	0	0	

(Number.)

State/agency	Number of incidents per bias motivation						Number of incidents per quarter				Population[1]
	Race/Ethnicity/Ancestry	Religion	Sexual orientation	Disability	Gender	Gender Identity	1st quarter	2nd quarter	3rd quarter	4th quarter	
Jessamine	0	0	0	1	0	0	0	0	1	0	
Kenton County Police Department	1	0	0	0	0	0	0	0	1	0	
Oldham County Police Department	2	0	0	0	0	0	0	2	0	0	
Pendleton	1	0	0	0	0	0	0	1	0	0	
Shelby	1	0	0	0	0	0	0	1	0	0	
Trigg	1	0	0	0	0	0	0	0	0	1	
Warren	3	0	0	0	0	0	0	0	0	3	
Nonmetropolitan Counties	27	4	3	1	7	0					
Anderson	0	1	0	0	0	0	0	0	1	0	
Bell	0	1	0	0	0	0	1	0	0	0	
Boyle	2	0	0	0	0	0	2	0	0	0	
Breckinridge	1	0	0	0	0	0	0	1	0	0	
Floyd	2	0	0	0	0	0	1	1	0	0	
Franklin	1	0	0	0	0	0	1	0	0	0	
Graves	1	0	0	0	0	0	1	0	0	0	
Knott	0	1	0	0	0	0	0	0	0	1	
Knox	1	0	0	0	0	0	0	1	0	0	
Laurel	1	0	0	0	0	0	0	1	0	0	
Lincoln	1	0	0	0	0	0	1	0	0	0	
Livingston	2	0	0	0	0	0	0	0	1	1	
Madison	0	0	1	0	0	0	1	0	0	0	
Marion	1	0	0	0	0	0	0	0	0	1	
Martin	1	0	0	0	0	0	1	0	0	0	
Mason	1	0	0	0	0	0	0	1	0	0	
McCracken	6	0	0	1	7	0	1	7	1	5	
Montgomery	2	1	1	0	0	0	0	2	2	0	
Ohio	1	0	0	0	0	0	0	0	1	0	
Rockcastle	0	0	1	0	0	0	0	0	1	0	
Simpson	1	0	0	0	0	0	0	1	0	0	
Taylor	1	0	0	0	0	0	0	1	0	0	
Wolfe	1	0	0	0	0	0	0	0	0	1	
State Police Agencies	22	2	1	3	1	0					
State Police											
Ashland	0	0	0	1	0	0	0	0	0	1	
Bowling Green	1	0	0	0	0	0	0	1	0	0	
Campbellsburg	0	1	1	0	0	0	1	0	0	1	
Cannabis Suppression Section	2	0	0	0	0	0	0	0	2	0	
Dry Ridge	1	0	0	0	0	0	0	1	0	0	
Elizabethtown	1	0	0	1	0	0	1	0	0	1	
Frankfort	2	0	0	0	0	0	1	0	1	0	
Harlan	1	0	0	0	0	0	0	0	1	0	
Hazard	3	0	0	0	0	0	1	0	1	1	
Henderson	1	0	0	0	0	0	0	0	0	1	
London	1	1	0	0	0	0	0	1	0	1	
Mayfield	2	0	0	1	1	0	2	1	1	0	
Morehead	3	0	0	0	0	0	0	0	0	3	
Pikeville	2	0	0	0	0	0	1	0	1	0	
Richmond	1	0	0	0	0	0	0	0	0	1	
West Drug Enforcement Branch	1	0	0	0	0	0	0	1	0	0	
Other Agencies	11	3	0	1	1	0					
Barren County Drug Task Force	3	0	0	0	0	0	1	1	1	0	
Cincinnati-Northern Kentucky International Airport	1	0	0	0	0	0	1	0	0	0	
Clark County School System	1	0	0	0	0	0	0	0	1	0	
Fayette County Schools	0	2	0	1	0	0	1	0	1	1	
Greater Hardin County Narcotics Task Force	1	0	0	0	0	0	0	1	0	0	
Jefferson County School District	1	1	0	0	1	0	1	1	0	1	
McCracken County Public Schools	1	0	0	0	0	0	0	0	0	1	
South Central Kentucky Drug Task Force	3	0	0	0	0	0	0	0	3	0	
LOUISIANA											
Total	14	11	1	0	0	0					
Cities	4	0	0	0	0	0					
Gretna	1	0	0	0	0	0	0	0	1	0	17,923

Table 13. Hate Crime Incidents Per Bias Motivation and Quarter, by Selected State and Agency, 2017—*Continued*

(Number.)

State/agency	Number of incidents per bias motivation						Number of incidents per quarter				Population[1]
	Race/ Ethnicity/ Ancestry	Religion	Sexual orientation	Disability	Gender	Gender Identity	1st quarter	2nd quarter	3rd quarter	4th quarter	
New Orleans	1	0	0	0	0	0			0	1	397,447
Shreveport	1	0	0	0	0	0	0	0	0	1	193,937
Vidalia	1	0	0	0	0	0	0		1		4,015
Universities and Colleges	1	0	0	0	0	0					
Louisiana State University, Baton Rouge	1	0	0	0	0	0	0	0	0	1	31,409
Metropolitan Counties	6	11	1	0	0	0					
Caddo	0	1	0	0	0	0	1	0	0	0	
Calcasieu	2	0	0	0	0	0	0	1	0	1	
Jefferson	1	0	0	0	0	0	0	1	0	0	
Lafourche	1	0	0	0	0	0	0	0	0	1	
St. Charles	0	10	0	0	0	0	3	2	3	2	
St. James	1	0	0	0	0	0	0	0	0	1	
St. John the Baptist	0	0	1	0	0	0	0	0	0	1	
St. Tammany	1	0	0	0	0	0	0	1	0	0	
Nonmetropolitan Counties	3	0	0	0	0	0					
Madison	2	0	0	0	0	0	0	0	2	0	
Washington	1	0	0	0	0	0	1	0	0	0	
MAINE											
Total	17	9	4	0	0	2					
Cities	16	5	2	0	0	1					
Augusta	0	1	0	0	0	0	1	0	0	0	18,394
Biddeford	1	0	1	0	0	0	0	0	2	0	21,378
Lewiston	1	0	0	0	0	0	0	0	0	1	36,067
Old Orchard Beach	2	0	0	0	0	0	0	1	1	0	8,842
Portland	7	2	1	0	0	0	6	3	1	0	67,079
Rumford	1	0	0	0	0	0	0	0	1	0	5,692
Saco	1	2	0	0	0	0	2	1	0	0	19,332
Sanford	3	0	0	0	0	1	1	1	2	0	20,963
Universities and Colleges	1	4	2	0	0	0					
University of Southern Maine	1	4	2	0	0	0	2	3	0	2	7,855
Nonmetropolitan Counties	0	0	0	0	0	1					
Waldo	0	0	0	0	0	1	0	1	0	0	
MARYLAND											
Total	24	12	6	0	0	6					
Cities	4	1	0	0	0	1					
Aberdeen	1	0	0	0	0	0	1	0	0	0	15,720
Annapolis	1	0	0	0	0	0	0	1	0	0	39,596
Baltimore	0	0	0	0	0	1	0	0	0	1	613,217
Laurel	0	1	0	0	0	0	0	1			25,997
Taneytown	1	0	0	0	0	0	1	0			6,762
Westminster	1	0	0	0	0	0	0	1			18,682
Universities and Colleges	4	4	0	0	0	0					
University of Maryland											
Baltimore County	0	3	0	0	0	0	1	1	1	0	13,640
College Park	4	1	0	0	0	0	0	1	2	2	39,083
Metropolitan Counties	15	6	4	0	0	5					
Anne Arundel County Police Department	5	1	2	0	0	1	4	3	2	0	
Baltimore County Police Department	5	1	0	0	0	4	6	1	3	0	
Harford	1	0	0	0	0	0	1	0	0		
Howard County Police Department	0	1	0	0	0	0	1	0			
Montgomery County Police Department	2	2	2	0	0	0	0	3	2	1	
Prince George's County Police Department	1	0	0	0	0	0	0	1			
Wicomico	1	1	0	0	0	0	0	2	0	0	
State Police Agencies	0	0	1	0	0	0					
State Police, Somerset County	0	0	1	0	0	0	0	0	1	0	

State/agency	Race/ Ethnicity/ Ancestry	Religion	Sexual orientation	Disability	Gender	Gender Identity	1st quarter	2nd quarter	3rd quarter	4th quarter	Population[1]
	Number of incidents per bias motivation						Number of incidents per quarter				
Other Agencies..	1	1	1	0	0	0					
State Fire Marshal..	0	1	0	0	0	0	1	0	0	0	
Transit Administration..	1	0	1	0	0	0	1	0	0	1	
MASSACHUSETTS											
Total	232	118	65	9	8	9					
Cities	185	110	60	9	8	9					
Acton............................	5	2	1	0	0	0	1	1	4	2	23,937
Agawam............................	1	0	0	0	0	0	1	0	0	0	28,839
Amherst[2]............................	1	0	1	0	2	0	0	1	1	1	40,313
Andover............................	1	2	0	0	0	0	0	1	0	2	35,898
Arlington............................	2	7	1	1	0	3	6	7	1	0	45,449
Ashburnham............................	1	0	0	0	0	0	0	1	0	0	6,255
Attleboro............................	1	0	0	0	0	0	0	1	0	0	44,607
Barnstable............................	2	0	0	0	0	0	0	1	0	1	44,142
Belmont............................	1	0	0	0	0	0	0	0	0	1	26,432
Beverly............................	1	0	0	0	0	0	1	0	0	0	41,678
Bolton............................	1	0	0	0	0	0	0	0	1	0	5,272
Boston[2]............................	79	28	33	0	0	1	29	42	36	33	682,903
Boxford............................	0	1	0	0	0	0	0	0	0	1	8,333
Braintree............................	4	1	0	0	0	2	3	3	0	1	37,579
Bridgewater............................	1	0	0	0	0	0	0	1	0	0	27,769
Brockton............................	1	0	0	0	0	0	0	0	0	1	96,016
Cambridge[2]............................	5	3	2	0	0	0	3	3	1	2	111,707
Chelmsford............................	0	1	1	0	0	0	1	0	1	0	35,392
Chelsea[2]............................	2	1	0	0	0	0	0	0	1	1	40,514
Concord............................	0	0	0	1	0	0	0	0	1	0	20,193
Danvers............................	0	2	0	1	0	0	0	1	0	2	28,168
Dracut............................	0	4	1	0	0	0	1	1	0	3	31,685
Duxbury............................	1	2	0	0	0	0	0	1	2	0	16,085
Edgartown............................	0	0	1	0	0	0	0	0	0	1	4,323
Everett............................	2	0	0	0	0	0	0	0	1	1	47,185
Fitchburg............................	1	0	0	0	0	0	1	0	0	0	40,445
Framingham............................	1	3	1	0	0	0	3	1	1	0	72,153
Grafton............................	2	0	0	0	0	0	0	1	1	0	18,763
Greenfield............................	1	0	0	0	0	0	0	0	0	1	17,462
Haverhill............................	2	1	0	0	0	0	1	0	1	1	63,244
Hingham............................	1	0	0	0	0	0	0	0	1	0	23,392
Holland............................	0	0	0	0	1	0	0	0	0	1	2,502
Hudson............................	0	2	0	0	0	0	0	0	1	1	19,963
Lexington............................	0	1	0	0	0	0	0	0	1	0	33,768
Lincoln............................	0	2	0	0	0	0	0	0	1	1	6,860
Lowell............................	0	1	1	0	0	0	0	1	1	0	111,294
Lynn[2]............................	5	0	2	0	0	0	4	0	1	1	93,140
Malden[2]............................	3	2	0	0	0	0	1	0	3	0	61,098
Manchester-by-the-Sea............................	0	0	0	1	0	0	1	0	0	0	5,435
Mansfield............................	1	0	0	0	0	0	0	0	0	1	23,847
Marblehead............................	0	1	0	0	0	0	0	1	0	0	20,618
Mashpee............................	0	1	0	0	0	0	0	0	1	0	14,272
Medford............................	5	1	0	1	0	0	2	3	0	2	57,418
Medway............................	1	0	0	0	0	0	0	0	0	1	13,407
Millbury............................	0	1	0	0	0	0	0	0	1	0	13,626
Milton............................	0	1	1	0	0	0	1	1	0	0	27,420
Nahant............................	0	1	0	0	0	0	0	0	1	0	3,500
Natick............................	0	1	0	0	0	0	1	0	0	0	36,705
New Bedford............................	0	0	1	0	0	0	0	1	0	0	95,107
Newburyport............................	0	1	0	0	0	0	0	0	1	0	18,092
Newton............................	3	7	2	0	0	0	5	4	1	2	89,736
North Andover............................	1	0	0	0	0	0	0	0	1	0	31,035
Northbridge............................	1	0	0	0	0	0	0	0	0	1	16,711
Northfield............................	0	4	4	0	0	0	0	0	0	8	2,966
Norwell............................	1	0	0	0	0	0	0	0	1	0	11,150
Pittsfield............................	0	1	0	0	0	0	1	0	0	0	42,546
Plymouth............................	0	1	0	0	0	0	1	0	0	0	59,803
Provincetown............................	1	0	1	0	0	0	0	1	0	1	2,993
Quincy[2]............................	8	2	1	0	0	0	2	1	4	3	93,966

(Number.)

State/agency	Number of incidents per bias motivation						Number of incidents per quarter				Population[1]
	Race/ Ethnicity/ Ancestry	Religion	Sexual orientation	Disability	Gender	Gender Identity	1st quarter	2nd quarter	3rd quarter	4th quarter	
Raynham	0	0	0	0	0	1	1	0	0	0	14,048
Reading	0	1	1	0	0	0	0	0	1	1	26,033
Revere	2	1	0	0	0	0	0	1	2	0	53,425
Rutland	0	1	0	0	0	0	0	0	1	0	8,687
Salem[2]	8	5	0	0	0	0	1	5	1	4	43,385
Salisbury	1	0	0	0	0	0	0	1	0	0	9,517
Saugus	1	0	0	0	0	0	1	0	0	0	28,241
Sharon	0	0	1	0	0	0	1	0	0	0	18,419
Shrewsbury	0	1	0	0	0	0	0	0	1	0	36,974
Somerville[2]	6	2	1	1	0	0	3	3	1	2	82,326
Southbridge	0	1	0	0	0	0	0	1	0	0	16,860
Springfield	5	1	1	0	0	1	4	2	1	1	154,562
Stoneham	0	0	0	1	0	0	1	0	0	0	22,077
Stoughton	0	1	0	0	0	0	0	0	0	1	28,678
Sudbury	0	1	0	0	0	0	0	0	1	0	19,120
Swampscott	0	1	0	0	1	0	2	0	0	0	15,016
Taunton	1	1	0	1	2	0	4	1	0	0	57,047
Tewksbury	1	0	0	0	0	0	0	1	0	0	31,245
Truro	1	0	0	0	0	0	0	0	0	1	2,018
Walpole	1	0	0	0	0	0	0	0	1	0	25,312
Waltham	1	1	1	1	2	0	0	3	1	2	63,413
Ware	1	0	0	0	0	0	0	0	1	0	9,907
Watertown	0	0	0	0	0	1	1	0	0	0	35,586
Webster	1	0	0	0	0	0	0	0	0	1	16,883
Westborough	0	1	0	0	0	0	0	1	0	0	19,074
Worcester[2]	5	1	0	0	0	0	2	2	0	1	185,107
Wrentham	0	1	0	0	0	0	0	0	0	1	11,838
Universities and Colleges	37	8	4	0	0	0					
Amherst College	0	0	2	0	0	0	2	0		0	1,849
Boston College	5	0	0	0	0	0	0			5	14,466
Boston University[2]	5	3	1	0	0	0	3	2	2	1	32,695
Clark University	0	2	0	0	0	0	2	0	0	0	3,298
College of the Holy Cross	0	0	1	0	0	0	0	0	0	1	2,720
Dean College	1	0	0	0	0	0	0	1	0	0	1,339
Framingham State University	8	0	0	0	0	0		0	0	8	5,977
Hampshire College	3	0	0	0	0	0	1	1	1	0	1,321
Harvard University	1	0	0	0	0	0	1				29,908
Massasoit Community College	0	1	0	0	0	0	1	0	0	0	7,471
Springfield Technical Community College	3	0	0	0	0	0	0	0	0	3	5,622
University of Massachusetts, Amherst	1	0	0	0	0	0	0	0	0	1	30,037
Westfield State University[2]	10	2	0	0	0	0	0	0	1	9	6,335
Other Agencies	10	0	1	0	0	0					
Massachusetts Bay Transportation Authority											
Middlesex County	1	0	0	0	0	0				1	
Suffolk County	4	0	0	0	0	0	1	1		2	
Massachusetts General Hospital	5	0	1	0	0	0			2	4	
MICHIGAN											
Total	311	78	57	2	8	0					
Cities	212	53	44	1	4	0					
Adrian	1	0	0	0	0	0	0	0	1	0	20,598
Albion	0	1	0	0	0	0	0	0	0	1	8,293
Ann Arbor	3	13	3	0	0	0	1	2	8	8	121,930
Bangor	1	0	0	0	0	0	0	1	0	0	1,839
Battle Creek	2	1	3	0	1	0	3	2	1	1	60,852
Bay City	1	0	0	0	0	0	1	0	0	0	33,286
Belleville	1	0	0	0	0	0	0	0	1	0	3,832
Benton Harbor	1	0	1	0	0	0	0	1	0	1	9,899
Berrien Springs-Oronoko Township	1	0	0	0	0	0	0	0	1	0	9,039
Birmingham	0	1	0	0	0	0	1	0	0	0	21,162
Blackman Township	23	0	0	0	0	0	1	4	3	15	36,908
Boyne City	1	1	0	0	0	0	1	1	0	0	3,741
Buena Vista Township	2	0	0	0	0	0	0	1	0	1	8,084
Burton	4	0	0	0	0	0	0	1	3	0	28,439

State/agency	Number of incidents per bias motivation						Number of incidents per quarter				Population[1]
	Race/ Ethnicity/ Ancestry	Religion	Sexual orientation	Disability	Gender	Gender Identity	1st quarter	2nd quarter	3rd quarter	4th quarter	
Cadillac	1	0	0	0	0	0	1	0	0	0	10,473
Canton Township	1	1	0	0	0	0	1	0	1	0	90,294
Carrollton Township	0	0	1	0	0	0	0	0	1	0	5,728
Center Line	2	0	0	0	0	0	1	1	0	0	8,304
Charlotte	2	0	0	0	0	0	0	0	1	1	9,053
Cheboygan	1	0	0	0	0	0	0	0	1	0	4,705
Chocolay Township	1	0	0	0	0	0	0	1	0	0	5,948
Clio	1	0	0	0	0	0	1	0	0	0	2,495
Dearborn	4	0	0	0	0	0	4	0	0	0	93,889
Dearborn Heights	1	1	1	0	0	0	1	1	0	1	55,454
Detroit	22	2	15	0	2	0	15	10	9	7	670,792
East Grand Rapids	1	0	0	0	0	0	0	0	0	1	11,812
East Lansing	2	1	0	0	0	0	0	1	2	0	48,920
Eastpointe	1	0	0	0	0	0	0	1	0	0	32,712
Ecorse	2	0	0	0	0	0	0	0	2	0	9,132
Escanaba	0	1	0	0	0	0	0	0	1	0	12,280
Farmington Hills	0	1	0	0	0	0	1	0	0	0	81,359
Ferndale	4	0	1	0	0	0	2	0	1	2	20,131
Flint	9	0	1	0	0	0	2	3	4	1	96,605
Fremont	1	0	0	0	0	0	0	0	1	0	4,020
Gaines Township	1	0	0	0	0	0	1	0	0	0	6,139
Galesburg	2	0	0	0	0	0	0	0	1	1	2,055
Gaylord	2	0	0	0	0	0	0	0	1	1	3,697
Grand Blanc	1	0	0	0	0	0	1	0	0	0	7,904
Grand Rapids	5	1	4	0	0	0	1	0	6	3	197,868
Grandville	0	2	0	0	0	0	0	1	1	0	16,108
Grosse Pointe	0	1	0	0	0	0	1	0	0	0	5,151
Grosse Pointe Farms	0	0	1	0	0	0	0	0	1	0	9,106
Hampton Township	1	0	0	0	0	0	1	0	0	0	9,522
Hamtramck	1	1	0	0	0	0	0	1	0	1	21,654
Hart	4	1	0	0	0	0	1	3	0	1	2,080
Highland Park	2	0	0	0	0	0	0	1	0	1	10,757
Holland	3	0	0	0	0	0	2	1	0	0	33,613
Huntington Woods	0	1	0	0	0	0	0	1	0	0	6,343
Huron Township	1	0	0	0	0	0	1	0	0	0	15,636
Independence Township	1	0	0	0	0	0	0	1	0	0	36,836
Inkster	1	0	0	0	0	0	1	0	0	0	24,324
Ionia	1	0	1	0	0	0	0	2	0	0	11,287
Iron River	1	0	0	0	0	0	0	0	0	1	2,838
Lansing	10	0	2	0	0	0	2	2	6	2	116,302
Lansing Township	0	0	1	0	0	0	0	1	0	0	8,150
Lapeer	0	1	0	0	0	0	1	0	0	0	8,735
Lincoln Park	2	0	0	0	0	0	0	0	2	0	36,502
Lincoln Township	1	0	0	0	0	0	1	0	0	0	14,460
Ludington	1	0	0	0	0	0	0	0	1	0	8,068
Madison Heights	1	0	0	0	0	0	1	0	0	0	30,152
Manistee	1	0	0	0	0	0	0	0	1	0	6,030
Meridian Township	2	1	6	0	0	0	2	0	6	1	42,878
Metro Police Authority of Genesee County	0	1	0	0	0	0	0	1	0	0	20,001
Midland	1	0	0	0	0	0	1	0	0	0	42,131
Millington	1	0	0	0	0	0	1	0	0	0	1,016
Monroe	1	0	0	0	0	0	1	0	0	0	19,868
Mount Pleasant	1	0	1	0	0	0	1	0	1	0	26,366
Muskegon	4	0	0	0	0	0	0	0	4	0	38,375
Northville Township	2	0	0	0	0	0	0	0	2	0	28,751
Oak Park	0	2	0	0	0	0	0	0	2	0	29,698
Ovid	1	0	0	0	0	0	0	0	1	0	1,615
Perry	2	0	0	0	0	0	0	2	0	0	2,094
Petoskey	1	0	0	0	0	0	0	0	1	0	5,764
Pinckney	0	0	0	1	0	0	0	0	1	0	2,463
Pittsfield Township	1	0	0	0	0	0	0	0	0	1	39,061
Pontiac	2	0	0	0	0	0	0	0	1	1	59,731
Portland	1	0	0	0	0	0	0	1	0	0	3,943
Raisin Township	1	0	0	0	0	0	1	0	0	0	7,619
Redford Township	1	0	0	0	0	0	0	1	0	0	46,867
Rochester Hills	1	2	1	0	0	0	1	0	0	3	73,827
Romulus	2	0	0	0	0	0	0	1	1	0	23,174

Table 13. Hate Crime Incidents Per Bias Motivation and Quarter, by Selected State and Agency, 2017—Continued

(Number.)

State/agency	Race/Ethnicity/Ancestry	Religion	Sexual orientation	Disability	Gender	Gender Identity	1st quarter	2nd quarter	3rd quarter	4th quarter	Population[1]
Roosevelt Park	0	1	0	0	0	0	0	0	1	0	3,826
Roseville	6	1	0	0	0	0	2	2	3	0	47,651
Royal Oak	1	0	0	0	0	0	0	0	1	0	59,303
Saginaw	3	0	0	0	0	0	0	0	2	1	48,589
Saginaw Township	2	0	0	0	0	0	1	0	0	1	39,319
Saline	1	0	0	0	0	0	0	0	1	0	9,207
Sault Ste. Marie	1	0	0	0	0	0	1	0	0	0	13,630
Schoolcraft	1	0	0	0	0	0	0	1	0	0	1,571
Shelby Township	4	2	0	0	0	0	2	1	2	1	79,217
Southfield	2	3	0	0	0	0	2	0	2	1	73,324
Southgate	4	0	0	0	0	0	0	0	0	4	28,939
Sparta	1	0	0	0	0	0	0	0	1	0	4,370
St. Joseph	1	0	0	0	0	0	0	0	1	0	8,276
Tawas	1	0	0	0	0	0	1	0	0	0	4,522
Taylor	3	0	0	0	0	0	0	2	1	0	60,882
Thomas Township	0	1	0	0	0	0	0	0	1	0	11,450
Traverse City	0	3	1	0	0	0	0	2	2	0	15,617
Trenton	0	1	0	0	0	0	1	0	0	0	18,161
Troy	3	0	0	0	1	0	0	2	2	0	84,086
Van Buren Township	2	0	0	0	0	0	1	0	1	0	27,911
Warren	1	0	0	0	0	0	1	0	0	0	135,303
Wayne	1	0	0	0	0	0	0	0	1	0	16,857
West Bloomfield Township	0	3	0	0	0	0	2	1	0	0	65,948
Westland	2	0	0	0	0	0	0	0	0	2	81,158
White Lake Township	1	0	0	0	0	0	0	1	0	0	31,016
Wyandotte	2	0	0	0	0	0	0	1	0	1	24,817
Wyoming	4	0	0	0	0	0	0	0	4	0	76,153
Universities and Colleges	14	5	4	0	1	0					
Eastern Michigan University	3	0	0	0	0	0	0	1	2	0	21,246
Grand Valley State University	0	0	2	0	0	0	0	0	2	0	25,460
Michigan State University	1	0	0	0	0	0	0	0	1	0	50,340
Oakland University	1	0	0	0	0	0	0	0	0	1	20,012
Saginaw Valley State University	0	0	0	0	1	0	0	0	0	1	9,105
University of Michigan											
Ann Arbor	9	4	2	0	0	0	4	0	5	6	44,718
Dearborn	0	1	0	0	0	0	0	1	0	0	9,131
Metropolitan Counties	15	10	2	0	0	0					
Eaton	1	0	0	0	0	0	0	0	1	0	
Genesee	2	2	0	0	0	0	1	1	0	2	
Jackson	0	2	0	0	0	0	0	2	0	0	
Kent	3	0	0	0	0	0	0	1	1	1	
Lapeer	0	1	0	0	0	0	0	1	0	0	
Midland	1	0	0	0	0	0	0	1	0	0	
Monroe	0	1	0	0	0	0	0	1	0	0	
Muskegon	0	0	1	0	0	0	1	0	0	0	
Ottawa	1	1	1	0	0	0	0	0	2	1	
Saginaw	0	1	0	0	0	0	0	1	0	0	
Van Buren	3	2	0	0	0	0	0	1	4	0	
Washtenaw	4	0	0	0	0	0	3	0	1	0	
Nonmetropolitan Counties	17	3	4	0	2	0					
Allegan	1	0	0	0	0	0	0	0	1	0	
Benzie	3	0	0	0	0	0	0	1	0	2	
Charlevoix	0	0	1	0	0	0	0	0	1	0	
Chippewa	1	1	1	0	0	0	0	1	1	1	
Clare	1	0	0	0	0	0	0	0	1	0	
Emmet	1	0	0	0	0	0	0	0	1	0	
Grand Traverse	2	0	0	0	0	0	0	1	1	0	
Gratiot	1	1	1	0	0	0	2	0	1	0	
Huron	1	0	0	0	0	0	0	1	0	0	
Mackinac	1	0	0	0	0	0	0	0	1	0	
Menominee	2	1	0	0	0	0	0	1	1	1	
Missaukee	1	0	0	0	0	0	0	0	1	0	
Newaygo	0	0	0	0	1	0	0	1	0	0	
Ontonagon	0	0	1	0	0	0	0	1	0	0	

Table 13. Hate Crime Incidents Per Bias Motivation and Quarter, by Selected State and Agency, 2017—Continued

(Number.)

State/agency	Number of incidents per bias motivation						Number of incidents per quarter				Population[1]
	Race/ Ethnicity/ Ancestry	Religion	Sexual orientation	Disability	Gender	Gender Identity	1st quarter	2nd quarter	3rd quarter	4th quarter	
Otsego	0	0	0	0	1	0	0	1	0	0	
Presque Isle	2	0	0	0	0	0	0	1	1	0	
State Police Agencies	50	6	3	1	1	0					
State Police											
Alpena County	2	0	0	0	0	0	0	0	2	0	
Barry County	3	0	0	0	0	0	0	0	3	0	
Bay County	2	0	1	0	0	0	0	1	2	0	
Berrien County	1	0	0	0	0	0	0	0	1	0	
Chippewa County	2	0	0	0	0	0	0	0	0	2	
Clare County	1	0	0	0	0	0	0	1	0	0	
Crawford County	1	0	0	0	0	0	0	0	0	1	
Eaton County	1	0	0	0	0	0	0	0	1	0	
Genesee County	1	0	0	0	0	0	0	0	1	0	
Gogebic County	2	0	0	0	0	0	1	0	1	0	
Isabella County	1	0	0	0	0	0	0	0	0	1	
Jackson County	3	0	1	0	0	0	1	1	1	1	
Kalamazoo County	2	0	0	0	0	0	0	1	0	1	
Kent County	3	0	0	0	0	0	0	0	1	2	
Lapeer County	1	1	0	0	0	0	0	0	1	1	
Livingston County	4	2	1	0	0	0	2	3	2	0	
Macomb County	1	0	0	0	0	0	0	0	0	1	
Mason County	0	1	0	0	0	0	0	0	0	1	
Monroe County	2	0	0	0	0	0	0	2	0	0	
Montcalm County	2	0	0	0	0	0	0	0	1	1	
Muskegon County	1	0	0	0	0	0	0	0	0	1	
Oakland County	2	0	0	1	0	0	0	2	1	0	
Oceana County	1	0	0	0	0	0	0	1	0	0	
Osceola County	1	0	0	0	0	0	0	0	1	0	
Saginaw County	2	1	0	0	0	0	0	1	1	1	
Shiawassee County	3	0	0	0	0	0	0	2	1	0	
St. Joseph County	1	0	0	0	0	0	0	1	0	0	
Van Buren County	0	1	0	0	1	0	2	0	0	0	
Washtenaw County	2	0	0	0	0	0	0	0	0	2	
Wayne County	1	0	0	0	0	0	1	0	0	0	
Wexford County	1	0	0	0	0	0	0	0	0	1	
Tribal Agencies	3	0	0	0	0	0					
Little River Band of Ottawa Indians	2	0	0	0	0	0	0	2	0	0	
Nottawaseppi Huron Band of Potawatomi	1	0	0	0	0	0	0	0	1	0	
Other Agencies	0	1	0	0	0	0					
Wayne County Airport	0	1	0	0	0	0	1	0	0	0	
MINNESOTA											
Total	92	34	22	0	0	0					
Cities	80	31	21	0	0	0					
Apple Valley	1	0	0	0	0	0	0	0	1	0	52,439
Belle Plaine	1	0	0	0	0	0	0	0	0	1	7,066
Blaine	3	0	0	0	0	0	1	1	0	1	63,857
Brooklyn Park	5	0	1	0	0	0	0	3	3	0	80,347
Burnsville	1	0	1	0	0	0	0	1	1	0	61,442
Clearbrook	1	0	0	0	0	0	0	1	0	0	522
Coon Rapids	0	1	0	0	0	0	0	0	1	0	62,495
Crookston	0	1	0	0	0	0	0	1	0	0	7,789
Duluth	1	0	1	0	0	0	1	0	1	0	86,306
Eden Prairie	1	0	0	0	0	0	0	0	0	1	64,429
Edina	0	1	0	0	0	0	0	0	1	0	51,923
Forest Lake	0	0	1	0	0	0	1	0	0	0	19,804
Fridley	0	0	1	0	0	0	0	0	1	0	27,516
Goodhue	1	0	0	0	0	0	0	0	0	1	1,186
Inver Grove Heights	4	1	0	0	0	0	0	3	0	2	35,254
Lakeville[2]	4	2	1	0	0	0	3	0	1	2	62,958
Mankato	1	0	0	0	0	0	0	0	0	1	42,047
Maple Grove	2	2	0	0	0	0	0	0	1	3	70,966
Maplewood	5	0	0	0	0	0	1	0	3	1	40,689

Table 13. Hate Crime Incidents Per Bias Motivation and Quarter, by Selected State and Agency, 2017—*Continued*

(Number.)

State/agency	Number of incidents per bias motivation						Number of incidents per quarter				Population[1]
	Race/Ethnicity/Ancestry	Religion	Sexual orientation	Disability	Gender	Gender Identity	1st quarter	2nd quarter	3rd quarter	4th quarter	
Minneapolis	16	7	8	0	0	0	10	9	8	4	418,971
Moorhead	2	0	1	0	0	0	3	0	0	0	42,999
New Brighton	1	0	0	0	0	0	0	0	1	0	22,772
Northfield	1	0	0	0	0	0	0	1	0	0	20,512
Oakdale	1	0	0	0	0	0	1	0	0	0	28,181
Plymouth	0	1	0	0	0	0	0	0	0	1	78,356
Rochester	10	3	0	0	0	0	3	3	3	4	115,228
Roseville	0	0	1	0	0	0	0	1	0	0	36,196
Sartell	0	0	1	0	0	0	0	0	1	0	17,353
Savage	1	0	1	0	0	0	1	0	1	0	31,491
Spring Lake Park	1	0	0	0	0	0	1	0	0	0	6,482
St. Anthony	1	0	0	0	0	0	0	0	0	1	9,159
St. Cloud	1	1	0	0	0	0	1	0	1	0	67,911
Stillwater	0	1	0	0	0	0	0	0	1	0	19,394
St. Louis Park[2]	3	4	2	0	0	0	3	1	2	2	49,355
St. Paul	11	5	1	0	0	0	5	8	2	2	306,696
Willmar	0	1	0	0	0	0	0	0	1	0	19,553
Universities and Colleges	3	2	0	0	0	0					
University of Minnesota, Twin Cities	3	2	0	0	0	0	2	2	1	0	51,579
Metropolitan Counties	9	0	1	0	0	0					
Benton	1	0	0	0	0	0	1	0	0	0	
Carver	5	0	0	0	0	0	1	1	2	1	
Ramsey	2	0	0	0	0	0	1	1	0	0	
Wright	1	0	1	0	0	0	1	0	0	1	
Nonmetropolitan Counties	0	1	0	0	0	0					
Otter Tail	0	1	0	0	0	0	1	0	0	0	
MISSISSIPPI											
Total	1	0	0	0	0	0					
Cities	1	0	0	0	0	0					
Gulfport	1	0	0	0	0	0	0	0	0	1	72,792
MISSOURI											
Total	79	11	13	0	1	1					
Cities	72	7	13	0	1	1					
Blue Springs	2	0	0	0	0	0	1	1	0	0	54,727
Branson	1	0	0	0	0	0	1	0	0	0	11,571
Camdenton	0	0	1	0	0	0	0	0	0	1	3,980
Cameron	3	0	0	0	0	0	0	2	0	1	9,765
Columbia	1	0	0	0	0	0	1	0	0	0	122,585
Crystal City	0	0	1	0	0	0	0	0	1	0	4,817
Festus	0	0	1	0	0	0	0	1	0	0	12,187
Gladstone	2	1	0	0	0	0	1	0	1	1	27,390
Grain Valley	2	0	0	0	0	0	0	0	1	1	13,825
Grandview	1	0	0	0	0	0	0	1	0	0	25,308
Independence	4	0	0	0	0	0	2	1	0	1	117,055
Joplin	0	0	1	0	0	0	0	0	0	1	52,412
Kansas City	34	5	6	0	1	1	6	19	16	6	484,948
Lee's Summit	1	0	0	0	0	0	1	0	0	0	96,855
Macon	1	0	0	0	0	0	0	0	1	0	5,360
Maryland Heights	1	0	0	0	0	0	0	0	0	1	27,083
Normandy	1	0	0	0	0	0	0	1	0	0	7,544
North Kansas City	1	0	0	0	0	0	0	1	0	0	4,407
Overland	1	0	0	0	0	0	0	1	0	0	15,760
Rolla	2	0	3	0	0	0	2	1	2	0	20,147
St. Louis	11	0	0	0	0	0	3	4	2	2	310,284
University City	1	0	0	0	0	0	0	1	0	0	34,601
Warrenton	1	0	0	0	0	0	0	1	0	0	8,168
Wentzville	1	0	0	0	0	0	0	1	0	0	38,876
Willard	0	1	0	0	0	0	0	1	0	0	5,452

Table 13. Hate Crime Incidents Per Bias Motivation and Quarter, by Selected State and Agency, 2017—Continued

(Number.)

State/agency	Number of incidents per bias motivation						Number of incidents per quarter				Population[1]
	Race/ Ethnicity/ Ancestry	Religion	Sexual orientation	Disability	Gender	Gender Identity	1st quarter	2nd quarter	3rd quarter	4th quarter	
Universities and Colleges	2	2	0	0	0	0					
St. Louis Community College, Meramec................	2	1	0	0	0	0	2	0	1	0	19,052
University of Missouri, Columbia...................	0	1	0	0	0	0	1	0	0	0	33,239
Metropolitan Counties	3	2	0	0	0	0					
Greene................	2	0	0	0	0	0	0	1	1	0	
St. Louis County Police Department...............	0	2	0	0	0	0	1	0	1	0	
Warren................	1	0	0	0	0	0	0	0	1	0	
Nonmetropolitan Counties..................	2	0	0	0	0	0					
Laclede................	1	0	0	0	0	0	0	0	0	1	
Taney................	1	0	0	0	0	0	1	0	0	0	
MONTANA											
Total	9	4	2	0	0	0					
Cities	3	2	0	0	0	0					
Bozeman................	0	2	0	0	0	0	1	0	1	0	46,728
Kalispell................	2	0	0	0	0	0	0	2	0	0	23,243
Whitefish................	1	0	0	0	0	0	0	0	1	0	7,446
Universities and Colleges	2	0	0	0	0	0					
Montana State University................	1	0	0	0	0	0	1	0	0	0	16,359
University of Montana................	1	0	0	0	0	0	0	0	0	1	12,419
Metropolitan Counties	3	1	1	0	0	0					
Cascade................	1	0	0	0	0	0	1	0	0	0	
Missoula................	1	1	0	0	0	0	0	0	2	0	
Yellowstone................	1	0	1	0	0	0	1	1	0	0	
Nonmetropolitan Counties..................	1	1	1	0	0	0					
Deer Lodge................	0	0	1	0	0	0	0	0	1	0	
Gallatin................	1	0	0	0	0	0	0	0	1	0	
Ravalli................	0	1	0	0	0	0	0	0	1	0	
NEBRASKA											
Total	34	6	4	1	0	0					
Cities	29	6	4	0	0	0					
Grand Island................	1	0	1	0	0	0	0	1	0	1	51,980
Kearney................	1	0	0	0	0	0	0	0	0	1	33,960
Lincoln................	21	5	3	0	0	0	3	5	10	11	284,063
Norfolk................	2	0	0	0	0	0	0	0	1	1	24,364
Omaha................	2	1	0	0	0	0	1	1	1	0	449,388
South Sioux City................	2	0	0	0	0	0	1	0	0	1	13,078
Metropolitan Counties	5	0	0	0	0	0					
Merrick................	4	0	0	0	0	0	0	0	2	2	
Saunders................	1	0	0	0	0	0	0	0	0	1	
Nonmetropolitan Counties..................	0	0	0	1	0	0					
Perkins................	0	0	0	1	0	0	0	0	0	1	
NEVADA											
Total	2	0	3	0	0	0					
Cities	1	0	3	0	0	0					
Henderson................	1	0	0	0	0	0	0	0	0	1	299,285
Reno................	0	0	3	0	0	0	1	2	0	0	248,531
Other Agencies................	1	0	0	0	0	0					
Clark County School District................	1	0	0	0	0	0	0	0	1	0	
NEW HAMPSHIRE											
Total	8	4	1	0	0	0					

Table 13. Hate Crime Incidents Per Bias Motivation and Quarter, by Selected State and Agency, 2017—Continued

(Number.)

State/agency	Number of incidents per bias motivation						Number of incidents per quarter				Population[1]
	Race/ Ethnicity/ Ancestry	Religion	Sexual orientation	Disability	Gender	Gender Identity	1st quarter	2nd quarter	3rd quarter	4th quarter	
Cities	7	4	0	0	0	0					
Concord	1	0	0	0	0	0	0	1	0	0	42,942
Dover..	1	0	0	0	0	0	1	0	0	0	31,344
Epping	0	1	0	0	0	0	1	0	0	0	6,978
Hudson..	1	0	0	0	0	0	1	0	0	0	25,212
Keene..	0	1	0	0	0	0	0	0	0	1	23,386
Laconia..	1	0	0	0	0	0	0	1	0	0	16,616
Manchester....................................	0	1	0	0	0	0	0	1	0	0	110,655
Pelham..	1	0	0	0	0	0	0	0	1	0	13,513
Plymouth	0	1	0	0	0	0	0	0	0	1	6,303
Rye	1	0	0	0	0	0	0	1	0	0	5,425
Seabrook	1	0	0	0	0	0	0	1	0	0	8,816
Universities and Colleges	0	0	1	0	0	0					
University of New Hampshire	0	0	1	0	0	0	0	0	0	1	15,188
State Police Agencies..........................	1	0	0	0	0	0					
State Police, Grafton County.....................	1	0	0	0	0	0	0	1	0	0	
NEW JERSEY											
Total	260	180	51	4	0	0					
Cities	241	163	41	3	0	0					
Aberdeen Township...........................	2	3	1	0	0	0	3	1	2	0	18,403
Belmar..	0	0	1	0	0	0	0	1	0	0	5,666
Belvidere.......................................	1	0	0	0	0	0	0	0	0	1	2,589
Bergenfield....................................	0	2	0	0	0	0	0	2	0	0	27,891
Berkeley Heights Township	1	0	0	0	0	0	0	0	1	0	13,654
Berkeley Township............................	0	1	0	0	0	0	0	0	1	0	42,036
Boonton	0	1	0	0	0	0	0	1	0	0	8,421
Bradley Beach	1	1	0	0	0	0	1	1	0	0	4,236
Brick Township	0	2	0	0	0	0	0	0	2	0	75,566
Bridgeton.......................................	1	0	0	0	0	0	0	1	0	0	24,937
Bridgewater Township	0	1	0	0	0	0	0	0	0	1	45,417
Brigantine......................................	0	1	0	0	0	0	0	0	1	0	8,976
Burlington Township	1	0	0	0	0	0	0	1	0	0	22,772
Carteret...	1	0	0	0	0	0	1	0	0	0	24,283
Chatham	0	1	0	0	0	0	0	1	0	0	9,011
Chatham Township............................	1	0	0	0	0	0	1	0	0	0	10,515
Cinnaminson Township.......................	2	3	1	0	0	0	2	3	0	1	16,696
Collingswood...................................	1	0	0	0	0	0	0	0	0	1	14,080
Colts Neck Township	2	0	0	0	0	0	2	0	0	0	9,936
Deal..	0	2	0	0	0	0	0	2	0	0	730
Delanco Township	2	0	0	0	0	0	2	0	0	0	4,528
Dover..	1	0	1	0	0	0	1	1	0	0	18,339
Eastampton Township........................	1	0	0	0	0	0	1	0	0	0	5,962
East Brunswick Township....................	11	13	0	0	0	0	4	13	5	2	49,019
East Hanover Township......................	2	1	0	0	0	0	1	2	0	0	11,284
East Orange....................................	1	1	0	0	0	0	0	1	1	0	65,160
East Windsor Township.......................	1	0	0	0	0	0	0	0	0	1	27,571
Eatontown......................................	0	0	1	0	0	0	0	0	0	1	12,258
Edison Township...............................	6	3	1	0	0	0	2	2	4	2	102,699
Egg Harbor Township	1	0	0	0	0	0	0	0	0	1	43,515
Elizabeth..	0	1	0	0	0	0	1	0	0	0	129,726
Elmwood Park..................................	1	0	0	0	0	0	0	0	0	1	20,515
Emerson...	0	1	0	0	0	0	0	1	0	0	7,747
Englewood	8	1	0	0	0	0	0	1	0	8	28,795
Evesham Township	10	7	0	1	0	0	2	4	5	7	45,314
Fair Lawn.......................................	0	0	1	0	0	0	0	0	0	1	33,759
Fort Lee...	1	0	1	0	0	0	0	1	1	0	38,095
Franklin Lakes.................................	1	5	0	0	0	0	0	1	0	5	10,939
Franklin Township, Somerset County	1	0	0	0	0	0	1	0	0	0	67,463
Freehold Borough	1	0	0	0	0	0	0	0	0	1	11,865
Freehold Township............................	2	0	1	0	0	0	2	0	1	0	35,531
Hackensack.....................................	4	4	1	0	0	0	1	0	2	6	45,226
Hackettstown	1	0	0	0	0	0	1	0	0	0	9,520

Table 13. Hate Crime Incidents Per Bias Motivation and Quarter, by Selected State and Agency, 2017—Continued

(Number.)

State/agency	Number of incidents per bias motivation						Number of incidents per quarter				Population[1]
	Race/ Ethnicity/ Ancestry	Religion	Sexual orientation	Disability	Gender	Gender Identity	1st quarter	2nd quarter	3rd quarter	4th quarter	
Haddonfield	1	0	0	0	0	0	1	0	0	0	11,445
Haddon Township	2	0	0	0	0	0	1	1	0	0	14,731
Hamilton Township, Mercer County	5	0	0	0	0	0	1	1	1	2	88,723
Hanover Township	1	4	0	0	0	0	4	1	0	0	14,904
Harrison Township	0	0	1	0	0	0	0	0	0	1	13,128
Haworth	0	2	0	0	0	0	0	0	0	2	3,491
High Bridge	0	1	0	0	0	0	0	1	0	0	3,524
Highland Park	2	2	0	0	0	0	1	1	1	1	14,287
Hightstown	2	0	0	0	0	0	1	1	0	0	5,522
Hillsborough Township	3	1	0	0	0	0	1	2	0	1	40,369
Hoboken	3	3	0	0	0	0	4	1	0	1	55,348
Hopewell Township	1	0	2	0	0	0	1	2	0	0	18,633
Howell Township	7	4	0	0	0	0	4	2	4	1	52,432
Interlaken	0	0	1	0	0	0	0	1	0	0	798
Jefferson Township	1	0	0	0	0	0	1	0	0	0	21,505
Jersey City	0	0	1	0	0	0	1	0	0	0	267,906
Keansburg	8	1	1	0	0	0	0	1	7	2	9,782
Kinnelon	1	0	0	0	0	0	0	1	0	0	10,275
Lakewood Township	7	15	0	0	0	0	4	6	7	5	102,759
Lawrence Township, Mercer County	0	2	0	0	0	0	0	1	0	1	32,929
Lindenwold	0	0	1	0	0	0	0	0	0	1	17,516
Livingston Township	2	1	0	0	0	0	1	1	0	1	29,987
Lodi	2	0	3	0	0	0	3	1	0	1	24,981
Lopatcong Township	0	1	0	0	0	0	1	0	0	0	8,298
Lumberton Township	0	1	0	0	0	0	0	0	1	0	12,286
Madison	1	2	0	0	0	0	1	1	0	1	16,175
Magnolia	2	0	0	0	0	0	1	1	0	0	4,310
Manalapan Township	4	4	0	0	0	0	1	2	4	1	40,177
Manasquan	2	0	0	0	0	0	1	0	1	0	5,804
Manchester Township	1	0	0	0	0	0	1	0	0	0	43,916
Mansfield Township, Warren County	0	1	0	0	0	0	0	1	0	0	7,435
Mantua Township	1	0	0	0	0	0	0	0	0	1	15,123
Maple Shade Township	1	2	0	0	0	0	1	1	0	1	18,797
Maplewood Township	0	1	0	0	0	0	1	0	0	0	24,863
Medford Lakes	1	1	0	0	0	0	0	0	2	0	4,038
Medford Township	3	2	2	0	0	0	1	1	0	5	23,503
Metuchen	0	0	0	1	0	0	1	0	0	0	13,981
Middlesex Borough	1	1	0	0	0	0	1	0	1	0	13,897
Millburn Township	0	1	0	0	0	0	0	0	0	1	20,421
Monmouth Beach	0	1	0	0	0	0	0	0	0	1	3,213
Monroe Township, Middlesex County	0	3	0	0	0	0	0	0	0	3	45,722
Montclair	2	0	0	0	0	0	0	0	1	1	39,029
Montvale	0	1	0	0	0	0	1	0	0	0	8,653
Moorestown Township	4	1	0	0	0	0	1	2	1	1	20,534
Mount Laurel Township	0	0	1	0	0	0	1	0	0	0	41,712
Mount Olive Township	1	0	1	0	0	0	0	0	0	2	29,410
Mullica Township	1	0	0	0	0	0	0	0	0	1	6,024
Neptune Township	6	0	1	0	0	0	4	1	0	2	27,757
New Brunswick	1	0	2	0	0	0	2		1		57,481
Newton	0	1	1	0	0	0	0	0	1	1	7,874
North Bergen Township	0	1	0	0	0	0	1	0	0	0	63,490
Northfield	1	0	0	0	0	0	1	0	0	0	8,376
Oakland	0	1	0	0	0	0	0	0	0	1	13,243
Ocean Township, Monmouth County	3	3	0	0	0	0	1	3	2	0	26,637
Old Bridge Township	2	0	0	0	0	0	1	0	1	0	67,162
Old Tappan	0	1	0	0	0	0	0	0	1	0	6,069
Oradell	0	2	0	0	0	0	0	2	0	0	8,291
Palmyra	1	0	1	0	0	0	0	1	0	1	7,217
Paramus	1	1	0	0	0	0	1	0	1	0	27,075
Passaic	1	1	1	0	0	0	0	0	2	1	71,053
Paulsboro	1	0	0	0	0	0	0	0	1	0	5,959
Pennsville Township	1	0	0	0	0	0	0	0	1	0	12,564
Pequannock Township	0	1	0	0	0	0	1	0	0	0	15,472
Piscataway Township	0	1	0	0	0	0	1	0	0	0	58,109
Plainfield	0	1	0	0	0	0	1	0	0	0	50,983
Point Pleasant	0	1	0	0	0	0	1	0	0	0	18,696
Pompton Lakes	1	0	0	0	0	0	0	0	0	1	11,176

State/agency	Number of incidents per bias motivation						Number of incidents per quarter				Population[1]
	Race/ Ethnicity/ Ancestry	Religion	Sexual orientation	Disability	Gender	Gender Identity	1st quarter	2nd quarter	3rd quarter	4th quarter	
Princeton	8	7	0	0	0	0	1	6	5	3	31,845
Ramsey	1	1	0	0	0	0	0	0	1	1	15,273
Randolph Township	4	4	0	0	0	0	4	2	0	2	25,950
Ridgewood	0	4	0	0	0	0	0	0	3	1	25,729
River Edge	0	1	0	0	0	0	0	1	0	0	11,744
Robbinsville Township	3	0	0	0	0	0	1	0	2	0	14,446
Roselle Park	1	0	0	0	0	0	0	0	1	0	13,747
Shrewsbury	0	1	0	0	0	0	0	1	0	0	4,178
South Brunswick Township	1	2	1	0	0	0	2	0	1	1	46,280
South Orange Village	4	1	1	0	0	0	3	0	1	2	16,407
South Plainfield	1	0	0	0	0	0	1	0	0	0	24,458
South River	1	0	0	0	0	0	0	1	0	0	16,399
Springfield Township, Union County	1	0	0	0	0	0	1	0	0	0	17,805
Stone Harbor	0	0	2	0	0	0	0	1	1	0	827
Summit	0	1	0	0	0	0	0	1	0	0	22,195
Teaneck Township	2	1	0	0	0	0	0	1	1	1	41,377
Tenafly	0	1	0	0	0	0	0	1	0	0	14,960
Toms River Township	1	3	0	0	0	0	2	1	1	0	92,543
Trenton	0	1	0	0	0	0	1	0	0	0	84,231
Union City	1	0	0	0	0	0	0	1	0	0	70,053
Union Township	1	0	0	0	0	0	1	0	0	0	59,051
Verona	1	0	0	0	0	0	1	0	0	0	13,584
Vineland	8	0	1	0	0	0	1	0	4	4	60,477
Voorhees Township	1	0	0	0	0	0	0	0	1	0	29,532
Washington Township, Gloucester County	1	0	1	0	0	0	0	1	1	0	48,088
Washington Township, Warren County	1	0	0	0	0	0	0	1	0	0	6,429
Waterford Township	2	0	0	0	0	0	1	0	1	0	10,817
Weehawken Township	2	0	0	0	0	0	0	0	0	2	15,683
Westampton Township	2	0	0	0	0	0	0	1	1	0	8,775
West Long Branch	1	0	1	0	0	0	1	0	0	1	7,944
West New York	1	0	0	0	0	0	0	0	1	0	54,156
West Windsor Township	1	1	0	0	0	0	2	0	0	0	28,495
Wildwood	1	0	0	0	0	0	0	0	1	0	5,087
Willingboro Township	0	2	0	0	0	0	0	0	2	0	31,726
Woodbridge Township	0	2	0	0	0	0	1	0	0	1	102,129
Woodbury	27	1	4	1	0	0	4	10	14	5	9,970
Universities and Colleges	12	15	10	0	0	0					
Montclair State University	3	1	1	0	0	0	2	1	2		20,987
Princeton University	3	0	0	0	0	0				3	8,181
Rutgers University											
Newark	0	2	0	0	0	0				2	12,321
New Brunswick	4	12	9	0	0	0	6	7	3	9	50,146
Stockton University	2	0	0	0	0	0			2		8,728
Metropolitan Counties	3	1	0	0	0	0					
Bergen	1	1	0	0	0	0	2				
Cape May	1	0	0	0	0	0		1			
Warren	1	0	0	0	0	0				1	
State Police Agencies	4	1	0	1	0	0					
New Jersey State Police	4	1	0	1	0	0	4			2	
NEW MEXICO											
Total	4	2	1	0	0	0					
Cities	4	2	1	0	0	0					
Albuquerque	4	2	1	0	0	0			4	3	561,375
NEW YORK											
Total	189	284	64	1	0	14					
Cities	127	194	55	1	0	13					
Albany	4	0	0	0	0	0	0	0	2	2	98,174
Ardsley Village	0	1	0	0	0	0	1	0	0	0	4,663
Auburn	1	0	0	0	0	0	0	1	0		26,686
Brighton Town	0	1	0	0	0	0	0	0	1	0	36,596

(Number.)

State/agency	Number of incidents per bias motivation						Number of incidents per quarter				Population[1]
	Race/ Ethnicity/ Ancestry	Religion	Sexual orientation	Disability	Gender	Gender Identity	1st quarter	2nd quarter	3rd quarter	4th quarter	
Buffalo..........	6	0	2	0	0	0	2	4	2	0	256,169
Clarkstown Town..........	0	2	0	0	0	0	0	1	0	1	81,810
Croton-on-Hudson Village	0	0	0	1	0	0	0	1	0	0	8,271
Fishkill Town..........	1	0	0	0	0	0	0	1	0	0	21,532
Fulton City..........	1	0	0	0	0	0	0	1	0	0	11,321
Gates Town	1	0	0	0	0	0	0	0	0	1	28,723
Greenburgh Town	0	1	0	0	0	1	1	0	1	0	45,923
Hamburg Town..........	1	0	0	0	0	0	0	0	1	0	46,040
Hastings-on-Hudson Village	0	3	0	0	0	0	0	1	1	1	7,987
Hempstead Village	0	0	1	0	0	0	0	1	0	0	55,807
Ilion Village..........	1	0	0	0	0	0	0	0	1	0	7,801
Ithaca	2	0	0	0	0	0	0	1	1	0	30,875
Johnson City Village..........	1	0	0	0	0	0	0	0	1	0	14,595
Liberty Village..........	1	0	0	0	0	0	0	0	1	0	4,050
Middletown..........	0	1	0	0	0	0	0	0	1	0	27,607
Monroe Village..........	2	0	0	0	0	0	0	0	2	0	8,636
Mount Vernon	2	0	0	0	0	0	0	0	1	1	68,507
New Castle Town..........	1	1	0	0	0	0	2				18,189
New Paltz Town and Village..........	0	1	0	0	0	0	1	0	0	0	14,125
New Rochelle..........	4	1	0	0	0	0	2	0	1	2	79,960
New York	88	173	46	0	0	11	96	82	68	72	8,616,333
Niagara Falls	3	0	0	0	0	0	0	1	2	0	48,385
Port Jervis	0	0	1	0	0	0	0		1	0	8,527
Poughkeepsie	1	0	0	0	0	1	0	0	1	1	30,159
Ramapo Town	0	4	0	0	0	0	0	2	2	0	94,019
Rochester..........	1	0	2	0	0	0	0	2	1	0	208,591
Schodack Town	1	0	0	0	0	0	0	1	0	0	11,685
Scotia Village	0	0	1	0	0	0	1	0	0	0	7,651
Southampton Town	1	1	1	0	0	0	1	0	1	1	50,987
Spring Valley Village..........	0	1	0	0	0	0	0	1	0	0	32,795
Troy..........	0	0	1	0	0	0	1	0	0	0	49,644
Utica..........	0	1	0	0	0	0	0	0	1	0	60,395
White Plains..........	1	0	0	0	0	0	0	1	0	0	58,461
Yonkers	2	2	0	0	0	0	2	0	2	0	201,554
Universities and Colleges	5	7	2	0	0	0					
State University of New York Police											
Buffalo State College	0	0	1	0	0	0	1	0	0	0	9,475
Cobleskill..........	1	0	0	0	0	0	0	0	1	0	2,287
Delhi..........	0	1	0	0	0	0	0	0	0	1	3,511
Geneseo	1	0	1	0	0	0	1	0	1	0	5,602
Morrisville	2	3	0	0	0	0	0	0	1	4	3,003
New Paltz	0	2	0	0	0	0	0	0	0	2	7,628
Plattsburgh	1	1	0	0	0	0	2	0	0	0	5,520
Metropolitan Counties	18	54	3	0	0	0					
Nassau..........	9	28	0	0	0	0	14	9	9	5	
Putnam..........	1	0	0	0	0	0	1	0	0	0	
Suffolk County Police Department	7	26	3	0	0	0	10	13	10	3	
Warren	1	0	0	0	0	0	0	0	0	1	
Nonmetropolitan Counties..........	1	1	0	0	0	0					
Cattaraugus..........	1	0	0	0	0	0	0	0	0	1	
Chenango..........	0	1	0	0	0	0	0	0	1		
State Police Agencies..........	22	16	4	0	0	1					
State Police											
Albany County	2	0	0	0	0	0	1	0	0	1	
Clinton County	6	0	0	0	0	0	0	2	2	2	
Columbia County	1	0	2	0	0	0	0	3	0	0	
Duchess County	1	2	0	0	0	0	2	0	0	1	
Franklin County	1	0	0	0	0	0	0	0	0	1	
Genesee County	1	0	0	0	0	0	1	0	0	0	
Greene County	1	0	0	0	0	0	0	1		0	
Hamilton County	1	0	0	0	0	0	0	0	0	1	
Lewis County	1	0	0	0	0	0	0	0	1	0	
Oneida County	0	1	0	0	0	0			1	0	

Table 13. Hate Crime Incidents Per Bias Motivation and Quarter, by Selected State and Agency, 2017—*Continued*

(Number.)

State/agency	Number of incidents per bias motivation						Number of incidents per quarter				Population[1]
	Race/ Ethnicity/ Ancestry	Religion	Sexual orientation	Disability	Gender	Gender Identity	1st quarter	2nd quarter	3rd quarter	4th quarter	
Onondaga County	0	1	0	0	0	0	0	0	0	1	
Orange County	0	1	0	0	0	0	0	0	1	0	
Oswego County	0	1	0	0	0	1	1	0	0	1	
Putnam County	0	1	1	0	0	0	0	1	0	1	
Saratoga County	1	0	0	0	0	0	1	0	0	0	
Steuben County	1	0	0	0	0	0	0	0	1	0	
Sullivan County	1	2	0	0	0	0	0	2	1	0	
Tioga County	0	1	0	0	0	0	0	0	0	1	
Tompkins County	0	1	0	0	0	0	1	0	0	0	
Ulster County	1	1	0	0	0	0	1	0	1	0	
Wayne County	1	1	0	0	0	0	0	1	0	1	
Westchester County	2	3	1	0	0	0	4	1	0	1	
Other Agencies	**16**	**12**	**0**	**0**	**0**	**0**					
New York City Metropolitan Transportation Authority	16	12	0	0	0	0	11	1	7	9	
NORTH CAROLINA											
Total	**114**	**24**	**24**	**4**	**0**	**0**					
Cities	**80**	**20**	**21**	**3**	**0**	**0**					
Albemarle	1	0	0	0	0	0	0	1	0	0	16,022
Apex	1	1	0	0	0	0	2	0	0	0	49,159
Asheville	4	2	1	0	0	0	3	2	2	0	90,103
Benson	0	1	0	0	0	0	1	0	0	0	3,764
Chapel Hill	5	0	4	0	0	0	2	3	3	1	59,553
Charlotte-Mecklenburg	17	9	5	1	0	0	7	9	11	5	914,609
Concord	1	0	0	0	0	0	0	0	0	1	91,756
Durham	13	1	2	0	0	0	3	4	6	3	269,088
Fayetteville	3	1	2	1	0	0	2	2	1	2	205,432
Greensboro	4	1	1	0	0	0	0	1	2	3	290,051
Hertford	1	0	0	0	0	0	0	0	1	0	2,122
High Point	1	0	0	0	0	0	0	0	0	1	112,368
Jacksonville	2	0	0	0	0	0	0	0	1	1	67,293
Kannapolis	1	0	0	0	0	0	0	1	0	0	48,754
Marion	1	2	0	0	0	0	0	2	0	1	7,819
Monroe	0	0	0	1	0	0	0	0	1	0	35,153
New Bern	1	0	0	0	0	0	1	0	0	0	30,191
Raleigh	12	2	3	0	0	0	2	7	5	3	468,261
Roanoke Rapids	1	0	0	0	0	0	0	1	0	0	15,083
Salisbury	2	0	0	0	0	0	0	1	0	1	34,085
Siler City	3	0	0	0	0	0	1	0	1	1	8,531
Waynesville	1	0	0	0	0	0	0	0	1	0	9,977
Wilmington	5	0	1	0	0	0	1	1	2	2	119,422
Wilson	0	0	2	0	0	0	0	1	1	0	49,686
Universities and Colleges	**3**	**0**	**1**	**0**	**0**	**0**					
East Carolina University	1	0	1	0	0	0	0	0	0	2	28,962
North Carolina Central University	1	0	0	0	0	0	0	0	0	1	8,094
University of North Carolina, Pembroke	1	0	0	0	0	0	0	1	0	0	6,268
Metropolitan Counties	**23**	**4**	**2**	**1**	**0**	**0**					
Brunswick	1	0	0	0	0	0	1	0	0	0	
Buncombe	1	1	0	0	0	0	0	0	0	2	
Burke	3	0	0	0	0	0	0	3	0	0	
Caldwell	1	0	0	0	0	0	0	0	0	1	
Forsyth	4	0	1	0	0	0	1	1	2	1	
Franklin	0	1	0	1	0	0	1	1	0	0	
Gaston County Police Department	3	0	1	0	0	0	1	1	0	2	
Guilford	1	0	0	0	0	0	0	0	1	0	
New Hanover	2	2	0	0	0	0	0	1	3	0	
Pitt	4	0	0	0	0	0	0	1	1	2	
Randolph	1	0	0	0	0	0	0	0	1	0	
Wake	2	0	0	0	0	0	0	1	0	1	
Nonmetropolitan Counties	**7**	**0**	**0**	**0**	**0**	**0**					
Jackson	3	0	0	0	0	0	1	2	0	0	
Martin	2	0	0	0	0	0	0	0	2	0	

Table 13. Hate Crime Incidents Per Bias Motivation and Quarter, by Selected State and Agency, 2017—Continued

(Number.)

State/agency	Number of incidents per bias motivation						Number of incidents per quarter				Population[1]
	Race/ Ethnicity/ Ancestry	Religion	Sexual orientation	Disability	Gender	Gender Identity	1st quarter	2nd quarter	3rd quarter	4th quarter	
Surry..........................	1	0	0	0	0	0	1	0	0	0	
Transylvania..................	1	0	0	0	0	0	0	1	0	0	
Other Agencies........................	1	0	0	0	0	0					
University of North Carolina Hospitals	1	0	0	0	0	0	1	0	0	0	
NORTH DAKOTA											
Total	8	5	2	0	0	0					
Cities	6	4	2	0	0	0					
Bismarck......................	2	1	1	0	0	0	0	3	1	0	74,397
Fargo .:.......................	1	2	0	0	0	0	0	0	3	0	123,430
Grand Forks..................	2	0	0	0	0	0	0	1	1	0	58,090
Minot	1	0	1	0	0	0	0	2	0	0	50,118
Wahpeton	0	1	0	0	0	0	0	0	0	1	7,841
Metropolitan Counties	2	0	0	0	0	0					
Cass..........................	1	0	0	0	0	0	0	1	0	0	
Morton	1	0	0	0	0	0	1	0	0	0	
Nonmetropolitan Counties.................	0	1	0	0	0	0					
McLean........................	0	1	0	0	0	0	0	0	1	0	
OHIO											
Total	259	35	53	31	0	2					
Cities	225	28	46	26	0	2					
Akron.........................	10	0	0	4	0	0	4	5	4	1	197,412
Amelia........................	1	1	0	0	0	0	0	2	0	0	4,982
Ashland.......................	1	0	0	0	0	0	0	0	0	1	20,485
Aurora........................	2	0	0	0	0	0	0	1	0	1	15,932
Austintown....................	1	0	0	0	0	0	0	1	0	0	35,303
Baltimore.....................	1	0	0	0	0	0	0	0	0	1	2,973
Barberton	2	0	0	0	0	0	0	0	1	1	26,050
Beavercreek	1	0	0	0	0	0	0	0	1	0	46,572
Beaver Township..............	1	0	0	0	0	0	0	1	0	0	6,427
Bellefontaine.................	1	0	0	0	0	0	0	0	1	0	13,144
Blue Ash	1	0	0	0	0	0	0	1	0	0	12,248
Boardman.....................	2	0	0	0	0	0	0	0	2	0	39,276
Brecksville	0	0	1	0	0	0	0	0	0	1	13,432
Butler Township...............	1	0	0	3	0	0	2	1	1	0	7,799
Canal Fulton	1	1	0	0	0	0	0	0	1	1	5,428
Cincinnati....................	31	5	4	1	0	0	6	15	13	7	299,116
Circleville	3	0	0	0	0	0	0	2	0	1	13,972
Cleveland.....................	12	0	0	0	0	0	1	1	5	5	385,351
Colerain Township.............	3	1	0	0	0	0	1	3	0	0	58,996
Columbus.....................	50	3	19	3	0	0	19	28	13	15	872,205
Copley Township	0	0	0	2	0	0	0	0	2	0	17,280
Dayton........................	1	0	1	0	0	0	0	1	1	0	140,171
Defiance	1	0	0	0	0	0	0	1	0	0	16,594
Englewood	0	0	1	1	0	0	1	1	0	0	13,504
Fairborn......................	2	0	0	0	0	0	1	1	0	0	33,936
Fairfax........................	1	0	0	0	0	0	0	0	0	1	1,702
Fairview Park	1	0	0	0	0	0	0	0	0	1	16,307
Findlay.......................	2	0	1	0	0	0	0	0	2	1	41,474
Forest Park	1	0	0	0	0	0	0	0	1	0	18,665
Franklin......................	3	0	0	0	0	0	1	0	2	0	11,779
Gahanna......................	1	1	0	0	0	1	1	1	1	0	35,243
Garrettsville	1	0	0	0	0	0	0	0	0	1	2,321
Georgetown...................	2	0	0	0	0	0	0	0	0	2	4,356
Green Township	3	0	0	0	0	0	0	1	2	0	58,853
Grove City	1	0	0	1	0	0	1	1	0	0	40,421
Groveport.....................	1	0	0	0	0	0	0	0	1	0	5,583
Hamilton......................	7	2	1	0	0	0	2	2	5	1	62,094
Hilliard.......................	1	1	0	0	0	0	2	0	0	0	36,144
Holland.......................	1	1	0	0	0	0	0	1	1	0	1,662
Howland Township	1	0	0	0	0	0	0	0	1	0	16,608

Table 13. Hate Crime Incidents Per Bias Motivation and Quarter, by Selected State and Agency, 2017—*Continued*

(Number.)

State/agency	Number of incidents per bias motivation						Number of incidents per quarter				Population[1]
	Race/ Ethnicity/ Ancestry	Religion	Sexual orientation	Disability	Gender	Gender Identity	1st quarter	2nd quarter	3rd quarter	4th quarter	
Huber Heights........................	0	0	0	1	0	0	0	0	1	0	37,996
Hudson.................................	1	0	1	1	0	0	0	0	1	2	22,248
Ironton	1	0	0	0	0	0	0	0	0	1	10,853
Jackson.................................	1	0	0	0	0	0	0	1	0	0	6,305
Jamestown............................	2	0	0	0	0	0	1	0	1	0	2,036
Lancaster..............................	1	0	0	0	0	0	0	0	0	1	40,026
Lima.....................................	6	1	1	0	0	0	1	4	1	2	37,220
Logan...................................	0	0	1	0	0	0	1	0	0	0	7,077
Lorain..................................	1	1	0	0	0	0	1	1	0	0	63,672
Louisville..............................	1	0	0	0	0	0	1	0	0	0	9,373
Loveland...............................	1	0	0	0	0	0	0	0	0	1	12,846
Lyndhurst..............................	2	1	0	0	0	0	0	1	1	1	13,586
Madison Township, Franklin County	0	1	0	1	0	0	1	1	0	0	18,661
Mansfield..............................	3	0	2	0	0	0	1	2	1	1	46,507
Marietta................................	1	0	2	0	0	0	0	1	0	2	13,582
Marysville.............................	0	0	1	0	0	0	1	0	0	0	23,622
Mason...................................	3	0	0	0	0	0	1	2	0	0	33,406
Massillon..............................	2	0	0	0	0	0	1	1	0		32,265
Medina Township	1	0	0	0	0	0	1	0	0		8,940
Mentor-on-the-Lake...............	0	1	0	0	0	0	1	0	0		7,359
Minster.................................	1	0	0	0	0	0	1	0			2,866
Montgomery..........................	0	1	0	0	0	0	0	1	0	0	10,638
Mount Healthy.......................	1	0	0	0	0	0	0	0	0	1	6,020
Mount Vernon........................	0	1	0	0	0	0	0	1	0	0	16,553
New Albany...........................	3	0	0	0	0	0	0	2	0	1	10,838
Newton Falls.........................	0	0	1	0	0	0	1	0	0	0	4,567
North Canton	1	1	1	0	0	0	2	0	1	0	17,348
Oak Harbor...........................	1	0	0	0	0	0	0	0	1	0	2,731
Ontario.................................	0	0	0	1	0	0	0	1	0	0	6,058
Oxford..................................	0	0	1	0	0	0	1	0	0	0	22,459
Parma...................................	1	0	0	0	0	0	0	0	1	0	79,340
Perkins Township....................	1	0	0	0	0	0	0	1	0	0	11,773
Perry Township, Franklin County	0	1	0	0	0	0	1	0	0	0	3,758
Pickerington..........................	0	1	0	0	0	0	0	0	0	1	20,373
Pierce Township.....................	1	0	0	0	0	0	1	0	0	0	11,623
Portsmouth............................	0	0	0	1	0	0	0	1	0	0	20,451
Powell...................................	1	0	0	0	0	0	0	0	0	1	13,029
Reading.................................	1	0	0	0	0	0	0	0	0	1	10,307
Reynoldsburg.........................	5	1	1	0	0	0	1	3	3	0	37,704
Rocky River...........................	0	0	0	1	0	0	0	0	1	0	20,342
Sabina...................................	2	0	0	0	0	0	0	2	0	0	2,534
Salem....................................	2	0	0	0	0	0	0	1	0	1	11,887
Shelby...................................	1	0	0	0	0	0	0	0	1	0	8,987
Sidney...................................	0	0	1	0	0	0	0	1	0	0	20,466
South Euclid..........................	0	0	0	1	0	0	0	0	1	0	21,628
Springfield Township, Hamilton County	1	0	2	0	0	1	0	1	0	3	36,571
Springfield Township, Summit County	1	0	0	0	0	0	1	0	0	0	14,434
St. Clair Township...................	0	0	0	1	0	0	0	0	0	1	7,583
Streetsboro............................	0	0	1	1	0	0	0	1	1	0	16,308
Sugarcreek Township...............	1	0	0	0	0	0	0	0	1	0	8,300
Sylvania Township...................	1	0	0	0	0	0	0	0	0	1	29,536
Tipp City..............................	0	1	0	0	0	0	0	0	0	1	9,957
Toledo..................................	2	0	0	0	0	0	1	0	0	1	277,116
Trotwood..............................	1	0	0	0	0	0	1	0	0	0	24,308
Upper Arlington.....................	1	0	0	0	0	0	0	1	0	0	35,214
Van Wert...............................	1	0	0	0	0	0	0	1	0	0	10,713
Wadsworth............................	3	0	1	0	0	0	1	0	1	2	23,388
West Chester Township	1	0	0	0	0	0	0	1	0	0	61,386
Westerville............................	1	0	0	0	0	0	0	0	1	0	39,418
Whitehall..............................	1	0	0	0	0	0	1	0	0	0	18,835
Willoughby............................	1	0	0	0	0	0	1	0	0	0	22,857
Wilmington...........................	2	0	0	0	0	0	1	0	1	0	12,416
Wooster.................................	0	0	0	1	0	0	0	1	0	0	27,172
Xenia....................................	1	0	0	0	0	0	1	0	0	0	26,331
Zanesville.............................	1	0	1	1	0	0	0	0	1	2	25,457
Universities and Colleges	6	1	2	0	0	0					
Bowling Green State University	2	0	0	0	0	0	2	0			17,644

Table 13. Hate Crime Incidents Per Bias Motivation and Quarter, by Selected State and Agency, 2017—Continued

(Number.)

State/agency	Race/ Ethnicity/ Ancestry	Religion	Sexual orientation	Disability	Gender	Gender Identity	1st quarter	2nd quarter	3rd quarter	4th quarter	Population[1]
Capital University	1	0	2	0	0	0	2	0	0	1	3,367
Columbus State Community College	0	1	0	0	0	0	0	0	1	0	27,109
Ohio State University, Columbus	3	0	0	0	0	0	1	0	1	1	59,482
Metropolitan Counties	14	4	2	3	0	0					
Belmont	1	0	0	0	0	0	0	0	0	1	
Butler	1	0	0	0	0	0	0	1	0	0	
Clark	1	1	0	0	0	0	0	1	1	0	
Clermont	1	0	0	0	0	0	0	0	0	1	
Fairfield	1	0	0	0	0	0	0	0	0	1	
Franklin	1	0	0	0	0	0	0	0	1	0	
Fulton	1	0	0	0	0	0	0	1	0	0	
Greene	0	1	0	0	0	0	0	0	1	0	
Hocking	0	1	0	0	0	0	0	0	0	1	
Lorain	1	0	0	0	0	0	0	0	1	0	
Lucas	2	0	0	0	0	0	0	1	1	0	
Madison	0	0	0	1	0	0	0	0	0	1	
Montgomery	3	0	2	0	0	0	1	2	0	2	
Perry	0	0	0	1	0	0	0	0	0	1	
Richland	1	0	0	0	0	0	0	0	0	1	
Stark	0	1	0	0	0	0	0	1	0	0	
Warren	0	0	0	1	0	0	0	1	0	0	
Nonmetropolitan Counties	11	2	3	1	0	0					
Ashland	3	0	0	0	0	0	2	0	1	0	
Athens	1	0	0	0	0	0	0	1	0	0	
Hardin	2	1	1	0	0	0	2	1	0	1	
Highland	1	0	0	0	0	0	0	0	1	0	
Logan	1	0	0	0	0	0	0	0	1	0	
Marion	0	0	1	1	0	0	1	1	0	0	
Ross	3	0	0	0	0	0	1	1	1	0	
Shelby	0	0	1	0	0	0	1	0	0	0	
Washington	0	1	0	0	0	0	0	1	0	0	
State Police Agencies	1	0	0	1	0	0					
Ohio State Highway Patrol	1	0	0	1	0	0	0	2	0	0	
Other Agencies	2	0	0	0	0	0					
Cleveland Metropolitan Park District	2	0	0	0	0	0	0	0	2	0	
OKLAHOMA											
Total	17	7	10	0	1	2					
Cities	10	5	7	0	1	1					
Catoosa	1	0	0	0	0	0	0	1	0	0	7,129
Chickasha	1	0	0	0	0	0	1	0	0	0	16,489
Collinsville	1	0	0	0	0	1	0	1	1	0	6,836
Fairland	0	1	0	0	0	0	1	0	0	0	1,051
Kellyville	0	0	1	0	0	0	0	0	0	1	1,147
Lawton	0	1	0	0	0	0	1	0	0	0	94,134
Luther	1	0	0	0	0	0	0	0	1	0	1,675
Marietta	0	1	0	0	0	0	1	0	0	0	2,782
Muldrow	1	0	1	0	0	0	0	1	1	0	3,250
Muskogee	1	0	0	0	0	0	1	0	0	0	38,199
Noble	0	0	1	0	0	0	0	0	1	0	6,799
Norman	1	0	1	0	1	0	1	0	1	1	124,074
Owasso	0	0	1	0	0	0	1	0	0	0	36,869
Sapulpa	0	1	0	0	0	0	0	0	1	0	21,062
Stillwater	0	1	1	0	0	0	0	2	0	0	50,159
Wagoner	1	0	0	0	0	0	0	0	1	0	8,931
Wewoka	1	0	1	0	0	0	0	1	0	1	3,390
Woodward	1	0	0	0	0	0	0	1	0	0	12,655
Universities and Colleges	1	0	0	0	0	1					
Langston University	0	0	0	0	0	1	0	0	0	1	2,420
Oklahoma State University, Main Campus	1	0	0	0	0	0	0	0	0	1	25,622

Table 13. Hate Crime Incidents Per Bias Motivation and Quarter, by Selected State and Agency, 2017—Continued

(Number.)

State/agency	Number of incidents per bias motivation						Number of incidents per quarter				Population[1]
	Race/ Ethnicity/ Ancestry	Religion	Sexual orientation	Disability	Gender	Gender Identity	1st quarter	2nd quarter	3rd quarter	4th quarter	
Metropolitan Counties	2	1	0	0	0	0					
Lincoln	1	0	0	0	0	0	0	1	0	0	
Tulsa	1	1	0	0	0	0	1	0	1	0	
Nonmetropolitan Counties	4	1	3	0	0	0					
Choctaw	0	0	1	0	0	0	0	0	0	1	
Delaware	0	1	2	0	0	0	1	1	1	0	
Kingfisher	2	0	0	0	0	0	0	1	0	1	
Marshall	1	0	0	0	0	0	0	0	1	0	
Payne	1	0	0	0	0	0	0	1	0	0	
OREGON											
Total	84	29	24	4	1	4					
Cities	79	29	20	3	1	4					
Albany	1	0	1	0	0	0	1	0	0	1	53,701
Ashland	1	1	1	0	0	0	1	0	1	1	21,908
Baker City	0	0	1	0	0	0	1	0	0	0	9,764
Beaverton	1	2	0	0	0	0	0	1	1	1	98,897
Canby	1	0	0	0	0	0	0	0	1	0	17,823
Central Point	1	0	0	0	0	0	0	1	0	0	18,525
Corvallis	3	0	1	0	0	0	0	2	1	1	57,576
Eugene	46	12	8	1	1	4	16	23	14	19	168,310
Gresham	0	0	1	1	0	0	0	1	1	0	112,466
Hillsboro	1	3	0	0	0	0	1	2	1	0	107,433
Klamath Falls	3	1	1	0	0	0	3	0	0	2	22,436
Newberg-Dundee	1	1	0	0	0	0	1	0	1	0	26,769
North Plains	1	0	0	0	0	0	0	0	1	0	2,158
Ontario	0	0	1	0	0	0	1	0	0	0	10,970
Oregon City	0	1	0	0	0	0	0	0	0	1	36,921
Portland	10	4	3	1	0	0	7	7	1	3	649,408
Salem	4	0	1	0	0	0	0	3	1	1	169,565
Sherwood	0	1	0	0	0	0	0	0	1	0	19,473
Springfield	1	0	0	0	0	0	0	0	0	1	62,318
Tigard	4	3	1	0	0	0	3	1	3	1	52,524
Universities and Colleges	0	0	1	0	0	0					
Portland State University	0	0	1	0	0	0	0	0	0	1	26,627
Metropolitan Counties	3	0	2	0	0	0					
Benton	1	0	0	0	0	0	0	0	0	1	
Columbia	1	0	0	0	0	0	0	0	1	0	
Lane	0	0	2	0	0	0	2	0	0	0	
Washington	1	0	0	0	0	0	0	1	0	0	
Nonmetropolitan Counties	0	0	1	1	0	0					
Crook	0	0	1	0	0	0	1	0	0	0	
Umatilla	0	0	0	1	0	0	1	0	0	0	
State Police Agencies	1	0	0	0	0	0					
State Police, Benton County	1	0	0	0	0	0	1	0	0	0	
Tribal Agencies	1	0	0	0	0	0					
Grand Ronde Tribal	1	0	0	0	0	0	0	1	0	0	
PENNSYLVANIA											
Total	52	17	6	0	0	3					
Cities	43	14	6	0	0	3					
Bethlehem	1	0	0	0	0	0	0	0	0	1	75,336
Carlisle	1	0	0	0	0	0	1	0	0	0	19,233
East Earl Township	1	0	0	0	0	0	0	1	0	0	6,838
Lower Windsor Township	1	0	0	0	0	0	1	0	0	0	7,500
Manor Township, Lancaster County	1	0	0	0	0	0	0	0	1	0	20,949
Murrysville	1	0	0	0	0	0	1	0	0	0	20,034
New Hope	0	0	1	0	0	0	0	0	0	1	2,492
Patton Township	1	0	0	0	0	0	0	0	1	0	16,100

(Number.)

State/agency	Number of incidents per bias motivation						Number of incidents per quarter				Population[1]
	Race/ Ethnicity/ Ancestry	Religion	Sexual orientation	Disability	Gender	Gender Identity	1st quarter	2nd quarter	3rd quarter	4th quarter	
Philadelphia	19	14	4	0	0	3	7	20	7	6	1,575,595
Pittsburgh	13	0	1	0	0	0	6	3	3	2	305,932
Richland Township, Cambria County	1	0	0	0	0	0	0	0	0	1	12,153
Selinsgrove	1	0	0	0	0	0	0	1	0	0	5,930
Washington Township, Franklin County	1	0	0	0	0	0	1	0	0	0	14,678
Wilkes-Barre	1	0	0	0	0	0	0	1	0	0	40,418
Universities and Colleges	4	2	0	0	0	0					
Elizabethtown College	1	0	0	0	0	0	0	0	0	1	1,784
Pennsylvania State University											
Brandywine	1	0	0	0	0	0	0	0	0	1	1,379
University Park	2	1	0	0	0	0	0	0	1	2	47,789
University of Pittsburgh, Pittsburgh	0	1	0	0	0	0	1	0	0	0	28,664
State Police Agencies	5	1	0	0	0	0					
State Police											
Centre County	1	0	0	0	0	0	0	0	1	0	
Chester County	1	0	0	0	0	0	0	1		0	
Cumberland County	1	0	0	0	0	0	0	0	1		
Erie County	1	0	0	0	0	0	0	0	1	0	
Skippack	1	1	0	0	0	0	0	1	0	1	
RHODE ISLAND											
Total	5	4	2	0	0	0					
Cities	5	4	2	0	0	0					
Coventry	1	0	0	0	0	0	0	0	1	0	35,083
East Providence	0	3	0	0	0	0	0	1	2	0	47,502
Johnston	1	0	0	0	0	0	0	1	0	0	29,375
Providence	3	1	2	0	0	0	1	2	3	0	179,854
SOUTH CAROLINA											
Total	63	11	12	1	0	0					
Cities	36	3	5	0	0	0					
Abbeville	0	0	1	0	0	0	0	0	0	1	5,153
Andrews	7	0	0	0	0	0	4	2	1	0	2,903
Beaufort	4	0	0	0	0	0	0	0	4	0	13,612
Cayce	3	0	0	0	0	0	0	3	0	0	14,434
Charleston	1	0	0	0	0	0	0	0	1	0	136,845
Chester	1	0	0	0	0	0	1	0	0	0	5,452
Denmark	3	0	0	0	0	0	0	0	0	3	2,942
Elloree	1	0	0	0	0	0	0	0	0	1	666
Greeleyville	1	0	0	0	0	0	1	0	0	0	400
Greenville	0	1	1	0	0	0	0	0	2	0	68,922
Hartsville	1	0	1	0	0	0	0	0	1	1	7,769
Irmo	1	0	0	0	0	0	0	0	1	0	12,353
Laurens	1	0	0	0	0	0	0	0	0	1	9,089
Moncks Corner	3	1	1	0	0	0	2	2	1	0	10,818
Myrtle Beach	0	0	1	0	0	0	0	0	1	0	33,167
North Charleston	1	0	0	0	0	0	0	0	0	1	111,305
Orangeburg	1	0	0	0	0	0	0	1	0	0	13,076
Pickens	1	0	0	0	0	0	0	0	1	0	3,201
St. George	1	0	0	0	0	0	0	0	1	0	2,181
Sullivans Island	0	1	0	0	0	0	0	1	0	0	1,961
Union	2	0	0	0	0	0	2	0	0	0	7,940
Westminster	1	0	0	0	0	0	0	0	0	1	2,514
Winnsboro	2	0	0	0	0	0	0	1	1	0	3,276
Universities and Colleges	4	0	0	0	0	0					
Benedict College	1	0	0	0	0	0	0	0	0	1	2,281
Clemson University	1	0	0	0	0	0	1	0	0	0	23,406
Medical University of South Carolina	1	0	0	0	0	0	1	0	0	0	2,986
The Citadel	1	0	0	0	0	0	0	1	0	0	3,602
Metropolitan Counties	5	2	4	0	0	0					
Beaufort	1	1	1	0	0	0	1	0	1	1	

Table 13. Hate Crime Incidents Per Bias Motivation and Quarter, by Selected State and Agency, 2017—Continued

(Number.)

State/agency	Number of incidents per bias motivation						Number of incidents per quarter				Population[1]
	Race/ Ethnicity/ Ancestry	Religion	Sexual orientation	Disability	Gender	Gender Identity	1st quarter	2nd quarter	3rd quarter	4th quarter	
Greenville	1	0	0	0	0	0	0	0	0	1	
Horry County Police Department	0	0	1	0	0	0	0	0	1	0	
Laurens	2	0	0	0	0	0	0	1	0	1	
Richland	1	1	1	0	0	0	1	0	1	1	
Sumter	0	0	1	0	0	0	1	0	0	0	
Nonmetropolitan Counties	17	6	3	1	0	0					
Abbeville	1	0	0	0	0	0	0	0	1	0	
Bamberg	0	4	0	0	0	0	2	1	0	1	
Chesterfield	4	0	0	0	0	0	1	3	0	0	
Clarendon	0	0	1	0	0	0	0	0	0	1	
Colleton	2	0	0	0	0	0	0	1	0	1	
Dillon	1	0	0	0	0	0	0	0	0	1	
Georgetown	0	1	0	0	0	0	0	0	0	1	
Greenwood	1	0	0	0	0	0	0	0	0	1	
Hampton	0	0	1	0	0	0	0	0	1	0	
Marion	0	0	1	0	0	0	0	0	0	1	
Orangeburg	7	1	0	1	0	0	3	1	2	3	
Williamsburg	1	0	0	0	0	0	1	0	0	0	
Other Agencies	1	0	0	0	0	0					
Lexington County Medical Center	1	0	0	0	0	0	0	0	0	1	
SOUTH DAKOTA											
Total	8	4	3	2	0	0					
Cities	5	2	2	0	0	0					
Brookings	2	0	0	0	0	0	0	1	0	1	24,198
Rapid City	1	0	0	0	0	0	0	1	0	0	74,986
Sioux Falls	1	2	2	0	0	0	2	2	0	1	177,888
Spearfish	1	0	0	0	0	0	1	0	0	0	11,697
Metropolitan Counties	3	0	1	1	0	0					
Custer	1	0	0	0	0	0	0	0	1	0	
McCook	0	0	1	0	0	0	0	0	0	1	
Minnehaha	1	0	0	0	0	0	1	0	0	0	
Pennington	1	0	0	0	0	0	0	0	0	1	
Union	0	0	0	1	0	0	1	0	0	0	
Nonmetropolitan Counties	0	2	0	1	0	0					
Brookings	0	2	0	1	0	0	0	0	3	0	
TENNESSEE											
Total	88	18	21	7	2	0					
Cities	61	9	21	6	2	0					
Adamsville	0	0	1	0	0	0	0	0	0	1	2,207
Alcoa	0	1	0	0	0	0	0	0	0	1	10,128
Bartlett	1	0	0	0	0	0	0	0	1	0	58,895
Bolivar	0	1	0	0	0	0	1	0	0	0	5,066
Brighton	1	0	0	0	0	0	1	0	0	0	2,949
Brownsville	1	0	0	0	0	0	1	0	0	0	9,698
Centerville	1	0	0	0	0	0	1	0	0	0	3,564
Chattanooga	3	0	1	0	0	0	2	1	1	0	178,753
Clarksville	2	0	2	0	0	0	1	1	2	0	153,294
Cleveland	7	0	0	0	0	0	0	3	0	4	44,778
Collierville	4	0	0	0	0	0	0	0	4	0	49,790
Covington	2	0	0	1	0	0	0	1	2	0	8,909
Crossville	1	0	0	0	0	0	0	1	0	0	11,555
Fairview	1	0	0	0	0	0	0	1	0	0	8,648
Germantown	1	0	0	0	1	0	0	1	0	1	39,086
Greenbrier	0	0	1	0	0	0	1	0	0	0	6,853
Greeneville	0	0	0	1	0	0	0	0	1	0	15,065
Jackson	3	0	2	0	0	0	1	3	1	0	67,031
Jamestown	0	0	1	1	0	0	1	0	1	0	1,964
Jonesborough	0	0	0	1	0	0	0	1	0	0	5,378

Table 13. Hate Crime Incidents Per Bias Motivation and Quarter, by Selected State and Agency, 2017—Continued

(Number.)

State/agency	Race/Ethnicity/Ancestry	Religion	Sexual orientation	Disability	Gender	Gender Identity	1st quarter	2nd quarter	3rd quarter	4th quarter	Population[1]
Knoxville	2	0	3	0	0	0	2	0	3	0	187,539
Lebanon	5	0	0	0	0	0	1	2	2	0	32,248
Manchester	1	0	0	0	0	0	0	0	0	1	10,702
McMinnville	1	1	0	0	0	0	0	1	1	0	13,786
Memphis	4	0	3	0	0	0	1	4	0	2	652,765
Milan	2	1	1	0	1	0	2	1	0	2	7,780
Millington	3	0	1	0	0	0	0	0	2	2	10,944
Morristown	3	0	0	0	0	0	0	1	2	0	29,774
Murfreesboro	0	0	0	1	0	0	1	0	0	0	136,102
Nashville Metropolitan	11	5	3	0	0	0	6	3	6	4	674,942
Ripley	0	0	1	0	0	0	0	0	1	0	8,067
Rogersville	1	0	0	0	0	0	0	0	1	0	4,367
Smyrna	0	0	1	0	0	0	0	0	0	1	50,091
White Bluff	0	0	0	1	0	0	0	1	0	0	3,483
Universities and Colleges	3	0	0	0	0	0					
Chattanooga State Community College	1	0	0	0	0	0	0	0	1	0	8,628
Tennessee Technological University	1	0	0	0	0	0	1	0	0	0	10,493
University of the South	1	0	0	0	0	0	0	0	0	1	1,815
Metropolitan Counties	10	5	0	0	0	0					
Anderson	1	0	0	0	0	0	0	1	0	0	
Cheatham	1	0	0	0	0	0	0	1	0	0	
Hamilton	1	2	0	0	0	0	0	0	3	0	
Hickman	0	1	0	0	0	0	0	0	1	0	
Knox	2	0	0	0	0	0	0	0	1	1	
Montgomery	0	1	0	0	0	0	0	0	0	1	
Rutherford	1	1	0	0	0	0	0	1	1	0	
Shelby	2	0	0	0	0	0	0	0	2	0	
Sullivan	1	0	0	0	0	0	0	0	1	0	
Washington	1	0	0	0	0	0	0	0	1	0	
Nonmetropolitan Counties	6	3	0	0	0	0					
Benton	0	2	0	0	0	0	0	0	2	0	
Claiborne	1	0	0	0	0	0	0	0	0	1	
Coffee	1	0	0	0	0	0	1	0	0	0	
Gibson	1	0	0	0	0	0	0	1	0	0	
Hardin	1	0	0	0	0	0	0	0	1	0	
McMinn	1	0	0	0	0	0	0	0	1	0	
Monroe	0	1	0	0	0	0	0	0	1	0	
Rhea	1	0	0	0	0	0	0	0	1	0	
State Police Agencies	8	1	0	0	0	0					
Department of Safety	8	1	0	0	0	0	0	2	5	2	
Other Agencies	0	0	0	1	0	0					
Tennessee Bureau of Investigation	0	0	0	1	0	0	0	0	1	0	
TEXAS											
Total	117	22	43	3	1	6					
Cities	104	20	38	3	0	6					
Abilene	3	0	0	0	0	0	0	1	2	0	122,981
Alvin	1	0	0	0	0	0	0	0	0	1	26,488
Arlington	4	2	1	0	0	0	0	1	0	6	397,377
Aubrey	0	0	1	0	0	0	1	0	0	0	3,535
Austin	10	3	4	0	0	1	5	4	4	5	971,949
Balch Springs	1	0	0	0	0	0	0	0	1	0	25,199
Beaumont	1	0	0	0	0	0	0	1	0	0	118,456
Bedford	1	0	0	0	0	0	1	0	0	0	49,947
Bellmead	1	0	0	0	0	0	0	1	0	0	10,371
Brownwood	1	0	0	0	0	0	1	0	0	0	19,133
Burkburnett	1	0	1	0	0	0	0	0	1	1	11,142
Burleson	2	0	0	0	0	0	1	0	0	1	46,531
Burnet	0	0	1	0	0	0	1	0	0	0	6,422
Cedar Park	2	0	0	0	0	0	0	1	1	0	72,143
Corsicana	0	0	1	0	0	0	0	0	0	1	24,011

(Number.)

State/agency	Number of incidents per bias motivation						Number of incidents per quarter				Population[1]
	Race/ Ethnicity/ Ancestry	Religion	Sexual orientation	Disability	Gender	Gender Identity	1st quarter	2nd quarter	3rd quarter	4th quarter	
Dallas	2	0	12	0	0	0	1	1	2	10	1,338,551
Decatur	1	0	0	0	0	0	0	0	0	1	6,755
Denton	1	1	2	0	0	0	0	0	3	1	136,836
Devine	3	0	0	0	0	0		0	0	3	4,847
Dumas	1	0	0	0	0	0	0	0	0	1	14,943
El Paso	4	0	0	0	0	0	4	0	0	0	688,667
Flower Mound	2	0	1	0	0	0	0	0	0	3	75,101
Fort Worth	7	2	4	0	0	0	2	1	7	3	873,069
Frisco	1	0	0	0	0	0	0	0	1	0	172,804
Galena Park	1	1	0	0	0	0	0	1		1	11,091
Galveston	2	0	1	0	0	0	0	3	0	0	51,021
Giddings	1	0	0	0	0	0	0	0	0	1	5,154
Greenville	1	0	0	0	0	0	0	0	1	0	27,434
Henderson	0	0	0	0	0	1	0	1	0	0	13,366
Hewitt	0	0	1	0	0	0	1	0	0	0	14,443
Hitchcock	1	0	0	1	0	0	0	0	0	2	7,949
Houston	2	3	1	0	0	2	2	1	2	3	2,338,235
Iowa Park	1	1	0	0	0	0	0	0	0	2	6,361
Jacksonville	1	0	0	0	0	0	0	0	0	1	14,955
Keene	2	0	0	0	0	0	1	1	0	0	6,334
Lacy-Lakeview	1	0	0	0	0	0	0	1	0	0	6,633
Lampasas	2	0	0	0	0	0	0	0	0	2	7,910
League City	3	0	0	0	0	0	1	1	0	1	105,351
Leon Valley	2	0	0	0	0	0		2	0		11,508
Longview[2]	1	2	3	0	0	1	0	3	0	3	82,303
Lubbock	2	0	0	0	0	0				2	256,335
Marble Falls	1	0	0	0	0	0	1	0	0	0	6,358
McKinney	4	1	0	0	0	0	2	1	2	0	179,934
Odessa	2	1	2	1	0	0	2	2	1	1	121,194
Palestine	1	0	0	0	0	0	0	0	0	1	18,316
Pampa	1	0	0	0	0	0	0	0	1	0	17,736
Pearland	1	0	0	0	0	0	0	1	0	0	117,869
Pflugerville	4	0	0	0	0	0			0	4	61,212
Plano	2	0	0	0	0	1	1	2	0	0	290,413
Rockwall	1	0	0	1	0	0	0	0	1	1	44,599
Round Rock	1	0	0	0	0	0	0	1	0	0	124,617
Rusk	2	0	0	0	0	0	0	0	1	1	5,576
Sachse	1	0	0	0	0	0	0	0	1	0	25,907
San Angelo	1	0	0	0	0	0	1	0	0	0	101,931
San Antonio	2	1	1	0	0	0	1	2	0	1	1,520,712
San Saba	0	1	0	0	0	0	0	0	0	1	3,071
Schulenburg	0	1	0	0	0	0	0	0	1	0	2,943
Seven Points	1	0	1	0	0	0	1	0	0	1	1,462
Silsbee	1	0	0	0	0	0	0	0	1	0	6,747
Temple	2	0	0	0	0	0	0	0	0	2	74,794
Thorndale	1	0	0	0	0	0	0	0	1	0	1,293
Victoria	1	0	0	0	0	0	0	1	0	0	68,544
Wolfforth	1	0	0	0	0	0	0	0	1	0	4,552
Universities and Colleges	0	0	2	0	0	0					
South Plains College	0	0	1	0	0	0	0	0	0	1	9,478
Texas Tech University, Lubbock	0	0	1	0	0	0			0	1	36,551
Metropolitan Counties	9	1	3	0	0	0					
Austin	1	0	0	0	0	0	0	0	1	0	
Fort Bend	3	0	0	0	0	0	1	1		1	
Kaufman	1	0	0	0	0	0	0	0	0	1	
Travis	2	1	3	0	0	0	2	2	0	2	
Webb	1	0	0	0	0	0	0	0	1	0	
Williamson	1	0	0	0	0	0	0	0	1	0	
Nonmetropolitan Counties	3	0	0	0	1	0					
Cherokee	1	0	0	0	0	0	0	0	1		
Floyd[2]	2	0	0	0	1	0	0	0	1	1	
Other Agencies	1	1	0	0	0	0					
Independent School District											

(Number.)

State/agency	Number of incidents per bias motivation						Number of incidents per quarter				Population[1]
	Race/Ethnicity/Ancestry	Religion	Sexual orientation	Disability	Gender	Gender Identity	1st quarter	2nd quarter	3rd quarter	4th quarter	
Austin	0	1	0	0	0	0	0	0	0	1	
Pflugerville	1	0	0	0	0	0			0	1	
UTAH											
Total	51	15	8	0	0	4					
Cities	32	10	4	0	0	2					
Bountiful	7	0	0	0	0	0	2	3	0	2	44,312
Draper	1	0	0	0	0	0	0	0	0	1	48,197
Kaysville	1	1	0	0	0	0	2	0	0	0	31,873
Layton	2	2	0	0	0	0	1	0	2	1	77,048
Logan	0	0	1	0	0	0	0	0	0	1	51,059
Moab	1	0	0	0	0	0	0	0	1	0	5,266
Ogden	2	1	1	0	0	0	1	1	2	0	87,323
Pleasant View	1	0	0	0	0	0	0	0	0	1	10,036
Price	1	1	0	0	0	2	2	2	0	0	8,313
Roosevelt	1	0	0	0	0	0	0	0	0	1	7,057
Roy	2	0	0	0	0	0	2	0	0	0	38,410
Salt Lake City	2	1	1	0	0	0	0	1	1	2	194,968
South Jordan	2	2	0	0	0	0	1	1	1	1	72,533
South Ogden	0	1	0	0	0	0	0	0	1	0	17,177
South Salt Lake	1	0	0	0	0	0	0	0	1	0	24,811
St. George	4	0	0	0	0	0	3	0	0	1	84,007
Washington	1	0	1	0	0	0	1	0	0	1	26,618
West Jordan	0	1	0	0	0	0	0	0	0	1	115,390
West Valley	3	0	0	0	0	0	0	1	2	0	137,762
Metropolitan Counties	1	3	1	0	0	0					
Davis	0	0	1	0	0	0	0	0	0	1	
Salt Lake County Unified Police Department	0	3	0	0	0	0	1	0	1	1	
Weber	1	0	0	0	0	0	0	0	1	0	
Nonmetropolitan Counties	5	1	2	0	0	0					
Carbon	0	1	1	0	0	0	0	0	0	2	
Duchesne	1	0	0	0	0	0	0	1	0	0	
Uintah	4	0	1	0	0	0	1	2	1	1	
Nonmetropolitan Counties	13	1	1	0	0	2					
Utah Transit Authority	11	1	1	0	0	2	4	5	3	3	
Weber Morgan Narcotics Strike Force	2	0	0	0	0	0	0	1	0	1	
VERMONT											
Total	18	6	8	3	0	0					
Cities	15	4	8	2	0	0					
Brattleboro[2]	2	0	1	0	0	0	1	0	1	0	11,536
Bristol	0	1	0	0	0	0	0	1	0	0	3,908
Burlington	4	1	2	0	0	0	1	1	5	0	42,230
Colchester	1	0	0	0	0	0	0	0	1	0	17,353
Dover	0	0	1	0	0	0	0	0	0	1	1,076
Essex	0	0	1	0	0	0	0	0	0	1	21,470
Hartford	1	0	0	1	0	0	0	0	1	1	9,628
Middlebury	1	0	0	0	0	0	0	0	0	1	8,681
Newport	0	0	1	0	0	0	0	1	0	0	4,287
Rutland	0	0	1	0	0	0	0	0	0	1	15,462
South Burlington	1	0	0	0	0	0	0	1	0	0	19,146
St. Albans	1	2	0	1	0	0	0	1	1	2	6,772
St. Johnsbury	1	0	0	0	0	0	0	1	0	0	7,196
Williston	3	0	0	0	0	0	3	0	0	0	9,731
Winooski	0	0	1	0	0	0	0	1	0	0	7,105
Universities and Colleges	2	2	0	1	0	0					
University of Vermont	2	2	0	1	0	0	1	2	1	1	13,105
Metropolitan Counties	1	0	0	0	0	0					
Franklin	1	0	0	0	0	0	0	0	0	1	

Table 13. Hate Crime Incidents Per Bias Motivation and Quarter, by Selected State and Agency, 2017—*Continued*

(Number.)

State/agency	Number of incidents per bias motivation						Number of incidents per quarter				Population[1]
	Race/ Ethnicity/ Ancestry	Religion	Sexual orientation	Disability	Gender	Gender Identity	1st quarter	2nd quarter	3rd quarter	4th quarter	
VIRGINIA											
Total	109	42	35	7	0	0					
Cities	41	10	9	1	0	0					
Alexandria..........	1	2	2	0	0	0	3	2	0	0	158,256
Altavista..........	0	0	1	0	0	0	1	0	0	0	3,470
Bedford..........	1	0	0	0	0	0	0	0	0	1	6,622
Blacksburg..........	0	1	0	0	0	0	1	0	0	0	45,443
Charlottesville..........	1	0	0	0	0	0	0	0	0	1	47,446
Chesapeake..........	6	0	0	0	0	0	1	0	1	4	240,119
Christiansburg..........	1	0	0	0	0	0	0	0	0	1	22,272
Emporia..........	1	0	0	0	0	0	1	0	0	0	5,201
Farmville..........	0	1	0	0	0	0	0	0	1	0	8,127
Front Royal..........	0	0	1	0	0	0	0	1	0	0	15,270
Hampton..........	3	0	0	0	0	0	0	1	1	1	134,929
Harrisonburg..........	2	0	0	0	0	0	0	2	0	0	53,717
Leesburg..........	4	2	0	0	0	0	1	3	1	1	54,393
Lynchburg..........	2	0	0	0	0	0	1	1	0	0	80,890
Manassas..........	1	0	0	0	0	0	1	0	0	0	41,995
Manassas Park..........	1	0	0	0	0	0	1	0	0	0	16,158
Marion..........	1	0	0	0	0	0	0	0	1	0	5,837
Newport News..........	2	1	1	0	0	0	3	0	1	0	181,738
Norfolk..........	1	0	1	0	0	0	0	0	1	1	245,190
Petersburg..........	1	0	0	0	0	0	1	0	0	0	31,739
Portsmouth..........	3	0	1	0	0	0	1	2	1	0	95,100
Purcellville..........	0	1	0	0	0	0	0	0	1	0	9,779
Richmond..........	2	0	0	0	0	0	1	0	0	1	226,236
Suffolk..........	1	0	2	0	0	0	0	1	2	0	89,922
Vienna..........	1	0	0	0	0	0	0	0	0	1	16,590
Vinton..........	0	1	0	0	0	0	0	0	1	0	8,207
Virginia Beach..........	5	1	0	1	0	0	2	4	1	0	454,353
Universities and Colleges	6	4	1	0	0	0					
George Mason University..........	3	0	0	0	0	0	0	1	2	0	34,909
Northern Virginia Community College..........	1	2	0	0	0	0	2	1	0	0	50,835
University of Mary Washington..........	0	2	1	0	0	0	1	0	2	0	4,726
Virginia Polytechnic Institute and State University.......	2	0	0	0	0	0	0	1	0	1	33,170
Metropolitan Counties	56	27	20	1	0	0					
Albemarle County Police Department..........	2	0	0	0	0	0	0	2	0	0	
Amelia..........	2	0	0	0	0	0	1	1	0	0	
Arlington County Police Department..........	2	2	0	0	0	0	1	1	2	0	
Bedford..........	0	0	0	1	0	0	0	1	0	0	
Chesterfield County Police Department..........	6	1	2	0	0	0	2	3	3	1	
Clarke..........	2	0	1	0	0	0	0	0	3	0	
Fairfax County Police Department	17	11	8	0	0	0	11	5	11	9	
Fauquier..........	3	0	0	0	0	0	1	0	1	1	
Franklin..........	1	0	1	0	0	0	0	0	2	0	
Frederick..........	2	0	0	0	0	0	0	1	0	1	
Gloucester..........	1	1	0	0	0	0	2	0	0	0	
Goochland..........	0	1	0	0	0	0	0	1	0	0	
Henrico County Police Department	1	0	0	0	0	0	1	0	0	0	
Loudoun..........	7	5	4	0	0	0	5	5	4	2	
Prince George County Police Department..........	0	0	1	0	0	0	0	0	0	1	
Prince William County Police Department..........	2	2	0	0	0	0	0	3	0	1	
Rockingham..........	1	0	1	0	0	0	0	1	1	0	
Spotsylvania..........	2	3	2	0	0	0	2	3	2	0	
Stafford..........	4	1	0	0	0	0	1	3	0	1	
York	1	0	0	0	0	0	0	1	0	0	
**Nonmetropolitan Counties..........	4	1	1	0	0	0					
King and Queen..........	1	0	0	0	0	0	1	0	0	0	
Louisa..........	1	0	0	0	0	0	0	0	1	0	
Madison	0	1	0	0	0	0	1	0	0	0	
Page	2	0	0	0	0	0	1	0	0	1	
Westmoreland..........	0	0	1	0	0	0	1	0	0	0	

(Number.)

State/agency	Race/ Ethnicity/ Ancestry	Religion	Sexual orientation	Disability	Gender	Gender Identity	1st quarter	2nd quarter	3rd quarter	4th quarter	Population[1]
State Police Agencies............................	2	0	4	5	0	0					
State Police											
Amherst County	0	0	0	3	0	0	0	0	2	1	
Frederick County..	0	0	1	0	0	0	0	1	0	0	
Halifax County..	0	0	0	1	0	0	1	0	0	0	
Harrisonburg..	0	0	1	0	0	0	0	0	0	1	
Henrico County...	0	0	1	0	0	0	0	0	0	1	
Rockbridge County	1	0	0	0	0	0	1	0	0	0	
Washington County....................................	0	0	1	0	0	0	0	1	0	0	
Westmoreland County................................	0	0	0	1	0	0	0	0	0	1	
Winchester	1	0	0	0	0	0	1	0	0	0	
WASHINGTON											
Total	323	88	79	1	6	16					
Cities	274	76	75	1	4	15					
Aberdeen......................................	0	0	1	0	0	0	0	1	0	0	16,243
Arlington......................................	1	0	0	0	0	0	0	1	0	0	19,302
Auburn...	4	0	1	0	0	0	0	3	2	0	78,718
Battle Ground..............................	1	0	0	0	0	0	1	0	0	0	20,516
Bellevue.......................................	11	4	0	0	0	1	3	3	6	4	143,703
Bellingham...................................	9	0	1	0	1	0	0	5	3	3	88,652
Bremerton....................................	0	0	1	0	0	0	1	0	0	0	41,173
Burien..	3	0	0	0	0	0	2	0	1		51,479
Centralia......................................	0	1	0	0	0	0	0	0	0	1	17,048
Darrington...................................	1	0	0	0	0	0	1	0	0	0	1,391
Dupont...	1	0	0	0	0	0	1	0	0	0	9,721
Edmonds......................................	6	0	0	0	0	0	1	4	0	1	42,197
Ellensburg....................................	0	1	0	0	0	0	0	0	0	1	20,026
Everett...	5	0	1	0	0	0	2	1	2	1	110,040
Federal Way.................................	0	1	0	0	0	0	0	0	1	0	98,014
Fife...	2	0	0	0	0	0	0	1	1	0	10,264
Forks..	1	0	0	0	0	0	0	0	0	1	3,822
Hoquiam.......................................	1	0	0	0	0	0	1	0	0	0	8,386
Issaquah.......................................	2	2	1	0	0	0	0	2	2	1	38,592
Kelso..	1	0	0	0	0	0	0	0	0	1	12,070
Kent..	13	2	0	0	0	0	5	5	3	2	128,990
Kirkland..	4	1	0	0	0	0	1	2	1	1	88,898
Lacey..	1	0	0	0	1	0	0	2	0	0	48,597
Lake Stevens................................	1	0	1	0	0	0	1	0	0	1	32,288
Lakewood.....................................	1	0	0	0	0	0	0	1	0	0	61,080
Lynnwood.....................................	1	0	0	0	0	0	1	0	0	0	38,469
Marysville....................................	2	2	0	0	0	0	1	2	1	0	68,950
Mill Creek....................................	0	0	1	0	0	1	0	1	0	1	20,664
Monroe...	3	1	0	0	0	0	0	1	2	1	18,596
Mount Vernon..............................	5	0	0	0	0	0	1	3	0	1	35,085
Mukilteo.......................................	0	1	0	0	0	0	0	1	0	0	21,662
Oak Harbor..................................	1	0	0	0	0	0	0	1	0	0	23,371
Olympia..	3	0	0	0	0	1	2	2	0	0	51,923
Orting..	2	2	0	0	0	0	2	0	1	1	7,863
Pasco...	1	0	0	0	0	0	1	0	0	0	72,146
Port Angeles................................	2	1	0	0	0	0	2	0	0	1	19,964
Pullman..	1	0	0	0	0	0	0	0	0	1	33,897
Puyallup.......................................	1	0	0	0	0	0	0	0	1	0	41,242
Redmond[2]...................................	1	2	2	0	0	0	1	1	1	0	63,889
Renton..	3	3	0	0	0	0	4	0	0	2	102,470
Richland.......................................	5	0	0	0	0	0	0	2	1	2	56,151
Seattle...	120	45	57	0	1	11	46	66	63	59	721,365
Shoreline......................................	1	0	1	0	0	0	1	0	1	0	55,703
Spokane..	22	2	3	0	1	0	16	8	0	4	217,066
Spokane Valley.............................	9	3	2	0	0	0	1	4	5	4	97,430
Tacoma...	7	1	0	0	0	0	2	2	4	0	213,504
Toppenish.....................................	1	0	0	0	0	0	0	0	1	0	8,974
Tukwila...	5	0	1	0	0	1	0	3	3	1	20,183
Tumwater......................................	1	0	0	0	0	0	0	1	0	0	22,961
Union Gap....................................	0	1	0	0	0	0	1	0	0	0	6,104
Vancouver....................................	1	0	0	0	0	0	0	0	1	0	176,884

Table 13. Hate Crime Incidents Per Bias Motivation and Quarter, by Selected State and Agency, 2017—*Continued*

(Number.)

State/agency	Number of incidents per bias motivation						Number of incidents per quarter				Population[1]
	Race/ Ethnicity/ Ancestry	Religion	Sexual orientation	Disability	Gender	Gender Identity	1st quarter	2nd quarter	3rd quarter	4th quarter	
Walla Walla	1	0	0	0	0	0	0	1	0	0	32,189
West Richland	0	0	0	1	0	0	1	0	0	0	14,603
Yakima	6	0	1	0	0	0	3	2	1	1	94,375
Universities and Colleges	4	1	1	0	2	1					
Eastern Washington University	0	0	0	0	1	1	1	0	1	0	12,279
Evergreen State College	1	0	0	0	0	0	0	1	0	0	4,089
University of Washington	3	0	0	0	1	0	1	0	1	2	45,591
Washington State University, Pullman	0	0	1	0	0	0	0	1	0	0	30,142
Western Washington University	0	1	0	0	0	0	0	0	0	1	15,574
Metropolitan Counties	41	9	3	0	0	0					
Cowlitz	1	0	0	0	0	0	0	0	0	1	
King	4	0	0	0	0	0	3	1	0		
Pierce	6	1	1	0	0	0	3	0	5	0	
Skagit	1	2	0	0	0	0	2	0	1	0	
Skamania	1	0	0	0	0	0	0	1	0	0	
Snohomish	6	2	1	0	0	0	2	2	3	2	
Spokane	8	3	0	0	0	0	3	4	3	1	
Thurston	2	0	0	0	0	0	0	1	1	0	
Whatcom[2]	5	1	1	0	0	0	0	0	5	1	
Yakima	7	0	0	0	0	0	1	2	3	1	
Nonmetropolitan Counties	1	0	0	0	0	0					
Clallam	1	0	0	0	0	0	0	0	0	1	
Tribal Agencies	1	0	0	0	0	0					
Lummi Tribal	1	0	0	0	0	0	0	1	0	0	
Other Agencies	2	2	0	0	0	0					
Port of Seattle	2	2	0	0	0	0	0	1	0	3	
WEST VIRGINIA											
Total	23	6	1	1	0	0					
Cities	10	4	1	0	0	0					
Barboursville	0	1	0	0	0	0	1	0	0	0	4,315
Bridgeport	1	0	0	0	0	0	1	0	0	0	8,401
Buckhannon	1	0	0	0	0	0	0	0	0	1	5,610
Charleston	3	0	1	0	0	0	1	0	2	1	48,788
Fairmont	1	0	0	0	0	0	1	0	0	0	18,604
Huntington	0	1	0	0	0	0	0	0	0	1	47,933
Martinsburg	0	1	0	0	0	0	0	0	0	1	17,761
Oak Hill	3	0	0	0	0	0	0	3	0	0	8,490
Parkersburg	1	0	0	0	0	0	0	1	0	0	30,475
White Sulphur Springs	0	1	0	0	0	0	0	1	0	0	2,417
Universities and Colleges	2	1	0	0	0	0					
Shepherd University	2	1	0	0	0	0	1	0	0	2	3,779
Metropolitan Counties	6	0	0	0	0	0					
Berkeley	3	0	0	0	0	0	0	1	1	1	
Brooke	1	0	0	0	0	0	1	0	0	0	
Fayette	1	0	0	0	0	0	0	0	0	1	
Jefferson	1	0	0	0	0	0	0	1	0	0	
Nonmetropolitan Counties	5	1	0	1	0	0					
Braxton	1	0	0	0	0	0	1	0	0	0	
Harrison	0	1	0	0	0	0	0	1	0	0	
Lewis	1	0	0	1	0	0	0	0	1	1	
Mason	1	0	0	0	0	0	0	0	1	0	
McDowell	2	0	0	0	0	0	0	1	0	1	
WISCONSIN											
Total	15	17	13	1	0	0					

Table 13. Hate Crime Incidents Per Bias Motivation and Quarter, by Selected State and Agency, 2017—*Continued*

(Number.)

State/agency	Number of incidents per bias motivation						Number of incidents per quarter				Population[1]
	Race/ Ethnicity/ Ancestry	Religion	Sexual orientation	Disability	Gender	Gender Identity	1st quarter	2nd quarter	3rd quarter	4th quarter	
Cities	14	12	11	1	0	0					
Appleton	1	3	0	0	0	0	0	0	1	3	74,660
Beloit	0	2	0	0	0	0	2	0	0		36,724
Eau Claire	1	0	0	0	0	0	1	0	0	0	68,687
Fond du Lac	0	1	0	0	0	0	0	0	1	0	42,929
Hudson..	1	3	8	0	0	0	2	3	6	1	13,788
Juneau..	0	0	0	1	0	0	0	1	0	0	2,703
Kaukauna	0	0	1	0	0	0	0	0	1	0	15,969
La Crosse	1	0	0	0	0	0	0	0	1	0	52,234
Madison	0	1	1	0	0	0	0	1	1	0	255,850
Manitowoc	1	0	0	0	0	0	1	0	0	0	32,813
Milwaukee	4	1	0	0	0	0	3	0	0	2	595,168
North Fond du Lac	1	0	0	0	0	0	0	1	0	0	5,038
Seymour	1	0	0	0	0	0	0	0	1	0	3,441
Sheboygan..	1	0	0	0	0	0	0	0	0	1	48,595
South Milwaukee	1	0	0	0	0	0	1	0	0	0	21,039
Tomahawk	0	1	0	0	0	0	0	1	0	0	3,169
West Allis..	1	0	0	0	0	0	0	0	0	1	60,043
Wisconsin Rapids	0	0	1	0	0	0	0	0	1	0	17,807
Metropolitan Counties	0	4	1	0	0	0					
Calumet...	0	1	0	0	0	0	0	0	0	1	
Columbia...	0	1	0	0	0	0	0	1	0	0	
Rock	0	0	1	0	0	0	0	0	1	0	
St. Croix...	0	2	0	0	0	0	1	1	0	0	
Nonmetropolitan Counties...................................	0	1	0	0	0	0					
Burnett	0	1	0	0	0	0	0	0	1	0	
Tribal Agencies	1	0	1	0	0	0					
Lac Courtes Oreilles Tribal	1	0	1	0	0	0	1	0	1	0	
WYOMING											
Total	1	1	2	0	0	0					
Cities	0	1	2	0	0	0					
Laramie..	0	1	1	0	0	0	0	0	0	2	32,632
Sheridan..	0	0	1	0	0	0	0	0	1	0	18,036
Universities and Colleges	1	0	0	0	0	0					
University of Wyoming....................................	1	0	0	0	0	0	0	1	0	0	12,366

[1]Population figures are published only for the cities. The figures listed for the universities and colleges are student enrollment and were provided by the United States Department of Education for the 2016 school year, the most recent available. The enrollment figures include full-time and part-time students.
[2]Includes one incident reported with more than one bias motivation.
[3]Student enrollment figures were not available.

Table 14. Participation Table, Number of Participating Agencies and Population Covered, by Population Group, 2017

(Number.)

Population group	Number of participating agencies	Population covered
Total	16,149	306,435,676
Group I (cities 250,000 and over)..	82	60,637,635
Group II (cities 100,000-249,999)...	218	32,396,880
Group III (cities 50,000-99,999)..	482	33,672,307
Group IV (cities 25,000-49,999)..	868	30,072,013
Group V (cities 10,000-24,999)...	1,786	28,545,233
Group VI1 (cities under 10,000)	8,290	23,637,355
Metropolitan counties[1]..	1,959	73,842,621
Nonmetropolitan counties[1]	2,464	23,631,632

[1]Includes universities and colleges, state police agencies, and/or other agencies to which no population is attributed.

METHODOLOGY

HATE CRIMES

The Federal Bureau of Investigation (FBI) began the procedures for implementing, collecting, and managing hate crime data after Congress passed the Hate Crime Statistics Act in 1990. This act required the collection of data "about crimes that manifest evidence of prejudice based on race, religion, sexual orientation, or ethnicity." Beginning in 2013, law enforcement agencies could submit hate crime data in accordance with a number of program modifications. In 1994, the Hate Crime Statistics Act was amended to include bias against persons with disabilities. The Church Arson Prevention Act, which was signed into law in July 1996, removed the sunset clause from the original statute and mandated that the collection of hate crime data become a permanent part of the UCR program. In 2009, Congress further amended the Hate Crime Statistics Act by passing the Matthew Shepard and James Byrd, Jr., Hate Crime Prevention Act. The amendment includes the collection of data for crimes motivated by bias against a particular gender and gender identity, as well as for crimes committed by, and crimes directed against, juveniles. In response to the Shepard/Byrd Act, the FBI modified its data collection so that reporting agencies could indicate whether hate crimes were committed by, or directed against, juveniles.

Definitions

Hate crimes include any crime motivated by bias against race, religion, sexual orientation, ethnicity/national origin, and/or disability. Because motivation is subjective, it is sometimes difficult to know with certainty whether a crime resulted from the offender's bias. Moreover, the presence of bias alone does not necessarily mean that a crime can be considered a hate crime. Only when law enforcement investigation reveals sufficient evidence to lead a reasonable and prudent person to conclude that the offender's actions were motivated, in whole or in part, by his or her bias should an incident be reported as a hate crime.

Starting with the 2015 data, incidents motivated by race and ethnicity are grouped in the new "Race/Ethnicity/Ancestry" single-bias category. New subcategories include anti-Arab, anti—Hispanic or Latino (the former ethnicity designation), and anti—other race/ethnicity/ancestry. Under "Anti-Religion," new subcategories include anti-Mormon, anti—Jehovah's Witness, anti—Eastern Orthodox (Russian/Greek/other), anti-Buddhist, anti-Hindu, and anti-Sikh.

Data Collection

The UCR (Uniform Crime Reporting) program collects data about both single-bias and multiple-bias hate crimes. A single-bias incident is defined as an incident in which one or more offense types are motivated by the same bias. A multiple-bias incident is defined as an incident in which more than one offense type occurs and at least two offense types are motivated by different biases.

A table enumerating selected places in the United States that did not report hate crimes in 2016 is available at https://ucr.fbi.gov/hate-crime/2016/tables/table-14/table_14_hate_crime_zero_data_submitted_per_quarter_by_state_and_agency_2016-.xls.xlsx/view.

Important Note: Rape

In 2013, the FBI UCR Program initiated the collection of rape data under a revised definition and removed the term "forcible" from the offense name. The changes bring uniformity to the offense in both the Summary Reporting System (SRS) and the National Incident-Based Reporting System (NIBRS) by capturing data (1) without regard to gender, (2) including penetration of any bodily orifice by any object or body part, and (3) including offenses where physical force is not involved. The UCR Program now defines rape as follows:

- **Rape (revised):** Penetration, no matter how slight, of the vagina or anus with any body part or object, or oral penetration by a sex organ of another person, without the consent of the victim. This includes the offenses of rape, sodomy, and sexual assault with an object.

- **Rape (legacy):** The carnal knowledge of a female forcibly and against her will.

The offenses of fondling, incest, and statutory rape are included in the Crimes Against Persons, Other category.

Beginning January 1, 2017, the UCR Program discontinued collecting rape data via the SRS according to the historical, legacy definition. Only rape data submitted under the revised definition will be published for 2017 and subsequent years. This change will not affect agencies that submit rape data via NIBRS.

Crimes Against Persons, Property, or Society

The UCR program's data collection guidelines stipulate that a hate crime may involve multiple offenses, victims, and offenders within one incident; therefore, the Hate Crime Statistics program is incident-based. According to UCR counting guidelines:

- One offense is counted for each victim in *crimes against persons*

- One offense is counted for each offense type in *crimes against property*

- One offense is counted for each offense type in *crimes against society*

Victims

In the UCR program, the victim of a hate crime may be an individual, a business, an institution, or society as a whole.

Offenders

According to the UCR program, the term *known offender* does not imply that the suspect's identity is known; rather, the term indicates that some aspect of the suspect was identified, thus distinguishing the suspect from an unknown offender. Law enforcement agencies specify the number of offenders, and when possible, the race of the offender or offenders as a group.

Race/Ethnicity

The UCR program uses the following racial designations in its Hate Crime Statistics program: White; Black; American Indian or Alaskan Native; Asian; Native Hawaiian or Other Pacific Islander; and Multiple Races, Group. In addition, the UCR program uses the ethnic designations of Hispanic or Latino and Not Hispanic or Latino.

The law enforcement agencies that voluntarily participate in the Hate Crime Statistics program collect details about an offender's bias motivation associated with 11 offense types already being reported to the UCR program: murder and nonnegligent manslaughter, rape, aggravated assault, simple assault, and intimidation (crimes against persons); and robbery, burglary, larceny-theft, motor vehicle theft, arson, and destruction/damage/vandalism (crimes against property). The law enforcement agencies that participate in the UCR program via the National Incident-Based Reporting System (NIBRS) collect data about additional offenses for *crimes against persons* and *crimes against property*. These data appear in the category of other. These agencies also collect hate crime data for the category called *crimes against society*, which includes drug or narcotic offenses, gambling offenses, prostitution offenses, and weapon law violations.

PART 7

Indicators of School Crime and Safety, 2018

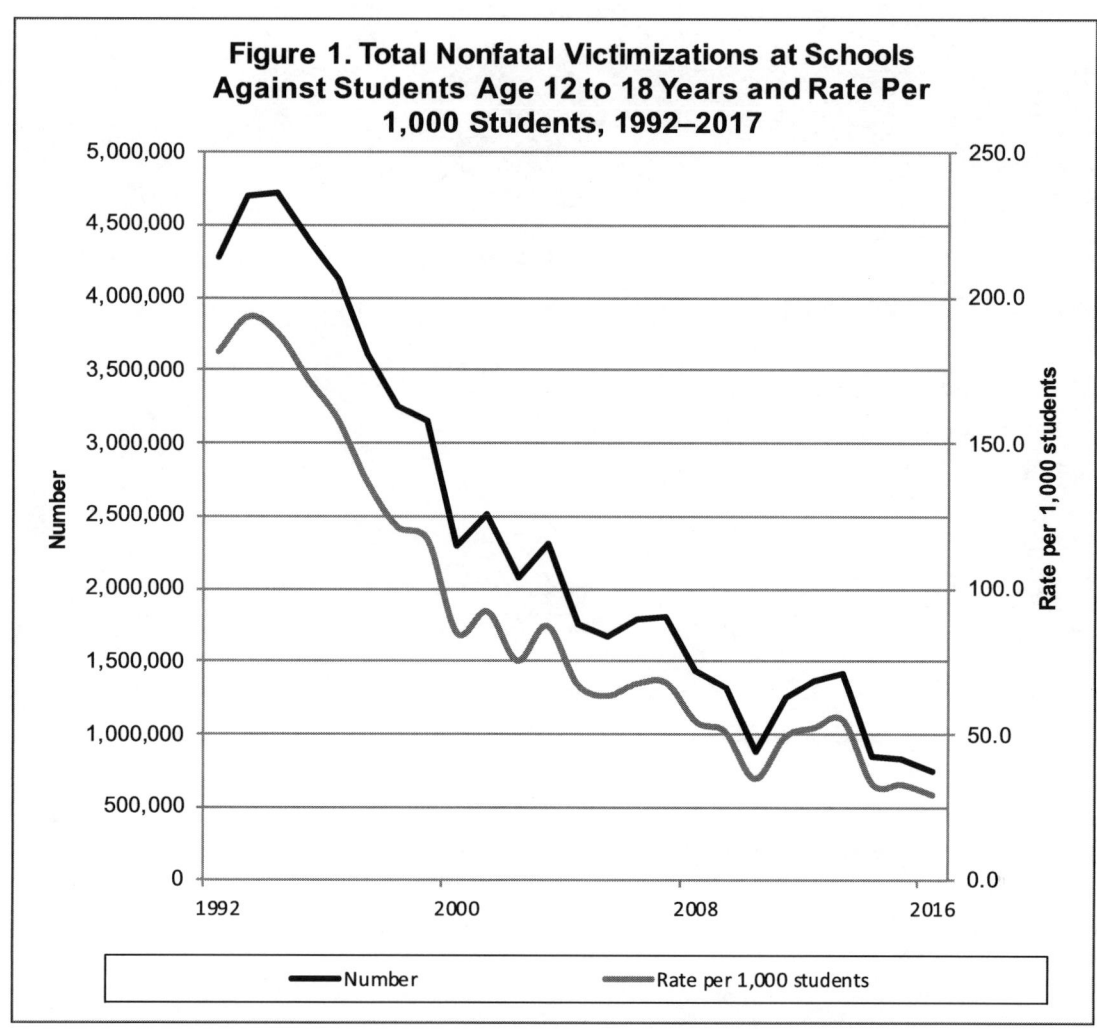

Figure 1. Total Nonfatal Victimizations at Schools Against Students Age 12 to 18 Years and Rate Per 1,000 Students, 1992–2017

- Approximately 827,000 victimization incidents of students age 12 to 18 years occurred in schools in 2017 (including theft and nonfatal victimizations and approximately 503,800 incidents occurred away from school.

- Between 2001 and 2017, the percentage of students ages 12 to 18 who reported that gangs were present at their school during the school year decreased overall (from 20 percent to 9 percent); this percentage also decreased for students from urban areas (from 29 percent to 11 percent), suburban areas (from 18 percent to 8 percent), and rural areas (from 13 percent to 7 percent).

- In 2017, about 6 percent of students ages 12 to 18 reported being called hate-related words at school during the

school year, representing a decrease from 12 percent in 2001. This percentage also decreased between 2001 and 2017 for male and female students and for White, Black, and Hispanic students. In 2017, about 23 percent of students reported seeing hate-related graffiti at school during the school year, representing a decrease from 36 percent in 2001.

- The percentage of students in grades 9–12 who reported that illegal drugs were made available to them on school property in the last 12 months decreased from 29 percent in 2001 to 20 percent in 2017.

Table 1. School-Associated Violent Deaths of All Persons, Homicides and Suicides of Youth Ages 5 to 18 Years at School, and Total Homicides and Suicides of Youth Ages 5 to 18 Years, by Type of Violent Death: 1992–1993 to 2015–2016

(Number.)

Year	School-associated violent deaths[1] of all persons (includes students, staff, and other nonstudents)						Homicides of youth age 5 to 18 years		Suicides of youth age 5 to 18 years	
	Total	Homicides	Suicides	Legal interventions	Unintentional firearm-related deaths	Undetermined violent deaths	Homicides at school[2]	Total homicides	Suicides at school[2]	Total suicides[3]
1992–1993	57	47	10	0	0	0	34	3,003	6	1,657
1993–1994	48	38	10	0	0	0	29	3,253	7	1,779
1994–1995	48	39	8	0	1	0	28	3,001	7	1,704
1995–1996	53	46	6	1	0	0	32	2,791	6	1,691
1996–1997	48	45	2	1	0	0	28	2,430	1	1,584
1997–1998	57	47	9	1	0	0	34	2,231	6	1,681
1998–1999	47	38	6	2	1	0	33	1,923	4	1,480
1999–2000	37[4]	26[4]	11[4]	0[4]	0[4]	0[4]	14[4]	1,694	8[4]	1,420
2000–2001	34[4]	26[4]	7[4]	1[4]	0[4]	0[4]	14[4]	1,636	6[4]	1,451
2001–2002	36[4]	27[4]	8[4]	1[4]	0[4]	0[4]	16[4]	1,593	5[4]	1,343
2002–2003	36[4]	25[4]	11[4]	0[4]	0[4]	0[4]	18[4]	1,658	10[4]	1,264
2003–2004	45[4]	37[4]	7[4]	1[4]	0[4]	0[4]	23[4]	1,620	5[4]	1,411
2004–2005	52[4]	40[4]	10[4]	2[4]	0[4]	0[4]	22[4]	1,720	8[4]	1,484
2005–2006	44[4]	37[4]	6[4]	1[4]	0[4]	0[4]	21[4]	1,859	3[4]	1,311
2006–2007	63[4]	48[4]	13[4]	2[4]	0[4]	0[4]	32[4]	1,906	9[4]	1,243
2007–2008	44[4]	39[4]	7[4]	2[4]	0[4]	0[4]	21[4]	1,858	5[4]	1,256
2008–2009	44[4]	29[4]	15[4]	0[4]	0[4]	0[4]	18[4]	1,720	7[4]	1,425
2009–2010	35[4]	27[4]	5[4]	3[4]	0[4]	0[4]	19[4]	1,551	2[4]	1,441
2010–2011	32[4]	26[4]	6[4]	0[4]	0[4]	0[4]	11[4]	1,436	3[4]	1,559
2011–2012	45[4]	26[4]	14	5[4]	0[4]	0[4]	15[4]	1,360	5[4]	1,541
2012–2013	53[4]	41[4]	11[4]	1[4]	0[4]	0[4]	31[4]	1,310	6[4]	1,608
2013–2014	48[4]	26[4]	20[4]	1[4]	0[4]	0[4]	12[4]	1,160	8[4]	1,638
2014–2015	47[4]	28[4]	17[4]	2[4]	0[4]	0[4]	20[4]	1,273	9[4]	1,882
2015–2016	38[4]	30[4]	7[4]	1[4]	0[4]	0[4]	18[4]	1,478	3[4]	1,941

Note: Unless otherwise noted, data are reported for the school year, defined as July 1 through June 30. Some data have been revised from previously published figures. Violent deaths for which the manner was undetermined; that is, the information pointing to one manner of death was no more compelling than the information pointing to one or more other competing manners of death when all available information was considered.
[1] A school-associated violent death is defined as "a homicide, suicide, or legal intervention (involving a law enforcement officer), in which the fatal injury occurred on the campus of a functioning elementary or secondary school in the United States," while the victim was on the way to or from regular sessions at school, or while the victim was attending or traveling to or from an official school-sponsored event.
[2] "At school" includes on school property, on the way to or from regular sessions at school, and while attending or traveling to or from a school-sponsored event.
[3] Excludes self-inflicted deaths among 5- to 9-year-olds. The number of self-inflicted deaths among 5- to 9-year-olds was generally less than 7 per year during the period covered by this table.
[4] Data from 1999–2000 onward are subject to change until interviews with school and law enforcement officials have been completed. The details learned during the interviews can occasionally change the classification of a case.

Table 2. Number of Nonfatal Victimizations Against Students Ages 12 to 18 Years and Rate of Victimization Per 1,000 Students, by Type of Victimization and Location, 1992–2017

(Number; rate per 1,000 students.)

Location and year	Number of nonfatal victimizations				Rate of victimization per 1,000 students			
			Violent				Violent	
	Total	Theft	All violent	Serious violent[1]	Total	Theft	All violent	Serious violent[1]
At School[2]								
1992	4,281,200	2,679,400	1,601,800	197,600	181.5	113.6	67.9	8.4
1993	4,692,800	2,477,100	2,215,700	535,500	193.5	102.1	91.4	22.1
1994	4,721,000	2,474,100	2,246,900	459,100	187.7	98.4	89.3	18.3
1995	4,400,700	2,468,400	1,932,200	294,500	172.2	96.6	75.6	11.5
1996	4,130,400	2,205,200	1,925,300	371,900	158.4	84.5	73.8	14.3
1997	3,610,900	1,975,000	1,635,900	376,200	136.6	74.7	61.9	14.2
1998	3,247,300	1,635,100	1,612,200	314,500	121.3	61.1	60.2	11.7
1999	3,152,400	1,752,200	1,400,200	281,100	117.0	65.1	52.0	10.4
2000	2,301,000	1,331,500	969,500	214,200	84.9	49.1	35.8	7.9
2001	2,521,300	1,348,500	1,172,700	259,400	92.3	49.4	42.9	9.5
2002	2,082,600	1,088,800	993,800	173,500	75.4	39.4	36.0	6.3
2003	2,308,800	1,270,500	1,038,300	188,400	87.4	48.1	39.3	7.1
2004	1,762,200	1,065,400	696,800	107,300	67.2	40.6	26.6	4.1
2005	1,678,600	875,900	802,600	140,300	63.2	33.0	30.2	5.3
2006[3]	1,799,900	859,000	940,900	249,900	67.5	32.2	35.3	9.4
2007	1,801,200	896,700	904,400	116,100	67.8	33.7	34.0	4.4
2008	1,435,500	648,000	787,500	128,700	54.3	24.5	29.8	4.9
2009	1,322,800	594,500	728,300	233,700	51.0	22.9	28.1	9.0
2010	892,000	469,800	422,300	155,000	34.9	18.4	16.5	6.1
2011	1,246,200	647,700	598,600	89,500	49.3	25.6	23.7	3.5
2012	1,364,900	615,600	749,200	89,000	52.4	23.6	28.8	3.4
2013	1,420,900	454,900	966,000	125,500	55.0	17.6	37.4	4.9
2014	850,100	363,700	486,400	93,800	33.0	14.1	18.9	3.6
2015	841,100	309,100	531,900	99,000	32.9	12.1	20.8	3.9
2016[4]	NA	NA	NA	NA	NA	NA	NA	NA
2017	827,000	306,500	520,500	110,600	32.7	12.1	20.6	4.4
Away from School								
1992	4,084,100	1,857,600	2,226,500	1,025,100	173.1	78.7	94.4	43.5
1993	3,835,900	1,731,100	2,104,800	1,004,300	158.2	71.4	86.8	41.4
1994	4,147,100	1,713,900	2,433,200	1,074,900	164.9	68.1	96.7	42.7
1995	3,626,600	1,604,800	2,021,800	829,700	141.9	62.8	79.1	32.5
1996	3,483,200	1,572,700	1,910,600	870,000	133.5	60.3	73.3	33.4
1997	3,717,600	1,710,700	2,006,900	853,300	140.7	64.7	75.9	32.3
1998	3,047,800	1,408,000	1,639,800	684,900	113.8	52.6	61.3	25.6
1999	2,713,800	1,129,200	1,584,500	675,400	100.8	41.9	58.8	25.1
2000	2,303,600	1,228,900	1,074,800	402,100	85.0	45.3	39.6	14.8
2001	1,780,300	961,400	819,000	314,800	65.2	35.2	30.0	11.5
2002	1,619,500	820,100	799,400	341,200	58.6	29.7	28.9	12.4
2003	1,824,100	780,900	1,043,200	412,800	69.1	29.6	39.5	15.6
2004	1,371,800	718,000	653,700	272,500	52.3	27.4	24.9	10.4
2005	1,429,000	637,700	791,300	257,100	53.8	24.0	29.8	9.7
2006[3]	1,413,100	714,200	698,900	263,600	53.0	26.8	26.2	9.9
2007	1,371,700	614,300	757,400	337,700	51.6	23.1	28.5	12.7
2008	1,132,600	498,500	634,100	258,600	42.8	18.9	24.0	9.8
2009	857,200	484,200	372,900	176,800	33.1	18.7	14.4	6.8
2010	689,900	378,800	311,200	167,300	27.0	14.8	12.2	6.5
2011	966,100	541,900	424,300	137,600	38.2	21.4	16.8	5.4
2012	991,200	470,800	520,400	169,900	38.0	18.1	20.0	6.5
2013	778,500	403,000	375,500	151,200	30.1	15.6	14.5	5.8
2014	621,300	288,900	332,400	165,000	24.1	11.2	12.9	6.4
2015	545,100	263,100	281,900	110,900	21.3	10.3	11.0	4.3
2016[4]	NA	NA	NA	NA	NA	NA	NA	NA
2017	503,800	188,600	315,200	145,300	19.9	7.4	12.4	5.7

Note: "Serious violent" victimization includes the crimes of rape, sexual assault, robbery, and aggravated assault. "All violent" victimization includes serious violent crimes as well as simple assault. "Theft" includes attempted and completed purse-snatching, completed pickpocketing, and all attempted and completed thefts, with the exception of motor vehicle thefts. Theft does not include robbery, which involves the threat or use of force and is classified as a violent crime. "Total victimization" includes theft and violent crimes. Data in this table are from the National Crime Victimization Survey (NCVS); due to differences in time coverage and administration between the NCVS and the School Crime Supplement (SCS) to the NCVS, data in this table cannot be compared with data in tables that are based on the SCS. Detail may not sum to totals because of rounding.
NA = Not available.
[1]Serious violent victimization is also included in all violent victimization.
[2]"At school" includes inside the school building, on school property, and on the way to and from school.
[3]Every 10 years, the survey sample is redesigned to reflect changes in the population. Due to the sample redesign and other methodological changes implemented in 2006, use caution when comparing 2006 estimates to other years.
[4]Every 10 years, the survey sample is redesigned to reflect changes in the population. Due to a sample increase and redesign in 2016, victimization estimates among youth in 2016 were not comparable to estimates for other years.

Table 3. Number of Nonfatal Victimizations Against Students Ages 12 to 18 Years and Rate of Victimization Per 1,000 Students, by Type of Victimization, Location, and Selected Student Characteristics, 2017

(Number; rate per 1,000 students.)

Location and year	Number of nonfatal victimizations				Rate of victimization per 1,000 students			
			Violent				Violent	
	Total	Theft	All violent	Serious violent[1]	Total	Theft	All violent	Serious violent[1]
At School[2]								
Total.........................	827,000	306,400	520,500	110,600	32.7	12.1	20.6	4.4
Sex								
Male	483,600	158,900	324,700	79,000	37.2	12.2	25.0	6.1
Female...................	343,400	147,600	195,900	31,600	27.8	12.0	15.9	2.6
Age								
12 to 14 years......................	468,500	131,200	337,300	79,400	37.9	10.6	27.3	6.4
15 to 18 years......................	358,500	175,200	183,300	31,200	27.7	13.5	14.1	2.4!
Race/ethnicity[3]								
White...........................	397,300	124,700	272,600	79,500	29.7	9.3	20.4	5.9
Black...........................	159,100	56,800	102,300	2,900	47.2	16.9	30.4	0.9!
Hispanic......................	187,800	79,800	108,000	19,700	30.8	13.1	17.7	3.2!
Other	82,800	45,100	37,700	8,500	33.5	18.3	15.2!	3.4!
Urbanicity[4]								
Urban.........................	377,400	133,300	244,100	24,800	49.5	17.5	32.0	3.2
Suburban	348,600	137,800	210,800	75,400	24.5	9.7	14.8	5.3
Rural	101,000	35,400	65,600	10,400	29.0	10.1	18.8	3.0
Household income[5]								
Less than $15,000.................	82,000	24,000	58,000	NA	39.5	11.5	27.9	NA
$15,000 to $29,999...............	211,500	54,300	157,200	24,900!	58.1	14.9	43.2	6.8!
$30,000 to $49,999...............	98,900	51,200	47,700	17,400!	19.5	10.1	9.4	3.4!
$50,000 to $74,999...............	194,100	60,500	133,600	44,900!	45.4	14.1	31.2	10.5!
$75,000 or more....................	240,600	116,400	124,100	22,500!	23.5	11.4	12.1	2.2!
Away from School								
Total.........................	503,800	188,600	315,200	145,300	19.9	7.4	12.4	5.7
Sex								
Male	295,100	90,700	204,500	106,500	22.7	7.0	15.7	8.2
Female...................	208,700	97,900	110,800	38,800	16.9	7.9	9.0	3.1
Age								
12 to 14 years......................	212,500	84,200	128,400	59,700	17.2	6.8	10.4	4.8
15 to 18 years......................	291,300	104,400	186,900	85,700	22.5	8.1	14.4	6.6
Race/ethnicity[3]								
White...........................	329,200	110,200	219,100	94,900	24.6	8.2	16.4	7.1
Black...........................	42,200	20,300	21,900!	5,600!	12.5	6.0	6.5	1.7!
Hispanic......................	103,200	39,800	63,400	36,100!	17.0	6.5	10.4	5.9!
Other	29,100	18,400	10,800!	8,600!	11.8	7.4	4.3!	3.5!
Urban/city[4]								
Urban...........................	173,700	67,300	106,400	57,600	22.8	8.8	13.9	7.6
Suburban	219,000	69,800	149,200	44,800	15.4	4.9	10.5	3.2
Rural	111,100	51,500	59,600	42,900!	31.9	14.8	17.1	12.3!
Household income[5]								
Less than $15,000..................	58,500	22,100	36,300	12,800!	28.2	10.6	17.5	6.1!
$15,000 to $29,999...............	123,500	43,900	79,700	43,700!	34.0	12.1	21.9	12.0!
$30,000 to $49,999...............	97,500	51,000	46,500	36,900!	19.2	10.0	9.1	7.3
$50,000 to $74,999...............	71,200	21,700	49,600	19,500!	16.6	5.1	11.6	4.5!
$75,000 or more....................	153,100	49,900	103,200	32,500	14.9	4.9	10.1	3.2

Note: "Serious violent" victimization includes the crimes of rape, sexual assault, robbery, and aggravated assault. "All violent" victimization includes serious violent crimes as well as simple assault. "Theft" includes attempted and completed purse-snatching, completed pickpocketing, and all attempted and completed thefts, with the exception of motor vehicle thefts. Theft does not include robbery, which involves the threat or use of force and is classified as a violent crime. "Total victimization" includes theft and violent crimes. Data in this table are from the National Crime Victimization Survey (NCVS) and are reported in accordance with Bureau of Justice Statistics standards. Detail may not sum to totals because of rounding and missing data on student characteristics. The population size for students ages 12–18 was 25,546,100 in 2016. Every 10 years, the survey sample is redesigned to reflect changes in the population. The sample redesign impacted the comparability of 2016 estimates to estimates for earlier years. Caution should be used when making comparisons to earlier years. For more information, see Criminal Victimization, 2016 (available at https://www.bjs.gov/index.cfm?ty=pbse&sid=6).
Source: U.S. Department of Justice, Bureau of Justice Statistics, National Crime Victimization Survey (NCVS), 2016. (This table was prepared August 2017.)
NA = Not available.
(!) = Interpret data with caution. Estimate based on 10 or fewer sample cases, or the coefficient of variation is greater than 50 percent.
[1] Serious violent victimization is also included in all violent victimization.
[2] "At school" includes inside the school building, on school property, and on the way to and from school.
[3] Race categories exclude persons of Hispanic ethnicity. "Other" includes Asians, Pacific Islanders, American Indians/Alaska Natives, and persons of two or more races.
[4] Refers to the Standard Metropolitan Statistical Area (MSA) status of the respondent's household as defined by the U.S. Census Bureau. Categories include "central city of an MSA (Urban)," "in MSA but not in central city (Suburban)," and "not MSA (Rural)."
[5] Income data for 2017 were imputed. For more information, see Criminal Victimization, 2017, available at https://www.bjs.gov/index.cfm?ty=pbse&sid=6.

Table 4. Percentage of Students Ages 12 to 18 Years Who Reported Criminal Victimization at School During the Previous 6 Months, by Type of Victimization and Selected Student and School Characteristics, Selected Years, 1995–2017

(Percent.)

Characteristic	1995	2001	2003	2005	2007	2009	2011	2013	2015	2017
Total	9.1	5.5	5.1	4.3	4.3	3.9	3.5	3.0	2.7	2.2
Sex										
Male	9.6	6.1	5.3	4.6	4.5	4.6	3.7	3.2	2.6	2.6
Female	8.5	4.9	4.8	3.9	3.9	3.2	3.4	2.8	2.8	1.8
Race/ethnicity[1]										
White	9.4	5.7	5.4	4.6	4.2	3.9	3.6	3.0	2.9	2.2
Black	9.6	6.1	5.1	3.9	4.3	4.4	4.6	3.2	2.2!	2.6
Hispanic	7.1	4.6	3.9	3.9	3.6	3.9	2.9	3.2	2.3	2.0
Asian/Pacific Islander	8.3	3.7	3.2	1.4!	3.4!	^	2.3!	2.4!	^	2.1!
Asian	NA	NA	3.3!	1.5!	3.6!	^	2.5!	2.6!	^	2.1!
Pacific Islander	NA	NA	^	^	^	^	^	^	^	^
American Indian/ Alaska Native	9.6!	^	^	^	^	^	^	^	^	11.!
Two or more races	NA	NA	9.8	^	10.1	^	4.9!	3.0	6.5!	^
Grade										
6th	8.8	5.9	3.8	4.6	3.9	3.7	3.8	4.1	3.1	3.1
7th	10.6	5.8	6.3	5.4	4.7	3.4	3.1	2.5	3.4	2.6
8th	10.1	4.3	5.2	3.6	4.4	3.8	3.8	2.3	2.3	1.8
9th	11.4	7.9	6.3	4.7	5.3	5.3	5.1	4.1	3.0	2.7
10th	8.7	6.5	4.7	4.3	4.4	4.2	3.0	3.3	1.6	2.7
11th	7.0	4.8	5.0	3.6	4.0	4.7	3.1	3.3	4.4	1.4
12th	5.8	2.9	3.6	3.7	2.7	2.0	2.9	2.0!	1.3!	1.4
Urbanicity[2]										
Urban	8.6	5.9	6.0	5.3	4.5	4.2	4.3	3.3	3.3	2.7
Suburban	9.9	5.6	4.7	4.2	4.1	4.0	3.3	3.2	2.8	2.1
Rural	8.1	4.7	4.7	2.8	4.4	3.1	2.8	2.0	1.5	1.6!
Control of school										
Public	9.3	5.7	5.1	4.4	4.5	4.1	3.7	3.1	2.8	2.3
Private	6.2	3.4	4.9	2.7	1.1!	1.8	1.9!	2.8	^	^
Theft	7.0	4.2	4.0	3.1	3.0	2.8	2.6	1.9	1.9	1.5
Sex										
Male	7.0	4.5	3.9	3.1	3.0	3.4	2.6	2.0	1.7	1.6
Female	7.0	3.8	4.1	3.2	3.0	2.1	2.6	1.8	2.0	1.3
Race/ethnicity[1]										
White	7.3	4.1	4.3	3.4	3.1	2.9	2.5	1.6	2.0	1.3
Black	6.9	5.0	3.8	2.7	3.1	2.5	3.7	2.7	1.3!	1.8
Hispanic	5.7	3.7	3.0	3.1	2.2	3.0	2.0	1.8	1.6	1.4
Asian/Pacific Islander	6.4	3.5	3.2	^	3.0!	^	2.3!	2.4!	^	2.1!
Asian	NA	NA	3.3!	^	3.2!	^	2.5!	2.6!	^	2.1!
Pacific Islander	NA	NA	^	^	^	^	^	^	^	^
American Indian/ Alaska Native	7.2!	^	^	^	^	^	^	^	^	7.2!
Two or more races	NA	NA	8.3	^	5.3	^	3.7!	^	4.3!	^
Grade										
6th	5.4	4.0	2.2	2.8	2.6	1.3	2.7	1.4!	1.6!	1.0!
7th	8.1	3.4	4.8	2.9	2.7	2.1	1.9	1.4	1.6!	1.3!
8th	7.8	3.3	4.1	2.4	2.5	2.0	2.0	1.0!	1.8	1.1!
9th	8.8	6.2	5.2	3.7	4.6	4.9	4.4	2.7	2.1	2.4
10th	7.6	5.7	3.7	3.8	3.6	3.5	2.1	2.6	1.4!	2.1
11th	5.4	3.8	4.1	2.8	2.6	3.3	2.7	2.3	3.4	1.1!
12th	4.5	2.3	3.1	3.4	1.9	1.5	2.4	1.6!	1.0!	1.2!
Urbanicity[2]										
Urban	6.4	4.5	4.5	3.6	2.8	2.9	3.0	2.4	2.3	1.8
Suburban	7.5	4.3	3.8	3.2	3.0	2.8	2.5	1.9	1.8	1.4
Rural	6.8	3.4	3.9	2.2!	3.2	2.3	2.0	0.8	1.2	0.9!
Control of school										
Public	7.2	4.4	4.0	3.3	3.2	2.9	2.7	1.9	1.9	1.6
Private	4.9	2.4	4.0	1.3!	1.1!	^	1.2!	2.0!	^	^
Violent	2.5	1.8	1.3	1.2	1.6	1.4	1.1	1.2	0.9	0.7
Sex										
Male	3.0	2.1	1.7	1.6	1.7	1.6	1.2	1.3	1.0	1.0
Female	2.0	1.4	0.9	0.8	1.4	1.1	0.9	1.1	0.9	0.5

(Percent.)

Characteristic	1995	2001	2003	2005	2007	2009	2011	2013	2015	2017
Race/ethnicity[1]										
White	2.5	2.0	1.4	1.3	1.5	1.2	1.2	1.5	1.0	0.9
Black	3.0	1.3!	1.5	1.3!	1.6!	2.3	1.1!	^	0.9	0.8!
Hispanic	2.0	1.5	1.1	0.9	1.4	1.3!	1.0	1.5	0.6	0.5!
Asian/Pacific Islander	2.2!	^	^	^	^	^	^	^	^	^
Asian	NA	NA	^	^	^	^	^	^	^	^
Pacific Islander	NA	NA	^	^	^	^	^	^	^	^
American Indian/ Alaska Native	^	^	^	^	^	^	^	^	^	^
Two or more races	NA	NA	^	^	5.3	^	^	^	3.6!	^
Grade										
6th	4.3	2.6	1.9	1.9	1.5	2.6!	1.3!	2.7	1.6!	2.1
7th	3.1	2.6	1.7	2.6	2.4	1.2!	1.2!	1.2!	1.9	1.4!
8th	2.7	1.3	1.4	1.4	2.1	2.0	2.1	1.4	0.6!	0.7!
9th	2.9	2.4	1.5	1.0	1.2!	0.9!	1.1!	1.4!	0.8!	^
10th	1.8	1.2	1.3	0.5!	1.2!	1.0!	0.9!	1.0!	^	0.7!
11th	1.6	1.6	0.9!	0.7!	1.5	1.5!	^	1.0!	1.3!	^
12th	1.6	0.9!	0.5!	^	0.8!	^	^	^	^	^
Urbanicity[2]										
Urban	2.6	1.7	1.8	1.8	2.0	1.8	1.4	0.9	1.0	0.9
Suburban	3.0	1.7	1.2	1.1	1.3	1.3	0.9	1.4	1.0	0.6
Rural	1.5	2.0!	0.9!	0.6!	1.7	0.8!	1.0!	1.1!	0.5!	0.7!
Control of school										
Public	2.6	1.8	1.4	1.2	1.7	1.4	1.1	1.2	1.0	0.8
Private	1.6	1.0	0.9!	1.4!	^	^	^	^	^	^
Serious Violent[3]	0.5	0.4	0.2	0.3	0.4	0.3	0.1	0.2	0.2	0.2
Sex										
Male	0.7	0.5	0.3!	0.3!	0.5!	0.6	0.2!	0.2!	0.2!	0.2!
Female	0.3	0.4!	^	0.3	0.2!	^	^	0.2!	^	0.2!
Race/ethnicity[1]										
White	0.5	0.4	0.2!	0.3!	0.2!	0.3!	0.2!	0.2!	0.3!	0.3!
Black	0.8!	0.5!	^	^	^	^	^	^	^	^
Hispanic	0.4!	0.8!	0.4!	0.4!	0.8!	^	^	0.4!	^	^
Asian/Pacific Islander	^	^	^	^	^	^	^	^	^	^
Asian	NA	NA	^	^	^	^	^	^	^	^
Pacific Islander	NA	NA	^	^	^	^	^	^	^	^
American Indian/ Alaska Native	^	^	^	^	^	^	^	^	^	^
Two or more races	NA	NA	^	^	^	^	^	^	^	^
Grade										
6th	1.2!	^	^	^	^	^	^	0.8!	^	^
7th	0.5!	0.6!	^	^	0.4!	^	0.5!	^	^	^
8th	0.6!	0.3!	^	^	^	^	*	^	^	^
9th	0.5!	0.8!	0.6!	^	^	^	^	^	^	^
10th	0.2!	0.4!	^	^	^	^	*	^	^	^
11th	0.3!	^	^	^	0.6!	^	*	^	^	^
12th	^	^	^	^	^	^	*	^	^	^
Urbanicity[2]										
Urban	0.9	0.5	0.3!	0.4!	0.7!	0.6!	^	0.3!	^	^
Suburban	0.4	0.4	0.1!	0.3!	0.2!	0.3!	^	0.2!	0.3!	0.2!
Rural	0.2!	0.5!	^	^	^	^	^	^	^	^
Control of school										
Public	0.5	0.5	0.2	0.3	0.4	0.4	0.1!	0.2!	0.2!	0.2!
Private	^	^	^	^	^	^	*	^	^	^

Note: "Total victimization" includes theft and violent victimization. A single student could report more than one type of victimization. In the total victimization section, students who reported both theft and violent victimization are counted only once. "Theft" includes attempted and completed purse-snatching, completed pickpocketing, and all attempted and completed thefts, with the exception of motor vehicle thefts. Theft does not include robbery, which involves the threat or use of force and is classified as a violent crime. "Serious violent victimization" includes the crimes of rape, sexual assault, robbery, and aggravated assault. "Violent victimization" includes the serious violent crimes as well as simple assault. "At school" includes in the school building, on school property, on a school bus, and, from 2001 onward, going to and from school. Some data have been revised from previously published figures.
NA = Not available.
* = Rounds to zero.
! = Interpret data with caution. The coefficient of variation (CV) for this estimate is between 30 and 50 percent.
^ = Reporting standards not met. Either there are too few cases for a reliable estimate or the coefficient of variation (CV) is 50 percent or greater.
[1]Race categories exclude persons of Hispanic ethnicity. Prior to 2003, separate data for Asian students, Pacific Islander students, and students of Two or more races were not collected.
[2]Refers to the Standard Metropolitan Statistical Area (MSA) status of the respondent's household as defined by the U.S. Census Bureau. Categories include "central city of an MSA (Urban)," "in MSA but not in central city (Suburban)," and "not MSA (Rural)."
[3]Serious violent victimization is also included in violent victimization.

Table 5. Number and Percentage of Public Teachers Who Reported That They Were Threatened with Injury or Physically Attacked by a Student from School During the Previous 12 Months, by Selected Teacher and School Characteristics, Selected Years, 1993–1994 Through 2015–2016

(Number; percent.)

Incident and year	Total	Sex		Race/ethnicity				Instructional level[1]	
		Male	Female	White	Black	Hispanic	Other[2]	Elementary	Secondary
					Number of teachers				
Threatened with Injury									
1993–1994	326,800	111,200	215,600	281,300	23,400	15,100	6,900	128,000	198,800
1999–2000	287,400	89,600	197,800	237,100	27,200	16,300	6,700	138,000	149,300
2003–2004	242,100	75,300	166,800	189,800	31,900	11,800	8,600	108,800	133,300
2007–2008	276,600	85,200	191,500	223,200	27,600	17,400	8,400	123,800	152,800
2011–2012	338,400	79,800	258,600	266,800	33,400	26,600	11,600	184,000	154,400
2015–2016	373,900	94,100	279,800	298,500	29,800	28,600	17,100	205,100	168,900
Physically Attacked									
1993–1994	112,400	28,700	83,700	96,300	7,600	5,900	2,600	71,600	40,700
1999–2000	125,000	29,100	95,900	103,100	11,000	8,400	2,500	94,400	30,600
2003–2004	121,400	21,700	99,700	95,500	14,800	6,400	4,700	85,100	36,300
2007–2008	146,400	33,400	113,000	124,100	11,600	7,800	2,800!	109,100	37,300
2011–2012	197,400	29,500	167,900	160,700	18,000	11,300	7,400	153,800	43,600
2015–2016	220,300	35,100	185,200	177,400	14,600	16,600	11,700	174,700	45,600
					Percent of teachers				
Threatened with Injury									
1993–1994	12.8	16.0	11.5	12.7	12.4	13.9	14.5	9.6	16.2
1999–2000	9.6	11.9	8.8	9.4	11.9	9.7	9.1	8.6	10.7
2003–2004	7.4	9.3	6.8	7.0	12.4	5.8	9.6	6.3	8.7
2007–2008	8.1	10.4	7.4	7.9	11.5	7.3	8.7	7.2	9.1
2011–2012	10.0	10.0	10.0	9.6	14.5	10.1	9.9	10.7	9.3
2015–2016	9.8	10.5	9.6	9.7	11.7	8.5	10.3	10.7	8.8
Physically Attacked									
1993–1994	4.4	4.1	4.5	4.3	4.0	5.4	5.4	5.4	3.3
1999–2000	4.2	3.9	4.3	4.1	4.8	5.0	3.4	5.9	2.2
2003–2004	3.7	2.7	4.1	3.5	5.8	3.2	5.3	5.0	2.4
2007–2008	4.3	4.1	4.4	4.4	4.9	3.3	3.0!	6.3	2.2
2011–2012	5.8	3.7	6.5	5.8	7.8	4.3	6.3	8.9	2.6
2015–2016	5.8	3.9	6.3	5.8	5.7	4.9	7.0	9.2	2.4

Note: Teachers who taught only prekindergarten students are excluded. Includes teachers in both traditional public schools and public charter schools. Instructional level divides teachers into elementary or secondary based on a combination of the grades taught, main teaching assignment, and the structure of the teachers' class(es). Race categories exclude persons of Hispanic ethnicity. Detail may not sum to totals because of rounding. Some data have been revised from previously published figures.
! = Interpret data with caution. The coefficient of variation (CV) for this estimate is between 30 and 50 percent.
[1]Teachers were classified as elementary or secondary on the basis of the grades they taught, rather than the level of the school in which they taught. In general, elementary teachers include those teaching prekindergarten through grade 6 and those teaching multiple grades, with a preponderance of the grades taught being kindergarten through grade 6. In general, secondary teachers include those teaching any of grades 7 through 12 and those teaching multiple grades, with a preponderance of the grades taught being grades 7 through 12 and usually with no grade taught being lower than grade 5.
[2]Includes American Indian/Alaska Native, Asian, and Pacific Islander; for 2003-04 and later years, also includes Two or more races.

Table 6. Percentage of Public Schools Recording Incidents of Crime at School and Reporting Incidents to Police, Number of Incidents, and Rate Per 1,000 Students, by Type of Crime, Selected Years, 1999–2000 Through 2015–2016

(Percent; number; rate per 1,000 students.)

Type of crime recorded or reported to police	Percent of schools						2015–2016		
	1999–2000	2003–2004	2005–2006	2007–2008	2009–2010	2013–2014[1]	Percent of schools	Number of incidents	Rate per 1,000 students
Recorded Incidents									
Total	86.4	88.5	85.7	85.5	85.0	NA	78.9	1,381,200	28.0
Violent Incidents	71.4	81.4	77.7	75.5	73.8	65.0	68.9	864,900	17.5
Serious violent incidents	19.7	18.3	17.1	17.2	16.4	13.1	15.5	40,800	0.8
Rape or attempted rape	0.7	0.8	0.3	0.8	0.5	0.2!	0.9	1,100	*
Sexual assault other than rape[2]	2.5	3.0	2.8	2.5	2.3	1.7	3.4	6,100	0.1
Physical attack or fight with a weapon	5.2	4.0	3.0	3.0	3.9	1.8	2.6	5,300	0.1
Threat of physical attack with a weapon	11.1	8.6	8.8	9.3	7.7	8.7	8.5	18,300	0.4
Robbery with a weapon	0.5!	0.6	0.4	0.4!	0.2	‡	0.5!	600	…
Robbery without a weapon	5.3	6.3	6.4	5.2	4.4	2.5	2.7	9,500	0.2
Physical attack or fight without a weapon	63.7	76.7	74.3	72.7	70.5	57.5	64.9	567,000	11.5
Threat of physical attack without a weapon	52.2	53.0	52.2	47.8	46.4	47.1	39.4	257,000	5.2
Theft[3]	45.6	46.0	46.0	47.3	44.1	NA	38.7	166,000	3.4
Other Incidents[4]	72.7	64.0	68.2	67.4	68.1	NA	58.5	350,400	7.1
Possession of a firearm/explosive device	5.5	6.1	7.2	4.7	4.7	NA	4.0	10,500!	0.2!
Possession of a knife or sharp object	42.6	NA	42.8	40.6	39.7	NA	38.4	70,600	1.4
Distribution of illegal drugs[5]	12.3	12.9	NA	NA	NA	NA	NA	NA	NA
Possession or use of alcohol or illegal drugs[5]	26.6	29.3	NA	NA	NA	NA	NA	NA	NA
Distribution, possession, or use of illegal drugs[6]	NA	NA	25.9	23.2	24.6	NA	24.9	112,100	2.3
Inappropriate distribution, possession, or use of prescription drugs[7]	NA	NA	NA	NA	12.1	NA	9.5	20,100	0.4
Distribution, possession, or use of alcohol[6]	NA	NA	16.2	14.9	14.1	NA	13.3	29,900	0.6
Sexual harassment	36.3	NA	NA	NA	NA	NA	NA	NA	NA
Vandalism	51.4	51.4	50.5	49.3	45.8	NA	33.4	107,200	2.2
Reported Incidents to Police									
Total	62.5	65.2	60.9	62.0	60.0	NA	47.4	448,900	9.1
Violent Incidents	36.0	43.6	37.7	37.8	39.9	NA	32.7	195,600	4.0
Serious violent incidents	14.8	13.3	12.6	12.6	10.4	NA	10.0	20,000	0.4
Rape or attempted rape	0.6	0.8	0.3	0.8	0.5	NA	0.7	900	*
Sexual assault other than rape[2]	2.3	2.6	2.6	2.1	1.4	NA	2.7	3,600	0.1
Physical attack or fight with a weapon	3.9	2.8	2.2	2.1	2.2	NA	1.3	2,500!	0.1!
Threat of physical attack with a weapon	8.5	6.0	5.9	5.7	4.5	NA	5.3	7,500	0.2
Robbery with a weapon	0.3!	0.6	0.4	0.4	0.2	NA	0.3!	400!	*
Robbery without a weapon	3.4	4.2	4.9	4.1	3.5	NA	1.9	5,000	0.1
Physical attack or fight without a weapon	25.8	35.6	29.2	28.2	34.3	NA	25.1	121,500	2.5
Threat of physical attack without a weapon	18.9	21.0	19.7	19.5	15.2	NA	12.9	54,200	1.1
Theft[3]	28.5	30.5	27.9	31.0	25.4	NA	18.1	71,600	1.5
Other Incidents[4]	52.0	50.0	50.6	48.7	46.3	NA	33.5	181,700	3.7
Possession of a firearm/explosive device	4.5	4.9	5.5	3.6	3.1	NA	1.9	7,500!	0.2!
Possession of a knife or sharp object	23.0	NA	25.0	23.3	20.0	NA	15.8	27,700	0.6
Distribution of illegal drugs[5]	11.4	12.4	NA	NA	NA	NA	NA	NA	NA
Possession or use of alcohol or illegal drugs[5]	22.2	26.0	NA	NA	NA	NA	NA	NA	NA
Distribution, possession, or use of illegal drugs[6]	NA	NA	22.8	20.7	21.4	NA	19.9	82,200	1.7
Inappropriate distribution, possession, or use of prescription drugs[7]	NA	NA	NA	NA	9.6	NA	7.4	15,100	0.3
Distribution, possession, or use of alcohol[6]	NA	NA	11.6	10.6	10.0	NA	8.6	17,800	0.4
Sexual harassment	14.7	NA	NA	NA	NA	NA	NA	NA	NA
Vandalism	32.7	34.3	31.9	30.8	26.8	NA	12.9	31,600	0.6

Note: Responses were provided by the principal or the person most knowledgeable about crime and safety issues at the school. "At school" was defined to include activities that happen in school buildings, on school grounds, on school buses, and at places that hold school-sponsored events or activities. Respondents were instructed to include incidents that occurred before, during, and after normal school hours or when school activities or events were in session. Detail may not sum to totals because of rounding and because schools that recorded or reported more than one type of crime incident were counted only once in the total percentage of schools recording or reporting incidents.
NA = Not available.
Source: U.S. Department of Education, National Center for Education Statistics, 1999–2000, 2003–04, 2005–06, 2007–08, and 2009–10 School Survey on Crime and Safety (SSOCS), 2000, 2004, 2006, 2008, and 2010; Fast Response Survey System (FRSS), "School Safety and Discipline: 2013-14," FRSS 106, 2014; and Common Core of Data (CCD), "Public Elementary/Secondary School Universe Survey," 2013-14. (This table was prepared September 2015.)
* = Rounds to zero.
! = Interpret data with caution. The coefficient of variation (CV) for this estimate is between 30 and 50 percent.
[1]Data for 2013–14 were collected using the Fast Response Survey System (FRSS), while data for all other years were collected using the School Survey on Crime and Safety (SSOCS). The 2013–14 FRSS survey was designed to allow comparisons with SSOCS data. However, respondents to the 2013–14 survey could choose either to complete the survey on paper (and mail it back) or to complete the survey online, whereas respondents to SSOCS did not have the option of completing the survey online. The 2013–14 survey also relied on a smaller sample. The smaller sample size and difference in survey administration may have impacted the 2013–14 results.
[2]Prior to 2015–2016, the wording of the survey item was "sexual battery other than rape."
[3]Theft/larceny (taking things worth over $10 without personal confrontation) was defined for respondents as "the unlawful taking of another person's property without personal confrontation, threat, violence, or bodily harm." This includes pocket picking, stealing a purse or backpack (if left unattended or no force was used to take it from owner), theft from a building, theft from a motor vehicle or motor vehicle parts or accessories, theft of a bicycle, theft from a vending machine, and all other types of thefts.
[4]Caution should be used when making direct comparisons of "Other incidents" between years because the survey questions about alcohol and drugs changed, as outlined in footnotes 5, 6, and 7.
[5]The survey items "Distribution of illegal drugs" and "Possession or use of alcohol or illegal drugs" appear only on the 1999–2000 and 2003–2004 questionnaires. Different alcohol- and drug-related survey items were used on the SSOCS questionnaires for later years.
[6]The survey items "Distribution, possession, or use of illegal drugs" and "Distribution, possession, or use of alcohol" appear only on the SSOCS questionnaires for 2005-2006 and later years.
[7]The survey item "Inappropriate distribution, possession, or use of prescription drugs" appears only on the 2009–2010 and 2015–2016 questionnaires.

Table 7. Percentage of Students Ages 12 to 18 Years Who Reported That Gangs Were Present at School During the School Year, by Sex, Race/Ethnicity, and Urbanicity, Selected Years, 2001–2017

(Percent.)

Year and urbanicity[2]	Total	Sex		Race/ethnicity[1]			Asian/Pacific Islander			American Indian/ Alaska Native	Two or more races
		Male	Female	White	Black	Hispanic	Total	Asian	Pacific Islander		
2001[3]											
Total	20.3	21.5	18.9	15.5	28.8	32.3	23.3	NA	NA	13.2!	NA
Urban	29.2	32.0	26.3	20.6	33.1	40.5	27.3	NA	NA	^	NA
Suburban	18.4	19.1	17.6	15.6	25.1	27.4	21.7	NA	NA	^	NA
Rural	13.3	14.1	12.5	12.0	22.8	16.8	^	NA	NA	^	NA
2003[3]											
Total	21.0	22.4	19.6	14.2	29.7	37.3	21.8	21.2	^	24.8!	22.3
Urban	31.0	32.2	29.8	19.8	33.1	42.8	31.4	30.4	^	^	29.4
Suburban	18.5	20.6	16.4	13.9	28.6	34.7	14.2	13.9	^	^	21.4
Rural	12.5	12.4	12.5	10.9	21.4!	12.8!	^	^	^	^	^
2005[3]											
Total	24.2	25.3	22.9	16.7	37.5	38.9	21.3	20.3	^	^	23.6
Urban	36.2	37.4	35.0	23.6	41.7	48.9	23.5	25.0	^	^	^
Suburban	20.8	22.4	19.1	15.9	36.2	32.1	20.5	18.3	^	^	18.8
Rural	16.4	16.1	16.7	14.1	24.4	26.2	^	^	^	^	^
2007											
Total	23.2	25.1	21.3	16.0	37.5	36.1	18.1	17.4	^	17.2!	28.3
Urban	32.3	35.3	29.2	23.4	39.5	40.4	20.7	18.4	^	^	31.4
Suburban	21.0	23.1	18.9	15.9	35.5	33.3	15.6	16.3	^	^	31.0
Rural	15.5	14.9	16.1	10.9	36.8	27.5!	^	^	^	^	^
2009											
Total	20.4	20.9	19.9	14.1	31.4	33.0	16.9	17.2	^	^	18.0
Urban	30.7	32.8	28.6	19.4	40.0	38.9	19.5	18.9	^	^	^
Suburban	16.6	17.2	16.0	13.5	20.2	28.3	13.8	14.5	^	^	16.3!
Rural	16.0	13.7	18.1	11.8	35.4	27.3!	^	^	^	^	^
2011											
Total	17.5	17.5	17.5	11.1	32.7	26.4	10.1	9.9	^	^	10.3
Urban	22.8	23.0	22.6	13.9	31.6	31.0	8.9	7.6	^	^	10.5!
Suburban	16.1	16.5	15.6	11.3	33.5	23.2	11.6	12.0	^	^	10.6!
Rural	12.1	10.2	14.1	7.7	34.5	22.1!	^	^	^	^	^
2013											
Total	12.4	12.9	12.0	7.4	18.6	20.1	9.8	9.4	^	18.3!	13.3
Urban	18.3	18.6	18.0	14.3	20.6	22.6	10.6	10.4	^	^	15.2!
Suburban	10.8	11.7	9.8	6.4	17.3	19.3	8.2	8.2!	^	^	13.8
Rural	6.8	5.7	7.9	4.1	16.1	9.4!	^	^	^	^	^
2015											
Total	10.7	10.9	10.4	7.4	17.1	15.3	5.0!	4.1!	^	^	13.5
Urban	15.3	14.8	15.8	12.3	19.3	17.8	6.8!	5.9!	^	^	17.7!
Suburban	10.2	10.7	9.6	7.1	19.3	14.7	3.8!	^	^	^	11.8!
Rural	3.9	4.2	3.7	3.5	3.4!	^	^	^	^	^	^
2017											
Total	8.6	7.9	9.3	5.3	16.6	12.3	2.4!		2.0!	^	9.7
Urban	11.3	9.8	12.8	8.0	17.2	13.4	^		^	^	11.2!
Suburban	7.6	7.8	7.4	4.9	14.8	12.6	^		^	^	6.5!
Rural	6.6	4.4	8.9	3.6	22.7	4.0	^		^	^	^

Note: All gangs, whether or not they are involved in violent or illegal activity, are included. "At school" includes in the school building, on school property, on a school bus, and going to and from school. Some data have been revised from previously published figures.
NA = Not available.
! = Interpret data with caution. The coefficient of variation (CV) for this estimate is between 30 and 50 percent.
^ = Reporting standards not met. Either there are too few cases for a reliable estimate or the coefficient of variation (CV) is 50 percent or greater.
[1]Race categories exclude persons of Hispanic ethnicity. In 2001, separate data for Asian students, Pacific Islander students, and students of Two or more races were not collected.
[2]"Urbanicity" refers to the Standard Metropolitan Statistical Area (MSA) status of the respondent's household as defined by the U.S. Census Bureau. Categories include "central city of an MSA (Urban)," "in MSA but not in central city (Suburban)," and "not MSA (Rural)."
[3]In 2005 and prior years, the period covered by the survey question was "during the last 6 months," whereas the period was "during this school year" beginning in 2007. Cognitive testing showed that estimates for earlier years are comparable to those for 2007 and later years.

Table 8. Percentage of Students in Grades 9 to 12 Who Reported That Illegal Drugs Were Made Available to Them on School Property During the Previous 12 Months, by Selected Student Characteristics, Selected Years, 1993–2015

(Percent.)

Student characteristic	1993	1995	1997	1999	2001	2003	2005	2007	2009	2011	2013	2015	2017
Total	24.0	32.1	31.7	30.2	28.5	28.7	25.4	22.3	22.7	25.6	22.1	21.7	19.8
Sex													
Male	28.5	38.8	37.4	34.7	34.6	31.9	28.8	25.7	25.9	29.2	24.5	24.2	20.9
Female	19.1	24.8	24.7	25.7	22.7	25.0	21.8	18.7	19.3	21.7	19.7	19.1	18.7
Race/ethnicity													
White	24.1	31.7	31.0	28.8	28.3	27.5	23.6	20.8	19.8	22.7	20.4	19.8	17.7
Black	17.5	28.5	25.4	25.3	21.9	23.1	23.9	19.2	22.2	22.8	18.6	20.6	18.9
Hispanic	34.1	40.7	41.1	36.9	34.2	36.5	33.5	29.1	31.2	33.2	27.4	27.2	25.4
Asian[1]	NA	NA	NA	25.7	25.7	22.5	15.9	21.0	18.3	23.3	22.6	15.3	17.7
Pacific Islander[1]	NA	NA	NA	46.9	50.2	34.7	41.3	38.5	27.6	38.9	27.7	30.1!	25.7
American Indian/Alaska Native	20.9	22.8	30.1	30.6	34.5	31.3	24.4	25.1	34.0	40.5	25.5	19.8	17.1
Two or more races[1]	NA	NA	NA	36.0	34.5	36.6	31.6	24.6	26.9	33.3	26.4	24.7	19.2
Sexual orientation[2]													
Heterosexual	NA	NA	NA	NA	NA	NA	NA	NA	NA	NA	NA	20.8	18.9
Gay, lesbian, or bisexual	NA	NA	NA	NA	NA	NA	NA	NA	NA	NA	NA	29.3	28.2
Not sure	NA	NA	NA	NA	NA	NA	NA	NA	NA	NA	NA	28.4	19.6
Grade													
9th	21.8	31.1	31.4	27.6	29.0	29.5	24.0	21.2	22.0	23.7	22.4	21.6	18.9
10th	23.7	35.0	33.4	32.1	29.0	29.2	27.5	25.3	23.7	27.8	23.2	21.9	20.3
11th	27.5	32.8	33.2	31.1	28.7	29.9	24.9	22.8	24.3	27.0	23.2	22.7	20.0
12th	23.0	29.1	29.0	30.5	26.9	24.9	24.9	19.6	20.6	23.8	18.8	20.3	19.6
Urban/city[3]													
Urban	NA	NA	31.2	30.3	32.0	31.1	NA	NA	NA	NA	NA	NA	NA
Suburban	NA	NA	34.2	29.7	26.6	28.4	NA	NA	NA	NA	NA	NA	NA
Rural	NA	NA	22.7	32.1	28.2	26.2	NA	NA	NA	NA	NA	NA	NA

Note: "On school property" was not defined for survey respondents. Race categories exclude persons of Hispanic ethnicity.

NA = Not available.

! = Interpret data with caution. The coefficient of variation (CV) for this estimate is between 30 and 50 percent.

[1]Before 1999, Asian students and Pacific Islander students were not categorized separately, and students could not be classified as Two or more races. Because the response categories changed in 1999, caution should be used in comparing data on race from 1993, 1995, and 1997 with data from later years.

[2]Students were asked which sexual orientation—"heterosexual (straight)," "gay or lesbian," "bisexual," or "not sure"—best described them.

[3]Refers to the Standard Metropolitan Statistical Area (MSA) status of the respondent's household as defined by the U.S. Census Bureau. Categories include "central city of an MSA (Urban)," "in MSA but not in central city (Suburban)," and "not MSA (Rural)."

Table 9. Percentage of Students Age 12 to 18 Years Who Reported Being the Target of Hate-Related Words and Seeing Hate-Related Graffiti at School During the School Year by Selected Student and School Characteristics and Location, Selected Years, 1999–2017

(Percent.)

Student/school characteristic	1999[1]	2001[1]	2003[1]	2005[1]	2007	2009	2011	2013	2015	2017
Hate-Related Words										
Total	13.3	12.3	11.8	11.2	9.7	8.7	9.1	6.6	7.2	6.4
Sex										
Male	12.4	12.9	12.1	11.7	9.9	8.5	9.0	6.6	7.8	6.0
Female	14.4	11.8	11.4	10.7	9.6	8.9	9.1	6.7	6.7	6.9
Race/Ethnicity[2]										
White	12.6	12.0	11.0	10.4	8.9	7.2	8.3	5.3	6.3	6.1
Black	16.6	14.1	14.3	15.0	11.4	11.1	10.7	7.8	9.4	7.4
Hispanic	12.1	11.1	11.4	10.5	10.6	11.2	9.8	7.4	6.5	6.3
Asian/Pacific Islander	13.9	13.0	11.4	10.7	10.5	10.9	9.6	9.8	11.2	4.7
Asian	NA	NA	11.4	11.0	11.1	10.7	9.0	10.3	10.8	4.8
Pacific Islander	NA	NA	^	^	^	^	^	^	^	^
American Indian/Alaska Native	28.5	17.4!	18.6!	^	^	^	^	^	^	^
Two or more races	NA	NA	19.4	10.6!	11.7	9.8!	11.1	13.5	8.5	11.4
Grade										
6th	13.1	12.2	11.9	11.1	12.1	8.3	9.0	6.7	10.1	6.7
7th	15.8	14.2	12.5	13.1	10.7	9.6	9.9	7.5	7.0	7.3
8th	16.1	13.0	12.9	11.2	11.0	10.9	8.4	7.4	9.2	7.0
9th	13.3	12.2	13.5	12.8	10.9	8.0	10.2	6.6	7.4	8.2
10th	11.9	13.2	11.7	10.9	9.0	9.7	9.6	6.4	6.5	6.3
11th	10.6	12.7	8.3	9.0	8.6	8.4	8.7	7.5	6.0	4.7
12th	11.8	8.0	10.9	9.7	6.0	5.8	7.5	4.1	5.4	4.6
Urban/city[3]										
Urban	14.2	12.0	13.3	12.2	9.7	9.9	8.0	7.2	6.5	6.8
Suburban	13.3	12.5	10.8	9.4	9.3	8.3	9.8	6.6	8.3	6.3
Rural	12.2	12.4	12.3	15.5	11.0	8.1	8.5	5.7	4.9	6.2
Control of School										
Public	13.9	12.7	11.9	11.6	10.1	8.9	9.3	6.6	7.6	6.6
Private	8.2	8.2	9.8	6.8	6.1	6.6	6.9	6.7	2.8!	3.8
Hate-Related Graffiti										
Total	36.6	36.0	36.9	38.4	35.0	29.2	28.4	24.6	27.2	23.2
Sex										
Male	34.0	35.4	35.6	37.7	34.5	29.0	28.6	24.1	26.3	22.6
Female	39.3	36.6	38.2	39.1	35.5	29.3	28.1	25.1	28.1	23.8
Race/Ethnicity[2]										
White	36.8	36.5	35.8	38.5	35.6	28.3	28.2	23.7	28.6	24.0
Black	38.0	34.0	38.7	37.9	33.7	29.0	28.1	26.3	24.9	24.8
Hispanic	35.8	35.6	40.9	38.0	34.9	32.2	29.1	25.6	26.7	21.0
Asian/Pacific Islander	30.9	33.5	27.7	34.5	28.5	29.9	29.8	20.8	19.5	15.2
Asian	NA	NA	26.8	34.7	28.2	31.2	29.9	20.8	17.5	14.6
Pacific Islander	NA	NA	^	^	^	^	^	^	^	^
American Indian/Alaska Native	47.1	31.5	35.9!	^	27.3	^	16.8!	22.0!	^	27.8!
Two or more races	NA	NA	40.8	47.7	41.9	30.3	27.4	31.1	29.1	35.0
Grade										
6th	30.7	35.2	36.1	34.0	35.6	28.1	25.9	21.9	30.0	20.6
7th	35.1	35.5	37.6	37.0	32.4	27.9	26.0	21.7	24.7	21.2
8th	35.9	37.2	35.1	35.7	33.5	30.8	25.9	24.0	27.2	22.4
9th	39.5	36.1	37.6	41.6	34.6	28.1	28.7	27.2	28.2	25.2
10th	39.3	36.8	41.4	40.7	36.5	31.0	33.3	26.0	28.6	27.0
11th	37.3	36.5	37.2	40.2	35.4	27.4	32.1	25.8	26.2	22.6
12th	35.8	33.5	32.6	37.8	37.7	30.4	25.7	24.2	26.1	22.2
Urban/City[3]										
Urban	37.4	36.3	39.2	40.9	34.6	31.1	27.5	27.8	26.4	23.6
Suburban	37.6	36.5	36.4	38.0	34.3	28.6	29.9	23.7	28.0	23.1
Rural	32.9	34.1	34.7	35.8	37.9	27.7	24.9	21.6	25.7	22.6
Control of School										
Public	38.3	37.8	38.5	40.0	36.5	30.7	29.7	25.6	28.3	24.6
Private	20.8	17.3	19.8	18.6	18.5	11.8	13.4	12.6	11.5	6.4

Note: "At school" includes in the school building, on school property, on a school bus, and, from 2001 onward, going to and from school. "Hate-related" refers to derogatory terms used by others in reference to students' personal characteristics. Some data have been revised from previously published figures.
NA = Not available.
! = Interpret data with caution. The coefficient of variation (CV) for this estimate is between 30 and 50 percent.
^ = Reporting standards not met. Either there are too few cases for a reliable estimate or the coefficient of variation (CV) is 50 percent or greater.
[1] In 2005 and prior years, the period covered by the survey question was "during the last 6 months," whereas the period was "during this school year" beginning in 2007. Cognitive testing showed that estimates for earlier years are comparable to those for 2007 and later years.
[2] Race categories exclude persons of Hispanic ethnicity. Prior to 2003, separate data for Asian students, Pacific Islander students, and students of Two or more races were not collected.
[3] Refers to the Standard Metropolitan Statistical Area (MSA) status of the respondent's household as defined by the U.S. Census Bureau. Categories include "central city of an MSA (Urban)," "in MSA but not in central city (Suburban)," and "not MSA (Rural)."

Table 10. Percentage of Students Age 12 to 18 Years Who Reported Being Bullied at School During the School Year, by Type of Bullying and Selected Student and School Characteristics, Selected Years, 2005–2017

(Percent.)

Student/school characteristic	Total bullied at school[1]	Type of bullying						
		Made fun of, called names, or insulted	Subject of rumors	Threatened with harm	Tried to make do things did not want to do	Excluded from activities on purpose	Property destroyed on purpose	Pushed, shoved, tripped, or spit on
2005[2]	28.5	18.9	14.9	4.9	3.5	4.6	3.5	9.2
2007	31.7	21.0	18.1	5.8	4.1	5.2	4.2	11.0
2009	28.0	18.8	16.5	5.7	3.6	4.7	3.3	9.0
2011	27.8	17.6	18.3	5.0	3.3	5.6	2.8	7.9
2013	21.5	13.6	13.2	3.9	2.2	4.5	1.6	6.0
2015	20.8	13.3	12.3	3.9	2.5	5.0	1.8	5.1
2017								
Total	20.2	13.0	13.4	3.9	1.9	5.2	1.4	5.3
Sex								
Male	16.7	10.3	9.3	4.2	1.9	3.5	1.3	6.1
Female	23.8	15.8	17.5	3.6	1.9	6.9	1.5	4.4
Race/Ethnicity								
White	22.8	15.0	15.2	4.2	2.1	6.7	1.8	5.4
Black	22.9	16.0	14.5	5.4	2.4	3.9	1.7	6.5
Hispanic	15.7	8.9	10.6	2.6	1.4	3.3	0.6!	4.6
Asian/Pacific Islander	7.3	5.3	4.7	^	^	^	^	1.6!
Asian	7.3	5.3	4.7	^	^	^	^	1.7!
Pacific Islander	^	^	^	^	^	^	^	^
American Indian/Alaska Native	27.2	14.7	^	^	^	^	^	17.0!
Two or more races	23.2	12.9	15.7	7.6	^	7.5	^	6.9
Grade								
6th	29.5	23.1	17.1	8.5	2.1	8.4	3.5	10.5
7th	24.4	17.7	14.2	4.9	3.0	7.6	1.7	8.2
8th	25.3	16.3	16.0	4.4	1.8	5.7	1.6	6.9
9th	19.3	12.5	12.3	3.7	2.2	4.3	1.1!	5.4
10th	18.9	9.4	16.1	3.6	2.1	4.4	1.5!	3.7
11th	14.7	9.5	9.6	2.5	1.6	3.2	0.9!	3.3
12th	12.2	6.0	9.1	1.3	0.4	3.5	0.5!	0.7!
Urban/city[3]								
Urban	18.3	12.5	11.3	4.3	2.1	5.0	1.0	5.0
Suburban	19.7	12.6	13.0	3.4	1.6	5.1	1.5	4.7
Rural	26.7	15.9	19.1	4.9	2.7	5.9	1.8	8.0
Control of School								
Public	20.6	13.2	13.6	4.0	1.9	5.1	1.5	5.3
Private	16.0	11.5	11.3	3.2	2.0	5.7	^	4.5!

Note: "At school" includes in the school building, on school property, on a school bus, and going to and from school. Race categories exclude persons of Hispanic ethnicity. Some data have been revised from previously published figures.
! = Interpret data with caution. The coefficient of variation (CV) for this estimate is between 30 and 50 percent.
^ = Reporting standards not met. Either there are too few cases for a reliable estimate or the coefficient of variation (CV) is 50 percent or greater.
[1]In the total for students bullied at school, students who reported more than one type of bullying were counted only once.
[2]In 2005, the period covered by the survey question was "during the last 6 months," whereas the period was "during this school year" beginning in 2007. Cognitive testing showed that estimates for 2005 are comparable to those for 2007 and later years.
[3]Refers to the Standard Metropolitan Statistical Area (MSA) status of the respondent's household as defined by the U.S. Census Bureau. Categories include "central city of an MSA (Urban)," "in MSA but not in central city (Suburban)," and "not MSA (Rural)."

METHODOLOGY

This annual report, a joint effort by the Bureau of Justice Statistics and the National Center for Education Statistics (NCES), provides the most current statistical information on the nature of crime in schools. It presents data on crime and safety at school from the perspectives of students, teachers, and principals. This report contains 23 indicators of crime and safety at school from a number of sources, including the National Crime Victimization Survey (NCVS), the School Crime Supplement to the NCVS, the Youth Risk Behavior Survey, the School Survey on Crime and Safety, and the School and Staffing Survey. Topics covered include victimization at school, teacher injury, bullying and cyber-bullying, school conditions, fights, weapons, availability and student use of drugs and alcohol, student perceptions of personal safety at school, and crime at postsecondary institutions. For more information or to access the full report, please see < https://nces.ed.gov/pubs2019/2019047.pdf>.

Data

The Bureau of Justice Statistics' (BJS) **National Crime Victimization Survey (NCVS)** is the nation's primary source of information on criminal victimization. The survey underwent a sample redesign in 2016; information is available in the *Criminal Victimization chapter*.

Nonresponse and Weighting Adjustments

Estimates in this report use data primarily from the 2016 NCVS data files. These data are weighted to produce annual estimates of victimization for persons age 12 or older living in U.S. households. Because the NCVS relies on a sample rather than a census of the entire U.S. population, weights are designed to adjust to known population totals and compensate for survey nonresponse and other aspects of the complex sample design.

NCVS data files include person, household, and victimization weights. Person weights provide an estimate of the population represented by each person in the sample. Household weights provide an estimate of the U.S. household population represented by each household in the sample. After proper adjustment, both household and person weights are also typically used to form the denominator in calculations of crime rates.

Victimization weights used in the analyses in this report account for the number of persons present during an incident and for high-frequency repeat victimizations (i.e., series victimizations). Series victimizations are similar in type but occur with such frequency that a victim is unable to recall each individual event or describe each event in detail. Survey procedures allow NCVS interviewers to identify and classify these similar victimizations as series victimizations and to collect detailed information on only the most recent incident in the series.

The weight counts series victimizations as the actual number of victimizations reported by the victim, up to a maximum of 10. Including series victimizations in national rates results in large increases in the level of violent victimization. However, trends in violent crime are generally similar, regardless of whether series victimizations are included. In 2016, series incidents accounted for fewer than 2 percent of all victimizations and fewer than 4 percent of all violent victimizations. Weighting series victimizations as the number of victimizations up to a maximum of 10 victimizations produces more reliable estimates of crime levels, while the cap at 10 minimizes the effect of extreme outliers on rates. Additional information on the enumeration of series victimizations is detailed in the report *Methods for Counting High-Frequency Repeat Victimizations in the National Crime Victimization Survey* (NCJ 237308, BJS web, April 2012).

The **School-Associated Violent Deaths Study (SAVD)** is an epidemiological study developed by the Centers for Disease Control and Prevention in conjunction with the U.S. Department of Education and the U.S. Department of Justice. SAVD seeks to describe the epidemiology of school-associated violent deaths, identify common features of these deaths, estimate the rate of school-associated violent deaths in the United States, and identify potential risk factors for these deaths. The study includes descriptive data on all school-associated violent deaths in the United States, including all homicides, suicides, or legal intervention deaths in which the fatal injury occurred on the campus of a functioning elementary or secondary school; while the victim was on the way to or from regular sessions at such a school; or while attending or on the way to or from an official school-sponsored event. Victims of such incidents include nonstudents, as well as students and staff members. SAVD includes descriptive information about the school, event, victim(s), and offender(s). The SAVD study has collected data from July 1, 1992, through the present.

SAVD uses a four-step process to identify and collect data on school-associated violent deaths. Cases are initially identified through a search of the LexisNexis newspaper and media database. Then law enforcement officials from the office that investigated the deaths are contacted to confirm the details of the case and to determine if the event meets the case definition. Once a case is confirmed, a law enforcement official and a school official are interviewed regarding details about the school, event, victim(s), and offender(s). A copy of the full law enforcement report is also sought for each case. The information obtained on schools includes school demographics, attendance/absentee rates, suspensions/expulsions and mobility, school history of weapon-carrying incidents, security measures, violence prevention activities, school response to the event, and school policies about weapon carrying. Event information includes the location of injury, the context of injury (while classes were being held, during break, etc.), motives for injury, method of injury, and school and community events happening around the time period. Information obtained on victim(s) and offender(s) includes demographics, circumstances of the event (date/time, alcohol or drug use, number of persons involved), types and origins of weapons, criminal history, psychological risk factors, school-related problems, extracurricular activities, and family history, including structure and stressors.

For some recent data, the interviews with school and law enforcement officials to verify case details have not been completed. The details learned during the interviews can occasionally change the classification of a case. Also, new cases may be identified because of the expansion of the scope of the media files used for case identification. Sometimes other cases not identified during earlier data years using the independent case finding efforts (which focus on nonmedia sources of information) will be discovered. Also, other cases may occasionally be identified while the law enforcement and school interviews are being conducted to verify known cases.

Created as a supplement to the NCVS and co-designed by the National Center for Education Statistics and Bureau of Justice Statistics, the School Crime Supplement (SCS) survey has been conducted in 1989, 1995, and biennially since 1999 to collect additional information about school-related victimizations on a national level. This report includes data from the 1995, 1999, 2001, 2003, 2005, 2007, 2009, 2011, 2013, 2015, and 2017 collections. The 1989 data are not included in this report as a result of methodological changes to the NCVS and SCS. The SCS was designed to assist policymakers, as well as academic researchers and practitioners at federal, state, and local levels, to make informed decisions concerning crime in schools. The survey asks students a number of key questions about their experiences with and perceptions of crime and violence that occurred inside their school, on school grounds, on the school bus, or on the way to or from school. Students are asked additional questions about security measures used by their school, students' participation in after-school activities, students' perceptions of school rules, the presence of weapons and gangs in school, the presence of hate-related words and graffiti in school, student reports of bullying and reports of rejection at school, and the availability of drugs and alcohol in school. Students are also asked attitudinal questions relating to fear of victimization and avoidance behavior at school.

The SCS survey was conducted for a 6-month period from January through June in all households selected for the NCVS (see discussion above for information about the NCVS sampling design and changes to the race/ethnicity variable beginning in 2003). Within these households, the eligible respondents for the SCS were those household members who had attended school at any time during the 6 months preceding the interview, were enrolled in grades 6–12, and were not homeschooled. In 2007, the questionnaire was changed and household members who attended school sometime during the school year of the interview were included. The age range of students covered in this report is 12–18 years of age. Eligible respondents were asked the supplemental questions in the SCS only after completing their entire NCVS interview. It should be noted that the first or unbounded NCVS interview has always been included in analysis of the SCS data and may result in the reporting of events outside of the requested reference period.

The **Youth Risk Behavior Surveillance System (YRBSS)** is an epidemiological surveillance system developed by the Centers for Disease Control and Prevention (CDC) to monitor the prevalence of youth behaviors that most influence health. The YRBSS focuses on priority health-risk behaviors established during youth that result in the most significant mortality, morbidity, disability, and social problems during both youth and adulthood. The YRBSS includes a national school-based Youth Risk Behavior Survey (YRBS) as well as surveys conducted in states and large urban school districts. This report uses 1993, 1995, 1997, 1999, 2001, 2003, 2005, 2007, 2009, 2011, 2013, 2015, and 2017 YRBSS data.

The national YRBS uses a three-stage cluster sampling design to produce a nationally representative sample of students in grades 9–12 in the United States. The target population consisted of all public and private school students in grades 9–12 in the 50 states and the District of Columbia. The first-stage sampling frame included selecting primary sampling units (PSUs) from strata formed on the basis of urbanization and the relative percentage of Black and Hispanic students in the PSU. These PSUs are either counties; subareas of large counties; or groups of smaller, adjacent counties. At the second stage, schools were selected with probability proportional to school enrollment size.

The final stage of sampling consisted of randomly selecting, in each chosen school and in each of grades 9–12, one or two classrooms from either a required subject, such as English or social studies, or a required period, such as homeroom or second period. All students in selected classes were eligible to participate. In surveys conducted before 2013, three strategies were used to oversample Black and Hispanic students: (1) larger sampling rates were used to select PSUs that are in high-Black and high- Hispanic strata; (2) a modified measure of size was used that increased the probability of selecting schools with a disproportionately high minority enrollment; and (3) two classes per grade, rather than one, were selected in schools with a high percentage of combined Black, Hispanic, Asian/Pacific Islander, or American Indian/Alaska Native enrollment. In 2013, only selection of two classes per grade was needed to achieve an adequate precision with minimum variance.

The **School Survey on Crime and Safety (SSOCS)** is managed by the National Center for Education Statistics (NCES) on behalf of the U.S. Department of Education. SSOCS collects extensive crime and safety data from principals and school administrators of U.S. public schools. Data from this collection can be used to examine the relationship between school characteristics and violent and serious violent crimes in primary schools, middle schools, high schools, and combined schools. In addition, data from SSOCS can be used to assess what crime prevention programs, practices, and policies are used by schools.

Definitions

General Terms

Crime Any violation of a statute or regulation or any act that the government has determined is injurious to the public, including felonies and misdemeanors. Such violation may or may not involve violence, and it may affect individuals or property.

Incident A specific criminal act or offense involving one or more victims and one or more offenders.

Multistage sampling A survey sampling technique in which there is more than one wave of sampling. That is, one sample of units is drawn, and then another sample is drawn within that sample. For example, at the first stage, a number of Census blocks may be sampled out of all the Census blocks in the United States. At the second stage, households are sampled within the previously sampled Census blocks.

Prevalence The percentage of the population directly affected by crime in a given period. This rate is based upon specific information elicited directly from the respondent regarding crimes committed against his or her person, against his or her property, or against an individual bearing a unique relationship to him or her. It is not based upon perceptions and beliefs

about, or reactions to, criminal acts.

School An education institution consisting of one or more of grades K–12.

School crime Any criminal activity that is committed on school property.

School year The 12-month period of time denoting the beginning and ending dates for school accounting purposes, usually from July 1 through June 30.

Stratification A survey sampling technique in which the target population is divided into mutually exclusive groups or strata based on some variable or variables (e.g., metropolitan area) and sampling of units occurs separately within each stratum.

Unequal probabilities A survey sampling technique in which sampled units do not have the same probability of selection into the sample. For example, the investigator may oversample rural students in order to increase the sample sizes of rural students. Rural students would then be more likely than other students to be sampled.

Specific Terms Used in Various Surveys

School-Associated Violent Deaths Study (SAVD)

Homicide An act involving a killing of one person by another resulting from interpersonal violence.

Legal intervention death An act involving the killing of one person by a law enforcement agent in the course of arresting or attempting to arrest a lawbreaker, suppressing a disturbance, maintaining order, or engaging in another legal action.

School-associated violent death A homicide or suicide in which the fatal injury occurred on the campus of a functioning elementary or secondary school in the United States, while the victim was on the way to or from regular sessions at such a school, or while the victim was attending or traveling to or from an official school-sponsored event. Victims included nonstudents as well as students and staff members.

Suicide An act of taking one's own life voluntarily and intentionally.

National Crime Victimization Survey (NCVS)

Aggravated assault Attack or attempted attack with a weapon, regardless of whether or not an injury occurs, and attack without a weapon when serious injury results.

At school (students) Inside the school building, on school property (school parking area, play area, school bus, etc.), or on the way to or from school.

Metropolitan Statistical Areas (MSAs) Geographic entities defined by the U.S. Office of Management and Budget (OMB) for use by federal statistical agencies in collecting, tabulating, and publishing federal statistics.

Rape Forced sexual intercourse including both psychological coercion as well as physical force. Forced sexual intercourse means vaginal, anal, or oral penetration by the offender(s). Includes attempts and verbal threats of rape. This category also includes incidents where the penetration is from a foreign object, such as a bottle.

Robbery Completed or attempted theft, directly from a person, of property or cash by force or threat of force, with or without a weapon, and with or without injury.

Serious violent victimization Rape, sexual assault, robbery, or aggravated assault.

Sexual assault A wide range of victimizations, separate from rape or attempted rape. These crimes include attacks or attempted attacks generally involving unwanted sexual contact between the victim and offender. Sexual assault may or may not involve force and includes such things as grabbing or fondling. Sexual assault also includes verbal threats.

Simple assault Attack without a weapon resulting either in no injury, minor injury, or an undetermined injury requiring less than 2 days of hospitalization. Also includes attempted assault without a weapon.

Theft Completed or attempted theft of property or cash without personal contact. Indicators of School Crime and Safety: 2015

Victimization A crime as it affects one individual person or household. For personal crimes, the number of victimizations is equal to the number of victims involved. The number of victimizations may be greater than the number of incidents because more than one person may be victimized during an incident.

Victimization rate A measure of the occurrence of victimizations among a specific population group. For personal crimes, the number of victimizations is equal to the number of victims involved. Each victimization that is reported by the respondents is counted, so there may be one incident with two victims, which would be counted as two victimizations. The number of victimizations may be greater than the number of incidents because more than one person may be victimized during an incident.

Violent victimization Includes serious violent victimization, rape, sexual assault, robbery, aggravated assault, or simple assault.

School Crime Supplement (SCS)

At school In the school building, on school property, on a school bus, or going to or from school.

Bullied Students were asked if any student had bullied them at school in one or more ways during the school year. Specifically, students were asked if another student had made fun of them, called them names, or insulted them; spread rumors about them; threatened them with harm; pushed, shoved, tripped, or spit on them; tried to make them to do something they did not want to do; excluded them from activities on purpose; or destroyed their property on purpose.

Gang Street gangs, fighting gangs, crews, or something else. Gangs may use common names, signs, symbols, or colors. All gangs, whether or not they are involved in violent or illegal activity, are included.

Hate-related graffiti Hate-related words or symbols written in school classrooms, school bathrooms, school hallways, or on the outside of the school building.

Hate-related words Students were asked if anyone called them an insulting or bad name at school having to do with their race, religion, ethnic background or national origin, disability, gender, or sexual orientation.

Serious violent victimization Rape, sexual assault, robbery, or aggravated assault.

Total victimization Combination of violent victimization and theft. If a student reported an incident of either type, he or she is counted as having experienced any victimization. If the student reported having experienced both, he or she is counted once under "total victimization."

Violent victimization Includes serious violent victimization, rape, sexual assault, robbery, aggravated assault, or simple assault.

Youth Risk Behavior Survey (YRBS)

On school property On school property is included in the question wording, but was not defined for respondents.

Rural school A school located outside a Metropolitan Statistical Area (MSA).

Suburban school A school located inside an MSA, but outside the "central city."

Urban school A school located inside an MSA and inside the "central city."

Weapon Examples of weapons appearing in the questionnaire include guns, knives, and clubs.

School Survey on Crime and Safety (SSOCS)

Gang An ongoing loosely organized association of three or more persons, whether formal or informal, that has a common name, signs, symbols, or colors, whose members engage, either individually or collectively, in violent or other forms of illegal behavior.

Hate crime A criminal offense or threat against a person, property, or society that is motivated, in whole or in part, by the offender's bias against a race, color, national origin, ethnicity, gender, religion, disability, or sexual orientation.

Intimidation To frighten, compel, or deter by actual or implied threats. It includes bullying and sexual harassment. (Intimidation was not defined in the front of the questionnaire in 2005–06.)

Physical attack or fight An actual and intentional touching or striking of another person against his or her will, or the intentional causing of bodily harm to an individual.

Rape Forced sexual intercourse (vaginal, anal, or oral penetration). Includes penetration from a foreign object.

Robbery The taking or attempting to take anything of value that is owned by another person or organization, under confrontational circumstances by force or threat of force or violence and/or by putting the victim in fear. A key difference between robbery and theft/larceny is that a threat or battery is involved in robbery.

Serious violent incidents Include rape, sexual battery other than rape, physical attacks or fights with a weapon, threats of physical attack with a weapon, and robbery with or without a weapon.

Sexual battery An incident that includes threatened rape, fondling, indecent liberties, child molestation, or sodomy. Principals were instructed that classification of these incidents should take into consideration the age and developmentally appropriate behavior of the offenders.

Sexual harassment Unsolicited, offensive behavior that inappropriately asserts sexuality over another person. The behavior may be verbal or nonverbal.

Theft/larceny Taking things valued at over $10 without personal confrontation. Specifically, the unlawful taking of another person's property without personal confrontation, threat, violence, or bodily harm. Included are pocket picking, stealing purse or backpack (if left unattended or no force was used to take it from owner), theft from a building, theft from a motor vehicle or motor vehicle parts or accessories, theft of bicycles, theft from vending machines, and all other types of thefts.

Vandalism The willful damage or destruction of school property, including bombing, arson, graffiti, and other acts that cause property damage. Includes damage caused by computer hacking.

Violent incidents Include rape, sexual battery other than rape, physical attacks or fights with or without a weapon, threats of physical attack with or without a weapon, and robbery with or without a weapon.

Weapon Any instrument or object used with the intent to threaten, injure, or kill. Includes look-alikes if they are used to threaten others.

PART 8

Jail Inmates in 2017

HIGHLIGHTS

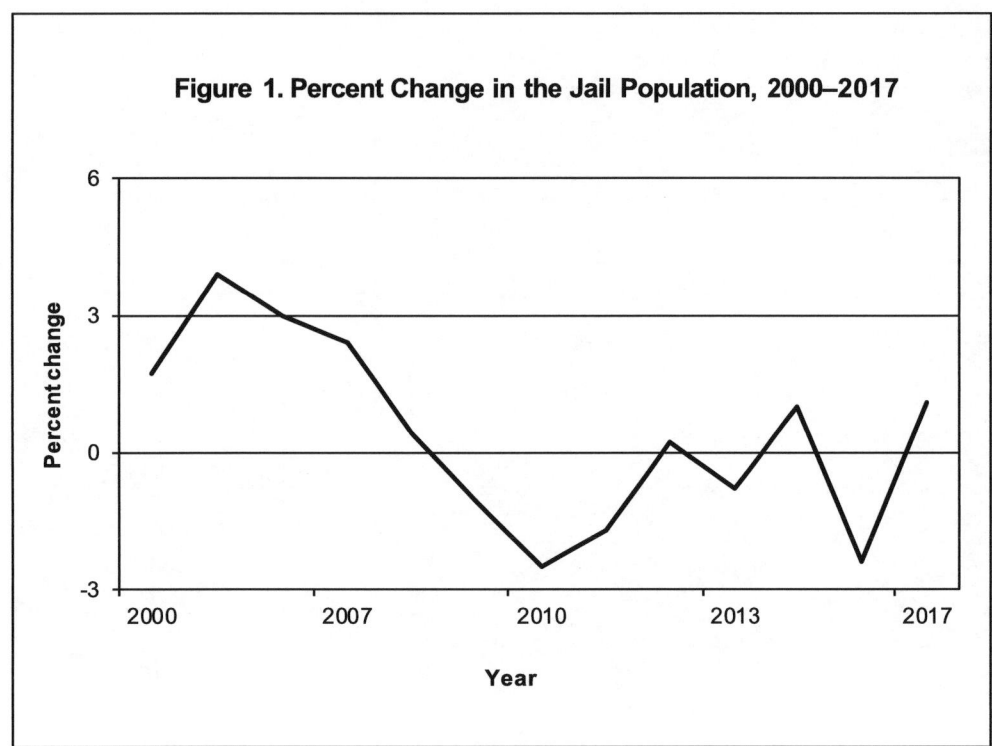

Figure 1. Percent Change in the Jail Population, 2000–2017

- The number of inmates confined in county and city jails was an estimated 740,700 at midyear 2016, lower than the peak of 776,600 inmates on an average day at midyear 2008.

- At midyear 2016, the jail incarceration rate had decreased from a peak of 259 per 100,000 U.S. residents at midyear to about 229 per 100,000 population.

- Approximately 10.6 million admissions to jail occurred in 2016, continuing the trend of steady decline that has been experienced since 2008.

- Fewer than 4,000 juveniles age 17 years or younger were held in local jails at midyear 2016; this was significantly below the peak of about 7,600 in 2000 and 2010.

- Approximately 80 percent of jail beds were occupied in 2016, down from 95 percent in 2007, while 17 percent of jails were operating at or above 100 percent of their operating capacity.

- At yearend 2016, non-Hispanic Blacks (599 per 100,000 Black residents) were incarcerated in jail at a rate 3.5 times that of non-Hispanic whites (171 per 100,000 White residents)

Table 1. Inmates Confined at Midyear, Average Daily Population and Incarceration Rates, 2005–2017

(Number; percent.)

Year	Confined inmates[1]	Average daily population[2]	Annual admissions[3]	Jail incarceration rate[4]
2005	747,500	733,400	12,100,000 B	253 B
2006	765,800 B	755,300	12,200,000 B	256 B
2007	780,200 B	773,100 B	13,100,000 B	259 B
2008	785,500 B	776,600 B	13,600,000 B	258 B
2009	767,400 B	768,100 B	12,800,000 B	250 B
2010	748,700	748,600 B	12,900,000 B	242 B
2011	735,600	735,600	11,800,000 B	236 B
2012	744,500	737,400	11,600,000 B	237 B
2013	731,200	731,400	11,700,000	231
2014	744,600	739,000	11,400,000 B	234
2015	727,400	719,500 B	10,700,000	227
2016	740,700	731,300	10,600,000	229
2017*				
Average Annual Percent Change				
2007–2017	-4.5	-3.6	-19.1	-11.6
2016–2017	0.6	1.9	0.0	-0.1

Note: Data are rounded to the nearest 100 for confined inmates and for average daily population (ADP) and to the nearest 100,000 for admissions. Results may differ from previous reports in the series due to data updates from jails.
* = Comparison year.
B = Difference with comparison year is significant at the 95% confidence level.
[1]Number of inmates held on the last weekday in June.
[2]The ADP is the sum of all inmates in jail each day for one year, divided by the number of days in the year. The ADP for 2015 and 2016 was calculated for the calendar year ending on December 31. The ADP for all other years was calculated for the 12-month period ending on June 30.
[3]Annual admissions in 2005 and 2007ñ2014 were estimated based on admissions during a one-week period in June. The 2006, 2015, and 2016 annual admissions were for the calendar year ending on December 31. The 2017 annual admissions were for the 12-month period ending on June 30, 2017.
[4]Number of confined inmates in local jails per 100,000 U.S. residents at midyear.

Table 2. Jail Incarceration Rates, by Sex, Race, and Hispanic Origin, Midyear 2005, and 2010–2017

(Number.)

Demographic characteristic	2005	2010	2011	2012	2013	2014	2015	2016[1]	2017*
Total[2]	253 B	242 B	236 B	237 B	231	233	226	229	229
Adults[3]	334 B	315 B	307 B	308 B	299	302	292	295	295
Sex[2]									
Male	448 B	431 B	419 B	418 B	404	405	394	398	394
Female	63 B	59 B	59 B	62 B	64 B	67	64 B	66 B	69
Race/Hispanic Origin									
White[4]	167 B	167 B	167 B	173 B	174 B	178 B	178 B	180	187
Black[4]	803 B	745 B	721 B	709 B	668 B	667 B	640	633	616
Hispanic	263 B	235 B	219 B	212 B	199 B	200 B	184	196 B	185
American Indian/Alaska Native[4]	339	426	410	401	437	443	378	379	366
Asian[4]	40 B	31 B	32 B	30 B	28	32 B	30 B	30 B	26
Other[4,5]	34	26 B	26 B	34	33	24 B	36	40	39

Note: Number of confined inmates in local jails per 100,000 U.S. residents (for total) or per 100,000 U.S. residents of a given demographic group, at midyear. Data are based on the inmate population confined on the last weekday in June. Results may differ from previous reports in the series due to data updates from jails.
* = Comparison year.
B = Difference with comparison year is significant at the 95% confidence level.
[1]In 2015 and 2016, the Annual Survey of Jails collected demographic data on inmate population at year-end instead of midyear. Jails typically hold fewer inmates at year-end than at midyear. In calculating midyear jail incarceration rates, the 2015 and 2016 inmate populations were adjusted for seasonal variation.
[2]Includes both adults and juveniles.
[3]Excludes persons age 17 or younger.
[4]Excludes persons of Hispanic/Latino origin (e.g., White refers to non-Hispanic Whites and Black refers to non-Hispanic Blacks).
[5]Includes Native Hawaiians, Other Pacific Islanders, and persons of two or more races.

Table 3. Percent of Confined Inmates in Local Jails, by Characteristics, 2005 and 2010–2017

(Percent.)

Characteristic	2005	2010	2011	2012	2013	2014	2015[1]	2016[1]	2017*
Sex									
Male	87.3[B]	87.8[B]	87.3[B]	86.8[B]	86.0[B]	85.3[B]	85.7[B]	85.5[B]	84.7
Female	12.7[B]	12.3[B]	12.7[B]	13.2[B]	14.0[B]	14.7[B]	14.3[B]	14.5[B]	15.3
Adult	99.1[B]	99.0[B]	99.2[B]	99.3[B]	99.4[B]	99.4[B]	99.5[B]	99.5	99.5
Male	86.5[B]	86.7[B]	86.6[B]	86.1[B]	85.4[B]	84.8[B]	85.3[B]	85.0[B]	84.3
Female	12.6[B]	12.3[B]	12.6[B]	13.2[B]	13.9[B]	14.6[B]	14.2[B]	14.5[B]	15.2
Juvenile[2]	0.9[B]	1.0[B]	0.8[B]	0.7[B]	0.6[B]	0.6[B]	0.5	0.5	0.5
Held as adult[3]	0.8[B]	0.8[B]	0.6[B]	0.6[B]	0.5[B]	0.5[B]	0.4	0.4	0.4
Held as juvenile	0.1[B]	0.3[B]	0.2[B]	0.1[B]	0.1[B]	0.1[B]	0.1	0.1[B]	Y
Race/Hispanic Origin									
White[4]	44.3[B]	44.3[B]	44.8[B]	45.8[B]	47.2[B]	47.4[B]	48.2[B]	48.2[B]	49.7
Black[4]	38.9[B]	37.8[B]	37.6[B]	36.9[B]	35.8[B]	35.4[B]	35.1[B]	34.4	33.6
Hispanic	15.0	15.8[B]	15.5[B]	15.1	14.8[B]	14.9	14.3	15.2	14.5
American Indian/Alaska Native[4]	1.0	1.3	1.3	1.2	1.4	1.4	1.2	1.2	1.2
Asian[4]	0.7[B]	0.6[B]	0.7	0.6	0.6[B]	0.7[B]	0.7[B]	0.7[B]	0.6
Other[4,5]	0.2[B]	0.2[B]	0.2[B]	0.3	0.3[B]	0.2[B]	0.3	0.4[B]	0.4
Conviction Status									
Convicted	38.0[B]	38.9[B]	39.4[B]	39.4[B]	38.0[B]	37.2[B]	37.5[B]	34.9	35.3
Unconvicted	62.0[B]	61.1[B]	60.6[B]	60.6[B]	62.0[B]	62.8[B]	62.5[B]	65.1	64.7
Most serious type of offense									
Felony	NC	NC	NC	NC	NC	NC	67.8	69.7	69.4
Misdemeanor	NC	NC	NC	NC	NC	NC	26.5	25.4	26.1
Other[6]	NC	NC	NC	NC	NC	NC	5.5	4.9	4.5

Note: Data are based on the inmate population confined on the last weekday in June, unless specified. Data are adjusted for non-response and rounded to the nearest 100. Details may not sum to totals due to rounding. Results may differ from previous reports in the series due to data updates from jails.
* = Comparison year.
B = Difference with comparison year is significant at the 95% confidence level.
NC = Not collected.
Y = Less than 0.05 percent.
[1]In 2015 and 2016, the Annual Survey of Jails collected demographic data on the inmate population at year-end instead of midyear. Jails typically hold fewer inmates at year-end than at midyear. The 2015 and 2016 inmate populations were adjusted for seasonal variation and represent estimated midyear counts.
[2]Persons age 17 or younger.
[3]Includes juveniles who were tried or awaiting trial as adults.
[4]Excludes persons of Hispanic/Latino origin (e.g., White refers to non-Hispanic Whites and Black refers to non-Hispanic Blacks).
[5]Includes Native Hawaiians, Other Pacific Islanders, and persons of two or more races.
[6]Includes civil infractions and unknown offenses.

Table 3A. Number of Confined Inmates in Local Jails, by Characteristics, 2005, and 2010–2017

(Number.)

Characteristic	2005	2010	2011	2012	2013	2014	2015[1]	2016[1]	2017*
Total	747,500	748,700	735,600	744,500	731,200	744,600	727,400	740,700	745,200
Sex									
Male..................	653,000[B]	656,400[B]	642,300	645,900	628,900	635,500	623,600	633,100	631,500
Female.................	94,600[B]	92,400[B]	93,300[B]	98,600[B]	102,400[B]	109,100[B]	103,800[B]	107,600[B]	113,700
Adult	740,800	741,200	729,700	739,100	726,600	740,400	723,800	736,800	741,600
Male.................	646,800[B]	649,300[B]	636,900	640,900	624,700	631,600	620,300	629,700	628,200
Female.................	94,000[B]	91,900[B]	92,800[B]	98,100[B]	101,900[B]	108,800[B]	103,500[B]	107,100[B]	113,400
Juvenile[2]...............	6,800[B]	7,600[B]	5,900[B]	5,400[B]	4,600[B]	4,200[B]	3,600	3,900	3,600
Held as adult[3]	5,800[B]	5,600[B]	4,600[B]	4,600[B]	3,500	3,700[B]	3,200	3,200	3,200
Held as juvenile.............	1,000[B]	1,900[B]	1,400[B]	900[B]	1,100[B]	500[B]	400	700[B]	300
Race/Hispanic Origin									
White[4]	331,000[B]	331,600[B]	329,400[B]	341,100[B]	344,900[B]	352,800[B]	351,600[B]	356.100[B]	370,100
Black[4].................	290,500[B]	283,200[B]	276,400[B]	274,600[B]	261,500	263,800[B]	255,200	254,600	250,100
Hispanic.................	111,900	118,100[B]	113,900	112,700	107,900	110,600	103,900	112,700	108,400
American Indian/Alaska Native[4]............	7,600	9,900	9,400	9,300	10,200	10,400	9,000	9,000	8,800
Asian[4]..................	4,900	4,400	4,800	4,700	4,500	5,400[B]	5,200	5,200[B]	4,800
Other[4,5]..................	1,500[B]	1,500[B]	1,600[B]	2,200[B]	2,200[B]	1,700[B]	2,500	2,900	2,900
Conviction Status									
Convicted.................	284,400[B]	291,300[B]	289,600[B]	293,100[B]	278,000[B]	277,100[B]	273,000	258,500	263,200
Unconvicted..................	463,200[B]	457,400[B]	446,000[B]	451,400[B]	453,200[B]	467,500	454,400[B]	482,100	482,000
Most serious type of offense									
Felony.................	NC	NC	NC	NC	NC	NC	494,100[B]	516,400	516,800
Misdemeanor.................	NC	NC	NC	NC	NC	NC	193,100	188,000	194,700
Other[6].................	NC	NC	NC	NC	NC	NC	40,200[B]	36,300	33,600

Note: Data are based on the inmate population confined on the last weekday in June, unless specified. Data are adjusted for non-response and rounded to the nearest 100. Details may not sum to totals due to rounding. Results may differ from previous reports in the series due to data updates from jails.
* = Comparison year.
B = Difference with comparison year is significant at the 95% confidence level.
NC = Not collected.
[1]In 2015 and 2016, the Annual Survey of Jails collected demographic data on the inmate population at year-end instead of midyear. Jails typically hold fewer inmates at year-end than at midyear. The 2015 and 2016 inmate populations were adjusted for seasonal variation and represent estimated midyear counts.
[2]Persons age 17 or younger.
[3]Includes juveniles who were tried or awaiting trial as adults.
[4]Excludes persons of Hispanic/Latino origin (e.g., White refers to non-Hispanic Whites and Black refers to non-Hispanic Blacks).
[5]Includes Native Hawaiians, Other Pacific Islanders, and persons of two or more races.
[6]Includes civil infractions and unknown offenses.

Table 4. Average Daily Jail Population, by Size of Jurisdiction, 2017

(Number; percent.)

Jail jurisdiction size	Jail jurisdictions		Total average daily population[1]		Mean average daily population
	Number	Percent	Number	Percent	
Total	2,828	100.0	745,600	100.0	263
49 or fewer....................................	972	34.4	21,600	2.9	22
50 to 99	516	18.3	35,500	4.8	69
100 to 249	677	24.0	111,300	14.9	164
250 to 499	305	10.8	109,200	14.6	358
500 to 999	205	7.2	144,500	19.4	705
1,000 to 2,499	121	4.3	172,700	23.3	1,431
2,500 and over......................	30	1.1	149,900	20.1	4,925

Note: Detail may not sum to total due to rounding.
[1]The average daily population is the sum of all inmates in jail each day for the calendar year divided by the number of days in the year.

Table 5. Jail Capacity, Midyear Population, and Percent of Capacity Occupied in Local Jails, 2005–2017

(Number; percent.)

Year	Jail capacity[1]	Midyear population[2]	Percent of capacity occupied[3]
2005..................................	787,000 [B]	747,500	95.0 [B]
2006..................................	795,000 [B]	765,800 [B]	96.3 [B]
2007..................................	810,500 [B]	780,200 [B]	96.3 [B]
2008..................................	828,700 [B]	785,500 [B]	94.8 [B]
2009..................................	849,900 [B]	767,400 [B]	90.2 [B]
2010..................................	857,900 [B]	748,700	87.3 [B]
2011..................................	870,400 [B]	735,600	84.5 [B]
2012..................................	877,400 [B]	744,500	84.9 [B]
2013..................................	872,900 [B]	731,200	83.8 [B]
2014..................................	890,500	744,600	83.6 [B]
2015..................................	901,400	727,400	80.7
2016..................................	915,400	740,700	80.9
2017*.................................	915,100	745,200	81.4

Note: Results may differ from previous reports in the series due to data updates from jails.
* = Comparison year.
B = Difference with comparison group is significant at the 95% confidence level.
[1]Maximum number of beds or inmates assigned by a rating official to a facility, excluding separate temporary holding areas.
[2]The number of inmates held on the last weekday in June.
[3]The midyear inmate population divided by the rated capacity.

Table 6. Percent of Jail Capacity Occupied, by Size of Jurisdiction, 2017

(Number; percent.)

Jail jurisdiction size	Midyear population[1]	Rated capacity[2]	Percent of capacity occupied at midyear[3]	Percent of jail jurisdictions operating at more than 100% of rated capacity at midyear
Total	745,200	915,100	81.4	20.0
49 or fewer....................................	21,300	36,300	58.7 [B]	11.0
50 to 99	36,400	49,900	72.8	26.6
100 to 249	109,000	128,100	85.1 [B]	22.6
250 to 499	111,400	127,600	87.3 [B]	30.4 [B]
500 to 999	144,100	178,100	80/9 [B]	22.7 [B]
1,000 to 2,499	174,400	203,500	85.7 [B]	19.0
2,500 or more*	148,800	191,600	77.6	17.1

Note: Jail jurisdiction size is based on the average daily population (ADP). Details may not sum to totals due to rounding.
* = Comparison group.
B = Difference with comparison group is significant at the 95% confidence level.
[1]The number of inmates held on the last weekday in June.
[2]Maximum number of beds or inmates assigned by a rating official to a facility, excluding separate temporary holding areas.
[3]The midyear population divided by the rated capacity.

Table 7. Inmate Turnover Rate and Expected Length of Stay, by Size of Jurisdiction, 2017

(Number; percent.)

Jail jurisdiction size	Average daily population[1]	Annual admissions	Weekly inmate turnover rate[2]	Expected average time in jail (days)[3]
Total	745,600	10,570,300	54.0	25.7
49 or fewer..............................	21,600	684,300	120.9[B]	11.5[B]
50 to 99	35,500	726,200	77.2[B]	17.8[B]
100 to 249	111,300	1,899,400	65[B]	21.4[B]
250 to 499	109,200	1,543,000	53.7[B]	25.8[B]
500 to 999	144,500	2,022,100	53.1[B]	26.1[B]
1,000 to 2,499	173,700	2,086,200	46.0[B]	30.4[B]
2,500 or more*	149,900	1,609,000	40.7	34.0

Note: Jail jurisdiction size is based on the average daily population (ADP). Details may not sum to totals due to rounding.
* = Comparison group.
B = Difference with comparison group is significant at the 95% confidence level.
[1]The sum of all inmates in jail each day for the 12-month period ending on June 30, divided by the number of days in the 12-month period.
[2]The sum of weekly admissions and releases, divided by the ADP. Weekly admissions and releases are calculated as the annual admissions and releases, divided by the number of weeks in the 12-month period.
[3]The ADP divided by the number of annual admissions, then multiplied by the number of days in a year.

Table 8. Persons Under Jail Supervision, by Confinement Status, 2006–2017

(Number.)

Year	Total	Held in jail	Supervised outside of a jail facility[1]
Midyear[2]			
2006...................................	826,000[B]	765,800[B]	60,200
2007...................................	848,400[B]	780,200[B]	68,200[B]
2008...................................	858,400[B]	785,500[B]	72,900[B]
2009...................................	837,600[B]	767,400[B]	70,200[B]
2010...................................	809,400	748,700	60,600
2011...................................	798,400	735,600	62,800[B]
2012...................................	808,600	744,500	64,100[B]
2013...................................	790,600	731,200	59,400
2014...................................	808,100	744,600	63,500[B]
2015[3]................................	782,300	727,400	54,900
2016[3]................................	794,900	740,700	54,200
2017*..................................	801,100	745,200	55,900

Note: Based on the number of inmates supervised on the last weekday in June, unless specified. Data are rounded to the nearest 100. Details may not sum to totals due to rounding.
* = Comparison year.
B = Difference with comparison year is significant at the 95% confidence level.
[1]Excludes persons supervised by a probation or parole agency. Includes offenders who serve their sentences of confinement on weekends only (i.e., Friday to Sunday); persons under electronic monitoring; persons in work release programs, work gangs, and other alternative work programs; and persons in drug, alcohol, mental health, and other medical treatment.
[2]In 2015 and 2016, the Annual Survey of Jails collected the number of persons supervised outside of a jail facility on December 31.

Table 9. Staff Employed in Local Jails, by Sex, Yearend 2016 and Midyear 2017

(Number; percent.)

Job function	Number		Percent	
	2016	2017*	2016	2017*
Job Function				
Total...	226,300	225,700	100.0	100.0
Correctional Officers[1]...	178,800	179,500	79.0	79.5
Male...	124,300	123,200	54.9	54.6
Female...	54,500	56,300	24.1	25.0
All Other Staff[2]...	47,500	46,200	21.0	20.5
Male...	21,000	20,300	9.3	9.0
Female...	26,500	25,900	11.7	11.5

Note: Details may not sum to totals due to rounding. Results may differ from previous reports in the series due to data updates from jails.
* = Comparison year.
[1]Includes deputies, monitors, and other custody staff who spend more than 50% of their time with the incarcerated population.
[2]Includes administrators, clerical and maintenance staff, educational staff, professional and technical staff, and other unspecified staff who spend more than 50% of their time in the facility.

Table 10. Prisoners Under Jurisdiction of State or Federal Correctional Authorities, by Jurisdiction and Sex, 2007–2017

(Number; percent.)

Year	Total	Federal[1]	State	Male	Female
2007...	1,596,835	199,618	1,397,217	1,482,524	114,311
2008...	1,608,282	201,280	1,407,002	1,493,670	114,612
2009...	1,615,487	208,118	1,407,369	1,502,002	113,485
2010...	1,613,803	209,771	1,404,032	1,500,936	112,867
2011...	1,598,968	216,362	1,382,606	1,487,561	111,407
2012...	1,570,397	217,815	1,352,582	1,461,625	108,772
2013...	1,576,950	215,866	1,361,084	1,465,592	111,358
2014...	1,562,319	210,567	1,351,752	1,449,291	113,028
2015...	1,526,603	196,455	1,330,148	1,415,112	111,491
2016[2]...	1,508,129	189,192	1,318,937	1,396,296	111,833
2017[3]...	1,489,363	183,058	1,306,305	1,378,003	111,360
Percent Change					
2007–2017...	-6.70	-8.30	-6.50	-7.10	-2.60
2016–2017...	-1.20	-3.20		-1.30	-0.40

Note: Jurisdiction refers to the legal authority of state or federal correctional officials over a prisoner, regardless of where the prisoner is held. Counts are for December 31 of each year.
[1]Includes prisoners held in non-secure, privately operated community corrections facilities and juveniles held in contract facilities.
[2]Counts from 2016 have been revised based on updated numbers and may differ from numbers in past reports. Total and state estimates include imputed counts for North Dakota, which did not submit 2016 National Prisoner Statistics (NPS) data.
[3]Total and state estimates for 2017 include imputed counts for New Mexico and North Dakota, which did not submit 2017 NPS data.

Table 11. Prisoners Under Jurisdiction of State or Federal Correctional Authorities, by Jurisdiction and Sex, 2016 and 2017

(Number; percent.)

Jurisdiction	2016			2017			Percent change, 2016–2017		
	Total	Male	Female	Total	Male	Female	Total	Male	Female
U.S. Total......................	1,508,129	1,396,296	111,833	1,489,363	1,378,003	111,360	-1.2	-1.3	-0.4
Federal[1]	189,192	176,495	12,697	183,058	170,525	12,533	-3.2	-3.4	-1.3
State[2]...............................	1,318,937	1,219,801	99,136	1,306,305	1,207,478	98,827			-0.3
Alabama[3]...........................	28,883	26,506	2,377	27,608	25,135	2,473	NC	NC	NC
Alaska[4]	4,434	4,024	410	4,399	4,011	388	-0.8	-0.3	-5.4
Arizona..............................	42,320	38,323	3,997	42,030	37,971	4,059	-0.7	-0.9	1.6
Arkansas............................	17,537	16,161	1,376	18,070	16,651	1,419	3.0	3.0	3.1
California[5].........................	130,084	124,198	5,886	131,039	125,180	5,859	0.7	0.8	-0.5
Colorado	19,981	18,078	1,903	19,946	18,044	1,902	-0.2	-0.2	-0.1
Connecticut[4].....................	14,957	13,892	1,065	14,040	13,069	971	-6.1	-5.9	-8.8
Delaware[4].........................	6,585	6,047	538	6,443	5,931	512	-2.2	-1.9	-4.8
Florida...............................	99,974	93,111	6,863	98,504	91,779	6,725	-1.5	-1.4	-2.0
Georgia	53,627	49,839	3,788	53,667	49,839	3,828	0.1	0.0	1.1
Hawaii[4]	5,602	4,934	668	5,630	5,006	624	0.5	1.5	-6.6
Idaho.................................	8,252	7,239	1,013	8,579	7,534	1,045	4.0	4.1	3.2
Illinois...............................	43,657	41,044	2,613	41,471	39,190	2,281	-5.0	-4.5	-12.7
Indiana	25,546	23,341	2,205	26,024	23,608	2,416	1.9	1.1	9.6
Iowa	9,031	8,210	821	9,024	8,218	806	-0.1	0.1	-1.8
Kansas...............................	9,920	9,051	869	9,971	9,069	902	0.5	0.2	3.8
Kentucky	23,022	20,080	2,942	23,543	20,522	3,021	2.3	2.2	2.7
Louisiana...........................	35,682	33,701	1,981	33,739	31,782	1,957	-5.4	-5.7	-1.2
Maine	2,404	2,169	235	2,404	2,177	227	0.0	0.4	-3.4
Maryland	19,994	19,172	822	19,367	18,519	848	-3.1	-3.4	3.2
Massachusetts	9,403	8,820	583	9,133	8,602	531	-2.9	-2.5	-8.9
Michigan	41,122	38,880	2,242	39,666	37,515	2,151	-3.5	-3.5	-4.1
Minnesota	10,592	9,818	774	10,708	9,974	734	1.1	1.6	-5.2
Mississippi.........................	19,192	17,823	1,369	19,103	17,688	1,415	-0.5	-0.8	3.4
Missouri............................	32,461	29,124	3,337	32,601	29,205	3,396	0.4	0.3	1.8
Montana............................	3,814	3,405	409	3,698	3,282	416	-3.0	-3.6	1.7
Nebraska	5,302	4,878	424	5,313	4,884	429	0.2	0.1	1.2
Nevada	13,757	12,490	1,267	13,671	12,405	1,266	-0.6	-0.7	-0.1
New Hampshire	2,818	2,591	227	2,750	2,524	226	-2.4	-2.6	-0.4
New Jersey.........................	19,786	18,952	834	19,585	18,811	774		-0.7	-7.2
New Mexico[5]	7,055	6,344	711	7,276	6,492	784	NC	NC	NC
New York	50,716	48,442	2,274	49,461	47,184	2,277	-2.5	-2.6	0.1
North Carolina...................	35,697	32,985	2,712	36,394	33,553	2,841	2.0	1.7	4.8
North Dakota[6,7].................	1,791	1,578	213	1,723	1,524	199	NC	NC	NC
Ohio	52,175	47,581	4,594	51,478	47,052	4,426	-1.3	-1.1	-3.7
Oklahoma[5,8]......................	29,916	26,452	3,464	28,143	24,952	3,191	-5.9	-5.7	-7.9
Oregon[5]............................	15,166	13,862	1,304	15,218	13,891	1,327	0.3	0.2	1.8
Pennsylvania	49,244	46,381	2,863	48,333	45,482	2,851	-1.8	-1.9	-0.4
Rhode Island[4]....................	3,103	2,927	176	2,861	2,690	171	-7.8	-8.1	-2.8
South Carolina...................	20,858	19,384	1,474	19,906	18,514	1,392	-4.6	-4.5	-5.6
South Dakota.....................	3,831	3,333	498	3,970	3,430	540	3.6	2.9	8.4
Tennessee..........................	28,203	25,481	2,722	28,980	25,969	3,011	2.8	1.9	10.6
Texas	163,703	149,368	14,335	162,523	148,565	13,958	-0.7	-0.5	-2.6
Utah[5]................................	6,175	5,769	406	6,443	5,951	492	4.3	3.2	21.2
Vermont[4]..........................	1,735	1,600	135	1,546	1,406	140	-10.9	-12.1	3.7
Virginia.............................	37,813	34,704	3,109	37,158	34,004	3,154	-1.7	-2.0	1.4
Washington.......................	19,104	17,446	1,658	19,656	17,914	1,742	2.9	2.7	5.1
West Virginia	7,162	6,286	876	7,092	6,274	818		-0.2	-6.6
Wisconsin	23,377	21,889	1,488	23,945	22,325	1,620	2.4	2.0	8.9
Wyoming	2,374	2,088	286	2,473	2,181	292	4.2	4.5	2.1

Note: Jurisdiction refers to the legal authority of state or federal correctional officials over a prisoner, regardless of where the prisoner is held. Counts are for December 31 of each year.
NC = Not calculated.
[1]Includes prisoners held in non-secure, privately operated community corrections facilities and juveniles held in contract facilities.
[2]Total and state estimates include imputed counts for New Mexico and North Dakota, which did not submit 2017 National Prisoner Statistics (NPS) data.
[3]Data from 2017 include offenders with Class D felonies and parole revocations and should not be compared to 2016 data.
[4]Prisons and jails form one integrated system. Data include total jail and prison populations.
[5]State submitted updated 2016 population counts.
[6]State did not submit 2017 NPS data. Counts were imputed for 2017 and should not be compared to 2016 counts.
[7]State did not submit 2016 NPS data. Counts were imputed for 2016 and should not be compared to 2017 counts.
[8]Includes persons who were waiting in county jails to be moved to state prison.

METHODOLOGY

Sampling Design

In years between the complete censuses of jails, the Bureau of Justice Statistics (BJS) conducts the Annual Survey of Jails (ASJ) to estimate the number and characteristics of the jail population in the United States. ASJ is a nationally representative survey of all county or city jail jurisdictions and all regional jails in the country. Federal jurisdiction and combined jail and prison systems in Alaska, Connecticut, Delaware, Hawaii, Rhode Island, and Vermont are not covered. These are included in BJS's prison collection. However, Alaska's 15 locally operated jails are covered.

A jail jurisdiction is a county (parish in Louisiana) or municipal government that administers one or more local jails and represents the entity responsible for managing jail facilities under its authority. Most jail jurisdictions consist of a single facility, but some have multiple facilities or multiple facility operators, called reporting units. For example, four reporting units in Allegheny County, Pennsylvania, represent a single jail jurisdiction. ASJ sample is drawn at the jurisdiction level. When a jail jurisdiction with multiple reporting units is sampled, data are collected from all reporting units within that jail jurisdiction. BJS collapses the reporting units into jail jurisdictions and reports statistics at the jurisdiction level.

The ASJ uses a strati ed probability sampling design based on jail population data collected through the most recent Census of Jails (2013). Jails in the ASJ sample are surveyed annually until the next sample refresh. The most recent sample refresh occurred in 2015. A sample of 876 jail jurisdictions were selected to represent the approximately 2,851 jail jurisdictions nationwide. In selecting the jails, all jurisdictions were grouped into 10 strata based on their average daily population (ADP) and presence of juveniles measured in the most recent Census of Jails. In 8 of the 10 strata, a random sample of jail jurisdictions was selected. The remaining two strata were certainty strata, where all jurisdictions were selected with a probability of 1. One certainty stratum consisted of all jails that were operated jointly by two or more jurisdictions (referred to as multijurisdictional jails). The other certainty stratum consisted of all jail jurisdictions that held juvenile inmates at the time of the 2013 Census of Jails and had an ADP of 500 or more inmates during the 12 months ending on December 31, 2013, held only adults and had an ADP of 750 or more, were located in California, or were known to be operating in 2015 and not included in the 2013 Census of Jails.

The ASJ sample includes all California jail jurisdictions. This sampling feature was introduced in 2013 in response to the enactment of California Assembly Bill (AB) 109 and AB 117, aimed to reduce the number of inmates housed in state prisons starting on October 1, 2011. After the enactment of these two laws, the jail population in California experienced an unusual increase that the rest of the United States did not experience. For this reason, the ASJ sampling design was modified to include all California jail jurisdictions in a certainty (self-representing) stratum. (See *Methodology* in *Jail Inmates at Midyear 2014*, NCJ 248629, BJS web, June 2015.) The inclusion of all California jail jurisdictions resulted in an additional 21 jurisdictions (California has 65 jurisdictions in total). The sample also includes in the certainty stratum six new jail jurisdictions that were known to be operating in 2015 and not represented in the sampling frame (2013 Census of Jails).

Nonresponse Weighting Adjustment

Nonresponse weighting was implemented to account for unit nonresponse. Using a simple weighting class method, a nonresponse weighting adjustment factor was calculated within each weighting class h as:

$$F_h = (\sum^{n_h} W_{hi} \times JURISA_{hi} \, F_h = i = 1) / (\sum^{n_h} W_{hi} \times JURISR_{hi} \, i = 1)$$

where

n_h = number of jurisdictions sampled in weighting class h,

W_{hi} = sampling weight for jurisdiction i in weighting class h,

$JURISA_{hi}$ = active status indicator for jurisdiction i in weighting class h (1 = active, 0 = out-of-scope), and

$JURISR_{hi}$ = response indicator of jurisdiction i in weighting class h (1 = respondent, 0=nonrespondent).

Final Weight

The final weight FW_{hi} for each jail jurisdiction is calculated as the product of the sampling weight, the weighting class adjustment within each weighting class, and the jurisdiction's response factor.

$$FW_{hi} = W_{hi} \times F_h \times JURISR_{hi}$$

Item Nonresponse Imputation

Item response rates ranged from 94 percent to 100 percent. For responding jail jurisdictions that were unable to provide some requested items, a weighted sequential hot-deck/cold-deck imputation procedure was used to impute values.

Midyear and Yearend Population Differences

Prior to 2015, the ASJ used midyear (last weekday in June) as the reference date in data collection. In 2015, ASJ changed the reference date to December 31. The 2016 ASJ continued to use the year-end reference date. Comparisons of year-end data with previous midyear data need to consider seasonal variations, as jails typically hold fewer inmates at year-end than at midyear.

Calculating Weekly Inmate Turnover Rates

The weekly jail inmate turnover rate is the sum of the average weekly admissions and releases divided by the ADP. The inmate turnover rate is an indicator of the fluctuation of the jail population.

Jail Functions

Jails in the ASJ include confinement facilities operated under the authority of a sheriff, police chief, or city or county administrator. They are intended for adults but may hold juveniles before or after they are adjudicated. Facilities include jails, detention centers, city or county correctional centers, special jail facilities (such as medical or treatment centers and pre-release centers) and temporary holding or lockup facilities that are part of the jail's combined function. Inmates sentenced to jail facilities usually have a sentence of 1 year or less.

Within the ASJ, jails:

- receive individuals pending arraignment and hold them awaiting trial, conviction, or sentencing

- re-admit probation, parole, and bail bond violators and absconders temporarily detain juveniles pending their transfer to juvenile authorities

- hold mentally ill persons pending their movement to appropriate mental health facilities

- hold individuals for the military, for protective custody, for contempt, and for the courts as witnesses

- release convicted inmates to the community on completion of sentence

- transfer inmates to federal, state, or other authorities house inmates for federal, state, or other authorities because of crowding of their facilities

- operate community-based programs as alternatives to incarceration.

For more information, please see https://www.bjs.gov/content/pub/pdf/ji16.pdf.

Terms and Definitions

Admissions: Persons who are officially booked and housed in jails by formal legal document and the authority of the courts or some other official agency. Jail admissions include persons sentenced to weekend programs and those who are booked into the facility for the first time. Excluded from jail admissions are inmates re-entering the facility after an escape, work release, medical appointment or treatment facility appointment, and bail and court appearances. BJS collects jail admissions for the last 7 days in June.

Average daily population (ADP): The average is derived by the sum of inmates in jail each day for a year, divided by the number of days in the year.

Average annual change: The mean average change across a 12-month time period.

Calculating annual admissions: Annual jail admissions are calculated by multiplying weekly admissions by the sum of 365 days divided by 7 days.

Calculating weekly jail turnover rate: This rate is calculated by adding admissions and releases and dividing by the average daily population.

Inmates confined: The number of inmates held in custody.

Jail incarceration rate: The number of inmates held in the custody of local jails, per 100,000 U.S. residents.

Percent of capacity occupied: This percentage is calculated by taking the number of inmates, dividing by the rated capacity, and multiplying by 100.

Rated capacity: The number of beds or inmates assigned by a rating official to a facility, excluding separate temporary holding areas.

Releases: Persons released after a period of confinement (e.g., sentence completion, bail or bond releases, other pretrial releases, transfers to other jurisdictions, and deaths). Releases include those persons who have completed their weekend program and who are leaving the facility for the last time. Excluded from jail releases are temporary discharges including work release, medical appointment or treatment center, court appearance, furlough, day reporting, and transfers to other facilities within the jail's jurisdiction.

Standard errors and tests of significance: As with any survey, the ASJ estimates are subject to error arising from sampling rather than using a complete enumeration of the jail population. A common way to express this sampling variability is to construct a 95 percent confidence interval around each survey estimate. Typically, multiplying the standard error by 1.96 and then adding or subtracting the result from the estimate produces the confidence interval. This interval expresses the range of values that could result among 95 percent of the different samples that could be drawn.

Under jail supervision but not confined: This classification includes all persons in community-based programs operated by a jail facility. These programs include electronic monitoring, house arrest, community service, day reporting, and work programs. The classification excludes persons on pretrial release and who are not in a community-based program run by the jail, as well as persons under supervision of probation, parole, or other agencies; inmates on weekend programs; and inmates who participate in work release programs and return to the jail at night.

Weekend programs: Offenders in these programs are allowed to serve their sentences of confinement only on weekends (i.e., Friday to Sunday).

Please note that some tables were derived from *Prisoners in 2017*, which encompasses much of the same material as this report.

PART 9

Law Enforcement Officers Killed and Assaulted, 2018

HIGHLIGHTS

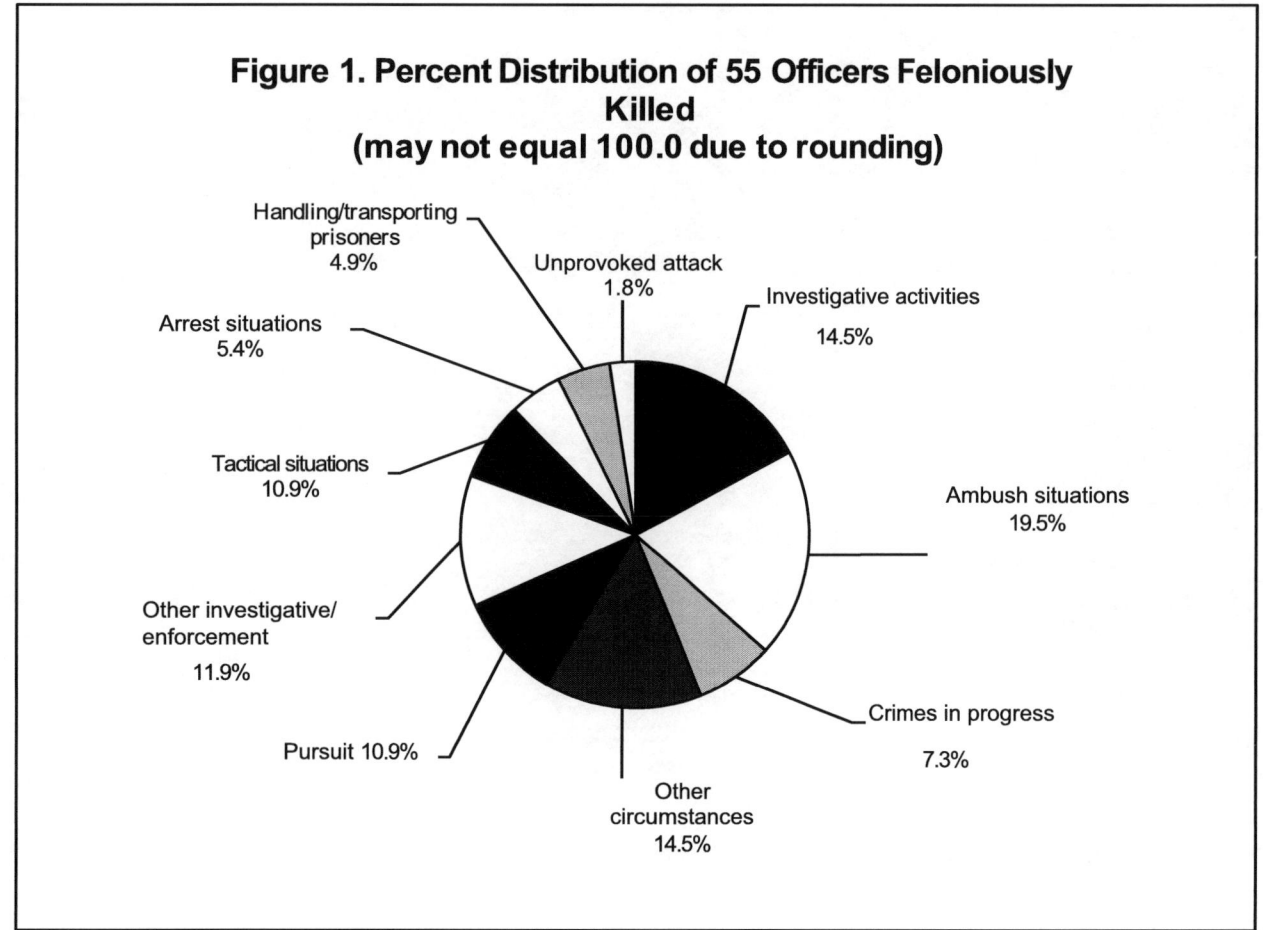

Figure 1. Percent Distribution of 55 Officers Feloniously Killed (may not equal 100.0 due to rounding)

- Handling/transporting prisoners 4.9%
- Unprovoked attack 1.8%
- Investigative activities 14.5%
- Arrest situations 5.4%
- Ambush situations 19.5%
- Tactical situations 10.9%
- Other investigative/enforcement 11.9%
- Crimes in progress 7.3%
- Pursuit 10.9%
- Other circumstances 14.5%

- In 2018, 55 law enforcement officers died from injuries incurred in the line of duty during felonious incidents. Of the officers feloniously killed, 28 were employed by city police departments, including 7 who were members of law enforcement agencies in cities with 250,000 or more inhabitants.

- Line-of-duty deaths in 2018 occurred in 27 states and Puerto Rico. By region, 26 officers were feloniously killed in the South, 12 officers in the Midwest, 12 officers in the West, 4 officers in the Northeast, and 1 officer in Puerto Rico.

- The average age of the officers who died in 2018 was 37 years old. The slain officers' average length of law enforcement service was 10 years. Of these officers, 52 were male and 3 were female.

- In 2018, 51 law enforcement officers died as the result of accidents that occurred in the line of duty. Accidental line-of-duty deaths of law enforcement officers occurred in 25 states. One officer was killed in an accident in Puerto Rico.

- Participating federal law enforcement agencies reported that 1,766 officers were nonfatally assaulted while performing their duties in 2018.

- Two federal law enforcement officers were feloniously killed in 2018. Of the 1,766 reported assaulted, 374 were reported as injured.

Table 1. Law Enforcement Officers Feloniously Killed, by Region, Geographic Division, and State/Territory, 2009–2018

(Number.)

Area	Total	2009	2010	2011	2012	2013	2014	2015	2016	2017	2018
Number of Victim Officers	510	48	55	72	49	27	51	41	66	46	55
Northeast	51	7	3	10	6	2	8	4	4	3	4
New England	9	0	1	0	2	1	1	0	1	0	3
Connecticut	0	0	0	0	0	0	0	0	0	0	0
Maine	1	0	0	0	0	0	0	0	0	0	1
Massachusetts	6	0	1	0	1	1	0	0	1	0	2
New Hampshire	2	0	0	0	1	0	1	0	0	0	0
Rhode Island	0	0	0	0	0	0	0	0	0	0	0
Vermont	0	0	0	0	0	0	0	0	0	0	0
Middle Atlantic	42	7	2	10	4	1	7	4	3	3	1
New Jersey	4	1	0	2	0	0	1	0	0	0	0
New York	18	0	0	4	2	1	5	2	1	2	1
Pennsylvania	20	6	2	4	2	0	1	2	2	1	0
Midwest	95	5	10	21	6	4	8	5	13	11	12
East North Central	57	2	8	12	2	3	5	3	6	8	8
Illinois	13	2	4	1	0	1	0	1	0	2	2
Indiana	10	0	0	2	0	1	3	0	1	1	2
Michigan	14	0	3	4	1	1	0	0	2	2	1
Ohio	14	0	1	4	1	0	1	1	2	2	2
Wisconsin	6	0	0	1	0	0	1	1	1	1	1
West North Central	38	3	2	9	4	1	3	2	7	3	4
Iowa	5	0	0	1	0	1	0	0	2	1	0
Kansas	10	1	0	1	2	0	1	0	2	0	3
Minnesota	7	1	2	1	1	0	1	1	0	0	0
Missouri	9	0	0	3	1	0	1	0	2	1	1
Nebraska	1	0	0	0	0	0	0	1	0	0	0
North Dakota	3	0	0	1	0	0	0	0	1	1	0
South Dakota	3	1	0	2	0	0	0	0	0	0	0
South	225	21	22	29	22	15	17	19	30	24	26
South Atlantic	100	7	11	18	10	5	10	3	13	8	15
Delaware	4	1	0	1	0	0	0	0	0	2	0
District of Columbia	0	0	0	0	0	0	0	0	0	0	0
Florida	29	3	4	6	2	2	4	1	0	3	4
Georgia	25	0	5	3	1	0	2	1	7	1	5
Maryland	7	0	1	0	0	1	0	0	2	1	2
North Carolina	13	3	1	2	3	0	2	0	1	0	1
South Carolina	9	0	0	2	1	0	1	1	1	0	3
Virginia	8	0	0	3	0	1	1	0	2	1	0
West Virginia	5	0	0	1	3	1	0	0	0	0	0
East South Central	39	5	4	6	5	3	0	5	4	1	6
Alabama	9	4	1	1	2	0	0	0	0	0	1
Kentucky	6	0	0	0	1	1	0	2	0	0	2
Mississippi	13	0	3	1	1	2	0	2	1	1	2
Tennessee	11	1	0	4	1	0	0	1	3	0	1
West South Central	86	9	7	5	7	7	7	11	13	15	5
Arkansas	9	1	2	1	0	0	1	1	1	2	0
Louisiana	22	0	3	0	2	1	1	6	4	4	1
Oklahoma	5	2	0	0	0	0	0	0	0	2	1
Texas	50	6	2	4	5	6	5	4	8	7	3
West	113	13	17	10	9	6	14	9	17	6	12
Mountain	55	2	10	5	5	1	7	7	8	4	6
Arizona	18	0	4	3	2	0	3	0	2	1	3
Colorado	12	1	1	2	1	0	0	2	2	1	2
Idaho	1	0	0	0	0	0	0	1	0	0	0
Montana	4	0	2	0	0	0	1	0	0	1	0
Nevada	6	0	1	0	1	0	2	1	0	1	0
New Mexico	6	1	0	0	0	0	0	3	2	0	0
Utah	8	0	2	0	1	1	1	0	2	0	1
Wyoming	0	0	0	0	0	0	0	0	0	0	0
Pacific	58	11	7	5	4	5	7	2	9	2	6
Alaska	5	0	2	0	0	0	2	0	1	0	0
California	39	5	5	3	2	5	5	2	6	2	4
Hawaii	1	0	0	0	0	0	0	0	0	0	1
Oregon	3	0	0	2	0	0	0	0	1	0	0
Washington	10	6	0	0	2	0	0	0	1	0	1

Table 1. Law Enforcement Officers Feloniously Killed, by Region, Geographic Division, and State/Territory, 2009–2018—*Continued*

(Number.)

Area	Total	2009	2010	2011	2012	2013	2014	2015	2016	2017	2018
Puerto Rico and other outlying areas.....	26	2	3	2	6	0	4	4	2	2	1
American Samoa.................................	0	0	0	0	0	0	0	0	0	0	0
Guam..	0	0	0	0	0	0	0	0	0	0	0
Mariana Islands	0	0	0	0	0	0	0	0	0	0	0
Puerto Rico......................................	25	2	3	2	5	0	4	4	2	2	1
U.S. Virgin Islands.............................	1	0	0	0	1	0	0	0	0	0	0

Table 2. Law Enforcement Officers Feloniously Killed, by Population Group/Agency Type, 2009–2018

(Number.)

Area	Total	2009	2010	2011	2012	2013	2014	2015	2016	2017	2018
Number of Victim Officers..........................	510	48	55	72	49	27	51	41	66	46	55
Group I (cities 250,000 and over)....................	95	15	12	13	6	4	8	10	12	8	7
Group II (cities 100,000–249,999)....................	41	3	3	9	4	2	6	2	8	2	2
Group III (cities 50,000–99,999).....................	33	4	3	9	2	2	2	1	2	4	4
Group IV (25,000–49,999).............................	34	1	6	4	2	3	2	4	6	2	4
Group V (cities 10,000–24,999)......................	35	3	2	5	3	2	4	2	5	2	7
Group VI (cities under 10,000).......................	58	6	5	10	4	3	5	5	8	8	4
Metropolitan counties...................................	106	8	9	14	11	6	11	5	15	7	20
Nonmetropolitan counties...............................	38	4	6	4	5	3	4	2	3	5	2
State agencies...	32	1	5	0	5	2	4	4	4	4	3
Federal agencies	12	1	1	2	1	0	1	2	1	2	1
Puerto Rico and other outlying areas..............	26	2	3	2	6	0	4	4	2	2	1

Table 3. Law Enforcement Officers Feloniously Killed, by Time of Incident, 2009–2018

(Number.)

Time of day	Total	2009	2010	2011	2012	2013	2014	2015	2016	2017	2018
Number of Victim Officers........................	510	48	55	72	49	27	51	41	66	46	55
Total A.M. hours..	223	21	23	36	24	13	20	22	28	17	19
12:01 a.m.–2 a.m..................................	48	3	7	7	5	3	4	4	7	4	4
2:01 a.m.–4 a.m....................................	38	1	4	9	3	3	6	6	3	2	1
4:01 a.m.–6 a.m....................................	22	2	3	2	3	3	3	1	1	1	3
6:01 a.m.–8 a.m....................................	26	5	2	5	3	0	1	1	1	5	3
8:01 a.m.–10 a.m..................................	39	8	1	3	4	1	0	8	10	2	2
10:01 a.m.–noon	50	2	6	10	6	3	6	2	6	3	6
Total P.M. hours	283	27	32	36	23	14	31	18	37	29	36
12:01 p.m.–2 p.m.	42	5	2	5	2	3	7	1	10	2	5
2:01 p.m.–4 p.m.	51	3	4	6	3	3	9	2	8	5	8
4:01 p.m.–6 p.m.	43	3	4	8	3	1	6	2	3	5	8
6:01 p.m.–8 p.m.	38	3	4	5	6	2	1	5	2	3	7
8:01 p.m.–10 p.m.	58	10	10	3	6	2	4	7	9	5	2
10:01 p.m.–midnight	51	3	8	9	3	3	4	1	5	9	6
Not reported..	4	0	0	0	2	0	0	1	1	0	0

Table 3A. Law Enforcement Officers Feloniously Killed, by Lighting and Weather/Environmental Conditions by Location of Incident, 2014–2018

(Number.)

Characteristic	Total	Commercial			Government		
		Inside of structure	Outside	Location not reported	Inside of structure	Outside	Location not reported
Number of Victim Officers...............................	259	17	22	0	6	5	0
Lighting							
Artificial	51	11	7	0	5	2	0
Dark...	64	1	5	0	0	0	0
Dawn..	5	0	2	0	0	0	0
Daylight	120	5	8	0	1	3	0
Dusk	13	0	0	0	0	0	0
Other	0	0	0	0	0	0	0
Not reported	6	0	0	0	0	0	0
Weather/environmental							
Blizzard	0	0	0	0	0	0	0
Blowing dirt/sand/soil	0	0	0	0	0	0	0
Clear...	164	0	19	0	0	5	0
Cloudy	15	0	2	0	0	0	0
Flooding..	0	0	0	0	0	0	0
Fog/smog/smoke	3	0	0	0	0	0	0
Hurricane	0	0	0	0	0	0	0
Rain	12	0	0	0	0	0	0
Severe crosswinds	0	0	0	0	0	0	0
Sleet/hail	0	0	0	0	0	0	0
Snow...	5	0	1	0	0	0	0
Tornado	0	0	0	0	0	0	0
Other	1	0	0	0	0	0	0
Unknown...	4	0	0	0	0	0	0
Not reported	9	0	0	0	0	0	0
Not applicable (indoors).................................	46	17	0	0	6	0	0

Table 3A. Law Enforcement Officers Feloniously Killed, by Lighting and Weather/Environmental Conditions by Location of Incident, 2014–2018—*Continued*

(Number.)

Characteristic	Public space[1]			Residential			Other		
	Inside of structure	Outside	Location not reported	Inside of structure	Outside	Location not reported	Inside of structure	Outside	Location not reported
Number of Victim Officers	1	117	0	22	66	1	0	2	0
Lighting									
Artificial	0	14	0	4	8	0	0	0	0
Dark	0	34	0	6	17	0	0	1	0
Dawn	0	1	0	0	2	0	0	0	0
Daylight	1	55	0	9	36	1	0	1	0
Dusk	0	10	0	0	3	0	0	0	0
Other	0	0	0	0	0	0	0	0	0
Not reported	0	3	0	3	0	0	0	0	0
Weather/environmental									
Blizzard	0	0	0	0	0	0	0	0	0
Blowing dirt/sand/soil	0	0	0	0	0	0	0	0	0
Clear	0	86	0	0	52	0	0	2	0
Cloudy	0	8	0	0	5	0	0	0	0
Flooding	0	0	0	0	0	0	0	0	0
Fog/smog/smoke	0	3	0	0	0	0	0	0	0
Hurricane	0	0	0	0	0	0	0	0	0
Rain	0	7	0	0	5	0	0	0	0
Severe crosswinds	0	0	0	0	0	0	0	0	0
Sleet/hail	0	0	0	0	0	0	0	0	0
Snow	0	2	0	0	1	1	0	0	0
Tornado	0	0	0	0	0	0	0	0	0
Other	0	0	0	0	1	0	0	0	0
Unknown	0	4	0	0	0	0	0	0	0
Not reported	0	7	0	0	2	0	0	0	0
Not applicable (indoors)	1	0	0	22	0	0	0	0	0

Note: Ten years of data for the topics presented in this table are not available at this time. A 10-year table is expected to be available for the publication of 2020 data.

[1]Examples of public space include, but are not limited to, alleys, highways, lakes, parks, rivers, roads, and sidewalks.

Table 4. Law Enforcement Officers Feloniously Killed, by Day of Incident, 2009–2018

(Number.)

Day of the week	Total	2009	2010	2011	2012	2013	2014	2015	2016	2017	2018
Number of Victim Officers......................	510	48	55	72	49	27	51	41	66	46	55
Sunday	75	9	5	13	7	2	9	5	13	8	4
Monday	62	5	5	12	5	3	7	6	4	8	7
Tuesday	70	6	11	11	10	5	5	6	6	3	7
Wednesday..	80	4	12	8	5	3	4	9	15	7	13
Thursday..	77	7	11	9	9	6	7	3	12	6	7
Friday...	67	4	6	11	5	5	8	4	7	9	8
Saturday	79	13	5	8	8	3	11	8	9	5	9

Table 5. Law Enforcement Officers Feloniously Killed, by Month of Incident, 2009–2018

(Number.)

Month	Total	2009	2010	2011	2012	2013	2014	2015	2016	2017	2018
Number of Victim Officers......................	510	48	55	72	49	27	51	41	66	46	55
January..	34	1	4	9	6	2	2	0	2	4	4
February	37	1	4	3	4	5	1	0	9	2	8
March...	52	6	5	9	1	1	8	6	5	4	7
April	37	8	1	9	4	3	1	0	1	4	6
May	47	0	7	3	3	1	9	10	3	7	4
June..	37	6	4	6	4	2	4	3	3	2	3
July...	50	7	7	8	2	1	4	1	10	4	6
August..	44	4	4	7	8	2	3	6	5	5	0
September..	36	4	1	1	5	4	6	4	3	2	6
October	39	2	4	5	1	1	4	4	9	5	4
November...	46	4	6	2	4	0	5	4	13	5	3
December...	51	5	8	10	7	5	4	3	3	2	4

Table 6. Law Enforcement Officers Feloniously Killed, by Age Group of Victim Officer, 2009–2018

(Number.)

Age group	Total	2009	2010	2011	2012	2013	2014	2015	2016	2017	2018
Number of Victim Officers............	510	48	55	72	49	27	51	41	66	46	55
Under 25 years	19	1	3	2	2	0	5	2	2	1	1
25–30 years.....................................	93	9	12	17	8	2	3	5	10	11	16
31–35 years.....................................	109	8	12	11	12	9	11	9	14	8	14
36–40 years.....................................	78	11	9	12	8	7	7	2	8	7	7
41–45 years.....................................	92	13	7	10	8	4	12	9	12	9	8
46–50 years.....................................	64	3	5	13	6	1	9	10	9	6	2
51–55 years.....................................	32	0	1	4	5	2	3	2	9	2	5
56–60 years.....................................	14	3	4	3	0	1	0	1	0	2	0
Over 60 years...................................	9	0	2	0	0	1	1	1	2	0	2
Average age (years).........................	39	38	38	38	38	39	39	40	40	38	37

Table 7. Law Enforcement Officers Feloniously Killed, by Years of Service of Victim Officer, 2009–2018

(Number.)

Years of service	Total	2009	2010	2011	2012	2013	2014	2015	2016	2017	2018
Number of Victim Officers	510	48	55	72	49	27	51	41	66	46	55
Less than 1	15	0	1	0	2	0	2	4	2	13	3
1–5	128	13	22	17	12	4	11	8	13	10	14
6–10	132	12	13	24	13	10	8	11	13	7	18
11–15	80	9	5	8	5	8	11	4	13	9	10
16–20	78	6	9	8	10	1	13	5	13	2	4
21–25	37	3	1	12	1	1	5	6	4	2	2
26–30	26	4	1	1	4	2	0	2	8	2	2
More than 30	9	0	3	2	1	1	1	0	0	0	1
Not reported	5	1	0	0	1	0	0	1	0	2	1
Average years of service	12	12	10	12	12	13	13	12	13	11	10

Table 8. Law Enforcement Officers Feloniously Killed, by Profile of Victim Officer, Averages, 1999–2018

(Number.)

Characteristic	2018	5-year averages		10-year averages	
		2009–2013	2014–2018	1999–2008	2009–2018
Age	37	38	39	37	39
Years of service	10	12	12	10	12
Height	5'10"	5'11"	5'10"	5'11"	5'11"
Weight	194	206	203	199	204

Note: The deaths of the 72 law enforcement officers that resulted from the events of September 11, 2001, are not included in this table.

Table 9. Law Enforcement Officers Feloniously Killed, by Race and Sex of Victim Officer, 2009–2018

(Number.)

Characteristic	Total	2009	2010	2011	2012	2013	2014	2015	2016	2017	2018
Number of Victim Officers	510	48	55	72	49	27	51	41	66	46	55
Race											
White	443	42	47	68	43	25	47	29	61	35	46
Black/African American	51	3	7	3	6	2	2	8	4	9	7
American Indian/Alaska Native	7	2	0	1	0	0	0	2	0	2	0
Asian/Native Hawaiian/Other Pacific Islander[1]	2	1	1	NA	NA	NA	NA	NA	NA	NA	NA
Asian[1]	5	NA	NA	0	0	0	2	2	1	0	0
Native Hawaiian/Other Pacific Islander[1]	2	NA	NA	0	0	0	0	0	0	0	2
Ethnicity[2]											
Hispanic or Latino	51	NA	NA	7	9	2	11	4	7	6	5
Not Hispanic or Latino	343	NA	NA	65	35	24	39	36	57	37	50
Not reported	116	48	55	0	5	1	1	1	2	3	0
Sex											
Male	486	47	53	69	44	25	51	38	64	43	52
Female	24	1	2	3	5	2	0	3	2	3	3

NA = Not available.
[1] For 2008, 2009, and 2010, the race categories "Asian" and "Native Hawaiian/Other Pacific Islander" were combined.
[2] Beginning in 2011, ethnicity was added to the data collection.

Table 10. Law Enforcement Officers Feloniously Killed, by Use of Weapon by Victim Officer, Assisting Officer, and Offender During Incident, 2009–2018

(Number; percent.)

Characteristic	Total	2009	2010	2011	2012	2013	2014	2015	2016	2017	2018
Number of victim officers.....................................	510	48	55	72	49	27	51	41	66	46	55
Average number of rounds fired by victim officers..............................	1.3	0.8	1.9	2.1	0.7	0.9	1.0	1.7	1.1	1.0	1.3
Average number of rounds fired by assisting officers[1].............................	9.9	8.6	6.7	11.3	8.1	2.8	12.8	9.0	14.9	9.4	10.2
Average number of rounds fired by offenders[2] ...	6.3	4.1	4.6	5.2	10.0	6.5	5.8	6.7	9.1	5.8	4.4
Number of victim officers who fired own weapon....................................	107	12	16	18	6	5	5	6	15	10	14
Average number of rounds fired by victim officers who fired own weapon.........................	6.9	4.1	7.5	9.7	6.0	5.8	9.6	11.2	6.1	4.7	5.2
Average number of victim officer's rounds that struck offenders	1.3	1.5	1.3	0.8	1.5	0.7	4.0	0.7	0.3	1.5	1.9
Percentage hit rate of victim officers' rounds striking offenders	19.3	50.0	19.6	6.3	40.0	13.3	41.7	6.0	1.4	28.6	43.4
Average number of rounds fired by assisting officers..............................	6.4	3.6	3.2	9.2	14.7	2.7	2.5	2.0	6.0	6.0	7.2
Average number of rounds fired by offenders	6.6	4.0	7.3	9.5	8.2	6.7	4.4	10.0	5.2	8.4	3.3
Number of victim officers who attempted to (but did not) use own firearm(s)	73	9	7	11	2	3	8	7	11	10	5
Average number of rounds fired by assisting officers..............................	15.8	14.2	12.4	5.8	0.0	1.0	15.2	23.0	14.8	15.7	33.5
Average number of rounds fired by offenders	6.2	8.8	3.3	3.6	2.0	2.3	9.3	3.4	11.2	3.1	9.5
Number of victim officers who did not use and did not attempt to use own firearm(s)	287	18	20	40	38	18	34	26	39	24	30
Average number of rounds fired by assisting officers..............................	9.7	4.4	7.2	12.9	6.4	3.0	12.5	3.8	19.4	8.1	7.3
Average number of rounds fired by offenders	6.3	4.7	4.2	4.4	9.1	7.3	4.7	7.0	10.2	6.1	4.2
Number of victim officers who did not use own firearm(s), but attempt to use own firearm(s) information was not reported.......	28	8	12	1	0	0	2	0	1	0	2
Average number of rounds fired by assisting officers[3].............................	12.4	15.2	4.8		0.0	0.0	41.0	0.0		0.0	
Average number of rounds fired by offenders[4] ...	4.9	3.3	4.0		0.0	0.0	15.0	0.0	3.0	0.0	1.0
Number of victim officers in which victim officer's use of firearm(s) was unknown or not reported	17	1	0	2	3	1	2	2	0	2	4

Note: When calculating the averages presented in this table, the FBI's Law Enforcement Officers Killed and Assaulted Program used all available data for each incident. For example, in a specific incident, if the number of rounds fired by the victim officer is known, but the number of rounds fired by the offender is not known, the known number was included in the calculation for the average number of rounds fired by victim officers.
[1] The number of rounds fired (1,100) during an incident in 2013 was excluded when calculating the average number of rounds fired by assisting officers to provide more accurate statistics.
[2] The number of rounds fired (1,046) during an incident in 2017 was excluded when calculating the average number of rounds fired by offenders to provide more accurate statistics.
[3] For 2011, 2016, and 2018, the victim officers were alone at the time of the incident; therefore, the number of rounds fired by assisting officers is not relevant.
[4] For 2011, number of rounds data were not available for inclusion in these averages.

Table 11. Law Enforcement Officers Feloniously Killed, by Victim Officer Killed with Own Weapon, Disarmed[1] of Weapon or Weapon Taken from Victim Officer, and Weapon Stolen[2] by Offender, 2009–2018

(Number.)

Characteristic	Total	2009	2010	2011	2012	2013	2014	2015	2016	2017	2018
Number of victim officers	510	48	55	72	49	27	51	41	66	46	55
Killed with own weapon	22	2	5	3	1	1	1	4	0	1	4
Disarmed of weapon/weapon taken from victim officer	22	2	5	3	1	1	1	4	0	1	4
Weapon stolen[3]	12	1	4	1	0	0	0	3	0	1	2
Weapon not stolen	10	1	1	2	1	1	1	1	0	0	2
Weapon stolen information not reported	0	0	0	0	0	0	0	0	0	0	0
Not disarmed of weapon/weapon not taken from victim officer	0	0	0	0	0	0	0	0	0	0	0
Weapon stolen	0	0	0	0	0	0	0	0	0	0	0
Weapon not stolen	0	0	0	0	0	0	0	0	0	0	0
Weapon stolen information not reported	0	0	0	0	0	0	0	0	0	0	0
Disarmed of weapon/weapon taken information not reported	0	0	0	0	0	0	0	0	0	0	0
Weapon stolen	0	0	0	0	0	0	0	0	0	0	0
Weapon not stolen	0	0	0	0	0	0	0	0	0	0	0
Weapon stolen information not reported	0	0	0	0	0	0	0	0	0	0	0
Killed with weapon other than own	487	45	50	69	48	26	50	37	66	45	51
Disarmed of weapon/weapon taken from victim officer	40	3	3	9	5	3	7	5	3	0	2
Weapon stolen	25	3	1	4	3	2	6	2	2	0	2
Weapon not stolen	15	0	2	5	2	1	1	3	1	0	0
Weapon stolen information not reported	0	0	0	0	0	0	0	0	0	0	0
Not disarmed of weapon/weapon not taken from victim officer	446	42	47	59	43	23	43	32	63	45	49
Weapon stolen	5	2	2	0	0	0	0	0	0	1	0
Weapon not stolen	440	40	44	59	43	23	43	32	63	44	49
Weapon stolen information not reported	1	0	1	0	0	0	0	0	0	0	0
Disarmed of weapon/weapon taken information not reported	1	0	0	1	0	0	0	0	0	0	0
Weapon stolen	0	0	0	0	0	0	0	0	0	0	0
Weapon not stolen	1	0	0	1	0	0	0	0	0	0	0
Weapon stolen information not reported	0	0	0	0	0	0	0	0	0	0	0
Killed with weapon information not reported	1	1	0	0	0	0	0	0	0	0	0
Disarmed of weapon/weapon taken from victim officer	1	1	0	0	0	0	0	0	0	0	0
Weapon stolen	1	1	0	0	0	0	0	0	0	0	0
Weapon not stolen	0	0	0	0	0	0	0	0	0	0	0
Weapon stolen information not reported	0	0	0	0	0	0	0	0	0	0	0
Not disarmed of weapon/weapon not taken from victim officer	0	0	0	0	0	0	0	0	0	0	0
Weapon stolen	0	0	0	0	0	0	0	0	0	0	0
Weapon not stolen	0	0	0	0	0	0	0	0	0	0	0
Weapon stolen information not reported	0	0	0	0	0	0	0	0	0	0	0
Disarmed of weapon/weapon taken information not reported	0	0	0	0	0	0	0	0	0	0	0
Weapon stolen	0	0	0	0	0	0	0	0	0	0	0
Weapon not stolen	0	0	0	0	0	0	0	0	0	0	0
Weapon stolen information not reported	0	0	0	0	0	0	0	0	0	0	0

Note: The term "weapon" includes all weapon types that may be issued to a law enforcement officer.

[1] The term "disarmed" indicates the victim officer was physically disarmed of one or more of his or her weapons by the offender(s) during the incident.

[2] The term "stolen" indicates a weapon issued to the victim officer was taken from the scene of the incident by the offender(s).

[3] One 2015 incident involved an offender(s) who commandeered the victim officer's patrol vehicle, fatally struck the victim officer with the patrol vehicle, and drove the patrol vehicle from the scene of the incident.

Table 12. Law Enforcement Officers Feloniously Killed with Own Weapons, by Victim Officer's Type of Weapon, 2009–2018

(Number.)

Type of weapon	Total	2009	2010	2011	2012	2013	2014	2015	2016	2017	2018
Number of Victim Officers Killed with Own Weapon.	22	2	5	3	1	1	1	4	0	1	4
Total, handgun	21	2	5	3	1	1	1	3	0	1	4
.38 caliber	1	0	0	1	0	0	0	0	0	0	0
.40 caliber	9	1	1	2	0	0	1	1	0	1	2
.45 caliber	1	0	1	0	0	0	0	0	0	0	0
9 millimeter	7	1	3	0	0	1	0	1	0	0	1
Not reported	3	0	0	0	1	0	0	1	0	0	1
Rifle, total	0	0	0	0	0	0	0	0	0	0	0
Shotgun, total	0	0	0	0	0	0	0	0	0	0	0
Other[1]	1	0	0	0	0	0	0	1	0	0	0

[1]One 2015 incident involved an offender(s) who fatally struck the victim officer with the officer's own patrol vehicle.

Table 13. Law Enforcement Officers Feloniously Killed, Time of Incident, by Type of Assignment, 2018

(Number.)

Characteristic and time	Total	2-officer patrol	1-officer patrol Alone	1-officer patrol Assisted	Investigative/detective Alone	Investigative/detective Assisted	Tactical assignment (uniformed) Alone	Tactical assignment (uniformed) Assisted	Plainclothes assignment Alone	Plainclothes assignment Assisted
Number of Victim Officers............	55	9	12	15	0	3	0	3	0	3
Total A.M. hours...............	19	1	6	6	0	1	0	1	0	1
12:01 a.m.–2 a.m...............	4	0	3	0	0	0	0	0	0	1
2:01 a.m.–4 a.m...............	1	0	0	0	0	0	0	1	0	0
4:01 a.m.–6 a.m...............	3	1	0	2	0	0	0	0	0	0
6:01 a.m.–8 a.m...............	3	0	2	0	0	1	0	0	0	0
8:01 a.m.–10 a.m...............	2	0	1	1	0	0	0	0	0	0
10:01 a.m.–noon	6	0	0	3	0	0	0	0	0	0
Total P.M. hours...............	36	8	6	9	0	2	0	2	0	2
12:01 p.m.–2 p.m...............	5	0	2	1	0	0	0	0	0	0
2:01 p.m.–4 p.m...............	8	1	1	1	0	0	0	2	0	1
4:01 p.m.–6 p.m...............	8	2	2	1	0	2	0	0	0	0
6:01 p.m.–8 p.m...............	7	1	0	3	0	0	0	0	0	1
8:01 p.m.–10 p.m...............	2	1	0	1	0	0	0	0	0	0
10:01 p.m.–midnight	6	3	1	2	0	0	0	0	0	0

Table 13. Law Enforcement Officers Feloniously Killed, Time of Incident, by Type of Assignment, 2018—Continued

(Number.)

Characteristic and time	Special assignment Alone	Special assignment Assisted	Undercover Alone	Undercover Assisted	Court/prisoner security Alone	Court/prisoner security Assisted	Other[1] Alone	Other[1] Assisted	Off duty
Number of Victim Officers............	0	2	0	0	0	2	0	2	4
Total A.M. hours...............	0	0	0	0	0	2	0	0	1
12:01 a.m.–2 a.m...............	0	0	0	0	0	0	0	0	0
2:01 a.m.–4 a.m...............	0	0	0	0	0	0	0	0	0
4:01 a.m.–6 a.m...............	0	0	0	0	0	0	0	0	0
6:01 a.m.–8 a.m...............	0	0	0	0	0	0	0	0	0
8:01 a.m.–10 a.m...............	0	0	0	0	0	0	0	0	0
10:01 a.m.–noon	0	0	0	0	0	2	0	0	1
Total P.M. hours...............	0	2	0	0	0	0	0	2	3
12:01 p.m.–2 p.m...............	0	0	0	0	0	0	0	0	2
2:01 p.m.–4 p.m...............	0	0	0	0	0	0	0	2	0
4:01 p.m.–6 p.m...............	0	0	0	0	0	0	0	0	1
6:01 p.m.–8 p.m...............	0	2	0	0	0	0	0	0	0
8:01 p.m.–10 p.m...............	0	0	0	0	0	0	0	0	0
10:01 p.m.–midnight	0	0	0	0	0	0	0	0	0

[1]Includes officers on overtime/extra duty activities and other types of assignments not listed.

Table 14. Law Enforcement Officers Feloniously Killed, by Circumstance Encountered by Victim Officer Upon Arrival at Scene of Incident, 2014–2018[1]

(Number.)

Circumstance	Total	2014	2015	2016	2017	2018
Number of victim officers..	259	51	41	66	46	55
Administrative assignment	4	0	1	0	1	2
Prisoner transport..	4	0	1	0	1	2
Other administrative assignment	0	0	0	0	0	0
Ambush (entrapment/premeditation)	53	11	7	19	5	11
Arrest situation	13	0	2	4	4	3
Attempting to control/handcuff/restrain offender(s).....................	6	0	2	0	1	3
Verbal advisement only	7	0	0	4	3	0
Assist another law enforcement officer	14	4	2	4	2	2
Deploying/providing equipment (traffic cones, flares, etc.)............	4	1	1	1	1	0
Foot pursuit..	3	0	1	0	0	2
Officer down (requiring emergency assistance)........................	0	0	0	0	0	0
Officer requiring emergency assistance (not pursuit)	1	0	0	1	0	0
Vehicular pursuit..	2	0	0	1	1	0
Other emergency circumstance	3	2	0	1	0	0
Other nonemergency circumstance	1	1	0	0	0	0
Assist motorist	2	1	1	0	0	0
Citizen complaint..	0	0	0	0	0	0
Animal bite..	0	0	0	0	0	0
Animal disturbance (barking dog, unleashed dog, etc.)................	0	0	0	0	0	0
Business check	0	0	0	0	0	0
Check on welfare of citizen..	0	0	0	0	0	0
Drug complaint	0	0	0	0	0	0
Traffic complaint..	0	0	0	0	0	0
Verbal complaint of noncriminal violation.............................	0	0	0	0	0	0
Disorder/disturbance..	11	5	1	2	1	2
Civil disorder (mass disobedience, riot, etc.).........................	0	0	0	0	0	0
Disturbance call (disorderly subject, fight, etc.)	6	4	0	1	0	1
Domestic disturbance (family quarrel, no assault).....................	2	0	0	1	1	0
Domestic violence	3	1	1	0	0	1
Encounter or assist an emotionally disturbed person	2	1	0	0	1	0
Investigative/enforcement...	109	20	17	28	21	23
Drug-related matter (drug bust, buy, etc.)	2	0	0	1	1	0
Handling person with mental illness	3	0	2	0	0	1
Investigate motor vehicle crash.......................................	1	0	0	0	1	0
Investigate possible DUI/DWI suspect (operating a vehicle)...........	1	1	0	0	0	0
Investigate suspicious person/circumstance...........................	31	6	5	11	6	3
Investigative activity..	19	2	1	6	2	8
Tactical situation	27	4	4	7	6	6
Traffic stop (felony traffic stop)......................................	2	1	0	0	1	0
Traffic stop (traffic violation stop)...................................	12	2	4	1	3	2
Undercover situation..	2	2	0	0	0	0
Wanted person	9	2	1	2	1	3
Pursuit..	24	4	4	4	6	6
Foot	14	1	2	4	3	4
Vehicular..	10	3	2	0	3	2
Respond to alarm...	0	0	0	0	0	0
Burglary	0	0	0	0	0	0
Robbery	0	0	0	0	0	0
Respond to crime in progress..	12	3	1	2	2	4
Assault..	1	1	0	0	0	0
Burglary	3	0	0	1	0	2
Larceny-theft..	0	0	0	0	0	0
Motor vehicle theft..	0	0	0	0	0	0
Person with firearm (no shots fired)	3	2	0	0	0	1
Robbery	2	0	0	1	1	0
Shooting/shots fired	2	0	1	0	1	0
Tampering with vehicle	0	0	0	0	0	0

Table 14. Law Enforcement Officers Feloniously Killed, by Circumstance Encountered by Victim Officer Upon Arrival at Scene of Incident, 2014–2018[1]—*Continued*

(Number.)

Circumstance	Total	2014	2015	2016	2017	2018
Other crime against person	0	0	0	0	0	0
Other crime against property	1	0	0	0	0	1
Respond to report of crime	1	1	0	0	0	0
Assault	0	0	0	0	0	0
Burglary	0	0	0	0	0	0
Homicide	0	0	0	0	0	0
Larceny-theft	0	0	0	0	0	0
Motor vehicle theft	0	0	0	0	0	0
Person with firearm (no shots fired)	1	1	0	0	0	0
Robbery	0	0	0	0	0	0
Shooting/shots fired	0	0	0	0	0	0
Tampering with vehicle	0	0	0	0	0	0
Other crime against person	0	0	0	0	0	0
Other crime against property	0	0	0	0	0	0
Traffic control (crash scene, directing traffic, etc.)	2	0	1	0	0	1
Unprovoked attack	11	1	3	3	3	1
Other	1	0	1	0	0	0

[1]Ten years of data for the topics presented in this table are not available at this time. A 10-year table is expected to be available for the publication of 2020 data.

Table 15. Law Enforcement Officers Feloniously Killed, by Specific Activity Being Performed by Victim Officer at Time of Attack, 2014–2018[1]

(Number.)

Circumstance	Total	2014	2015	2016	2017	2018
Number of victim officers	259	51	41	66	46	55
Administrative assignment	7	0	4	0	1	2
Prisoner transport	4	0	1	0	1	2
Other administrative assignment	3	0	3	0	0	0
Ambush (entrapment/premeditation)	0	0	0	0	0	0
Arrest situation	37	4	5	7	9	12
Attempting to control/handcuff/restrain offender(s)	25	2	5	4	5	9
Verbal advisement only	12	2	0	3	4	3
Assist another law enforcement officer	10	3	1	2	2	2
Deploying/providing equipment (traffic cones, flares, etc.)	4	1	1	1	1	0
Foot pursuit	1	0	0	0	0	1
Officer down (requiring emergency assistance)	1	0	0	0	0	1
Officer requiring emergency assistance (not pursuit)	0	0	0	0	0	0
Vehicular pursuit	0	0	0	0	0	0
Other emergency circumstance	3	2	0	1	0	0
Other nonemergency circumstance	1	0	0	0	1	0
Assist motorist	2	0	1	0	1	0
Citizen complaint	3	0	1	0	0	2
Animal bite	0	0	0	0	0	0
Animal disturbance (barking dog, unleashed dog, etc.)	0	0	0	0	0	0
Business check	0	0	0	0	0	0
Check on welfare of citizen	3	0	1	0	0	2
Drug complaint	0	0	0	0	0	0
Traffic complaint	0	0	0	0	0	0
Verbal complaint of noncriminal violation	0	0	0	0	0	0
Disorder/disturbance	11	4	1	4	0	2
Civil disorder (mass disobedience, riot, etc.)	0	0	0	0	0	0
Disturbance call (disorderly subject, fight, etc.)	5	3	0	1	0	1
Domestic disturbance (family quarrel, no assault)	2	1	0	1	0	0
Domestic violence	4	0	1	2	0	1
Encounter or assist an emotionally disturbed person	1	1	0	0	0	0
Investigative/enforcement	119	22	18	33	22	24
Drug-related matter (drug bust, buy, etc.)	1	0	0	1	0	0
Handling person with mental illness	3	1	1	0	0	1
Investigate motor vehicle crash	1	0	0	0	1	0
Investigate possible DUI/DWI suspect (operating a vehicle)	1	0	0	1	0	0
Investigate suspicious person/circumstance	33	6	6	12	5	4
Investigative activity	20	2	1	6	5	6
Tactical situation	36	4	6	9	7	10
Traffic stop (felony traffic stop)	3	1	0	1	0	1
Traffic stop (traffic violation stop)	16	4	3	3	4	2
Undercover situation	2	2	0	0	0	0
Wanted person	3	2	1	0	0	0
Pursuit	27	7	2	8	5	5
Foot	21	5	1	7	4	4
Vehicular	6	2	1	1	1	1
Respond to alarm	0	0	0	0	0	0
Burglary	0	0	0	0	0	0
Robbery	0	0	0	0	0	0
Respond to crime in progress	13	2	2	3	3	3
Assault	0	0	0	0	0	0
Burglary	3	0	0	1	0	2
Larceny-theft	0	0	0	0	0	0
Motor vehicle theft	0	0	0	0	0	0
Person with firearm (no shots fired)	4	2	1	0	0	1
Robbery	3	0	1	1	1	0
Shooting/shots fired	3	0	0	1	2	0
Tampering with vehicle	0	0	0	0	0	0

Table 15. Law Enforcement Officers Feloniously Killed, by Specific Activity Being Performed by Victim Officer at Time of Attack, 2014–2018[1]—Continued

(Number.)

Circumstance	Total	2014	2015	2016	2017	2018
Other crime against person	0	0	0	0	0	0
Other crime against property	0	0	0	0	0	0
Respond to report of crime	1	1	0	0	0	0
Assault	0	0	0	0	0	0
Burglary	0	0	0	0	0	0
Homicide	0	0	0	0	0	0
Larceny-theft	0	0	0	0	0	0
Motor vehicle theft	0	0	0	0	0	0
Person with firearm (no shots fired)	1	1	0	0	0	0
Robbery	0	0	0	0	0	0
Shooting/shots fired	0	0	0	0	0	0
Tampering with vehicle	0	0	0	0	0	0
Other crime against person	0	0	0	0	0	0
Other crime against property	0	0	0	0	0	0
Traffic control (crash scene, directing traffic, etc.)	6	0	1	4	0	1
Unprovoked attack	0	0	0	0	0	0
Other	22	7	5	5	3	2

[1]Ten years of data for the topics presented in this table are not available at this time. A 10-year table is expected to be available for the publication of 2020 data.

Table 16. Law Enforcement Officers Feloniously Killed During Traffic-Related Incidents,[1] by Circumstance at Scene of Incident, by Type of Assignment, 2014–2018

(Number.)

Location of offender	Total	Approaching offender(s)	Approaching suspect vehicle		Returning to victim officer's vehicle	Seated in victim officer's vehicle	
			On driver's side	On passenger's side		Prior to approaching suspect vehicle	After obtaining contact with offenders
Number of victim officers killed during traffic-related incidents	4	0	0	0	0	0	0
Prone	0	0	0	0	0	0	0
On ground	0	0	0	0	0	0	0
On vehicle/object	0	0	0	0	0	0	0
Seated	2	0	0	0	0	0	0
In suspect's vehicle	2	0	0	0	0	0	0
In victim officer's vehicle	0	0	0	0	0	0	0
Seated outside in vicinity of suspect's vehicle	0	0	0	0	0	0	0
Front driver's side	0	0	0	0	0	0	0
Front passenger's side	0	0	0	0	0	0	0
Rear driver's side	0	0	0	0	0	0	0
Rear passenger's side	0	0	0	0	0	0	0
Seated outside in vicinity of victim officer's vehicle	0	0	0	0	0	0	0
Front driver's side	0	0	0	0	0	0	0
Front passenger's side	0	0	0	0	0	0	0
Rear driver's side	0	0	0	0	0	0	0
Rear passenger's side	0	0	0	0	0	0	0
Standing in vicinity of suspect's vehicle	0	0	0	0	0	0	0
Front driver's side	0	0	0	0	0	0	0
Front passenger's side	0	0	0	0	0	0	0
Rear driver's side	0	0	0	0	0	0	0
Rear passenger's side	0	0	0	0	0	0	0
Standing in vicinity of victim officer's vehicle	0	0	0	0	0	0	0
Front driver's side	0	0	0	0	0	0	0
Front passenger's side	0	0	0	0	0	0	0
Rear driver's side	0	0	0	0	0	0	0
Rear passenger's side	0	0	0	0	0	0	0
Unrestricted movement	1	0	0	0	0	0	0
Outside of suspect's vehicle	0	0	0	0	0	0	0
Outside of victim officer's vehicle	1	0	0	0	0	0	0
Other	1	0	0	0	0	0	0
Multiple locations due to multiple offenders	0	0	0	0	0	0	0
Not reported	0	0	0	0	0	0	0

Note: For 2018, 2 of the 4 victim officers who were feloniously killed during traffic-related incidents contacted radio dispatchers prior to or during the attack.
[1]Traffic-related incidents include traffic stops (felony traffic stops and traffic violation stops), investigating possible DUI/DWI suspects, and assisting motorists.

Table 16. Law Enforcement Officers Feloniously Killed During Traffic-Related Incidents,[1] by Circumstance at Scene of Incident, by Type of Assignment, 2014–2018—*Continued*

(Number.)

Location of offender	Standing in vicinity of suspect's vehicle				Standing in vicinity of victim officer's vehicle				Not reported
	Front driver's side	Front passenger's side	Rear driver's side	Rear passenger's side	Front driver's side	Front passenger's side	Rear driver's side	Rear passenger's side	
Number of victim officers killed during traffic-related incidents	2	0	0	0	0	0	1	0	1
Prone	0	0	0	0	0	0	0	0	0
On ground	0	0	0	0	0	0	0	0	0
On vehicle/object	0	0	0	0	0	0	0	0	0
Seated	2	0	0	0	0	0	0	0	0
In suspect's vehicle	2	0	0	0	0	0	0	0	0
In victim officer's vehicle	0	0	0	0	0	0	0	0	0
Seated outside in vicinity of suspect's vehicle	0	0	0	0	0	0	0	0	0
Front driver's side	0	0	0	0	0	0	0	0	0
Front passenger's side	0	0	0	0	0	0	0	0	0
Rear driver's side	0	0	0	0	0	0	0	0	0
Rear passenger's side	0	0	0	0	0	0	0	0	0
Seated outside in vicinity of victim officer's vehicle	0	0	0	0	0	0	0	0	0
Front driver's side	0	0	0	0	0	0	0	0	0
Front passenger's side	0	0	0	0	0	0	0	0	0
Rear driver's side	0	0	0	0	0	0	0	0	0
Rear passenger's side	0	0	0	0	0	0	0	0	0
Standing in vicinity of suspect's vehicle	0	0	0	0	0	0	0	0	0
Front driver's side	0	0	0	0	0	0	0	0	0
Front passenger's side	0	0	0	0	0	0	0	0	0
Rear driver's side	0	0	0	0	0	0	0	0	0
Rear passenger's side	0	0	0	0	0	0	0	0	0
Standing in vicinity of victim officer's vehicle	0	0	0	0	0	0	0	0	0
Front driver's side	0	0	0	0	0	0	0	0	0
Front passenger's side	0	0	0	0	0	0	0	0	0
Rear driver's side	0	0	0	0	0	0	0	0	0
Rear passenger's side	0	0	0	0	0	0	0	0	0
Unrestricted movement	0	0	0	0	0	0	1	0	0
Outside of suspect's vehicle	0	0	0	0	0	0	0	0	0
Outside of victim officer's vehicle	0	0	0	0	0	0	1	0	0
Other	0	0	0	0	0	0	0	0	1
Multiple locations due to multiple offenders	0	0	0	0	0	0	0	0	0
Not reported	0	0	0	0	0	0	0	0	0

Note: For 2018, 2 of the 4 victim officers who were feloniously killed during traffic-related incidents contacted radio dispatchers prior to or during the attack.

[1] Traffic-related incidents include traffic stops (felony traffic stops and traffic violation stops), investigating possible DUI/DWI suspects, and assisting motorists.

Table 17. Law Enforcement Officers Feloniously Killed, by Type of Weapon, 2009–2018

(Number.)

Type of weapon	Total	2009	2010	2011	2012	2013	2014	2015	2016	2017	2018
Number of Victim Officers........................	510	48	55	72	49	27	51	41	66	46	55
Total firearms..	471	45	54	63	44	26	46	38	62	42	51
Handgun...	335	28	38	49	34	18	33	29	37	32	37
Rifle	108	15	15	7	7	5	10	7	23	9	10
Shotgun..	23	2	1	6	3	3	3	1	1	1	2
Multiple firearms used by offender(s), unable to determine which caused fatal injury[1]	2	NA	NA	1	0	0	0	0	1	0	0
Type of firearm unknown..........................	1	0	0	0	0	0	0	1	0	0	0
Type of firearm not reported	2	0	0	0	0	0	0	0	0	0	2
Knife or other cutting instrument[2].................	0	0	0	NA	NA	NA	NA	NA	NA	NA	NA
Knife[2]...	3	NA	NA	1	1	0	0	0	0	1	0
Other cutting instrument[2]..........................	0	NA	NA	0	0	0	0	0	0	0	0
Bomb...	0	0	0	0	0	0	0	0	0	0	0
Blunt instrument	0	0	0	0	0	0	0	0	0	0	0
Personal weapons (hands, feet, fists, etc.)	5	0	0	2	2	0	1	0	0	0	0
Vehicle..	31	3	1	6	2	1	4	3	4	3	4
Other..	0	0	0	0	0	0	0	0	0	0	0
Number of Victim Officers Who Had Prior Knowledge That a Weapon Might Be Involved in the Incident..............................	172	21	20	25	6	8	15	17	26	11	23

NA = Not available.
[1] Beginning in 2011, a new option was added: "Multiple firearms used by offender(s), unable to determine which caused fatal injury."
[2] For 2009 and 2010, the type of weapon categories "Knife" and "Other cutting instrument" were combined.

Table 18. Law Enforcement Officers Feloniously Killed, by Number of Victim Officers Wearing Uniform, Body Armor, or Holster, 2009–2018

(Number.)

Characteristic	Total	2009	2010	2011	2012	2013	2014	2015	2016	2017	2018
Number of Victim Officers......................	510	48	55	72	49	27	51	41	66	46	55
Wearing body armor.................................	368	36	37	52	25	19	40	30	51	35	43
In uniform	344	32	34	47	25	18	40	28	50	33	37
Not in uniform	24	4	3	5	0	1	0	2	1	2	6
Wearing holster	481	45	52	69	43	27	48	37	65	44	51
In uniform..	422	39	45	61	38	20	43	35	59	39	43
Not in uniform	52	6	7	8	2	7	5	2	4	5	6
Wearing uniform not reported	7	0	0	0	3	0	0	0	2	0	2

Table 19. Law Enforcement Officers Feloniously Killed, Age Group of Known Offender, 2009–2018

(Number.)

Age group	Total	2009	2010	2011	2012	2013	2014	2015	2016	2017	2018
Number of Known Offenders	532	45	80	76	51	28	60	37	56	44	55
Under 18	17	2	1	5	1	0	3	0	3	1	1
18–24	127	14	24	20	14	9	13	4	12	3	14
25–30	131	6	23	19	15	7	18	14	6	10	13
31–35	94	9	12	9	6	6	10	10	10	12	10
36–40	52	5	8	7	4	2	9	1	6	5	5
41–45	36	5	6	3	5	0	1	1	5	6	4
46–50	26	1	0	5	2	3	3	2	6	3	1
51–55	21	2	3	4	1	1	1	3	2	1	3
56–60	14	0	2	4	0	0	2	2	3	0	1
Over 60	10	1	1	0	1	0	0	0	1	3	3
Not reported	4	0	0	0	2	0	0	0	2	0	0
Average age	32	31	31	32	31	31	31	34	35	36	33

Table 20. Law Enforcement Officers Feloniously Killed, by Profile of Known Offender, Averages, 1999–2018

(Number.)

Characteristic	2018	5-year averages		10-year averages	
		2009–2013	2014–2018	1999–2008	2009–2018
Age	33	31	34	30	32
Height	5'10"	5'10"	5'10"	5'10"	5'10"
Weight	183	181	185	177	183

Note: The 14 known offenders involved in the events of September 11, 2001, are not included in this table.

Table 21. Law Enforcement Officers Feloniously Killed, by Race, Ethnicity, and Sex of Known Offender, 2009–2018

(Number.)

Characteristic	Total	2009	2010	2011	2012	2013	2014	2015	2016	2017	2018
Number of Known Offenders	532	45	80	76	51	28	60	37	56	44	55
Race											
White	302	28	32	44	32	15	43	18	33	26	31
Black/African American	201	17	39	28	17	12	14	18	17	16	23
American Indian/Alaska Native	12	0	4	2	1	0	2	1	1	1	0
Asian/Native Hawaiian/Other Pacific Islander[1]	2	0	2	NA	NA	NA	NA	NA	NA	NA	NA
Asian[1]	3	NA	NA	1	0	0	1	0	0	1	0
Native Hawaiian/Other Pacific Islander[1]	2	NA	NA	0	1	0	0	0	0	0	1
Not reported	10	0	3	1	0	1	0	0	5	0	0
Ethnicity[2]											
Hispanic or Latino	63	NA	NA	7	7	3	19	3	9	5	10
Not Hispanic or Latino	326	NA	NA	68	41	23	39	33	41	38	43
Not reported	143	45	80	1	3	2	2	1	6	1	2
Sex											
Male	517	43	78	74	50	27	55	37	56	44	53
Female	15	2	2	2	1	1	5	0	0	0	2

NA = Not available.
[1] For 2009 and 2010, the race categories "Asian" and "Native Hawaiian/Other Pacific Islander" were combined.
[2] Beginning in 2011, ethnicity was added to the data collection.

Table 22. Law Enforcement Officers Feloniously Killed, by Status of Known Offender at Time of Incident, 2009–2018

(Number.)

Characteristic	Total	2009	2010	2011	2012	2013	2014	2015	2016	2017	2018
Number of Known Offenders	532	45	80	76	51	28	60	37	56	44	55
Under judicial supervision	137	13	19	19	12	6	12	11	15	18	18
Total	145	13	19	19	12	6	12	11	15	18	20
Conditional release, pending criminal prosecution	27	3	·1	5	2	2	1	3	1	3	6
Escapee from penal institution	2	0	1	0	0	0	0	0	0	0	1
Halfway house	2	0	0	1	0	0	0	0	0	1	0
Parole	40	3	8	4	4	2	5	3	3	5	3
Probation	62	7	9	7	5	2	5	4	10	5	8
Serving time in penal institution[1]	1	NA	NA	0	0	0	0	0	0	1	0
Other judicial supervision[1]	10	NA	NA	2	1	0	1	1	1	3	1
Multiple forms of judicial supervision	1	0	0	0	0	0	0	0	0	0	1
Known to agency as											
Controlled substance dealer	61	5	7	9	6	4	12	2	4	2	10
Controlled substance possessor	62	2	12	9	5	2	10	2	9	1	10
Controlled substance user	87	10	19	13	6	3	8	2	12	4	10
Known or suspected gang member[2]	34	NA	NA	8	4	2	7	4	7	0	2
Known or suspected terrorist (domestic or international)[2]	2	NA	NA	1	0	0	0	0	0	1	0
Other[2]	82	NA	NA	11	2	7	6	7	12	15	22
Use of alcohol and/or controlled substance											
Under influence	112	3	17	12	13	4	13	13	16	6	15
Alcohol	27	2	6	4	3	3	2	3	1	1	2
Controlled substance[3]	11	1	10	NA	NA	NA	NA	NA	NA	NA	NA
Amphetamines/methamphetamines	11	NA	NA	0	0	1	3	0	4	1	2
Barbiturates	1	NA	NA	0	0	0	1	0	0	0	0
Cocaine (all forms except Crack)	1	NA	NA	0	1	0	0	0	0	0	0
Crack/cocaine	1	NA	NA	0	0	0	1	0	0	0	0
Hashish	0	NA	NA	0	0	0	0	0	0	0	0
Heroin	2	NA	NA	0	0	0	0	2	0	0	0
LSD	0	NA	NA	0	0	0	0	0	0	0	0
Marijuana	21	NA	NA	2	2	0	3	2	4	2	6
Morphine	0	NA	NA	0	0	0	0	0	0	0	0
Opium	0	NA	NA	0	0	0	0	0	0	0	0
PCP	1	NA	NA	0	0	0	1	0	0	0	0
Other depressants not listed	0	NA	NA	0	0	0	0	0	0	0	0
Other hallucinogens not listed	0	NA	NA	0	0	0	0	0	0	0	0
Other narcotics not listed	0	NA	NA	0	0	0	0	0	0	0	0
Other stimulants not listed	1	NA	NA	0	0	0	0	0	0	0	1
Other dangerous drug/substance	2	NA	NA	1	0	0	0	0	1	0	0
Multiple forms of substances	33	0	1	5	7	0	2	6	6	2	4
Not under influence	53	10	10	11	3	3	4	2	3	3	4
Use of alcohol/controlled substance unknown	329	26	48	48	28	20	42	19	31	35	32
Use of alcohol/controlled substance not reported	38	6	5	5	7	1	1	3	6	0	4
Known to agency as having prior mental disorders	29	3	2	7	2	2	1	3	2	2	5
Relationship between victim officer and offender											
Prior relationship through law enforcement (arrest, investigation, etc.)	54	3	8	11	4	3	3	4	10	3	5
Prior relationship through non-law enforcement (acquaintance, neighbor, relative, etc.)	4	0	1	0	0	2	0	0	0	0	1
No known relationship	457	33	66	65	47	23	57	33	45	40	48
Not reported	17	9	5	0	0	0	0	0	1	1	1

NA = Not available.
[1] Beginning in 2011, new options were added, including: "Serving time in penal institution" and "Other judicial supervision."
[2] Beginning in 2011, new options were added, including: "Known or suspected gang member" and "Known or suspected terrorist (domestic or international)."
[3] Beginning in 2011, new options were added to indicate the type of controlled substance the offender had used at the time of the incident.

Table 23. Law Enforcement Officers Feloniously Killed, by Judicial History of Known Offender Prior to Incident, 2009–2018

(Number.)

Judicial history prior to incident	Total	2009	2010	2011	2012	2013	2014	2015	2016	2017	2018
Number of Known Offenders	532	45	80	76	51	28	60	37	56	44	55
Previously arrested	450	35	71	64	41	20	51	32	47	40	49
Convicted on prior criminal charge[1]	83	28	55	NA	NA	NA	NA	NA	NA	NA	NA
Conviction as adult[2]	263	NA	NA	48	29	13	35	28	39	34	37
Conviction as juvenile	104	8	10	18	6	2	10	9	14	12	15
Halfway house[3]	9	NA	NA	1	1	0	2	0	1	2	2
House arrest[3]	0	NA	NA	0	0	0	0	0	0	0	0
Incarceration in penal institution[3]	92	NA	NA	19	4	4	9	10	11	13	22
Parole or probation[4]	67	26	41	NA	NA	NA	NA	NA	NA	NA	NA
Parole[4]	81	NA	NA	14	7	3	12	12	13	11	9
Probation[4]	191	NA	NA	37	17	8	26	18	31	22	32
Prior arrest for:											
Assault on law enforcement officer/resisting arrest[5]	29	9	20	NA	NA	NA	NA	NA	NA	NA	NA
Assault on law enforcement officer[5]	43	NA	NA	10	1	1	7	5	7	7	5
Crime of violence (includes arrests for aggravated assault, murder, rape, and robbery)[6]	67	23	44	NA	NA	NA	NA	NA	NA	NA	NA
Drug law violation	238	13	39	27	20	8	34	15	27	22	33
Murder	24	2	7	1	2	0	1	3	4	2	2
Other crime of violence (includes arrests for aggravated assault, rape, and robbery)[6]	208	NA	NA	38	19	12	22	24	35	30	28
Resisting arrest[5]	97	NA	NA	19	9	3	15	11	14	13	13
Weapons violation	214	18	40	32	15	7	26	19	21	16	20

NA = Not available.
[1] For 2009 and 2010, adult and juvenile convictions were combined into one category, "Convicted on prior criminal charge."
[2] In 2011, "Conviction as adult" was added as an option for judicial history.
[3] In 2011, new options for judicial history were added, including: "Halfway house," "House arrest," and "Incarceration in penal institution."
[4] For 2009 and 2010, the judicial history categories "Parole" and "Probation" were combined.
[5] For 2009 and 2010, the prior arrests categories "Assault on law enforcement officer" and "Resisting arrest" were combined.
[6] For 2009 and 2010, "Crime of violence" counts for prior arrests included prior murders. Beginning in 2011, "Crime of violence" was renamed to "Other crime of violence" since "Murder" is listed separately.

Table 24. Law Enforcement Officers Feloniously Killed, by Disposition of Known Offender, 2007–2016

(Number.)

Disposition	2007–2011	2012–2016	2007–2016
Number of Known Offenders	309	232	541
Fugitive	3	0	3
Arrested and charged	204	137	341
Guilty of murder	137	82	219
Received death sentence	23	9	32
Received life imprisonment	82	49	131
Received prison term (ranging from 8.75 years to 999 years)	32	24	56
Guilty of lesser offense related to murder	22	8	30
Guilty of crime other than murder	13	8	21
Acquitted/dismissed/nolle prosequi	21	3	24
Indeterminate charge and sentence	1	0	1
Committed to psychiatric institution	4	8	12
Case pending/disposition unknown	5	27	32
Died in custody prior to sentencing	1	1	2
Not arrested	102	95	197
Justifiably killed	63	58	121
Justifiably killed by victim officer	20	12	32
Justifiably killed by person(s) other than victim officer	43	46	89
Committed suicide	33	29	62
Killed by civilian(s)	1	1	2
Died under other circumstance	2	4	6
Died by unknown cause	0	1	1
Other	3	2	5

Table 25. Law Enforcement Officers Accidentally Killed, by Region, Geographic Division, and State/Territory, 2009–2018

(Number.)

Area	Total	2009	2010	2011	2012	2013	2014	2015	2016	2017	2018
Number of Victim Officers.................	511	48	72	53	48	49	45	45	52	48	51
Northeast............................	65	6	8	8	9	5	8	5	5	6	5
New England..................	15	2	3	2	4	0	1	0	1	1	1
Connecticut..................	3	0	2	0	0	0	0	0	0	0	1
Maine...........................	2	0	0	1	0	0	0	0	0	1	0
Massachusetts.............	9	2	1	1	3	0	1	0	1	0	0
New Hampshire............	0	0	0	0	0	0	0	0	0	0	0
Rhode Island...............	1	0	0	0	1	0	0	0	0	0	0
Vermont........................	0	0	0	0	0	0	0	0	0	0	0
Middle Atlantic..............	50	4	5	6	5	5	7	5	4	5	4
New Jersey...................	16	0	4	1	1	0	2	3	2	1	2
New York......................	23	3	1	5	2	3	3	0	2	3	1
Pennsylvania................	11	1	0	0	2	2	2	2	0	1	1
Midwest..............................	79	9	14	7	3	4	4	6	12	9	11
East North Central...........	52	6	7	3	3	4	3	4	8	6	8
Illinois.........................	15	0	3	0	1	2	1	1	2	2	3
Indiana.........................	6	2	2	0	0	0	1	0	0	0	1
Michigan......................	13	2	0	1	0	1	1	2	2	2	2
Ohio.............................	11	1	1	2	1	1	0	0	3	1	1
Wisconsin.....................	7	1	1	0	1	0	0	1	1	1	1
West North Central.........	27	3	7	4	0	0	1	2	4	3	3
Iowa.............................	4	0	0	1	0	0	0	0	3	0	0
Kansas..........................	3	0	2	0	0	0	0	0	1	0	0
Minnesota....................	1	0	0	0	0	0	0	0	0	1	0
Missouri.......................	15	2	4	3	0	0	1	2	0	1	2
Nebraska......................	2	1	0	0	0	0	0	0	0	1	0
North Dakota...............	1	0	0	0	0	0	0	0	0	0	1
South Dakota...............	1	0	1	0	0	0	0	0	0	0	0
South.................................	272	21	39	27	28	31	19	29	24	27	27
South Atlantic.................	118	12	16	16	14	9	4	12	8	14	13
Delaware......................	0	0	0	0	0	0	0	0	0	0	0
District of Columbia.....	1	0	1	0	0	0	0	0	0	0	0
Florida.........................	23	1	4	1	2	1	1	1	4	4	4
Georgia........................	28	2	3	6	4	2	1	5	2	2	1
Maryland......................	12	0	3	2	3	0	0	3	1	0	0
North Carolina.............	18	3	0	4	2	1	1	0	1	0	6
South Carolina.............	14	2	2	1	0	2	0	2	0	4	1
Virginia........................	20	3	3	2	3	3	1	1	0	3	1
West Virginia...............	2	1	0	0	0	0	0	0	0	1	0
East South Central..........	50	4	6	3	3	7	7	9	1	5	5
Alabama.......................	13	1	0	2	1	3	2	2	0	1	1
Kentucky......................	7	0	1	0	1	0	0	2	0	1	2
Mississippi...................	15	2	2	0	0	4	2	2	0	1	2
Tennessee....................	15	1	3	1	1	0	3	3	1	2	0
West South Central.........	104	5	17	8	11	15	8	8	15	8	9
Arkansas......................	7	1	0	0	0	4	0	0	1	1	0
Louisiana.....................	24	1	3	3	2	3	1	2	5	1	3
Oklahoma....................	12	1	1	0	2	2	2	1	0	2	1
Texas...........................	61	2	13	5	7	6	5	5	9	4	5
West..................................	90	12	11	10	8	9	13	5	9	6	7
Mountain........................	40	8	4	4	6	4	4	2	5	2	1
Arizona........................	11	1	1	2	1	2	2	0	2	0	0
Colorado......................	9	0	0	0	4	0	1	2	1	0	1
Idaho...........................	2	2	0	0	0	0	0	0	0	0	0
Montana.......................	2	1	0	1	0	0	0	0	0	0	0
Nevada.........................	4	2	0	0	0	1	0	0	0	1	0
New Mexico.................	7	2	1	0	0	1	1	0	1	1	0
Utah.............................	4	0	2	0	1	0	0	0	1	0	0
Wyoming......................	1	0	0	1	0	0	0	0	0	0	0
Pacific.............................	50	4	7	6	2	5	9	3	4	4	6
Alaska..........................	1	0	0	0	0	1	0	0	0	0	0
California.....................	41	3	6	5	0	3	9	2	4	4	5
Hawaii..........................	3	0	0	1	2	0	0	0	0	0	0
Oregon.........................	1	0	0	0	0	0	0	1	0	0	0
Washington..................	4	1	1	0	0	1	0	0	0	0	1

Table 25. Law Enforcement Officers Accidentally Killed, by Region, Geographic Division, and State/Territory, 2009–2018—Continued

(Number.)

Area	Total	2009	2010	2011	2012	2013	2014	2015	2016	2017	2018
Puerto Rico and other outlying areas.....	5	0	0	1	0	0	1	0	2	0	1
American Samoa..............................	0	0	0	0	0	0	0	0	0	0	0
Guam...	0	0	0	0	0	0	0	0	0	0	0
Mariana Islands	0	0	0	0	0	0	0	0	0	0	0
Puerto Rico....................................	5	0	0	1	0	0	1	0	2	0	1
U.S. Virgin Islands..........................	0	0	0	0	0	0	0	0	0	0	0

Table 26. Law Enforcement Officers Accidentally Killed, by Population Group/Agency Type, 2009–2018

(Number.)

Area	Total	2009	2010	2011	2012	2013	2014	2015	2016	2017	2018
Number of Victim Officers.....................	511	48	72	53	48	49	45	45	52	48	51
Group I (cities 250,000 and over)...............	60	4	9	5	9	5	6	4	4	4	10
Group II (cities 100,000–249,999).................	30	3	3	3	3	4	1	3	3	2	5
Group III (cities 50,000–99,999).................	26	3	2	5	1	5	2	3	2	0	3
Group IV (25,000–49,999)......................	27	1	6	3	6	1	2	1	1	1	5
Group V (cities 10,000–24,999).................	16	1	2	0	1	3	2	1	1	4	1
Group VI (cities under 10,000)......................	61	4	4	7	2	6	7	7	10	7	7
Metropolitan counties.............................	107	10	13	11	12	10	10	10	12	9	10
Nonmetropolitan counties.........................	58	11	9	3	4	5	7	4	4	8	3
State agencies....................................	97	10	19	12	6	8	5	12	9	13	3
Federal agencies	24	1	5	3	4	2	2	0	4	0	3
Puerto Rico and other outlying areas...........	5	0	0	1	0	0	1	0	2	0	1

Table 27. Law Enforcement Officers Accidentally Killed, by Time of Incident, 2009–2018

(Number.)

Time of day	Total	2009	2010	2011	2012	2013	2014	2015	2016	2017	2018
Number of Victim Officers.....................	511	48	72	53	48	49	45	45	52	48	51
Total A.M. hours......................................	240	23	39	22	25	16	26	17	25	25	22
12:01 a.m.–2 a.m....................................	54	8	10	5	6	3	6	2	6	4	4
2:01 a.m.–4 a.m......................................	48	2	8	9	5	5	4	4	5	3	3
4:01 a.m.–6 a.m......................................	29	4	4	3	4	1	1	2	3	4	3
6:01 a.m.–8 a.m......................................	49	3	5	3	5	3	7	4	5	7	7
8:01 a.m.–10 a.m.....................................	25	2	4	1	4	2	3	2	1	3	3
10:01 a.m.–noon	35	4	8	1	1	2	5	3	5	4	2
Total P.M. hours	258	25	32	31	23	30	19	27	24	22	25
12:01 p.m.–2 p.m....................................	39	4	4	6	3	3	4	4	6	2	3
2:01 p.m.–4 p.m......................................	38	3	5	6	5	4	4	4	3	3	1
4:01 p.m.–6 p.m......................................	40	3	3	7	2	4	3	5	5	4	4
6:01 p.m.–8 p.m......................................	38	3	5	4	2	3	2	2	3	5	9
8:01 p.m.–10 p.m.....................................	52	8	6	3	5	10	2	5	4	5	4
10:01 p.m.–midnight	51	4	9	5	6	6	4	7	3	3	4
Not reported..	13	0	1	0	0	3	0	1	3	1	4

Table 28. Law Enforcement Officers Accidentally Killed, by Day and Time of Incident, 2009–2018

(Number.)

Time of day	Total	Sunday	Monday	Tuesday	Wednesday	Thursday	Friday	Saturday
Number of Victim Officers.....................	51	8	6	4	6	8	10	9
Total A.M. hours..........................	22	5	1	1	1	3	6	5
12:01 a.m.–2 a.m..........................	4	2	0	0	0	1	1	0
2:01 a.m.–4 a.m..........................	3	0	0	0	0	0	1	2
4:01 a.m.–6 a.m..........................	3	0	0	1	0	0	0	2
6:01 a.m.–8 a.m..........................	7	2	0	0	1	1	2	1
8:01 a.m.–10 a.m..........................	3	0	1	0	0	0	2	0
10:01 a.m.–noon	2	1	0	0	0	1	0	0
Total P.M. hours	25	2	5	2	4	4	4	4
12:01 p.m.–2 p.m..........................	3	0	0	1	0	2	0	0
2:01 p.m.–4 p.m..........................	1	0	1	0	0	0	0	0
4:01 p.m.–6 p.m..........................	4	0	0	1	0	1	1	1
6:01 p.m.–8 p.m..........................	9	1	3	0	2	1	1	1
8:01 p.m.–10 p.m..........................	4	1	0	0	1	0	2	0
10:01 p.m.–midnight	4	0	1	0	1	0	0	2
Not reported..........................	4	1	0	1	1	1	0	0

Table 29. Law Enforcement Officers Accidentally Killed, by Day of Incident, 2009–2018

(Number.)

Day of the week	Total	2009	2010	2011	2012	2013	2014	2015	2016	2017	2018
Number of Victim Officers.....................	511	48	72	53	48	49	45	45	52	48	51
Sunday	75	5	11	7	6	6	9	6	10	7	8
Monday	69	8	8	7	7	6	5	12	7	3	6
Tuesday	67	5	7	10	5	7	9	3	6	11	4
Wednesday	52	7	8	2	2	6	4	5	7	5	6
Thursday	72	9	10	10	8	4	5	6	7	5	8
Friday	90	7	17	7	8	12	8	4	8	9	10
Saturday	86	7	11	10	12	8	5	9	7	8	9

Table 30. Law Enforcement Officers Accidentally Killed, by Month of Incident, 2009–2018

(Number.)

Month	Total	2009	2010	2011	2012	2013	2014	2015	2016	2017	2018
Number of Victim Officers.....................	511	48	72	53	48	49	45	45	52	48	51
January..........................	48	9	8	4	4	1	6	6	2	6	2
February..........................	32	4	9	4	1	0	2	1	1	6	4
March..........................	46	2	3	8	3	5	2	5	9	3	6
April	40	5	6	1	3	5	5	5	1	5	4
May..........................	54	6	4	8	4	9	6	2	3	6	6
June..........................	48	3	15	5	4	2	1	5	5	4	4
July..........................	38	3	3	5	8	6	1	3	4	3	2
August..........................	36	4	4	3	2	3	1	5	5	6	3
September	45	2	6	4	6	3	5	3	9	4	3
October	46	4	10	2	4	5	6	2	7	2	4
November..........................	34	2	1	3	5	3	4	5	4	1	6
December..........................	44	4	3	6	4	7	6	3	2	2	7

Table 31. Law Enforcement Officers Accidentally Killed, by Age Group of Victim Officer, 2009–2018

(Number.)

Age group	Total	2009	2010	2011	2012	2013	2014	2015	2016	2017	2018
Number of Victim Officers......................	511	48	72	53	48	49	45	45	52	48	51
Under 25	40	7	2	3	2	1	4	7	2	1	11
25–30	95	13	15	9	6	6	7	10	12	11	6
31–35	86	8	15	3	9	5	9	4	12	11	10
36–40	79	7	13	11	6	11	8	7	6	6	4
41–45	71	4	5	8	13	11	5	7	5	5	8
46–50	60	7	8	9	8	5	3	2	7	4	7
51–55	39	2	6	5	3	8	5	3	4	1	2
56–60	21	0	5	2	1	2	2	3	1	5	0
Over 60	16	0	2	3	0	0	2	1	2	4	2
Not reported	4	0	1	0	0	0	0	1	1	0	1
Average age (years)................................	39	35	39	41	40	41	39	37	38	40	36

Table 32. Law Enforcement Officers Accidentally Killed, by Years of Service of Victim Officer, 2009–2017

(Number.)

Years of service	Total	2009	2010	2011	2012	2013	2014	2015	2016	2017	2018
Number of Victim Officers......................	511	48	72	53	48	49	45	45	52	48	51
Less than 1	35	2	4	2	2	2	5	4	6	3	5
1–5	154	20	24	13	9	9	14	18	14	16	17
6–10	112	12	18	13	14	12	13	3	9	10	8
11–15	68	4	8	7	9	8	3	7	8	7	7
16–20	59	4	8	6	8	7	3	9	5	3	6
21–25	27	2	2	5	3	5	0	2	2	3	3
26–30	31	4	4	3	3	3	5	2	5	1	1
More than 30	20	0	4	4	0	2	2	0	2	5	1
Not reported	5	0	0	0	0	1	0	0	1	0	3
Average years of service................................	11	9	11	13	12	13	10	9	11	12	10

Table 33. Law Enforcement Officers Accidentally Killed, by Profile of Victim Officer, Averages, 1999–2018

(Number.)

Characteristic	2018	5-year averages		10-year averages	
		2009–2013	2014–2018	1999–2008	2009–2018
Age	36	39	38	38	39
Years of service................................	10	12	11	10	11
Height	5'10"	5'11"	5'11"	5'11"	5'11"
Weight	211	210	210	197	210

Table 34. Law Enforcement Officers Accidentally Killed, by Race, Ethnicity, and Sex of Victim Officer, 2009–2018

(Number.)

Characteristic	Total	2009	2010	2011	2012	2013	2014	2015	2016	2017	2018
Number of Victim Officers.......................	511	48	72	53	48	49	45	45	52	48	51
Race											
White..	425	44	60	45	36	43	43	33	40	42	39
Black/African American	64	4	8	7	10	6	0	9	9	3	8
American Indian/Alaska Native	9	0	2	0	0	0	0	0	2	2	3
Asian/Native Hawaiian/Other Pacific Islander[1]	1	0	1	NA	NA	NA	NA	NA	NA	NA	NA
Asian[1]...	6	NA	NA	0	2	0	2	0	0	1	1
Native Hawaiian/Other Pacific Islander[1] .	2	NA	NA	1	0	0	0	1	0	0	0
Not reported	4	0	1	0	0	0	0	2	1	0	0
Ethnicity[2]											
Hispanic or Latino..................................	38	NA	NA	4	6	2	7	3	7	3	6
Not Hispanic or Latino............................	343	NA	NA	46	40	47	38	40	43	44	45
Not reported	130	48	72	3	2	0	0	2	2	1	0
Sex											
Male	486	48	67	50	46	49	42	41	50	46	47
Not reported	25	0	5	3	2	0	3	4	2	2	4

NA = Not available.
[1] For 2009 and 2010, the race categories "Asian" and "Native Hawaiian/Other Pacific Islander" were combined.
[2] Beginning in 2011, ethnicity was added to the data collection.

Table 35. Law Enforcement Officers Accidentally Killed, Time of Incident, by Type of Assignment, 2018

(Number.)

Characteristic and time	Total	2-officer patrol	1-officer patrol		Investigative/detective		Tactical assignment (uniformed)		Plain clothes assignment	
			Alone	Assisted	Alone	Assisted	Alone	Assisted	Alone	Assisted
Number of Victim Officers.............	51	5	25	10	1	0	0	1	1	0
Total A.M. hours...............................	22	0	11	4	1	0	0	1	0	0
12:01 a.m.–2 a.m..........................	4	0	1	2	0	0	0	0	0	0
2:01 a.m.–4 a.m..........................	3	0	1	1	0	0	0	0	0	0
4:01 a.m.–6 a.m..........................	3	0	2	0	0	0	0	0	0	0
6:01 a.m.–8 a.m..........................	7	0	3	1	1	0	0	1	0	0
8:01 a.m.–10 a.m.........................	3	0	2	0	0	0	0	0	0	0
10:01 a.m.–noon	2	0	2	0	0	0	0	0	0	0
Total P.M. hours	25	5	12	5	0	0	0	0	1	0
12:01 p.m.–2 p.m.	3	0	1	0	0	0	0	0	1	0
2:01 p.m.–4 p.m.	1	0	1	0	0	0	0	0	0	0
4:01 p.m.–6 p.m.	4	2	2	0	0	0	0	0	0	0
6:01 p.m.–8 p.m.	9	3	5	1	0	0	0	0	0	0
8:01 p.m.–10 p.m.	4	0	3	1	0	0	0	0	0	0
10:01 p.m.–midnight	4	0	0	3	0	0	0	0	0	0
Not reported...................................	4	0	2	1	0	0	0	0	0	0

Table 35. Law Enforcement Officers Accidentally Killed, Time of Incident, by Type of Assignment, 2018—*Continued*

(Number.)

Characteristic and time	Special assignment		Undercover		Court/prisoner security		Other[1]		Off duty
	Alone	Assisted	Alone	Assisted	Alone	Assisted	Alone	Assisted	
Number of Victim Officers	2	3	0	0	0	0	1	1	1
Total A.M. hours	1	2	0	0	0	0	0	1	1
12:01 a.m.–2 a.m.	1	0	0	0	0	0	0	0	0
2:01 a.m.–4 a.m.	0	1	0	0	0	0	0	0	0
4:01 a.m.–6 a.m.	0	1	0	0	0	0	0	0	0
6:01 a.m.–8 a.m.	0	0	0	0	0	0	0	0	1
8:01 a.m.–10 a.m.	0	0	0	0	0	0	0	1	0
10:01 a.m.–noon	0	0	0	0	0	0	0	0	0
Total P.M. hours	1	1	0	0	0	0	0	0	0
12:01 p.m.–2 p.m.	0	1	0	0	0	0	0	0	0
2:01 p.m.–4 p.m.	0	0	0	0	0	0	0	0	0
4:01 p.m.–6 p.m.	0	0	0	0	0	0	0	0	0
6:01 p.m.–8 p.m.	0	0	0	0	0	0	0	0	0
8:01 p.m.–10 p.m.	0	0	0	0	0	0	0	0	0
10:01 p.m.–midnight	1	0	0	0	0	0	0	0	0
Not reported	0	0	0	0	0	0	1	0	0

[1]Includes officers on overtime/extra duty activities and other types of assignments not listed.

Table 36. Law Enforcement Officers Accidentally Killed, by Lighting and Weather/Environmental Conditions by Location of Incident, 2014–2018

(Number.)

Characteristic	Total	Aircraft accident	Drowning	Fall	Firearm-related incident	Motor vehicle crash	Pedestrian officer struck by vehicle	Other
Number of Victim Officers	241	4	9	3	9	171	40	5
Lighting	15	0	0	0	3	6	6	0
Artificial	92	1	5	1	1	70	13	1
Dark	11	0	0	0	0	7	4	0
Dawn	95	3	3	2	4	68	14	1
Daylight	8	0	1	0	0	7	0	0
Dusk	0	0	0	0	0	0	0	0
Other	1	0	0	0	0	0	0	1
Not reported	19	0	0	0	1	13	3	2
Weather/environmental	0	0	0	0	0	0	0	0
Blizzard	0	0	0	0	0	0	0	0
Blowing dirt/sand/soil	147	3	4	3	4	108	24	1
Clear	23	0	0	0	0	19	4	0
Cloudy	5	0	5	0	0	0	0	0
Flooding	4	0	0	0	0	3	1	0
Fog/smog/smoke	1	0	0	0	0	1	0	0
Hurricane	27	0	0	0	0	22	5	0
Rain	0	0	0	0	0	0	0	0
Severe crosswinds	0	0	0	0	0	0	0	0
Sleet/hail	4	0	0	0	0	2	2	0
Snow	0	0	0	0	0	0	0	0
Tornado	2	0	0	0	0	0	1	1
Other	1	1	0	0	0	0	0	0
Not reported	21	0	0	0	0	16	3	2
Not applicable (indoors)	6	0	0	0	5	0	0	1

Note: Ten years of data for the topics presented in this table are not available at this time. A 10-year table is expected to be available for the publication of 2020 data.

Table 37. Federal Law Enforcement Officers Killed and Assaulted, Department and Agency, by Number of Victim Officers and Known Offenders, 2017–2018

(Number.)

Department and agency	Victim officers		Known offenders	
	2017	2018	2017	2018
Number of victim officers/known offenders	1,784	1,768	604	1,049
Amtrak (National Railroad Passenger Corporation)[1]				
Total		0		0
Office of Inspector General		0		0
Architect of the Capitol[1]				
Total		0		0
Office of Inspector General		0		0
Corporation for National and Community Service[1]				
Total		0		0
Office of Inspector General		0		0
Federal Deposit Insurance Corporation[1]				
Total		0		0
Office of Inspector General		0		0
Library of Congress[1]				
Total		0		0
Office of Inspector General		0		0
National Aeronautics and Space Administration[1]				
Total		0		0
Office of Inspector General		0		0
Pension Benefit Guaranty Corporation[1]				
Total		0		0
Office of Inspector General		0		0
Smithsonian Institution[1]				
Total		0		0
Office of Inspector General		0		0
Tennessee Valley Authority Police[1]				
Total		0		0
Office of Inspector General		0		0
U.S. Agency for International Development[1]				
Total		0		0
Office of Inspector General		0		0
U.S. Capitol Police	16	18	12	12
U.S. Department of Agriculture[1]				
Total		8		8
U.S. Forest Service, Law Enforcement and Investigations		8		8
Office of Inspector General		0		0
U.S. Department of Commerce[1]				
Total		0		0
Office of Inspector General		0		0
U.S. Department of Defense				
Total	23	16	11	13
Defense Criminal Investigative Service[1]		0		0
Defense Intelligence Agency Police[1]		0		0
Defense Logistics Agency[1]		0		0
National Security Agency	0	1	0	1
Pentagon Force Protection Agency	0	1	0	1
U.S. Department of the Air Force	0	0	0	0
U.S. Department of the Army	0	12	0	9
U.S. Department of the Navy[2]	23	2	11	2
Commander, Navy Installations Command		2		2
Naval Criminal Investigative Service		0		0

Table 37. Federal Law Enforcement Officers Killed and Assaulted, Department and Agency, by Number of Victim Officers and Known Offenders, 2017–2018—*Continued*

(Number.)

Department and agency	Victim officers 2017	Victim officers 2018	Known offenders 2017	Known offenders 2018
U.S. Department of Health and Human Services[1]				
Total		3		2
National Institutes of Health Police		3		2
Office of Inspector General		0		0
U.S. Department of Homeland Security				
Total	687	751	95	403
Federal Emergency Management Agency, Mount Weather Police[1]		0		0
Federal Protective Service[1]		22		17
Office of Inspector General[1]		0		0
Transportation Security Administration, Law Enforcement/Federal Air Marshal Service[1]		0		0
U.S. Coast Guard[1]		0		0
U.S. Customs and Border Protection (CBP)	506	634		315
CBP, Air and Marine Operations[3]	12	30		6
CBP, Office of Field Operations[3]	62	75		55
CBP, U.S. Border Patrol[3]	432	529		254
U.S. Immigration and Customs Enforcement	159	75	76	54
U.S. Secret Service	22	20	19	17
U.S. Department of the Interior				
Total	724	689	311	414
Bureau of Indian Affairs	609	511	307	408
Bureau of Land Management	4	6	4	3
National Park Service[4]	98	167		
U.S. Fish and Wildlife Service (FWS)	13	5	0	3
FWS, Division of Refuge Law Enforcement[5]	13	5		3
FWS, Office of Law Enforcement	0	0	0	0
U.S. Department of Justice				
Total	333	271	172	191
Bureau of Alcohol, Tobacco, Firearms and Explosives	18	13	16	17
Federal Bureau of Investigation	16	15	13	10
U.S. Drug Enforcement Administration[6]	10	16		14
U.S. Marshals Service	289	227	143	150
U.S. Department of Labor[1]				
Total		0		0
Office of the Assistant Secretary for Administration and Management, Division of Protective Operations		0		0
U.S. Department of State[1]				
Total		0		0
Office of Inspector General		0		0
U.S. Department of Transporation[1]				
Total		0		0
National Highway Traffic Safety Administration, Office of Odometer Fraud Investigations		0		0
Office of Inspector General		0		0
U.S. Department of the Treasury				
Total	1	1	3	1
Bureau of Engraving and Printing Police[1]		0		0
Internal Revenue Service[7]	1		3	
Office of Special Inspector General for the Troubled Asset Relief Program[1]		0		0
Office of Inspector General[1]		0		0
Treasury Inspector General for Tax Administration	0	0	0	0
U.S. Mint Police[1]		1		1
U.S. Department of Veterans Affairs[1]				
Total		0		0
Office of Inspector General		0		0
U.S. Environmental Protection Agency[1]				
Total		0		0
Criminal Investigation Division		0		0
Office of Inspector General, Office of Investigations		0		0

Table 37. Federal Law Enforcement Officers Killed and Assaulted, Department and Agency, by Number of Victim Officers and Known Offenders, 2017–2018—*Continued*

(Number.)

Department and agency	Victim officers		Known offenders	
	2017	2018	2017	2018
U.S. General Services Administration[1]				
Total		0		0
Office of Inspector General, Office of Investigations		0		0
U.S. Government Publishing Office[1]				
Total		0		0
Uniformed Police Branch		0		0
U.S. National Archives and Records Administration[1]				
Total		0		0
Office of Inspector General		0		0
U.S. Office of Personnel Management[1]				
Total		0		0
Office of Inspector General		0		0
U.S. Postal Service				
Total	0	11	0	5
Office of Inspector General[1]		0		0
U.S. Postal Inspection Service (including the U.S. Postal Police)	0	11	0	5

[1] For 2017, data were not reported by these departments, agencies, or offices.
[2] For 2017, data reported by the U.S. Department of the Navy were aggregated and not submitted separately.
[3] For 2017, known offender data were not reported by the CBP, Air and Marine Operations; the CBP, Office of Field Operations; and the CBP, U.S. Border Patrol to 2017 data.
[4] For 2017 and 2018, known offender data were not reported by the National Park Service.
[5] For 2017, known offender data were not reported by the FWS, Division of Refuge Law Enforcement.
[6] For 2017, known offender data were not reported by the U.S. Drug Enforcement Administration.
[7] For 2018, data were not reported by the Internal Revenue Service.

Table 38. Federal Law Enforcement Officers Killed and Assaulted, Department and Agency, by Number of Victim Officers Killed and Injured, 2018

(Number.)

Department and agency	Killed		Injured	
	Firearms	Other weapons	Firearms	Other weapons
Number of Victim Officers...	2	0	11	363
U.S. Capitol Police...	0	0	0	3
U.S. Department of Agriculture				
Total	0	0	0	0
U.S. Forest Service, Law Enforcement and Investigations........................	0	0	0	0
U.S. Department of Defense				
Total	0	0	0	5
National Security Agency..	0	0	0	1
Pentagon Force Protection Agency	0	0	0	0
U.S. Department of the Army...................................	0	0	0	3
U.S. Department of the Navy, Commander, Navy Installations Command..	0	0	0	1
U.S. Department of Health and Human Services				
Total	0	0	0	3
National Institutes of Health Police	0	0	0	3
U.S. Department of Homeland Security				
Total	0	0	1	218
Federal Protective Service	0	0	0	20
U.S. Customs and Border Protection (CBP)...................	0	0	1	161
CBP, Air and Marine Operations................................	0	0	0	3
CBP, Office of Field Operations.................................	0	0	0	24
CBP, U.S. Border Patrol..	0	0	1	134
U.S. Immigration and Customs Enforcement	0	0	0	30
U.S. Secret Service...	0	0	0	7
U.S. Department of the Interior				
Total	0	0	3	80
Bureau of Indian Affairs...	0	0	2	70
Bureau of Land Management....................................	0	0	1	2
National Park Service	0	0	0	8
U.S. Fish and Wildlife Service, Division of Refuge Law Enforcement	0	0	0	0
U.S. Department of Justice				
Total	2	0	7	45
Bureau of Alcohol, Tobacco, Firearms and Explosives...........................	0	0	2	0
Federal Bureau of Investigation................................	0	0	2	5
U.S. Drug Enforcement Administration	0	0	1	3
U.S. Marshals Service..	2	0	2	37
U.S. Department of the Treasury				
Total	0	0	0	0
U.S. Mint Police..	0	0	0	0
U.S. Postal Service				
Total	0	0	0	9
U.S. Postal Inspection Service (including the U.S. Postal Police)..............	0	0	0	9

Note: This table includes federal agencies that indicated one or more of their law enforcement officers were killed or assaulted.

Table 39. Federal Law Enforcement Officers Killed and Assaulted, Department and Agency, by Extent of Injury of Victim Officer, 2014–2018

(Number.)

Department and agency	2014 Killed	2014 Injured	2014 Not injured	2015 Killed	2015 Injured	2015 Not injured	2016 Killed	2016 Injured	2016 Not injured	2017 Killed	2017 Injured	2017 Not injured	2018 Killed	2018 Injured	2018 Not injured
Number of Victim Officers..........................	0	170	867	1	176	814	1	324	1,122	0	426	1,358	2	374	1,392
U.S. Capitol Police..	0	0	3	0	5	8	0	4	21	0	9	7	0	3	15
U.S. Department of Agriculture[1]															
Total													0	0	8
U.S. Forest Service, Law Enforcement and Investigations													0	0	8
U.S. Department of Defense[2]															
Total										0	2	21	0	5	11
National Security Agency...............										0	0	0	0	1	0
Pentagon Force Protection Agency										0	0	0	0	0	1
U.S. Department of the Army...............										0	0	0	0	3	9
U.S. Department of the Navy[3]...............										0	2	21	0	1	1
Commander, Navy Installations Command													0	1	1
U.S. Department of Health and Human Services[1]															
Total													0	3	0
National Institutes of Health Police													0	3	0
U.S. Department of Homeland Security															
Total	0	39	123	0	36	103	0	146	357	0	225	462	0	219	532
Federal Protective Service[1]													0	20	2
U.S. Customs and Border Protection (CBP)...............	0	18	109	0	24	81	0	139	345	0	137	369	0	162	472
CBP, Air and Marine Operations...............	0	0	11	0	0	19	0	0	19	0	5	7	0	3	27
CBP, Office of Field Operations...............	0	18	98	0	24	62	0	7	61	0	29	33	0	24	51
CBP, U.S. Border Patrol[4,5]...............							0	132	265	0	103	329	0	135	394
U.S. Immigration and Customs Enforcement[6]	0	7	1	0	4	4	0	0	0	0	76	83	0	30	45
U.S. Secret Service...............	0	14	13	0	8	18	0	7	12	0	12	10	0	7	13
U.S. Department of the Interior															
Total	0	84	523	0	85	485	0	117	504	0	124	600	0	83	606
Bureau of Indian Affairs...............	0	69	481	0	74	431	0	86	418	0	105	504	0	72	439
Bureau of Land Management...............	0	1	4	0	1	2	0	0	4	0	0	4	0	3	3
National Park Service...............	0	13	34	0	7	47	0	31	76	0	15	83	0	8	159
U.S. Fish and Wildlife Service, Division of Refuge Law Enforcement	0	1	4	0	3	5	0	0	6	0	4	9	0	0	5
U.S. Department of Justice															
Total	0	46	211	1	49	214	1	57	240	0	66	267	2	52	217
Bureau of Alcohol, Tobacco, Firearms and Explosives.	0	5	5	0	1	10	0	0	11	0	0	18	0	2	11
Federal Bureau of Investigation...............	0	3	8	0	9	17	0	5	11	0	4	12	0	7	8
U.S. Drug Enforcement Administration...............	0	0	6	0	1	10	0	2	3	0	1	9	0	4	12
U.S. Marshals Service...............	0	38	192	1	38	177	1	50	215	0	61	228	2	39	186
U.S. Department of the Treasury															
Total	0	0	1	0	0	1	0	0	0	0	0	1	0	0	1
Internal Revenue Service[7]...............	0	0	1	0	0	0	0	0	0	0	0	1			
Treasury Inspector General for Tax Administration	0	0	0	0	0	1	0	0	0	0	0	0	0	0	0
U.S. Mint Police[1]...............													0	0	1
U.S. Postal Service															
Total	0	1	6	0	1	3	0	0	0	0	0	0	0	9	2
U.S. Postal Inspection Service (including the U.S. Postal Police)...............	0	1	6	0	1	3	0	0	0	0	0	0	0	9	2

Note: This table includes federal agencies that indicated one or more of their law enforcement officers were killed or assaulted.

[1] For 2014, 2015, 2016, and 2017, data were not reported by the U.S. Department of Agriculture, the U.S. Department of Health and Human Services, the Federal Protective Service, and the U.S. Mint Police.
[2] For 2014, 2015, and 2016, data were not reported by the U.S. Department of Defense.
[3] For 2014, extent of injury data for 373 victim officers were not reported by the CBP, Office of Border Patrol.
[4] For 2017, data reported by the U.S. Department of the Navy were aggregated and not submitted separately.
[5] For 2014, extent of injury data for 373 victim officers were not reported by the CBP, U.S. Border Patrol.
[6] For 2015, extent of injury data for 349 victim officers were not reported by the CBP, U.S. Border Patrol.
[7] For 2014, 2015, and 2016, data requests to the U.S. Immigration and Customs Enforcement (ICE) were inadvertently received and addressed by entities within ICE that did not possess the appropriate resources to provide comprehensive and complete data; therefore, caution must be taken when comparing 2014, 2015, and 2016 data to 2017 and 2018 data.

Table 40. Federal Law Enforcement Officers Killed and Assaulted, by Region, Geographic Division, and State/Territory, 2018

(Number.)

Area	Total	Firearm	Knife or other cutting instrument	Bomb	Blunt instrument	Personal weapons	Vehicle	Other
Number of Victim Officers................................	1768	133	57	0	12	797	106	663
Northeast....................................	77	7	3	0	3	45	5	14
New England.............................	11	1	1	0	0	3	1	5
Connecticut...........................	2	0	0	0	0	1	1	0
Maine.....................................	0	0	0	0	0	0	0	0
Massachusetts........................	9	1	1	0	0	2	0	5
New Hampshire......................	0	0	0	0	0	0	0	0
Rhode Island..........................	0	0	0	0	0	0	0	0
Vermont.................................	0	0	0	0	0	0	0	0
Middle Atlantic..........................	66	6	2	0	3	42	4	9
New Jersey.............................	3	0	0	0	3	0	0	0
New York................................	34	3	0	0	0	27	3	1
Pennsylvania..........................	29	3	2	0	0	15	1	8
Midwest....................................	307	13	4	0	0	57	8	225
East North Central.....................	55	7	0	0	0	17	3	28
Illinois...................................	15	5	0	0	0	0	1	9
Indiana..................................	7	2	0	0	0	3	0	2
Michigan................................	23	0	0	0	0	8	2	13
Ohio.......................................	8	0	0	0	0	5	0	3
Wisconsin...............................	2	0	0	0	0	1	0	1
West North Central...................	252	6	4	0	0	40	5	197
Iowa.......................................	3	0	0	0	0	3	0	0
Kansas...................................	1	0	0	0	0	1	0	0
Minnesota..............................	16	0	0	0	0	16	0	0
Missouri.................................	23	5	2	0	0	8	5	3
Nebraska................................	2	0	0	0	0	2	0	0
North Dakota.........................	86	0	0	0	0	3	0	83
South Dakota.........................	121	1	2	0	0	7	0	111
South..	476	45	18	0	3	258	35	117
South Atlantic...........................	139	13	10	0	2	78	6	30
Delaware................................	0	0	0	0	0	0	0	0
District of Columbia...............	77	1	4	0	0	54	1	17
Florida...................................	16	1	2	0	0	8	1	4
Georgia..................................	8	5	0	0	0	2	1	0
Maryland................................	9	0	0	0	1	3	2	3
North Carolina.......................	7	0	0	0	0	5	1	1
South Carolina.......................	5	4	0	0	0	0	0	1
Virginia..................................	14	1	3	0	1	6	0	3
West Virginia..........................	3	1	1	0	0	0	0	1
East South Central....................	38	10	1	0	0	21	3	3
Alabama.................................	2	1	0	0	0	0	1	0
Kentucky................................	7	1	0	0	0	6	0	0
Mississippi.............................	8	3	0	0	0	3	1	1
Tennessee..............................	21	5	1	0	0	12	1	2
West South Central...................	299	22	7	0	1	159	26	84
Arkansas................................	5	1	1	0	0	0	0	3
Louisiana...............................	0	0	0	0	0	0	0	0
Oklahoma...............................	15	4	0	0	0	8	2	1
Texas......................................	279	17	6	0	1	151	24	80
West...	893	66	32	0	5	432	55	303
Mountain..................................	518	48	21	0	4	283	26	136
Arizona..................................	298	22	7	0	2	167	13	87
Colorado................................	24	5	0	0	0	18	0	1
Idaho.....................................	7	0	0	0	0	6	0	1
Montana................................	8	0	0	0	0	6	0	2
Nevada...................................	28	6	3	0	1	10	1	7
New Mexico............................	119	12	7	0	1	61	6	32
Utah.......................................	16	2	0	0	0	8	3	3
Wyoming................................	18	1	4	0	0	7	3	3
Pacific.......................................	375	18	11	0	1	149	29	167
Alaska....................................	1	0	0	0	0	0	0	1
California...............................	311	18	7	0	1	116	23	146
Hawaii....................................	1	0	0	0	0	0	0	1
Oregon..................................	22	0	3	0	0	8	1	10
Washington............................	40	0	1	0	0	25	5	9

Table 40. Federal Law Enforcement Officers Killed and Assaulted, by Region, Geographic Division, and State/Territory, 2018—*Continued*

(Number.)

Area	Total	Firearm	Knife or other cutting instrument	Bomb	Blunt instrument	Personal weapons	Vehicle	Other
Puerto Rico and other outlying areas......................	6	0	0	0	1	3	0	2
American Samoa...	0	0	0	0	0	0	0	0
Guam..	0	0	0	0	0	0	0	0
Mariana Islands...	0	0	0	0	0	0	0	0
Puerto Rico..	2	0	0	0	0	0	0	2
U.S. Virgin Islands...	4	0	0	0	1	3	0	0
Foreign	6	2	0	0	0	2	1	1
Costa Rica..	1	0	0	0	0	0	0	1
Douala, Cameroon...	2	0	0	0	0	2	0	0
Jamaica..	1	0	0	0	0	0	1	0
Mexico...	1	1	0	0	0	0	0	0
Santo Domingo, Dominican Republic...................	1	1	0	0	0	0	0	0
Location not reported	3	0	0	0	0	0	2	1

Note: Location data for 3 victim officers who were assaulted with "Other" weapons were not reported by the National Park Service.

METHODOLOGY

This year, the LEOKA program is releasing the 2017 publication on a new schedule. Also, due to a technical refresh, this year's publication includes additional details about incidents in which officers are killed and assaulted.

Officers Killed

When an officer is killed in the line of duty, the FBI gathers data about circumstances pertaining to the death. The data come from various sources:

- City, university and college, county, state, tribal, and federal law enforcement agencies participating in the Uniform Crime Reporting Program may report line-of-duty deaths that occur in their jurisdictions

- FBI field offices report line-of-duty deaths of law enforcement officers that occur in the United States and its outlying areas

- Several nonprofit organizations, such as the Concerns of Police Survivors and the National Law Enforcement Officers Memorial Fund, which provide various services to the families of fallen officers, also furnish information about line-of-duty deaths

When the FBI receives notification of a line-of-duty death, the Law Enforcement Officers Killed and Assaulted (LEOKA) Program's staff works with FBI field offices to contact the fallen officer's employing agency and request additional details about the fatal incident. The LEOKA staff also obtains criminal history data from the FBI's Interstate Identification Index about individuals who are identified in connection with line-of-duty felonious deaths.

Officers Assaulted

The Uniform Crime Reporting (UCR) Program collects information monthly about assaults on duly sworn city, university and college, county, state, and tribal law enforcement officers. The agencies that employ these officers collect and submit data either through their state UCR Programs or, for non-Program states, directly to the FBI. For assault data to be included in this publication, law enforcement agencies must have submitted information for all 12 months of 2015 regarding their sworn officers who were assaulted as well as the number of officers and civilians their agencies employed full time for the reporting year.

Law enforcement agencies report to the UCR Program the number of assaults resulting in injuries to their officers or instances in which an offender used a weapon that could have caused injury or death. Law enforcement agencies report other assaults (i.e., those not causing injury) if they involved more than verbal abuse or minor resistance to an arrest.

The data in this report pertain to felonious deaths, accidental deaths, and assaults of duly sworn law enforcement officers who, at the time of the incident, met the following criteria. These law enforcement officers:

- Wore/carried a badge (ordinarily).

- Carried a firearm (ordinarily).

- Were duly sworn and had full arrest powers.

- Were members of a law enforcement agency.

- Were acting in an official capacity, whether on or off duty, at the time of incident.

- If killed, the deaths were directly related to the injuries received during the incident.

An exception to the above criteria includes individuals who were killed or assaulted while acting in a law enforcement capacity at the request of a law enforcement agency whose officers meet the LEOKA criteria. (See below for further explanation in reference to this exception.)

Exclusions from the LEOKA Program's Data Collection

Deaths resulting from the following are not included in the LEOKA Program's statistics:

- Natural causes, such as, heart attack, stroke, aneurism, etc.

- On duty, but death is attributed to their own personal situation, such as, domestic violence, neighbor conflict, etc.

- Suicide

Examples of job positions not typically included in the LEOKA Program's statistics (unless they meet the above exception):

- Corrections/correctional officers

- Bailiffs

- Probation/parole officers

- Federal judges

- U.S. and Assistant U.S. Attorneys

- Bureau of Prison Officers

- Private Security Officers

In September 2014, the LEOKA Program expanded its collection criteria to include the data of individuals who are killed or assaulted while temporarily serving as a law enforcement officer at the request of a law enforcement agency whose officers meet the general current collection criteria. These individuals must be under the supervision of a certified law enforcement officer from the requesting agency at the time of the incident, but they are not required to be in the physical presence of the supervisory officer while they are working an assigned duty. The data of individuals who met this exception and were submitted in 2015 are included in this publication.

Example of permitted exception: An unpaid reserve officer responded to a structure fire along with a law enforcement officer. As the reserve officer exited the patrol unit, he was immediately confronted in an ambush-style attack and was fatally shot by the offender.

Example of permitted exception: A correctional officer was fatally shot while assisting local law enforcement agencies who were tracking a man wanted for murdering his parents. The officer was a canine handler at a local correctional facility and was asked to assist during the incident based on the need for the canine. (If the correctional officer was working in his/her normal capacity as a correctional officer when killed, that correctional officer would not be counted in the LEOKA Program's statistics.)

Federal Law Enforcement Officers Killed and Assaulted

Data published by the FBI concerning federal officers who were killed or assaulted in the line of duty are provided by the following six federal departments:

- U.S. Capitol Police

- U.S. Department of Defense

- U.S. Department of Homeland Security

- U.S. Department of the Interior

- U.S. Department of Justice

- U.S. Department of the Treasury

- U.S. Postal Inspection Service

Within these departments are the agencies, bureaus, and services that employ most of the personnel who are responsible for protecting government officials and enforcing and investigating violations of federal law. Every year, the FBI contacts these agencies and requests information about the officers who were killed or assaulted in the line of duty.

The information concerning federal officers differs slightly from the data regarding assaults on city, university and college, county, state, and tribal law enforcement officers. First, the data regarding federal officers include all reports of assaults regardless of the extent (or the absence) of personal injury. Second, the circumstance categories are tailored to represent the unique duties of federal law enforcement personnel.

Data Considerations

When reviewing the tables, charts, and summaries presented in this publication, readers should be aware of certain features of the LEOKA data collection process that could affect their interpretation of the information.

- The data in the tables and charts reflect the number of victim officers, not the number of incidents or weapons used.

- The UCR Program considers any parts of the body that can be used as weapons (such as hands, fists, or feet) to be personal weapons and designates them as such in its data.

- Law enforcement agencies use a different methodology for collecting and reporting data about officers who were killed than the methodology used for those who were assaulted. As a result, information about officers killed and information about officers assaulted reside in two separate databases, and the data are not comparable.

- Because the information in the tables of this publication is updated each year, the FBI cautions readers against making comparisons between the data in this publication and those in prior editions.

Caution Against Comparisons with Data from Other Organizations

The FBI's LEOKA Program is one of a number of entities that report information concerning line-of-duty deaths and/or assaults of law enforcement officers in the United States. Each organization has its own purpose and may use different methods to collect and report information or focus on somewhat different aspects of these important topics. Therefore, care should be taken not to compare LEOKA data to data provided by other entities, such as the Officer Down Memorial Page, National Law Enforcement Officers Memorial Fund, and others. More information about the LEOKA Program's mission and history is included at https://ucr.fbi.gov/leoka/2017/home.

History

Beginning in 1937, the FBI's UCR Program collected and published statistics on law enforcement officers killed in the line of duty in its annual publication, *Crime in the United States*. Statistics regarding assaults on officers were added in 1960. In June 1971, executives from the law enforcement conference, "Prevention of Police Killings," called for an increase in the FBI's involvement in preventing and investigating officers' deaths. In response to this directive, the UCR Program expanded its collection of data to include more details about the incidents in which law enforcement officers were killed and assaulted.

Using this comprehensive set of data, the FBI began in 1972 to produce two reports annually, the *Law Enforcement Officers Killed Summary* and the *Analysis of Assaults on Federal Officers*. These two reports were combined in 1982 to create the annual publication, *Law Enforcement Officers Killed and Assaulted*.

Definitions

Type of Incident

Feloniously Killed – Incident type in which an officer, while engaged in or on account of the performance of their official duties, was fatally injured as a direct result of a willful and intentional act by an offender.

Accidentally Killed – Incident type in which an officer was fatally injured as a result of an accident or negligence that occurred while the officer was acting in an official capacity. Due to the hazardous nature of the law enforcement profession, deaths of law enforcement officers are considered accidental if the act causing the death is found not to be willful and intentional.

Assaulted – An unlawful attack by one person upon another for the purpose of inflicting severe or aggravated bodily injury. This type of assault is accompanied by the use of a weapon or by a means likely to produce death or great bodily injury.

Detailed Assault Data – The detailed data collection is limited to officers who are assaulted and injured with firearms or knives/other cutting instruments. – Incident type in which an officer, while engaged in or on account of the performance of their official duties, received nonfatal injuries as a direct result of a willful and intentional act by an offender.

Race

White – A person having origins in any of the original peoples of Europe, the Middle East, or North Africa.

Black/African American – A person having origins in any of the black racial groups of Africa. Terms such as "Haitian" or "Negro" can be used in addition to "Black or African American."

Asian – Included within "Asian/Pacific Islander" in LEOKA publication tables referring to Race – A person having origins in any of the original peoples of the Far East, Southeast Asia, or the Indian subcontinent, including, for example, Cambodia, China, India, Japan, Korea, Malaysia, Pakistan, the Philippine Islands, Thailand, and Vietnam.

Native Hawaiian/Other Pacific Islands – Included within "Asian/Pacific Islander" in LEOKA publication tables referring to Race – A person having origins in any of the original peoples of Hawaii, Guam, Samoa, or other Pacific Islands, e.g., individuals who are Carolinian, Fijian, Kosraean, Melanesian, Micronesian, Northern Mariana Islander, Palauan, Papua New Guinean, Ponapean (Pohnpelan), Polynesian, Solomon Islander, Tahitian, Tarawa Islander, Tokelauan, Tongan, Trukese (Chuukese), and Yapese. (NOTE: The term "Native Hawaiian" does not include individuals who are native to the state of Hawaii simply by virtue of being born there.)

American Indian/Alaska Native – A person having origins in any of the original peoples of North and South America (including Central America), and who maintains tribal affiliation or community attachment.

Type of Assignment

2-Officer vehicle – An assignment where the officer is on patrol and is accompanied by another law enforcement officer(s) in the agency's marked patrol vehicle.

1-Officer vehicle – An assignment where the officer is on patrol and is not accompanied by another officer in the agency's marked patrol vehicle.

Foot patrol – An assignment where the officer is patrolling a designated route on foot.

Administrative – Included within "Other" in LEOKA publication tables referring to Type of Assignment – An assignment in which an officer is working management, performance, or executive duties of the local, state, or federal jurisdiction. Examples include, but are not limited to:

- handling, transporting, or maintaining custody of persons who are in the custodial care of a law enforcement agency subsequent to an arrest and/or while dealing with persons who are being detained in accordance with the law;

- attending community meetings, crime preventive programs, or other organized functions as an official representative of a law enforcement agency;

- performing duties and recreational activities associated with agency sanctioned programs such as D.A.R.E., Boys and Girls Clubs, or other youth programs; or

- serving of writs, notices, summonses, subpoenas, hearing notices, notifications, and other civil processes; and transporting of papers, equipment, or persons associated with official agency sanctioned activities, functions, and programs.

Investigative/detective – Included within "Other" in LEOKA publication tables referring to Type of Assignment – An officer whose occupation is mainly to investigate and solve crimes.

Plainclothes assignment – Included within "Other" in LEOKA publication tables referring to Type of Assignment – A non-uniformed assignment where the officer's role and identity as a sworn law enforcement officer is not intended to be confidential or clandestine.

Tactical assignment (uniformed) – Included within "Other" in LEOKA publication tables referring to Type of Assignment – A uniformed assignment where an officer is strategically deployed in order to achieve a specific goal or objective. These are typically high-risk assignments.

Undercover – Included within "Other" in LEOKA publication tables referring to Type of Assignment – A non-uniformed assignment where the officer requires anonymity or blending into a group or environment to gather evidence or intelligence. The disclosure of the officer's identity would pose a significant safety risk.

Off duty – An officer who is off duty at the time of incident, but is acting in such a way which is sanctioned by, recognized by, or derived from authority.

Circumstances at Scene of Incident

Disturbance (bar fight, person with firearm, etc.) – A breach of the peace type of circumstance resulting in a call for law enforcement to respond. Examples include, but are not limited to: curfew violations, disorderly persons, drinking in public, fights, fireworks violations, gambling in public space, persons under the influence, landlord/tenant disputes, loitering, loud noise of any type (excluding animal disturbance complaints by a citizen), littering, nuisance complaints, prostitution offenses, trespassing or unwanted guests, vagrancy violations, and verbal altercations.

Domestic disturbance (family quarrel, etc.) – A breach of the peace or crime against a person occurring within a family, families, or other relatives or members of the household. Examples include, but are not limited to: family disputes, family intimidations, family arguments, and assisting citizens with the removal of legally owned possessions at locations where prior domestic disturbances or other related offenses have occurred. (Family includes a current or former spouse, parent, or guardian of the victim; a person with whom the victim shares a child in common; a person who is or has been in a

social relationship of a romantic or intimate nature with the victim; a person who is cohabiting with or has cohabited with the victim as a spouse, parent, or guardian; or by a person who is or has been similarly situated to a spouse, parent, or guardian of the victim.)

Domestic violence – Included within "Domestic disturbance (family quarrels, etc.)" in LEOKA publication tables referring to Circumstance at Scene of Incident – The use, attempted use, or threatened use of physical force, or a weapon; or the use of coercion or intimidation; or committing a crime against property by a current or former spouse, parent, or guardian of the victim; a person with whom the victim shares a child in common; a person who is or has been in a social relationship of a romantic or intimate nature with the victim; a person who is cohabiting with or has cohabited with the victim as a spouse, parent, or guardian; or by a person who is or has been similarly situated to a spouse, parent, or guardian of the victim.

Burglary – The unlawful entry of a structure with the intent to commit a felony or a theft.

Burglary in progress/pursuing burglary suspect – Situation where an officer is pursuing, arresting, or attempting to arrest an offender involved in a burglary.

Robbery – The taking, or attempting to take, anything of value under confrontational circumstances from the care, custody, or control of a person by force, threat of force, or violence and/or by putting the victim in fear of immediate harm.

Robbery in progress/pursuing robbery suspect – Situation where an officer is pursuing, arresting, or attempting to arrest an offender involved in a robbery.

Drug-related matter – Situation where an officer is pursuing, arresting, or attempting to arrest an offender involved in a drug-related matter, such as, drug busts, buys, etc.

Drug complaint – Included within "Drug-related matter" in LEOKA publication tables referring to Circumstance at Scene of Incident – Incident where a citizen reports the use or presence of illegal drugs or drug paraphernalia. Examples include, but are not limited to, the possession, buying, or selling of illegal drugs or drug paraphernalia.

Attempting other arrest – Situation where an officer is arresting or attempting to arrest an offender either through verbal advisement or through physical contact, such as, attempting to restrain, control, or handcuff the offender.

Civil disorder (mass disobedience, riot, etc.) – An activity where an officer is to control, disperse, or terminate a riot or mass disobedience.

Handling, transporting, custody of prisoner – Situation where an officer is handling, transporting, or maintaining custody of persons who are in the custodial care of a law enforcement agency subsequent to an arrest and/or while dealing with persons who are being detained in accordance with the law.

Investigating suspicious person/circumstance – An activity where an officer's intent is to investigate an unusual occurrence, an out-of-the-ordinary condition, or a suspicious person or circumstance.

Ambush – Situation where an officer is assaulted, unexpectedly, as the result of premeditated design by the perpetrator.

Ambush (entrapment/premeditation) – Situation where an unsuspecting officer was targeted or lured into danger as the result of conscious consideration and planning by the offender.

Unprovoked attack – An attack on an officer not prompted by official contact at the time of the incident between the officer and the offender.

Investigative activity (surveillance, search, interview, etc.) – An activity where an officer is making official inquiries relating to prior criminal offenses and/or perpetrators. Examples include, but are not limited to, obtaining follow-up information or additional information relating to any crime (excluding drug offense complaints) or interviewing a citizen relating to any criminal matter (excluding drug offenses).

Handling person with mental illness – Situation where an officer is handling a person who is known or suspected to be suffering from a mental illness that impairs judgment, behavior, perceptions of reality, or their ability to cope with the ordinary demands of life. Examples include, but are not limited to: mental patients, suicidal persons, service of commitment orders, and calls to investigate persons or activities where it is suspected that a person is suffering from a mental illness.

Felony vehicle stop – A vehicle stop made by an officer that is considered to be high-risk in nature.

Traffic violation stop – A vehicle stop made by an officer due to a motorist's violation of traffic rules and regulations.

Tactical situation (barricaded offender, hostage taking, high-risk entry, etc.) – Situation where an officer is strategically deployed in order to achieve a specific goal or objective. Examples include, but are not limited to: serving search warrants, hostage situations, barricaded offenders, search warrants for drug violations, and any other situations that could be deemed "high-risk," such as, serving an arrest warrant on a known armed felon.

PART 10

Probation and Parole, 2016

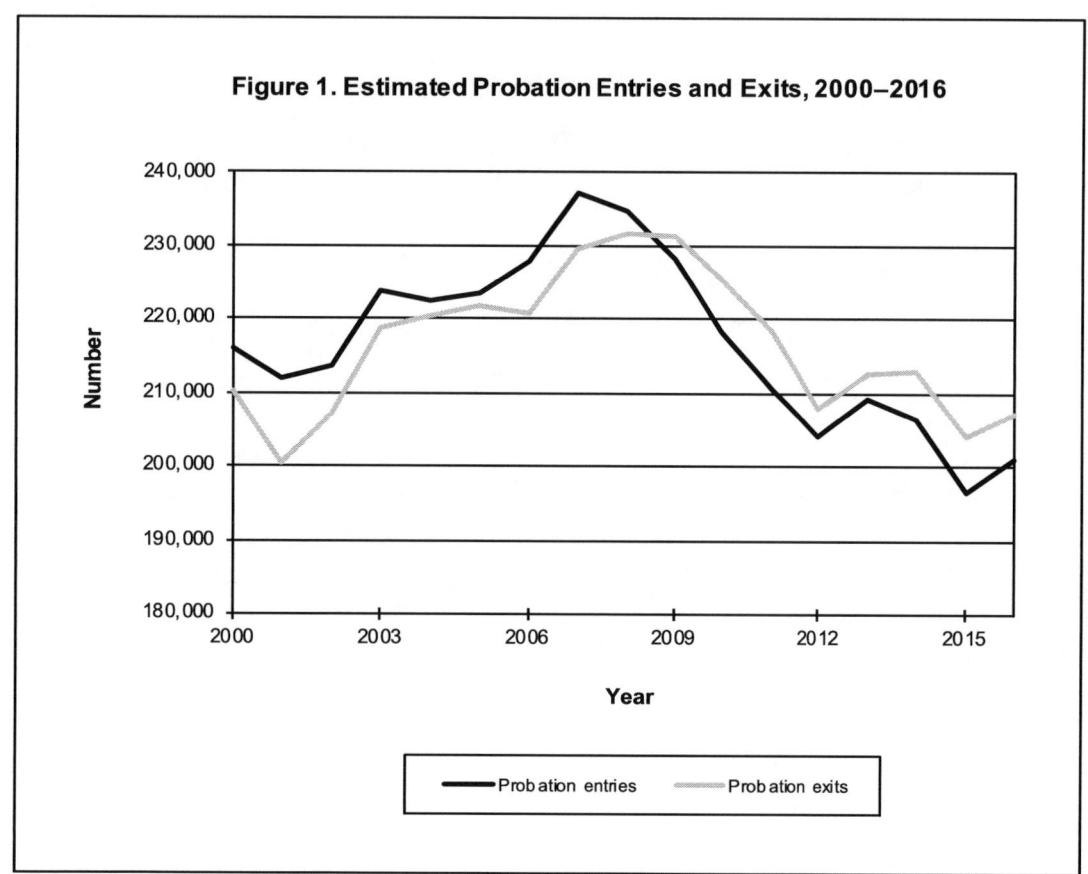

Figure 1. Estimated Probation Entries and Exits, 2000–2016

- At yearend 2016, an estimated 4,537,100 adults were under community supervision, down by about 49,800 offenders (1.1 percent) from January 1, 2016; the total community supervision population in 2016 was at its lowest level since 1999.

- Approximately 1 in 55 adults in the United States was under community supervision at yearend 2016.

- Between yearend 2015 and 2016, the adult probation population declined by approximately 1.4 percent (about 52,500 offenders), dropping to an estimated 3,673,100 offenders at yearend 2015.

- The adult parole population increased by 0.5 percent (4,300 offenders) between yearend 2015 and 2016 to an estimated 874,800 offenders.

- Parole exits decreased from an estimated 463,700 in 2015 to 456,000 in 2016, while probation exits increased from 2,043,200 in 2015 to 2,071,400 in 2016.

Table 1. Adults Under Community Supervision on Probation or Parole, 2000–2016

(Number; percent.)

Year	Total	Probation	Parole
2000	4,564,900	3,839,400	725,500
2001	4,665,700	3,934,500	731,100
2002	4,748,100	3,995,000	753,100
2003	4,847,300	4,073,800	773,500
2004	4,916,300	4,140,400	775,900
2005	4,946,600	4,162,300	784,400
2006	5,035,000	4,236,800	798,200
2007	5,119,000	4,293,000	826,100
2008	5,093,400	4,271,200	826,100
2009	5,019,900	4,199,800	824,600
2010	4,888,500	4,055,900	840,800
2011	4,818,300	3,973,800	855,500
2012	4,790,700	3,944,900	858,400
2013	4,749,800	3,912,900	849,500
2014	4,713,200	3,868,400	857,700
2015	4,650,900	3,789,800	870,500
2016			
January 1, 2016	4,586,900	3,725,600	870,700
December 31, 2016	4,537,100	3,673,100	874,800
Percent change, 2000–2016	-0.6	-4.3	-20.6
Percent change, 1/1/16–12/31/16	-1.1	-1.4	-0.5

Note: Counts are rounded to the nearest 100. Detail may not sum to total due to rounding. Estimates are based on most recent data and may differ from previously published statistics. Reporting methods for some probation agencies changed over time. From 2008 to 2016, detail may not sum to total because total was adjusted to exclude parolees who were also on probation.

Table 2. Rates of U.S. Adult Residents on Community Supervision, Probation, and Parole, 2000, 2005, 2010–2015

(Number; rate.)

Year	Number per 100,000 U.S. adult residents			U.S. adult residents on:		
	Community supervision[1,2]	Probation	Parole	Community supervision[1]	Probation	Parole
2000	2,162	1,818	344	1 in 46	1 in 53	1 in 285
2005	2,215	1,864	351	1 in 45	1 in 54	1 in 285
2010	2,067	1,715	356	1 in 48	1 in 58	1 in 281
2011	2,017	1,663	358	1 in 50	1 in 60	1 in 279
2012	1,984	1,634	356	1 in 50	1 in 61	1 in 281
2013	1,946	1,603	348	1 in 51	1 in 62	1 in 287
2014	1,911	1,568	348	1 in 52	1 in 64	1 in 288
2015	1,872	1,526	350	1 in 53	1 in 66	1 in 285
2016	1,811	1,467	349	1 in 55	1 in 68	1 in 287

Note: Rates are based on most recent data available and may differ from previously published statistics. Rates are based on the total community supervision, probation, and parole population counts as of December 31 of the reporting year and were computed using the estimates of the U.S. resident population of persons age 18 or older from the U.S. Census Bureau for January 1 of the following year.
[1]Includes adults on probation and adults on parole.
[2]For 2008 to 2016, detail may not sum to total because the community supervision rate was adjusted to exclude parolees who were also on probation.

Table 3. Parolees on Probation Excluded from the January 1 and December 31 Community Supervision Populations, 2008–2016

(Number.)

Year	January 1	December 31
2008	3,562	3,905
2009	3,905	4,959
2010	8,259	8,259
2011	8,259	10,958
2012	10,958	12,672
2013	12,672	12,511
2014	12,511	12,919
2015	12,919	9,375
2016	9,375	10,822

Note: Counts are based on most recent data and may differ from previously published statistics. Individuals being supervised on both probation and parole are excluded from community supervision population to avoid double counting. For 2011 through 2016, data are based on the December 31 count of the prior reporting year. For 2010, the December 31, 2010, count was used as a proxy because additional states reported these data in 2010.

Table 4. One-Day Difference Based on Reporting Changes for Probation and Parole, 2000–2016

(Number.)

Year	Probation population difference from December 31 to January 1 of the following year	Parole population difference from December 31 to January 1 of the following year
2000	-13,320	-1,630
2001	-2,980	1,190
2002	28,900	-2,210
2003	18,860	23,610
2004	3,150	-4,020
2005	4,260	-3,740
2006	-21,660	1,670
2007	-59,280	-4,920
2008	-33,670	1,390
2009	-73,120	13,700
2010	-2,400	-80
2011	9,770	-2,830
2012	2,960	-23,640
2013	20,980	540
2014	9,750	170
2015	-64,150	130

Note: Counts are rounded to the nearest 10. Calculated as the difference between December 31 of the year displayed and January 1 of the following year.

Table 5. Adults Under Community Supervision, 2016

(Number; percent; rate.)

Jurisdiction	Community supervision population[1]		Entries		Exits		Community supervision population, 12/31/16[1]	Change, 2016		Number under community supervision per 100,000 adult residents, 12/31/16[3]
	December 31, 2015	January 1, 2016	Reported	Estimated[2]	Reported	Estimated[2]		Number	Percent	
U.S. Total	4,650,900	4,586,900	1,997,600	2,469,300	2,356,700	2,527,400	4,537,100	-49,800	-1.1	1,810
Federal	132,800	133,100	53,700	53,700	57,300	57,300	131,700	-1,400		53
State	4,518,100	4,453,900	1,943,900	2,415,600	2,299,400	2,470,100	4,405,400	-48,400	-1.1	1,758
Alabama	64,600	59,600	17,000	17,000	16,100	16,100	60,700	1,200	2	1,609
Alaska	U	8,600	7,700	7,700	7,800	7,800	8,400	-200	-2	1,520
Arizona	83,300	83,300	35,600	35,600	34,100	34,100	84,800	1,500	2	1,587
Arkansas[4]	51,500	51,400	22,200	22,200	19,400	19,400	51,500	100	0	2,246
California[4]	349,600	325,000	164,900	192,000	159,400	181,700	333,300	8,300	1	1,100
Colorado[4]	89,200	88,800	63,200	63,600	61,100	61,600	90,900	2,200	2	2,106
Connecticut	45,300	45,000	24,100	24,100	23,100	23,100	44,700	-300		1,580
Delaware	16,100	16,100	12,600	12,600	12,900	12,900	15,800	-300	-2	2,101
District of Columbia	9,900	9,900	5,900	5,900	6,100	6,100	9,600	-200	-3	1,709
Florida[4]	225,400	226,100	134,300	150,200	142,600	156,300	218,600	-7,400	-3.3	1,315
Georgia[4]	451,800	430,800	U	U	U	U	U	U	U	U
Hawaii	22,500	22,400	5,000	5,000	5,600	5,600	21,900	-500	-2	1,949
Idaho	37,800	37,800	15,500	15,500	15,800	15,800	37,500	-300		2,980
Illinois	151,300	151,800	66,900	66,900	76,200	76,200	143,400	-8,300	-6	1,451
Indiana	122,500	121,100	84,700	84,700	89,100	89,100	116,700	-4,400	-4	2,300
Iowa	35,600	35,500	19,300	19,300	19,700	19,700	35,100	-400	-1.2	1,456
Kansas	20,900	20,900	26,000	26,000	25,400	25,400	21,500	600	3	978
Kentucky	70,600	68,800	27,900	35,900	29,700	40,800	63,800	-5,000	-7	1,858
Louisiana	71,900	72,000	28,800	28,800	29,800	29,800	71,000	-1,100	-1.5	1,985
Maine	6,700	6,700	3,300	3,300	3,300	3,300	6,800	100	2	634
Maryland	87,400	87,400	37,800	37,800	42,300	42,300	82,800	-4,600	-5	1,770
Massachusetts	66,900	66,900	67,900	67,900	71,200	71,200	63,600	-3,300	-4.9	1,167
Michigan[4]	193,900	192,200	U	U	U	U	U	U	U	U
Minnesota	105,100	105,000	54,400	54,400	55,400	55,400	103,900	-1,000		2,447
Mississippi[4]	44,800	44,800	16,400	16,400	23,400	23,400	37,700	-7,000	-16	1,660
Missouri[4]	62,600	62,400	38,400	38,400	39,200	39,300	61,600	-800		1,305
Montana	9,700	9,900	5,000	5,000	4,700	4,700	10,200	300	3	1,247
Nebraska	13,700	13,700	11,500	11,500	13,900	13,900	14,600	900	6.6	1,013
Nevada	19,200	19,200	9,400	9,400	9,300	9,300	19,000	-200	-1.3	831
New Hampshire	6,300	6,300	4,000	4,000	3,900	3,900	6,400	100	1	592
New Jersey	151,300	151,300	38,000	38,000	33,600	33,600	155,700	4,400	2.9	2,231
New Mexico	16,800	15,400	8,700	14,900	16,000	16,000	15,500	100	0.8	973
New York	145,600	146,400	46,900	46,900	50,900	50,900	142,400	-4,000	-3	913
North Carolina	97,400	97,400	62,600	62,600	64,600	64,600	95,200	-2,200	-2	1,205
North Dakota	6,900	7,000	6,100	6,100	6,000	6,000	7,100	200	2	1,228
Ohio[4]	262,000	254,700	130,400	143,900	130,200	144,500	256,400	1,700	1	2,842
Oklahoma	33,400	33,400	13,400	13,400	11,300	11,300	35,500	2,100	6	1,193
Oregon	U	60,000	37,600	37,600	36,200	36,200	61,400	1,400	2	1,887
Pennsylvania	296,200	296,200	155,300	155,300	159,900	159,900	291,600	-4,600	-2	2,880
Rhode Island	24,400	24,400	200	4,900	200	6,000	23,200	-1,100	-4.6	2,735
South Carolina	38,500	38,300	15,900	15,900	17,600	17,600	36,700	-1,600	-4	944
South Dakota	9,800	9,600	5,100	5,100	5,400	5,400	9,300	-300	-4	1,420
Tennessee	75,400	75,900	27,100	27,100	27,800	27,800	74,700	-1,200	-2	1,443
Texas	488,800	488,400	179,500	179,500	184,300	184,300	482,900	-5,500	-1.1	2,328
Utah	15,700	15,700	8,300	8,300	8,000	8,000	15,900	300	2	740
Vermont	6,300	6,200	U	3,500	U	3,900	5,800	-400	-6.5	1,153
Virginia	57,000	57,000	34,600	34,600	38,100	38,100	62,500	5,400	10	952
Washington[4]	104,700	105,100	43,800	47,300	42,700	51,600	100,600	-4,400	-4.2	1,763
West Virginia	10,100	10,100	2,100	3,200	3,200	3,200	10,100	-100		692
Wisconsin[4,5]	65,600	66,400	U	29,500	7,800	31,000	64,900	-1,500	-2	1,442
Wyoming	5,900	5,600	3,300	3,300	3,400	3,400	5,500	-100	-2.4	1,235

Note: Counts are rounded to the nearest 100. Detail may not sum to total due to rounding. Data quality may vary across jurisdictions for counts of entries and exits; therefore, the population on December 31, 2016, does not equal the population on January 1, 2016, plus entries, minus exits.
U = Not known.
[1]The December 31, 2015, and January 1, 2016, population excludes 9,375 offenders and the December 31, 2016, population excludes 10,822 offenders under community supervision who were on both probation and parole. See Methodology for more detail on dual status.
[2]Reported data will equal estimated data in cases where no imputation was required.
[3]Rates were computed using the estimated U.S. adult resident population in each jurisdiction on January 1, 2017.
[4]See Methodology for more detail.
[5]Exits reported were deaths and absconders.

Table 6. Adults on Probation, 2016

(Number; percent; rate.)

Jurisdiction	Probation population December 31, 2015	Probation population January 1, 2016	Entries Reported	Entries Imputed[1]	Exits Reported	Exits Imputed[1]	Probation population, 12/31/16	Change, 2016 Number	Change, 2016 Percent	Number on probation per 100,000 adult residents, 12/31/16[2]
U.S. Total......................	3,789,785	3,725,638	1,574,587	2,012,200	1,928,687	2,071,400	3,673,120	-52,518	-1.4	1,466
Federal	18,368	18,320	8,240	8,240	9,155	9,155	17,284	-1,036	-5.7	7
State............................	3,771,417	3,707,318	1,566,347	2,003,900	1,919,532	2,062,300	3,655,836	-51,482	-1.4	1,459
Alabama......................	56,700	51,694	14,477	14,477	13,994	13,994	52,177	483	0.9	1,382
Alaska.........................	U	6,513	6,942	6,900	6,834	6,800	6,621	108	1.7	1,193
Arizona.......................	76,005	76,005	24,136	24,136	22,768	22,768	77,373	1,368	1.8	1,447
Arkansas......................	28,900	29,003	11,328	11,328	9,450	9,450	30,881	1,878	6.5	1,347
California[3,4]................	263,531	238,911	138,876	138,876	136,166	136,166	239,735	824	1	791
Colorado[4]	78,883	78,810	55,501	56,000	53,701	54,200	80,740	1,930	2.4	1,870
Connecticut	42,346	42,064	21,483	21,483	20,920	20,920	41,311	-753	-1.8	1,461
Delaware	15,646	15,646	12,463	12,463	12,714	12,714	15,395	-251	-1.6	2,049
District of Columbia......	5,536	5,546	4,576	4,576	4,284	4,284	5,838	292	5.3	1,034
Florida[4]....................	220,769	221,446	128,167	144,100	136,484	150,100	214,066	-7,380	-3.3	1,288
Georgia[4,5]	432,235	410,964	U	U	U	U	U	U	U	U
Hawaii	20,912	20,912	4,400	4,400	4,796	4,796	20,516	-396	-1.9	1,828
Idaho	32,898	32,898	12,480	12,480	12,969	12,969	32,409	-489	-1.5	2,578
Illinois	122,125	122,125	42,970	43,000	51,106	51,100	113,989	-8,136	-6.7	1,154
Indiana	113,076	111,709	77,640	77,640	81,047	81,047	108,302	-3,407	-3	2,135
Iowa	29,875	29,819	15,502	15,502	16,067	16,067	29,254	-565	-1.9	1,213
Kansas	16,588	16,588	21,493	21,493	21,427	21,427	16,654	66	0.4	758
Kentucky	54,049	52,266	17,125	25,100	17,834	28,900	48,457	-3,809	-7.3	1,411
Louisiana	40,764	40,959	12,875	12,875	13,660	13,660	40,174	-785	-1.9	1,124
Maine	6,708	6,702	3,290	3,290	3,307	3,307	6,817	115	1.7	632
Maryland	76,505	76,505	33,494	33,494	37,470	37,470	72,529	-3,976	-5.2	1,550
Massachusetts	64,934	64,934	65,772	65,772	68,917	68,917	61,789	-3,145	-4.8	1,133
Michigan[4]	175,965	175,189	U	U	U	U	U	U	U	U
Minnesota	98,258	98,165	47,266	47,266	48,579	48,579	96,852	-1,313	-1.3	2,280
Mississippi[4]	36,333	36,333	9,753	9,753	17,019	17,019	29,067	-7,266	-20	1,280
Missouri[4]...................	44,876	44,762	25,127	25,200	26,090	26,100	43,799	-963	-2.2	928
Montana......................	8,610	8,818	4,444	4,444	4,143	4,143	9,132	314	3.6	1,115
Nebraska	12,626	12,626	9,951	9,951	12,425	12,425	13,489	863	6.8	937
Nevada	13,724	13,724	5,724	5,724	5,414	5,414	13,724	0	...	601
New Hampshire	3,861	3,861	2,508	2,508	2,430	2,430	3,939	78	2	366
New Jersey...................	136,137	136,137	32,456	32,456	28,004	28,004	140,589	4,452	3.3	2,015
New Mexico..................	15,048	13,778	6,288	12,600	13,615	13,615	12,714	-1,064	-7.7	798
New York	100,996	101,789	26,494	26,494	30,355	30,355	97,928	-3,861	-3.8	628
North Carolina	85,634	85,634	48,995	48,995	52,163	52,163	82,466	-3,168	-3.7	1,044
North Dakota................	6,303	6,343	4,591	4,591	4,593	4,593	6,341	-2	...	1,090
Ohio[4]........................	243,710	236,375	122,295	135,800	123,450	137,800	236,754	379	0.2	2,624
Oklahoma....................	31,281	31,281	13,004	13,004	10,723	10,723	33,562	2,281	7.3	1,129
Oregon	U	35,938	28,028	28,000	27,308	27,300	36,658	720	2	1,127
Pennsylvania	183,868	183,868	94,091	94,091	97,467	97,467	180,492	-3,376	-1.8	1,783
Rhode Island	23,920	23,920	U	4,700	U	5,800	22,781	-1,139	-4.8	2,680
South Carolina..............	33,843	33,652	13,483	13,483	14,501	14,501	32,634	-1,018	-3	839
South Dakota................	7,118	6,959	3,311	3,311	3,660	3,660	6,610	-349	-5	1,009
Tennessee....................	62,325	62,829	23,703	23,703	23,431	23,431	62,609	-220	-0.4	1,209
Texas	378,937	378,514	144,055	144,055	148,284	148,284	374,285	-4,229	-1.1	1,805
Utah	12,181	12,164	5,616	5,616	5,551	5,551	12,229	65	0.5	568
Vermont	5,170	5,164	U	2,900	U	3,200	4,904	-260	-5	969
Virginia	55,472	55,472	33,897	33,897	37,532	37,532	60,821	5,349	9.6	927
Washington[4]...............	93,535	93,953	37,969	41,600	37,108	46,000	89,317	-4,636	-4.9	1,565
West Virginia	7,008	7,008	U	1,100	1,539	1,539	6,523	-485	-6.9	448
Wisconsin[4,6]	46,144	46,183	U	22,900	6,351	24,600	44,489	-1,694	-3.7	988
Wyoming	5,113	4,860	2,564	2,564	2,758	2,758	4,666	-194	-4	1,046

Note: Data quality may vary across jurisdictions for counts of entries and exits; therefore, the population on December, 31, 2016, does not equal the population on January 1, 2016, plus entries, minus exits. Counts may not be actual as reporting agencies may provide estimates on some or all detailed data.
... = Less than 0.05%.
U = Not known.
[1]Reported data will equal estimated data in cases where no imputation was required.
[2]Rates were computed using the estimated U.S. adult resident population in each jurisdiction on January 1, 2017.
[3]January 1, 2016, reflects a reporting change resulting in a decrease of 24,650 from the population reported for December 31, 2015.
[4]See Probation: Explanatory Notes in Methodology for more detail.
[5]January 1, 2016, reflects a reporting change resulting in a decrease of 21,271 from the population reported for December 31, 2015.
[6]Exits reported were deaths and absconders.

Table 7. Adults Exiting Probation, by Type of Exit, 2016

(Number.)

Jurisdiction	Total reported	Completion	Incarcerated				Absconder	Discharged to warrant or detainer	Other unsatisfactory	Death	Other[1]	Unknown or not reported
			With new sentence	Under current sentence	To receive treatment	Other/ unknown						
U.S. Total	1,928,687	971,498	64,177	98,698	4,678	65,650	49,159	11,958	262,418	12,367	80,106	307,978
Federal	9,155	7,714	0	800	0	0	0	0	118	90	0	433
State	1,919,532	963,784	64,177	97,898	4,678	65,650	49,159	11,958	262,300	12,277	80,106	307,545
Alabama*	13,994	10,880	1,603	486	0	0	0	1	0	322	2	700
Alaska*	6,834	1,300	1,936	2,201	U	U	630	U	U	55	U	712
Arizona*	22,768	16,176	U	4,893	X	0	U	U	1,268	331	100	0
Arkansas*	9,450	5,150	449	1,802	567	0	0	24	1,269	183	6	0
California*	136,166	58,090	0	0	0	0	0	0	53,388	0	24,688	0
Colorado*	53,701	34,115	256	927	0	6,589	5,065	0	165	394	5,007	1,183
Connecticut*	20,920	15,985	U	U	U	U	371	4,564	U	U	U	0
Delaware*	12,714	7,720	337	976	U	U	U	U	1,634	119	1,928	0
District of Columbia	4,284	3,345	0	0	0	725	0	0	94	45	75	0
Florida*	136,484	72,412	13,236	19,974	17	132	304	1,308	3,134	1,017	81	24,869
Georgia*	294,357	137,526	U	U	U	U	U	U	156,831	U	U	0
Hawaii*	4,796	3,502	236	533	U	453	U	U	U	68	4	0
Idaho*	12,969	3,123	U	19	1,203	26	6	3	U	60	U	8,529
Illinois*	51,106	37,435	427	6,090	X	X	X	X	7,154	X	X	0
Indiana*	81,047	50,271	8,287	9,452	U	U	7,077	U	U	U	5,960	0
Iowa	16,067	11,014	1,431	258	0	0	15	0	3,193	125	31	0
Kansas*	21,427	13,363	X	X	X	130	2,472	U	2,970	U	2,492	0
Kentucky*	17,834	9,969	1,502	3,699	0	1,974	88	0	37	384	181	0
Louisiana*	13,660	8,187	1,394	2,708	X	16	X	X	1,085	221	49	0
Maine	3,307	2,532	U	U	U	589	U	U	U	U	U	186
Maryland	37,470	23,736	3,533	3,231	U	X	U	U	4,949	550	1,063	408
Massachusetts*	68,917	U	U	U	U	U	U	U	U	U	U	68,917
Michigan*	94,767	39,203	1,831	2,677	208	204	155	716	4,295	229	1,764	43,485
Minnesota	48,579	U	U	U	U	U	U	U	U	U	U	48,579
Mississippi	17,019	12,855	889	2,017	0	585	0	0	0	70	573	30
Missouri	26,090	11,102	935	3,701	939	18	8,766	U	U	431	U	198
Montana*	4,143	1,570	310	753	4	54	17	0	0	56	188	1,191
Nebraska	12,425	9,727	1,694	10	0	0	0	0	789	56	148	1
Nevada*	5,414	2,794	0	0	0	0	14	0	2,201	405	0	0
New Hampshire	2,430	2,242	U	170	X	X	U	U	X	18	U	0
New Jersey	28,004	U	U	U	U	U	6	U	U	20	U	27,978
New Mexico*	13,615	8,585	U	732	U	U	2,907	1,092	U	73	4	222
New York	30,355	17,973	U	U	U	U	U	U	U	447	U	11,935
North Carolina	52,163	27,407	3,015	3,825	X	X	8,275	X	8,078	656	X	907
North Dakota	4,593	2,304	736	1,156	U	U	314	0	U	69	0	14
Ohio*	123,450	53,984	3,033	8,290	1,722	1,125	3,849	2,288	5,380	958	5,880	36,941
Oklahoma*	10,723	8,458	463	785	U	U	U	U	109	146	U	762
Oregon*	27,308	7,391	479	4,010	0	0	125	0	134	142	1,373	13,654
Pennsylvania*	97,467	73,891	10,954	3,390	0	0	1,127	35	619	1,122	6,329	0
Rhode Island	U	U	U	U	U	U	U	U	U	U	U	U
South Carolina	14,501	10,856	478	2,876	0	0	0	0	0	227	64	0
South Dakota*	3,660	1,922	U	U	U	735	U	U	U	U	U	1,003
Tennessee*	23,431	15,055	3,051	4,216	0	0	325	0	0	457	327	0
Texas*	148,284	96,279	U	U	U	44,697	U	U	X	1,727	5,581	0
Utah	5,551	2,097	381	362	0	0	8	0	1,636	112	955	0
Vermont	U	U	U	U	U	U	U	U	U	U	U	U
Virginia	37,532	15,584	0	0	0	7,414	0	80	0	589	13,691	174
Washington*	37,108	15,211	811	589	18	184	11	1,847	1,740	185	1,545	14,967
West Virginia*	1,539	U	323	558	U	U	658	U	U	U	U	0
Wisconsin[2]	6,351	U	U	U	U	U	6,176	U	U	175	U	U
Wyoming	2,758	1,463	167	532	0	0	398	0	148	33	17	0

Note: Based on reported data only.
* = Some or all data were estimates.
U = Not known.
X = Not applicable.
[1]Includes 21,578 probationers who transferred to another jurisdiction and 58,528 probationers who exited supervision for other reasons.
[2]Exits reported were deaths and absconders.

Table 8. Characteristics of Adults on Probation, 2000, 2015, and 2016

(Percent.)

Characteristic	2000	2015	2016
Total	100.0	100.0	100.0
Sex	100.0	100.0	100.0
Male	78.0	75.0	75.0
Female	22.0	25.0	25.0
Race/Hispanic origin[1]	100.0	100.0	100.0
White	54.0	55.0	55.0
Black/African American	31.0	30.0	28.0
Hispanic/Latino	13.0	13.0	14.0
American Indian/Alaska Native	1.0	1.0	1.0
Asian/Native Hawaiian/Other Pacific Islander	1.0	1.0	1.0
Two or more races	NA	...	...
Status of supervision	100.0	100.0	100.0
Active	76.0	76.0	75.0
Residential/other treatment program	NA	1.0	1.0
Financial conditions remaining	NA	2.0	2.0
Inactive	9.0	4.0	4.0
Absconder	9.0	7.0	7.0
Supervised out of jurisdiction	3.0	2.0	2.0
Warrant status	NA	5.0	5.0
Other	3.0	4.0	4.0
Type of offense	100.0	100.0	100.0
Felony	52.0	57.0	59.0
Misdemeanor	46.0	41.0	40.0
Other infractions	2.0	2.0	2.0
Most serious offense	100.0	100.0	100.0
Violent	NA	20.0	20.0
Domestic violence	NA	4.0	4.0
Sex offense	NA	4.0	4.0
Other violent offense	NA	13.0	13.0
	NA		
Property	NA	28.0	26.0
Drug	24.0	25.0	24.0
Public order	24.0	15.0	17.0
DWI/DUI	18.0	13.0	14.0
Other traffic offense	6.0	2.0	2.0
Other[2]	52.0	12.0	13.0

Note: Characteristics are based on probationers with a known status. Detail may not sum to total due to rounding.
... = Less than 0.5%.
NA = Not available.
[1]Excludes persons of Hispanic or Latino origin, unless specified.
[2]Includes violent and property offenses in 2000 because those data were not collected separately.

Table 9. Adults on Parole, 2016

(Number; percent; rate.)

Jurisdiction	Parole population December 31, 2015	Parole population January 1, 2016	Entries Reported	Entries Estimated[1]	Exits Reported	Exits Estimated[1]	Parole population, 12/31/16	Change, 2016 Number	Change, 2016 Percent	Number on parole per 100,000 adult residents, 12/31/16[2]
U.S. Total..........................	870,526	870,657	422,975	457,100	428,022	456,000	874,777	4,120	0.5	349
Federal	114,471	114,746	45,469	45,469	48,108	48,108	114,385	-361	-0.3	46
State.................................	756,055	755,911	377,506	411,700	379,914	407,900	760,392	4,481	0.6	303
Alabama............................	8,138	8,150	2,515	2,515	2,103	2,103	8,562	412	5.1	227
Alaska...............................	U	2,100	717	700	1,005	1,000	1,812	-288	-13.7	326
Arizona.............................	7,379	7,379	11,481	11,481	11,360	11,360	7,500	121	1.6	140
Arkansas............................	23,093	22,910	10,868	10,868	9,902	9,902	23,792	882	3.8	1,038
California[3]........................	86,053	86,053	26,007	53,100	23,212	45,600	93,598	7,545	8.8	309
Colorado	10,269	9,953	7,657	7,657	7,424	7,424	10,186	233	2.3	236
Connecticut	2,939	2,939	2,591	2,591	2,151	2,151	3,379	440	15	119
Delaware...........................	425	425	129	129	167	167	387	-38	-8.9	52
District of Columbia..........	4,594	4,548	1,330	1,330	1,853	1,853	4,025	-523	-11.5	713
Florida..............................	4,611	4,611	6,110	6,110	6,155	6,155	4,566	-45		27
Georgia	24,130	24,413	9,434	9,434	11,461	11,461	22,386	-2,027	-8.3	285
Hawaii	1,540	1,479	629	629	822	822	1,367	-112	-7.6	122
Idaho................................	4,875	4,875	3,055	3,055	2,876	2,876	5,054	179	3.7	402
Illinois	29,146	29,629	23,889	23,889	25,083	25,083	29,428	-201	-0.7	298
Indiana.............................	9,434	9,420	7,056	7,056	8,091	8,091	8,385	-1,035	-11	165
Iowa	5,918	5,901	3,810	3,810	3,660	3,660	6,051	150	2.5	251
Kansas	4,331	4,331	4,465	4,465	3,966	3,966	4,830	499	11.5	220
Kentucky	16,563	16,536	10,757	10,757	11,910	11,910	15,383	-1,153	-7	448
Louisiana	31,187	31,187	15,888	15,888	16,168	16,168	30,907	-280	-0.9	864
Maine...............................	21	21	1	1	1	1	21	0	...	2
Maryland	10,887	10,887	4,295	4,295	4,877	4,877	10,305	-582	-5.3	220
Massachusetts	1,978	1,995	2,111	2,111	2,255	2,255	1,851	-144	-7.2	34
Michigan	17,909	U	U	U	U	U	U	U	U	216
Minnesota	6,808	6,810	7,129	7,129	6,864	6,864	7,075	265	3.9	167
Mississippi.........................	8,424	8,424	6,597	6,597	6,376	6,376	8,645	221	2.6	381
Missouri............................	17,694	17,657	13,255	13,255	13,120	13,120	17,792	135	0.8	377
Montana............................	1,092	1,092	533	533	551	551	1,074	-18	-1.6	131
Nebraska	1,043	1,050	1,537	1,537	1,499	1,499	1,088	38	3.6	76
Nevada	5,507	5,507	3,635	3,635	3,881	3,881	5,261	-246	-4.5	230
New Hampshire	2,451	2,451	1,461	1,461	1,476	1,476	2,436	-15	-0.6	226
New Jersey.........................	15,180	15,180	5,539	5,539	5,591	5,591	15,128	-52	-0.3	217
New Mexico........................	2,888	2,763	2,384	2,384	2,367	2,367	2,780	17	0.6	175
New York	44,562	44,562	20,443	20,443	20,579	20,579	44,426	-136	-0.3	285
North Carolina	11,744	11,744	13,647	13,647	12,388	12,388	12,726	982	8.4	161
North Dakota....................	644	634	1,545	1,545	1,375	1,375	804	170	26.8	138
Ohio.................................	18,284	18,284	8,085	8,085	6,735	6,735	19,634	1,350	7.4	218
Oklahoma..........................	2,116	2,116	383	383	604	604	1,895	-221	-10.4	64
Oregon..............................	U	24,077	9,561	9,600	8,927	8,900	24,711	634	2.6	760
Pennsylvania	112,351	112,351	61,179	61,179	62,443	62,443	111,087	-1,264	-1.1	1,097
Rhode Island.....................	433	441	239	239	220	220	460	19	4.3	54
South Carolina..................	5,021	4,963	2,460	2,460	3,076	3,076	4,347	-616	-12.4	112
South Dakota....................	2,652	2,673	1,788	1,788	1,774	1,774	2,687	14	0.5	410
Tennessee.........................	13,093	13,063	3,353	3,353	4,324	4,324	12,092	-971	-7.4	234
Texas	111,892	111,892	35,398	35,398	36,003	36,003	111,287	-605	-0.5	537
Utah.................................	3,506	3,502	2,640	2,640	2,435	2,435	3,707	205	5.9	172
Vermont............................	1,090	1,083	U	600	U	700	935	-148	-13.7	185
Virginia	1,576	1,576	711	711	601	601	1,650	74	4.7	25
Washington	11,198	11,131	5,782	5,782	5,591	5,591	11,322	191	1.7	198
West Virginia	3,123	3,123	2,113	2,113	1,686	1,686	3,550	427	13.7	244
Wisconsin[4]......................	19,453	20,241	U	6,500	1,450	6,400	20,401	160	0.8	453
Wyoming	812	783	691	691	632	632	842	59	7.5	189

Note: Data quality may vary across jurisdictions for counts of entries and exits; therefore, the population on December, 31, 2016, does not equal the population on January 1, 2016, plus entries, minus exits. Counts may not be actual as reporting agencies may provide estimates on some or all detailed data.
... = Less than 0.05%.
U = Not known.
[1]Reported data will equal estimated data in cases where no imputation was required.
[2]Rates were computed using the estimated U.S. adult resident population in each jurisdiction on January 1, 2017.
[3]Includes Post-Release Community Supervision and Mandatory Supervision parolees: 44,687 parolees on January 1, 2016; and 27,093 entries, 22,343 exits, and 49,437 parolees on December 31, 2016.
[4]Exits reported were deaths and absconders.

Table 10. Adults Entering Parole, by Type of Entry, 2016

(Number.)

Jurisdiction	Total reported	Discretionary[1]	Mandatory[2]	Reinstatement[3]	Term of supervised release[4]	Other[5]	Unknown or not reported
U.S. Total..................................	422,975	187,341	116,303	11,575	75,974	5,026	26,756
Federal.......................................	45,469	289	0	0	45,180	0	0
State...	377,506	187,052	116,303	11,575	30,794	5,026	26,756
Alabama*..................................	2,515	2,506	9	U	U	0	0
Alaska*.....................................	717	143	325	249	X	0	0
Arizona.....................................	11,481	27	11,374	80	0	0	0
Arkansas*..................................	10,868	9,085	1,783	0	0	0	0
California*.................................	26,007	U	U	U	U	0	26,007
Colorado	7,657	2,727	3,305	1,475	0	150	0
Connecticut..............................	2,591	1,235	0	0	1,356	0	0
Delaware*.................................	129	U	U	U	U	0	129
District of Columbia.....................	1,330	199	0	0	1,131	0	0
Florida	6,110	34	5,363	0	700	13	0
Georgia*....................................	9,434	9,434	0	0	0	0	0
Hawaii*	629	629	0	0	X	0	0
Idaho*......................................	3,055	1,701	U	1,347	U	7	0
Illinois*.....................................	23,889	18	23,006	90	X	559	216
Indiana	7,056	0	7,056	0	0	0	0
Iowa	3,810	3,810	0	0	0	0	0
Kansas.......................................	4,465	0	3	153	4,215	34	60
Kentucky*..................................	10,757	6,618	4,138	0	0	1	0
Louisiana	15,888	575	14,974	285	26	28	0
Maine*......................................	1	0	0	1	0	0	0
Maryland*..................................	4,295	1,962	2,333	U	U	0	0
Massachusetts	2,111	1,998	0	113	0	0	0
Michigan	U	U	U	U	U	U	U
Minnesota*................................	7,129	2	6,659	0	0	468	0
Mississippi..................................	6,597	4,770	621	0	0	862	344
Missouri*...................................	13,255	10,142	837	1,248	X	1,028	0
Montana....................................	533	533	0	0	0	0	0
Nebraska*..................................	1,537	1,320	0	211	X	6	0
Nevada*....................................	3,635	2,271	1,209	155	X	0	0
New Hampshire*.........................	1,461	785	0	573	X	103	0
New Jersey..................................	5,539	3,339	2,200	X	0	0	0
New Mexico*..............................	2,384	U	U	U	2,133	251	0
New York	20,443	5,272	6,439	0	7,867	865	0
North Carolina*..........................	13,647	31	281	X	13,335	0	0
North Dakota..............................	1,545	1,545	0	0	0	0	0
Ohio	8,085	72	7,809	204	0	0	0
Oklahoma*.................................	383	383	X	X	X	0	0
Oregon......................................	9,561	2,294	7,186	4	11	66	0
Pennsylvania*.............................	61,179	57,542	0	3,637	0	0	0
Rhode Island*.............................	239	239	X	X	X	0	0
South Carolina............................	2,460	809	1,651	0	0	0	0
South Dakota*............................	1,788	500	1,175	U	20	93	0
Tennessee...................................	3,353	3,267	6	75	0	5	0
Texas	35,398	34,110	403	509	X	376	0
Utah	2,640	2,452	0	77	0	111	0
Vermont	U	U	U	U	U	U	U
Virginia	711	258	453	0	0	0	0
Washington................................	5,782	224	5,134	424	0	0	0
West Virginia*............................	2,113	2,071	42	0	0	0	0
Wisconsin	U	U	U	U	U	U	U
Wyoming	691	615	0	76	0	0	0

* = Some or all data were estimates.
U = Not known.
X = Not applicable.
[1]Includes persons entering due to a parole board decision.
[2]Includes persons whose release from prison was not decided by a parole board and persons entering due to determinate sentencing, good-time provisions, or emergency releases.
[3]Includes persons returned to parole after serving time in a prison due to a parole violation. Depending on the reporting jurisdiction, reinstatement entries may include only parolees who were originally released from prison through a discretionary release, mandatory release, or a combination of both types. May also include those originally released through a term of supervised release.
[4]Includes persons sentenced by a judge to a fixed period of incarceration based on a determinate statute immediately followed by a period of supervised release in the community.
[5]See https://www.bjs.gov/content/pub/pdf/ppus16.pdf for examples of commonly provided categories.

Table 11. Adults Exiting Parole, by Type of Exit, 2016

(Number.)

Jurisdiction	Total reported	Completion	Returned to incarceration — With new sentence	Returned to incarceration — With revocation	Returned to incarceration — To receive treatment	Returned to incarceration — Other/ unknown	Absconder	Other unsatisfactory	Death	Other[1]	Unknown or not reported
U.S. Total.................................	428,022	242,154	31,831	69,855	2,757	11,982	7,925	5,395	6,214	17,760	32,149
Federal..	48,108	28,906	0	11,276	0	0	0	285	801	0	6,840
State...	379,914	213,248	31,831	58,579	2,757	11,982	7,925	5,110	5,413	17,760	25,309
Alabama*.....................................	2,103	1,513	415	58	U	U	U	U	90	27	0
Alaska*..	1,005	446	190	369	U	U	U	U	U	U	0
Arizona*......................................	11,360	7,682	16	2,472	0	0	37	1,094	59	0	0
Arkansas*....................................	9,902	3,665	262	5,741	0	0	0	0	196	38	0
California*...................................	23,212	U	U	U	U	U	U	U	U	U	23,212
Colorado	7,424	4,027	827	2,397	0	2	0	0	104	67	0
Connecticut.................................	2,151	1,094	0	0	0	878	179	0	0	0	0
Delaware*....................................	167	54	2	6	U	U	U	6	2	97	0
District of Columbia.................	1,853	789	0	0	0	653	0	198	54	159	0
Florida	6,155	3,957	337	764	0	0	0	0	1	791	305
Georgia*......................................	11,461	8,675	304	22	U	2,235	0	0	120	0	105
Hawaii*..	822	293	0	336	0	0	75	0	7	111	0
Idaho*...	2,876	748	373	U	6	U	186	U	33	154	1,376
Illinois*..	25,083	15,533	1,770	6,570	X	X	50	9	297	854	0
Indiana*.......................................	8,091	3,830	389	1,985	0	0	1,491	0	65	331	0
Iowa	3,660	1,967	713	789	0	0	4	145	41	1	0
Kansas..	3,966	3,201	162	0	0	0	404	0	32	167	0
Kentucky*....................................	11,910	5,513	486	2,093	X	3,631	X	X	187	X	0
Louisiana*....................................	16,168	7,059	1,439	1,232	X	1,396	X	1,539	245	3,258	0
Maine...	1	0	1	0	0	0	0	0	0	0	0
Maryland	4,877	2,990	493	516	U	X	U	614	119	44	101
Massachusetts*............................	2,255	1,749	68	408	0	14	0	0	16	0	0
Michigan	U	U	U	U	U	U	U	U	U	U	U
Minnesota*..................................	6,864	3,646	299	2,883	0	0	0	0	36	0	0
Mississippi*.................................	6,376	1,142	1,621	0	0	392	0	0	51	3,170	0
Missouri.......................................	13,120	4,982	1,004	3,439	692	1,478	1,266	X	238	X	21
Montana......................................	551	306	22	206	0	0	0	0	14	3	0
Nebraska*....................................	1,499	1,063	X	416	X	13	X	X	7	X	0
Nevada*.......................................	3,881	2,574	304	525	X	390	35	0	53	0	0
New Hampshire	1,476	679	U	797	X	X	U	U	U	U	0
New Jersey...................................	5,591	3,961	98	1,387	X	0	~	0	113	32	0
New Mexico*...............................	2,367	672	196	1,172	0	276	0	0	42	9	0
New York	20,579	10,571	1,318	6,362	2,056	0	0	X	272	X	0
North Carolina*...........................	12,388	9,184	931	397	X	0	1,590	163	123	X	0
North Dakota...............................	1,375	1,011	72	239	U	0	40	U	13	0	0
Ohio...	6,735	4,251	1,595	127	0	0	275	0	224	263	0
Oklahoma*...................................	604	555	14	10	X	X	X	X	25	X	0
Oregon...	8,927	4,661	862	2,041	3	0	5	885	163	172	135
Pennsylvania*..............................	62,443	41,664	6,293	5,302	0	0	765	299	793	7,327	0
Rhode Island...............................	220	167	8	41	0	0	0	0	4	0	0
South Carolina............................	3,076	2,740	32	212	0	0	0	0	40	52	0
South Dakota*.............................	1,774	916	172	583	X	79	0	X	24	X	0
Tennessee....................................	4,324	2,603	887	704	0	0	0	0	130	0	0
Texas	36,003	27,855	5,400	1,273	X	469	X	X	941	16	49
Utah	2,435	425	274	1,547	0	0	0	142	34	13	0
Vermont	U	U	U	U	U	U	U	U	U	U	U
Virginia	601	101	105	35	0	0	0	0	8	349	3
Washington..................................	5,591	3,799	892	760	0	76	0	0	64	0	0
West Virginia*.............................	1,686	1,172	58	272	0	0	152	0	32	0	0
Wisconsin[2].................................	1,450	U	U	U	U	U	1,339	U	111	U	U
Wyoming	632	417	27	133	0	0	32	16	4	1	2

* = Some or all data were estimates.
U = Not known.
X = Not applicable.
[1]Includes 2,239 parolees who were transferred to another state and 15,521 parolees who exited for other reasons.
[2]Exits reported were deaths and absconders.

Table 12. Characteristics of Adults on Parole, 2000, 2015, and 2016

(Percent.)

Characteristic	2005	2014	2015
Total	100.0	100.0	100.0
Sex	100.0	100.0	100.0
Male	88.0	87.0	87.0
Female	12.0	13.0	13.0
Race/Hispanic origin[1]	100.0	100.0	100.0
White	38.0	44.0	45.0
Black/African American	40.0	38.0	38.0
Hispanic/Latino	21.0	16.0	15.0
American Indian/Alaska Native	1.0	1.0	1.0
Asian/Native Hawaiian/other Pacific Islander	...	1.0	1.0
Two or more races	NA	...	...
Status of supervision	100.0	100.0	100.0
Active	83.0	83.0	82.0
Inactive	4.0	5.0	5.0
Absconder	7.0	6.0	7.0
Supervised out of state	5.0	4.0	4.0
Financial conditions remaining	...	...	...
Other	1.0	3.0	2.0
Maximum sentence to incarceration	100.0	100.0	100.0
Less than 1 year	3.0	6.0	6.0
1 year or more	97.0	94.0	94.0
Most serious offense	100.0	100.0	100.0
Violent	NA	32.0	30.0
Sex offense	NA	8.0	8.0
Other violent offense	NA	24.0	22.0
Property	NA	21.0	21.0
Drug	NA	31.0	31.0
Weapon	NA	4.0	4.0
Other[2]	NA	13.0	13.0

... = Less than 0.5%.
NA = Not available.
[1]Excludes persons of Hispanic or Latino origin, unless specified.
[2]Includes public order offenses.

METHODOLOGY

About the Data

The Bureau of Justice Statistics' (BJS) Annual Probation Survey and Annual Parole Survey began in 1980 and collect data from probation and parole agencies in the United States that supervise adults. In these data, adults are persons subject to the jurisdiction of an adult court or correctional agency. Juveniles prosecuted as adults in a criminal court are considered adults. Juveniles under the jurisdiction of a juvenile court or correctional agency are excluded from these data.

The National Criminal Justice Information and Statistics Service of the Law Enforcement Assistance Administration, BJS's predecessor agency, began a statistical series on parole in 1976 and on probation in 1979. The two surveys collect data on the total number of adults supervised in the community on January 1 and December 31 each year, the number of entries and exits to supervision during the reporting year, and characteristics of the population at yearend.

Both surveys cover all 50 states, the District of Columbia, and the federal system. BJS depends on the voluntary participation of state central reporters and separate state, county, and court agencies for these data. During 2016, RTI International served as BJS's collection agent for the 50 states and the District of Columbia. Data for the federal system were provided directly to BJS from the Office of Probation and Pretrial Services, Administrative Office of the United States Courts, through the Federal Justice Statistics Program.

Probation

The 2016 Annual Probation Survey was sent to 456 agencies, four fewer than on the 2015 population frame. Because two local Michigan probation agencies merged, their individual listings were removed from the 2016 population frame. Also, one local Michigan probation agency was added based on a review of the list of supervising agencies. In addition, three local Ohio probation agencies were removed due to consolidation of agency reporting. One local Florida probation agency changed from being privately run to county run.

The 456 respondents included 42 central state agencies and the District of Columbia; 414 separate state, county, or court agencies; and the federal system. States with multiple state agencies included Alabama (3), Colorado (8), Florida (42), Georgia (2), Idaho (2), Kentucky (3), Michigan (129), Missouri (2), Montana (4), New Mexico (2), Ohio (181), Oklahoma (3), Pennsylvania (2), Tennessee (3), and Washington (32). Pennsylvania

and Georgia are both included as central state agencies, but each provides data from two departments within the state government. Of the 456 agencies in the population frame, 1 locality in Colorado, 5 in Florida, 17 in Michigan, 1 in Missouri, 11 in Ohio, and 4 in Washington did not provide data for the 2016 collection. The final response rate was 91 percent.

The Michigan Department of Corrections was unable to provide data for 2016 because of staffing changes. At the state's request, the December 31, 2015, population count for Michigan was used as an estimate for both January 1, 2016, and December 31, 2016. Estimates for December 31, 2016, have been included in national and state totals. The Georgia Department of Community Supervision, Adult Felony Probation Supervision, requested that the December 31, 2015, population count be used as an estimate for the January 1, 2016 count. They provided the total population count for December 31, 2016, but did not provide any additional data for 2016.

Probation: Explanatory Notes

Probation agencies vary in their ability to provide counts consistent with Bureau of Justice Statistics (BJS) definitions on an annual basis. Some agencies report the number of cases, while others report the number of individuals they supervise. Because an individual can have multiple probation sentences, counting cases can artificially inflate probation totals. BJS requests that agencies report the number of individuals under supervision, and each year some agencies make the conversion, resulting in what appears to be a large decrease from previous years' data. BJS documents these and other reporting anomalies below:

Alabama— The Alabama Board of Pardons and Paroles, in preparation for a new data management system, found many errors in older records that required reconciliation.

California—Reporting changes from 2015 to 2016—data are not comparable to those reported in previous years, most likely as the result of one county changing from reporting the number of probation cases to individuals. Other counties made minor adjustments at year-end; however, those changes are small in comparison to the major correction from reporting cases to individuals. This change resulted in a decrease of 24,650 probationers on January 1, 2016 (238,911), compared to December 31, 2015 (263,561).

Colorado—Nonreporting agencies in 2016—one local agency did not report data. The most recently available December 31 population count for this agency was used to estimate January

1, 2016, and December 31, 2016. Another agency was unable to report the January 1, 2016, and December 31, 2016, population but was able to provide other data for 2016.*

Florida—Nonreporting agencies in 2016—five local agencies did not report data. The most recently available December 31 population count was used to estimate January 1, 2016, and December 31, 2016, counts for this agency.* Data cleanup by local agencies resulted in an increase of 3,666 probationers on January 1, 2016 (221,446), compared to December 31, 2015 (217,780).

Georgia—Nonreporting agency in 2016—a state agency in Georgia requested that the December 31, 2015, population count be used as an estimate for the January 1, 2016, count. They provided the total population count for December 31, 2016 but did not provide additional data for 2016. Counts for December 31, 2016, have been included in national and combined state totals.*

Reporting changes between 2015 and 2016—data are not comparable to those reported in previous years as the result of one reporter. The Georgia Department of Community Supervision provided counts based on summary counts submitted by independent local probation agencies. It switched from reporting cases to individuals in 2016, resulting in a decrease of 21,271 on January 1, 2016 (410,964), compared to December 31, 2015 (432,235).

Kentucky—One agency was required to estimate their population due to an update in computer systems.

Michigan—Nonreporting agencies in 2016—the Michigan DOC was unable to provide data for 2016 because of staffing changes. At the state's request, the December 31, 2015, population count was used as an estimate for January 1, 2016, and December 31, 2016. Estimates for December 31, 2016, have been included in national and "all state" totals.*

Mississippi—Reporting changes between 2015 and 2016—the state agency closed the records of individuals who had been on inactive supervision. This change resulted in an increase of 4,019 offenders exiting probation in 2016.

Missouri—Nonreporting agency—one agency that made up fewer than 0.5 percent of the state's population total did not report. For the nonreporting agency, December 31, 2015, population counts were used to estimate January 1, 2016, and December 31, 2016, populations.*

New Mexico—One agency updated their estimates due to a new case-management system.

Ohio—Nonreporting agencies in 2016—eleven local agencies did not report data. The most recently available December 31

population count was used to estimate January 1, 2016, and December 31, 2016, populations for these agencies.*

Washington—Nonreporting agencies in 2016—four local agencies did not report data. December 31, 2015, population counts were used to estimate January 1, 2016, and December 31, 2016, populations for these agencies.*

Wisconsin— The state probation agency, overseeing the entire state probation population, was able to report the number of probationers who died or absconded, but it was not able to report the total number of exits or entries to probation during 2016. Total entries and exits were imputed for 2016.*

(* = See https://www.bjs.gov/content/pub/pdf/ppus16.pdf for more information.)

The number of probation agencies included in the survey expanded in 1998 and continued to expand through 1999 to include misdemeanor probation agencies in a few states that fell within the scope of this survey. For a discussion of this expansion, see *Probation and Parole in the United States, 2010* (NCJ 236019, BJS web, November 2011).

Parole

The 2016 Annual Parole Survey was sent to 53 agencies: 50 central state reporters, which included the state parole agency in Pennsylvania (which also provided data for its 65 counties), the District of Columbia, and the federal system. In this report, federal parole includes a term of supervised release from prison, mandatory release, parole, military parole, or special parole. A federal judge orders a term of supervised release at the time of sentencing, and it is served after release from a federal prison sentence.

The California Department of Corrections and Rehabilitation did not provide data on the parole population for 2016. To produce the national year-end population estimates, data for December 31, 2016, reported on the California Department of Corrections and Rehabilitation Website were used to estimate the December 31, 2016, state parole population. Additional information about the data collection instruments is available on the BJS website.

Parole: Explanatory Notes

Each year, changes in legislation or offender management systems require states to alter previously submitted data or the data they can currently submit. The Bureau of Justice Statistics documents these changes as reported by the data respondents:

Arkansas—Reporting changes from 2015 to 2016—legislation changes in July 2015 required Arkansas Community

Corrections to track suspended imposition of sentence (SIS) cases, resulting in a substantial increase in the number of SIS cases under parole supervision. This is reflected in the total number of dual parole and SIS cases. It includes 2,641 dual parole and SIS, 546 dual parole and probation, and 6 dual boot camp and probation cases.

California— The state agency was not able to provide data on the 2016 parole population. To produce the national year-end population estimates, data for December 31, 2016, reported in *Parole Counts for Parole Statuses by Parole Region, District, and Units for December 31, 2016* (http://www.cdcr.ca.gov/Reports_Research/Offender_Information_Services_Branch/Monthly/PAROLE/PAROLEd1612.pdf) were used to estimate the December 31, 2016, state parole population. Estimates of state entries and exits were based on data reported by the state on the 2015 Annual Parole Survey, using the reported December 31, 2015, counts and data from *Parole Counts for Parole Statuses by Parole Region, District, and Units for December 31, 2016.*

Colorado—Reporting changes between 2015 and 2016—the Department of Corrections (DOC) noted the 2015 submission included interstate compact cases supervised by the DOC for another state. They corrected this for 2016, and data no longer include these cases. These changes resulted in a decrease of 1,600 parolees from 2015. Data may not be comparable to previous years.

Wisconsin— The state probation agency, overseeing the entire state probation population, was able to report the number of probationers who died or absconded but was not able to report the total number of exits or entries to probation during 2016. Entries and exits were imputed for 2016.*

(* = See https://www.bjs.gov/content/pub/pdf/ppus16.pdf for more information.)

Estimating change in population counts

Technically, the change in the probation and parole populations from the beginning of the year to the end of the year should equal the difference between entries and exits during the year. However, those numbers may not be equal. Some probation and parole information systems track the number of cases that enter and exit community supervision, not the number of offenders. This means that entries and exits may include case counts as opposed to counts of individuals, while the beginning and yearend population counts represent individuals. Some individuals are being supervised for more than one charge or case simultaneously. Additionally, all of the data on entries and exits may not have been logged into the information systems, or the information systems may not have fully processed all of the data before the data were submitted to BJS.

As a result, the January 1, 2016, population, plus entries, minus exits, is 6,682 persons less than the published December 31 population at the national level. For parolees, the calculated total is 3,020 fewer persons than the published December 31 population. (Estimates of annual change reported in appendix tables 1,2, and 4 were calculated as the difference between the January 1 and December 31 populations within the reporting year.)

Jurisdiction counts reported for January 1 may differ from December 31 counts reported in the previous year. As a result, the direction of change based on year-end data could be in the opposite direction of the within-year change.

For more information on the imputation of probation and parole entries, as well as on the changes made in 2016 please see https://www.bjs.gov/content/pub/pdf/ppus16.pdf.

Types of Federal Offenders Under Community Supervision

Since the Sentencing Reform Act of 1984 was enacted on November 1, 1987, offenders sentenced to federal prison are no longer eligible for parole but are required to serve a term of supervised release following release from prison. Those sentenced to prison prior to November 1, 1987, continue to be eligible for parole, as do persons violating laws of the District of Columbia, military offenders, and foreign treaty transfer offenders.

In 2008, the Annual Parole Survey included a new type of entry-to-parole category—term of supervised release—to better classify the large majority of entries to parole reported by the federal system. It is a fixed period of release to the community that follows a fixed period of incarceration based on a determinate sentencing statute. Both are determined by a judge at the time of sentencing. For details about estimating methods used to analyze national trends for all types of entry to parole, see *Probation and Parole in the United States, 2010* (NCJ 236019, BJS web, November 2011).

The Sentencing Reform Act also required the adoption and use of sentencing guidelines, which took effect on the same day. Many offenses for which probation had been the typical sentence prior to this date, particularly property and regulatory offenses, subsequently resulted in sentences to prison. Changes in how federal offenders are supervised in the community were first described in the BJS report *Federal Offenders Under Community Supervision, 1987-96* (NCJ 168636, BJS web, August 1998) and updated in *Federal Criminal Case Processing, 2002: With Trends 1982-2002, Reconciled Data* (NCJ 207447, BJS web, January 2005).

PART 11

Update on Prisoner Recidivism: A 9-Year Follow-Up Period (2005–2014)

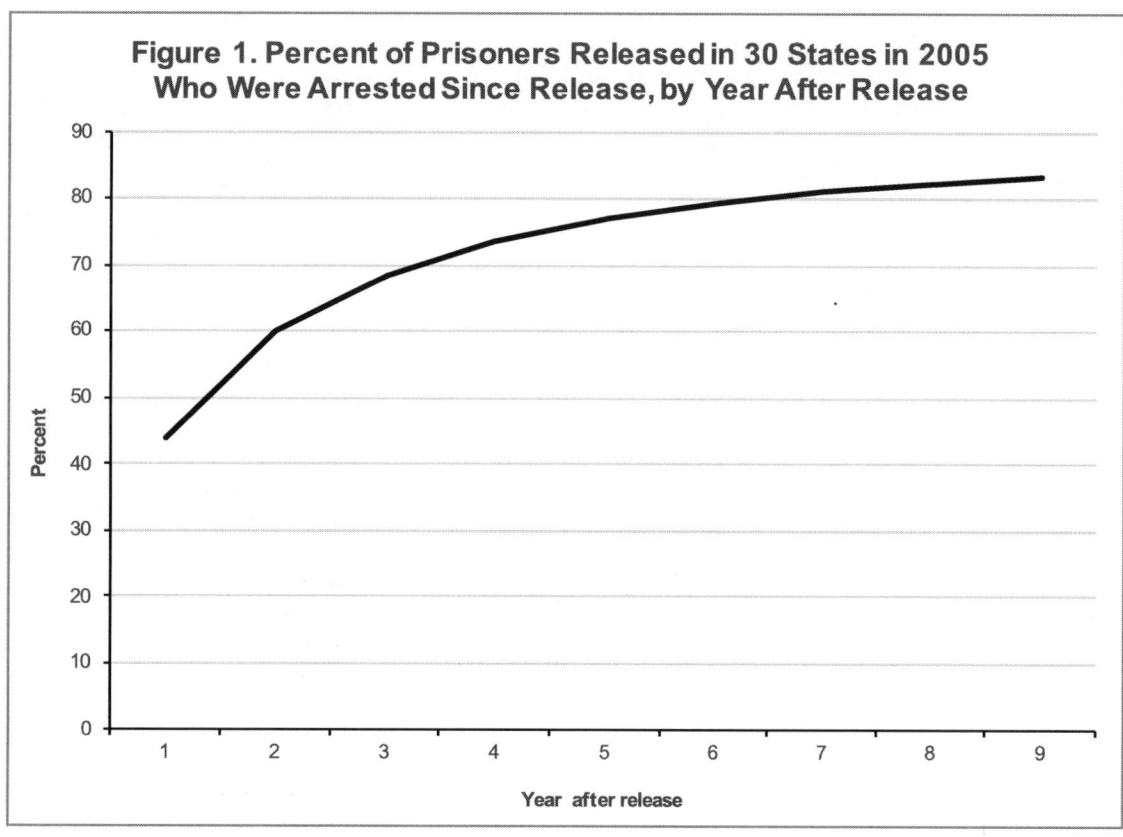

Figure 1. Percent of Prisoners Released in 30 States in 2005 Who Were Arrested Since Release, by Year After Release

- The 30 states studied accounted for 77 percent of all state prisoners released nationwide in 2005 and compares prisoners whose most serious commitment offenses were rapes and sexual assaults to other released prisoners. Statistics were measured for up to nine years following the prisoners' releases in 2005.

- Approximately 401,288 state prisoners released in 2005 had 1,994,000 arrests during the 9-year period, an average of 5 arrests per released prisoner. Sixty percent of these arrests occurred during years 4 through 9.

- An estimated 68 percent of released prisoners were arrested within 3 years, 79 percent within 6 years, and 83 percent within 9 years; eighty-two percent of prisoners arrested during the 9-year period were arrested within the first 3 years.

- Almost half (47 percent) of prisoners who did not have an arrest within 3 years of release were arrested during years 4 through 9; approximately forty-four percent of released prisoners were arrested during the first year following release, while 24 percent were arrested during year 9.

- Rape and sexual assault offenders were less likely than other released prisoners to be arrested, but they were more likely than other released prisoners to be arrested for rape or sexual assault; released sex offenders were more than three times as likely as other released prisoners to be arrested for rape or sexual assault (7.7 percent versus 2.3 percent)

Table 1. Characteristics of Prisoners Released in 30 States in 2005

(Percent; number.)

Characteristic	Percent	Most serious commitment offense		
		Rape/sexual assault	Assault	Other than rape/sexual assault
Total	100.0	100.0	100.0	100.0
Sex				
Male	89.3	98.4	93.0	88.8
Female	10.7	1.6	7.0	11.2
Race/Hispanic origin				
White[1]	39.7	52.1	36.1	39.1
Black/African American[1]	40.1	27.2	38.0	40.8
Hispanic/Latino	17.7	17.2	22.5	17.7
Other[1,2]	2.4	3.5	3.4	2.4
Age at release				
24 or younger	17.7	12.3	19.4	18.0
25–29	19.4	15.9	21.3	19.6
30–34	16.0	14.1	17.1	16.1
35–39	15.7	14.0	14.9	15.8
40 or older	31.2	43.8	27.3	30.6
Median (years)	34	38	32	34
Mean	35.0	38.8	34.0	34.8
Type of release				
Conditional	74.1	67.9	75.3	74.4
Unconditional	25.9	32.1	24.7	25.6
Maximum sentence length[3]				
1–2 years	19.2	10.5	12.9	19.6
2–5 years	44.7	34.2	56.3	45.3
5–10 years	22.1	28.0	20.4	21.8
10 years or more	14.0	27.3	10.4	13.3
Median (months)	36	60	36	36
Number of prior arrests per released prisoner[4]				
4 or fewer	24.8	52.4	25.0	23.4
5–9	30.3	26.6	30.2	30.5
10 or more	44.9	21.0	44.8	46.2
Median (arrests)	9	4	9	9
Mean	11.0	6.3	10.8	11.3
At least one prior arrest for:				
Drug offense	70.7	30.5	57.9	72.8
Property offense	81.3	55.8	78.0	82.6
Number of released prisoners	401,288	20,195	38,468	381,093

Note: Persons could have been in prison for more than one offense, the most serious of which is reported. Percentages exclude missing data. Data on prisoners' age at release were reported for 100% of cases; race/Hispanic origin, for 99.86%; type of prison release, for 98.19%; and maximum sentence length, for 99.72%. Details may not sum to totals due to rounding.
[1]Excludes persons of Hispanic/Latino origin (e.g., White refers to non-Hispanic Whites and Black refers to non-Hispanic Backs).
[2]Includes Asians, Native Hawaiians, and Other Pacific Islanders; American Indians and Alaska Natives; and persons of two or more races.
[3]Based on the released prisoners' total maximum sentence length for all commitment offenses. Study excludes prisoners sentenced to less than one year.
[4]Includes arrests for any type of crime prior to the prisoners' date of release in 2005.

Table 2. Prisoners Released in 30 States in 2005 Who Were Arrested Within 9 Years Following Release, by Most Serious Commitment Offense and Types of Post-Release Arrest Charges

(Percent.)

Most serious commitment offense	Any offense	Violent post-release arrest offense					Other post-release arrest offense		
		Total violent[1]	Homicide	Rape/sexual assault	Robbery	Assault	Property	Drug	Public order
All prisoners.........................	83.3	39.1	1.2	2.6	7.8	31.3	48.0	48.0	68.4
Violent[1]............................	78.1	43.4	1.4	4.0	9.2	34.1	39.6	36.7	65.0
Homicide........................	60.0	29.5	2.7	1.9	4.3	23.1	24.4	26.1	45.8
Rape/sexual assault.............	66.9	28.1	0.2	7.7	3.8	18.7	24.2	18.5	58.9
Robbery	84.1	47.2	1.5	3.4	16.8	34.3	47.7	45.3	67.1
Assault	82.9	50.7	1.4	2.8	7.7	44.2	44.3	43.2	69.6
Property............................	87.8	40.3	1.0	2.5	9.1	31.9	63.5	48.4	72.4
Drug	83.7	34.0	1.1	1.6	5.8	28.0	42.4	60.4	66.9
Public order	81.8	39.8	1.3	2.4	6.7	32.5	42.5	38.8	70.1
Rape/sexual assault*	66.9	28.1	0.2	7.7	3.8	18.7	24.2	18.5	58.9
Offense other than rape/sexual assault[2].....	84.1[B]	39.6[B]	1.2[B]	2.3[B]	8.0[B]	31.9[B]	49.2[B]	49.6[B]	68.9[B]

Note: Detail may not sum to total due to rounding. The numerator for each percentage is the number of persons arrested for that offense during the 9-year follow-up period, and the denominator is the number released after serving time for each type of commitment offense. Persons could have been in prison for more than one offense, the most serious of which is reported. Details may not sum to totals because a person may be arrested more than once for different types of offenses and each arrest may involve more than one offense.
* = Comparison group.
B = Difference with comparison group (rape/sexual assault) is significant at the 95% confidence level.
[1]Includes other miscellaneous violent offenses that are not shown separately.
[2]Includes the 381,093 prisoners whose most serious commitment offense was an offense other than rape or sexual assault.

Table 3. Cumulative Percent of Prisoners Released in 30 States in 2005 Who Were Arrested Following Release, by Year Following Release and Most Serious Commitment Offense

(Percent.)

Year after release	All prisoners		Most serious commitment offense					
			Rape/sexual assault		Assault		Offense other than rape/sexual assault	
	Year of first arrest	Cumulative arrest percentage	Year of first arrest	Cumulative arrest percentage	Year of first arrest	Cumulative arrest percentage	Year of first arrest	Cumulative arrest percentage
1..........................	43.8	43.8	29.0	29.0	43.2	43.2	44.5	44.5
2..........................	16.2	60.0	12.9	41.9	16.2	59.4	16.4	60.9
3..........................	8.3	68.3	7.0	48.9	8.5	67.9	8.4	69.3
4..........................	5.1	73.4	4.9	53.8	5.6	73.5	5.2	74.4
5..........................	3.5	76.9	4.4	58.2	4.1	77.5	3.5	77.9
6..........................	2.3	79.3	3.6	61.8	2.1	79.6	2.3	80.2
7..........................	1.7	80.9	2.0	63.8	1.5	81.2	1.7	81.8
8..........................	1.3	82.3	1.9	65.7	1.1	82.3	1.3	83.1
9..........................	1.0	83.3	1.2	66.9	0.7	82.9	1.0	84.1

Note: Persons could have been in prison for more than one offense, the most serious of which is reported.

Table 4. Cumulative Percent of Prisoners Released in 29 States in 2005 After Serving a Sentence for Rape/ Sexual Assault or Assault Who Had an Arrest That Led to a Conviction After Release

(Percent.)

Year after release	All prisoners	Most serious commitment offense	
		Rape/sexual assault	Assault
1..	25.4	12.8	22.4
2..	39.6	22.3	37.7
3..	49.0	28.4	46.4
4..	55.3	34.2	53.5
5..	59.8	38.5	58.3
6..	63.1	42.2	62.1
7..	65.7	45.2	65.1
8..	67.8	48.1	67.7
9..	69.2	49.6	68.8

Note: Estimates based on time from release to first arrest that led to a conviction among prisoners released in 29 of the study's 30 states (all but Louisiana). Persons could have been in prison for more than one offense, the most serious of which is reported.

Table 5. Cumulative Percent of Prisoners Released in 30 States in 2005 After Serving a Sentence for Rape/Sexual Assault Who Were Arrested for Rape/Sexual Assault After Release, by Age and Year After Release

(Percent.)

Most serious commitment offense	Year 1	Year 2	Year 3	Year 4	Year 5	Year 6	Year 7	Year 8	Year 9
All prisoners	0.5	0.9	1.2	1.5	1.8	2.0	2.2	2.4	2.6
Prisoners released after serving a sentence for rape/sexual assault..........................	1.9	3.5	4.4	5.1	5.9	6.3	6.9	7.6	7.7
Age at release									
24 or younger........................	2.5	7.1	9.4	9.7	10.3	10.5	11.2	11.7	11.8
25–39......................................	2.8	3.8	4.3	4.9	6.3	6.8	7.5	8.2	8.4
40 or older	0.8	2.2	3.0	3.9	4.2	4.5	5.0	5.8	5.9
Race/Hispanic origin									
White[1]	1.6	2.6	3.2	3.9	4.6	5.1	5.5	5.8	6.2
Black/African American[1].............	1.7	4.4	4.6	6.0	6.5	6.8	7.7	9.7	9.7
Hispanic/Latino	3.3	4.9	7.5	7.5	8.1	8.1	8.6	8.6	8.6
Other[1,2]...................................	1.0	2.6	3.8	4.1	4.5	4.7	6.7	6.7	6.9

Note: Persons could have been in prison for more than one offense, the most serious of which is reported. Data on prisoners' sex and age at release were known for 100% of cases, and race/Hispanic origin was known for 99.86%. Details may not sum to total due to rounding.
[1]Excludes persons of Hispanic/Latino origin (e.g., White refers to non-Hispanic Whites and Black refers to non-Hispanic Blacks).
[2]Includes Asians, Native Hawaiians, and Other Pacific Islanders; American Indians and Alaska Natives; and persons of two or more races.

Table 6. Cumulative Percent of Prisoners Released in 30 States in 2005 After Serving a Sentence for Rape/Sexual Assault or Assault Who Were Arrested Outside Their State of Release, by Year of Release

(Percent.)

Year after release	All prisoners	Most serious commitment offense	
		Rape/sexual assault	Assault
1..	3.3	2.1	3.6
2..	5.7	3.4	6.4
3..	7.7	5.2	8.4
4..	9.3	6.7	10.2
5			
....	10.8	8.2	11.9
6..	12.1	9.4	13.1
7..	13.3	10.1	14.4
8..	14.4	10.6	15.6
9..	15.4	11.4	16.7

Note: Persons could have been in prison for more than one offense, the most serious of which is reported.

Table 7. Annual Arrest Percentage of Prisoners Released in 30 States in 2005 After Serving a Sentence for Rape/Sexual Assault or Assault, by Prisoner Characteristics

(Number; percent.)

Characteristic	Number of released prisoners	Total arrested within 9 years	Year 1	Year 2	Year 3	Year 4	Year 5	Year 6	Year 7	Year 8	Year 9
All prisoners	401,288	83.3	43.8	37.6	34.2	31.9	30.0	27.9	27.2	25.9	24.0
Prisoners released after serving a sentence for rape/sexual assault	20,195	66.9	29.0	26.6	24.2	19.3	20.2	19.5	17.6	17.3	16.1
Age at release											
24 or younger	2,486	83.8	42.9	37.5	29.7	21.2	26.9	21.9	25.5	27.5	18.7
25–39	8,867	72.0	32.7	30.4	27.5	21.7	23.1	22.5	19.3	17.5	17.5
40 or older	8,842	57.1	21.3	19.7	19.2	16.3	15.3	15.7	13.7	14.3	14.0
Race/Hispanic origin											
White[1]	10,499	61.3	23.8	22.0	20.1	16.7	16.4	17.2	14.0	15.9	12.8
Black/African American[1]	5,482	78.6	35.0	34.1	30.1	24.8	27.4	21.6	26.0	25.3	25.7
Hispanic/Latino	3,459	64.9	34.9	26.6	27.1	16.4	20.9	22.4	15.1	9.2	11.2
Other[1,2]	713	66.9	25.4	31.7	19.7	24.3	11.6	17.2	13.6	11.5	9.8
Prisoners released after serving a sentence for assault	38,468	82.9	43.2	38.1	34.0	32.4	31.3	29.0	29.0	28.4	24.8
Age at release											
24 or younger	7,468	87.3	50.9	43.5	35.4	31.0	35.5	29.1	25.8	29.1	27.4
25–39	20,511	85.2	44.1	39.1	36.1	33.8	32.2	30.0	32.1	30.8	26.7
40 or older	10,489	75.4	35.9	32.4	28.9	30.7	26.5	27.1	25.3	23.4	19.2
Race/Hispanic origin											
White[1]	13,841	80.3	38.8	34.5	32.5	29.7	30.9	29.7	27.5	26.6	23.1
Black/African American[1]	14,562	86.4	45.2	41.4	35.7	35.0	31.2	30.3	29.9	28.9	25.6
Hispanic/Latino	8,629	80.6	46.0	37.5	32.8	33.0	31.7	24.9	28.8	28.7	25.4
Other[1,2]	1,312	85.0	47.0	44.6	34.6	29.5	34.0	32.6	33.1	37.6	24.8

Note: Persons could have been in prison for more than one offense, the most serious of which is reported. Percentages exclude missing data. Data on prisoners' age at release were reported for 100% of cases, and race/Hispanic origin was known for 99.86%.
[1]Excludes persons of Hispanic/Latino origin (e.g., White refers to non-Hispanic Whites and Black refers to non-Hispanic Blacks).
[2]Includes Asians, Native Hawaiians, and Other Pacific Islanders; American Indians and Alaska Natives; and persons of two or more races.

Table 8. Annual Arrest Percentage of Prisoners Released in 30 States in 2005 After Serving a Sentence for Rape/Sexual Assault or Assault, by Types of Post-Release Arrest Offenses

(Percent.)

Most serious commitment offense and type	Number of released prisoners	Year 1	Year 2	Year 3	Year 4	Year 5	Year 6	Year 7	Year 8	Year 9
Commitment offense: rape or sexual assault										
Post-release arrest offense										
Violent	28.1	6.6	6.4	5.3	5.4	5.3	3.7	4.1	3.0	2.6
Property	24.2	5.7	5.7	4.7	4.0	4.7	3.8	4.2	4.5	3.1
Drug	18.5	4.2	4.5	3.8	1.9	3.3	3.0	3.1	3.1	3.3
Public order	58.9	23.4	20.9	19.5	15.3	14.7	14.7	13.9	13.4	13.0
Commitment offense: rape or sexual assault										
Post-release arrest offense										
Violent	50.7	12.9	13.1	10.4	11.1	11.6	8.1	8.6	8.6	7.5
Property	44.3	12.5	10.7	11.1	8.8	7.9	8.0	8.7	8.9	8.3
Drug	43.2	11.5	12.1	7.8	9.2	8.7	8.1	8.7	9.0	8.0
Public order	69.6	30.9	25.1	23.2	22.4	20.0	19.3	19.2	19.6	16.3

Note: Persons could have been in prison for more than one offense, the most serious of which is reported.

Table 9. Types of Offenses for Which Prisoners Were Arrested Within 9 Years Following Release in 30 States in 2005, by Most Serious Commitment Offense

(Number; percent.)

Post-release arrest offense	Number of post-release arrest offenses	Most serious commitment offense							
		Violent							
		Homicide	Rape/sexual assault	Robbery	Assault	Other violent	Year 7	Year 8	Year 9
Any arrest after release									
All released prisoners	43.9	37.7	34.3	31.9	30.1	28.0	27.4	25.9	24.0
Violent*	38.9	33.7	30.4	28.1	27.2	25.0	25.2	24.1	21.4
Property	50.8 A	41.6 A	38.3 A	36.5 A	33.2 A	31.3 A	30.6 A	29.3 A	27.6 A
Drug	42.8 A	38.5 A	34.9 A	31.8 A	30.2 A	37.6 A	26.7 A	25.0	23.4 A
Public order	40.5	34.3	31.2	28.9	28.0	27.0 A	25.8	23.8	22.5
Violent arrest after release									
All released prisoners	9.0	8.3	7.6	7.6	7.2	6.5	6.6	6.0	5.2
Violent*	11.0	10.2	8.4	8.8	8.9	6.8	6.9	6.5	5.8
Property	9.3 A	7.8 A	7.7	7.8 A	6.9 A	7.1	7.2	6.2	5.7
Drug	6.8 A	7.2 A	6.7 A	6.2 A	6.2 A	5.3 A	5.7 A	5.4 A	4.4 A
Public order	9.7	8.6 A	8.3	8.1	7.3 A	7.2	6.6	6.4	5.3
Arrest after release for same type as most serious commitment offense[1]									
All released prisoners	21.0	18.0	15.6	14.5	13.7	12.2	11.8	11.5	10.6
Violent	11.0	10.2	8.4	8.8	8.9	6.8	6.9	6.5	5.8
Property	25.0	20.6	17.6	16.9	15.6	14.2	14.1	13.9	12.6
Drug	22.0	19.6	17.2	15.0	13.8	12.2	11.5	11.4	11.0
Public order	29.2	23.8	21.1	19.2	18.4	18.2	17.0	16.0	14.5
Arrest after release for different type as most serious commitment offense[2]									
All released prisoners	36.1	30.9	28.0	26.3	24.6	23.1	22.8	21.5	20.0
Violent	35.2	30.4	27.6	25.1	23.9	22.7	22.8	22.0	19.5
Property	42.4	34.4	31.6	30.6	27.6	26.0	25.6	24.1	23.0
Drug	34.8	31.3	27.9	26.0	24.6	22.7	22.2	20.7	19.1
Public order	26.3	22.6	20.7	19.8	18.7	17.9	18.0	16.6	16.0

Note: Persons could have been in prison for more than one offense; the most serious one is reported in this table. Each arrest may include more than one type of offense. "Type of offense" refers to the categories of violent, property, drug, and public order. Public order includes 0.8% of cases in which prisoners' most serious offense was unspecified.

* = Comparison group.

A = Difference with comparison group is significant at the 95% confidence level.

[1,2]Percentages in these two categories do not sum to the "any arrest after release" category because categories overlap.

Table 10. Characteristics of Male Prisoners Released in 30 States in 2005, by Most Serious Commitment Offense

(Number; percent.)

Characteristic	All male prisoners	Most serious commitment offense		
		Rape/sexual assault	Assault	Other than rape/sexual assault
Total	100.0	100.0	100.0	100.0
Race/Hispanic origin				
White[1]	38.4	51.7	36.1	37.6
Black/African American[1]	40.9	27.4	37.2	41.7
Hispanic/Latino	18.4	17.3	23.2	18.4
Other[1,2]	2.4	3.6	3.4	2.3
Age at release				
24 or younger	18.3	12.3	19.6	18.7
25–29	19.7	15.9	21.7	20.0
30–34	15.9	14.0	17.1	16.0
35–39	15.2	13.9	14.7	15.3
40 or older	30.8	44.0	26.9	30.1
Median (years)	34	38	32	34
Mean	34.9	38.9	34.0	34.6
Type of prison release				
Conditional	74.3	68.0	76.0	74.7
Unconditional	25.7	32.0	24.0	25.3
Maximum sentence length[3]				
1–2 years	18.1	10.4	12.4	18.6
2–5 years	44.6	34.4	56.4	45.2
5–10 years	22.5	27.8	20.5	22.2
10 years or more	14.7	27.4	10.7	14.0
Median (months)	39	60	36	36
Number of prior arrests per released prisoner[4]				
4 or fewer	24.5	52.0	24.2	22.8
5–9	30.4	26.8	30.2	30.6
10 or more	45.2	21.2	45.6	46.6
Median (arrests)	9	4	9	9
Mean	11.0	6.4	10.9	11.3
At least one prior arrest for:				
Drug offense	70.5	30.6	58.5	72.9
Property offense	81.2	56.1	78.6	82.7
Number of released prisoners	358,398	19,871	35,771	338,527

Note: Persons could have been in prison for more than one offense, the most serious of which is reported. Percentages exclude missing data. Data on male prisoners' age at release were reported for 100% of cases; race/Hispanic origin, for 99.85%; type of prison release, for 98.21%; and maximum sentence length, for 99.72%.
[1]Excludes persons of Hispanic/Latino origin (e.g., White refers to non-Hispanic Whites and Black refers to non-Hispanic Clacks).
[2]Includes Asians, Native Hawaiians, and Other Pacific Islanders; American Indians and Alaska Natives; and persons of two or more races.
[3]Based on the released prisoners' total maximum sentence length for all commitment offenses. Study excludes prisoners sentenced to less than one year.
[4]Includes arrests for any type of crime prior to the prisoners' date of release in 2005.

Table 11. Characteristics of Female Prisoners Released in 30 States in 2005, by Most Serious Commitment Offense

(Number; percent.)

Characteristic	All female prisoners	Most serious commitment offense	
		Rape/sexual assault	Assault
Total	100.0	100.0	100.0
Race/Hispanic origin			
White[1]	51.0	75.9	35.5
Black/African American[1]	33.9	14.3	47.9
Hispanic/Latino	12.3	8.6	13.0
Other[1,2]	2.9	1.2	3.6
Age at release			
24 or younger	12.0	15.0	17.2
25–29	16.6	15.9	16.0
30–34	17.1	20.1	17.4
35–39	19.7	16.1	17.6
40 or older	34.6	32.8	31.8
Median (years)	36	34	35
Mean	36.0	35.7	34.8
Type of prison release			
Conditional	71.9	62.7	66.8
Unconditional	28.1	37.3	33.2
Maximum sentence length[3]			
1–2 years	27.8	17.8	19.8
2–5 years	45.8	21.6	55.2
5–10 years	18.3	36.6	18.3
10 years or more	8.1	24.0	6.7
Median (months)	36	60	36
Number of prior arrests per released prisoner[4]			
4 or fewer	28.0	78.9	35.5
5–9	29.3	12.6	30.7
10 or more	42.7	8.5	33.8
Median (arrests)	8	2	6
Mean	10.8	3.8	9.0
At least one prior arrest for:			
Drug offense	72.0	27.4	49.8
Property offense	81.8	36.4	69.8
Number of released prisoners	42,890	324	2,697

Note: Persons could have been in prison for more than one offense, the most serious of which is reported. Percentages exclude missing data. Data on female prisoners' age at release were reported for 100% of cases; race/Hispanic origin, for 99.97%; and maximum sentence length, for 99.68%.
[1]Excludes persons of Hispanic/Latino origin (e.g., White refers to non-Hispanic Whites and Black refers to non-Hispanic Clacks).
[2]Includes Asians, Native Hawaiians, and Other Pacific Islanders; American Indians and Alaska Natives; and persons of two or more races.
[3]Based on the released prisoners' total maximum sentence length for all commitment offenses. Study excludes prisoners sentenced to less than one year.
[4]Includes arrests for any type of crime prior to the prisoners' date of release in 2005.

Table 12. Cumulative Arrest Percentage of Male Prisoners Released in 30 States in 2005 After Serving a Sentence for Rape/Sexual Assault or Assault Who Were Arrested After Release, by Year of Release

(Percent.)

Year after release	All male prisoners	Most serious commitment offense	
		Rape/sexual assault	Assault
1..	44.8	29.0	44.1
2..	61.1	42.0	60.3
3..	69.4	49.1	68.9
4..	74.4	53.9	74.5
5..	77.9	58.4	78.5
6..	80.2	62.0	80.6
7..	81.8	64.0	82.1
8..	83.1	65.9	83.1
9..	84.0	67.1	83.8

Note: Persons could have been in prison for more than one offense, the most serious of which is reported.

Table 13. Cumulative Arrest Percentage of Female Prisoners Released in 30 States in 2005 After Serving a Sentence for Rape/Sexual Assault or Assault Who Were Arrested After Release, by Year of Release

(Percent.)

Year after release	All female prisoners	Most serious commitment offense	
		Rape/sexual assault	Assault
1..	35.1	28.8	31.5
2..	50.8	38.1	47.0
3..	59.2	40.2	54.9
4..	64.7	44.6	60.3
5..	68.9	47.0	64.4
6..	71.4	50.0	67.1
7..	73.6	53.8	69.0
8..	75.3	53.8	70.9
9..	76.7	54.4	71.7

Note: Persons could have been in prison for more than one offense, the most serious of which is reported.

METHODOLOGY

Measuring Recidivism

Recidivism measures require three characteristics:

1. a starting event, such as a release from prison

2. a measure of failure following the starting event, such as a subsequent arrest, conviction, or return to prison

3. an observation or follow-up period that generally extends from the date of the starting event to a predefined end date (e.g., 6 months, 1 year, 3 years, 5 years, or 9 years).

This study used four outcome measures to examine the recidivism patterns of former state prisoners. Arrest data were used because they provided the offense details needed to produce these four measures for prisoners from all 30 states in the study.

1. Cumulative arrest percentage is the percentage of prisoners who had been arrested at least once at various points in the follow-up period. For example, the cumulative arrest percentage for year-5 is the percentage of all released prisoners who had at least one arrest during the 5-year period. BJS previously examined the cumulative percentage of prisoners who had a subsequent conviction or returned to prison within 5 years following release. The return-to-prison analysis for the 5-year follow-up study was limited to 23 of the study's 30 states with the data needed to identify returns to prison during the entire observation period.

2. Annual percentage of first arrests is the percentage of prisoners who had their first arrest following release during a specific year in the follow-up period. The denominator for each annual first-arrest percentage from years 1 through 9 is the total number of prisoners released in the 30 states during 2005. The numerators are the number of prisoners arrested for the first time during each of those years (i.e., they had not been arrested during a prior year in the follow-up period). The sum of the annual first-arrest percentages during a follow-up period equals the cumulative arrest percentage for the same period.

3. Annual arrest percentage of released prisoners includes those who were arrested at least once during a particular year within the follow-up period. The denominator for each percentage from years 1 through 9 is the total number of prisoners released in the 30 states during 2005. The numerators are the number of prisoners arrested during the particular year, regardless of whether they had been arrested during a prior year.

4. Annual volume of arrests is the total number of arrests of released prisoners during a particular year in the follow-up period. The total volume of arrests is the sum of each annual volume of arrests during the entire follow-up period. A prisoner may have had multiple arrests during a year or in the follow-up period, and a single arrest may have involved charges for more than one crime.

Measuring Desistance

Desistance is measured as the percentage of prisoners who, after a particular year, had no subsequent arrests during the remainder of the 9-year follow-up period. For example, if a prisoner was arrested during year-3 but was not arrested during years 4 through 9, the prisoner would be classified as having desisted during year-3. While recidivism is a measure of arrest at any point during the follow-up period, desistance is a measure of the absence of arrest between a particular point within the follow-up period and the end of the follow-up period.

Importance of Recidivism and Desistance Measures

Measures of recidivism and desistance provide information relevant to a deeper understanding of criminal behavior and the administration of justice in a wide range of policy areas. For example, law enforcement officials interested in the amount of crime committed by released prisoners can turn to statistics on the annual volume of arrests. Parole and probation agencies interested in the involvement of various types of former prisoners in criminal activities after release may focus on variations in cumulative arrest percentages. Treatment providers looking for measures of program effectiveness will be interested in desistance patterns. Additionally, task forces and policymakers examining the movement of criminals across state borders will be interested in the types of released prisoners most likely to commit new crimes (i.e., recidivate) in other states.

Sampling

This study estimates the recidivism patterns of persons released in 2005 from state prisons in 30 states. States were included in this study if the state departments of corrections could provide the prisoner records and the FBI or state identification numbers on persons released from prison during 2005. The fingerprint-based identification numbers were required to obtain the criminal history records on released prisoners. The prisoner records—obtained from the state departments of corrections through the Bureau of Justice Statistics' (BJS) National Corrections Reporting Program (NCRP)—also included each prisoner's sex, race, Hispanic origin, date of birth, confinement offenses, sentence length, type of prison release, and date of release. The 30 states whose departments of corrections submitted the NCRP data on prisoners released in 2005 included Alaska, Arkansas, California, Colorado, Florida, Georgia, Hawaii, Iowa, Louisiana, Maryland, Michigan, Minnesota, Missouri, Nebraska, Nevada, New Jersey, New York, North Carolina, North Dakota, Ohio, Oklahoma, Oregon, Pennsylvania, South Carolina, South Dakota, Texas, Utah, Virginia, Washington, and West Virginia.

Across the 30 states in 2005, a total of 412,731 prisoners were released and were eligible for this study. That number excludes 131,997 prisoners (for a total of 544,728) who were sentenced to less than one year, transferred to the custody of another authority, died in prison, were released on bond, were released to seek or participate in an appeal of a case, or escaped from prison or were absent without official leave. The first release during 2005 was used for those prisoners released multiple times during the year.

From the universe of persons released from prison in the 30 states in 2005 in this study, all males and females who were in prison for homicide were selected with certainty into the study. Analyses were done to determine the number of non-homicide prisoners that would be needed from each state's universe of released prisoners to yield a statistically sound estimate of that state's recidivism and desistance rates. As a result, states contributed different numbers of records to the final sample. To achieve the desired state-level samples, lists of all males and females imprisoned for a non-homicide offense were sorted separately by the county in which the sentence was imposed, race, Hispanic origin, age, and most serious commitment offense. The within-state sampling rate for female prisoners was double that of males to improve the precision of female recidivism and desistance estimates. The combined number of persons in the 30 state samples totaled 70,878 individuals who were representative of all state prisoners released in those states during 2005. (This number dropped to 67,966 after accounting for those who died during the subsequent 9 years, lacked criminal history records, or had invalid release records.) Each prisoner in the sample was assigned a weight based on the probability of selection within the state.

Collecting and Processing Criminal Records for Recidivism Research

In 2008, BJS entered into a data-sharing agreement with the FBI's Criminal Justice Information Services Division and the International Justice and Public Safety Network (Nlets) to allow BJS access to criminal history records through the FBI's Interstate Identification Index (III).

The FBI's III is an automated pointer system that allows authorized agencies to determine whether any state repository has criminal history records on an individual. Nlets is a computer-based network that is responsible for interstate transmissions of federal and state criminal history records. It allows authorized users to query III and send requests to states holding criminal history records on an individual. The FBI also maintains criminal history records for which it has sole responsibility for disseminating, such as information on federal arrests. The identification bureaus that operate the central repositories in each state respond automatically to requests over the Nlets network with an individual's criminal history record. Put together, these requests represent the individual's national criminal history record.

Once BJS received approval from the FBI's Institutional Review Board to conduct this recidivism study on prisoners released in 2005, Nlets transmitted the state and FBI identification numbers on the sampled prisoners to the FBI's III system to collect the criminal history records on behalf of BJS. The criminal history records include information from the state of release and all other states in which the sampled prisoners had been arrested both prior to the release in 2005 and afterward.

Nlets parsed the fields from individual criminal history records into a relational database consisting of state- and federal-specific numeric codes and text descriptions (e.g., criminal statutes and case outcome information) into a uniform record layout. NORC at the University of Chicago assisted BJS with standardizing the content of the relational database into a uniform coding structure to support national-level recidivism research.

BJS conducted a series of data-quality checks on the criminal history records to assess the accuracy and completeness of the information, including an examination of the response messages and the identification numbers that failed to match a record in III. To ensure that the correct records were received on the released prisoners using their fingerprint-based identification numbers, BJS compared other individual identifiers in the NCRP data to those reported in the criminal history records. For 98 percent of cases, a released prisoner's date of birth in the NCRP data exactly matched the prisoner's birthdate in the criminal history records. Nearly 100 percent (99.9 percent) of the NCRP and criminal history records matched prisoner sex, race, and Hispanic origin.

BJS reviewed the criminal history records for differences and inconsistencies in reporting practices and noticed some variations across states. During data processing and analysis, steps were taken to standardize the information and to minimize the impact these variations had on the overall recidivism and desistance estimates. For example, administrative (e.g., a criminal registration or the issuance of a warrant) and procedural (e.g., transferring a suspect to another jurisdiction) records embedded in the criminal history data that did not refer to an actual arrest were identified and removed. Traffic offenses (except for vehicular manslaughter, driving while intoxicated, and hit-and-run) were also excluded because the reporting of these events in the criminal history records varied widely by state.

Deaths During the Follow-Up Period

BJS documented that 2,173 of the 70,878 sampled prisoners died during the 9-year follow-up period, and BJS removed these cases from the recidivism and desistance analysis along with four additional cases that were determined to be invalid release records. The fingerprint-verified death notices obtained through the FBI's III system were used to identify some of the sampled prisoners who died within the 9 years following release in 2005. Additional deaths were identified through the Social Security Administration's (SSA) public Death Master File (DMF). While the public DMF provided a more complete source of death information than the FBI's III system, the public DMF provided death information only for the years 2005 to 2011. Therefore, the identification of those who died between 2012 and 2014 was limited to the FBI's III data, which included only fingerprint-verified deaths. The number of released prisoners who were identified as dead between 2005 and 2011 in the public DMF is an undercount of the actual number of deaths within the sample. Due to state disclosure laws, the public DMF does not include information on certain protected state death records received via SSA's contracts with the states. Beginning in 2011, the SSA removed more than 4 million state-reported death records from the public DMF and began adding fewer records to the public DMF. As a result, the public DMF contains an undercount of annual deaths.

The extent to which the public DMF undercounts the annual number of deaths is not exactly known. Analyses of deaths in the public DMF compared to those reported by the Centers for Disease Control and Prevention's (CDC) mortality counts suggest that the public DMF undercounted the overall number of deaths in the United States by about 10 percent in 2005. The undercount increased during succeeding years, and as of 2010, the public DMF contained less than half (45 percent) of the deaths reported by the CDC. If the number of released prisoners who died during the follow-up period and were removed from the recidivism and desistance analysis were adjusted to account for this undercount, the estimated cumulative recidivism rate would likely increase by about one percentage point.

Missing Criminal History Records

Among the 68,701 sampled prisoners not identified as deceased during the follow-up period, BJS did not receive criminal history records on 735 prisoners, either because the state departments of correction were unable to provide their FBI or state identification number or because the prisoner had an identification number that did not link to a criminal history record either in the FBI or state record repositories. To account for the missing criminal history records and to ensure the recidivism and desistance statistics were representative of all 68,701 prisoners in the analysis, BJS developed weighting class adjustments to account for those prisoners without criminal history information to reduce nonresponse bias.

To create the statistical adjustments, the 68,701 sampled prisoners were stratified into groups by crossing the two categories of sex (male or female), five categories of age at release (24 or younger, 25 to 29, 30 to 34, 35 to 39, or 40 or older), four categories of race/Hispanic origin (non-Hispanic White, non-Hispanic Black, Hispanic, or other race), and four categories of the most serious commitment offense (violent, property, drug, or public order). Within each of the subgroups, statistical weights were applied to the data of the 67,966 prisoners with criminal history information to allow their data to represent the 735 prisoners without criminal history information.

Conducting Tests of Statistical Significance

This study was based on a sample, not a complete enumeration, so the estimates are subject to sampling error. One measure of the sampling error associated with an estimate is the standard error. The standard error can vary from one estimate to the next. In general, an estimate with a smaller standard error provides a more reliable approximation of the true value than an estimate with a larger standard error. Estimates with relatively large standard errors should be interpreted with caution. BJS conducted tests to determine whether differences in the estimates were statistically significant once sampling error was taken into account.

All differences discussed in this report are statistically significant at the 95 percent confidence interval level. Standard errors were generated using Stata, a statistical so ware package that calculates sampling errors for data from complex sample surveys.

Offense Definitions

Violent offenses include homicide, rape or sexual assault, robbery, assault, and other miscellaneous or unspecified violent offenses.

Property offenses include burglary, fraud or forgery, larceny, motor vehicle the, and other miscellaneous or unspecified property offenses.

Drug offenses include possession, trafficking, and other miscellaneous or unspecified drug offenses.

Public order offenses include violations of the peace or order of the community or threats to the public health or safety through unacceptable conduct, interference with a governmental authority, or the violation of civil rights or liberties. This category includes weapons offenses, driving under the influence, probation and parole violation, obstruction of justice, commercialized vice, disorderly conduct, and other miscellaneous or unspecified offenses.

Arrests for probation and parole violations

In this report, arrests for probation and parole violations were included as public order offenses. Excluding arrests for probation and parole violations from the analysis would have had only a small impact on the recidivism rates. Excluding probation and parole violations from the annual arrest percentages, 39.5 percent of prisoners released in 30 states in 2005 were arrested in year-1, 34.3 percent were arrested in year-2, 31.5 percent in year-3, 29.7 percent in year-4, 28.2 percent in year-5, 25.9 percent in year-6, 25.9 percent in year-7, 24.6 percent in year-8, and 23.0 percent in year-9. Overall, excluding probation and parole violations, 82.4 percent of prisoners released in 30 states in 2005 were arrested within 9 years. In other words, 99 percent of prisoners who were arrested during the 9-year follow-up period were arrested for an offense other than a probation or parole violation.

PART 12

Victims of Identity Theft, 2016

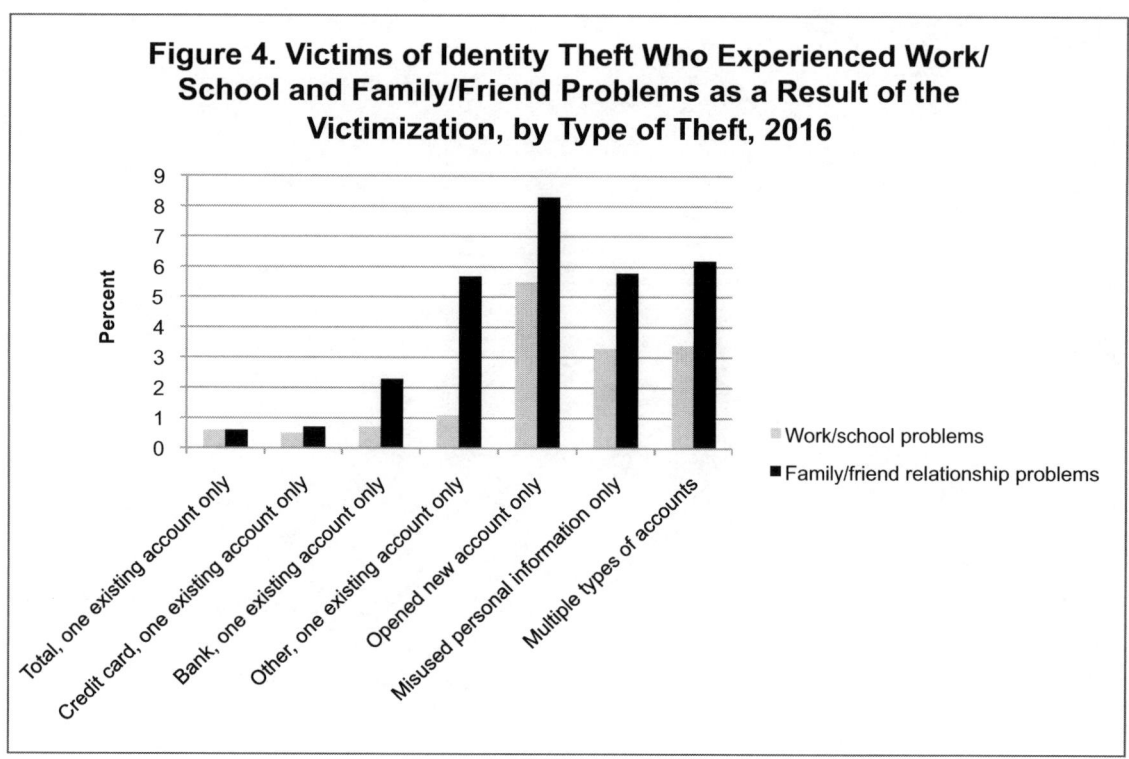

Figure 4. Victims of Identity Theft Who Experienced Work/School and Family/Friend Problems as a Result of the Victimization, by Type of Theft, 2016

- In 2016, 10 percent of persons age 16 or older had been victims of identity theft during the prior 12 months.

- For 85 percent of identity-theft victims, the most recent incident involved the misuse or attempted misuse of only one type of existing account, such as a credit card or bank account.

- One percent of persons age 16 or older had experienced the opening of a new account or misuse of personal information apart from misuse of an existing credit card or bank account or other existing account.

- An estimated 12 percent of identity-theft victims had out-of-pocket losses of $1 or more; 88 percent either had no out-of-pocket losses or had losses of less than $1.

- More than half (55 percent) of identity-theft victims who resolved associated financial or credit problems did so in one day or less.

Table 1. Prevalence of Identity Theft in Continuing Counties and Full Sample, by Type of Identity Theft, 2014 and 2016

(Percent.)

Type of identity theft	Continuing National Crime Victimization Survey sample counties		Full National Crime Victimization Survey sample	
	2014*	2016	2014**	2016
Total	7.4	9.7 B	7.0	10.2 B
Existing account				
Credit card...............................	3.3	4.1 B	3.4	5.3 B
Bank	3.7	5.3 B	3.2	4.7 B
Other	0.6	0.7 B	0.6	0.8 B
Opened new account...................	0.5	0.6 B	0.4	0.6 B
Misused personal information..........	0.3	0.4 B	0.3	0.5 B

Note: Details do not sum to totals because persons could experience more than one type of identity theft.
* = Comparison year. Continuing sample counties for 2014 are compared to continuing sample counties for 2016.
** = Comparison year. Full sample for 2014 is compared to full sample for 2016.
B = Significant difference from comparison year at 95% confidence level.

Table 2. Persons Age 16 or Older Who Had Experienced at Least One Identity-Theft Incident During the Past 12 Months, by Victim Characteristics and Type of Theft, 2016

(Number; percent.)

Victim characteristic	Total identity theft		Misuse of existing credit card			Misuse of existing bank account			Opened a new account or misused personal information[1]	
	Number of victims	Percent of all persons	Number of victims	Percent of all persons	Percent of all persons with a credit card	Number of victims	Percent of all persons	Percent of all persons with a bank account	Number of victims	Percent of all persons
Total	25,952,400	10.2	13,422,800	5.3	7.5	11,950,100	4.7	5.4	2,610,000	1.0
Sex										
Male*	12,496,400	10.1	6,816,400	5.5	7.9	5,342,200	4.4	5.0	1,215,400	1.0
Female	13,456,000 B	10.3	6,606,400	5.0 B	7.1 B	6,517,900 B	5.0 B	5.7 B	1,394,600	1.1
Race/Hispanic origin[2]										
White*	19,425,200	11.8	10,661,500	6.5	8.4	8,476,000	5.1	5.6	1,639,700	1.0
Black...	2,314,800 B	7.4 B	756,100 B	2.4 B	4.5 B	1,424,000 B	4.6 B	5.9	398,900 B	1.3 B
Hispanic.....................................	2,538,300 B	6.3 B	1,026,200 B	2.5 B	4.5 B	1,427,500 B	3.5 B	4.7 B	354,600 B	0.9
Other[3]......................................	1,307,900 B	8.4 B	839,200 B	5.4 B	7.0 B	393,3000 B	2.5 B	2.9 B	162,300 B	1.0
Two or more races	366,200 B	12.0	139,700 B	4.6 B	8.1	229,300 B	7.5 B	8.8 B	54,500 B	1.8 A
Age										
16–17 years	81,400 B	1.0 B	13,700!	0.2! B	2.5! B	50,500 B	0.6 B	1.6 B	2,000! B	--! B
18–24 years	1,997,500 B	6.6 B	537,800 B	1.8 B	4.1 B	1,379,700 B	4.5 B	5.7 B	192,400 B	0.6 B
25–34 years	4,781,700 B	10.8 B	2,030,100 B	4.6 B	6.5 B	2,521,000 B	5.7	6.6	463,300 B	1.1 A
35–49 years*	7,541,200	12.4	3,809,500	6.2	8.3	3,592,600	5.9	6.6	781,000	1.3
50–64 years	7,480,000	11.8	4,235,000 B	6.7	8.4	3,115,900 B	4.9 B	5.4 B	800,300	1.3
65 years or older	4,070,600 B	8.5 B	2,796,700 B	5.9	7.3 B	1,290,500 B	2.7 B	2.9 B	371,000 B	0.8 B
Household income										
$24,999 or less	3,273,300 B	6.2 B	1,053,600 B	2.0 B	4.2 B	1,831,200 B	3.5 B	4.6 B	548,000 B	1.0
$25,000–$49,999	5,315,600 B	8.0 B	2,349,000 B	3.5 B	5.4 B	2,800,400 B	4.2 B	4.9 B	588,600 B	0.9 B
$50,000–$74,999	4,623,300 B	10.2 B	2,212,900 B	4.9 B	6.4 B	2,285,700 B	5.1 A	5.6	374,700 B	0.8 B
$75,000 or more*	12,740,300	14.1	7,807,300	8.6	10.2	5,032,900	5.6 B	6.0	1,098,700	1.2

Note: Estimates are based on the most recent incident of identity theft. Percentages are based on the number of persons in each category. Missing data for household income were imputed. Details do not sum to totals because persons could experience more than one type of identity theft.
* = Comparison group.
-- = Less than 0.05 percent.
! = Interpret with caution. Estimate is based on 10 or fewer sample cases, or coefficient of variation is greater than 50%.
A = Significant difference from comparison group at 90% confidence level.
B = Significant difference from comparison group at 95% confidence level.
[1]Includes the misuse of personal information to open a new account or for other fraudulent purposes apart from misuse of an existing credit card or bank account or other existing account.
[2]White, Black, other race, and persons of two or more race categories exclude persons of Hispanic/Latino origin.
[3]Includes persons identifying as Asian, Native Hawaiian, or Other Pacific Islander; or American Indian or Alaska Native.

Table 3. The Most Recent Incident of Identity Theft, by Type of Theft, 2016

(Number; percent.)

Type of identity theft	Number of victims	Percent of all persons	Percent of all victims
Total	25,952,400	10.2	100.0
Only one type of existing account	22,179,200	8.7	85.5
Credit card*	11,077,600	4.3	42.7
Bank	9,828,600 B	3.9 B	37.9 B
Other	1,272,900 B	0.5 B	4.9 B
Opened new account only	873,400 B	0.3 B	3.4 B
Misused personal information only....................	838,600 B	0.3 B	3.2 B
Multiple types..	2,061,300 B	0.8 B	7.9 B
Existing account[1].....................................	1,441,000 B	0.6 B	5.6 B
Other[2]...	620,300 B	0.2 B	2.4 B

Note: In 2016, there were 255 million persons age 16 or older living in noninstitutionalized, residential settings in the United States. Details may not sum to totals due to rounding.
* = Comparison group.
B = Significant difference from comparison year at 95% confidence level.
[1]Includes victims who experienced two or more of the following: misuse of a credit card, bank account, or other existing account.
[2]Includes victims who experienced two or more of the following: misuse of an existing account, personal information to open a new account, or personal information for other fraudulent purposes.

Table 4. The Most Common Ways Victims Had Discovered Identity Theft, by Type of Theft, 2016

(Percent.)

Way victims discovered identity theft	Any identity theft	Misuse of existing account*[1]	Other identity theft[2]
Total	100.0	100.0	100.0
Contacted by financial institution about suspicious activity..........................	47.6	50.8	15.4 B
Noticed fraudulent charges on account................	18.7	20.0	6.1 B
Noticed money missing from account	8.0	8.6	2.0 B
Contacted financial institution to report a theft......	6.1	6.5	1.8 B
Credit card declined, check bounced, or account closed due to insufficient funds	4.7	5.0	1.9 B
Notified by company or agency........................	4.6	3.0	21.2 B
Received a bill or contacted about an unpaid bill......	2.9	2.0	12.6 B
Problems with applying for a loan, government benefits, or with income taxes	1.6	0.4	13.8 B
Discovered through credit report or credit monitoring service.............................	1.4	0.8	7.3 B
Received merchandise or card that victim did not order or did not receive product ordered.........	0.6	0.4	2.4 B
Notified by police......................................	0.5	0.1	4.3 B
Notified by family member............................	0.4	0.4	0.7 !
Another way[3]...	2.9	2.1	10.7 B

Note: Estimates are based on the most recent incident of identity theft.
* = Comparison group.
! = Interpret with caution. Estimate is based on 10 or fewer sample cases, or coefficient of variation is greater than 50%.
B = Significant difference from comparison year at 95% confidence level.
[1]Includes identity-theft incidents involving only the misuse of one type of existing account or the misuse of multiple types of existing accounts.
[2]Includes the following identity-theft incidents: the misuse of at least one type of existing account and the misuse of personal information to open a new account or for another fraudulent purpose; and the misuse of personal information to open a new account or for another fraudulent purpose.
[3]Includes someone other than a family member notified the victim; victim noticed account information was missing or stolen; victim noticed from suspicious computer activity, including hacked email; victim noticed from suspicious contact, including phishing; and discovery in other ways.

Table 5. Identity Theft Victims Who Knew Something About the Offender, by Type of Theft, 2016

(Number; percent.)

Type of identity theft	Victim knew something about offender
Total	6.2
Only one type of existing account	5.0[B]
Credit card*	3.1[B]
Bank	6.1[B]
Other	13.0[B]
Opened new account only	13.2[A]
Misused personal information only	16.4
Multiple types	11.8
Existing account[1]	8.2[B]
Other[2]	20.1

Note: Estimates are based on the most recent incident of identity theft. Details do not sum to totals.
* = Comparison group.
B = Significant difference from comparison year at 95% confidence level.
[1]Includes victims who experienced two or more of the following: misuse of a credit card, bank account, or other existing account.
[2]Includes victims who experienced two or more of the following: unauthorized use of an existing account, personal information to open a new account, or personal information for other fraudulent purposes.

Table 6. Financial Loss Among Victims Who Had Experienced at Least One Attempted or Successful Identity-Theft Incident in the Past 12 Months, by Type of Loss and Theft, 2016

(Dollars; percent.)

Victim characteristic	Total identity theft	Only one type of existing account				Opened new account only	Misused personal information	Multiple types		
		Total*	Credit card	Bank	Other			Total	Existing accounts[1]	Other[2]
Any loss[3]										
Mean	$850	$680	$730	$630	$700	$3,460[B]	$2,620[B]	$1,680[B]	$970	$3,470
Median	$300	$200	$200	$200	$200	$800	$600	$400	$400	$800
Percent experiencing a loss	67.4	69.3	70.1	71.7	45.0	41.6[B]	26.7[B]	73.9[B]	75.8	69.5
Direct[4,5]										
Mean	$850	$680	$740	$610	$720	$3,430[B]	$3,530[B]	$1,660[B]	$950	$3,500
Median	$300	$200	$200	$200	$200	$900	$1,900	$400	$300	$800
Percent experiencing a loss	66.2	68.4	69.4	70.7	42.3	39.8[B]	19.4[B]	73.0[B]	75.4	67.3
Indirect[6]										
Mean	$250	$200	$110	$250	$170	$850[A]	$150	$360[B]	$270	$450
Median	$20	$20	$10	$20	$50	$100	$50	$40	$10	$200
Percent experiencing a loss	5.4	4.7	3.3	6.1	6.3	8.3[B]	11.7[B]	8.7[B]	6.3	14.1
Total out of pocket										
Mean	$690	$540	$470	$600	$480	$1,390[A]	$1,3260[B]	$1,070[B]	$650	$1,690
Median	$100	$70	$50	$80	$200	$400	$200	$300	$200	$500
Percent experiencing a loss	11.8	10.6	7.0	13.7	17.0	16.2[B]	16.9[B]	20.4[B]	17.5	27.2
Number of victims	25,952,400	22,179,200	11,077,600	9,828,600	1,272,900	873,400	838,600	2,061,300	1,441,000	620,300

Note: Estimates are based on the most recent incident of identity theft. Details do not sum to totals.
* = Comparison group. Compared to opened new account only, personal information only, and multiple types total.
A = Significant difference from comparison group at 90% confidence level.
B = Significant difference from comparison group at 95% confidence level.
[1]Includes victims who experienced two or more of the following: misuse of a credit card, bank account, or other existing account.
[2]Includes victims who experienced two or more of the following: misuse of an existing account, personal information to open a new account, or personal information for other fraudulent purposes.
[3]Includes any direct or indirect loss of $1 or more.
[4]Includes victims who had a direct loss of $1 or more and no indirect loss and victims who had both direct and indirect losses of $1 or more.
[5]Mean amounts for direct loss could be greater than any mean loss amounts due to top coding, a procedure used to protect respondents with loss amounts from disclosure risk.
[6]Includes victims who had an indirect loss of $1 or more and no direct loss and victims who had both direct and indirect losses of $1 or more.

Table 7. Victims Who Had Experienced Financial or Legal Problems as a Result of Identity Theft, by Type of Theft, 2016

(Percent.)

Type of problem	Any identity theft	Misuse of existing account[1]	Other identity theft[2]
Credit related[3]	2.1	1.3	10.2 B
Debt collectors	1.9	1.1	9.9 B
Banking problems[4]	1.5	1.2	4.8 B
Utilities cut off or new services denied	0.4	0.3	2.4 B
Legal[5]	0.3	0.2	1.5 B
Other[6]	0.6	0.2	4.5 B

Note: Estimates are based on the most recent incident of identity theft.
* = Comparison group.
B = Significant difference from comparison year at 95% confidence level.
[1]Includes identity-theft incidents involving only the misuse of an existing account or the misuse of multiple types of existing accounts.
[2]Involves the following types of incidents: the misuse of at least one type of existing account and the misuse of personal information to open a new account or for another fraudulent purpose; and the misuse of personal information to open a new account or for another fraudulent purpose.
[3]Includes having to correct the same information on a credit report repeatedly, being turned down for credit or loans, or paying higher interest rates.
[4]Includes being turned down for a checking account or having checks bounce.
[5]Includes being the subject of a lawsuit or other criminal proceedings, or being arrested.
[6]Includes being turned down for a job, losing a job, or problems with income taxes.

Table 8. Identity-Theft Victims Who Had Experienced Emotional Distress, by Type of Theft, 2016

(Percent.)

Type of problem	Total	None	Mild	Moderate	Severe
Total	100.0	20.6	45.9	23.8	9.7
Only one type of existing account	100.0	21.6 B	45.8 B	22.6 B	8.0 B
Credit card	100.0	23.6 B	51.2 B	20.3 B	4.9 B
Bank	100.0	19.1 B	44.6 B	25.2 B	11.1 B
Other	100.0	22.9 B	43.9 B	22.0 B	11.2 B
Opened new account only	100.0	16.9 B	35.6 A	28.5	19.0 B
Misused personal information only	100.0	12.4	28.9	36.8	21.9
	100.0				
Multiple types	100.0	15.2	36.7	29.4	18.6
Existing account[1]	100.0	17.8 B	40.5 B	27.3 A	14.4 B
Other[2]	100.0	9.3	27.9	34.4	28.4

Note: Estimates are based on the most recent incident of identity theft. Details may not sum to totals due to rounding. Excludes less than 1% of identity-theft victims who had missing data on emotional distress.
* = Comparison group.
A = Significant difference from comparison year at 90% confidence level.
B = Significant difference from comparison year at 95% confidence level.
[1]Includes victims who experienced two or more of the following: misuse of a credit card, bank account, or other existing account.
[2]Includes victims who experienced two or more of the following: misuse of an existing account, personal information to open a new account, or personal information for other fraudulent purposes.

Table 9. Victims Who Did and Did Not Report Identity Theft to Police, by Type of Theft and Reason for Not Reporting, 2016

(Percent.)

Victim response	Total identity theft	Only one type of existing account				Opened new account only	Misused personal information	Multiple types		
		Total	Credit card	Bank	Other			Total	Existing accounts[1]	Other[2]
Reported to police	6.8	4.7 B	2.9 B	6.6 B	5.6 B	18.4 B	29.3	15.1 B	8.9 B	29.3
Did not report to police................................	93.1	95.2 B	97.0 B	93.2 B	94.1 B	81.4 B	70.2	84.9 B	91.1 B	70.7 B
Handled it another way[3]............................	67.8	69.5 B	72.2 B	68.8 B	51.3	50.3	47.4	61.3 B	63.7 B	54.0
Not important enough[4]	18.2	18.4 A	17.6	18.3	27.0 B	20.5 A	13.9	16.2	16.6	15.0
Did not think about or know how[5]..........	16.8	16.5	16.4	16.3	18.6	16.9	20.5	19.9	19.6	20.6
Did not think police could help[6]..............	12.4	11.8 B	11.0 B	11.7 B	20.1	20.6	26.0	12.0 B	10.9 B	15.0 B
Personal reasons[7]	2.0	1.5 B	1.2 B	1.6 B	3.7	8.4	5.5	4.6	3.2	8.9
Other[8]	1.9	1.5 B	1.6 B	1.3 B	2.4 B	3.0! B	8.5	3.1 B	2.5 B	5.0! B

Note: Estimates are based on the most recent incident of identity theft. Details do not sum to totals because persons could report multiple reasons for not contacting police.
* = Comparison group.
! = Interpret with caution. Estimate is based on 10 or fewer sample cases, or coefficient of variation is greater than 50%.
A = Significant difference from comparison group at 90% confidence level.
B = Significant difference from comparison group at 95% confidence level.
[1]Includes victims who experienced two or more of the following: misuse of a credit card, bank account, or other existing account.
[2]Includes victims who experienced two or more of the following: misuse of an existing account, personal information to open a new account, or personal information for other fraudulent purposes.
[3]Includes victims who reported it to a credit card company, bank, insurance company, or other organization; taking care of it themselves; a credit card company, bank, or other organization took care of problem; they thought that a credit card company, bank, or other organization would handle the problem; and a family member took care of the problem.
[4]Includes victims who did not lose any money, reported that the incident was an attempt, thought that it was not important enough to report, or experienced a small monetary loss.
[5]Includes victims who did not know they could report the incident, did not think about reporting the incident, or did not know what agency was responsible for identity-theft crimes.
[6]Includes victims who did not think the police would do anything, did not want to bother police, thought it was too late for police to help, and could not identify the offender or provide much information that would be helpful to police.
[7]Includes victims who were afraid to report the incident, did not want to get the offender in trouble, were embarrassed, and reported that it was too inconvenient to report.
[8]Includes victims who stated that the incident occurred in another state or outside of the United States, they were not sure it was a crime or if it was a mistake, law enforcement made first contact, the incident just occurred or was still an ongoing problem and they planned to report it soon, and other reasons.

Table 10. Identity-Theft Victims, by Type of Theft and Type of Organization Contacted, 2016

(Percent; number.)

Type of organization contact	Total identity theft	Only one type of existing account				Opened new account only	Misused personal information only[1]	Multiple types		
		Total	Credit card*	Bank	Other			Total	Existing accounts[2]	Other[3]
Credit card company or bank............................	88.4	91.9	95.2	94.0	47.3 B	61.9 B	24.4 B	88.1 B	93.8	74.8 B
Credit bureau	7.9	5.2	4.8	5.2	8.4 B	35.4 B	25.1 B	17.8 B	11.5 B	32.7 B
Credit-monitoring services	5.7	3.9	4.0	3.6	5.5	24.6 B	13.8 B	13.1 B	7.6 B	25.9 B
Document-issuing agency[4]	2.1	1.1	0.7	1.3 B	2.7 B	7.0 B	14.3 B	5.5 B	2.7 B	12.0 B
Consumer agency[5]	1.5	0.8	0.5	0.9 A	2.2 B	5.3 B	7.2 B	5.6 B	2.0 B	14.0 B
Federal Trade Commission	0.9	0.4	0.2!	0.5	1.3! A	5.7 B	5.3 B	3.0 B	1.3! A	6.9 B
Victim services agency[6]	0.9	0.6	0.5	0.6	1.1!	1.9! A	4.0 B	2.3 B	1.1!	5.1! B
Attorney	0.7	0.5	0.3	0.8 B	0.3!	1.7! A	0.8!	2.0 B	0.9!	4.7! B
Other...	0.2	0.1	--	0.2! B	0.3!	1.0!	1.5! B	0.5!	0.4!	0.5!
Number of victims..	25,952,400	22,179,200	11,077,600	9,828,600	1,272,900	873,400	838,600	2,061,300	1,441,000	620,300

Note: Details do not sum to totals, as victims could have contacted multiple organizations. Estimates are based on the most recent incident of identity theft.
* = Comparison group.
-- = Less than 0.05 percent.
! = Interpret with caution. Estimate is based on 10 or fewer sample cases, or coefficient of variation is greater than 50%.
A = Significant difference from comparison group at 90% confidence level.
B = Significant difference from comparison group at 95% confidence level.
[1]Includes crimes such as providing false information to law enforcement when charged with a crime or traffic violation.
[2]Includes victims who experienced two or more of the following: unauthorized use of a credit card, bank account, or other existing account.
[3]Includes victims who experienced two or more of the following: unauthorized use of an existing account, misuse of personal information to open a new account, or misuse of personal information for other fraudulent purposes.
[4]Includes agencies that issue drivers' licenses or Social Security cards.
[5]Includes state or local consumer affairs agencies, such as the State Attorney General's office, and consumer agencies, such as the Better Business Bureau.
[6]Includes agencies other than the police that deal with victims of crime.

Table 11. Identity-Theft Victims Who Contacted a Credit Bureau, by Type of Theft and Action Taken, 2016

(Percent.)

Action taken	Total identity theft	Only one type of existing account				Opened new account only	Misused personal information only[1]	Multiple types		
		Total	Credit card*	Bank	Other			Total	Existing accounts[2]	Other[3]
Placed a fraud alert on their credit report	72.0	66.4	63.8	67.0	76.3	85.4 B	82.0 B	72.8	58.8	84.3 B
Requested a credit report	64.6	59.6	58.6	62.2	52.0	73.2 B	71.4 A	68.9 A	59.5	76.6 B
Placed a freeze on their credit report	41.8	37.5	35.7	36.8	49.2	48.9 B	38.3	51.6 B	31.7	67.9 B
Requested corrections to their credit report	36.9	31.5	31.2	27.7	51.0 B	48.9 B	19.9 A	53.6 B	34.1	69.5 B
Provided a police report to the credit bureau	19.0	12.0	8.2	15.2 A	15.4 !	27.5 B	17.4 A	34.6 B	21.5 B	45.2 B

Note: Details do not sum to totals, as victims could have taken multiple actions with a credit bureau. Estimates are based on the most recent incident of identity theft.
* = Comparison group.
A = Significant difference from comparison group at 90% confidence level.
B = Significant difference from comparison group at 95% confidence level.
[1]Includes crimes such as providing false information to law enforcement when charged with a crime or traffic violation.
[2]Includes victims who experienced two or more of the following: unauthorized use of a credit card, bank account, or other existing account.
[3]Includes victims who experienced two or more of the following: unauthorized use of an existing account, misuse of personal information to open a new account, or misuse of personal information for other fraudulent purposes.

Table 12. Actions Persons Age 16 or Older Had Taken During the Past 12 Months to Reduce the Risk of Identity Theft, by Whether the Action Was Taken in Response to Experiencing Identity Theft, 2016

(Percent.)

Type of action	Total	Non-victims*	During the past 12 months, victims of identity theft:		
			Total	Took action in response to experiencing identity theft	Took action independent of experiencing identity theft
Any	85.8	84.5	97.6 B	11.2 B	86.4 B
Checked bank or credit statements	75.6	73.7	92.9 B	25.9 B	67.0 B
Shredded or destroyed documents with personal information	67.5	66	80.3 B	13.8 B	66.5
Checked credit report	44.3	42.3	61.7 B	16.8 B	44.9 B
Changed passwords on financial accounts	36.8	33.8	63.3 B	24.7 B	38.7 B
Used identity-theft security program on computer	16.2	15.2	25.9 B	6.6 B	19.3 B
Purchased identity-theft insurance or credit monitoring service	11.7	10.4	23.2 B	10.6	12.6 B
Purchased identity-theft protection	4.7	4.2	9.3 B	4.7 A	4.6

Note: Details do not sum to totals because persons could take multiple preventable actions.
* = Comparison group.
A = Significant difference from comparison group at 90% confidence level.
B = Significant difference from comparison group at 95% confidence level.

Table 13. Persons Age 16 or Older Who Experienced Identity Theft in Their Lifetime, by Type of Identity Theft Experienced Outside the past Year and Ongoing problems from Identity Theft, 2016

(Number; percent.)

Identity theft during lifetime and outside past 12 months	Number of victims	Percent of total age-16-or-older population	Percent of victims whose problems resulting from identity theft were unresolved[1]
At least one incident of identity theft during lifetime	49,493,000	19.4	7.0
At least one incident of identity theft outside of the past 12 months	29,182,600	11.4	6.3
Only one type of existing account	22,365,800 B	8.8 B	3.4 B
Credit card*	13,000,700 B	5.1 B	2.5 B
Bank	8,428,000 B	3.3 B	4.3 B
Other	937,100 B	0.4 B	7.7 B
Opened new account only	1,943,400 B	0.8 B	14.2 B
Misused personal information only	2,588,800 B	1.0 B	15.8 B
Multiple types	2,258,500	0.9	17.9
Existing account*[2]	1,077,600	0.4	7.8 B
Other[3]	1,181,000	0.5	27.1

Note: Details do not sum to totals due to a small number of victims who did not know the type of identity theft they experienced outside of the past 12 months. In 2016, there were 255 million persons age 16 or older living in non-institutionalized, residential settings in the United States.
* = Comparison group.
B = Significant difference from comparison year at 95% confidence level.
[1]Based on number of persons who experienced the identity theft.
[2]Includes victims who experienced two or more of the following: misuse of a credit card, bank account, or other existing account.
[3]Includes victims who experienced two or more of the following: misuse of an existing account, personal information to open a new account, or personal information for other fraudulent purposes.

METHODOLOGY

The 2016 Identity Theft Supplement (ITS) was administered as a supplement to the National Crime Victimization Survey (NCVS), a collection by the Bureau of Justice Statistics (BJS). From January 1, 2016, to June 30, 2016, approximately 125,200 persons age 16 or older received the ITS at the end of their NCVS interview.

The NCVS sample was redesigned in 2016. (Please see *Criminal Victimization, 2016,* on the BJS Web site for more information.) From 2015 to 2016, the NCVS sample size increased by 41 percent (from 95,760 to 134,690 households interviewed) to facilitate the ability to produce state- and local-level victimization estimates for the largest 22 states. At the same time, the sample was adjusted to reflect the U.S. population counts in the U.S. Census Bureau's 2010 decennial census (rather than being based on the 2000 decennial census, as was the case from 2006 through 2015).

Given these changes to the sample design, BJS examined changes in identity theft between 2014 (the most recent iteration of the ITS) and 2016 both overall and for continuing counties—those that were included in the sample in 2014 and remained in the sample in 2016. This report focuses primarily on the level and nature of identity theft in 2016 and is based on the full sample unless otherwise specified. Data users should use caution when comparing 2016 estimates to those from previous years.

Identity-theft victims are persons age 16 or older who experienced one or more of the following:

Misuse of an existing account—completed or attempted unauthorized use of one or more existing accounts, such as a credit card, debit card, checking, savings, telephone, mortgage, or insurance account.

Misuse of a new account—completed or attempted unauthorized use of personal information to open a new account, such as a credit card or debit card, checking, savings, telephone, online, mortgage, or insurance account.

Misuse of personal information—completed or attempted unauthorized use of personal information for fraudulent purposes, such as getting medical care, a job, or government benefits; renting an apartment or house; or providing false information to law enforcement when charged with a crime or traffic violation. This excludes the completed or attempted unauthorized use of personal information to open a new account or to misuse an existing account.

Data Collection

The Identity Theft Supplement (ITS) was administered as a supplement to the Bureau of Justice Statistics' National Crime Victimization Survey (NCVS). The NCVS collects data on crime reported and not reported to police against persons age 12 or older from a nationally representative sample of U.S. households. The sample includes persons living in group quarters (such as dormitories, rooming houses, and religious group dwellings). It excludes persons living in military barracks and institutional settings (such as correctional or hospital facilities) and persons who are homeless.

From January 1, 2016, to June 30, 2016, 125,200 persons age 16 or older in sampled NCVS households received the ITS at the end of the NCVS interview. Proxy respondents did not receive the ITS. If the NCVS interview was conducted in some language other than English, the ITS interview was allowed to be conducted in that language by either the interviewer or a reliable translator. All NCVS and ITS interviews were conducted using computer-assisted personal interviewing by telephone or personal visit. A final sample size of about 96,100 persons of the original NCVS-eligible respondents completed the ITS questionnaire, a person response rate of 77 percent.

The combined ITS response rate, computed as a product of the NCVS household response rate and ITS person response rate, was about 61 percent. Because of the level of non-response, a bias analysis was conducted. The result of the non-response bias analysis suggested that there was little or no bias of substantive importance due to non-response in the ITS estimates.

The ITS collected individual data on the prevalence of and victim response to attempted or successful misuse of an existing account, misuse of personal information to open a new account, or misuse of personal information for other fraudulent purposes. Respondents were asked whether they experienced any of these types of misuse during the 12 months prior to the interview.

Persons who reported experiencing one or more incidents of identity theft over the prior 12 months were asked questions about the incident and their response to the incident, such as how they discovered the identity theft; financial, credit, and other problems resulting from the incident; time spent resolving associated problems; and reporting to police and credit bureaus. For most sections of the survey instrument, the ITS asked victims who experienced more than one incident during the 12-month reference period to describe only the most recent incident when answering questions about details of the identity-theft incident. It asked victims who experienced multiple incidents of identity theft during the year to provide details on the total financial losses they experienced as a result of all incidents. It also asked all respondents a series of questions about identity theft they experienced outside of the 12-month reference period and about measures they took to avoid or minimize the risk of becoming an identity-theft victim.

Changes in BJS Identity-Theft Statistics Over Time

In 2008, the Bureau of Justice Statistics (BJS) conducted the first ITS to the NCVS. Prior to that year, BJS reports on identity theft used household-level data from the core NCVS. Data were reported for the household as a whole rather than for individual respondents, and the questions were more limited, providing less detail on the characteristics of the incident and the victim response. For additional information, see Identity Theft, 2005 (NCJ 219411, BJS web, November 2007); Identity Theft Reported by Households, 2007 Statistical Tables

(NCJ 230742, BJS web, June 2010); and Identity Theft Reported by Households, 2005-2010 (NCJ 236245, BJS web, November 2011).

The 2008 collection, like the 2012 and 2014 ITS collections, gathered detailed information on victim experiences with identity theft from persons age 16 or older. For more information, see Victims of Identity Theft, 2008 (NCJ 231680, BJS web, December 2010). Following the administration of the 2008 ITS, BJS made substantial changes to the survey instrument, making it difficult to compare estimates from the 2008 ITS to estimates from later iterations of the ITS. For details on these changes, see Victims of Identity Theft, 2012 (NCJ 243779, BJS web, December 2013).

From 2015 to 2016, the NCVS sample size increased by 41 percent to facilitate the ability to produce state- and local-level victimization data for the largest 22 states. At the same time, the sample was adjusted to reflect the U.S. population counts in the U.S. Census Bureau's 2010 decennial census. During January through June 2016 when the ITS was administered, 55 percent of the ITS households were new to the sample. In a normal data collection year, roughly 14 percent of these households would be new to the sample. Due to these changes, comparisons between 2012 or 2014 and 2016 ITS data should be made with caution.

In-Depth Defining of Identity Theft

As with many other crime types, there is no standard definition of identity theft used nationwide. The ITS was developed in

conjunction with the Federal Trade Commission (FTC)—the U.S. government's consumer protection agency—in addition to a range of government and private experts from the criminal justice and financial fields. The definition used for the supplement follows from the FTC's general definition of identity theft: a fraud that is committed or attempted using a person's identifying information without authority. (Fair and Accurate Credit Transactions Act of 2003, P.L. 108-159.)

Many state legal codes use a similar definition of identity theft, though the codes vary from one state to the next in terms of how personal information is defined and the type of misuse that must occur. For example, the California Penal Code specifies that identity theft occurs when an individual "willfully obtains personal identifying information, as defined in subdivision (b) of Section 530.55, of another person, and uses that information for any unlawful purpose, including to obtain, or attempt to obtain, credit, goods, services, real property, or medical information without the consent of that person." The list of personal identifying information includes, "any name, address, telephone number, health insurance number, taxpayer identification number, school identification number, state or federal driver's license, or identification number, social security number, place of employment, employee identification number, professional or occupational number, mother's maiden name, demand deposit account number, savings account number, checking account number, PIN (personal identification number) or password, alien registration number, government passport number, date of birth, unique biometric data including fingerprint, facial scan identifiers, voiceprint, retina or iris image, or other unique physical representation, unique electronic data including information identification number assigned to the person, address or routing code, telecommunication identifying information or access device, information contained in a birth or death certificate, or credit card number of an individual person, or an equivalent form of identification." (California Penal Code Part 1. Title 13. Chapter 8. Section 530.5. and California Penal Code Part 1. Title 13. Chapter 8. Section 530.55.)

The Pennsylvania Code defines identifying information as "any document, photographic, pictorial or computer image of another person, or any fact used to establish identity, including, but not limited to, a name, birth date, Social Security number, driver's license number, non-driver governmental identification number, telephone number, checking account number, savings account number, student identification number, employee or payroll number or electronic signature." It specifies that identity theft occurs when a person "possesses or uses, through any means, identifying information of another person without the consent of that other person to further any unlawful purpose." (Pennsylvania Code Title 18. Section 4120.)

The primary categories of identity theft used in the ITS were modeled after a survey on identity theft conducted by the FTC in 2005 and 2006. The categories of identity theft identified in the initial FTC survey were the misuse of an existing credit card or credit card account, the misuse of an existing non-credit card account, and the misuse of personal information to open new accounts or to engage in types of fraud other than the misuse of existing or new financial accounts. The ITS splits the latter category into two separate groups.

Possible Overreporting of Losses from Jointly Held Accounts

Persons may have experienced the unauthorized use of a jointly held account. Joint accounts present a difficulty with counting financial harm or loss because of the potential for double-counting loss (e.g., both account holders report the same $500 loss). Because financial loss was not attributed to a particular type of identity theft, victims of multiple types of identity theft may have experienced some financial loss from a joint account and an independently held account. Therefore, it was not possible to correct for potential overreporting due to joint account-holders who may have been double-counted.

Standard Error Computations

When national estimates are derived from a sample, caution must be taken when comparing one estimate to another. Although one estimate may be larger than another, estimates based on a sample have some degree of sampling error. The sampling error of an estimate depends on several factors, including the amount of variation in the responses, the size of the sample, and the size of the subgroup for which the estimate is computed. When the sampling error around the estimates is taken into consideration, the estimates that appear different may not be statistically different.

One measure of the sampling error associated with an estimate is the standard error. The standard error may vary from one estimate to the next. In general, for a given metric, an estimate with a smaller standard error provides a more reliable approximation of the true value than an estimate with a larger standard error. Estimates with relatively large standard errors are associated with less precision and reliability and should be interpreted with caution.

The U.S. Census Bureau produces generalized variance function (GVF) parameters for BJS. The GVFs take into account aspects of the NCVS's complex sample design and represent the curve fitted to a selection of individual standard errors based on the Jackknife Repeated Replication technique. Except where otherwise noted, the GVF parameters were used to generate standard errors for each point estimate (e.g., numbers or percentages) in the report.

BJS conducted tests to determine whether differences in estimated numbers and percentages were statistically significant once sampling error was taken into account. Using statistical programs developed specifically for the NCVS, all comparisons in the text were tested for significance. The primary test procedure used was Student's t-statistic, which tests the difference between two sample estimates. The significance level was set at the 95 percent confidence level to ensure observed difference between estimates were larger than what was expected due to sampling variation.

Data users may employ estimates and standard errors of the estimates provided in this report to generate a confidence interval around the estimate as a measure of the margin of error. The following example illustrates how standard errors may be used to generate confidence intervals:

According to the ITS, in 2016 an estimated 10.2 percent of persons age 16 or older experienced identity theft. Using GVFs, BJS determined that the estimate has a standard error of 0.18. A confidence interval around the estimate was generated by multiplying the standard errors by ±1.96 (the t-score of a normal, two-tailed distribution that excludes 2.5 percent at either end of the distribution). Therefore, the confidence interval around the estimate is 10.2 ± (0.18 × 1.96) or 9.85 percent to 10.55 percent. In other words, if BJS used the same sampling method to select different samples and computed an interval estimate for each sample, the true population parameter (percent of identity-theft victims) would be expected to fall within the interval estimates 95 percent of the time.

BJS also calculated a coefficient of variation (CV) for all estimates, representing the ratio of the standard error to the estimate. CVs provide a measure of reliability and a means to compare the precision of estimates across measures with differing levels or metrics. In cases where the CV was greater than 50 percent, or the unweighted sample had 10 or fewer cases, the estimate was noted with a "!" symbol (interpret data with caution; estimate is based on 10 or fewer sample cases, or the CV exceeds 50 percent).

Many variables examined in this report may be related to one another and to other variables not included in the analyses. Complex relationships among variables were not fully explored and warrant more extensive analysis. Readers are cautioned not to draw causal inferences based on the results presented.

For more information, please see http://www.bjs.gov/index.cfm?ty=pbdetail&iid=6467

APPENDIX A: SOURCES FOR TABLES

Part 1. Capital Punishment, 2016

1	Bureau of Justice Statistics, National Prisoner Statistics program (NPS-8), 2016
2	Bureau of Justice Statistics, National Prisoner Statistics program (NPS-8), 2016
3	Bureau of Justice Statistics, National Prisoner Statistics program (NPS-8), 2016
4	Bureau of Justice Statistics, National Prisoner Statistics program (NPS-8), 2016
5	Bureau of Justice Statistics, National Prisoner Statistics program (NPS-8), 2016
6	Bureau of Justice Statistics, National Prisoner Statistics program (NPS-8), 2016
7	Bureau of Justice Statistics, National Prisoner Statistics program (NPS-8), 1930–2016
8	Bureau of Justice Statistics, National Prisoner Statistics program (NPS-8), 1953–2016
9	Bureau of Justice Statistics, National Prisoner Statistics program (NPS-8), 1973–2016
10	Bureau of Justice Statistics, National Prisoner Statistics program (NPS-8), 1968–2016

Part 2. Crimes Against Persons with Disabilities, 2009–2015

1	Bureau of Justice Statistics, National Crime Victimization Survey, 2011–2015; and U.S. Census Bureau, American Community Survey, 2011–2015.
2	Bureau of Justice Statistics, National Crime Victimization Survey, 2011–2015; and U.S. Census Bureau, American Community Survey, 2011–2015
3	Bureau of Justice Statistics, National Crime Victimization Survey, 2011–2015; and U.S. Census Bureau, American Community Survey, 2011–2015
4	Bureau of Justice Statistics, National Crime Victimization Survey, 2011–2015; and U.S. Census Bureau, American Community Survey, 2011–2015
5	Bureau of Justice Statistics, National Crime Victimization Survey, 2011–2015; and U.S. Census Bureau, American Community Survey, 2011–2015
6	Bureau of Justice Statistics, National Crime Victimization Survey, 2011–2015
7	Bureau of Justice Statistics, National Crime Victimization Survey, 2011–2015; and U.S. Census Bureau, American Community Survey, 2011–2015.
8	Bureau of Justice Statistics, National Crime Victimization Survey, 2011–2015
9	Bureau of Justice Statistics, National Crime Victimization Survey, 2011–2015
10	Bureau of Justice Statistics, National Crime Victimization Survey, 2011–2015
11	Bureau of Justice Statistics, National Crime Victimization Survey, 2011–2015
12	Bureau of Justice Statistics, National Crime Victimization Survey, 2011–2015
13	Bureau of Justice Statistics, National Crime Victimization Survey, 2011–2015

Part 3. Crime in the United States, 2017

1	United States Department of Justice, Federal Bureau of Investigation, Uniform Crime Reports, 2018
2	United States Department of Justice, Federal Bureau of Investigation, Uniform Crime Reports, 2018
3	United States Department of Justice, Federal Bureau of Investigation, Uniform Crime Reports, 2018
4	United States Department of Justice, Federal Bureau of Investigation, Uniform Crime Reports, 2018
5	United States Department of Justice, Federal Bureau of Investigation, Uniform Crime Reports, 2018
6	United States Department of Justice, Federal Bureau of Investigation, Uniform Crime Reports, 2018
7	United States Department of Justice, Federal Bureau of Investigation, Uniform Crime Reports, 2018
8	United States Department of Justice, Federal Bureau of Investigation, Uniform Crime Reports, 2018
9	United States Department of Justice, Federal Bureau of Investigation, Uniform Crime Reports, 2018
10	United States Department of Justice, Federal Bureau of Investigation, Uniform Crime Reports, 2018
11	United States Department of Justice, Federal Bureau of Investigation, Uniform Crime Reports, 2018
12	United States Department of Justice, Federal Bureau of Investigation, Uniform Crime Reports, 2018

13   United States Department of Justice, Federal Bureau of Investigation, Uniform Crime Reports, 2018
14   United States Department of Justice, Federal Bureau of Investigation, Uniform Crime Reports, 2018
15   United States Department of Justice, Federal Bureau of Investigation, Uniform Crime Reports, 2018
16   United States Department of Justice, Federal Bureau of Investigation, Uniform Crime Reports, 2018
17   United States Department of Justice, Federal Bureau of Investigation, Uniform Crime Reports, 2018
18   United States Department of Justice, Federal Bureau of Investigation, Uniform Crime Reports, 2018
19   United States Department of Justice, Federal Bureau of Investigation, Uniform Crime Reports, 2018
20   United States Department of Justice, Federal Bureau of Investigation, Uniform Crime Reports, 2018
21   United States Department of Justice, Federal Bureau of Investigation, Uniform Crime Reports, 2018
22   United States Department of Justice, Federal Bureau of Investigation, Uniform Crime Reports, 2018
23   United States Department of Justice, Federal Bureau of Investigation, Uniform Crime Reports, 2018
24   United States Department of Justice, Federal Bureau of Investigation, Uniform Crime Reports, 2018
25   United States Department of Justice, Federal Bureau of Investigation, Uniform Crime Reports, 2018
26   United States Department of Justice, Federal Bureau of Investigation, Uniform Crime Reports, 2018
27   United States Department of Justice, Federal Bureau of Investigation, Uniform Crime Reports, 2018
28   United States Department of Justice, Federal Bureau of Investigation, Uniform Crime Reports, 2018
29   United States Department of Justice, Federal Bureau of Investigation, Uniform Crime Reports, 2018
30   United States Department of Justice, Federal Bureau of Investigation, Uniform Crime Reports, 2018
31   United States Department of Justice, Federal Bureau of Investigation, Uniform Crime Reports, 2018
32   United States Department of Justice, Federal Bureau of Investigation, Uniform Crime Reports, 2018
33   United States Department of Justice, Federal Bureau of Investigation, Uniform Crime Reports, 2018
34   United States Department of Justice, Federal Bureau of Investigation, Uniform Crime Reports, 2018
35   United States Department of Justice, Federal Bureau of Investigation, Uniform Crime Reports, 2018
36   United States Department of Justice, Federal Bureau of Investigation, Uniform Crime Reports, 2018
37   United States Department of Justice, Federal Bureau of Investigation, Uniform Crime Reports, 2018
38   United States Department of Justice, Federal Bureau of Investigation, Uniform Crime Reports, 2018
39   United States Department of Justice, Federal Bureau of Investigation, Uniform Crime Reports, 2018
40   United States Department of Justice, Federal Bureau of Investigation, Uniform Crime Reports, 2018
41   United States Department of Justice, Federal Bureau of Investigation, Uniform Crime Reports, 2018
42   United States Department of Justice, Federal Bureau of Investigation, Uniform Crime Reports, 2018
43   United States Department of Justice, Federal Bureau of Investigation, Uniform Crime Reports, 2018
44   United States Department of Justice, Federal Bureau of Investigation, Uniform Crime Reports, 2018
45   United States Department of Justice, Federal Bureau of Investigation, Uniform Crime Reports, 2018
46   United States Department of Justice, Federal Bureau of Investigation, Uniform Crime Reports, 2018
47   United States Department of Justice, Federal Bureau of Investigation, Uniform Crime Reports, 2018
48   United States Department of Justice, Federal Bureau of Investigation, Uniform Crime Reports, 2018
49   United States Department of Justice, Federal Bureau of Investigation, Uniform Crime Reports, 2018
50   United States Department of Justice, Federal Bureau of Investigation, Uniform Crime Reports, 2018
51   United States Department of Justice, Federal Bureau of Investigation, Uniform Crime Reports, 2018
52   United States Department of Justice, Federal Bureau of Investigation, Uniform Crime Reports, 2018
53   United States Department of Justice, Federal Bureau of Investigation, Uniform Crime Reports, 2018

Part 4. *Criminal Victimization*, 2017

1   Bureau of Justice Statistics, National Crime Victimization Survey, 2015, 2016, and 2017 Public-Use Files
2   Bureau of Justice Statistics, National Crime Victimization Survey, 2015, 2016, and 2017 Public-Use Files
3   Bureau of Justice Statistics, National Crime Victimization Survey, 2015, 2016, and 2017 Public-Use Files
4   Bureau of Justice Statistics, National Crime Victimization Survey, 2015, 2016, and 2017 Public-Use Files
5   Bureau of Justice Statistics, National Crime Victimization Survey, 2015, 2016, and 2017 Public-Use Files
6   Bureau of Justice Statistics, National Crime Victimization Survey, 2015, 2016, and 2017 Public-Use Files
7   Bureau of Justice Statistics, National Crime Victimization Survey, 2015, 2016, and 2017 Public-Use Files
8   Bureau of Justice Statistics, National Crime Victimization Survey, 2015, 2016, and 2017 Public-Use Files
9   Bureau of Justice Statistics, National Crime Victimization Survey, 2015, 2016, and 2017 Public-Use Files
10   Bureau of Justice Statistics, National Crime Victimization Survey, 2015, 2016, and 2017 Public-Use Files
11   Bureau of Justice Statistics, National Crime Victimization Survey, 2015, 2016, and 2017 Public-Use Files

12   Bureau of Justice Statistics, National Crime Victimization Survey, 2015, 2016, and 2017 Public-Use Files
13   Bureau of Justice Statistics, National Crime Victimization Survey, 2015, 2016, and 2017 Public-Use Files

Part 5. *Federal Justice Statistics, 2015–2016*

1   Bureau of Justice Statistics, based on data from the Administrative Office of the U.S. Courts, Probation and Pretrial Services, Probation and Pretrial Services Automated Case Tracking System; U.S. Marshals Service, Justice Detainee Information System; and Federal Bureau of Prisons, SENTRY database, fiscal year-end 2006, 2015, and 2016

2   Bureau of Justice Statistics, based on data from the U.S. Marshals Service, Justice Detainee Information Systems, fiscal years 2015 and 2016

3   Bureau of Justice Statistics, based on data from the Executive Office for U.S. Attorneys, National Legal Information Office Network System database, fiscal years 2006, 2014, 2015, and 2016

4   Bureau of Justice Statistics, based on data from the Executive Office for U.S. Attorneys, National Legal Information Office Network System database, fiscal year 2016

5   Bureau of Justice Statistics, based on data from the Administrative Office of the U.S. Courts, Probation and Pretrial Services, Probation and Pretrial Services Automated Case Tracking System, fiscal year 2016

6   Bureau of Justice Statistics, based on data from the Administrative Office of the U.S. Courts, Criminal Master File, fiscal year 2016

7   Bureau of Justice Statistics, based on data from the Administrative Office of the U.S. Courts, Criminal Master File, fiscal year 2016

8   Bureau of Justice Statistics, based on data from the Federal Bureau of Prisons, SENTRY database, fiscal year-end 2006, 2015, and 2016

9   Bureau of Justice Statistics, based on data from the Administrative Office of the U.S. Courts, Probation and Pretrial Services, Probation and Pretrial Services Automated Case Tracking System, fiscal year-end 2016

Part 6. Hate Crime Statistics, 2017

1   Federal Bureau of Investigation, Hate Crime Statistics, 2017
2   Federal Bureau of Investigation, Hate Crime Statistics, 2017
3   Federal Bureau of Investigation, Hate Crime Statistics, 2017
4   Federal Bureau of Investigation, Hate Crime Statistics, 2017
5   Federal Bureau of Investigation, Hate Crime Statistics, 2017
6   Federal Bureau of Investigation, Hate Crime Statistics, 2017
7   Federal Bureau of Investigation, Hate Crime Statistics, 2017
8   Federal Bureau of Investigation, Hate Crime Statistics, 2017
9   Federal Bureau of Investigation, Hate Crime Statistics, 2017
10   Federal Bureau of Investigation, Hate Crime Statistics, 2017
11   Federal Bureau of Investigation, Hate Crime Statistics, 2017
12   Federal Bureau of Investigation, Hate Crime Statistics, 2017
13   Federal Bureau of Investigation, Hate Crime Statistics, 2017
14   Federal Bureau of Investigation, Hate Crime Statistics, 2017

Part 7. Indicators of School Crime and Safety, 2018

1   Centers for Disease Control and Prevention (CDC), 1992-2016 School-Associated Violent Death Surveillance System (SAVD-SS) (partially funded by the U.S. Department of Education, Office of Safe and Healthy Students), previously unpublished tabulation; and CDC, National Center for Health Statistics, 1992-2016 National Vital Statistics System (NVSS), previously unpublished tabulation prepared by CDC's National Center for Injury Prevention and Control. (This table was prepared October 2018.)

2   U.S. Department of Justice, Bureau of Justice Statistics, National Crime Victimization Survey (NCVS), 1992 through 2017. (This table was prepared October 2018.)

3   U.S. Department of Justice, Bureau of Justice Statistics, National Crime Victimization Survey (NCVS), 2017. (This table was prepared October 2018.)

4   U.S. Department of Justice, Bureau of Justice Statistics, School Crime Supplement (SCS) to the National Crime Victimization Survey, 1995 through 2017. (This table was prepared September 2018.)

5   U.S. Department of Education, National Center for Education Statistics, Schools and Staffing Survey (SASS), "Public School Teacher Data File," 1993-94, 1999-2000, 2003-04, 2007-08, and 2011-12; "Charter School Teacher Data File," 1999-2000; and National Teacher and Principal Survey (NTPS), "Public School Teacher Data File," 2015-16. (This table was prepared August 2017.)

6   U.S. Department of Education, National Center for Education Statistics, 1999–2000, 2003–04, 2005–06, 2007–08, 2009–10, and 2015–16 School Survey on Crime and Safety (SSOCS), 2000, 2004, 2006, 2008, 2010, and 2016; and Fast Response Survey System (FRSS), "School Safety and Discipline: 2013–14," FRSS 106, 2014.

7   U.S. Department of Justice, Bureau of Justice Statistics, School Crime Supplement (SCS) to the National Crime Victimization Survey, 2001 through 2017. (This table was prepared September 2018.)

8   Centers for Disease Control and Prevention, Division of Adolescent and School Health, Youth Risk Behavior Surveillance System (YRBSS), 1993 through 2017. (This table was prepared June 2018.)

9   U.S. Department of Justice, Bureau of Justice Statistics, School Crime Supplement (SCS) to the National Crime Victimization Survey, 1999 through 2017. (This table was prepared October 2018.)

10   U.S. Department of Justice, Bureau of Justice Statistics, School Crime Supplement (SCS) to the National Crime Victimization Survey, selected years, 2005 through 2017. (This table was prepared September 2018.)

Part 8. Jail Inmates in 2017

1   Bureau of Justice Statistics, Annual Survey of Jails, 2006–2017; Census of Jail Inmates, 2005; Mortality in Correctional Institutions (formerly Deaths in Custody Reporting Program), 2006 (admissions only); and U.S. Census Bureau, Population Estimates by Age, Sex, Race, and Hispanic Origin for the United States: January 1, 2005, to January 1, 2018.

2   Bureau of Justice Statistics, Annual Survey of Jails, 2010–2017, and Census of Jail Inmates, 2005.

3   Bureau of Justice Statistics, Annual Survey of Jails, 2010–2017, and Census of Jail Inmates, 2005.

3A   Bureau of Justice Statistics, Annual Survey of Jails, 2010–2017, and Census of Jail Inmates, 2005.

4   Bureau of Justice Statistics, Annual Survey of Jails, 2017.

5   Bureau of Justice Statistics, Annual Survey of Jails, 2017.

6   Bureau of Justice Statistics, Annual Survey of Jails, 2017.

7   Bureau of Justice Statistics, Annual Survey of Jails, 2017.

8   Bureau of Justice Statistics, Annual Survey of Jails, 2006–2017.

9   Bureau of Justice Statistics, Annual Survey of Jails, 2016 and 2017.

10   Bureau of Justice Statistics, Annual Survey of Jails, 2006–2017; Census of Jail Inmates, 2005; Mortality in Correctional Institutions (formerly Deaths in Custody Reporting Program), 2006 (admissions only); and U.S. Census Bureau, Population Estimates by Age, Sex, Race, and Hispanic Origin for the United States: January 1, 2005, to January 1, 2018.

11   Bureau of Justice Statistics, Annual Survey of Jails, 2006–2017; Census of Jail Inmates, 2005

Part 9. Law Enforcement Officers Killed and Assaulted, 2018

1   United States Department of Justice, Federal Bureau of Investigation, Uniform Crime Reports, 2018

2   United States Department of Justice, Federal Bureau of Investigation, Uniform Crime Reports, 2018

3   United States Department of Justice, Federal Bureau of Investigation, Uniform Crime Reports, 2018

4   United States Department of Justice, Federal Bureau of Investigation, Uniform Crime Reports, 2018

5   United States Department of Justice, Federal Bureau of Investigation, Uniform Crime Reports, 2018

6   United States Department of Justice, Federal Bureau of Investigation, Uniform Crime Reports, 2018

7   United States Department of Justice, Federal Bureau of Investigation, Uniform Crime Reports, 2018

8   United States Department of Justice, Federal Bureau of Investigation, Uniform Crime Reports, 2018

9   United States Department of Justice, Federal Bureau of Investigation, Uniform Crime Reports, 2018

10   United States Department of Justice, Federal Bureau of Investigation, Uniform Crime Reports, 2018

11   United States Department of Justice, Federal Bureau of Investigation, Uniform Crime Reports, 2018

12   United States Department of Justice, Federal Bureau of Investigation, Uniform Crime Reports, 2018

13   United States Department of Justice, Federal Bureau of Investigation, Uniform Crime Reports, 2018

14   United States Department of Justice, Federal Bureau of Investigation, Uniform Crime Reports, 2018

15 United States Department of Justice, Federal Bureau of Investigation, Uniform Crime Reports, 2018
16 United States Department of Justice, Federal Bureau of Investigation, Uniform Crime Reports, 2018
17 United States Department of Justice, Federal Bureau of Investigation, Uniform Crime Reports, 2018
18 United States Department of Justice, Federal Bureau of Investigation, Uniform Crime Reports, 2018
19 United States Department of Justice, Federal Bureau of Investigation, Uniform Crime Reports, 2018
20 United States Department of Justice, Federal Bureau of Investigation, Uniform Crime Reports, 2018
21 United States Department of Justice, Federal Bureau of Investigation, Uniform Crime Reports, 2018
22 United States Department of Justice, Federal Bureau of Investigation, Uniform Crime Reports, 2018
23 United States Department of Justice, Federal Bureau of Investigation, Uniform Crime Reports, 2018
24 United States Department of Justice, Federal Bureau of Investigation, Uniform Crime Reports, 2018
25 United States Department of Justice, Federal Bureau of Investigation, Uniform Crime Reports, 2018
26 United States Department of Justice, Federal Bureau of Investigation, Uniform Crime Reports, 2018
27 United States Department of Justice, Federal Bureau of Investigation, Uniform Crime Reports, 2018
28 United States Department of Justice, Federal Bureau of Investigation, Uniform Crime Reports, 2018
29 United States Department of Justice, Federal Bureau of Investigation, Uniform Crime Reports, 2018
30 United States Department of Justice, Federal Bureau of Investigation, Uniform Crime Reports, 2018
31 United States Department of Justice, Federal Bureau of Investigation, Uniform Crime Reports, 2018
32 United States Department of Justice, Federal Bureau of Investigation, Uniform Crime Reports, 2018
33 United States Department of Justice, Federal Bureau of Investigation, Uniform Crime Reports, 2018
34 United States Department of Justice, Federal Bureau of Investigation, Uniform Crime Reports, 2018
35 United States Department of Justice, Federal Bureau of Investigation, Uniform Crime Reports, 2018
36 United States Department of Justice, Federal Bureau of Investigation, Uniform Crime Reports, 2018
37 United States Department of Justice, Federal Bureau of Investigation, Uniform Crime Reports, 2018
38 United States Department of Justice, Federal Bureau of Investigation, Uniform Crime Reports, 2018
39 United States Department of Justice, Federal Bureau of Investigation, Uniform Crime Reports, 2018
40 United States Department of Justice, Federal Bureau of Investigation, Uniform Crime Reports, 2018

Part 10. Probation and Parole, 2016

3 Bureau of Justice Statistics, Annual Survey of Jails, 2006–2017; Census of Jail Inmates, 2005
4 Bureau of Justice Statistics, Annual Survey of Jails, 2006–2017; Census of Jail Inmates, 2005
5 Bureau of Justice Statistics, Annual Probation Survey and Annual Parole Survey, 2016
6 Bureau of Justice Statistics, Annual Probation Survey and Annual Parole Survey, 2016
7 Bureau of Justice Statistics, Annual Probation Survey, 2016
8 Bureau of Justice Statistics, Annual Probation Survey, 2000, 2015, and 2016
9 Bureau of Justice Statistics, Annual Parole Survey, 2016.
10 Bureau of Justice Statistics, Annual Parole Survey, 2016
11 Bureau of Justice Statistics, Annual Parole Survey, 2016
12 Bureau of Justice Statistics, Annual Parole Survey, 2000, 2015, and 2016

Part 11. 2018 Update on Prisoner Recidivism: A 9-Year Follow-up Period (2005-2014)

1 Bureau of Justice Statistics, Recidivism of State Prisoners Released in 2005 data collection, 2005–2014
2 Bureau of Justice Statistics, Recidivism of State Prisoners Released in 2005 data collection, 2005–2014
3 Bureau of Justice Statistics, Recidivism of State Prisoners Released in 2005 data collection, 2005–2014
4 Bureau of Justice Statistics, Recidivism of State Prisoners Released in 2005 data collection, 2005–2014
5 Bureau of Justice Statistics, Recidivism of State Prisoners Released in 2005 data collection, 2005–2014
6 Bureau of Justice Statistics, Recidivism of State Prisoners Released in 2005 data collection, 2005–2014
7 Bureau of Justice Statistics, Recidivism of State Prisoners Released in 2005 data collection, 2005–2014

8   Bureau of Justice Statistics, Recidivism of State Prisoners Released in 2005 data collection, 2005–2014
9   Bureau of Justice Statistics, Recidivism of State Prisoners Released in 2005 data collection, 2005–2014
10   Bureau of Justice Statistics, Recidivism of State Prisoners Released in 2005 data collection, 2005–2014
11   Bureau of Justice Statistics, Recidivism of State Prisoners Released in 2005 data collection, 2005–2014
12   Bureau of Justice Statistics, Recidivism of State Prisoners Released in 2005 data collection, 2005–2014
13   Bureau of Justice Statistics, Recidivism of State Prisoners Released in 2005 data collection, 2005–2014

Part 12. Victims of Identity Theft, 2016

1   Bureau of Justice Statistics, National Crime Victimization Survey, Identity Theft Supplement, 2016
2   Bureau of Justice Statistics, National Crime Victimization Survey, Identity Theft Supplement, 2016
3   Bureau of Justice Statistics, National Crime Victimization Survey, Identity Theft Supplement, 2016
4   Bureau of Justice Statistics, National Crime Victimization Survey, Identity Theft Supplement, 2016
5   Bureau of Justice Statistics, National Crime Victimization Survey, Identity Theft Supplement, 2016
6   Bureau of Justice Statistics, National Crime Victimization Survey, Identity Theft Supplement, 2016
7   Bureau of Justice Statistics, National Crime Victimization Survey, Identity Theft Supplement, 2016
8   Bureau of Justice Statistics, National Crime Victimization Survey, Identity Theft Supplement, 2016
9   Bureau of Justice Statistics, National Crime Victimization Survey, Identity Theft Supplement, 2016
10   Bureau of Justice Statistics, National Crime Victimization Survey, Identity Theft Supplement, 2016
11   Bureau of Justice Statistics, National Crime Victimization Survey, Identity Theft Supplement, 2016
12   Bureau of Justice Statistics, National Crime Victimization Survey, Identity Theft Supplement, 2016
13   Bureau of Justice Statistics, National Crime Victimization Survey, Identity Theft Supplement, 2016

INDEX